Blending a balanced, four-skills approach with contemporary multimedia, this proven program works better than ever.

Focused on building linguistic skills and comprehension through creative introductions to contemporary life and cultures in German-speaking countries, ***Wie geht's?*** Tenth Edition effectively prepares your students to communicate in German—in and beyond your classroom.

One of the most popular introductory German programs in the country, ***Wie geht's?*** continues to meet the World Language Standards of the American Council on the Teaching of Foreign Languages (the 5 C's → Communication, Connections, Comparisons, Cultures, Communities), the need for a balanced, communicative approach complemented by a strong grammar presentation and supported by an abundance of activities. As the authors, native Germans, show students how the German language actually works, they encourage cultural awareness and the acquisition of functional vocabulary that effectively prepares students to continue their study of German.

Highlights of *Wie geht's?* Tenth Edition:

- Uses a structured, balanced approach proven to be effective
- Addresses the communicative skills speaking, listening, reading, writing, and comprehension in an integrated program
- Encourages cultural awareness that engages students in learning
- Supports instructors and students with a comprehensive technology package, including **iLrn™: Heinle Learning Center**, new end-of-chapter *Rückschau* sections featuring chapter vocabulary lists, review activities, and online activities through iLrn.

PREVIEW

Turn the page for a closer look at how ***Wie geht's?*** works.

It works . . .

by providing a thematic and cultural context for learning with communicative, meaningful, and mechanical materials.

The ***Wie geht's?*** program features fifteen chapters and five introductory pre-units *(Schritte)*. Each chapter's content is organized around a different theme.

Lernziele: chapter objectives at a glance. Each chapter is enhanced by video, audio, and a variety of activities available online at the **iLrn™: Heinle Learning Center**.

Kapitel 3

Im Restaurant

Lernziele In this chapter you will learn about:

Zum Thema
Food *(continued)* and restaurants

Fokus
Where to eat, cafés and coffee houses, regional specialties, wines, table manners, friends and acquaintances

Struktur
- Verbs with vowel changes
- The dative case

Einblicke
Lesetext: Man ist, was man isst.

Rückschau
Kapitalwortschatz
Zum Schluss

RESSOURCEN
iLrn Video
Audio SAM

Bergrestaurant oberhalb von Innsbruck mit Blick aufs (view of) *weite Land*

82

Vorschau Eating In and Out

Until the end of World War II, cooking in the German-speaking countries varied substantially from region to region, as each region's cuisine was noticeably influenced by its neighbors. Austrian cooking, for example, had a strong Hungarian component, and Bavarian cooks in turn borrowed from Austria. Swiss-German cuisine however, incorporated many aspects of French and Italian culinary traditions. As in many other countries, cooking shows have become quite popular on German television.

While retaining its regional flavors, modern German cooking has been influenced by cuisines from around the world. Indeed, Germans have developed a sophisticated palate and a sharp awareness of variety and quality in their diet. Health-food shops **(Reformhäuser)** and organic food stores **(Bio-Läden)** can be found almost everywhere. Those Germans who prefer to eat out can choose from a wide range of international restaurants, including Greek, Italian, Spanish, Chinese, and Thai. However, fast food is also very popular. Pizza delivery and American hamburger outlets are available in almost every city; other favorite ethnic fast foods include Turkish döner kebabs, Lebanese falafel, and shawarma. The traditional German **Imbiss** continues to offer a quick snack of sausage with potato salad **(Bratwurst mit Kartoffelsalat).**

Restaurant customs in Germany, Austria, and Switzerland differ somewhat from those of North America. Guests usually seat themselves. Before eating, diners wish each other a pleasant meal **(Guten Appetit!** or **Mahlzeit!).** The appropriate response is **Danke, gleichfalls!** *(Thanks, the same to you!)*. Salads generally are not eaten before, but with the main course. Germans, like most Europeans, don't drink coffee with a meal, only afterward. Also, water is never served automatically (and not with ice); guests are expected to order mineral water or another beverage. There are no free refills. Service **(die Bedienung)** and the value-added tax are included in the price of the meal. Although a tip **(das Trinkgeld)** is not necessary, it is customary to round up the total; how much is added depends on the friendliness and the quality of service. After asking for the bill **(Zahlen, bitte!)**, diners give the money, including the tip, directly to the server. Often diners are asked if they want to pay the whole bill or split it **(Zusammen oder getrennt?).** If you intend to pay by credit card, ask if they are accepted before you start your meal; if they are, it's likely to be the electronic debit card **(die EC-Karte).**

First introduced by Turkish immigrants, the **Dönerkebab** is extremely popular in Europe. The classical **Döner** consists of pita bread split open and filled with shredded lettuce, red onion, cucumber, tomatoes, green pickled chilis, and red chili sauce, as well as long strips of freshly carved, thinly sliced, pieces of lamb preferably cooked on a revolving spit. Dönerkebabs generally taste nothing like gyros in the United States. Gyros are seasoned quite differently.

Fragen: 1. Was haben sie hier zu essen? 2. Was ist besonders billig? 3. Essen Sie das gern oder essen Sie lieber *(rather)* Schnitzel? 4. Was kostet das Schnitzel mit Champignonsoße *(mushroom gravy)*? 5. Gibt es hier ein deutsches Restaurant? Wenn ja, wie heißt es? 6. Ist es da billig oder teuer?

83

The *Vorschau* section provides the cultural background for the chapter's topic or the subject geographic region.

It works. . .
with a structured approach to building vocabulary.

Zum Thema promotes the acquisition of vocabulary and the development of communicative skills, focusing on words and phrases related to the chapter theme. A variety of exercises and activities offer the practice that is essential to learning and communication.

Zum Thema

Gespräche

Im Restaurant

■ Listen to the dialogue. Then act out the dialogue with a partner. ■

AXEL Herr Ober, die Speisekarte bitte!
OBER Hier bitte!
AXEL Was empfehlen Sie heute?
OBER Die Menüs sind alle sehr gut.
AXEL Gabi, was nimmst du?
GABI Ich weiß nicht. Was nimmst du?
AXEL Ich glaube, ich nehme Menü 1: Schnitzel und Kartoffelsalat.
GABI Und ich hätte gern Menü 2: Rindsrouladen mit Kartoffelklößen.
OBER Möchten Sie etwas trinken?
GABI Ein Glas Apfelsaft, und du?
AXEL Mineralwasser. *(Der Ober kommt mit dem Essen.)* Guten Appetit!
Danke, gleichfalls . . . Hm, das schmeckt.

© Cengage Learning

Lively and authentic dialogues introduce the featured topic in each chapter. Functioning as models for conversation, they reinforce previously learned vocabulary and introduce some new words in context.

Fokus Cafés and Coffee Houses

Cafés and pastry shops **(Konditoreien)** are favorite places for conversation or for breaks in shopping excursions. They serve coffee, tea, and hot chocolate, along with a great variety of delicious cakes and pastries. In Austria, many people have a favorite café **(das Kaffeehaus)** where they can relax over such items as a **Melange** *(half coffee, half frothed milk)* or a piece of **Linzertorte** *(jam-filled tart)*. The tradition of the coffee house goes back to the early 1700s. Since then, it has been the preferred meeting place not only of the literati, reformers, artists, and philosophers but also of middle-class society.

Wortschatz 1 presents a list of new active vocabulary. These sections have been revised to ensure that the vocabulary is natural and current.

Fokus cultural notes, interspersed throughout each chapter, expand on the *Vorschau,* amongst others comparing and contrasting the differences between life in North America and German-speaking countries.

■ In upscale restaurants, the server is usually referred to as **der Kellner / die Kellnerin** or **der Ober**. Diners usually say **Herr Ober!, Entschuldigen Sie!, Hallo!, Bedienung bitte!** or use a hand signal to catch a server's attention. There is no equivalent to **Ober** for a female server. Don't use **Oberin** for *waitress*, as that means *Mother Superior* and also *head nurse*!

■ **Die Speisekarte** *(à la carte menu)* is not the same thing as **das Menü** *(complete, fixed-price menu, usually including soup and dessert).*

■ **Eis** means both *ice* and *ice cream*. If you ask for **Eis** in a restaurant, you will get ice cream. Ice water is generally not served in German-speaking countries.

■ **Die [pom frits],** BUT **die [pommes]**

■ ALSO: **Was gibt's zu kaufen (sehen, sagen . . .)?**

■ **Viel Obst** *(sg. collective noun)*, **Wie viel Obst?** BUT: **Viele Äpfel, Wie viele Äpfel?**

■ Ich bin **zu Hause.** BUT: Ich gehe **nach Hause.** (See Struktur 3.2–3.)

■ The verbs **zahlen** and **bezahlen** are mostly used interchangeably. They both mean *to pay for* as well as *to pay*: **Er (be)zahlt die Rechnung.** Although most Germans would say **Zahlen bitte!**, you might also hear **Ich möchte (be)zahlen.**

Wortschatz 1

Das Restaurant, -s *(restaurant)*

der Kellner, -	*waiter*	die Bedienung	*server; service*
Ober, -		Gabel, -n	*fork*
Löffel, -	*spoon*	Mensa	*student cafeteria*
Teller, -	*plate*	Rechnung, -en	*check; bill*
		Serviette, -n	*napkin*
das Café, -s	*café*	Speisekarte, -n	*menu*
Messer, -	*knife*		

Das Essen *(food; meal)*

der Nachtisch	*dessert*	das Eis	*ice cream*
Pfeffer	*pepper*	Salz	*salt*
Pudding	*pudding*	Frühstück	*breakfast*
Reis	*rice*	Mittagessen	*lunch, midday meal*
Zucker	*sugar*		
		Abendessen	*supper*
die Kartoffel, -n	*potato*	Suppe, -n	*soup*
Nudel, -n	*noodle*	die Pommes (frites) *(pl.)*	*(French) fries*
Pizza, -s	*pizza*		

Verschiedenes

Herr Ober!	*Waiter!*
Bedienung!	*Waiter! / Waitress!*
Was gibt's zum Frühstück / Mittagessen?	*What's for breakfast / lunch?*
Was gibt's zu essen / trinken?	*What is there to eat / drink?*
Guten Appetit!	*Enjoy your meal!*
Danke, gleichfalls!	*Thanks, the same to you!*
etwas (zu essen)	*something (to eat)*
nichts (zu trinken)	*nothing (to drink)*
noch ein(e)	*another*
viel / viele	*much / many*
wie viel? / wie viele?	*how much? / how many?*
zu Hause / nach Hause	*at home / (toward) home*
bestellen	*to order*
(be)zahlen	*to pay (for)*
bleiben	*to remain, stay*
bringen	*to bring*
empfehlen	*to recommend*
frühstücken	*to eat breakfast*
schmecken	*to taste*
Das schmeckt (gut)!	*That's good!, That tastes good!*
Das schmeckt (mir).	*I like it., i.e., I like the way it tastes.*
Ich mag kein(e/en) . . . (+ *acc.*)	*I don't like (any) . . .*
Ich möchte / hätte gern . . .	*I would like to have . . .*
(Ich möchte) zahlen bitte!	*I'd like to pay.*

Zum Erkennen: das (Tages)menü, -s *(daily special)*; das Schnitzel, - *(veal cutlet)*; die Rindsroulade, -n *(stuffed beef roll)*; der Kloß, ¨-e *(dumpling)*; einmal (here: *one order of*); AUCH: der Dativ; das Objekt, -e; die Präposition, -en; zurück *(back)*; backen *(to bake)*, braten *(to fry)*, grillen, kochen *(to cook)*

Übungen zum Thema

A. Was passt nicht?

1. der Teller—das Messer—die Speisekarte—die Gabel
2. das Frühstück—der Nachtisch—das Mittagessen—das Abendessen
3. das Salz—der Zucker—der Pfeffer—die Serviette
4. die Rechnung—die Kartoffeln—die Nudeln—der Reis
5. das Café—der Appetit—das Restaurant—die Mensa
6. bestellen—empfehlen—sein—zahlen

B. Was bedeuten die Wörter und was sind die Artikel?

Frühstückstisch	Teelöffel	Schokoladenpudding
Kaffeetasse	Suppenlöffel	Joghurteis
Fleischgabel	Suppenteller	Zitroneneis
Buttermesser	Kartoffelsuppe	

C. Was passt?

_____ 1. Die Suppe ist aber kalt.
_____ 2. Die Bratwurst schmeckt prima.
_____ 3. Möchtest du nichts trinken?
_____ 4. Und etwas zum Nachtisch?
_____ 5. Guten Appetit!

a. Das Brot auch.
b. Wirklich?
c. Na klar!
d. Das finde ich auch.
e. Ja, bitte.
f. Ja, lecker *(delicious)*!
g. Doch, eine Tasse Kaffee.
h. Nein, danke.
i. Ja, fantastisch!
j. Ja, gern.
k. Ja, ich hätte gern ein Eis.
l. Danke, gleichfalls.
m. Ein Glas Orangensaft bitte!
n. . . .

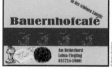

In der schönen Lausitz
Bauernhofcafé
Am Reiherhorst
Lohsa-Tiegling
035724-59001

© Beatrix Brockman

D. Was noch? *(What else?)* With a partner, see how many items you can find for each word or phrase below. Compare your results with those of others.

BEISPIEL ein Stück . . .
Ich möchte ein Stück Brot.

1. ein Stück . . .
2. ein Glas . . .
3. eine Tasse . . .
4. ein paar . . .
5. etwas . . .
6. ein Pfund . . .
7. viel . . .
8. viele . . .

E. Kombinieren Sie! With your partner, make compound nouns with the following words. Then compare your list with that of others.

BEISPIEL der Kuchen
der Kirschkuchen, die Kuchengabel

1. die Wurst
2. der Pudding
3. die Suppe
4. der Wein
5. das Obst
6. der Kaffee

Zum Erkennen presents words and phrases, intended for recognition only, from the dialogue and exercises.

Contemporary activities in the *Übungen zum Thema* follow the vocabulary presentation, encouraging communication and reinforcing the verbal interaction introduced in the dialogues.

PREVIEW

It works…
with a clear presentation of grammar.

Following the vocabulary presentation, each chapter's *Struktur* section teaches the basic elements of German grammar, providing a strong linguistic foundation.

Throughout the section, explanations in English are followed by activities (*Übungen*) that offer opportunities to practice grammar points in exercises that incorporate the communicative skills reading, writing, speaking, and listening.

Struktur

3.1 Verbs with vowel changes

Some very common verbs have a stem-vowel change in the SECOND and THIRD PERSON singular. These changes will be clearly noted in all vocabulary lists like this: **sprechen (spricht).**

	e → i **sprechen** *to speak*	e → ie **sehen** *to see*	a → ä **fahren** *to drive*	au → äu **laufen** *to walk, run*
ich	spreche	sehe	fahre	laufe
du	**sprichst**	**siehst**	**fährst**	**läufst**
er	**spricht**	**sieht**	**fährt**	**läuft**
wir	sprechen	sehen	fahren	laufen
ihr	sprecht	seht	fahrt	lauft
sie	sprechen	sehen	fahren	laufen

Siehst du Dresden auf der Landkarte?
Dieter **fährt** nach Dresden.

A few verbs in this group have additional consonant changes:

	nehmen *to take*	**werden** *to become, get*
ich	nehme	werde
du	**nimmst**	**wirst**
er	**nimmt**	**wird**
wir	nehmen	werden
ihr	nehmt	werdet
sie	nehmen	werden

You need to know the following common verbs with stem-vowel changes:

empfehlen	**empfiehlt**	*to recommend*
essen	**isst**	*to eat*
fahren	**fährt**	*to drive*
geben	**gibt**	*to give*
gefallen	**gefällt**	*to please, be pleasing to*
helfen	**hilft**	*to help*
laufen	**läuft**	*to walk; to run*
lesen	**liest**	*to read*
nehmen	**nimmt**	*to take; to have (food)*
sehen	**sieht**	*to see*
sprechen	**spricht**	*to speak*
tragen	**trägt**	*to carry; to wear*
werden	**wird**	*to become, get*

Note that the second and third person singular forms of **essen** and **lesen** are identical **(du/er isst, du/er liest).** As you know from Chapter 1, the **du**-form of verbs with a stem ending in any s-sound **(-s, -ß, ss, -tz, -z)** adds only a **t**-ending instead of an **-st:** lese → du lies**t**; heißen → du heiß**t.**

Übungen

A. Bilden Sie Sätze! Create sentences with one word from each column making all necessary adjustments. You can also add your own words to each column.

BEISPIEL Du liest gern.

ich	fahren	ein paar Bücher
du	nehmen	schon wieder
der Herr	werden	einen Mantel
die Frau	empfehlen	das Omelett
das Kind	sehen	kein Salz
Axel und ich	sprechen	Deutsch
ihr	helfen	schnell
die Leute	lesen	müde
	essen	gern
	laufen	laut
	tragen	nichts
		nicht

B. Was tun sie? Answer the questions in your own words to tell what others do. Use pronouns and stem-changing verbs in your answers.

BEISPIEL Ich esse schnell. Und Ihr Großvater?
Er isst sehr langsam.

1. Ich helfe gern. Und Ihr Nachbar?
2. Ich nehme Apfelstrudel. Und Gabi?
3. Ich empfehle den Schweinebraten. Und der Ober?
4. Ich laufe viel. Und Ihr Bruder oder Ihre Schwester?
5. Ich lese gern. Und Ihre Mutter?
6. Ich fahre im Sommer nach Deutschland. Und Ihre Familie?
7. Ich sehe alles. Und Ihr Nachbar?
8. Ich gebe der Bedienung normalerweise 20 Prozent Trinkgeld *(tip)*. Und Ihr Vater / Ihre Mutter?

C. Und du? Choose a classmate whom you don't know well and find out what he/she likes. Follow the model and try to vary your responses. At the end, report to the class what you found out.

1. **Was isst du gern?** Before doing this exercise, glance at the menu and the food vocabulary in this chapter and in Chapter 2.

BEISPIEL
S1 Ich esse gern . . . (z. B. Fischbrötchen). Und du, isst du gern . . . ?
S2 Ja, ich esse gern . . . / Nein, ich esse nicht gern . . .
S1 Magst du . . . (z. B. Erbsensuppe)?
S2 Ja, ich mag . . . / Nein, ich mag kein(e/en) . . .
S1 Was magst du auch nicht gern?
S2 Ich mag auch kein(e/en) . . .

2. **Was trägst du gern?** You might first review the list of clothing in *Schritt 3*.

BEISPIEL
S1 Ich trage gern . . . (z. B. Jeans). Und du, trägst du auch gern . . . ?
S2 Natürlich trage ich gern . . . (z. B. Jeans). / Nein, ich trage keine . . . (z. B. Jeans).
S1 Was trägst du noch / nicht gern?
S2 Ich trage (nicht) gern . . . / Ich mag kein(e/en) . . . / Ich hasse *(hate)* . . .

iLrn

Visit the ***Wie geht's?*** iLrn website for more review and practice of the grammar points you have just learned.

Zusammenfassung

N. Guten Appetit: Was fehlt? Complete the articles and contractions if needed.

1. Zu____ Essen braucht man ein____ Messer und ein____ Gabel. 2. Suppe isst man mit ein____ Esslöffel *(tablespoon)* und für d____ Kaffee braucht man ein____ Kaffeelöffel. 3. D____ Restaurant gefällt d____ Studenten *(pl.)*. 4. Aber sie haben etwas gegen d____ Preise. 5. Wir sprechen von d____ Professor und von d____ Prüfung. 6. Ich bestelle noch ein____ Cola. 7. Hier trinke ich d____ Cola aus ein____ Glas, aber zu Hause aus d____ Flasche *(f., bottle)*. 8. Da kommt der Ober mit d____ Rechnung. 9. Ohne d____ Rechnung geht's nicht. 10. Danke für d____ Mittagessen!

O. Gabi und Axel im Restaurant Create complete sentences.

BEISPIEL Axel / sprechen / mit / Ober
Axel spricht mit dem Ober.

1. Ober / bringen / Studenten *(pl.)* / Speisekarte
2. er / empfehlen / Student / Menü eins
3. Axel / nehmen / Schnitzel
4. Studentin / schmecken / Rindsroulade *(f.)*
5. Axel und Gabi / danken / Ober / für / Empfehlung *(f.)*
6. zu / Essen / trinken / Gabi / Glas Mineralwasser
7. Axel / helfen / Ober / mit / Rechnung
8. außer / Brötchen *(sg.)* / sein / alles / auf / Rechnung
9. Gabi / geben / Ober / 40 Euro

A grammar summary activity section provides review and asks students to synthesize and apply the grammar points presented in the chapter. Additional practice and review of targeted structures are available in the **Student Activities Manual** and **iLrn™: Heinle Learning Center**.

It works…

with reading-skills development that fosters cultural understanding.

Each chapter's *Einblicke* section features a reading passage (e.g., *Lesetext, Dialog, Brief, Bericht*, etc.) related to cultural aspects of the chapter theme. Various skills are recycled and reinforced as students are exposed to new cultural facts and topics. These readings are recorded on the **SAM Audio Program**.

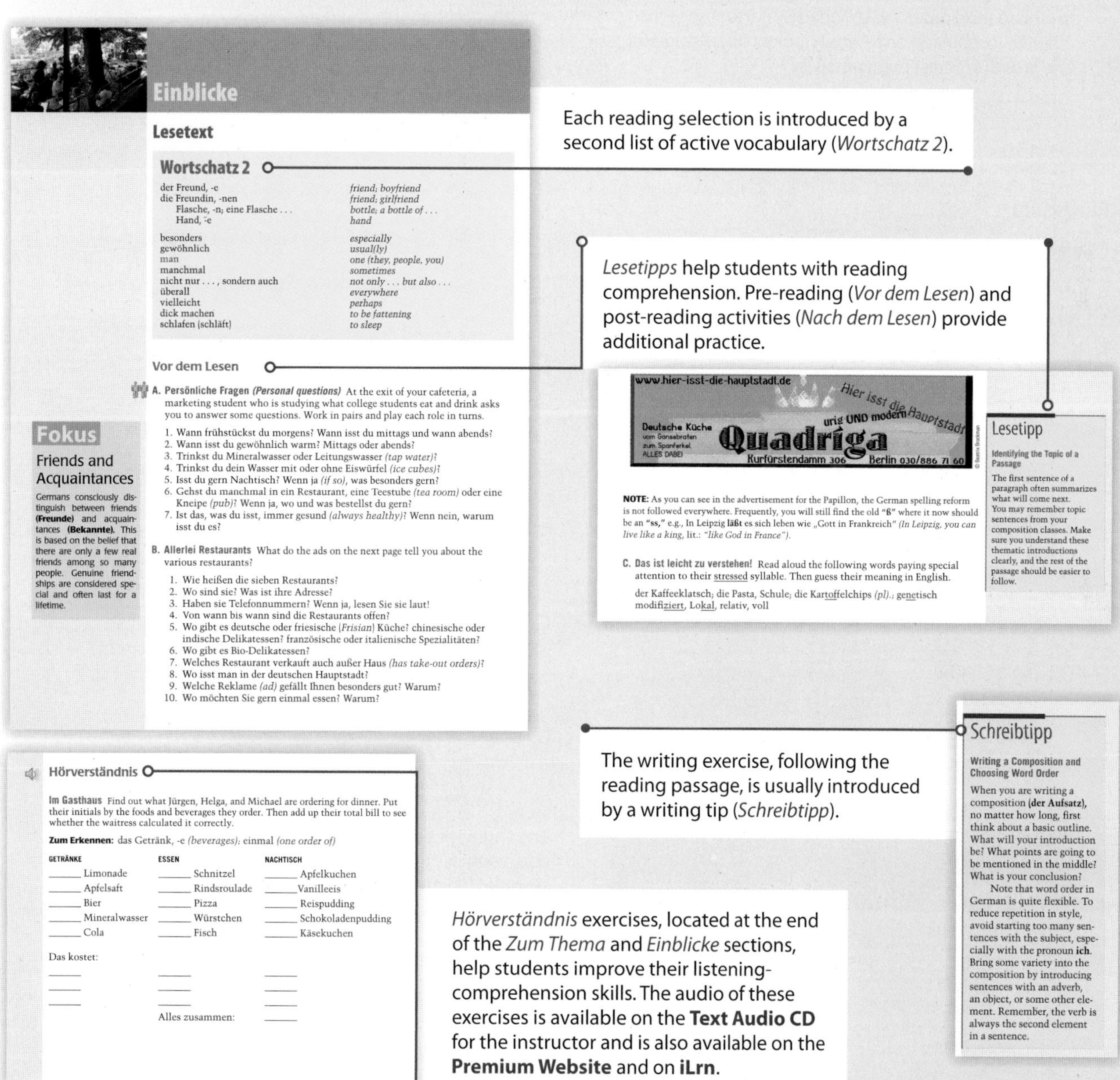

Einblicke

Lesetext

Wortschatz 2

der Freund, -e	*friend; boyfriend*
die Freundin, -nen	*friend; girlfriend*
Flasche, -n; eine Flasche …	*bottle; a bottle of …*
Hand, ¨-e	*hand*
besonders	*especially*
gewöhnlich	*usual(ly)*
man	*one (they, people, you)*
manchmal	*sometimes*
nicht nur …, sondern auch	*not only … but also …*
überall	*everywhere*
vielleicht	*perhaps*
dick machen	*to be fattening*
schlafen (schläft)	*to sleep*

Each reading selection is introduced by a second list of active vocabulary (*Wortschatz 2*).

Vor dem Lesen

A. Persönliche Fragen *(Personal questions)* At the exit of your cafeteria, a marketing student who is studying what college students eat and drink asks you to answer some questions. Work in pairs and play each role in turns.

1. Wann frühstückst du morgens? Wann isst du mittags und wann abends?
2. Wann isst du gewöhnlich warm? Mittags oder abends?
3. Trinkst du Mineralwasser oder Leitungswasser *(tap water)*?
4. Trinkst du dein Wasser mit oder ohne Eiswürfel *(ice cubes)*?
5. Isst du gern Nachtisch? Wenn ja *(if so)*, was besonders gern?
6. Gehst du manchmal in ein Restaurant, eine Teestube *(tea room)* oder eine Kneipe *(pub)*? Wenn ja, wo und was bestellst du gern?
7. Ist das, was du isst, immer gesund *(always healthy)*? Wenn nein, warum isst du es?

B. Allerlei Restaurants What do the ads on the next page tell you about the various restaurants?

1. Wie heißen die sieben Restaurants?
2. Wo sind sie? Was ist ihre Adresse?
3. Haben sie Telefonnummern? Wenn ja, lesen Sie sie laut!
4. Von wann bis wann sind die Restaurants offen?
5. Wo gibt es deutsche oder friesische (*Frisian*) Küche? chinesische oder indische Delikatessen? französische oder italienische Spezialitäten?
6. Wo gibt es Bio-Delikatessen?
7. Welches Restaurant verkauft auch außer Haus *(has take-out orders)*?
8. Wo isst man in der deutschen Hauptstadt?
9. Welche Reklame *(ad)* gefällt Ihnen besonders gut? Warum?
10. Wo möchten Sie gern einmal essen? Warum?

Fokus

Friends and Acquaintances

Germans consciously distinguish between friends **(Freunde)** and acquaintances **(Bekannte)**. This is based on the belief that there are only a few real friends among so many people. Genuine friendships are considered special and often last for a lifetime.

Lesetipps help students with reading comprehension. Pre-reading (*Vor dem Lesen*) and post-reading activities (*Nach dem Lesen*) provide additional practice.

NOTE: As you can see in the advertisement for the Papillon, the German spelling reform is not followed everywhere. Frequently, you will still find the old "ß" where it now should be an "**ss**," e.g., In Leipzig **läßt** es sich leben wie „Gott in Frankreich" *(In Leipzig, you can live like a king*, lit.: *"like God in France")*.

C. Das ist leicht zu verstehen! Read aloud the following words paying special attention to their stressed syllable. Then guess their meaning in English.

der Kaffeeklatsch; die Pasta, Schule; die Kartoffelchips *(pl).*; genetisch modifiziert, Lokal, relativ, voll

Lesetipp

Identifying the Topic of a Passage

The first sentence of a paragraph often summarizes what will come next. You may remember topic sentences from your composition classes. Make sure you understand these thematic introductions clearly, and the rest of the passage should be easier to follow.

Hörverständnis

Im Gasthaus Find out what Jürgen, Helga, and Michael are ordering for dinner. Put their initials by the foods and beverages they order. Then add up their total bill to see whether the waitress calculated it correctly.

Zum Erkennen: das Getränk, -e *(beverages)*; einmal *(one order of)*

GETRÄNKE	ESSEN	NACHTISCH
______ Limonade	______ Schnitzel	______ Apfelkuchen
______ Apfelsaft	______ Rindsroulade	______ Vanilleeis
______ Bier	______ Pizza	______ Reispudding
______ Mineralwasser	______ Würstchen	______ Schokoladenpudding
______ Cola	______ Fisch	______ Käsekuchen

Das kostet:

______	______	______
______	______	______
______	______	______
	Alles zusammen:	______

The writing exercise, following the reading passage, is usually introduced by a writing tip (*Schreibtipp*).

Schreibtipp

Writing a Composition and Choosing Word Order

When you are writing a composition **(der Aufsatz)**, no matter how long, first think about a basic outline. What will your introduction be? What points are going to be mentioned in the middle? What is your conclusion?

Note that word order in German is quite flexible. To reduce repetition in style, avoid starting too many sentences with the subject, especially with the pronoun **ich**. Bring some variety into the composition by introducing sentences with an adverb, an object, or some other element. Remember, the verb is always the second element in a sentence.

Hörverständnis exercises, located at the end of the *Zum Thema* and *Einblicke* sections, help students improve their listening-comprehension skills. The audio of these exercises is available on the **Text Audio CD** for the instructor and is also available on the **Premium Website** and on **iLrn**.

PREVIEW

Starting with Chapter 8, each *Einblicke* section also includes one or two pieces of authentic literature (*Literatur*), chosen to help students make connections between language and culture. Literary selections are introduced by a brief biography and accompanied by pre- and postreading questions. A recording of these selections is available on the **Text Audio CD**, on the **Premium Website**, and on **iLrn**.

It works…

with an engaging multimedia review, synthesis, and application of skills.

The new **Rückschau** segments at the end of each chapter combine the vocabulary from **Wortschatz 1**, **Wortschatz 2**, and the **Struktur** sections for quick access and also provide review activities which reinforce the learned material from the chapters.

In alphabetical order and grouped by parts of speech, chapter vocabulary can be easily looked up by students and is useful for test preparation.

The review activities reinforce grammatical concepts and practice skills introduced in the chapter.

Rückschau

Kapitelwortschatz

Hauptwörter

das Abendessen	*supper*
die Bedienung	*server; service*
das Café, -s	*café*
das Eis	*ice cream*
das Essen	*food; meal*
die Flasche, -n; eine Flasche . . .	*bottle; a bottle of . . .*
der Freund, -e	*male friend; boyfriend*
die Freundin, -nen	*female friend; girlfriend*
das Frühstück	*breakfast*
die Gabel, -n	*fork*
die Hand, ¨-e	*hand*
die Kartoffel, -n	*potato*
der Kellner, -	*waiter*
der Löffel, -	*spoon*
die Mensa	*student cafeteria*
das Messer, -	*knife*
das Mittagessen	*lunch, midday meal*
der Nachtisch	*dessert*
die Nudel, -n	*noodle*
der Ober, -	*waiter*
der Pfeffer	*pepper*
die Pizza, -s	*pizza*
die Pommes (frites) *(pl.)*	*(French) fries*
der Pudding, -s	*pudding*
die Rechnung, -en	*check; bill*
der Reis	*rice*
das Restaurant, -s	*restaurant*
das Salz	*salt*
die Serviette, -n	*napkin*
die Speisekarte, -n	*menu*
die Suppe, -n	*soup*
der Teller, -	*plate*
der Zucker	*sugar*

Verben

antworten	*to answer*
bestellen	*to order*
(be)zahlen	*to pay (for)*
bleiben	*to remain, stay*
bringen	*to bring*
danken	*to thank*
dick machen	*to be fattening*
empfehlen	*to recommend*
essen	*to eat*
fahren	*to drive*
frühstücken	*to eat breakfast*
geben	*to give*
gefallen	*to please, be pleasing to*
gehören	*to belong to*
glauben	*to believe*
helfen	*to help*
laufen	*to walk; to run*
lesen	*to read*
nehmen	*to take; to have (food)*
schlafen	*to sleep*
schmecken	*to taste*
sehen	*to see*
sprechen	*to speak*
tragen	*to carry; to wear*
werden	*to become, get*

Präpositionen

aus *(+ dat.)*	*out of; from* (a place of origin)
außer *(+ dat.)*	*besides*
bei *(+ dat.)*	*at, for* (a company); *near, by; at the home of, with* (a person)
mit *(+ dat.)*	*with; together with*
nach *(+ dat.)*	*after* (time); *to* (cities, countries, continents); *to* (in certain expressions)
seit *(+ dat.)*	*since; for* (duration)
von *(+ dat.)*	*of; from; by* (creator, doer of action)
zu *(+ dat.)*	*to* (in the direction of); *at* (in certain expressions); *for* (purpose)

Verschiedenes

Bedienung!	*Waiter! / Waitress!*
besonders	*especially*
Danke, gleichfalls!	*Thanks, the same to you!*
Das schmeckt (gut)!	*That's good!, That tastes good!*
Das schmeckt (mir).	*I like it.*, i.e., *I like the way it tastes.*
etwas (zu essen)	*something (to eat)*
gewöhnlich	*usual(ly)*
Guten Appetit!	*Enjoy your meal!*
Herr Ober!	*Waiter!*
Ich mag kein(e/en) . . .	*I don't like (any) . . .*
Ich möchte / hätte gern . . .	*I would like to have . . .*
(Ich möchte) zahlen bitte!	*I'd like to pay.*
man	*one (they, people, you)*
manchmal	*sometimes*
nach Hause	*(toward) home*
nicht nur . . . , sondern auch	*not only . . . but also*
nichts (zu trinken)	*nothing (to drink)*
noch ein(e)	*another*
überall	*everywhere*
viel / viele	*much / many*
vielleicht	*perhaps*
Was gibt's zum Frühstück / Mittagessen?	*What's for breakfast / lunch?*
Was gibt's zu essen / trinken?	*What is there to eat / drink?*
wie viel? / wie viele?	*how much? / how many?*
zu Hause	*at home*

Zum Schluss

1. **Wer sind Sie?** Answer the following questions about your likes and dislikes. Add a few more questions of your own! Incorporate at least three new verbs from the chapter.
   a. Was essen Sie gern? Was essen Sie in der Mensa gern? Wo essen Sie gern?
   b. Was tragen Sie gern? Was tragen Sie heute?
   c. Mit wem sprechen Sie Deutsch?
   d. Wohnen Sie bei den Eltern?
   e. Was gefällt Ihnen an der Universität?
   f. . . .
   g. . . .
   h. . . .
2. **Wer ist wer?** Now, ask your classmates the same questions. How do their answers compare with yours?
3. **Kombinieren Sie!** How many sentences can you create with the following elements? Use the **Wortschatz** from this chapter and from earlier chapters to create complete sentences. Pay attention to case!

antworten	fahren	lesen	aus
arbeiten	geben	nehmen	außer
bestellen	gefallen	schlafen	bei
(be)zahlen	gehen	schmecken	mit
bringen	gehören	sehen	nach
danken	glauben	sprechen	seit
empfehlen	helfen	tragen	von
essen	kommen	wohnen	zu

4. **Das gefällt mir! Und das gefällt mir nicht!** Now, complete the following sentences.
   a. Ich mag kein(e/en) . . .
   b. Ich möchte . . .
   c. . . . gefällt mir (nicht).
   d. Ich esse kein(e/en) . . .
5. **Erzählen Sie!** Describe your favorite restaurant to a classmate. What kind of food do they serve? What do you like to eat there? What do you dislike there? Why? How often do you eat there? Compare answers! Make sure to include clarifying words: **besonders**, **gewöhnlich**, **manchmal**, **nicht nur . . .**, **sondern auch**, **vielleicht**.

iLrn **Onlineaktivitäten** Visit iLrn for online activities related to this chapter. There you will find additional resources, such as a memory game (**Gedächtnisspiel**), a crossword puzzle (**Kreuzworträtsel**), audio flash cards (**Vokabelblitz**), a tutorial quiz (**Mini-Quiz**), and the active vocabulary (**Wortschatz**) for this chapter.

The **Onlineaktivitäten** sections present activities and resources that are available on **iLrn**, including **Google™ Earth coordinates** for virtual trips to locations in the German-speaking countries.

Beginnen wir die Reise ins Märchenland!

Sie können Ihre gesamte Reise in Einzelschritten oder einfacher über das Internet-Portal der *Deutschen Märchenstraße* planen.

Sie planen, mit dem Flugzeug von Ihrem Heimatland nach Frankfurt am Main zu fliegen. Frankfurt ist Deutschlands größter internationaler Flughafen und liegt gar nicht weit von Hanau, dem Geburtsort der Gebrüder Grimm. Anstatt sich ein Auto zu mieten, fahren sie lieber mit dem Zug von Frankfurt nach Hanau!

Märchen-Freilichtbühne in Gudensberg, südlich von Kassel

Reiseplanung

Hanau

Aufgabe 1. Suchen Sie im Internet eine Zugverbindung vom Frankfurter Flughafen nach Hanau heraus! Gehen Sie dazu auf die Website der Deutschen Bundesbahn!

1. Finden Sie die Website der Deutschen Bundesbahn. Was kann man dort alles machen?
2. Sie kommen um 13 Uhr in Frankfurt an. Wann fährt der nächste Zug nach

A new travel guide section called "*Eine Reise ins Märchenland*" completes the new edition of ***Wie Geht's?*** It is an eight-page tour through the locales, scenery, and history of Grimms' fairy tales. Students are introduced to the "*Deutsche Märchenstraße*" and are tasked with planning a real or virtual trip along the life stations of the Brothers Grimm and through the regions of various German legends and fairy tales. This section reinforces and combines what students have learned about travel, finding lodging, ordering food, going to cultural events, and so on, in Germany.

Practical, efficient, and easy to use!

Go to www.cengage.com/ilrn for a 30-day trial.

This dynamic all-in-one online environment saves you time and enhances your students' language-learning experience!

Students access all learning components through one site, including:

- An audio- and video-enhanced **eBook**
- Assignable, integrated **textbook activities**
- **Companion videos** with pre- and post-viewing activities
- **eBook smart activity icons** with due dates and scores
- Assignable **voice-recorded activities** for multiple students
- An online **Student Activities Manual** with **audio**
- Interactive **practice activities**
- A **diagnostic study tool** with personalized study plan
- And much more!

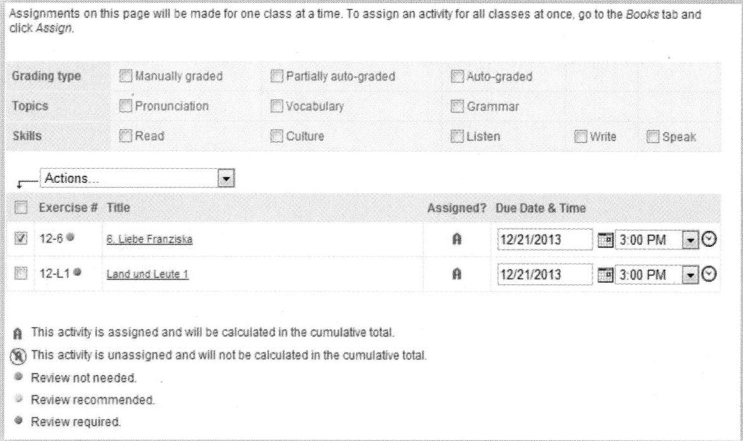

FOR SIGNIFICANT SAVINGS,
package access to **iLrn™: Heinle Learning Center** with new copies of this text. Use **ISBN: 978-1-305-12165-2** when placing your textbook order. Contact your local Cengage Learning representative for additional packaging and pricing information.

Go to www.cengage.com/ilrn

PREVIEW

Integrated Teaching and Learning Components

ONLINE RESOURCES AND VIDEO

iLrn™: Heinle Learning Center
Printed Access Card ISBN: 978-1-2857-6025-4

See preceding page for details. Access card required.

Video on DVD
ISBN: 978-1-2857-3815-4

Shot on location in Germany, Austria, and Switzerland, this new two-tier video is closely correlated to each chapter.

Premium Website
Printed Access Card ISBN: 978-1-2857-6127-5

The **Premium Website** makes it easy for you and your students to access all of the available resources. You will find the complete **Audio Program** and the complete **Video Program here**.

FOR INSTRUCTORS

Annotated Instructor's Edition + DVD + Text Audio CDs
ISBN: 978-1-2857-3819-2

On-page annotations offer answers to **all** discrete-point exercises, supplemental exercises, and teaching tips. The Front Matter also contains scripts of the listening comprehension activities and chapter vocabulary lists.

SAM Audio Script (with Answer Key)

This is available online on iLrn™ and the Instructor's side of the **Premium Website.**

Testing Audio CD and Instructor's Resource materials

This invaluable resource, located on the **Premium Website,** provides one ready-to-use test for each chapter and an extensive bank testing activities, grammar PowerPoints, and a set of situation cards and guide. The Testing Audio Program includes audio recordings of real conversations that serve as listening comprehension activities. The Testing Audio Program is also available as a standalone CD-ROM.

FOR STUDENTS

Student Text
ISBN: 978-1-2857-3360-9

Student Activities Manual (SAM) *Arbeitsbuch*
ISBN: 978-1-2857-3712-6

This essential study tool provides additional listening, speaking, and writing practice.

Text and SAM Audio Program

The **Text** audio and the **SAM** audio are available online on the **Premium Website** and on iLrn™.

Please contact your local Cengage Learning representative for additional information about these resources.

In Memoriam

Dieter H. Sevin (1938–2012)

Dr. Dieter Sevin (1938–2012) was the former chair of the Department of Germanic and Slavic Languages at Vanderbilt University; he died of pancreatic cancer on July 29, 2012. A specialist in language pedagogy and the literature of the former East Germany, Dr. Sevin published extensively, taught German language and literature for over 44 years, and has been a co-author of ***Wie geht's?*** since its first edition in 1980.

Born near Wittenberg, Germany, Dr. Sevin follow his dream as a 19-year-old and emigrated by boat from Bremerhaven to New York. With little money to his name, his enterprising spirit and work ethic enabled him to finance his undergraduate studies at San Jose State College (now University). After their marriage in 1963, he and his wife moved to Seattle to pursue graduate studies at the University of Washington. He received his Ph.D. in German and History in 1968, and then accepted a position at Vanderbilt University. In 1969, Dr. Sevin was instrumental in launching the Vanderbilt-in-Germany program with Regensburg University. In subsequent years, he served as the program's director and also helped establish a summer exchange program with the Free University of Berlin. In 2007, he was awarded the *Bundesverdienstkreuz* (Cross of the Order of Merit of the Federal Republic of Germany). The Atlanta-based German Consul General remarked on the occasion, "Dieter Sevin is a beacon of German language teaching in the U.S. His entire career has been dedicated to promoting the knowledge of German language, literature, and culture in the United States." Convinced that travel, studies, and/or work in different countries widens perspectives and enriches lives, he saw himself as a cultural mediator between the United States and Germany and worked enthusiastically to enable others to participate in intercultural exchange. He also was active in Nashville's Sister City partnership with Magdeburg, Germany, and the German-American Chamber of Commerce.

To those who knew him, Dieter Sevin was a unique human being, always positive and willing to help. Quick with a laugh and sound advice, he was always ready to listen, mentor, and inspire. He loved his work, his colleagues, and his students; he enjoyed traveling, reading, music and the arts; but most of all, he cherished spending time with family and friends. He will be missed by his wife of 49 years, his children Sonja and Karen, his grand-children Caroline, Anna, and Sasha, and all those who knew him.

To the Instructor

About the Program and the Authors

Welcome to the tenth edition of ***Wie geht's?***, an introductory German program that has proven itself to be one of the leading German programs in the country! Thousands of students have learned German with ***Wie geht's?***, and it's no surprise why teachers adopt this program. Plainly put by its users: "IT WORKS!" The goal of ***Wie geht's?*** is simple: the program presents a well-integrated package of material that focuses on speaking, listening, reading, writing, and comprehension, combined with an introduction to life and culture in the German-speaking countries today. The approach is student-oriented, manageable, and up-to-date. Students will communicate in meaningful ways after only one year and also be provided with significant cultural insights.

Dieter Sevin (1938–2012), a native of Germany, was Professor of German and Chair of the Department of Germanic and Slavic Languages at Vanderbilt University. During his lifetime, he went back to Europe regularly to travel, do research, and take part in an exchange program with the University in Regensburg. He received grants from organizations, such as the American Philosophical Association, American Council of Learned Societies, German Academic Exchange Service, and the Vanderbilt Research Council. He authored several academic books on exile literature and East German literature, wrote numerous articles in professional journals, and was a frequent speaker at professional meetings.

Ingrid Sevin, a native of Germany, received her BA and MA from the University of Washington and has taught German and French at the high school and college level in the United States and in Germany. From 1987 to 2002, she was the editor of the German audio-magazine *Schau ins Land.* She also co-authored the German conversation text *Zur Diskussion* and *Stimmen der Zeit, An Audio-History of Germany in the 20th Century.*

Beatrix Brockman, a native of Germany, is Assistant Professor of Languages and Literature at Austin Peay State University in Clarksville, TN. She received her BA in Translations from the *Institut für Fremdsprachen und Auslandskunde* at the *Universität Erlangen-Nürnberg,* her BA and MA in English from Austin Peay State University in Clarksville, TN, and her PhD in German from Vanderbilt University in Nashville, TN. She travels to Germany on a regular basis to do research and keep in touch with the changes occurring in social, political, or cultural facets of Germany. Recently, she has published a book on the Poetics of East German poet Eva Strittmatter *("Nur fliegend fängt man Worte ein", Eva Strittmatters Poetik)* and, a poet herself, several collections of poetry.

General Course Objectives

Listening Students should be able to understand German spoken at a moderate conversational speed as long as the conversation deals with everyday occurrences. The lab program, the video program, the Student Activities Manual (SAM), and the summary of pronunciation in the main text all complement ***Wie geht's!*** in enhancing students' listening skills. The Text Audio Program has a recording of all listening comprehension sections *(Hörverständnis)* as well as the original pieces of literature presented in the book.

Speaking Students should be able to engage in simple conversations with other speakers of German. Each *Schritt* and *Kapitel* provides ample opportunity for oral practice in meaningful contexts.

Reading Students should be able to read nontechnical German of moderate difficulty. These skills are developed through the study of dialogues, various reading texts accompanied by a *Lesetipp* margin note, original pieces of literature, as well as exercises in the Student Activities Manual.

Writing Students should be able to write simple sentences correctly on the topics presented in the text. Written exercises extend and reinforce oral exercises. The textbook and the Student Activities Manual provide ample suggestions for writing dialogues and compositions on each chapter topic. The writing activity in the post-reading section of the chapter's reading passage, accompanied by a *Schreibtipp* margin note, offers important writing tips and an opportunity to apply them.

Highlights of the Program

The tenth edition has retained the following core features:

Schritte The purpose of these *Schritte* is to acquaint students with the German language and the language-learning process by focusing on listening and speaking ***before*** any grammar is officially introduced.

Vorschau This section previews the culture for each chapter and supplies the necessary background information.

Fokus These cultural notes are interspersed throughout each chapter. They point out or explain differences between life in North America and in the German-speaking countries.

Zum Thema This section contains:

- the dialogues that focus on the chapter theme and function as models for conversation.
- *Wortschatz 1,* a longer list of active topical vocabulary followed by a brief list of passive vocabulary *(Zum Erkennen),* and a variety of exercises and activities on the chapter theme *(Übungen zum Thema),* including practice on pronunciation *(Aussprache).*
- a short listening-comprehension section *(Hörverständnis).*

Struktur This section teaches the basics of German grammar. After the *Schritte* and then every 3 to 4 chapters, it is followed by a review *(Rückblick)* in the Student Activities Manual that sums up and practices points of structure. It is intended for reference and as preparation and review for quizzes and tests.

Einblicke This section is introduced by a second active vocabulary list *(Wortschatz 2)* and pre-reading activities *(Vor dem Lesen),* and is followed by post-reading activities *(Nach dem Lesen).* It always has an author-generated reading passage *(Lesetext)* that features one or more cultural aspects related to the chapter topic. It is usually accompanied by special instructions on reading German texts *(Lesetipps).*

Starting with Chapter 8, the main reading passage is followed by a short poem or story *(Literatur)* for students' enrichment and enjoyment. Each text is introduced by biographical data *(Biographisches)* and accompanied by pre- and post-reading activities.

Hörverständnis This exercise, at the end of the *Zum Thema* and *Lesetext* sections, should improve listening-comprehension skills. A supplementary listening-comprehension section *(Verstehen Sie?)* can be found in the corresponding chapter of the Student Activities Manual.

Note: A new final section, called *Rückschau*, provides a cumulative list of all the active vocabulary in the chapter, organized mainly by part of speech, followed by practice exercises that review the active vocabulary and the chapter's grammar points. See more information under *New to this Edition.*

Planning the Course

Wie geht's? is designed for a one-year college-level course. In planning the schedule, take into consideration the number of class hours available per week as well as student background and motivation. Those who have only three hours of instruction time per week, or who feel that some grammar topics are better left for the second year, may prefer to spread the work over three semesters.

In most situations, there will be enough time to complete the book, read the literature, watch the videos, do the virtual trip on the Märchenstraße, and use the Student Activities Manual materials. Remember, however, that the literature reading is no substitute for the reading texts and their accompanying *Wortschatz 2*. The video presentations are intended as an enrichment, some of which can be done on the students' own time.

It is important not to regard a schedule as unchangeable, but to remain flexible and respond to the special needs of a class. Overly strict adherence to a schedule can be detrimental to the success of the course. Below are scheduling suggestions for the quarter, two-semester, and three-semester system. Normally, 1½ days per *Schritt* and 1½ weeks per *Kapitel* should be appropriate.

The Quarter System

Week	1st Qtr.	Week	2nd Qtr.	Week	3rd Qtr.
1	S1–S5, R	1	6	1	11, R
2		2		2	
3	1 + 2	3	7, R	3	12
4		4		4	
5		5	Test, 8	5	13, Test
6	3, R, Test	6		6	
7		7	9	7	14
8	4 + 5	8		8	
9		9	10	9	15, R
10		10		10	
	Final		Final		Final

The Two-Semester System

Week	1st Semester	Week	2nd Semester
1	S1–S5, R	1	
2		2	8 + 9
3		3	
4	1 + 2	4	
5		5	10 + 11
6	3, R, Test	6	
7		7	R, Test
8		8	
9	4 + 5	9	12 + 13
10		10	
11		11	
12	6 + 7	12	14 + 15
13		13	
14	R	14	R
	Final		Final

The Three-Semester System

1st Semester		2nd Semester		3rd Semester	
Week	Chapter	Week	Chapter	Week	Chapter 1
1	S1-S3	1	6	1	12
2	S4-S5	2		2	
3	R, Test	3	7	3	
4	1	4		4	13
5		5	8	5	
6	2	6		6	
7		7	R, Test	7	Test
8	3	8	9	8	14
9		9		9	
10	R, Test	10	10	10	
11	4	11		11	15
12		12	11	12	
13	5	13		13	
14		14	R	14	R
	Final	15	Final	15	Final

* **NOTE:** With the three-semester system, use the *Rückblick* after Chapter 7 and include Chapter 8 as well.

New to this Edition

- All materials have been thoroughly updated and many new illustrations have been added.
- Five new literary pieces have been added: one poem by Tabea Vahlenkamp and four prose texts by Jutta Strzalka, Jörg Zschocke, Evelyne Weissenbach, and Gisela Reuter.
- An entirely new two-page review section *(Rückschau)* has been added containing the active chapter vocabulary, some grammar review activities, and a list of the online activities related to each chapter on iLrn. These resources include a memory game *(Gedächtnisspiel)*, a crossword puzzle *(Kreuzworträtsel)*, audio flash cards *(Vokabelblitz)*, a tutorial quiz *(Mini-Quiz)*, and the active vocabulary *(Wortschatz)* for the chapter.
- The video activities from the media spread in the ninth edition have been compiled and combined with the Video Interviews in the Student Activities Manual under the heading *Zum Sehen*. In the textbook, these video activities are referenced next to the second *Hörverständnis* of each chapter of the textbook.
- A new travel guide called *Eine Reise ins Märchenland* completes the new addition of ***Wie Geht's!*** It is an eight-page tour through the locales, scenery, and history of Grimms' fairy tales. Students are introduced to the *Deutsche Märchenstraße* and are tasked with planning a real or virtual trip along the life stations of the Brothers Grimm and through the regions of various German legends and fairy tales. This section reinforces and combines what students have learned about travel, finding lodging, ordering food, going to cultural events, and so on, in Germany.

Some Dos and Don'ts of Language Learning

- Make maximum use of German.
- Speak distinctly and accurately.
- Use words and constructions that are within the students' comprehension.
- Organize each class meeting into a variety of activities.
- Make it clear when one activity ends and another begins.
- Maintain a fairly lively pace, especially in choral responses.
- Be flexible, imaginative, and attentive. Take advantage of special situations and student interests.
- Be well prepared.
- Be honest.
- Encourage all students to participate actively.
- Praise good performances and originality. Positive feedback makes all the difference!
- Ignore minor mistakes if the answer is original. Repeat a correct version for the rest of the class.
- Be tactful in correcting mistakes; some students are very sensitive. Gently remind them that they are all in the same boat, that only "practice makes perfect" *(Es ist noch kein Meister vom Himmel gefallen)*. They are all there to learn and help one another learn.
- Address questions to the entire class before asking individual students. This will get everyone thinking.
- Stop an exercise when all students understand and know the material.
- Be clear and strict with assignments.
- Spot-check frequently.

- Don't constantly lapse into English.
- Don't speak too slowly, since students need to get used to German spoken at a normal conversational speed.
- Don't use German that is beyond their current level.
- Don't stretch any activity beyond students' attention span.
- Don't confuse students by suddenly asking them to do something else without clear instructions.
- Don't let one student hold up the class too long. Special discussions that don't benefit the entire class should be saved until after class.
- Don't give the impression that it is impossible to deviate from your plan and that there is no time for anything else.
- Don't be caught without things to do.
- Don't make mistakes by improvising. Sometimes students will have to wait a whole day for an answer; that's better than telling them something incorrect.
- Don't monopolize class time yourself.
- Don't take special efforts for granted.
- Don't discuss every little mistake. That only inhibits the students.
- Don't put students on the spot, unless they habitually don't pay attention.
- Don't bore students.
- Don't accept sloppy work.

Resources

Besides the textbook specific resources described in the previous pages, you may find sources of supplementary materials through the German Consulate in your area, the German Information Center, the various Offices of Tourism, and the International Film Bureau. You might check the extensive list of links on the ***Wie geht's?*** Companion Website.

AATG
American Assoc. of Teachers of German, Inc.
112 Haddontowne Court #104
Cherry Hill, N.J. 08034-3668
Tel.: 856-795-5553
e-mail: headquarters@aatg.org
Website: http://www.aatg.org

Presse- und Informationsamt der Bundesregierung
Dorotheenstr. 84
10117 Berlin
Tel.: (0)30 182720
e-mail: postmaster@bpa.bund.de
Website: http://www.bundesregierung.de

Deutsche Zentrale für Tourismus e.V.
Beethovenstr. 69
60325 Frankfurt am Main
Tel.: (0)69-974640-287
Website: http://www.germany-tourism.de

German National Tourist Office
122 East 42nd Street, Suite 2000
New York, NY 10168-0072
Tel.: (212) 661-7200
Website: www.germanyinnyc.org

Goethe-Institut
Kundenmanagement
Goethestr. 20
D-80336 München
e-mail: deutsch@goethe.de
Tel.: USA/CANADA: 1-8884Goethe
Website: http://www.goethe.de

Deutscher Akademischer Austauschdienst
Kennedyallee 50
53175 Bonn
Tel.: (0)228-882-0
e-mail: postmaster@daad.de
Website: http://www.daad.de

Script for the *Hörverständnis* Sections

Schritte

Das Klassenzimmer — p. 26

Das Klassenzimmer ist sehr groß. Es hat zwei Türen und fünf Fenster. Die Wände sind grau, die Türen sind braun und die Stühle sind rot. Die Tafel ist nicht schwarz; sie ist weiß. Der Professor heißt Oskar Thieme. Er hat drei Bleistifte. Sie sind blau, grün und rot. Er schreibt an die Tafel. Wir haben sieben Bilder von Deutschland. Sie sind sehr schön. Der Professor fragt und wir antworten. Wir lernen Deutsch. Bitte sprechen Sie laut und langsam, Professor Thieme! Wir verstehen Sie nicht.

Kapitel 1

A. Guten Morgen! — p. 36

PROFESSOR Guten Morgen! Ich bin Professor Hugo Schmidt.
STUDENTIN Guten Morgen, Herr Professor! Ich heiße Monika Müller.
PROFESSOR Ach ja, Frau Müller. Sie sind Studentin hier, nicht wahr? Wie geht's?
STUDENTIN Sehr gut, danke.
PROFESSOR Sie sprechen Spanisch, nicht?
STUDENTIN Ja. Ich spreche Deutsch, Englisch und Spanisch.
PROFESSOR Prima! Woher kommen Sie?
STUDENTIN Ich bin aus Venezuela. Mein Vater ist aus Deutschland und meine Mutter ist Amerikanerin.
PROFESSOR Und wie alt sind Sie?
STUDENTIN Ich bin 22.

PROFESSOR	Gut. Hören Sie! Ich brauche eine Assistentin: Montag, Mittwoch und Freitag von zwei Uhr bis sechs Uhr.
STUDENTIN	Oh, wunderbar! Ich brauche Arbeit.
PROFESSOR	Wie lange sind Sie denn hier?
STUDENTIN	Zwei Jahre.

B. Europäer in Deutschland p. 53

1. Guten Tag! Mein Name ist Vittorio. Ich bin 21 Jahre alt und Student hier in Kiel. Meine Eltern sind Italiener; sie sind aus Florenz. Meine Eltern wohnen schon 24 Jahre in Deutschland. Wir sprechen Deutsch, aber meine Großeltern und ich sprechen Italienisch. Ich studiere Physik. Wir finden es prima hier in Kiel, aber Italien ist auch sehr schön. In Italien ist es warm und die Sonne scheint.
2. Ich heiße Wlodzimierz. Meine Frau und ich sind aus Polen. Wir wohnen schon ein Jahr in Hamburg. Ich bin zuerst Hamburger, dann Europäer und dann Pole.
3. Mein Name ist Maria. Ich bin 20. Meine Familie wohnt schon 16 Jahre hier in Düsseldorf. Ich habe zwei Brüder. Meine Eltern sind aus Griechenland. Es ist komisch: In Griechenland sind wir Deutsche und in Deutschland sind wir Griechen.
4. Ich heiße José und komme aus Portugal. Ich bin schon 24 Jahre hier. Ich bin Professor hier in Bonn. Meine Frau ist Berlinerin. Wir haben drei Kinder. Die Kinder sprechen hier Deutsch, aber die Kinder und meine Eltern sprechen Portugiesisch. Wir finden es hier alle sehr schön.

Kapitel 2

A. Essen und Trinken p. 62

1. Tag! Ich heiße Hanjo Schulz. Was ich gern esse und trinke? Also, ich esse sehr gern Obst: Äpfel, Orangen, Bananen, Erdbeeren usw. Ich esse auch gern Fisch. Und was trinke ich gern? Ach, Cola oder Saft, manchmal auch ein Bier.
2. Guten Tag! Ich bin Martina Schneider. Ich esse gern Fleisch, Kartoffeln und Gemüse—und natürlich Kuchen: Käsekuchen, Erdbeerkuchen, Apfelkuchen. Ich trinke gern Tee, aber ich finde Kaffee furchtbar.
3. Mein Name ist Dirk Taeger. Was esse und trinke ich nicht gern? Ich esse nicht gern Gemüse—Karotten, Erbsen, Gurken. Und ich trinke nicht gern Milch oder Cola.

B. Neu in Regensburg p. 79

CLAUDIA	Guten Morgen! Bist du Ursula?
URSULA	Ja, und wie heißt du?
CLAUDIA	Ich bin Claudia.
URSULA	Freut mich.
CLAUDIA	Wie lange wohnst du schon hier in Regensburg?
URSULA	Schon zwei Jahre. Bist du neu hier?
CLAUDIA	Ja, ich bin aus Passau. Sag mal, wo gibt es hier billig Jeans und Sweatshirts?
URSULA	Ich gehe heute Nachmittag einkaufen. Ich brauche auch Jeans und einen Rock. Gehen wir zusammen?
CLAUDIA	Ach, gern. Wann gehst du?
URSULA	So um drei. Und danach gehen wir in ein Café und essen ein Stück Kuchen.
CLAUDIA	Prima! Bis später dann!

Kapitel 3

A. Im Gasthaus p. 88

Jürgen, Helga und Michael, drei Studenten, sind zum Abendessen im Restaurant. Sie essen hier gern, denn das Essen ist sehr gut und nicht teuer. Sie kommen früh und finden einen Tisch. Eine Kellnerin bringt die Speisekarten. Jürgen bestellt eine Cola, Helga Apfelsaft und Michael Mineralwasser. Die Kellnerin bringt die Getränke und fragt, was sie essen möchten. Helga bestellt Schnitzel mit Pommes frites, Jürgen Pizza und Michael Würstchen mit Sauerkraut. Zehn Minuten später bringt die Kellnerin das Essen. Die Studenten haben wirklich Hunger und alles schmeckt prima. Zum Nachtisch bestellt Michael Vanilleeis. Jürgen möchte Schokoladenpudding und Helga Käsekuchen. Die Kellnerin kommt wieder und Jürgen sagt: „Wir möchten zahlen bitte!" Die Kellnerin schreibt die Rechnung: eine Cola 1,75 €, ein Apfelsaft 1,50 €, ein Mineralwasser 1,20 €, einmal Schnitzel 7,50 €, Pizza 5 €,–, Würstchen 6,25 €, ein Eis 2,50 €, Schokoladenpudding 1,40 € und Käsekuchen 2,00 €. Die Kellnerin sagt: „Das macht zusammen 29,92 €." Ist das richtig?

B. Gäste zum Wochenende

p. 105

KAI Du, wann kommen Ruth und Uwe?
SANDRA Am Samstag um vier.
KAI Also zum Kaffee sind sie schon hier. Kaufen wir Kuchen oder machst du etwas?
SANDRA Ich glaube, ich mache einen Erdbeerkuchen. Der schmeckt Ruth so gut.
KAI Prima! Haben wir Kaffee?
SANDRA Oh ja!—Zum Abendessen gibt's Käsefondue, Weißbrot und Wein.
KAI Zum Frühstück machen wir Eier. Wir haben genug Wurst, Käse und Marmelade.
SANDRA Richtig. Aber wir brauchen Schwarzbrot und Joghurt. Uwe isst gern Joghurt.
KAI Und was gibt's zum Mittagessen?
SANDRA Vielleicht Fisch?
KAI Mit Kartoffeln, Salat und Bohnen?
SANDRA Warum nicht? Zum Nachtisch gibt's Eis, oder machen wir Obstsalat?
KAI Obstsalat. Ich kaufe Orangen, Äpfel und Bananen.
SANDRA Ich glaube, wir brauchen auch Mineralwasser.
KAI Richtig. Wann gehen wir einkaufen?
SANDRA Morgen früh. Fährst du zum Supermarkt? Ich gehe zum Markt und kaufe Eier, Obst, Gemüse und Blumen.
KAI Gut.

Kapitel 4

A. Die Geburtstagsparty

p. 117

ANKE Hallo, hier Anke Müller.
PAUL Tag, Anke! Hier Paul.
ANKE Tag, Paul! Wie geht's denn?
PAUL Gut, danke. Du, am zehnten Oktober hat Claire Geburtstag und Peter am zwölften. Geben wir eine Party?
ANKE Ja, gute Idee! Aber wann?
PAUL Am Wochenende? Samstag ist der 9.
ANKE Ich glaube, Claire arbeitet samstags bis um drei. Aber Samstagabend geht's sicher. Wir haben ja noch zwei Wochen Zeit.
PAUL Richtig. Und wo geben wir die Party?
ANKE Bei mir, mein Zimmer ist schön groß.
PAUL Super! Ich bringe meine CDs und etwas zu essen und Klaus bringt etwas zu trinken.
ANKE Toll! Und ich telefoniere mit Peter und Claire.
PAUL Um wie viel Uhr beginnen wir mit der Party?
ANKE Vielleicht um acht, oder ist das zu spät?
PAUL Nein, das ist gut. Also am neunten um 8 Uhr.
ANKE Schön. Mach's gut!
PAUL Du auch. Tschüss! Bis später!

B. Das Straßenfest

p. 135

MATTHIAS Tag, Bibi! Was gibt's?
BIBI Eigentlich nichts Besonderes. Warum?
MATTHIAS Ich bin am Samstag bei euch gewesen, aber niemand hat die Tür geöffnet.
BIBI Wir haben Straßenfest gehabt und da haben wir etwas geholfen.
MATTHIAS Ach so.
BIBI Vater hat mit den Tischen und Stühlen geholfen und Mutter hat Würstchen und Cola verkauft.
MATTHIAS Was haben sie noch verkauft?
BIBI Ach, Bücher, Bilder, Kleidung und Krimskrams.
MATTHIAS Und du, was hast du getan?
BIBI Ich habe mit den Kindern Spiele gespielt.
MATTHIAS Hat's Spaß gemacht?
BIBI Ja, das ist eigentlich immer sehr schön. Alle Nachbarn sind da gewesen, Jung und Alt. Und abends haben wir dann noch ein bisschen getanzt.
MATTHIAS Toll! Du, ich habe nicht viel Zeit. Mach's gut!
BIBI Ich auch nicht. Tschüss, Matthias!

Kapitel 5

A. Touristen in Innsbruck

p. 143

TOURIST Entschuldigung! Können Sie uns sagen, wo das Goldene Dachl ist?
INNSBRUCKERIN Ja, natürlich. Möchten Sie mit dem Bus fahren oder zu Fuß gehen?
TOURIST Ist es weit?
INNSBRUCKERIN Nein, nein. Sie können leicht zu Fuß gehen. Sehen Sie die Brücke da drüben? Dort beginnt die Fußgängerzone. Gehen Sie immer geradeaus und dann ist links das Dachl.
TOURIST Können Sie uns auch sagen, wo der Dom ist? Da ist später ein Konzert. Das möchten wir hören.
INNSBRUCKERIN Der Dom ist ganz in der Nähe vom Dachl. Fragen Sie dort noch einmal! Wann beginnt denn das Konzert?
TOURIST Um fünf.
INNSBRUCKERIN Oh, da haben Sie noch viel Zeit. Es ist ja erst halb vier.
TOURIST Hm, was machen wir bis fünf?
TOURIST Wo können wir eine Tasse Kaffee und ein Stück Kuchen bekommen?
INNSBRUCKERIN In der Nähe vom Dachl ist ein Café.
TOURIST Und dann können wir noch etwas die Maria-Theresia-Straße entlanglaufen.
INNSBRUCKERIN Ja, von dort sehen Sie die Berge wunderbar. Aber gehen Sie nicht zu spät zum Dom! Da sind heute sicher furchtbar viele Leute.
TOURIST Vielen Dank für die Information!
TOURIST Ja, danke!
INNSBRUCKERIN Bitte, bitte. Viel Spaß!

B. Schon lange nicht mehr gesehen!

p. 163

UWE Tag, Erika!
ERIKA Tag, Uwe! Ich habe dich ja schon lange nicht mehr gesehen. Wo bist du denn immer?
UWE Jürgen und ich sind eine Woche in Österreich gewesen.
ERIKA In Österreich? Super! Wie ist es denn gewesen?
UWE Einfach wunderbar! Mit dem Wetter haben wir auch Glück gehabt. Es hat nur einmal geregnet.
ERIKA Wo seid ihr denn gewesen?
UWE Wir sind nach Maria Alm gefahren. Von dort haben wir ein paar tolle Bergwanderungen gemacht.
ERIKA Maria Alm? Wo ist denn das?
UWE In der Nähe von Salzburg.
ERIKA Prima! Was habt ihr denn noch gemacht?
UWE Wir sind natürlich auch in Salzburg gewesen.
ERIKA Salzburg finde ich wunderschön. Habt ihr die Burg besichtigt?
UWE Natürlich. Wir haben den Dom besichtigt und sind zu Fuß zur Burg gelaufen. Von dort kann man Salzburg ganz toll sehen.
ERIKA Ja, ich weiß. Seid ihr auch in Wien gewesen?
UWE Nein, wir wollen im Oktober nach Wien, wenn meine Eltern kommen.
ERIKA Ja, Wien musst du wirklich sehen. Du, mach's gut! Ich muss in meine Vorlesung. Sie beginnt in fünf Minuten.
UWE Tschüss, Erika! Bis später!

Kapitel 6

A. Hier Müller!

p. 172

FRAU MÜLLER Hier Müller!
INGE Hallo, Mutti!
FRAU MÜLLER Tag, Inge! Wie geht's?
INGE Oh, mir geht's gut. Ich will dir nur sagen, dass ich ein Zimmer gefunden habe.
FRAU MÜLLER Das ist ja prima. Wo denn?
INGE In der Schillerstraße, Schillerstraße 23. Die Telefonnummer ist 68 91.
FRAU MÜLLER Und wie hast du das Zimmer gefunden?
INGE Du weißt ja, wie lange ich schon gesucht habe. Aber die Wohnungen sind viel zu teuer. Vor ein paar Tagen habe ich Horst in einer Vorlesung gesehen und er hat mir gesagt, dass in seiner Wohngemeinschaft ein Platz frei geworden ist.
FRAU MÜLLER In einer Wohngemeinschaft?
INGE Ja. Er und ein paar Freunde haben ein Haus gemietet. Jens, Gisela und Renate sind auch Studenten. Sie sind wirklich nett. Wir haben vier Schlafzimmer. Ein Zimmer ist sehr groß und Gisela und ich teilen es.

Frau Müller	Was bezahlst du denn?
Inge	Weil wir ein Zimmer teilen, bezahle ich nur € 175,– im Monat.
Frau Müller	Ist es weit zur Uni?
Inge	Nein, nein. Wir gehen zu Fuß oder fahren mit dem Fahrrad.
Frau Müller	Na gut. Das freut mich sehr. Wann kommst du mal nach Hause?
Inge	Ich weiß noch nicht, in zwei oder drei Wochen.
Frau Müller	Prima! Tschüss dann!
Inge	Tschüss, Mutti! Bis bald!

B. Die Großeltern kommen. p. 191

Kinder, ich muss heute bis um sechs arbeiten und kann nicht einkaufen oder kochen. Ihr wisst, dass die Großeltern heute Abend kommen. Ihr müsst mir helfen.

Sebastian, fahr bitte zum Supermarkt und kauf zwei Pfund Bratwurst und etwas Käse zum Abendessen! Nimm € 20,–! Geld ist im Schreibtisch. Bring die Mineralwasserflaschen zum Supermarkt! Stell auch zwei Flaschen Wein in den Kühlschrank!

Mareike, bitte mach einen Schokoladenpudding zum Nachtisch und koch Kartoffeln für den Kartoffelsalat!

Julia, fahr mit dem Fahrrad zum Blumengeschäft und kauf ein paar Blumen! Stell sie auf den Tisch im Esszimmer! Wenn die Großeltern kommen, zeig ihnen, wo sie schlafen, und häng ihre Kleidung in den Schrank!

Sagt Vati, dass ich um halb sieben nach Hause komme. Spielt das Radio bitte nicht zu laut! Und esst den Apfelkuchen nicht—er ist nämlich für morgen! Also tschüss, bis bald!

Kapitel 7

A. Eine Busfahrt p. 201

Professor	So, passen Sie auf! Wir wollen am Montag um 7 Uhr abfahren. Montag bis Mittwoch sind wir in der Schweiz und Donnerstag bis Samstag in Österreich. Haben Sie Fragen?
Student 1	Ja. Wo kann man hier Geld umtauschen?
Professor	Am besten an einem Geldautomaten. Da stecken Sie Ihre Karte rein und bekommen das Geld in der Währung des Landes, wo Sie sind.
Student 1	Das geht aber auch mit Kreditkarten, oder?
Professor	Ja, aber das kostet etwas mehr.
Student 2	Wie viel Geld sollen wir umtauschen?
Professor	Nicht viel. Die Reise ist inklusive Übernachtungen, Mahlzeiten und Eintrittskarten.
Student 3	Wir brauchen also Bargeld nur, wenn wir etwas kaufen wollen?
Professor	Ja, für Getränke, Eis, Postkarten oder Briefmarken zum Beispiel. Viele Geschäfte nehmen natürlich auch Ihre Kreditkarte. Vergessen Sie nicht etwas Kleingeld für Toiletten!
Student 1	Alles klar! Bis bald!
Student 2	Bis Montag!

B. Hotel Lindenhof p. 217

Rezeption	Hier Hotel Lindenhof.
Baumann	Guten Morgen! Hier Baumann. Meine Familie und ich kommen im Sommer an den Bodensee und wir suchen ein Hotel.
Rezeption	Von wann bis wann?
Baumann	Wir wollen am 10. Juli ankommen und eine Woche bleiben.
Rezeption	Und für wie viele Personen brauchen Sie Zimmer?
Baumann	Für vier. Wir möchten ein Doppelzimmer für meine Frau und mich, und eins für unsere Töchter.
Rezeption	Einen Moment! Lassen Sie mich bitte sehen, ob wir dann noch etwas frei haben!
Baumann	Danke! . . .
Rezeption	Hallo, Herr Baumann!
Baumann	Ja.
Rezeption	Sie haben Glück. Wir haben noch zwei Doppelzimmer für die sieben Tage im Juli, beide mit Bad.
Baumann	Die Kinder können doch bei Ihnen schwimmen?
Rezeption	Aber natürlich. Wir haben ein Schwimmbad. Ganz in der Nähe kann man auch Minigolf und Tennis spielen und zum See ist's auch nicht weit.
Baumann	Das klingt gut. Sagen Sie, wo liegen die Zimmer?
Rezeption	Im 2. Stock. Vom Balkon haben sie einen Blick auf den See und die Alpen. Wir sind sehr ruhig gelegen.
Baumann	Haben sie ein Restaurant?

Rezeption Ja, wir haben ein Restaurant im Haus.
Baumann Sehr schön.
Rezeption Darf ich die Zimmer dann reservieren?
Baumann Ja, bitte.

Kapitel 8

A. Mit dem Glacier Express durch die Schweizer Alpen

p. 228

Bill Na, Claudia, habt ihr Spaß gehabt?
Claudia Und ob! In der Schweiz gibt's so viel zu sehen, aber die Reise durch die Alpen vergesse ich nie.
Bill Echt? Erzähl mal!
Claudia Am Montag sind wir mit dem Glacier Express von St. Moritz nach Andermatt gefahren, ein Dorf mit malerischen Häusern und Gassen. Dienstagvormittag sind wir auf der Sonnenseite des Tales etwas gewandert und nachmittags dann weitergefahren nach Zermatt.
Bill Und dann?
Claudia Die Panoramafahrt durch die Alpen im Herzen der Schweiz ist wunderschön. Es geht über Berge und Brücken, durch Tunnel, Täler, Wälder und Weiden.
Bill Und wie lange dauert so eine Fahrt?
Claudia Ungefähr sieben Stunden, aber das macht nichts, denn die Sitze sind sehr bequem. Man hat uns das Mittagessen sogar direkt am Platz serviert.
Bill Nicht schlecht! Ich bin sicher, dass das auch ein bisschen was gekostet hat.
Claudia Das stimmt.
Bill Habt ihr die Plätze reservieren müssen?
Claudia Ja, schon drei Monate vorher.
Bill Und was gibt's in Zermatt zu sehen?
Claudia Da kann man mit einer Zahnradbahn auf den Gornergrat fahren. Der Blick von dort auf das Matterhorn ist unglaublich.
Bill Hast du viel fotografiert?
Claudia Na klar!

B. Im Reisebüro

p. 246

Ulrike Guten Morgen!
Dame Guten Morgen! Was kann ich für Sie tun?
Ulrike Meine Freundin und ich möchten im März ein paar Tage zum Skilaufen in die Schweiz fahren.
Dame Wissen Sie schon, wohin?
Ulrike Ja, ins Berner Oberland oder in die Gegend von Interlaken.
Dame Und wann möchten Sie reisen?
Ulrike Vom 8. bis zum 15. März.
Dame Schön. Lassen Sie mich mal sehen! . . . Ja, hier ist etwas: eine Woche in Grindelwald im Hotel Alpina, inklusive Frühstück, pro Person 900 Franken. Oder . . . Hotel Alpenrose in Wengen, 1 170 Franken die Woche, inklusive Halbpension, Skipass, Benützung der Eisbahn und des Solebads.
Ulrike Hotel Alpenrose in Wengen klingt gut.
Dame Brauchen Sie auch Zugfahrkarten?
Ulrike Ja, bitte.
Dame Einen Moment . . . Sie fahren von hier über Zürich nach Bern; in Bern müssen Sie in den Zug nach Interlaken umsteigen. Abfahrt von hier um 8.25 Uhr, Abfahrt von Zürich um 10.30 Uhr, Ankunft in Bern um 11.10 Uhr und in Interlaken um 12.16 Uhr. Der Bus nach Wengen fährt um 12.30 Uhr ab und ist um ein Uhr dort.
Ulrike Ja, das ist gut. Und wie ist es mit der Rückfahrt?
Dame Am 15. März um 14.00 Uhr; Ankunft hier um 18.44 Uhr.
Ulrike Gut.
Dame Soll ich Zugplätze reservieren?
Ulrike Ja, bitte.
Dame Okay, ich reserviere dann also das Hotel Alpenrose in Wengen und Fahrkarten für zwei Personen. Soll ich Ihnen die Karten mit der Post schicken oder wollen Sie sie abholen?
Ulrike Ich komme nächste Woche wieder hier vorbei.
Dame Gut. Vielen Dank! Auf Wiedersehen!
Ulrike Auf Wiedersehen!

Kapitel 9

A. Beim Arzt p. 257

ARZT Guten Morgen, Frau Heller!
KIM Guten Morgen, Herr Doktor!
ARZT Was bringt Sie zu mir?
KIM Mein rechtes Knie tut mir so weh.
ARZT Lassen Sie mich mal sehen. Na, das Knie ist ganz schön dick. Wie ist denn das passiert?
KIM Ich bin mit meiner Freundin zum Skilaufen im Harz gewesen. Alles war wunderschön, aber am letzten Tag bin ich gefallen und nun tut mir das ganze Bein weh. Mein Ellbogen ist auch ganz blau.
ARZT Das tut mir leid. Ich glaube Ihnen gern, dass das wehtut. Sie dürfen ein paar Tage nicht laufen. Legen Sie das Bein hoch! Wenn Sie wollen, können Sie auch Eis auf Ihr Knie tun—aber nicht zu lange, nur zwanzig Minuten. Zeigen Sie mir auch mal Ihren Ellbogen! . . . Ja, der ist wirklich blau. Tut das weh?
KIM Au! Ja, das tut sehr weh. Können Sie mir Schmerztabletten geben?
ARZT Ja, ich gebe Ihnen ein paar Tabletten mit.
KIM Ich kann doch wieder Skilaufen gehen?
ARZT Natürlich, aber nicht vorm Herbst. Aber Sie können bald wieder schwimmen oder spazieren gehen.
KIM Na gut.
ARZT Wenn Ihnen das Bein in einer Woche immer noch wehtut, kommen Sie bitte wieder!
KIM Mach' ich. Vielen Dank! Auf Wiedersehen!
ARZT Auf Wiedersehen!

B. Eine tolle Radtour p. 275

Ich sitze jeden Tag lange genug im Büro. Da habe ich während der Ferien keine Lust, auch noch stundenlang im Auto zu sitzen. Da muss ich einfach etwas ganz anderes tun. Im Frühling habe ich mit ein paar Freunden eine fantastische Radtour gemacht. Wir sind mit der Bahn nach Romanshorn am Bodensee gefahren, wo wir unsere Mietfahrräder abgeholt haben. Wir sind auf Fahrradwegen am See entlang nach Rorschach gefahren und dann mit der Zahnradbahn bis nach Heiden im Appenzeller Land. Ein tolles Panorama! In Heiden haben wir auch übernachtet. Am zweiten Tag hat uns eine schnelle Talfahrt durch Weindörfer zurück an den See gebracht und dann sind wir durchs Rheindelta über Bregenz bis Lindau gefahren. Dort sind wir gemütlich durch die Straßen gebummelt und haben abends in einem kleinen Restaurant schön gegessen. Am dritten Tag sind wir bis nach Friedrichshafen gekommen, wo uns eine Fähre dann zurück nach Romanshorn gebracht hat. In drei Tagen durch drei Länder, und das alles für nur 322 Franken. Nicht schlecht, was? Nur das Mittagessen hat extra gekostet. Meistens haben wir gepicknickt. So eine Radtour macht wirklich Spaß und man hält sich fit.

Kapitel 10

A. *Biedermann und die Brandstifter* p. 287

FRAU WEISS Hier Weiß.
CHRISTIAN Guten Tag, Frau Weiß! Hier ist Christian Kolb. Kann ich mal eben mit Daniel sprechen?
FRAU WEISS Natürlich. Einen Moment, bitte!
DANIEL Christian? Was gibt's?
CHRISTIAN Hör zu! Mein Cousin hat mir gerade zwei Theaterkarten für heute Abend gegeben. Hast du Lust mitzukommen?
DANIEL Was steht denn auf dem Programm?
CHRISTIAN Max Frisch, *Biedermann und die Brandstifter.* Die Inszenierung soll ausgezeichnet sein. Die Plätze sind auch gut, dritte Reihe im Parkett.
DANIEL Na klar, das sehen wir uns an. Wer sind die Schauspieler?
CHRISTIAN Ulrich Hoening und Dirk Meinhart spielen die Hauptrollen.
DANIEL Toll! Wann fängt die Vorstellung an?
CHRISTIAN Um 20.30 Uhr.
DANIEL Jetzt ist es schon halb sieben. Du, Christian, ich muss mich noch rasieren und duschen; und essen möchte ich auch was.
CHRISTIAN Wenn du dich beeilst, können wir schnell zusammen was essen.
DANIEL Wo wollen wir uns treffen?
CHRISTIAN Beim U-Bahnausgang in der Breslauer Straße.
DANIEL Gut. Ich bin um Viertel nach sieben dort. Vielen Dank für die Einladung!
CHRISTIAN Bitte, bitte. Bis gleich! Tschüss!

B. Pläne für den Abend

p. 303

STEFAN Na, Kinder, was machen wir heute Abend?
MONIKA Habt ihr Lust, ins Theater zu gehen?
FELIX Woran denkst du denn?
MONIKA Die Komödie *Jahre später, gleiche Zeit*, von Bernhard Slate, soll ganz gut sein.
STEFAN Das habe ich auch gehört.
FELIX Ja, die möchte ich schon lange mal sehen.
STEFAN Ich auch.
MONIKA Soll ich mal schnell anrufen und fragen, ob es noch Karten für heute Abend gibt?
FELIX Ja, tu das!
MONIKA (*Sound of the telephone dialing*) . . . Hallo? Sagen Sie, hätten Sie noch Karten für heute Abend? . . . Gar nichts mehr? . . . Vielen Dank! . . . Schade, alles ausverkauft!
STEFAN Wie wär's mit einem Kabarett?
FELIX Klingt gut. Hier sind zwei Anzeigen. Gehen wir zur DISTEL oder zum KARTOON?
STEFAN Beim KARTOON gibt es eine Kneipe. Da können wir dann auch gleich essen.
MONIKA Wann beginnt denn die Vorstellung?
FELIX Um 21 Uhr.
STEFAN Ich rufe mal an. Vielleicht können wir einen Tisch bestellen. Wann wollen wir denn essen?
MONIKA Um halb acht?
FELIX Schön. Wisst ihr, wie wir dorthin kommen?
MONIKA Keine Ahnung!
STEFAN Ich kann ja gleich mal fragen, wenn ich anrufe.
FELIX Gut.

Kapitel 11

A. Leute sind verschieden.

p. 315

1. Martin kenne ich schon lange. Wir sind zusammen in die Schule gegangen. In der Schule war er faul und hat seine Hausaufgaben oft nicht gemacht. Im Sport war er eine Katastrophe. Er konnte weder laufen noch Ball spielen; er konnte nicht einmal Rad fahren. Aber er hat schon immer toll Klavier gespielt. Jetzt komponiert er Musik für Fernsehfilme und ist damit reich und erfolgreich geworden.
2. Oliver ist mein Cousin, ein netter Mann, blond, groß und schlank. Er studiert Medizin in Tübingen. Das Studium findet er nicht schwer. Schon in der Schule war er immer sehr gut. Er sagt nicht viel, wenn er mit seinen Freunden zusammen ist. Er hat aber viele Freunde und Freundinnen.
3. Sabine ist eine gute Freundin. Ich finde sie prima. Sie studiert Psychologie in Hamburg. Im Winter besucht sie mich und wir gehen zusammen Skilaufen. Sie treibt viel Sport: Sabine schwimmt fast jeden Tag und spielt viel Tennis. Wir verstehen uns sehr gut—was mir natürlich wichtig ist. Sie kann gut zuhören, wenn man ihr etwas erzählt. Sie zieht sich schick an und lacht viel.

B. Vier berühmte Märchen

p. 333

MÄRCHEN 1: Sie gingen durch den Wald, bis sie ein kleines Häuschen fanden. Das Häuschen war aus Kuchen und Brot und die Fenster aus Zucker. Da brachen sie ein Stück Kuchen ab und fingen an zu essen.

MÄRCHEN 2: Da musste nun das Mädchen von morgens bis abends schwer arbeiten, früh aufstehen, Wasser tragen, Feuer machen, kochen und waschen. Die Schwestern lachten nur über sie und schütteten ihr Erbsen und Linsen in die Asche. Die musste sie dann wieder auslesen. Abends, wenn sie müde war, hatte sie kein Bett, sondern musste sich in die Asche legen und war darum immer schmutzig.

MÄRCHEN 3: Es geschah, dass an dem Tag, als das Mädchen 15 Jahre alt wurde, der König und die Königin nicht zu Hause waren. Da wanderte das Mädchen im Schloss herum, sah in alle Kammern und kam dann auch zu einem alten Turm. Sie ging die Treppe hinauf, kam zu einer kleinen Tür und machte sie auf. Da saß eine alte Frau an einem Spinnrad. „Guten Tag, du altes Mütterchen", sagte die Königstochter. „Was machst du da?" „Ich spinne", sagte die Alte. „Was ist das?" sprach das Mädchen und nahm die Spindel und wollte auch spinnen. Kaum aber hatte sie die Spindel in der Hand, so erfüllte sich der Zauberspruch. Das Mädchen stach sich in den Finger, fiel auf ein Bett und schlief sofort ein.

MÄRCHEN 4: Das Mädchen lief durch den Wald, solange die Füße es tragen wollten, bis es fast Abend war. Da sah es ein kleines Häuschen und ging hinein, um sich auszuruhen. In dem Häuschen war alles klein, aber sehr schön und sauber. Da stand ein Tischchen mit sieben kleinen Tellern, jedes Tellerchen mit seinem Löffelchen, sieben Messerchen, Gäbelchen und sieben Gläschen. An der Wand standen sieben Bettchen. Das Mädchen war so hungrig und durstig. Also aß es von jedem Tellerchen ein bisschen und trank aus jedem Gläschen ein bisschen Wein. Danach, weil sie so müde war, wollte sie sich hinlegen, aber kein Bettchen war lang genug. So legte sie sich quer über alle Betten und schlief ein.

Kapitel 12

A. Was bin ich? p. 344

1. Ich bin Mädchen für alles: Putzfrau, Köchin, Lehrerin, Beraterin, Sekretärin und Chauffeur. Meine Arbeit hat kein Ende, sie fängt immer wieder neu an. Dabei verdiene ich nichts, nur ab und zu ein Dankeschön. Was bin ich?
2. In meinem Beruf habe ich mit vielen jungen Menschen zu tun. Viele meinen, dass mein Beruf leicht ist, weil ich so viele Ferien habe. Aber mein Beruf ist manchmal sehr anstrengend. Meine Arbeit geht zu Hause weiter, weil ich viel lesen und korrigieren muss. Was bin ich?
3. Ich bin viel unterwegs. Wenn es eine Katastrophe oder etwas Besonderes gibt, bin ich da. Ich spreche mit Politikern, Wissenschaftlern, Rechtsanwälten, Polizisten, Menschen aus allen Berufen, mit den Leuten auf der Straße. Ich hoffe, dass Sie dann meine Artikel in der Zeitung lesen. Was bin ich?
4. Viele Leute kommen zu mir nur, wenn ihnen etwas wehtut. Meistens kommen sie nicht gern, weil sie denken, dass ich ihnen noch mehr wehtue. Aber da haben sie unrecht. Sie kommen mit Schmerzen, setzen sich in meinen gemütlichen Stuhl, öffnen ihren Mund und bald sind die Schmerzen weg. Was bin ich?

B. Zwei Lebensläufe p. 361

1. LEBENSLAUF: Ich heiße Wolf Wicke und bin am 23. November 1995 in Bremen als jüngstes Kind von Norbert und Ursula Wicke geboren. Mein Vater ist Vorarbeiter bei der Firma Eggebrecht; meine Mutter ist Lebensmittelverkäuferin. Meine Eltern sind geschieden. Ich lebe bei meiner Mutter und habe zwei ältere Schwestern. Vom September 2001 bis Juli 2005 habe ich die Grundschule besucht. Danach ging ich bis Juli 2010 zur Hauptschule. Seit 1. September 2010 mache ich eine Lehre als Automechaniker bei VW. Außerdem gehe ich zweimal die Woche zur Berufsschule. Danach gehe ich zum Militär. In meiner Freizeit spiele ich gern Fußball.
2. LEBENSLAUF: Mein Name ist Kristina Bayer. Ich bin am 31. Januar 1991 als zweites Kind von Richard und Susanne Bayer in Bayreuth geboren. Mein Vater war Journalist; er ist 1996 bei einem Autounfall gestorben. Meine Mutter ist Architektin. Ich habe einen fünf Jahre älteren Bruder. Nach vier Jahren Grundschule besuchte ich das Gymnasium in Bayreuth. Im Juni 2010 habe ich mein Abitur gemacht, mit der Note „sehr gut". Seit Oktober 2010 studiere ich Medizin an der Universität Heidelberg. In meiner Freizeit höre ich gern Musik. Außerdem spiele ich Tennis und Golf.

Kapitel 13

A. Ein guter Start p. 371

Der MBA, kurz für Master of Business Administration, ist nicht nur ein Privileg amerikanischer Universitäten. Man kann ihn auch in Deutschland—zum Beispiel am Europa-Institut in Saarbrücken, an der Fachhochschule in Berlin oder an der privaten Wissenschaftlichen Hochschule in Koblenz—bekommen. Die Studenten kommen nicht nur aus Deutschland, sondern aus anderen europäischen Nachbarländern, aus Asien und den USA. Die 26-jährige Terry Furman hat in Deutschland ihr Abitur gemacht und dann in England Jura studiert. Jetzt möchte sie ihre wirtschaftswissenschaftlichen Kenntnisse verbessern. Der 24-jährige Franzose Dominique Laurent hofft, mit dem MBA bessere Berufschancen als Ingenieur zu haben.

An der Fachhochschule für Wirtschaft in Berlin können Vollzeitstudenten das 1. Semester in Spanien, Finnland, Frankreich oder Berlin studieren. Im 2. Semester nehmen sie dann MBA-Vorlesungen an der South Bank University in London. Danach beginnt das „Company Project", ein Praktikum mit Abschlussarbeit. Billig ist so ein MBA natürlich nicht. Trotzdem ist der Titel populär, denn er verspricht einen guten Start für eine internationale Karriere.

B. Zwei Briefe p. 389

1. **An das Reisebüro Eckhardt in Würzburg**
   Sehr geehrter Herr Eckhardt, in Ihrem Stellenangebot suchen Sie eine Reiseleiterin mit Auslandserfahrung, Fremdsprachenkenntnissen und Organisationstalent. Diese Wünsche kann ich erfüllen. Ich habe einen guten Mittelschulabschluss, drei Jahre Auslandserfahrung—ein Jahr in den USA, ein Jahr in Frankreich und ein Jahr in Italien. Meine Muttersprache ist Deutsch, aber ich spreche auch Englisch, Französisch und Italienisch. Mein Mann ist Italiener. Ich kann gut selbstständig arbeiten, habe Computerkenntnisse und arbeite sehr gern mit Menschen. Seit drei Jahren arbeite ich beim ADAC in Wiesbaden. Meinen Lebenslauf habe ich dem Brief beigelegt. Dürfte ich mich bei Ihnen vorstellen? Mit freundlichem Gruß, Dagmar Schröder.

2. **An die Carl-Duisberg Gesellschaft in Köln**
Sehr geehrte Damen und Herren, nach meinem Studium in Betriebswirtschaft und Deutsch an der University of California in Santa Barbara würde ich gern ein Praktikum in Deutschland absolvieren. Von Freunden habe ich gehört, dass es möglich ist, bei Ihnen Geschäftsdeutsch zu belegen und dass Sie danach auch Praktika in Deutschland vermitteln. Ich wäre Ihnen sehr dankbar, wenn Sie mir weitere Informationen und Formulare dazu schicken könnten. Mit freundlichen Grüßen, Joe Jackson.

Kapitel 14

A. Mit dem Fahrrad durch Berlin p. 399

Es gibt viele Möglichkeiten, Berlin kennen zu lernen. Man könnte mit dem Auto oder mit einem Taxi durch die Stadt fahren. Eine Stadtrundfahrt mit einem der vielen Tourbusse dürfte auch recht informativ sein. Viele dieser Busse sind Doppeldeckerbusse, wo man von oben einen guten Blick hat und schöne Fotos machen kann. An den verschiedenen Haltepunkten kann man aussteigen, die Fahrt unterbrechen, um sich alles in Ruhe anzuschauen, und dann wieder einsteigen. Eine Bootsfahrt auf der Spree gäbe noch eine ganz andere Perspektive. Das alles ist interessant und vielleicht für das erste Mal keine schlechte Idee, aber besser gefallen würde mir ein Stadtbummel zu Fuß und mit der U-Bahn. Da wäre man völlig unabhängig und hätte man Zeit, sich auch mal ins Café zu setzen oder in ein Museum zu gehen. Wenn Sie aber einmal was ganz anderes erleben möchten, dann sollten Sie an einer Radtour teilnehmen. Das hab' ich getan, als ich das letzte Mal in Berlin war. Mit dem Fahrrad unterwegs und einem guten Stadtführer dabei bekommt man doch ein ganz anderes Bild der Stadt. Die Tour dauerte ungefähr vier Stunden. Also mir hat das unheimlich Spaß gemacht. Was mich das nächste Mal interessieren würde ist die Afternoon-Clubtour, wo ein DJ die Clubkultur der Hauptstadt präsentiert, oder die Nightseeing-Tour. Wenn es Nacht wird, hat Berlin eine ganz besondere Atmosphäre und man erlebt den Zauber einer Stadt, die nie schläft.

B. Realität und Hoffnung p. 447

Nachdem die Mauer gefallen war, meinte Bundeskanzler Helmut Kohl, dass aus den neuen Bundesländern „blühende Landschaften" würden. Das geschah und geschah auch nicht.

Seit der Wiedervereinigung hat sich dort viel verändert. Diese Länder haben heute eine moderne Infrastruktur und viele Städte sind wieder wunderschön restauriert. Der Tourismus blüht: von den Ferienorten an der Ostsee mit ihren alten Bädern bis hin zur Sächsischen Schweiz mit ihren Schlössern sowie in Städten wie Potsdam, Erfurt oder Leipzig. Alte Industriezentren sind neu entstanden. In Sachsen-Anhalt, zum Beispiel, produziert das Bayer-Werk in Bitterfeld Aspirin für ganz Europa. Aus Dresden liefert die amerikanische Firma AMD heute Computerchips in alle Welt. BMW, Volkswagen, Opel und Porsche haben in Sachsen Fabriken gebaut, deren Produktivität international konkurrieren kann. Firmen wie Zeiss (Optik) und der Buchverlag Reclam, die bis zur Wiedervereinigung in Ost und West koexistierten, arbeiten wieder zusammen.

All das ist positiv. Und doch, trotz dieser Entwicklung und all dem Geld, das der Westen in den Osten gepumpt hat und immer noch pumpt, sind östlich der Elbe immer noch mehr Menschen arbeitslos als im Westen. Und warum? Mit dem Zusammenbruch der DDR-Wirtschaft verschwand ein Großteil der Industrie und die neuen Investoren sparen an Personalkosten, um weltweit konkurrieren zu können.

Um zu vermeiden, dass immer mehr junge Leute in den Westen ziehen und um für junge qualifizierte Menschen attraktiv zu bleiben, hat man viel in Forschung und Wissenschaft investiert. Man hofft, dass regionale wissenschaftliche Zentren oder Clusters, die mit den Hochschulen und der Geschäftswelt zusammenarbeiten, ein Magnet für Wissenschaftler sein werden.

Kapitel 15

A. Habitat Wattenmeer p. 428

Das flache Vorland der Nordseeküste heißt Watt oder Wattenmeer. Es grenzt an mehrere Länder und ist die größte Wattlandschaft der Erde. Alle sechs Stunden wechselt es von Ebbe zu Flut. Bei Ebbe kann man weit ins Meer hinauswandern und Muscheln suchen. So eine Wanderung ist unheimlich interessant, denn überall gibt es Leben. Es ist ein wahres Paradies für Vögel und Fische. Beim Wandern durchs Watt kann es natürlich auch passieren, dass mal eine Krabbe am Fuß knabbert; aber da muss man einfach ein bisschen aufpassen. Wer eine längere Wanderung machen möchte, muss das gut planen, denn man möchte nicht von der Flut überrascht werden. Die Wanderung von Cuxhaven nach Neuwerk zum Beispiel ist 12 Kilometer lang. Wer zu faul ist zu laufen, kann mit dem Pferdewagen fahren. Zurück geht es mit dem Schiff. Auf diese Weise erlebt man Ebbe und Flut und kann sicherlich auch Seehunde beobachten, was Spaß macht.

Das Wattenmeer hat ein sehr empfindliches Ökosystem. Die größten Gefahren sind die Verschmutzung des Meeres durch Öl und Giftstoffe von Schiffen, aber auch durch Düngemittel in der Landwirtschaft entlang der Küste. Deshalb haben Deutschland, Dänemark und die Niederlande sich zum gemeinsamen Schutz dieser Landschaft entschieden. Deutschlands Watt ist heute Naturschutzgebiet, wo man die Natur allein lässt und einfach nichts tut. Menschen, die dort an der Küste zu Hause sind, sehen dieses Nichtstun aber oft mit anderen Augen. Seit Generationen leben sie vom Meer und seinem Vorland und sind darum weniger interessiert, es nur als schöne Landschaft zu sehen. Als Kompromiss hat man für sie in den 90er Jahren einige Stellen als besonderes Reservat erklärt, wo Fischfang erlaubt ist, aber nur sehr begrenzt. Man ist auch hier viel umweltbewusster geworden.

B. Europa-Schulen

p. 444

Wie kann man Kinder zu Europäern statt zu Deutschen, Luxemburgern, Belgiern oder Italienern erziehen? Nun, man kann sie in eine internationale Schule schicken; die meisten Schüler sind allerdings Kinder von Leuten, die für die EU arbeiten. Die Europäische Union oder EU hat internationale Schulen in den verschiedensten europäischen Ländern. Die größte dieser Schulen ist in Brüssel, mit Kindern vom Kindergarten bis zur 12. Klasse. Andere Schulen sind zum Beispiel in München, Karlsruhe und in Luxemburg.

Juan, ein Junge aus Spanien, ist 15 und Schüler an der Brüsseler Schule. Er lernt Literatur, Mathematik, Naturwissenschaften und Religion auf Spanisch und Geschichte und Geographie auf Englisch. Dreimal pro Woche hat er Französisch. Mit seinem Sportlehrer spricht er nur Französisch. Seine Klassenkameradin Greta ist aus Dänemark. Sie lernt Geschichte und Geographie auf Französisch und spricht in der Musikstunde Englisch. Mit ihrem Freund Carlo spricht sie Italienisch.

Alle Schüler lernen wenigstens drei Sprachen. Sie lernen auch, ihr eigenes Land objektiver zu sehen. Geschichte zum Beispiel haben sie immer in einer Fremdsprache. Leider gibt es keine internationalen Lehrbücher in Geschichte; darum haben sie Geschichtsbücher aus dem Land, in dessen Sprache sie Geschichte lernen. So lernen zum Beispiel Schüler aus England aus einem französischen Buch, dass ihre Kultur lange nicht so hoch steht wie die französische Kultur. Schüler aus Belgien, den Niederlanden oder Luxemburg lernen, dass ihre Länder in deutschen, französischen oder englischen Lehrbüchern kaum zu finden sind. Nicht nur die Schüler, sondern auch die Lehrer lernen dadurch und werden weniger chauvinistisch. Ein Lehrer aus England zum Beispiel findet es unmöglich, seinen spanischen Schülern stolz zu sagen, dass Nelson bei Trafalgar die spanische Flotte zerstört hat. So konzentriert er sich in seinen Klassen weniger auf die Kriege und mehr auf den Frieden.

Active Vocabulary List

This section will help you prepare tests and supplementary practice. Nouns are grouped by gender and alphabetically within that group. Words preceded by G are introduced in the grammar section. The symbol (—) is used to mark the beginning of *Wortschatz 2*.

Ch.	Nouns		Verbs	Adjectives	Other
S1	der Herr	die Frau	heißen	gut / schlecht	auch Auf Wiedersehen! Bis später! danke / bitte Es geht mir . . . Freut mich. Guten Abend / Morgen / Tag! Ich bin . . . Ich heiße / Sie heißen . . . ja / nein Mach's gut! Mein Name ist . . . nicht Tschüss! und Verschiedenes wie? Wie geht's (dir)? Wie geht es Ihnen? Wie heißt du? Wie heißen Sie?
S2	der Bleistift Kuli Stuhl Tisch das Bild Buch Fenster Heft Papier Zimmer	die Farbe Kreide Tafel Tür Wand	antworten fragen hören lernen lesen sagen sein wiederholen	richtig / falsch rot . . .	auf Deutsch / Englisch Das ist (nicht) . . . für morgen hier / da noch einmal Was bedeutet . . . ? Was ist das? Weiteres Welche Farbe hat . . . ? Wie sagt man . . . ? Wo ist . . . ?
S3	der Cent Euro Mantel Pulli Pullover (Pulli) Rock das Gegenteil Hemd Kleid T-Shirt Sweatshirt	die Bluse Hose Jacke Jeans (*pl.*) Kleidung Zahl . . .	brauchen kosten nehmen zählen	dick / dünn groß / klein lang / kurz langsam / schnell neu / alt sauber / schmutzig teuer / billig	aber Das kostet . . . oder Was kostet/kosten . . . ? wie viel(e)? zu
S4	der Frühling . . . Januar . . . Monat Montag . . . Tag das Jahr Wetter	die Uhrzeit Woche	finden	furchtbar heiß / kalt prima schön super toll warm / kühl windig	Das finde ich auch. Die Sonne scheint. Die Woche hat . . . Es ist . . . Es regnet. Es schneit. heute / morgen Ich bin im . . . geboren. Ich finde es . . . nicht wahr? nur Schade! schon wieder sehr Wann sind Sie geboren? wirklich

Ch.	Nouns		Verbs	Adjectives	Other
S5	der Kurs Student die Minute Sekunde Studentin Stunde Uhr Vorlesung Zeit		beginnen essen gehen haben Tennis spielen	fertig	Bitte! Das verstehe ich nicht. Es ist ein (. . .) Uhr. Es ist eins (. . .). Ich habe eine Frage. Ich habe keine Zeit. Ich weiß nicht. jetzt morgens . . . Öffnen Sie das Buch auf Seite . . . ! Schreiben Sie das bitte! (Sprechen Sie) bitte langsam! (um) Viertel nach . . . (um) halb . . . (um) Viertel vor . . . Wie bitte? Wie spät ist es? Wie viel Uhr ist es?
1	der Ausländer Berg Bruder Cousin Deutsche . . . Fluss Großvater Junge Onkel Mann Satz See Sohn Vater das Deutsch . . . Deutschland . . . Kind Land Mädchen die Deutsche . . . Eltern *(pl.)* EU Familie Frage	die Frau Geschwister *(pl.)* Großeltern *(pl.)* Großmutter Hauptstadt Kusine Landkarte Leute *(pl.)* Mutter Prüfung Schwester Sprache Stadt Tante Tochter — der Mensch Nachbar Staat Teil die Nachbarin	kommen liegen wohnen — arbeiten	amerikanisch kanadisch — wichtig	Ich bin / komme aus . . . im Norden . . . mein/dein/Ihr nördlich . . . von woher? — so . . . wie ungefähr
2	der Apfel Fisch Joghurt Kaffee Käse Kuchen Saft Salat (Super)markt Tee Verkäufer Wein das Bier Brot Brötchen Ei Fleisch Gemüse Geschäft Kaufhaus Obst Pfund Plätzchen Stück Wasser	die Bäckerei Banane Bohne Buchhandlung Butter Cola Erbse Erdbeere Gurke Karotte Lebensmittel *(pl.)* Limo(nade) Marmelade Milch Orange Tomate Wurst Zitrone G: Franzose, Herr, Junge, Mensch, Nachbar, Student	glauben machen suchen (ver)kaufen G: sein, haben	frisch — offen / zu	allerlei (Das ist) alles. dann doch es gibt etwas . . . Ich esse / trinke gern . . . Ich hätte / möchte gern . . . natürlich was für (ein . . . ? Was / Wo gibt's . . . ? zusammen G: durch, für, gegen, ohne, um G: kein / nicht G: aber, denn, oder, und — Bitte, bitte! ein paar Ich gehe . . . einkaufen Ich habe Durst / Hunger. montags . . . Na klar! warum?

Ch.	Nouns		Verbs	Adjectives	Other
2 (cont.)		— der Durst / Hunger Laden das Frühstück Glas Würstchen die Apotheke Blume Drogerie Tasse			
3	der Kellner Ober Löffel Nachtisch Pfeffer Pudding Reis Teller Zucker das Café Eis Essen Abendessen Mittagessen Frühstück Messer Restaurant Salz die Bedienung Gabel Kartoffel Mensa Nudel Pizza Pommes (frites) *(pl.)*	die Rechnung Serviette Speisekarte Suppe — der Freund die Freundin Flasche Hand	bestellen (be)zahlen bleiben bringen empfehlen frühstücken schmecken G: essen, empfehlen, fahren, geben, gefallen, helfen, laufen, lesen, nehmen, sehen, sprechen, tragen, werden G: antworten, danken, gefallen, gehören, glauben, helfen — dick machen schlafen		Danke. gleichfalls! Das schmeckt (gut/mir). etwas (zu essen) Guten Appetit! Herr Ober! Ich mag kein(e/en) . . . (Ich möchte) zahlen bitte! Ich möchte / hätte gern . . . nichts (zu trinken) noch ein(e) viel(e) Was gibt's zu essen? Was gibt's zum . . . ? wie viel(e)? zu / nach Hause G: aus, außer, bei, mit, nach seit, von, zu — besonders gewöhnlich man manchmal nicht nur . . ., sondern auch überall vielleicht
4	der Feiertag Geburtstag Sekt das Datum Fest Geschenk die Feier Ferien *(pl.)* (Ordinal)zahl . . . Party Überraschung — das Lied die Kerze		bekommen dauern denken feiern gratulieren nennen schenken singen tanzen tun überraschen G: danken, gefallen, gehören, scheinen . . . — fallen Glück / Pech haben Spaß machen studieren	— laut lustig verrückt	Alles Gute (. . .)! am Wochenende Bitte / Danke schön! Das gibt's doch nicht! Die Ferien sind vom . . . bis zum . . . Ein gutes neues Jahr! (Ein) schönes Wochenende! Frohe / Fröhliche Weihnachten! gerade gestern / vorgestern morgen / übermorgen Gute Besserung! Herzlichen Glückwunsch! Heute ist . . . Ich bin 1960 geboren. Ich bin am . . . geboren. Ich gratuliere dir . . . ! Ich habe am . . . Geburtstag. Ich wünsche dir . . . ! Nichts zu danken! noch sicher So eine Überraschung! Übermorgen / vorgestern Vielen / Herzlichen Dank! Viel Glück! vom . . . bis . . . vor einer Woche Wann haben Sie Geburtstag? Wann sind Sie geboren? Welches Datum ist . . . ? Wie lange? zu (Weihnachten . . .) G: bevor, dass, ob, obwohl, weil, wenn

Ch.	Nouns		Verbs	Adjectives	Other
4 (cont.)					— Das macht mir Spaß. dort eigentlich Glück / Pech gehabt! immer (noch) nie
5	der Bahnhof Bus Dom Park Platz Stadtplan Tourist Weg das Auto Fahrrad Hotel Kino Museum Rathaus Schloss Taxi Theater die Bank Bibliothek Brücke Dame Haltestelle Kirche Post Schule Straße Straßenbahn	die Touristin U-Bahn Uni(versität)	besichtigen halten zeigen zu Fuß gehen — bummeln	nah/weit — bekannt gemütlich interessant lieb	an/am . . . vorbei bis Sie . . . sehen da drüben dorthin die erste Straße links/rechts (den Fluss) entlang Entschuldigen Sie / Entschuldigung / Verzeihung! Es tut mir leid. Fahren Sie mit dem Bus! gegenüber von Gibt es hier in der Nähe . . .? Ich möchte zum/zur . . . (immer) geradeaus in der Nähe von Können Sie mir sagen, wo . . . ist? Sie können zu Fuß gehen. sondern Wie kommt man von hier zum/ zur . . .? G: aber, sondern — (ein)mal genug hoffentlich leider stundenlang . . .
6	der Balkon Baum Dachboden Fernseher Flur Garten Keller Kühlschrank Schrank Sessel Stuhl Teppich Tisch Vorhang das Bad Bett Dach Haus Problem Radio Regal Sofa Studentenwohnheim Telefon (. . .)zimmer	die Ecke Garage Kommode Küche Lampe Möbel *(pl.)* Toilette Wohnung — das Reihenhaus die Arbeit Eigentumswohnung	baden duschen hängen kochen legen liegen setzen sitzen stehen stellen (ver)mieten waschen G: (imperative) G: wissen, kennen — bauen leben lieben sparen	hell/dunkel praktisch (un)bequem — ausgezeichnet leicht / schwer	Auf Wiederhören! (Das ist) kein Problem. (Das) klingt gut. (Das) stimmt. ein bisschen im Erdgeschoss / Parterre / Dachgeschoss im ersten Stock im Monat im Wohnzimmer in der Küche oben / unten sogar ziemlich G: an, auf, hinter, in, neben, über, unter, vor, zwischen G: wo? wohin? — am Abend / Tag Erdgeschoss aufs Land / auf dem Land(e) außerdem fast mitten in noch nicht trotzdem

Ch.	Nouns		Verbs	Adjectives	Other
7	der Aus-/ Eingang Ausweis Dollar Gast Geldautomat Koffer Pass Scheck Schlüssel das Bargeld Kleingeld Doppelzimmer Einzelzimmer Gepäck Hotel die Bank Kasse Kreditkarte Nacht Nummer Tasche Uhrzeit — der Gasthof Wald die Jugendherberge Pension Reise		einlösen lassen umtauschen unterschreiben wechseln G: anrufen aufmachen aufpassen aufschreiben aufstehen ausgehen einkaufen mitbringen mitgehen mitkommen mitnehmen umtauschen vorbeigehen zuhören zumachen zurückkommen — ankommen annehmen kennenlernen packen reisen reservieren übernachten	frei geöffnet geschlossen laut / ruhig möglich — einfach	auf / zu bald Das glaube ich nicht. Das ist doch nicht möglich! Das kann doch nicht wahr sein! einen Moment Halt! Pass auf! . . . Quatsch! Vorsicht! Wann machen Sie auf/zu? Warte! . . . G: der, dieser, jeder, mancher, solcher, welche; mein . . . G: prefixes G: aber, denn, doch, ja — Das kommt darauf an. meistens
8	der Absender Aufenthalt Bahnsteig Brief Briefkasten Fahrplan Flug Flughafen Schalter Wagen Zug das Flugzeug Gleis Handy Paket Postfach die Abfahrt Adresse Ankunft (Ansichts)karte Bahn Briefmarke E-Mail (Hin- und Rück) fahrkarte Fahrt	die Post Postleitzahl Reise SMS Telefonkarte Telefonnummer Vorwahl G: Franzose, Herr, Junge, Mensch, Nachbar, Student, Tourist, Name — des Dorf die Gegend Geschichte	abfahren abfliegen aussteigen einsteigen umsteigen besuchen erzählen fliegen landen schicken telefonieren mit . . . fahren — hinauffahren weiterfahren	— herrlich	Ach du meine Güte! Das freut mich (für dich). Das ist doch egal. Das macht nichts. Das sieht dir (. . .) ähnlich. Gott sei Dank! in einer (Drei)viertelstunde in einer halben Stunde Na und? G: (an)statt, trotz, während, wegen G: morgen früh, heute Morgen, Montagmorgen; täglich . . . ; montags, montagmorgens; Anfang / Ende der Woche, Mitte des Monats; jeden Tag; diese Woche; einen Monat; eines Tages
9	der Arm Bauch Finger Fußball Hals Kopf Körper Mund Rücken Sport Zahn	— der Urlaub das Leben die Musik	angeln, backen faulenzen, fernsehen, fotografieren kochen, malen Rad fahren, sammeln, schwimmen (gehen), Ski laufen (gehen), spazieren gehen,	gesund/krank fantastisch — ander- beliebt ganz	Ach so. andere / die anderen Bis bald / gleich! Ja, sicher. Lust haben, zu . . . / Ich habe (keine) Lust, . . . zu spielen. Nein, das geht (heute) nicht. nichts Besonderes Schmerzen haben / Ich habe (Kopf)schmerzen. Was gibt's (Neues)?

Ch.	Nouns		Verbs	Adjectives	Other
9 (cont.)	das Auge Bein Gesicht Haar Hobby Klavier Knie Ohr Spiel die CD DVD Freizeit Gitarre Hand Idee Karte Nase		Schach spielen (Freunde) treffen Sport treiben wandern G: s. fragen, treffen; s. wünschen . . . G: s. anhören, ansehen, anschauen ausziehen, umziehen, baden, beeilen, duschen, erkälten, (wohl) fühlen, (hin)legen, kämmen, konzentrieren, (die Zähne / Nase) putzen, rasieren, (hin)setzen, waschen — ausgeben s. entspannen s. erholen erleben s. fit halten s. langweilen vorziehen		Was ist los? wehtun/Mir tut der Hals weh. zuerst/danach — anders etwas (ganz) anderes (genauso) wie . . .
10	der Anfang Autor Chor Film Komponist Krimi Maler Roman Schauspieler das Ballett Ende Gemälde Konzert Orchester Stück die Kunst Oper Pause Vorstellung Unterhaltung Werbung Zeitschrift Zeitung	— der Bürger Einfluss Zuschauer das Fernsehen Programm die Art (von) Auswahl (an) Nachricht Sendung	anfangen anmachen s. erholen klatschen lächeln lachen weinen malen vergessen G: denken an, schreiben an, s. freuen auf, s. vorbereiten auf, warten auf, s. ärgern über, s. entscheiden für / gegen, s. informieren über lächeln über s. interessieren für erzählen von, halten von sprechen von/über	dumm folgend komisch langweilig nächst-/letzt- spannend traurig monatlich . . . — öffentlich/privat	am Anfang / Ende Das ärgert mich. (Das ist) klasse / spitze! Das ist zu ... (Das ist doch) unglaublich! (Das ist) unheimlich interessant. (Das ist ja) Wahnsinn! diesmal ein Blick (in/auf) Keine Ahnung! Jetzt habe ich aber genug. Na gut. vor kurzem Was gibt's im Fernsehen? G: dafür . . . ; wofür . . . — etwa sowieso vor allem weder . . . noch
11	der Hund Partner Vogel Wunsch das Pferd Tier Vertrauen	der König das Gold Märchen die Königin Welt	ein·laden heiraten meinen passieren träumen von vergleichen s. verlieben in verlieren s. verloben mit versuchen	attraktiv charmant eigen- ernst / lustig fleißig / faul geschieden gut aussehend hübsch / hässlich intelligent / dumm	beide damals jemand Wenn du meinst. G: als, wann, wenn G: nachdem

Ch.	Nouns		Verbs	Adjectives	Other
11 (cont.)	die Anzeige Beziehung Ehe Eigenschaft Freundschaft Hochzeit Katze Liebe Scheidung		— geschehen hereinkommen spinnen springen sterben vergleichen verlieren versprechen	jung ledig lieb nett reich/arm schick schlank schrecklich süß unternehmungslustig verliebt in verlobt mit verständnisvoll vielseitig (un)ehrlich (un)freundlich (un)gebildet (un)geduldig (un)glücklich (un)kompliziert (un)musikalisch (un)selbstständig (un)sportlich (un)sympathisch (un)talentiert (un)verheiratet (un)zuverlässig zärtlich — allein froh voll	— das 1. Mal zum 1. Mal niemand nun plötzlich sofort
12	der Architekt Arzt Beruf Betriebswirt Geschäftsmann Hausmann Ingenieur Journalist Krankenpfleger Künstler Kurs Lehrer Plan Polizist Rechtsanwalt Reiseleiter Sekretär Wissenschaftler Zahnarzt das Büro Einkommen Geschäft die Ausbildung Erfahrung Firma Geschäftsfrau Hausfrau Klasse Krankenschwester Schule	die Sicherheit Stelle Stunde Verantwortung Zukunft G: Angestellte, Bekannte, Deutsche, Kranke, Verlobte, Beamte — der Arbeiter Bereich Handel Ort Rat das Praktikum Unternehmen die Arbeitslosigkeit Berufswahl Entscheidung (Fach)kenntnis	anbieten s. bewerben um erklären s. gewöhnen an glauben an recht haben verdienen werden — aussehen (wie) bitten hoffen s. Sorgen machen um s. vorstellen	anstrengend arbeitslos früher gleich hoch / hoh- (un)sicher — unbedingt	Ach was! Ich will . . . werden. momentan Nun/also/na ja/tja, . . . Überhaupt/Gar kein Problem! Unsinn! Was willst du (mal) werden? G: gern, groß, gut, hoch, nah, viel (mehr, meist-) . . .; genauso . . . wie; nicht so . . . wie; . . . als; immer . . .; je . . . desto . . . — darum Ich stelle mir vor, dass . . . im / ins Ausland jedoch unter *(among)*

Ch.	Nouns		Verbs	Adjectives	Other
13	der Abschluss Hörsaal Mitbewohner Professor Schein Student das Fach Haupt-/Nebenfach Labor Referat Quartal Semester Seminar Stipendium Studium System die Fachrichtung Note (Natur) wissenschaft (Seminar)arbeit		(das Studium) abschließen ausfüllen belegen etwas dagegen haben holen lehren eine Prüfung machen eine Prüfung bestehen (bei einer Prüfung) durchfallen ein Referat halten teilnehmen (an) — Angst haben vor annehmen aufhören teilen	schwierig — ausländisch	Hast du etwas dagegen, wenn . . . ? Mal sehen. Na klar. wieso? — an deiner Stelle auf diese Weise bestimmt Das geht (nicht). deshalb jedenfalls so dass sowieso überhaupt/gar nicht wahrscheinlich
14	der Frieden Krieg Spitzname Turm das Gebäude Volk die Kneipe Mauer Umgebung	— der Gedanke das Tor die Grenze Heimat Insel Jugend Luft Macht (Wieder)vereinigung	berichten erinnern an s. erinnern an führen (s.) verändern verschwinden vorbeiführen an — austauschen erkennen verlassen	einmalig historisch wunderschön — berühmt leer vereint	irgendwo jede Menge kaum oder? Und ob! seitdem — einst
15	der Abfall Behälter Bau Müll Schutz das Denkmal (Naturschutz)gebiet die Erhaltung Küste Landschaft Mülltonne Natur Rede Sammelstelle Umwelt Verschmutzung — die Bevölkerung		abreißen (wieder) aufbauen finanzieren garantieren planen reden mit/über renovieren restaurieren retten schaden schonen schützen trennen verbieten verwenden wegwerfen zerstören — verbinden (zusammen)wachsen	umweltbewusst — einzeln gefährlich gemeinsam stolz auf typisch	allerdings schließlich übrigens — endlich inzwischen

Wie geht's?

An Introductory German Course

TENTH EDITION

Dieter Sevin
Vanderbilt University

Ingrid Sevin

Beatrix Brockman
Austin Peay State University

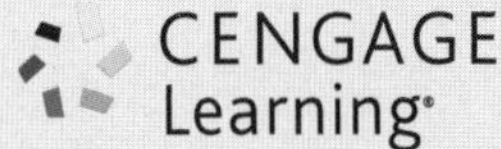

Australia • Brazil • Japan • Korea • Mexico • Singapore • Spain • United Kingdom • United States

Wie geht's?: An Introductory German Course, Tenth Edition
Dieter Sevin, Ingrid Sevin, Beatrix Brockman

Product Director: Beth Kramer

Senior Product Manager: Martine Edwards

Managing Developer: Katie Wade

Senior Content Developer: Isabelle Alouane

Senior Content Project Manager: Esther Marshall

Associate Content Developer: Greg Madan

Managing Media Developer: Patrick Brand

Executive Marketing Manager: Ben Rivera

Manufacturing Planner: Betsy Donaghey

Production Service: PreMediaGlobal

Text Designer: PreMediaGlobal

Intellectual Property Analyst: Jessica Elias

Senior Art Director: Linda Jurras

Cover Designer: Harold Burch

Cover Image: ©Science Photo Library/SuperStock

Compositor: PreMediaGlobal

Library of Congress Control Number: 2013958264

Student Edition:

ISBN-13: 978-1-285-73360-9

ISBN-10: 1-285-73360-6

Annotated Instructor's Edition:

ISBN-13: 978-1-285-73819-2

ISBN-10: 1-285-73819-5

Cengage Learning
20 Channel Center Street
Boston, MA 02210
USA

Cengage Learning is a leading provider of customized learning solutions with office locations around the globe, including Singapore, the United Kingdom, Australia, Mexico, Brazil and Japan. Locate your local office at: **international.cengage.com/region**

Cengage Learning products are represented in Canada by Nelson Education, Ltd.

For your course and learning solutions, visit **www.cengage.com**

Purchase any of our products at your local college store or at our preferred online store **www.cengagebrain.com**

Printed in the United States of America
1 2 3 4 5 6 7 18 17 16 15 14

Inhalt

Kapitel 2: Lebensmittel und Geschäfte 56

Zum Thema

Struktur

Einblicke

Rückschau

Kapitel 3: Im Restaurant 82

Zum Thema

Struktur

Einblicke

Rückschau

Kapitel 4: Feiertage und Feste 108

Zum Thema

Struktur

Einblicke

Kapitel 11: Beziehungen 308

Kapitel 12: Wege zum Beruf 338

Kapitel 13: Das Studium 366

Kapitel 14: Berlin: Damals und heute 394

Kapitel 15: Deutschland, Europa und die Umwelt 422

To the Student

Welcome to ***Wie geht's?***, a program for Introductory German that focuses on all four skills—listening, speaking, reading, and writing—and promotes cultural proficiency.

Organization of *Wie geht's?*

The main text is divided into five pre-units *(Schritte)*, fifteen chapters *(Kapitel)*, and an Appendix *(Anhang)*.

The Pre-Units *(Schritte)*

The purpose of the *Schritte* is to acquaint you with the German language and the language learning process by focusing on listening and speaking. When you have completed the last *Schritt*, you should be able to greet each other, describe your classroom and your clothes, use numbers, discuss the weather, and tell time, all in German.

The Fifteen Chapters *(Kapitel)*

Each chapter opens with a summary of the learning objectives *(Lernziele)*. This is followed by a cultural preview in English *(Vorschau)* that provides you with background information on the chapter topic. The first section of the learning material is **Zum Thema.** It introduces the topic through one or two dialogues that function as models for conversation and recycle structures taught in previous chapters. These dialogues are all recorded and, for your reference, translated in the Appendix.

Wortschatz 1, which contains most of the new chapter vocabulary, is arranged thematically, with nouns listed in alphabetical order according to gender. This list of active vocabulary is followed by a brief list of vocabulary intended for recognition only *(Zum Erkennen)* containing words and phrases from the dialogue and exercises that might make it easier to keep classroom conversation in German. The vocabulary list is followed by exercises and activities on the chapter topic *(Übungen zum Thema)* that foster communication and help you learn the new words and expressions. A pronunciation section *(Aussprache)*, recorded in your lab program, is included as well and is coordinated with more extensive practice in the supplementary summary of pronunciation *(Zur Aussprache)* in the front of this book. At the end of *Übungen zum Thema*, and again after the reading text, you will find an activity *(Hörverständnis)* that will help improve your listening comprehension. To complete it, you will need to listen to the text audio files that are posted on the ***Wie geht's!*** Premium Website.

The **Struktur** section introduces two or three major grammar points. A variety of exercises *(Übungen)* directly follow each grammar presentation. Additional exercises are also available in the ***Arbeitsbuch*** **(Student Activities Manual, SAM).**

Each chapter has an **Einblicke** section that focuses on a variety of author-generated reading passages *(Lesetext)*. It is introduced by a second active vocabulary list *(Wortschatz 2)*, accompanied by reading strategies *(Lesetipp)* and a pre-reading section *(Vor dem Lesen)* with activities. The reading passage itself features one or more cultural aspects related to the chapter topic. It offers additional examples of the new grammar and a review of the chapter vocabulary. The post-reading exercises and activities *(Nach dem Lesen)* are designed to check comprehension and provide additional grammar, speaking, and writing practice. A second listening activity *(Hörverständnis)* concludes this section. Starting with Chapter 8, a literature section *(Literatur)* is also included. It offers short literary readings or poems for your enrichment and enjoyment.

Finally, each chapter ends with a new two-page **Rückschau** section, where you can find all of the active chapter vocabulary, a few grammar review exercises, and a list of online activities that can be found on the iLrn™: Heinle Learning Center.

Cultural notes *(Fokus)* appear throughout each *Kapitel*, as well as the *Schritte*. They point out or explain differences between life in North America and in countries where German is spoken.

In each chapter, you will also find references to the iLrn™: Heinle Learning Center pointing to additional practice. Using all of the videos, the ***Wie geht's!*** Premium Website, and the iLrn™: Heinle Learning Center will enrich your language learning, add to cultural insights, and open new vistas of direct contact to the German-speaking countries.

Eine Reises ins Märchenland

A new travel guide called *Eine Reise ins Märchenland* completes the new addition of ***Wie Geht's!*** It is an eight-page tour through the locales, scenery, and history of Grimms' fairy tales. Students are introduced to the *Deutsche Märchenstraße* and are tasked with planning a real or virtual trip along the life stations of the Brothers Grimm and through the regions of various German legends and fairy tales. This section reinforces and combines what students have learned about travel, finding lodging, ordering food, going to cultural events, and so on, in Germany.

The Appendix

The Appendix includes information on predicting the gender of some nouns, a grammar summary in chart form, tables of all basic verb forms, lists of irregular verbs, translations of dialogues, supplementary charts for the information-gap activities *(Hoppla, hier fehlt was!)*, a German-English and English-German vocabulary, and a grammar index.

Icons for *Wie geht's?*

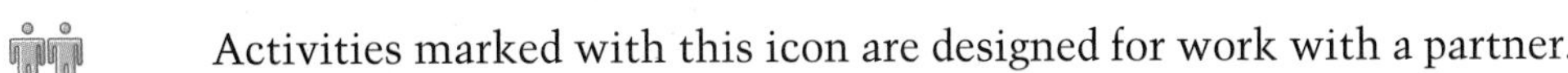

Activities marked with this icon are designed for work with a partner.

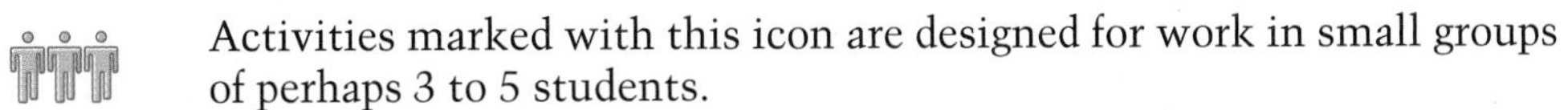

Activities marked with this icon are designed for work in small groups of perhaps 3 to 5 students.

This icon points to audio material available in mp3 format on the ***Wie geht's!*** Premium Website, including *Hörverständnis* and various pieces of original literature featured in Chapters 8–15.

This icon indicates a writing activity.

This icon marks a reference to activities that can be found in the ***Arbeitsbuch*** **(Student Activities Manual, SAM)**

This icon marks a reference to the ***Wie geht's!*** video and the video activities in the ***Arbeitsbuch*** video. Downloadable video mp4 files are available on the Premium Website.

This icon marks a reference to Internet activities.

iLrn This logo marks references to the iLrn™: Heinle Learning Center.

Student Program Components

- The ***Arbeitsbuch*** **(Student Activities Manual, SAM)** contains practice for the various *Schritte* and *Kapitel*. Each *Kapitel* consists of three components:

    a) **Zum Hören** — This section provides activities correlated to the ***Arbeitsbuch*** Audio program. It contains instructions and examples of the recorded activities.

    b) **Zum Sehen** — This section provides activities to both parts of each chapter's video, *Video-Szenen and Video-Interviews*. Video clips can be viewed and downloaded through the ***Wie geht's?*** Premium Website.

    c) **Zum Schreiben** — This section focuses on vocabulary building, grammar practice, and cultural enrichment.

After the *Schritte,* as well as after *Kapitel* 3, 7, 11, and 15, you will find review sections (*Rückblicke*) that summarize the grammatical structures you have learned in the last few chapters. They are accompanied by extensive exercises to review vocabulary and grammar. An answer key for the *Rückblicke* exercises can be found at the end of the ***Arbeitsbuch.***

- The ***Arbeitsbuch*** **Audio program,** available on the Premium Website, provides additional practice in listening and speaking. In the program, you will find the chapter dialogues and pronunciation practices, supplementary grammar activities, the chapter reading text, a dictation, and a listening-comprehension exercise *(Verstehen Sie?).*
- The two-tier **Video** program consists of *Video-Szenen* that present cultural insights into the various aspects of life in the German-speaking countries, and *Video-Interviews* in which individual speakers respond to a particular question about themselves or chapter-related themes. Activities to accompany both the *Video-Szenen* and the *Video-Interviews* are in the ***Arbeitsbuch.***
- The ***Wie geht's?*** Premium Website offers the audio and video programs for each chapter.
- iLrn™: Everything you need to master the skills and concepts of the course is built right into this dynamic audio- and video-enhanced learning environment: online activities specifically tailored to the book, including additional resources, such as a memory game *(Gedächtnisspiel),* a crossword puzzle (*Kreuzworträtsel*), audio flash cards *(Vokabelblitz),* a tutorial quiz *(Mini-Quiz),* the active vocabulary *(Wortschatz),* diagnostic activities, an audio-enhanced **e-Book** with integrated activities, companion **videos,** an interactive **VoiceBoard,** an online ***Arbeitsbuch*** with audio, interactive enrichment **activities,** and access to online tutoring with a German teaching expert through **NetTutor.**)

We hope that you will find the ***Wie geht's?*** program enjoyable. You will be surprised at the rapid progress you will make in just one year. Many students have been able to study abroad after their first year of studying German!

Acknowledgments

We would like to thank the following colleagues who reviewed the manuscript during its various stages of development:

Zsuzsanna Abrams,
University of Texas at Austin

Gabriela Appel,
Pennsylvania State University

Prisca Augustyn,
Florida Atlantic University

Shana Bell,
Arizona State University – Tempe

John Blair,
University of West Georgia

Stephanie Borst,
Texas Tech University

Elise Brayton,
California State University – San Diego

Francis Brévart,
University of Pennsylvania

Johannes Bruestle,
Grossmont College

Bettina F. Cothram,
Georgia Technical University

Christopher Dolmetsch,
Marshall University

James Dunn,
San Antonio College

Karl-Georg Federhofer,
University of Michigan

Shelley French,
Eastern Illinois University

Ingrid Fry,
Texas Tech University

Julia Karolle,
Purdue University

Susanne Kelley,
Kennesaw State University

Yvonne Ivory,
Duke University

Peter Meister,
University of Alabama – Huntsville

George Mower,
Allegheny County Community College

Eva Norling,
Bellevue Community College

Lisa Parkes,
University of California – Los Angeles

Julia Pittman,
Auburn University

Hartmut Rastalsky,
University of Michigan

Simone Schlichting-Artur,
Drexel University

Barbara Smith,
North Georgia College & State University

Bruce Spencer,
University of Iowa

Cordelia Stroinigg,
University of Cincinnati

Christine Staininger,
San Diego University

John Sundquist,
Purdue University

Ingrid Wollank,
Long Beach City College

We would like to thank Beth Kramer, Product Director, for putting together such an excellent team and for her support of the ***Wie geht's?*** project. The great professional support we received from members of the Cengage editorial staff is hereby gratefully acknowledged. We are especially appreciative of Martine Edwards, Isabelle Alouane, and Esther Marshall.

Our thanks also go to the service and freelancers who worked on the different stages of the production, in particular: Peggy Potter, the development editor; Sandra Mercado, Aravinda Doss, Carly Bergey, and Sylvie Pittet from PMG; Maki Wiering, the proofreader; Jamie Rankin for writing the test bank; Jessica Riviere for the native read of the test bank and web search activities.

Last but not least, we would like to express our appreciation to Kathryn McEwen and Jessica Riviere for the invaluable help in creating the new *Rückschau* pages.

Zur Aussprache *(Summary of Pronunciation)*

Pronunciation is a matter of learning not just to hear and pronounce isolated sounds or words, but to understand entire phrases and sentences, and to say them in such a way that a native speaker of German can understand you. You will need to practice this continuously as you study German.

This section summarizes and reviews the production of individual sounds. We have tried to keep it simple and nontechnical, and to provide ample practice of those German sounds that are distinctly different from American English. Often we have used symbols of pronunciation in a simplified phonetic spelling. Upon completing this section, you should hear the difference between somewhat similar English and German words (*builder* / **Bilder**) and between somewhat similar German words (**schon** / **schön**).

To develop good German pronunciation—or at least one without a heavy American accent—you will have to keep three things in mind: First, you must resist the temptation of responding to German letters with American sounds. Second, at the outset you will probably feel a bit odd when speaking German with a truly German accent; however, nothing could give you a better start in your endeavor. (Imposing a German accent on your English may be hilarious, but it is also very good practice!) Third, you will have to develop new muscular skills. Germans move their jaws and lips more vigorously and articulate more precisely than Americans. After a good practice session your face should feel the strain of making unaccustomed sounds.

We will point out those cases where English sounds are close enough to German to cause no distortion. However, we purposely avoid trying to derive German sounds from English because such derivations often do more harm than good. Listen carefully to your instructor and the tape or CD. If you can record your own voice in the language lab, do so, and compare how you sound with the voice of the native speaker. With patience and practice, you should be able to develop new speech habits quite rapidly. You will also find that German spelling reflects pronunciation very well.

I. Word Stress

In both English and German, one syllable of a word receives more stress than others. In English, stress can even signal the difference between two words *(ob'ject / object')*. In native German words, the accent is on the stem of the word, which is usually the first syllable (**Hei'rat, hei'raten**) or the syllable following an unstressed prefix (**verhei'ratet**). Words borrowed from other languages are less predictable; frequently the stress falls on the last or next-to-last syllable (**Universität', Muse'um**). You will find such words marked for stress in the German-English vocabulary at the end of the textbook.

II. Vowels

One of the most important differences between English and German is that in English most vowels are to some degree glides. This means that while they are being pronounced, there occurs a shift from one vowel sound to another *(so, say)*. German vowel sounds do not glide, and they do not change quality. The jaw does not shift while a German vowel is being produced (**so, See**). Three German vowels occur with two dots over them (**ä, ö, ü**). These vowels are called *umlauts*. Short and long **ä** sounds like short and long **e**, but **ö** and **ü** represent distinct sounds.

Certain vowels appear in combinations (**ei, ey, ai, ay; au; äu, eu**) called *diphthongs*. While diphthongs in American English may be drawn out or drawled, the German diphthongs are short.

Pay special attention to the length of a vowel. In many words, the length of the stressed vowel is the only clue to their meaning. When spoken, **Rate!** with a long **a** [a:] means *Guess!*, whereas **Ratte** with a short **a** [a] means *rat*.

A. Short Vowels [i, e, a, u, o,]

Keep these vowels really short!

1. [i] **in, immer,** Z**i**mmer, K**i**nd, W**i**nter, F**i**nger, b**i**tte, d**i**ck
2. [e] **es, essen,** F**e**nster, schn**e**ll, M**ä**rz, L**ä**nder, S**ä**tze
3. [a] **alt,** k**a**lt, Kl**a**sse, T**a**sse, T**a**nte, W**a**nd, w**a**nn, m**a**n
4. [u] **um, und,** M**u**nd, M**u**tter, B**u**tter, St**u**nde, Sek**u**nde
5. [o] **oft, O**nkel, S**o**nne, S**o**mmer, S**o**nntag, m**o**rgen, k**o**mmen, k**o**sten
6. [a] and [o] Be sure to dinstinguish clearly between these sounds.

K**a**mm / K**o**mm!	*comb / Come!*	F**a**ll / v**o**ll	*fall / full*
B**a**nn / B**o**nn	*ban / Bonn*	B**a**ss / B**o**ss	*bass / boss*

7. [e] Don't forget that **ä** doesn't sound like [a], but like [e].

Kamm / K**ä**mme / S**e**mmel	*comb / combs / roll*
Schwamm / Schw**ä**mme / Schw**e**mme	*sponge / sponges / watering place*
Fall / F**ä**lle / F**e**lle	*fall / falls / furs*
Mann / M**ä**nner / M**e**sser	*man / men / knife*

8. Unstressed short **e** [ə] In unstressed syllables [a], [i], [o], and [u] retain their basic quality in German, whereas in English they become rather neutral (**Amerika'ner** / *Amer¢ican;* **Aro'ma** / *aro'ma*). The German unstressed short **e** [ə], however, becomes neutral, too.

   heut**e**, Leut**e**, frag**e**n, sag**e**n, b**e**ginn**e**n, G**e**sicht, G**e**schenk, G**e**burtstag

9. Final **er** [ʌ] When **r** occurs after a vowel at the end of a syllable or word, and especially in the ending **-er,** it sounds like a weak **a** [ʌ]. It requires a good deal of attention and practice for speakers of American English not to pronounce the **r.** The German sound resembles the final vowel in the word *comma.*

   Vat**er**, Mutt**er**, Kind**er**, d**er**, w**ir**, vi**er**, Uh**r**, Oh**r**, schw**er**, Donn**er**stag, wund**er**bar, **er**zählen, **ver**stehen

10. [ə] and [ʌ] Listen carefully to the difference between these two sounds.

bitt**e** / bitt**er**	*please / bitter*	zeig**e** / Zeig**er**	*I show / watch hand*
ess**e** / Ess**er**	*I eat / eater*	dies**e** / dies**er**	*these / this*
leid**e** / leid**er**	*I suffer / unfortunately*		

B. Long Vowels [i: / a: / u: / e: / o:]

Be sure to stretch these vowels until they are really long.

11. [i:] Draw your lips far back.
    pr**i**ma, m**i**nus, Mus**i**k, **ih**n, **ih**m, **ih**nen, d**ie**, w**ie**, w**ie**der, s**ie**ben, stud**ie**ren, Pap**ie**r, Biolog**ie**
12. [a:] H**aa**re, S**aa**l, J**a**hr, Z**ah**l, Z**ah**n, s**a**gen, fr**a**gen, N**a**me, N**a**se
13. [u:] Round your lips well.
    d**u**, g**u**t, K**u**li, J**u**li, Min**u**te, Bl**u**se, Sch**uh**, St**uh**l, **Uh**r, T**ou**r
14. [e:] and [o:] These two vowels need particular attention. Listen carefully for the differences between English and German.

say / S**ee**	*vain* / w**e**n	*boat* / B**oo**t
bait / B**ee**t	*tone* / T**o**n	*pole* / P**o**l

15. [e:] Draw your lips back and hold the sound steady.
    S**ee**, T**ee**, Id**ee**, z**eh**n, n**eh**men, g**eh**en, s**eh**en, Z**äh**ne, M**ä**dchen, K**ä**se, l**e**sen, sp**ä**t, Universit**ä**t, Qualit**ä**t
16. [o:] Purse your lips and don't let the sound glide off.
    Z**oo**, B**oo**t, **Oh**r, **oh**ne, B**oh**ne, w**oh**nen, s**o**, r**o**t, **o**ben, H**o**se, h**o**len

C. Contrasting Short and Long Vowels

As you were practicing the short and long vowels, you probably discovered that spelling provides some clues to the length of the stressed vowel. Here are the most reliable signals. Some apply only to the dictionary forms of words, not to the inflected forms.

The stressed vowel is *short*, . . .

- when followed by a double consonant.
  immer, essen, alle, Butter, Tennis, Lippe, Mütter
- usually when followed by two or more consonants, including **ch** and **sch.**
  Winter, Fenster, kalt, unten, Kopf, Hände, Wünsche, Gesicht, Tisch
- in many common one-syllable words before a single consonant.
  mit, es, an, um, von

The stressed vowel is *long*, . . .

- when doubled.
  Idee, Haar, Zoo
- **i** and **u** cannot be doubled, but **i** followed by **e** is always long.
- die, sie, wie, viel, vier, Fantasie
- when followed by **h, h** is silent; after a vowel it is strictly a spelling device to signal length.
  ihn, ihm, sehen, nehmen, Zahn, Zahl, Uhr, Schuh
- usually when followed by a single consonant.
  Kino, lesen, Tafel, Bluse, Väter, Türen, hören

17. [i] and [i:]

innen / ihnen	*inside / to them*	still / Stil	*quiet / style*
im / ihm	*in / him*		

18. [e] and [e:]

denn / den	*for / the*	Wellen / Wählen	*waves / to choose*
Betten / beten	*beds / to pray*		

19. [a] and [a:]

Stadt / Staat	*city / state*	nasse / Nase	*wet / nose*
Kamm / kam	*comb / came*		

20. [u] and [u:]

muss / Mus	*must / mush*	Sucht / sucht	*mania / looks for*
Busse / Buße	*busses / repentance*		

21. [o] and [o:]

offen / Ofen	*open / oven*	Motte / Mode	*moth / fashion*
Wonne / wohne	*delight / I live*		

D. Umlauts

There are also a long and short **ü** and **ö.**

22. [i:] and [ü:] To make the [ü:], say [i:], keep your tongue and jaw in this position, and round your lips firmly.

diene / Düne	*I serve / dune*	liegen / lügen	*to lie / to (tell a) lie*
Biene / Bühne	*bee / stage*	diese / Düse	*these / nozzle*

23. [ü:] Note that the German letter **y** is pronounced like **ü.**
    über, übrigens, müde, Füße, kühl, Frühling, grün, natürlich, Typ, typisch

24. [u:] and [ü] Observe the change in tongue position as you shift from one sound to the other.

Fuß / Füße	*foot / feet*	Kuh / Kühe	*cow / cows*
Stuhl / Stühle	*chair / chairs*	Hut / Hüte	*hat / hats*

25. [u] and [ü] To make the [ü], begin by saying [i], then round your lips.

Kissen / küssen	*pillow / to kiss*	Kiste / Küste	*box / coast*
missen / müssen	*to miss / must*	sticke / Stücke	*embroider / pieces*

26. [ü] dünn, fünf, hübsch, Glück, zurück, Flüsse, München, Nymphe

27. [u] and [ü] Be aware of the movements of your tongue as you shift from one sound to the other.

Busch / Büsche	*bush / bushes*	Kuss / Küsse	*kiss / kisses*
Fluss / Flüsse	*river / rivers*	Kunst / Künste	*art / arts*

28. [ü:] and [ü]

Hüte / Hütte	*hats / hut*	fühle / fülle	*I feel / I fill*
Wüste / wüsste	*desert / would know*	Düne / dünne	*dune / thin*

29. [e:] and [ö:] To make the [ö:], begin by saying [e:]. Keep your tongue in this position, then round your lips firmly for [ö:].

Hefe / Höfe	*yeast / courts*	Sehne / Söhne	*tendon / sons*
lesen / lösen	*to read / to solve*	Besen / bösen	*broom / bad*

30. [o:] schön, Möbel, hören, möglich, Brötchen, französisch, Österreich

31. [o:] and [ö:] Observe the tongue position as you shift from one sound to the other.

Ofen / Öfen	*oven / ovens*	Sohn / Söhne	*son / sons*
Ton / Töne	*tone / tones*	Hof / Höfe	*court / courts*

32. [e] and [ö] Begin by saying [e], then round your lips.

kennen / können	*to know / can*	fällig / völlig	*due / total*
Helle / Hölle	*light / hell*	Zelle / Zölle	*cell / tolls*

33. [ö] öffnen, östlich, zwölf, Wörter, Töchter

34. [o] and [ö] Observe the tongue position as you shift from one sound to the other.

Kopf / Köpfe	*head / heads*	Stock / Stöcke	*stick / sticks*
Rock / Röcke	*skirt / skirts*	konnte / könnte	*was able to / could*

35. [ö:] and [ö]

Höhle / Hölle	*cave / hell*	Röslein / Rösslein	*little rose / little horse*
Schöße / schösse	*laps / I'd shoot*		

36. [ü:] vs. [ö:] and [ü] vs. [ö]

Sühne / Söhne	*repentance / sons*	Hülle / Hölle	*cover / hell*
Güte / Goethe	*grace / Goethe*	Stücke / Stöcke	*pieces / sticks*
blüht / blöd	*blooms / stupid*	rücke / Röcke	*move / skirts*

E. Diphthongs

German diphthongs are short. They are not drawled.

37. [ai] eins, zwei, drei, mein, dein, kein, Seite, Kreide, Meyer, Mai, Bayern, Haydn

38. [oi] neu, neun, heute, Leute, teuer, deutsch, träumen, Häuser, toi, toi, toi!

39. [au] auf, Auge, Haus, Frau, grau, faul, auch, Bauch, brauchen

40. Remember that **ie** [i:] is not a diphthong.

Wien / Wein	*Vienna / wine*	Biene / Beine	*bee / legs*
Lied / Leid	*song / suffering*	Lieder / leider	*songs / unfortunately*

41. Can you pronounce these words correctly without hesitation?
Schreiben, schrieb, hieß, heiß, wieder, weiter, sei, Sie, wie, wieso, weiß, Beispiel, wie viel

F. Glottal Stops

Both English and German use a glottal stop (+) to avoid running words together. German uses it much more frequently than English, where the last consonant of one word is often linked with the first vowel of the next (**mit +einem +Eis**, *with an ice cream*). A good way to become aware of the glottal stop is to say *Oh oh!* as if in dismay.

42. Use the glottal stop where indicated:
    +Am +Abend +essen wir +in +einem Restaurant.
    Wir sitzen +in +einer kleinen +Ecke.
    Der +Ober bringt +uns +ein +Eis.
    Wir +erzählen von der +Uni.
    Hans beobachtet +andere Leute.

III. Consonants

A. Single Letters

1. **f, h, k, m, n, p, t, x:** These are pronounced alike in both languages.
   fün**f**, **h**aben, **k**aufen, **m**üde, **n**ei**n**, **P**ark, **T**ag, e**x**tra
2. **j**: It is pronounced like the English *y*.
   ja, **J**ahr, **J**anuar, **J**uni, **J**uli, **j**ung, **j**etzt
3. **b, d, g:** They usually sound like their English counterparts (**g** as in *garden*).
   bitte, **d**anke, **g**ut
   However, when they occur at the end of a word or syllable, or before *s* or *t*, they sound like [p], [t], [k], respectively.
   [p] o**b**, gel**b**, hal**b**, a**b**hängig, gi**b**st, ge**b**t
   [t] un**d**, Mun**d**, Bil**d**, aben**d**s, Sta**d**t
   [k] Ta**g**, tä**g**lich, we**g**, genu**g**, lie**g**st, lie**g**t

[p] vs. [b]	[t] vs. [d]	[k] vs. [g]
ha**b**t / ha**b**en	Kin**d** / Kin**d**er	sa**g**t / sa**g**en
gi**b**st / ge**b**en	Wan**d** / Wän**d**e	fra**g**st / fra**g**en
sie**b**zig / sie**b**en	aben**d**s / Aben**d**e	Zu**g** / Zü**g**e

4. **v:** It usually sounds like [f], but in words of foreign origin it is pronounced [v] unless it is at the end of the word.
   [f] **v**ier, **v**on, **v**erstehen, **V**ater, **V**olkswagen, relati**v**, intensi**v**
   [v] **V**okabeln, **V**ase, **V**ision, **V**ariation, No**v**ember, Re**v**olution
5. **w:** It is pronounced [v] in German.
   was, **w**o, **w**er, **w**ie, **w**arum, **w**elche, **w**omit, **w**underbar
6. **s, ss, ß:** The pronunciation of the letter *s* depends on its position of the word. If preceeds a vowel, it is pronounced [z] as in the English *fuzz*. Otherwise it is pronounced [s] as in the English *fuss*.
   [z] **s**ehen, **S**ofa, **S**alat, Gemü**s**e, Na**s**e, le**s**en
   [s] wa**s**, da**s**, au**s**, Bu**s**, Ei**s**, Gla**s**, Hal**s**, al**s**
   ss and **ß** are also pronounced [s]. ß [Estset] is used after long vowels **(Füße).** According to the spelling reform, however, short vowels are always followed by an **ss** (muss, lässt).
   Ta**ss**e, Wa**ss**er, be**ss**er, wi**ss**en, Profe**ss**or, lä**ss**t; Gru**ß** Grü**ß**e, hei**ß**, hei**ß**en, gro**ß**, Grö**ß**e; lä**ss**t, wei**ß**t
7. **z:** It is pronounced [ts] as in English *rats*.
   [ts] **z**u, **Z**oo, **Z**ahn, **Z**eit, **z**wischen, De**z**ember, Medi**z**in, du**z**en, Mär**z**, schwar**z**, Tan**z**, Toleran**z**, **z**ick**z**ack
8. **s** and **z:** Watch the contrast between these two letters.

so / **Z**oo	*so/ zoo*	**s**iegen / **Z**iegen	*to win / goats*
sauber / **Z**auber	*clean / magic*	**s**agen / **z**agen	*to stay / hesitate*

9. **l:** There is an important difference between English and German in the pronunciation of the letter **l.** When an American pronounces [l], the tongue forms a hump toward the back of the mouth, which makes the [l] sound "dark." For the German [l], the tongue is flat and touches just behind the front teeth; it is very "light" sound. Listen for the difference between American and German [l]:

   feel / vie**l**   *felt* / fä**ll**t   *built* / Bi**l**d

   [l] **l**aut, **l**ernen, **l**ogisch, **L**imo, K**l**asse, ka**l**t, Fi**l**m, he**ll**, Hote**l**, Apri**l**, wi**ll**, küh**l**

10. **r:** To avoid a noticeable American accent in German, don't use the American [r]. In German you can either use a tongue-tip trill or a uvular trill. (The uvula is the little skin flap in the back of your mouth that vibrates when you gargle.) Listen for the difference between American and German [r]:

    rest / **R**est   *fry* / f**r**ei   *ring* / **R**ing   *wrote* / **r**ot

    [r] **r**ot, **R**ose, **R**adio, **R**athaus, **R**eis, **R**hein, fah**r**en, hö**r**en, o**r**ange, Bü**r**o, F**r**age, K**r**eide, b**r**aun, g**r**au, g**r**ün

    Remember that **r** after a vowel at the end of a syllable or word, especially in the ending **-er,** is usually pronounced [ʌ].

    [ʌ] Bild**er**, Kind**er**, ab**er**, Zimm**er**, Körp**er**, Lehr**er**, schw**er**, Papi**er**, di**r**, ih**r**

B. Letter Combinations

11. **sch:** This sound [š] resembles the English *sh*, but in German the lips protrude more.

    Scheck, **Sch**ach, **Sch**iff, **Sch**ule, **Sch**okolade, **sch**reiben, **sch**wer, wa**sch**en, Ti**sch**, Fi**sch**

12. **st, sp:** At the beginning of a word or word stem, they are pronounced [št] and [šp].

    [št] **St**ock, **St**ein, **st**ill, **St**adt, **St**atistik, Früh**st**ück, ver**st**ehen

    [šp] **Sp**ort, **sp**ät, **sp**ielen, **Sp**rache, ver**sp**rechen, Ge**sp**räch

    Otherwise they sound the same as in English.

    [st] i**st**, bi**st**, O**st**en, We**st**en, Fen**st**er, Ga**st**, Po**st**, Pro**st**

    [sp] We**sp**e, Ka**sp**ar, li**sp**eln

13. **ch:** There are no English equivalents for the two German sounds [x] and [ç]

    - [x]—the "**ach**-sound"—is produced in the same place as [k]. However, for [k] the breath stops, whereas for [x] it continues to flow through a narrow opening in the back of the throat, **ch** is pronounced [x] after a, o, u, and au.

      a**ch**, Ba**ch**, a**ch**t, Na**ch**t, ma**ch**en, la**ch**en, no**ch**, do**ch**, Wo**ch**e, su**ch**en, Ku**ch**en, Bau**ch**, au**ch**

      Be sure to distinguish clearly between [k] and [x].

A**k**t / a**ch**t	*act / eight*	Do**ck** / do**ch**	*dock / indeed*
na**ck**t / Na**ch**t	*naked / night*	bu**k** / Bu**ch**	*baked / book*

    - [ç]—the "**ich**-sound"—is produced much farther forward in the mouth. The sound **ch** is pronounced [ç] after the vowels e, i, ä, ö, ü, the dipthongs ei (ai) and eu (äu), and the consonants l, n, and r.

      The diminutive suffix **-chen** is also pronounced [çen]. The ending **-ig** is always pronounced [iç]. You can learn to make this sound by whispering loudly *you* or *Hugh.*

      i**ch**, mi**ch**, ni**ch**t, schle**ch**t, spre**ch**en, lä**ch**eln, mö**ch**ten, Bü**ch**er, Zei**ch**nung, Bäu**ch**e, Mil**ch**, Mün**ch**en, fur**ch**tbar, Mäd**ch**en, ri**ch**tig, ruhi**g**, brummi**g**

      Be sure not to substitute [s] for [ç].

mi**ch** / mi**sch**	*me / mix*	Männ**ch**en / Men**sch**en	*dwarf / people*
fi**ch**t / fi**sch**t	*fights / fisher*		

      Often [x] and [ç] alternate automatically in different forms of the same word.

Bu**ch** / Bü**ch**er	*book / books*	Bau**ch** / Bäu**ch**e	*belly / bellies*
Na**ch**t / Nä**ch**te	*night / nights*		

14. **chs:** It is pronounced [ks].
    se**chs**, Wa**chs**
15. **ck:** It sounds like [k]
    di**ck**, Pickni**ck**, Ro**ck**, Ja**ck**e, pa**ck**en, Sche**ck**
16. **ph:** It sounds like [f]. In fact, according to the new spelling, many words can now be spelled or are routinely spelled with an **f.**
    Philosophie, **Ph**ysik, **ph**ysisch, **f**otografieren, **F**antasie
17. **th:** It sounds like [t].
    Thema, **Th**eater, **Th**eologie, **Th**eorie, Ma**th**ematik, Biblio**th**ek
18. **tz:** It sounds like [ts].
    Sa**tz**, Pla**tz**, se**tz**en, tro**tz**, Hi**tz**e
    ALSO: Na**t**ion, Informa**t**ion, Por**t**ion, Varia**t**ion
19. **qu:** It must be pronounced [kv].
    Quatsch, **Qu**äker, **Qu**alität, **Qu**antität, **Qu**artier, **Qu**ote
20. **ng:** It always is pronounced [nj] as in English *sing*, not [ng] as in *finger*
    la**ng**, e**ng**lisch, si**ng**en, Fi**ng**er, Hu**ng**er, Übu**ng**, Prüfu**ng**
21. **pf:** Both letters are pronounced: [pf].
    pfui, **Pf**effer, **Pf**ennig, **Pf**efferminz, **pf**lanzen, Ko**pf**, Dummko**pf**
22. **ps:** Both letters are pronounced: [ps].
    Psychologie, **Ps**ychologe, **ps**ychologisch, **Ps**ychiater, **Ps**alm, **Ps**eudonym
23. **kn, gn:** They sound just as they are spelled: [kn gn].
    Knie, **Kn**oten, **Kn**ackwurst, **Kn**irps
    Gnu, **Gn**eis, Ver**gn**ügen

Elevation in meters
2000+
500–2000
200–500
0–200
Sea Level
DÄNEMARK
die Ostsee
Flensburg
Rügen
Stralsund
Helgoland
die Nordsee
Kiel
SCHLESWIG-HOLSTEIN
Rostock
Lübeck
MECKLENBURG-VORPOMMERN
die Ostfriesischen Inseln
Schwerin
HAMBURG
Hamburg
Bremerhaven
Neubrandenburg
die Elbe
die NIEDERLANDE
Oldenburg
BREMEN
Bremen
BRANDENBURG
die Oder
POLEN
die Ems
NIEDERSACHSEN
die Havel
BERLIN
Berlin
der Mittelland kanal
Hannover
Wolfsburg
Potsdam
Frankfurt
Braunschweig
Hildesheim
die Weser
Hameln
Magdeburg
der Teutoburger Wald
Münster
SACHSEN-ANHALT
Wittenberg
Dessau
Cottbus
der Rhein
der HARZ
Dortmund
Essen
die Ruhr
Göttingen
Halle
die Spree
die Neiße
Kassel
Leipzig
die Elbe
Düsseldorf
NORDRHEIN-WESTFALEN
THÜRINGEN
die Saale
Dresden
Köln
Eisenach
Weimar
SACHSEN
Aachen
HESSEN
Erfurt
Jena
Chemnitz
Bonn
Marburg
der THÜRINGER WALD
die Lahn
die Fulda
die Werra
das ERZGEBIRGE
BELGIEN
Koblenz
der TAUNUS
die Elbe
die Mosel
Wiesbaden
Frankfurt
Mainz
LUXEMBURG
der Main
Bayreuth
TSCHECHIEN
Würzburg
Trier
RHEINLAND-PFALZ
Mannheim
Fürth
Nürnberg
SAARLAND
Ludwigshafen
Saarbrücken
Heidelberg
Rothenburg
die FRÄNKISCHE ALB
der BÖHMERWALD
Karlsruhe
BADEN-WÜRTTEMBERG
Regensburg
der BAYERISCHE WALD
die Saar
Stuttgart
die Donau
FRANKREICH
Tübingen
die SCHWÄBISCHE ALB
BAYERN
die Isar
Landshut
Passau
der Rhein
der SCHWARZWALD
Ulm
Augsburg
die Donau
der Inn
der Neckar
die VOGESEN
München
ÖSTERREICH
Freiburg
Meilen
0
80
der Chiemsee
Friedrichshafen
Konstanz
Lindau
der Rhein
der Bodensee
die ALPEN
Garmisch-Partenkirchen
Kilometer
0
80
die SCHWEIZ
die ZUGSPITZE 2.963 m

ÖSTERREICH
Hauptstadt
Landeshauptstadt
Stadt
Berg
Tunnel/Pass
TSCHECHIEN
DEUTSCHLAND
Passau
der Inn
NIEDERÖSTERREICH
die SLOWAKEI
die Donau
Linz
Melk
WIEN
Pressburg
OBERÖSTERREICH
St.Pölten
Wien
Steyr
Salzburg
Wiener Neustadt
Eisenstadt
der Bodensee
die ZUGSPITZE 2.963 m
Kitzbühel
die Enns
BURGENLAND
der Neusiedler See
Bregenz
VORARLBERG
A L P E N
der DACHSTEIN 2.995m
Leoben
die Salzach
Vaduz
der Inn
Innsbruck
SALZBURG
STEIERMARK
TIROL
Graz
LIECHTENSTEIN
der GROSSGLOCKNER 3.798 m
der TAUERN TUNNEL
die Mur
UNGARN
die SCHWEIZ
der BRENNER PASS
(Zu Tirol)
KÄRNTEN
Lienz
der Wörther See
Villach
Klagenfurt
die Drau
Meilen
0 50
Kilometer
0 50
ITALIEN
SLOWENIEN
DIE SCHWEIZ
Hauptstadt
Landeshauptstadt
Stadt
Berg
Tunnel/Pass
der Rhein
DEUTSCHLAND
SCHAFFHAUSEN
Schaffhausen
BASEL-STADT
der Bodensee
Frauenfeld
Basel
AARGAU
ZÜRICH
THURGAU
Liestal
Winterthur
St. Gallen
die Aare
Delémont
BASEL-LAND
Aarau
Zürich
Herisau
APPENZELL AUSSERRHODEN
JURA
Appenzell
der Zürichsee
APPENZELL INNERRHODEN
SOLOTHURN
FRANKREICH
Solothurn
Zug
SANKT GALLEN
LIECHTENSTEIN
Biel
SCHWYZ
der Bieler See
LUZERN
ZUG
Vaduz
ÖSTERREICH
BERN
Glarus
NEUENBURG
Neuenburg
Schwyz
Luzern
Bern
GLARUS
der Neuenburger See
die Aare
Sarnen
Stans
der Vierwaldstätter See
NIDW.
Altdorf
Chur
Freiburg
UNTERWALDEN OBW.
URI
der Rhein
Davos
Thun
A L P E N
GRAUBÜNDEN
WAADT
Interlaken
FREIBURG
der Thuner See
Grindelwald
der Inn
Lausanne
die JUNGFRAU 4.158 m
der ST. GOTTHARD-TUNNEL
St. Moritz
der Genfer See
Montreux
TESSIN
ITALIEN
die Rhône
der SIMPLON-TUNNEL
GENF
WALLIS
Bellinzona
Sion
Locarno
Genf
Saas-Fee
Meilen
das MATTERHORN 4.478 m
Zermatt
der Lago Maggiore
Lugano
0 40
Kilometer
der MONT BLANC 4.807 m
FRANKREICH
ITALIEN
0 40

EUROPA und NORDAFRIKA
Hauptstadt
Landeshauptstadt
Stadt
Arctic Circle
ISLAND
Reykjavik
der ATLANTIK
NORWEGEN
SCHWEDEN
FINNLAND
Oslo
Stockholm
Helsinki
St. Petersburg
Tallinn
ESTLAND
RUSSLAND
LETTLAND
Riga
Moskau
LITAUEN
Vilnius
Minsk
die NORDSEE
SCHOTTLAND
NORDIRLAND
Edinburgh
Belfast
Dublin
IRLAND
GROSSBRITANNIEN
DÄNEMARK
Kopenhagen
die OSTSEE
Königsberg
(ZU RUSSLAND)
BELARUS
WALES
ENGLAND
Cardiff
London
die NIEDERLANDE
Amsterdam
Den Haag
Berlin
POLEN
Warschau
der ÄRMELKANAL
Brüssel
Bonn
BELGIEN
DEUTSCHLAND
LUXEMBURG
Luxemburg
Paris
Prag
TSCHECHIEN
Kiew
die UKRAINE
die SLOWAKEI
FRANKREICH
LIECHTENSTEIN
Bern
Vaduz
die SCHWEIZ
Wien
Bratislava
ÖSTERREICH
Budapest
UNGARN
MOLDAU
Chisinau
SLOWENIEN
Ljubljana
Zagreb
KROATIEN
RUMÄNIEN
Belgrad
Bukarest
BOSNIEN-HERZEGOWINA
Sarajevo
ITALIEN
PORTUGAL
Madrid
Lissabon
SPANIEN
KORSIKA
MALLORCA
Rom
SERBIEN
BULGARIEN
Sofia
MONTENEGRO
Skopje
MAZEDONIEN
Tirana
ALBANIEN
das SCHWARZE MEER
Istanbul
Ankara
die TÜRKEI
SARDINIEN
GRIECHENLAND
die STRASSE von GIBRALTAR
Rabat
Algier
SIZILIEN
Athen
Tunis
das MITTELMEER
MAROKKO
ALGERIEN
TUNESIEN
KRETA
Tripoli
LIBYEN
Meilen
0
400
Kilometer
0
400
AFRIKA

Schritte

Beginnen wir!

Lernziele *(Learning objectives)* The *Schritte ("pre-units")* will help you take your first steps in German.

You will learn to:

- introduce yourself and greet others.
- say the alphabet and spell.
- describe your classroom, clothing, and other things around you.
- count, tell prices, and do math.
- talk about the calendar, the weather, and time.

Fokus

The German language and its place in the world, greetings and leave-taking, **du** or **Sie**?, German climate, benefits of learning German, and descendants of German-speaking immigrants in North America

Rückschau

Kapitelwortschatz

RESSOURCEN

iLrn  Video

Audio   SAM

Hallo, wie geht's? Studentengruppe vor dem Reichstagsgebäude in Berlin.

Vorschau The German Language

Close to 120 million people worldwide speak German as their native tongue. It is the official language in Germany, Austria, and Liechtenstein as well as one of the official languages of Switzerland and Luxembourg. It is also spoken in parts of eastern Belgium and in Italy's South Tyrol region. In addition, there are significant German-speaking minorities in Denmark (northern Schleswig), France (Alsace), Poland (Silesia), the Czech Republic, and Hungary as well as in Estonia, Lithuania, Latvia, Bosnia and Herzegovina, Russia, and the Ukraine. German is also the native tongue of many people in Australia, Canada, the United States, and some South American countries.

The purpose of the *Vorschau* and all *Fokus* notes is to give students a quick and easy introduction to the various cultural points. They are intended just for enrichment and enjoyment.

German belongs to the Germanic branch of the Indo-European language family and is closely related to Dutch, English, the Scandinavian languages, Flemish, Frisian, Yiddish, and Afrikaans. For various political, literary, and linguistic reasons, we speak of Germans and the German language as dating from around the year 800. At that time, at least six major dialects with numerous variations were spoken. During the twelfth and thirteenth centuries, efforts were made to write a standardized form of German; thus, the years 1170–1250 saw great literary achievements. However, this use of German as a literary language declined and Latin was preferred for writing important documents. Around the year 1500, Martin Luther's translation of the Bible into German and Johann Gutenberg's invention of the printing press were major impetuses toward the development of a common, written German language. Nonetheless, Latin remained the sole language of instruction at German universities until the 1700s. Because of political fragmentation, a standard language was slow to develop in Germany. As late as the early 1900s, many people spoke only their regional dialects. The use of standard German (**Hochdeutsch**) in both newspapers and magazines and in radio and television broadcasts helped foster the widespread use of standard German, but regional accents and dialects are still common (see *Fokus* note in Chapter 6).

Because German and English are members of the same branch of the Indo-European language family, they share a considerable number of words. Some of these related words, called *cognates*, are identical in spelling in both languages (e.g., **Arm, Hand, Finger**), while others are similar (e.g., **Vater, Mutter, Haus**). As the two languages developed, certain cognates acquired different meanings, such as **Hose** (in German, *a pair of pants*) versus "hose" (in English, *nylon stockings*). For those cognates that came to be spelled differently, the differences between English and German often developed systematically. Note the following patterns:

	English	German
t → z	*ten*	zehn
	salt	Salz
p → pf	*pound*	Pfund
	apple	Apfel
t → ss	*water*	Wasser
	white	weiß
p → f	*ship*	Schiff
	help	helfen
k → ch	*book*	Buch
	make	machen
d → t	*bed*	Bett
	dance	tanzen
th → d	*bath*	Bad
	thank	danken

What are the English equivalents of these cognates? What other words do you know in English that are derived from German? For additional practice, see the *Zum Schreiben* section of the *Arbeitsbuch* (SAM).

Schritt 1

Practice reading these dialogues aloud in class. You might start by reading one role and students the other. Then let students practice in pairs. Finally, call on individual groups to recite them.

Draw two faces or stick figures on the board; label one **Herr Sanders** and one **Frau Lehmann.** Point to each figure while introducing the first dialogue and have students repeat after you. Then walk around the room and greet several students using the patterns they have just heard. Begin by saying in German who you are **(Ich heiße . . .),** then write your name on the board. Repeat **Ich heiße . . .** and ask a student **Wie heißen Sie?** Repeat until students understand and can respond.

■ Note the difference in verb form and pronoun when you address someone casually **(Wie heißt du?)** or formally **(Wie heißen Sie?).** This will be explained later. So for now, just learn these phrases as idioms.

■ The following dialogues are recorded for you on the ***Wie geht's?*** Premium Website and iLrn. Listen to them and read them aloud until you can do so fluently. Then answer questions about them. If necessary, consult the translations in the Appendix. ■

Gespräche

Guten Tag!

HERR SANDERS	Guten Tag!
FRAU LEHMANN	Guten Tag!
HERR SANDERS	Ich heiße Sanders, Willi Sanders. Und Sie, wie heißen Sie?
FRAU LEHMANN	Mein Name ist Erika Lehmann.
HERR SANDERS	Freut mich. Wie geht es Ihnen?
FRAU LEHMANN	Danke, gut. Und Ihnen?
HERR SANDERS	Danke, es geht mir auch gut.

LUCA SEIBEL	Guten Tag!
EVA BACH	Tag!
LUCA SEIBEL	Ich heiße Luca Seibel. Und du, wie heißt du?
EVA BACH	Mein Name ist Eva Bach.
LUCA SEIBEL	Freut mich. Und wie geht es dir?
EVA BACH	Ach, nicht schlecht.

HEIDI	Hallo, Ute! Wie geht's?
UTE	Tag, Heidi! Ach, ich bin müde.
HEIDI	Ich auch. Zu viel Stress. Bis später!
UTE	Tschüss! Mach's gut!

Fragen: 1. Willi Sanders, Luca Seibel 2. Erika Lehmann, Eva Bach, Heidi, Ute 3. gut 4. müde 5. *(answer varies)*

Fragen *(Questions)* Answer these questions about the dialogues.

1. Wie heißen die zwei *(two)* Herren?
2. Wie heißen die vier *(four)* Frauen?
3. Wie geht es Frau Lehmann? Frau Lehmann geht es . . .
4. Wie geht es Ute und Heidi? Ute und Heidi sind *(are)* . . .
5. Und wie geht es Ihnen?

Fokus Greetings and Leave-taking

When greeting someone, **Guten Morgen!** is usually used until about 10 A.M., **Guten Tag!** between then and early evening, and **Guten Abend!** from about 5 P.M. on. Casual greetings (equivalent to *Hi!*) include **Tag!, Hallo!,** and **Grüß dich!** In Switzerland and Liechtenstein, people also say **Grüezi!,** and in southern Germany and Austria, **Servus!** or **Grüß Gott!** (lit. *Greetings in the name of God!*). The parting expressions **Tschüss!** or **Ciao [Tschau]!** are more informal than **Auf Wiedersehen!** Note that **Gute Nacht!** *(Good night!)* is never used for leave-taking but rather to wish someone a good night's sleep.

When you ask **Wie geht's?** or **Wie geht es Ihnen?,** expect a detailed answer about the other person's well-being. This is different from the English question *How are you?,* which elicits only a short response. Most German speakers pose this question only to people they already know well.

Wortschatz *(Vocabulary)*

■ You are responsible for knowing all the vocabulary of the *Wortschatz* (literally, "treasure of words"), including the headings. Be sure to learn the gender and plural forms of nouns! Words and phrases listed under *Zum Erkennen* are intended for comprehension only; you will not be asked to produce them actively. ■

- In German, all nouns are capitalized.
- The pronoun **ich** *(I)* is not capitalized unless it occurs at the beginning of a sentence. The formal pronoun **Sie** *(you)* is always capitalized.

Wie geht's? (casual: *How are you?*)

Wie geht es dir? (familiar: *How are you?*)

Wie geht es Ihnen? (formal: *How are you?*)

der Herr, die Herren *(pl.)* — *Mr.; gentleman*
die Frau, die Frauen *(pl.)* — *Mrs., Ms.; woman; wife*
Guten Tag! — *Hello.*
Guten Morgen! — *Good morning.*
Guten Abend! — *Good evening.*

Wie heißt du? — *What's your name?* (familiar)
Wie heißen Sie? — *What's your name?* (formal)
Mein Name ist . . . — *My name is . . .*
heißen — *to be called*
Ich heiße . . . — *My name is . . .*
Du heißt . . . — *Your name is . . .* (familiar)
Sie heißen . . . — *Your name is . . .* (formal)
Freut mich. — *Pleased to meet you.*
Es geht mir gut. — *I'm fine.*
gut / schlecht — *good; fine, well / bad(ly)*
wunderbar — *wonderful(ly), great*
Ich bin müde. — *I'm tired.*
ja / nein — *yes / no*
danke / bitte — *thank you / please; you're welcome*
auch — *also, too*
nicht — *not*
und — *and*
Auf Wiedersehen! — *Good-bye!*
Tschüss! — *Good-bye!; Bye!* (colloquial)
Mach's gut! — *Take care!* (colloquial)
Bis später! — *See you later!* (colloquial)

■ In modern German, the title **Frau** *(Mrs., Ms.)* is generally used for any adult woman regardless of her age or marital status.

Again, draw students' attention to the difference in verb form and pronoun when you address someone casually **(Wie geht es dir?)** or formally **(Wie geht es Ihnen?).** Also point out the different verb endings in **Ich heiße, Du heißt,** and **Sie heißen.**

Point out the difference between **Es geht mir gut** *(I feel good)* and **Er ist gut** *(He's a good person).* **Es geht mir gut** is an idiom, and as such it has a meaning that is different from its literal translation.

If students ask: *all right* **sehr gut, ganz gut;** *so-so* **nicht so gut, so lala;** *I am exhausted* **ich bin k.o.;** *I am sick* **ich bin krank**

Zum Erkennen: Hallo! *(Hi! Hello!)*; Tag! *(Hi!)*; ach *(oh)*; ich auch *(me too)*; zu viel Stress *(too much stress)*; AUCH: das Beispiel, -e *(example)*; Lesen Sie laut! *(Read aloud!)*; Wie schreibt man das? *(How do you write that?)*; Buchstabieren Sie auf Deutsch! *(Spell in German!)*; Was sagen sie? *(What do they say? / What are they saying?)*

■ The words in *Zum Erkennen* are for recognition only, that is, passive vocabulary. They are listed in order of appearance in the dialogue(s). Following "AUCH" are a few other words or expressions that will facilitate classroom instruction in German.

Lerntipp

Experiencing a New Language

Learning another language is much like learning to play a musical instrument or a sport. Just as you can't learn to play the piano or swim by reading about it, you can't learn a foreign language by thinking or reading about it. You must practice. Listen to your instructor, to recordings, and to the answers of your fellow students. Use every chance you get to speak German. Whenever possible, read the language aloud and write it.

Remember, too, that you are still improving your English; so don't expect immediate perfection in another language. Just as you made mistakes while learning English, when you are learning a foreign language, mistakes are also inevitable. With daily practice, however, your fluency in German will rapidly increase.

Mündliche Übungen *(Oral exercises)*

A. Das Alphabet: Lesen Sie laut! *(Read aloud.)*

Germans would say **äh, öh, üh** rather than **a-umlaut, o-umlaut,** or **u-umlaut.** The [ts] in the pronunciation of **c** and **z** is like the *ts* in *cats* or the *z* in *pizza*.

a ah	**g** geh	**m** emm	**s** ess	**y** üppsilon
b beh	**h** hah	**n** enn	**t** teh	**z** tsett
c tseh	**i** ih	**o** oh	**u** uh	**ä** äh (a-umlaut)
d deh	**j** yot	**p** peh	**v** fau	**ö** öh (o-umlaut)
e eh	**k** kah	**q** kuh	**w** veh	**ü** üh (u-umlaut)
f eff	**l** ell	**r** err	**x** iks	**ß** ess-tsett

For capital letters, say **großes A (B, C . . .)**, for lowercase letters, **kleines D (E, F . . .)**. For further explanation of the **ß**-sound, see Part III A.6 in the Summary of Pronunciation section in the front of this book. Note that there is also a specific pronunciation section (**Aussprache**) for each *Schritt* on the ***Wie geht's?*** Premium Website and iLrn, each focusing on particular vowels and consonants. Make it a point to listen to it and to repeat what you hear.

A B C D E F G
H I J K L M N O P
Q R S T U V W
X Ypsilon Z, juchhe!
Das ist das ganze ABC.

B. Wie schreibt man das? *(How do you write that?)* Ask your partner to spell the following words in German.

BEISPIEL S1 Wie schreibt man Autobahn?
S2 A-U-T-O-B-A-H-N.

Audi	Gesundheit
Mercedes	Strudel
Volkswagen	Zwieback
Kindergarten	Zeitgeist

C. Schreiben Sie, was ich buchstabiere! *(Write down what I am spelling.)* Pick one of the words from the *Wortschatz* or the name of a famous German-speaking person and spell it. A partner listens, writes down what you spell, and reads it back to you. Take turns.

You might ask if there is anyone with a German name in this class. If so, have it spelled in German.

Aufgaben *(Assignments)*

A. Wie heißt du? Ask classmates for their name and then how to spell it.

BEISPIEL S1 Wie heißt du?
S2 Ich heiße . . .
S1 Wie schreibt man das? *(How does one spell that?)*
S2 . . . *(Spell that name in German.)*

B. Wie geht's? In pairs, ask each other how you are doing.

S1 Hallo, . . . ! Wie geht's?
S2 Tag, . . . ! . . .
S1 . . .
S2 Tschüss!
S1 Mach's gut! . . .

■ Prepare all assignments so that you can answer fluently in class.

A: This also would lend itself to a chain reaction in which students ask each other.

Aussprache *(Pronunciation):* a, e, er, i, o, u

■ The words listed below are either familiar words, cognates (words related to English), or proper names **(Erika, Amerika).** A simplified phonetic spelling for each sound is given in brackets. The colon (:) following a vowel means that the vowel is long. Pay particular attention to word stress as you hear it from your instructor or the recording. For a while, you may want to mark words for stress. ■

Hören Sie zu und wiederholen Sie! ***(Listen and repeat.)***

1. [a:] **A**bend, T**a**g, Ban**a**ne
2. [a] **A**nna, **A**lbert, w**a**s
3. [e:] **E**rika, P**e**ter, Am**e**rika
4. [e] **E**llen, H**e**rmann, **e**s
5. [ə] (*unstressed* **e**) Ut**e**, dank**e**, heiß**e**
6. [ʌ] (*final* **-er**) Diet**er** Fiedl**er**, Rain**er** Mei**er**
7. [i:] **Ih**nen, Mar**i**a, Sab**i**ne
8. [i] b**i**n, b**i**tte
9. [o:] M**o**nika, H**o**se, s**o**
10. [o] **O**skar, **o**ft, M**o**rgen
11. [u:] **U**te, G**u**drun, g**u**t
12. [u] **u**nd, w**u**nderbar, Ges**u**ndheit

As you may have noticed, double vowels **(Tee, Boot),** vowels followed by **h (geht, Schuh),** and the combination **ie (wie, Sie)** are long. Vowels followed by double consonants (two identical consonants as in **Anna, Sommer**) are short.

■ The *Aussprache* section is closely tied to the Summary of Pronunciation in the front of this book. Be sure to see Part II, subsections 1–21.

Remember to assign the *Zum Hören* sections in the *Arbeitsbuch* (SAM) for each pre-unit and chapter; they are recorded on the ***Wie geht's?*** Premium Website and iLrn.

For extra practice of specific sounds, add some examples of your own.

Fokus *Du* or *Sie*?

German has more than one way of saying *you.* **Du,** corresponding in form to the archaic English word *thou,* is used primarily for addressing children, family members, friends, and animals. **Sie** is used with adults who are not close friends or relatives. Today, young people and university students tend to address each other automatically with the informal **du**-form; but it is still considered rude to address older people, or even colleagues, with **du.** When in doubt, use **Sie.** The general custom is that it is up to the person of higher age or status to suggest **Duzen** instead of **Siezen.** Similarly, you address a German speaker "on a first-name basis" only after you begin using the **du**-form. Up to that point, it is **Herr** . . . or **Frau** . . . to you.

Schritt 2

Gespräch

Was und wie ist das?

Warm-ups: 1. **Guten Tag! Ich heiße . . . Wie heißen Sie? Heißen Sie . . . ? Ja / Nein . . .** 2. **Wie geht's? Geht es Ihnen gut? Ja / Nein . . .** 3. **Ich sage „Guten Tag!" Was sagen Sie?**— These *Warm-ups* are meant as a quick review and should not take much time.

With all of these *Warm-ups*, you might ask the first question, and then let students continue asking their classmates.

Act out the dialogue as you introduce it, so that students understand most of it without reference to the English translation in the Appendix. Bring a yellow pencil, a light-blue notebook, and a blue ballpoint pen.

DEUTSCHPROFESSORIN Hören Sie jetzt gut zu und antworten Sie auf Deutsch! Was ist das?
JIM MILLER Das ist der Bleistift.
DEUTSCHPROFESSORIN Welche Farbe hat der Bleistift?
SUSAN SMITH Gelb.
DEUTSCHPROFESSORIN Bilden Sie bitte einen Satz!
SUSAN SMITH Der Bleistift ist gelb.
DEUTSCHPROFESSORIN Ist das Heft auch gelb?
DAVID JENKINS Nein, das Heft ist nicht gelb. Das Heft ist hellblau.
DEUTSCHPROFESSORIN Gut!
SUSAN SMITH Was bedeutet *hellblau*?
DEUTSCHPROFESSORIN *Hellblau* bedeutet *light blue* auf Englisch.
SUSAN SMITH Und wie sagt man *dark blue*?
DEUTSCHPROFESSORIN *Dunkelblau.*
SUSAN SMITH Ah, der Kuli ist dunkelblau.
DEUTSCHPROFESSORIN Richtig! Das ist alles für heute. Für morgen lesen Sie bitte das Gespräch noch einmal und lernen Sie auch die Wörter!

Fragen

Fragen: 1. Jim Miller, Susan Smith, David Jenkins 2. Deutsch 3. der Bleistift; das Heft; der Kuli 4. das Gepräch noch einmal 5. die Wörter

1. Wie heißen die drei *(three)* Studenten?
2. Was lernen *(learn)* die Studenten?
3. Was ist gelb? hellblau? dunkelbau?
4. Was lesen die Studenten für morgen noch einmal? Für morgen lesen die Studenten . . .
5. Was lernen die Studenten für morgen? Für morgen lernen die Studenten . . .

Wortschatz

- In English, the DEFINITE ARTICLE has just one form: *the*. The German singular definite article has three forms: **der, das, die.** Some nouns take **der** and are called MASCULINE; some take **das** and are called NEUTER; and some take **die** and are called FEMININE. This is a grammatical distinction and has little to do with biological gender, although it is true that most nouns referring to female beings are feminine and most referring to male beings are masculine.

  der Mann, **die** Frau, BUT **das** Kind *(child)*

  Objects without biological gender, such as *table, book*, and *blackboard*, are by no means necessarily neuter. Many inanimate objects are masculine and many others are feminine.

  das Buch, BUT **der** Tisch, **die** Tafel

  Because the gender of many nouns is unpredictable, you must always learn the article with the noun.

Point out that modern German has acquired many words from English and that there, too, the article is a "multiple guess": e.g., **der** Bestseller, Computer, Boss, Job, Trend, Mausklick; **das** Design, Happening, Image, Make-up, Team; **die** Publicity, Show, Story.

- The PLURAL OF NOUNS is formed in various ways that are often unpredictable. You must, therefore, learn the plural together with the article and the noun. In vocabulary lists and in dictionaries, plurals are given in an abbreviated form. These are the most common plural forms and their abbreviations:

ABBREVIATION	LISTING	PLURAL FORM
- *(add nothing)*	das Fenster, **-**	die Fenster
¨ *(add umlaut)*	der Mantel, **¨**	die M**ä**ntel
-e (*add* e)	der Tisch, **-e**	die Tisch**e**
¨e (*add umlaut* + e)	der Stuhl, **¨e**	die St**ü**hl**e**
-er (*add* er)	das Bild, **-er**	die Bild**er**
¨er (*add umlaut* + er)	das Buch, **¨er**	die B**ü**ch**er**
-n (*add* n)	die Farbe, **-n**	die Farbe**n**
-en (*add* en)	die Frau, **-en**	die Frau**en**
-nen (*add* nen)	die Professorin, **-nen**	die Professorin**nen**
-s (*add* s)	der Kuli, **-s**	die Kuli**s**

To make sure students understand the plural abbreviations, write some of the new words with their plurals on the board: **Zimmer, Bleistifte, Kulis, Stühle,** and so on.

NOTE: The PLURAL ARTICLE for all nouns is **die.** In this book, when the noun being taught is not followed by one of the plural endings, it either does not have a plural or the plural is rarely used.

Die Farbe, -n *(color)*

Optional colors, if students ask: *beige* **beige;** *colorful* **bunt;** *khaki* **khaki;** *lavender* **flieder;** *natural* **natur;** *olive* **oliv;** *plum* **pflaume;** *purple* **lila;** *rust-colored* **rost;** *turquoise* **türkis;** *wine-red* **weinrot**

There is a great deal of vocabulary taught in *Schritt 2.* Help students learn it by reviewing for several days the names of objects and colors around you. Don't expect students to master all of it overnight.

Das Zimmer, - *(room)*

der Bleistift, -e	*pencil*	das Heft, -e	*notebook*
Kuli, -s	*pen*	Papier, -e	*paper*
Stuhl, ¨e	*chair*	die Kreide	*chalk*
Tisch, -e	*table*	Tafel, -n	*blackboard*
das Bild, -er	*picture*	Tür, -en	*door*
Buch, ¨er	*book*	Wand, ¨e	*wall*
Fenster, -	*window*		

These vocabulary sections are organized by topic, with the nouns listed alphabetically by gender.

Lerntipp

Techniques for Building New Vocabulary

To remember vocabulary, you must use it. Name things in German as you see them in the course of your day. Label objects in your room or home using sticky notes. Practice new words aloud—the use of your auditory and motor memory will greatly enhance your learning efficiency. Be sure to learn the gender and plural with each noun. For some, the gender and plural are predictable; study Part 1 in the Appendix.

Verschiedenes *(Different words and phrases)*

auf Deutsch / auf Englisch	*in German / in English*
für morgen	*for tomorrow*
hier / da	*here / there*
noch einmal	*again, once more*
richtig / falsch	*correct(ly), right(ly) / wrong; false(ly)*
Was ist das?	*What is that?*
Das ist (nicht) . . .	*That is (not) . . .*
Welche Farbe hat . . . ?	*What color is . . . ?*
Was bedeutet . . . ?	*What does . . . mean?*
Wie sagt man . . . ?	*How does one say . . . ?*
Wo ist . . . ?	*Where is . . . ?*
antworten	*to answer*
fragen	*to ask*
hören	*to hear*
lernen	*to learn; to study*
lesen	*to read*
sagen	*to say*
wiederholen	*to repeat*
sein	*to be*
ich bin	*I am*
du bist	*you* (familiar) *are*
es ist	*it is*
sie sind	*they are*
Sie sind	*you* (formal) *are*

Zum Erkennen: Hören Sie gut zu! *(Listen carefully!)*; Bilden Sie einen Satz! *(Form a sentence.)*; hell(grün) / dunkel(blau) *(light[green] / dark[blue])*; Das ist alles für heute. *(That's all for today.)*; das Gespräch, -e *(dialogue, conversation)*; das Wort, ¨-er *(word)*; AUCH: der Artikel, - (von) *(article [of])*; der Plural, -e (von) *(plural [of])*; Alle zusammen! *(All together!)*

Mündliche Übungen

A. Fragen und Antworten *(Questions and answers)*

A: Modify the sentences to fit your particular surroundings.

1. –Ist das Papier weiß?
   –Ja, das Papier ist weiß.
   –Ist das Buch gelb? die Tafel grün? die Kreide weiß? der Kuli rot? . . .
2. –Ist die Kreide grün?
   –Nein, die Kreide ist nicht grün.
   –Ist die Tafel rot? der Bleistift weiß? das Buch rosa? das Papier braun? . . .
3. –Die Kreide ist weiß. Ist das richtig? *(Is that correct?)*
   –Ja, das ist richtig.
   –Das Heft ist schwarz. Ist das richtig?
   –Nein, das ist nicht richtig.
   –Das Papier ist weiß. Die Tür ist orange. Der Kuli ist blau. Das Buch ist rosa.
   –Der Tisch ist braun . . .

4. –Ist das richtig? Ask a partner whether certain items are indeed the color you say they are. Take turns.

B. Wiederholung *(Review)*

1. **Was sagen sie?**

a.

b.

c.

© Cengage Learning

B.1: a. **Guten Abend!** b. **Ich bin müde.** c. **Auf Wiedersehen! / Tschüss! / Mach's gut!**

2. **Wie schreibt man das?** Ask a partner to spell the names of the following animals in German.

Elefant	Maus	Tiger	Löwe
Katze	Hund	Giraffe	Hamster
Ratte	Goldfisch	Dinosaurier	Känguru

3. **Was buchstabiere ich? *(What am I spelling?)*** Think of any German word or name and spell it in German without saying the word. Let your partner write it down and read it back to you.

Play the "Alphabet Game." Assign each student a letter of the alphabet, including those with an umlaut. As you say a particular word (e.g., **Farbe**), one "letter" after the other will stand up and "identify itself" **(F, A, R, B, E).** Then the whole class repeats the word.

Aufgaben

A. Artikel, Plurale und Farben

1. **Was ist der Artikel?** Tür → die Tür
   Zimmer, Bleistift, Bild, Kreide, Kuli, Stuhl, Tafel, Buch, Tisch, Fenster, Farbe, Papier, Wand, Heft, Wort, Herr, Frau
2. **Was ist der Plural?** Kuli → die Kulis
   Tür, Bild, Bleistift, Buch, Heft, Tisch, Fenster, Tafel, Stuhl, Wort, Farbe
3. **Welche Farben** hat das Deutschbuch?

Besides knowing the articles and plurals of these words, also know how to pronounce and write them.

A.1: das Zimmer, der Bleistift, das Bild, die Kreide, der Kuli, der Stuhl, die Tafel, das Buch, der Tisch, das Fenster, die Farbe, das Papier, die Wand, das Heft, das Wort, der Herr, die Frau

A.2: Türen, Bilder, Bleistifte, Bücher, Hefte, Tische, Fenster, Tafeln, Stühle, Wörter, Farben

B. Jetzt sind Sie dran! *(Now it's your turn!)* Now that you are familiar with the new vocabulary in the *Wortschatz*, be ready to create your own dialogue with a partner. Take turns pointing at and identifying things and telling their colors.

BEISPIEL S1 Was ist das?
S2 Das ist die Tafel.
S1 Richtig! Welche Farbe hat die Tafel?
S2 Die Tafel ist grün.
S1 Richtig!

Aussprache: e, ä, ö, ü, eu, au, ai, ei, ie

Hören Sie zu und wiederholen Sie!

1. [e:] **E**rika, K**ä**the, g**e**ht
2. [e] W**ä**nde, H**ä**nde, h**ä**ngen
3. [ö:] **Ö**l, h**ö**ren, **Ö**sterreich
4. [ö] **Ö**tker, P**ö**ppel, W**ö**rter
5. [ü:] T**ü**r, f**ü**r, St**ü**hle
6. [ü] J**ü**rgen M**ü**ller, G**ü**nter, m**ü**ssen
7. [oi] D**eu**tsch, fr**eu**t, **Eu**ropa
8. [au] Fr**au** P**au**la B**au**er, **au**f, **au**ch
9. [ai] R**ai**ner, Kr**ei**de, w**ei**ß

Pay special attention to the pronunciation of **ei** and **ie** (as in *Einstein's niece*):

10. [ai] h**ei**ßen, H**ei**di M**ei**er
    [i:] S**ie**, w**ie**, W**ie**dersehen
    [ai / i:] B**ei**sp**ie**l, H**ei**nz F**ie**dler

For further review, see the Summary of Pronunciation in the front of this book. Study Part II, subsections 22–36 and 37–41.

Aussprache: For most speakers, **Erika** and **Käthe** have the same long vowel [e:]. The easiest way to learn to say [ö:] and [ü:] is to start from the tongue position for [e:] and [i:] and then round the lips. [ü:] and [ö:] need to be reviewed regularly. Students find it hard to hear and make these sounds.

Schritt 3

Gespräche

Im Kaufhaus

Warm-ups: 1. **Guten Tag! Wie geht es Ihnen?** 2. **Was ist das?** *Point to various items in the classroom.* 3. **Welche Farbe hat . . . ?** *Ask for colors.* 4. **Welche Wörter beginnen mit B (F, H, T, . . .)?**

© Cengage Learning

VERKÄUFERIN Na, wie ist die Hose?
CHRISTIAN Zu groß und zu lang.
VERKÄUFERIN Und der Pulli?
MEIKE Zu teuer.
CHRISTIAN Aber die Farben sind toll. Schade!

VERKÄUFERIN Guten Tag! Was darf's sein?
SILVIA Ich brauche ein paar Bleistifte und Papier. Was kosten die Bleistifte?
VERKÄUFERIN Fünfundfünfzig Cent (0,55 €).
SILVIA Und das Papier hier?
VERKÄUFERIN Zwei Euro vierzig (2,40 €).
SILVIA Gut. Ich nehme sechs Bleistifte und das Papier.
VERKÄUFERIN Ist das alles?
SILVIA Ja, danke.
VERKÄUFERIN Fünf Euro siebzig (5,70 €).

Fragen

Fragen: 1. zu groß und zu lang 2. der Pulli 3. Ja, die Farben sind toll. 4. ein paar Bleistifte und Papier 5. 5,70 €

1. Wie ist die Hose?
2. Was ist zu teuer?
3. Sind die Farben schön?
4. Was braucht *(needs)* Silvia? Silvia braucht . . .
5. Was kosten die Bleistifte und das Papier?

Fokus The Benefits of Learning German

Learning German will bring you benefits you may not have thought of before. In professional terms, you will be at an advantage regardless of whether your interests are in business, law, or academics. After all, the German economy is the largest and the strongest in Europe. Germany and Austria are active partners in the European Union, and many fields (such as music, art, literature, archaeology, philosophy, physics—to name just a few) reflect the creative work of artists and researchers from the German-speaking world. In personal terms, knowing German will open the doors to another culture. Because German and English are closely related Germanic languages, it is probable that in the course of your studies you will gain new insights into your own language as well.

Wortschatz

Die Zahl, -en *(number)*

1	eins	11	elf	21	ei**nu**ndzwanzig	0	null
2	zwei	12	zwölf	22	zweiundzwanzig	10	zehn
3	drei	13	dreizehn	30	drei**ß**ig	100	hundert
4	vier	14	vierzehn	40	vierzig	101	hunderteins
5	fünf	15	fünfzehn	50	fünfzig	200	zweihundert
6	sechs	16	se**chz**ehn	60	se**chz**ig	1 000	tausend
7	sieb**en**	17	sie**bz**ehn	70	sie**bz**ig	1 001	tausendeins
8	acht	18	achtzehn	80	achtzig	10 000	zehntausend
9	neun	19	neunzehn	90	neunzig	100 000	hunderttausend
10	zehn	20	zwanzig	100	hundert	1 000 000	eine Million

To reduce confusion with **drei,** speakers sometimes use the term **zwo** as a substitute for **zwei,** especially on the phone.

You might want to point out the irregularities with the numbers 16, 17, 30, 60, and 70, and explain why they happen.

As a memory aid, note these similarities between English and German:

-zehn = *-teen* **vierzehn** = *fourteen* **-zig** = *-ty* **vierzig** = *forty*

- 21–29, 31–39, and so on to 91–99 follow the pattern of "four-and-twenty **(vierundzwanzig)** blackbirds baked in a pie."
- German numbers above twelve are seldom written out, except on checks. When they are written out, however, they are written as one word, no matter how long:

  234 567: **zweihundertvierunddreißigtausendfünfhundertsiebenundsechzig**
- Where English uses a decimal point, German uses a comma ($2.75 BUT 2,75 €). In larger numbers, where English uses a comma, German uses a space or a period ($1,600.00 BUT 1 600,00 € or 1.600,00 €).
- The numbers 1 and 7 are written differently, as shown at right.

1 7

EINS SIEBEN

Die Kleidung *(clothing)*

Note that **die Hose** is singular in German; **die Jeans**, however, is plural.

If students ask: *blazer* **der Blazer, -;** *boot* **der Stiefel, -;** *cap* **die Kappe, -s;** *cardigan* **die Strickjacke, -n;** *denim skirt* **der Jeansrock, ¨-e;** *miniskirt* **der Minirock, ¨-e;** *overall* **die Latzhose, -n;** *sandal* **die Sandale, -n;** *sneaker* **der Tennisschuh, -e;** *lady's suit* **das Kostüm, -e;** *pants suit* **der Hosenanzug, ¨-e;** *sports shoe* **der Sportschuh, -e;** *turtleneck sweater* **der Rollkragenpullover, -;** *vest* **die Weste, -n**

There is a great deal of vocabulary taught in *Schritt 3*. Don't expect students to master all of it overnight. Help students learn it by reviewing the numbers and articles of clothing around them for several days.

Das Gegenteil, -e *(opposite)*

dick / dünn	*thick; fat / thin, skinny*
groß / klein	*tall; big, large / short; small, little*
lang / kurz	*long / short*
langsam / schnell	*slow(ly) / fast, quick(ly)*
neu / alt	*new / old*
sauber / schmutzig	*clean, neat / dirty*
teuer / billig	*expensive / inexpensive, cheap*

Verschiedenes

aber	*but, however*
oder	*or*
zu	*too* (with adjective or adverb)
wie viel? / wie viele?	*how much? / how many?*
kosten	*to cost, come to (a certain amount)*
Was kostet / kosten . . . ?	*How much is / are . . . ?*
Das kostet . . .	*That comes to . . .*
brauchen	*to need*
nehmen	*to take*
zählen	*to count*
ich zähl**e**	*I count*
wir } zähl**en**	*we count*
sie } zähl**en**	*they count*
Sie } zähl**en**	*you* (formal) *count*
der Cent, -s (ein Cent, fünf Cent)	*cent (one cent, five cents)*
der Euro, -s (ein Euro, zehn Euro)	*euro (one euro, ten euros)*

Zum Erkennen: im Kaufhaus *(in the department store);* der Verkäufer, - / die Verkäuferin, -nen *(salesclerk);* na *(well);* toll *(super);* Schade! *(Too bad!);* Was darf's sein? *(May I help you?);* ein paar *(a couple of);* Ist das alles? *(Is that all?);* AUCH: von . . . bis *(from . . . to);* die Seite, -n *(page);* auf Seite . . . *(on page . . .)*

Mündliche Übungen

You could introduce Exercise A on the first day by repeating several times in chorus the numbers from 1 to 12, 13 to 20, 21 to 30, 31 to 100, and do Exercise B the next day. Continue reviewing numbers. To sharpen listening skills, say a few numbers every day and let students write them as numerals.

A. Hören Sie gut zu und wiederholen Sie!

1. Wir zählen von eins bis zehn: eins, zwei, drei, vier, fünf, sechs, sieben, acht, neun, zehn.
2. Wir zählen von zehn bis zwanzig: zehn, elf, zwölf, dreizehn, vierzehn, fünfzehn, sechzehn, siebzehn, achtzehn, neunzehn, zwanzig.
3. Wir zählen von zwanzig bis dreißig: zwanzig, einundzwanzig, zweiundzwanzig, dreiundzwanzig, vierundzwanzig, fünfundzwanzig, sechsundzwanzig, siebenundzwanzig, achtundzwanzig, neunundzwanzig, dreißig.
4. Wir zählen von zehn bis hundert: zehn, zwanzig, dreißig, vierzig, fünfzig, sechzig, siebzig, achtzig, neunzig, hundert.
5. Wir zählen von hundert bis tausend: hundert, zweihundert, dreihundert, vierhundert, fünfhundert, sechshundert, siebenhundert, achthundert, neunhundert, tausend.

B. Zahlen

1. **Seitenzahlen *(Page numbers)*** Lesen Sie laut auf Deutsch!

   Seite 1, 7, 8, 9, 11, 12, 17, 21, 25, 32, 43, 54, 66, 89, 92, 101

2. **Preise *(Prices)*** Lesen Sie laut!

   0,25 € / 0,75 € / 1,10 € / 2,50 € / 8,90 € / 30,00 € / 45,54 € / 80,88 €

Show some euros and explain their value in relation to the dollar. Point out that when reading **1,10** as a number, it is read as **eins Komma zehn;** but when read as a price, the **eins** becomes **ein: 1,10 € (ein Euro zehn).**

3. **Inventar** With an employee, played by a partner, take inventory of the items you have in stock in your store.

   BEISPIEL Jacke / 32 —**Wie viele Jacken?**
   —*Zweiunddreißig Jacken.*

   a. Pullover / 42
   b. Rock / 14
   c. Hemd / 66
   d. Kleid / 19
   e. Hose / 21
   f. Jeans / 102
   g. Sweatshirt / 89
   h. T-Shirt / 37
   i. Schuh / 58

When counting, Germans use the thumb (not the index finger) to indicate number 1. Have students count students, women, men, fingers, feet, windows, chairs, etc.

4. **Telefonnummern *(Telephone numbers)***

   a. **Im Telefonbuch** Ask about the phone number of the people listed below.

   BEISPIEL Wie ist die Telefonnummer von *(of)* Jutta Scheurer?
   Die Nummer ist 4 27 18 12 (vier zwei sieben eins acht eins zwei or *vier siebenundzwanzig achtzehn zwölf)*

Note: The phrase **Wie ist** (or **Wie lautet) die Telefonnummer?** seems to be just as common among native speakers nowadays as **Was ist die Telefonnummer? Was ist . . . ?** actually is an Anglicism.

Scheufler Heike, Schiller-2	8 02 25 75	**Schewe Cornelia,** Tannen-3	8 80 82 35
-Gisela, Dresdner-51	8 41 26 74	**-Uwe,** Blumen-1	2 81 34 51
-Gustav, Schumann-8	4 11 65 75	**Schibalski Paul,** Bach-2a	4 21 94 83
Scheumann Ulf, Zwingli-7	4 27 29 69	**Schicht Carsten,** Haupt-27	4 40 16 69
Scheurer Ingo, Schul-20b	2 84 48 43	**-Eberhard,** Azaleenweg-3	8 38 72 78
-Jutta, Wolfszug-33	4 27 18 12	**Schick Bettina,** Görlitzer-12	8 36 33 78
-Werner, Meißner- 8	4 41 46 40	**Schicke Detlef,** Kant-16	2 01 24 71
Scheurich Sven, Neue-5b	4 16 04 71	**-Oliver,** Schäfer-10	2 61 01 96
Scheuring Jan, Scheriner-9	2 59 15 91	**Schickedanz Ute,** Bach-17	4 12 48 75
-Jochen, Böttger-4	8 03 12 63	**Schickmann Udo,** Park-31	4 11 26 61

Note that in German telephone books a hyphen following a name usually indicates "street", e.g., **Bach- = Bachstraße.**

   b. **Wie ist deine *(your)* Telefonnummer?** Ask other students about their phone number.

   BEISPIEL S1 Wie ist deine Telefonnummer?
   S2 Meine Telefonnummer ist 781-555-4601.

If you prefer not to use your own phone number, just make one up.

C. Wiederholung

1. **Wie schreibt man das?** Ask your partner how to spell the following names. You can also add names of your own to the list.

Mozart	Dürer	Nietzsche	Röntgen
Beethoven	Barlach	Aichinger	Zeppelin
Strauß	Kandinsky	Wohmann	Schwarzenegger

2. **Fragen und Antworten** Ask each other the following questions.

   a. Wie geht's? Bist du müde?
   b. Wie heißt du? Heißt du . . . ?
   c. Was ist das? Ist das . . . ? *(Point to items in the classroom.)*
   d. Welche Farbe hat der Tisch? die Tafel? . . .
   e. Was ist auch grün? blau? . . .

Aufgaben

A. Artikel, Plurale und Gegenteile Ask your classmates questions about the articles, plurals, and opposites below.

A: 1. Der Mantel, die Kleidung, der Pulli, die Bluse, das Hemd, der Rock, die Hose, das Kleid, die Jacke, der Schuh, das T-Shirt 2. Schuhe, Jacken, Röcke, Kleider, Hemden, Blusen, Pullover, Mäntel 3. falsch, neu, gut, langsam, teuer, dünn, ja, bitte, klein, schmutzig.

1. Was ist der Artikel von Mantel? Kleidung? Pulli? Bluse? Hemd? Rock? Hose? Kleid? Jacke? Schuh? T-Shirt?
2. Was ist der Plural von Schuh? Jacke? Rock? Kleid? Hemd? Bluse? Pullover? Mantel?
3. Was ist das Gegenteil von richtig? alt? schlecht? schnell? billig? dick? nein? danke? groß? sauber?

Optional chain reaction: **Wie geht's weiter?** a. 100 – 10 = 90 – 10 = ___ b. 70 – 7 = 63 – 7 = ___

B. Wie viel ist das? Lesen Sie laut!

BEISPIEL 4 + 4 = 8 *Vier plus vier ist acht.*
8 – 4 = 4 *Acht minus vier ist vier.*

a. 3 + 2 = 5
b. 7 + 3 = 10
c. 1 + 1 = 2
d. 8 + 1 = 9
e. 10 – 2 = 8
f. 9 – 4 = 5
g. 8 – 2 = 6
h. 7 – 6 = 1
i. 5 – 5 = 0

C. Jetzt sind Sie dran! Now that you are familiar with the new vocabulary in the *Wortschatz*, read the dialogue in the left-hand column below. Then be prepared to act out a similar dialogue with a partner using objects in the classroom.

S1 Ist das die Tafel?	S1 Ist das . . . ?
S2 Nein, das ist nicht die Tafel. Das ist die Wand.	S2 Nein, das ist nicht . . . Das ist . . .
S1 Wo ist die Tafel?	S1 Wo ist . . . ?
S2 Da ist die Tafel.	S2 Da . . .
S1 Welche Farbe hat die Tafel?	S1 Welche Farbe hat . . . ?
S2 Die Tafel ist grün.	S2 . . . ist . . .
S1 Was ist auch grün?	S1 Was ist auch . . . ?
S2 Das Buch ist auch grün.	S2 . . . ist auch . . .
S1 Wie ist das Buch? Ist das Buch alt?	S1 Wie ist . . . ?
S2 Nein, das Buch ist neu.	S2 . . .

Aussprache: l, s, st, sp, sch, f, v, z

Hören Sie gut zu und wiederholen Sie!

1. [l] **l**ernen, **l**esen, Pu**ll**over
2. [z] **s**ie **s**ind, **s**ieben, **s**auber
3. [s] Profe**ss**orin, hei**ß**en, Prei**s**
4. [st] Fen**st**er, ko**st**en, i**st**
5. [št] **St**efan, **St**uhl, **St**ein
6. [šp] **Sp**ort, Bei**sp**iel, Ge**sp**räch
7. [š] **sch**nell, **sch**lecht, **sch**warz
8. [f] **f**ünf, **f**ün**f**zehn, **f**ün**f**zig
   [f] **v**ier, **v**ierzehn, **v**ierzig
9. [ts] **Z**immer, **Z**ahl, **z**ählen
10. [z / ts] **s**ieben, sieb**z**ig, siebenund**s**ieb**z**ig

For further review, see the Summary of Pronunciation in the front of this book. Study Part III, subsections 1, 4, 6–9, and 11–12.

Initial **z** [ts] is difficult for language learners. Point out to students that they have no trouble with [ts] in *rats* or *pizza* and that initial **z** is the same sound.

Schritt 4

Gespräche

Das Wetter im April

Norbert Es ist schön heute, nicht wahr?
Julia Ja, wirklich. Die Sonne scheint wieder!
Rudi Nur der Wind ist kühl.
Julia Ach, das macht nichts.
Norbert Ich finde es toll.

Hannes Mensch, so ein Sauwetter! Es schneit schon wieder.
Martin Na und?
Hannes In Mallorca ist es schön warm.
Martin Wir sind aber hier und nicht in Mallorca.
Hannes Schade!

Lea Das Wetter ist furchtbar, nicht wahr?
Heiko Das finde ich auch. Es regnet und regnet!
Sara Und es ist wieder so kalt. Nur 7 Grad!
Heiko Ja, typisch April.

Warm-ups: 1. **Was ist das?** *Point to various articles of clothing.* 2. **Welche Farbe hat . . . ?** *Tell something about your clothes.* 3. **Was sage ich?** *Write down numerals, prices, or telephone numbers that others say in German.* 4. **Wie viel ist . . . ?** *Solve simple arithmetic problems that you hear.* 5. **Was ist das Gegenteil von . . . ?**

Inverted word order will be presented in Chapter 1.

Fragen

1. Wie finden Norbert und Julia das Wetter im April?
2. Was scheint?
3. Was ist kühl?
4. Was sagt *(says)* Hannes, wenn *(when)* es schneit? Hannes sagt . . .
5. Wo ist es schön warm?

Fragen: 1. schön, toll 2. die Sonne 3. der Wind 4. So ein Sauwetter! 5. in Mallorca

Es ist wieder Frühling und schön warm.

Wortschatz

Das Jahr, -e *(year)*
Die Jahreszeit, -en *(season)*

Note that the names of the **Jahreszeiten** are all masculine.

der Frühling

der Sommer

der Herbst

der Winter

© Cengage Learning

Tage und Monate *(days and months)*

Note that the names of the **Tage** and **Monate** are all masculine.

For *Saturday*, people in northern and central Germany generally use **Sonnabend,** while those in southern Germany say **Samstag** (derived from the Hebrew word *Sabbat*).

der Tag, -e	*day*	der Monat, -e	*Month*
Montag	*Monday*	Januar	*January*
Dienstag	*Tuesday*	Februar	*February*
Mittwoch	*Wednesday*	März	*March*
Donnerstag	*Thursday*	April	*April*
Freitag	*Friday*	Mai	*May*
Samstag	*Saturday*	Juni	*June*
Sonntag	*Sunday*	Juli	*July*
		August	*August*
		September	*September*
		Oktober	*October*
		November	*November*
		Dezember	*December*

If students ask: *cloudy* **bewölkt;** *foggy* **neblig;** *humid* **schwül;** *stormy* **stürmisch;** *sunny* **sonnig;** *wet* **nass;** *It's pouring.* **Es gießt.;** *It's thundering.* **Es donnert.;** *There's lightning.* **Es blitzt.**

Das Wetter *(weather)*

Es ist . . .	*It's . . .*	heiß / kalt	*hot / cold*
Es regnet.	*It's raining.*	warm / kühl	*warm / cool*
Es schneit.	*It's snowing.*	furchtbar	*awful(ly), terrible, terribly*
Die Sonne scheint.	*The sun is shining.*	prima	*great, wonderful*
		schön	*nice; beautiful*
		super	*superb, super*
		toll	*great, terrific*
		windig	*windy*

Verschiedenes

Im is used with the names of the months and seasons: **im Mai, im Winter.**

die Woche, -n	*week*	nicht wahr?	*isn't it?, isn't that right?*
Die Woche hat sieben Tage.	*The week has seven days.*	Wann bist du geboren?	*When were you* (familiar) *born?*
heute / morgen	*today / tomorrow*	Ich bin im Mai geboren.	*I was born in May.*
nur	*only*	finden	*to find*
sehr	*very*	Ich finde es . . .	*I think it's . . .*
(schon) wieder	*again*	Das finde ich auch.	*I think so, too.*
wirklich	*really, indeed*		
Schade!	*Too bad!*		

Zum Erkennen: der Wind *(wind);* Das macht nichts. *(It doesn't matter. That's okay.);* Mensch, so ein Sauwetter! *(Man, what lousy weather!);* Na und? *(So what?);* wir sind *(we are);* Grad *(degrees);* typisch *(typically);* AUCH: Hören Sie gut zu! *(Listen carefully!)*

Mündliche Übungen

A. Wie heißen die Jahreszeiten, Monate und Tage?

1. Die Jahreszeiten heißen . . .
2. Die Monate heißen . . .
3. Die Tage heißen . . .

B. Fragen

1. Wie ist das Wetter hier im Winter? im Sommer? im Frühling? im Herbst?
2. Wie heißen die vier Jahreszeiten?
3. Wie heißen die Wintermonate? die Frühlingmonate? die Sommermonate? die Herbstmonate?
4. Welcher Tag ist heute? morgen?
5. Wie viele Tage hat die Woche? Wie heißen die Tage?
6. Wie viele Tage hat der September? der Oktober? der Februar?
7. Wie viele Monate hat das Jahr? Wie heißen die Monate?

C. Kettenreaktion *(Chain reaction)* Ask each other when and where you were born.

1. Ich bin im [Mai] geboren. Und du?
2. Ich bin in [Seattle] geboren. Und du?

D. Wiederholung

1. **Antworten Sie mit JA!**

   BEISPIEL Wiederholen Sie das noch einmal?
   Ja, ich wiederhole das noch einmal.

   a. Lesen Sie das auf Deutsch?
   b. Lernen Sie das für morgen?
   c. Brauchen Sie das Buch?
   d. Nehmen Sie das Heft?

2. **Antworten Sie mit NEIN!**

   BEISPIEL Ist das die Kreide?
   Nein, das ist nicht die Kreide.

   a. Ist das die Wand?
   b. Ist das der Pulli?
   c. Sind das die Schuhe?
   d. Sind das die Klassenzimmer?

   BEISPIEL Ist die Kreide gelb?
   Nein, die Kreide ist nicht gelb.

   e. Ist die Antwort richtig?
   f. Ist die Farbe schön?
   g. Ist das Wetter gut?
   h. Ist das typisch?

3. **Wie geht's weiter?** One person states an addition or subtraction problem. A classmate gives the answer, then turns to another student and adds or subtracts another number. Follow the model.

   BEISPIEL S1 Sieben plus vier?
   S2 Sieben plus vier ist elf. Elf minus acht?
   S3 Elf minus acht ist drei. Drei plus . . . ?

A: Read and practice in chorus several times. 1. der Frühling, der Sommer, der Herbst, der Winter 2. Januar, Februar, März, April, Mai, Juni, Juli, August, September, Oktober, November, Dezember 3. Montag, Dienstag, Mittwoch, Donnerstag, Freitag, Samstag, Sonntag

B: 2 Frühling, Sommer, Herbst, Winter 3. Winter: Dezember, Januar, Februar Frühling: März, April, Mai Sommer: Juni, Juli, August Herbst: September, Oktober, November 5. sieben: Montag, Dienstag, Mittwoch, Donnerstag, Freitag, Samstag, Sonntag 6. September: 30; Oktober: 31; Februar: 28/29; 7: 12: Januar, Februar, März, April, Mai, Juni, Juli, August, September, Oktober, November, Dezember

D: After the students have mastered this pattern, you could ask students all sorts of questions that they would answer with *yes* or *no*. You might follow up by having students ask each other questions and give their own answers.

D.1: a. Ja, ich lese das auf Deutsch. b. Ja, ich lerne das für morgen. c. Ja, ich brauche das Buch. d. Ja, ich nehme das Heft.

D.2: a. Nein, das ist nicht die Wand. b. Nein, das ist nicht der Pulli. c. Nein, das sind nicht die Schuhe. d. Nein, das sind nicht die Klassenzimmer.

e. Nein, die Antwort ist nicht richtig. f. Nein, die Farbe ist nicht schön. g. Nein, das Wetter ist nicht gut. h. Nein, das ist nicht typisch.

Optional practice: **Was kostet das?** Write prices on the board for students to read aloud.

4. **Gegenteile** Choose the pair of German adjectives that describe each drawing.

__e__ kurz / lang __a__ neu / alt __b__ schmutzig / sauber

__c__ dünn / dick __d__ klein / groß

Aufgaben

A. Temperaturen ***(Temperatures)*** European thermometers use the Celsius scale. On that scale, water freezes at 0°C and boils at 100°C. Normal body temperature is about 37°C, and fever starts at about 37.6°C. To convert Fahrenheit units into Celsius, subtract 32, multiply by 5, then divide by 9. To convert Celsius degrees into Fahrenheit, multiply by 9, divide by 5, then add 32.

A.1: 38°C, 36°C, 29°C, 20°C, 5°C, −5°C, −20°C, −25°C

1. **Wie viel Grad Celsius** ***(degrees Celsius)*** **sind das?** Use the thermometer as a reference.

   BEISPIEL 32°F = 0°C
   Zweiunddreißig Grad Fahrenheit sind null Grad Celsius.

   100°F, 96°F, 84°F, 68°F, 41°F, 23°F, −4°F, −13°F

A.2: 21°C = **schön,** 0°C = **kalt,** 30°C = **sehr schön,** 38°C = **heiß,** −10°C = **sehr kalt,** −25°C = **furchtbar kalt**

2. **Wie ist das Wetter?** ***(What's the weather like?)***

   BEISPIEL 12°C (zwölf Grad Celsius) *Es ist kühl.*

   21°C, 0°C, 30°C, 38°C, −10°C, −25°C

Winter am Königssee in Süddeutschland

TEMPERATUREN

GRAD

Fahrenheit	Celsius	
100	38	Körpertemperatur
98.6	37 ←	
96	36	
95	35	
94	34	
90	32	
86	30	
84	29	
82	28	
79	26	
77	25	
72	22	
70	21	
68	20	
64	18	
59	15	
53	12	
50	10	
46	8	
41	5	Gefrierpunkt
37	3	
32	0 ←	
28	−2	
23	−5	
14	−10	
5	−15	
−4	−20	
−13	−25	

 **B. Jetzt sind Sie dran!** Based on the new vocabulary in the *Wortschatz*, create your own dialogue talking about the weather and how you like it.

BEISPIEL S1 Es ist . . . heute, nicht wahr?
S2 Ja, . . . / Nein, . . .
S1 Ich finde es . . .
S2 Typisch . . . , nicht wahr?
S1 . . .

Aussprache: r; p, t, k; final b, d, g; j, h

For further review, see the Summary of Pronunciation in the front of this book. Study Part III, subsections 1–3, 10, and 17.

Hören Sie zu und wiederholen Sie!

1. [r] **r**ichtig, **r**egnet, **r**ot
2. [ʌ] wi**r**, vie**r**, nu**r** BUT [ʌ / r] Tür / Tü**r**en; Papie**r** / Papie**re**; Jah**r** / Jah**re**
3. [p] **P**ulli, **P**lural, **p**lus AND [p] Her**b**st, Jako**b**, gel**b** BUT [p / b] gel**b** / gel**be**
4. [t] **Th**eo, **T**ür, Doro**th**ea AND [t] un**d**, tausen**d**, Bil**d** BUT [t / d] Bil**d** / Bil**d**er
5. [k] **k**ühl, **k**urz, **K**uli, dan**k**e AND [k] sa**g**t, fra**g**t, Ta**g** BUT [k / g] sa**g**t / sa**g**en; fra**g**t / fra**g**en; Ta**g** / Ta**g**e
6. [j] **j**a, **J**ahr, **J**anuar
7. [h] **h**ören, **h**eiß, **h**at
8. [:] z**äh**len, n**eh**men, **Ih**nen

The **r** requires substantial practice. For additional examples, use German names: Renate, Rita, Robert, Andreas, Sara, Laura, Moritz. . . .

Point out that **th** in German is [t]: **Ruth.** Final **b, d,** and **g** must be practiced repeatedly.

Fokus The German Climate

Although Germany lies between the 47th and 55th parallel north, roughly as far north as northern New England and southern Canada, its climate is generally far milder because of the effect of the warming Gulf Stream. Overall, Germany enjoys a temperate climate, ample rainfall throughout the year, and an absence of extreme heat and cold. In the northwest, summers tend to be cool and winters mild. Toward the east and south, the climate becomes more continental, with greater temperature differences between day and night, and summer and winter. Average daytime temperatures in Berlin are 30°F in January and 64°F in July; in Munich, they are 33°F in January and 73°F in July. Autumns are usually mild, sunny, and drier than other seasons. Between December and March, the mountainous regions of Germany can always expect snow. At the **Zugspitze,** the highest point in the German Alps, snow may pile up from 13 to 16 feet. In the Black Forest, it may average 5 feet. (Find the current weather in Germany on a German weather website.)

Looking at the weather map, have students ask each other what the weather is like in various places of Europe. **Das Wetter in Europa: 1. Wo scheint die Sonne? 2. Wo regnet es? 3. Wie warm ist es in . . . ? Ist das heiß (schön warm, kühl) oder kalt?**

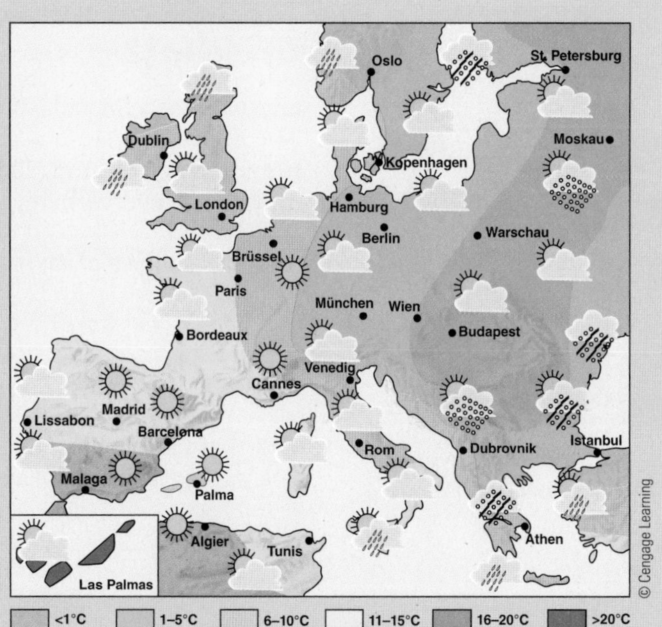

In Norwegen bringt stürmischer Wind, Schnee und Regen und auch im Südosten Europas ist es winterlich. Viel Sonne steht dagegen von Warschau über Paris bis Malaga auf dem Programm – dazu in Südspanien 20°C.

Schritt 5

Gespräche

Warm-ups: 1. **Welcher Tag ist heute?** 2. **Wie ist das Wetter heute?** 3. **Wie viel ist das?** *Write larger numbers on the board and have students say them in German.* 4. **Welche Wörter beginnen mit A (B, D, E, . . .)** 5. **Was ist dick / dünn (groß / klein, kurz / lang, neu / alt, sauber / schmutzig, teuer / billig)?**

Wie spät ist es?

RITA Hallo, Axel! Wie spät ist es?
AXEL Hallo, Rita! Es ist zehn vor acht.
RITA Oje, in zehn Minuten habe ich Philosophie.
AXEL Dann mach's gut, tschüss!
RITA Ja, tschüss!

Point out that the flavoring particle **denn** conveys what English expresses through gestures and intonation. Flavoring particles often have no exact English equivalent (see Chapter 7, Section 7.3).

PHILLIP Hallo, Steffi! Wie viel Uhr ist es denn?
STEFFI Tag, Phillip! Es ist halb zwölf.
PHILLIP Gehen wir jetzt essen?
STEFFI Okay, die Vorlesung beginnt erst um Viertel nach eins.

ANTON Wann bist du denn heute fertig?
PAUL Um zwei. Warum?
ANTON Spielen wir heute Tennis?
PAUL Ja, prima! Es ist jetzt halb eins. Um Viertel vor drei dann?
ANTON Gut! Bis später!

Fragen

Fragen: 1. Philosophie 2. Phillip und Steffi gehen essen. 3. um Viertel nach eins 4. um zwei 5. um Viertel vor drei

1. Was hat Rita in zehn Minuten?
2. Was tun *(do)* Phillip und Steffi?
3. Wann beginnt die Vorlesung?
4. Wann ist Paul heute fertig?
5. Wann spielen Paul und Anton Tennis?

Uhr am Rathausturm* (city hall tower) *in Passau

Wortschatz

- German has a formal (see Chapter 7) and informal way of telling time. The informal system is used in everyday speech and varies somewhat from region to region. The standard system below is certain to be understood everywhere.

die Uhrzeit, -en *(time of day)*

Es ist ein Uhr. Es ist eins.

Es ist zwei Uhr. Es ist zwei.

Es ist Viertel nach zwei.

Es ist halb drei.

Es ist Viertel vor drei.

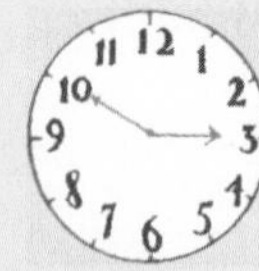

Es ist zehn (Minuten) vor drei.

Es ist fünf nach vier.

Es ist zwanzig (Minuten) nach sieben.

die Minute, -n	*minute*	morgens	*in the morning*
Sekunde, -n	*second*	mittags	*at noon*
Stunde, -n	*hour*	nachmittags	*in the afternoon*
Uhr, -en	*watch, clock; o'clock*	abends	*in the evening*
		Wie spät ist es?	*How late is it?*
Zeit, -en	*time*	Wie viel Uhr ist es?	*What time is it?*

Stunde refers to *duration* or to a *particular class:* **Eine Stunde hat 60 Minuten. Die Deutschstunde ist von acht bis neun.** The noun **Uhr** refers to clock time: **Es ist 9 Uhr.** *It is nine o'clock.*

Verschiedenes

der Student, -en	*student* (male)
die Studentin, -nen	*student* (female)
der Kurs, -e	*course*
die Vorlesung, -en	(*university*) *lecture, class*
Es ist ein Uhr (zwei Uhr).	*It's one o'clock (two o'clock).*
Es ist eins (zwei).	*It's one (two).*
(um) eins	*(at) one o'clock*
(um) Viertel nach eins, 1.15	*(at) quarter past one, 1:15*
(um) halb zwei, 1.30	*(at) half past one, 1:30*
(um) Viertel vor zwei, 1.45	*(at) quarter to two, 1:45*
fertig	*finished, done*
jetzt	*now*
Bitte!	here: *You're welcome.*
beginnen	*to begin*
essen	*to eat*
gehen	*to go*
Tennis spielen	*to play tennis*
haben	*to have*
ich habe	*I have*
du hast	*you* (familiar) *have*
es hat	*it has*
wir haben	*we have*
sie haben	*they have*
Sie haben	*you* (formal) *have*
Ich habe eine Frage.	*I have a question.*
Ich habe keine Zeit.	*I don't have time.*

Ein Uhr, BUT **Um eins.**

Expressions of time used to be punctuated differently in German than in English: *1:30* vs. **1.30.** Today both styles are used in German. While digital clocks separate hours from minutes with a colon, newspapers and magazines commonly use a simple period.

Zum Erkennen: Oje! *(Oh, no!);* denn *(flavoring particle used for emphasis);* erst *(only, not until);* warum? *(why?)*

Mündliche Übungen

A. Wie spät ist es?

1. 1.00: **Es ist** ein **Uhr.**
   3.00, 5.00
2. 1.05: **Es ist** fünf **nach** eins.
   3.05, 9.10
3. 1.15: **Es ist Viertel nach** eins.
   2.15, 6.15
4. 1.30: **Es ist halb** zwei.
   4.30, 6.30
5. 1.40: **Es ist** zwanzig **vor** zwei.
   5.40, 9.50
6. 1.45: **Es ist Viertel vor** zwei.
   3.45, 9.45
7. 9.00: **Die Vorlesung ist um** neun.
   12.15, 1.30

A: It would be helpful to have a model clock or to draw a clock face on the board to show **eins, Viertel nach eins, halb zwei, Viertel vor zwei,** and so on. You might also write some extra examples of time on the board.

B. Die Zeit

B.2: a sechzig Sekunden
b. sechzig Minuten
c.vierundzwanzig Stunden
d. vier Jahreszeiten

1. **Wie spät ist es?** Lesen Sie laut!
   8.45, 9.30, 10.15, 1.05, 2.20, 2.45, 6.59
2. **Wie viele?**
   a. Wie viele Sekunden hat die Minute?
   b. Wie viele Minuten hat die Stunde?
   c. Wie viele Stunden hat der Tag?
   d. Wie viele Jahreszeiten hat das Jahr?

iLrn

Visit the ***Wie geht's?*** iLrn website for more review and practice.

C. Wiederholung

C.1: a. Es ist heiß. b. Es ist schön. c. Es ist windig. d. Es ist (sehr / furchtbar) kalt.

1. **Wie ist das Wetter?**

a.

b.

c.

d.

C.2: a. Wie geht's? / Wie geht es Ihnen? b. Welche Farbe hat das Buch? c. Heißen Sie Fiedler? / Sie heißen Fiedler, nicht wahr? d. Wo ist die Tür? e. Sprechen Sie langsam? f. Was / Wie viel kostet das Papier? g. Wie ist das Wetter heute? h. Wie finden Sie das? i. Wie viel ist 5 + 16? j. Ist heute Sonntag, Mittwoch . . . ?

2. **Wie fragen Sie?** Formulate a logical question for each answer.

   BEISPIEL Ja, ich bin müde.
   Sind Sie müde?

   a. Danke, gut.
   b. Das Buch ist grau.
   c. Nein, ich heiße nicht Fiedler.
   d. Da ist die Tür.
   e. Ja, ich spreche langsam.
   f. Das Papier kostet 1,50 €.
   g. Heute ist es furchtbar heiß.
   h. Ich finde das nicht schön.
   i. Fünf plus sechzehn ist einundzwanzig.
   j. Nein, heute ist Dienstag.

3. **Und du?** Answer, then ask someone else.

   a. S1 Wie alt bist du?
      S2 Ich bin _____. Und du?
   b. S1 Wo bist du geboren?
      S2 Ich bin in _____ geboren. Und du?
   c. S1 Wann bist du geboren?
      S2 Ich bin im _____ *[month]* geboren. Und du?

Aufgaben

A. Meine Kurse Read the cue lines below. Then use them to ask about your partner's schedule and to relate your own.

In German, as a rule, the first syllable is stressed. In this exercise, if the stressed syllable differs from that rule, it is underlined.

Biologie, Chemie, Deutsch, Englisch, Französisch *(French)*, Geographie, Geologie, Geschichte *(history)*, Informatik *(computer science)*, Kunst *(art)*, Latein, Mathe(matik), Musik, Philosophie, Physik, Politik, Psychologie, Religion, Soziologie, Spanisch, Sport

S1 Welche Kurse hast du heute?
S2 Ich habe heute . . .
S1 Und morgen? Welche Kurse hast du morgen?
S2 Ich habe morgen . . .
S1 Wann hast du . . . ?
S2 Ich habe . . . um . . .

S1 Wie heißt der Professor / die Professorin?
S2 Er / Sie heißt . . .
S1 Ist der . . .kurs gut?
S2 . . .
S1 Wann bist du heute fertig?
S2 Ich bin heute um . . . fertig.

B. Spiel: Unterschreibe bitte hier! ***(Game: Please sign here!)*** Circulate around the room asking other students the following questions. As soon as someone truthfully answers **Ja,** ask for his or her signature. When someone answers **Nein,** thank him or her and ask someone else the same question until someone answers **Ja.** The first person with signatures for all questions wins.

BEISPIEL S1 Geht es dir gut?
S2 Ja. / Nein.
S1 Unterschreibe bitte hier! / Danke!

1. Geht es dir gut?
2. Bist du müde?
3. Hast du viel Stress?
4. Ist das Wetter heute schön?
5. Bist du im [Juli] geboren?
6. Bist du in [Tennessee] geboren?
7. Findest du Deutsch toll?

B: Students can supply their own paper for the signatures. In case students ask, point out that **Unterschreibe!** is the familiar imperative form of *unterschreiben.*

C. Praktische Ausdrücke im Klassenzimmer ***(Useful classroom expressions)***

You should be able to use the following phrases.

Das verstehe ich nicht.	*I don't understand that.*
Ich habe eine Frage.	*I have a question.*
Ich weiß nicht.	*I don't know.*
Ist das richtig?	*Is that correct?*
Öffnen Sie das Buch auf Seite . . . !	*Open the book to page . . .*
Sagen Sie das bitte noch einmal!	*Say that again, please.*
Schreiben Sie das bitte!	*Please write that!*
(Sprechen Sie) bitte langsam!	*(Speak) slowly please!*
Was bedeutet . . . ?	*What does . . . mean?*
Wie bitte?	*I beg your pardon?*
Wiederholen Sie das bitte!	*Please repeat that!*
Wie sagt man . . . auf Deutsch?	*How do you say . . . in German?*
Wie schreibt man das?	*How do you spell that?*

A vertical bar to the left of a list signals that the material is important and must be learned as active vocabulary. You already know most of these expressions. Those in **boldface** are new.

Was sagen Sie wann? Read again the classroom expressions. Then decide what you would say in each of the situations listed here.

1. You got called on in class and didn't hear the question.
2. You were unable to follow your instructor's explanation.
3. You have to ask your instructor to repeat something.
4. You want to let your instructor know that you have a question.
5. You have asked your new neighbor for his/her telephone number, but he/she is speaking much too fast.
6. You also did not understand his/her name and ask him/her to spell it.
7. In a conversation, the word **Geschwindigkeitsbegrenzung** keeps coming up. You want to ask for clarification.
8. You want to know how to say *first name* and *last name* in German.
9. You try to repeat the word and want to make sure that what you said is right.
10. You don't know whether something is correct.

C: 1. Wie bitte? 2. Das verstehe ich nicht. 3. Wiederholen Sie das bitte! / Sagen Sie das bitte noch einmal! 4. Ich habe eine Frage. 5. (Sprechen Sie) bitte langsam! 6. Wie heißen Sie? Wie schreibt man das? 7. Was bedeutet *Geschwindigkeitsbegrenzung*? 8. Wie sagt man *first name* und *last name* auf Deutsch? 9. Ist das richtig? 10. Ich weiß nicht.

Aussprache: ch, ig, ck, ng, gn, kn, qu, pf, ps, w

Hören Sie gut zu und wiederholen Sie!

■ For further review, see the Summary of Pronunciation in the front of this book. Study Part III, subsections 5, 13–15, 19, and 20–23.

1. [k] **Ch**ristine, **Ch**ristian, **Ch**aos
2. [x] a**ch**t, au**ch**, brau**ch**en
3. [ç] i**ch**, ni**ch**t, wirkli**ch**
4. [iç] richt**ig**, wind**ig**, bill**ig**
5. [ks] se**chs**, se**chs**undsechzig
6. [k] Ja**ck**e, Ro**ck**, Pickni**ck**
7. [ŋ] Englisch, Frühli**ng**, la**ng**
8. [gn] re**gn**et, resi**gn**ieren, Si**gn**al
9. [kn] **Kn**irps, **Kn**ie
10. [kv] **Qu**alität, **Qu**antität, **Qu**artett
11. [pf] **Pf**efferminz, A**pf**el
12. [ps] **Ps**ychologie, **Ps**ychiater, **Ps**ychoanalyse
13. [v] **W**ort, **w**ie, **w**as

Hörverständnis

The recordings for the *Hörverständnis* sections can be found on the ***Wie geht's?*** Premium Website and iLrn. The script can be found in the Annotated Instructor's Edition front matter.

■ The ***Hörverständnis*** listening comprehension activities go with the Text Audio files. These activities let you listen to natural language by native speakers. Listen to each recording several times. Note that it is not essential to understand every word in order to follow the gist of the conversation or report and answer the questions. ■

Das Klassenzimmer Listen to the description of this class and classroom. Then select the correct response from those given below.

1. Das Klassenzimmer ist ___b___.
   a. kühl b. groß c. schmutzig
2. Das Zimmer hat ___c___ Fenster.
   a. zwei b. drei c. fünf
3. Die Wände sind ___a___.
   a. grau b. blau c. schwarz
4. Die ___c___ sind rot.
   a. Türen b. Bücher c. Stühle
5. Der Professor heißt ___b___.
   a. Theo Seidl b. Oskar Thieme c. Otto Brockmann
6. Die Bilder sind ___b___.
   a. alt b. schön c. furchtbar

For further practice, an optional two-part video (**Szenen** and **Interviews**) is available on the ***Wie geht's?*** Premium Website and in iLrn, with corresponding questions and activities in the *Arbeitsbuch* (SAM).

There is a review section following the *Schritte* in the *Arbeitsbuch* (SAM). The accompanying exercises and answer key will help you prepare for the test.

Fokus Descendants of German-speaking Immigrants in North America

German-speaking immigrants are one of the largest ethnic groups in the United States and Canada. Names of such towns as Frankfort, Bremen, Dresden, Heidelberg, Hanover, Berlin, Zurich, and Salzburg bear witness to their influence. The role played by German-speaking immigrants in shaping US and Canadian life has been enormous: Anheuser, Boeing, Eisenhower, Guggenheim, Hammerstein, Heinz, Hershey, Pershing, Rockefeller, Sousa, Steinway, Weyerhaeuser, Westinghouse—the list of companies with German, Austrian, or Swiss names goes on and on. Blue jeans? Thank German immigrant Levi Strauss for them. The hamburger? It is generally attributed to German-Americans in St. Louis. The Republicans' elephant, the Democrats' donkey, and Uncle Sam himself? They sprang from the pen of Thomas Nast, a German-born cartoonist whose drawing of Santa Claus has delighted many over the years. The values of hard work and thrift, commitment to workers' rights, interest in the arts, and love of good living are all attributed to those immigrants, who have all left indelible marks on US and Canadian society.

The first organized group of German immigrants to come to the New World founded Germantown, now part of Philadelphia, in 1683. Thirteen Mennonite families had fled religious persecution in Germany. Their descendants came to be known as the Pennsylvania "Dutch," a misconstrual of the word **Deutsch.** Many other German speakers followed in the years to come, primarily for economic reasons, although religion and politics sometimes played roles as well. While the great majority of German immigrants were farmers, baking, brewing, and carpentry were also prominent skills among these new Americans. Between 1820 and 1930, 5.9 million people of German descent came to North America. By 1900, a quarter of all Chicago residents had been born in Germany or had parents who had been born in Germany. Between 1933 and 1937, there was a large exodus of German emigrants fleeing from Hitler's fascist regime to the United States and Canada, including **Bauhaus** architect Walter Gropius, physicist Albert Einstein, authors Thomas Mann and Bertolt Brecht, and composers Arnold Schönberg and Paul Hindemith. During the 1950s and 1960s, another large wave of immigrants from Germany, Austria, and Switzerland entered the United States and Canada, hoping for a fresh start abroad.

Opened in 2005, the German Emigration Center (**Deutsches Auswandererhaus**) in Bremerhaven recounts the story of the 7 million European emigrants who left by boat from this North Sea port for North America between 1830 and 1974.

Today, we find German descendants not only in cities with a traditionally high German-speaking population, such as Milwaukee, Cincinnati, St. Louis, Toronto, and Vancouver, but in every state of the Union and in all Canadian provinces. Nearly one-fourth of the US population claims some German ancestry; in Canada, Germans are the third largest ethnic group after the English and the French.

Bildarchiv, Preussischer Kulturbesitz/ Art Resource, NY

Jetzt geht's nach Amerika! Abfahrt von (departure from) *Bremerhaven.*

Fokus: You might show students the Santa Claus drawing of Thomas Nast, or refer them to the Internet.

Rückschau

Kapitelwortschatz

Hauptwörter *(Nouns)*

das Bild, -er	*picture*
der Bleistift, -e	*pencil*
die Bluse, -n	*blouse*
das Buch, ¨-er	*book*
der Cent, -s (ein Cent, fünf Cent)	*cent (one cent, five cents)*
der Euro, -s (ein Euro, zehn Euro)	*euro (one euro, ten euros)*
die Farbe, -n	*color*
das Fenster, -	*window*
(die) Frau, die Frauen (*pl.*)	*Mrs., Ms.; woman; wife*
der Frühling	*spring*
das Gegenteil, -e	*opposite*
das Heft, -e	*notebook*
das Hemd, -en	*shirt*
der Herbst	*fall*
(der) Herr, die Herren (*pl.*)	*Mr.; gentleman*
die Hose , -n	*pants*
die Jacke, -n	*jacket*
das Jahr, -e	*year*
die Jahreszeit, -en	*season*
die Jeans (*pl.*)	*jeans*
das Kleid, -er	*dress*
die Kleidung	*clothing*
die Kreide	*chalk*
der Kuli, -s	*pen*
der Kurs, -e	*course*
der Mantel, ¨	*coat*
die Minute, -n	*minute*
der Monat, -e	*month*
das Papier, -e	*paper*
der Pulli, -s	*sweater*
der Pullover, -	*sweater*
der Rock, ¨-e	*skirt*
der Schuh, -e	*shoe*
die Sekunde, -n	*second*
der Sommer	*summer*
der Student, -en	*student* (male)
die Studentin, -nen	*student* (female)
der Stuhl, ¨-e	*chair*
die Stunde, -n	*hour*
das Sweatshirt, -s	*sweatshirt*
das T-Shirt, -s	*t-shirt*
die Tafel, -n	*blackboard*
der Tag, -e	*day*
der Tisch, -e	*table*
die Tür, -en	*door*
die Uhr, -en	*watch, clock; o'clock*
die Uhrzeit, -en	*time of day*
die Vorlesung, -en	*(university) lecture, class*
die Wand, ¨-e	*wall*
das Wetter	*weather*
der Winter	*winter*
die Woche, -n	*week*
die Zahl, -n	*number*
die Zeit, -en	*time*
das Zimmer, -	*room*

Monate *(Months)*

Januar	*January*
Februar	*February*
März	*March*
April	*April*
Mai	*May*
Juni	*June*
Juli	*July*
August	*August*
September	*September*
Oktober	*October*
November	*November*
Dezember	*December*

Tage der Woche *(Days of the week)*

Montag	*Monday*
Dienstag	*Tuesday*
Mittwoch	*Wednesday*
Donnerstag	*Thursday*
Freitag	*Friday*
Samstag	*Saturday*
Sonntag	*Sunday*

Verben *(Verbs)*

antworten	*to answer*
beginnen	*to begin*
brauchen	*to need*
essen	*to eat*
finden	*to find*
fragen	*to ask*
gehen	*to go*
haben	*to have*
heißen	*to be called*
hören	*to hear*
kosten	*to cost, come to (a certain amount)*
lernen	*to learn; to study*
lesen	*to read*
nehmen	*to take*
sagen	*to say*
sein	*to be*
Tennis spielen	*to play tennis*
wiederholen	*to repeat*
zählen	*to count*

heißen

Ich heiße . . .	*My name is . . .*
Du heißt . . .	*Your name is . . .* (familiar)
Sie heißen . . .	*Your name is . . .* (formal)

zählen

ich zähle	*I count*
wir zählen	*we count*
sie zählen	*they count*
Sie zählen	*you* (formal) *count*

sein

ich bin	*I am*
du bist	*you* (familiar) *are*
es ist	*it is*
sie sind	*they are*
Sie sind	*you* (formal) *are*

haben

ich habe	*I have*
du hast	*you* (familiar) *have*
es hat	*it has*
wir haben	*we have*
sie haben	*they have*
Sie haben	*you* (formal) *have*

Adjektive und Adverbien *(Adjectives and adverbs)*

alt — *old*
billig — *inexpensive, cheap*
dick — *thick; fat*
dünn — *thin, skinny*
falsch — *wrong; false(ly)*
fertig — *finished, done*
furchtbar — *awful(ly), terrible, terribly*
groß — *tall; big, large*
gut — *good; fine, well*
heiß — *hot*
kalt — *cold*
klein — *short; small, little*
kühl — *cool*
kurz — *short*
lang — *long*
langsam — *slow(ly)*
neu — *new*
prima — *great, wonderful*
richtig — *correct(ly), right(ly)*
sauber — *clean, neat*
schlecht — *bad(ly)*
schmutzig — *dirty*
schnell — *fast, quick(ly)*
schön — *nice; beautiful*
super — *superb, super*
teuer — *expensive*
toll — *great, terrific*
warm — *warm*
windig — *windy*
wunderbar — *wonderful(ly), great*

Farben *(Colors)*

blau — *blue*
braun — *brown*
gelb — *yellow*
grau — *grey*
grün — *green*
orange — *orange*
rosa — *pink*
rot — *red*
schwarz — *black*
weiß — *white*

Verschiedenes *(Different words and phrases)*

abends — *in the evening*
aber — *but, however*
auch — *also, too*
auf Deutsch / auf Englisch — *in German / in English*
Auf Wiedersehen! — *Good-bye!*
Bis später! — *See you later!* (colloquial)
bitte — *please; you're welcome*
danke — *thank you*
Das finde ich auch. — *I think so, too.*
Das ist (nicht) . . . — *That is (not) . . .*
Das kostet . . . — *That comes to . . . , That costs . . .*
Das verstehe ich nicht. — *I don't understand.*
Die Sonne scheint. — *The sun is shining.*
Die Woche hat sieben Tage. — *The week has seven days.*
Es geht mir gut. — *I'm fine.*
Es ist . . . — *It's . . .*
Es ist ein Uhr (zwei Uhr). — *It's one o'clock (two o'clock).*
Es ist eins (zwei). — *It's one (two).*
Es ist fünf nach vier. — *It's five after four (time).*
Es ist zehn (Minuten) vor drei. — *It's ten (minutes) to three.*
Es ist zwanzig (Minuten) nach sieben. — *It's twenty (minutes) after seven.*
Es regnet. — *It's raining.*
Es schneit. — *It's snowing.*
Freut mich. — *Pleased to meet you.*
für morgen — *for tomorrow*
Guten Abend! — *Good evening.*
Guten Morgen! — *Good morning.*
Guten Tag! — *Hello.*
heute — *today*
hier / da — *here / there*
Ich bin im Mai geboren. — *I was born in May.*
Ich bin müde. — *I'm tired.*
Ich finde es . . . — *I think it's . . .*
Ich habe eine Frage. — *I have a question.*
Ich habe keine Zeit. — *I don't have time.*
Ich weiß nicht. — *I don't know.*
Ist das richtig? — *Is that correct?*
ja — *yes*
jetzt — *now*
Mach's gut! — *Take care!* (colloquial)
Mein Name ist . . . — *My name is . . .*
mittags — *at noon*
morgen — *tomorrow*
morgens — *in the morning*
nachmittags — *in the afternoon*
nein — *no*
nicht — *not*
nicht wahr? — *isn't it?, isn't that right?*
noch einmal — *again, once more*
nur — *only*
oder — *or*
Öffnen Sie das Buch auf Seite . . . ! — *Open the book to page . . .*
Sagen Sie das bitte noch einmal! — *Say that again, please.*
Schade! — *Too bad!*
(schon) wieder — *again*
Schreiben Sie das bitte! — *Please write that!*
sehr — *very*
(Sprechen Sie) bitte langsam! — *(Speak) slowly please!*
Tschüss! — *Good-bye!; Bye!* (colloquial)
(um) eins — *(at) one o'clock*
(um) halb zwei, 1.30 — *(at) half past one, 1:30*
(um) Viertel nach eins, 1.15 — *(at) quarter past one, 1:15*
(um) Viertel vor zwei, 1.45 — *(at) quarter to two, 1:45*
und — *and*
Wann bist du geboren? — *When were you born?* (familiar)
Was bedeutet . . . ? — *What does . . . mean?*
Was ist das? — *What is that?*
Was kostet / kosten . . . ? — *How much is / are . . . ?*
Welche Farbe hat . . . ? — *What color is . . . ?*
Wie bitte? — *I beg your pardon?*
Wiederholen Sie das bitte! — *Please repeat that!*
Wie geht es dir? — *How are you?* (familiar)
Wie geht es Ihnen? — *How are you?* (formal)
Wie geht's? — *How are you?* (casual)
Wie heißt du? — *What's your name?* (familiar)
Wie heißen Sie? — *What's your name?* (formal)
Wie sagt man . . . (auf Deutsch)? — *How does one say . . . (in German)?*
Wie schreibt man das? — *How do you spell that?*
Wie spät ist es? — *How late is it?*
Wie viel Uhr ist es? — *What time is it?*
wie viel? / wie viele? — *how much? / how many?*
wirklich — *really, indeed*
Wo ist . . . ? — *Where is . . . ?*
zu — *too* (with adjective or adverb)

Kapitel 1

Familie, Länder, Sprachen

Lernziele In this chapter you will learn about:

Zum Thema

The family, geographical terms, country names, nationalities, and languages

Fokus

Germany, the Goethe Institute, German in Europe and throughout the world, the EU, and Frankfurt am Main

Struktur

- The present tense of regular verbs
- The nominative case
- Sentence structure
- Compound nouns

Einblicke

Lesetext: Deutschland in Europa

Rückschau

Kapitelwortschatz
Zum Schluss

RESSOURCEN

 iLrn
Video
 Audio
SAM

© Peggy Setje-Eilers

Bootsfahrt auf der Spree in Berlin. Wir lernen hier Deutsch.

Vorschau Spotlight on Germany

The purpose of the *Vorschau* and all *Fokus* notes is to give students a quick and easy introduction to the various cultural points. They are intended just for enrichment and enjoyment.

Ask students which German cities they have visited. As an extra activity, you could look at the blank map of Germany in the *Zum Schreiben* section of the *Arbeitsbuch* (SAM) and fill it in together.

Size: Approximately 135,800 square miles, comparable to the size of Montana; divided into 16 federal states (**Bundesländer**).

Population: 81.8 million (including 10.7 million migrants). After Russia, Germany is the most populous country of Europe, followed by France, the United Kingdom, and Italy.

Religion: 30% Catholic, 29% Protestant, 5% Muslim, 36% unaffiliated or other (see *Fokus* note in Chapter 4, "Diversity in Religious Traditions"). Close to four million Muslims now form the largest non-Christian group in Germany; about 63% of them are Turkish or of Turkish descent.

Geography: Divided into three major regions: the flat lowlands in the north, the central mountain region, and the southern highlands, including a narrow band of the Alps.

Currency: Euro, 1 € = 100 cents.

Capital: Berlin (pop. 3.5 million).

Germany's sometimes turbulent history spans nearly 2,000 years. Unlike its neighbors, it did not become a centralized nation until relatively recently. Originally, the population of what is now Germany consisted of various Germanic tribes, and even now their heritage gives the different regions of Germany their particular identity. The Holy Roman Empire, a loose federation of states under an emperor, lasted from 962 to 1806. During this time, the country was divided further until there were almost 350 individual political entities, some of them minuscule. During the reign of Napoleon I, they were consolidated into about 40 states. In 1871, under Prussian Chancellor Otto von Bismarck, Germany became a unified state for the first time. This monarchy lasted until the end of World War I, when Germany became a republic (**die Weimarer Republik,** 1919–1933).

After the Nazi dictatorship led Germany to ruin in World War II, the country was divided into the Federal Republic of Germany or FRG (**die B**undes**r**epublik **D**eutschland = **BRD**) in the west, and the German Democratic Republic or GDR (**die D**eutsche **D**emokratische **R**epublik = **DDR**) in the east. The line between the West and Communist Europe, a heavily fortified border, ran through the middle of Germany. The symbol of this division, the infamous Berlin Wall built in 1961 by the GDR, fell on November 9, 1989. On October 3, 1990, the two Germanys were officially reunited. Since then, Germans have been trying to overcome more than 40 years of living in diametrically opposed political and economic systems. The cost of reunification, both socially and economically, has been much higher than anticipated. In the East, the closing of obsolete socialist enterprises had resulted in massive unemployment and westward migration of workers; in the West, taxes have increased in order to finance the high cost of reunification. The federal government signed a "Solidarity Pact" with the new **Bundesländer** granting them a total of 250 billion euros, to be distributed through 2019. The massive transfer of public funds is finally showing results. Infrastructures have been completely rebuilt, all important steps in the economic development of eastern Germany. The region's long-struggling economy is now competing with other European and Asian regions and attracting investors, especially in technology-intensive industries. Most German cities have their own website. A simple browser search will get you there.

Lesen Sie die Tabelle *(chart)*! Wie viele Einwohner *(inhabitants)* hat . . . (Duisburg, Dresden usw.)? z. B. Duisburg hat 488 000 Einwohner. Lesen Sie die Einwohnerzahlen laut auf Deutsch!

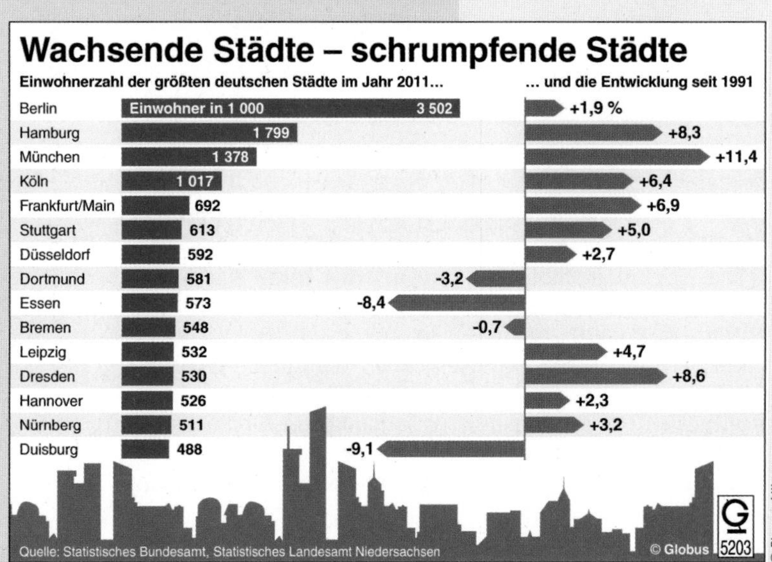

© Picture-Alliance

Zum Thema

Gespräche

Am Goethe-Institut

■ Listen to the dialogue. Then, with a partner, act out the dialogue together. ■

■ The basic purpose of these dialogues is to present the chapter topic, not the grammar! If your teacher does *Warm-up* activities with you, their basic purpose is to review material you have already learned; they are not related to the dialogues.

Warm-ups: 1. **Wie ist das Wetter heute? Wie geht es Ihnen / dir?** 2. **Was ist das?** *Point to objects in the classroom and ask to have them identified.* 3. **Wie ist . . . ?** *Ask about the color of various items.* 4. **Ist . . . groß oder klein** (dick / dünn, kurz / lang, schnell / langsam, neu / alt, sauber / schmutzig, teuer / billig, heiß / kalt, warm / kühl / kalt)? *Ask about various items, people, the weather, etc.* 5. **Wie schreibt man das?** *Ask to have various German words spelled out.*

SHARON Roberto, woher kommst du?
ROBERTO Ich bin aus Rom. Und du?
SHARON Ich komme aus Sacramento, aber jetzt wohnt meine Familie in Seattle.
ROBERTO Hast du Geschwister?
SHARON Ja, ich habe zwei Schwestern und zwei Brüder. Und du?
ROBERTO Ich habe nur eine Schwester. Sie wohnt in Montreal, in Kanada.
SHARON Wirklich? So ein Zufall! Mein Onkel wohnt auch da.

© Cengage Learning

Später

ROBERTO Sharon, wann ist die Prüfung?
SHARON In zehn Minuten. Du, wie heißen ein paar Flüsse in Deutschland?
ROBERTO Im Norden ist die Elbe, im Osten die Oder, im Süden . . .
SHARON . . . die Donau?
ROBERTO Richtig! Und im Westen der Rhein. Wo liegt Düsseldorf?
SHARON Düsseldorf? Hm. Wo ist eine Landkarte?
ROBERTO Oh, hier. Im Westen von Deutschland, nördlich von Bonn, am Rhein.
SHARON Ach ja, richtig! Na, viel Glück!

■ Note that there is no apostrophe in the German possessive, e.g., *Sharon's family* BUT **Sharons Familie.**

A. Alles verstanden?

1. Woher kommt Roberto? 2. Woher kommt Sharon? 3. Wo wohnt Sharons Familie? 4. Wie groß ist Sharons Familie? 5. Wann ist die Prüfung? 6. Was sind die Elbe, die Oder, die Donau und der Rhein? 7. Wo ist die Elbe? die Oder? die Donau? der Rhein? 8. Wo liegt Düsseldorf?

A: 1. aus Rom 2. aus Sacramento 3. in Seattle 4. zwei Schwestern und zwei Brüder 5. in zehn Minuten 6. Flüsse (in Deutschland) 7. im Norden / Osten / Süden / Westen 8. Im Westen von Deutschland, nördlich von Bonn, am Rhein.

B. Jetzt sind Sie dran! Use the dialogue above as a model and the *Wortschatz* that follows to create your own dialogue with a partner. Talk about geography or about your family and where they live.

BEISPIEL S1 Woher kommst du?
S2 Ich bin aus . . . Und du?

You may wish to introduce the *Wortschatz* formally before asking students to create their own dialogues.

Fokus The Goethe Institute

The Goethe Institute **(Goethe-Institut Inter Nationes)** is the official representative of German culture abroad. With over 150 branches in 92 countries, it offers German language courses and organizes lectures, exhibitions, film screenings, and readings by poets and authors. The combination of language instruction and lively cultural exchange makes the Goethe Institutes important intermediaries in international dialogue and in communicating a comprehensive image of Germany. (For further information, visit their website.)

© Goethe-Institut Boston

Wortschatz 1

Die Familie, -n *(family)*

der Bruder, ¨	*brother*	die Schwester, -n	*sister*
der Cousin, -s	*cousin* (male)	die Kusine, -n / Cousine, -n	*cousin* (female)
der Junge, -n	*boy*	das Mädchen, -	*girl*
der Mann, ¨er	*man; husband*	die Frau, -en	*woman; wife*
der Onkel, -	*uncle*	die Tante, -n	*aunt*
der Sohn, ¨e	*son*	die Tochter, ¨	*daughter*
der Vater, ¨	*father*	die Mutter, ¨	*mother*
der Großvater, ¨	*grandfather*	die Großmutter, ¨	*grandmother*
das Kind, -er	*child*		
die Geschwister *(pl.)*	*siblings; brother and/or sister*		
die Eltern *(pl.)*	*parents*		
die Großeltern *(pl.)*	*grandparents*		

■ In case you're curious: *Dad / Mom / Grandma / Grandpa* = **Vati, Papa / Mutti, Mama / Oma / Opa;** *half-* = **Halb- (Halbbruder, Halbschwester);** *step-* = **Stief- (Stiefbruder, Stiefschwester,** etc.); *-in-law* = **Schwieger- (Schwiegervater, Schwiegermutter,** etc.), BUT **Schwager, -** *(brother-in-law)* and **Schwägerin, -nen** *(sister-in-law); nephew / niece* = **Neffe, -n / Nichte, -n;** *grandchild* = **Enkelkind, -er;** *great-grand-* = **Urgroß- (Urgroßeltern).**

Das Land, ¨er *(country, state)*	**Die Leute *(pl.)* *(people)***	**Die Sprache, -n *(language)***
Deutschland	der Deutsche, -n / die Deutsche, -n	Deutsch
Frankreich	der Franzose, -n / die Französin, -nen	Französisch
Österreich	der Österreicher, - / die Österreicherin, -nen	Deutsch
die Schweiz	der Schweizer, - / die Schweizerin, -nen	Deutsch, Französisch, Italienisch
Italien	der Italiener, - / die Italienerin, -nen	Italienisch
Spanien	der Spanier, - / die Spanierin, -nen	Spanisch
England	der Engländer, - / die Engländerin, -nen	Englisch
Amerika	der Amerikaner, - / die Amerikanerin, -nen	Englisch
Kanada	der Kanadier, - / die Kanadierin, -nen	Englisch, Französisch

■ ARTICLES: All countries and cities are neuter unless indicated otherwise **(die Schweiz).**

■ Many feminine nouns can be derived from masculine nouns by adding **-in**, in which case their plurals end in **-nen (der Schweizer > die Schweizerin, -nen).** BUT: **der Deutsche > die Deutsche, -n; der Franzose > die Französin, -nen.**

■ Adjectives denoting nationality are not capitalized: Typisch **deutsch!** *(Typically German!)*, BUT: Ich spreche **Deutsch** *(the German language).* Antworten Sie auf **Deutsch** *(in German)*!

Verschiedenes

der Satz, ¨e	*sentence*	die Frage, -n	*question*
Berg, -e	*mountain*	Landkarte, -n	*map*
Fluss, ¨e	*river*	Prüfung, -en	*test, exam*
See, -n	*lake*	Stadt, ¨e	*city*
		Hauptstadt, ¨e	*capital city*

kommen	*to come*
liegen	*to lie; to be located*
wohnen	*to live, reside*
amerikanisch / kanadisch	*American / Canadian*
woher?	*from where?*
Ich bin / komme aus . . .	*I'm from . . . (a native of)*
im Norden / Süden / Osten / Westen	*in the north / south / east / west*
nördlich / südlich / östlich / westlich von	*north / south / east / west of*
mein(e)	*my*
dein(e) / Ihr(e)	*your* (informal / formal)

■ **Im** is used with months, seasons, and points of the compass **(im Mai, im Winter, im Norden); in** is used with names of cities, countries, and continents **(in Berlin, in Deutschland, in Europa).**

■ **Mein, dein,** and **Ihr** have no ending when used before masculine and neuter nouns that are sentence subjects: **mein Vater, dein Bruder, Ihr Kind.** Before feminine and plural nouns, **meine, deine,** and **Ihre** are used: **meine Mutter, deine Schwester, Ihre Eltern.**

Zum Erkennen: So ein Zufall! *(What a coincidence!);* Na, viel Glück! *(Well, good luck!);* Dir auch! *(To you, too!);* AUCH: das Pronomen, - *(pronoun);* das Subjekt, -e *(subject);* fehlen *(to be missing);* z. B. = zum Beispiel *(e.g., for example).*

Übungen zum Thema *(Topical activities)*

A. Was passt? *(What fits?)* For each question or statement on the left, select one or more appropriate responses from the right-hand column, or give your own.

_d, h_ 1. Woher kommst du?

_a, i_ 2. Wie groß ist deine Familie?

_c, j_ 3. Meine Schwester wohnt in Seattle.

_e, f, k_ 4. Wann ist die Prüfung?

_g, k_ 5. Wo liegt Erfurt?

a. Sehr klein. Ich habe keine Geschwister.
b. Am Rhein.
c. Mein Onkel wohnt auch da.
d. Aus Seattle, und du?
e. Um Viertel nach zehn.
f. In zwanzig Minuten.
g. Westlich von Weimar.
h. Ich bin aus Rom.
i. Wir sind sechs.
j. Wirklich?
k. Ich weiß nicht.
l. . . .

B. Kombinieren Sie! Create sentences by combining items from the three columns and then filling in the blanks with the proper country, the people of that country, and their language. You can use the map of Europe on the inside cover of the book as reference.

BEISPIEL Nördlich von Deutschland liegt Dänemark. Die Dänen sprechen Dänisch.

Südlich von	Deutschland	
Im Süden von	England	
Nördlich von	Frankreich	
Im Norden von	Italien	liegt ____. Die ____ sprechen ____.
Östlich von	Österreich	
Im Osten von	Spanien	
Westlich . . .		

C. Was sind sie? Identify the following people.

CAUTION: Unlike English, German does not use an indefinite article before nationalities or references to membership in a group: **Sie ist Amerikanerin** *(an American);* **Sie ist Studentin** *(a student);* **Er ist Berliner** *(a Berliner).*

1. **Ländernamen**

BEISPIEL Juan ist Spanier. Und Juanita?
Juanita ist Spanierin.

a. Antonio ist Italiener. Und Luisa?
b. Hugo ist Österreicher. Und Lilo?
c. Walter ist Schweizer. Und Monique?
d. Pierre ist Franzose. Und Claire?

2. **Städtenamen**

BEISPIEL Uwe und Margit sind aus Frankfurt.
Uwe ist Frankfurter und Margit ist Frankfurterin.

a. Robert und Evi sind aus Berlin.
b. Klaus und Inge sind aus Hamburg.
c. Rolf und Katrin sind aus Wien.
d. Bert und Romy sind aus Zürich.

C.1: a. **Luisa ist Italienerin.** b. **Lilo ist Österreicherin.** c. **Monique ist Schweizerin.** d. **Claire ist Französin.**

Be prepared to supply students with forms that might not necessarily follow the **-er(in)** pattern.

C.2: a. **Robert ist Berliner und Evi ist Berlinerin.** b. **Klaus ist Hamburger und Inge ist Hamburgerin.** c. **Rolf ist Wiener und Katrin ist Wienerin.** d. **Bert ist Züricher und Romy ist Züricherin.**

3. **Kettenreaktion *(Chain reaction):* Was sind Sie?** Ask your classmates where they are from.

BEISPIEL S1 Ich bin aus Amerika und wohne in New York. Ich bin Amerikaner(in) und New Yorker(in). Und du?
S2 Ich bin . . .

D. Familien

1. **Elkes Stammbaum** Look at Elke's family tree and explain who each person is.

BEISPIEL *Elke ist die Tochter von Jens und Ute.*
Elke ist Arndts Schwester.

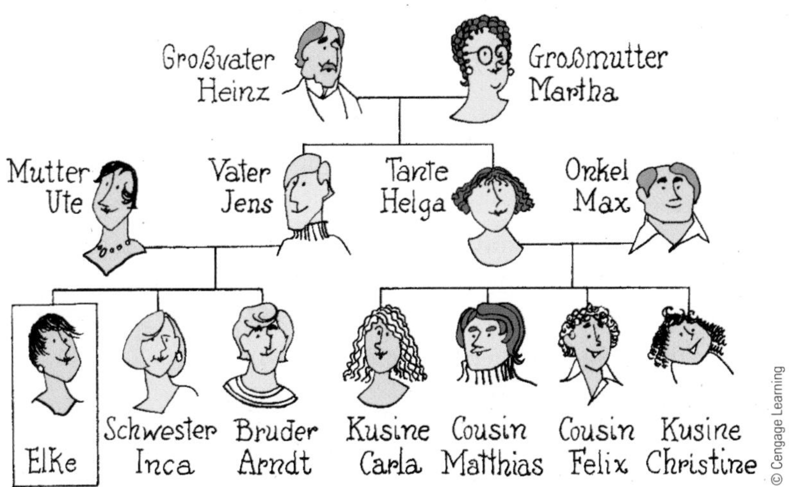

More questions about Elke's family: 1. **Wie viele Kinder sind in Elkes Familie? Wie heißen sie?** 2. **Wie heißt Elkes Vater? Elkes Mutter?** 3. **Wie heißen die Großeltern?** 4. **Wie viele Geschwister / Cousins und Kusinen hat sie? Wie heißen sie?** 5. **Wer ist Onkel Max?** 6. **Wie heißt die Schwester von Elkes Vater?** 7. **Wie heißt der Mann von Ute?** 8. **Wie viele Enkelkinder** *(grandchildren)* **haben die Großeltern? wie viele Jungen? wie viele Mädchen?**

2. **Familiennamen: Wer ist das?** Write down various names of your immediate and extended family and pass the list on to your partner, who then asks who these different people are. Take turns inquiring about each other's family. For extra vocabulary, see the list next to *Wortschatz 1*.

3. **Zwei Familien**

D.3: Jot down your classmate's information on a separate piece of paper.

a. **Meine Familie** Taking turns, ask your partner details about his/her family, covering questions like the ones below.

Wie heißt du?
Woher kommst du? *(name of your state/country)*
Wie groß ist deine Familie? Wie heißen sie und wie alt sind sie?
Wo in . . . *(name of your state/country)* wohnt deine Familie?
Wo liegt . . . *(name of your state/country)*? (z. B. **Kalifornien liegt südlich von Oregon.**)
Wie heißt die Hauptstadt von . . . *(name of your state/country)*?
Wie schreibt man das? *(spell the name of your capital)*
Ist . . . *(name of your city)* groß oder klein? Wie viele Leute wohnen da?
Ist da ein Fluss oder ein See? der Ozean *(ocean)*? Wenn ja, wie heißt der Fluss / See / Ozean?
Sind da Berge? Wenn ja, wie heißen die Berge?
Wie ist das Wetter da im Frühling? im Sommer? im Herbst? im Winter? (z. B. **kalt, warm, wunderbar,** . . .)
Wie findest du es *(how do you like it)* in . . . *(name your city or state/ country)*? (z. B. **schön, langweilig, toll,** . . .)

b. **Deine Familie** Take turns reporting what you found out about your partner's family.

For further review, see the Summary of Pronunciation in the front of this book. Study Part II, subsections 1, 3–4, 11–13, 17, and 19–20.

All pronunciation exercises have been recorded and can be found on the ***Wie geht's?*** Premium Website and iLrn. See the *Zum Hören* section of the *Arbeitsbuch* (SAM).

Aussprache: i, a, u

A. Laute *(Sounds)*

1. [i:] **Ih**nen, l**ie**gen, w**ie**der, W**ie**n, Berl**i**n
2. [i] b**i**n, b**i**tte, K**i**nd, Geschw**i**ster
3. [a:] Fr**a**ge, Spr**a**che, Amerik**a**ner, Sp**a**nier, V**a**ter
4. [a] St**a**dt, L**a**nd, K**a**n**a**d**a**, S**a**tz, T**a**nte
5. [u:] g**u**t, Br**u**der, K**u**li, Min**u**te, d**u**
6. [u] St**u**nde, J**u**nge, M**u**tter, Fl**u**ss, schm**u**tzig, k**u**rz

B. Wortpaare

1. still / Stil
2. Stadt / Staat
3. Kamm / komm
4. Schiff / schief
5. Rum / Ruhm
6. Ratte / rate

Hörverständnis

Guten Morgen! Listen to the conversation between Hugo Schmidt and Monika Müller. Then decide whether the statements below are true (**r**) or false (**f**) according to the dialogue. Remember that you may listen as often as you wish.

Zum Erkennen: die Assistentin, -nen; die Arbeit *(work)*

__r__ 1. Hugo Schmidt ist Professor.
__r__ 2. Monika spricht *(speaks)* Deutsch, Englisch und Spanisch.
__f__ 3. Monikas Mutter ist aus Deutschland.
__f__ 4. Monika ist 23.
__r__ 5. Der Professor braucht Monika von 2 Uhr bis 6 Uhr.
__r__ 6. Monika braucht Arbeit.

Lerntipp

Developing Listening and Comprehension Skills

Being able to understand spoken German is probably your most important skill. You cannot learn to speak German unless you understand it. Use class time well and listen carefully to your instructor and your classmates. Play the Lab and Text Audio as often as you need to in order to understand the dialogues and listening comprehension texts, and to complete the exercises correctly. Be sure to listen to the reading texts with the book closed. Watch each chapter's videos and listen to the songs on iTunes. Take advantage of opportunities to hear German spoken at the German Club or German House on campus. Listen to German CDs and watch plays or movies (some can be rented in video stores). Even if you can't understand much of it in the beginning, you will be able to pick out key words and learn to "tune in" to German.

Schiffe auf dem Rhein beim Lorelei-Felsen **(rock)**

Struktur

1.1 The present tense of regular verbs

1. You are already familiar with some of the PERSONAL PRONOUNS; there are three others: **er, sie,** and **ihr.**

	SINGULAR	PLURAL	SINGULAR/PLURAL
1st person	ich *(I)*	wir *(we)*	
2nd person	**du** (*you*, fam.)	**ihr** (*you*, fam.)	Sie (*you*, formal)
3rd person	**er** / es / **sie** *(he, it, she)*	sie *(they)*	

- **du** and **ihr** are intimate forms of address used with family members, close friends, fellow students, children, and animals.
- **Sie,** which is always capitalized when it means *you*, is used with strangers, casual acquaintances, and people addressed with a title, e.g., **Herr** and **Frau.** It is used to address one or more persons. **Sie** (*you*, capitalized) and **sie** (*they*, not capitalized) can be distinguished in conversation only through context.

  Herr Schmidt, wo wohnen **Sie**? Und Ihre Eltern, wo wohnen **sie**?

  Mr. Schmidt, where do you live? And your parents, where do they live?
- The subject pronouns **sie** *(she, it)* and **sie** *(they)* can be distinguished through the personal endings of the verb.

  Sie komm**t** im Mai und **sie** komm**en** im Juni.

  She comes in May, and they come in June.

2. The infinitive is the form of the verb that has no subject and takes no personal ending (e.g., *to learn*). Almost every German infinitive ends in **-en: lernen, antworten.** The stem of the verb is the part that precedes the infinitive ending **-en.** Thus, the stem of **lernen** is **lern-,** and that of **antworten** is **antwort-.**

   English verbs have at most one personal ending in the present tense, *-s: I (you, we, they) learn*, but *he (it, she) learns*. In German, endings are added to the verb stem for all persons.

   stem + personal ending = present tense verb form

   German verb endings vary, depending on whether the subject is in the FIRST, SECOND, OR THIRD PERSON and in the SINGULAR OR PLURAL. The verb must agree with the subject. You have already learned the endings used for some persons. Here is the complete list of endings:

	SINGULAR	PLURAL	FORMAL *(SG. / PL.)*
1st person	ich lern**e**	wir lern**en**	
2nd person	du lern**st**	ihr lern**t**	Sie lern**en**
3rd person	er / es / sie lern**t**	sie lern**en**	

NOTE: The verb forms for formal *you* (**Sie**) and plural *they* (**sie**) are identical. The same holds true for **er / es / sie.**

To give students experience in using **du** and **Sie,** have them address you with **Sie** and one another with **du.** Address them with **Sie.**

Lerntipp

Studying Grammar

Don't let the idea of grammar scare you. It is a shortcut to learning, providing you with the patterns native speakers follow when they use the language. The fact that German and English are closely related will be very helpful. However, you must make sure to note the instances when German patterns differ from English. As a bonus, your study of German will make you more aware of the fine points of English grammar. To freshen up on grammar terminology, you might consider buying a reference book, e.g., *English Grammar for Students of German*, by Cecile Zorach and Charlotte Melin.

German speakers find it rude if, when talking about yourself and others, you name yourself first, e.g., *I and my brother.* You yourself should always come last in the list, e.g., **Mein Bruder, meine Schwester und ich.**

Caution: Students cannot yet be expected to use these verbs to write their own sentences, since most require objects to make a meaningful statement.

The following verbs, which you already know from the *Schritte* and from this chapter, follow the model of **lernen.** Be sure to review them:

beginnen	*to begin*	sagen	*to say; to tell*
brauchen	*to need*	schreiben	*to write*
fragen	*to ask*	spielen	*to play*
gehen	*to go*	verstehen	*to understand*
hören	*to hear*	wiederholen	*to repeat; to review*
kommen	*to come*	wohnen	*to live, reside*
liegen	*to lie; to be located*	zählen	*to count*

NOTE: Remember that the bar on the left signals that a list is important.

Here is the entire rule: Insert an **-e-** if the infinitive stem ends in **-m** or **-n** preceded by a consonant other than **l, m, n,** or **r,** or simple **h** (e.g., **atmet, regnet,** BUT **qualmt, kommt, nennt, lernt, nehmt**). If the **h** is part of a consonant cluster, such as **ch, sch,** or **th,** then the extra **-e-** is inserted (e.g., **rechnet**). At this level, this much detail is unnecessarily complicated for most classes.

3. When a verb stem ends in **-d** or **-t** (**antwort-, find-**), or in certain consonant combinations with **-m** or **-n** (**öffn-, regn-**), an **-e** is inserted between the stem and the **-st** and **-t** endings.

	SINGULAR	PLURAL	FORMAL *(SG. / PL.)*
1st person	ich antworte	wir antworten	
2nd person	du antwort**e**st	ihr antwort**e**t	Sie antworten
3rd person	er / es / sie antwort**e**t	sie antworten	

These familiar verbs follow the model of **antworten:**

finden	*to find*
kosten	*to cost*
öffnen	*to open*
regnen	*to rain*

4. The **du-**form of verbs with a stem ending in any **s-**sound (**-s, -ss, -ß, -tz, -z**) adds only a **-t** instead of **-st: ich heiße, du heißt.** Thus, the **du-**form is identical with the **er-**form of these verbs: **du heißt, er heißt.**

5. German has only one verb form to express what can be said in English in several ways.

Ich wohne in Köln. — *I live in Cologne.* / *I'm living in Cologne.* / *I do live in Cologne.*

Wo wohnst du? — *Where are you living?* / *Where do you live?*

6. Even more than in English, in German the present tense is very frequently used to express future time, particularly when a time expression clearly indicates the future.

In dreißig Minuten **gehe** ich in die Stadt.	*I'm going downtown in thirty minutes.*
Er **kommt** im Sommer.	*He'll come in the summer.*

Übungen

For additional exercises on any of the grammar topics, see the exercises in the *Arbeitsbuch* (SAM).

A. *Du, ihr* oder *Sie?* How would you generally address these people: in the singular familiar, the plural familiar, or in a formal fashion?

BEISPIEL your brother
(I would address him with) ***du***

1. your father 2. members of your family 3. your German professor 4. a store clerk 5. two police officers 6. your roommate 7. friends of your three-year-old niece 8. your classmates 9. a group of strangers who are older than you

A: 1. du 2. ihr 3. Sie 4. Sie 5. Sie 6. du 7. ihr 8. ihr 9. Sie

B. Ersetzen Sie das Subjekt! Replace the subject by using the words in parentheses.

BEISPIEL Ich sage das noch einmal. (wir, Maria)
Wir sagen das noch einmal.
Maria sagt das noch einmal.

1. Wir antworten auf Deutsch. (Roberto, du, ich, die Mutter)
2. Ich wiederhole die Frage. (er, wir, ihr, Sie)
3. Ihr lernt die Wörter. (ich, du, die Kinder, wir)
4. Du öffnest das Buch auf Seite 3. (der Franzose, ich, ihr, sie/*sg.*)
5. Lea Bauer geht an die Tafel. (ihr, sie/*pl.*, ich, du)
6. Brauchst du Papier und Bleistifte? (wir, ich, Sie, ihr)
7. Wie finden Sie das? (ihr, du, Ihre Familie, die Leute)

B: 1. antwortet, antwortest, antworte, antwortet 2. wiederholt, wiederholen, wiederholt, wiederholen 3. lerne, lernst, lernen, lernen 4. öffnet, öffne, öffnet, öffnet 5. geht, gehen, gehe, gehst 6. brauchen, brauche, brauchen, braucht 7. findet, findest, findet, finden

C. Was fehlt? *(What's missing?)* Fill in the missing verb forms.

C: After students complete the dialogue, have them use it as a model for a role-playing activity.

SVEN Danny und Laura, woher ___kommt___ ihr? (kommen)
LAURA Ich ___komme___ aus Heidelberg. (kommen)
DANNY Und ich ___bin___ aus Berlin. (sein)
SVEN Wirklich? Meine Großmutter ___kommt___ auch aus Berlin. (kommen) Aber sie ___wohnt___ jetzt in Hamburg. (wohnen) Wie ___findet___ ihr es hier? (finden)
LAURA Wir ___finden___ es hier in Bregenz prima. (finden)
DANNY Ich ___finde___ den Bodensee wunderbar. (finden)
SVEN Ich auch!

D. Kombinieren Sie! Create sentences by combining items from each column.

BEISPIEL *Er kommt aus Kanada.*

1	2	3
ich	beginnen	auf Deutsch
du	brauchen	auf Englisch
er	hören	aus . . .
es	kommen	(das) nicht
sie	kosten	Deutsch
das	lernen	heute
die Deutschvorlesung	regnen	in . . .
das Mädchen	schreiben	jetzt
wir	spielen	morgen
ihr	wohnen	(nicht) gut
Sie	zählen	Tennis
sie		um . . . Uhr
		vier Euro
		von zehn bis zwanzig

1.2 The nominative case

To show the function of nouns or pronouns in a sentence, German uses a system called CASE. There are four cases in German: nominative, accusative, dative, and genitive. The NOMINATIVE CASE is the case of the subject and of the predicate noun. (The predicate noun is discussed in section 1.3–2 below).

In the English sentence *The boy asks the father*, the SUBJECT of the sentence is *the boy;* he does the asking. We know that *the boy* is the subject of the sentence because in English the subject precedes the verb. This is not always true in German, where the function of a word or phrase frequently depends on its form rather than on its position. In the sentence **Der Junge fragt den Vater,** the phrase **der Junge** indicates the subject, whereas **den Vater** represents a direct object (more about this in Chapter 2). In dictionaries and vocabulary lists, nouns are given in the nominative. The nominative answers the questions *who?* for persons or *what?* for objects and ideas.

Der Junge fragt den Vater.	*The boy asks the father.*
Der See ist schön.	*The lake is beautiful.*

1. The forms of the INTERROGATIVE PRONOUNS are **wer?** *(who?)* and **was?** *(what?)*.

	PERSONS	THINGS AND IDEAS
nom.	wer?	was?

Wer fragt die Tante?	→	**Der Junge.**
Who is asking the aunt?	→	*The boy.*
Was ist schön?	→	**Der See.**
What is beautiful?	→	*The lake.*

2. The nominative forms of the DEFINITE ARTICLE **der, das, die** *(the)* are already familiar. Note that the INDEFINITE ARTICLE **ein** *(a, an)* is the same for masculine and neuter nouns; it has no ending. It also has no plural: *I have a pencil*, but *I have pencils.*

This table will be augmented gradually and used to teach cases.

	SINGULAR			PLURAL	
	masc.	**neut.**	**fem.**		
nom.	der	das	die	die	*the*
	ein	ein	eine	—	*a, an*
	kein	kein	keine	keine	*no, not a, not any*

Point out the capital **I** on the possessive adjective **Ihr.**

The POSSESSIVE ADJECTIVES **mein** *(my)*, **dein** *(your)*, and **Ihr** (*your*, formal) follow the pattern of **ein** and **kein.**

Die Frau, der Junge und das Mädchen sind aus Österreich.

Mein Onkel und **meine** Tante wohnen auch da. Wo wohnen **deine** Eltern?

3. Nouns can be replaced by personal pronouns. In English, we replace persons with *he, she,* or *they*, and objects and ideas with *it* or *they*. In German, the pronoun used depends on the gender of the noun.

Wer ist **der Mann?**	**Er** heißt Max.	*He's called Max.*
Wie heißt **das Kind?**	**Es** heißt Susi.	*She's called Susi.*
Wer ist **die Frau?**	**Sie** heißt Ute.	*She's called Ute.*
Wie ist **der See?**	**Er** ist groß.	*It's big.*
Wie ist **das Land?**	**Es** ist klein.	*It's small.*
Wie heißt **die Stadt?**	**Sie** heißt Ulm.	*It's called Ulm.*

- Note that German uses three pronouns **(er, es, sie)** for things where English uses only one *(it)*.
- Note also how similar these pronouns are to the forms of the articles:

der → er; das → es; die → sie

- In the plural, there are no gender distinctions, as the definite article for all plural nouns is **die.** The pronoun for all plural nouns is **sie.**

die Männer, die Kinder, die Frauen } **sie** *(they)*
die Seen, die Länder, die Städte } **sie** *(they)*

According to *Duden:* **das Mädchen, das Kind** = **es.** However, in everyday speech you also hear **sie** for **das Mädchen** and **er** or **sie** for **das Kind: Er heißt Felix. Sie heißt Susi.**

Übungen

E. Ersetzen Sie die Wörter mit Pronomen *(pronouns)*!

BEISPIEL Fritz — *er*
die Landkarte — *sie*

der Vater er	der Bleistift er	Deutschland es
der Berg er	der Pulli er	das Kind es
das Land es	Österreich es	die Geschwister sie
die Großmutter sie	der Österreicher er	die Töchter sie
der Junge er	die Schweiz sie	die Söhne sie
die Stadt sie	die Schweizerin sie	

F. Die Geographiestunde

1. **Was ist das?** Describe some features of Europe, using a word from the boxed vocabulary with the appropriate form of **ein.** You can also add to the features below.

BEISPIEL Dresden — *Dresden ist eine Stadt.*

Stadt See Sprache Land Fluss Berg

die Schweiz, der Main, die Elbe, Österreich, Berlin, Französisch, die Donau, Bremen, Luxemburg, Italienisch, das Matterhorn, der Bodensee *(Lake Constance)* . . .

F.1: Die Schweiz ist ein Land. Der Main ist ein Fluss. Die Elbe ist ein Fluss. Österreich ist ein Land. Berlin ist eine Stadt. Französisch ist eine Sprache. Die Donau ist ein Fluss. Bremen ist eine Stadt. Luxemburg ist ein Land. Italienisch ist eine Sprache. Das Matterhorn ist ein Berg. Der Bodensee ist ein See.

F.2a: Frankfurt kein Fluss / eine Stadt; Frankreich keine Sprache / ein Land; Heidelberg kein Berg / eine Stadt; der Rhein keine Stadt / ein Fluss; die Schweiz kein See / ein Land; Spanien keine Sprache / ein Land; Bonn kein Land / eine Stadt; die Zugspitze kein See / ein Berg

2. **Ist das richtig?**

a. **Geographische Namen in Europa** Ask and answer some questions about Europe, using the appropriate form of **kein.**

BEISPIEL die Donau / Land
Ist die Donau ein Land?
Nein, die Donau ist kein Land. Die Donau ist ein Fluss.

Frankfurt / Fluss; Frankreich / Sprache; Heidelberg / Berg; der Rhein / Stadt; die Schweiz / See; Spanien / Sprache; Bonn / Land; Zugspitze / See

b. **Geographische Namen irgendwo *(anywhere)*** Make your own statements about any geographical location and have your classmates react to them.

BEISPIEL Die Smokys sind Berge. *Ja, das sind Berge.*
Der Hudson ist ein See. *Nein, das ist kein See. Das ist ein Fluss.*

G. Ersetzen Sie das Subjekt!

1. **Antworten Sie mit JA!** A curious neighbor asks you questions about the new family in the neighborhood. Answer positively, using pronouns.

BEISPIEL Die Eltern kommen aus Italien, nicht wahr?
Ja, sie kommen aus Italien.

a. Der Sohn antwortet auf Italienisch, nicht wahr? — Ja, __er__ antwortet auf Italienisch.
b. Die Tochter versteht Deutsch, nicht wahr? — Ja, __sie__ versteht Deutsch.
c. Das Kind ist fünf Jahre alt, nicht wahr? — Ja, __es__ ist fünf Jahre alt.
d. Die Großmutter heißt Maria, nicht wahr? — Ja, __sie__ heißt Maria.
e. Der Großvater wohnt auch da, nicht wahr? — Ja, __er__ wohnt auch da.
f. Die Familie kommt aus Rom, nicht wahr? — Ja, __sie__ kommt aus Rom.

G.2: This could be done as group competition. Whichever team answers correctly first, gets a point. For a more communicative variation, show items or pictures as cues.

2. **Blitzreaktionen *(Fast responses)*** Say one of the German nouns you have learned. Someone else will quickly repeat the word with its article and make a statement about it, using the proper pronoun.

BEISPIEL Hemd
Das Hemd. Es ist weiß.

3. **Antworten mit Pronomen** Ask another student the following types of questions, which can vary. He or she answers and then returns the question.

BEISPIEL S1 Wann beginnt . . . (z. B. dein Tag)?
S2 Mein Tag? Er beginnt morgens um sechs. Und dein Tag?
S1 Er beginnt morgens um halb sieben.

a. Wann beginnt . . . (z. B. die Deutschvorlesung)?
b. Wie heißt . . . (z. B. das Deutschbuch)?
c. Welche Farbe hat . . . (z. B. dein Kuli / deine Jacke)?
d. Wo ist . . . (z. B. das Fenster)?
e. Wie viele . . . hat . . . (z. B. Monate / das Jahr)?

Fokus German in Europe

As a result of geography, history, and economics, German is one of the principal languages of Europe, with some 99 million Europeans who are native speakers and millions more who speak German as a second language. In Greece, Spain, and Turkey, German is also widely spoken, mainly because of southern European "guest workers" **(Gastarbeiter)** who have brought German back to their countries, and also as a result of the millions of German tourists who flock to the Mediterranean every year.

Farther east, German has a long tradition. The Austro-Hungarian Empire, in which German was the official language, encompassed large areas of central and eastern Europe. Today, after decades of Soviet domination, young people in Poland, the Czech Republic, Slovakia, and Hungary are rediscovering old links to German culture.

© cluckva/Shutterstock

Of course, the opportunities offered by the powerful economies of neighboring Austria and Germany are an added incentive to learn German. In Russia alone, 2.3 million students are learning German; in the rest of Eastern Europe, German is generally the most frequently studied second language.

At the beginning of the 20th century, German—not English—was the primary language of science, philosophy, and psychology. Although the German language has since seen growing competition from English, it still remains one of the most widely understood languages in Europe.

1.3 Sentence structure

1. In English, the subject usually precedes the verb, and more than one element may do so.

   1 2
   *They **are learning** German at the Goethe Institute.*
   *At the Goethe Institute they **are learning** German.*

   In German statements and information questions, the verb is always the second sentence element.

   1 2
   Sie **lernen** Deutsch am Goethe-Institut.
   Was **lernen** sie?

   In contrast to English, however, only one sentence element may precede the verb, and this element is not necessarily the subject. If an element other than the subject precedes the verb, *the verb stays* in the second position and *the subject follows* the verb. This pattern is called INVERTED WORD ORDER.

   2 1
   Deutsch **lernen** sie am Goethe-Institut.
   Am Goethe-Institut **lernen** sie Deutsch.

Inverted word order is very common. The first sentence element either functions as connector to the previous sentence or draws attention to a particular concept.

2. The verbs **sein** *(to be)* and **heißen** *(to be called)* are LINKING VERBS. They normally link two words referring to the same person or thing, both of which are in the nominative: the first is the subject, the other a PREDICATE NOUN.

subject	predicate noun
Der Herr **ist**	Schweizer.
Er **heißt**	Stefan Wolf.

The verbs **sein** and **heißen** work like an equal sign: **Er ist Schweizer (Er = Schweizer). Er heißt Stefan Wolf (Er = Stefan Wolf).** This is the best time to practice this concept and the absence of **ein** before nationalities. Practice sentences like *He's an Austrian. I'm an American.*

The verb **sein** can be complemented not only by a predicate noun but also by a PREDICATE ADJECTIVE. Both are considered part of the verb phrase. This is an example of a typical and important feature of German sentence structure: when the predicate consists of more than one part, the inflected part (V1)—that is, the part of the verb that takes a personal ending—is the second element in the sentence, as always. However, the uninflected part (V2) stands at the very end of the sentence as a verb complement.

Stefan Wolf **ist** auch **Schweizer.**

Er **ist** heute **sehr müde.**

V1 V2

REMEMBER: In German, no indefinite article is used before nationalities: **Er ist Schweizer** *(a citizen of Switzerland).*

Katja ist Deutsche und Monique Französin.

H: Draw students' attention to the change in meaning or nuance that is a consequence of the change in word order. 1. Jetzt bin ich am Goethe-Institut. 2. Hier sprechen die Leute nur Deutsch. 3. In zehn Minuten haben wir eine Prüfung in Geographie. 4. Auf Seite 6 findest du die Landkarte. 5. Im Süden ist die Donau. 6. Nördlich von Bonn liegt Düsseldorf. 7. Mir geht es gut. 8. Um halb drei spielen wir Tennis. 9. Im April regnet es oft. 10. Heute scheint die Sonne wieder.

Übungen

H. Sagen Sie es anders *(differently)*! Begin each sentence with the word or phrase in boldface.

BEISPIEL Mein Cousin kommt **morgen.**
Morgen kommt mein Cousin.

1. Ich bin **jetzt** am Goethe-Institut.
2. Die Leute sprechen **hier** nur Deutsch.
3. Wir haben **in zehn Minuten** eine Prüfung in Geographie.
4. Du findest die Landkarte **auf Seite 6.**
5. Die Donau ist **im Süden.**
6. Düsseldorf liegt **nördlich von Bonn.**
7. Es geht **mir** gut.
8. Wir spielen **um halb drei** Tennis.
9. Es regnet oft **im April.**
10. Die Sonne scheint **heute** wieder.

I: 1. Schon fünf Jahre wohnt Jürgen in Lübeck. 2. Da wohnt seine Schwester auch. 3. Heute ist das Wetter schön und . . . 4. Nur 75 km südwestlich von Lübeck liegt Hamburg. 5. Da wohnen die Eltern. 6. In zwei Wochen besucht er sie. 7. Oft kommen sie nach Lübeck. 8. Das finden er und seine Schwester schön.

I. Noch einmal bitte! Make the following sentences more interesting by starting with the boldfaced words or phrases.

1. Jürgen wohnt **schon fünf Jahre** in Lübeck. 2. Seine Schwester wohnt auch **da.** 3. Das Wetter ist **heute** schön und sie gehen segeln *(sailing).* 4. Hamburg liegt **nur 75 km südwestlich von Lübeck.** 5. Die Eltern wohnen **da.** 6. Er besucht *(visits)* sie **in zwei Wochen.** 7. Sie kommen **oft** *(often)* nach Lübeck. 8. Er und seine Schwester finden **das** schön.

1.4 Compound nouns

In German, two or three simple words are frequently combined to create a new one, like **Fingerhut** (a "hat" that protects your finger = *thimble*), **Menschenfreund** (a friend of human beings = *philanthropist*), or **Stinktier** (an animal that stinks = *skunk*). The last component determines the gender and the plural form.

das Land + **die Karte** = **die** Land**karte, -n**
die Kinder + **das Mädchen** = **das** Kinder**mädchen, -**
der Arm + das Band + **die Uhr** = **die** Armband**uhr, -en**
schreiben + **der Tisch** = **der** Schreib**tisch, -e**
klein + **die Stadt** = **die** Klein**stadt, ¨-e**

For additional practice on word compounds, see the *Zum Schreiben* section in Chapters 1 and 7 of the *Arbeitsbuch* (SAM).

Students can form many other compound nouns, e.g., **Wintermantel (Sommer-, Regen-), Deutschkurs (Französisch-, Englisch-), Kinderbuch (-bild, -pullover).** This sort of exercise can be done throughout the course. Additional vocabulary-building exercises are found in the various *Zum Schreiben* sections of the *Arbeitsbuch* (SAM).

Übung

J. Was bedeuten die Wörter und was sind die Artikel? Determine the meaning and gender of the following words.

BEISPIEL Sprachkurs *der Sprachkurs; language course*

_____ Wochentag	_____ Wörterbuch	_____ Hemdbluse
_____ Neujahr	_____ Sprechübung	_____ Hausschuh
_____ Sommerbluse	_____ Familienvater	_____ Handschuh
_____ Herbstwetter	_____ Jungenname	_____ Deutschstunde
_____ Altstadt	_____ Zimmertür	_____ Wanduhr
_____ Bergsee	_____ Hosenrock	_____ Uhrzeit

J: *weekday* **(der)**, *New Year's* **(das)**, *summer blouse* **(die)**, *fall weather* **(das)**, *old center of town* **(die)**, *mountain lake* **(der)**, *dictionary* **(das)**, *oral exercise* **(die)**, *father of the family* **(der)**, *boy's name* **(der)**, *room door* **(die)**, *culottes* **(der)**, *shirt-like blouse* **(die)**, *house shoe, slipper* **(der)**, *glove* **(der)**, *German class* **(die)**, *wall clock* **(die)**, *time* **(die)**

Fokus Frankfurt am Main

Located on the Main River, Frankfurt is Germany's principal transportation hub. The city has been valued for its strategic position since Roman times. Beginning in 1356, the emperors of the Holy Roman Empire were crowned here. The poet Johann Wolfgang von Goethe (1749–1832), for whom the city's university is named, was born in Frankfurt, and the first German national assembly met here in Saint Paul's Church in 1848.

The city's airport is one of the busiest in Europe. Nicknamed "Mainhattan" because of its modern skyline, Frankfurt is one of Europe's leading financial centers. More than 300 banks (including the seat of the European Central Bank), 75 consulates, and more than 3,000 international businesses have set up shop in the Frankfurt area. Frankfurt's cosmopolitan atmosphere is reflected in its population, eight international schools, and 180 non-German professional and cultural clubs. Almost one-third of its residents have non-German passports. Thanks to its central location, every fall Frankfurt hosts two trade shows of major international importance: the **Frankfurter Buchmesse** *(Frankfurt Book Fair)* and the **Internationale Automobil-Ausstellung** *(IAA, Frankfurt Motor Show)*. Visitors from around the world attend these shows annually.

Frankfurt ist alt und modern. Hier wohnen viele Menschen aus aller Welt.

Visit the ***Wie geht's?*** iLrn website for more review and practice.

Deutschland

DIE ZEITSCHRIFT IN 15 SPRACHEN
- **DEUTSCH**
- **ENGLISCH**
- **FRANZÖSISCH**
- **PORTUGIESISCH**
- **SPANISCH**
- **POLNISCH**
- **RUMÄNISCH**
- **UNGARISCH**
- **RUSSISCH**
- **UKRAINISCH**
- **TÜRKISCH**
- **ARABISCH**
- **CHINESISCH**
- **JAPANISCH**

AUSSERDEM IM INTERNET:
http://www.magazine-deutschland.de

INTERNET-SERVICE IN:
- **ENGLISCH**
- **FRANZÖSISCH**
- **SPANISCH**

Source: Deutschland Magazine

Zusammenfassung *(Summary)*

K. Hoppla, hier fehlt was! *(Oops, something is missing here!)*

■ This is the first of several activities throughout the book in which you will try to find missing information with the help of a partner. Each of you has a chart—one appears below, the other in Section 11 of the Appendix. Each chart has information the other person needs. Do not look at your partner's chart! Always start by asking about the first blank on the left; fill it in, and then proceed to the next. Take turns asking questions until both charts are complete. ■

Wer sind sie? Take turns asking each other for the missing names, nationalities, places of residence, and ages of the persons listed. Follow the model.

BEISPIEL S1 Wer ist Schweizer?
S2 Toni ist Schweizer. Und woher kommt Toni?
S1 Toni kommt aus Bern. Wie alt ist er?
S2 Er ist 32.

NAME	NATIONALITÄT	WOHNORT	ALTER
Toni	Schweizer	Bern	32
Katja	Deutsche	Ulm	21
Pia	Österreicherin	Bregenz	61
Nicole	Französin	Lyon	26
Pierre	Franzose	Dijon	52
Mario	Italiener	Rimini	25
Maria	Spanierin	Madrid	17
Tom	Kanadier	Halifax	28
Amy	Amerikanerin	Miami	49

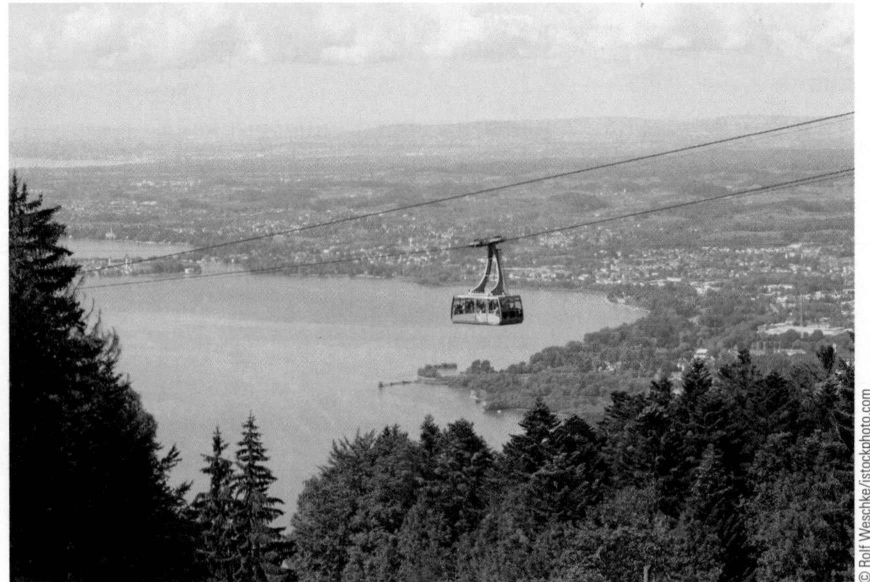

Bregenz am Bodensee

L. Sprachstudenten: Auf Deutsch bitte!

■ The translation exercises in this summary section always include material introduced in this chapter and possibly previous ones. Watch carefully for differences between English and German patterns. ■

1. Tomorrow my parents are coming. 2. My father is (a) French(man), and my mother is (an) Austrian. 3. In France they speak French, and in Austria they speak German. 4. France is west of Germany, and Austria is south of Germany. 5. I do understand French and German, but I answer in English. 6. Where are you *(fam.)* from? 7. I'm from Texas. 8. There's Thomas. Thomas is (an) American. 9. He's also learning German. 10. I think it's beautiful here, but I am very tired.

L: 1. Morgen kommen meine Eltern. 2. Mein Vater ist Franzose und meine Mutter ist Österreicherin. 3. In Frankreich sprechen sie Französisch und in Österreich sprechen sie Deutsch. 4. Frankreich ist (liegt) westlich von Deutschland und Österreich ist (liegt) südlich von Deutschland. 5. Ich verstehe Französisch und Deutsch, aber ich antworte auf Englisch. 6. Woher kommst du? 7. Ich bin (komme) aus Texas. 8. Da ist Thomas. Thomas ist Amerikaner. 9. Er lernt auch Deutsch. 10. Ich finde es hier schön (schön hier), aber ich bin sehr müde.

Dein Christus ein **Jude,**
dein Auto ein **Japaner,**
deine Pizza *italienisch,*
deine Demokratie GRIECHISCH,
dein Kaffee brasilianisch,
dein Urlaub ***türkisch,***
deine Zahlen **arabisch,**
deine Schrift *lateinisch,*
und dein Nachbar nur ein Ausländer?

Fokus Germany and the European Union

Germany is part of the European Union, which encompasses 28 member countries, with Croatia being the last to join, in July 2013. The EU's population now totals more than 507 million, compared with close to 312 million in the United States, and its gross domestic product ranks first in the world.

European integration, which began in the 1950s, has gone farthest in the economic sphere: Since 2002, Germany and 16 other EU members have a common currency, called the euro **(der Euro).** This means that capital, services, and goods can move freely, without restrictions, within **Euroland.** Today, EU citizens can travel, study, and work in other EU countries. The EU has been less successful in coordinating its members' foreign policy; individual countries are still reluctant to have their sovereignty infringed upon. Following the failure by some member states to ratify a new EU constitution in 2004, the Treaty of Lisbon was signed in December 2007. It will have to be ratified by all 27 member states before it can come into force. Its main objectives are to make the EU more democratic in terms of accountability, transparency, and participation; and to make the EU more efficient and able to tackle today's global challenges, such as climate change, security, and sustainable development. Some observers believe that the expanded EU is getting too large and diverse to work well. Though inspired by the US federal model in its search for political unity, Europe is working on its own model for unification with respect for its richest asset: the historical, cultural, and linguistic diversity of the European nations. Since the 2008 global financial crisis, Euroland has also been under pressure, due to large national debts especially in Greece, Ireland, Italy, Spain, and Portugal. The austerity measures instituted by the EU under the leadership of German chancellor Merkel have not been welcomed in these countries.

Einblicke *(Insights)*

Lesetipp

Reading German Texts

The first time you read a passage, you should just try to get the gist of what is being communicated. Then reread carefully and always finish a paragraph, or at least a sentence, before looking up an unfamiliar word or phrase. Look up as little as possible; it is often possible to determine meaning from context. Underline and pronounce the words in question, but do not scribble the English translation into the text. It will only distract you from the German. Finally, read the text a third time, after having guessed or looked up all the underlined words. See how many of them you remember. Try to learn them now, at least passively, to avoid looking them up repeatedly. If a word or phrase still remains unclear, circle it and ask your instructor instead of spending more time on it.

Lesetext

■ The reading texts expand on the chapter topic. All vocabulary that is to become active is listed under *Wortschatz 2*. Learn these words well; they will recur in future exercises and activities. Following *Wortschatz 2*, a pre-reading activity *(Vor dem Lesen)* introduces each reading selection. It proceeds from one to several activities composed of all sorts of general and personal questions to *Das ist leicht zu verstehen!*, a short set of cognates and compounds from the reading that you should be able to pronounce and recognize but do not have to master actively. The post-reading section *(Nach dem Lesen)* includes a variety of exercises related to the reading, followed by *Weiteres* whose activities go beyond that and focus on the chapter topic as a whole, including a brief conversation, a writing exercise, and a listening-comprehension activity. ■

Wortschatz 2

der Ausländer, -	*foreigner*
Mensch, -en	*human being, person;* (pl.) *people*
Nachbar, -n / die Nachbarin, -nen	*neighbor*
Staat, -en	*state*
Teil, -e	*part*
die Europäische Union (EU)	*European Union (EU)*
arbeiten	*to work*
so . . . wie . . .	*as . . . as . . .*
ungefähr	*approximately, about*
wichtig	*important*

Vor dem Lesen *(Pre-reading section)*

If students ask: the forms **von der Schweiz, von der Tschechischen Republik,** or **von den Niederlanden,** are explained in Chapter 3.

A. Die Deutschlandkarte Looking at the map of Germany on the inside cover of the book, answer the following questions.

1. Wie viele Nachbarn hat Deutschland? Wie heißen sie und was sind ihre *(their)* Hauptstädte?
2. Welche Flüsse und Berge gibt es *(are there)* in Deutschland? *(Name three each.)*
3. Wo liegt der Bodensee? die Nordsee? die Ostsee?
4. Wo liegt . . . ? *(Ask about the location of various towns or places in Germany.)*

A: To foster listening skills, have students look only at the map while you read the questions aloud. Point out the difference between **der See** (*lake*, e.g., der Bodensee) and **die See** (*sea*, e.g., die Nordsee, Ostsee); **die See** is not active vocabulary!

1. Dänemark (Kopenhagen), Polen (Warschau), Tschechien (Prag), Österreich (Wien), die Schweiz (Bern), Frankreich (Paris), Luxemburg (Luxemburg), Belgien (Brüssel), die Niederlande (Amsterdam) 2. *(answers vary)* 3. im Süden, im Nordwesten, im Norden 4. *(answers vary)*

B. Das ist leicht zu verstehen! *(That's easy to understand!)* Read aloud the following words, paying special attention to their stressed syllable. Then guess their meaning in English.

der Bankier, Europäer, Großteil, Partner, Service, Tourismus; (das) Europa, Kapital, Osteuropa, Sprachenlernen, Zentrum; die Politik; *(pl.)* die Millionen, Personen, USA; Dänisch, Finnisch, Flämisch, Griechisch, Holländisch, Luxemburgisch, Norwegisch, Polnisch, Portugiesisch, Schwedisch, Tschechisch, Ungarisch; studieren; europäisch, interessant, lange, traditionell

■ In German, as a rule, the first syllable is stressed. In this exercise, if the stressed syllable differs from that rule, it is underlined.

Deutschland in Europa

Europa hat viele Länder und viele Sprachen. In Deutschland hören Sie natürlich° Deutsch, aber die Nachbarn im Norden sprechen Dänisch, Schwedisch, Norwegisch und Finnisch. Die Nachbarn im Osten sprechen Polnisch und Tschechisch und im Westen sprechen sie Holländisch, Flämisch und Französisch. Im Süden von Europa sprechen die Menschen Italienisch, Spanisch, Portugiesisch und Griechisch; und das sind noch lange nicht° alle Sprachen!

Deutsch ist sehr wichtig. Ungefähr 98 Millionen Europäer sprechen Deutsch als° Muttersprache: die Deutschen, Österreicher, Liechtensteiner, ein Großteil der° Schweizer und ein Teil der Luxemburger und Belgier. Viele Ausländer arbeiten oder studieren in Deutschland, Österreich und in der Schweiz und lernen so° auch Deutsch. Sehr viele Menschen in Europa sprechen zwei oder drei Sprachen. Sie finden das interessant und auch wichtig für Tourismus, Handel° und Politik.

Die Europäische Union (EU) hat jetzt 28 Mitgliedstaaten° und eine Bevölkerung° von mehr als° 500 Millionen Menschen. Das sind mehr Menschen als in den° USA, in Kanada und in Mexiko zusammen. Deutschland liegt im° Zentrum von Europa. Es ist ein Tor zu° den traditionellen Handelspartnern° in Westeuropa und zu den Wachstumsmärkten° in Osteuropa. Kapital und Service bewegen sich frei° in der EU.

Viele Deutsche arbeiten im Ausland° und viele Ausländer arbeiten in Deutschland. Ein Beispiel ist Familie Breughel. Marcel Breughel erzählt°: „Ich bin aus Brüssel und meine Frau Nicole ist Französin. Sie ist Dolmetscherin° und ich bin Bankier. Wir wohnen schon zwei Jahre in Frankfurt. Wir finden es hier sehr schön. Wir haben zwei Kinder, Maude und Dominique. Sie sprechen zu Hause° Französisch, aber in der Schule° sprechen sie fließend° Deutsch. Das finde ich toll. Das Sprachenlernen ist heute so wichtig wie nie zuvor°."

of course
by far not
as
of the
this way
trade
member states
population / more than
in the / in the
gate to / trade partners
growth markets
move freely
abroad
tells
interpreter
at home
in school / fluently
as never before

Nach dem Lesen *(Post-reading Section)*

A. Alles verstanden?

1. Wo in Europa sprechen die Leute auch Deutsch als Muttersprache?
2. Warum *(Why)* lernen so viele Europäer zwei oder drei Sprachen?
3. Wie viele Mitgliedstaaten hat die EU?
4. Wie viele Menschen leben *(live)* in der EU?
5. Wo arbeiten viele Deutsche?
6. Wo wohnt die Familie Breughel und woher kommen sie?
7. Was tun *(do)* sie da?
8. Was sprechen die Kinder zu Hause und was sprechen sie in der Schule?

A: 1. in Österreich, Liechtenstein, Luxemburg, Belgien, in der Schweiz 2. interessant, wichtig 3. 28 4. mehr als 500 Millionen 5. im Ausland 6. in Frankfurt; aus Brüssel 7. Sie ist Dolmetscherin. Er ist Bankier. 8. Französisch; Deutsch

Optional practice: 1. **z. B. (das) Europa = es.** (Deutschland, Berlin, Menschen, Norden, Deutsch, Sprache, Nachbar, Europäerin) 2. **Was bedeuten die Wörter und was sind die Artikel?** Menschenzahl, Nachbarland, Zimmernachbar, Satzteil, Stadtteil, Teilzeit, Stadtmensch. 3. **z. B. Herr und Frau Watzlik sind aus Warschau. Er ist Warschauer / Pole; sie ist Warschauerin / Polin.** Okko und Antje sind aus Amsterdam. Pierre und Nadine sind aus Paris. Björn und Christina sind aus Oslo; etc. 4. **Wie viele Menschen wohnen in** Bonn (Köln, Frankfurt/Main, Düsseldorf, Stuttgart, Leipzig, Dresden)?

B. Noch einmal: Deutschland heute Using the following key words taken from the reading text, summarize the passage in five or six sentences.

Sprachen
wichtig
Europa
Europäer
Ausländer
im Zentrum von
im Ausland
EU
studieren
Menschen
lernen
sprechen
wohnen
arbeiten
Nachbarn

Schreibtipp

Writing a Summary

When writing a summary, keep the following in mind: (1) Be brief and try not to be repetitious. (2) Include key words from the passage. (3) Use pronouns where appropriate: *Viele Europäer sprechen zwei oder drei Sprachen.* ***Sie*** *finden das interessant.*

You can use this realia for spelling practice.

© Alberto Masnovo/Shutterstock

Weiteres

C. Die EU-Karte Look at the map of Europe showing the old and new members of the EU, then answer the following questions.

1. **Länder und Sprachen**
   a. Wie heißen die alten EU-Mitgliedstaaten (beige)?
   b. Wie heißen die neuen EU-Mitgliedstaaten (grün)?
   c. Welche Länder sind nicht in der EU?
   d. Welche Sprachen sprechen die Menschen in der Europäischen Union? *(Name 5–7.)*

■ **Rumänien** and **Bulgarien** (marked in a lighter green) became EU members in 2007. Croatia **(Kroatien)** became a member in 2013. Turkey **(die Türkei)** has applied for membership in the EU. Keep up to date!

2. **Was liegt wo?** Ask your classmates to describe the location of the various European countries. You can vary the type of question asked.

BEISPIEL	Wo liegt Portugal?	*Portugal liegt westlich von Spanien.*
	Was liegt westlich von Spanien?	*Portugal!*

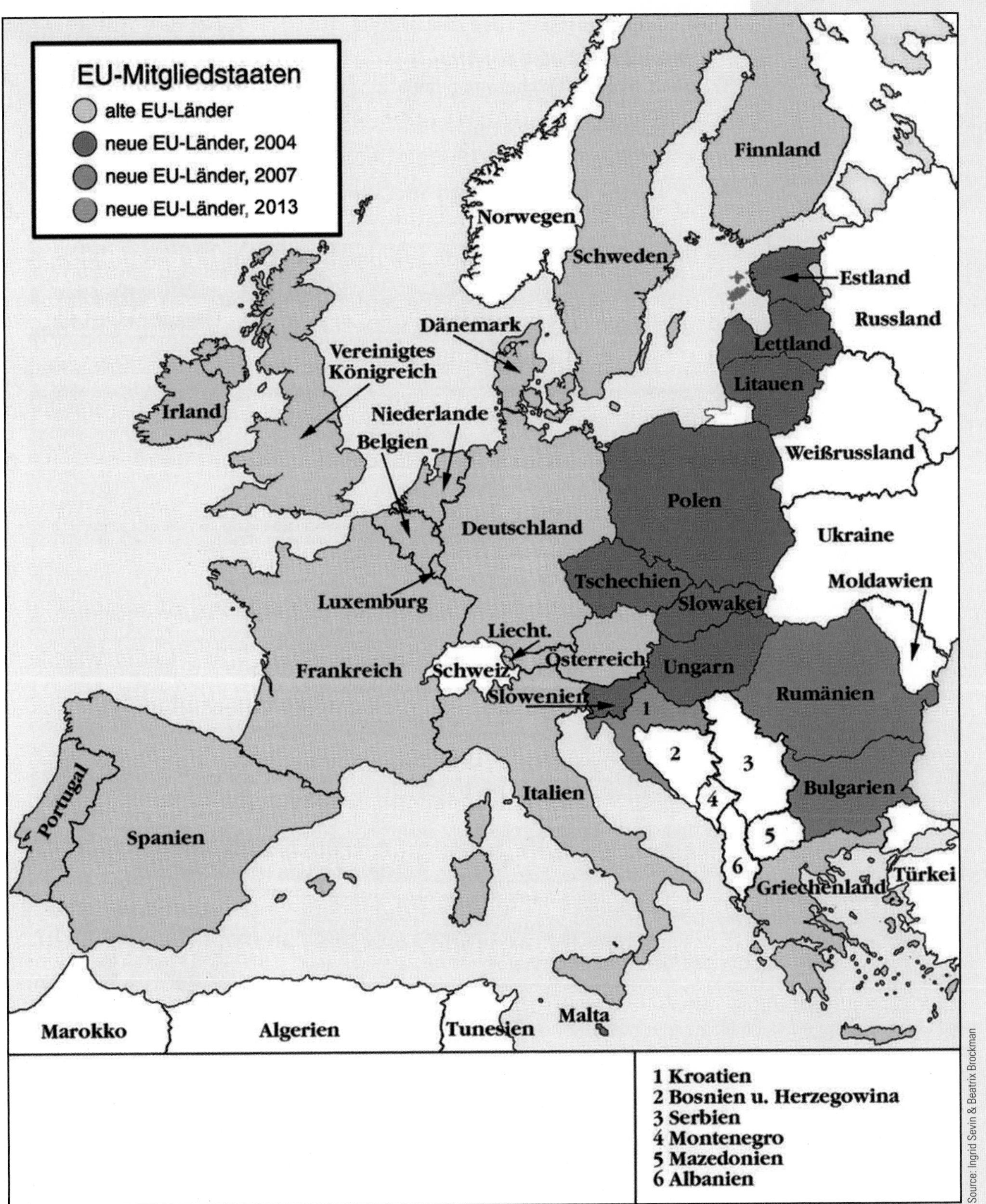

Source: Ingrid Sevin & Beatrix Brockman

C.1: a. Schweden, Finnland, Dänemark, Deutschland, Österreich, Liechtenstein, Italien, Griechenland, Portugal, Spanien, Frankreich, Luxemburg, Belgien, die Niederlande (Holland), Vereinigtes Königreich (Großbritannien + Nordirland), Irland b. Estland, Lettland, Litauen, Polen, Tschechien, die Slowakei, Ungarn, Slowenien, Zypern, Malta, Rumänien, Bulgarien, Kroatien c. die Schweiz, Norwegen, die Türkei, Bosnien u. Herzegowina, Serbien, Montenegro, Mazedonien, Albanien. *Please update students if this should change.* d. Here students might need some help: Estnisch, Lettisch, Litauisch, Polnisch, Tschechisch, Slowakisch, Ungarisch, Slowenisch, Griechisch, Türkisch.

1 km² = 247.1 acres = 0.3861 square miles.

Note that **Tschechien** is also called **die Tschechische Republik** and **Slowakien die Slowakische Republik.** Note also: die Tschechische Republik, **in der** Tschechische**n** Republik; die Slowakei, **in der** Slowakei.

D. Die EU-Mitgliedstaaten seit *(since)* 2004

1. **Wie groß sind die Länder?** Read aloud in German the numbers relating to their size **(die Fläche)** and population **(die Bevölkerung).**

BEISPIEL Fläche: 65.000 km²
Litauen hat fünfundsechzigtausend Quadratkilometer.

Bevölkerung: 3,5 Mio.
Litauen hat drei Komma fünf Millionen Menschen.

Bulgarien
Fläche: 111.900 km²
Bevölkerung: 7,7 Mio.
Polen
Fläche: 312.678 km²
Bevölkerung: 38,2 Mio.
Slowakei
Fläche: 49.030 km²
Bevölkerung: 5,4 Mio.
Kroatien
Fläche: 56.500 km²
Bevölkerung: 4,5 Mio.
Tschechien
Fläche: 78.866 km²
Bevölkerung: 10,2 Mio.
Slowenien
Fläche: 20.723 km²
Bevölkerung: 2,0 Mio.
Zypern
Fläche: 9.251 km²
Bevölkerung: 778,700
Estland
Fläche: 45.227 km²
Bevölkerung: 1,4 Mio.
Litauen
Fläche: 65.000 km²
Bevölkerung: 3,5 Mio.
Lettland
Fläche: 64.597 km²
Bevölkerung: 2,3 Mio.
Rumänien
Fläche: 238.400 km²
Bevölkerung: 21,5 Mio.
Malta
Fläche: 316 km²
Bevölkerung: 385.000
Ungarn
Fläche: 93.000 km²
Bevölkerung: 10,2 Mio.

2. **Welche Farben haben ihre Flaggen?** Ask each other about the colors of their flags.
   a. Welche Flaggen haben drei Farben? (Die Flagge von . . . hat . . .) Welche Farben haben sie?
   b. Welche Flaggen haben zwei Farben? Welche Farben haben sie?

Fokus German throughout the World

Even though Germany was never an important colonial power, German language and culture have reached all regions of the globe. Looking for new opportunities, millions of Germans emigrated to the Americas, especially to the United States, Canada, Chile, Argentina, and Brazil. Nearly a fourth of the US population claims German ancestry, and some 300 German-language periodicals are still published here.

In Asia, German language, literature, and philosophy continue to be popular subjects at universities; thousands of exchange scholars and students from the Far East have studied in Germany. When Japan opened up to the West in the late 1800s, it borrowed heavily from German law and science. At the turn of the century, the Chinese city of Qingdao was under German administration and consequently has many German buildings—and the best beer in China.

Although Germany only briefly controlled a handful of African colonies—Togo, Cameroon, and Namibia (formerly South-West Africa)—the effect of those years, as well as the influence of German missionaries and doctors, is still noticable in some regions. German is taught at all levels throughout Africa. Worldwide, 17 million people are learning German as a second language.

Die Christuskirche in Windhoek, Namibia

Carlos-Gomes-Theater in Blumenau, Brasilien

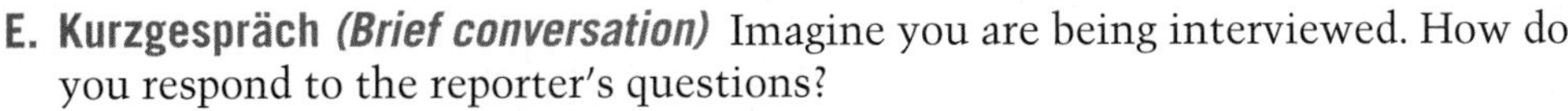

E. Kurzgespräch *(Brief conversation)* Imagine you are being interviewed. How do you respond to the reporter's questions?

1. Guten Tag! Wie heißen Sie?
2. Woher kommen Sie?
3. Was ist Ihre Muttersprache?
4. Sprechen Ihre Eltern oder Großeltern Deutsch?
5. Sprechen Sie noch andere Sprachen?
6. Wie heißt Ihr Deutschbuch?
7. Wie heißt Ihr Professor?
8. Lernen Sie viel?
9. Wie finden Sie Deutsch?

Hörverständnis

Europäer in Deutschland Many foreign nationals have chosen to live in Germany. Listen to the four speakers, and then circle the letter of the response that correctly completes the statement.

Zum Erkennen: zuerst *(first of all)*; komisch *(strange)*

VITTORIO

1. Vittorio ist __c__.
   a. 20 b. 29 c. 21
2. Seine Eltern sind aus __b__.
   a. Portugal b. Italien c. Spanien

WLODZIMIERZ

3. Wlodzimierz ist aus __a__.
   a. Polen b. Portugal c. Italien
4. Er wohnt schon __a__ Jahr(e) in Deutschland.
   a. 1 b. 2 c. 5

MARIA

5. Maria wohnt in __c__.
   a. Frankfurt b. Dresden c. Düsseldorf
6. Sie und ihre Familie sind __a__.
   a. Griechen b. Italiener c. Türken

JOSÉ

7. José ist Professor in __b__.
   a. Frankfurt b. Bonn c. Düsseldorf
8. Seine Frau ist aus __a__.
   a. Berlin b. Erfurt c. Köln

For further practice, an optional two-part video (**Szenen** and **Interviews**) is available on the ***Wie geht's?*** Premium Website and in iLrn, with corresponding questions and activities in the *Arbeitsbuch* (SAM).

As an optional activity with Google Earth, visit Frankfurt or any city mentioned in this chapter, and also visit any country in Europe.

Rückschau

Kapitelwortschatz

Hauptwörter

(das) Amerika	*America*
der Amerikaner, -	*the American* (male)
die Amerikanerin, -nen	*the American* (female)
der Ausländer, -	*foreigner*
der Berg, -e	*mountain*
der Bruder, ¨	*brother*
der Cousin, -s	*cousin* (male)
die Cousine, -n	*cousin* (female)
(das) Deutsch	*German* (language)
der Deutsche, -n	*the German* (male)
die Deutsche, -n	*the German* (female)
(das) Deutschland	*Germany*
die Eltern (*pl.*)	*parents*
(das) England	*England*
der Engländer, -	*Englishman*
die Engländerin, -nen	*Englishwoman*
(das) Englisch	*English*
die Europäische Union (EU)	*European Union (EU)*
die Familie, -n	*family*
der Fluss, ¨e	*river*
die Frage, -n	*question*
(das) Frankreich	*France*
der Franzose, -n	*Frenchman*
die Französin, -nen	*Frenchwoman*
(das) Französisch	*French* (language)
die Frau, -en	*woman; wife*
die Geschwister (*pl.*)	*siblings; brothers and/or sisters*
die Großeltern (*pl.*)	*grandparents*
der Großvater, ¨	*grandfather*
die Großmutter, ¨	*grandmother*
die Hauptstadt, ¨e	*capital city*
(das) Italien	*Italy*
der Italiener, -	*the Italian* (male)
die Italienerin, -nen	*the Italian* (female)
(das) Italienisch	*Italian* (language)
der Junge, -n	*boy*
(das) Kanada	*Canada*
der Kanadier, -	*the Canadian* (male)
die Kanadierin, -nen	*the Canadian* (female)
das Kind, -er	*child*
die Kusine, -n	*cousin* (female)
das Land, ¨er	*country, state*
die Landkarte, -n	*map*
die Leute (*pl.*)	*people*
das Mädchen, -	*girl*
der Mann, ¨er	*man; husband*
der Mensch, -en	*human being, person;* (pl.) *people*
die Mutter, ¨	*mother*
der Nachbar, -n	*neighbor* (male)
die Nachbarin, -nen	*neighbor* (female)
(das) Österreich	*Austria*
der Österreicher, -	*the Austrian* (male)
die Österreicherin, -nen	*the Austrian* (female)
der Onkel	*uncle*
die Prüfung, -en	*test, exam*
der Satz, ¨e	*sentence*
die Schweiz	*Switzerland*
der Schweizer, -	*the Swiss* (male)
die Schweizerin, -nen	*the Swiss* (female)
die Schwester, -n	*sister*
der See, -n	*lake*
der Sohn, ¨e	*son*
(das) Spanien	*Spain*
der Spanier, -	*Spaniard* (male)
die Spanierin, -nen	*Spaniard* (female)
(das) Spanisch	*Spanish* (language)
die Sprache, -n	*language*
der Staat, -en	*state*
die Stadt, ¨e	*city*
die Tante, -n	*aunt*
der Teil, -e	*part*
die Tochter, ¨	*daughter*
der Vater, ¨	*father*

Verben

antworten	*to answer*
arbeiten	*to work*
beginnen	*to begin*
brauchen	*to need*
finden	*to find*
fragen	*to ask*
gehen	*to go*
hören	*to hear*
kommen	*to come*
kosten	*to cost*
lernen	*to learn; to study*
liegen	*to lie; to be located*
öffnen	*to open*
regnen	*to rain*
sagen	*to say; to tell*
schreiben	*to write*
spielen	*to play*
verstehen	*to understand*
wiederholen	*to repeat; to review*
wohnen	*to live, reside*
zählen	*to count*

Adjektive und Adverbien

amerikanisch	*American*
kanadisch	*Canadian*
wichtig	*important*

Verschiedenes

dein(e)	*your* (familiar)
der/das/die	*the*
ein(e)	*a, an*
Ihr(e)	*your* (formal)
Ich bin / komme aus . . .	*I'm from (a native of) . . .*
im Norden / Süden / Osten / Westen	*in the north / south / east / west*
kein(e)	*no, not a, not any*
mein(e)	*my*
nördlich / südlich / östlich / westlich von	*north / south / east / west of*
so . . . wie . . .	*as . . . as . . .*
ungefähr	*approximately, about*
Was?	*what?*
Wer?	*who?*
Woher?	*from where?*

Zum Schluss *(Conclusion)*

1. **Wer sind Sie?** Pretend you are a historical or fictional figure to answer the following questions. Use full sentences in the present tense. Be creative!

   a. Woher kommen Sie?

   b. Wie ist das Wetter da im Frühling? im Sommer? im Herbst? im Winter?

   c. Was ist Ihre Muttersprache?

   d. Sprechen Sie noch andere Sprachen?

   e. Wie groß ist Ihre Familie? Wie heißen die Familienmitglieder (*family members*) und wie alt sind sie?

2. **Wer ist wer?** Are you part of a study group? If so, share your responses with your classmates. Can they guess who you are? Can you guess who they are?

3. **Sätze schreiben**

   a. Create sentences by combining items from each column. Add a few additional words of your own to each column.

1	2	3
ich	arbeiten	Amerikaner(in)
du	antworten	auf Spanisch
der Vater	beginnen	aus . . .
die Stadt	hören	Deutsch
das Kind	kommen	im Osten von . . .
mein Bruder und ich	liegen	in . . .
ihr	verstehen	(nicht) gut
Sie		nördlich von
die Eltern		um . . . Uhr

   b. Now rewrite three sentences so that they begin with a word or phrase other than the subject.

   c. Take a look at your sentences. Can you replace any subjects with pronouns? Rewrite at least three sentences, replacing the subject with the appropriate pronoun.

4. **Etwas** (*A little*) **Geographie** Describe some of the features of the area you are from to a classmate, using the appropriate form of ***ein*** and ***kein***. Check the chapter vocabulary for ideas!

5. **Wortkombinationen** How many compound nouns can you create from vocabulary in the chapter? Brainstorm with a partner. Make sure to include the correct article! Check your compounds in a dictionary!

iLrn **Onlineaktivitäten** Visit iLrn for online activities related to this chapter. There you will find additional resources, such as a memory game (**Gedächtnisspiel**), a crossword puzzle (**Kreuzworträtsel**), audio flash cards (**Vokabelblitz**), a tutorial quiz (**Mini-Quiz**), and the active vocabulary (**Wortschatz**) for this chapter.

Kapitel 2

Lebensmittel und Geschäfte

Lernziele In this chapter you will learn about:

Zum Thema

Food and grocery shopping

Fokus

Shopping styles, weights and measures, breads and cold cuts, flower power, the euro, pedestrian areas, and Regensburg

Struktur

- The present tense of **sein** *(to be)* and **haben** *(to have)*
- The accusative case and *n*-nouns
- Sentence structure *(continued)*

Einblicke

Dialog: Geschäfte und Einkaufen

Rückschau

Kapitalwortschatz
Zum Schluss

RESSOURCEN

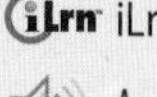 iLrn
 Video
Audio
 SAM

Ich gehe gern jeden* (each) *Tag einkaufen.

Vorschau Shopping and Store Hours

As much as the development of American-style supermarkets and discount chains has changed the way Europeans shop, customs still differ considerably from those in North America. Many people shop daily or several times a week, frequently going on foot or by bicycle rather than by car. With competition from supermarket chains, grocery sections in department stores, shopping centers **(Einkaufszentren)**, and discount stores, the traditional corner grocery store is disappearing rapidly. However, specialty stores, such as butcher shops, bakeries, fruit and vegetable stores, and organic and health food stores **(Bioläden)** continue to thrive. Many towns also have retained open-air farmers' markets. Consumers value the freshness of the products and the personal atmosphere. They usually bring their own reusable cloth shopping bags **(Einkaufstaschen)** to stores and markets rather than buy plastic bags **(Plastiktüten)** at the checkout counter. They also bag their purchases themselves. Grocery store clerks sit rather than stand when checking out customers. The amount shown on the price tag always includes a value-added tax **(die Mehrwertsteuer)**. People generally pay in cash **(das Bargeld)**. In big cities, credit cards are becoming increasingly accepted, but it is still preferable to ask before ordering a meal or shopping in a store. The most popular piece of plastic is the EC-debit card **(die EC [Eurocheque]-Karte)**.

In 1991, Germany introduced a package recycling program **(Der Grüne Punkt)** that has proven very successful. Basically, every package in the country carries a green dot indicating that the manufacturer contributes to the recovery and recycling system. In addition, there is a comprehensive deposit system for beverage packaging **(das Pfandsystem)** on plastic bottles, aluminum cans, and glass bottles.

Until 1996, store hours in Germany were regulated by Europe's most restrictive closing law. Over vigorous opposition from owners of small shops, retail workers, and trade unions, the law was finally liberalized. Stores can now be open from 6 A.M. to 8 P.M., Monday through Saturday, and many shops and supermarkets in bigger cities are doing that. However, quite a few small neighborhood stores still close earlier in the evening and even for one or two hours around lunchtime. Sunday and holiday shopping has been banned since 1891, although pharmacies, bakeries, pastry shops, and news and flower stands were exempt. The only stores that can do around-the-clock business are at airports, train stations, and gas stations.

Ask students whether they know of any products from German-speaking countries being sold in supermarkets or specialty stores. Maybe they or you could bring in some labels of such products. Any kind of German, Swiss, or Austrian food advertisement as well as catalogues might also be of interest.

Fragen: 1. Das Delikatessengeschäft links verkauft Salate, Wurst *(sausage)* und Gurken *(pickles)*. Essen Sie gern Wurst und Gurken? 2. Wo kaufen Sie Ihr Obst und Gemüse? 3. Kaufen Sie Ihr Gemüse frisch oder gefroren *(frozen)*? 4. Was verkauft der Obst- und Gemüsestand unten (*below*)? 5. Was möchten Sie hier gern kaufen? 6. Wie ist das Wetter? 7. Was tragen die Leute? 8. Welche Jahreszeit ist das vielleicht? Was denken Sie?

You might want to wait until you are more into the chapter to ask more questions.

Ein Obst- und Gemüsestand. Hier ist alles besonders frisch.

Einkaufen in Regensburg

Zum Thema

Gespräche

Warm-ups: 1. **Wo sprechen die Leute was?** z. B. Deutschland: In Deutschland sprechen sie Deutsch 2. **Wie geht's weiter?** z. B. April > Mai (Juli, September, . . .) 3. **Was ist der Plural!** z. B. der Deutsche: die Deutschen (Engländer, Franzose, Französin, Amerikaner, Student, Studentin, Sprache, Land, Stadt, Fluss, See, Berg) 4. **Wie spät ist es?**

Have various times already written on the board. Or, take a homemade cardboard clock to class and adjust the hands to different times to quiz the students.

Students may be curious about **im Lebensmittelgeschäft** vs. **in der Bäckerei.** Don't try to explain; tell them they will learn the reasons for this difference later.

Im Lebensmittelgeschäft

■ Listen to the dialogue. Then act out the dialogue with a partner. ■

VERKÄUFER Guten Tag! Was darf's sein?
OLIVER Ich hätte gern etwas Obst. Haben Sie denn keine Bananen?
VERKÄUFER Doch, da drüben.
OLIVER Was kosten sie?
VERKÄUFER 90 Cent das Pfund.
OLIVER Und die Orangen?
VERKÄUFER 45 Cent das Stück.
OLIVER Gut, zwei Pfund Bananen und sechs Orangen bitte!
VERKÄUFER Sonst noch etwas?
OLIVER Ja, zwei Kilo Äpfel bitte!
VERKÄUFER 8,10 € bitte! Danke! Auf Wiedersehen!

In der Bäckerei

VERKÄUFERIN Guten Morgen! Was darf's sein?
SIMONE Guten Morgen! Ein Schwarzbrot und sechs Brötchen bitte!
VERKÄUFERIN Sonst noch etwas?
SIMONE Ja, ich brauche etwas Kuchen. Ist der Apfelstrudel frisch?
VERKÄUFERIN Natürlich, ganz frisch.
SIMONE Gut, dann nehme ich vier Stück.
VERKÄUFERIN Ist das alles?
SIMONE Ich möchte auch ein paar Plätzchen. Was für Plätzchen haben Sie heute?
VERKÄUFERIN Zitronenplätzchen, Schokoladenplätzchen, Butterplätzchen . . .
SIMONE Hm . . . Ich nehme 300 Gramm Schokoladenplätzchen.
VERKÄUFERIN Noch etwas?
SIMONE Nein, danke. Das ist alles.
VERKÄUFERIN Das macht dann 9,55 € bitte.

A: 1. etwas Obst 2. 90 Cent das Pfund, 45 Cent das Stück 3. 2 Pfund Bananen, 6 Orangen 4. 2 Kilo Äpfel 5. 8,10 Euro 6. 6 Brötchen 7. der Apfelstrudel 8. 4 Stück 9. Schokoladenplätzchen 10. nein

A. Alles verstanden?

1. Was braucht Oliver? 2. Was kosten die Bananen? die Orangen? 3. Wie viele Bananen und wie viele Orangen kauft er? 4. Was kauft er noch? 5. Was kostet alles zusammen? 6. Wie viele Brötchen möchte Simone? 7. Was ist ganz frisch? 8. Wie viel Stück Apfelstrudel kauft sie? 9. Was für Plätzchen kauft sie? 10. Kauft sie sonst noch etwas?

B. Jetzt sind Sie dran! Working with a partner, use the dialogues above as models and the *Wortschatz* that follows to create your own dialogue between a customer and a salesperson.

BEISPIEL S1 Guten Tag! Was darf's sein?
S2 Ich möchte . . . / Ich hätte gern etwas . . .
S1 Noch etwas?

Wortschatz 1

Die Lebensmittel *(pl.)* *(groceries)*

der Apfel, ¨	*apple*
Fisch, -e	*fish*
Jog(h)urt, -s	*yog(h)urt*
Kaffee, -s	*coffee*
Käse, -	*cheese*
Kuchen, -	*cake*
Saft, ¨e	*juice*
Salat, -e	*lettuce; salad*
Tee, -s	*tea*
Wein, -e	*wine*
das Bier, -e	*beer*
Brot, -e	*bread*
Brötchen, -	*roll*
Ei, -er	*egg*
Fleisch	*meat*
Gemüse, -	*vegetable(s)*
Obst	*fruit*
Plätzchen, -	*cookie*
Wasser	*water*
die Banane, -n	*banana*
Bohne, -n	*bean*
Butter	*butter*
Cola	*cola drink*
Erbse, -n	*pea*
Erdbeere, -n	*strawberry*
Gurke, -n	*cucumber*
Karotte, -n	*carrot*
Limonade, -n	*soft drink*
Limo, -s	
Marmelade, -n	*jam*
Milch	*milk*
Orange, -n	*orange*
Tomate, -n	*tomato*
Wurst, ¨e	*sausage*
Zitrone, -n	*lemon*

Verschiedenes

der Markt, ¨e	*(farmers') market*
Supermarkt, ¨e	*supermarket*
Verkäufer, -	*salesperson*
das Geschäft, e	*store*
das Kaufhaus, ¨er	*department store*
Pfund, -e; ein Pfund	*pound; one pound (of)*
Stück, -e; ein Stück	*piece; one piece (of)*
die Bäckerei, -en	*bakery*
Buchhandlung, -en	*bookstore*
allerlei	*all sorts of, various*
alles	*everything, all*
dann	*then* (temporal)
Das ist alles.	*That's all., That's it.*
doch	*yes, sure, certainly, of course* (response to negative question or statement)
es gibt	*there is, there are*
Was / Wo gibt's . . . ?	*What / Where do you (they) have . . . ?*
etwas . . .	*a little, some . . .* (used with sg. collective nouns)
frisch	*fresh(ly)*
gern	*gladly*
Ich esse / trinke gern . . .	*I like to eat / drink . . .*
Ich esse / trinke nicht gern . . .	*I don't like to eat / drink . . .*
Ich hätte gern . . .	*I would like (to have) . . .*
Ich möchte (gern) . . .	*I would like (to have) . . .*
glauben	*to believe; to think*
kaufen / verkaufen	*to buy / to sell*
machen	*to make; to do*
suchen	*to look for*
natürlich	*of course*
was für (ein) . . . ?	*what kind of (a) . . . ?*
zusammen	*together*

Zum Erkennen: Was darf's sein? *(May I help you?)*; da drüben *(over there)*; Sonst noch etwas? *(Anything else?)*; das Kilo / zwei Kilo *(kilogram / two kilos)*; der Apfelstrudel *(apple strudel)*; ein paar *(a couple of)*; AUCH: der Akkusativ, -e; verneinen *(to negate)*

Cola can also be neuter. In southern Germany, Austria, and Switzerland, **Joghurt** is frequently used with **das.** It can also be spelled as **Jogurt.**

Limonade (or **Limo**) is a carbonated soft drink similar to Sprite or 7-UP. It is quite different from North American *lemonade*. What North Americans call *lemonade* is **Zitronensaft.**

In case you are curious: *apricot* **die Aprikose, -n**; *asparagus* **der Spargel**; *broccoli* **der Brokkoli, die Brokkoli, *pl.***; *fancy cake* **die Torte, -n**; *cherry* **die Kirsche, -n**; *chocolate* **die Schokolade, -n**; *hot chocolate* **der Kakao**; *corn* **der Mais**; *cornflakes* **die Cornflakes, *pl.***; *grape* **die Traube, -n**; *grapefruit* **die Grapefruit, -s**; *liver sausage / liverwurst* **die Leberwurst**; *melon* **die Melone, -n**; *oatmeal* **die Haferflocken, *pl.***; *onion* **die Zwiebel, -n**; *pancake* **der Pfannkuchen, -**; *peach* **der Pfirsich, -e**; *peanut butter* **die Erdnussbutter**; *pear* **die Birne, -n**; *pineapple* **die Ananas, -**; *spinach* **der Spinat**; *waffle* **die Waffel, -n**; *whole-grain granola* **das Müsli**

Point out that units of measure are always in the singular **(ein Pfund, ein Stück),** even with a plural noun: **zwei Pfund Fleisch, drei Stück Kuchen.** This applies to money as well: **vier Euro.**

To express that you like or dislike doing something, use **(nicht) gern** + verb: **Ich esse gern Obst. Sie trinkt nicht gern Milch.**

Möchte and **hätte** are subjunctive verb forms that will be explained in Chapters 13–14.

Fokus Weights and Measures

In the German-speaking countries—as in most of the world—the metric system is used to measure distance, volume, and weight. One exception is the older measurement, **das Pfund,** which is half a kilogram (500 grams), or a little more than a US pound (454 grams). For a quick approximation, deduct 10% from US pounds to get European pounds (120 lbs − 12 = 108 lbs) or, vice versa, add 10% to European pounds to get US pounds (108 lbs + 11 = 119 lbs). Liquids are measured by the liter (a little more than a quart). In cooking or baking, scales are preferred over cups and spoons, as weighing is more precise. Here is a quick-and-easy guide for converting US measures to the metric system: 1 oz = 28.35g; 1 lb = 454 g; 2.2 lbs = 1 kg; 4 cups = 1 liter, 1 US gallon = 3.79 liters.

A: *bean salad* **(der)**, *buttermilk* **(die)**, *deli store* **(das)**, *strawberry jam* **(die)**, *fish sandwich* **(das)**, *(coffee) creamer* **(die)**, *café au lait* **(der)**, *fruit salad* **(der)**, *orange softdrink* **(die)**, *lemon softdrink* **(die)**, *lemon juice / lemonade* **(der)**, *stationery store* **(das)**, *water for tea* **(das)**, *open sausage sandwich* **(das)**.

Fragen: 1. Wo ist das Pfannkuchen-Haus? Lesen Sie laut die Adresse und die Telefonnummer! 2. Gibt es hier auch ein Pfannkuchenhaus? Wie heißt es? 3. Essen Sie gern Pfannkuchen oder Waffeln? 4. Wie essen Sie sie gern: mit *(with)* Butter und Syrup, mit Marmelade oder Nutella, mit Puderzucker *(powdered sugar)* oder Zimtzucker *(cinnamon sugar)*, mit Erdbeeren oder Blaubeeren und Schlagsahne *(whipped cream)*?

Übungen zum Thema

A. Was bedeuten die Wörter und was sind die Artikel? Determine the English meaning and the gender of these words.

Bohnensalat, Buttermilch, Delikatessengeschäft, Erdbeermarmelade, Fischbrötchen, Kaffeemilch, Milchkaffee, Obstsalat, Orangenlimonade, Zitronenlimonade, Zitronensaft, Schreibwarengeschäft, Teewasser, Wurstbrot

B. Was passt nicht? Which item does not belong in each list?

1. die Butter—der Käse—die Milch—die Bohne
2. das Brötchen—die Zitrone—das Plätzchen—der Kuchen
3. die Karotte—die Erdbeere—die Gurke—der Salat
4. das Gemüse—der Apfel—die Orange—die Banane
5. das Obst—das Gemüse—der Salat—der Tee
6. der Wein—das Bier—die Erbse—die Milch
7. das Geschäft—die Lebensmittel—die Bäckerei—das Kaufhaus

C. Im Pfannkuchen-Haus. Was passt?

bdh 1. Möchten Sie ein paar Pfannkuchen?

ai 2. Die Waffeln sind auch sehr gut.

eg 3. Sind die Erdbeeren frisch?

cik 4. Ich nehme Waffeln mit Nutella.

bhj 5. Sonst noch etwas?

a. Prima!
b. Ich weiß nicht.
c. Wir auch.
d. Ja, gern.
e. Nein.
f. Schade.
g. Ja, natürlich.
h. Nein, danke.
i. Wirklich?
j. Nein, das ist alles.
k. Wie bitte?
l. Freut mich.

D. Allerlei Lebensmittel und anderes durcheinander In the basket below, you will find various groceries and a few other items thrown all together that need to be grouped. One person starts by reading aloud one of the items. Someone else quickly responds by adding the proper article and putting it into the correct category. Whoever gives the fastest correct response will pick the next item. Go through the whole list, crossing off each word placed. On a separate sheet, keep track of how many items you finally listed in each category (see margin).

Optional **Alphabetspiel: Welche Lebensmittel gibt es mit . . . ?** Name a certain letter and ask students to respond quickly with a few German words that start with that letter, e.g., **B: Brot, Butter, Banane,** etc.

Obst
Gemüse
Getränke
Milchprodukte
Backwaren *(baked goods)*
Fleischwaren *(meats)*
Schreibwaren *(stationery)*

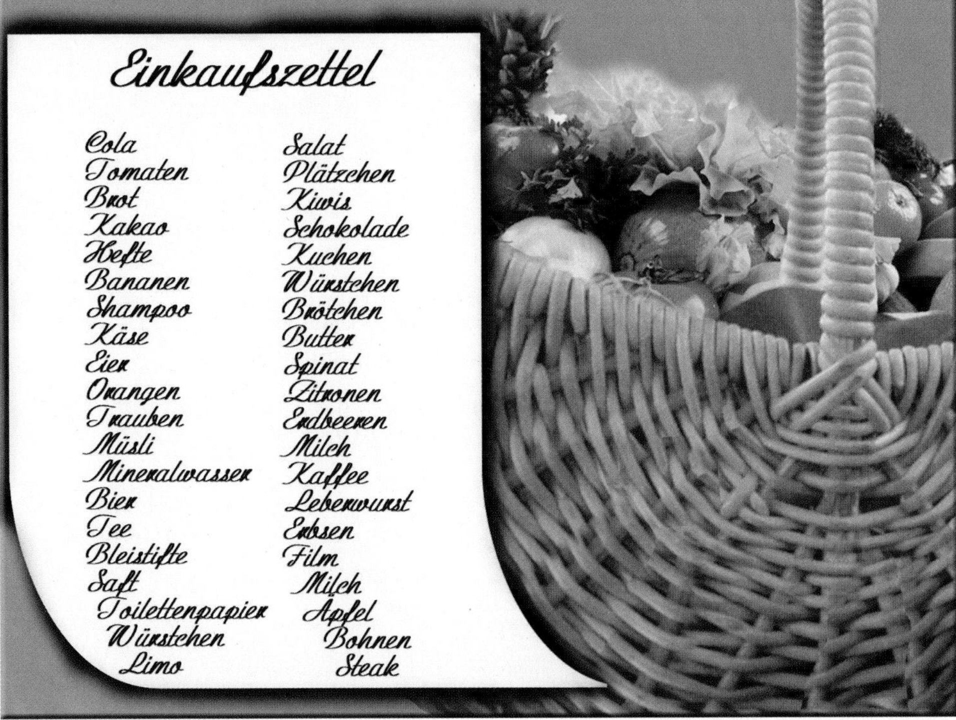

Einkaufszettel
Cola
Tomaten
Brot
Kakao
Hefte
Bananen
Shampoo
Käse
Eier
Orangen
Trauben
Müsli
Mineralwasser
Bier
Tee
Bleistifte
Saft
Toilettenpapier
Würstchen
Limo
Salat
Plätzchen
Kiwis
Schokolade
Kuchen
Würstchen
Brötchen
Butter
Spinat
Zitronen
Erdbeeren
Milch
Kaffee
Leberwurst
Erbsen
Film
Milch
Apfel
Bohnen
Steak

Fokus Breads, Sausages, and Cheeses

When Germans think of **Brot,** they probably think first of a firm, heavy loaf of rye bread **(Schwarzbrot)** and not of the soft white bread so common in North America. In Germany, white loaves and rolls are prized for their crisp crust. There are more than 300 varieties of bread in Central Europe, including bread made from a mixture of wheat and rye **(Graubrot)** or of cracked rye and wheat grains **(Vollkornbrot),** as well as bread with flaxseed **(Leinsamenbrot)** or sunflower seeds **(Sonnenblumenkernbrot).**

For Germans, bread is the most important staple and the central focus of both the morning and evening meals. On average they eat four slices of bread and one roll per day. The traditional German supper, appropriately called **das Abendbrot,** usually consists of bread with cheese, sausage, or cold cuts **(der Aufschnitt).** Germany offers a wide variety of cheeses and sausages, which often carry the name of their place of origin: **Emmentaler** *(cheese),* **Frankfurter, Thüringer** *(both sausages).* Others are named after ingredients: **Butterkäse, Kräuterkäse** *(cheese with herbs),* **Leberwurst.** Many Germans also eat bread, cold cuts, and cheese for breakfast.

In der Bäckerei. Die Deutschen, Österreicher und Schweizer essen gern Brot.

Aussprache: e, o

A. Laute

1. [e:] g**e**h**en**, n**eh**men, K**ä**se, G**e**genteil, Am**e**rika, T**ee**
2. [e] **e**s, spr**e**chen, Gesch**ä**ft, M**e**nsch, H**e**md
3. [o:] **oh**ne B**oh**nen, **o**der, gr**o**ß, **O**bst, Br**o**t
4. [o] k**o**mmen, d**o**ch, **O**sten, N**o**rden, S**o**nne

For further review, see the Summary of Pronunciation in the front of this book. Study Part II, subsections 2, 5, 14–16, 18, and 21.

B. Wortpaare

1. *gate* / geht
2. *shown* / schon
3. zähle / Zelle
4. den / denn
5. Ofen / offen
6. Bonn / Bann

Hörverständnis

Essen und Trinken Listen to three students tell what they like and don't like to eat and drink. Then note which foods and beverages each student mentions. Write **H** for Hanjo, **M** for Martina, and **D** for Dirk. Not all the available slots will be filled.

Zum Erkennen: also *(well)*; manchmal *(sometimes)*; die Kartoffel, -n *(potato)*

ESSEN				TRINKEN			
gern		**nicht gern**		**gern**		**nicht gern**	
H	Äpfel	D	Gemüse	M	Tee	M	Kaffee
H	Bananen	D	Gurken	___	Kaffee	___	Bier
M	Kartoffeln	D	Karotten	___	Kakao	___	Wein
M	Kuchen	D	Erbsen	___	Milch	D	Milch
H	Erdbeeren	___	Fisch	H	Saft	D	Cola
H	Orangen	___	Bananen	H	Bier	___	Wasser
M	Gemüse	___	Jogurt	H	Cola	___	Tee
H	Fisch	___	Pizza	___	Mineralwasser	___	Kakao
M	Fleisch	___	Käsebrot	___	Limonade	___	Eiswasser

Fokus Flower Power

Germans are very fond of having fresh flowers in their homes. When invited for coffee, tea, or dinner, guests usually bring their hosts a bouquet **(der Strauß, ¨-e).** The flowers, however, have to be carefully chosen: red roses, for example, carry the message of romantic love, while white chrysanthemums are considered funeral flowers. The gift of flowers (or some other small present) eliminates the need for a thank-you note, but a follow-up telephone call is very much appreciated.

***Blumen sind immer ein schönes Geschenk* (present).**

Struktur

2.1 The present tense of *sein* (to be) and *haben* (to have)

	sein		**haben**	
1st person	ich bin	wir sind	ich habe	wir haben
2nd person	du bist	ihr seid	du hast	ihr habt
3rd person	er/es/sie ist	sie sind	er hat	sie haben

Übung

A. Ersetzen Sie das Subjekt!

BEISPIEL Haben Sie Zeit? (du)
Hast du Zeit?

1. Ich bin schon fertig. (er, wir, sie/*sg.*)
2. Sind Sie müde? (du, ihr, sie/*pl.*)
3. Sie hat die Landkarte. (ich, er, wir)
4. Haben Sie Papier? (sie/*sg.*, ihr, du)
5. Wir sind Amerikaner. (er, sie/*pl.*, ich)
6. Er hat eine Frage. (ich, wir, Sie)
7. Seid ihr aus Düsseldorf? (Sie, du, sie/*sg.*)
8. Er hat Orangensaft. (sie/*pl.*, ich, ihr)

A: 1. er ist, wir sind, sie ist 2. bist du, seid ihr, sind sie 3. ich habe, er hat, wir haben 4. hat sie, habt ihr, hast du 5. er ist, sie sind, ich bin 6. ich habe, wir haben, Sie haben 7. sind Sie, bist du, ist sie 8. sie haben, ich habe, ihr habt

Fokus The Euro

In January 2002, the euro **(der Euro)** was introduced as the common currency of the European Union. There are seven denominations of bills (5, 10, 20, 50, 100, 200, and 500 euros) and eight different coins (1, 2, 5, 10, 20, 50 cents, as well as 1 and 2 euros). The bills **(Scheine)** have different colors and increase in size along with their value; they are the same throughout the EU. On one side, they show all sorts of historic arches symbolizing bridges to be built between the nations; on the other side, they show a variety of national windows and portals symbolizing Europe as gateway to the rest of the world. With the coins, only the front (showing a map of Europe) is the same for all countries; the back side differs reflecting national diversity.

While a few of the EU countries will be introducing the euro by stages, 17 EU nations already enjoy the benefits of a single market using the same currency **(die Währung).** This represents a tremendous advantage for consumers when traveling or buying goods or services abroad, as well as for the new economy founded on e-commerce. A single currency also allows investors to do business throughout the euro area **(das Euroland)** with minimal disruptions and to take advantage of a more stable economic environment.

2.2 The accusative case and *n*-nouns

The accusative case has two major functions: it is the case of the direct object and it follows certain prepositions.

1. In the English sentence *The boy asks the father*, the DIRECT OBJECT of the sentence is *the father*. He is being asked; he is the target of the verb's action. We determine the direct object by asking *who* or *what* is directly affected by the verb's action. In other words, the person you see, hear, or ask, or the thing you have, buy, or eat, is the direct object.

Der Junge fragt **den Vater.**	*The boy asks the father.*
Ich kaufe **den Kuchen.**	*I buy the cake.*

a. The accusative forms of the INTERROGATIVE PRONOUN are **wen?** *(whom?)* and **was?** *(what?)*. You now know two cases for this pronoun.

	PERSONS	THINGS AND IDEAS
nom.	wer?	was?
acc.	**wen?**	**was?**

Wen fragt der Junge?	→	**Den Vater.**
Whom does the boy ask?	→	*The father.*
Was kaufe ich?	→	**Den Kuchen.**
What am I buying?	→	*The cake.*

b. Of the articles, only those for masculine nouns have special forms for the accusative. In the other genders, the nominative and the accusative forms are identical.

	SINGULAR			PLURAL
	masc.	**neut.**	**fem.**	
nom.	der	das	die	die
	ein	ein	eine	—
	kein	kein	keine	keine
acc.	**den**	**das**	**die**	**die**
	einen	**ein**	**eine**	**—**
	keinen	**kein**	**keine**	**keine**

PETER Der Käse, das Obst, die Wurst und die Brötchen sind frisch.
KATJA Dann kaufe ich **den** Käse, **das** Obst, **die** Wurst und **die** Brötchen.
PETER Aber wir brauchen **keinen** Käse, **kein** Obst, **keine** Wurst und **keine** Brötchen!

This pattern is true of all possessive adjectives, but these are the only ones introduced so far.

- The POSSESSIVE ADJECTIVES **mein, dein,** and **Ihr** follow the pattern of **ein** and **kein:**

  Brauchen Sie mein**en** Bleistift?

  Nein danke, ich brauche Ihr**en** Bleistift nicht.

c. German has a few masculine nouns that have an **-n** or **-en** ending in all cases (singular and plural) except in the nominative singular. They are called *N*-NOUNS. Note how they are listed in vocabularies and dictionaries: the first ending refers to the singular for cases other than the nominative, the second one to the plural.

You are already familiar with all of the *n*-nouns below.

der Franzose, **-n,** -n	*Frenchman*
Herr, **-n,** -en	*gentleman*
Junge, **-n,** -n	*boy*
Mensch, **-en,** -en	*human being, person*
Nachbar, **-n,** -n	*neighbor*
Student, -**en**, -en	*student*

	SINGULAR	PLURAL
nom.	der Student	die Studenten
acc.	**den Studenten**	die Studenten

Der Herr heißt Müller. Fragen Sie Herr**n** Müller!

Da kommt ein Student. Fragen Sie den Student**en!**

d. Verbs that elicit accusative objects are called TRANSITIVE. (Some verbs are INTRANSITIVE, i.e., they cannot take a direct object: **gehen** *to go.*) Here are some familiar transitive verbs.

brauchen	*to need*	mögen / möcht-	*would like*
essen	*to eat*	nehmen	*to take*
finden	*to find*	öffnen	*to open*
fragen	*to ask*	sagen	*to say*
haben	*to have*	schreiben	*to write*
hören	*to hear*	sprechen	*to speak; to talk*
kaufen	*to buy*	suchen	*to look for*
lernen	*to learn*	trinken	*to drink*
lesen	*to read*	verkaufen	*to sell*
machen	*to make; to do*	verstehen	*to understand*
es gibt	*there is, there are*		

Sie kauft den Rock und die Bluse.
Schreiben Sie den Satz!
Ich esse einen Apfel und eine Banane.
Wir haben einen Supermarkt und ein Kaufhaus.
Das Geschäft verkauft keinen Fisch und kein Fleisch.

- The idiom **es gibt** is always followed by the accusative case in the singular or in the plural.

  Es gibt einen Markt in Altdorf. *There's a market in Altdorf.*
  Es gibt auch Lebensmittelgeschäfte. *There are also grocery stores.*

  The pronoun **es** is the subject of the sentence. What "there is," is in the accusative. **Es gibt** implies a general, unspecified existence—unlike **hier ist** or **da ist,** which points to a specific item.

  Gibt es einen Markt in Altdorf? *Is there a market in Altdorf?*
  Ja, es gibt einen Markt. *Yes, there's a market.*
  Und wo ist der Markt? *And where is the market?*
  Da ist der Markt. *There's the market. (There it is.)*

REMINDER: The bar on the left of a vocabulary list signals that the list is important. **All new words will be boldfaced;** learn these as active vocabulary before you do the exercises that follow!

ALSO: der Asiate, Chinese, Däne, Este, Finne, Grieche, Ire, Lette, Pole, Portugiese, Rumäne, Russe, Schotte, Schwede, Serbe, Slowake, Slowene, Tscheche, Türke, Vietnamese . . .

Students cannot yet use **essen, lesen,** or **nehmen** in the 2nd and 3rd person singular (see Chapter 3).

Many students need to develop a sense of the accusative case. It may help to go through the list of these verbs. Point out that they take or even require objects in English, too. If you say *I need* or *I would like*, someone is bound to ask *What?* What you need, buy, sell, take, etc., is the direct object of the verb.

Have students identify the accusatives in each example.

© Cengage Learning

2. ACCUSATIVE PREPOSITIONS are always followed by the accusative case. Here are the ones used most frequently.

durch	*through*	Britta kommt **durch die Tür.**
für	*for*	Das Obst ist **für den Kuchen.**
gegen	*against*	Was hast du **gegen meinen Bruder?**
ohne	*without*	Ich esse das Brötchen **ohne den Käse.**
um	*around*	Wir gehen **um den See.**
	at (time)	Sie kommen **um 12 Uhr.**

- Some prepositions may be contracted with the definite article. These forms are especially common in everyday speech.

durch + das = **durchs**
für + das = **fürs**
um + das = **ums**

NOTE: A sentence can contain two accusatives, one the direct object and the other the object of a preposition.

Sie kauft den Fisch für den Fischsalat.

Übungen

B: 1. (k)einen Rock, (k)ein Kleid, (k)eine Bluse 2. (k)ein Hemd, (k)eine Hose, (k)einen Pullover 3. (k)ein Brötchen, (k)eine Wurst, (k)einen Salat 4. (k)einen Herrn, (k)eine Frau, (k)ein Mädchen 5. (k)eine Tür, (k)ein Fenster

B. Wiederholen Sie die Sätze noch einmal mit *ein* und *kein*!

BEISPIEL Er kauft den Bleistift, das Buch und die Landkarte.
Er kauft einen Bleistift, ein Buch und eine Landkarte.
Er kauft keinen Bleistift, kein Buch und keine Landkarte.

1. Sie möchte den Rock, das Kleid und die Bluse.
2. Du brauchst das Hemd, die Hose und den Pullover.
3. Ich esse das Brötchen, die Wurst und den Salat.
4. Wir fragen den Herrn, die Frau und das Mädchen.
5. Öffnen Sie bitte die Tür und das Fenster!

C: 1. das Gemüse / das Obst / das Schwarzbrot 2. Die Marmelade / die Tomate / Die Gurke 3. keine Limonade, keine Cola, kein Wasser 4. einen Markt, ein Delikatessengeschäft, Kaufhäuser 5. den Jungen, den Studenten, die Studenten 6. Die Verkäuferin, Den Nachbarn, Den Menschen, Das Kind 7. keinen Saft, keine Eier, keine Limo

If students have difficulties with Exercises C and E because they can't remember the genders of the nouns used, point out how crucial it is to learn the article with the noun. Ask them to state the article of each noun before giving the accusative form.

C. Einkaufen You're making small talk while shopping with friends. Substitute the nouns in parentheses.

BEISPIEL Wir kaufen den Saft. (Salat)
Wir kaufen den Salat.

1. Möchtest du das Fleisch? (Gemüse, Obst, Schwarzbrot)
2. Die Wurst essen wir nicht. (Marmelade, Tomate, Gurke)
3. Meine Schwester trinkt keinen Saft. (Limonade, Cola, Wasser)
4. Gibt es hier eine Buchhandlung? (Markt, Delikatessengeschäft, Kaufhäuser)
5. Fragen Sie den Herrn! (Junge, Student, Studenten/*pl.*)
6. Den Verkäufer verstehe ich nicht! (Verkäuferin, Nachbar, Mensch, Kind)
7. Haben Sie keinen Joghurt? (Saft, Eier, Limo)

D. Umzug *(Moving)* You are giving instructions to the movers who are bringing your belongings into your new apartment. Use the cues.

BEISPIEL durch / Zimmer
Durch das Zimmer bitte!

1. gegen / Wand
2. um / Tisch
3. ohne / Bücher
4. durch / Tür
5. ohne / Stuhl
6. für / Kinderzimmer *(pl.)*
7. gegen / Fenster *(sg.)*
8. um / Ecke *(f.)*

D: 1. gegen die Wand 2. um den Tisch 3. ohne die Bücher 4. durch die Tür 5. ohne den Stuhl 6. für die Kinderzimmer 7. gegen das Fenster 8. um die Ecke

E. Sagen Sie es noch einmal! Replace the noun following the preposition with another noun.

BEISPIEL Ich suche etwas für meinen Vater. (Mutter, Kind)
Ich suche etwas für meine Mutter.
Ich suche etwas für mein Kind.

1. Wir gehen durch die Geschäfte. (Supermarkt, Kaufhaus, Bäckerei)
2. Er kommt ohne das Bier. (Wein, Cola, Kaffee, Käsebrot, Salat)
3. Was haben Sie gegen den Herrn? (Verkäuferin, Mädchen, Junge, Nachbarin)
4. Wiederholen Sie das für Ihren Großvater! (Bruder, Schwester, Nachbar, Eltern)

E: 1. den Supermarkt, das Kaufhaus, die Bäckerei 2. den Wein, die Cola, den Kaffee, das Käsebrot, den Salat 3. die Verkäuferin, das Mädchen, den Jungen, die Nachbarin 4. Ihren Bruder, Ihre Schwester, Ihren Nachbarn, Ihre Eltern

F. Was darf's sein? Kombinieren Sie! You are a salesperson in a clothing store. Ask your customers—(a) a friend, (b) a stranger, and (c) two of your relatives—what kind of items they need.

BEISPIEL *Was für einen Pullover möchtest du?*
Was für einen Pullover möchten Sie?
Was für Pullover möchtet ihr?

1	2	3	4
was für (ein)	Rock	brauchen	du
	Hemd	möchten	ihr
	Jacke	suchen	Sie
	Schuhe		
	. . .		

Optional practice: Play a memory game. Write the title of a recipe on the board, e.g., for a salad **(ein Salat):** Begin with the question **Was kaufen Sie für den Salat?** One student answers **Ich kaufe Tomaten für den Salat.** He / She then asks a classmate **Was kaufen Sie / kaufst du noch?** He / She might continue, **Ich kaufe Tomaten und Gurken für den Salat,** etc. Students keep adding to the list.

G. Was kaufen Sie? Working with a partner, answer each question with four to six items, drawing on all the vocabulary you have had so far. Use articles whenever necessary.

BEISPIEL S1 Sie sind im Supermarkt. Was kaufen Sie?
S2 Wir kaufen einen Kuchen, eine Cola, ein Pfund Erdbeeren, ein Stück Käse, etwas Obst, etwas Joghurt . . .

1. Sie sind in der Bäckerei. Was kaufen Sie?
2. Sie sind im Kaufhaus. Was kaufen Sie?
3. Sie sind in der Buchhandlung. Was kaufen Sie?

G: This also could be done as a competition between groups of students. Who can find the most items?

H.1: a. Wer hört den Nachbarn? Wen hört der Vater? b. Wer fragt Tante Martha? Wen fragt Matthias? c. Wer kauft Obst? Was kauft die Mutter? d. Wer möchte einen Apfel? Was möchten die Kinder? e. Wer versteht die Engländer nicht? Wen verstehen Helga und Britta nicht? f. Wer lernt Deutsch? Was lernen wir? g. Wer sucht eine Landkarte? Was suche ich / Was suchst du?

H. Wie bitte?

1. **Großvater hört schlecht.** Your grandfather, who is hard of hearing and forgetful, always wants you to repeat whatever you say. What questions does he ask?

   BEISPIEL Benjamin hat heute eine Prüfung.
   Wer hat eine Prüfung?
   Was hat Benjamin?

   a. Vater hört den Nachbarn.
   b. Matthias fragt Tante Martha.
   c. Die Mutter kauft Obst.
   d. Die Kinder möchten einen Apfel.
   e. Helga und Britta verstehen die Engländer nicht.
   f. Wir lernen Deutsch.
   g. Ich suche eine Landkarte.

Optional activity: **Was hast du dabei?** *(What did you bring along?)* Have students ask each about the contents of their (hand) bag. By using **Ich habe . . . ,** they'll automatically use the accusative. Be prepared to help with certain vocabulary.

2. **Auch Sie hören schlecht.** You are having difficulty understanding your partner. As he or she makes statements about shopping or anything else, ask for details.

   BEISPIEL Bei *(at)* ALDI gibt es heute Vollkornbrot für 99 Cent.
   Wo gibt es Brot?
   Was für Brot gibt es?
   Was kostet es?

2.3 Sentence structure *(continued)*

1. **Verb complements**

   As you know from Chapter 1, predicate nouns and predicate adjectives are verb complements (V2). Sometimes objects or another verb also become part of the verb phrase, i.e., VERB COMPLEMENTS, and in that combination they complete the meaning of the main verb (V1). Verb complements usually stand at the end of the sentence.

Sie **sprechen Deutsch.**	Wir **gehen essen.**
Sie **sprechen** gut **Deutsch.**	Wir **gehen** gern **essen.**
Sie **sprechen** (V1) wirklich gut **Deutsch.** (V2)	Wir **gehen** (V1) mittags gern **essen.** (V2)

2. **Negation**

   a. **Kein**

   Kein *(no, not a, not any)* is the negative of **ein** and, therefore, takes the same endings as **ein.** It negates nouns that in an affirmative statement or question would be preceded by **ein** or by no article at all.

preceded by **ein:**	Hast du **einen** Bleistift?
	Nein, ich habe **keinen** Bleistift.
	No, I don't have a pencil.
unpreceded:	Haben Sie Geschwister?
	Nein, ich habe **keine** Geschwister.
	No, I don't have any brothers or sisters.

b. **Nicht**

Nicht ***(not)*** is used when **kein** cannot be used. It can negate an entire sentence or just part of it. Its position is determined as follows:

- When negating an entire statement, **nicht** generally stands at the end of that sentence or clause. It always follows the *subject and verb;* also, it usually follows *noun and pronoun objects* and expressions of *definite time.*

subject and verb:	*Sie schreiben* **nicht.**
noun object:	Ich brauche *die Landkarte* **nicht.**
pronoun object:	Ich brauche *sie* **nicht.**
definite time:	Ich brauche sie *heute* **nicht.**

- When **nicht** negates a particular sentence element, it usually comes right before that element. Such elements commonly include: *adverbs,* including adverbs of general time, *prepositional phrases,* and *verb complements (V2).*

adverbs:	Ich kaufe das **nicht** *gern.*
	Ich kaufe das **nicht** *hier.*
	Ich kaufe das **nicht** *oft.*
prepositional phrase:	Ich kaufe das **nicht** *im Geschäft.*
	Ich kaufe das **nicht** *auf dem Markt.*
verb complements:	Ich gehe heute **nicht** *essen.*
	Ich spiele heute **nicht** *Tennis.*
	Ich heiße **nicht** *Beyer.*
	Das ist **nicht** *mein Buch.*
	Das Obst ist **nicht** *billig.*

Ich kaufe das nicht gern. Similarly, **Ich kaufe Käse nicht gern.** (emphasizing that you don't really like to buy cheese). The more common way is **Ich kaufe nicht gern Käse.** (emphasizing that you don't particularly care to buy cheese). Both sentences are acceptable, but there is a fine difference in emphasis. The word at the end of the sentence is emphasized the most.

If students ask, explain that the function of **Tennis** as a verb complement overrides its function as a direct object—hence **Tennis** is the final element rather than **nicht.**

- The following summary chart shows the most frequent pattern for the placement of **nicht.** Note, however, that very rarely do all of these elements appear in one sentence.

S V1 O definite time expression other adverbs or adverbial phrases V2.

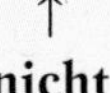

nicht

c. **Kein** vs. **nicht**

- Use **kein** when the noun has an indefinite article or no article at all.

noun + indefinite article:	Ich kaufe *ein Brot.*
	Ich kaufe ***kein*** *Brot.*
unpreceded noun:	Ich kaufe *Milch.*
	Ich kaufe ***keine*** *Milch.*

- Use **nicht** when the noun is preceded by a definite article or a possessive adjective.

noun + definite article:	Ich kaufe *das Brot.*
	Ich kaufe *das Brot* ***nicht.***
noun + possessive adjective:	Das ist *mein Buch.*
	Das ist ***nicht*** *mein Buch.*

d. **Ja, nein, doch**

COMPARE:	Hast du das Buch?	**Ja!**	*Yes.*
		Nein!	*No.*
	Hast du das Buch **nicht?**	**Doch!**	*Of course, I do.*

- **Doch** is an affirmative response to a negative question or statement.

Wohnt Erika Schwarz **nicht** in Salzburg?	**Doch!**
Haben Sie **keine** Swatch-Uhren?	**Doch,** hier sind sie.
Ich glaube, sie sind **nicht** teuer.	**Doch,** sie sind teuer.

3. **Coordinating conjunctions**

Two independent clauses can be joined into one sentence by using COORDINATING CONJUNCTIONS. Each of the two clauses keeps the original word order.

aber	*but; however*	Wir essen Fisch, aber sie essen Fleisch.
denn	*because, for*	Sie kauft Obst, denn es ist frisch.
oder	*or*	Nehmen Sie Brot oder möchten Sie Brötchen?
und	*and*	Ich kaufe Wurst und er kauft Käse.

Übungen

I: 1. keine Erdbeeren 2. keinen Gurkensalat 3. keine Limo 4. keinen/kein Joghurt 5. kein Stück Graubrot 6. kein Wurstbrötchen 7. kein Glas Milch 8. keinen Apfel

I. Die Nachbarin Every time you visit your elderly neighbor, she insists that you eat or drink something. Politely refuse, using the negative **kein.**

BEISPIEL Möchten Sie eine Banane?
Nein, danke, ich möchte keine Banane.

1. Nehmen Sie Erdbeeren? 2. Essen Sie Gurkensalat? 3. Trinken Sie Limo? 4. Essen Sie Joghurt? 5. Möchten Sie ein Stück Graubrot? 6. Nehmen Sie ein Wurstbrötchen? 7. Trinken Sie ein Glas Milch? 8. Möchten Sie einen Apfel?

J. Das stimmt nicht! *(That's not true!)* A recent acquaintance has confused you with someone else. Correct his/her misconceptions using **nicht.** Act out this situation with a partner, then switch roles. You may use the cues in brackets or your own.

BEISPIEL Ihr Name ist [Fiedler], nicht wahr?
Nein, mein Name ist nicht [Fiedler]. Mein Name ist [Fiedel].

1. Sie heißen [Watzlik], nicht wahr?
2. Sie kommen aus [Polen], nicht wahr?
3. Ihre Familie wohnt in [Sachsen], nicht wahr?
4. Ihr Onkel und Ihre Tante sprechen [Sächsisch], nicht wahr?
5. Ihr Bruder wohnt in [Thüringen], nicht wahr?
6. Sie studieren [Musik], nicht wahr?
7. Sie trinken gern [Tomatensaft], nicht wahr?
8. Sie essen gern [Fleischsalat], nicht wahr?

K. Nein!!!

1. **Mein kleiner Bruder verneint alles.** To get your attention, your little brother—played by your partner—contradicts everything you say. Use either **nicht** or **kein.**

   BEISPIEL S1 Heute ist es heiß.
   S2 Nein, heute ist es nicht heiß.

   a. Die Sonne scheint. b. Da drüben *(over there)* ist ein Geschäft. c. Das Geschäft verkauft Limonade und Eistee. d. Die Cola ist kalt. e. Ich möchte ein Käsebrötchen. f. Ich esse das Käsebrötchen! g. Ich bin Vegetarier *(vegetarian)*. h. Ich esse gern Käse. i. Käse ist gesund *(healthy / healthful)*. j. Wir gehen jetzt in eine Buchhandlung. k. Vater braucht eine Landkarte und einen Stadtplan *(city map)*. l. Er braucht die Landkarte. m. Ich finde das Amerikabuch schön. n. Wir haben Zeit. o. Ich lese gern Bücher. p. Das ist ein Spanischbuch. q. Heinz lernt Spanisch. r. Er studiert in Madrid. s. Ich brauche einen Kalender *(calendar)*. t. Ich finde den Städtekalender gut. u. Der Kalender ist billig. v. Ich möchte den Kalender. w. Wir brauchen Bleistifte und Kulis.

2. **Meinst du? *(Do you think so?)*** This time, make your own statements, which your partner may confirm or contradict. Take turns.

K.1: a. scheint nicht b. kein Geschäft c. keine Limonade und keinen Eistee d. nicht kalt e. kein Käsebrötchen f. das Käsebrötchen nicht g. kein Vegetarier h. nicht gern i. nicht gesund j. in keine Buchhandlung / nicht in eine Buchhandlung k. keine Landkarte und keinen Stadtplan l. die Landkarte nicht m. nicht schön n. keine Zeit o. nicht gern p. kein Spanischbuch q. nicht Spanisch r. nicht in Madrid s. keinen Kalender t. nicht gut u. nicht billig v. den Kalender nicht w. keine Bleistifte und keine Kulis

L. *Ja, nein* oder *doch*?

Looking at the advertisement for the Juice Bar store, answer the questions with *Ja!, Nein!*, or *Doch!*

BEISPIEL Heißt das Geschäft Saftbar? *Ja, es heißt Saftbar.*
Heißt das Geschäft Saftladen? *Nein, es heißt nicht Saftladen.*
Es heißt nicht Saftbar, oder? *Doch, es heißt Saftbar.*

1. Verkauft das Geschäft Obst und Gemüse?
2. Es verkauft Obstsäfte und Gemüsesäfte, nicht wahr?
3. Das Geschäft ist nicht in Oldenburg, oder?
4. Verkaufen sie auch Säfte in der Heerstraße?
5. Montags ist die Saftbar nicht offen *(open)*.
6. Auch sonntags ist das Geschäft offen, oder?
7. Tomatensaft und Selleriesaft sind keine Gemüsesäfte, oder?
8. Hier in . . . *(name your town)* gibt es keine Saftbars, oder? Wenn ja, wo?

L: 1. Nein, es verkauft kein Obst und Gemüse. 2. Ja, es verkauft Obstsäfte und Gemüsesäfte. 3. Doch, es ist in Oldenburg. 4. Ja, da verkaufen sie auch Säfte. 5. Doch, montags ist die Saftbar offen. 6. Nein, sonntags ist es nicht offen. 7. Doch, Tomatensaft und Selleriesaft sind Gemüsesäfte. 8. *(answer varies)*

Fokus Pedestrian Areas

Most European cities have developed a pedestrian area **(die Fußgängerzone)** in the center of town. Since cars are prohibited, these areas are free of traffic noise and exhaust fumes—a great improvement in the quality of life in dense urban centers. During business hours, and especially on Saturdays, pedestrian areas are packed with shoppers. During the summer, cafés spill out onto the sidewalks, and street musicians add to the atmosphere. The prime real-estate market along pedestrian areas has provided property owners with an incentive to refurbish older buildings, which typically combine apartments in the upper stories and businesses on the ground floor.

Fußgängerzone in Trier

iLrn

Visit the ***Wie geht's?*** iLrn website for more review and practice of the grammar points you have just learned.

M. Blitzreaktionen *(Quick reactions)* Ask your partner all sorts of questions, which he/she quickly answers with **ja, nein,** or **doch.**

BEISPIEL S1 Du kommst aus . . . , nicht wahr?
S2 Ja! / Nein!
S1 Du hast keine Geschwister, oder?
S2 Doch! / Nein!

N: 1. denn ich habe keine Zeit 2. und ich lerne auch sehr viel 3. aber sie verstehen nicht viel Deutsch 4. oder wir gehen in die Stadt

N. Eine Postkarte After your first week in Bremen, you are writing a brief postcard to a friend. Join the two sentences with the conjunctions indicated.

Hallo Frank,

1. Ich schreibe nicht viel. Ich habe keine Zeit. *(for)*
2. Ich finde es hier schön. Ich lerne auch sehr viel. *(and)*
3. Meine Mitbewohner *(roommates)* kommen aus Kanada und sprechen Französisch. Sie verstehen nicht viel Deutsch. *(but)*
4. Am Sonntag spielen wir zusammen Minigolf. Wir gehen in die Stadt. *(or)*

O: 1. Was möchten Sie? / Was darf's sein? 2. Was für Gemüse haben Sie heute? 3. Ich glaube, ich nehme zwei Pfund Bohnen. 4. Die Eier sind frisch, nicht wahr? –Natürlich! 5. Wir brauchen keine Eier. 6. Aber wir brauchen etwas Fisch und Salat. 7. Ich esse keinen Fisch. 8. Hast du / Haben Sie Karottensaft? 9. Trinkst du / Trinken Sie nicht gern Karottensaft? –Nein! 10. Hast du / Haben Sie Cola? Ich trinke gern Cola. 11. Sie kauft eine Cola und etwas Orangensaft. 12. Ist das alles? –Nein, ich möchte auch zwei Stück Erdbeerkuchen.

Zusammenfassung

O. Auf dem Marktplatz: Auf Deutsch bitte!

1. What would you like? 2. What kind of vegetables do you have today? 3. I think I'll take two pounds of beans. 4. The eggs are fresh, aren't they?—Of course. 5. We don't need (any) eggs. 6. But we need some fish and lettuce. 7. I'm not eating any fish. 8. Do you have any carrot juice? 9. Don't you like (to drink) carrot juice? —No! 10. Do you have any Coke? I like to drink Coke. 11. She's buying a Coke and some orange juice. 12. Is that all? —No, I'd also like two pieces of strawberry cake.

P. Hoppla, das haben sie hier wohl nicht! ***(Oops, it looks as if they don't have that here!)*** You and your partner are looking for certain groceries in the supermarket but discover that you can't find them right away. Ask your partner questions about items that might or might not be visible in the picture below. Take turns and keep track of what you find.

BEISPIEL S1 Hier gibt es kein Brot, oder?
S2 Doch, hier gibt es Brot. Aber ich sehe keinen Wein.
S1 Nein, ich sehe auch keinen Wein. Gibt es hier . . . ?

Hier gibt es . . .	Hier gibt es kein/keine/keinen . . .
__________	__________
__________	__________
__________	__________
__________	__________

Einblicke

Dialog

Wortschatz 2

der Durst	*thirst*
Hunger	*hunger*
Laden, ¨	*store*
das Frühstück	*breakfast*
Glas, ¨er; ein Glas	*glass; a glass (of)*
Würstchen, -	*hot dog*
die Apotheke, -n	*pharmacy*
Blume, -n	*flower*
Drogerie, -n	*drugstore*
Tasse, -n; eine Tasse	*cup; a cup (of)*
Bitte, bitte!	*You're welcome.*
ein paar	*a few, some* (used with plural nouns)
montags (dienstags . . .)	*on Mondays (Tuesdays, . . .)*
Na klar!	*Of course!*
offen / zu	*open / closed*
warum?	*why?*
Ich gehe . . . einkaufen.	*I go shopping . . .*
Ich habe Hunger / Durst.	*I'm hungry / thirsty.*

All nouns ending in the suffix **-chen** are neuter **(das Würstchen).** The suffix makes diminutives of nouns, i.e., it makes them smaller. They often have an umlaut, but no additional plural ending: **die Tasse, das Tässchen,** *(pl.)* **zwei Tässchen.**

An **Apotheke** sells prescription and nonprescripton drugs and is staffed by a university-trained pharmacist **(Apotheker/in)** and trained assistants. A **Drogerie** sells over-the-counter drugs, toiletries, and other items found in US drugstores and is headed by a druggist **(Drogist/in)** trained in a three-year apprenticeship.

Ein paar Tomaten, ein paar Äpfel *(pl.)*; BUT **etwas Kaffee, etwas Butter** *(sg., collective noun).*

A.1: Sie hat noch etwas Butter (Marmelade, Wurst . . .) und ein paar Brötchen (Eier, Bananen . . .). Sie braucht kein Fleisch (Gemüse, Papier), keine Brötchen (Butter, Marmelade . . .) und keinen Fisch (Salat, Saft . . .). 2. Sie hat kein Brot, keine Würstchen (Tomaten) und keinen Käse (Kaffee, Kuchen). Sie kauft ein paar Würstchen (Tomaten), ein Pfund Orangen und etwas Käse (Kaffee, Kuchen).

Vor dem Lesen

A. Die Einkaufsliste In the following text you will meet Susan, an American student in Germany. Consult her shopping list, where she has checked what she needs, and then complete the sentences. Several correct answers are possible.

Supermarkt
S
√ Brot
Brötchen
Butter
Marmelade
√ Käse
Eier
Durst
√ Würstchen
Fleisch
Fisch
Bananen
√ Orangen
Gemüse
√ Tomaten
Gurken
Salat
√ Kaffee
Milch
Saft
Tee
√ Kuchen
Plätzchen
Blumen
Papier
Wir lieben Lebensmittel.

1. Was hat Susan und was braucht sie nicht? Sie hat noch etwas _____ und ein paar _____. Sie braucht kein(e/en) _____.
2. Was hat sie nicht und was kauft sie? Susan hat kein(e/en) ___________. Sie kauft ein paar ___________, ein Pfund ___________ und etwas ___________.

B. Allerlei Geschäfte Ask your partner questions about the various stores. Take turns.

1. Wohin gehst du, wenn du ein paar Blumen brauchst? Wo ist der Blumenladen? Wie viele Tage im Jahr ist er offen? Was ist die Webseite? Buchstabieren Sie bitte die E-Mail-Adresse!
2. Wo gibt es Medizin? Von wann bis wann ist die Apotheke offen? Wie ist die Telefonnummer? Lesen Sie das laut!
3. Wo verkaufen sie Wein? Kannst du das buchstabieren? Wo ist das Geschäft? Wie ist die Telefonnummer? Lesen Sie das laut!
4. Wo ist die Teestube? Gibt es hier auch Teeläden, wo die Leute ihren Tee trinken oder Tee kaufen? Wenn ja, wo?
5. Auf dieser Seite sehen Sie Reklame *(advertisement)* für nur ein paar Geschäfte. Für welche Geschäfte sehen wir hier keine Reklame? Wohin gehen Sie oft und was kaufen Sie da?

© Beatrix Brockman

© Beatrix Brockman

© Beatrix Brockman

© Beatrix Brockman

C. Das ist leicht zu verstehen! Read aloud the following words paying special attention to their stressed syllable. Then guess their meaning in English.

der Bus; das Auto, Café, Einkaufszentrum, Restaurant, Spezialgeschäft; die Boutique; fantastisch, romantisch

Hörtipp

Understanding Spoken Language

Your listening comprehension will only improve when you learn to listen without relying on the written word at all. First do the *Vor dem Lesen* activities and study the vocabulary in *Wortschatz 2*. Then listen to the dialogue in the audio program available on the ***Wie geht's?*** Premium Website or in iLrn, books closed, without looking at the written text. You will be surprised at how much you understand. Now read along as you listen one more time to the audio text. Then do the post-reading activities *(Nach dem Lesen)*.

Geschäfte und Einkaufen

Susan ist Studentin. Sie studiert ein Jahr in Regensburg. In der Studentenwohnheimküche° trifft° sie zwei Regensburger Studenten, Ursula und Florian.

SUSAN Guten Morgen! Mein Name ist Susan.
URSULA Hallo! Das ist Florian und ich heiße Ursula.
FLORIAN Guten Morgen, Susan! Woher kommst du?
SUSAN Ich komme aus Colorado.
FLORIAN Du, wir frühstücken gerade°. Möchtest du eine Tasse Kaffee?
SUSAN Ja, gern.
URSULA Auch ein Stück Brot, etwas Butter und Marmelade?
SUSAN O, das klingt gut°. Ich habe echt° Hunger.
FLORIAN Etwas Milch für den Kaffee?
SUSAN Ja, bitte.
FLORIAN Auch ein Ei?
SUSAN Nein, danke.—Hm, das Brot ist gut! . . . Wo gibt's denn hier Geschäfte?
URSULA Wir haben hier in der Nähe° einen Supermarkt, eine Bäckerei und einen Buchladen.
SUSAN O ja?
URSULA Ja, aber wir gehen meistens° in die Stadt°. Am Bahnhof° gibt's die Arcaden. Das Einkaufszentrum ist super! Da findest du alles, was du brauchst: Restaurants, Bäckereien, Spezialgeschäfte, ein Kaufhaus und Kaufland. Bei° Kaufland sind die Lebensmittel sehr billig.
SUSAN Gibt's da auch eine Apotheke und eine Drogerie?
URSULA Na klar!
FLORIAN Du, Regensburg ist echt schön. Es ist alt und romantisch, aber hier gibt's wirklich alles.
URSULA Um den Dom° findest du auch viele Boutiquen.
FLORIAN Ich finde die Fußgängerzone fantastisch, denn da gibt es keine Autos, nur Fußgänger.
SUSAN Gibt's von hier einen Bus in die Stadt?
FLORIAN Ja natürlich und auch einen Altstadtbus direkt in die Fußgängerzone.
SUSAN Toll!
URSULA Manchmal gehen wir da auch gern in ein Café oder in eine Teestube°.
FLORIAN Oder an die Donau zur° „Wurstküche" und essen ein paar Würstchen.
URSULA Samstags ist Markt. Da verkaufen die Bauern° Obst, Gemüse, Eier und Blumen. Alles ist sehr frisch.
SUSAN Und von wann bis wann sind die Läden offen?
FLORIAN Hier draußen° sind die Geschäfte Montag bis Freitag von halb neun bis um sechs offen, samstags nur bis um zwei.
URSULA Die Kaufhäuser in der Stadt° sind von neun bis acht offen; Kaufland ist sogar° schon um sieben offen. Die meisten Läden sind aber abends um halb sieben zu.
SUSAN Gut, dann gehe ich morgen früh° bei Kaufland einkaufen.
FLORIAN Nein, das geht nicht°.
SUSAN Warum nicht?

dorm kitchen / meets
are just eating breakfast
that sounds good / really
nearby
mostly / into town / train station
At
Around the cathedral
tearoom
to the
farmers
Out here
in town
even
tomorrow morning
that won't work

URSULA Morgen ist Sonntag. Sonntags sind die Geschäfte zu.
SUSAN Aber nicht die Kaufhäuser, oder?
FLORIAN Doch!
SUSAN Ach, dann gehe ich jetzt noch schnell einkaufen. Danke fürs Frühstück!
FLORIAN Bitte, bitte!
URSULA Ciao, ciao!
SUSAN Tschüss!

Nach dem Lesen

A. Alles verstanden?

1. Woher kommt Susan?
2. Wen trifft sie in der Studentenwohnheimküche?
3. Was tun sie gerade und was geben sie Susan?
4. Was für Geschäfte gibt es in der Nähe?
5. Wo gehen Florian und Ursula meistens einkaufen?
6. Warum finden sie die Fußgängerzone so schön?
7. Wohin gehen sie auch gern?
8. Wann ist Markt? Was verkaufen die Bauern da?
9. Von wann bis wann sind die Kaufhäuser in der Stadt offen?
10. Warum geht Susan jetzt noch schnell einkaufen?

A: 1. aus Colorado 2. Florian und Ursula 3. frühstücken, eine Tasse Kaffee, ein Stück Brot, etwas Butter, Marmelade, (Kaffee) Milch 4. einen Supermarkt, eine Bäckerei, einen Buchladen 5. bei Kaufland, in der Stadt 6. keine Autos 7. in ein Café, eine Teestube, zur Wurstküche 8. samstags, Obst, Gemüse, Eier, Blumen 9. von morgens um sieben bis abends um acht 10. Morgen sind die Läden zu.

B. Bei *Weltbild-plus* im Regensburger Einkaufszentrum Looking at the picture of the *Weltbild-plus* store, answer the following questions about it with **nein** or **kein,** and give a proper answer.

1. Ist *Weltbild-plus* eine Drogerie?
2. Verkaufen sie da nur Bücher?
3. Gibt es da momentan *(right now)* sehr viele Leute?
4. Gibt's bei *Weltbild-plus* ein Café, eine Teestube oder ein Restaurant?
5. Wie finden Sie das Geschäft?
6. Haben Sie in . . . *(name your city)* auch solche *(such)* Läden? Wie heißen sie? Gibt es da ein Café oder eine Teestube?

B: 1. keine Drogerie 2. nicht nur Bücher 3. nicht sehr viele Leute 4. kein Café, keine Teestube, kein Restaurant 5. *(answer varies)* 6. *(answer varies)*

Stellen Sie Fragen mit *wer, wen* oder *was*! z. B. Susan ist Studentin: **Wer ist Studentin? Was ist Susan?** (Ursula trifft Susan in der Studentenwohnheimküche. Florian und Ursula frühstücken gerade. In der Nähe gibt es auch eine Apotheke. Die Bauern verkaufen Obst, Gemüse und Blumen.)

© Ingrid Sevin

Der Buchladen hat alles. Hier braucht man Zeit.

Fokus Regensburg

Regensburg (pop. 135,000) is one of the few larger medieval cities in Germany not seriously damaged during World War II. Founded by the Celts around 500 B.C.E., it was later the site of a Roman military outpost called *Castra Regina*, dating back to C.E. 179. During the Middle Ages, the imperial diet of the Holy Roman Empire held occasional sessions there. After 1663, the city was the seat of a perpetual diet, the first attempt to establish a permanent German parliament.

Today Regensburg's old city center is largely intact and contains fine examples of Romanesque, Gothic, and baroque architecture. Its two most famous landmarks are the Gothic cathedral and a twelfth-century stone bridge that spans the Danube. The city's main sources of income are tourism, the electronics industry, and a BMW plant. The university, founded in 1962, has a significant impact on the cultural and economic life of the city.

Regensburg ist alt und liegt an der Donau.

Schreibtipp

Writing a Dialogue

When writing a dialogue in German, make sure the speakers use the appropriate form of address, i.e., the **du-**, **ihr-**, or **Sie-** forms. Note that responses in dialogues are sometimes brief (**Freut mich. / Ja, gern. / Warum nicht? / Doch!**) or colloquial (**Prima! / Na und! / Ach nein!**). This is appropriate for authentic spoken language.

D: This game should be played at the end of the chapter. You can make as many tasks as you want, and also add to the items on the list. In order to complete the task, some students might have to go to various stores. The first person to buy everything wins. This exercise should help force students to say "Haben Sie . . . ? / Ja, ich habe . . . / Nein, das verkaufe ich nicht. / Was brauchen Sie? / Ich brauche . . . / Das kostet . . ."

C. Dialog: Hallo, wie geht's? Write a brief dialogue that includes answers to the following questions about Regensburg.

Wie geht's? Wie findest du Regensburg? Sind die Studenten nett *(nice)*? Gibt es eine Fußgängerzone? Was für Geschäfte gibt es da? Wie lange sind sie abends offen? Sind sie sonntags offen? Gibt es auch einen Markt? Wenn ja, wann und was gibt es da? . . .

Weiteres

D. Einkaufsspiel Different occasions need different preparations. Read the tasks below, and then choose which role you will play. Some of you will be buyers, others sellers. While shopping, keep track of what you spend. At the end, tell what you bought (**Ich habe hier . . .**) and how much money you have left (**Ich habe noch . . .**).

1. **Sie spielen den Käufer:**
   a. **Ihr Nachbar hat eine Gartenparty.** Sie bringen Limo, Obstsalat, Brötchen und Bratwurst. Sie brauchen noch: 3 Äpfel, 2 Pfund Trauben, 2 Pfund Erdbeeren, Käse, 20 Brötchen, 20 Bratwürstchen und 3 Flaschen *(bottles of)* Cola . . . Sie haben 50 Euro.
   b. **Morgen kommen die Eltern aus Milwaukee.** Sie brauchen noch: 1 Brot, 1 Glas Marmelade, 4 Joghurt, Leberwurst, 1 Paket Kaffee, 1 Flasche *(bottle of)* Orangensaft und 2 CDs . . . Sie haben 50 Euro.
   c. **Sie geben eine Dinnerparty für acht.** Sie brauchen noch: 2 Flaschen Wein, 2 Kilo Schweinefilet *(pork tenderloin)*, 2 Pfund Kartoffeln, Kuchen, Servietten *(napkins)*, 2 Kerzen *(candles)* und Blumen . . . Sie haben 85 Euro.

2. **Sie spielen den Verkäufer:**

WILLIS BIO-LADEN	
Äpfel	0,50 € / Stück
Bananen	0,40 € / Stück
Erdbeeren	2,50 € / kg
Orangen	1,00 € / Stück
Trauben	3,00 € / kg
Gurken	0,80 € / Stück
Kartoffeln	2,50 € / kg
Bio-Tomaten	2,00 € / kg

BÄCKEREI ENGELKE	
Weißbrot	3,00 €
Schwarzbrot	3,00 €
Vollkornbrot	3,50 €
Brötchen	0,30 € / Stück
Apfelkuchen	2,50 € / Stück
Schokokuchen	2,50 € / Stück
Käsekuchen	18,00 €
Plätzchen	5,00 € / Paket

GISELAS BLUMENLADEN	
Rosen	1,50 € / Stück
Tulpen *(tulips)*	0,60 € / Stück
Osterglocken *(daffodils)*	1,00 € / Stück

TONIS DELIKATESSEN	
Butterkäse	2,50 € / 200 g
Bio Bergkäse	4,20 € / 200 g
Joghurt	0,50 €
Salami	3,50 € / Stück
Leberwurst	2,00 € / 200 g
Bratwürstchen	1,00 € / Stück
Schweinefilet	10,00 € / kg
Marmelade	1,50 € / Glas

MECKIS GETRÄNKEMARKT	
Kaffee	4,00 € / Paket
Orangensaft	1,20 € / Flasche
Cola	2,50 € / Flasche
Mineralwasser	0,50 € / Flasche
Weißwein	9,00 € / Flasche
Rotwein	10,00 € / Flasche

BUCHHANDLUNG PUSTET	
CD	12,00 €
DVD	15,00 €
Kerzen	2,50 € / Stück
Servietten	2,00 € / Paket

Hörverständnis

Neu in Regensburg Listen to the conversation between two students. Decide whether the statements are true or false according to the information in the dialogue.

Zum Erkennen: Sag mal! *(Say!)*; nachher *(afterward)*

f 1. Ursula wohnt schon zwanzig Jahre in Regensburg.

r 2. Claudia ist aus Passau.

f 3. Claudia braucht Schuhe.

r 4. Ursula geht heute Nachmittag einkaufen.

r 5. Sie geht um drei Uhr.

f 6. Ursula braucht Jeans und ein Sweatshirt.

f 7. Dann gehen sie ein paar Würstchen essen.

For further practice, an optional two-part video (**Szenen** and **Interviews**) is available on the ***Wie geht's?*** Premium Website and in iLrn, with corresponding questions and activities in the *Arbeitsbuch* (SAM).

As a optional activity, with Google Earth you could visit Regensburg or any city in the German-speaking countries to check out stores.

Rückschau

Kapitelwortschatz

Hauptwörter

der Apfel, ¨	*apple*
die Apotheke, -n	*pharmacy*
die Bäckerei, -en	*bakery*
die Banane, -n	*banana*
die Bohne, -n	*bean*
das Bier, -e	*beer*
die Blume, -n	*flower*
das Brot, -e	*bread*
das Brötchen, -	*roll*
die Buchhandlung, -en	*bookstore*
die Butter	*butter*
die Cola	*cola drink*
die Drogerie, -n	*drugstore*
der Durst	*thirst*
das Ei, -er	*egg*
die Erbse, -n	*pea*
die Erdbeere, -n	*strawberry*
der Fisch, -e	*fish*
das Fleisch	*meat*
das Frühstück	*breakfast*
das Gemüse, -	*vegetable(s)*
das Geschäft, -e	*store*
das Glas, ¨er; ein Glas	*glass; a glass (of)*
die Gurke, -n	*cucumber; pickle*
der Hunger	*hunger*
der Jog(h)urt, -s	*yog(h)urt*
der Kaffee, -s	*coffee*
die Karotte, -n	*carrot*
der Käse, -	*cheese*
das Kaufhaus, ¨er	*department store*
der Kuchen, -	*cake*
der Laden, ¨	*store*
die Lebensmittel (*pl.*)	*groceries*
die Limonade, -n (die Limo, -s)	*soft drink*
der Markt, ¨e	*(farmers') market*
die Marmelade, -n	*jam*
die Milch	*milk*
das Obst	*fruit*
die Orange, -n	*orange*
das Pfund, -e; ein Pfund	*pound; one pound (of)*
das Plätzchen, -	*cookie*
der Saft, ¨e	*juice*
der Salat, -e	*lettuce; salad*
das Stück, -e; ein Stück	*piece; one piece (of)*
der Supermarkt, ¨e	*supermarket*
die Tasse, -n; eine Tasse	*cup; a cup (of)*
der Tee, -s	*tea*
die Tomate, -n	*tomato*
der Verkäufer, -	*salesperson*
das Wasser	*water*
der Wein, -e	*wine*
die Wurst, ¨e	*sausage*
das Würstchen, -	*hot dog*
die Zitrone, -n	*lemon*

Verben

glauben	*to believe; to think*
haben	*to have*
kaufen	*to buy*
machen	*to make; to do*
sein	*to be*
suchen	*to look for*
verkaufen	*to sell*

Adjektive und Adverbien

frisch	*fresh(ly)*
offen	*open*
zu	*closed*

Präpositionen

durch (+ *acc*)	*through*
für (+ *acc*)	*for*
gegen (+ *acc*)	*against*
ohne (+ *acc*)	*without*
um (+ *acc*)	*around; at* (time)

Verschiedenes

aber	*but; however*
allerlei	*all sorts of, various*
alles	*everything, all*
Bitte, bitte!	*You're welcome.*
dann	*then* (temporal)
Das ist alles.	*That's all., That's it.*
denn	*because, for*
doch	*yes, sure, certainly, of course* (response to negative question or statement)
ein paar	*a few, some* (used with plural nouns)
es gibt	*there is, there are*
etwas . . .	*a little, some . . .* (used with sg. collective nouns)
gern	*gladly*
Ich esse / trinke gern . . .	*I like to eat / drink . . .*
Ich esse / trinke nicht gern . . .	*I don't like to eat / drink . . .*
Ich gehe . . . einkaufen.	*I go shopping . . .*
Ich habe Hunger / Durst.	*I'm hungry / thirsty.*
Ich hätte gern . . .	*I would like (to have) . . .*
Ich möchte (gern) . . .	*I would like (to have) . . .*
kein	*no, not a, not any*
montags (dienstags . . .)	*on Mondays (Tuesdays, . . .)*
Na klar!	*Of course!*
natürlich	*of course*
nicht	*not*
oder	*or*
und	*and*
Warum?	*Why?*
Was / Wo gibt's . . . ?	*What / Where do you (they) have . . . ?*
Was für (ein) . . . ?	*What kind of (a) . . . ?*
Wen?	*Whom?*
zusammen	*together*

Zum Schluss

1. **Wer sind Sie?** Answer the following questions about what you like to eat. Use as many new words as you can!
   a. Was für Obst essen Sie gern?
   b. Was für Gemüse essen Sie gern?
   c. Was essen Sie nicht (gern)?
   d. Sie haben Durst. Was trinken Sie?
   e. Essen Sie kein Brot? kein Sauerkraut?

2. **Wer ist wer?** Now, ask a classmate the same questions. How do his/her answers compare with yours? How do you think your answers compare with what Germans like to eat?

3. **Kombinieren Sie!** You are planning a party with some friends. Using the words you have learned, discuss with them what you will need, find, buy, make, or look for. Try to use the prepositions you have learned.

   BEISPIEL *Ich kaufe etwas Käse für den Salat.*
   Sie kommen um zwei.

1	2	3	4
ich	brauchen	durch	Der Apfel, der Joghurt . . .
du	finden	für	Das Ei, das Wasser . . .
er/es/sie	kaufen	gegen	Die Cola, die Lebensmittel . . .
wir	machen	ohne	
ihr	geben	um	
sie/Sie	suchen		

4. **Noch einmal!** Uh oh! Your friends are all sick. Now you will not need what you were looking for. Rewrite your sentences, saying what you will not need, find, buy, make, or look for.

   BEISPIEL *Ich kaufe keinen Käse für den Salat.*
   Es gibt keinen Salat.

iLrn **Onlineaktivitäten** Visit iLrn for online activities related to this chapter. There you will find additional resources, such as a memory game (**Gedächtnisspiel**), a crossword puzzle (**Kreuzworträtsel**), audio flash cards (**Vokabelblitz**), a tutorial quiz (**Mini-Quiz**), and the active vocabulary (**Wortschatz**) for this chapter.

Kapitel 3

Im Restaurant

Lernziele In this chapter you will learn about:

Zum Thema

Food *(continued)* and restaurants

Fokus

Where to eat, cafés and coffee houses, regional specialties, wines, table manners, friends and acquaintances

Struktur

- Verbs with vowel changes
- The dative case

Einblicke

Lesetext: Man ist, was man isst.

Rückschau

Kapitalwortschatz
Zum Schluss

RESSOURCEN

 iLrn · Video · Audio · SAM

© Bernd-Uwe Sevin

Bergrestaurant oberhalb von Innsbruck mit Blick aufs* (view of) *weite Land

Vorschau Eating In and Out

Until the end of World War II, cooking in the German-speaking countries varied substantially from region to region, as each region's cuisine was noticeably influenced by its neighbors. Austrian cooking, for example, had a strong Hungarian component, and Bavarian cooks in turn borrowed from Austria. Swiss-German cuisine however, incorporated many aspects of French and Italian culinary traditions. As in many other countries, cooking shows have become quite popular on German television.

While retaining its regional flavors, modern German cooking has been influenced by cuisines from around the world. Indeed, Germans have developed a sophisticated palate and a sharp awareness of variety and quality in their diet. Health-food shops (**Reformhäuser**) and organic food stores (**Bio-Läden**) can be found almost everywhere. Those Germans who prefer to eat out can choose from a wide range of international restaurants, including Greek, Italian, Spanish, Chinese, and Thai. However, fast food is also very popular. Pizza delivery and American hamburger outlets are available in almost every city; other favorite ethnic fast foods include Turkish döner kebabs, Lebanese falafel, and shawarma. The traditional German **Imbiss** continues to offer a quick snack of sausage with potato salad (**Bratwurst mit Kartoffelsalat**).

Restaurant customs in Germany, Austria, and Switzerland differ somewhat from those of North America. Guests usually seat themselves. Before eating, diners wish each other a pleasant meal (**Guten Appetit!** or **Mahlzeit!**). The appropriate response is **Danke, gleichfalls!** *(Thanks, the same to you!)*. Salads generally are not eaten before, but with the main course. Germans, like most Europeans, don't drink coffee with a meal, only afterward. Also, water is never served automatically (and not with ice); guests are expected to order mineral water or another beverage. There are no free refills. Service (**die Bedienung**) and the value-added tax are included in the price of the meal. Although a tip (**das Trinkgeld**) is not necessary, it is customary to round up the total; how much is added depends on the friendliness and the quality of service. After asking for the bill (**Zahlen, bitte!**), diners give the money, including the tip, directly to the server. Often diners are asked if they want to pay the whole bill or split it (**Zusammen oder getrennt?**). If you intend to pay by credit card, ask if they are accepted before you start your meal; if they are, it's likely to be the electronic debit card (**die EC-Karte**).

Ask students what German, Austrian, or Swiss dishes they know, which ones they like, and which ones they don't like. Try to bring in pictures from magazines or show German menus. Maybe somebody in the class could bake something from a German recipe, or you could go to a German restaurant. Which food items are cognates?

First introduced by Turkish immigrants, the **Dönerkebab** is extremely popular in Europe. The classical **Döner** consists of pita bread split open and filled with shredded lettuce, red onion, cucumber, tomatoes, green pickled chilis, and red chili sauce, as well as long strips of freshly carved, thinly sliced, pieces of lamb preferably cooked on a revolving spit. Dönerkebabs generally taste nothing like gyros in the United States. Gyros are seasoned quite differently.

Fragen: 1. Was haben sie hier zu essen? 2. Was ist besonders billig? 3. Essen Sie das gern oder essen Sie lieber *(rather)* Schnitzel? 4. Was kostet das Schnitzel mit Champignonsoße *(mushroom gravy)*? 5. Gibt es hier ein deutsches Restaurant? Wenn ja, wie heißt es? 6. Ist es da billig oder teuer?

Later in the chapter, you might ask students on various other German foods they like.

Zum Thema

Gespräche

Warm-ups: 1. **Welche Getränke und Lebensmittel beginnen mit F, B, K, S, E, W?** (z. B. **F: Fisch**). 2. **Was ist das Gegenteil von** kaufen, offen, frisch, billig, klein, langsam, im Süden, Westen? 3. **Was ist der Artikel von** Blume, Glas, Tasse, Markt, Geschäft, Bäckerei, Kaufhaus, Zeit, Familie, Tag, Woche, Jahr, Kleidung, Farbe? 4. **Welche Länder gibt es** in Europa? Wie heißen die Hauptstädte? Welche Sprachen sprechen welche Leute? 5. **Wie alt sind Sie? Haben Sie Geschwister?** Wie viele? Wie heißen sie?

Im Restaurant

■ Listen to the dialogue. Then act out the dialogue with a partner. ■

AXEL Herr Ober, die Speisekarte bitte!
OBER Hier bitte!
AXEL Was empfehlen Sie heute?
OBER Die Menüs sind alle sehr gut.
AXEL Gabi, was nimmst du?
GABI Ich weiß nicht. Was nimmst du?
AXEL Ich glaube, ich nehme Menü 1: Schnitzel und Kartoffelsalat.
GABI Und ich hätte gern Menü 2: Rindsrouladen mit Kartoffelklößen.
OBER Möchten Sie etwas trinken?
GABI Ein Glas Apfelsaft, und du?
AXEL Mineralwasser. *(Der Ober kommt mit dem Essen.)* Guten Appetit!
GABI Danke, gleichfalls . . . Hm, das schmeckt.
AXEL Das Schnitzel auch.

Später

GABI Wir möchten zahlen, bitte!
OBER Ja, bitte. Alles zusammen?
GABI Ja. Geben Sie mir die Rechnung bitte!
AXEL Nein, nein, nein!
GABI Doch, Axel! Heute bezahle ich.
OBER Also, einmal Menü 1, einmal Menü 2, ein Apfelsaft, ein Mineralwasser, zwei Tassen Kaffee. Sonst noch etwas?
AXEL Ja, ein Brötchen.
OBER Das macht 30,30 € bitte.
GABI *(Sie gibt dem Ober 40,– €)* 32 Euro bitte.
OBER Und acht Euro zurück. Vielen Dank!

A: 1. der Ober 2. die Menüs 3. Axel bestellt Menü 1 und Gabi Menü 2. 4. Gabi trinkt (ein Glas) Apfelsaft und Axel Mineralwasser. 5. die Rechnung 6. Gabi 7. 30,30 € 8. 1,70 €, das ist nicht viel. 9. Ich gebe normalerweise . . .

A. Alles verstanden?

1. Wer bringt die Speisekarte?
2. Was empfiehlt der Ober?
3. Was bestellen Gabi und Axel?
4. Was trinken sie?
5. Was bringt der Ober am Ende?
6. Wer zahlt?
7. Was kostet alles zusammen?
8. Wie viel Trinkgeld *(tip)* gibt *(gives)* Gabi dem Ober? Ist das viel?
9. Wie viel Trinkgeld geben Sie normalerweise *(normally)*? **(Ich gebe normalerweise . . . Prozent.)**

Beim Berliner Rathaus **(City Hall)**

B. Im Rathaus Café

Speisekarte

Tagesmenü:

I. Nudelsuppe, Schnitzel und Kartoffelsalat, Eis	€	12,20
II. Gemüsesuppe, Rindsrouladen mit Kartoffelklößen, Eis		14,60

Tagesspezialitäten

Bratwurst, Sauerkraut und Kartoffeln	7,50
Marinierter Hering mit Zwiebeln, Äpfeln, Gurken und Kartoffeln	8,90
Omelett mit Schinken, Bratkartoffeln und Salat	9,--
Putensteak mit Mais, Preiselbeeren und Pommes frites	10,80
Kalbsleber, Erbsen mit Karotten und Kartoffelbrei	10,75
Hühnchen mit Weinsoße, Reis und Salat	12,50
Schweinebraten, Kartoffelklöße und Rotkraut	13,20
Sauerbraten, Spätzle und Salat	14,75
Gemischte Fischplatte, Kartoffeln und Salat	14,25

Suppen

Gulaschsuppe, Bohnensuppe, Erbsensuppe, Linsensuppe, Kartoffelsuppe, Tomatensuppe	3,50

Salate:

Grüner Salat, Tomatensalat, Gurkensalat, Bohnensalat	3,80

Getränke:

Mineralwasser	1,–	Tee	1,80
Apfelsaft	1,75	Kaffee	2,–
Limonade	2,25	Espresso	3,50
Cola	2,50	Cappuccino	4,50
Bier (0,2l)	2,40		
Wein (0,2l)	3,20		

Nachtisch:

Schokoladenpudding	2,80	Käsekuchen	3,55
Apfelkompott	2,30	Apfelstrudel	3,80
Vanilleeis mit Erdbeeren	3,50	Kirschtorte	4,60
Rote Grütze mit Sahne	4,25	Sachertorte	4,80

1. **Wir möchten bestellen!** ***(We would like to order!)*** In groups of two to four students, take turns ordering from the menu. One student plays the server and writes the orders down.

2. **Zahlen bitte!** Ask for the check. Tell the server what you had, e.g., **Einmal Bratwurst . . . ,** and let him/her figure out what you owe. Round up your bill to include an appropriate tip.

■ In case you are curious: **die Rindsroulade**, -n *(stuffed beef roll)*; **der Kloß, ¨-e** *(dumpling)* **der marinierte Hering, -e** *(marinated herring)*; **das Omelett, -s** *(omelet)*; **der Schinken, -** *(ham)*; **die Bratkartoffeln *(pl.)*** *(fried potatoes)*; **das Putensteak, -s** *(turkey steak)*; **die Preiselbeeren *(pl.)*** *(type of cranberries)*; **die Kalbsleber** *(calf's liver)*; **das Hühnchen, -** *(chicken)*; **die Soße, -n** *(sauce, gravy)*; **der Schweinebraten** *(pork roast)*; **der Rotkohl** *(red cabbage)*; **der Kartoffelbrei** *(mashed potatoes)*; **der Sauerbraten** *(marinated pot roast)*; **die Spätzle *(pl.)*** *(tiny Swabian dumplings)*; **die . . . -platte, -n** *(. . . platter)*; **die Linsen *(pl.)*** *(lentils)*; **der Espresso, -s; der Cappuccino, -s; das Kompott, -e** *(stewed fruit)*; **die Rote Grütze** *(berries in a thick sauce)*; **Rotkraut** *(red cabbage)*; **die (Schlag)Sahne** *([whipped] cream)*.

■ A liter is a little more than a quart. Therefore, 0,2 liters of beer is approximately three-fourths of a cup.

If students ask: *bacon* **der Speck;** *doughnut* **der Krapfen, -;** *pancake* **der Pfannkuchen, -;** *boiled egg* **das gekochte Ei, -er;** *fried egg* **das Spiegelei, -er;** *scrambled egg* **das Rührei, -er;** *hamburger* **der Hamburger, -;** *honey* **der Honig**; *mustard* **der Senf**; *open-faced sandwich* **das belegte Brot, -e / Brötchen, -;** *toast* **das Toastbrot, -e**

Fragen: 1. Was ist Menü eins? Menü zwei? Was haben die Menüs zum Nachtisch? 2. Was für Suppen gibt es? was für Salate? was für Getränke? 3. Was kostet eine Tasse Kaffee? ein Cappuccino? ein Glas Apfelsaft / Limo? ein Teller Suppe? ein Salat? 4. Was finden Sie besonders gut / nicht gut auf der Speisekarte?

In upscale restaurants, the server is usually referred to as **der Kellner / die Kellnerin** or **der Ober**. Diners usually say **Herr Ober!, Entschuldigen Sie!, Hallo!, Bedienung bitte!** or use a hand signal to catch a server's attention. There is no equivalent to **Ober** for a female server. Don't use **Oberin** for *waitress*, as that means *Mother Superior* and also *head nurse*!

Die Speisekarte *(à la carte menu)* is not the same thing as **das Menü** *(complete, fixed-price menu, usually including soup and dessert)*.

Eis means both *ice* and *ice cream*. If you ask for **Eis** in a restaurant, you will get ice cream. Ice water is generally not served in German-speaking countries.

Die [pom frits], BUT **die [pommes]**

ALSO: **Was gibt's zu kaufen (sehen, sagen . . .)?**

Viel Obst *(sg. collective noun)*, **Wie viel Obst?** BUT: **Viele Äpfel, Wie viele Äpfel?**

Ich bin **zu Hause.** BUT: Ich gehe **nach Hause.** (See Struktur 3.2–3.)

The verbs **zahlen** and **bezahlen** are mostly used interchangeably. They both mean *to pay for* as well as *to pay*: **Er (be)zahlt die Rechnung.** Although most Germans would say **Zahlen bitte!**, you might also hear **Ich möchte (be)zahlen.**

Wortschatz 1

Das Restaurant, -s *(restaurant)*

der Kellner, -	*waiter*	die Bedienung	*server; service*
Ober, -		Gabel, -n	*fork*
Löffel, -	*spoon*	Mensa	*student cafeteria*
Teller, -	*plate*	Rechnung, -en	*check; bill*
		Serviette, -n	*napkin*
das Café, -s	*café*	Speisekarte, -n	*menu*
Messer, -	*knife*		

Das Essen *(food; meal)*

der Nachtisch	*dessert*	das Eis	*ice cream*
Pfeffer	*pepper*	Salz	*salt*
Pudding	*pudding*	Frühstück	*breakfast*
Reis	*rice*	Mittagessen	*lunch, midday meal*
Zucker	*sugar*		
		Abendessen	*supper*
die Kartoffel, -n	*potato*	Suppe, -n	*soup*
Nudel, -n	*noodle*	die Pommes (frites) *(pl.)*	*(French) fries*
Pizza, -s	*pizza*		

Verschiedenes

Herr Ober!	*Waiter!*
Bedienung!	*Waiter! / Waitress!*
Was gibt's zum Frühstück / Mittagessen?	*What's for breakfast / lunch?*
Was gibt's zu essen / trinken?	*What is there to eat / drink?*
Guten Appetit!	*Enjoy your meal!*
Danke, gleichfalls!	*Thanks, the same to you!*
etwas (zu essen)	*something (to eat)*
nichts (zu trinken)	*nothing (to drink)*
noch ein(e)	*another*
viel / viele	*much / many*
wie viel? / wie viele?	*how much? / how many?*
zu Hause / nach Hause	*at home / (toward) home*
bestellen	*to order*
(be)zahlen	*to pay (for)*
bleiben	*to remain, stay*
bringen	*to bring*
empfehlen	*to recommend*
frühstücken	*to eat breakfast*
schmecken	*to taste*
Das schmeckt (gut)!	*That's good!, That tastes good!*
Das schmeckt (mir).	*I like it., i.e., I like the way it tastes.*
Ich mag kein(e/en) . . . (+ *acc.*)	*I don't like (any) . . .*
Ich möchte / hätte gern . . .	*I would like to have . . .*
(Ich möchte) zahlen bitte!	*I'd like to pay.*

Zum Erkennen: das (Tages)menü, -s *(daily special)*; das Schnitzel, - *(veal cutlet)*; die Rindsroulade, -n *(stuffed beef roll)*; der Kloß, ¨-e *(dumpling)*; einmal (here: *one order of*); AUCH: der Dativ; das Objekt, -e; die Präposition, -en; zurück *(back)*; backen *(to bake)*, braten *(to fry)*, grillen, kochen *(to cook)*

Übungen zum Thema

A. Was passt nicht?

1. der Teller—das Messer—die Speisekarte—die Gabel
2. das Frühstück—der Nachtisch—das Mittagessen—das Abendessen
3. das Salz—der Zucker—der Pfeffer—die Serviette
4. die Rechnung—die Kartoffeln—die Nudeln—der Reis
5. das Café—der Appetit—das Restaurant—die Mensa
6. bestellen—empfehlen—sein—zahlen

Point out that many families have shallow soup bowls the size of a dinner plate; hence the term **der Suppenteller**. BUT *Bring me a bowl of soup.* **Bringen Sie mir einen Teller Suppe!**

B. Was bedeuten die Wörter und was sind die Artikel?

Frühstückstisch	Teelöffel	Schokoladenpudding
Kaffeetasse	Suppenlöffel	Joghurteis
Fleischgabel	Suppenteller	Zitroneneis
Buttermesser	Kartoffelsuppe	

B: *breakfast table* **(der)**, *(coffee) cup* **(die)**, *meat fork* **(die)**, *butter knife* **(das)**, *teaspoon* **(der)**, *soup spoon* **(der)**, *soup plate* **(der)**, *potato soup* **(die)**, *chocolate pudding* **(der)**, *frozen yogurt* **(das)**, *lemon sherbet* **(das)**

C. Was passt?

bd 1. Die Suppe ist aber kalt.
adfi 2. Die Bratwurst schmeckt prima.
ghm 3. Möchtest du nichts trinken?
cehjk 4. Und etwas zum Nachtisch?
l 5. Guten Appetit!

a. Das Brot auch.
b. Wirklich?
c. Na klar!
d. Das finde ich auch.
e. Ja, bitte.
f. Ja, lecker *(delicious)*!
g. Doch, eine Tasse Kaffee.
h. Nein, danke.
i. Ja, fantastisch!
j. Ja, gern.
k. Ja, ich hätte gern ein Eis.
l. Danke, gleichfalls.
m. Ein Glas Orangensaft bitte!
n. . . .

C: After students have completed this exercise, they could expand it into a real conversation.

In der schönen Lausitz
Bauernhofcafé
Am Reiherhorst
Lohsa-Tiegling
035724-59001

© Beatrix Brockman

D. Was noch? *(What else?)* With a partner, see how many items you can find for each word or phrase below. Compare your results with those of others.

BEISPIEL ein Stück . . .
Ich möchte ein Stück Brot.

1. ein Stück . . .	3. eine Tasse . . .	5. etwas . . .	7. viel . . .
2. ein Glas . . .	4. ein paar . . .	6. ein Pfund . . .	8. viele . . .

D: 1. ein Stück Käse, Kuchen, Brot, Fleisch, Wurst 2. ein Glas Saft, Wein, Bier, Wasser, Cola, Milch, Limonade 3. eine Tasse Kaffee, Milch, Tee 4. ein paar Bilder, Bücher, Stühle, Kinder, Minuten, Äpfel, Brötchen, Eier, Bohnen, Blumen, Kartoffeln . . . 5. etwas Butter, Gemüse, Obst, Wurst, Salz, Zucker, Reis, Pfeffer, Marmelade, Milch, Wasser, Eis, Joghurt, Kaffee, Suppe, Pudding, Fleisch . . . 6. ein Pfund Kartoffeln, Reis, Zucker . . . 7. viel Kuchen, Brot, Wurst, Käse . . . 8. viele Äpfel, Tomaten, Eier, Plätzchen . . .

E. Kombinieren Sie! With your partner, make compound nouns with the following words. Then compare your list with that of others.

BEISPIEL der Kuchen
der Kirschkuchen, die Kuchengabel

1. die Wurst	3. die Suppe	5. das Obst
2. der Pudding	4. der Wein	6. der Kaffee

E: You might give a time limit to make this more competitive.

Fokus Deciding Where to Eat

In smaller towns, hotels are often the best place to eat. A **Gasthof** or **Gasthaus** can be a restaurant or a hotel that has a restaurant serving complete meals. Since many restaurants serve hot food only at lunch and dinner times, the selection in the afternoon or late at night is usually limited. Whereas older people still like to have coffee and cake in cafés **(das Café, -s)** and pastry shops **(die Konditorei, -en),** young people flock to pubs **(die Kneipe, -n)** for a drink or small meal, or to tearooms **(die Teestube, -n)** for a cup of tea. To avoid fancy places with astronomical prices, check the menus that are usually posted outside by the entrance.

Aussprache: ü

■ For further review, see the Summary of Pronunciation in the front of this book. Study Section II, subsections 22–28.

A. Laute

1. [ü:] **ü**ber, T**ü**r, f**ü**r, Fr**üh**ling, Pr**ü**fung, Gem**ü**se, s**ü**dlich, gr**ü**n, nat**ü**rlich, m**ü**de
2. [ü] Fl**ü**sse, W**ü**rste, St**ü**ck, J**ü**rgen M**ü**ller, M**ü**nchen, f**ü**nf, f**ü**nfundf**ü**nfzig

■ Optional tongue twisters **(Zungenbrecher):** 1. Selten ess' ich Essig *(vinegar).* Ess' ich Essig, ess' ich Essig mit Salat. 2. Klaus Knopf liebt Knödel, Klöße, Klöpse *(meat balls).* Knödel. Klöße, Klöpse liebt Klaus Knopf.

B. Wortpaare

1. vier / für
2. missen / müssen
3. Stuhl / Stühle
4. Mutter / Mütter
5. fühle / Fülle
6. Goethe / Güte

Hörverständnis

Im Gasthaus Find out what Jürgen, Helga, and Michael are ordering for dinner. Put their initials by the foods and beverages they order. Then add up their total bill to see whether the waitress calculated it correctly.

Zum Erkennen: das Getränk, -e *(beverages);* einmal *(one order of)*

GETRÄNKE		ESSEN		NACHTISCH	
______	Limonade	H	Schnitzel	______	Apfelkuchen
H	Apfelsaft	______	Rindsroulade	M	Vanilleeis
______	Bier	J	Pizza	______	Reispudding
M	Mineralwasser	M	Würstchen	J	Schokoladenpudding
J	Cola	______	Fisch	H	Käsekuchen

Das kostet:

1,75 €	7,50 €	2,50 €
1,50	5,–	1,40
1,20	6,25	2,–
	Alles zusammen:	29,10 €

Struktur

3.1 Verbs with vowel changes

Some very common verbs have a stem-vowel change in the SECOND and THIRD PERSON singular. These changes will be clearly noted in all vocabulary lists like this: **sprechen (spricht).**

	e → i **sprechen** ***to speak***	**e → ie** **sehen** ***to see***	**a → ä** **fahren** ***to drive***	**au → äu** **laufen** ***to walk, run***
ich	spreche	sehe	fahre	laufe
du	**sprichst**	**siehst**	**fährst**	**läufst**
er	**spricht**	**sieht**	**fährt**	**läuft**
wir	sprechen	sehen	fahren	laufen
ihr	sprecht	seht	fahrt	lauft
sie	sprechen	sehen	fahren	laufen

Siehst du Dresden auf der Landkarte?
Dieter **fährt** nach Dresden.

A few verbs in this group have additional consonant changes:

	nehmen ***to take***	**werden** ***to become, get***
ich	nehme	werde
du	**nimmst**	**wirst**
er	**nimmt**	**wird**
wir	nehmen	werden
ihr	nehmt	werdet
sie	nehmen	werden

You need to know the following common verbs with stem-vowel changes:

empfehlen	**empfiehlt**	*to recommend*
essen	**isst**	*to eat*
fahren	**fährt**	*to drive*
geben	**gibt**	*to give*
gefallen	**gefällt**	*to please, be pleasing to*
helfen	**hilft**	*to help*
laufen	**läuft**	*to walk; to run*
lesen	**liest**	*to read*
nehmen	**nimmt**	*to take; to have (food)*
sehen	**sieht**	*to see*
sprechen	**spricht**	*to speak*
tragen	**trägt**	*to carry; to wear*
werden	**wird**	*to become, get*

Note that the second and third person singular forms of **essen** and **lesen** are identical **(du/er isst, du/er liest).** As you know from Chapter 1, the **du-**form of verbs with a stem ending in any s-sound **(-s, -ß, ss, -tz, -z)** adds only a **t-**ending instead of an **-st:** lese → du lies**t;** heißen → du heiß**t.**

Übungen

A. Bilden Sie Sätze! Create sentences with one word from each column making all necessary adjustments. You can also add your own words to each column.

BEISPIEL Du liest gern.

ich	fahren	ein paar Bücher
du	nehmen	schon wieder
der Herr	werden	einen Mantel
die Frau	empfehlen	das Omelett
das Kind	sehen	kein Salz
Axel und ich	sprechen	Deutsch
ihr	helfen	schnell
die Leute	lesen	müde
	essen	gern
	laufen	laut
	tragen	nichts
		nicht

B: 1. er hilft 2. sie nimmt 3. er empfiehlt 4. sie laufen 5. sie liest 6. sie fährt 7. er sieht 8. er/sie gibt

B. Was tun sie? Answer the questions in your own words to tell what others do. Use pronouns and stem-changing verbs in your answers.

BEISPIEL Ich esse schnell. Und Ihr Großvater?
Er isst sehr langsam.

1. Ich helfe gern. Und Ihr Nachbar?
2. Ich nehme Apfelstrudel. Und Gabi?
3. Ich empfehle den Schweinebraten. Und der Ober?
4. Ich laufe viel. Und Ihr Bruder oder Ihre Schwester?
5. Ich lese gern. Und Ihre Mutter?
6. Ich fahre im Sommer nach Deutschland. Und Ihre Familie?
7. Ich sehe alles. Und Ihr Nachbar?
8. Ich gebe der Bedienung normalerweise 20 Prozent Trinkgeld *(tip)*. Und Ihr Vater / Ihre Mutter?

C. Und du? Choose a classmate whom you don't know well and find out what he/she likes. Follow the model and try to vary your responses. At the end, report to the class what you found out.

C.1: Before doing this exercise, ask students to glance at the menu and the food vocabulary in this chapter and in Chapter 2.

1. **Was isst du gern?** Before doing this exercise, glance at the menu and the food vocabulary in this chapter and in Chapter 2.

BEISPIEL
S1 Ich esse gern . . . (z. B. Fischbrötchen). Und du, isst du gern . . . ?
S2 Ja, ich esse gern . . . / Nein, ich esse nicht gern . . .
S1 Magst du . . . (z. B. Erbsensuppe)?
S2 Ja, ich mag . . . / Nein, ich mag kein(e/en) . . .
S1 Was magst du auch nicht gern?
S2 Ich mag auch kein(e/en) . . .

2. **Was trägst du gern?** You might first review the list of clothing in *Schritt 3*.

BEISPIEL
S1 Ich trage gern . . . (z. B. Jeans). Und du, trägst du auch gern . . . ?
S2 Natürlich trage ich gern . . . (z. B. Jeans). / Nein, ich trage keine . . . (z. B. Jeans).
S1 Was trägst du noch / nicht gern?
S2 Ich trage (nicht) gern . . . / Ich mag kein(e/en) . . . / Ich hasse *(hate)* . . .

D. Umfrage *(Survey)* In small groups, ask the following questions. Then report back to the class. (Note: *everybody* = **jeder,** *nobody* = **niemand.**)

1. Wer spricht hier . . . (z. B. Französisch, Spanisch, Chinesisch)?
2. Wer liest den/das/die . . . ? *(Ask for a familiar local or national newspaper.)*
3. Wer sieht gern . . . ? *(Ask for a familiar TV show.)*
4. Wer läuft gern . . . (z. B. Ski, Wasserski . . .)?
5. Wer trägt heute . . . (z. B. Lila, Gelb . . .)?
6. Wer isst gern . . . (z. B. Bratwurst, Pommes frites . . .)?
7. Wer isst nicht gern . . . (z. B. Fisch, Sauerkraut . . .)?
8. Wer trinkt gern . . . (z. B. Latte, Cappuccino . . .)?
9. Wer trinkt kein(e/n) . . . (z. B. Buttermilch, Cola, Alkohol . . .)?

Biergarten in München

Ask students whether there are beer gardens or garden restaurants in their town, where they and their friends love to hang out, and what they usually order.

3.2 The dative case

The dative case has three major functions in German: it is the case of the INDIRECT OBJECT, it follows certain verbs, and it follows certain prepositions.

1. In English the INDIRECT OBJECT is indicated in two ways:
   - through word order: *The boy gives* ***the father*** the plate.
   - with a preposition: *The boy gives the plate* ***to the father.***

In German this function is expressed through case and word order. You can determine the indirect object by asking *for whom* or *in reference to whom* (or occasionally *what*) the action of the verb is taking place.

Point out that students have already used the dative forms of **ich (mir)** and **Sie (Ihnen).**

Der Junge gibt **dem Vater** den Teller.

The boy gives the father the plate.

a. The dative form of the INTERROGATIVE PRONOUN is **wem?** *(to whom?).*

	PERSONS	THINGS AND IDEAS
nom.	wer?	was?
acc.	wen?	was?
dat.	**wem?**	

You may wish to point out the colloquial English phrase *Who does the boy give the plate to?*

Wem gibt der Junge den Teller? → **Dem Vater.**
To whom does the boy give the plate? → *To the father.*

b. The dative forms of the DEFINITE and INDEFINITE ARTICLES are as follows:

	SINGULAR			PLURAL
	masc.	**neut.**	**fem.**	
nom.	der ein kein	das ein kein	die eine keine	die — keine
acc.	den einen keinen			
dat.	**dem** **einem** **keinem**	**dem** **einem** **keinem**	**der** **einer** **keiner**	**den** — **keinen**

Der Ober empfiehlt **dem** Vater, **der** Mutter und **den** Kindern das Schnitzel. Er bringt **dem** Kind einen Löffel, aber er gibt **einem** Kind kein Messer und keine Gabel.

- The POSSESSIVE ADJECTIVES **mein, dein, sein** *(his)*, and **Ihr** follow the pattern of **ein** and **kein:**

  Was empfiehlt er Ihr**em** Vater und Ihr**er** Mutter?
  Er empfiehlt mein**em** Vater und mein**er** Mutter den Fleischsalat.

The dative-plural **n**-ending needs a lot of practice. Give students familiar nouns and have them give you the dative-plural form in short sentences.

- In the dative plural, all nouns add an **-n** ending, unless the plural form already ends in **-n** or **-s.**

  die Kinder / den Kinder**n**
  die Äpfel / den Äpfel**n**
  BUT: die Eltern / den Elter**n**
  die Kulis / den Kuli**s**

- *N*-nouns also have an **-n** or **-en** ending in the dative singular, as they do in the accusative singular:

  Das Eis schmeckt dem Herr**n** und dem Student**en.**

Such verbs include **bringen, empfehlen, geben, kaufen, öffnen, sagen, schreiben, verkaufen.** Point out that the verbs listed here can have two objects in English, too. Give English sample sentences and have students identify the dative and the accusative object.

c. Many verbs can have both accusative and dative objects.

Der Ober bringt dem Kind den Apfelstrudel.
The waiter brings the child the apple strudel.

Er empfiehlt der Studentin den Sauerbraten.
He recommends the marinated pot roast to the student.

Note the difference in meaning:

Der Onkel trägt der Tante die Lebensmittel. BUT Der Onkel trägt die Tante.

d. In sentences with two objects, the direct object, if it is a noun, generally follows the indirect object.

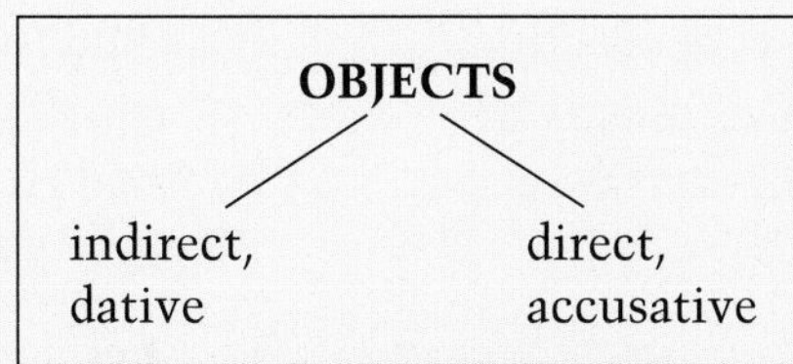

Der Kellner bringt dem Herrn den Tee.

2. Dative verbs

Some verbs take only dative objects; a few such verbs are

Remind students that boldface words are new; others are being reviewed.

antworten	*to answer*	**glauben**	*to believe*
danken	*to thank*	helfen	*to help*
gefallen	*to please, be pleasing to*	schmecken	*to taste*
gehören	*to belong to*		

You might point out that **glauben** is not strictly a dative verb, since you can say **Ich glaube das nicht.**

CAUTION: Gefallen is usually not used to talk about food but rather to say that a city, a picture, an item of clothing, or a person is pleasing to you. **Schmecken** is used with food and beverages.

Der Bruder antwortet der Kusine.	*The brother answers (gives an answer to) the cousin.*
Alex dankt der Kellnerin.	*Alex thanks (gives thanks to) the waitress.*
Der Mantel gehört dem Mädchen.	*The coat belongs to the girl.*
Ich glaube dem Jungen.	*I believe the boy.*
Ich helfe dem Nachbarn.	*I'm helping (giving help to) the neighbor.*
Die Mensa gefällt den Studenten.	*The students like the cafeteria (the cafeteria pleases the students).*
Das Schnitzel schmeckt den Leuten.	*People like the schnitzel (i.e., the way it tastes).*

3. Dative prepositions

The following prepositions are always followed by the dative case:

Students can very easily memorize the list of dative prepositions, if you sing it with them to the tune of the waltz "The Blue Danube."

Point out that **nach Hause** does not follow the rule that "**nach** is used for cities, countries, continents."

Seit translates as *for* in English when it expresses a duration of time (e.g., three minutes, one year) that began in the past and continues into the present: *They have been living there for three years.*

aus	*out of* *from* (a place of origin)	Sie kommt **aus** dem Geschäft. Er ist **aus** Berlin.
außer	*besides*	**Außer** dem Café ist alles zu.
bei	*at, for* (a company) *near, by* *at the home of, with* (a person)	Sie arbeitet **bei** VW. Die Drogerie ist **beim** Markt. Er wohnt **bei** Familie Angerer.
mit	*with* *together with*	Ich schreibe **mit** einem Kuli. Alex kommt **mit** Gabi.
nach	*after* (time) *to* (cities, countries, continents) *to* (in certain expressions)	Kommst du **nach** dem Mittagessen? Fahrt ihr auch **nach** Österreich? Gehen Sie **nach** Hause!
seit	*since* *for* (duration)	Sie wohnen **seit** Mai in Ulm. Sie wohnen **seit** drei Tagen da.
von	*of* *from* *by* (creator, doer of action)	Das Gegenteil **von** billig ist teuer. Wir fahren **von** Ulm nach Hamburg. Das Bild ist **von** Albrecht Dürer.
zu	*to* (in the direction of) *at* (in certain expressions) *for* (purpose)	Sie fährt **zum** Supermarkt. Sie sind **zu** Hause. Was gibt es **zum** Nachtisch?

- Some dative prepositions are frequently contracted with the definite article.

bei + dem = **beim**	zu + dem = **zum**
von + dem = **vom**	zu + der = **zur**

- Pay particular attention to the contrasting use of these pairs of prepositions:

Sie fährt **zum** *(to the)* Supermarkt.
Fahrt ihr **nach** *(to)* Deutschland?
Wir fahren **von** *(from)* Ulm **nach** München.
Er kommt **aus** *(from)* Salzburg.
Gehen Sie **nach** Hause *(home)*!
Sie sind nicht **zu** Hause *([at] home)*.

Übungen

E. Ersetzen Sie das Dativobjekt!

E: 1. dem Bruder / dem Spanier / der Schweizerin 2. der Schwester, dem Herrn, der Frau 3. den Leuten / den Amerikanern / den Studenten 4. meinem Nachbarn, meinen Eltern, meiner Familie 5. der Schwester, dem Franzosen, den Leuten 6. meiner Mutter, meinen Kusinen, meinen Cousins

BEISPIEL Die Bedienung bringt dem Kind ein Eis. (Großmutter)
Die Bedienung bringt der Großmutter ein Eis.

1. Die Kellnerin empfiehlt dem Vater die Rouladen. (Bruder, Spanier, Schweizerin)
2. Der Junge gibt der Mutter ein Bild. (Schwester, Herr, Frau)
3. Der Ober bringt den Eltern das Essen. (Leute, Amerikaner/*pl.*, Studenten/*pl.*)
4. Die Drogerie gehört meiner Großmutter. (Nachbar, Eltern, Familie)
5. Axel dankt dem Bruder. (Schwester, Franzose, Leute)
6. Meine Großmutter hilft meinem Vater. (Mutter, Kusinen, Cousins)

F. Sagen Sie es noch einmal! Replace the nouns following the prepositions with the words in parentheses.

BEISPIEL Eva geht zum Lebensmittelgeschäft. (Apotheke)
Eva geht zur Apotheke.

1. Kevin kommt aus dem Kaufhaus. (Drogerie, Café, Mensa)
2. Seit Sonntag ist er wieder hier. (zwei Tage, eine Woche, ein Monat)
3. Er spricht gern Deutsch mit dem Großvater. (Frau, Mädchen, Großeltern)
4. Er wohnt bei meinen Eltern. (Bruder, Schwester, Familie)
5. Außer meinem Bruder sind wir alle hier im Restaurant. (Vater, Mutter, Tante, Geschwister)
6. Wir bestellen einen Salat zu den Rouladen. (Schnitzel, Suppe, Würstchen/ *pl.*, Fleisch)

If students have difficulties with Exercise F because they can't remember the genders of the nouns used, remind them how crucial it is to learn the article with the noun. Ask them to state the article of each noun before giving the dative form.

F: 1. aus der Drogerie, dem Café, der Mensa 2. Seit zwei Tagen, einer Woche, einem Monat 3. mit der Frau, dem Mädchen, den Großeltern 4. bei meinem Bruder, meiner Schwester, meiner Familie 5. Außer meinem Vater, meiner Mutter, meiner Tante, meinen Geschwistern 6. zu dem (zum) Schnitzel, der (zur) Suppe, den Würstchen, dem (zum) Fleisch

G. Hm, lecker *(delicious)*! Restate the sentences making the phrases in boldface plural.

BEISPIEL Ich spreche mit **dem Studenten.**
Ich spreche mit den Studenten.

1. Die vier Amerikaner sind seit **einer Woche** [sechs] in Deutschland und wohnen bei **einer Gastfamilie.**
2. Mit **der Familie** sprechen sie nur Deutsch, aber mit **dem Nachbarn** auch Englisch.
3. Die Brezeln schmecken **der Studentin,** aber John mag keine Brezeln.
4. Berlin gefällt **dem Studenten und der Studentin.**
5. Sie sprechen von **einem Berliner** und von **einem Café.**
6. Im Deutschkurs sind außer **dem Amerikaner und der Amerikanerin** natürlich auch Leute aus anderen *(other)* Ländern.

© Ingrid Sevin

G: 1. sechs Wochen, Gastfamilien 2. den Familien, den Nachbarn 3. den Studentinnen 4. den Studenten und (den) Studentinnen 5. den Berlinern, den Cafés 6. den Amerikanern und (den) Amerikanerinnen

H. *Wer, wem* oder *was*? You are talking to a friend at a graduation party. Because of the loud music, you can't hear him/her very well. Ask what he/she said three different ways and provide the answer he/she gives for each one.

BEISPIEL Oskar gibt dem Bruder die Bücher.
— Wer gibt dem Bruder die Bücher?
— Oskar!
— Wem gibt Oskar die Bücher?
— Dem Bruder!
— Was gibt Oskar dem Bruder?
— Die Bücher!

1. Der Nachbar verkauft Onkel Willi den BMW.
2. Onkel Willi gibt dem Jungen den BMW.
3. Großmutter empfiehlt Irene ein paar Tage Ferien *(vacation)*.
4. Die Kinder zahlen der Mutter die Hotelrechnung.
5. Der Vater glaubt den Leuten die Geschichte *(story)* nicht.

H: 1. Wer verkauft Onkel Willi den BMW? Wem verkauft der Nachbar den BMW? Was verkauft der Nachbar Onkel Willi? 2. Wer gibt dem Jungen den BMW? Wem gibt Onkel Willi den BMW? Was gibt Onkel Willi dem Jungen? 3. Wer empfiehlt Irene ein paar Tage Ferien? Wem empfiehlt (die) Großmutter ein paar Tage Ferien? Was empfiehlt (die) Großmutter Irene? 4. Wer zahlt der Mutter die Hotelrechnung? Wem zahlen die Kinder die Hotelrechnung? Was zahlen die Kinder der Mutter? 5. Wer glaubt den Leuten die Geschichte nicht? Wem glaubt der Vater die Geschichte nicht? Was glaubt der Vater den Leuten nicht?

Fokus Cafés and Coffee Houses

Cafés and pastry shops **(Konditoreien)** are favorite places for conversation or for breaks in shopping excursions. They serve coffee, tea, and hot chocolate, along with a great variety of delicious cakes and pastries. In Austria, many people have a favorite café **(das Kaffeehaus)** where they can relax over such items as a **Melange** *(half coffee, half frothed milk)* or a piece of **Linzertorte** *(jam-filled tart)*. The tradition of the coffee house goes back to the early 1700s. Since then, it has been the preferred meeting place not only of the literati, reformers, artists, and philosophers but also of middle-class society.

Pflaumenkuchen* (plum cake) *mit Schlagsahne

I. Hoppla, hier fehlt was! Freunde helfen auspacken. You and your partner are helping another friend unpack after a family move. Work together to figure out what belongs to whom. One of you looks at and completes the chart below, the other one works with the chart in Section 11 of the Appendix.

BEISPIEL S1 Wem gehören die Hausschuhe?
S2 Die Hausschuhe gehören dem Vater. Und wem gehört das Bild?
S1 Das Bild gehört dem Bruder.

S1:

Was gehört wem?

	BRUDER	SCHWESTER	MUTTER	VATER	GROSSELTERN
Bild	x				
Bücher					x
Tennishose				x	
Hausschuhe				x	
Pulli		x			
Ringe *(pl.)*			x		
T-Shirts		x			
Mantel			x		
Messer *(sg.)*	x				
Gläser					x

J: 1. der Tante, der Großmutter, den Kindern, den Geschwistern, dem Studenten, der Studentin, den Studenten 2. der Frau, den Leuten, dem Nachbarn, den Herren — Point out that the phrases with dative pronouns should be treated as idioms for now. Personal pronouns (including dative) will be presented in Chapter 5.

J. Was gefällt wem? Replace the dative object.

1. Das Restaurant gefällt dem Onkel. (Tante, Großmutter, Kinder, Geschwister, Student, Studentin, Studenten)
2. Die Preise gefallen der Familie nicht. (Frau, Leute, Nachbar, Herren)

K. Was kaufen wir wem? The holiday season is approaching, and you and your partner are coming up with ideas for presents for the whole family: brothers and sisters, parents and grandparents, uncles and aunts, as well as friends **(der Freund / die Freundin)**. Draw on all the vocabulary you have learned so far plus any from the gift box below. Respond to each other's suggestions.

BEISPIEL S1 Braucht deine Mutter Schreibpapier?
S2 Nein. Sie hat Schreibpapier. Ich kaufe meiner Mutter kein Schreibpapier.
S1 Möchte dein Vater vielleicht ein Kochbuch?
S2 Ja, vielleicht. Gut, dann kaufe ich meinem Vater ein Kochbuch.

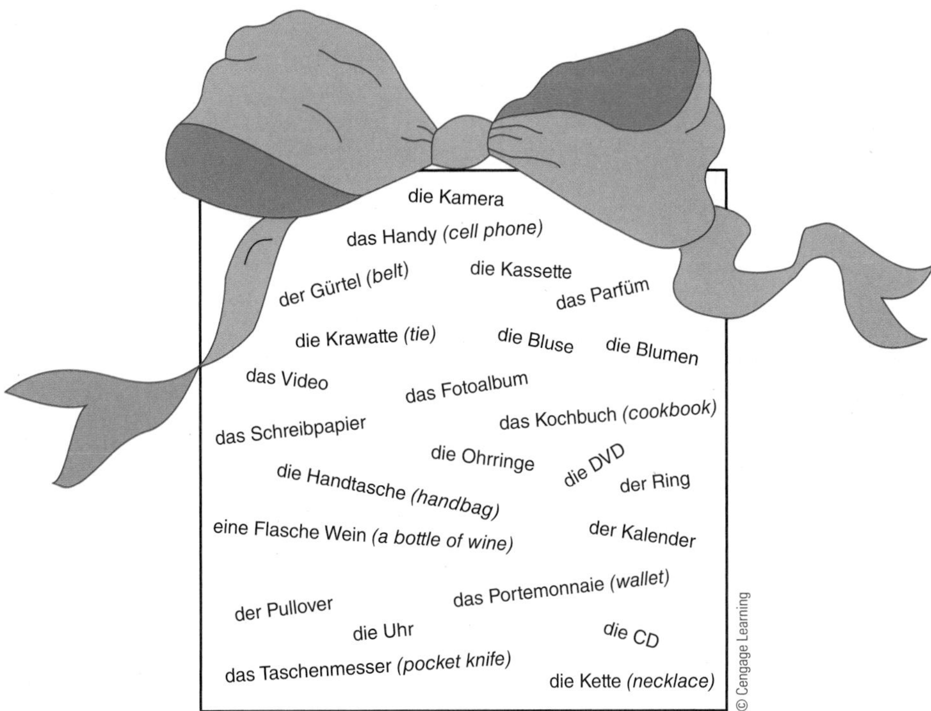

die Kamera
das Handy (cell phone)
der Gürtel (belt)
die Kassette
das Parfüm
die Krawatte (tie)
die Bluse
die Blumen
das Video
das Fotoalbum
das Schreibpapier
das Kochbuch (cookbook)
die Ohrringe
die DVD
der Ring
die Handtasche (handbag)
eine Flasche Wein (a bottle of wine)
der Kalender
der Pullover
das Portemonnaie (wallet)
die Uhr
die CD
das Taschenmesser (pocket knife)
die Kette (necklace)

L. *Nach Hause* und *zu Hause*

1. **Was fehlt?**
   a. Heute essen wir __zu Hause__.
   b. Jürgen ist noch nicht __zu Hause__.
   c. Er kommt am Montag oft spät __nach Hause__.
   d. Morgen bleibt er __zu Hause__.
   e. Er arbeitet gern __zu Hause__.
   f. Ich bringe jetzt die Großeltern __nach Hause__.

2. **Umfrage *(Survey)*** In small groups, ask these questions and then report back to the class. In case you need it: *everybody* = **jeder,** *nobody* = **niemand.**
   a. Wer wohnt bei den Eltern?
   b. Wer hat zu Hause einen Hund *(dog)*? eine Katze *(cat)*? einen Vogel *(bird)*?
   c. Wer hilft zu Hause gern in der Küche *(in the kitchen)*?
   d. Wer arbeitet zu Hause viel im Garten *(in the yard)*?
   e. Wer schreibt oder emailt viel nach Hause?
   f. Wer geht zu Hause für die Familie einkaufen?
   g. Wem schmeckt das Essen zu Hause nicht?

The animals are not active vocabulary!

L.2: For question b, you might want to ask them some specifics about their pets, including the name, age, etc. When asking **Haben Sie einen Vogel?,** point out that that also means Are you nuts / crazy?

Using those same prepositions, now ask students to ask each other similar questions regarding where he/she is from, where he/she lives and works, and what he/she does in the summer.

M. Allerlei Fragen Complete the following dialogue with the prepositions ***aus, bei, mit, nach, von,*** or ***zu.*** Use contractions when appropriate.

S1 Gehst du auch ___zum___ Kaufhaus? *(to the)*
S2 Nein, ich gehe ___zur___ Apotheke. *(to the)*
S1 Die Apotheke ist ___beim___ Rathaus *(city hall, n.)*. *(by)*
S2 Sag mal *(say)*, kommst du ___aus___ Norddeutschland? *(from)*
S1 Nein, ich komme ___aus___ Wiesbaden. *(from)*
S2 Wohnst du noch ___bei___ den Eltern? *(at the home of)*
S1 Nein, ich wohne nicht mehr ___zu___ Hause. Ich wohne ___bei___ Familie Dinkelacker. *(at / at the home of)*
S2 Wo arbeitest du und ___von___ wann bis wann? *(from)*
S1 Ich arbeite ___bei___ McDonalds ___von___ sechs bis zwölf. *(at / from)*
S2 Arbeitest du auch im Sommer?
S1 Nein, ich fahre ___mit___ den Eltern ___nach___ Italien. *(together with / to)*
S2 Toll!

iLrn

Visit the ***Wie geht's?*** iLrn website for more review and practice of the grammar points you have just learned.

Zusammenfassung

N. Guten Appetit: Was fehlt? Complete the articles and contractions if needed.

1. Zu__m__ Essen braucht man ein__—__ Messer und ein__e__ Gabel. 2. Suppe isst man mit ein__em__ Esslöffel *(tablespoon)* und für d__en__ Kaffee braucht man ein__en__ Kaffeelöffel. 3. D__as__ Restaurant gefällt d__en__ Studenten *(pl.)*. 4. Aber sie haben etwas gegen d__ie__ Preise. 5. Wir sprechen von d__em__ Professor und von d__er__ Prüfung. 6. Ich bestelle noch ein__—/e__ Cola. 7. Hier trinke ich d__as/ie__ Cola aus ein__em__ Glas, aber zu Hause aus d__er__ Flasche *(f., bottle)*. 8. Da kommt der Ober mit d__er__ Rechnung. 9. Ohne d__ie__ Rechnung geht's nicht. 10. Danke für d__as__ Mittagessen!

O: Explain synthetic exercises. Tell students that they will have to modify the verbs and add articles to the key words given in order to make complete sentences.
1. Der Ober bringt den Studenten die Speisekarte. 2. Er empfiehlt dem Studenten (das) Menü eins. 3. Axel nimmt ein Schnitzel. 4. Die Rindsroulade schmeckt der Studentin. (Der Studentin schmeckt die Rindsroulade.) 5. Axel und Gabi danken dem Ober für die Empfehlung. 6. Zum Essen trinkt Gabi ein Glas Mineralwasser. 7. Axel hilft dem Ober mit der Rechnung. 8. Außer dem Brötchen ist alles auf der Rechnung. 9. Gabi gibt dem Ober 40 Euro. 10. Das Restaurant gefällt den Studenten.

O. Gabi und Axel im Restaurant Create complete sentences.

BEISPIEL Axel / sprechen / mit / Ober
Axel spricht mit dem Ober.

1. Ober / bringen / Studenten *(pl.)* / Speisekarte
2. er / empfehlen / Student / Menü eins
3. Axel / nehmen / Schnitzel
4. Studentin / schmecken / Rindsroulade *(f.)*
5. Axel und Gabi / danken / Ober / für / Empfehlung *(f.)*
6. zu / Essen / trinken / Gabi / Glas Mineralwasser
7. Axel / helfen / Ober / mit / Rechnung
8. außer / Brötchen *(sg.)* / sein / alles / auf / Rechnung
9. Gabi / geben / Ober / 40 Euro
10. Restaurant / gefallen / Studenten *(pl.)*

Fokus Regional Specialties

"Food and drink are the glue that keep body and soul together," claims an old Viennese saying. This sentiment is popular in all German-speaking countries.

German cooking has many regional specialties. In addition to excellent hams and sausages, there are numerous fish dishes, such as Helgoland lobster, **Hamburger Matjestopf** *(pickled herring with sliced apples and onion rings in a sour-cream sauce),* Berlin eel soup, and Black Forest trout. Other regional dishes include **Sauerbraten** *(marinated pot roast)* from the Rhineland, **Kasseler Rippchen** *(smoked loin of pork),* Bavarian **Spanferkel** *(suckling pig),* and **Leberkäs** *(meat loaf made with minced meat and liver, eggs, and spices).* In the South, dumplings and pasta dishes (e.g., **Spätzle**) are popular. Germany also boasts a large variety of pastries, such as **Schwarzwälder Kirschtorte** *(Black Forest cake),* **Frankfurter Kranz** *(a rich cake ring decorated with whipped cream and nuts),* and **Thüringer Mohnkuchen** *(poppy-seed cake).* A favorite summer dessert is **Rote Grütze** *(berries and their juices thickened with sago starch and served with vanilla sauce or cream).*

Most famous among Austrian dishes are **Schnitzel, Gulasch,** and a variety of salted and smoked meats, as well as dumplings. But desserts such as **Strudel, Palatschinken** *(dessert crêpes),* **Kaiserschmarren** *(pancakes pulled to pieces and sprinkled with powdered sugar and raisins),* and **Sachertorte** delight visitors even more. Swiss cooking has also developed many specialties of its own, such as **Geschnetzeltes** *(minced veal in a cream sauce),* **Berner Platte** *(dish with a variety of hams and sausages),* and **Rös(ch)ti** *(fried potatoes with bacon cubes).* The most famous Swiss dish is probably cheese fondue **(Käsefondue),** a reminder that Switzerland produces a great variety of excellent cheeses (e.g., **Gruyère, Emmentaler, Appenzeller**).

P. In der Mensa: Auf Deutsch bitte!

1. Paul and Helga are walking to the cafeteria.
2. Paul lives with *(at the home of)* a family, and Helga lives at home.
3. Helga, what are you having?
4. I think I'll take the roast **(der Braten),** peas, carrots, and a glass of juice.
5. Would you *(formal)* like a piece of cake for dessert?
6. No, I'm not eating any cake, because I am on a diet **(auf Diät).**
7. I have no knife, no fork, and no spoon.
8. Paul brings the student *(f.)* a knife, a fork, a spoon, and (some) ice cream.
9. Whose ice cream is that? (To whom does the ice cream belong?)
10. Would you *(fam.)* like some ice cream with a cookie?
11. She thanks the student *(m.).*

Lerntipp

Reviewing for Tests

If you have taken full advantage of all class sessions, kept up with your work, and reviewed your lessons regularly, you should not have to spend much time preparing for tests. Concentrate on the areas that give you the most trouble. Use the *Rückblicke* sections in the *Arbeitsbuch* (SAM) for efficient reviewing. Go over the vocabulary lists of the chapters that will be covered by the test; make sure you know genders and plurals of nouns. Mark any words you seem to have trouble remembering; review them again. Begin your review early enough so that you can clarify any questions with your instructor.

© Silke's Cafe in Clarksville, TN

Schwarzwälder Kirschtorte

© Gerda Häusler

Kaiserschmarren

Paul und Helga gehen zur Mensa. 2. Paul wohnt bei einer Familie und Helga wohnt zu Hause. 3. Helga, was nimmst du? glaube, ich nehme den Braten, Erbsen und Karotten und ein Glas Saft. 5. Möchten Sie ein Stück Kuchen zum Nachtisch? in, ich esse keinen Kuchen, denn ich bin auf Diät. 7. Ich habe kein Messer, keine Gabel und keinen Löffel. 8. Paul bringt tudentin ein Messer, eine Gabel, einen Löffel und etwas Eis. 9. Wem gehört das Eis? 10. Möchtest du etwas Eis mit einem chen? 11. Sie dankt dem Studenten.

Einblicke

Lesetext

Wortschatz 2

der Freund, -e	*friend; boyfriend*
die Freundin, -nen	*friend; girlfriend*
Flasche, -n; eine Flasche . . .	*bottle; a bottle of . . .*
Hand, ¨-e	*hand*
besonders	*especially*
gewöhnlich	*usual(ly)*
man	*one (they, people, you)*
manchmal	*sometimes*
nicht nur . . . , sondern auch	*not only . . . but also . . .*
überall	*everywhere*
vielleicht	*perhaps*
dick machen	*to be fattening*
schlafen (schläft)	*to sleep*

Make students aware that the German pronoun **man** is used only in the singular: *one speaks, they speak, people speak* = **man spricht.** They should not confuse man with the noun **der Mann: Hier spricht man Deutsch.** *Here one speaks German.* **Der Mann spricht Deutsch.** *The man speaks German.*

Vor dem Lesen

A. Persönliche Fragen *(Personal questions)* At the exit of your cafeteria, a marketing student who is studying what college students eat and drink asks you to answer some questions. Work in pairs and play each role in turns.

1. Wann frühstückst du morgens? Wann isst du mittags und wann abends?
2. Wann isst du gewöhnlich warm? Mittags oder abends?
3. Trinkst du Mineralwasser oder Leitungswasser *(tap water)*?
4. Trinkst du dein Wasser mit oder ohne Eiswürfel *(ice cubes)*?
5. Isst du gern Nachtisch? Wenn ja *(if so)*, was besonders gern?
6. Gehst du manchmal in ein Restaurant, eine Teestube *(tea room)* oder eine Kneipe *(pub)*? Wenn ja, wo und was bestellst du gern?
7. Ist das, was du isst, immer gesund *(always healthy)*? Wenn nein, warum isst du es?

Fokus

Friends and Acquaintances

Germans consciously distinguish between friends **(Freunde)** and acquaintances **(Bekannte).** This is based on the belief that there are only a few real friends among so many people. Genuine friendships are considered special and often last for a lifetime.

B. Allerlei Restaurants What do the ads on the next page tell you about the various restaurants?

1. Wie heißen die sieben Restaurants?
2. Wo sind sie? Was ist ihre Adresse?
3. Haben sie Telefonnummern? Wenn ja, lesen Sie sie laut!
4. Von wann bis wann sind die Restaurants offen?
5. Wo gibt es deutsche oder friesische (*Frisian*) Küche? chinesische oder indische Delikatessen? französische oder italienische Spezialitäten?
6. Wo gibt es Bio-Delikatessen?
7. Welches Restaurant verkauft auch außer Haus *(has take-out orders)*?
8. Wo isst man in der deutschen Hauptstadt?
9. Welche Reklame *(ad)* gefällt Ihnen besonders gut? Warum?
10. Wo möchten Sie gern einmal essen? Warum?

© Beatrix Brockman

© Beatrix Brockman

© Beatrix Brockman

© Beatrix Brockman

© Beatrix Brockman

© Beatrix Brockman

© Beatrix Brockman

NOTE: As you can see in the advertisement for the Papillon, the German spelling reform is not followed everywhere. Frequently, you will still find the old **"ß"** where it now should be an **"ss,"** e.g., In Leipzig **läßt** es sich leben wie „Gott in Frankreich" *(In Leipzig, you can live like a king*, lit.: *"like God in France")*.

C. Das ist leicht zu verstehen! Read aloud the following words paying special attention to their stressed syllable. Then guess their meaning in English.

der Kaffeeklatsch; die Pasta, Schule; die Kartoffelchips *(pl)*.; genetisch modifiziert, Lokal, relativ, voll

Lesetipp

Identifying the Topic of a Passage

The first sentence of a paragraph often summarizes what will come next. You may remember topic sentences from your composition classes. Make sure you understand these thematic introductions clearly, and the rest of the passage should be easier to follow.

The serial comma before **und** is not used in German: **Die Deutschen, Österreicher und Schweizer ...**

Man ist, was man isst.

Die Deutschen, Österreicher und Schweizer beginnen den Tag gewöhnlich mit einem guten° Frühstück. Zum Frühstück gibt es Brot oder Brötchen, Butter, Marmelade, vielleicht auch ein Ei, etwas Schinken oder Käse und manchmal auch etwas Joghurt oder Müsli. Dazu° trinkt man Kaffee, Milch, Obstsaft, Tee oder Kakao.

Mittags isst man warm. Um die Zeit sind viele Schulen aus und die Kinder kommen dann zum Mittagessen nach Hause. Manche Büros° machen mittags zu. Viele Leute essen mittags zu Hause. Andere° gehen nicht nach Hause, sondern in die Kantine° oder in ein Restaurant. Im Restaurant gibt es gewöhnlich ein Tagesmenü. Das ist oft besonders gut und billig. Außer Bratwurst, Omelett oder Hähnchen° findet man natürlich auch Lokalspezialitäten, wie zum Beispiel Hamburger Matjestopf° oder bayrische Schweinshax'n° mit Knödeln°. Zum Mittagessen trinkt man gern Saft, Limonade oder Mineralwasser, vielleicht auch ein Glas Wein oder Bier, aber kein Leitungswasser° und auch keinen Kaffee. Kaffee trinkt man manchmal nach dem Essen. Egal wo°, überall findet man etwas Besonderes°. Probieren° Sie die Spezialitäten und probieren Sie auch, wie die Europäer mit Messer und Gabel zu essen! Nehmen Sie das Messer in die rechte° Hand und die Gabel in die linke° Hand, und dann Guten Appetit!

Fürs Mittagessen braucht man gewöhnlich Zeit. Leute mit nur wenig° Zeit gehen zur Imbissbude°. Da gibt es Bratwurst, Fischbrötchen, Tacos, Burritos, Pizza, Pasta, Döner° oder Hamburger mit Pommes frites. Schnell essen ist manchmal nicht schlecht, aber ein Mittagessen ist das für die meisten° Leute nicht.

Nachmittags sieht man viele Menschen in Cafés. Da sitzen sie gemütlich° bei einer Tasse Kaffee und reden°. Kaffeeklatsch gibt es aber nicht nur im Café oder einer Konditorei, sondern auch zu Hause. Besonders sonntags kommt man oft mit Freunden zusammen zu einer Tasse Kaffee und einem Stück Kuchen.

Abends zum Abendbrot° isst man gewöhnlich kalt und nicht so viel wie mittags. Man sagt: Mit einem vollen Bauch° schläft man schlecht; und was man abends isst, macht dick. So gibt es nur etwas Brot mit Quark° oder Käse, Wurst oder Fisch, ein paar Tomaten oder saure Gurken. Dazu gibt es vielleicht eine Tasse Tee oder ein Bier. Abends öffnet man auch gern eine Flasche Wein für Freunde. Dazu gibt es Salzstangen° oder Kartoffelchips.

Den meisten Deutschen, Österreichern und Schweizern ist wichtig, was sie essen. Wie bei uns° essen sie relativ viel Obst, Salat und Gemüse. Auch haben sie etwas gegen Farbstoffe° und Konservierungsmittel°. Genetisch modifizierte Lebensmittel sind unbeliebt°—und das nicht nur in Deutschland, sondern auch in den anderen EU-Ländern. Was man isst, ist heute wichtig. Wie heißt es? „Man ist, was man isst!"

good
With it
Some offices
Others
company cafeteria
(grilled) chicken
pickled herring / Bavarian pig's knuckles / dumplings
tap water
no matter where
something special / try
right
left
little
fast-food stand
gyros
most
leisurely
talk
evening meal
full stomach
curd cheese
pretzel sticks
as we do here
food coloring / preservatives
unpopular

Nach dem Lesen

A. Alles verstanden?

1. Was essen die Deutschen, Österreicher und Schweizer gewöhnlich zum Frühstück? Was trinken sie gern dazu?
2. Wann isst man gewöhnlich warm, mittags oder abends?
3. Warum sind Tagesmenüs in Restaurants populär?
4. Was für Lokalspezialitäten gibt es?
5. Wohin gehen die Leute manchmal, wenn sie nicht viel Zeit haben?
6. Wohin gehen sie gern zum Kaffeeklatsch?
7. Warum isst man abends gewöhnlich nicht warm? Was isst man dann gern?
8. Was ist unbeliebt und warum?

A: 1. Brot, Brötchen, Butter, Marmelade, Ei, Schinken, Käse, Joghurt, Müsli, Kaffee, Milch, Obstsaft, Tee, Kakao 2. mittags 3. sind gut und billig 4. Hamburger Matjestopf, bayrische Schweinshax'n mit Knödel 5. zur Imbissbude 6. ins Café 7. Dann schläft man schlech. Das macht dick. 8. Farbstoffe, Konservierungsmittel und genetisch modifizerte Lebensmittel, ungesund. Man ist, was man isst.

B. Guten Appetit! What's missing?

1. Ich beginne den Tag gewöhnlich mit ein<u>em</u> guten Frühstück: mit ein<u>em</u> Brötchen, ein<u>em</u> Ei und ein<u>er</u> Tasse Tee. 2. Gehst du mittags <u>nach</u> Hause? 3. Ja, <u>zu</u> Hause ist es nicht so teuer. 4. Bei d<u>en</u> Preisen esse ich gern <u>zu</u> Hause. 5. Warum gehst du nicht zu<u>r</u> Mensa? 6. D<u>as</u> Essen schmeckt mir nicht. 7. Manchmal gehe ich zu ein<u>er</u> Imbissbude *(f.)*. 8. Dann esse ich nichts außer ein<u>er</u> Bratwurst und die Cola trinke ich schnell aus d<u>er</u> Flasche. 9. Oft habe ich kein<u>en</u> Hunger. 10. Dann esse ich nur ein<u>en</u> Apfel oder ein<u>e</u> Banane. 11. Möchtest du etwas Brot mit ein<u>em</u> Stück Käse? 12. Es ist von d<u>em</u> Bio-Laden und hat kein<u>e</u> Konservierungsmittel *(pl.)*!

Optional **Artikelspiel: Der, das oder die?** Name certain foods or other new vocabulary from this chapter without their articles. If an item is masculine, only the men will say **der;** if feminine, the women will say **die;** if neuter, they'll all reply with **das.**

C. Zusammengesetzte Wörter *(Compound nouns)* Welche finden Sie im Lesetext? Was sind ihre Artikel?

BEISPIEL Mittagessen
der Mittag + das Essen = das Mittagessen

Compound nouns can be either plain **(Obstsaft)** or linked **(Tagesmenü, Konservierungsmittel).** The **-es-** or **-s-** are genitive links. There are also **-e-**, **-en-**, and **-n-** links for plural forms. Which link will be used in a compound is not predictable (See *Arbeitsbuch* [SAM], Chapter 8).

C: das Obst + der Saft = der Obstsaft; der Tag + das Menü = das Tagesmenü; der Kaffee + der Klatsch = der Kaffeeklatsch; der Abend + das Brot = das Abendbrot; die Farbe + der Stoff = der Farbstoff; die Konservierung + das Mittel = das Konservierungsmittel

D. Textanalyse

1. Welche Sätze im Text beginnen mit dem Subjekt? Finden Sie fünf!

   BEISPIEL *Die Deutschen, Österreicher und Schweizer beginnen den Tag mit einem guten Frühstück.*

2. Welche Sätze beginnen mit . . . ?
   a. einem Adverb: z. B. **Mittags** isst man gewöhnlich warm.
   b. einem Objekt: z. B. **Kaffeeklatsch** gibt es aber nicht nur im Café.
   c. etwas anderem *(something else)*: **So** gibt es nur etwas Brot.

E. Wie isst man das? Working in groups or pairs, show each other how you would eat the following foods.

Suppe, Salat, Bratwurst, Hähnchen, Putenfleisch *(turkey meat)*, Sauerbraten, Schnitzel, Spagetti, Erbsen, Spargel *(asparagus)*, Kartoffelbrei *(mashed potatoes)*, Fondue, Eis, Erdbeeren

Wine from Franconia is sold in a special bottle called a **Bocksbeutel,** and no other wine may be sold in a bottle that has this shape. Look it up on the Internet!

Fokus Wines from Germany, Austria, and Switzerland

All in all, there are 13 German wine-growing regions, but most of Germany's wine is produced in western and southwestern Germany. The wines from the Rhine and Moselle rivers **(Rheinwein and Moselwein),** as well as from Franconia **(Franken)** and Baden-Württemberg, are especially famous around the world. In Switzerland, 18 of the 23 cantons grow wine. It seems that wine is to the Swiss what beer is to the Bavarians. In Austria, there are excellent vineyards along the Danube around Vienna. Wines are classified as **Tafelwein** *(table or ordinary wine)*, **Qualitätswein** *(quality wine)*, or **Qualitätswein mit Prädikat** *(superior wine)*.

Optional practice: 1. **Ersetzen Sie das Subjekt!** (Ich schlafe schlecht. Mittags essen wir warm. Sie nehmen die Gabel in die linke Hand. Ich sehe keine Imbissbude.) 2. **Sagen Sie es anders!** (Viele Leute essen **mittags** in der Kantine. Das Tagesmenü ist **gewöhnlich** gut und billig. Man geht **natürlich** manchmal auch zur Imbissbude. Man braucht manchmal viel Zeit **fürs Mittagessen.** Qualität ist **den Deutschen** oft wichtiger als Quantität.)

F. Die Pizzeria Taking turns, ask your partner about MARIO's pizza ad, and find out how he/she likes pizza.

1. Wie heißt die Pizzeria?
2. Wie ist die Telefonnummer?
3. Was macht das Pizza-Taxi?
4. Wann ist die Pizzeria offen?
5. Bestellen Sie manchmal auch eine Pizza per Telefon? Wenn ja, wo?
6. Welche Pizza bestellen Sie gern?
7. Was kostet so eine Pizza?
8. Essen Sie Pizza mit Gabel und Messer oder mit der Hand?

Bistro - Pizzeria
MARIO
Haus-Service
Pizza-Taxi
05112-1470
Öffnungszeiten:
Mo.-So. 12.00-14.00 Uhr und 16.00-23.00 Uhr
Kein Ruhetag

Weiteres

G. Kurzgespräche Working with a partner, prepare one of the following brief dialogues. Then present it to the class.

1. **An der Uni** You have just met a student in the cafeteria for the first time and inquire how he/she likes it here. Very much, he/she answers. The other student then asks you whether the soup tastes good. You reply that it is not bad, but . . . *(add your own comment)*. You ask how your fellow student likes the chicken. He/She replies that . . . *(let him/her add their own comment)*.

2. **Im Restaurant** You and a friend are in a German restaurant. The server asks what you would like, and you ask what he/she recommends. He/She mentions a particular dish. Both you and your friend order, each choosing a soup, a main dish, and a salad. The server asks what you would like to drink, and you order beverages. Use the menu on page 83.

Fokus Table Manners

Whenever Europeans eat something that needs to be cut, they hold the knife in the right hand and the fork in the left throughout the meal—rather than shifting the fork to the right hand after cutting. (It is said that American spies during World War II could be identified by their different food-cutting habits.) If no knife is needed, the left hand rests on the table next to the plate, not in the lap. To signal that a person is finished eating, the knife and fork are placed parallel and diagonally on the plate.

H. Aufsatz: Meine Essgewohnheiten *(My eating habits)* Pretend you are explaining your eating habits to someone from Germany. Write 8–10 sentences describing what you usually like and dislike eating and drinking at various meals. Include these key words: **nachmittags, vielleicht, abends, gewöhnlich, manchmal, morgens, nicht nur . . . sondern auch, mittags.**

© SH-Vector/Shutterstock

Schreibtipp

Writing a Composition and Choosing Word Order

When you are writing a composition **(der Aufsatz)**, no matter how long, first think about a basic outline. What will your introduction be? What points are going to be mentioned in the middle? What is your conclusion?

Note that word order in German is quite flexible. To reduce repetition in style, avoid starting too many sentences with the subject, especially with the pronoun **ich**. Bring some variety into the composition by introducing sentences with an adverb, an object, or some other element. Remember, the verb is always the second element in a sentence.

Hörverständnis

Gäste zum Wochenende Listen to Kai and Sandra's plans for their weekend guests, Ruth and Uwe. Then read the questions and select the correct response.

Zum Erkennen: die Forelle, -n *(trout)*; genug *(enough)*

1. Ruth und Uwe kommen am __b__.
   a. Sonntag um vier
   b. Samstagnachmittag
   c. Sonntag zum Kaffee
2. Sandra macht einen __c__.
   a. Quarkkuchen
   b. Apfelkuchen
   c. Erdbeerkuchen
3. Zum Abendessen gibt es __b__.
   a. Kartoffelsalat und Würstchen
   b. Fondue, Brot und Wein
   c. Eier, Wurst und Käse
4. Uwe isst gern __a__.
   a. Joghurt
   b. Schwarzbrot
   c. Erdbeerkuchen
5. Zum Mittagessen machen sie __c__.
   a. eine Nudelsuppe
   b. Fleisch und Gemüse
   c. Fisch mit Kartoffeln

© Cengage Learning

For further practice, an optional two-part video (**Szenen** and **Interviews**) is available on the ***Wie geht's?*** Premium Website and in iLrn, with corresponding questions and activities in the *Arbeitsbuch* (SAM).

As an optional activity, with Google Earth you could visit any city in the German-speaking countries to check out restaurants and cafés.

Following this chapter, there is an extensive review section in the *Arbeitsbuch* (SAM) *(Rückblick: Kapitel 1–3)*. The accompanying exercises and answer key should help you prepare for the test.

Rückschau

Kapitelwortschatz

Hauptwörter

das Abendessen	*supper*
die Bedienung	*server; service*
das Café, -s	*café*
das Eis	*ice cream*
das Essen	*food; meal*
die Flasche, -n; eine Flasche . . .	*bottle; a bottle of . . .*
der Freund, -e	*male friend; boyfriend*
die Freundin, -nen	*female friend; girlfriend*
das Frühstück	*breakfast*
die Gabel, -n	*fork*
die Hand, ¨-e	*hand*
die Kartoffel, -n	*potato*
der Kellner, -	*waiter*
der Löffel, -	*spoon*
die Mensa	*student cafeteria*
das Messer, -	*knife*
das Mittagessen	*lunch, midday meal*
der Nachtisch	*dessert*
die Nudel, -n	*noodle*
der Ober, -	*waiter*
der Pfeffer	*pepper*
die Pizza, -s	*pizza*
die Pommes (frites) *(pl.)*	*(French) fries*
der Pudding, -s	*pudding*
die Rechnung, -en	*check; bill*
der Reis	*rice*
das Restaurant, -s	*restaurant*
das Salz	*salt*
die Serviette, -n	*napkin*
die Speisekarte, -n	*menu*
die Suppe, -n	*soup*
der Teller, -	*plate*
der Zucker	*sugar*

Verben

antworten	*to answer*
bestellen	*to order*
(be)zahlen	*to pay (for)*
bleiben	*to remain, stay*
bringen	*to bring*
danken	*to thank*
dick machen	*to be fattening*
empfehlen	*to recommend*
essen	*to eat*
fahren	*to drive*
frühstücken	*to eat breakfast*
geben	*to give*
gefallen	*to please, be pleasing to*
gehören	*to belong to*
glauben	*to believe*
helfen	*to help*
laufen	*to walk; to run*
lesen	*to read*
nehmen	*to take; to have (food)*
schlafen	*to sleep*
schmecken	*to taste*
sehen	*to see*
sprechen	*to speak*
tragen	*to carry; to wear*
werden	*to become, get*

Präpositionen

aus *(+ dat.)*	*out of; from* (a place of origin)
außer *(+ dat.)*	*besides*
bei *(+ dat.)*	*at, for* (a company); *near, by; at the home of, with* (a person)
mit *(+ dat.)*	*with; together with*
nach *(+ dat.)*	*after* (time); *to* (cities, countries, continents); *to* (in certain expressions)
seit *(+ dat.)*	*since; for* (duration)
von *(+ dat.)*	*of; from; by* (creator, doer of action)
zu *(+ dat.)*	*to* (in the direction of); *at* (in certain expressions); *for* (purpose)

Verschiedenes

Bedienung!	*Waiter! / Waitress!*
besonders	*especially*
Danke, gleichfalls!	*Thanks, the same to you!*
Das schmeckt (gut)!	*That's good!, That tastes good!*
Das schmeckt (mir).	*I like it.*, i.e., *I like the way it tastes.*
etwas (zu essen)	*something (to eat)*
gewöhnlich	*usual(ly)*
Guten Appetit!	*Enjoy your meal!*
Herr Ober!	*Waiter!*
Ich mag kein(e/en) . . .	*I don't like (any) . . .*
Ich möchte / hätte gern . . .	*I would like to have . . .*
(Ich möchte) zahlen bitte!	*I'd like to pay.*
man	*one (they, people, you)*
manchmal	*sometimes*
nach Hause	*(toward) home*
nicht nur . . . , sondern auch	*not only . . . but also*
nichts (zu trinken)	*nothing (to drink)*
noch ein(e)	*another*
überall	*everywhere*
viel / viele	*much / many*
vielleicht	*perhaps*
Was gibt's zum Frühstück / Mittagessen?	*What's for breakfast / lunch?*
Was gibt's zu essen / trinken?	*What is there to eat / drink?*
wie viel? / wie viele?	*how much? / how many?*
zu Hause	*at home*

Zum Schluss

1. **Wer sind Sie?** Answer the following questions about your likes and dislikes. Add a few more questions of your own! Incorporate at least three new verbs from the chapter.
   a. Was essen Sie gern? Was essen Sie in der Mensa gern? Wo essen Sie gern?
   b. Was tragen Sie gern? Was tragen Sie heute?
   c. Mit wem sprechen Sie Deutsch?
   d. Wohnen Sie bei den Eltern?
   e. Was gefällt Ihnen an der Universität?
   f. . . .
   g. . . .
   h. . . .

2. **Wer ist wer?** Now, ask your classmates the same questions. How do their answers compare with yours?

Alternative: Have students answer the questions as if they were a historical or fictional figure, or even one of their fellow students! Tell them to be creative!

3. **Kombinieren Sie!** How many sentences can you create with the following elements? Use the **Wortschatz** from this chapter and from earlier chapters to create complete sentences. Pay attention to case!

antworten	fahren	lesen	aus
arbeiten	geben	nehmen	außer
bestellen	gefallen	schlafen	bei
(be)zahlen	gehen	schmecken	mit
bringen	gehören	sehen	nach
danken	glauben	sprechen	seit
empfehlen	helfen	tragen	von
essen	kommen	wohnen	zu

4. **Das gefällt mir! Und das gefällt mir nicht!** Now, complete the following sentences.
   a. Ich mag kein(e/en) . . .
   b. Ich möchte . . .
   c. . . . gefällt mir (nicht).
   d. Ich esse kein(e/en) . . .

5. **Erzählen Sie!** Describe your favorite restaurant to a classmate. What kind of food do they serve? What do you like to eat there? What do you dislike there? Why? How often do you eat there? Compare answers! Make sure to include clarifying words: **besonders**, **gewöhnlich**, **manchmal**, **nicht nur . . .**, **sondern auch**, **vielleicht**.

iLrn **Onlineaktivitäten** Visit iLrn for online activities related to this chapter. There you will find additional resources, such as a memory game (**Gedächtnisspiel**), a crossword puzzle (**Kreuzworträtsel**), audio flash cards (**Vokabelblitz**), a tutorial quiz (**Mini-Quiz**), and the active vocabulary (**Wortschatz**) for this chapter.

Kapitel 4

Feiertage und Feste

Lernziele In this chapter you will learn about:

Zum Thema

Ordinal numbers, dates, holidays, and congratulations

Fokus

Holiday customs, vacations, celebrations, diversity in religious traditions, tourist destinations

Struktur

- The present perfect with **haben**
- The present perfect with **sein**
- Subordinating conjunctions

Einblicke

Bericht: Da macht das Feiern Spaß!

Rückschau

Kapitelwortschatz
Zum Schluss

RESSOURCEN

iLrn  Video

Audio  SAM

Weihnachtsmarkt vor dem Wiener Rathaus

Vorschau Holidays and Vacations

One of the most pleasant aspects of life in Germany, Switzerland, and Austria is the large number of secular and religious holidays **(Feiertage)**, on which stores are closed and people don't work. There are, for example, two vacation days each for Christmas and for Easter. When these holidays are combined with a weekend or a couple of vacation days, Germans find it easy to visit family in other parts of the country, to go skiing, or to go to the countryside for a few days.

Secular holidays include New Year's Eve **(Silvester)** and New Year's Day **(Neujahr)**, May Day or Labor Day **(Maifeiertag** or **Tag der Arbeit)**, and national holidays marked by parades, speeches, and fireworks. On October 3 **(Tag der deutschen Einheit)**, Germany commemorates its reunification in 1990. Austria, in turn, celebrates its independence from the Allied occupation in 1955 on October 26 **(Nationalfeiertag)**. Switzerland's **Bundesfeiertag** on August 1 is based on the country's founding in 1291. Besides Christmas **(Weihnachten)**, Good Friday **(Karfreitag)**, and Easter **(Ostern)**, religious holidays include Ascension Day **(Christi Himmelfahrt)** and Pentecost **(Pfingsten)**. Additional religious holidays, such as Epiphany **(Heilige Drei Könige)** and All Saints' Day **(Allerheiligen)** are observed only in those states and areas where the majority of the population is Catholic. Reformation Day **(Reformationstag)** is a public holiday in the predominantly Protestant areas, that is, in the northern and eastern parts of Germany.

The combination of generous paid vacation **(der Urlaub)** allowances—up to 30 work days of vacation for nonsalaried employees—and many holidays has reduced the average number of working days in Germany to fewer than 200 per year, considerably fewer than in the US or Canada. Germans feel that frequent holidays and generous vacations improve efficiency and productivity. Recently, however, some concerns have arisen about the competitiveness of German workers in the global economy, especially as some unions have have been able to reduce the workweek to less than 40 hours.

German enthusiasm for travel has created some problems, such as overcrowding on highways when school vacations **(Ferien)** begin and end. To alleviate this situation, a system of rotating and staggered school vacations was developed in the various federal states, so that no state—with the exception of Bavaria—always has very late or very early vacations.

Möchten Sie ein paar gebrannte Mandeln?

Weihnachtssterne für die Weihnachtszeit

Ask on which holidays schools, shops, banks, etc. are closed in this country. How much vacation does the average worker get here? How does that affect families whose children are off for a long summer?

You might mention that **Christi Himmelfahrt** is also **Vatertag,** and in some parts of the country people use the occasion to celebrate with picnics and libations.

The **Reformationstag** commemorates the reformation of the church by Martin Luther in the 16th century, which led to the formation of a new religious group, the Protestant-Lutheran Church.

Fragen: 1. Die Frau verkauft gebrannte Mandeln. Wie heißen *gebrannte Mandeln* auf Englisch? 2. Gibt es hier bei Ihnen auch gebrannte Mandeln? Wenn ja, wo? 3. Essen Sie gern gebrannte Mandeln?

Zum Thema

Gespräche

Am Telefon

© Cengage Learning

Warm-ups: 1. Frau X ist im Supermarkt, in der Bäckerei, auf dem Markt. **Was kauft sie?** 2. Zum Mittagessen sind Sie im Restaurant. **Was möchten Sie?** 3. **Was ist der Artikel von** Suppenlöffel, Nudelsuppe, Obstsalat, Saftflasche, Käsebrot, Wurstbrötchen? . . . 4. **Wie geht's weiter?** ein Stück . . . ; etwas / viel . . . ; ein Glas / eine Flasche / ein Pfund . . . 5. **Nach Hause** oder **zu Hause?** Wir gehen . . . ; Jetzt sind wir . . . ; . . . sprechen wir Deutsch.

NADJA Hallo, Simon!
SIMON Hallo, Nadja! Wie geht's dir denn?
NADJA Nicht schlecht, danke. Was machst du am Wochenende?
SIMON Nichts Besonderes. Warum?
NADJA Erik hat übermorgen Geburtstag und wir geben eine Party.
SIMON Super! Aber bist du sicher, dass Erik übermorgen Geburtstag hat? Ich glaube, sein Geburtstag ist am siebten Mai.
NADJA Quatsch! Erik hat am dritten Mai Geburtstag. Und Samstag ist der dritte.
SIMON Na gut. Wann und wo ist die Party?
NADJA Samstag um sieben bei mir. Aber nichts sagen! Es ist eine Überraschung.
SIMON Okay! Also, bis dann!
NADJA Tschüss! Mach's gut!

As in previous chapters, you could have students act out the dialogue with a partner.

Erik klingelt bei Nadja.

NADJA Grüß dich, Erik! Herzlichen Glückwunsch zum Geburtstag!
ERIK Wie bitte?
SIMON Ich wünsche dir alles Gute zum Geburtstag.
ERIK Tag, Simon! . . . Hallo, Silke! Tobias und Sabine, ihr auch?
ALLE Wir gratulieren dir zum Geburtstag!
ERIK Danke! So eine Überraschung! Aber ich habe nicht heute Geburtstag, mein Geburtstag ist am siebten.
NADJA Echt? Na, dann hat Simon doch recht gehabt. Ach, das macht nichts. Wir feiern heute.

A: 1. Erik 2. am Samstag, bei Nadja 3. eine Überraschung 4. Simon, Silke, Tobias und Sabine; sie gratulieren Erik 5. nein, am 7. Mai

A. Alles verstanden?

1. Wer hat Geburtstag?
2. Wann und wo ist die Party?
3. Warum sagen sie nichts zu Erik?
4. Wer kommt zur Geburtstagsparty und was tun sie alle?
5. Ist Eriks Geburtstag wirklich am 3. Mai?

Preferably you would do Exercise B after the students are more familiar with the new vocabulary. However, having the original dialogue close by might help. That's why **Jetzt sind Sie dran!** was placed here.

B. Jetzt sind Sie dran! With a partner, create your own dialogue. Talk about weekend plans and any upcoming events, possibly a birthday party.

Fokus Congratulations

Herzlichen Glückwunsch! (or its plural, **Herzliche Glückwünsche!**) suits almost any occasion, be it a birthday, an engagement, a wedding, the birth or christening of a baby, church confirmation or communion, or an anniversary. Germans put a lot of emphasis on the celebration of birthdays. Contrary to US custom, the "birthday kid" in Germany is expected to throw his or her own party. Surprise parties, however, are popular with students. Coming-of-age and special birthdays (18, 25, 30, 40, 50, and so forth) are considered particularly important—the older you get, the more elaborate the celebration. Other occasions for congratulations are **Muttertag** and **Vatertag.** While the **Muttertag** tradition is similar to that in North America, **Vatertag** in Germany is celebrated on Ascension Day, a federal holiday. Regionally, it is also called men's day, **Männertag**, or gentlemen's day, **Herrentag.**

Wortschatz 1

Die (Ordinal)zahl, -en *([ordinal] number)*

1. erste	9. neunte	17. **siebzehnte**
2. zweite	10. zehnte	18. achtzehnte
3. **dritte**	11. elfte	19. neunzehnte
4. vierte	12. zwölfte	20. zwanzigste
5. fünfte	13. dreizehnte	21. einundzwanzigste
6. sechste	14. vierzehnte	22. zweiundzwanzigste
7. **siebte**	15. fünfzehnte	30. dreißigste
8. **achte**	16. **sechzehnte**	

From 1 to 19, the ordinal numbers have a **-te** ending. Starting with 20, they end in **-ste.** Note the boldface irregularities within the numbers.

Das Datum, die Daten *(calendar date)*

Welches Datum ist heute?	*What's the date today?*
Heute ist der erste Mai (1.5.).	*Today is the first of May (5/1).*
Wann haben Sie Geburtstag?	*When is your birthday?* (formal)
Ich habe am ersten Mai (1.5.) Geburtstag.	*My birthday is on the first of May.*
Wann sind Sie geboren?	*When were you born?* (formal)
Ich bin 1993 geboren.	*I was born in 1993.*
Ich bin am 1.5.1993 geboren.	*I was born on May 1, 1993.*
Die Ferien sind vom . . . bis zum . . .	*The vacation is from . . . until . . .*

In writing dates, Americans give the month and then the day. Germans give the day first and then the month. The ordinal number is followed by a period: **1.5. (1. Mai), 5.1. (5. Januar).** Thus **1.5.** reads **der erste Mai,** and **5.1.** reads **der fünfte Januar.** Note the **-en** after **am, vom,** and **zum: am ersten Mai,** vom neunt**en** Juli bis zum achtzehnt**en** August.

German does not use a preposition when simply naming a year: **Ich bin 1993 geboren.** *I was born in 1993.*

Das Fest, -e *(fest, festival)*

der Feiertag, -e	*holiday*	die Feier, -n	*celebration*
Geburtstag, -e	*birthday*	Party, -s	*party*
Sekt	*champagne*	Überraschung, -en	*surprise*
das Geschenk, -e	*present, gift*	die Ferien *(pl.)*	*vacation*
bekommen	*to get, receive*	singen	*to sing*
dauern	*to last, take* (duration)	tanzen	*to dance*
denken	*to think*	tun	*to do*
feiern	*to celebrate, party*	überraschen	*to surprise*
gratulieren	*to congratulate*	wünschen	*to wish*
nennen	*to name, call*		
schenken	*to give* (a gift)		

Feiertag refers to a special day, a holiday, and can be in either the singular or the plural, whereas **Ferien** (always in the plural) refers to school or university vacation time. A (paid) vacation from work is **der Urlaub.**

The present tense forms of **tun** are: **ich tue, du tust, er tut, wir tun, ihr tut, sie tun.**

Verschiedenes

gerade	*just, right now*
noch	*still; else*
sicher	*sure(ly), certain(ly)*
gestern / vorgestern	*yesterday / the day before yesterday*
morgen / übermorgen	*tomorrow / the day after tomorrow*
am Wochenende	*on the weekend*
Wie lange?	*How long?*
vor einer Woche	*a week ago*
Das gibt's doch nicht!	*I don't believe it!, That's impossible!*
Echt?	*Really?*
So eine Überraschung!	*What a surprise!*
Vielen / Herzlichen Dank!	*Thank you very much!*
Danke schön! / Bitte schön!	*Thanks a lot! / You're welcome!*
Nichts zu danken!	*You're welcome!, My pleasure!*
zu Ostern / Weihnachten / Silvester	*at/for Easter / Christmas / New Year's Eve*
zum Geburtstag	*on/for one's birthday*
Alles Gute!	*All the best!*

vor meaning *ago* is PREpositional rather than POST-positional as it is in English: **vor einer Woche** *(a week ago)*, **vor zwei Tagen** *(two days ago)*.

anniversary **das Jubiläum, Jubiläen;** *graduation* **Abschluss, ¨-e;** colloquial for *party* **die Fete, -n**

Alles Gute zum Geburtstag!	*Happy birthday!*
Herzlichen Glückwunsch (zum Geburtstag)!	*Congratulations (on your birthday)!*
Ich gratuliere dir/Ihnen . . . !	*Congratulations . . . !*
Ich wünsche dir/Ihnen . . . !	*I wish you . . . !*
Herzliche Glückwünsche!	*Best wishes!*
Viel Glück!	*Good luck!*
Gute Besserung!	*Get well soon!*
Frohe / Fröhliche Weihnachten!	*Merry Christmas!*
Ein gutes neues Jahr!	*Have a good New Year!*
(Ein) schönes Wochenende!	*Have a nice weekend!*

Zum Erkennen: nichts Besonderes *(nothing special)*; Quatsch! *(Nonsense!)*; na gut *(all right)*; klingeln (here: *to ring the doorbell*); recht haben *(to be correct)*; AUCH: das Partizip, -ien *(participle)*; der Infinitiv, -e; der Nebensatz, ¨-e *(subordinate clause)*; verbinden *(to connect)*

■ Check the Internet for an American version of Nuremberg's Christmas in Chicago.

Fokus The Christmas Season

During the weeks before Christmas, outdoor Christmas markets add to the flair of the season in many cities. The Nuremberg **Christkindlmarkt** is the most famous one in Germany. In the month before Christmas, more than 2 million visitors from all over the world stroll by the market's booths, which offer Christmas decorations, candy, and toys. The smell of mulled wine, toasted almonds, and roasted chestnuts is in the air, as well as the festive music of choirs and instrumentalists. Nuremberg is home to the fancy gingerbread called **Nürnberger Lebkuchen.** The traditional **Weihnachtsplätzchen** *(Christmas cookies)* and **Stollen**—a buttery yeast bread filled with almonds, currants, raisins, and candied fruit—are other favorites at Christmas.

The celebration of Saint Nicholas falls on December 6. Until the 16th century, it was **Sankt Nikolaus** who brought children gifts on this holiday, a custom still followed in the Netherlands. In some areas, he was accompanied by his fearsome helper **(Knecht Ruprecht)** who would ensure that children who had misbehaved during the year got a good spanking or even disappeared into the big sack he carried. When Saint Nicholas was unable to deliver his presents in person, children would put their shoes in front of the door, where they would be filled the night of December 5. During the Reformation, German Protestants, in an effort to suppress devotion to saints, tried to transfer their children's adoration from Saint Nicholas to the Christ Child by letting Him bring Christmas presents on Christmas Eve. Today, the **Christkind** is more likely to bring gifts in the predominantly Catholic South, while the **Weihnachtsmann** brings gifts in the predominantly Protestant North. During the four weeks before Christmas, the Advent wreath **(der Adventskranz)** with its four candles is a symbol of preparation for the birth of Christ. In the German-speaking countries, Christmas Eve **(Heiligabend)** stands at the center of the Christmas celebration. Many attend late-afternoon or midnight church services on this day, and gifts are exchanged in the evening.

The Christmas tree **(der Tannenbaum)** is traditionally lit for the first time on Christmas Eve and remains up until January 6 **(Heilige Drei Könige).** December 25 and 26 are holidays when everything is closed, freeing time for family and friends.

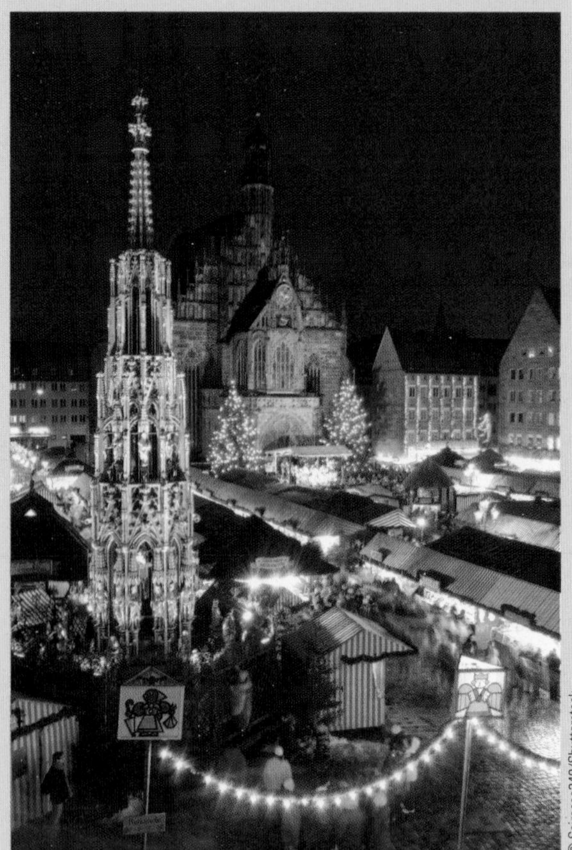

Abends auf dem Christkindlmarkt in Nürnberg

Übungen zum Thema

A. Was passt nicht?

1. feiern—gratulieren—dauern—wünschen
2. schenken—bekommen—danken—tragen
3. gehören—singen—tanzen—lesen
4. Silvester—Überraschung—Weihnachten—Ostern
5. das Fest—die Feier—die Bedienung—der Feiertag
6. der Saft—der Sekt—die Serviette—der Tee
7. Natürlich!—Na klar!—Sicher!—Schade!

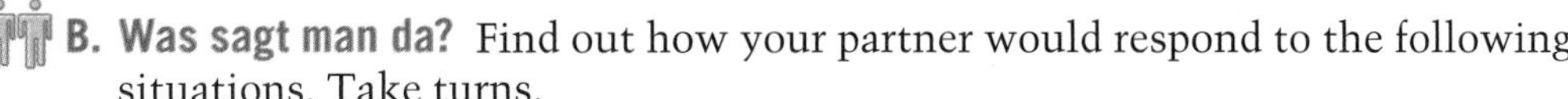

B. Was sagt man da? Find out how your partner would respond to the following situations. Take turns.

1. Ihr Freund hat Geburtstag. Was sagen Sie zu ihm?
2. Viele Leute kommen zu seiner Party. Ihr Freund weiß nichts von der Party. Was sagt er?
3. Die Geschenke gefallen ihm. Was sagt er?
4. Ihre Zimmernachbarin hilft Ihnen mit den Mathematikhausaufgaben. Was sagen Sie?
5. Sie hilft wirklich gern. Was sagt sie?
6. Zum Wochenende fährt die Nachbarin in die Berge. Was sagen Sie zu ihr?
7. Ihr Freund hat in zehn Minuten eine Prüfung. Was wünschen Sie ihm?
8. Sie schreiben Ihrer Tante und Ihrem Onkel zu Weihnachten eine Karte. Was wünschen Sie ihnen?
9. Ihre Freundin fragt, wie es Ihnen geht. Was sagen Sie?
10. Es geht Ihnen nicht besonders gut. Was wünscht sie Ihnen?

You can also add other familiar expressions.

B: 1. Herzlichen Glückwunsch / Alles Gute / Herzliche Glückwünsche zum Geburtstag!, Ich gratuliere dir zum Geburtstag! 2. Das gibt's doch nicht!, So eine Überraschung! 3. Vielen (herzlichen) Dank! 4. Danke (schön)!, Vielen Dank! 5. Bitte schön!, Bitte bitte!, Nichts zu danken! 6. Viel Spaß! 7. Viel Glück! 8. Frohe / Fröhliche Weihnachten (und ein gutes neues Jahr)! 9. Danke, gut! 10. Gute Besserung!

C. Allerlei Daten

1. **Kettenreaktion *(Chain reaction):* Das Datum heute, morgen und übermorgen** Start with any date, then name the next two.

   BEISPIEL Heute ist der 2. Juli.
   Morgen ist der 3. Juli und übermorgen ist der 4. Juli.

2. **Nationalfeiertage in Europa** Say when these European countries celebrate their national holidays.

   BEISPIEL Irland (3.3.)
   Der Nationalfeiertag in Irland ist am dritten März.

   a. Griechenland (25.3.)
   b. England (23.4.)
   c. Italien (2.6.)
   d. Dänemark (5.6.)
   e. Portugal (10.6.)
   f. Luxemburg (23.6.)
   g. Frankreich (14.7.)
   h. Belgien (21.7.)
   i. Deutschland (3.10.)
   j. Spanien (12.10.)

Before doing Exercise C, write several dates on the board (**31.12., 1.4., 7.6.,** etc.) and have the students repeat the dates after you. Then point to the dates at random and let individual students read them. Instead of **Welches Datum ist heute?,** the following two expressions are also quite common (but a little more difficult): **Was für ein Datum ist heute? Der Wievielte ist heute? Den Wievielten haben wir heute?**

D. Geburtstage und Sternzeichen *(Signs of the zodiac)* Find out about your partner's birthday and those of other family members. What are their signs of the zodiac?

D: You could also ask students to report findings to the class. Note: students can report to the class about family members only if they use proper names: **Martins Mutter / Vater / Bruder ist . . . ; sein/ihr** is new.

S1 Wann hast du Geburtstag und was bist du?
S2 Ich habe am . . . Geburtstag. Ich bin . . . *(sign of the zodiac)*. Und du?
S1 Mein Geburtstag ist am . . . Ich bin . . .
S2 Wann ist dein(e) . . . *(name a relative)* geboren?
S1 Mein(e) . . . *(the same relative)* ist am . . . geboren. Er/Sie ist . . . *(sign of the zodiac)*.

Note **die Waage, die Jungfrau,** but all other signs of the zodiac are masculine.

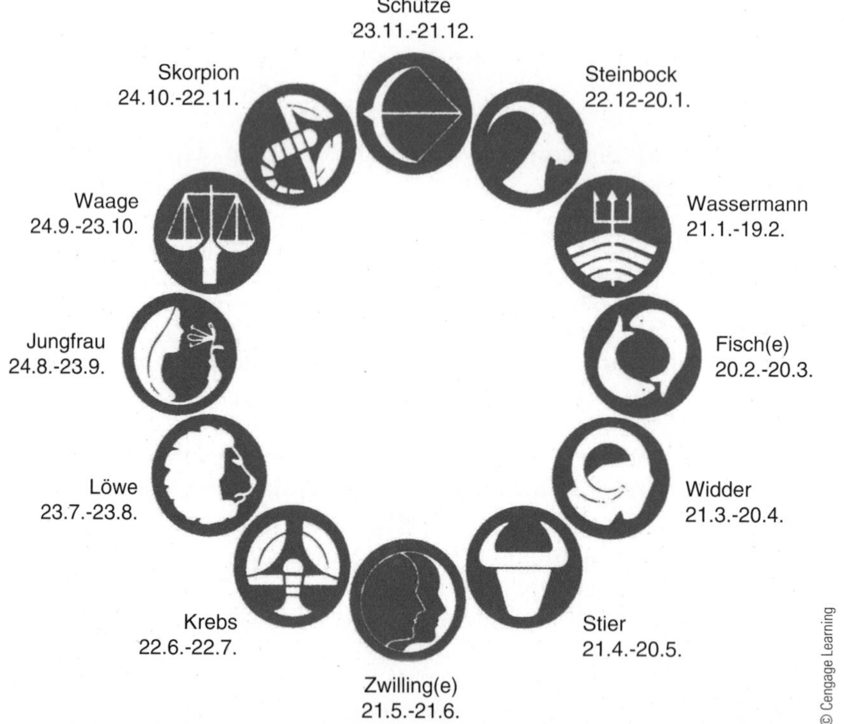

Musizieren macht Spaß. Zwei Musikanten mit Gitarre und Akkordeon.

E. Ferienzeit

1. **Ferien in Deutschland** Looking at the vacation schedule, ask each other about vacations in Germany. Take turns.
   a. Von wann bis wann sind die Osterferien in Bayern und Baden-Württemberg?
   b. Von wann bis wann sind die Pfingstferien in Sachsen und Sachsen-Anhalt?
   c. Von wann bis wann sind die Sommerferien in Brandenburg und Mecklenburg-Vorpommern?
   d. Von wann bis wann sind die Herbstferien in Niedersachsen und Thüringen?
   e. Von wann bis wann sind die Weihnachtsferien in Hessen und Rheinland-Pfalz?
   f. Welche Länder haben keine Winterferien und auch keine Pfingstferien?

E.1: a. Bayern: 17.4.–29.4. Baden-Württemberg: 25.4.–29.4. b. Sachsen: 10.6.–13.6. Sachsen-Anhalt: 2.6.–10.6. c. Brandenburg: 20.7.–2.9. Mecklenburg-Vorpommern: 20.7.–30.8. d. Niedersachsen: 19.10.–1.11. Thüringen: 16.10.–21.10. e. Hessen: 27.12.–13.1. Rheinland-Pfalz: 22.12.–5.1. f. keine Winterferien: Baden-Württemberg, Bayern, Bremen, Hamburg, Hessen, Niedersachsen, Rheinland-Pfalz, Saarland, Schleswig-Holstein; keine Pfingstferien: Brandenburg, Bremen, Hessen, Nordrhein-Westfalen, Rheinland-Pfalz, Saarland, Schleswig-Holstein

Land	Winter	Ostern	Pflingsten	Sommer	Herbst	Weihnachten
Baden-Württemberg	–	25.04. – 29.04.	02.06 – 13.06.	27.07. – 09.09.	02.11 – 03.11.	23.12 – 05.01.
Bayern	–	17.04. – 29.04.	13.06 – 24.06.	27.07 – 11.09.	30.10 – 04.11.	27.12 – 08.01.
Berlin	29.01. – 09.02.	20.04. – 06.05.	02.06./10.06. – 13.06.	20.07. – 02.09.	28.10 – 04.11.	23.12 – 02.01.
Brandenburg	31.01. – 12.02.	25.04. – 04.05.	–	20.07 – 02.09.	30.10 – 04.11.	23.12 – 02.01.
Bremen	–	03.04. – 25.04.	–	13.07. – 26.08.	23.10. – 01.11.	22.12. – 06.01.
Hamburg	–	06.03. – 18.03.	29.05. – 03.06.	20.07. – 30.08.	16.10 – 28.10.	21.12. – 02.01.
Hessen	–	10.04. – 20.04.	–	23.06. – 04.08.	02.10. – 14.10.	27.12. – 13.01.
Mecklenburg-Vorp.	07.02. – 19.02.	15.04. – 25.04.	09.06. – 13.06.	20.07. – 30.08.	23.10. – 28.10.	20.12. – 02.01.
Niedersachsen	–	14.04. – 29.04.	02.06. – 13.06.	13.07. – 23.08.	19.10. – 01.11.	22.12. – 06.01.
Nordrhein-Westfalen	–	17.04. – 29.04.	–	29.06. – 12.08.	02.10. – 14.10.	22.12. – 06.01.
Rheinland-Pfalz	–	17.04. – 28.04.	–	23.06. – 04.08.	02.10. – 13.10.	22.12. – 05.01.
Saarland	–	14.04. – 29.04.	–	22.06. – 02.08.	02.10. – 14.10.	23.12. – 06.01.
Sachsen	14.02. – 26.02.	20.04. – 28.04.	10.06. – 13.06.	13.07. – 23.08.	16.10. – 27.10.	22.12. – 02.01.
Sachsen-Anhalt	07.02. – 26.02.	17.04 – 20.04.	02.06. – 10.06.	13.07. – 23.08.	23.10. – 30.10.	27.12. – 02.01.
Schleswig-Holstein	–	08.04. – 25.04.	–	20.07. – 02.09.	23.10. – 04.11.	27.12. – 06.01.
Thüringen	07.02. – 12.02.	17.04. – 29.04.	10.06. – 13.06.	13.07. – 23.08.	16.10. – 21.10.	22.12. – 06.01.

2. **Ferien hier bei uns** Answer a few questions about our vacations here.
   a. Welche Ferien gibt es hier (in den USA, in Kanada . . .)? Wann sind sie gewöhnlich und wie lange dauern sie?
   b. Ist die Ferienzeit überall gleich *(at the same time)*?
   c. Wann beginnen hier die nächsten *(next)* Ferien? Wann enden sie? Was tun Sie dann?

F. Deutsche Länder und Hauptstädte Now that you have checked out the vacations in the various federal states of Germany, take turns asking each other questions about their location and respective capitals.

BEISPIEL S1 Wo liegt Brandenburg?
S2 Brandenburg liegt südlich von Mecklenburg-Vorpommern und östlich von Sachsen-Anhalt.
S1 Und was ist die Hauptstadt von Brandenburg?
S2 Potsdam!

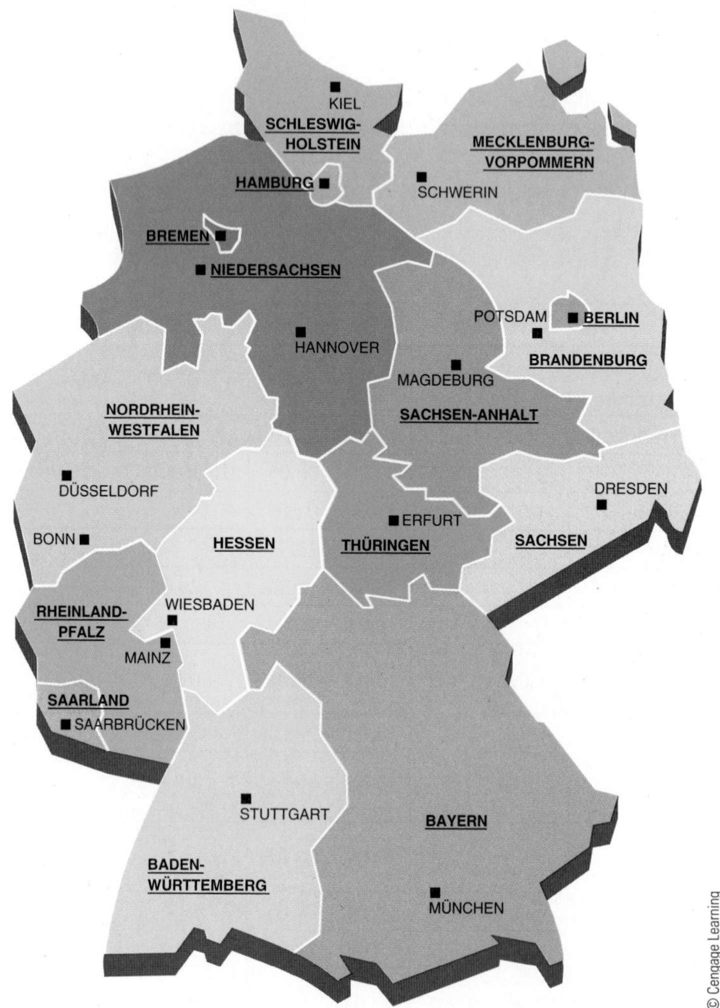

Aussprache: ch, ck

A. Laute

1. [ç] i**ch**, ni**ch**t, fur**ch**tbar, viellei**ch**t, man**ch**mal, spre**ch**en, Re**ch**nung, Mäd**ch**en, Mil**ch**, dur**ch**, gewöhnli**ch**, ri**ch**tig, wi**ch**tig
2. [x] a**ch**, a**ch**t, ma**ch**en, Weihna**ch**ten, au**ch**, brau**ch**en, Wo**ch**e, no**ch**, do**ch**, Bu**ch**, Ku**ch**en, Ba**ch**, Ba**ch**ara**ch**
3. [ks] se**chs**, se**chs**te
4. [k] di**ck**, Zu**ck**er, Bä**ck**er, Ro**ck**, Ja**ck**e, Frühstü**ck**, schme**ck**en

For further review, see the Summary of Pronunciation in the front of this book. Study section II, subsections 13–15.

B. Wortpaare

1. mich / misch	3. nickt / nicht	5. Nacht / nackt
2. Kirche / Kirsche	4. lochen / locken	6. möchte / mochte

Hörverständnis

Die Geburtstagsparty Listen to the conversation between Anke and Paul. Then answer the questions below by jotting down key words.

Zum Erkennen: Gute Idee! *(That's a good idea!)*; es geht sicher *(it's probably all right)*; also *(well)*

1. Wer hat am 10. Oktober Geburtstag? ___Claire___
2. Wer hat am 12. Oktober Geburtstag? ___Peter___
3. Was möchte Paul machen? ___eine Party geben___
4. Was tut Claire samstags bis um drei? ___arbeiten___
5. Wo wollen sie feiern? ___bei Anke___
6. Was bringt Paul? ___CDs___ und ___etwas zu essen___
7. Was bringt Klaus? ___etwas zu trinken___
8. Wer telefoniert mit Peter und Claire? ___Anke___
9. Wann beginnt die Party? ___um 8 Uhr___

You might want to suggest to the students to search YouTube for a variety of different songs Germans sing on the occasion of a birthday, e.g., "**Hoch soll er leben!**" "**Zum Geburtstag viel Glück!**", or "**Alles Gute zum Geburtstag!**"

Fokus Diversity in Religious Traditions

Germany has traditionally been a predominantly Christian society; for this reason, almost all official holidays are of Christian origin. Today, as a result of immigration, new ethnic and religious communities have settled in Germany, each bringing its own traditions with it. These include about 4.3 million Muslims, 1.5 million Eastern Orthodox, 245,000 Buddhists, more than 200,000 people of the Jewish faith, and 97,000 Hindus.

Muslims constitute the largest non-Christian group in Germany today. They have come to Germany from many countries, notably Turkey. The most important date in the Muslim calendar is the three-day celebration of Id al-Fitr **(Fest des Fastenbrechens),** which occurs at the end of the month of Ramadan. The once-thriving Jewish community in Germany celebrates numerous holidays: Passover **(Pessach)** in the spring; Yom Kippur (**Jom Kippur,** the day of atonement) and Rosh Hashanah (**Rosch ha-Schanah,** Jewish New Year), both observed in the fall; and Hanukkah (**Chanukka,** the festival of lights) in December. The German Constitution allows for religious education to be taught in the public schools. Because non-Christian celebrations are not official holidays in Germany, Muslim and Jewish students in public schools can request a day off from school to attend religious celebrations.

On the basis of a long-standing agreement between church and state, a special tax levy of 8–10 percent of an individual's income tax is collected by the state for the "established churches." However, only major Christian denominations and the Jewish faith are recognized as "established churches." Having a choice, some people discontinued their affiliation with a church. In the East, where the communist regime had discouraged church membership, many people never rejoined after reunification. They often continue the East German ritual of a non-religious dedication of young people **(die Jugendweihe)** instead of the traditional religious confirmation ceremony **(die Konfirmation).** The families of these young people are among the 32 percent of Germans who are officially unaffiliated with any church and, thus, are not required to pay the church tax collected from all church members.

Denkmal von Heinz Kudalla in Braunschweig

Struktur

4.1 The present perfect with *haben*

1. The German PRESENT PERFECT corresponds closely in form to the English present perfect. In both languages it consists of an inflected auxiliary verb (or "helping verb") and an unchanging past participle.

*You **have learned** that well.*	Du **hast** das gut **gelernt.**
*She **has brought** the books.*	Sie **hat** die Bücher **gebracht.**
*We **haven't spoken** any English.*	Wir **haben** kein Englisch **gesprochen.**

2. In the use of this tense, however, there is a considerable difference between English and German. In everyday conversation, English makes more use of the simple past, whereas German prefers the present perfect.

Du **hast** das gut **gelernt.**	*You **learned*** that well.
Sie **hat** die Bücher **gebracht.**	*She **brought*** the books.
Wir **haben** kein Englisch **gesprochen.**	*We **didn't speak*** any English.

The German present perfect corresponds to four past-tense forms in English:

Wir haben das gelernt. {
We have learned that.
We learned that.
We did learn that.
We were learning that.
}

3. Most German verbs form the present perfect by using the present tense of **haben** (V1) with the past participle (V2). The past participle is placed at the end of the sentence or clause.

ich	**habe**	. . . gelernt	wir	**haben**	. . . gelernt
du	**hast**	. . . gelernt	ihr	**habt**	. . . gelernt
er/es/sie	**hat**	. . . gelernt	sie/Sie	**haben**	. . . gelernt

4. German has two groups of verbs that form their past participles in different ways:

- *T*-VERBS (also called "WEAK VERBS") with the participle ending in **-t (gelernt).**
- *N*-VERBS (also called "STRONG VERBS") with the participle ending in **-en (gesprochen).**

Any verb not specifically identified as an irregular *t*-verb or as an *n*-verb can be assumed to be a regular *t*-verb.

a. The majority of German verbs are regular *t*-verbs. They form their past participles with the prefix **ge-** and the ending **-t.** They correspond to such English verbs as *learn, learned,* and *ask, asked.*

ge + STEM + **t**   lernen →   ge lern t

Familiar verbs that follow this pattern include: brauchen, danken, dauern, feiern, fragen, glauben, hören, kaufen, machen, sagen, schenken, schmecken, spielen, suchen, tanzen, wohnen, zählen.

Although lists of familiar verbs such as these are not printed in boldface, they are important. Please review these verbs.

- Verbs with stems ending in **-d, -t,** or with certain consonant combinations with **-m** or **-n** insert an **-e-.**

ge + STEM + **et**	kosten →	ge kost et

Other familiar verbs that follow this pattern include: antworten, arbeiten, öffnen, regnen.

- A few *t*-verbs are IRREGULAR (MIXED VERBS), i.e., they usually change their stem. They can be compared to such English verbs as *bring, brought,* and *think, thought.*

ge + STEM *(change)* + **t**	bringen →	ge brach t

Here are the participles of familiar irregular *t*-verbs:

bringen	**gebracht**	haben	**gehabt**
denken	**gedacht**	nennen	**genannt**

b. A smaller but extremely important group of verbs, the N-VERBS, form their past participles with the prefix **ge-** and the ending **-en.** They correspond to such English verbs as *write, written,* and *speak, spoken.* The *n*-verbs frequently have a stem change in the past participle. Their forms are not predictable and therefore must be memorized. Many of them also have a stem change in the second and third person singular of the present tense: **sprechen, du sprichst, er spricht.**

NOTE: Those that do have this change are always *n*-verbs.

ge + STEM *(change)* + **en**	geben → finden →	ge geb en ge fund en

You will need to learn the past participles of these *n*-verbs:

essen	**gegessen**	schlafen	**geschlafen**
finden	**gefunden**	schreiben	**geschrieben**
geben	**gegeben**	sehen	**gesehen**
heißen	**geheißen**	singen	**gesungen**
helfen	**geholfen**	sprechen	**gesprochen**
lesen	**gelesen**	tragen	**getragen**
liegen	**gelegen**	trinken	**getrunken**
nehmen	**genommen**	tun	**getan**
scheinen	**geschienen**		

For a complete alphabetical listing, see Appendix, Section 7.

5. Two groups of verbs have no **ge**-prefix for the past participle.

- Inseparable-prefix verbs

  In English as in German, many verbs have been formed by the use of inseparable prefixes, e.g., *to belong, to impress, to proceed.* In both languages, the stress is on the verb, not on the prefix. The German inseparable prefixes are **be-, emp-, ent-, er-, ge-, ver-,** and **zer-.**

NOTE: These verbs do not have a **ge**-prefix.

bestellen	→	be stell t
verstehen	→	ver stand en

Familiar *t*-verbs that also follow this pattern include: bedeuten, bezahlen, gehören, verkaufen, überraschen, wiederholen.

You will need to learn the past participles of these familiar *n*-verbs:

beginnen	**begonnen**	gefallen	**gefallen**
bekommen	**bekommen**	verstehen	**verstanden**
empfehlen	**empfohlen**		

Other **-ieren** verbs: kombinieren, telefonieren, dekorieren, addieren, multiplizieren, dividieren, reservieren, reparieren, praktizieren, operieren, analysieren, hypnotisieren, etc.

- Verbs ending in **-ieren** (all of which are *t*-verbs):

gratulieren	**gratuliert**
studieren	**studiert**

Übungen

A. Nennen Sie das Partizip!

BEISPIEL fragen *gefragt*

A: 1. gedauert, gefeiert, gedankt, gewohnt, getanzt, geantwortet, bedeutet, gekostet, geöffnet, geregnet, geschmeckt, verkauft, bezahlt, gratuliert, gedacht, gebracht, genannt, studiert

A: 2. gegessen, gefunden, getan, geholfen, gelesen, geheißen, getrunken, geschlafen, geschienen, gesungen, bekommen, empfohlen, begonnen, gefallen, verstanden

1. dauern, feiern, danken, wohnen, tanzen, antworten, bedeuten, kosten, öffnen, regnen, schmecken, verkaufen, bezahlen, gratulieren, denken, bringen, nennen, studieren
2. essen, finden, tun, helfen, lesen, heißen, trinken, schlafen, scheinen, singen, bekommen, empfehlen, beginnen, gefallen, verstehen

B. Ersetzen Sie das Subjekt!

B: 1. habt, hat, habe 2. haben, hast, hat 3. habt, haben, habe 4. habe, hat, hast 5. hast, habt, haben

BEISPIEL Ich habe ein paar Kuchen gekauft. (er)
Er hat ein paar Kuchen gekauft.

1. Du hast Klaus gratuliert. (ihr, man, ich)
2. Ich habe ein Lied gesungen. (wir, du, er)
3. Er hat Klaus eine Geburtstagstorte und eine Flasche Sekt gebracht. (ihr, sie/*pl.*, ich)
4. Ihr habt Kaffee getrunken. (ich, sie/*sg.*, du)
5. Wir haben auf Deutsch gefeiert. (du, ihr, Marko und Silva)

Geburtstagskuchen

C. Was fehlt? Complete the report on a birthday celebration with the appropriate past participles.

Am. 21. Juni hat mein Vater Geburtstag ___gehabt___. Weil Mutter an dem Tag keine Zeit ___gehabt___ hat, haben wir den Geburtstag am 24. Juni mit einer Party ___gefeiert___. Da haben wir ihn echt ___überrascht___, weil er da nicht mehr an seinen Geburtstag ___gedacht___ hat. Alle haben ihm ___gratuliert___ und alles Gute ___gewünscht___. Er hat viele Geschenke ___bekommen___ und man hat ihm auch viele Karten ___geschrieben___. Natürlich hat es Kaffee und Kuchen ___gegeben___ und wir haben auch „Happy birthday!" ___gesungen___. Zum Abendessen hat Mutter einen Tisch in einem Restaurant ___bestellt / reserviert___ und da haben wir alle gut ___gegessen___ und Wein ___getrunken___. Ich habe meine Cousins und Kusinen, Onkel und Tanten schon lange nicht mehr ___gesehen___. Das Wiedersehen hat richtig Spaß ___gemacht___.

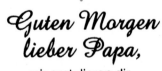

Guten Morgen
lieber Papa,
wir gratulieren dir
ganz herzlich zu deinem
50. Geburtstag
Wir wünschen dir alles Liebe
und Gute, vor allem aber
Gesundheit.
Deine Lieben

D. Fragen zum Geburtstag Ask each other about your last birthday and how you celebrated it, using only verbs that form the present perfect with **haben.** Be creative!

BEISPIEL S1 Was hast du zum Geburtstag bekommen?
S2 Ich habe . . . bekommen. Und du?
S1 . . .
S2 Hast du groß gefeiert?
S1 . . . Und du?
S2 . . .

Fokus Tourist Destinations

While most of Germany's annual celebrations are rooted firmly in its long history, some of the best-known ones play an important role in the nation's tourism industry, which contributes significantly to the German economy.

Each year, millions of visitors flock to Munich's **Oktoberfest,** the world's largest beer festival—which actually starts at the end of September. The Munich Oktoberfest offers visitors the chance to order **eine Maß** (a large glass holding about one liter of beer) and enjoy sausage and sauerkraut, grilled chicken, or fish, while listening to Bavarian music. Some Oktoberfest celebrations take place annually elsewhere in Germany and throughout the German-speaking world (even in the United States!), but on a much smaller scale.

One of the largest annual events in Germany is **Karneval** (as it is known in the North; it is called **Fasching** or **Fastnacht** in the South). The best-known carnival celebrations are in Cologne and Mainz, both of which draw tourists from around the world. Carnival time (celebrated as Mardi Gras by North Americans in New Orleans) takes place the last few weeks before Ash Wednesday, which occurs sometime in February or March, six weeks before Easter. The celebration has its roots in a rite from the pre-Christian era, intended to cast out the demons of winter. In Cologne, carnival time is a holiday. Revelers at carnival often dress up in costumes, engage in merrymaking in the streets, and enjoy the annual parade on **Rosenmontag** (the Monday before Ash Wednesday).

In late summer and early autumn, there are many wine festivals **(Winzerfeste)** in towns along the Rhine, Main, and Moselle rivers—areas where wine production plays an important economic role.

Karneval in Köln

If students ask: **Eine Maß** weighs more than 4.4 lbs. The **Bedienung** normally carries 8 such large glasses at a time, sometimes even 12 to a thirsty table. The beer comes from Munich's breweries and is brewed specially for the 16-day event.

4.2 The present perfect with *sein*

Whereas most German verbs use **haben** as the auxiliary in the perfect tenses, a few common verbs use **sein.** You will probably find it easiest to memorize **sein** together with the past participles of those verbs requiring it. However, you can also determine which verbs take **sein** by remembering that they must fulfill two conditions:

- They are INTRANSITIVE, i.e., they cannot take an accusative (direct) object. Examples of such verbs are: **gehen, kommen,** and **laufen.**
- They express a CHANGE OF PLACE OR CONDITION.

Wir **sind** nach Hause **gegangen.**
We went home.

Er **ist** müde **geworden.**
He got tired.

Note that **sein** and **bleiben** are exceptions to this rule: Ich **bin** zu Hause **geblieben.** *(I stayed home.)*; Er **ist** müde **gewesen.** *(He was tired.)*

CAUTION: A change in prefix or the addition of a prefix may cause a change in auxiliary because the meaning of the verb changes.

Ich **bin** nach Hause **gekommen.** *I came home.*
Ich **habe** ein Geschenk **bekommen.** *I received a present.*

The present perfect of the following *n*-verbs is formed with the present tense of **sein** (V1) and the past participle (V2).

sein	**ist gewesen**	kommen	**ist gekommen**
bleiben	**ist geblieben**	laufen	**ist gelaufen**
fahren	**ist gefahren**	werden	**ist geworden**
gehen	**ist gegangen**		

ich **bin**	. . . gekommen	wir **sind**	. . . gekommen
du **bist**	. . . gekommen	ihr **seid**	. . . gekommen
er **ist**	. . . gekommen	sie **sind**	. . . gekommen

Occasionally, **fahren** takes an object. In that case, the auxiliary **haben** is used:

Sie **sind** nach Hause **gefahren.** — *They drove home.*
Sie **haben** mein Auto nach Hause **gefahren.** — *They drove my car home.*

Übungen

E: hat gegessen, hat gebracht, ist geworden, ist gewesen, hat gefallen, ist geblieben, hat gelegen, hat gesprochen, ist gelaufen, hat geholfen

E. *Sein* oder *haben:* Nennen Sie das Partizip und das Hilfsverb *(auxiliary)*!

BEISPIEL empfehlen *hat empfohlen*
gehen *ist gegangen*

essen, bringen, werden, sein, gefallen, bleiben, liegen, sprechen, laufen, helfen

F. Hoppla, hier fehlt was! Wie ist das gewesen? Yesterday's party went very late, and you don't remember all the details. With a partner, piece together the picture. One of you looks at and completes the chart below, the other works with the chart in Section 11 of the Appendix.

BEISPIEL S1 Was hat Kai gemacht?
S2 Kai hat mit dem Essen geholfen und etwas getanzt. Und Eva?
S1 Eva hat . . .

S1:

	KAI	EVA	MAX	SVEN	ICH	PARTNER/IN
an alles denken		x				
mit dem Essen helfen	x					x
Getränke bringen			x		x	
den Sekt öffnen		x				
viel essen			x		x	
viel trinken			x			
schön singen				x		
etwas tanzen	x					x
mit allen sprechen						x
nichts tun				x		
nicht lange bleiben				x	x	

G. Ferien

G.1: bin . . . gefahren, habe . . . genommen . . . gewohnt, hat . . . gelegen, hat . . . gefallen, bin . . . gelaufen, sind . . . gegangen, hat . . . gehört, hat . . . geholfen, hat . . . empfohlen, hat . . . geschmeckt, habe . . . bekommen, hat . . . gebracht, hat . . . geregnet, haben . . . gelesen . . . gehört, ist . . . gewesen . . . sind geworden

1. **Michaels Sommerferien** Michael is explaining what he did during his last summer vacation. Use the present perfect. In each case, decide whether to use the auxiliary **haben** or **sein.**

   BEISPIEL Im August habe ich Ferien.
   Im August habe ich Ferien gehabt.

   In den Ferien **fahre** ich nach Zell in Österreich. Ich **nehme** zwei Wochen frei und **wohne** bei Familie Huber. Das Haus **liegt** direkt am See. Zell **gefällt** mir gut. Nachmittags **laufe** ich gewöhnlich in die Stadt. Manchmal **gehen** Renate und ich auch in ein Café. Das Café **gehört** der Familie. Mittwochs **hilft** Renate da. Sie **empfiehlt** mir die Kuchen. Der Apfelstrudel **schmeckt** besonders gut. Ich **bekomme** alles umsonst *(for free)*. Renate **bringt** auch oft Kuchen nach Hause. Leider *(unfortunately)* **regnet** es viel. Wir **lesen** viel und **hören** Musik. Renate **ist** dann in den Winterferien bei uns und wir **werden** gute Freunde.

2. **Meine Ferien** Tell your partner what you did during your last vacation, using the present perfect with **haben** or **sein.**

   BEISPIEL *Ich bin nach Miami geflogen und habe da bei Freunden gewohnt.*

4.3 Subordinating conjunctions

You already know how to join sentences with a coordinating conjunction **(aber, denn, oder, und).** Clauses can also be joined with SUBORDINATING CONJUNCTIONS. Subordinating conjunctions introduce a subordinate or dependent clause, i.e., a statement with a subject and a verb that cannot stand alone as a complete sentence.

because *it's his birthday*

that *they have left already*

Coordinating conjunctions do not affect word order, but subordinating conjunctions do. German subordinate clauses are always set off by a comma, and the inflected verb (V1) stands at the very end.

1. Six common subordinating conjunctions are

bevor	*before*
dass	*that*
ob	*if, whether*
obwohl	*although*
weil	*because*
wenn	*if; when(ever)*

When it is possible to replace *if* with *whether*, use **ob**; otherwise use **wenn.**

In case students ask, both **denn** and **weil** mean *because*. Whereas **denn** (Ch. 1) is a coordinating conjunction and has no effect on word order, **weil** is a subordinating conjunction that influences the position of the main verb. **Denn** cannot begin a sentence, but **weil** can.

Ich kaufe ein Geschenk.
Ich frage Helga, **bevor** ich ein Geschenk **kaufe.**
I'll ask Helga before I buy a present.

Klaus hat Geburtstag.

Sie sagt, **dass** Klaus morgen Geburtstag **hat.**

She says that Klaus has his birthday tomorrow.

Ist sie sicher?

Ich frage, **ob** sie sicher **ist.**

I'll ask whether she is sure.

Sie hat nicht viel Zeit.

Sie kommt zur Party, **obwohl** sie nicht viel Zeit **hat.**

She's coming to the party although she doesn't have much time.

Er trinkt gern Sekt.

Wir bringen eine Flasche Sekt, **weil** er gern Sekt **trinkt.**

We are bringing a bottle of champagne because he likes to drink champagne.

Ich habe Zeit.

Ich komme auch, **wenn** ich Zeit **habe.**

I'll come, too, if I have time.

NOTE: The subject of the dependent clause almost always follows the subordinating conjunction. When a sentence with inverted word order becomes a dependent clause, the subject moves to the position immediately after the conjunction.

Morgen hat **Klaus** Geburtstag.

Ich glaube, dass **Klaus morgen** Geburtstag hat.

2. Information questions can become subordinate clauses by using the question word (**wer? was? wie? wo?** etc.) as a conjunction and putting the verb last.

Wie schmeckt der Sekt?

Sie fragt, **wie** der Sekt **schmeckt.**

She asks how the champagne tastes.

Wo sind die Brötchen?

Sie fragt, **wo** die Brötchen **sind.**

She asks where the rolls are.

Note the similarity with English:

Where are the rolls?

*She asks **where** the rolls **are.***

3. Yes/No questions require **ob** as a conjunction.

Schmeckt der Sekt gut?

Sie fragt, **ob** der Sekt gut **schmeckt.**

She asks whether the champagne tastes good.

Sind die Würstchen heiß?

Sie fragt, **ob** die Würstchen heiß **sind.**

She asks whether the franks are hot.

Lerntipp

Having the Last Word

When listening or reading, pay special attention to the end of the sentence, which often contains crucial sentence elements. As Mark Twain wrote in *A Connecticut Yankee in King Arthur's Court:* "Whenever the literary German dives into a sentence, that is the last we are going to see of him till he emerges on the other side of the Atlantic with his verb in his mouth."

4. Subordinate clauses as the first sentence element

If the subordinate clause precedes the main clause, the inflected verb of the main clause—the second sentence element—comes right after the comma. In that case, the entire subordinate clause is the first sentence element.

1 2
Ich **komme,** wenn ich Zeit habe.
Wenn ich Zeit habe, **komme** ich.

5. The present perfect in subordinate clauses

In subordinate clauses in the present perfect, the inflected verb **haben** or **sein** (V1) stands at the end of the sentence.

Er hat eine Geburtstagskarte bekommen.
Er sagt, **dass** er eine Geburtstagskarte bekommen **hat.**

Er ist überrascht gewesen.
Er sagt, **dass** er überrascht gewesen **ist.**

Übungen

H. Verbinden Sie die Sätze!

BEISPIEL Eva ist zur Drogerie gegangen. Sie braucht noch etwas Shampoo. *(because)*
Eva ist zur Drogerie gegangen, weil sie noch etwas Shampoo braucht.

1. Der Verkäufer hat Eva gefragt. Kommt sie aus den USA? *(whether)*
2. Sie hat ihm geantwortet. Sie ist aus Sarasota. *(that)*
3. Florida gefällt den Deutschen. Es ist da im Winter schön warm. *(because)*
4. Sie spielen gern Tennis. Sie sind nicht am Strand *(at the beach). (when)*
5. Sie schlafen viel oder lesen Bücher. Es regnet. *(if)*
6. Sie kaufen gern Kleidung. Sie fliegen *(fly)* wieder nach Hause. *(before)*
7. Sie kaufen besonders gern Jeans. Es gibt auch zu Hause Jeans. *(although)*
8. Sie sagen, die Jeans in den USA sind nicht so teuer. *(that)*

H.1: Though the word **Amerika** *(sg., n.)* is commonly used for the United States of America, especially among Germans, the politically more correct version is **die Vereinigten Staaten / USA** *(pl).*

H: 1. ob sie aus den USA kommt 2. dass sie aus Sarasota ist 3. weil es da im Winter schön warm ist 4. wenn sie nicht am Strand sind 5. wenn es regnet 6. bevor sie wieder nach Hause fliegen 7. obwohl es auch zu Hause Jeans gibt 8. dass die Jeans in den USA nicht so teuer sind

I. Beginnen Sie mit dem Nebensatz *(subordinate clause)*!

BEISPIEL Ich trinke Wasser, wenn ich Durst habe.
Wenn ich Durst habe, trinke ich Wasser.

1. Ich habe gerade eine Currywurst bestellt, weil ich Hunger habe.
2. Ich verstehe nicht, warum es zum Essen so viele Pommes frites gibt.
3. Ich habe alles gegessen, obwohl das viel zu viel gewesen ist.
4. Ich weiß nicht, ob ich noch einmal zu der Imbissbude gehe.
5. Man wird müde, wenn man so viel isst.

I: 1. Weil ich Hunger habe, habe ich . . . 2. Warum es zum Essen so viele Pommes frites gibt, verstehe ich . . . 3. Obwohl das viel zu viel gewesen ist, habe ich . . . 4. Ob ich noch einmal zu der Imbissbude gehe, weiß ich . . . 5. Wenn man so viel isst, wird man . . .

J. Sagen Sie die Sätze noch einmal mit den Konjunktionen!

1. **Er sagt, dass . . .** A friend has just come back from Luxembourg. Tell the class what he has observed. Follow the model.

   BEISPIEL Luxemburg ist wirklich schön.
   Er sagt, dass Luxemburg wirklich schön ist.

   a. Die Luxemburger sprechen Französisch, Deutsch und Letzeburgisch.
   b. Er hat den Geburtstag auf einer Burg *(in a castle)* gefeiert.
   c. Das ist einfach toll gewesen.
   d. In Luxemburg gibt es viele Banken.
   e. Den Leuten geht es wirklich sehr gut.
   f. Überall sieht man BMWs.

2. **Sie fragt, . . .** Your mother wants to know about Carla's graduation party. Follow the model.

   BEISPIEL Wer ist Carla?
   Sie fragt, wer Carla ist.

   a. Wo wohnt Carla? b. Wie viele Leute sind da gewesen? c. Wie lange hat die Party gedauert? d. Was habt ihr gegessen und getrunken? e. Mit wem hast du getanzt? f. Wie bist du nach Hause gekommen?

3. **Sie fragt, ob . . .** Your parents are celebrating their 30th anniversary, and your sister is in charge of the party. Now she asks whether you and your brothers have completed the tasks she assigned a week ago.

   BEISPIEL Hast du Servietten gekauft?
   Sie fragt, ob du Servietten gekauft hast.

   a. Seid ihr gestern einkaufen gegangen? b. Hat Alfred Sekt gekauft? c. Haben wir jetzt alle Geschenke? d. Habt ihr den Kuchen beim Bäcker *(baker)* bestellt? e. Hat Peter mit den Nachbarn gesprochen? f. Hat Alfred die Kamera gefunden?

J.1: Er sagt, . . . a. dass die Luxemburger Französisch . . . sprechen b. dass er den Geburtstag auf einer Burg gefeiert hat c. dass das einfach toll gewesen ist d. dass es in Luxemburg viele Banken gibt e. dass es den Leuten wirklich sehr gut geht f. dass man überall BMWs sieht

J.2: Sie fragt, . . . a. wo Carla wohnt b. wie viele Leute da gewesen sind c. wie lange die Party gedauert hat d. was ihr (wir) gegessen und getrunken habt (haben) e. mit wem du (ich) getanzt hast (habe) f. wie du (ich) nach Hause gekommen bist (bin)

J.3: Sie fragt, . . . a. ob ihr gestern einkaufen gegangen seid b. ob Alfred Sekt gekauft hat c. ob wir jetzt alle Geschenke haben d. ob ihr (wir) den Kuchen beim Bäcker bestellt habt (haben) e. ob Peter mit den Nachbarn gesprochen hat f. ob Alfred die Kamera gefunden hat

K. Interview Find out the following information from a classmate and then tell the class what he/she said.

1. wann er/sie gestern ins Bett *(to bed)* gegangen ist
2. ob er/sie gut geschlafen hat und wie lange
3. was er/sie heute zum Frühstück gegessen und getrunken hat
4. wie er/sie zur Uni(versität) gekommen ist, ob er/sie gelaufen oder gefahren ist
5. wie viele Kurse er/sie heute schon gehabt hat und welche

K: To help students go through several items of this interview, demonstrate how they must transform the indirect questions into direct ones.

Zusammenfassung

L. Rückblick auf die Gespräche Together with your partner, pick one dialogue from the *Schritte* or *Kapitel* you have read so far and report what people talked about.

KAPITEL 1: *Sharon hat Roberto gefragt, woher er kommt. Er hat gesagt, dass er aus Rom kommt und dass er eine Schwester in Montreal hat. Dann hat Roberto Sharon gefragt, wann die Prüfung ist. Sie hat gesagt, dass sie in zehn Minuten ist und sie hat Roberto viel Glück gewünscht.*

iLrn

Visit the ***Wie geht's?*** iLrn website for more review and practice of the grammar points you have just learned.

L: You might assign different chapters for each of the partners.

Fokus Traditional Folk Celebrations

Germans don't have a Thanksgiving holiday with traditional foods such as cranberry sauce and pumpkin pie. Instead, churches and rural communities celebrate Harvest Thanksgiving **(Erntedankfest)** with special services and harvest wreaths.

Some towns attract visitors by recreating historical events in their carefully preserved surroundings. The **Meistertrunk** in Rothenburg ob der Tauber recalls an event from the Thirty Years' War (1618–1648). Landshut recruits many of its residents in the reenactment of the 1475 wedding of the son of Duke Ludwig to a Polish princess **(die Fürstenhochzeit).** The "Rattenfänger von Hameln" *("The Pied Piper of Hamelin")* commemorates the Children's Crusade of 1284, when 130 of the town's children mysteriously vanished.

While no longer everyday attire, traditional folk costumes **(Trachten)** are still worn in rural areas of Germany, Switzerland, and Austria for church holidays, weddings, and other special occasions. Special clubs **(Trachtenvereine)** endeavor to keep the tradition alive.

M: 1. habe . . . studiert, (habe) . . . gewohnt 2. sind . . . gewesen 3. haben . . . geholfen 4. haben . . . gegessen, sind . . . gegangen 5. haben gesprochen, habe . . . gelernt 6. sind gelaufen, haben . . . gegessen 7. hat . . . gefallen

M. Vor einem Jahr Susan reads what she wrote a year ago. Using the present perfect, how would she tell about it today?

1. Ich studiere in Regensburg und wohne in einem Studentenheim.
2. Ursula und Florian sind besonders nett *(nice)*.
3. Sie helfen mir viel.
4. Morgens essen wir gewöhnlich zusammen Frühstück und nachmittags gehen wir oft in die Stadt.
5. Wir sprechen nur Deutsch und ich lerne viel von ihnen.
6. Wir laufen gern durch die Fußgängerzone und essen manchmal Fischbrötchen bei Nordsee.
7. Es gefällt mir da wirklich gut.

N. Das habe ich gestern gemacht. Schreiben Sie 8–10 Sätze im Perfekt!

BEISPIEL *Ich habe bis 10 Uhr geschlafen. Dann . . .*

O. Die Abschlussparty

1. **Wir planen eine Abschlussparty.** With one or several partners, work out a plan for your cousin's graduation party. Be prepared to outline your ideas.

   Sagen Sie, . . . !

   a. wann und wo die Party ist
   b. wie lange sie dauert
   c. wer kommt
   d. was Sie trinken und essen
   e. was Sie noch brauchen

2. **Wie ist die Party gewesen?** Describe what happened at the party.

P. Die Geburtstagsfeier: Auf Deutsch bitte!

1. The day before yesterday I gave a birthday party.
2. Did Volker and Bettina come?
3. Yes, they came, too.
4. My friends brought presents.
5. My father opened some bottles of wine.
6. How long did you *(pl. fam.)* celebrate?
7. Until three o'clock. We danced, ate well, and drank a lot of Coke.
8. The neighbors said that the music was too loud **(laut).**
9. Did you *(sg. fam.)* hear the music?
10. Yesterday a neighbor came and spoke with my parents.
11. I liked the party.

P: 1. Vorgestern habe ich eine Geburtstagsparty/-feier gegeben. 2. Sind Volker und Bettina gekommen? 3. Ja, sie sind auch gekommen. 4. Meine Freunde haben Geschenke gebracht. 5. Mein Vater hat ein paar Flaschen Wein geöffnet. 6. Wie lange habt ihr gefeiert? 7. Bis um drei. Wir haben getanzt, gut gegessen und viel Cola getrunken. 8. Die Nachbarn haben gesagt, dass die Musik zu laut gewesen ist. 9. Hast du die Musik gehört? 10. Gestern ist ein Nachbar/eine Nachbarin gekommen und hat mit meinen Eltern gesprochen. 11. Die Party / Feier hat mir gefallen.

Du bist super!
Du bist toll!
Du bist einfach wundervoll!
Alles Gute zum Geburtstag!

Einblicke

Bericht *(Report)*

Wortschatz 2

das Lied, -er	*song*
die Kerze, -n	*candle*
dort	*(over) there*
eigentlich	*actual(ly)*
immer	*always*
laut	*loud, noisy*
lustig	*funny, amusing*
(noch) nie	*never (before)*
verrückt	*crazy*
fallen (fällt), ist gefallen	*to fall*
studieren	*to study a particular field, be a student at a university*
Glück / Pech haben	*to be lucky / unlucky.*
Glück / Pech gehabt!	*I was (you were, she was, etc.) lucky / unlucky.*
Spaß machen	*to be fun*
Das macht (mir) Spaß.	*That's fun.*

Ich studiere *(I am a student)* in Heidelberg. **Ich studiere** Kunst (i.e., *art is my major).* BUT **Ich lerne** Deutsch (i.e., *I'm taking German).* **Ich lerne** die Vokabeln (i.e., *I'm learning / studying the vocabulary, possibly for a test).*

Learn this as an idiom: **Lesen macht Spaß.** *(Reading is fun.)* **Das macht mir/ihm/uns/ ihnen Spaß.** *(I/he/ we/they love [to do] it.)*; **Macht es dir Spaß?** *(Do you enjoy [doing] it?)*

Vor dem Lesen

A. Fragen

1. Was für Feste feiert man in . . . (z. B. den USA, Kanada)? 2. Gibt es hier historische Feste? Wenn ja, welche? 3. Wann oder wo gibt es hier Karussells, Buden *(booths)*, Spaß für alle? 4. Gehen Sie gern zu Veranstaltungen *(events)*, wo es viele Leute gibt? Warum (nicht)?

Weihnachtsmarkt in Dresden mit Karussell und Buden

B. Wohin gehen wir? There are all sorts of musical entertainment during the Christmas season. Look at the Leipzig calendar of events and then discuss with your partner what performances might interest you and why. Compare the program with what is typically offered in your home town or on campus during that time.

BEISPIEL S1 Wohin möchtest du gehen, in die Leipziger Oper oder ins Gewandhaus?

S2 Ich möchte . . . sehen. / Ich möchte keine Oper sehen, aber ich gehe gern in ein(e/en) . . .

Spielpläne

Oper Leipzig

29. 11.	19.30 Uhr	**Les Contes d'Hoffmann**
30. 11.	10.30 Uhr	**Salome**
1. 12.	19.00 Uhr	**Bruckner 8** *(Ballet)*
2. 12.	18.00 Uhr	**Tannhäuser**
5. 12.	19.30 Uhr	**Hänsel und Gretel**
6. 12.	19.30 Uhr	**Bruckner 8** *(Ballet)*
7. 12.	19.30 Uhr	**Hänsel und Gretel**
8. 12.	19.00 Uhr	**Bruckner 8** *(Ballet)*
9. 12.	18.00 Uhr	**Salome**
12. 12.	19.30 Uhr	**Bruckner 8** *(Ballet)*
13. 12.	19.30 Uhr	**Rigoletto**
14. 12.	19.30 Uhr	**Salome**
15. 12.	19.00 Uhr	**Carmen**
16. 12.	11.00 Uhr	**Hänsel und Gretel**
	17.00 Uhr	**Hänsel und Gretel**
20. 12.	19.30 Uhr	**Schwanensee** *(Ballet)*
21. 12.	19.30 Uhr	**Hänsel und Gretel**
22. 12.	17.00 Uhr	**Hänsel und Gretel**
23. 12.	18.00 Uhr	**Schwanensee** *(Ballet)*

Neues Gewandhaus

1. 12.	16.00 Uhr	**Salonorchester CAPPUCCINO** Vorweihnachtliche Impressionen
	17.00 Uhr	**Orgelstunde zum 1. Advent**
2. 12.	11.00 Uhr	**Salonorchester CAPPUCCINO** Vorweihnachtliche Impressionen
	20.00 Uhr	**Großes Konzert für UNICEF**
3. 12.	16.00 Uhr	**Adventskonzert**
6./7./8. 12.	19.30 Uhr	**Großes Konzert**
	19.00 Uhr	G. F. Händel: Messias (Teil I – III)
8. 12.	16.00 Uhr	**Orgelstunde zum 2. Advent**
9. 12.	18.00 Uhr	**Kammermusik**
10. 12.	16.00 Uhr	**Adventskonzert**
12. 12.	20.00 Uhr	**Konzert für den American Football Club „Leipzig Lions"** J. S. Bach: Weihnachtsoratorium (I–III)
15. 12.	16.00 Uhr	**Familienkonzert: Hänsel und Gretel**
16. 12.	18.00 Uhr	**Kammermusik**
17. 12.	16.00 Uhr	**Adventskonzert**
20./21. 12.	20.00 Uhr	**Musik aus Hollywood-Filmen**

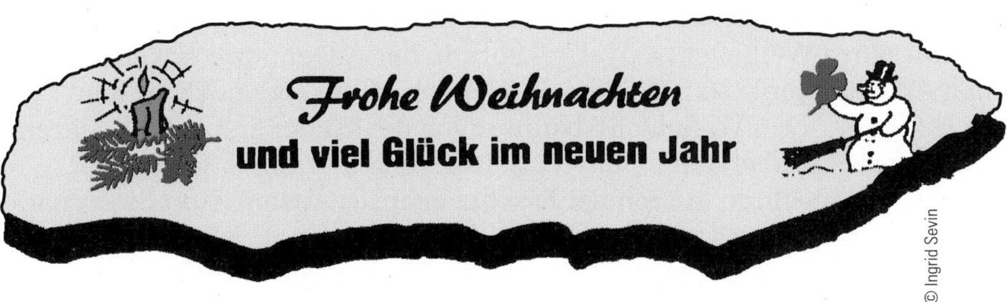

Frohe Weihnachten
und viel Glück im neuen Jahr

C. Das ist leicht zu verstehen! Read aloud the following words paying special attention to their stressed syllable. Then guess their meaning in English.

der Engel, Prinz, Studentenball, Vampir, Walzer; das Kostüm, Musikinstrument; die Adventszeit, Kontaktlinse, Konversationsstunde, Prinzessin, Partyzone, Tradition, Weihnachtsdekoration; ins Bett fallen; enorm viel, gigantisch, historisch, rund, wunderschön

Lesetipp

Understanding a Text Through Images

In this text, Susan talks about her exchange year in Germany. She uses pictures to illustrate her presentation. Use the pictures to better understand the text. What do the images tell you about the different events Susan describes?

Da macht das Feiern Spaß!

(Susan berichtet° für die Konversationsstunde.)

Wie ihr gehört habt, habe ich gerade ein Jahr in Deutschland studiert. Ich habe viel gesehen und gelernt. Heute habe ich ein paar Bilder mitgebracht° . . .

Im September bin ich mit Freunden beim Winzerfest°in Bacharach am Rhein gewesen. Da hat man viel Wein getrunken und gesungen. Ich habe immer gedacht, dass die Deutschen etwas steif° sind. Aber nicht, wenn sie feiern! So lustig und verrückt habe ich sie noch nie gesehen. Zwei Wochen später sind wir zum Oktoberfest nach München gefahren. Im Bierzelt° haben wir Brezeln gegessen und natürlich auch ein Bier getrunken. Die Musik ist sehr laut gewesen. Was mir aber besonders gefallen hat, war° der Trachtenzug° zur Wies'n°.

Im Oktoberfestzelt

Im Februar gibt's den Fasching. Das ist so etwas wie° Mardi Gras in New Orleans, mit Umzügen° und Kostümen. Ich bin als° Vampir zu einem Studentenball gegangen. Wir haben lange getanzt und morgens bin ich dann todmüde° ins Bett gefallen. Halloween kommt in Deutschland auch immer mehr in Mode°, jedenfalls° in den Geschäften. Das finde ich lustig.

Außer diesen° Festen gibt's natürlich noch viele Feiertage. Weihnachten war besonders schön. Auf dem Christkindlmarkt in Nürnberg gibt es viele Buden mit Weihnachtsdekorationen, Kerzen, Lebkuchen° und Glühwein°. Ich habe mir einen Weihnachtsengel gekauft. In der Adventszeit haben viele nur einen Adventskranz° und Weihnachtsdekorationen, aber noch keinen° Weihnachtsbaum°. Den Weihnachtsbaum sehen die Kinder erst am 24. Dezember, am Heiligabend, aber dann bleibt er gewöhnlich bis zum 6. Januar im Zimmer. Zu Weihnachten bin ich bei Familie Fuchs gewesen. Zum Essen hat es Gans° mit Rotkraut° und Knödeln gegeben. Die Plätzchen von Frau Fuchs haben mir besonders gut geschmeckt. Am 25. und 26. Dezember sind alle Geschäfte zu gewesen. Das finde ich eigentlich ganz gut°, weil die Menschen dann mehr Zeit für ihre Familie und für Freunde haben.

Silvester habe ich mit Freunden in Wien gefeiert. Da ist die ganze° Altstadt eine gigantische Partyzone. Um Mitternacht° haben die Glocken geläutet° und die Leute haben Walzer getanzt. So etwas habe ich noch nie gesehen! Mit Sekt, „Prost Neujahr!"° und einem Feuerwerk° haben wir dann das neue Jahr begonnen.

Das Bild hier ist von der Landshuter Hochzeit°. Dort bin ich im Juni gewesen. Die rund 2 300 Teilnehmer° sind alles Landshuter Bürger°. Sie tragen historische Kleidung und alles ist dann wie im Mittelalter°: die Ritter°, Prinzen und Prinzessinnen, die Musikinstrumente und Turniere°. Übrigens° habe ich Glück gehabt, weil man das Fest nur alle° vier Jahre feiert.

Ich habe immer gedacht, dass die Deutschen viel arbeiten. Das tun sie, aber sie haben auch enorm viele Feiertage. Da macht das Feiern Spaß!

reports
brought along
vintage festival
stiff
. . . tent
was / parade in traditional garb / festival grounds
like
parades / as
dead-tired
into vogue / at least
these
gingerbread / mulled wine
Advent wreath / still no
. . . tree
goose / red cabbage
pretty good
entire
at midnight / rang
Happy New Year! / fireworks
wedding
participants / citizens
the Middle Ages / knights
tournaments / by the way
every

Auf der Landshuter Hochzeit

Nach dem Lesen

A. Alles verstanden?

1. Wo ist Susan zum Winzerfest gewesen und was hat man da gemacht?
2. Was hat Susan beim Oktoberfest besonders gefallen und was nicht?
3. Wo ist sie zum Fasching gewesen und als was?
4. Was gibt es auf den Christkindlmärkten? Was hat Susan da gekauft?
5. Wie lange haben die Deutschen gewöhnlich ihren Weihnachtsbaum?
6. Warum sind am 26. Dezember die Geschäfte zu?
7. Was hat Susan zu Silvester in Wien so gut gefallen?
8. Was ist so besonders bei der Landshuter Hochzeit?

A: 1. in Bacharach am Rhein, Wein getrunken und viel gesungen 2. der Trachtenumzug, zu laut 3. auf einem Studentenball, als Vampir 4. Buden, Weihnachtsdekorationen, Kerzen, Lebkuchen, Glühwein 5. vom 24. 12.–6.1. 6. ein Feiertag für Familie und Freunde 7. eine gigantische Partyzone, Glockenläuten, Walzer, Sekt, Feuerwerk 8. Alles ist dann wie im Mittelalter.

B. Feiern in Deutschland

Complete these sentences with the appropriate verb in the present perfect. Use each verb only once.

bringen	feiern	haben	studieren
essen	gefallen	kaufen	tanzen
fahren	gehen	sein	

Susan ___hat___ ein Jahr in Deutschland ___studiert___. Es ___ist___ wunderschön ___gewesen___. Sie ___hat___ ein paar Bilder zur Deutschstunde ___gebracht___. Im September ___ist___ sie mit Freunden zum Winzerfest nach Bacharach am Rhein ___gefahren___. Zum Fasching ___ist___ sie als Vampir zu einem Studentenball ___gegangen___. Die Weihnachtszeit ___hat___ Susan besonders gut ___gefallen___. In Nürnberg ___hat___ sie einen Weihnachtsengel ___gekauft___. Am Heiligabend ___hat___ sie bei Familie Fuchs Gans, Rotkraut und Knödel ___gegessen___. Silvester ___hat___ sie in Wien ___gefeiert___, wo die Leute in der Fußgängerzone Walzer ___getanzt___ ___haben___. Mit der Landshuter Hochzeit ___hat___ sie Glück ___gehabt___, weil man das Fest nur alle vier Jahre feiert.

Optional practice: **Nennen Sie das Partizip!** z. B. geben: hat gegeben (hören, werden, sehen, lernen, sprechen, trinken, singen, denken, Spaß machen, essen, heißen, fallen, bleiben, dekorieren, haben, finden, schmecken, beginnen, liegen, tragen, arbeiten)

Weiteres

If students ask: **der Schlips, -e** *tie;* **Gürtel, -** *belt;* **Schlafanzug, ¨-e** *pajamas;* **das Nachthemd, -en** *nightgown;* **Parfüm, -e** *perfume;* **die Rose, -n; Kassette, -n; CD, -s; DVD, -s**

C. Interview: Fragen Sie einen Nachbarn / eine Nachbarin, . . . ! Ask your classmate about the following holidays.

1. was er/sie gewöhnlich zum Vatertag, zum Muttertag und zum Valentinstag, zu Weihnachten (Chanukka ...) macht
2. was für Geschenke er/sie gern bekommt und was er/sie gern der Familie schenkt
3. zu welchem Fest oder Feiertag er/sie gern einmal in Deutschland oder in . . . sein möchte und warum
4. wie und wo er/sie das letzte *(last)* Silvester gefeiert hat

D. Kurzgespräche With a partner, prepare a brief dialogue using one of the situations. Then role-play your dialogue to the class.

1. **Krankenbesuch *(Call on someone who is ill)***

   One of your very best friends has been quite sick. You stop by to visit. Your friend expresses his/her surprise. You have also brought a little present (e.g., a book, flowers, cookies). Your friend is very pleased and thanks you. You respond appropriately and wish him/her a speedy recovery.

2. **Ich komme!**

   Your mom calls you and asks whether you have plans for the weekend. She is driving through the town where you are studying and would like to see you **(dich).** You are surprised and pleased. It is your mother's birthday, and you wish her a happy birthday. Tell her you have bought a present and that she will get it when she comes. You conclude the conversation.

Schreibtipp

Writing a Postcard

Greetings to friends and relatives usually start with *Dear . . .* **(Liebe Eva / Lieber Axel)** or *Hi . . .* **(Hallo Luca),** and mostly end with *Greetings, your . . .* **(Viele [liebe] Grüße, Dein(e)/ Euer(e) . . .).**

Other informal good-byes are *Bye.!!!* **(Tschüss!),** *See you then!* **(Bis dann!),** or *See you soon!* **(Bis bald!).**

In addressing the postcard, you may use the person's name alone, or else precede it with **Herrn** or **Frau.** A card might also be addressed **An Familie [Norbert Fuchs].** Note the last line of the address shows the country code + postal code + the name of the city. Common country codes are **D** for Germany **(Deutschland), A** for Austria **(Österreich),** and **CH** for Switzerland **(Confoederatio Helvetica = Schweiz).**

E. Eine Postkarte: Gruß aus München Read the following postcard written to a friend you know in Germany, Austria, or Switzerland. Your friend mentions some of the experiences with holiday celebrations described in the text. Using her postcard as a model, write your own postcard.

Lieber Axel,
meine Freunde und ich sind gerade in München und haben viel Spaß. Die Stadt ist echt interessant, das Wetter ist prima und die Leute sind nett. Gestern sind wir beim Oktoberfest gewesen. Verrückt! So viel Bier und Brezeln habe ich schon lange nicht mehr gesehen. Der Trachtenzug zur Wies'n hat mir besonders gefallen. Wenn ihr Deutschen feiert, feiert ihr richtig. Habe viele Fotos gemacht.
Viele Grüße,
Deine Michelle

Herrn
Axel Fitzke
Am Neuen Teiche 37
D–31139 Hildesheim

Printed in Germany

51-H3275

Hörverständnis

Das Straßenfest Listen to what Bibi tells Matthias about their local street fair. Then select the correct response from those given below.

Zum Erkennen: Was gibt's? *(What's up?)*; niemand *(nobody)*; der Krimskrams *(this and that)*; das Spiel, -e *(game)*; Jung und Alt *(all ages, young and old)*

1. Matthias ist bei Bibi gewesen, aber niemand hat __c__ geöffnet.
   a. das Fenster
   b. die Garage
   c. die Tür
2. Bei Bibi hat es am __b__ ein Straßenfest gegeben.
   a. Freitag
   b. Samstag
   c. Sonntag
3. Bibi findet das eigentlich __b__ sehr schön.
   a. nie
   b. immer
   c. noch
4. Bibi hat mit __b__ beim Straßenfest geholfen.
   a. Matthias
   b. den Eltern
   c. dem Bruder
5. Der Vater hat __c__.
   a. Würstchen verkauft
   b. mit den Kindern gespielt
   c. mit den Tischen und Stühlen geholfen
6. Abends haben die Leute __b__.
   a. Pech gehabt
   b. getanzt
   c. geschlafen

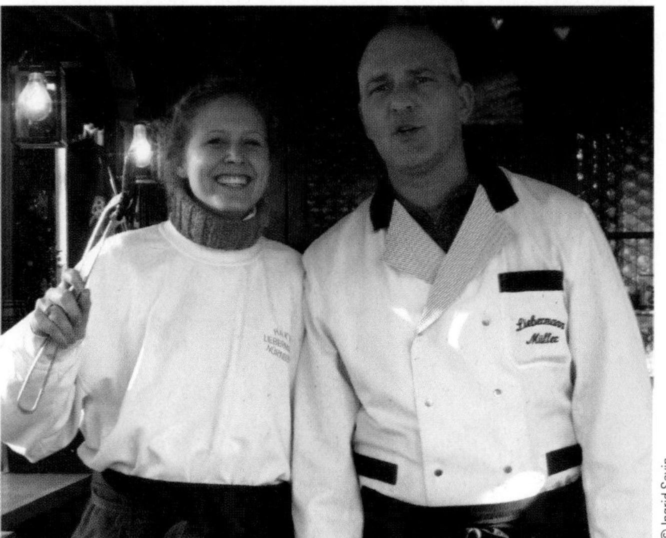

© Ingrid Sevin

Würstchenverkauf beim Straßenfest

© Cengage Learning

The Turkish Feast of the Sacrifice **(Opferfest)** is a religious holiday in December, remembering the event when Abraham sacrificed a ram in place of his son Ismail. (In the Bible, it is Isaac who was almost sacrificed.)

For further practice, an optional two-part video (**Szenen** and **Interviews**) is available on the ***Wie geht's?*** Premium Website and in iLrn, with corresponding questions and activities in the *Arbeitsbuch* (SAM).

As an optional activity, with Google Earth you could visit any of the cities where the celebrations mentioned in this chapter take place, for example Cologne, Munich, or Landshut.

Rückschau

Kapitelwortschatz

Hauptwörter

das Datum, die Daten	*calendar date*
die Feier, -n	*celebration*
der Feiertag, -e	*holiday*
die Ferien *(pl.)*	*vacation*
das Fest, -e	*fest, festival*
der Geburtstag, -e	*birthday*
das Geschenk, -e	*present, gift*
die Kerze, -n	*candle*
das Lied, -er	*song*
die (Ordinal)zahl, -en	*(ordinal) number*
die Party, -s	*party*
der Sekt, -e	*champagne*
die Überraschung, -en	*surprise*

Verben

bekommen	*to get, receive*
dauern	*to last, take* (duration)
denken	*to think*
fallen	*to fall*
feiern	*to celebrate, party*
Glück haben	*to be lucky*
gratulieren	*to congratulate*
nennen	*to name, call*
Pech haben	*to be unlucky*
schenken	*to give* (a gift)
singen	*to sing*
Spaß machen	*to be fun*
studieren	*to study a particular field; to be a student at a university*
tanzen	*to dance*
tun	*to do*
überraschen	*to surprise*
wünschen	*to wish*

Adjektive und Adverbien

laut	*loud(ly), noisy, noisily*
lustig	*funny, amusing*
verrückt	*crazy*

Konjunktionen

bevor	*before*
dass	*that*
ob	*if, whether*
obwohl	*although*
weil	*because*
wenn	*if; when(ever)*

Verschiedenes

Alles Gute zum Geburtstag!	*Happy birthday!*
Alles Gute!	*All the best!*
am Wochenende	*on the weekend*
Bitte schön!	*You're welcome!*
Danke schön!	*Thanks a lot!*
Das gibt's doch nicht!	*I don't believe it!, That's impossible!*
Das macht (mir) Spaß.	*That's fun.*
Die Ferien sind vom . . . bis zum . . .	*The vacation is from . . . until . . .*
dort	*(over) there*
Echt?	*Really?*
eigentlich	*actual(ly)*
Ein gutes neues Jahr!	*Have a good New Year!*
(Ein) schönes Wochenende!	*Have a nice weekend!*
Frohe / Fröhliche Weihnachten!	*Merry Christmas!*
gerade	*just, right now*
gestern	*yesterday*
Glück gehabt!	*I was (you were, she was, etc.) lucky.*
Gute Besserung!	*Get well soon!*
Herzliche Glückwünsche!	*Best wishes!*
Herzlichen Glückwunsch (zum Geburtstag)!	*Congratulations (on your birthday)!*
Heute ist der erste Mai (1.5.).	*Today is the first of May (5/1).*
Ich bin 1993 geboren.	*I was born in 1993.*
Ich bin am 1.5.1993 geboren.	*I was born on May 1, 1993.*
Ich gratuliere dir / Ihnen . . . !	*Congratulations . . . !*
Ich habe am ersten Mai (1.5.) Geburtstag.	*My birthday is on the first of May.*
Ich wünsche dir / Ihnen . . . !	*I wish you . . . !*
immer	*always*
morgen	*tomorrow*
Nichts zu danken!	*You're welcome!, My pleasure!*
noch	*still; else*
(noch) nie	*never* (before)
Pech gehabt!	*I was (you were, she was, etc.) unlucky.*
sicher	*sure(ly), certain(ly)*
So eine Überraschung!	*What a surprise!*
Viel Glück!	*Good luck!*
Vielen / Herzlichen Dank!	*Thank you very much!*
vor einer Woche	*a week ago*
vorgestern	*the day before yesterday*
Wann haben Sie Geburtstag?	*When is your birthday?* (formal)
Wann sind Sie geboren?	*When were you born?* (formal)
Welches Datum ist heute?	*What's the date today?*
Wie lange?	*How long?*
übermorgen	*the day after tomorrow*
zu Ostern / Weihnachten / Silvester	*at/for Easter / Christmas / New Year's Eve*
zum Geburtstag	*on/for one's birthday*

Zum Schluss

Die Partys

1. **Was haben Sie gemacht?** Answer the following questions about the last party you planned. Use the present perfect when you describe what happened.
   a. Was für eine Party haben Sie gehabt?
   b. Wann ist die Party gewesen?
   c. Mit wem haben Sie gefeiert?
   d. Was haben Sie für die Party eingekauft? Was hat es zum Essen und zum Trinken gegeben?
2. **Wer hat auch eine Party gehabt?** Now ask a classmate the same questions. What was the same? What was different? Practice telling the story of their party.
3. **Feiern macht keinen Spaß!** Imagine you are someone who does not like going to parties. Explain your reasoning to someone else, using as many subordinating conjunctions as possible: **bevor, dass, ob, obwohl, wenn, weil.**
   a. Ich mag keine Partys, weil . . .
   b. Ich tanze nicht gern, bevor . . .
   c. Ich weiß nicht, ob . . .
   d. Die Gäste sprechen nicht mit mir, obwohl . . .
   e. Mir gefällt es nicht, wenn . . .
   f. Ich finde, dass . . .
4. **Allerlei Wünsche**
   a. **Alles Gute!** You are leaving school on Friday, December 23rd, and you're saying good-bye to your friend, whose birthday is on December 28th. Neither of you will be back at school until January 3rd. Write a dialogue in which you use a lot of greetings and wishes with each other.
   b. **Noch Einmal!** Now repeat your greetings, only this time, you are speaking with your supervisor, Frau Doktor Schneider. Use the formal form of address.

iLrn **Onlineaktivitäten** View iLrn for online activities related to this chapter. There you will find additional resources, such as a memory game (**Gedächtnisspiel**), a crossword puzzle (**Kreuzworträtsel**), audio flash cards (**Vokabelblitz**), a tutorial quiz (**Mini-Quiz**), and the active vocabulary (**Wortschatz**) for this chapter.

Kapitel 5 In der Stadt

Lernziele In this chapter you will learn about:

Zum Thema

Viennese landmarks and asking for directions

Fokus

Austria, Viennese life, music, art, architecture, sights, and history

Struktur

- Personal pronouns
- Modal auxiliary verbs
- **Sondern** vs. **aber**

Einblicke

Brief: Grüße aus Wien

Rückschau

Kapitalwortschatz
Zum Schluss

RESSOURCEN

iLrn iLrn   Video
Audio    SAM

© ArTo/Fotolia

Schloss Belvedere in Wien

Vorschau Spotlight on Austria

Area: Approximately 32,400 square miles, about the size of Maine.

Population: About 8.4 million, 98% German-speaking; ethnic minorities include some 56,000 Croats in the Burgenland, 20,000 Slovenes in southern Carinthia *(Kärnten),* and small groups of Hungarians, Czechs, Slovaks, and Italians.

Religion: 74% Catholic, 5% Protestant, 4% Muslim, 17% other

Geography: The Alps are the dominant physical feature, covering all of the narrow western part of the country and much of its central and southern regions. The Danube Valley and the Vienna Basin lie in the northeastern part of the country.

Currency: Euro, 1 € = 100 Cents.

Principal cities: Vienna (*Wien*, pop. 1.7 million, capital); Graz (pop. 261,000), Linz (pop. 189,000); Salzburg (pop. 148,000); Innsbruck (pop. 120,000).

Ask students whether they have been to Austria and what they associate with the different cities mentioned here. What prominent Austrians do they know? In the *Zum Schreiben* section of the *Arbeitsbuch* (SAM), there is also a blank map of Austria. Let them fill in the blanks to check their knowledge of geography.

The history of Austria and of the Habsburg family, who ruled Austria through much of its history, were closely linked for more than 650 years. Rudolf von Habsburg started the dynasty in 1273 when he was elected Emperor of the Holy Roman Empire (which existed in some form from 962 until 1806). Over the course of several centuries, the Habsburg empire grew to include Flanders, Burgundy, Bohemia, Hungary, and large areas of the Balkans. These acquisitions were made not only through war, but also through shrewdly arranged marriages **(Heiratspolitik)** with other European ruling houses. The Holy Roman Empire ended with the Napoleonic wars in the early 1800s, yet members of the Habsburg family ruled until the end of World War I. In 1918, the defeated Austro-Hungarian Empire was divided into independent countries: Austria, Hungary, Czechoslovakia, Yugoslavia, and Romania. In 1938, after several political and economic crises, Hitler annexed the young Austrian republic into the Third Reich. After World War II, the country was occupied by the Allies until 1955, when Austria regained its sovereignty and pledged neutrality. During the Cold War, the country belonged neither to the Warsaw Pact nor to NATO.

Since the end of World War II, Austria has been actively involved in international humanitarian efforts. Hungary's decision in 1989 to allow East German refugees to cross its border into Austria was a contributing factor in the fall of the Berlin Wall. In 1995, the country became a member of the European Union. Most Austrian cities have their own website. A simple browser search will get you there.

Blick auf Salzburg von oben auf der Festung **(fortress)**

Getreidegasse in Salzburg

Fragen: 1. Wie viele Brücken *(bridges)* über die Salzach sehen Sie auf dem Bild von Salzburg? 2. Wie viele Kirchen *(churches)* sehen Sie? 3. Welche Farbe haben viele Türme *(towers)*? 4. Wie ist das Wetter an dem Tag in Salzburg? 5. Warum sieht man auf dem Bild von der Kärntner Straße keine Autos? 6. Was gibt es da? 7. Was tragen die Leute?

Zum Thema

Gespräche

Entschuldigen Sie! Wo ist . . . ?

Hotel Sacher is probably the best-known hotel in Vienna. One of the reasons for its popularity is its famous café, for which a rich, delicious cake **(die Sachertorte)** is named.

Warm-ups: 1. **Welches Datum ist das?** Ist das Ihr Geburtstag? z. B. Das ist der 1. Mai. Ich habe am 3. August Geburtstag. *(Write various dates on the board; have students answer.)* 2. **Was ist das Partizip?** (arbeiten, bekommen, beobachten, bedeuten, bleiben, denken, gefallen, fahren, fallen, finden, gehen, gratulieren, helfen, laufen, lesen, nennen, singen, tragen, tun, überraschen)

TOURIST Entschuldigen Sie! Können Sie mir sagen, wo das Hotel Sacher ist?
WIENER Erste Straße links hinter der Staatsoper.
TOURIST Und wie komme ich von da zum Stephansdom?
WIENER Geradeaus, die Kärntner Straße entlang.
TOURIST Wie weit ist es zum Dom?
WIENER Nicht weit. Sie können zu Fuß gehen.
TOURIST Danke!
WIENER Bitte schön!

© Cengage Learning

Da drüben!

TOURIST Entschuldigung! Wo ist das Burgtheater?
HERR Es tut mir leid. Ich bin nicht aus Wien.
TOURIST Verzeihung! Ist das das Burgtheater?
DAME Nein, das ist nicht das Burgtheater, sondern die Staatsoper. Fahren Sie mit der Straßenbahn zum Rathaus! Gegenüber vom Rathaus ist das Burgtheater.
TOURIST Und wo hält die Straßenbahn?
DAME Da drüben links.
TOURIST Vielen Dank!
DAME Bitte sehr!

A: 1. hinter der Staatsoper 2. geradeaus, die Kärntner Straße entlang 3. einen Herrn 4. nein 5. mit der Straßenbahn 6. da drüben links 7. das Rathaus

A. Alles verstanden?

1. Wo ist das Hotel Sacher? 2. Wie kommt man von der Staatsoper zum Stephansdom? 3. Wen fragt der Tourist im zweiten Gespräch? 4. Ist der Herr Wiener? 5. Wie kommt der Tourist zum Burgtheater? 6. Wo ist die Haltestelle? 7. Was ist gegenüber vom Burgtheater?

Fokus Viennese Landmarks

Vienna, the capital of Austria, is an old city, filled with reminders of its history. It is also a very walkable city, and its residents are frequently reminded of its past by the famous buildings that they pass each day. In addition to the Sacher Hotel with its famous café—for which the delicious **Sachertorte** was named—the three following famous landmarks are mentioned in the dialogue.

- Vienna's Opera **(die Staatsoper),** inaugurated in 1869, was built in the style of the early French Renaissance and is one of the foremost European opera houses.
- A masterpiece of Gothic architecture, Saint Stephen's Cathedral **(der Stephansdom)** dates from the 12th century. Its roof of colored tiles and its 450-feet-high spire (nicknamed "Steffi") make it the principal landmark of Vienna. There is an excellent panoramic view of the city at the top of the spire's 438 steps. It is possible to take an elevator from the lower, unfinished tower to the top, which houses the **Pummerin,** a bell that weighs over 4 tons. It was made out of the metal melted down from the cathedral's former bells, all of which were smashed to the ground during World War II.
- In 1776, Emperor Joseph II declared Vienna's **Burgtheater** Austria's national theater. The Burgtheater has always devoted itself to classical drama. Over the years, its actors have developed a stylized mode of diction that gives an aura of conservatism to their performances. Most of the ensemble, numbering more than a hundred, have lifetime contracts.

 **B. Jetzt sind Sie dran!** With a partner, create your own dialogue asking for directions to any place in your city.

BEISPIEL S1 Entschuldigung. Wo ist . . . ?
S2 . . .

Wortschatz 1

Der Stadtplan, ¨-e *(city map)*

der Bahnhof, ¨-e	*train station*	die Bank, -en	*bank*
Bus, -se	*bus*	Bibliothek, -en	*library*
Dom, -e	*cathedral*	Brücke, -n	*bridge*
Park, -s	*park*	Haltestelle, -n	(*bus,* etc.) *stop*
Platz, ¨-e	*place; square*	Kirche, -n	*church*
Weg, -e	*way; trail*	Post	*post office*
das Auto, -s	*car*	Schule, -n	*school*
Fahrrad, ¨-er	*bike*	Straße, -n	*street*
Hotel, -s	*hotel*	Straßenbahn, -en	*streetcar*
Kino, -s	*movie theater*	**U-Bahn**	*subway*
Museum, Museen	*museum*	Universität, -en	*university*
Rathaus, ¨-er	*city hall*	Uni, -s *(coll.)*	
Schloss, ¨-er	*palace*		
Taxi, -s	*taxi*		
Theater, -	*theater*		

Verschiedenes

die Dame, -n	*lady*
der Tourist, -en, -en	*tourist* (male)
die Touristin, -nen	*tourist* (female)
besichtigen	*to tour, visit (a palace,* etc.*)*
halten (hält), gehalten	*to stop; to hold*
zeigen	*to show*
zu Fuß gehen	*to walk*
Entschuldigen Sie! / Entschuldigung! / Verzeihung!	*Excuse me!*
Es tut mir leid.	*I'm sorry.*
Ich möchte zum/zur . . .	*I would like to go to . . .*
Können Sie mir sagen, wo . . . ist?	*Can you tell me where . . . is?*
Wie kommt man von hier zum/zur . . . ?	*How do you get from here to . . . ?*
Gibt es hier in der Nähe . . . ?	*Is there . . . nearby?*
in der Nähe von (+ *dat.*)	*near, in the vicinity of*
die erste Straße links / rechts	*first street to the left / right*
(immer) geradeaus	*(keep) straight ahead*
an/am . . . vorbei	*past the . . .*
(den Fluss) entlang	*along (the river)*
bis Sie . . . sehen	*until you see . . .*
da drüben	*over there*
dorthin	*to there*
gegenüber von (+ *dat.*)	*across from*
nah / weit	*nearby, close / far*
sondern	*but, on the contrary, rather*
Sie können zu Fuß gehen.	*You can walk.*
Fahren Sie mit dem Bus!	*Take the bus!*

Zum Erkennen: hinter *(behind);* die Oper, -n *(opera house);* AUCH: das Hauptwort, ¨-er *(noun);* das Modalverb, -en *(modal auxiliary)*

■ **U-Bahn** stands for **Untergrundbahn,** and **S-Bahn** for **Schnellbahn** *(a suburban commuter train).*

■ When **halten** is intransitive (that is, without an accusative object), it means *to come to a stop:* **Der Bus hält da drüben.** When it is transitive, it means *to hold:* **Halten Sie mir bitte das Buch!**

The difference between **sondern** and **aber** will be discussed in *Struktur 5.3.*

Point out that **fahren** expresses *to go* when a vehicle is involved.

Das Wiener Burgtheater

Übungen zum Thema

A: *cathedral square* **(der)**, *bicycle path* **(der)**, *palace hotel* **(das)**, *tourist town* **(die)**, *church festival* **(das)**, *school vacation* **(die)**, *student cinema* **(das)**, *train station drugstore* **(die)**, *university parking lot* **(der)**, *parking meter* **(die)**

A. Was bedeuten die Wörter und was sind die Artikel?

Domplatz, Fahrradweg, Schlosshotel, Touristenstadt, Kirchenfest, Schulferien, Studentenkino, Bahnhofsdrogerie, Universitätsparkplatz, Parkuhr

B. Was passt nicht?

1. der Bus—das Taxi—das Fahrrad—das Kino
2. das Theater—der Weg—das Museum—die Bibliothek
3. die U-Bahn—die Bank—die Post—das Rathaus
4. die Straße—die Brücke—der Stadtplan—der Platz
5. da drüben—gegenüber von—in der Nähe von—schade
6. fahren—zu Fuß gehen—halten—laufen

If students ask: *building* **das Gebäude, -;** *dorm* **das Studentenwohnheim, -e;** *gym* **die Turnhalle, -n;** *lab* **das Labor, -s;** *office* **das Büro, -s;** *parking lot* **der Parkplatz, ¨-e;** *stadium* **das Stadion, Stadien.**

C. Wo ist . . . ? Working with a partner, ask each other and give directions to various places on campus.

S1 Entschuldigen Sie! Wo ist . . . ?
S2 . . .
S1 Und wie komme ich dorthin?
S2 . . .
S1 Vielen Dank!
S2 . . . !

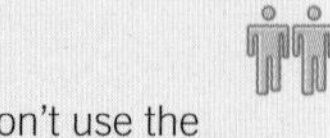

The Swiss don't use the letter **ß**; therefore, the spelling is **Strasse** instead of **Straße.**

D. Fragen zum Stadtplan von Winterthur You are on a short trip from Austria to Switzerland and visit Winterthur. With your partner, using the formal **Sie,** practice asking for and giving directions from one place to another. Start out at the information office at the train station. Then reverse roles.

BEISPIEL S1 Entschuldigung! Können Sie mir sagen, wie ich zum Technikum *(technical university)* komme?
S2 Das Technikum ist in der Technikumstrasse. Gehen Sie am Bahnhof vorbei und links in die Technikumstrasse. Dann gehen Sie immer geradeaus, bis Sie rechts das Technikum sehen.

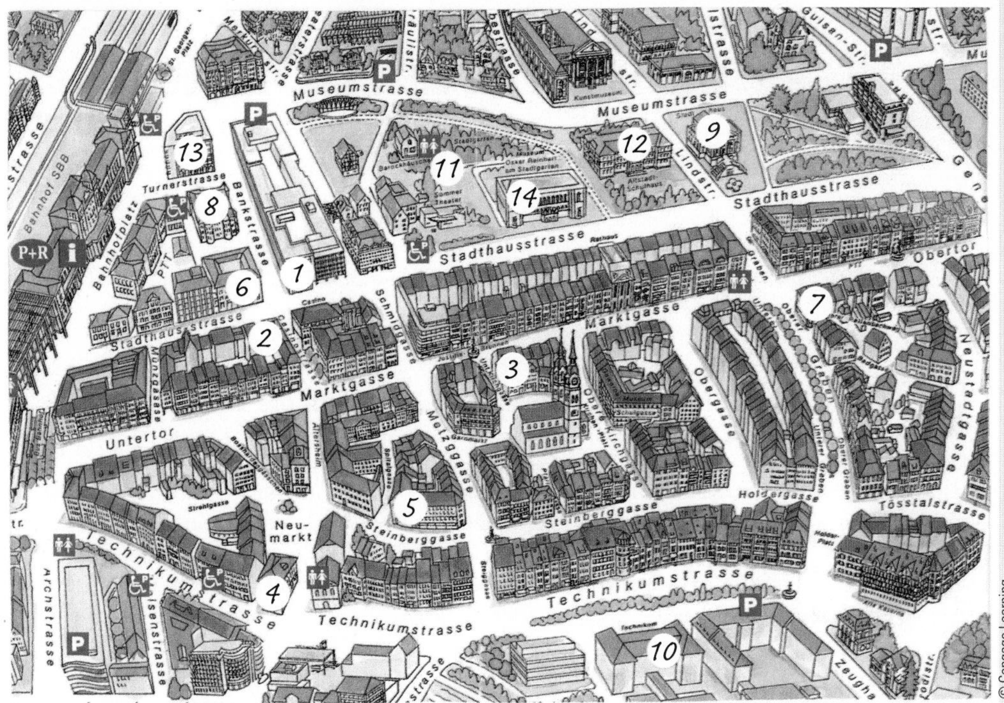

1. Kaufhaus 2. Supermarkt 3. Möbelladen 4. Hotel 5. Fotogeschäft 6. Sportgeschäft 7. Drogerie 8. Bank 9. Theater 10. Technikum 11. Stadtpark 12. Schule 13. Post 14. Museum

Aussprache: ö

For further review, see the Summary of Pronunciation at the front of this book. Study Part II, subsections 29–36.

A. Laute

1. [ö:] **Ö**sterreich, Br**ö**tchen, G**oe**the, sch**ö**n, gew**öh**nlich, franz**ö**sisch, h**ö**ren
2. [ö] **ö**ffnen, **ö**stlich, k**ö**nnen, L**ö**ffel, zw**ö**lf, n**ö**rdlich, m**ö**chten

B. Wortpaare

1. kennen / können
2. Sehne / Söhne
3. große / Größe
4. schon / schön
5. Sühne / Söhne
6. Höhle / Hölle

Hörverständnis

Touristen in Innsbruck Listen to this conversation between two tourists and a woman from Innsbruck. Then complete the sentences below with the correct information from the dialogue.

Zum Erkennen: uns *(us)*; das Goldene Dachl *(The Golden Roof, a 15th-century burgher house)*; das Konzert *(concert)*; erst *(only)*; Viel Spaß! *(Have fun!)*

1. Die Touristen fragen, wo ___das Goldene Dachl___ ist.
2. Bei der Brücke ___beginnt___ die Fußgängerzone.
3. Der Dom ist ___in der Nähe vom___ Dachl.
4. Das Konzert beginnt ___um fünf___.
5. Vor dem Konzert möchten die Touristen ___die Maria-Theresia-Straße entlanglaufen___.
6. Von der Maria-Theresia-Straße sieht man wunderbar ___die Berge___.

Struktur

5.1 Personal pronouns

1. In English the PERSONAL PRONOUNS are *I, me, you, he, him, she, her, it, we, us, they*, and *them*. Some of these pronouns are used as subjects, others as direct or indirect objects, or objects of prepositions.

SUBJECT:	**He** *is coming.*
DIRECT OBJECT:	*I see* **him.**
INDIRECT OBJECT:	*I give* **him** *the book.*
OBJECT OF A PREPOSITION:	*We'll go without* **him.**

Encourage students to use pronouns whenever possible. Have them practice the forms of the personal pronouns regularly over several days in simple sentences, e.g., **Das ist für euch** *(for us, for them, for me, etc.).*

The German personal pronouns are likewise used as subjects, direct or indirect objects, or objects of prepositions. Like the definite and indefinite articles, personal pronouns have special forms in the various cases. You already know the nominative case of these pronouns. Here are the nominative, accusative, and dative cases together.

	SINGULAR					PLURAL			SG. / PL.
nom.	ich	du	er	es	sie	wir	ihr	sie	Sie
acc.	**mich**	**dich**	**ihn**	**es**	**sie**	**uns**	**euch**	**sie**	**Sie**
dat.	**mir**	**dir**	**ihm**	**ihm**	**ihr**	**uns**	**euch**	**ihnen**	**Ihnen**

SUBJECT:	**Er** kommt.
DIRECT OBJECT:	Ich sehe **ihn.**
INDIRECT OBJECT:	Ich gebe **ihm** das Buch.
OBJECT OF A PREPOSITION:	Wir gehen ohne **ihn.**

- Note the similarities between the definite article of the noun and the pronoun that replaces it.

	MASC.	NEUT.	FEM.	PL.
nom.	de**r** Mann = e**r**	da**s** Kind = e**s**	di**e** Frau = si**e**	di**e** Leute = si**e**
acc.	de**n** Mann = ih**n**	da**s** Kind = e**s**	di**e** Frau = si**e**	di**e** Leute = si**e**
dat.	de**m** Mann = ih**m**	de**m** Kind = ih**m**	de**r** Frau = ih**r**	de**n** Leuten = ih**nen**

2. As in English, the indirect object usually precedes the direct object, unless the direct object is a pronoun. If that is the case, the direct object pronoun comes first.

Ich gebe **dem Studenten**	den Kuli.	*I'm giving the student the pen.*
Ich gebe **ihm**	den Kuli.	*I'm giving him the pen.*
Ich gebe ihn	**dem Studenten.**	*I'm giving it to the student.*
Ich gebe ihn	**ihm.**	*I'm giving it to him.*

It might help to explain the arrow in this chart: If the direct object is a pronoun, it gets "kicked" in front of the indirect object.

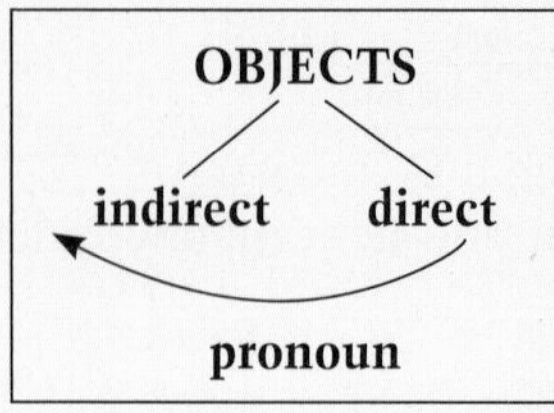

Übungen

A. Ersetzen Sie die Hauptwörter durch Pronomen! Replace each noun with a pronoun in the appropriate case.

BEISPIEL den Bruder *ihn*

1. der Vater, dem Mann, den Großvater, dem Freund, den Ober
2. die Freundin, der Großmutter, der Dame, die Frau, der Familie
3. die Eltern, den Herren, den Frauen, die Freundinnen, den Schweizern
4. für die Mutter, mit den Freunden, gegen die Studenten, außer dem Großvater, ohne den Ober, von den Eltern, zu dem Mädchen, bei der Großmutter

A: 1. er, ihm, ihn, ihm, ihn
2. sie, ihr, ihr, sie, ihr
3. sie, ihnen, ihnen, sie, ihnen
4. für sie, mit ihnen, gegen sie, außer ihm, ohne ihn, von ihnen, zu ihm/ihr, bei ihr

B. Kombinieren Sie mit den Präpositionen! Was sind die Akkusativ- und Dativformen?

BEISPIEL ich (ohne, mit) *ohne mich, mit mir*

1. er (für, mit)
2. wir (durch, von)
3. Sie (gegen, zu)
4. du (ohne, bei)
5. ihr (für, außer)
6. sie/*sg.* (um, nach)
7. sie/*pl.* (für, aus)
8. es (ohne, außer)

B: 1. für ihn, mit ihm 2. durch uns, von uns 3. gegen Sie, zu Ihnen 4. ohne dich, bei dir 5. für euch, außer euch 6. um sie, nach ihr 7. für sie, aus ihnen 8. ohne es, außer ihm.

As optional practice, you can also have students put these phrases into complete sentences, e.g., **Tun Sie das ohne mich!**

C. Was fehlt? Working with a partner, complete the following sentences.

S1 Siehst du ___sie___? *(them)*
S2 Nein, aber sie sehen ___uns___. *(us)*
S1 Gehört das Buch ___dir___? *(you*/sg. fam.*)*
S2 Nein, es gehört ___ihm___. *(him)*
S1 Glaubst du ___ihm___? *(him)*
S2 Nein, aber ich glaube ___euch___. *(you*/pl. fam.*)*
S1 Sie sucht ___dich___. *(you*/sg. fam.*)*
S2 Ich suche ___sie___. *(her)*
S1 Hilft er ___uns___? *(us)*
S2 Nein, aber er hilft ___ihnen___. *(them)*
S1 Zeigst du ___uns___ das Goldene Dachl? *(us)*
S2 Ja, ich zeige es ___euch___ gern. *(you*/pl. fam.*)*

© Dieter Sevin

Blick auf das Goldene Dachl in Innsbruck

D: 1. der Dom, er; das Rathaus, es; die Apotheke, sie 2. die Kirche, sie; das Geschäft, es; der Platz, er 3. dem Mann, ihm; den Leuten, ihnen; der Frau, ihr 4. dem Kind, ihm; den Damen, ihnen; der Nachbarin, ihr 5. den Bus, ihn; die U-Bahn, sie; das Taxi, es 6. das Hotel, es; die Universität, sie; der Park, er

D. Antworten Sie und ersetzen Sie die Hauptwörter!

BEISPIEL Wo ist **das Hotel? Es** ist da drüben. (Bank)
*Wo ist **die Bank? Sie** ist da drüben.*

1. Wo ist **die Post?** Da ist **sie.** (Dom, Rathaus, Apotheke)
2. Ist **das Museum** weit von hier? Nein, **es** ist nicht weit von hier. (Kirche, Geschäft, Platz)
3. Zeigen Sie **dem Mädchen** den Weg? Ja, ich zeige **ihr** den Weg. (Mann, Leute, Frau)
4. Helfen Sie **dem Herrn?** Ja, ich helfe **ihm.** (Kind, Damen, Nachbarin)
5. Haben Sie **die Straßenbahn** genommen? Ja, ich habe **sie** genommen. (Bus, U-Bahn, Taxi)
6. Wie hat dir **die Stadt** gefallen? **Sie** hat mir gut gefallen. (Hotel, Universität, Park)

E. Im Wiener Café With your partner, read the following dialogue about the picture in the café. Then reread it, using pronouns for the boldfaced words.

© Ingrid Sevin

E: wir/euch, ihn, sie, ihm, ihr, Er, ihnen/Es, sie/ihnen, sie, uns/euch/Ihm, ihr/Sie

S1 Siehst du die sechs Leute am Tisch? Das sind **unser Professor, seine Frau, meine Freunde und ich.**

S2 Ja, ich sehe **dich und deine Freunde** und auch **den Professor** und **seine Frau.** Du hast schon viel von **dem Professor** und von **seiner Frau** gesprochen. **Der Professor** geht gern mit **seinen Studenten** ins Café, nicht wahr?

S1 Ja. Hier sind wir im Café Central. **Das Café** ist aus dem Jahr 1868. Da haben schon Arthur Schnitzler, Franz Kafka und andere bekannte *(famous)* Leute wie **diese Autoren** ihren Kaffee getrunken.

S2 Und da siehst du Kaiser *(emperor)* Franz Joseph und Kaiserin Elisabeth. Von **Franz Joseph und Elisabeth** habe ich schon viel gehört. Die Österreicher haben **Elisabeth** Sissi genannt. Vielleicht kannst du **meinen Eltern und mir** das Café auch einmal zeigen.

S1 Ja, gern. Ich glaube, dass es **dir und deinen Eltern** da gefällt.

S2 **Meinem Vater** bestellen wir dann einen Mokka und **meiner Mutter** einen Apfelstrudel.

S1 Ja, und dir ein Stück Linzertorte! **Die Torte** schmeckt hier besonders gut.

F. Fragen und Antworten mit Pronomen Ask your partner all sorts of questions which he/she answers freely with the proper pronouns. Take turns.

BEISPIEL S1 Wie geht es . . . (dir, deiner Freundin)?
S2 Es geht mir gut. / Es geht ihr nicht so gut.

1. Wie geht es . . . (Andreas, Stefanie, Mario und Antje usw.)?
2. Hast du mit . . . (Kevin, Miriam, Sabine und Karin usw.) gesprochen?
3. Wie gefällt/gefallen dir . . . (die Uni, Björn, Paul und Paula usw.)?
4. Wie findest du . . . (die Restaurants, Toni, Tobias und Anne usw.)?
5. Habt ihr schon einmal . . . (den Park, das Rathaus, die Museen usw.) besichtigt?
6. Zeigst du . . . (deinem Onkel, deinem Onkel und deiner Tante, Sara und mir usw.) die Stadt?
7. Glaubst du alles, was . . . (ich, wir, er, die Leute usw.) sage/sagt/sagen?

F: 1. Wie geht es ihm / ihr / ihnen? 2. Hast du mit ihm / ihr / ihnen gesprochen? 3. Wie gefällt sie / er dir? Wie gefallen sie dir? 4. Wie findest du sie / ihn / sie? 5. Habt ihr ihn / es / sie . . . besichtigt? 6. Zeigst du ihm / ihnen / uns die Stadt? 7. Glaubst du alles, was ich sage / wir sagen / er sagt / sie sagen?

G. Wer bekommt was?

1. **Wem gibt sie was?** Susan has just cleaned out her closet and is going to give away all the souvenirs from her trip to Europe. Explain to whom she is going to give them.

BEISPIEL ihrer Schwester / die Bilder
Sie gibt ihrer Schwester die Bilder.
Sie gibt ihr die Bilder.
Sie gibt sie ihrer Schwester.
Sie gibt sie ihr.

a. ihrem Vater / den Stadtplan
b. ihren Großeltern / die Landkarte
c. ihrer Mutter / den Zuckerlöffel
d. ihrer Schwester / das Kleingeld *(small change)*
e. Max / den Gürtel *(belt)*
f. Tina / die Bluse
g. Eva / die CD von Mariah Carey
h. Moritz und Merle / die Poster *(pl.)*
i. der Nachbarin / das Wien-Buch
j. dir / das T-Shirt
k. mir / den Pulli
l. uns / die Bilder

G.1: a. Sie gibt ihrem Vater den Stadtplan (ihm den Stadtplan, ihn ihrem Vater, ihn ihm). b. Sie gibt ihren Großeltern die Landkarte (ihnen die Landkarte, sie ihren Großeltern, sie ihnen). c. Sie gibt ihrer Mutter den Zuckerlöffel (ihr den Zuckerlöffel, ihn ihrer Mutter, ihn ihr). d. Sie gibt ihrer Schwester das Kleingeld (ihr das Kleingeld, es ihrer Schwester, es ihr). e. Sie gibt Max den Gürtel (ihm den Gürtel, ihn Max, ihn ihm). f. Sie gibt Tina die Bluse (ihr die Bluse, sie Tina, sie ihr). g. Sie gibt Eva die CD (ihr die CD, sie Eva, sie ihr). h. Sie gibt Moritz und Merle die Poster (ihnen die Poster, sie Moritz und Merle, sie ihnen). i. Sie gibt der Nachbarin das Buch (ihr das Buch, es der Nachbarin, es ihr). j. Sie gibt dir das T-Shirt (es dir). k. Sie gibt mir den Pulli (ihn mir). l. Sie gibt uns die Bilder (sie uns).

2. **Wem schenkst du was?** Ask your partner what presents he/she is giving for Christmas, Hanukkah, or other holiday. Follow the pattern.

BEISPIEL S1 Was schenkst du deinem Vater?
S2 Ich schenke ihm ein Wörterbuch.

Susan schenkt ihrer Großmutter die Kuhglocken **(cow bells).**

Fokus Viennese Landmarks *(continued)*

In addition to the places mentioned in the *Zum Thema* section, numerous other Viennese landmarks are known around the world.

- The **Hofburg** is almost a self-contained city within the city of Vienna. Although originally it was a medieval castle, later it became the imperial palace of the Habsburgs, who resided there until 1918. It now houses several museums, such as the Museum of Fine Arts, the Museum of Ethnology, the portrait collection of the National Library **(die Nationalbibliothek),** the Imperial Treasury **(die Schatzkammer),** the Spanish Riding Academy **(die Spanische Hofreitschule),** as well as the Federal Chancellor's residence.
- **Schönbrunn** was the favorite summer residence of the Empress Maria Theresa, who ruled Austria, Hungary, and Bohemia from 1740 to 1780. Her daughter Marie Antoinette, who became queen of France, spent her childhood there. It was at Schönbrunn where Mozart dazzled the empress with his talents. During the wars of 1805 and 1809, Napoleon used it as his headquarters. Franz Joseph I, emperor of Austria from 1848 to 1916, was born and died at Schönbrunn, and Charles I, the last of the Habsburgs, abdicated there in 1918, when Austria became a republic. To this day, the parks of Schönbrunn feature some of the best-preserved French-style baroque gardens in the world.
- The **Prater** is a large amusement park with a 220-feet-tall Ferris wheel and many modern rides, a stadium, fairgrounds, race tracks, bridle paths, pools, and ponds.

Das Riesenrad im Wiener Prater

5.2 Modal auxiliary verbs

1. Both English and German have a small group of MODAL AUXILIARY VERBS that modify the meaning of another verb. Modal verbs express such ideas as permission, ability, necessity, obligation, or desire to do something.

dürfen	*to be allowed to, may*	**sollen**	*to be supposed to*
können	*to be able to, can*	**wollen**	*to want to*
müssen	*to have to, must*	**mögen**	*to like*

- The German modals are irregular in the singular of the present tense:

Möchte(n) is the subjunctive form of **mögen.** Students are already learning several ways to express liking: **gefallen, gern** + verb, **etwas schön / gut finden.** For additional practice, give students English cues: *I like to sleep, I like the city, I would like a cup of tea, I would like an apple, I like the store, I like to read, etc.*

	dürfen	**können**	**müssen**	**sollen**	**wollen**	**mögen / möchten**	
ich	**darf**	**kann**	**muss**	**soll**	**will**	**mag**	**möchte**
du	**darfst**	**kannst**	**musst**	**sollst**	**willst**	**magst**	**möchtest**
er	**darf**	**kann**	**muss**	**soll**	**will**	**mag**	**möchte**
wir	dürfen	können	müssen	sollen	wollen	mögen	möchten
ihr	dürft	könnt	müsst	sollt	wollt	mögt	möchtet
sie	dürfen	können	müssen	sollen	wollen	mögen	möchten

- The **möchte**-forms of **mögen** occur more frequently than the **mag**-forms.

Ich **möchte** eine Tasse Tee.	*I would like (to have) a cup of tea.*
Ich **mag** Kaffee nicht.	*I don't like coffee.*

2. Modals are another example of the two-part verb phrase. In statements and information questions, the modal is the inflected second element of the sentence (V1). The modified verb (V2) appears at the very end of the sentence in its infinitive form.

V1	V2	
Er **geht** nach Hause.		*He's going home.*
Er **darf** nach Hause	gehen.	*He may (is allowed to) go home.*
Er **kann** nach Hause	gehen.	*He can (is able to) go home.*
Er **muss** nach Hause	gehen.	*He must (has to) go home.*
Er **soll** nach Hause	gehen.	*He is supposed to go home.*
Er **will** nach Hause	gehen.	*He wants to go home.*
Er **möchte** nach Hause	gehen.	*He would like to go home.*

If students use the English equivalents *to be able to, to have to,* and *to be allowed to* rather than *can, must,* and *may,* they'll avoid certain problems, e.g., **Ich muss gehen.** *I have to go.;* **Ich muss nicht gehen.** *I don't have to go,* NOT: *I must not go;* **Du darfst gehen.** *You're allowed to go.;* **Du darfst nicht gehen.** *You're not allowed to go. = You must not go.*

Ihr sollt gehen always expresses *you're supposed to go* (outer compulsion), NOT: *you should go* (inner compulsion). *Should* must be avoided at this point, since it is a subjunctive form. Students may grasp this if you refer to the Bible: *Thou shalt not kill* (a command), NOT: *you shouldn't kill* (an appeal to one's conscience).

CAUTION

- The English set of modals is frequently supplemented by such forms as *is allowed to, is able to, has to.* The German modals, however, do not use such supplements. They follow the pattern of *may, can,* and *must:*
  Ich muss gehen. *(I must go.)*
- The subject of the modal and of the infinitive are always the same:
  Er möchte nach Hause gehen. *(He would like to go home.)*
  The English construction *to want somebody to do something,* e.g., *He would like you to go home,* cannot be duplicated in German. The correct way to express this idea is **Er möchte, dass du nach Hause gehst.**

3. Modals can be used without an infinitive, provided the omitted infinitive can be inferred from the context. This structure is common with verbs of motion.

Musst du zum Supermarkt?	—Ja, ich **muss,** aber ich **kann** nicht.
Do you have to (go) to the supermarket?	*—Yes,* ***I have to,*** *but I* ***can't.***

Because modals use two different forms in the present perfect, we have avoided sentences with modals in that tense. The simple past of the modals will be discussed in Chapter 11.

4. Watch these important differences in meaning:

   a. ***Gern* vs. *möchten***

   Ich **esse gern** Kuchen. BUT Ich **möchte** ein Stück Kuchen **(haben).**

   The first sentence says that I am generally fond of cake *(I like to eat cake).* The second sentence implies a desire for a piece of cake at this particular moment *(I'd like a piece of cake).*

   b. ***Wollen* vs. *möchten***

   Note the difference in tone and politeness between these two sentences: Ich **will** Kuchen. BUT Ich **möchte** Kuchen.

   The first might be said by a spoiled child *(I want cake),* the second by a polite adult *(I would like cake).*

If students ask: **Ich möchte gern ein Stück Kuchen (haben).** *I really would like (to have) a piece of cake.*

5. Modals in subordinate clauses

a. Remember that the inflected verb stands at the very end of clauses introduced by subordinate conjunctions such as **bevor, dass, ob, obwohl, wenn,** and **weil.**

Sie sagt, **dass** du nach Hause gehen **kannst.**
Du kannst nach Hause gehen, **wenn** du **möchtest.**

b. If the sentence starts with the subordinate clause, then the inflected verb of the main sentence (the modal) follows right after the comma.

In a dependent clause, two-part verb structures appear in the sequence V2 V1.

Du **kannst** nach Hause gehen, wenn du möchtest.
Wenn du möchtest, **kannst** du nach Hause gehen.

Übungen

H. Ersetzen Sie das Subjekt!

H: 1. er will, sie wollen, du willst, ich will 2. ich muss, ihr müsst, du musst, Vater muss 3. er darf, ihr dürft, die Kinder dürfen, ich darf 4. sie möchten, du möchtest, er möchte, das Mädchen 5. Kannst du, Könnt ihr, Kann er, Können die Damen

BEISPIEL Wir sollen zum Markt fahren. (ich)
Ich soll zum Markt fahren.

1. Wir wollen zu Hause bleiben. (er, sie/*pl.*, du, ich)
2. Sie müssen noch die Rechnung bezahlen. (ich, ihr, du, Vater)
3. Du darfst zum Bahnhof kommen. (er, ihr, die Kinder, ich)
4. Möchtet ihr ein Eis haben? (sie/*pl.*, du, er, das Mädchen)
5. Können Sie mir sagen, wo das ist? (du, ihr, er, die Damen)

I. Was tun sie am Wochenende?

I: 1. wollen . . . bleiben
2. möchte . . . fahren
3. muss . . . bezahlen
4. soll . . . helfen
5. können . . . besichtigen
6. dürfen . . . spielen

BEISPIEL Teckla geht in den Prater. (wollen)
Teckla will in den Prater gehen.

1. Frank und Margit bleiben gemütlich zu Hause. (wollen)
2. Christoph fährt mit ein paar Freunden an den Neusiedler See in der Nähe von Wien. (möchten)
3. Janina bezahlt Rechnungen. (müssen)
4. Ronny hilft seinem Vater bei einem Projekt *(n.)*. (sollen)
5. Herr und Frau Ahrendt besichtigen Schloss Belvedere. (können)
6. Die Kinder spielen Minigolf. (dürfen)

J. Besucher *(Visitors)*

J.1: Heike fragt, ob . . .
a. ihr . . . finden könnt
b. ihr . . . haben wollt
c. ihr . . . gehen möchtet
d. ich . . . bringen soll
e. ihr . . . müsst

1. **Stadtbesichtigung *(Sightseeing in town)*** Mitzi and Sepp are visiting their friends Heike and Dirk in Salzburg. Dirk tells Mitzi and Sepp what Heike wants to know.

Beginnen Sie mit **Heike fragt, ob . . . !**

a. Könnt ihr den Weg in die Stadt allein finden?
b. Wollt ihr einen Stadtplan haben?
c. Möchtet ihr zu Fuß gehen?
d. Soll ich euch mit dem Auto zum Stadtzentrum bringen?
e. Müsst ihr noch zur Bank?

Fokus The **Sezessionsstil** Movement

Known as *Art Nouveau* in France and as **Jugendstil** in Germany, the Austrian variant on this modern art movement was the **Sezessionsstil,** or the *Vienna Secession.* It was so called because its practitioners hoped to break off entirely ("to secede") from traditional art conventions. It was a style of art that emerged toward the end of the 19th century and flourished until World War I. It broke with previous historical styles, combining romantic and almost sentimental fidelity to nature with symbolic and abstract ornamentation. The school's influence brought about changes not only in art but also in the applied arts, including fashion, architecture, jewelry, sculpture, poetry, music, theater, and dance. Munich, Darmstadt, Brussels, Paris, Nancy, and Vienna were all centers of the movement. Gustav Klimt emerged as the leader of the Secession in Austria from 1897 until 1905, when he broke off from the Secession to develop his own style.

Sylvain Grandadam/age fotostock

Der Kuss **von Gustav Klimt (Österreichische Gallerie, Wien)**

Übungen

N. *Sondern* oder *aber*? Insert the appropriate conjunction.

© Peggy Setje-Eilers

1. Diese Studenten sind keine Deutschen, __sondern__ Amerikaner.
2. Sie studieren gerade in Berlin, __aber__ nur im Sommer.
3. Das macht Spaß, __aber__ sie müssen auch viel lernen.
4. Sie schreiben hier keine Briefe, __sondern__ machen eine Prüfung.
5. Sie sitzen nicht an einem Tisch, __sondern__ auf dem Fußboden (*floor*).
6. Das ist nicht sehr bequem (*comfortable*), __aber__ sie tun das nicht stundenlang.
7. Die Wohnung gehört nicht der Universität, __sondern__ ihrem Professor.
8. Die Studenten haben schon viel gesehen, __aber__ noch lange nicht alles.
9. Sie gehen viel zu Fuß, __aber__ fahren auch oft mit der U-Bahn.
10. Sie besichtigen nicht nur Museen, __sondern__ bummeln auch gern durch die Stadt.

O. Wie geht's weiter? Complete the following sentences in your own words, adding also the conjunction **aber** or **sondern.**

1. Wenn ich Lebensmittel brauche, gehe ich gewöhnlich zu . . . *(name a store),* ___aber___ *(but)* nicht zu . . .
2. Bei . . . sind die Lebensmittel gut, ___aber___ *(but)* . . .
3. Ich gehe dann nicht zu Fuß, ___sondern___ *(but)* . . .
4. Hier in der Nähe gibt es ein paar Restaurants, ___aber___ *(but)* . . .
5. Im Einkaufszentrum gibt es nicht nur Geschäfte, ___sondern___ *(but)* auch . . .
6. Manchmal gehe ich ins Kino, aber nicht allein, ___sondern___ *(but)* mit . . .
7. Das Theater hat mir gut gefallen, ___aber___ *(but)* . . . nicht.
8. Nach dem Kino gehen wir oft nicht direkt nach Hause, ___sondern___ *(but)* . . .

Visit the *Wie geht's?* iLrn website for more review and practice of the grammar points you have just learned.

Zusammenfassung

P. Kombinieren Sie! Create questions by combining items from each column. Then ask different classmates and have them give you an answer using a modal.

BEISPIEL S1 Wann möchtet ihr essen gehen?
S2 Ich möchte jetzt gehen. Und ihr?
S3 Wir möchten um halb eins gehen.

1	2	3	4
wann	dürfen	du	nach Österreich fahren
warum	können	man	nach Hause gehen
was	möchten	wir	in die Stadt (Mensa . . .) gehen
wer	müssen	ihr	schön (billig . . .) essen
wie lange	sollen	Sie	zu Fuß gehen
	wollen	das	mit dem Bus fahren
		. . .	jetzt tun
			kommen
			. . .

Q: Let each student offer at least six sentences that use **aber** and **sondern** correctly. Students may use the sentences in Ex. Q as patterns but should try to communicate something about themselves, e.g., **Ich esse nicht gern Fisch, aber ich esse gern Gemüse.**

Q. Beenden Sie die Sätze! Use the statements below as models to complete a thought logically using the conjunction **aber** or **sondern.**

BEISPIEL Ich esse nicht gern Karotten, aber . . .
Ich esse nicht gern Karotten, aber Bohnen finde ich gut.

1. Ich trinke nicht gern Cola, aber . . .
2. Wir besichtigen nicht das Museum, sondern . . .
3. Die Straßenbahn hält nicht hier, sondern . . .
4. Es gibt keinen Bus, aber . . .
5. Er kann uns heute die Stadt nicht zeigen, aber . . .
6. Ich bin nicht in Wien geblieben, sondern . . .
7. Ihr lernt nicht Spanisch, sondern . . .
8. Es tut mir leid, aber . . .
9. Sie möchte nicht zu Fuß gehen, sondern . . .
10. Ich darf nicht lange schlafen, aber . . .
11. Man geht nicht geradeaus, sondern . . .
12. Das ist nicht das Theater, sondern . . .

R. Die Bank: Auf Deutsch bitte!

1. Excuse me *(formal)*, can you tell me where there's a bank?
2. I'm sorry, but I'm not from Vienna.
3. Whom can I ask?
4. Who can help me?
5. May I help you?
6. I'd like to find a bank.
7. Near the cathedral (there) is a bank.
8. Can you tell me whether that's far from here?
9. You can walk (there), but the banks close (are closed) in 20 minutes.
10. Take the subway or a taxi!

R: 1. Entschuldigen Sie, können Sie mir sagen, wo eine Bank ist / wo es eine Bank gibt? 2. Es tut mir leid, aber ich bin nicht aus Wien. 3. Wen kann ich fragen? 4. Wer kann mir helfen? 5. Darf / kann ich Ihnen helfen? 6. Ich möchte eine Bank finden. 7. In der Nähe vom Dom ist / gibt es eine Bank. 8. Können Sie mir sagen, ob das weit von hier ist? 9. Sie können zu Fuß gehen / laufen, aber die Banken sind in zwanzig Minuten zu. 10. Fahren Sie mit der U-Bahn oder mit einem Taxi!

Fokus The Gateway City

Originally, Vienna **(Wien)** was a Roman settlement. The city's fate was linked to its geographic location on the Danube and at the gateway to the plains of eastern Europe. Here merchants met where ancient trade routes crossed; crusaders passed through on their way to the Holy Land; and in 1683, at the walls and gates of this city, the Turks abandoned their hopes of conquering the heart of Europe.

The center of Vienna **(die Innenstadt)** dates back to medieval times. As late as the 1850s, it was surrounded by horseshoe-shaped walls. The city reached its zenith of power and wealth as the capital of the Austro-Hungarian Empire during the reign of Emperor Franz Joseph (1848–1916), when it developed into one of Europe's most important cultural centers. Composers such as Haydn, Mozart, Beethoven, Schubert, Brahms, Bruckner, Johann and Richard Strauss, Mahler, and Schönberg have left a lasting imprint on the city's cultural life. The psychoanalyst Freud, the writers Schnitzler, Zweig, and von Hofmannsthal, as well as the painters Klimt, Schiele, and Kokoschka, laid the intellectual and artistic foundation of the 20th century.

Today, Vienna ranks among the leading convention cities in the world. It houses the headquarters for the International Atomic Energy Agency (IAEA), the Organization of Petroleum Exporting Countries (OPEC), and the United Nations Industrial Development Organization (UNIDO). It is also one of the three headquarters of the United Nations, along with New York City and Geneva.

Fußgängerzone am Wiener Stephansdom

Einblicke

Brief *(letter)*

Wortschatz 2

bekannt	*well-known*
(ein)mal	*once, (at) one time*
gemütlich	*pleasant, convivial; cozy*
genug	*enough*
hoffentlich	*hopefully; I hope*
interessant	*interesting*
leider	*unfortunately*
lieb	*dear; lovingly, tenderly*
stundenlang	*for hours*
bummeln, ist gebummelt	*to stroll*

Einmal *(once)*, **zweimal** *(twice)*, **dreimal** *(three times)*, etc.; BUT: Ich habe ihr **mal** geschrieben; sie hat auch **mal** geantwortet. *I wrote her once; she also answered at one time.*

Liebe Eltern, liebe Elisabeth, lieber Michael

Like **stundenlang:** jahrelang, monatelang, wochenlang, tagelang, etc.

Vor dem Lesen

A. Auf Reisen *(Traveling)* Read the list below and pick out the five most important things you like to do when you travel. Compare your travel interests with those of your partner. What do you have in common? Where do you differ?

_____ zu Fuß durch die Stadt gehen
_____ mit Leuten sprechen
_____ Souvenirs kaufen
_____ in Museen gehen
_____ in Restaurants gehen
_____ ins Konzert gehen
_____ zum Park gehen
_____ Kirchen besichtigen
_____ Karten schreiben
_____ fotografieren
_____ ins Theater gehen
_____ lange schlafen

Kloster Melk an der Donau

B. Wohin gehen wir? Look over the following entertainment offers with your partner. Then tell each other where you would like to go and why.

BEISPIEL S1 Ich möchte in die Dinner Show gehen. Ich tanze gern. Und du?
S2 Ich möchte zum Burggarten gehen. Schmetterlinge sind toll!

As an additional reading exercise, you might ask students to find examples of informal language in the letter before reading it.

Mozart! was a musical production by the Vereinigte Bühnen Wien GmbH, which also delighted its viewers with musicals like *Elisabeth, Tanz der Vampire* and *Rebecca."*

Lesetipp

Reading a Personal Letter

Personal letters tend to be conversational in tone and often use informal language. As you read this letter, look for examples of informal language, such as abbreviations or casual idioms.

C. Das ist leicht zu verstehen! Read aloud the following words, paying special attention to their stressed syllable; then guess their meaning in English.

der Sport, Stopp, Walzer; das Gästehaus; die Studentengruppe, Winterresidenz; fantastisch, zentral

Grüße° aus Wien

Greetings

Liebe Eltern!

Jetzt muss ich euch aber wirklich wieder mal schreiben! Ich habe so viel gesehen, dass ich nicht weiß, wo ich beginnen soll. Vor einer Woche bin ich mit unserer Studentengruppe noch in Passau gewesen. Von dort sind wir mit dem Schiff die Donau hinuntergefahren°. Wir haben einen Stopp in Linz gemacht und die Stadt, das Schloss und den Dom besichtigt. Dann sind wir mit dem Schiff weiter bis nach Wien gefahren. Die Weinberge°, Burgen° und besonders das Kloster° Melk haben mir sehr gut gefallen. Das Wetter ist auch sehr schön gewesen. Glück gehabt!

traveled down

vineyards / castles / monastery

Oh
reach / Just
in the
(flavoring particle)
elevator
went to the top of the tower
Magic Flute

Jetzt sind wir schon ein paar Tage in Wien. Ach°, ich finde es toll hier! Unser Gästehaus liegt sehr zentral und wir können alles zu Fuß oder mit der U-Bahn erreichen°. Einfach° super! So viel bin ich noch nie gelaufen! Am Freitag sind wir stundenlang durch die Innenstadt gebummelt. Die Geschäfte in der° Kärntner Straße sind sehr teuer, aber man muss ja° nichts kaufen. Wir haben natürlich auch den Stephansdom besichtigt und sind mit dem Aufzug° im Turm hinaufgefahren°. Von dort kann man Wien gut sehen. Am Abend haben wir Mozarts *Zauberflöte*° in der Oper gesehen. Fantastisch!

of the / emperors
(a breed of white horses)
riding / art
small restaurant

Am Samstag haben wir die Hofburg besichtigt. Das ist einmal die Winterresidenz der° Habsburger Kaiser° gewesen. Dort ist auch die Spanische Hofreitschule und man kann die Lipizzaner° beim Training sehen. Das haben wir auch getan. Wirklich prima! Da ist das Reiten° kein Sport, sondern Kunst°. Am Abend sind wir mit der Straßenbahn nach Grinzing gefahren und haben dort Marks Geburtstag mit Musik und Wein gefeiert. Die Weinstube° ist sehr gemütlich gewesen.

■ Search for a YouTube video of the **Spanische Hofreitschule**. You will be amazed to see the elegant movements of horses and riders accompanied by beautiful Viennese music.

Schloss Schönbrunn, Wien

Johann-Strauss-Denkmal

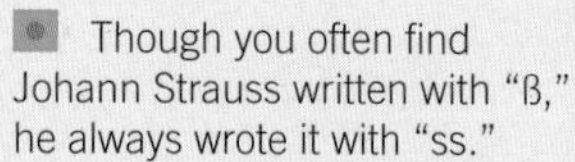

■ Though you often find Johann Strauss written with "ß," he always wrote it with "ss."

well
Ferris wheel
almost over
monuments
traffic
Hungary
we get going again

Tja°, und heute gehen wir ins Museum. Später wollen ein paar von uns noch zum Prater. Das Riesenrad° dort soll toll sein. Morgen früh wollen wir noch zum Schloss Schönbrunn, der Sommerresidenz der Habsburger; und dann ist unsere Zeit in Wien auch schon fast um°. Schade!

Wien ist wirklich interessant. Überall findet man Denkmäler° oder Straßen mit bekannten Namen wie Mozart, Beethoven, Johann Strauss usw. Aber ihr dürft nicht denken, dass man hier nur Walzer hört und alles romantisch ist. Wien ist auch eine Großstadt mit vielen Menschen und viel Verkehr°. Es gefällt mir hier so gut, dass ich gern noch ein paar Tage bleiben möchte. Das geht leider nicht, weil wir nicht nur Wien sehen wollen, sondern auch Salzburg und Innsbruck. Eine Woche ist einfach nicht lange genug für so eine Reise. Nach Budapest können wir leider auch nicht, aber hoffentlich komme ich im Frühling einmal nach Ungarn°.

So, jetzt muss ich aber schnell frühstücken und dann geht's wieder los°! Tschüss und viele liebe Grüße!

Euer Michael

Fokus Heurigen Wine

Because of the relatively mild climate, vineyards flourish on the hillsides of the Danube valley north of Vienna. There you can find the traditional **Heurige,** the young, fresh wine sold by wine growers in their courtyards or houses. Some of these places, identified by a wreath of vines or a branch hanging over the door, have been turned into restaurants **(Weinstuben** or **Heurigenschänken).** The more tourist-oriented ones also have **Schrammelmusik** with violins, guitars, and accordions. Located on the outskirts of Vienna, Grinzing is probably the best-known **Heurigen** wine village.

"Hier gibt's Gemütlichkeit beim Heurigenwein mit Musik."

Nach dem Lesen

A. Alles verstanden?

1. Wem schreibt Michael?
2. Wo ist er vor einer Woche noch gewesen?
3. Wie sind sie von dort nach Wien gekommen?
4. Warum findet er das Gästehaus in Wien so toll?
5. Warum hat er in der Kärntner Straße nichts gekauft?
6. Was hat er da natürlich auch besichtigt?
7. Welche Oper haben sie am Abend gesehen?
8. Wie heißt die Winterresidenz der Habsburger Kaiser und wo haben sie im Sommer gewohnt?
9. Was kann man in der Spanischen Hofreitschule sehen?
10. Wo und wie haben sie den Geburtstag von Mark gefeiert?
11. Was findet man überall in Wien?
12. Wohin wollen sie auch noch fahren, aber wohin kommen sie leider nicht?

A: 1. den/seinen Eltern 2. in Passau 3. mit dem Schiff 4. sehr zentral, können alles zu Fuß oder mit der U-Bahn erreichen 5. Die Geschäfte sind teuer. 6. den Stephansdom 7. *Die Zauberflöte* 8. die Hofburg, Schloss Schönbrunn 9. die Lipizzaner beim Training 10. in Grinzing in einer Weinstube 11. Denkmäler und Straßen mit bekannten Namen 12. nach Salzburg und Innsbruck, nach Budapest

B. *Sondern* oder *aber*? Insert the appropriate conjunction.

1. Das Gästehaus ist nicht sehr elegant, __aber__ es liegt zentral.
2. Wir sind nicht mit dem Bus gefahren, __sondern__ viel gelaufen.
3. Bei der Spanischen Hofreitschule ist das Reiten kein Sport, __sondern__ eine Kunst.
4. Die Geschäfte in der Kärntner Straße sind teuer, __aber__ sie gefallen mir.

C: 1. soll . . . beginnen 2. wollen . . . machen 3. kann . . . sehen 4. wollen . . . bleiben 5. soll . . . geben 6. muss . . . haben 7. darf . . . laufen 8. möchte . . . bummeln

Passau is a German city situated at the border with Austria. It is the starting point for regular steamer service down the Danube to Vienna and the Black Sea.

C. Fahrt *(Trip)* nach Österreich Mr. Schubach is talking about his travel plans. Phrase his statements using the modal verbs in parentheses.

BEISPIEL Ihr fahrt mit uns mit dem Schiff bis nach Wien. (müssen)
Ihr müsst mit uns mit dem Schiff bis nach Wien fahren.

1. Unsere Fahrt beginnt in Passau. (sollen)
2. In Linz machen wir einen Stopp. (wollen)
3. Vom Schiff sieht man viele Weinberge und Burgen. (können)
4. Wir bleiben fünf Tage in Wien. (wollen)
5. Dort gibt es viel zu sehen. (sollen)
6. Man hat natürlich bequeme *(comfortable)* Schuhe. (müssen)
7. Ich laufe aber nicht so viel. (dürfen)
8. Meine Frau bummelt gemütlich durch die Kärntner Straße. (möchten)

Weiteres

D. 1. Deutschland nordwestlich, Tschechien nördlich, dir Slowakie östlich, Ungarn östlich, Slowenien südlich, Italien südwestlich, die Schweiz westlich, Liechtenstein westlich 2. *(answer varies)*; Wien 3. *(answer varies)*; Wien / die Donau, Salzburg / die Salzach, Innsbruck / der Inn, Linz / die Donau, Graz / die Mur 4. der Bodensee; der Neusiedlersee; am Wörthersee

D. Landkarte von Österreich: Beantworten Sie die Fragen!

1. Wie viele Nachbarländer hat Österreich? Wie heißen sie und wo liegen sie?
2. Wie heißen ein paar Städte in Österreich? Wie heißt die Hauptstadt?
3. Welche Flüsse gibt es in Österreich? An welchem Fluss liegt Wien? Salzburg? Innsbruck? Linz? Graz? **(. . . liegt am / an der . . .)**
4. Welcher See liegt nicht nur in Österreich, sondern auch in Deutschland und in der Schweiz? Welcher See liegt zum Teil in Österreich und zum Teil in Ungarn? An welchem See liegt Klagenfurt?
5. Wo liegt der Brenner-Pass?

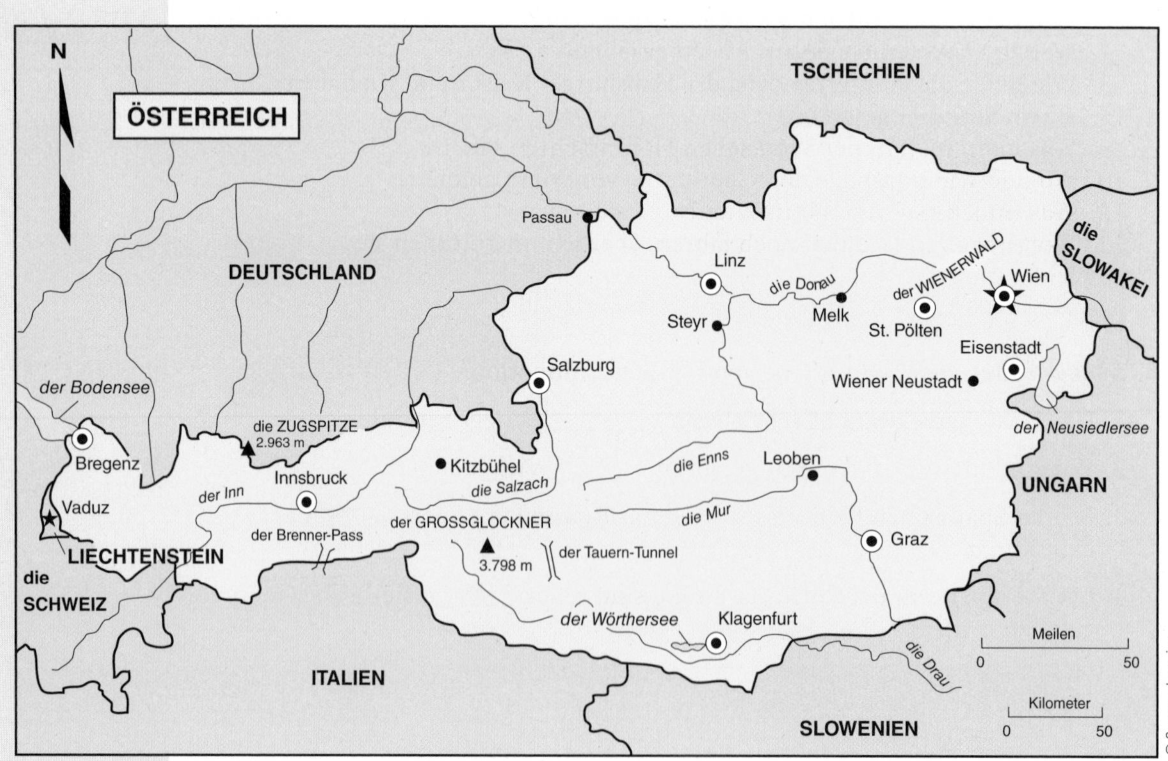

Straße über den Brenner-Pass

Fußgängerzone in Kitzbühel

E. Interview: Fragen Sie einen Partner / eine Partnerin, . . . !

E: Have students work in pairs or use the questions as guideline's for a written assignment.

1. ob er/sie schon einmal in Wien gewesen ist; wenn ja, was ihm/ihr in Wien besonders gut gefallen hat **(Was hat dir . . . ?)**; wenn nein, was er/sie einmal in Wien sehen möchte
2. wie die Hauptstadt in seinem/ihrem Bundessstaat oder in seiner/ihrer Provinz heißt
3. ob die Stadt eine Altstadt hat und ob sie schön ist
4. ob es dort eine Straßenbahn, eine U-Bahn oder Busse gibt
5. welche Denkmäler und Straßen mit bekannten Namen es gibt
6. was ihm/ihr dort besonders gefällt und was nicht

F. Kurzgespräche With a partner, choose one of the situations and prepare a brief dialogue. Then present it to the class.

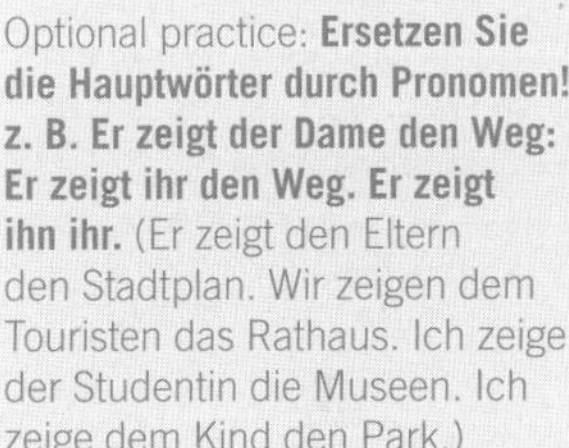
Optional practice: **Ersetzen Sie die Hauptwörter durch Pronomen! z. B. Er zeigt der Dame den Weg: Er zeigt ihr den Weg. Er zeigt ihn ihr.** (Er zeigt den Eltern den Stadtplan. Wir zeigen dem Touristen das Rathaus. Ich zeige der Studentin die Museen. Ich zeige dem Kind den Park.)

1. **Im Kaffeehaus** You and a friend are in a Viennese coffee house. Your friend suggests visiting the *Kunsthistorische Museum*. You ask someone at the table next to yours where the museum is located. You find out that it is not too far away, but that unfortunately it is closed today. You respond politely. Your friend suggests an alternative activity (strolling along the *Kärntner Straße*, visiting the *Spanische Hofreitschule* or the *Stephansdom*, etc.). Discuss how to reach your destination. Then consider what you might want to do in the evening **(heute Abend):** Perhaps go to *Grinzing* or the *Prater*?

Das Kunsthistorische Museum

Schreibtipp

Writing a Letter

Letters should start with the name of the city and a date. Less formal letters may begin with the salutation **Liebe(r) . . .** followed by a name, but more formal letters start with **Sehr geehrte Frau Schulz / Sehr geehrter Herr Schulz / Sehr geehrte Damen und Herren).** If either salutation is followed by a comma, the first word of the paragraph that follows is not capitalized.

End your letter with a closing, such as **Mit freundlichem Gruß! Ihr(e)/ Dein(e)/Euer(e)** + your name. Until the spelling reform a few years ago, the 2nd person familiar **du** and **ihr,** as well as all cases of those pronouns, were always capitalized in letters. It is no longer necessary to capitalize them, but many people still prefer to do so. Note that, on the envelope, the return address is always preceded by **Abs.** (= **Absender).**

2. **Souvenirs aus Wien** Before leaving Vienna, you and a friend are hunting for souvenirs but have a hard time finding something. What could one bring home? You might end up buying some **Mozartkugeln** or a piece of **Sachertorte,** but instead of taking them home, you eat them yourselves. You decide that's O.K. and that they were delicious. Some postcards **(Karten)** would be fine, too, but of what?

G. Brief: Grüße an die Gastfamilie in Regensburg Pretend you are with Michael's group in Vienna. Write eight to ten sentences to your host family in Regensburg, using the format of the letter below.

Wien, den 11. 9. 2014

Liebe Familie Fuchs,

jetzt wird es Zeit, dass ich Ihnen einmal schreibe. Wir sind schon eine Woche in Wien. Alles ist sehr interessant. Bin noch nie so viel gelaufen! Wir haben viele Museen besichtigt und sind auch einmal in die Oper gegangen. Sie haben "Die Zauberflöte" gespielt. Fantastisch! Heute Abend wollen wir in Grinzing gemütlich Geburtstag feiern. Morgen fahren wir nach Salzburg und Innsbruck und dann geht es wieder nach Hause. Wir sind Samstagnachmittag um 4 Uhr 15 wieder in Regensburg.

Viele liebe Grüße!

Ihr Oliver

Abs. Oliver Smith
Singerstraße 11
A-1010 Wien

An Familie
Norbert Fuchs
Bogenstraße 30
D-93051 Regensburg

Hörverständnis

Schon lange nicht mehr gesehen! Listen to the conversation between Uwe and Erika; then answer the questions. You do not need to write complete sentences.

Zum Erkennen: schon lange nicht mehr *(not for a long time)*; die Bergwanderungen *(mountain hikes)*

1. Wo ist Uwe gewesen? in Österreich
2. Mit wem ist er gefahren? mit Jürgen
3. Wie ist das Wetter gewesen? wunderbar, es hat nur einmal geregnet
4. Wo ist Maria Alm? in der Nähe von Salzburg
5. Was haben sie dort gemacht? Bergwanderungen
6. Wo sind sie noch gewesen? in Salzburg
7. Was haben sie dort besichtigt? die Burg und den Dom
8. Wann will Uwe nach Wien? im Oktober
9. Warum muss Erika gehen? Ihre Vorlesung beginnt in fünf Minuten.

For further practice, an optional two-part video (**Szenen** and **Interviews**) is available on the ***Wie geht's?*** Premium Website and in iLrn, with corresponding questions and activities in the *Arbeitsbuch* (SAM).

As an optional activity, with Google Earth you could visit Vienna, Salzburg, or any other Austrian city, or even follow Michael down the Danube from Passau to Vienna on a River Cruise.

Schloss Mirabell mit seinem Garten und Blick auf die Festung Hohensalzburg

Rückschau

Kapitelwortschatz

Hauptwörter

das Auto, -s	*car*
der Bahnhof, ¨e	*train station*
die Bank, -en	*bank*
die Bibliothek, -en	*library*
die Brücke, -n	*bridge*
der Bus, -se	*bus*
die Dame, -n	*lady*
der Dom, -e	*cathedral*
das Fahrrad, ¨er	*bike*
die Haltestelle, -n	(*bus,* etc.) *stop*
das Hotel, -s	*hotel*
das Kino, -s	*movie theater*
die Kirche, -n	*church*
das Museum, Museen	*museum*
der Park, -s	*park*
der Platz, ¨e	*place; square*
die Post	*post office*
das Rathaus, ¨er	*city hall*
das Schloss, ¨er	*palace*
die Schule, -n	*school*
der Stadtplan, ¨e	*city map*
die Straße, -n	*street*
die Straßenbahn, -en	*streetcar*
das Taxi, -s	*taxi*
das Theater, -	*theater*
der Tourist, -en, -en	*tourist* (male)
die Touristin, -nen	*tourist* (female)
die U-Bahn	*subway*
die Universität, -en	*university*
die Uni, -s	*university* (coll.)
der Weg, -e	*way; trail*

Verben

besichtigen	*to tour, visit* (*a palace,* etc.)
bummeln	*to stroll*
halten	*to stop; to hold*
zeigen	*to show*
zu Fuß gehen	*to walk*

Modalverben

dürfen	*to be allowed to, may*
können	*to be able to, can*
mögen	*to like*
müssen	*to have to, must*
sollen	*to be supposed to*
wollen	*to want to*

Adjektive und Adverbien

bekannt	*well-known*
gemütlich	*pleasant, convivial; cozy*
genug	*enough*
hoffentlich	*hopefully; I hope*
interessant	*interesting*
leider	*unfortunately*
lieb	*dear; lovingly, tenderly*
nah	*nearby, close*
stundenlang	*for hours*
weit	*far*

Verschiedenes

aber	*but; however*
an/am . . . vorbei	*past the . . .*
bis Sie . . . sehen	*until you see . . .*
da drüben	*over there*
dorthin	*to there*
die erste Straße links / rechts	*first street to the left / right*
(den Fluss) entlang	*along (the river)*
(ein)mal	*once, (at) one time*
Entschuldigen Sie!	*Excuse me!*
Entschuldigung!	*Excuse me!*
Es tut mir leid.	*I'm sorry.*
Fahren Sie mit dem Bus!	*Take the bus!*
gegenüber von	*across from*
Gibt es hier in der Nähe . . .?	*Is there . . . nearby?*
Ich möchte zum/zur . . .	*I would like to go to . . .*
(immer) geradeaus	*(keep) straight ahead*
in der Nähe von	*near, in the vicinity of*
Können Sie mir sagen, wo . . . ist?	*Can you tell me where . . . is?*
Sie können zu Fuß gehen.	*You can walk.*
sondern	*but, on the contrary, rather*
Verzeihung!	*Excuse me!*
Wie kommt man von hier zum/ zur . . . ?	*How do you get from here to . . . ?*

Zum Schluss

1. Schreiben Sie!

a. **Besuchen Sie uns!** (*Come and visit us!*) Pretend you could invite anyone you like—your favorite band, favorite celebrity, a fictional or historical figure—to visit your city. How would you convince them to visit? Write a letter describing the sights and landmarks in your city. Where might they like to visit? Where would you like to take them? Refer to the examples from this chapter, along with the **Wortschatz**, to write at least eight to ten sentences.

b. **Ersetzen Sie die Hauptwörter!** Now, read through your letter and replace some of the nouns with pronouns. Don't forget to pay attention to case and proper word order!

2. Kombinieren Sie!

a. How many sentences can you create with the following elements? Work with your study group to use vocabulary from this chapter and earlier chapters to create complete sentences. Again, pay attention to case and proper word order!

1	2	3	4	5
wann	besichtigen	ich	das Auto	(immer) geradeaus
warum	bummeln	du	die Bibliothek	in der Nähe von (+ *dat.*)
was	dürfen	er	das Fahrrad	an/am . . . vorbei
wer	empfehlen	es	der Stadtplan	da drüben
wem	geben	sie	der Tourist	dorthin
wie lange	können	wir	die Touristen	gegenüber von (+ *dat.*)
	möchten	ihr	die Universität (Uni)	nah/weit
	müssen	sie	. . .	stundenlang
	sollen	Sie	. . .	nach Österreich fahren
	wollen	. . .	. . .	in die Stadt gehen
	zeigen	. . .	. . .	zu Fuß gehen
	. . .	. . .	. . .	sondern / aber

b. **Ersetzen Sie die Hauptwörter!** Again, read through your sentences. How many nouns can you replace with pronouns? Rewrite at least three sentences using the appropriate pronouns.

3. Rat geben (*Giving advice*) What advice would you give, if a friend came to you with the following problems? Use the modal verbs from this chapter to make suggestions. Compare your answers with a classmate. What would he/she advise?

a. Ich bin so müde, aber morgen habe ich eine Prüfung.

b. Ich verstehe die Fragen einfach nicht.

c. Ich habe Hunger, aber ich habe nichts zu Hause.

d. Meine Freunde kommen und wollen mit mir in die Stadt gehen. Sie verstehen nicht, dass ich keine Zeit habe.

e. Wir sind spät durch die Stadt gebummelt und jetzt fährt kein Bus mehr.

iLrn **Onlineaktivitäten** View iLrn for online activities related to this chapter. There you will find additional resources, such as a memory game (**Gedächtnisspiel**), a crossword puzzle (**Kreuzworträtsel**), audio flash cards (**Vokabelblitz**), a tutorial quiz (**Mini-Quiz**), and the active vocabulary (**Wortschatz**) for this chapter.

Kapitel 6

Wohnen

Lernziele In this chapter you will learn about:

Zum Thema

Homes and home furnishings

Fokus

Housing and living arrangements, Friedensreich Hundertwasser, public transportation and city life, High German and German dialects

Struktur

- Two-way prepositions
- Imperatives
- **Wissen** vs. **kennen**

Einblicke

Lesetext: Schaffen, sparen, Häuschen bauen

Rückschau

Kapitalwortschatz
Zum Schluss

RESSOURCEN

 iLrn
Video
 Audio
 SAM

Alle Wohnungen in diesem Eckhaus **(corner building)** ***haben große Fenster und sind schön hell.***

Vorschau Housing

After World War II, West Germany suffered an acute housing shortage, not only because so many buildings had been destroyed but also because of the large number of refugees coming from the east. Rebuilding in the 1960s and 1970s created high-rise apartment clusters (**Wohnsilos**) that mushroomed around the old cities, often contrasting sharply with the traditional architecture. Fortunately, urban planning has rediscovered the beauty of older buildings and given priority to eco-friendly construction, and subsidies and tax incentives have made it possible to restore and modernize housing. Strict zoning and building regulation laws have attempted to harmonize housing construction and renovation with the surroundings and to conform to local building styles. Home investment and rehabilitation is encouraged by various forms of governmental help, such as tax incentives. But contrary to the situation in North America, home ownership in Germany is only about 51 percent.

With the end of the Cold War and the collapse of the economy in the former East Germany, another wave of people moved west, which again created a housing crisis. Students, young couples, and large families often have difficulties finding affordable accommodations, especially in the larger cities of southern Germany, such as Stuttgart and Munich.

Ask students what they expect to be included in a furnished apartment where they live, and what supplementary expenses they expect to have to pay.

Two-thirds of the housing units in the former German Democratic Republic (GDR, East Germany) dated back to the time before World War II, often lacking modern sanitary facilities and heating systems. In the early 1970s, the GDR started a housing program of standardized pre-fabricated high-rise apartment buildings on the outskirts of towns, the so-called **Plattenbauten** made with concrete sheets. These cheaply and quickly produced apartments came as a solution to the housing shortage and created uniform satellite cities, typical for Soviet Union urban planning. For most families, they were a luxury, because they provided central heating and bathroom facilities. After reunification, however, more and more people have been leaving these housing projects to move into newly renovated prewar buildings (**Altbauwohnungen**) or newly built modern homes and apartments, leaving 30 percent of the cheap GDR apartments empty—many of them being either left abandoned or torn down; a few are being rehabilitated.

Fragen: 1. Sind die Wohnungen auf dem Bild links alt oder modern? 2. Wie viele Stockwerke *(floors)* sieht man hier? 3. Auf dem Balkon von einigen *(some)* Wohnungen und auch vor dem Haus gibt es Grünpflanzen *(. . . plants)*. Haben Sie da, wo Sie jetzt wohnen, auch einen Balkon mit Blumen oder Grünpflanzen? 4. Wie gefällt Ihnen das Haus unten *(below)*? Warum? 5. Wo möchten Sie gern wohnen, in einer Altbauwohnung von dem Haus links oder in dem Haus unten? Warum?

Apartments are advertised by the number of rooms. Those who want to rent a three-bedroom apartment with a living room and a dining room need a **Fünfzimmerwohnung;** bathroom and kitchen are excluded from the room count. Furnished apartments are relatively rare. "Unfurnished" is usually to be taken literally, since there are no built-in closets, kitchen cabinets, appliances, light fixtures, or other such conveniences. Tenants are responsible for furnishing and maintaining their apartments (including interior painting and decorating) and usually have to pay monthly maintenance fees. Heat may or may not be included in the rent or maintenance fees, and the apartment is advertised accordingly as being either **warm** or **kalt.**

Haus mit Garten in Österreich

Zum Thema

Gespräche

Wohnung zu vermieten

Warm-ups: 1. **Was ist der Artikel von . . . ?** *Refer to clothing and food.* 2. **Was ist der Plural von** Bus, Brücke, Kino, Museum, . . . ? 3. **Können Sie mir sagen,** wie spät es ist? welches Datum heute ist? was für ein Tag heute ist? auf welcher Seite vom Buch wir sind?

ANNA Hallo, mein Name ist Anna Moser. Ich habe gehört, dass Sie eine Zweizimmerwohnung zu vermieten haben. Stimmt das?
VERMIETER Ja, in der Nähe vom Dom, mit Blick auf den Marktplatz.
ANNA Wie alt ist die Wohnung?
VERMIETER Ziemlich alt, aber sie ist renoviert und schön groß und hell. Sie hat sogar einen Balkon.
ANNA Ein Balkon? Das ist ja toll! Ich habe viele Pflanzen. In welchem Stock liegt sie?
VERMIETER Im dritten Stock.
ANNA Ist sie möbliert oder unmöbliert?
VERMIETER Unmöbliert.
ANNA Und was kostet die Wohnung?
VERMIETER 550 Euro.
ANNA Ist das kalt oder warm?
VERMIETER Kalt.
ANNA Oje, das ist mir ein bisschen zu teuer. Na ja, vielen Dank! Auf Wiederhören!
VERMIETER Auf Wiederhören!

Point out that, as mentioned in the *Vorschau*, **kalt** means "without heating and with a monthly maintenance fee." The renter pays for that.

In der WG (Wohngemeinschaft)

ANNA Euer Haus gefällt mir!
JÖRG Wir haben noch Platz für dich. Komm, ich zeige dir alles! . . . Hier links ist unsere Küche. Sie ist klein, aber praktisch.
ANNA Wer kocht?
JÖRG Wir alle: Benno, Verena und ich.
ANNA Und das ist das Wohnzimmer?
JÖRG Ja. Es ist ein bisschen dunkel, aber das ist okay.
ANNA Eure Sessel gefallen mir.
JÖRG Sie sind alt, aber echt bequem . . . So, und hier oben sind dann vier Schlafzimmer und das Bad.
ANNA Mm, die Schlafzimmer sind sehr gemütlich, aber nur ein Bad?
JÖRG Ja, leider! Aber unten ist noch eine Toilette.
ANNA Was bezahlt ihr im Monat?
JÖRG Jeder 200 Euro.
ANNA Nicht schlecht! Und wie kommst du zur Uni?
JÖRG Kein Problem. Ich gehe zu Fuß.
ANNA Klingt gut!

A. Alles verstanden?

A: 1. in der Nähe vom Dom 2. eine Zweizimmerwohnung / Altbauwohnung. 3. im 3. Stock 4. der Balkon 5. zu teuer 6. in einer WG 7. 4 Schlafzimmer, 1 Bad 8. 200 Euro 9. (sehr) gut 10. laufen / zu Fuß gehen

1. Wo gibt es eine Wohnung zu vermieten? 2. Was für eine Wohnung ist es? 3. In welchem Stock liegt sie? 4. Was gefällt Anna an der Wohnung? 5. Warum will sie sie nicht nehmen? 6. Wo wohnen Jörg, Benno und Verena? 7. Wie viele Schlafzimmer und Bäder hat die Wohngemeinschaft? 8. Was muss jeder im Monat zahlen? 9. Wie gefällt Anna die Wohnung? 10. Wie kann sie von dort zur Uni kommen?

 **B. Jetzt sind Sie dran!** With a partner, create your own dialogue. Pretend you are hunting for an apartment or house. Talk about prices, individual rooms, whether utilities are included or not, location, and how to get from there to the university.

Fokus Shared Living Arrangements

Rooms in dormitories **(Studentenwohnheime)** are typically quite scarce and often allocated by lottery, so students and other young people often choose instead to live in **WGs** or **Wohngemeinschaften** (*shared housing or "co-ops"*). Moving into an apartment or a house with others—who are often complete strangers—is quite common, since even studio apartments are often too expensive for student budgets.

Wortschatz 1

Das Haus, ¨er *(house)*

Das Studentenwohnheim, -e *(dorm)*

Die Wohnung, -en *(apartment)*

der Balkon, -s	*balcony*	die Ecke, -n	*corner*
Baum, ¨e	*tree*	Garage, -n	*garage*
Flur, -e	*hallway*	Küche, -n	*kitchen*
Garten, ¨	*garden, yard*	Toilette, -n	*toilet*
Keller, -	*basement, cellar*		
das Bad, ¨er	*bathroom*		
Dach, ¨er	*roof*	im Bad / in der Küche	*in the bathroom / kitchen*
Zimmer, -	*room*		
Arbeitszimmer, -	*study*	im Keller	*in the basement*
Esszimmer, -	*dining room*	im Parterre / Erdgeschoss	*on the first floor (ground floor)*
Schlafzimmer, -	*bedroom*		
Wohnzimmer, -	*living room*	im ersten Stock	*on the second floor*

Das Parterre, BUT **der** Stock.

Die Möbel *(pl.) (furniture)*

der Fernseher, -	*TV set*	das Bett, -en	*bed*
Kühlschrank, ¨e	*refrigerator*	Radio, -s	*radio*
Schrank, ¨e	*closet, cupboard*	Regal, -e	*shelf, bookcase*
Schreibtisch, -e	*desk*	Sofa, -s	*sofa*
Sessel, -	*armchair*	Telefon, -e	*telephone*
Stuhl, ¨e	*chair*	die Kommode, -n	*dresser*
Teppich, -e	*carpet*	Lampe, -n	*lamp*
Tisch, -e	*table*		
Vorhang, ¨e	*curtain*		

Verschiedenes

ein bisschen	*a little bit (of), some*
im Monat	*per month*
oben / unten	*up(stairs) / down(stairs)*
hell / dunkel	*light; bright(ly) / dark*
praktisch	*practical(ly)*
(un)bequem	*(un)comfortable; (in)convenient*
sogar	*even*
ziemlich	*quite, rather*
baden	*to take a bath; to swim*

Note that translations in these lists focus on the use of these words in the dialogue, e.g., ***sogar*** could be translated in many other ways.

There are two verbs with the infinitive ***hängen.*** The *t*-verb means *to hang (up)* something somewhere; the *n*-verb, that something *is hanging* somewhere.

duschen	*to take a shower*
hängen, gehängt	*to hang (up)*
hängen, gehangen	*to hang (be hanging)*
kochen	*to cook*
legen	*to lay, put (flat)*
liegen, gelegen	*to lie (be lying flat)*
mieten / vermieten	*to rent / to rent out*
setzen	*to set, put*
sitzen, gesessen	*to sit (be sitting)*
stehen, gestanden	*to stand (be standing)*
stellen	*to stand, put (upright)*
waschen (wäscht), gewaschen	*to wash*
das Problem, -e	*problem*
(Das ist) kein Problem.	*(That's) no problem.*
(Das) klingt gut!	*(That) sounds good.*
(Das) stimmt!	*(That's) true.; (That's) right.*
Auf Wiederhören!	*Good-bye!* (on the phone)

Zum Erkennen: renoviert *(renovated);* (un)möbliert *([un]furnished);* die WG, -s / Wohngemeinschaft, -en *(shared housing);* Oje! *(Oh no! Good gracious!);* na ja *(oh well, all right then);* jeder *(each one);* AUCH: der Imperativ, -e; der Blick auf *(+ acc.) (view of);* im Dachgeschoss *(in the attic)*

Übungen zum Thema

A. Was bedeuten die Wörter? Was ist ihr Artikel und ihr Plural?

Balkontür, Bücherregal, Dachgeschosswohnung, Duschvorhang, Elternschlafzimmer, Kinderbad, Farbfernseher, Küchenfenster, Kochecke, Liegestuhl, Schlafsofa, Schreibtischlampe, Sitzecke, Stehlampe, Wandlampe, Waschecke, Wohnzimmerteppich

A: *balcony door* (**die** / -türen), *bookshelf* (**das** / -regale), *attic apartment* (**die** / -wohnungen), *shower curtain* (**der** / -vorhänge), *master bedroom* (**das** / -zimmer), *children's bath* (**das** / -bäder), *color TV* (**der** / -fernseher), *kitchen window* (**das** / -fenster), *cook's nook / cooking area* (**die** / -ecken), *lounge chair* (**der** / -stühle), *sofa sleeper* (**das** / -sofas), *desk lamp* (**die** / -lampen), *corner bench seating arrangement* (**die** / -ecken), *floor lamp* (**die** / -lampen), *wall lamp* (**die** / -lampen), *vanity area* (**die** / -ecken), *livingroom carpet* (**der** / -teppiche)

Fokus Homes and Houses

When German-speakers say "first floor" **(erste Etage** or **erster Stock),** they mean what North Americans usually call the *second floor.* Either **das Parterre** or **das Erdgeschoss** is used to denote the ground floor, or North American first floor. In elevators, remember to press "E" (for **Erdgeschoss**) or "0" to get to the exit.

Homes and apartments usually have a foyer **(die Diele)** and a hallway **(der Flur),** with doors leading to the various rooms. For the sake of privacy and to conserve energy, many Germans prefer to keep doors shut—this also holds true in the workplace and in such institutions as like the university, where people prefer to work with doors closed. Sheer, pretty curtains **(Gardinen)** are also a typical feature that permits people to see out, but prevents others from looking in. In addition, some houses have outside shutters **(Rolläden** or **Rollos)** that can be rolled down over the windows at night. Traditional half-timbered houses **(Fachwerkhäuser)** often have colorful shutters that swing shut on hinges.

Das Fachwerkhaus ist alt, aber innen sehr gemütlich.

B. Beschreiben Sie die Wohnung! With a partner, take turns describing what furniture you see in the various rooms of this apartment. Don't forget to use the accusative case!

BEISPIEL *Im Wohnzimmer gibt es einen Esstisch, . . .*

C. Kein Haus / keine Wohnung ohne Maschinen Working in small groups, report what machines or appliances you have or don't have, what you need, and what you would like to have in your house or apartment.

D. Interview: Fragen Sie einen Nachbarn / eine Nachbarin, . . . !

1. ob er/sie eine Wohnung hat oder ob er/sie zu Hause, im Studentenwohnheim oder in einer WG wohnt; wenn nicht zu Hause, wie viel Miete er/sie im Monat bezahlt
2. ob er/sie Mitbewohner *(housemates)*, einen Zimmerkollegen oder eine Zimmerkollegin *(roommate)* hat; wenn ja, wie sie heißen
3. wie sein/ihr Zimmer ist und was für Möbel er/sie im Zimmer hat
4. ob er/sie eine Küche hat; wenn ja, was es in der Küche gibt und wer kocht
5. wie lange er/sie schon da wohnt
6. wie er/sie zur Uni kommt

In case you are curious: *answering machine* **der Anrufbeantworter, -;** *bathtub* **die Badewanne, -n;** *cell phone* **das Handy, -s;** *computer* **der Computer, -;** *dining room cabinet* **das Büfett, -s;** *dishwasher* **die Spülmaschine, -n;** *elevator* **der Aufzug, ¨-e;** *fireplace* **der Kamin, -e;** *kitchen cabinet* **der Küchenschrank, ¨-e;** *microwave* **die Mikrowelle, -n *(coll.)*;** *mirror,* **der Spiegel, -;** *MP3 player* **der MP3-Spieler, -;** *nightstand* **der Nachttisch, -e;** *oven* **der Ofen ¨-;** *patio* **die Terrasse, -n;** *personal digital assistant* **der persönliche digitale Assistent, -en, (PDA);** *piano* **das Klavier, -e;** *pool* **der Swimmingpool, -s;** *range, cooktop* **der Herd, -e;** *shower* **die Dusche, -n;** *(bathroom) sink* **das Waschbecken, -;** *(kitchen) sink* **das Spülbecken, -;** *stairwell* **das Treppenhaus;** *toaster* **der Toaster, -;** *wardrobe / armoire* **der Kleiderschrank, ¨-e**

For Exercises B and C encourage students to check the list in the margin as well. Exercise C might be fun, but if you feel that it has too much passive vocabulary, just skip it.

Aussprache: ei, au, eu, äu

A. Laute

1. [ai] w**ei**t, l**ei**der, **ei**gentlich, z**ei**gen, f**ei**ern, bl**ei**ben
2. [au] **au**f, bl**au**gr**au**, B**au**m, K**au**fh**au**s, br**au**chen, l**au**fen
3. [oi] **eu**ch, h**eu**te, t**eu**er, L**eu**te, Fr**eu**nde, H**äu**ser, B**äu**me

B. Wortpaare

1. *by* / bei
2. *Troy* / treu
3. *mouse* / Maus
4. Haus / Häuser
5. aus / Eis
6. euer / Eier

For further review, see the Summary of Pronunciation in the front of this book. Study Part II, subsections 37–39.

Hörverständnis

Hier Müller! Listen to the conversation between Inge and Mrs. Müller. Then decide whether the statements below are true or false according to the dialogue.

Zum Erkennen: nett *(nice);* teilen *(to share);* na gut *(well, good);* Bis bald! *(See you soon!)*

	Das stimmt.	Das stimmt nicht.
1. Inge ist Frau Müllers Tochter.	✓	___
2. Frau Müller hat ihr ein Zimmer gefunden.	___	✓
3. Das Zimmer ist in der Schillerstraße.	✓	___
4. Inges Telefonnummer ist 91 68.	___	✓
5. Wohnungen sind ein bisschen teuer.	✓	___
6. Inge hat Horst vor ein paar Tagen gesehen.	✓	___
7. Sie teilt jetzt ein Zimmer mit Horst.	___	✓
8. Inge zahlt 140 Euro im Monat.	___	✓
9. Sie kann mit dem Fahrrad zur Uni fahren.	✓	___
10. Am Wochenende kommt sie nach Hause.	___	✓

Mensch, klingt das nicht interessant?

Struktur

6.1 Two-way prepositions

You have learned some prepositions that are always followed by the dative and some that are always followed by the accusative. You will now learn a set of prepositions that sometimes take the dative (location) and sometimes the accusative (change of place or destination).

1. Below are the basic meanings of the nine TWO-WAY PREPOSITIONS:

an	*to; up to; at (the side of); on* (vertical surface)
auf	*on, on top of; onto* (horizontal surface)
hinter	*behind*
in	*in; into; inside of*
neben	*beside, next to*
über	*over; above; about*
unter	*under; below*
vor	*before; in front of*
zwischen	*between*

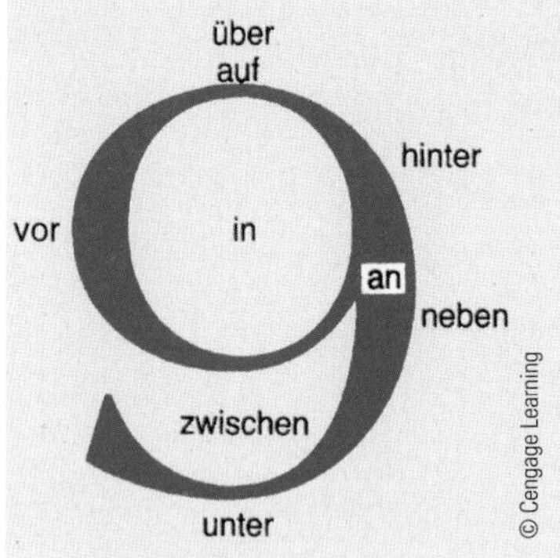

© Cengage Learning

Most of these prepositions may be contracted with articles in colloquial German. The following are the most common contractions that are acceptable even in written German:

an + das = **ans**	in + das = **ins**
an + dem = **am**	in + dem = **im**
auf + das = **aufs**	

To practice the meaning of the prepositions, give students sentences in English and have them state the appropriate German preposition: 1. *My car is in front of the house.* **(vor)** 2. *I left my books on top of the car.* **(auf)** 3. *I saw them when I went to the window.* **(an)**

You might also mention the contractions **vorm** and **vors**, but these are strictly colloquial.

CAUTION: Be careful to distinguish between **vor** and **bevor.** The preposition **vor** precedes a noun **(vor dem Haus).** The conjunction **bevor** introduces a clause **(. . . , bevor du das Haus mietest).**

2. **Wo?** vs. **wohin?**

   a. German has two words to ask *where:* **wo?** *(in what place?)* and **wohin?** *(to what place?).* **Wo** asks about LOCATION, where something is or an activity within a place. **Wohin** asks about DESTINATION or a CHANGE OF PLACE.

LOCATION:	**Wo** ist Horst?	*Where's Horst? (in what place)*
DESTINATION:	**Wohin** geht Horst?	*Where's Horst going? (to what place)*

   b. The difference between location and destination also plays a role in determining the case following two-way prepositions. If the question is **wo?,** the *dative* is used. If the question is **wohin?,** the *accusative* is used.

■ **woher** *(from where),* introduced in Chapter 1, denotes origin.

Demonstrate the difference between ACTIVITY IN A PLACE by walking back and forth in the classroom, then CHANGE OF PLACE by walking out of the room.

Wo ist Horst?	→ In **der** Küche.	*Where's Horst?*	→ *In the kitchen.*
Wohin geht Horst?	→ In **die** Küche.	*Where's Horst going?*	→ *To the kitchen.*

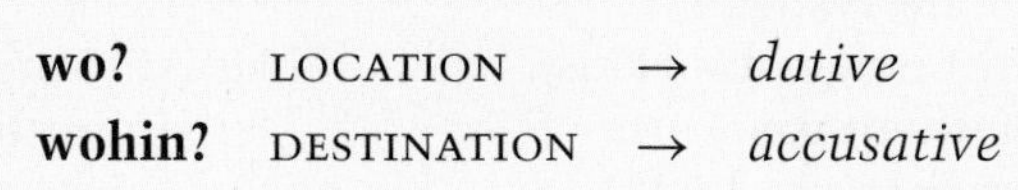

wo?	LOCATION	→	*dative*
wohin?	DESTINATION	→	*accusative*

To give students practice in determining whether the *dative* or the *accusative* must be used, give them English sentences and have them state the proper case in German: e.g., *The library is next to the dorm. She's going into the cafeteria. He sits down next to a friend.*

3. The difference lies entirely with the verb!

   - Some verbs denoting LOCATION OR ACTIVITY WITHIN A PLACE (**wo?** → *dative*) are hängen, kaufen, kochen, lesen, liegen, schlafen, sein, sitzen, spielen, stehen, studieren, tanzen, trinken, wohnen.
   - Typical verbs implying DESTINATION OR A CHANGE OF PLACE OR MOTION TOWARD a point (**wohin?** → *accusative*) are bringen, fahren, gehen, hängen, kommen, laufen, legen, setzen, stellen, tragen.

4. Some important verb pairs

N*-VERBS / LOCATION → *DATIVE	***T*-VERBS / CHANGE OF PLACE → *ACCUSATIVE***
hängen, gehangen *(to be hanging)*	hängen, gehängt *(to hang up)*
liegen, gelegen *(to be lying [flat])*	legen, gelegt *(to lay down, put [flat])*
sitzen, gesessen *(to be sitting)*	setzen, gesetzt *(to set/put down)*
stehen, gestanden *(to be standing)*	stellen, gestellt *(to put [upright])*

   - Note that the four *n*-verbs are all intransitive (that is, they do not take a direct object). The four *t*-verbs, in contrast, are transitive (that is, they do take a direct object).

Der Mantel hat **im** Schrank gehangen.
Ich habe den Mantel **in den** Schrank gehängt.

CAUTION: Although **legen, setzen,** and **stellen** are all sometimes translated as *to put*, they are *not interchangeable!*

Sie **stellt** den Stuhl an die Wand. *(upright position)*
Sie **legt** das Heft auf den Tisch. *(flat position)*
Er **setzt** das Kind auf den Stuhl. *(sitting position)*

As an optional activity, you could act out situations: 1. Ich gehe an die Tafel. Ich stehe . . . 2. Ich lege das Buch auf den Tisch. Es liegt . . . 3. Ich stelle den Stuhl hinter den Tisch. Er steht . . . 4. Ich werfe das Papier in den Papierkorb. Es liegt . . . 5. Ich hänge das Bild an die Wand. Es hängt . . . 6. Ich lege das Heft unter das Buch. Es liegt . . . 7. Die Kreide fällt vom Tisch. Sie liegt vor (unter, auf . . .) 8. Ich gehe zwischen den Tisch und die Tafel. Ich stehe . . .

5. Summary

WOHIN?	**WO?**
Die Tante hängt den Teppich **über das** Balkongeländer *(. . . banister)*.	Der Teppich hängt **über dem** Balkongeländer.
Die Mutter stellt die Leiter *(ladder)* **an die** Wand.	Die Leiter steht **an der** Wand.
Das Auto fährt **neben das** Haus.	Das Auto steht **neben dem** Haus.
Der Hund läuft **vor das** Auto.	Der Hund steht **vor dem** Auto.
Der Großvater nimmt die Pfeife *(pipe)* **in den** Mund *(mouth)*.	Der Großvater hat die Pfeife **im** Mund.

■ ALSO: Das Kind legt den Teddy auf die Bank *(bench)*. Der Teddy liegt auf der Bank. / Das Huhn läuft unter die Bank. Es sitzt unter der Bank.

Note also these uses of **an, auf,** and **in.** You are already familiar with most of them:

Die Stadt liegt **am** Rhein / **an der** Donau.	*The city is on the Rhine / on the Danube.*
Sie spielen **auf der** Straße.	*They're playing in the street.*
Sie leben **in** Deutschland / **in der** Schweiz.	*They live in Germany / in Switzerland.*
Sie leben **in** Stuttgart / **im** Süden.	*They live in Stuttgart / in the South.*
Sie wohnen **in der** Schillerstraße.	*They live on Schiller Street.*
Sie wohnen **im** Parterre / **im** ersten Stock.	*They live on the first / second floor.*

- With feminine or plural names of countries, **in** is used rather than **nach** to express *to.*

  Wir fahren **in die Schweiz / in die Bundesrepublik.**
  Wir fahren **in die USA / in die Vereinigten Staaten.**
  BUT: Wir fahren **nach Österreich / nach Deutschland.**

Be aware that there are also a few cases, where a masculine name of a country uses **in** to express *to,* such as **Ich reise *(travel)* in den Iran, in den Irak.**

- If you plan to see a film or play, or to attend a church service, **in** must be used; **zu** implies going *in the direction of, up to,* BUT NOT *into a place.*

Wir gehen **zum Kino.**	*(To go just to look outside and see what's playing, or to meet somebody there)*
Wir gehen **ins Kino.**	*(To go inside to see a movie)*

The preposition **zu** was introduced in Chapter 3.

Übungen

A. Sagen Sie es noch einmal! Replace the nouns following the prepositions with the words suggested.

BEISPIEL Der Bleistift liegt unter dem Papier. (Jacke)
Der Bleistift liegt unter der Jacke.

1. Die Post ist neben der Bank. (Bahnhof, Kino, Apotheke)
2. Melanie kommt in die Wohnung. (Küche, Esszimmer, Garten)
3. Die Mäntel liegen auf dem Bett. (Sofa, Kommode, Stühle)
4. Mein Schlafzimmer ist über der Küche. (Wohnzimmer, Garage, Bad)
5. Willi legt den Pullover auf die Kommode. (Bett, Schreibtisch, Sessel)
6. Stellen Sie das Fahrrad hinter die Terrasse! (Haus, Baum, Garage)

A: Remind students that most nouns end in **-n** in the dative plural.

A: 1. neben dem Bahnhof, dem Kino, der Apotheke 2. in die Küche, das Esszimmer, den Garten 3. auf dem Sofa, der Kommode, den Stühlen 4. über dem Wohnzimmer, der Garage, dem Bad 5. auf das Bett, den Schreibtisch, den Sessel 6. hinter das Haus, den Baum, die Garage

B: 1. Bücher bekommt man in der Bibliothek. Silvia geht in die Bibliothek. 2. CDs bekommt man im Kaufhaus. Oliver geht ins Kaufhaus. 3. Shampoo bekommt man in der Drogerie. Bettina geht in die Drogerie. 4. Schuhe bekommt man im Schuhgeschäft. Maren geht ins Schuhgeschäft. 5. Regale bekommt man im Möbelgeschäft. Christian geht ins Möbelgeschäft. 6. Kaffee und Kuchen bekommt man im Café. Oma Schütz geht ins Café. 7. Medizin bekommt man in der Apotheke. Andreas geht in die Apotheke.

Optional practice: **Fragen an die Studenten:** 1. Wo schläft man? 2. Wo kocht man? 3. Wohin tut man Lebensmittel wie Milch, Butter und Käse? 4. Wo essen Sie gewöhnlich? 5. Wo machen Sie Ihre Hausaufgaben? 6. Wo sitzen Sie gewöhnlich mit Ihren Freunden?

B. Wo bekommt man das? Starting with the boldface phrase repeat the information by saying where each of the people below is going to get those items.

BEISPIEL Frau Müller braucht etwas **Butter und Käse.** (Supermarkt)
Butter und Käse bekommt man im Supermarkt.
Frau Müller geht in den Supermarkt.

1. Silvia sucht ein paar **Bücher.** (Bibliothek)
2. Oliver will ein paar **CDs.** (Kaufhaus)
3. Bettina braucht ein bisschen **Shampoo.** (Drogerie)
4. Maren sucht ein paar **Schuhe.** (Schuhgeschäft)
5. Christian hat viele Bücher, aber keine **Regale.** (Möbelgeschäft)
6. Oma Schütz ist müde vom Einkaufen und möchte eine Tasse **Kaffee und Kuchen.** (Café)
7. Andreas braucht **Medizin.** (Apotheke)

C. Wo sind Sie wann? Report where you are at certain times. You may use the locations in the last column or come up with ideas of your own.

BEISPIEL morgens
Morgens bin ich gewöhnlich in der Bibliothek.

1	2	3	4	5
morgens	fahren	gern	an	Badewanne *(f.)*
mittags	gehen	gemütlich	auf	Berge
abends	liegen	gewöhnlich	in	Bett
am Wochenende	sein	manchmal	vor	Bibliothek
(über)morgen	sitzen	nicht		Computer *(m.)*
im Sommer / Winter	sprechen	oft		Fernseher
wenn ich Hunger habe	. . .	stundenlang		Garten
wenn ich faul *(lazy)* bin		tagelang		Garten
wenn ich lernen muss		. . .		Sofa
wenn ich baden will				Kühlschrank
wenn ich müde bin				Swimmingpool
wenn ich keine Zeit habe				Kino
. . .				Vorlesung(en)
				. . .

D. Wieder zu Hause After you and your family come home from a camping trip, your mother has many questions. Form her questions with **wo** or **wohin.**

BEISPIEL Vater ist in der Garage. — *Wo ist Vater?*
Jochen geht in den Garten. — *Wohin geht Jochen?*

1. Das Handy ist im Auto.
2. Der Teppich liegt im Flur.
3. Sandra legt die Röcke aufs Bett.
4. Kristina hängt den Mantel über den Stuhl.
5. Die Regenmäntel sind auf dem Balkon.
6. Die Jacken liegen in der Ecke.
7. Kristina und Niels haben die Lebensmittel in die Küche gebracht.
8. Niels hat die Milch in den Kühlschrank gestellt.

D: 1. Wo ist das Handy? 2. Wo liegt der Teppich? 3. Wohin legt Sandra die Röcke? 4. Wohin hängt Kristina den Mantel? 5. Wo sind die Regenmäntel? 6. Wo liegen/sind die Jacken? 7. Wohin haben Kristina und Niels die Lebensmittel gebracht? 8. Wohin hat Niels die Milch gestellt?

E. Ein paar Fragen, bevor Sie gehen! Before you leave for vacation, answer the questions your house sitter is asking you.

BEISPIEL Wo ist das Telefon? (an / Wand)
An der Wand!

1. Wo darf ich schlafen? (auf / Sofa; in / Arbeitszimmer)
2. Wohin soll ich meine Kleider hängen? (in / Schrank; an / Wand; über / Stuhl)
3. Wo gibt es ein Lebensmittelgeschäft? (an / Ecke; neben / Bank; zwischen / Apotheke und Café)
4. Wo können die Kinder spielen? (hinter / Haus; unter / Baum; auf / Spielplatz)
5. Wohin gehen sie gern? (in / Park; an / Fluss; in / Kino)
6. Wohin soll ich die Katze bringen? (vor / Tür *[outside]*; in / Garten; auf / Balkon; in / Garage)

E: 1. auf dem Sofa, im Arbeitszimmer 2. in den Schrank, an die Wand, über den Stuhl 3. an der Ecke, neben der Bank, zwischen der Apotheke und dem Café 4. hinter dem Haus, unter dem Baum, auf dem Spielplatz 5. in den Park, an den Fluss, ins Kino 6. vor die Tür, in den Garten, auf den Balkon, in die Garage

Additional questions: 1. **Wohin geht man,** wenn man Geld braucht? einen Film sehen will? duschen möchte? . . . 2. **Wo liegt . . . ?** (Ask about various geographic locations, using **in, in der, im, an der, am** . . .)

F. Wir bekommen Besuch Your visitors will arrive soon. You still have a lot to prepare. Fill in the blanks with the correct preposition and the correct form of the definite article. Use contractions where possible.

1. Die Gläser sind __in der__ Küche. *(in the)*
2. Ich muss die Gläser __ins__ Wohnzimmer bringen und sie __auf den__ Tisch stellen. *(into the; on the)*
3. Der Wein ist unten __im__ Keller. *(in the)*
4. Wir müssen die Gläser __neben die__ Teller *(pl.)* stellen. *(next to the)*
5. Ich muss __in die__ Küche gehen und die Wurst und den Käse __auf den__ Teller *(sg.)* legen. *(into the; on the)*
6. Haben wir Blumen __im__ Garten? *(in the)*
7. Wir stellen die Blumen __auf das__ Tischchen *(sg.)* __vor dem__ Sofa. *(on the; in front of the)*
8. Sind die Kerzen oben __im__ Schrank? *(in the)*
9. Nein, sie stehen __auf der__ Kommode. *(on the)*

G. Bei Lotte

1. **Was ist wo?** Make ten statements about the picture of Lotte's house, telling where things are standing, lying, or hanging.

   BEISPIEL *Der Schreibtisch steht an der Wand.*

2. **Wo sind nur meine Schlüssel?** Lotte has lost her keys. Looking at the drawing of the house, work with a partner to help her find them. One of you plays Lotte and the other asks her about specific places she may have left them. Lotte will answer each question negatively until you finally get it right. Ask at least five questions using two-way prepositions.

   BEISPIEL S1 Hast du sie auf den Schreibtisch gelegt?
   S2 Nein, sie liegen nicht auf dem Schreibtisch.

H. Mensch, wo ist mein Handy *(cell phone)*?

Your partner can't find his/her cell phone. Looking at the drawing of Lotte's home or just simply around the classroom, ask him/her about specific places where it might have been put. Your partner will answer each question negatively until you finally guess right. Ask at least five questions using two-way prepositions.

BEISPIEL S1 Hast du es neben die Blumen im Flur gelegt?
S2 Nein, es liegt nicht neben den Blumen im Flur.

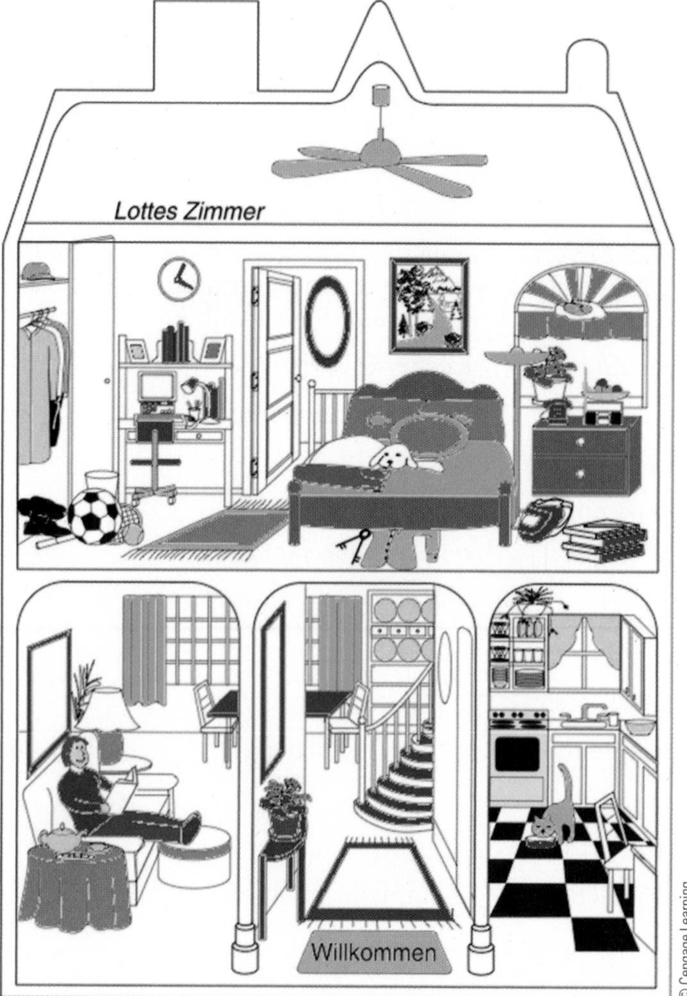

Fokus Friedensreich Hundertwasser

Friedensreich Hundertwasser, born Friedrich Stowasser (1928–2000), was a well-known Austrian painter, graphic artist, and architect. In his ecologically oriented writings, he vehemently protested against contemporary architecture, which he described as "an aesthetic void," "a desert of uniformity," and as having a "criminal sterility." Since no straight lines exist in nature, he also rejected them in his art, referring to them as "something cowardly drawn with a ruler, without thought or feeling." His architecture echoes that conviction, as exemplified by the Hundertwasser House in Vienna and the Hundertwasser Church in Bärnbach near Graz, the exterior of which is uneven and constructed of various materials that symbolize the vicissitudes of life. Its processional path leads through multiple gates that bear symbols taken from a variety of religions, their inclusion intended to show respect for all faiths.

I. Mein Zimmer / Meine Wohnung / Mein Studentenwohnheim Describe your room, apartment, or dorm in 8 to 10 sentences. Use a two-way preposition in each sentence.

BEISPIEL *Mein Schreibtisch steht neben der Tür.*

6.2 Imperatives

You are already familiar with the FORMAL IMPERATIVE, which addresses one individual or several people. You know that the verb is followed by the pronoun **Sie:**

Herr Schmidt, **lesen Sie** das bitte!

Herr und Frau Müller, **kommen Sie** bitte später wieder!

1. The FAMILIAR IMPERATIVE has two forms: one for the singular and one for the plural.

   a. The singular usually corresponds to the **du**-form of the verb *without* the pronoun **du** and *without* the **-st** ending:

du schreibst	du tust	du antwortest	du fährst	du nimmst	du isst	du liest
Schreib!	**Tu!**	**Antworte!**	**Fahr!**	**Nimm!**	**Iss!**	**Lies!**

NOTE: **Lesen** and **essen** retain the **s** or **ss** of the verb stem. **Lies! Iss!**

- Verb stems ending in **-d, -t, -ig,** or in certain other consonant combinations, *usually* have an **-e** ending in the **du**-form.

  Finde es! **Antworte** ihm! **Entschuldige** bitte! **Öffne** die Tür!

- Verbs with vowel changes from **a** → **ä** in the present singular *do not* make this change in the imperative. Verbs that change from **e** → **i(e)** do retain this change, however.

  Fahr langsam! **Lauf** schnell!

  Komm, **gib** mir deine Hand! **Nimm** das!

  Iss nicht so viel! **Sprich** Deutsch! **Lies** laut! **Sieh** mal!

Here is the rule according to *Duden:* Always add an **-e**, if the infinitive stem ends in **-d**, **-t**, **-el**, or **-er: Finde! Rate! Samm(e)le! Wandere!** Always add an **-e** if it ends in **-m** or **-n** preceded by a consonant *other than* **l, m, n,** or **r**, or simple **h** (e.g., **Atme!, Rechne!**). Usually add an **-e** if the stem ends in any other "hard" consonant: **Entschuldige!** Optionally add an **-e** in all other cases (**Komm(e)! Fahr(e)!**, with the following exception. Never add an **-e** if the verb has a stem vowel change in the 3rd person singular present from **e** to **i / ie: Gib! Sieh!**

b. The plural corresponds to the **ihr**-form of the verb without the pronoun **ihr.**

ihr schreibt	ihr tut	ihr antwortet	ihr fahrt	ihr nehmt	ihr esst	ihr lest
Schreibt!	**Tut!**	**Antwortet!**	**Fahrt!**	**Nehmt!**	**Esst!**	**Lest!**

Legt den Teppich vor das Sofa! — *Put the carpet in front of the couch.*
Stellt die Kommode an die Wand! — *Put the dresser against the wall.*
Hängt das Bild neben die Tür! — *Hang the picture next to the door.*

2. English imperatives beginning with *Let's* . . . are expressed in German as follows:

Sprechen wir Deutsch! — *Let's speak German.*
Gehen wir nach Hause! — *Let's go home.*

3. Here is a summary chart of the imperative.

FORMAL	FAMILIAR (SG.)	FAMILIAR (PL.)	LET'S!
Schreiben Sie!	Schreib!	Schreibt!	Schreiben wir!
Antworten Sie!	Antworte!	Antwortet!	Antworten wir!
Fahren Sie!	**Fahr!**	Fahrt!	Fahren wir!
Nehmen Sie!	**Nimm!**	Nehmt!	Nehmen wir!
Essen Sie!	**Iss!**	Esst!	Essen wir!
Lesen Sie!	**Lies!**	Lest!	Lesen wir!

In case questions arise, the imperatives of **sein** and **werden** are **Seien Sie! Seid! Sei! / Werden Sie! Werdet! Werde!** If you like, you could introduce these.

Frau Schmidt, **schreiben Sie** mir!
Helga, **schreib** mir!
Kinder, **schreibt** mir!
Schreiben wir Lisa!

Note that an INFINITIVE can be used as an impersonal imperative, especially in recipes and on signs: **Drei Minuten kochen. Langsam fahren! Nicht mit dem Fahrer sprechen!**

NOTE: The German imperative is usually followed by an EXCLAMATION POINT.

Übungen

J. Nennen Sie den Imperativ! First form the singular and then the plural familiar.

BEISPIEL Bleiben Sie bitte hier!
Bleib bitte hier!
Bleibt bitte hier!

1. Fragen Sie ihn!
2. Entschuldigen Sie bitte!
3. Bitte helfen Sie uns!
4. Zeigen Sie uns den Weg!
5. Geben Sie mir die Landkarte!
6. Fahren Sie immer geradeaus!
7. Wiederholen Sie das bitte!
8. Halten Sie da drüben!
9. Hören Sie mal!
10. Schlafen Sie gut!
11. Essen Sie einen Apfel!
12. Trinken Sie eine Cola!

J: 1. Frag, Fragt 2. Entschuldige, Entschuldigt 3. Hilf, Helft 4. Zeig, Zeigt 5. Gib, Gebt 6. Fahr, Fahrt 7. Wiederhol, Wiederholt 8. Halte, Haltet 9. Hör, Hört 10. Schlaf, Schlaft 11. Iss, Esst 12. Trink, Trinkt

Additional practice: bitte kommen, jetzt beginnen, Golf spielen, schön feiern, zusammen singen, auch tanzen, nicht so schnell laufen, im See baden, schwimmen gehen, das wieder finden, auf Deutsch antworten, nicht so viel arbeiten, die Wohnung mieten, ihm danken, den Dom besichtigen, die Suppe empfehlen, mal sehen, nicht so viel essen, den Imperativ nennen

Tu was für
deine Gesundheit!
Iss jeden Tag
einen Apfel!

K. Geben Sie Befehle! Form formal and familiar commands, using the phrases below.

> **BEISPIEL** an die Tafel gehen
> *Gehen Sie bitte an die Tafel!*
> *Geh bitte an die Tafel!*
> *Geht bitte an die Tafel!*

1. die Kreide nehmen 2. ein Wort auf Deutsch schreiben 3. von 1 bis 10 zählen 4. wieder an den Platz gehen 5. das Deutschbuch öffnen 6. auf Seite 150 lesen 7. mit dem Nachbarn auf Deutsch sprechen 8. mir einen Kuli geben 9. nach Hause gehen 10. das nicht tun

K: 1. Nehmen Sie, Nimm, Nehmt 2. Schreiben Sie, Schreib, Schreibt 3. Zählen Sie, Zähl, Zählt 4. Gehen Sie, Geh, Geht 5. Öffnen Sie, Öffne, Öffnet 6. Lesen Sie, Lies, Lest 7. Sprechen Sie, Sprich, Sprecht 8. Geben Sie, Gib, Gebt 9. Gehen Sie, Geh, Geht 10. Tun Sie, Tu, Tut —To vary this exercise, you could have students call out whom they want addressed and the others adjust the command accordingly, e.g., Tom!—Tom, geh bitte an die Tafel!; Laura und Vivian! —Laura und Vivian, geht bitte an die Tafel!

L. Was tun? Decide with your friend what to do with the rest of the day.

> **BEISPIEL** zu Hause bleiben *Bleiben wir zu Hause!*

1. in die Stadt gehen 2. an den See fahren 3. durch die Geschäfte bummeln 4. eine Pizza essen 5. das Schloss besichtigen 6. eine Wohnung mieten

L: 1. Gehen wir 2. Fahren wir 3. Bummeln wir 4. Essen wir 5. Besichtigen wir 6. Mieten wir

M. Bitte tu, was ich sage! Ask your partner to do what you say. Give each other 5–10 different classroom commands that are to be followed, for example, opening the book to a certain page, reading something fast or slowly, counting in German, and so forth.

M: We already did something similar at the end of the *Schritte*, but now students understand what they recognized only as "useful classroom instructions" before. Also, they can now use the **du-** and **ihr**-forms of the imperative.

6.3 *Wissen* vs. *kennen*

In German, two verbs correspond to the English *to know.*

kennen, gekannt	*to know, to be acquainted with (a person, place, or thing)*
wissen, gewusst	*to know (a fact)* (The fact is most often expressed in a subordinate clause.)

If you notice students mixing them, remind them not to confuse the forms of **kennen** and **können.**

Whereas **kennen** is regular in the present tense, the forms of **wissen** are very similar to the forms of the modals.

ich	weiß
du	weißt
er	weiß
wir	wissen
ihr	wisst
sie	wissen

Ich **kenne** das Buch.
Ich **kenne** den Lehrer.

Ich **weiß, dass** es gut ist.
Ich **weiß, dass** er aus Graz ist.
Ich **weiß** seine Telefonnummer.

WO BITTE GEHT'S HIER ZUR GESUNDHEIT?

IHR APOTHEKER KENNT DEN WEG.

© Beatrix Brockman

© Beatrix Brockman

Übungen

Optional practice: Have students indicate whether to use **kennen** or **wissen** in the following sentences: 1. Do you know Dr. Schumann? 2. No, I don't know him. 3. But I know that he works here. 4. What else do you know about him? 5. Do you know where to find him? 6. No, I don't know. 7. I don't know the university that well.

N. *Kennen* oder *wissen*? These young people are looking for a place to eat in Vienna. Fill in the appropriate forms in the dialogue.

ANGELIKA Entschuldigen Sie! __Wissen__ Sie, wo die Wipplinger Straße ist?

DAME Nein. Ich __kenne__ Wien gut, aber das __weiß__ ich nicht.

MICHAEL Danke! Du, Angelika, __weißt__ du, wie spät es ist?

ANGELIKA Nein, aber ich __weiß__, dass ich Hunger habe.

MICHAEL Hallo, Holger und Sabine! Sagt mal, __kennt__ ihr Angelika?

SABINE Ja, natürlich.

MICHAEL Wir haben Hunger. __Wisst__ ihr, wo es hier ein Restaurant gibt?

HOLGER Ja, da drüben ist das „Bastei Beisl" Wir __kennen__ es nicht, aber wir __wissen__, dass es gut sein soll.

MICHAEL __Wisst__ ihr was? Gehen wir essen!

Fokus Public Transportation and City Life

Visitors from North America are often astounded by the efficient and extensive public transportation networks in German cities. Their existence is one reason why Germans consume only two-thirds of the per capita energy used by Americans. Most large cities have extensive subway lines **(U-Bahn-Linien)** that connect with suburban commuter trains **(die S-Bahn).** Bikes are usually permitted on trains and subways during off-peak hours. Train stations as well as the trains themselves are generally clean and safe.

German urban transportation operates on the honor system. Passengers are required to validate their own tickets **(Fahrkarten entwerten)** by inserting them into machines that stamp the time and date. People who evade paying **(Schwarzfahrer)** have to reckon with random checks by plainclothes employees and stiff fines. Monthly and yearly tickets are available with reduced rates for students and senior citizens. Bigger firms also offer their employees a reduced transportation ticket. Buses and streetcars complement the subway system, making for dense networks that reach outlying suburbs. Most large cities also have night buses **(Nachtbusse),** which run on special routes all night long.

All cities have some form of public transportation, usually heavily subsidized in an effort to limit pollution and congestion in city centers. In major cities, the German Railways even provides a very well-organized and popular bike-sharing system, known by its English description as **Call a Bike.**

Das Fahren mit der U-Bahn ist bequem und schnell.

O. Was weißt du und wen kennst du? Ask your partner ten questions about certain people or certain things, which he/she will answer in a complete German sentence. Also include questions in the present perfect.

These "certain people" might be any politicians, movie stars, the chancellor of the university, teachers, and so forth.

BEISPIEL S1 Kennst du den Mann da?
S2 Natürlich kenne ich ihn.
S1 Weißt du, dass er gut Deutsch spricht?
S2 Nein, das habe ich nicht gewusst.

Zusammenfassung

iLrn

Visit the ***Wie geht's?*** iLrn website for more review and practice of the grammar points you have just learned.

P. Am Schweizer Platz Read aloud the following passage and then tell what case follows the two-way prepositions and why.

BEISPIEL	
Hier sehen wir **auf einen Platz.**	auf + *acc. (destination)*
Auf dem Platz ist viel los.	auf + *dat. (location)*

© Ingrid Sevin

1. **Auf dem Bild** sehen wir den Schweizer Platz in Frankfurt **am** Main.
2. Die Rolltreppe *(escalator)* rechts bringt die Leute **unter den Platz** zur U-Bahn.
3. **Unter dem Platz** gibt's auch Geschäfte.
4. Links **neben der Rolltreppe** ist ein U-Bahn-Schild *(sign, n.)* und **über dem Schild** eine Uhr.
5. Rechts **neben der Rolltreppe** sieht man eine Frau mit einem Kind.
6. **An dem Baum** vor ihr stehen Fahrräder.
7. Die Autos **hinter den Rädern** fahren um den Platz.
8. **Zwischen den beiden Häusern** kommt gerade eine Straßenbahn und fährt **auf die Insel** *(island, f.)* **mitten auf** *(in the middle of)* **dem Platz.**
9. Im Parterre von den Häusern **auf der anderen Seite** sind Geschäfte.
10. Wenn Sie **in die Stadt** ziehen *(move)*, ist alles **in der Nähe.**

P: 1. auf + *dat. (L)*, an + *dat. (L)* 2. unter + *acc. (D)* 3. unter + *dat. (L)* 4. neben + *dat. (L)*, über + *dat. (L)* 5. neben + *dat. (L)* 6. an + *dat. (L)* 7. hinter + *dat. (L)* 8. zwischen + *dat. (L)*, auf + *acc. (D)*, mitten auf + *dat. (L)* 9. im + *dat. (L)*, auf + *dat. (L)* 10. in + *acc. (D)*, in + *dat. (L)*

Q. Hoppla, kannst du mir mit den Möbeln helfen?

MÖBEL: Sessel, Tischchen, Esstisch, Stuhl, Fernseher, Regal, Bücher, Blumen, Elternbett, Nachttisch, Lampe, Kommode, Bild, Kinderbett, Schreibtisch, Kleiderschrank, Spiegel (*mirror*, m.), Computer, Eckbank *(corner bench)*, Küchentisch, Küchenstuhl, Kühlschrank . . .

1. **Wohin soll das?** You and a friend—your partner—are each moving into a new house and are helping each other. With both of you looking at the floor plan in this exercise, your partner will tell you where to put things (being as specific as possible and keeping track of all instructions), and you then write the name or abbreviation of each item into the spot where it should go. Then reverse roles with both of you looking at the similar, but different floor plan in the Appendix.

   BEISPIEL S1 Wohin soll der Teppich?
   S2 Leg den Teppich ins Wohnzimmer vor das Sofa!
   S1 Und die Lampe?
   S2 Stell die Lampe rechts neben das Sofa!

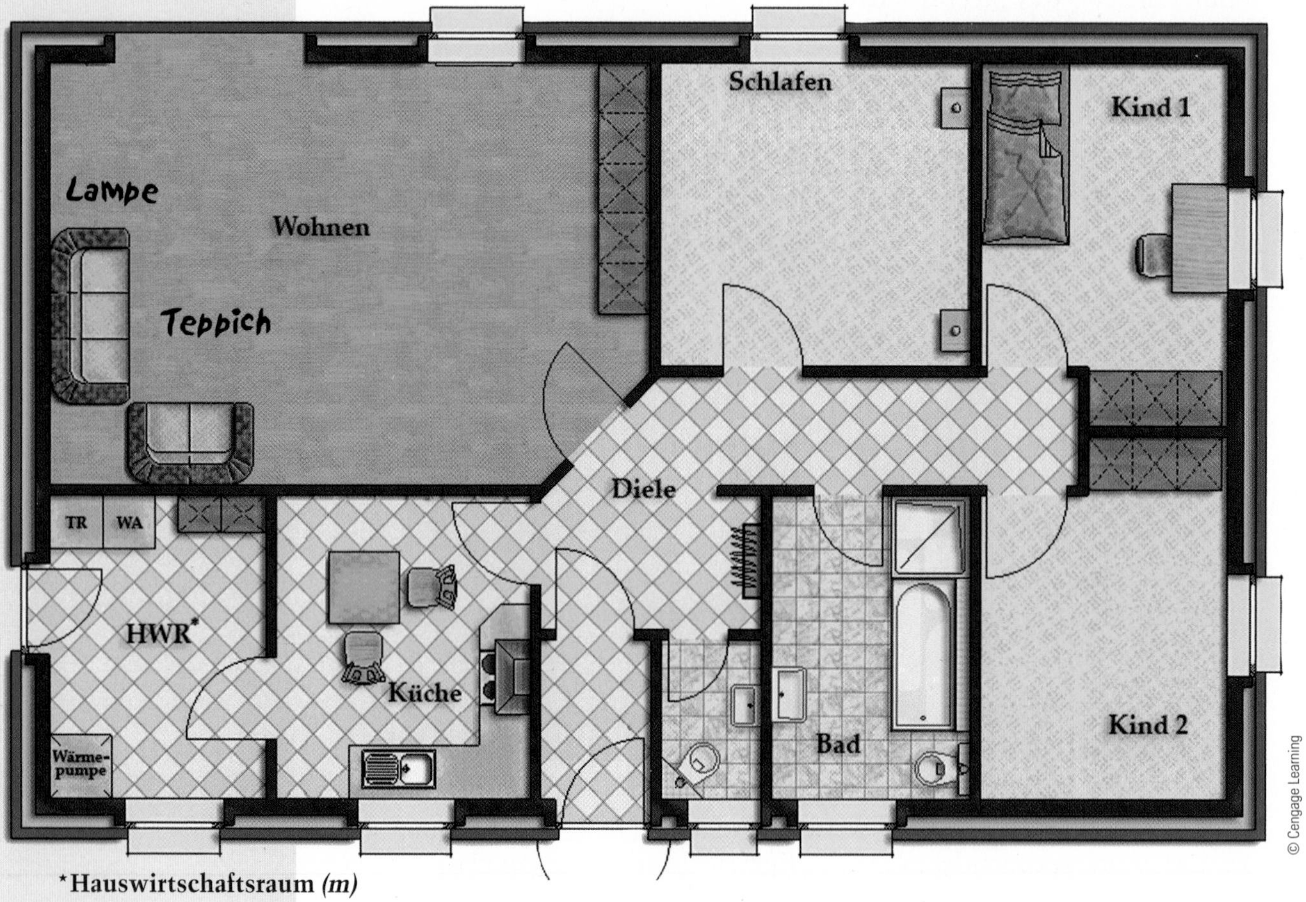

*Hauswirtschaftsraum *(m)*

2. **Ist alles da, wo es sein soll?** When you are finished furnishing both places, each partner checks with the other, whether directions have been followed for each of the respective homes.

   BEISPIEL S1 Liegt der Teppich im Wohnzimmer vor dem Sofa?
   S2 Ja, ich habe den Teppich ins Wohnzimmer vor das Sofa gelegt.
   S1 Steht die Lampe rechts neben dem Sofa?
   S2 Ja, ich habe die Lampe rechts neben das Sofa gestellt. (*OR* Nein, ich habe die Lampe links neben das Sofa gestellt.)

R. Wohnungsanzeigen *(Apartment classified ads)* Read the rental ads at right, then choose one and pretend you are the landlord. Your partner is looking for an apartment and will inquire about it. Answer his/her questions based on the ad. If some of the information is not given in the ad, make it up. Then reverse roles.

S1 Ich habe gelesen, dass Sie eine Wohnung zu vermieten haben. Wo ist die Wohnung?
S2 . . .
S1 Können Sie mir die Wohnung etwas beschreiben?
S2 Ja, gern. Sie hat . . .
S1 Gibt es auch . . . ?
S2 . . .
S1 Wie weit ist es zu . . . ?
S2 . . .
S1 Und was kostet die Wohnung?
S2 . . .

VERMIETUNGEN
1-Zi-Whg in Uninähe, 25 qm, möbl., schön u. hell, Dusche/WC, 200,— warm. 0941 / 70 63 22
1-Zi-Neubauwhg an Student/in, ca. 29 qm, teilmöbl., zentral, 250,— kalt, ab 1.11.11. 0941 / 4 28 62
2 Zi-Dachgeschoss, Altstadt, ca. 50 qm, 315,— kalt, ab Februar '11. 0941 / 99 06 86
2 1/2 Zi-Whg, Neubau, 60 qm, Balkon, ruhig, 280,—. 0941 / 4 63 61 45
3-ZKB, Balkon, 72 qm, auch an WG 3 Pers., 425,—, zum 1.12.11 frei. 0941 / 5 17 76
3-ZKB, Terrasse, 98 qm, Gäste-WC, Garage, Keller, Kaltmiete 550,—. 0941 / 44 98 69
Bungalow, 120 qm, 4-ZKB, Garten, Terrasse, Sauna, 750,—. 0941 / 4 70 04
2-Zi-Whg auf Bauernhof, 50 qm, Garten, Tiere kein Problem, gegen 10 Stunden Arbeit pro Woche. 0941 / 57 65 98

R: In case students ask: **Whg** = **Wohnung, qm** = **Quadratmeter** *(square meter)*, **teilmöbliert** *(partly furnished)*, **ruhig** *(quiet)*, **WC** = **Wasserklosett** *(toilet)*, **ZKB** = **Zimmer Küche Bad, Bauernhof** *(farm)*, **pro Woche** *(per week)*

S. An der Uni: Auf Deutsch bitte!

1. Hello, Hans! Where have you been?
2. I've been in the dorm.
3. Where are you going? —To the library.
4. I'd like to live in a dorm, too.
5. Where do you live now?
6. In an apartment. Unfortunately it's above a club **(der Klub)** and next to a restaurant.
7. Tell me, are the rooms in the dorm nice?
8. I like my room, but I don't like the furniture.
9. On which floor do you live? —On the third floor.
10. Do you know how much it costs? —240 Euro a month.
11. There's Rico.
12. Who's that? From where am I supposed to know him? (Where am I supposed to know him from?)
13. I didn't know that you don't know him.
14. Let's say hello.

S: 1. Hallo, Hans! Wo bist du gewesen? 2. Ich bin im Studentenwohnheim gewesen. 3. Wohin gehst du? —In die / Zur Bibliothek. 4. Ich möchte auch in einem Studentenwohnheim wohnen. 5. Wo wohnst du jetzt? 6. In einer Wohnung. Leider ist sie über einem Klub und neben einem Restaurant. 7. Sag mal / Sag mir, sind die Zimmer im Studentenwohnheim schön? 8. Mein Zimmer gefällt mir, aber die Möbel gefallen mir nicht. 9. In welchem Stock wohnst du? —Im zweiten Stock. 10. Weißt du, wie viel es kostet? —240 Euro im Monat. 11. Da ist Rico. 12. Wer ist das? Woher soll ich ihn kennen? 13. Ich habe nicht gewusst, dass du ihn nicht kennst. 14. Sagen wir „Hallo!" / „Guten Tag!"

Mittagspause im Studentenwohnheim

Einblicke

Lesetext

Wortschatz 2

das Reihenhaus, ¨-er	*townhouse, row house*
die Arbeit	*work*
die Eigentumswohnung, -en	*condominium*
am Abend	*in the evening*
am Tag	*during the day*
aufs Land / auf dem Land(e)	*into the country(side) / in the country(side)*
ausgezeichnet	*excellent*
außerdem	*besides, in addition* (adverb)
fast	*almost*
leicht	*easy, easily* (lit. *light*)
schwer	*hard, difficult* (lit. *heavy*)
mitten in (+ *acc./dat.)*	*in the middle of*
noch nicht	*not yet*
trotzdem	*nevertheless, in spite of that*
bauen	*to build*
leben	*to live*
lieben	*to love*
sparen	*to save*

Komm aufs Land!

Note the difference between ***leben*** (*to live*, literally: *to be alive*) and **wohnen** *(to reside)*: **Dürer lebt nicht mehr. Er hat in dem Haus da drüben gewohnt.**

Vor dem Lesen

A. Fragen

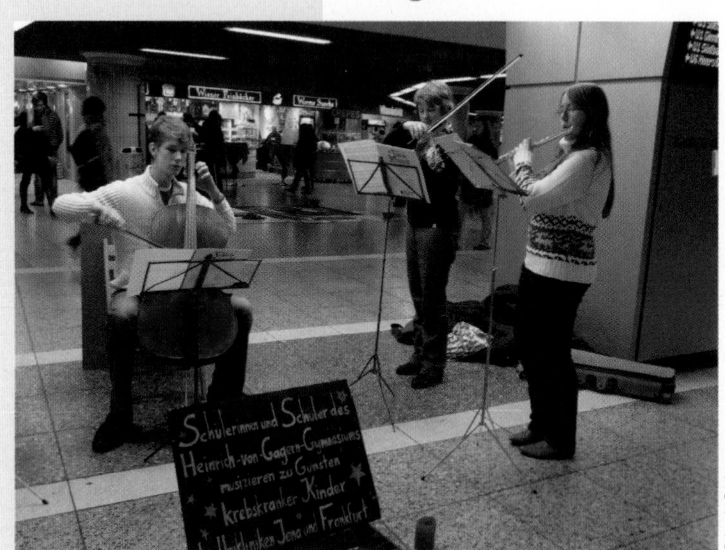

1. Leben die meisten Leute *(most people)* in Ihrer Stadt in Wohnungen oder in Häusern mit Garten?
2. Wo ist Bauland *(building lot[s])* teuer? Wissen Sie, wo es nicht so teuer ist?
3. Was für öffentliche Verkehrsmittel *(public transportation)* gibt es hier?
4. Wie kommen die meisten Leute zur Arbeit? Wie kommen Sie zur Uni? Braucht man hier unbedingt *(necessarily)* ein Auto?
5. Gibt es hier Schlafstädte *(bedroom communities)*, von wo die Leute morgens in die Stadt und abends wieder nach Hause fahren?
6. Wohin gehen oder fahren die Leute hier am Wochenende?

B. Das ist leicht zu verstehen! Read aloud the following words paying special attention to their stressed syllable, then guess their meaning in English.

der Arbeitsplatz, Biergarten, Clown, Dialekt, Musiker, Spielplatz, Wanderweg; das Boot, Feld; die Energie, Mietwohnung, Wirlichkeit; frei, idyllisch, pünktlich; Ball spielen, eine Pause machen, picknicken

Lesetipp

Analyzing Comparisons and Contrasts

This passage compares life in the city with life in the country. As you read, make note of the arguments it makes for and against each lifestyle.

Schaffen, sparen, Häuschen bauen

„Schaffe, spare, Häusle baue" ist ein Spruch° aus Schwaben°. Auf Hochdeutsch° heißt es „Schaffen°, sparen, Häuschen bauen." Der Spruch aus Schwaben ist nicht nur für die Schwaben typisch, sondern für viele Deutsche, Österreicher und Schweizer.

In den drei Ländern leben viele Menschen, aber es gibt nur wenig° Land. Die meisten° wohnen in Wohnungen und träumen von° einem Haus mit Garten. Oft bleibt das aber nur ein Traum°, denn in den Städten ist Bauland sehr teuer. Es gibt auch nicht genug Bauland, weil man nicht überall bauen darf.

Oft muss man an den Stadtrand° oder aufs Land ziehen°, wo mehr Platz ist und wo Land noch nicht so teuer ist. Aber nicht alle möchten so weit draußen° wohnen und stundenlang hin- und herpendeln°. Das kostet Energie, Zeit und Geld°. Abends kommt man auch nicht so leicht ins Kino oder ins Theater. Das Leben auf dem Land ist oft idyllisch, aber nicht immer sehr bequem.

In der Stadt kann man eigentlich sehr gut leben. Die Wohnungen sind oft schön und gemütlich. Man braucht nicht unbedingt ein Auto, weil alles in der Nähe liegt. Fast überall gibt es Bürgersteige° und Fahrradwege und die öffentlichen Verkehrsmittel sind ausgezeichnet. Die Busse kommen relativ oft und pünktlich. In Großstädten gibt es auch Straßenbahnen, U-Bahnen und S-Bahnen. Damit° können Sie nicht nur aus der Stadt oder durch die Stadt, sondern auch mitten ins Zentrum, in die Fußgängerzone fahren, wo die Leute am Tag einkaufen und am Abend gern bummeln gehen. Man sieht ein bisschen in die Schaufenster° und geht vielleicht in eine Bar oder ein Café. Auf den Straßen ist im Sommer fast immer etwas los°. Es gibt Straßenkünstler°, Musiker und Clowns.

Wenn man in der Stadt wohnt, kann man aber auch leicht aufs Land fahren. Viele tun das gern und oft. Am Wochenende fährt man gern einmal an die See° oder in die Berge. Überall zwischen Wäldern° und Feldern gibt es Wanderwege und Fahrradwege. Dort findet man auch leicht ein Restaurant, wo man gemütlich Pause machen kann.

Man muss aber nicht unbedingt aufs Land fahren, wenn man ins Grüne° will. Fast alle Städte, ob groß oder klein, haben Stadtparks. Die Münchner z. B. lieben ihren Englischen Garten. Dort gibt es nicht nur Wanderwege, sondern auch Spielplätze und Bänke, Biergärten, Wiesen° zum Picknicken und zum Ballspielen und einen See mit Booten.

Die meisten leben eigentlich gern in der Stadt, entweder in einer Eigentumswohnung oder einer Mietwohnung. In der Stadt gibt es viel zu sehen und zu tun. Alles ist ziemlich nah, nicht nur der Arbeitsplatz, die Geschäfte und die Schulen, sondern auch die Theater, Kinos, Museen und Parks. Viele träumen trotzdem von einem Haus mit Garten. Sie wissen, dass sie schwer arbeiten und sparen müssen, wenn der Traum Wirklichkeit werden soll. Und das tun auch viele.

saying / Swabia / standard German
work hard
little
most / dream of
dream
to the outskirts / move
out(side)
commute back and forth
money
sidewalks
with them
goes window-shopping
there's something going on / street artists
ocean
forests
out into nature
meadows

A: 1. Da leben viele Menschen. 2. Sie wohnen in Wohnungen in der Stadt. 3. Das kostet Energie, Zeit, Geld und ist oft unbequem 4. Es gibt Bürgersteige, Fahrradwege und öffentliche Verkehrsmittel. 5. Man fährt gern aufs Land, in die Berge oder an die See. 6. Es gibt Wanderwege und Fahrradwege. 7. Sie können in einen Park gehen. 8. Alles ist in der Nähe: die Arbeitsplätze, Schulen und Geschäfte. 9. Sie träumen von einem Häuschen mit Garten. 10. Sie müssen schwer arbeiten und sparen.

Optional activity: **Was ist das?** 1. Bauland 2. eine Wohnung 3. ein Bürgersteig 4. öffentliche Verkehrsmittel 5. eine Fußgängerzone 6. ein Straßenkünstler 7. die Innenstadt 8. ein Häuschen im Grünen

Nach dem Lesen

A. Alles verstanden?

1. Warum gibt es in den Städten in Deutschland, in Österreich und in der Schweiz nicht viel Bauland?
2. Wo wohnen die meisten Leute?
3. Warum wollen viele Leute nicht aufs Land ziehen?
4. Warum braucht man nicht unbedingt ein Auto, wenn man in der Stadt wohnt?
5. Wohin fährt man gern am Wochenende?
6. Was gibt's überall zwischen Wäldern und Feldern?
7. Wohin können die Leute in der Stadt leicht gehen, wenn sie mal ins Grüne wollen?
8. Was ist in der Stadt in der Nähe?
9. Was für einen Traum haben die Menschen oft trotzdem?
10. Was müssen sie tun, wenn der Traum Wirklichkeit werden soll?

B. Haus oder Wohnung? Fill in the appropriate two-way prepositions and articles. Use contractions where possible.

1. Die meisten Deutschen wohnen __in einer__ Wohnung.
2. __In (den)__ Städten ist Bauland sehr teuer.
3. Der Traum vom Häuschen mit Garten hat viele __an den__ Stadtrand (*sg. m.*) oder __aufs__ Land gebracht.
4. __Auf den__ Feldern stehen jetzt Reihenhäuser.
5. Die Reihenhäuser sind manchmal direkt __an der__ Straße.
6. Morgens fahren viele __in die__ Stadt.
7. Das Leben __auf dem__ Land kann unbequem sein.
8. Viele bleiben __in der__ Stadt, weil dort alles __in der__ Nähe ist.
9. __Nach der__ Arbeit fahren sie dann noch einmal __ins__ Zentrum (*n.*)
10. __Im__ Zentrum ist fast immer etwas los.

C. *Kennen* oder *wissen*?

1. __Kennen__ Sie den Spruch „Schaffe, spare, Häusle baue"?
2. __Wissen__ Sie, wie viele Leute in Deutschland auf dem Land leben?
3. __Kennen__ Sie den Englischen Garten?
4. __Wisst__ ihr, dass es überall Fahrradwege gibt?
5. Ich habe nicht __gewusst__, dass es in der Stadt so viele Fußgängerwege gibt.
6. __Kennst__ du Herrn Jakob? Nein, aber Hans __kennt__ ihn.
7. __Weißt__ du, dass er mit seinen 80 Jahren immer noch viel wandert?

D. In der Großstadt You have never been to Frankfurt/Main before. Ask questions about the city, using **wo** or **wohin.**

BEISPIEL In Großstädten gibt es eine U-Bahn.
Wo gibt es eine U-Bahn?

1. Mit der U-Bahn kann man mitten in die Fußgängerzone fahren.
2. Im Zentrum kann man wunderschön bummeln.
3. Abends kann man ins Kino oder ins Theater gehen.
4. Wenn man ins Grüne will, geht man vielleicht in den Palmengarten *(botanical garden).*
5. Am Main gibt es überall Wege und Bänke.

D: 1. Wohin kann man mit der U-Bahn fahren? 2. Wo kann man wunderschön bummeln? 3. Wohin kann man abends gehen? 4. Wohin kann man gehen, wenn man ins Grüne will? 5. Wo gibt es überall Wege?

Weiteres

E. Was ist typisch auf dem Land und in der Stadt? Work in groups of three. Some groups list the advantages of city life and the disadvantages of country life, while the others do the reverse. Then compare. Which group has the most convincing arguments?

BEISPIEL *Auf dem Land kann man (nicht) . . . / Auf dem Land gibt es (kein-) . . .*
In der Stadt kann man (nicht) . . . / In der Stadt gibt es (kein-). . .

Don't forget to consider how age or family life could influence your decision, i.e., where it is easier to live when you are older or have a family.

Optional tongue twister **(der Zungenbrecher):** Wer nichts weiß und weiß, dass er nichts weiß, weiß mehr als der, der *(the one who)* nichts weiß und nicht weiß, dass er nichts weiß.

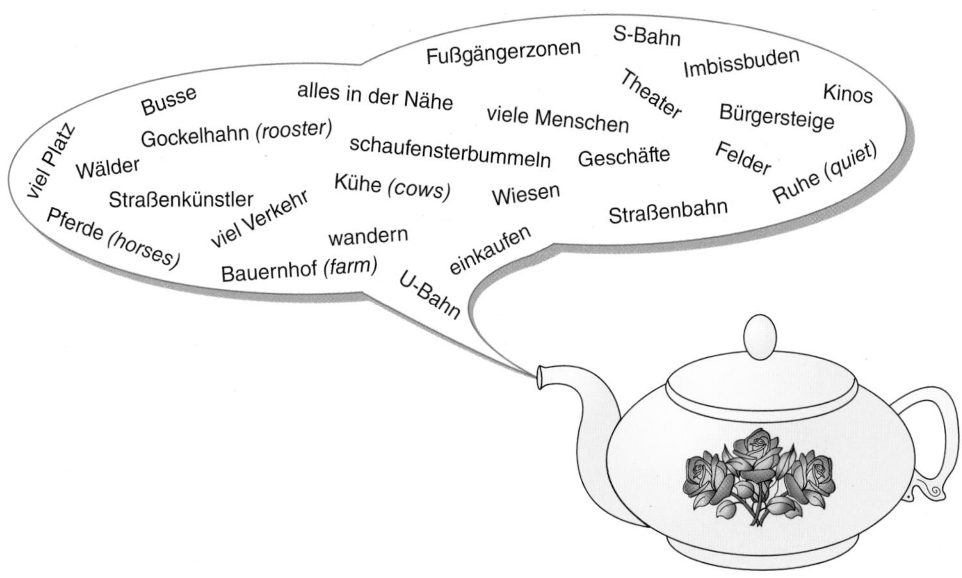

S-Bahn
Fußgängerzonen
Imbissbuden
Busse
alles in der Nähe
Theater
Kinos
viele Menschen
Bürgersteige
viel Platz
Gockelhahn (rooster)
schaufensterbummeln
Geschäfte
Felder
Wälder
Ruhe (quiet)
Straßenkünstler
Kühe (cows)
Wiesen
viel Verkehr
Straßenbahn
Pferde (horses)
wandern
einkaufen
Bauernhof (farm)
U-Bahn

F. Kurzgespräche With a partner, choose one of the situations and prepare a brief dialogue. Then present it to the class.

1. **Einladung zum Mittagessen**
You have been invited to a classmate's house for dinner, but you are quite late. You introduce yourself to his/her mother, who asks you to come in **(herein).** You apologize repeatedly for being so late, while she maintains it doesn't matter. When you hand her the flowers you have brought, she thanks you and says that dinner is ready.

© Ingrid Sevin

Knochenhauer Amtshaus, Hildesheim

Schreibtipp

Responding to an Ad

Real estate ads are typically full of abbreviations that people tend to adopt when talking about properties. For example, **2. OG** means that an apartment is upstairs (**Obergeschoss**) on the third floor (the second above ground level). The expression **u.v.m.** means **und viel mehr.**

A **2-Zimmer-Wohnung** has two rooms in addition to the kitchen and bathroom. Note that measurements are given in square meters (**qm**); **91 qm (91 m²)** would equal approximately 1000 square feet. In responding to the ad and e-mail from Christian, be sure to ask specific questions. Rephrase any real estate jargon to be sure that you have understood all about the condominium.

2. **Wo ist das Knochenhauer Amtshaus?**
You are visiting Hildesheim and want to see the well-known *Knochenhauer Amtshaus,* a 16th-century guild house. You stop a Hildesheimer and ask where the building is. He/She replies that it is at the *Marktplatz,* across from city hall. Your informant asks whether you see the pedestrian area over there; he/she directs you to walk along that street and turn right at the pharmacy. The *Marktplatz* is nearby. You thank the stranger and say good-bye.

G. Eine E-Mail: Eigentumswohnung in Hildesheim Pretend you are Ryan or Tiffany. Read through the condominium ad and Christian's e-mail. Write a brief response congratulating him on his discovery and ask some questions about it. Then tell him that you are also looking for a place. Describe what you have in mind and how much something like that would cost in your town.

© Ingrid Sevin and Beatrix Brockman

Datum: Sonntag, 20. September, 20:50
Thema: Eigentumswohnung
Von: "Armin Schuetz" schuetzarmin@web.de
An: "Ryan Bloxom" ryanbloxom@yahoo.com

Hallo Ryan und Tiffany,

wie geht's euch? Ich glaube, ich habe in Hildesheim eine Eigentumswohnung gefunden: „Wohnen am Kalenberger Graben." Eine Altbauwohnung im 2. Stock, sogar mit Fahrstuhl, 91 qm, total renoviert und möbliert, Parkettfußböden, Wohnzimmer, Schlafzimmer, Einbauküche, Bad und Gäste WC. Das alles mitten im Zentrum gegenüber vom Kalenberger Graben — einem See mit Park und Wanderwegen. Alles ist ganz in der Nähe und man kann von dort überall zu Fuß hingehen. Zur Arbeit laufe ich nur 15 Minuten. Ist das nicht toll? Und der Preis der Wohnung? 158.000 Euro. Wie findet ihr das? Gibt's das bei euch auch?

Armin

© Cengage Learning

Hörverständnis

© Cengage Learning

Die Großeltern kommen. Listen to the message that Mrs. Schmidt has left for her children on the answering machine. Then indicate which chores each child has been asked to do; write **S** for Sebastian, **M** for Mareike, and **J** for Julia. Finally, note briefly what the children are *not* supposed to do.

1. **Wer soll was tun?**
   - S zum Supermarkt fahren
   - M einen Schokoladenpudding machen
   - S Bratwurst und Käse kaufen
   - J zum Blumengeschäft fahren
   - M Kartoffeln kochen
   - J Blumen ins Esszimmer stellen
   - J die Kleidung der *(of the)* Großeltern in den Schrank hängen
   - S Wein in den Kühlschrank stellen
2. **Was sollen die Kinder nicht tun?**
   a. das Radio nicht zu laut spielen
   b. den Apfelkuchen nicht essen

For further practice, an optional two-part video (**Szenen** and **Interviews**) is available on the ***Wie geht's?*** Premium Website and in iLrn, with corresponding questions and activities in the *Arbeitsbuch* (SAM).

As an optional activity with Google Earth, you could take a closer look at cities along the Rhine or visit Stuttgart or any other place mentioned in the chapter.

You could point out on a map where dialects such as **Schwäbisch, Bayrisch, Fränkisch, Thüringisch, Sächsisch, Westfälisch, Mecklenburgisch,** or **Friesisch** are spoken.

Fokus High German and Dialects

The German language has numerous dialects. Generally, these dialects have existed much longer than High German **(Hochdeutsch),** the standard form of German spoken everywhere in Germany and used in schools and businesses. Austria and Switzerland have standard versions and dialects of German as well. The German spoken in Austria is similar to that of Germany for the most part, whereas Swiss German diverges greatly. The differences between regional dialects are often so great, for example, that someone from Münster in the north speaking Westphalian **(Westfälisch)** won't be understood by someone from Munich in the south.

With the European Union's growth in importance, greater interest has developed in local traditions and history and has led to the creation of movements to keep regional dialects alive. North German Radio, for example, broadcasts short daily sermons in Low German **(Plattdeutsch),** while some Bavarian newspapers include regular features in Bavarian **(Bayrisch).** Some dialects are staging a comeback in song, literature, and theater. In areas where a dialect is spoken, children learn it automatically at home before starting school. Once in school, however, they need to master standard German in order to succeed both in their education and, later, professionally.

„Joden Dach, wie jeit es Ihne?" sagt der Kölner.
„Tachchen, wie jeht et Ihnen?" sagt der Berliner.
„Moin, moin, wie geiht Di dat?" sagt der Hamburger.
„Griaß Gott, wia geht's Eana?" sagt der Bayer.

© Cengage Learning

Rückschau

Kapitelwortschatz

Hauptwörter

die Arbeit	*work*
das Arbeitszimmer, -	*study*
das Bad, ¨er	*bathroom*
der Balkon, -s	*balcony*
der Baum, ¨e	*tree*
das Bett, -en	*bed*
das Dach, ¨er	*roof*
die Ecke, -n	*corner*
die Eigentumswohnung, -en	*condominium*
das Esszimmer, -	*dining room*
der Fernseher, -	*TV set*
der Flur, -e	*hallway*
die Garage, -n	*garage*
der Garten, ¨	*garden, yard*
das Haus, ¨er	*house*
der Keller, -	*basement, cellar*
die Kommode, -n	*dresser*
die Küche, -n	*kitchen*
der Kühlschrank, ¨e	*refrigerator*
die Lampe, -n	*lamp*
die Möbel *(pl.)*	*furniture*
das Problem, -e	*problem*
das Radio, -s	*radio*
das Regal, -e	*shelf, bookcase*
das Reihenhaus, ¨er	*townhouse, row house*
das Schlafzimmer, -	*bedroom*
der Schrank, ¨e	*closet, cupboard*
der Schreibtisch, -e	*desk*
der Sessel, -	*armchair*
das Sofa, -s	*sofa*
das Studentenwohnheim, -e	*dorm*
der Stuhl, ¨e	*chair*
das Telefon, -e	*telephone*
der Teppich, -e	*carpet*
der Tisch, -e	*table*
die Toilette, -n	*toilet*
der Vorhang, ¨e	*curtain*
die Wohnung, -en	*apartment*
das Wohnzimmer, -	*living room*
das Zimmer, -	*room*

Verben

baden	*to take a bath; to swim*
bauen	*to build*
duschen	*to take a shower*
hängen, gehangen	*to hang (be hanging)*
hängen, gehängt	*to hang (up)*
kennen	*to know, to be acquainted with (a person, place, or thing)*
kochen	*to cook*
leben	*to live*
legen	*to lay (down), put (flat)*
lieben	*to love*
liegen	*to lie (be lying flat)*
mieten	*to rent*
setzen	*to set, put (down)*
sitzen	*to sit (be sitting)*
sparen	*to save*
stehen	*to stand (be standing)*
stellen	*to stand, put (upright)*
vermieten	*to rent out*
waschen	*to wash*
wissen	*to know (a fact)*

Adjektive und Adverbien

ausgezeichnet	*excellent(ly)*
dunkel	*dark*
hell	*light; bright(ly)*
leicht	*easy, easily* (lit. *light[ly]*)
praktisch	*practical(ly)*
schwer	*difficult, hard* (lit. *heavy*), *with difficulty*
(un)bequem	*(un)comfortable; (in) convenient*

Präpositionen

an *(+ acc./dat.)*	*to; up to; at (the side of); on* (vertical surface)
auf *(+ acc./dat.)*	*on, on top of; onto* (horizontal surface)
hinter *(+ acc./dat.)*	*behind*
in *(+ acc./dat.)*	*in; into; inside of*
neben *(+ acc./dat.)*	*beside, next to*
über *(+ acc./dat.)*	*over; above; about*
unter *(+ acc./dat.)*	*under; below*
vor *(+ acc./dat.)*	*before, in front of*
zwischen *(+ acc./dat.)*	*between*

Verschiedenes

am Abend	*in the evening*
am Tag	*during the day*
Auf Wiederhören!	*Good-bye!* (on the phone)
aufs Land / auf dem Land(e)	*into the country(side) / in the country(side)*
außerdem	*besides, in addition, as well* (adverb)
(Das ist) kein Problem.	*(That's) no problem.*
(Das) klingt gut!	*(That) sounds good.*
(Das) stimmt!	*(That's) true.; (That's) right.*
ein bisschen	*a little bit (of), some*
fast	*almost*
im Bad / im Keller / in der Küche	*in the bathroom / basement / kitchen*
im Erdgeschoss	*on the ground level*
im Parterre	*on the first floor*
im ersten Stock	*on the second floor*
im Monat	*per month*
mitten in	*in the middle of*
noch nicht	*not yet*
oben	*up(stairs)*
sogar	*even*
trotzdem	*nevertheless, in spite of that*
unten	*down(stairs)*
wo	*where*
wohin	*where to*
ziemlich	*quite, rather*

Zum Schluss

1. **Wo sind Sie?** Describe the room you are in now. Where is it? Explain how the objects in the room are positioned relative to one another. Are there other people in the room with you? What are they doing? Use examples from the chapter, along with the **Wortschatz**, to write at least eight to ten sentences.

2. **Wohin gehen Sie?** Where will you go after you are done studying? What will you do there? Use the words below to get you started.

   BEISPIEL: Nach dem Lernen gehe ich gern in das Café am Marktplatz.

1	2	3	4
gehen	sogar	gegenüber von	die Mensa
fahren	trotzdem	hinter	die Bibliothek
liegen	gern	neben	der Supermarkt
sitzen	langsam/schnell	in	das Café
stehen	manchmal	vor	der Park
stellen	gemütlich	zwischen	das Sofa

3. **Erfolgstipps** (*Success strategies*)

   a. ***Was tun?*** A friend comes to you for advice. He/She is having a hard time in college but knows you are doing well. Share your advice with him/her by suggesting what to do. How should he/she spend time? What should he/she eat? What should he/she be careful (***vorsichtig sein***) about? Give your friend your top ten pieces of advice. Use the imperative.

   b. ***Toll!*** Your advice was so good, your friend put it on the Internet. It went viral! Now you are an invited speaker all over Germany. Give the same advice, but since you do not know your audience, use the formal address.

Mein Traumhaus (*dream house*) Describe your dream house. Would it be in the country or the city? Why? Would it be big or small? What would you have in it? Be as detailed as you can.

iLrn **Onlineaktivitäten** View iLrn for online activities related to this chapter. There you will find additional resources, such as a memory game (**Gedächtnisspiel**), a crossword puzzle (**Kreuzworträtsel**), audio flash cards (**Vokabelblitz**), a tutorial quiz (**Mini-Quiz**), and the active vocabulary (**Wortschatz**) for this chapter.

Kapitel 7

Auf der Bank und im Hotel

Lernziele In this chapter you will learn about:

Zum Thema

Official time, banking, and hotels

Fokus

History of German currency, credit cards, hotels, youth hostels, and Luxembourg

Struktur

- **Der-** and **ein-**words
- Separable-prefix verbs
- Flavoring particles

Einblicke

Lesetext: Übernachtungsmöglichkeiten

Rückschau

Kapitelwortschatz
Zum Schluss

RESSOURCEN

iLrn iLrn  Video
Audio SAM

Hier kann man gemütlich Kaffee trinken oder auch übernachten **(stay overnight).**

Vorschau The History of German Currency

Although West Germany experienced a postwar economic boom that lasted almost forty years, Germans have always had a fear of inflation. The concern is rooted in the conditions that plagued Germany after World War I, when it experienced what was probably the worst inflation of any modern industrialized country. The German unit of currency, **the Reichsmark (RM),** had so little value at the time that people needed pushcarts to transport the piles of money needed to buy groceries; a single loaf of bread cost billions of marks. In the aftermath of World War II, to hold inflation in check, to reduce the enormous war debt, and to instill economic confidence, the Western Allies replaced the **Reichsmark** with the **Deutsche Mark (DM).** The Soviet Union followed suit with the introduction of the **Mark (M)** in the Soviet-controlled East German zone. Boosted by the Marshall Plan, the West German economy experienced dramatic growth, while the Soviets stripped East German factories of machinery and shipped it east. Nevertheless, the economy of the German Democratic Republic (GDR) became one of the strongest in the East bloc. Yet in spite of that, it always lagged behind the free-enterprise economy in the West. The disparity in economic efficiency widened in the two decades before the collapse of the GDR in 1989.

On July 2, 1990, three months before German reunification, the West German government in Bonn undertook one of the biggest financial bailouts in history by establishing a currency union **(die Währungsunion)** with East Germany. GDR citizens were allowed to exchange up to 6,000 Eastmark (M) for DM at a rate of 1:1; savings above these amounts were converted at a rate of 2:1. This meant that after the exchange **(der Umtausch),** the average savings of a three-member GDR household of 27,000 M became DM 13,500. The introduction of the much-desired, strong West German Mark had a devastating effect on the East German economy by making much of its industry noncompetitive overnight and throwing large numbers of employees out of work. The situation required huge cash infusions from West to East, increasing inflationary pressure in all of Germany. The staunchly independent German Central Bank **(die Bundesbank),** which is charged with ensuring monetary stability, raised interest rates to the highest level in decades. The bank reluctantly lowered them only after a deep recession in the early 1990s.

The introduction in 1999 of the **Euro**—the new currency—for institutional transactions meant the beginning of the end for the **Deutsche Mark,** symbol of German economic power and stability in the second half of the twentieth century. At the beginning of 2002, the euro replaced the DM in everyday transactions, making room for a large, single market with a common currency (see *Fokus*, Chapter 2). As the world's largest exporter, Germany was hit especially hard by the sudden economic downturn in 2008 but has been recuperating better than other EU-members.

Children up to the age of 14 were allowed to exchange up to 2,000 DM at a rate of 1:1, people aged 15–59 up to 4,000 DM, and people older than 60 up to 6,000 DM. All salaries and pensions were also converted at a rate of 1:1.

Fragen: 1. Beschreiben Sie das Bild auf der linken Seite. Wie gefällt es Ihnen? 2. Haben Sie schon einmal so ein Haus gesehen? Wenn ja, wo? 3. Was für alte Münzen sehen Sie unten rechts? 4. Wie viel ist der Schein *(banknote)* wert *(worth)*. 5. Welche Farben haben die Euroscheine unten? 6. Wie viele Euromünzen liegen auf den Scheinen?

In case you are curious: *bell tower* **der Glockenturm;** *bench* **die Bank, ⸗e;** *bill* **der Schein, -e;** *cross* **das Kreuz,-e;** *hill* **der Hügel, -;** *pot* **der Topf;** *rooster* **der Gockelhahn;** *sun umbrella* **der Sonnenschirm, -e**

Neue EU-Währung (currency)

Alte deutsche Währung

Zum Thema

Gespräche

Auf der Bank

Warm-ups: 1. **Was ist das Gegenteil von** immer, oben, links, bequem, hell, leicht, nah, offen, schnell, Tag, mitten, zu Fuß gehen? 2. **Welche Zimmer gibt es in einem Haus?** Was gibt es im Wohnzimmer, in der Küche . . . ? 3. **Was ist der Plural von** Bank, Fahrrad, Museum, Haus, Wohnung, Studentenwohnheim, Bad, Bett, Ecke, Kommode, Regal, Schrank, Telefon, Teppich, Vorhang, Dach, Keller?

If you have some Swiss francs or euros, bring them to class. Ask students to check the current exchange rate of the dollar to the euro.

TOURISTIN Guten Tag! Wo kann ich hier Dollar umtauschen?
ANGESTELLTE Haben Sie eine Kreditkarte?
TOURISTIN Ja, eine Kreditkarte und eine Debitkarte aus Kanada.
ANGESTELLTE Nun, dann gehen Sie am besten da drüben oder draußen am Eingang an den Geldautomaten. Mit der Debitkarte ist der Wechselkurs etwas besser.
TOURISTIN Vielen Dank!
ANGESTELLTE Bitte, bitte!

An der Rezeption im Hotel

EMPFANGSDAME Guten Abend!
GAST Guten Abend! Haben Sie ein Einzelzimmer frei?
EMPFANGSDAME Für wie lange?
GAST Für zwei oder drei Nächte; wenn möglich ruhig und mit Bad.
EMPFANGSDAME Leider haben wir heute nur noch ein Doppelzimmer, und das nur für eine Nacht. Aber morgen wird ein Einzelzimmer frei. Wollen Sie das Doppelzimmer sehen?
GAST Ja, gern.
EMPFANGSDAME Zimmer Nummer 12, im ersten Stock rechts. Hier ist der Schlüssel.
GAST Sagen Sie, kann ich meinen Koffer einen Moment hier lassen?
EMPFANGSDAME Ja, natürlich. Stellen Sie ihn da drüben in die Ecke!
GAST Danke! Noch etwas, wann machen Sie abends zu?
EMPFANGSDAME Um 24.00 Uhr. Wenn Sie später kommen, müssen Sie klingeln.

A: 1. die Touristin 2. aus den USA 3. an den Geldautomaten 4. draußen am Eingang 5. der Wechselkurs 6. ein Einzelzimmer 7. für 2 oder 3 Nächte 8. ein Doppelzimmer, im 1. Stock 9. den Schlüssel 10. um 24.00 Uhr

You might also ask students to narrate the events of the dialogues.

A. Alles verstanden?

1. Wer möchte Geld umtauschen?
2. Woher kommt die Touristin?
3. Wohin soll sie gehen?
4. Wo gibt es einen Geldautomaten?
5. Was ist mit der Debitkarte besser?
6. Was für ein Zimmer möchte der Hotelgast?
7. Für wie lange braucht er es?
8. Was für ein Zimmer nimmt er und wo liegt es?
9. Was gibt die Dame an der Rezeption dem Gast?
10. Wann macht das Hotel zu?

B. Jetzt sind Sie dran! With a partner, create your own dialogue of interaction at a bank counter or the reception desk of a hotel.

Wortschatz 1

Die Uhrzeit *(time of day)*

The formal (official) time system in German-speaking countries is like the one used by the military. The hours are counted from 0 to 24, with 0 to 11 referring to A.M. and 12 to 24 referring to P.M. The system is commonly used in timetables for trains, buses, planes, etc., on radio and television, and to state business hours of stores and banks.

16.05 Uhr = sechzehn Uhr fünf	*4:05 P.M.*
16.15 Uhr = sechzehn Uhr fünfzehn	*4:15 P.M.*
16.30 Uhr = sechzehn Uhr dreißig	*4:30 P.M.*
16.45 Uhr = sechzehn Uhr fünfundvierzig	*4:45 P.M.*
17.00 Uhr = siebzehn Uhr	*5:00 P.M.*
24.00 Uhr = vierundzwanzig Uhr	*midnight*

In newspapers and advertisements, German traditionally separates hours and minutes by a period instead of a colon (**16.05 Uhr** = *4:05 P.M.*). However, with the popularity of digital clocks, the use of the colon has also become very common (**16:05 Uhr** AND *4:05 P.M.*). Note that *midnight* can be referred to as **24.00 Uhr** or **0.00 (null) Uhr.**

Die Bank, -en *(bank)*

der Ausweis, -e	*identification card (ID)*	das Geld	*money*
Dollar, -(s)	*dollar*	Bargeld	*cash*
Geldautomat, -en, -en	*ATM machine*	Kleingeld	*change*
Pass, ¨-e	*passport*	die Kasse, -n	*cashier's window*
Scheck, -s	*check*	Kreditkarte, -n	*credit card*

Das Hotel, -s *(hotel)*

der Ausgang, ¨-e	*exit*	das Einzelzimmer, -	*single room*
Eingang, ¨-e	*entrance*	Doppelzimmer, -	*double room*
Gast, ¨-e	*guest*	Gepäck	*baggage, luggage*
Koffer, -	*suitcase*	die Nacht, ¨-e	*night*
Schlüssel, -	*key*	Nummer, -n	*number*
		Tasche, -n	*bag; pocket*

Verschiedenes

der Blick (in / auf + *acc.*)	*view (of)*
die Lage	*location*
bald	*soon*
frei	*free(ly); available*
auf / zu	*open / closed*
geöffnet / geschlossen	*open / closed*
laut / ruhig	*loud(ly), noisy, noisily / quiet(ly)*
möglich	*possible*
einen Moment	*(for) just a minute*
Wann machen Sie auf / zu?	*When do you open / close?*
wechseln	*to change; to exchange*
lassen (lässt), gelassen	*to leave (behind)*
unterschreiben, unterschrieben	*to sign*
Das glaube ich nicht.	*I don't believe that.*
Das ist doch nicht möglich!	*That's impossible* (lit. *not possible*)!
Das kann doch nicht wahr sein!	*That can't be true!*
Quatsch!	*Nonsense!*
Vorsicht!	*Careful!*
Pass auf! / Passt auf! / Passen Sie auf!	*Watch out!*
Warte! / Wartet! / Warten Sie!	*Wait!*
Halt!	*Stop!*

Die Geschäfte **sind** alle **auf / zu (offen, geöffnet / geschlossen).** Sie **machen** bald **auf / zu** (BUT NOT **offen / geschlossen**).

Zum Erkennen: die Angestellte, -n *(clerk, employee, f.)*; umtauschen *(to exchange)*; nun *(well)*; der Wechselkurs *(exchange rate)*; besser *(better)*; die Empfangsdame, -n *(receptionist)*; klingeln *(here: to ring the doorbell)*

A: 1. *exit door* **(die)**, *guest pass* **(der)**, *money exchange* **(der)**, *piece of luggage* **(das)**, *handbag* **(die)**
2. *hotel entrance* **(der)**, *suitcase key* **(der)**, *night-time pharmacy* **(die)**, *nightgown* **(das)**, *night person* **(der)**
3. *passport number* **(die)**, *checkbook* **(das)**, *lake / ocean view* **(der)**, *savings book* **(das)**, *pocket money* **(das)**, *flashlight* **(die)**

Übungen zum Thema

A. Was bedeuten die Wörter und was sind die Artikel?

1. Ausgangstür, Gästeausweis, Geldwechsel, Gepäckstück, Handtasche
2. Hoteleingang, Kofferschlüssel, Nachtapotheke, Nachthemd, Nachtmensch
3. Passnummer, Scheckbuch, Seeblick, Sparbuch, Taschengeld, Taschenlampe

B. Ich brauche Kleingeld. With a partner, practice asking for a place where you can get change. Take turns and vary your responses.

S1 Ich habe kein Kleingeld. Kannst du mir . . . wechseln?
S2 Nein, . . .
S1 Schade!
S2 Aber du kannst . . .
S1 Wo ist . . . ?
S2 . . .
S1 Danke schön!
S2 . . .

Fokus Exchange Offices and Credit Cards

Currency can be exchanged and traveler's checks cashed at banks and post offices during business hours. However, currency exchange bureaus **(Wechselstuben)** are open daily at all major railroad stations, airports, and border crossings.

Credit cards are increasingly popular in the German-speaking countries, although many small businesses and restaurants still do not accept them. Electronic bank cards **(EC-Karten)** are used by Europeans to withdraw cash at banks or ATMs **(Geldautomaten)** and to pay bills in shops, restaurants, and hotels throughout Europe. If you have a four-digit PIN, you can use most US credit cards in European ATMs, but the banks usually charge a hefty transaction fee and the current interest rate on the date of transaction. Even though the exchange rate might be good, it is usually more advantageous to exchange traveler's checks at a bank.

Allerlei Kleingeld

C. Im Hotel Thüringer Hof With a partner, practice inquiring about a hotel room. Take turns and be sure to vary your responses.

Before doing this exercise, have a quick look at the chapter dialogue („An der Rezeption"), and also read through the advertisement for this hotel.

HOTEL THÜRINGER HOF
EISENACH

❖ *2 Übernachtungen*
Thüringer Spezialitätenmenü am 1. Tag
3-Gang Überraschungsmenü am 2. Tag
freier Eintritt ins Bach- und Lutherhaus
Besuch der Wartburg

pro Person im Doppelzimmer	*165,- €*
Einzelzimmer	*232,- €*

3 für 2 – Die Feiertage genießen

❖ *3 Übernachtungen*

pro Person im Doppelzimmer	*ab 119,- €*
Einzelzimmer	*ab 198,- €*

Alle Preise inklusive Frühstücksbuffet, Sauna und Fitnessraum

S1 Guten . . . ! Haben Sie noch . . . frei?
S2 Wie lange wollen Sie bleiben?
S1 . . .
S2 Wir haben noch . . . im . . .
S1 Das ist inklusive . . . und . . . , nicht wahr?
S2 Ja, auch inklusive Eintritt *(entrance fee)* ins . . . und Besichtigung von der . . .
S1 . . . Und was kostet das?
S2 . . .
S1 Kann ich das Zimmer sehen?
S2 . . . Hier ist der Schlüssel, Zimmernummer . . .
S1 Sagen Sie, wo kann ich . . . lassen?
S2 . . .
S1 Und wann machen Sie abends zu?
S2 . . .

D. Wie spät ist es? Ralf loves his new digital watch. Lea prefers her old-fashioned one with hands. As Ralf says what time it is, Lea confirms it in a more casual way. Work with a classmate. Take turns.

BEISPIEL 14.15
S1 Auf meiner Uhr ist es vierzehn Uhr fünfzehn.
S2 Bei mir ist es Viertel nach zwei.

1. 8.05	5. 14.30	9. 22.50
2. 11.10	6. 17.37	10. 23.59
3. 12.30	7. 19.40	11. 00.01
4. 13.25	8. 20.45	12. 02.15

D: 1. acht Uhr fünf, fünf nach acht 2. elf Uhr zehn, zehn nach elf 3. zwölf Uhr dreißig, halb eins 4. dreizehn Uhr fünfundzwanzig, fünf vor halb zwei 5. vierzehn Uhr dreißig, halb drei 6. siebzehn Uhr siebenunddreißig, sieben nach halb sechs 7. neunzehn Uhr vierzig, zwanzig vor acht 8. zwanzig Uhr fünfundvierzig, Viertel vor neun 9. zweiundzwanzig Uhr fünfzig, zehn vor elf 10. dreiundzwanzig Uhr neunundfünfzig, eine Minute vor zwölf / Mitternacht 11. null Uhr eins, eine Minute nach zwölf / Mitternacht 12. zwei Uhr fünfzehn, Viertel nach zwei

E: 1. von elf bis sechs (achtzehn Uhr) 2. um neun (einundzwanzig Uhr) 3. um sieben (neunzehn Uhr) 4. ein Sonntagsbrunch von zehn bis zwei (vierzehn Uhr) 5. nein 6. vom 1. November bis zum 30. Juni

E. Öffnungszeiten im Restaurant Marienburg Answer the following questions about this restaurant in the Marienburg Castle near Hildesheim. Give both official and unofficial clock times, where applicable.

1. Von wann bis wann ist das Restaurant sonntags bis mittwochs geöffnet?
2. Wann macht es donnerstags bis samstags zu?
3. Wann gibt es mittwochs etwas Besonderes?
4. Was haben sie am Sonntag von wann bis wann?
5. Hat das Restaurant einen Tag in der Woche geschlossen?
6. Wann ist das Restaurant ganz geschlossen? *(Give specific date!)*

F. Was sagen Sie? Working with a partner, react to the following situations with an appropriate expression, using each expression only once. Take turns.

Some familiar expressions of disbelief are: **Stimmt das?**, **Echt?**, **Wirklich?**, or **Das gibt's doch nicht!** Other helpful ones might be: **Du spinnst (wohl)!** *(You're crazy!)*, **Mach keine Witze!** *(Stop joking!)*, or **Achtung!** *(Watch out!)*.

BEISPIEL S1 Da kommt ein Auto wie verrückt um die Ecke!
S2 Vorsicht!

1. Hier kostet ein Hotelzimmer 110 Euro.
2. Ich habe ein Zimmer für 240 Euro im Monat gefunden.
3. Du, die Vorlesung beginnt um 14.15 Uhr und es ist schon 14.05 Uhr!
4. Sie bummeln mit einem Freund durch die Stadt. Ihr Freund will bei Rot *(at a red light)* über die Straße laufen.
5. Sie sind auf einer Party und es macht Ihnen viel Spaß. Aber morgen ist eine Prüfung und es ist schon zwei Uhr.
6. Sie lernen auf einer Party einen Studenten kennen. Sie hören, dass sein Vater und Ihr Vater zusammen in Heidelberg studiert haben.
7. Sie stehen mit einer Tasse Kaffee an der Tür. Die Tür ist zu. Ein Freund möchte hereinkommen.
8. Ein Freund aus Deutschland will die Kerzen auf seinem Weihnachtsbaum anzünden *(light)*. Sie sind sehr nervös.

G. Interview: Fragen Sie einen Nachbarn / eine Nachbarin, . . . !

1. wo man hier Bargeld oder Kleingeld bekommt
2. wo man hier Franken *(Swiss currency)* oder Euros bekommen kann
3. ob er/sie weiß, wie viele Franken/Euros man ungefähr für einen Dollar bekommt
4. wie er/sie bezahlt, wenn er/sie einkaufen geht: bar, mit einem Scheck oder mit einer Kreditkarte
5. wie er/sie bezahlt, wenn er/sie reist *(travels)*
6. was er/sie tut, wenn er/sie kein Geld mehr hat

Aussprache: ei, ie

For further review, see the Summary of Pronunciation in the front of this book. Study Part II, subsections 37, 40–41.

A. Laute

1. [ei] seit, weißt, bleibst, leider, frei, Rainer Meyer, Bayern
2. [ie] wie, wie viel, nie, lieben, liegen, mieten, lies, sieh, Dienstag
3. vielleicht, Beispiel, bleiben / blieben, heißen / hießen, Wien / Wein, Wiese / weiß

B. Wortpaare

1. See / Sie
2. beten / bieten
3. biete / bitte
4. Miete / Mitte
5. leider / Lieder
6. Mais / mies

Hörverständnis

Eine Busfahrt Listen to the conversation between these American exchange students in Tübingen and their professor before taking a bus trip early in their stay. Then complete the statements below based on the dialogue.

Zum Erkennen: ab·fahren *(to depart);* stecken in *(+acc.)(to put into);* die Währung *(currency);* die Reise, -n *(trip);* die Übernachtung, -en *(overnight stay);* die Mahlzeit, -en *(meal);* also *(in other words);* die Briefmarke, -n *(stamp);* vergessen *(to forget)*

1. Der Professor und die Studenten wollen ___am Montag___ um ___7 Uhr___ abfahren.
2. Von ___Montag___ bis ___Mittwoch___ sind sie in der Schweiz.
3. Sie sind von ___Donnerstag___ bis ___Samstag___ in Österreich.
4. Wenn man seine Kreditkarte in einen Geldautomaten steckt, bekommt man das ___Geld___ in der Währung von dem ___Land___, wo man ist.
5. Die Reise ist inklusive Übernachtungen, ___Essen / Mahlzeiten___ und Eintrittskarten.

Struktur

7.1 *Der-* and *ein*-words

Point out that students already know the endings for the **der**- and **ein**-words.

1. **Der**-words

   This small but important group of limiting words is called DER-WORDS, because their case endings are the same as those of the definite articles **der, das, die.**

alle	*all* (pl.)
der, das, die	*the; that* (when stressed)
dieser, -es, -e	*this; these*
jeder, -es, -e	*each, every* (sg. only)
mancher, -es, -e	*many a* (sg.); *several, some* (usually pl.)
solcher, -es, -e	*such* (usually pl.)
welcher, -es, -e	*which*

The plural of **jeder** is **alle,** which takes the same endings as the definite article in the plural.

CAUTION: In everyday speech, the singular of **solcher** usually is **so ein**, which is not a **der**-word but an **ein**-word: **so ein Hotel** (*such a hotel*) BUT **solche Hotels** (*such hotels*).

Compare the endings of the definite article and the **der**-words.

<table>
<tr><th></th><th>masc.</th><th>neut.</th><th>fem.</th><th>pl.</th></tr>
<tr><td>nom.</td><td>der
dieser
welcher</td><td rowspan="2">das
dieses
welches</td><td rowspan="2">die
diese
welche</td><td rowspan="2">die
diese
welche</td></tr>
<tr><td>acc.</td><td>den
diesen
welchen</td></tr>
<tr><td>dat.</td><td>dem
diesem
welchem</td><td>dem
diesem
welchem</td><td>der
dieser
welcher</td><td>den
diesen
welchen</td></tr>
</table>

It might be helpful to translate these sentences into English. They can be used in reverse (English to German) during the next period as warm-up.

nom. —Wo ist **der** Schlüssel?
—**Welcher** Schlüssel?
—**Dieser** Schlüssel?

acc. —Hast du **den** Kofferschlüssel gesehen?
—Wie soll ich **jeden** Schlüssel kennen?

dat. —Kannst du den Koffer mit **dem** Schlüssel öffnen?
—Mit **welchem** Schlüssel?

plural —Gib mir **die** Schlüssel!
—Hier sind **alle** Schlüssel. **Manche** Schlüssel sind vom Haus, **solche** Schlüssel zum Beispiel.

BUT —Der Kofferschlüssel ist **so ein** Schlüssel. Hast du **so einen** Schlüssel?

2. **Ein**-words

POSSESSIVE ADJECTIVES are called **ein**-words because their case endings are the same as those of the indefinite article **ein** and the negative **kein.**

mein	*my*	**unser**	*our*
dein	*your* (sg. fam.)	**euer**	*your* (pl. fam.)
sein	*his/its*	**ihr**	*their*
ihr	*her/its*	**Ihr**	*your* (sg./pl. formal)

Compare the endings of the indefinite article and the **ein**-words.

	masc.	neut.	fem.	pl.
nom.	ein mein unser	ein mein unser	ein**e** mein**e** unser**e**	kein**e** mein**e** unser**e**
acc.	ein**en** mein**en** unser**en**			
dat.	ein**em** mein**em** unser**em**	ein**em** mein**em** unser**em**	ein**er** mein**er** unser**er**	kein**en** mein**en** unser**en**

CAUTION: The **-er** of uns**er** and eu**er** is not an ending!

- **Ein**-words have no endings in the masculine singular nominative and in the neuter singular nominative and accusative.

nom.	Hier ist **ein** Pass. Ist das **mein** Pass oder **dein** Pass?
acc.	Braucht er **keine** Kreditkarte? —Wo hat er **seine** Kreditkarte? Hat sie **einen** Ausweis? —Natürlich hat sie **ihren** Ausweis. Haben Sie **Ihren** Ausweis?
dat.	In welcher Tasche sind die Schlüssel? —Sie sind in **meiner** Tasche. Oder sind die Schlüssel in **einem** Koffer? —Sie sind in **Ihrem** Koffer.
plural	Wo sind die Schecks? —Hier sind **unsere** Schecks und da sind **eu(e)re** Schecks.

If students need help in telling whether **ihr** is a dative pronoun or a possessive adjective (and which one of the two), give them examples such as the following: 1. Ich gebe **ihr** das Buch. Ich habe **ihr** Buch. 2. Sie bringen **ihr** Blumen. Sie bringen **ihre** Blumen. 3. Das ist Ruth. Ich habe **ihr** Heft. 4. Wir fahren zu Müllers. Wo ist **ihre** Adresse? 5. Guten Tag, Herr Fiedler! Wie geht es **Ihrer** Frau?

Translate into English! This can be used in reverse (or as a quiz) in the next period.

When **unser** and **euer** have an ending, the **-e-** is often dropped **(unsre, eure),** especially in colloquial speech.

Übungen

A. Ersetzen Sie die Artikel!

1. ***Der*-Wörter**

BEISPIEL die Tasche *(this)*
diese Tasche

a. das Gepäck *(every, which, this)*
b. der Ausweis *(this, every, which)*
c. die Nummer *(which, each, this)*
d. die Nächte *(some, such, these)*
e. an der Kasse *(this, every, which)*
f. mit den Schecks *(these, some, all)*

A.1–2: Use variations of these exercises during several class periods until students have mastered the **der**- and **ein**-words.

A.1: a. jedes, welches, dieses
b. dieser, jeder, welcher
c. welche, jede, diese
d. manche, solche, dieses
e. dieser, jeder, welcher
f. diesen, manchen, allen

A.2: a. mein, ihr, kein, sein b. unser, ihr, kein c. meine, uns(e)re, deine / eu(e)re / Ihre d. deinen / eu(e)ren / Ihren, uns(e)ren, ihren e. keinem, seinem, deinem / eu(e)rem, Ihrem f. deinen / eu(e)ren / Ihren, meinen, ihren

To make the practice of the possessive adjective more meaningful, do it with some of your own and the students' belongings: e.g., **Ist das Ihr Bleistift? Nein, das ist sein Bleistift.**

A.3: a. vor ihrem / diesem / uns(e)rem / Ihrem Hotel b. Alle / Diese / Uns(e)re / Eu(e)re Zimmer c. Manche / Ihre / uns(e)re / ihre Betten d. seine / solche / alle / manche Gäste e. meine / ihre / eu(e)re / ihre Kreditkarte f. diesen / uns(e)ren / seinen / meinen Schlüssel g. Uns(e)re / Alle / Meine / Ihre Taschen h. deinen, eu(e)ren, Ihren / jeden / alle / uns(e)re Koffer

2. ***Ein*-Wörter**

BEISPIEL die Gäste *(your/3×)*
deine / eu(e)re / Ihre Gäste

a. der Pass *(my, her, no, his)*
b. das Bargeld *(our, her, no)*
c. die Wohnung *(my, our, your/3×)*
d. neben den Koffer *(your/3×, our, their)*
e. in dem Doppelzimmer *(no, his, your/3×)*
f. mit den Schlüsseln *(your/3×, my, her)*

3. **Was für ein Hotel!** Repeat the following sentences with the appropriate ***der-*** or ***ein-***words.

BEISPIEL **Den** Leuten gefällt das Hotel nicht. *(these)*
Diesen Leuten gefällt das Hotel nicht.

a. Die Straße vor **dem** Hotel ist zu laut. *(their, this, our, your/formal)*
b. **Die** Zimmer sind sehr klein. *(all, these, our, your/pl. fam.)*
c. **Die** Betten sind unbequem. *(some, your/formal, our, their)*
d. Der Mann an der Rezeption kennt **die** Gäste. *(his, such, all, some)*
e. Er möchte jetzt **die** Kreditkarte sehen. *(my, her, your/pl. fam, their)*
f. Soll ich **den** Schlüssel hier lassen? *(this, our, his, my)*
g. **Die** Taschen stehen schon am Ausgang. *(our, all, my, her)*
h. Der Portier bringt **den** Koffer zum Auto. *(your/3×, each, all, our)*

B. Was fehlt? Complete the sentences about the photo in front of a German ATM machine.

Auf ___diesem___ *(this)* Bild seht ihr zwei Freunde von ___meinen___ *(my)* Eltern vor einem Geldautomaten. Sie sind zwei Jahre ___uns(e)re___ *(our)* Nachbarn gewesen. In ___welcher___ *(which)* Stadt ist ___dieser___ *(this)* Automat? Er ist in Augsburg neben ___ihrem___ *(their)* Supermarkt. ___Solche___ *(Such)* Automaten gibt es aber überall und in ___jeder___ *(each)* Stadt. Bei euch fahren ___manche___ *(some)* Leute ja sogar mit ___ihrem___ *(their)* Auto direkt zum Automaten, wo man schnell Geld bekommt. Wenn man ___keine___ *(no)* Zeit hat oder die Bank geschlossen ist, ist ___so ein___ *(such a)* Automat sehr praktisch.

C. Ruck, zuck! Wem gehört das? One person claims to own everything. Quickly correct him/her and tell whose property it is. You may mention the items suggested or think of your own.

BEISPIEL Das ist mein Buch. (Heft, Bleistift, Jacke, Tasche, Schlüssel usw.)
Quatsch! Das ist nicht dein Buch; das ist mein (ihr, sein) Buch.

Fokus Hotel Names

Germany, Austria, and Switzerland have many small hotels (**Gasthöfe** or **Gasthäuser**), a type of accommodation that first appeared around monasteries toward the end of the Middle Ages. Many of these hotels still have names of biblical origin: *Gasthof Engel* (angel); *Gasthof Drei Könige* (the Three Kings, representing travel); *Gasthof Rose* or *Gasthof Lilie* (both flowers represent the Virgin Mary); *Gasthof Lamm* (the Lamb of God). After a postal system began to develop in the 1400s, names such as *Gasthof Alte Post / Neue Post / Zur Post* became common.

7.2 Separable-prefix verbs

1. English has a number of two-part verbs that consist of a verb and a preposition or an adverb.

Watch out! Hurry up! Come back!

In German, such verbs are called SEPARABLE-PREFIX verbs. You are already familiar with two of them:

Passen Sie **auf! Hören** Sie **zu!**

Their infinitives are **aufpassen** and **zuhören.** The prefixes **auf** and **zu** carry the main stress: **auf'·passen, zu'·hören.** From now on, we will identify such separable-prefix verbs with a raised dot (·) between the prefix and the verb in vocabulary lists: **auf·passen, zu·hören.**

- These verbs are separated from the prefixes when the inflected part of the verb is the first or second sentence element: in imperatives, questions, and statements.

Kick the separable prefix to the end of the sentence or clause, just like the soccer player.

Hören Sie bitte **zu!**
Hören Sie jetzt **zu?**
Warum **hören** Sie nicht **zu?**
Wir **hören** immer gut **zu.**
V1 ... V2

- These verbs are not separated from the prefix when the verb stands at the end of a sentence or clause with modals, in the present perfect, and in subordinate clauses. Note, however, that in the present perfect the **-ge-** of the past participle is inserted between the stressed prefix and the participle.

  Ich soll immer gut **zuhören.**
  Ich habe immer gut **zugehört.**
  Ich weiß, dass ich immer gut **zuhöre.**
  Ich weiß, dass ich immer gut **zuhören** soll.
  Ich weiß, dass ich immer gut **zugehört** habe.

2. Knowing the basic meanings of some of the most frequent separable prefixes will help you derive the meanings of some of the separable-prefix verbs.

ab-	*away; off*	**nach-**	*after; behind; later*
an-	*to; up to*	**um-**	*around; over; from one to the other*
auf-	*up; open*		
aus-	*out; out of*	**vor-**	*ahead; before*
ein-	*into*	**vorbei-**	*past, by*
her-	*toward (the speaker)*	**zu-**	*closed, shut*
hin-	*away from (the speaker)*	**zurück-**	*back*
mit-	*together with, along with*		

an·kommen	*to arrive (come to)*
her·kommen	*to come (toward the speaker)*
herein·kommen	*to come in (toward the speaker)*
heraus·kommen	*to come out (toward the speaker)*
hin·kommen	*to get there (away from the point of reference)*
mit·kommen	*to come along*
vorbei·kommen	*to come by*
zurück·kommen	*to come back*

You may want to point out that there are numerous compounds with **hin-** and **her-:** Ich gehe **hinaus (hinauf, hinein, hinüber).** Er kommt **heraus (herauf, herein, herüber).** In colloquial speech: **raus, rauf, rein, rüber.**

You will need to learn these common separable-prefix verbs:

Point out that students already know the endings for the **der-** and **ein-** words

an·rufen, angerufen	*to call, phone*
auf·machen	*to open*
auf·passen	*to pay attention, watch (out)*
auf·schreiben, aufgeschrieben	*to write down*
auf·stehen, ist aufgestanden	*to get up*
aus·gehen, ist ausgegangen	*to go out*
ein·kaufen	*to shop*
mit·bringen, mitgebracht	*to bring along*
mit·gehen, ist mitgegangen	*to go along*
mit·kommen, ist mitgekommen	*to come along*
mit·nehmen, mitgenommen	*to take along*
um·tauschen	*to exchange*
vorbei·gehen, ist vorbeigegangen (an, bei)	*to pass (by)*
zu·hören (+ *dat.*)	*to listen*
zu·machen	*to close*
zurück·kommen, ist zurückgekommen	*to come back*

CAUTION: Not all verbs with prefixes are separable, for example, **unterschreiben, wiederholen.** Here the main stress is on the verb, not on the prefix: **unterschrei'ben, wiederho'len.** Remember also the inseparable prefixes **be-, ent-, er-, ge-, ver-,** and so on. (Chapter 4, *Struktur 4.1*). They never stand alone.

Übungen

D. Was bedeuten diese Verben? Knowing the meanings of the basic verbs and the prefixes, can you tell what these separable-prefix verbs mean?

1. abgeben, abnehmen
2. ansprechen
3. aufbauen, aufgeben, aufstehen, aufstellen
4. ausarbeiten, aushelfen, aus(be)zahlen
5. heraufkommen, herauskommen, herüberkommen, herunterkommen
6. hinaufgehen, hinausgehen, hineingehen, hinuntergehen
7. mitgehen, mitfahren, mitfeiern, mitsingen, mitspielen
8. nachkommen, nachlaufen, nachmachen
9. vorbeibringen, vorbeifahren, vorbeikommen
10. zumachen
11. zurückbekommen, zurückbleiben, zurückbringen, zurückgeben, zurücknehmen, zurücksehen

D: 1. *to hand in, to take off* 2. *to address/speak to* 3. *to build up, to give up, to get up, to put in place* 4. *to work out, to help out, to pay out* 5. *to come up, to come out, to come over, to come down* 6. *to go up, to go out, to go in, to go down* 7. *to go along, to drive along, to join in celebrating, to sing along, to join in playing* 8. *to follow, to run after, to imitate* 9. *to bring by, to drive by, to come by* 10. *to close* 11. *to get back, to stay back, to bring back, to give back, to take back, to look back*

E. Noch einmal Repeat these sentences without a modal.

BEISPIEL Margit soll Gisela gut zuhören.
Margit hört Gisela gut zu.

1. Margit soll am Wochenende auf Giselas Haus aufpassen.
2. Gisela will ihr alle Telefonnummern aufschreiben.
3. Morgens muss Margit früh aufstehen und die Tiere füttern *(feed the animals)*.
4. Frank und die Kinder wollen auch mitkommen.
5. Die Kinder dürfen ein paar Videos mitbringen.
6. Am Samstag will Margit mit ihrer Tochter einkaufen.
7. Ein paar Freunde können auch vorbeikommen.
8. Frank soll morgens alle Fenster aufmachen.
9. Abends muss er alle Türen zumachen.
10. Gisela will am Montag wieder zurückkommen.

E: 1. Margit passt . . . auf 2. Gisela schreibt . . . auf 3. Morgens steht Margit . . . auf und füttert . . . 4. Frank und die Kinder kommen . . . mit 5. Die Kinder bringen . . . mit 6. Am Samstag kauft Margit . . . ein 7. Ein paar Freunde kommen . . . vorbei 8. Frank macht . . . auf 9. Abends macht er . . . zu 10. Gisela kommt . . . zurück

F. Am Telefon Report to a brother what your mother is telling or asking you about tomorrow's family reunion.

BEISPIEL Sie möchte wissen, ob Rainer und Wolfgang die Kinder mitbringen.
Bringen Rainer und Wolfgang die Kinder mit?

Sie sagt, dass die Tante auch mitkommt.
Die Tante kommt auch mit.

1. Sie sagt, dass wir abends alle zusammen ausgehen.
2. Sie möchte wissen, ob du deine Kamera mitbringst.
3. Sie möchte wissen, wann die Bank aufmacht.
4. Sie sagt, dass sie schnell noch etwas Geld umtauscht.
5. Sie sagt, dass sie dann hier vorbeikommt.

F: 1. Wir gehen abends alle zusammen aus. 2. Bringst du deine Kamera mit? 3. Wann macht die Bank auf? 4. Sie tauscht noch schnell etwas Geld um. 5. Sie kommt dann hier vorbei.

G. Das tut man gewöhnlich. Say what one usually does before checking out of a hotel.

BEISPIEL früh aufstehen *Man steht früh auf.*

1. die Koffer zumachen 2. das Gepäck zur Rezeption mitnehmen 3. die Rechnung unterschreiben 4. den Schlüssel zurückgeben 5. vielleicht ein Taxi anrufen

G: 1. Man macht die Koffer zu. 2. Man nimmt das Gepäck zur Rezeption mit. 3. Man unterschreibt die Rechnung. 4. Man gibt den Schlüssel zurück. 5. Man ruft vielleicht ein Taxi an.

Optional practice: **Natürlich, immer!** Have students (possibly in chorus) reply in the present tense, e.g., Haben Sie das Deutschbuch mitgebracht? **Natürlich, ich bringe das Deutschbuch immer mit.** Haben Sie gut zugehört? Haben Sie alles aufgeschrieben? Sind Sie heute früh aufgestanden? Sind Sie am Wochenende ausgegangen? Haben Sie etwas Geld mitgenommen? Sind Sie spät zurückgekommen?

H. Hoppla, hier fehlt was: Wer hat was getan? Work with a partner to find out whether various family members have finished their tasks. Take turns asking questions until you have both completed your lists. One list is below, the other in Section 11 of the Appendix.

BEISPIEL S1 Ist Vater bei der Bank vorbeigegangen?
S2 Ja, er ist gestern bei der Bank vorbeigegangen. Haben die Kinder den Fernseher ausgemacht?
S1 Ja, sie haben den Fernseher ausgemacht.

S1:

WER?	WAS TUN?	JA. / NEIN.
Vater	bei der Bank vorbeigehen	Ja, gestern.
Vater	Geld umtauschen	Ja.
Mutter	die Kamera mitbringen	Ja, ich glaube.
Mutter	die Nachbarn anrufen	Nein.
Thomas	die Telefonnummer aufschreiben	Ja, ich glaube.
Thomas	die Garagentür zumachen	Nein, noch nicht.
Carla	bei der Post vorbeigehen	Ja, gestern.
Carla	die Fenster zumachen	Nein, noch nicht.
Kinder	den Fernseher ausmachen *(turn off)*	Ja.
Kinder	die Lichter *(lights)* ausmachen	Nein, noch nicht.
ich	ein paar Bücher mitnehmen	Ja.

I: 1. Fahren Sie / Fahr / Fahrt / Fahren wir mit ihnen! 2. Kaufen Sie / Kauf / Kauft / Kaufen wir bei Aldi ein! 3. Nehmen Sie / Nimm / Nehmt / Nehmen wir ein paar Einkaufstaschen mit! 4. Bringen Sie / Bring / Bringt / Bringen wir die Flaschen zum Getränkemarkt zurück! 5. Gehen Sie / Geh / Geht / Gehen wir auch bei der Bank vorbei! 6. Bringen Sie / Bring / Bringt / Bringen wir etwas Bargeld zurück!

I: To vary this exercise, you could have students call out whom they wish to address and the others adjust the command accordingly, e.g., Karen! —Karen, hör gut zu!; Karen und Charlie! —Karen und Charlie, hört gut zu!

I. Nennen Sie alle vier Imperative!

BEISPIEL gut zuhören
Hören Sie gut zu!
Hör gut zu!
Hört gut zu!
Hören wir gut zu!

© Ingrid Sevin

1. mit ihnen mitfahren
2. bei Aldi einkaufen
3. ein paar Einkaufstauschen *(. . . bags)* mitnehmen
4. die Flaschen zum Getränkemarkt zurückbringen
5. auch bei der Bank vorbeigehen
6. etwas Bargeld zurückbringen

J. Nein, das tue ich nicht! Your partner is not very cooperative and makes all sorts of statements that he/she won't do this or that. You plead with him/her not to be so stubborn and do it anyway. Create sentences with the verbs listed in *Struktur 7.2* of this chapter. Follow the example. Take turns.

BEISPIEL anrufen
S1 Nein, ich rufe sie nicht an!
S2 Ach, ruf(e) sie doch bitte an! Du hast sie doch immer angerufen.

 **K. Interview: Fragen Sie einen Nachbarn / eine Nachbarin, . . . !**

1. wann er/sie heute aufgestanden ist
2. wann er/sie gewöhnlich am Wochenende aufsteht
3. wohin er/sie gern geht, wenn er/sie ausgeht
4. wo er/sie einkauft (z.B. Lebensmittel, Kleidung usw.)
5. was er/sie heute zur Uni mitgebracht hat (drei Beispiele bitte!)

7.3 Flavoring particles

In everyday speech, German speakers use many FLAVORING WORDS (or intensifiers) to convey what English often expresses through gestures or intonation, for example, surprise, admiration, or curiosity. When used in these contexts, flavoring particles have no exact English equivalent. Here are some examples:

At this level, do not expect students always to use flavoring particles correctly.

aber	*expresses admiration, or intensifies a statement*
denn	*expresses curiosity, interest (usually in a question)*
doch	*expresses concern, impatience, assurance*
ja	*adds emphasis*

Euer Haus gefällt mir **aber!**	*I do like your house.*
Die Möbel sind **aber** schön!	*Isn't this furniture beautiful!*
Was ist **denn** das?	*What (on earth) is that?*
Wie viel kostet **denn** so etwas?	*(Just) how much does something like that cost?*
Das weiß ich **doch** nicht.	*That I don't know.*
Frag **doch** Julia!	*Why don't you ask Julia!*
Du kennst **doch** Julia?	*You do know Julia, don't you?*
Euer Garten ist **ja** super!	*(Wow,) your garden is great!*
Ihr habt **ja** sogar einen Pool!	*(Hey,) you even have a pool!*

Read these examples aloud to make students aware of how varying intonation and gestures can express admiration, curiosity, impatience, assurance, or emphasis in English.

Übung

Note that your answers might differ from those of your classmates. That's typical for these flavoring particles. Just be aware that these particles are frequenly used in conversation and add a certain flavor to the sentence.

L. Im Hotel Read aloud the following sentences and determine what is expressed through the use of certain flavoring particles. What might their translation be?

BEISPIEL Dieses Hotel ist ja wunderschön!
Emphasis: Isn't this hotel beautiful?

1. Haben Sie denn noch Zimmer frei?
2. Der Blick *(view)* vom Balkon ist aber toll!
3. Es gibt ja sogar einen See!
4. Wir gehen aber noch aus, nicht wahr?
5. Wohin gehen wir denn?
6. Hast du denn keinen Hunger?
7. Komm doch mit!
8. Wann kommst du denn?
9. Ich komme ja schon!
10. Es ist doch schon acht Uhr.
11. Du bist aber heute ungemütlich.
12. Wir haben doch Ferien.

L: 1. Curiosity: You do still have rooms available, don't you? 2. Admiration: Isn't the view from the balcony fantastic? 3. Emphasis: (Wow,) there's even a lake. 4. Intensifies: (Hey,) we are still going out, right? 5. Curiosity: (Just) where are we going to go? 6. Curiosity: Aren't you hungry (at all)? 7. Concern: Why don't you come along? 8. Impatience: When are your you coming? 9. Assurance: I'm coming (, I'm coming). 10. Impatience: (Hey,) it's already eight o'clock. 11. Intensifies: (Boy,) you are impatient today. 12. Impatience: We are on vacation (after all).

Fokus Accommodations and Tourist Information

When looking for accommodations in a German city, you can choose from a wide range of prices and comfort levels, from campgrounds to luxury hotels. A **Pension** usually offers a simple room with a private bath; sometimes shared toilets and showers are down the hall. Homes offering inexpensive **Fremdenzimmer,** or rooms for tourists, are common in rural areas and can be spotted by a sign saying **Zimmer frei.** Breakfast is usually included in the price of accommodation, regardless of the price category. In the interest of public safety, hotel guests are required by law to fill out a form providing home address, date of birth, and other personal information.

To find accommodations, travelers can rely on a town's tourist information office (**die Touristeninformation** or **das Fremdenverkehrsbüro**). Usually located in the train station or city center, this office provides tourists with the usual sightseeing information, as well as help them with lodging (**die Zimmervermittlung**) in hotels or private homes.

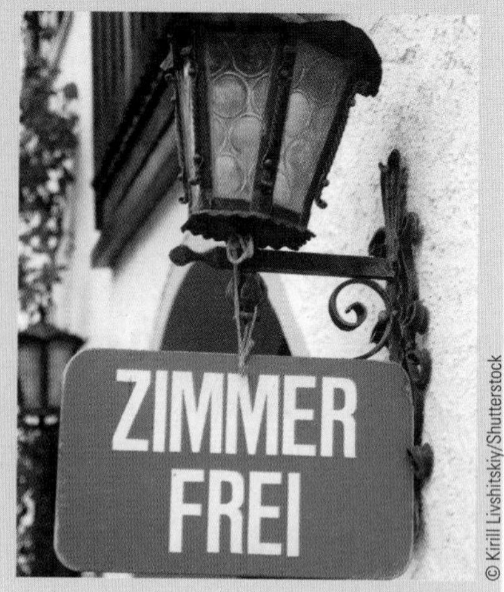

Zusammenfassung

iLrn

Visit the ***Wie geht's?*** iLrn website for more review and practice of the grammar point you have just learned.

M. Bilden Sie Sätze! Create sentences using the verb forms indicated in parentheses.

BEISPIEL Eva / anrufen / Laura *(present perf.)*
Eva hat Laura angerufen.
Laura / einkaufen gehen / heute / in / Stadt *(present tense)*
Laura geht heute in die Stadt einkaufen.

1. vorbeikommen / du / bei / eine / Apotheke? *(present tense)*
2. können / du / mir / bitte / mitbringen / etwas Medizin? *(present tense)*
3. wann / zumachen / denn / Apotheke? *(present tense)*
4. bitte / anrufen / doch / schnell! *(imperative / sg. fam.)*
5. sie / zumachen / leider schon *(present perf.)*
6. sie / aufmachen / morgen um 9.00 Uhr / wieder *(present tense)*
7. dann / vorbeigehen / bitte / morgen / und / mitbringen / mir / das! *(imperative/sg. fam.)*
8. du / aufschreiben / alles? *(present perf.)*
9. mein / Eltern / wieder / aus / Schweiz / zurückkommen *(present perf.)*
10. sie *(pl.)* / mitbringen / mir / ein Buch *(present perf.)*
11. leider / ich / lesen / es / schon *(present perf.)*
12. ich / gehen / heute / in / Stadt / und / es / umtauschen *(present tense)*

M: 1. Kommst du bei einer Apotheke vorbei? 2. Kannst du mir bitte etwas Medizin mitbringen? 3. Wann macht denn die Apotheke zu? 4. Bitte ruf doch mal schnell an! 5. Sie hat leider schon zugemacht. 6. Sie machen morgen um 9.00 Uhr wieder auf. 7. Dann geh bitte morgen vorbei und bring mir das mit! 8. Hast du alles aufgeschrieben? 9. Meine Eltern sind wieder aus der Schweiz zurückgekommen. 10. Sie haben mir ein Buch mitgebracht. 11. Leider habe ich es schon gelesen. 12. Ich gehe heute in die Stadt und tausche es um.

N. Gedächtnisspiel *(Memory game)* In a small group, one of your classmates starts with a statement using a verb, such as **mitbringen** or **umtauschen.** The next student repeats the statement and adds to it, and so on. When your memory fails, or if you forget to add the separable prefix, you are out of the game. Let's see who wins!

BEISPIEL *Ich bringe Blumen mit.*
Ich bringe Blumen und Wein mit.
Ich bringe Blumen, Wein und Salzstangen mit.

O. An der Rezeption: Auf Deutsch bitte!

1. All (the) hotels are full **(voll).**
2. That can't be true!
3. Wait, there's another hotel.
4. Why don't you *(sg. fam.)* ask at Hotel Engel?
5. Do you *(formal)* still have rooms available?
6. Just a minute. Yes, one room with (a) bath on the second floor.
7. Can we see it?
8. Yes, here is a key.
9. We'll be right back **(zurückkommen).**
10. We like this room.
11. You do take credit cards, don't you? —Of course.
12. Did you see our restaurant? —Which restaurant?
13. This restaurant. From every table you have a view of the water.
14. You don't find a restaurant like this (such a restaurant) everywhere.

O: 1. Alle Hotels sind voll. 2. Das kann doch nicht wahr sein! 3. Warte, da ist noch ein Hotel! 4. Warum fragst du nicht bei Hotel Engel? 5. Haben Sie noch Zimmer frei? 6. Einen Moment. Ja, ein Zimmer mit Bad im ersten Stock. 7. Können wir es sehen? 8. Ja, hier ist der Schlüssel. 9. Wir kommen gleich wieder zurück. 10. Das Zimmer gefällt uns. 11. Sie nehmen doch Kreditkarten? —Natürlich. 12. Haben Sie unser Restaurant gesehen? —Welches Restaurant? 13. Dieses Restaurant. Von jedem Tisch haben Sie einen Blick aufs Wasser. 14. Sie finden so ein Restaurant nicht überall.

Fokus Youth Hostels

Youth hostels (**Jugendherbergen**) are immensely popular among budget-minded travelers in Germany, Switzerland, and Austria. There are 556 of them in Germany and around 150 in Austria and Switzerland combined. These are open to individual travelers, groups, and families. There is generally no upper age limit, but during peak season, young people under 25 have priority. Accommodation is usually dormitory-style, with bunk beds and shared bathrooms. Many youth hostels offer laundry facilities, dining halls, and common rooms. Although they are not real hotels–many are closed during the day and have a curfew–youth hostels have reached a relatively high level of comfort for the price. Students and backpackers have come to value the hostels as places to meet other young people from around the world. If you plan on "hosteling," remember to purchase a membership card (**der Jugendherbergsausweis**) before traveling overseas. You can find organizations in the US, Canada, and Europe, where you can obtain the card, on the Web.

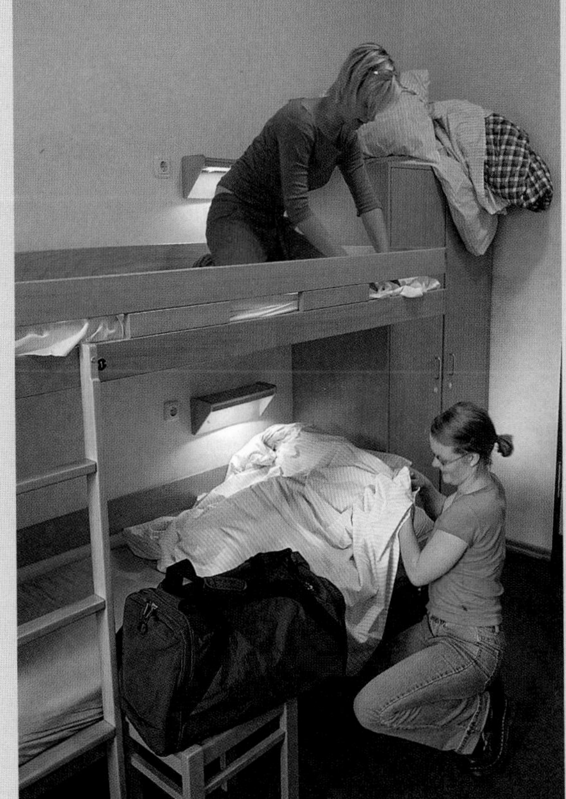

Beim Bettenmachen in der Jugendherberge

Einblicke

Lesetext

© Hiro1775 | Dreamstime.com

Two-way prepositions take the dative with **ankommen: Er ist am Bahnhof / in der Stadt angekommen.**

Point out that **übernachten** works like **wiederholen** and **unterschreiben;** here, **über-** is an inseparable prefix.

Wortschatz 2

der Gasthof, ¨-e	*small hotel*
Wald, ¨-er	*forest, woods*
die Jugendherberge, -n	*youth hostel*
Pension, -en	*boarding house; hotel*
Reise, -n	*trip*
einfach	*simple, simply*
meistens	*mostly, usually*
an·kommen, ist angekommen	*to arrive*
an·nehmen, angenommen	*to accept*
kennen·lernen	*to get to know; meet*
packen	*to pack*
reisen, ist gereist	*to travel*
reservieren	*to reserve*
übernachten	*to spend the night*
Das kommt darauf an.	*That depends.*

Vor dem Lesen

A. Allerlei Hotels: Wo möchten Sie übernachten? With your partner, compare the various hotels listed below and decide which one to recommend to your parents, who are going to visit you in Regensburg.

HOTEL	ADRESSE	TEL.	PREIS	
Adler	Steinweg 10	5 54 54	55,00	TV P
Am Berg	Taunusweg 15	93 50-0	80,00	TV BAR
Astor	Mainzerstr. 8	64 85-0	49,00	TV MINI BAR P
Engel	Rathausplatz 2	9 20 20	98,00	TV MINI BAR BAR P
Schäfer	Schillerstr. 50	57 34-0	110,00	TV MINI BAR
Sonne-Post	Müllergasse 12	59 20 07	85,00	TV BAR
Waldsee	Wormserstr. 33	58 31 3	145,00	TV MINI BAR P

SYMBOLE: = Fahrstuhl (elevator) = Aircondition = Modemanschluss (...connection) = Nachtportier = Frühstücksbüfett = Sauna + Solarium = Radio

© Ingrid Sevin

B. Fragen

1. Wo kann man in den USA / in Kanada gut übernachten?
2. Wie heißen ein paar Hotels oder Motels?
3. Was gibt es in einem Hotelzimmer?
4. Was ungefähr kostet ein Zimmer in einem Luxushotel in New York oder Vancouver?
5. Haben Sie schon einmal in einer Jugendherberge übernachtet? Wenn ja, wo?
6. Gehen Sie gern campen? Wenn ja, warum; wenn nein, warum nicht?

Lesetipp

Looking for Conjunctions

Being aware of verb-last word order after subordinating conjunctions can help your reading comprehension. In this reading, note that while some sentences start out with the dependent clause, in others, the dependent clause follows after the main clause and a comma. Pay special attention to the position of the verb in the dependent clauses. How many examples of dependent clauses can you find?

Jugendherberge Burg Stahleck in Bacharach am Rhein

C. Das ist leicht zu verstehen! Read aloud the following words paying special attention to their stressed syllable. Then guess their meaning in English.

der Campingplatz, Evangelist; das Formular, Symbol; die Adresse, Attraktion, Bibel, Übernachtungsmöglichkeit; ausfüllen; international, luxuriös, primitiv, privat

Übernachtungsmöglichkeiten

Wo kann man gut übernachten? Nun°, das kommt darauf an, ob das Hotel elegant oder einfach sein soll, ob es zentral liegen muss oder weiter draußen° sein darf. Wer will, kann auch Gast in einem Schloss oder einer Burg sein.

Wie in den USA und in Kanada gibt es viele Hotels mit gleichen° Namen, weil sie zu einer Hotelkette° gehören, z. B. Holiday Inn oder Hilton. Bei diesen Hotels weiß man immer, was man hat, wenn man hineingeht. In Deutschland, Österreich und in der Schweiz gibt es außerdem noch andere Hotels mit gleichen Namen, z. B. Hotel zur Sonne oder Gasthof Post. Das bedeutet aber nicht, dass solche Hotels innen gleich sind°. Im Gegenteil°! Sie sind meistens sehr verschieden, weil sie zu keiner Kette gehören. Ihre Namen gehen oft bis ins Mittelalter zurück. Sie sagen gewöhnlich etwas über° ihre Lage°, z. B. Berghotel, Pension Waldsee. Andere° Namen—wie z. B. Gasthof zum Löwen, zum Adler° oder zum Stier°—sind aus der Bibel genommen. Sie sind Symbole für die Evangelisten Markus, Johannes und Lukas.

Manche Hotels sind sehr luxuriös und teuer, andere sind einfach und billig. Wenn Sie zum Beispiel in einem Gasthof oder Gasthaus ankommen, gehen Sie zur Rezeption. Dort müssen Sie meistens ein Formular ausfüllen und bekommen dann Ihr Zimmer.

Well
farther out
same
chain
are alike inside / On the contrary
about / location
Other / eagle
bull

included
day off

Das Frühstück ist gewöhnlich im Preis inbegriffen°. Übrigens hat jeder Gasthof seinen Ruhetag°. Dann ist das Restaurant geschlossen und man nimmt keine neuen Gäste an. An der Rezeption kann man Ihnen auch Geschäfte und Attraktionen in der Stadt empfehlen und manchmal auch Geld umtauschen. Aber Vorsicht! Das Beste ist immer noch ein Geldautomat. Die gibt es überall und da ist der Wechselkurs besser.

in advance

Note that youth hostels and small **Pensionen** or **Gasthöfe** usually don't accept credit cards.

Sie können ein Zimmer vorher° durchs Internet reservieren oder eine Übernachtungsmöglichkeit durch die Touristeninformation am Hauptbahnhof finden. Hier gibt es nicht nur Adressen von Hotels, sondern auch von Privatzimmern und Pensionen, wo eine Übernachtung gewöhnlich nicht sehr teuer, aber sauber und gut ist.

for that

Haben Sie schon einmal in einer Jugendherberge oder einem Jugendgästehaus übernachtet? Sie brauchen dafür° einen Jugendherbergsausweis. So einen Ausweis können Sie aber schon vorher in Amerika oder Kanada bekommen. Fast jede Stadt hat eine Jugendherberge, manchmal in einem modernen Haus, manchmal in einer Burg oder in einem Schloss. Jugendherbergen und Jugendgästehäuser sind in den Ferien meistens schnell voll, denn viele Gruppen reservieren schon vorher.

experience
disadvantage
rather
only

Das Übernachten in einer Jugendherberge kann ein Erlebnis° sein, weil man oft interessante Leute kennenlernt. Jugendherbergen haben nur einen Nachteil°: Sie machen gewöhnlich abends um 22.00 Uhr zu. Wenn Sie später zurückkommen, haben Sie Pech gehabt. In fast allen Großstädten gibt es Jugendgästehäuser. Wenn Sie schon vorher wissen, dass Sie fast jeden Abend ausgehen und spät nach Hause kommen, dann übernachten Sie lieber° in einem Jugendgästehaus, denn diese machen erst° um 24.00 oder 1.00 Uhr zu, und in manchen Gästehäusern kann man sogar einen Hausschlüssel bekommen.

in other ways / tent
on the road

Man kann natürlich auch anders° übernachten, z. B. im Zelt° auf einem Campingplatz. Das macht Spaß, wenn man mit dem Fahrrad unterwegs° ist. Ob im Hotel oder auf dem Campingplatz, in einer Pension oder Jugendherberge, überall wünschen wir Ihnen viel Spaß auf Ihrer Reise durch Europa.

Nach dem Lesen

A: 1. alle gleich; man weiß, was man bekommt; vielleicht nicht so interessant. 2. das Frühstück 3. Wechselkurs nicht so gut 4. durchs Internet, bei der Touristeninformation am Hauptbahnhof. 5. billig, Leute kennenlernen; machen abends um 22.00 Uhr zu. 6. auf dem Campingplatz; nicht immer sehr bequem, man braucht ein Zelt

Optional practice: **Was ist das?** 1. eine Hotelkette 2. die Rezeption 3. ein Gasthof 4. eine Jugendherberge 5. eine Pension 6. ein Waldsee 7. ein Hausschlüssel 8. Glück

A. Alles verstanden?

1. Was ist bei Hotelketten gut und nicht so gut?
2. Was ist bei Gasthöfen und Pensionen gewöhnlich im Preis inbegriffen?
3. Warum ist es manchmal besser, das Geld nicht im Hotel umzutauschen?
4. Wo kann man auch Übernachtungsmöglichkeiten finden?
5. Was ist gut und nicht so gut beim Übernachten in einer Jugendherberge?
6. Wo kann man sonst noch *(. . . else)* noch übernachten? Warum ist das aber nicht für alle zu empfehlen?

B. Wo sollen wir übernachten? Match each lodging with the corresponding description.

a. Campingplatz
b. Gasthof
c. Jugendgästehaus
d. Jugendherberge
e. Luxushotel
f. Pension

__f__ 1. Diese Übernachtungsmöglichkeit ist meistens nicht teuer, aber doch gut. Man kann sie z. B. durch die Touristeninformation am Bahnhof finden.
__a__ 2. Hier ist es besonders billig, aber wenn es viel regnet, kann es sehr ungemütlich sein.
__e__ 3. Wenn man viel Geld hat, ist es hier natürlich wunderbar.
__c__ 4. Diese Möglichkeit ist für junge Leute. Sie ist nicht teuer und man kann abends spät zurückkommen oder einen Schlüssel bekommen.
__b__ 5. Das Übernachten kann hier sehr bequem und gemütlich sein; das Frühstück kostet nichts extra. Am Ruhetag kann man dort nicht essen.
__d__ 6. Hier können Leute mit Ausweis billig übernachten, aber man darf abends nicht nach elf zurückkommen.

Optional practice: **Nennen Sie alle vier Imperative!** (bei der Information fragen, die Namen lesen, in einer Pension übernachten, ein Zimmer reservieren, ein Formular ausfüllen, Geld umwechseln, jetzt frühstücken, Ihre Tasche mitnehmen)

C. Übernachtungsmöglichkeiten What's missing?

1. In __diesem__ Hotel kann man gut übernachten, aber das kann man nicht von __jedem__ Hotel sagen. *(this, every)*
2. Bei __so einem__ Hotel wissen Sie immer, wie es innen aussieht. *(such a)*
3. __Manche__ Hotels sind sehr luxuriös und teuer, __dieses__ Hotel zum Beispiel. *(some, this)*
4. __Unser__ Hotel ist sehr schön gewesen. *(our)*
5. Hast du schon einmal von __dieser__ Pension gehört? *(this)*
6. Wie gefällt es euch in __eu(e)rer__ Jugendherberge? *(your)*
7. __Uns(e)re__ Jugendherberge ist in einer Burg. *(our)*
8. In __dieser__ Jugendherberge gibt es noch Platz. *(this)*
9. Wollen wir auf __diesem__ Campingplatz übernachten? *(this)*
10. __Welchen__ Campingplatz meinst du *(do you mean)*? *(which)*

D. In der Jugendherberge Repeat these sentences without a modal auxiliary, (a) in the present tense and (b) in the present perfect.

BEISPIEL Du kannst in den Ferien vorbeikommen.
Du kommst in den Ferien vorbei.
Du bist in den Ferien vorbeigekommen.

1. Wann möchtet ihr ankommen?
2. In der Jugendherberge könnt ihr Leute kennenlernen.
3. Du musst natürlich einen Jugendherbergsausweis mitbringen.
4. Wollt ihr abends spät ausgehen?
5. Die Jugendherberge soll abends um zehn zumachen.
6. Wer spät zurückkommen möchte, kann Pech haben.

D: 1. kommt ihr an / seid ihr angekommen 2. lernt ihr . . . kennen / habt ihr . . . kennengelernt 3. du bringst . . . mit / du hast . . . mitgebracht 4. geht ihr . . . aus / seid ihr . . . ausgegangen 5. macht . . . zu / hat . . . zugemacht 6. zurückkommt / zurückgekommen ist; hat Pech / hat Pech gehabt

Fokus Luxembourg

The Grand Duchy of Luxembourg (**Luxemburg**, pop. 517,000), half the size of Delaware, is one of Europe's oldest and smallest independent countries and lies between Germany, France, and Belgium. Although it is one of the world's most industrialized nations, its heavy industry—mainly iron and steel production—has not spoiled the natural beauty of the country's rolling hills and dense forests.

Most of the population is Catholic, and there is a high percentage of foreigners (Italians, French, Germans, Belgians, and Portuguese. Almost all Luxembourgers speak Letzeburgish, a German dialect. French, German, and Letzeburgish are all taught in schools and used in public life. Despite close ties to their neighbors, the people of Luxembourg maintain an independent spirit, as expressed in the words of their national anthem: *Mir wölle bleiwe wat mir sin* **(Wir wollen bleiben, was wir sind).** The French statesman Robert Schuman (1886–1963) was born in Luxembourg. He was one of the formulators of the cooperative effort, known as the Schuman Plan, by which the coal and steel industries of Germany, Italy, Belgium, Luxembourg, and the Netherlands became economically linked into a Common Market in 1958.

Luxembourg's capital by the same name (pop. 100,000) is a big financial and banking center and home to several European institutions. Luxembourg joined the euro currency zone in 1999.

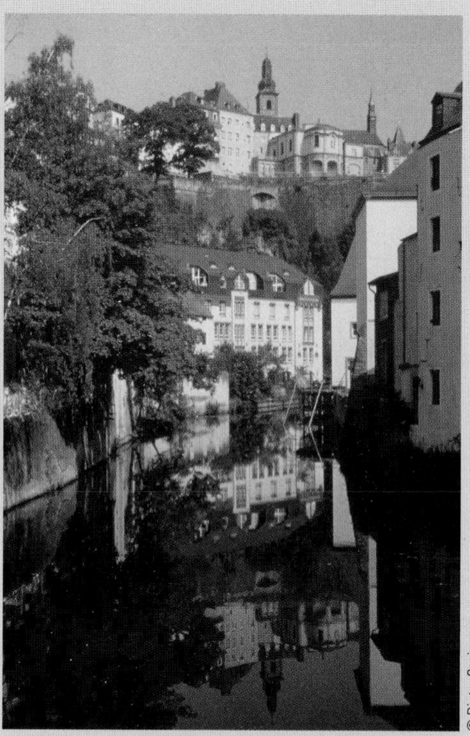

Blick auf Luxemburg von der Unterstadt an der Alzette

Weiteres

E. Kurzgespräche With a partner, choose one of the situations and prepare a brief dialogue. Then present it to the class.

1. **Überraschung in Heidelberg**

   You are visiting your aunt in Heidelberg. As you tour the castle, you see a German student whom you got to know while you both stayed at a youth hostel in Aachen. Call out to the German student. Both of you express your disbelief that you have met again. Your friend is studying in Heidelberg; you explain why you are there. You ask whether your friend would like to go for a coffee or a soft drink, and he/she agrees.

2. **Hotelsuche in Luxemburg**

   You and a friend are in Luxembourg and are looking for a hotel room. You have both inquired in several places. All the hotels you saw had no rooms available at all; in desperation your friend has taken a double room that will cost you 120 euros for one night. You both express your disbelief at your bad luck.

Schreibtipp

Doing Free Writing in German

Keep your German writing simple. Never start by writing your composition in English, then translating it. Rather, focus on what you know how to express in German. Review recently learned vocabulary and structures and try to include them in your writing. This composition does not require the use of the past tense.

F. Aufsatz: Deutsche reisen in Nordamerika Pretend you are a German who is writing an article for a German travel guide about travel in the United States or Canada. What is it like traveling as a German in North America? How is traveling in North America different from traveling in Germany?

G. Ein Brief: Hotel Hansablick Pretend you are working in this hotel and respond to the email below. Use your imagination.

From: Jürgen Marmein
Date: 02.12.2013
Subject: Unterkunft im Alsterblick
To: info@alsterblick.de

Sehr geehrte Damen und Herren,

meine Frau und ich planen eine Reise nach Hamburg. Haben Sie vom 26.12. bis zum 1.1. noch ein Zimmer frei? Wenn ja, was für ein Zimmer und wie viel kostet es? Ist das Frühstück inbegriffen? Ist Ihr Hotel zentral gelegen und doch ruhig? Haben Sie einen Parkplatz? Wie weit ist es zur U-Bahn oder S-Bahn? Können Sie Musical-Karten für uns besorgen?

Bitte lassen Sie uns sobald wie möglich wissen, ob wir buchen können!

Mit freundlichem Gruß,

Jürgen Marmein

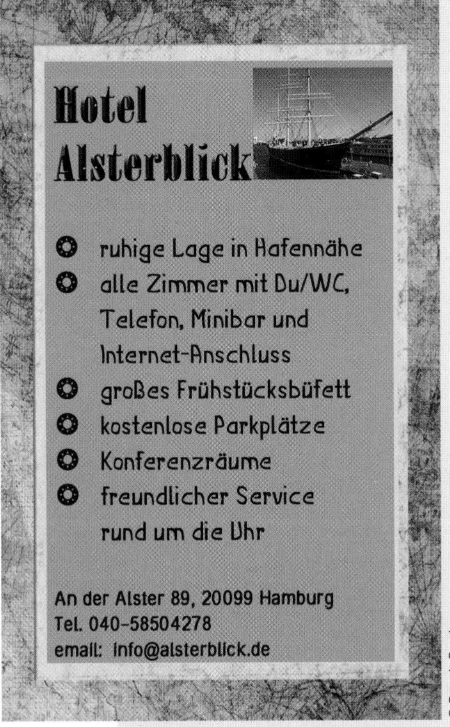

Hotel
Alsterblick
ruhige Lage in Hafennähe
alle Zimmer mit Du/WC, Telefon, Minibar und Internet-Anschluss
großes Frühstücksbüfett
kostenlose Parkplätze
Konferenzräume
freundlicher Service rund um die Uhr
An der Alster 89, 20099 Hamburg
Tel. 040-58504278
email: info@alsterblick.de

There is an extensive review section following this chapter in the *Arbeitsbuch* (SAM). The accompanying exercises and answer key will help you prepare for the test.

For further practice, an optional two-part video (**Szenen** and **Interviews**) is available on the ***Wie geht's?*** Premium Website and in iLrn, with corresponding questions and activities in the *Arbeitsbuch* (SAM).

As an optional activity with Google Earth, you could check out hotels in Luxembourg or in any of the German-speaking countries.

Hörverständnis

Hotel Lindenhof Mr. Baumann calls the reception of Hotel Lindenhof on Lake Constance. Listen to the conversation. Then complete the sentences with the correct information from the dialogue.

Zum Erkennen: die Person, -en *(person)*; das Frühstücksbüfett *(breakfast buffet)*; das Schwimmbad *(pool)*; Minigolf *(miniature golf)*

1. Herr Baumann und seine Familie fahren im Sommer an den ___Bodensee___. 2. Sie wollen am ___10. Juli___ ankommen und ___eine Woche___ bleiben. 3. Sie brauchen Zimmer für ___vier___ Personen, also ___zwei___ Zimmer. 4. Die Zimmer kosten ___85 Euro___ pro Tag. 5. Das Frühstückbüfett kostet ___nichts___ extra. 6. Herr Baumannn findet das nicht ___(zu) teuer___. 7. Die Kinder können dort ___schwimmen___ und in der Nähe auch ___Minigolf___ und ___Tennis___ spielen. 8. Zum See ist es auch nicht ___weit___.
9. Vom Balkon hat man einen Blick auf den ___See___ und die ___Alpen___. 10. Er ___nimmt / reserviert___ die Zimmer.

Rückschau

Kapitelwortschatz

Hauptwörter

der Ausgang, -¨e	*exit*
der Ausweis, -e	*identification card (ID)*
die Bank, -en	*bank*
das Bargeld	*cash*
der Blick (in / auf)	*view (of)*
der Dollar, -(s)	*dollar*
das Doppelzimmer, -	*double room*
die Eingang, -¨e	*entrance*
das Einzelzimmer, -	*single room*
der Gast, -¨e	*guest*
der Gasthof, -¨e	*small hotel*
das Geld	*money*
der Geldautomat, -en, -en	*ATM machine*
das Gepäck	*baggage, luggage*
das Hotel, -s	*hotel*
die Jugendherberge, -n	*youth hostel*
die Kasse, -n	*cashier's window*
das Kleingeld	*change*
der Koffer, -	*suitcase*
die Kreditkarte, -n	*credit card*
die Lage	*location*
die Nacht, -¨e	*night*
die Nummer, -n	*number*
der Pass, -¨e	*passport*
die Pension, -en	*boarding house; hotel*
die Reise, -n	*trip*
der Scheck, -s	*check*
der Schlüssel, -	*key*
die Tasche, -n	*bag; pocket*
die Uhrzeit	*time of day*
der Wald, -¨er	*forest, woods*

Verben

an·kommen	*to arrive (come to)*
an·nehmen	*to accept*
an·rufen	*to call, phone*
auf·machen	*to open*
auf·passen	*to pay attention, watch (out)*
auf·schreiben	*to write down*
auf·stehen	*to get up*
aus·gehen	*to go out*
ein·kaufen	*to shop*
kennen·lernen	*to get to know; meet*
lassen	*to leave (behind)*
mit·bringen	*to bring along*
mit·gehen	*to go along*
mit·kommen	*to come along*
mit·nehmen	*to take along*
packen	*to pack*
reisen	*to travel*
reservieren	*to reserve*
übernachten	*to spend the night*
um·tauschen	*to exchange*
unterschreiben	*to sign*
vorbei·gehen	*to pass (by)*
wechseln	*to change; to exchange*
zu·hören	*to listen*
zu·machen	*to close*
zurück·kommen	*to come back*

Adjektive und Adverbien

einfach	*simple, simply*
frei	*free(ly); available*
geöffnet	*open*
geschlossen	*closed*
laut	*loud(ly), noisy, noisily*
meistens	*mostly, usually*
möglich	*possible*
ruhig	*quiet(ly)*

Der-Wörter

alle	*all* (pl.)
das, der, die	*the; that* (when stressed)
dieser, -es, -e	*this; these*
jeder, -es, -e	*each, every* (sg. only)
mancher, -es, -e	*many a* (sg.); *several, some* (usually pl.)
solcher, -es, -e	*such* (usually pl.)
welcher, -es, -e	*which*

Ein-Wörter

dein	*your* (sg. fam.)
euer	*your* (pl. fam.)
ihr	*her/its*
ihr	*their* (pl.)
Ihr	*your* (sg./pl. formal)
mein	*my*
sein	*his/its*
unser	*our*

Trennbare Vorsilben *(Separable prefixes)*

ab-	*away; off*
an-	*to; up to*
auf-	*up; open*
aus-	*out; out of*
ein-	*into*
her-	*toward* (*the speaker*)
hin-	*away from* (*the speaker*)
mit-	*together with, along with*
nach-	*after; behind; later*
um-	*around; over; from one to the other*
vor-	*ahead; before*
vorbei-	*past, by*
zu-	*closed, shut*
zurück-	*back*

Verschiedenes

auf	*open*
bald	*soon*
Das glaube ich nicht.	*I don't believe that.*
Das ist doch nicht möglich!	*That's impossible* (lit. *not possible)!*
Das kann doch nicht wahr sein!	*That can't be true!*
Das kommt darauf an.	*That depends.*
einen Moment	*(for) just a minute*
Halt!	*Stop!*
Pass auf! / Passt auf! / Passen Sie auf!	*Watch out!*
Quatsch!	*Nonsense!*
Vorsicht!	*Careful!*
Wann machen Sie auf / zu?	*When do you open / close?*
Warte! / Wartet! / Warten Sie!	*Wait!*
zu	*closed*

Zum Schluss

1. **Erzählen Sie!**

   a. **Eine Reise** Describe one of your favorite vacations to a classmate. Where did you go? How long were you gone? Describe where you stayed, what kinds of restaurants you visited, and some of your favorite foods. Was the trip expensive? Did you have to visit the bank often? How does your trip compare with your classmate's favorite vacation?

   b. **Eine Traumreise** (*A dream trip*) Now, pretend that you could plan a trip where money is no object. Where would you visit? How long would you be gone? Where would you stay? What sights would you want to see? Where would you want to eat? What would you want to avoid? Compare your answers!

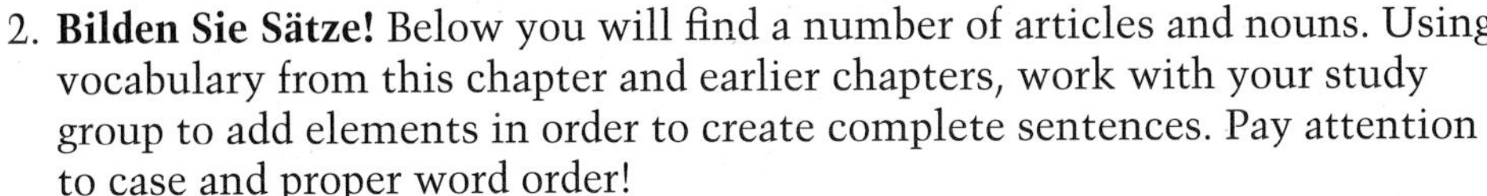

2. **Bilden Sie Sätze!** Below you will find a number of articles and nouns. Using vocabulary from this chapter and earlier chapters, work with your study group to add elements in order to create complete sentences. Pay attention to case and proper word order!

alle (*pl.*)	der Ausweis
der, das, die	die Bank
dein-	das Einzelzimmer
dieser, -es, -e	der Geldautomat
ein-	das Hotel
jeder, -es, -e	der Koffer
mancher, -es, -e	die Kreditkarte
mein, -e	die Nacht
solcher, -es, -e	der Pass
unser-	die Reise
welcher, -es, -e	der Schlüssel

3. **Eine Postkarte schreiben**

   a. **Grüße aus den Ferien!** Pretend you are on vacation in Germany. Write a postcard of five to seven sentences to your best friend back at home. Use at least five of the following verbs.

an·kommen	auf·schreiben	mit·bringen	zu·hören
an·nehmen	auf·stehen	mit·gehen	zu·machen
an·rufen	aus·gehen	mit·kommen	zurück·kommen
auf·machen	ein·kaufen	mit·nehmen	
auf·passen	kennen·lernen	um·tauschen	

   b. **Noch einmal!** Now rewrite your postcard to incorporate flavoring participles where appropriate.

iLrn **Onlineaktivitäten** Visit iLrn for online activities related to this chapter. There you will find additional resources, such as a memory game (**Gedächtnisspiel**), a crossword puzzle (**Kreuzworträtsel**), audio flash cards (**Vokabelblitz**), a tutorial quiz (**Mini-Quiz**), and the active vocabulary (**Wortschatz**) for this chapter.

Kapitel 8

Post und Reisen

Lernziele In this chapter you will learn about:

Zum Thema

Postal service, telephones, and travel

Fokus

Switzerland, phone and postal service, modes of travel, and Wilhelm Tell

Struktur

- The genitive case
- Time expressions
- Sentence structure *(continued)*

Einblicke

Interviews: Touristen in der Schweiz
Literatur: Hermann Hesse, „Im Nebel"

Rückschau

Kapitelwortschatz
Zum Schluss

RESSOURCEN

 iLrn Video

 Audio SAM

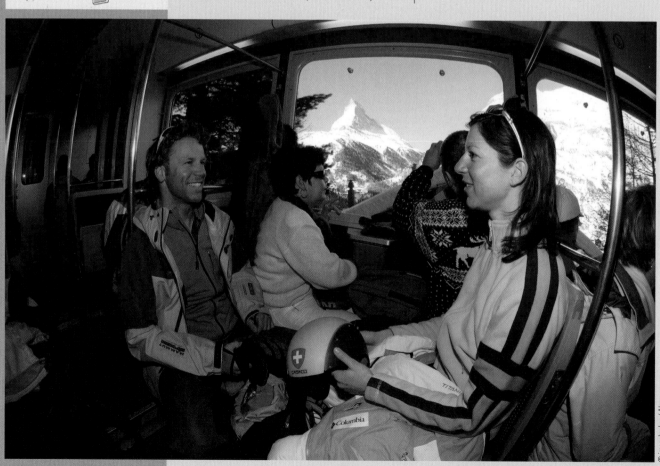

Von der Gornergratbahn kann man das Matterhorn sehen.

Vorschau Spotlight on Switzerland

Area: Approximately 16,000 square miles, about half the size of Indiana.
Population: About 7.9 million.
Religion: 39% Catholic, 31% Protestant, 10% other, and 20% declared no religion.
Geography: This landlocked country is clearly defined by three natural regions: the *Alpine ranges* that stretch from the French border south of Lake Geneva diagonally across the southern half of Switzerland and include the world-renowned resorts of the Bernese Uplands **(Berner Oberland),** Zermatt and St. Moritz in the Inn River valley; the plateaus and valleys of the *midland* between Lake Geneva and Lake Constance; and the mountains of the *Jura* in the northernmost section of the Alps.
Currency: Schweizer Franken, 1 sfr = 100 Rappen or Centimes.
Principal cities: Capital Berne (*Bern*, pop. 124,400), Zurich (*Zürich*, pop. 373,000), Geneva (*Genf*, pop. 187,500), Basel (pop. 163,500), Lausanne (pop. 128,000), Winterthur (pop. 101,000).

Switzerland was founded in 1291, when the cantons (states) of Uri, Schwyz, and Unterwalden formed an alliance against the ruling House of Habsburg. Over time, the original confederation grew into a nation of 26 cantons. These cantons maintain considerable autonomy, with their own constitutions and legislatures. The 1848 constitution merged the old confederation into a single federal state by eliminating all commercial barriers and establishing a common postal service, military, legislature, and judiciary.

Despite its small size, few natural resources, and ethnic diversity, Switzerland is one of the most stable nations in the world. Its stability can be attributed to its high standard of living and the country's neutrality in the two world wars. Switzerland has stubbornly adhered to the principle of neutrality—to the extent of staying out of NATO and the European Union; it joined the United Nations (UN) only in 2002, with a narrow margin of 12 cantons voting for and 11 against the approval. In December 2008, it joined the European passport-free travel zone, called the Schengen Area. Switzerland's stability and bank-secrecy law have attracted capital from all over the world. However, revelations during the 1990s about the role of Swiss banks in holding gold stolen by the Nazis during World War II, and the 2008 investigation of Swiss banks for helping Americans evade taxes have presented a challenge to these renowned financial institutions.

Switzerland is home to many United Nations organizations, such as the UN's Economic and Social Council, the International Labor Organization, the World Health Organization, as well as the International Olympic Committee, and the International Red Cross. Founded in Geneva in 1864, the Red Cross derived its universally recognized symbol from the inverse of the Swiss flag, which consists of a white cross on a red background. Most Swiss cities have their own website. A simple browser search will get you there.

Genf

Ask students what products they associate with Switzerland and which famous Swiss nationals they know about. Do they know of any Swiss companies in this country or any Swiss people in their own community? Students could also look for articles about Switzerland or use the Web to access Swiss newspapers or magazines. Ask them to find out about the exchange rate of the Swiss franc to the dollar. In the *Zum Schreiben* section of the *Arbeitsbuch*, there is also a blank map of Switzerland. Let students fill in the blanks to check their geography knowledge.

Switzerland's official name is Confoederatio Helvetica (CH).

Fragen: 1. Wo sitzen diese Skifahrer? 2. Was sieht man auf dem Helm der Frau? 3. Welche Farben haben ihre Anoraks und warum tragen sie so bunte Jacken? 4. Denken Sie, dass die zwei Leute am Fenster auch Skifahrer sind? Warum (nicht)? 5. Wie heißt der bekannte Berg im Hintergrund *(background)*? 6. Von welcher Stadt ist das Bild unten? 7. Was sieht man auf diesem Bild? In case you are curious: *boat* **das Boot,-e**; *harbor* **der Hafen**; *light tower* **der Leuchtturm**; *pier* **das Kai**; *swan* **der Schwan**

Zum Thema

Gespräche

Warm-ups: 1. **Können Sie mir sagen,** wie spät es ist? welches Datum heute ist? wo ich . . . lassen kann? *In a chain reaction, ask students where you can leave certain things, e.g.,* **Wo kann ich das Buch lassen? — Legen Sie es auf den Tisch!** *Whoever answers, asks the next question with the* ***du****-form.*
2. **Welche Verben beginnen mit** an-, auf-, ein-, mit-, um-, vor-, bei-, zu-, zurück-; be-, emp-, ent-, ge-, über-, ver-, wieder-?
3. **Was ist die Imperativform von** hier bleiben, bitte entschuldigen, langsam sprechen, schön schlafen, nicht so viel essen, laut lesen, hier unterschreiben?

Auf der Post am Bahnhof

HERR Grüezi!
UTA Grüezi! Ich möchte dieses Paket nach Amerika schicken.
HERR Normal oder per Luftpost?
UTA Per Luftpost. Wie lange dauert das denn?
HERR Ungefähr eine Woche. Füllen Sie bitte diese Paketkarte aus! . . . Moment, hier fehlt noch Ihr Absender.
UTA Ach ja! . . . Noch etwas. Ich brauche eine Telefonkarte.
HERR Für fünf, zehn, zwanzig oder fünfzig Franken?
UTA Für zwanzig Franken. Vielen Dank!

Ask students to find out how many francs equal one dollar.

Am Fahrkartenschalter in Zürich

ANNE Wann fährt der nächste Zug nach Interlaken?
FRAU In 10 Minuten. Abfahrt um 11.28 Uhr, Gleis 2.
ANNE Ach du meine Güte! Und wann kommt er dort an?
FRAU Ankunft in Interlaken um 14.16 Uhr.
ANNE Muss ich umsteigen?
FRAU Ja, in Bern, aber Sie haben Anschluss zum InterCity mit nur 24 Minuten Aufenthalt.
ANNE Gut. Geben Sie mir bitte eine Hin- und Rückfahrkarte nach Interlaken!
FRAU Erster oder zweiter Klasse?
ANNE Zweiter Klasse.

As in previous chapters, you could have students act out the dialogue with a partner.

Zug									
		IC 118 4 ✕	518 ✕	1720		IC 120 4 ✕	1520	1822	4
Zürich HB		10 03	10 07	10 28		11 03	11 07	11 28	
Baden				10 45				11 45	
Brugg (Aargau)				10 53				11 53	
Aarau			10 35	11 07			11 35	12 07	
Olten 24016 O			10 44	11 15			11 44	12 15	
Olten 24000			10 47				11 47		
Biel/Bienne O			11 33				12 33		
Lausanne O							13 48		
Genève O			13 05						
Zug	IC 721		2521		EC 73 7 ✕		1866 4		IC 725
Basel SBB	10 00		10 11	*10 29*	11 00			*11 29*	12 00
Liestal			10 21	*10 46*				*11 46*	
Olten O	10 26		10 43	*11 11*	11 26			*12 11*	12 26
Olten	10 28		10 48	11 17	11 28			12 17	12 28
Langenthal			11 00	11 29				12 29	
Herzogenbuchsee			11 06	11 35				12 35	
Burgdorf			11 18	11 47				12 47	
Bern O	11 10	11 14	11 35	12 04	12 10	12 14		13 04	13 10
Bern 24004	11 28			12 28		*12 28*			13 28
Interlaken West O	12 16			13 16		*13 16*			14 16

A. Alles verstanden?

1. Wo ist die Post? 2. Wohin will Uta ihr Paket schicken? 3. Wie schickt sie es? 4. Wie lange soll das dauern? 5. Was muss man bei einem Paket ins Ausland *(abroad)* ausfüllen? 6. Was fehlt auf der Paketkarte? 7. Was braucht Uta noch? 8. Was kosten Telefonkarten? 9. Wohin will Anne fahren? 10. Wann fährt der Zug ab und wann kommt er in Interlaken an? 11. Wo muss Anne umsteigen? 12. Was für eine Karte kauft sie?

A: 1. am Bahnhof 2. in die USA 3. per Luftpost 4. ungefähr eine Woche 5. eine Paketkarte 6. der Absender 7. eine Telefonkarte 8. 5, 10, 20 oder 50 Franken 9. nach Interlaken 10. in 5 Minuten / Abfahrt 11.28 Uhr, Ankunft 14.16 Uhr 11. in Bern 12. eine Hin- und Rückfahrkarte zweiter Klasse

B. Jetzt sind Sie dran! Diesmal *(this time)* sind Sie an einem Flughafenschalter. Bereiten Sie Ihr eigenes Gespräch *(Prepare your own dialogue)* mit Ihrem Partner / Ihrer Partnerin vor und präsentieren Sie es dann vor der Klasse!

S1 Wann gehen Flüge nach . . . ?
S2 Zu welcher Tageszeit möchten Sie denn fliegen?
S1 Ich muss um . . . in . . . sein.
S2 Es gibt einen Flug um . . .
S1 Hat er eine Zwischenlandung?
S2 Ja, in . . . Dort haben Sie . . . Aufenthalt.
S1 Muss ich umsteigen?
S2 . . .
S1 . . . Dann geben Sie mir bitte eine Hin- und Rückflugkarte nach . . . !

If students ask: *collect call* **das R-Gespräch, -e;** *mail carrier* **der Briefträger, - / Postbote, -n, -n;** *plain postcard* **die Postkarte, -n.** Also: **das Internet; das Ticket, -s**

Wortschatz 1

Die Post *(post office, mail)*
Das Telefon, -e *(telephone)*

der Absender, -	*return address*	die Adresse, -n	*address*
Brief, -e	*letter*	(Ansichts)karte, -n	*(picture) postcard*
Briefkasten, ¨	*mailbox*	Briefmarke, -n	*stamp*
		E-Mail, -s	*e-mail*
das Handy, -s	*cell phone*	Postleitzahl, -en	*zip code*
Paket, -e	*package, parcel*	SMS, -	*text message* (on cell phone)
Postfach, ¨er	*PO box*	Telefonkarte, -n	*telephone card*
		Telefonnummer, -n	*telephone number*
		Vorwahl, -en	*area code*

Die Reise, -n *(trip)*

der Aufenthalt, -e	*stopover, stay*	das Flugzeug, -e	*plane*
Bahnsteig, -e	*platform*	Gleis, -e	*track*
Fahrplan, ¨e	*schedule*	die Abfahrt, -en	*departure*
Flug, ¨e	*flight*	Ankunft, ¨e	*arrival*
Flughafen, ¨	*airport*	Bahn, -en	*railway, train*
Schalter, -	*counter, ticket window*	Fahrkarte, -n	*ticket*
Wagen, -	*car; railroad car*	(Hin- und) Rückfahrkarte, -n	*round-trip ticket*
Zug, ¨e	*train*	Fahrt, -en	*trip, drive*

Although Germans say **Briefmarken** for stamps, foreigners will often look in vain for the word in a German post office, where the official word **Postwertzeichen** is more common.

Note **die SMS** in Germany, but in Austria and Switzerland also **das SMS.** The German verb meaning to text *(send a text message)* is **simsen.**

der **Wagen**, BUT das Auto

Like **mit dem Zug fahren: mit dem Bus / mit dem Fahrrad / mit der U-Bahn fahren** *to go by bus / bike / subway*

Verschiedenes

ab·fahren (fährt ab), ist abgefahren (von)	*to leave, depart (from)*
ab·fliegen, ist abgeflogen (von)	*to take off, fly (from)*
aus·steigen, ist ausgestiegen	*to get off/out*
ein·steigen, ist eingestiegen	*to get on/in*
um·steigen, ist umgestiegen	*to change (trains,* etc.*)*
besuchen	*to visit*
erzählen	*to tell*
fehlen	*to be missing / lacking*
fliegen, ist geflogen	*to fly*
landen, ist gelandet	*to land*
schicken	*to send*
telefonieren	*to call up, phone*
in einer Viertelstunde	*in a quarter of an hour*
in einer halben Stunde	*in half an hour*
in einer Dreiviertelstunde	*in three-quarters of an hour*
mit dem Zug / der Bahn fahren, ist gefahren	*to go by train*
Ach du meine Güte!	*My goodness!*
Na und?	*So what?*
Das ist doch egal. / Das macht nichts.	*It's all the same to me.; That doesn't matter.*
Das sieht dir (ihm, ihr, ihnen) ähnlich.	*That's typical of you (him, her, them).*
Das freut mich (für dich).	*I'm happy (for you).*
Gott sei Dank!	*Thank God!*

Zum Erkennen: normal *(regular)*; per Luftpost *(by airmail)*; die Paketkarte, -n *(parcel form)*; aus•füllen *(to fill out)*; noch etwas *(one more thing, something else)*; der nächste / letzte Zug nach *(the next / last train to)*; der Anschluss, ¨-e *(connection)*; die Klasse, -n; AUCH: der Genitiv; die Gruppe, -n *(group)*; die Liste, -n; benutzen *(to use)*; ergänzen *(to add to)*; jemandem eine Frage stellen *(to ask sb. a question)*; heraus•finden *(to find out)*

Fokus Phoning and Postal Services

Since the liberalization of the telecommunication market in 1998, telephoning in German-speaking countries has become very inexpensive, and there is a broad selection of companies offering flat rates or discount rates for local or long-distance calls. Germany has become a major player in the telecommunications market, with T-Mobile being one of Europe's largest mobile operators. People are using cell phones **(Handys)** everywhere, a popular version being one with a prepaid card that is especially "handy" for travelers abroad. In Europe, incoming calls to a cell phones are free, but the cost of placing a call is higher. It is illegal to use cell phones while driving, unless you're using a hands-free cell phone car kit.

Most public phone booths **(Telefonzellen),** which have become rather rare, require a phone card **(Telefonkarte)** to operate. The **deutsche Telekom** offers a prepaid telephone card that can be used with any telephone, whether phone booth, landline, or cell phone. After inputting an access number and an access code, calls will be charged to the phone card. Phone cards can be bought at post offices or newspaper stands. Since hotels usually add a substantial surcharge for phone calls, travelers often find it cheaper to use a long-distance calling card or to place calls from a post office. Post offices in European countries offer a far greater range of services than in the United States or Canada. For example, it is possible to open a bank account with the post office, wire money, buy traveler's checks, and send a telegram. However, the postal service and its express delivery DHL no longer have a monopoly on mail-delivery services; UPS and FedEx trucks have become a familiar sight in Europe.

Übungen zum Thema

A. Allerlei Fragen

1. Was kostet es, wenn man einen Brief innerhalb von *(within)* den USA oder von Kanada schicken will? Wie lange braucht ein Brief innerhalb der Stadt? nach Europa?
2. Was muss man auf alle Briefe, Ansichtskarten und Pakete schreiben? Schreiben Sie oft Briefe? Wenn ja, wem? Schicken Sie oft E-Mails oder eine SMS an Ihre Freunde? Was ist Ihre E-Mail-Adresse?
3. In Deutschland sind Briefkästen gelb. Welche Farbe haben die Briefkästen hier? Wo findet man sie?
4. Wo kann man hier telefonieren? Gibt es Telefonkarten? Wenn ja, wo bekommt man sie?
5. Haben Sie ein Handy? Wenn ja, wann und wie oft benutzen Sie es?
6. Benutzen Sie Ihr Handy beim Autofahren? Ist das Telefonieren beim Autofahren gefährlich *(dangerous)*? Warum (nicht)?
7. Wie reisen Sie gern und wie nicht? Warum?
8. Wohin sind Sie zuletzt *(the last time)* gereist? Sind Sie geflogen oder mit dem Wagen gefahren?

A: Have students prepare answers in small groups, then ask the class some of these questions. When students of the same age speak to each other, they should address each other with **du**! If they don't want to give their e-mail address, they can invent one.

Additional questions: 1. Was ist das Gegenteil von abfahren? abfliegen? einsteigen? Abfahrt? Abflug? 2. Wie heißt der Ort *(place)*, wo Züge abfahren und ankommen? wo Flugzeuge abfliegen und landen? wo Busse halten?

B. Was bedeuten diese Wörter und was sind ihre Artikel?

1. Adressbuch, Abfahrtszeit, Ankunftsfahrplan, Bahnhofseingang, Busbahnhof
2. Busfahrt, Flugkarte, Flugschalter, Flugsteig, Gepäckkarte, Mietwagen
3. Nachtzug, Paketschalter, Postfachnummer, Speisewagen, Telefonrechnung

B: 1. *address book* **(das)**, *departure time* **(die)**, *schedule of arrivals* **(der)**, *train station entrance* **(der)**, *bus depot* **(der)** 2. *bus trip* **(die)**, *plane ticket* **(die)**, *flight ticket counter* **(der)**, *gate* **(der)**, *luggage claim ticket* **(die)**, *rental car* **(der)** 3. *night train* **(der)**, *parcel post counter* **(der)**, *PO box number* **(die)**, *dining car* **(der)**, *telephone bill* **(die)**

Fokus Train Travel

Trains are a popular means of transportation in Europe, not only for commuting but also for long-distance travel. The rail network is extensive, and trains are generally clean, comfortable, and on time. Domestic InterCity **(IC)** and international EuroCity **(EC)** trains connect all major western European cities. In Germany, the high-speed InterCityExpress **(der ICE),** which travels at speeds up to 280 km/h (175 mph), is an attractive alternative to congested highways. Businesspeople can make or receive phone calls on board and even rent conference rooms equipped with fax machines. Non-European residents can benefit from a *Eurailpass,* which permits unlimited train—and some bus and boat—travel in most European countries. Alternatively, the traveler should consider a German Railpass, which is less expensive but limited to Germany plus two selected adjacent countries. Both passes must be purchased outside Europe. Larger train stations provide a wide range of services for the traveler, including coin-operated lockers **(Schließfächer)** or checked-luggage rooms **(die Gepäckaufgabe).** The stations in large cities even have a wide range of restaurants and retail establishments.

Auf dem Bahnsteig im Bahnhof

C. Was fehlt? Finden Sie die Antworten auf dem Fahrplan!

km	Stuttgart–Zürich	Zug	E 3504	D 83 R3)	D 381 R3)	D 383		D 85 R4) ◆	D 389 R2)	D 87 50 ◆	D 385 R1) ◆1)	E 3309 R1) ◆1)	D 387 R1) ◆1) 73
0	**Stuttgart** Hbf 740			6 48	7 31	9 34		12 44	14 26	17 32	18 26	20 06	
26	Böblingen			|	7 53	9 56		13 06	14 48	17 55	18 48	20 29	
67	Horb			7 34	8 20	10 24		13 33	15 15	18 21	19 15	21 00	
110	Rottweil			8 05	8 59	10 54		14 02	15 52	18 51	19 45	21 36	
138	Tuttlingen			8 26	9 17	11 13		14 21	16 11	19 09	20 11	21 55	
172	Singen (Hohentwiel) ⊞	O		8 49	9 42	11 37		14 45	16 35	19 32	20 35	22 22	
		Zug		⊞	⊞	⊞	D 2162	✕1) ⊞	⊞	⊞	⊞	⊞	
	Singen (Hohentwiel) 730		6 31	8 55	9 49	11 44	12 43	14 51	16 44	19 37	20 44		22 44
192	Schaffhausen ⊞	O	6 49	9 10	10 05	12 00	12 58	15 07	17 00	19 52	21 00		23 00
		Zug	1559 ✕	(EC 83)			IC 357	(EC 85)	✕	(IC 87)	[bed]		
	Schaffhausen 24032		7 02	9 12	10 09	12 09	13 09	15 09	17 09	19 55	21 09		23 09
238	**Zürich HB**	O	57 7 47	9 47	10 47	12 47	13 47	15 47	17 47	20 31	21 47		23 47

NOTE: 1 km = 0.62 miles. Here is an easy and fairly accurate way to convert kilometers to miles: divide the km figure in half, and add a quarter of that to the half. Thus, 80 km ÷ 2 = 40 + 10 = 50 miles.

1. Von Stuttgart nach Zürich sind es ___238___ Kilometer.
2. Der erste Zug morgens fährt um ___6.48___ Uhr und der letzte *(last)* Zug abends um ___20.06___ Uhr.
3. Die Reise von Stuttgart nach Zürich geht über ___Singen / Schaffhausen___.
4. Wenn man um 6.48 Uhr von Stuttgart abfährt, ist man um ___9.47___ Uhr in Zürich.
5. Die Fahrt dauert ungefähr ___drei___ Stunden.

D. Jeder hat Probleme

So geht's! *(That's the way it goes!)* Bevor Sie die Übung machen, lesen Sie auch die Ausdrücke am Rand *(expressions in the margins)* und dann laut die folgenden *(following)* Sätze! Was sagen Sie zu Daniels Glück und Pech? Wechseln Sie sich ab *(take turns)*!

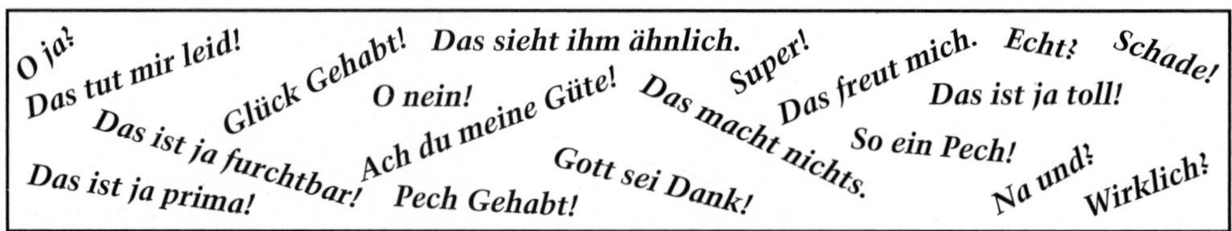

O ja!
Das tut mir leid!
Glück Gehabt!
Das sieht ihm ähnlich.
Super!
Das freut mich.
Echt?
Schade!
O nein!
Ach du meine Güte!
Das macht nichts.
Das ist ja toll!
Das ist ja furchtbar!
So ein Pech!
Gott sei Dank!
Das ist ja prima!
Pech Gehabt!
Na und?
Wirklich?

ALSO: Klasse! *(Great!)*, Super!, Fantastisch!, Schrecklich! *(Awful!)*, Verflixt nochmal! *(Darn it!)*, Das gibt's doch nicht!, Das kann doch nicht wahr sein!, Das tut mir leid!

1. Daniel hat von seinen Eltern zum Geburtstag ein Auto bekommen.
2. Das Auto ist nicht ganz neu.
3. Aber es fährt so schön ruhig und schnell, dass er gleich am ersten Tag einen Strafzettel *(ticket)* bekommen hat.
4. Am Wochenende ist er in die Berge gefahren, aber es hat immer nur geregnet.
5. Es hat ihm trotzdem viel Spaß gemacht, weil er dort eine Studentin kennengelernt hat.
6. Auf dem Weg zurück ist ihm jemand in sein Auto gefahren. Totalschaden *(total wreck)*!
7. Er hat übrigens seit ein paar Tagen eine Wohnung mitten in der Stadt. Sie ist gar nicht teuer.
8. Er möchte das Mädchen aus den Bergen wiedersehen, aber er kann sein Adressbuch mit ihrer Telefonnummer nicht finden.

E. Kofferpacken: Was nimmst du mit? Working in groups of three or four students, make a list of what you would take along on vacation to the following destinations. Then compare.

1. ans Meer 2. in die Berge 3. nach Europa

BEISPIEL *Ich nehme eine Sonnenbrille mit. Und du?*
Ich nehme eine Sonnenbrille und meine Kamera mit.

E: This probably is done best as a class activity using the board. You could also have a **Gedächtnisspiel** with this vocabulary.

These words are not active vocabulary!

Fokus Car Travel

In Switzerland and Austria, a toll **(die Maut)** is charged for using the express highway **(die Autobahn).** In Germany, a GPS-reliant toll system for large truck travel went into effect in 2005. The 12,000 km of *autobahn* covered is about 1.5 times the 8,000 km of toll roads in the US and approximately the length of all the freeways in California and Texas combined. Large trucks are not allowed on German roads on Sundays or holidays, or on Saturdays during peak vacation times.

Many traffic signs are identical to those in the United States and Canada; some of the different ones are self-explanatory, but others must be learned. Unless otherwise indicated, the driver approaching from the right has the right of way. As a rule, right turns at a red light are prohibited, as is passing on the right. The speed limit **(das Tempolimit** or **die Geschwindigkeitsbegrenzung)** in cities and towns is generally 50 km/h (31 mph), and on the open highway 100 km/h (62 mph). Except for certain stretches, there is no official speed limit on the freeway, but drivers are recommended **(die Richtgeschwindigkeit)** not to exceed 130 km/h (81 mph). German drivers are generally more aggressive than those in North America. But watch out! The police in Germany often use radar speed checks to catch drivers who break the speed limit. There are also a number of radar speed boxes installed on some roads. Driving too fast on German roads is expensive and can also mean a temporary loss of driving privileges.

For further review, see the Summary of Pronunciation in the front of this book. Study Part II, subsections 8–10.

Aussprache: e, er

A. Laute

1. [ə] Adress**e**, Eck**e**, Haltestell**e**, bekomm**e**n, besuch**e**n, ein**e** halb**e** Stund**e**
2. [ʌ] ab**er**, saub**er**, schw**er**, eu**er**, uns**er**, Zimm**er**numm**er**, Uh**r**, vo**r**, nu**r**, unt**er**, üb**er**, auß**er**, wied**er**holen

B. Wortpaare

1. Studenten / Studentin	3. diese / dieser	5. lese / Leser
2. Touristen / Touristin	4. arbeiten / Arbeitern	6. mieten / Mietern

Hörverständnis

Mit dem Glacier Express durch die Schweizer Alpen

Zum Erkennen: das Dorf *(village);* umgeben von *(surrounded by);* wandern *(to hike);* der Tunnel, -; die Weide, -n *(pasture);* der Sitz, -e *(seat);* vorher *(in advance);* die Zahnradbahn *(rack-railway);* fotografieren *(to take pictures)*

Was fehlt?

1. Claudia ist mit dem Glacier Express von St. ___Moritz___ nach Zermatt gefahren. 2. Die Fahrt im ___Panorama___-wagen hat ihr sehr gut ___gefallen___. 3. Von da kann man alles schön ___sehen___. 4. In Andermatt haben sie übernachtet und sind dann morgens etwas ___gewandert___. 5. Von Zermatt kann man mit einer Zahnradbahn auf den Gornergrat ___fahren___. 6. Der Blick von dort auf das ___Billig___ ist fantastisch. 7. ___Matterhorn___ ist die Reise natürlich nicht und man muss die Plätze auch vorher ___reservieren___. 8. Es hat aber ___Spaß___ gemacht und Claudia hat viel ___fotografiert___.

Mit dem Glacier Express über Brücken und durch Tunnel

Struktur

8.1 The genitive case

The genitive case has two major functions: (1) it expresses possession or another close relationship between two nouns, or (2) it follows certain prepositions.

1. The English phrases *the son's letter* and *the date of the letter* are expressed by the same genitive construction in German.

Das ist **der Brief des Sohnes.**	*That's the son's letter.*
Was ist **das Datum des Briefes?**	*What's the date of the letter?*

a. The genitive form of the INTERROGATIVE PRONOUN **wer** is **wessen** *(whose)*. The chart that follows shows all four cases of the interrogative pronouns.

	PERSONS	THINGS AND IDEAS
nom.	wer?	was?
acc.	wen?	was?
dat.	wem?	—
gen.	**wessen?**	—

Wessen Brief ist das?	*Whose letter is that?*
Der Brief des Sohnes!	*The son's letter.*

The interrogative pronoun **wessen** is always followed (eventually) by a noun: **Wessen Sohn? Wessen (furchtbar langer) Brief?**

b. The genitive forms of the DEFINITE and INDEFINITE ARTICLES complete this chart of articles.

<table>
<tr><th></th><th colspan="3">SINGULAR</th><th>PLURAL</th></tr>
<tr><th></th><th>masc.</th><th>neut.</th><th>fem.</th><th></th></tr>
<tr><td>nom.</td><td>der
ein
kein</td><td rowspan="2">das
ein
kein</td><td rowspan="2">die
eine
keine</td><td rowspan="2">die
—
keine</td></tr>
<tr><td>acc.</td><td>den
einen
keinen</td></tr>
<tr><td>dat.</td><td>dem
einem
keinem</td><td>dem
einem
keinem</td><td rowspan="2">der
einer
keiner</td><td>den
—
keinen</td></tr>
<tr><td>gen.</td><td>des
eines
keines</td><td>des
eines
keines</td><td>der
—
keiner</td></tr>
</table>

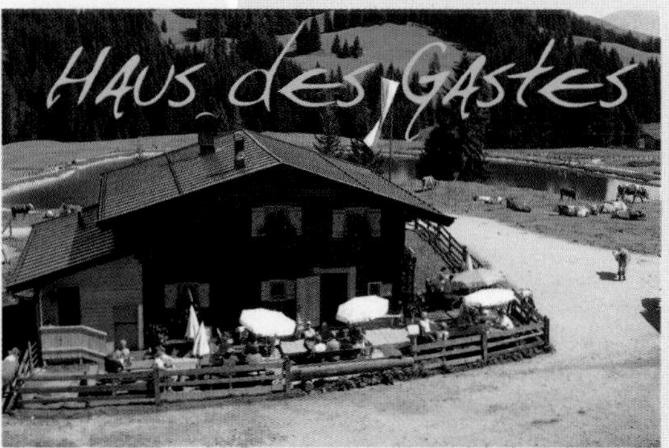

© Ingrid Sevin

c. The genitive case is signaled not only by the forms of the articles, but also by a special ending for MASCULINE and NEUTER nouns in the singular.

- Most one-syllable nouns and nouns ending in **-s, -ss, -ß, -z, -tz,** or **-zt,** add **-es:**

der Zug	das Geld	der Ausweis	der Pass	der Platz
des Zug**es**	**des** Geld**es**	**des** Ausweis**es**	**des** Pass**es**	**des** Platz**es**

The only exception to this rule about NO apostrophe for the genitive occurs when a proper name ends in **-s**, **-z**, **-tz**, or **-x**: **Hans' Adresse.** In written language, such genitives of names also take the ending **-ens**: **Schulzens Auto, Lorenzens Reisepläne.**

Note also: die Deutsche, der Deutsche**n**

- Nouns with more than one syllable add only an **-s:**

des Flughafen**s**	*of the airport, the airport's*
des Wagen**s**	*of the car, the car's*

NOTE: German uses NO apostrophe for the genitive!

- *N*-nouns have an **-n** or **-en** ending *in all cases except in the nominative singular*. A very few *n*-nouns have a genitive **-s** as well.

der Deutsche, **-n**, -n	**des** Deutsche**n**
Franzose, **-n**, -n	Franzose**n**
Herr, **-n**, -en	Herr**n**
Junge, **-n**, -n	Junge**n**
Geldautomat, **-en**, -en	Geldautomat**en**
Mensch, **-en**, -en	Mensch**en**
Nachbar, **-n**, -n	Nachbar**n**
Student, **-en**, -en	Student**en**
Tourist, **-en**, -en	Tourist**en**
Name, **-n(s)**, -n	Name**ns**

Note how *n*-nouns are listed in vocabularies and dictionaries: the first ending usually refers to the accusative, dative, and genitive singular; the second one to the plural.

d. Regular FEMININE NOUNS and PLURAL NOUNS have no special endings in the genitive.

NOMINATIVE	GENITIVE
die Reise	**der** Reise
die Idee *(idea)*	**der** Idee
die Reisen	**der** Reisen
die Ideen	**der** Ideen

e. Proper names usually add a final **-s.**

Annemarie**s** Flug	*Annemarie's flight*
Frau Strobel**s** Fahrt	*Ms. Strobel's trip*
Wien**s** Flughafen	*Vienna's airport*

In colloquial speech, however, **von** is frequently used instead of the genitive of a name: **die Adresse von Hans.**

f. Nouns in the genitive normally follow the nouns they modify, whereas proper names precede them.

Er liest den Brief **der Tante.**
Er liest **Annemaries** Brief.
Er liest **Herrn Hunkelers** Brief.

CAUTION: Even though the use of the possessive adjectives **mein, dein,** and so on inherently show possession, they still have the genitive case along with the noun.

Das ist **mein** Onkel.	*That's my uncle.*
Das ist der Koffer **meines Onkels.**	*That's my uncle's suitcase (the suitcase of my uncle).*
Er ist der Bruder **meiner Mutter.**	*He's my mother's brother (the brother of my mother).*

2. These prepositions are followed by the genitive case.

(an)statt	*instead of*	Ich nehme oft den Bus **(an)statt der U-Bahn.**
trotz	*in spite of*	**Trotz des Wetters** bummele ich gern durch die Stadt.
während	*during*	**Während der Mittagspause** gehe ich in den Park.
wegen	*because of*	Heute bleibe ich **wegen des Regens** *(rain)* hier.

In colloquial speech, **trotz** and **wegen** are also used with the dative, e.g., **trotz dem Wetter, wegen dem Regen.**

Während is also used as a subordinating conjunction: **Während ich hier bin, lerne ich viel Deutsch.**

Übungen

A. Im Reisebüro *(At the travel agency)* Überprüfen Sie *(check)* noch einmal, ob Ihr Assistent die Reise nach Bern auch gut vorbereitet hat!

BEISPIEL Wo ist die Liste der Touristen? (Hotel/*pl.*)
Wo ist die Liste der Hotels?

1. Wie ist der Name des Reiseführers *(tour guide)*? (Schloss, Dom, Museum, Straße, Platz, Tourist, Touristin, Franzose, Französin, Deutsche/*m.*, Deutsche/*f.*)
2. Wo ist die Telefonnummer des Hotels? (Gästehaus, Pension, Gasthof, Jugendherberge)
3. Wo ist die Adresse dieser Dame? (Gast, Mädchen, Junge, Herr, Herren, Student, Studenten)
4. Wann ist die Ankunft unserer Gruppe? (Bus, Zug, Flugzeug, Reiseführerin, Gäste)
5. Haben Sie wegen des Zimmers angerufen? (Schlüssel/*sg.*, Gepäck, Adresse, SMS, Theaterkarten)
6. Wir fahren trotz des Wetters. (Regen/*m.*, Eis, Feiertag, Ferien)
7. Christiane Binder kommt statt ihrer Mutter mit. (Vater, Bruder, Onkel, Tante, Nachbar, Nachbarin, Geschwister)
8. Die Lage des Hotels ist sehr zentral. (Bahnhof, Studentenwohnheim, Apotheke, Geschäfte)

A: 1. des Schlosses, des Domes, des Museums, der Straße, des Platzes, des Touristen, der Touristin, des Franzosen, der Französin, des Deutschen, der Deutschen 2. des Gästehauses, der Pension, des Gasthofs, der Jugendherberge 3. dieses Gastes, dieses Mädchens, dieses Jungen, dieses Herrn, dieser Herren, dieses Studenten, dieser Studenten 4. unseres Busses, unseres Zuges, unseres Flugzeugs, unserer Reiseführerin, unserer Gäste 5. des Schlüssels, Gepäcks, der SMS, der Theaterkarten 6. des Regens, des Eises, des Feiertags, der Ferien 7. ihres Vaters, ihres Bruders, ihres Onkels, ihrer Tante, ihres Nachbarn, ihrer Nachbarin, ihrer Geschwister 8. des Bahnhofs, des Studentenheims, der Apotheke, der Geschäfte

Simple introductory exercise: **z. B. das Buch: des Buches** 1. das Heft, der Pass, die Reise, der Scheck, das Taxi, der Ausweis, die Nacht, der Name 2. welche Bank, dieses Hotel, jeder Wagen, alle Flughäfen, manche Studenten, solche Leute 3. deine Geschwister, ihre Tante, unser Auto, euer Haus, sein Telefon, seine Telefonkarte, so ein Wagen, so eine Bahn

B. Bilden Sie Sätze mit dem Genitiv! Benutzen Sie Wörter von jeder Liste!

BEISPIEL *Die Abfahrt des Zuges ist um 19.05 Uhr.*

1	2	3		4	5
die Farbe	d-	Wagen	Gasthof	ist	________
der Name	dies-	Bus	Ausweis	gefällt	
die Adresse	mein-	Zug	Pass	. . .	
die Nummer	unser-	Bahnsteig	Scheck		
das Zimmer	. . .	Koffer	Flug		
das Gepäck		Tasche	Frau		
die Abfahrt		Haus	Herr		
der Preis		Wohnung	Freund(in)		
die Lage *(location)*		Hotel	Tourist(in)		
. . .		Pension	Gäste		
		Berge	. . .		
		Postfach			
		. . .			

B: Have each student write five sentences (e.g., **Die Farbe des Wagens ist rot.**), and then share them with the class. Column 5 can be various things: an adjective, a noun, a name, a pronoun, or a phrase.

C: 1. mein Bruder 2. meine Großmutter 3. meine Schwester, (ich) 4. meine Geschwister und ich 5. mein Großvater 6. mein Urgroßvater 7. meine Tante 8. mein Onkel 9. meine Mutter, (meine Tante)

C: When students are familiar with the genitive, you can reverse this exercise: **Wer ist Ihr Großvater? Er ist der Vater meines Vaters.**

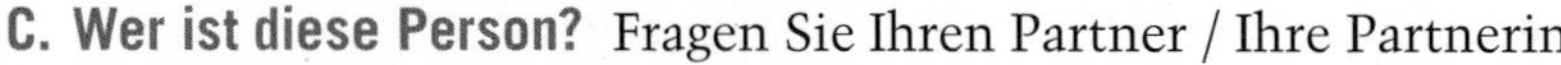

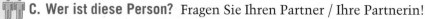

C. Wer ist diese Person? Fragen Sie Ihren Partner / Ihre Partnerin!

BEISPIEL S1 Wer ist der Vater deiner Mutter?
S2 Der Vater meiner Mutter ist mein Großvater.

1. Wer ist der Sohn deines Vaters? 2. Wer ist die Mutter deiner Mutter? 3. Wer ist die Tochter deiner Mutter? 4. Wer sind die Söhne und Töchter deiner Eltern? 5. Wer ist der Sohn deines Urgroßvaters *(great-grandfather)*? 6. Wer ist der Großvater deiner Mutter? 7. Wer ist die Schwester deiner Mutter? 8. Wer ist der Mann deiner Tante? 9. Wer ist die Tochter deines Großvaters?

D: First ask questions such as these of individual students, using anything they have with them or on them. Then have them form pairs or small groups, and ask each other similar questions.

D. Wem gehört das? Fragen Sie Ihren Partner / Ihre Partnerin!

BEISPIEL S1 Gehört die Jacke deinem Freund?
S2 Nein, das ist nicht die Jacke meines Freundes. Das ist meine Jacke.

Gehört das Hemd deinem Bruder? Gehört die Uhr deiner Mutter? Gehört das Buch deinem Professor? Gehört die Tasche deiner Freundin? Gehört die Post deinem Nachbarn? Gehört der Kuli Frau . . . *(name a student)*? Gehört das Heft Herrn . . . *(name a student)*? usw.

8.2 Time expressions

1. Adverbs of time

   a. To refer to SPECIFIC TIMES, such as *yesterday evening* or *tomorrow morning*, combine one word from group A with another from group B. The words in group A can be used alone, whereas those in group B must be used in combinations: **gestern Abend, morgen früh.**

All boldfaced vocabulary items in these lists are new and must be learned!

A		B	
vorgestern	*the day before yesterday*	**früh**, Morgen[1]	*early, morning*
gestern	*yesterday*	**Vormittag**[2]	*midmorning (9 A.M.–noon)*[4]
heute	*today*	**Mittag**	*noon (12–2 P.M.)*
morgen	*tomorrow*	**Nachmittag**	*afternoon (2–6 P.M.)*
übermorgen	*the day after tomorrow*	Abend[3]	*evening (6–10 P.M.)*
		Nacht[3]	*night (after 10 P.M.)*[4]

Morgen früh bin ich in Basel.

Übermorgen fahre ich nach Schaffhausen.

Montagabend besuche ich Krauses in St. Gallen.

[1]**Heute früh** and **heute Morgen** both mean *this morning,* BUT *Tomorrow morning* is always **morgen früh.**

[2]The expressions in this column are commonly combined with the days of the week. In that combination—except for **früh**—they combine to make a compound noun: **Montagmorgen, Dienstagvormittag, Donnerstagabend,** BUT **Montag früh.**

[3]German distinguishes clearly between **Abend** and **Nacht:** Wir sind **gestern Abend** ins Kino gegangen. Ich habe **gestern Nacht** schlecht geschlafen. **Heute Nacht** can mean *last night* or *tonight* (whichever is closer), depending on context.

[4]The times may vary somewhat, but these are close approximations.

b. Adverbs such as **montags** and **morgens** don't refer to specific time (a specific *Monday* or *morning*), but rather imply that events usually occur (more or less regularly), for example, *on Mondays* or *in the mornings, most mornings*. The following new expressions also belong to this group: **täglich** *(daily)*, **wöchentlich** *(weekly)*, **monatlich** *(monthly)*, and **jährlich** *(yearly, annually)*.

montags, dienstags, mittwochs, donnerstags, freitags, samstags, sonntags; morgens, vormittags, mittags, nachmittags, abends, nachts, montagmorgens, dienstagabends, **täglich, wöchentlich, monatlich, jährlich**

Note the difference in spelling: Kommst du **Dienstagabend?** Nein, **dienstagabends** kann ich nicht.

Sonntags tue ich nichts, aber **montags** arbeite ich schwer.

Morgens und **nachmittags** gehe ich zur Uni. **Mittags** spiele ich Tennis.

Freitagabends gehen wir gern aus und **samstagmorgens** stehen wir dann nicht so früh auf.

Ich muss für die Wohnung **monatlich** 500 Euro zahlen.

2. Other time expressions

a. The accusative of time

To refer to a DEFINITE point in time **(wann?)** or length of time **(wie lange?)**, German often uses time phrases in the accusative, without any prepositions. Here are some of the most common expressions.

WANN?		WIE LANGE?	
jeden Tag	*every day; each day*	zwei Wochen	*for two weeks*
diese Woche	*this week*	einen Monat	*for one month*

Haben Sie **diese Woche** Zeit?	*Do you have time this week?*
Die Fahrt dauert **zwei Stunden.**	*The trip takes two hours.*
Ich bleibe **zwei Tage** in Davos.	*I'll be in Davos for two days.*

b. The genitive of time

To refer to an INDEFINITE point in time (in the past or future), German uses the genitive.

eines Tages *one day, someday*

Eines Tages habe ich eine E-Mail bekommen.	*One day, I got an e-mail.*
Eines Tages fahre ich in die Schweiz.	*Someday, I'll go to Switzerland.*

The following new expressions also belong in this group:

Anfang / Ende der Woche	*at the beginning / end of the week*
Mitte des Monats	*in the middle of the month*

Anfang / Mitte / Ende **des Monats** BUT: Anfang / Mitte / Ende **Mai**

c. Prepositional time phrases

You are already familiar with the following phrases.

an	am Abend, am Wochenende, am Montag, am 1. April
bis	bis morgen, bis (um) 2.30 Uhr, bis (zum) Freitag, bis (zum) Januar
für	für morgen, für Freitag, für eine Nacht
in	im Juli, im Sommer, in einem Monat; in 10 Minuten, in einer Viertelstunde, in einer Woche, in einem Jahr
nach	nach dem Essen, nach einer Stunde
seit	seit einem Jahr, seit September
um	um fünf (Uhr)
von . . . bis	vom 1. Juni bis (zum) 25. August; von Juli bis August
vor	vor einem Monat, vor ein paar Tagen
während	während des Sommers, während des Tages

- Two-way prepositions usually use the dative in time expressions: Wir fahren **in einer Woche** in die Berge. **Am Freitag** fahren wir ab.
- German uses **seit** plus the present tense to describe an action or condition that began in the past and still continues in the present. English uses the present perfect or present perfect progressive to express the same thing: **Er wohnt seit zwei Jahren hier.** *(He has lived / has been living here for two years.)*

Übungen

E. Ein Besuch *(Visit)* Was fehlt?

1. Sven und seine Frau sind __vor einer Woche__ bei uns in Luzern angekommen. *(one week ago)*
2. Sie sind __Donnerstagabend um zehn (Uhr),__ abgereist und haben __neun Stunden__ im Zug gesessen. *(Thursday evening at 10 o'clock, for nine hours)*
3. Sven schläft __morgens__ gewöhnlich nicht lange. *(in the morning)*
4. Aber er hat __heute Morgen bis um elf (Uhr)__ geschlafen. *(this morning until 11 o'clock.)*
5. Die beiden bleiben ungefähr __eine Woche__ hier. *(for one week)*
6. __Vorgestern__ haben wir einen Bummel *(stroll)* durch die Stadt gemacht. *(The day before yesterday)*
7. __Heute Abend__ gehen wir ins Konzert. *(This evening)*
8. __Morgen früh__ kommen Meike und Thomas vorbei. *(Tomorrow morning)*
9. __Morgen Mittag__ gehen wir alle essen. *(Tomorrow at noon)*
10. __Am Nachmittag__ machen wir eine Fahrt auf dem Vierwaldstätter See. *(In the afternoon)*
11. Was wir __übermorgen__ machen, wissen wir noch nicht. *(the day after tomorrow)*
12. __Jeden Tag / Täglich__ machen wir etwas Besonderes. *(Every day)*

F. Bei mir Erzählen Sie Ihrer Gruppe, wie das bei Ihnen ist! Was tun Sie gewöhnlich? Was haben Sie neulich *(recently)* getan? Benutzen Sie Wörter von den Listen oder ergänzen Sie, was Sie brauchen!

BEISPIEL *Morgens trinke ich gewöhnlich Kaffee, aber heute Morgen habe ich Tee getrunken.*

1	2	3	4	5	6
morgens	gewöhnlich	ausgehen	aber	letzte Woche	zu Hause bleiben
(nach)mittags	manchmal	in der Bibliothek arbeiten		diese Woche	meine Familie besuchen
(freitag)abends	meistens	die Wohnung putzen		vor ein paar Tagen	ins Konzert gehen
sonntags	oft	fernsehen *(watch TV)*		(vor)gestern	ein Buch lesen
während der Woche	immer	einkaufen gehen		gestern Abend	Tee trinken
am Wochenende	nie	E-Mails schreiben		heute Morgen	Musik hören
jeden Tag	. . .	im Internet surfen		(über)morgen	. . .
. . .		Kaffee trinken		. . .	
		. . .			

G. Allerlei Märkte in Bern Finden Sie mit Ihrem Partner / Ihrer Partnerin heraus, wann es welchen Markt wo gibt! Geben Sie die Antwort auf Deutsch und auf Englisch!

BEISPIEL Weihnachtsmarkt
täglich / jeden Tag / im Dezember
every day in December

Berner Märkte
Alpenveilchen
Flohmarkt auf dem Mühlenplatz: von Mai bis Oktober jeden dritten Samstag des Monats.
Obst-, Gemüse- und Blumenmarkt auf dem Bundes- und Bärenplatz: ganzjährlich Dienstag und Mittwoch vormittags; von April bis Oktober täglich.
Fleischmarkt in der Münstergasse: Dienstag und Samstag vormittags.
Warenmarkt auf dem Waisenhausplatz: ganzjährlich dienstags und samstags; von April bis Oktober auch donnerstags mit Abendvorverkauf.
Weihnachtsmarkt auf dem Münster- und Waisenhausplatz: täglich im Dezember.
www.marktbern.ch

Fokus Switzerland's Mountain World

Not surprisingly, Switzerland has a number of popular and fashionable mountain resorts. The glacier village of **Grindelwald** in the Bernese Uplands is a favorite base for mountain climbers and skiers. **St. Moritz,** south of Davos, is nestled in the Upper Inn Valley next to a lake. Twice host to the Winter Olympics (1928 and 1948), the resort has become a jet-set sports mecca. Another fashionable area is **Saas-Fee**, northeast of Zermatt. The village allows no motor vehicles to spoil its magnificent setting facing the great Fee glacier.

Besides the **Matterhorn** (14,692 ft.), the most famous Swiss peaks are the **Jungfrau, Mönch,** and **Eiger** (all ca. 13,000 ft.). A tunnel, almost 4.5 miles long, leads steeply up to the **Jungfraujoch** terminus (11,333 ft.). Its observation deck offers a superb view of the surrounding mountains and the lakes of central Switzerland. From there, on a very clear day, even the Black Forest in southern Germany can be seen.

Blick aufs Matterhorn vom Gornergrat

8.3 Sentence structure *(continued)*

1. Types of adverbs

   You have already encountered various adverbs and adverbial phrases. They are usually divided into three major groups.

   a. ADVERBS OF TIME, answering the questions **wann? wie lange?**
   am Abend, am 2. April, am 4. Montag, Anfang März, bis Mai, eine Woche, eines Tages, ein paar Minuten, Ende des Monats, heute, im Juni, immer, jetzt, manchmal, meistens, montags, Mitte Juli, morgens, nie, oft, stundenlang, täglich, um zwölf, vor einer Woche, während des Winters usw.

   Since **stundenlang** means *for hours*, let students figure out the meaning of **tagelang, wochenlang, monatelang, jahrelang.**

   b. ADVERBS OF MANNER, answering the question **wie?**
   gemütlich, langsam, laut, mit der Bahn, ohne Geld, schnell, zu Fuß, zusammen usw.

   c. ADVERBS OF PLACE, answering the questions **wo? wohin? woher?**
   auf der Post, bei uns, da, dort, hier, im Norden, zu Hause, mitten in der Stadt, überall, nach Berlin, nach Hause, auf die Post, zur Uni, aus Kanada, von Amerika, aus dem Flugzeug usw.

2. Sequence of adverbs

   If two or more adverbs or adverbial phrases occur in one sentence, they usually follow the sequence TIME, MANNER, PLACE.

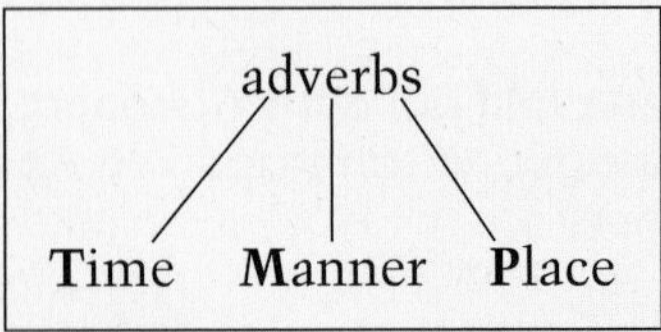

Er kann das Paket **morgen** **mit dem Auto** **zur Post** bringen.
T M P

- If there is more than one time expression, general time references precede specific time references:

  Er bringt das Paket **morgen** **um zehn Uhr** zur Post.

- Like other sentence elements, adverbs and adverbial phrases may precede the verb.

Morgen kann er das Paket mit dem Auto zur Post bringen.
Mit dem Auto kann er das Paket morgen zur Post bringen.
Zur Post kann er das Paket morgen mit dem Auto bringen.

3. Position of **nicht**

As you already know from Chapter 2, Section 2.3, **nicht** usually comes *after adverbs of definite time* but *before other adverbs, such as adverbs of manner or place.*

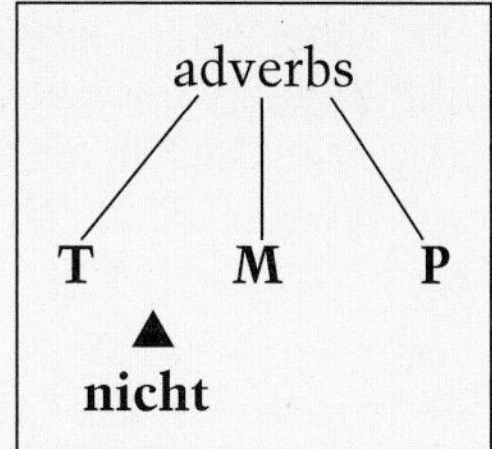

Er bringt das Paket ▲.
Er bringt das Paket ▲ mit.
Er kann das Paket ▲ mitbringen.
Er kann das Paket **morgen** ▲ mitbringen.
Er kann das Paket **morgen** ▲ **mit dem Auto** mitbringen.
Er kann das Paket **morgen** ▲ **mit dem Auto zur Post** bringen.

Übungen

H. Sagen Sie das noch einmal! Benutzen Sie die adverbialen Ausdrücke *(adverbial expressions)* in der richtigen Reihenfolge *(sequence)*! Beginnen Sie jeden Satz mit dem Subjekt!

BEISPIEL Ich kaufe die Briefmarken. (auf der Post, morgen)
Ich kaufe die Briefmarken morgen auf der Post.

1. Sie kommen an. (heute Abend, in Chur, mit dem Bus)
2. Wir gehen. (zu Fuß, in die Stadt, morgen früh)
3. Ich kaufe Eier und Blumen. (samstags, auf dem Markt, gern frisch)
4. Wir wollen ins Konzert gehen. (zusammen, morgen Abend)
5. Sie reisen. (am Sonntag, nach Italien, ohne die Kinder)
6. Sie lassen sie in Chur. (bei den Großeltern, ein paar Tage)
7. Die Bahnfahrkarten liegen auf dem Sofa. (da drüben, seit drei Tagen)
8. Sie wollen zurückkommen. (zu uns, Dienstagabend, mit dem Zug)

I. So kann man's auch sagen. Beginnen Sie jeden Satz mit dem fettgedruckten *(boldfaced)* Satzteil und sagen Sie ihn dann auf Englisch!

BEISPIEL Wir bleiben **während der Ferien** gewöhnlich zu Hause.
Während der Ferien bleiben wir gewöhnlich zu Hause.
During vacations, we usually stay home.

1. Wir haben gewöhnlich keine Zeit **für Reisen.**
2. Patrick hat **gerade** mit seiner Schwester in Amerika gesprochen.
3. Sie ist **seit einer Woche** bei ihrem Bruder in Florida.
4. Wir wollen sie alle **am Wochenende** besuchen *(visit)*.

H: 1. Sie kommen heute Abend mit dem Bus in Chur an. 2. Wir gehen morgen früh zu Fuß in die Stadt. 3. Ich kaufe Eier und Blumen samstags gern frisch auf dem Markt. 4. Wir wollen morgen Abend zusammen ins Konzert gehen. 5. Sie reisen am Sonntag ohne die Kinder nach Italien. 6. Sie lassen sie ein paar Tage bei den Großeltern in Chur. 7. Die Bahnfahrkarten liegen seit drei Tagen da drüben auf dem Sofa / auf dem Sofa da drüben. 8. Sie wollen Dienstagabend mit dem Zug zu uns zurückkommen.

H: As an extra practice, you might have students repeat these sentences by starting with one of the adverbs or adverbial phrases.

I: 1. Für Reisen haben wir gewöhnlich keine Zeit. *For trips we usually have no time.* 2. Gerade hat Patrick mit seiner Schwester in Amerika gesprochen. *Patrick just talked with his sister in America.* 3. Seit einer Woche ist sie bei ihrem Bruder in Florida. *Since one week, she's been with her brother in Florida.* 4. Am Wochenende wollen wir sie alle besuchen. *On the weekend, we want to visit them all.*

Fokus Switzerland and Its Languages

European motor vehicles usually carry a small sticker indicating the country of origin: *D* stands for Germany, *A* for Austria, and *CH* for Switzerland. The abbreviation *CH* stands for the Latin *Confoederatio Helvetica,* a reference to the Celtic tribe of the Helvetii who settled the territory of modern Switzerland when Julius Caesar prevented them from moving to Gaul (today's France). The neutral choice of *CH* is a good example of how the Swiss avoid giving preference to one of their four national languages.

Roughly 70% of the Swiss speak a dialect of Swiss-German **(Schwyzerdütsch);** 20% speak French; 9% Italian; and a tiny minority (1%) speaks Romansh **(Rätoromanisch).** Most Swiss people understand two or three—some even all four—of these languages. This quadrilingualism goes back to the time when the Romans colonized the area. Over time, tribes from present-day Italy, France, and Germany migrated to the region. Romansh is a Romance language that has evolved little from Vulgar Latin and is spoken mainly in the remote valleys of the Grisons (canton *Graubünden*). Although it became one of the four official languages in 1938, Romansh has been under constant pressure from the other major languages in surrounding areas. The fact that Romansh is not one language but a group of dialects (including **Ladin**) makes it even harder to preserve.

Fokus: For the general location of where these languages are spoken, see the map in the pre-reading section **(Vor dem Lesen).**

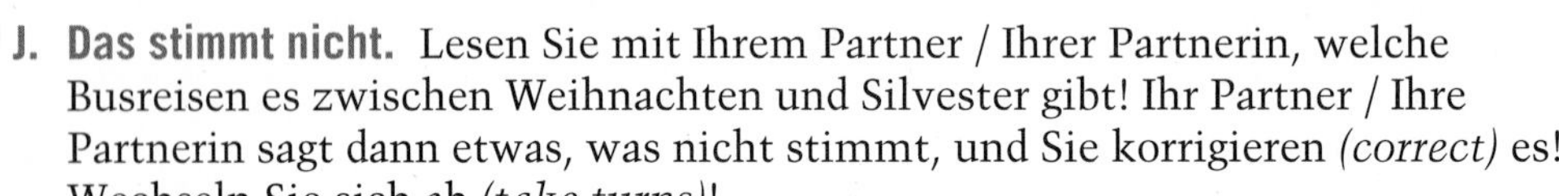

J. Das stimmt nicht. Lesen Sie mit Ihrem Partner / Ihrer Partnerin, welche Busreisen es zwischen Weihnachten und Silvester gibt! Ihr Partner / Ihre Partnerin sagt dann etwas, was nicht stimmt, und Sie korrigieren *(correct)* es! Wechseln Sie sich ab *(take turns)*!

BEISPIEL S1 Die 7-Tage-Busreise zu Silvester in die Schweiz kostet 299 Euro.
S2 Nein, sie kostet nicht 299 Euro, sondern 460 Euro.

Busreisen Weihnachten & Silvester

❖ **7 Tage Skiferien in Österreich**
4 Sterne Hotel in Lech am Arlberg, Hallenbad und Sauna,
22. Dez. - 28. Dez. €420 / Silvester 29. Dez.- 4. Jan. €485

❖ **7 Tage im Salzburger Land**
Hotel Alpenrose, Kufstein, Halbpension mit allem Komfort,
22. Dez. - 28. Dez. €400

❖ **5 Tage Skiurlaub in der Schweiz**
4x Übernachtung bei Familie Schmidhuber in St. Moritz,
Halbpension, zentral, ruhig und gemütlich
23. - 27. Dez. €385 / Silvester 30. Dez. - 3. Jan. €425

❖ **7 Tage über Silvester im Berner Oberland**
4 Sterne Hotel, Grindelwald, 6x Übernachtung,
Halbpension, Musik, Silvesterball mit Stars
29. Dez.- 4. Jan., €460

❖ **7 Tage Winterferien im Tessin**
Lugano, 6x Übernachtung, Wellness, Spa, Tanz, Musik
23. Dez. - 29. Dez. €510 / Silvester 29. Dez. - 4. Jan. €580

Reisebüro Herold 0800 / 49 13 22 0

K. Ferienwünsche Verneinen Sie *(Negate)* die Sätze mit **nicht**!

TANJA Ich möchte diesen Winter in die Berge fahren.
LARS Gefallen dir die Berge?
TANJA Das habe ich gesagt. Warum fliegen wir diesen Winter nach Korsika? 279 Euro, das ist sehr teuer.
LARS Ich weiß.
TANJA Im Flugzeug wird man so müde.
LARS Ich fliege gern.
TANJA Ich möchte aber mit dem Auto fahren.
LARS In Korsika kannst du den ganzen Tag in der Sonne liegen.
TANJA Morgens und nachmittags ist die Sonne so heiß.
LARS In den Bergen ist es so langweilig.
TANJA Gut. Wenn wir nach Korsika fliegen, komme ich mit.

K: nicht in die Berge; die Berge nicht; nicht gesagt, nicht diesen Winter (diesen Winter nicht), nicht sehr teuer; weiß nicht; nicht so müde; nicht gern; nicht mit dem Auto; nicht den ganzen Tag nicht so heiß; nicht so langweilig; nicht nach Korsika, nicht mit

If students need more practice, have them negate: Hast du die Paketkarte ausgefüllt? Haben Sie das Fax geschickt? Haben Sie Petras E-Mail-Adresse? Sie hat den Brief mit Luftpost geschickt. Wollen wir zu Fuß zum Bahnhof gehen? Sie fahren gern mit dem Bus. Er kann morgen kommen. Olaf hat Tante Irma besucht. Dieser Zug fährt nach Basel.

Zusammenfassung

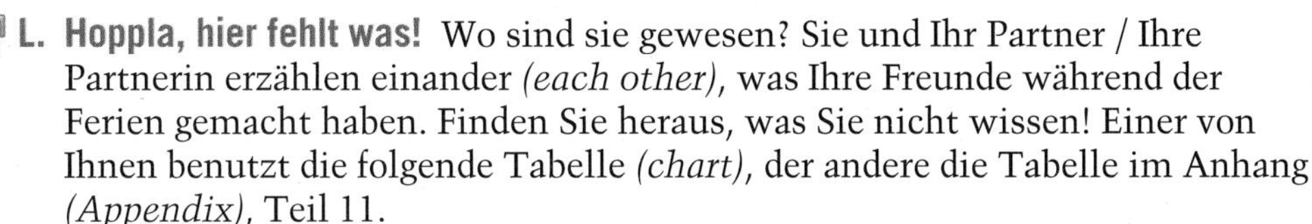

L. Hoppla, hier fehlt was! Wo sind sie gewesen? Sie und Ihr Partner / Ihre Partnerin erzählen einander *(each other)*, was Ihre Freunde während der Ferien gemacht haben. Finden Sie heraus, was Sie nicht wissen! Einer von Ihnen benutzt die folgende Tabelle *(chart)*, der andere die Tabelle im Anhang *(Appendix)*, Teil 11.

Visit the ***Wie geht's?*** iLrn website for more review and practice of the grammar points you have just learned.

BEISPIEL S1 Ich weiß, dass Lucian gemütlich durch Italien gereist ist. Aber wann?
S2 Das weiß ich nicht genau. Ich weiß nur, dass er ein paar Wochen gereist ist. Und hast du gehört, was Christl gemacht hat? Sie ist . . .

S1:

WER	WANN / WIE LANGE	WIE / OBJ. + PRÄPOSITION	WO UND WAS
Lucian	ein paar Wochen	gemütlich	durch Italien reisen
Christl	ein- Monat	bei einer Gastfamilie	in Amerika sein
Steffi	dies- Sommer	wegen ihrer Prüfung	zu Hause bleiben
Nina + Kim	während der Ferien	mit dem Schiff	von Passau bis Wien fahren
Ben + Michi	jed- Nachmittag	zusammen	in einer Pizzeria arbeiten
Günther	im August	trotz des Wetters / dem Wetter	auf der Insel Rügen campen
Jutta	vom 1. bis 31. Juli	als Au-Pair	in London arbeiten
Nicole	vor einer Woche	wieder	von Griechenland zurückkommen
Yvonne	morgens	meistens	im Fitnessstudio trainieren
Jochen	mittags	gewöhnlich	im Restaurant jobben

M: 1. Die Tante unserer Freunde lebt hier in Bern. 2. Leider weiß ich die Adresse dieser Tante nicht. 3. Der Name der Frau ist Köchli. 4. Wegen dieses Namens kann ich Frau Köchli nicht finden. 5. Statt einer Köchli gibt es viele Köchlis. 6. Weißt du die Telefonnummer eu(e)rer Freunde nicht? 7. Die Nummer steht im Adressbuch meiner Frau. 8. Ich kann Inges Adressbuch nicht finden. 9. Eines Tages findet Inge es hoffentlich wieder. 10. Könnt ihr mir den Namen eines Hotels sagen? 11. Trotz der Preise brauchen wir ein Hotelzimmer. 12. Während der Feiertage hast du Probleme wegen der Touristen.

M. Frau Köchli Bilden Sie Sätze!

BEISPIEL Hauptstadt / Schweiz / sein / Bern
Die Hauptstadt der Schweiz ist Bern.

1. Tante / unsere Freunde / leben / hier in Bern
2. leider / ich / nicht / wissen / die / Adresse / diese Tante
3. Name / Frau / sein / Köchli
4. wegen / dieser Name / ich / nicht / können / finden / Frau Köchli
5. statt / eine Köchli / es gibt / viele Köchlis
6. du / nicht / wissen / Telefonnummer / euere Freunde?
7. Nummer / stehen / in / Adressbuch / meine Frau
8. ich / nicht / können / finden / Inge / Adressbuch
9. ein Tag / Inge / es / hoffentlich / wieder / finden
10. können / ihr / mir / sagen / Name / ein Hotel?
11. trotz / Preise *(pl.)* / wir / brauchen / Hotelzimmer
12. während / Feiertage / du / haben / Probleme *(pl.)* / wegen / Touristen *(pl.)*

N. Mein Alltag *(My daily life)* Schreiben Sie 8–10 Sätze über *(about)* Ihren Alltag, zum Beispiel wann Sie aufstehen, wann Sie essen, wann Sie zur Schule / Uni gehen, welche Vorlesungen Sie wann haben, was Sie abends und am Wochenende tun usw.! Benutzen Sie so viele Zeitausdrücke wie möglich *(as possible)*!

BEISPIEL *Ich bin fast jeden Tag an der Uni. Morgens stehe ich um sechs auf . . .*

Fokus Wilhelm Tell

William Tell **(Wilhelm Tell)** is a legendary Swiss folk hero and a universal symbol of resistance to oppression. In 1307, he purportedly refused to obey the commands of the tyrannical Austrian bailiff, Gessler, who then forced him to shoot an arrow through an apple on his son's head. Tell did so, but later took revenge by killing Bailiff Gessler. That event was the beginning of a general uprising of the Swiss against the Habsburgs, the ruling dynasty since 1273. In 1439, when the Habsburgs tried to bring Switzerland back under Austrian rule, the Confederation broke free of the Empire. The story of Tell's confrontation with Gessler inspired Friedrich Schiller's drama *Wilhelm Tell* (1804) and Rossini's opera *Guillaume Tell* (1829).

Wilhelm-Tell-Denkmal in Altdorf

Einblicke

Interviews

Wortschatz 2

das Dorf, ¨er	*village*
die Gegend, -en	*area, region*
Geschichte, -n	*history; story*
herrlich	*wonderful (ly), great*
beschreiben, beschrieben	*to describe*
hinauf·fahren (fährt hinauf), ist hinaufgefahren	*to go / drive up (to)*
weiter·fahren (fährt weiter), ist weitergefahren	*to drive on, keep on driving*

Since **weiterfahren** means *to drive on, to keep on driving,* let students guess what these words mean: **weitergehen, weitergeben, weiterfliegen, weiterlesen, weiterreisen, weiterschlafen.**

Vor dem Lesen

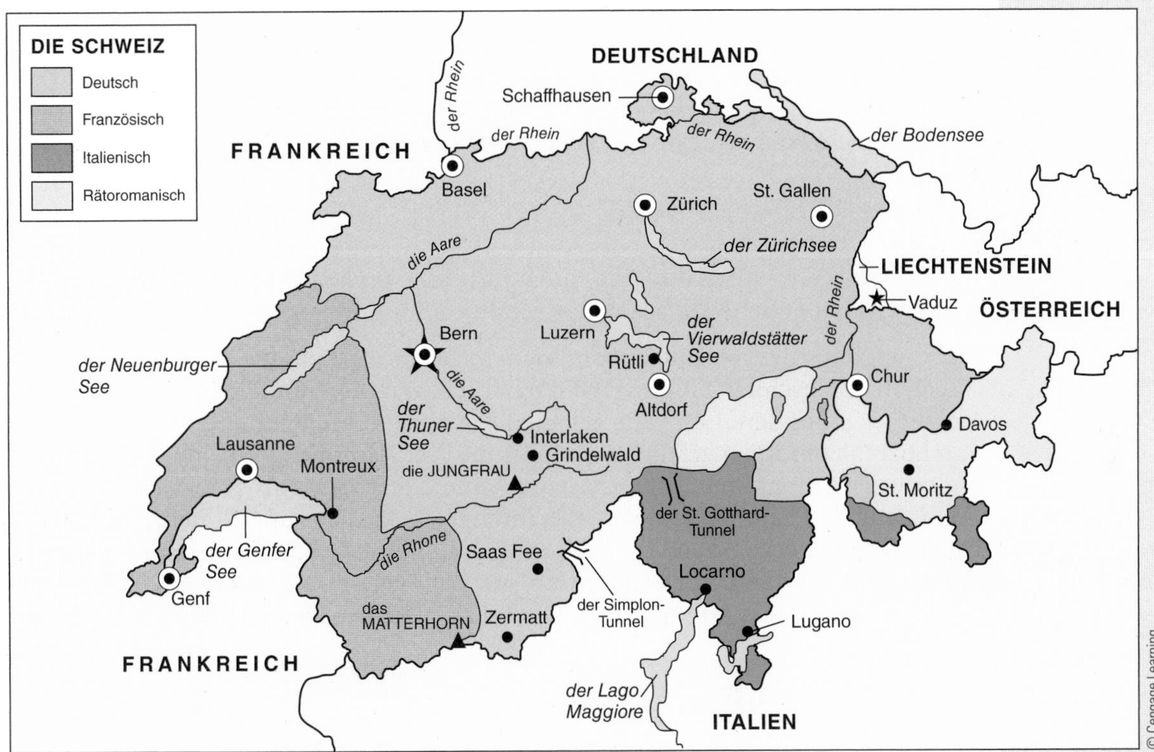

A. Etwas Geographie Sehen Sie auf die Landkarte der Schweiz und beantworten Sie die Fragen!

1. Wie heißen die Nachbarländer der Schweiz? Wo liegen sie?
2. Wie heißt die Hauptstadt der Schweiz?
3. Nennen Sie ein paar Schweizer Flüsse, Seen und Berge! Welcher Fluss fließt weiter *(flows on)* nach Deutschland / nach Frankreich? Welcher See liegt zwischen der Schweiz und Deutschland / Italien / Frankreich?
4. Wo liegt Bern? Basel? Zürich? Luzern? Genf? Lausanne? Zermatt? Lugano? St. Moritz? Davos? Saas-Fee? Grindelwald? Chur? Schaffhausen?
5. Wo spricht man Deutsch? Französisch? Italienisch? Rätoromanisch?
6. Was assoziieren Sie mit der Schweiz?

A: 1. Deutschland, Liechtenstein, Österreich, Italien, Frankreich 2. Bern 3. die Aare, die Rhone, der Rhein; der Vierwaldstätter See, der Zürichsee, der Neuenburger See, der Genfer See, die Jungfrau, das Matterhorn; der Rhein > Deutschland, die Rhone > Frankreich; der Bodensee, der Lago Maggiore, der Genfer See 4–6. *(answers vary)*

B. Besuch in Bern Lesen Sie mit Ihrem Partner / Ihrer Partnerin, wie man als Tourist Bern zu Fuß oder mit dem Schlauchboot *(inflatable raft)* kennenlernen kann! Stellen Sie einander *(each other)* Fragen und beantworten Sie sie!

BEISPIEL S1 Wo beginnt die Stadtrundfahrt mit dem Schlauchboot?
S2 Sie beginnt am Schwellenmätteli.

Altstadtbummel

Auf dem Spaziergang durch die Berner Altstadt (UNESCO Welterbe) sehen Sie alle Attraktionen der Bundesstadt. Ihr(e) Stadtführer(in) spricht Ihre Sprache.

1.6.–30.9.	täglich	**11.00 Uhr**
Preis	*Erwachsene*	*CHF 16.–*
	Kinder 6–16 Jahre	*CHF 8.–*
Dauer	*1-1/2 Stunden*	

Treffpunkt: Tourist Center im Bahnhof

Stadtrundfahrt im Schlauchboot

Bern aus einer anderen Perspektive! Vom Schlauchboot sehen Sie die alten Sandsteinbrücken und blumengeschmückten Häuser der Stadt.

2.6.–30.9.	Di, Do, Sa, So	**17.00 Uhr**
Preis	*Erwachsene*	*CHF 32.–*
	Kinder 6–16 Jahre	*CHF 20.–*
Dauer	*1-1/2 Stunden*	

Treffpunkt: Schwellenmätteli

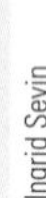

C. Das ist leicht zu verstehen! Lesen Sie laut die folgenden Wörter und raten Sie *(guess)*, was sie auf Englisch bedeuten.

der Film, Besucher, Kanton, Wintersport; das Kurzinterview; die Alpenblume, Arkade, Bergbahn, Konferenz, Nation, Rückreise, Schneeszene, Viersprachigkeit; bergsteigen gehen, faszinieren, filmen; autofrei, elegant

Touristen in der Schweiz

In Kurzinterviews mit Touristen in Altdorf, Bern und Saas-Fee hören wir, was Besuchern in der Schweiz besonders gefällt:

FELIX: Ich finde die Gegend um den Vierwaldstätter See besonders interessant wegen ihrer Geschichte. Gestern bin ich in Luzern gewesen und auch über die Holzbrücke° aus dem Jahr 1408 gelaufen. Heute früh bin ich mit dem Schiff von Luzern zum Rütli gefahren, wo 1291 die drei Kantone Uri, Schwyz und Unterwalden ihren Bund gemacht haben° und die Schweiz als eine Nation begonnen hat. Dann bin ich weitergefahren nach Altdorf zum Wilhelm-Tell-Denkmal und heute Abend gehe ich zu den Wilhelm-Tell-Freilichtspielen°. Dieses Wochenende ist hier auch Bundesfeier° mit Umzügen° und Feuerwerk. Dann geht's wieder zurück mit dem Zug. Die Fahrt durch die Berge ist einfach herrlich.

wooden bridge
created their confederation
outdoor performances
national holiday / parades

Lesetipp

Looking for Genitives

Note the use of genitive constructions in this reading. How many examples of the genitive case can you find? In each case, determine whether the genitive is being used to express a close relationship between two nouns or whether it follows a certain preposition.

Die alte Kapellbrücke mit dem 8-eckigen Wasserturm in Luzern

Zürich mit Blick auf die Limmat

FRAU WEBER: Mir gefällt Bern wegen seiner Arkaden und Brunnen°. Mein Mann und ich fahren fast jedes Jahr im Juni oder Juli in die Schweiz. Auf unserer Fahrt kommen wir gewöhnlich durch Bern und bleiben ein paar Tage dort. Wenn wir Glück haben, ist dann gerade Flohmarkt° oder Handwerksmarkt°. Da haben wir schon manches Schnäppchen° gemacht. Morgen fahren wir weiter nach Grindelwald ins Berner Oberland. Wir wollen mit der Bergbahn zum Jungfraujoch hinauffahren und von dort oben den Blick auf die Berge genießen°. Trotz der vielen Touristen ist das Berner Oberland immer wieder schön. Haben Sie gewusst, dass man fast alle Schneeszenen der James-Bond-Filme im Berner Oberland gefilmt hat? Auf der Rückreise haben wir Aufenthalt in Zürich, wo mein Mann mit den Banken zu tun hat. Der See mit dem Panorama der Berge ist herrlich. Während der Konferenzen meines Mannes bummle ich gern durch die Stadt. Die Geschäfte in der Bahnhofstraße sind elegant, aber teuer.

fountains
flea market / crafts fair
bargain
enjoy

FRAU LORENZ: Die Viersprachigkeit der Schweiz fasziniert uns. Unsere Reise hat in Lausanne begonnen, wo wir Französisch gesprochen haben. Jetzt sind wir hier in Saas-Fee bei Freunden. Mit uns sprechen sie Hochdeutsch, aber mit der Familie Schwyzerdütsch. Saas-Fee ist nur ein Dorf, aber wunderschön. Es ist autofrei und in den Bergen kann man überall wandern und bergsteigen gehen. Wegen der Höhenlage° gibt es viele Alpenblumen und Gämsen° und oben auf den Gletschern kann man sogar während des Sommers immer noch Ski laufen gehen. Übermorgen fahren wir weiter nach St. Moritz, wo man viel Rätoromanisch hört. Am Ende der Reise wollen wir noch nach Lugano, wo das Wetter fast immer schön sein soll und die Leute Italienisch sprechen. Vier Sprachen in einem Land, das ist schon toll.

altitude / mountain goats

Nach dem Lesen

A: 1. wegen ihrer Geschichte 2. 1291 3. Umzüge, ein Feuerwerk 4. wegen der Arkaden und Brunnen 5. zum Jungfraujoch 6. im Berner Oberland 7. wegen der Banken 8. die Viersprachkigkeit 9. Französisch, Hochdeutsch 10. Rätoromanisch, Italienisch

A. Alles verstanden?

1. Warum findet Felix die Gegend um den Vierwaldstätter See so interessant?
2. Wann hat die Schweiz als Nation begonnen?
3. Was gibt's bei der Bundesfeier in Altdorf?
4. Warum gefällt Frau Weber Bern so gut?
5. Wohin wollen sie mit einer Bergbahn fahren?
6. Wo hat man fast alle Schneeszenen der James-Bond-Filme gefilmt?
7. Warum muss Frau Webers Mann auch nach Bern?
8. Was fasziniert die Familie Lorenz in der Schweiz?
9. Welche Sprache haben sie in Lausanne gesprochen? Was sprechen ihre Freunde in Saas-Fee mit ihnen?
10. In St. Moritz hört man nicht nur Deutsch, sondern auch welche Sprache? Was spricht man in Lugano?

B: 1. Wegen ihrer Geschichte findet Felix die Gegend um den Vierwaldstätter See interessant. 2. Von Luzern is Felix mit einem Schiff zum Rütli gefahren. 3. 1291 haben die drei Kantone Uri, Schwyz und Unterwalden ihren Bund am Rütli geschlossen. 4. Natürlich wollen viele Touristen Wilhelm Tells Denkmal sehen. 5. Jedes Jahr am 1. August feiert man in der Schweiz die Bundesfeier. 6. Wegen dieses Festes ist Felix noch einen Tag geblieben.

B. Die Eidgenossenschaft *(The Swiss Confederacy)* Sagen Sie es anders!

BEISPIEL Viele Touristen fahren **jedes Jahr** in die Schweiz.
Jedes Jahr fahren viele Touristen in die Schweiz.

1. Felix findet die Gegend um den Vierwaldstätter See **wegen ihrer Geschichte** interessant.
2. Felix ist mit einem Schiff **von Luzern** zum Rütli gefahren.
3. Die drei Kantone Uri, Schwyz und Unterwalden haben ihren Bund **1291** am Rütli geschlossen.
4. Viele Touristen wollen **natürlich** Wilhelm Tells Denkmal sehen.
5. In der Schweiz feiert man **jedes Jahr am 1. August** die Bundesfeier.
6. Felix ist **wegen dieses Festes** noch einen Tag geblieben.

Schiff auf dem Vierwaldstätter See

Weiteres

C: This exercise practices reading dates, which was presented in Chapter 4, *Wortschatz*.

C. Etwas Geschichte Lesen Sie laut!

Im Jahr 1291 schlossen Uri, Schwyz und Unterwalden am Rütli einen Bund. Luzern ist 1332 dazu gekommen (here: *joined it*) und Zürich 1351. 1513 hat es 13 Kantone gegeben. Heute, im Jahr 20 ____ *(add current year)*, sind es 26 Kantone. 1848 ist die Schweiz ein Bundesstaat geworden. Im 1. Weltkrieg (1914–1918) und im 2. Weltkrieg (1939–1945) ist die Schweiz neutral geblieben. Trotz ihrer Tradition von Demokratie können die Frauen der Schweiz erst seit 1971 in allen Kantonen wählen *(vote)*. Seit 1981 gibt es offiziell auch keine Diskriminierung der Frau mehr.

D. Kurzgespräche Erzählen Sie den anderen von Ihrer Reise! Was sagen sie dazu *(to that)*?

1. **Die Heimreise** *(Trip home)*

   The weather was awful. Your plane arrived two hours late **(mit zwei Stunden Verspätung)** and departed only **(erst)** five hours later. You arrived at two o'clock in the morning. Your suitcase wasn't there. There were no buses into town. You didn't have enough cash for a taxi. You phoned your father. You got home at 4 A.M. You were very tired.

2. **Im Schwyzerhüsli**

   Staying overnight: You and your friend arrived in Schaffhausen on the Rhine. You inquired at three hotels, but they had no rooms available. They sent you to the *Schwyzerhüsli*. There they had some rooms. Since you were very tired, you went to bed early **(ins Bett).** There was a party in the hotel until midnight. Then cars kept driving by. It was very loud. At 4 A.M. your neighbors got up, talked in the hallway, and got into their car. You couldn't sleep anymore, so you got up too, and left. What a night!

E. Wer möchte mit uns tauschen *(trade)*? Lesen Sie die Anzeige und schreiben Sie zurück! Sagen Sie, dass Sie gern einmal tauschen möchten, und beschreiben Sie, was Sie zu bieten haben *(have to offer)*!

WOHNUNGSTAUSCH IN DEN FERIEN
ZEIT: 20. JULI BIS 30. AUGUST

Wir bieten:
Unsere Wohnung in der Nähe von Zürich: Wohnzimmer, Küche, Bad, 2 Schlafzimmer, Balkon, Blick auf die Berge, 15 Minuten Fahrt mit der S-Bahn ins Zentrum von Zürich.

Wir suchen:
Wohnung in Amerika oder Kanada, wenn möglich im Zentrum und nicht weit zur Universität.

Wer möchte mit uns tauschen?

Nadine und Martin Hunkeler
Erlenstrasse 10
8134 Adliswil
Schweiz

Schreibtipp

Choosing Subject Pronouns

Avoid switching back and forth between *one* **(man)** and *you* **(Sie)**; try to be consistent. Also, vary your sentence structure, and don't start too many sentences with **ich.** If you are using a compound subject that includes you, never name yourself first: Write **Mein Freund und ich . . . ,** *not* **Ich und mein Freund . . . !** Remember: **„Der Esel nennt sich selbst zuerst: Iah!"** (literally: *The donkey names itself first: Hee-haw!*)

Hörverständnis

For further practice, an optional two-part video (**Szenen** and **Interviews**) is available on the ***Wie geht's?*** Premium Website and in iLrn, with corresponding questions and activities in the *Arbeitsbuch* (SAM).

As an optional activity with Google Earth, you could visit Switzerland and have a closer look at Lake Geneva **(Genfer See)**, check out various places around it or any other Swiss sites mentioned in this chapter.

Im Reisebüro Was stimmt?

Zum Erkennen: inbegriffen *(included);* die Broschüre, -n *(brochure)*

1. Ulrike und Steffi möchten im ___b___ reisen.
   a. August
   b. März
   c. Januar
2. Sie wollen ___c___.
   a. wandern
   b. bergsteigen gehen
   c. Ski laufen gehen
3. Ulrike reserviert ein Zimmer im Hotel ___a___.
   a. Alpenrose
   b. Alpina
   c. Eiger
4. Ulrike und Steffi fahren mit der Bahn bis ___b___.
   a. Bern
   b. Interlaken
   c. Grindelwald
5. Sie kommen um ___c___ Uhr an ihrem Ziel *(destination)* an.
   a. 12.16
   b. 12.30
   c. 13.00
6. Sie fahren am ___a___ um ______ nach Hause zurück.
   a. 15. / vierzehn
   b. 14. / drei
   c. 16. / sechs

Literatur

■ Beginning with this chapter, there will be a brief section with original literature **(die Literatur)** by one or two authors, introduced by a biographical note on the author(s) and accompanied by pre- and post-reading exercises. This section is optional and not a replacement for the reading text with **Wortschatz 2.** ■

Biographisches

Hermann Hesse (1899–1962) was awarded the Nobel Prize for literature in 1946. Although born in Germany, he became a Swiss citizen at the outbreak of World War I. The first stage of his writing began with his romantic rendering of the artist as a social outcast. At the beginning of the war, the strain of his pacifist beliefs and domestic crises led him to undergo psychoanalysis, which gave a new dimension to his work. The novels *Demian, Siddhartha,* and *Steppenwolf* were influenced by his readings of Nietzsche, Dostoyevsky, Spengler, and Buddhist mysticism and are based on his conviction that people must discover their own nature. A third phase began in 1930, balancing the artist's rebellion against the constraints of social behavior. After 1943, when his name was put on the Nazi blacklist, he quit writing novels and concentrated on poems, stories, and essays that articulated a humanistic spirit reminiscent of Goethe's **Weltbürgertum** *(world citizenship).* Hesse's works also reflect his faith in the spirituality of all mankind, for which he coined the term **Weltglaube.**

Vor dem Lesen

Allgemeine *(general)* Fragen

1. Lesen Sie gern Gedichte *(poems)*? Warum (nicht)?
2. Haben Sie einen Lieblingsdichter *(favorite poet)* oder ein Lieblingsgedicht? Wenn ja, welches Gedicht / welchen Dichter?
3. Warum sind Gedichte oft so zeitlos *(timeless)*?
4. Haben Sie schon mal ein Gedicht auswendig *(by heart)* gelernt? Wenn ja, welches? Können Sie es heute noch auswendig?
5. Dieses Gedicht spricht von Einsamkeit *(loneliness)*. Welche Adjektive und Hauptwörter *(nouns)* im Gedicht sind typisch für das Thema?

The text in the *Literatur* section is considered optional or extra reading and not a substitute for the *Einblicke* reading text, which is closely tied to the chapter grammar and also introduces active vocabulary. Begin by reading the poem aloud, so that students get a feel for the rhythm and intonation. You could also play the recorded version on the text audio CD that accompanies your Annotated Instructor's Edition.

Im Nebel

Seltsam°, im Nebel° zu wandern!	strange / fog
Einsam° ist jeder Busch und Stein,	lonely
Kein Baum sieht den andern,	
Jeder ist allein.	
Voll von Freunden war° mir die Welt°,	was / world
Als° noch mein Leben licht° war;	When / light
Nun, da der Nebel fällt,	
Ist keiner mehr sichtbar°.	visible
Wahrlich°, keiner ist weise°,	Truly / wise
Der nicht das Dunkel kennt,	
Das unentrinnbar° und leise°	inescapably / quietly
Von allen ihn trennt°.	separates
Seltsam, im Nebel zu wandern!	
Leben ist Einsamkeit.	
Kein Mensch kennt den andern,	
Jeder ist allein.	
Hermann Hesse	

Nach dem Lesen

A. Fragen zum Gedicht

1. Was ist typisch, wenn es neblig *(foggy)* ist?
2. Wo sind oft die Freunde im Nebel des Lebens?
3. Wie ist das Leben ohne Freunde?
4. Warum ist eine Zeit der Dunkelheit manchmal auch wichtig?
5. Wie ist die Stimmung *(mood)* dieses Gedichts?
6. Wie gefällt Ihnen das Gedicht? Warum?

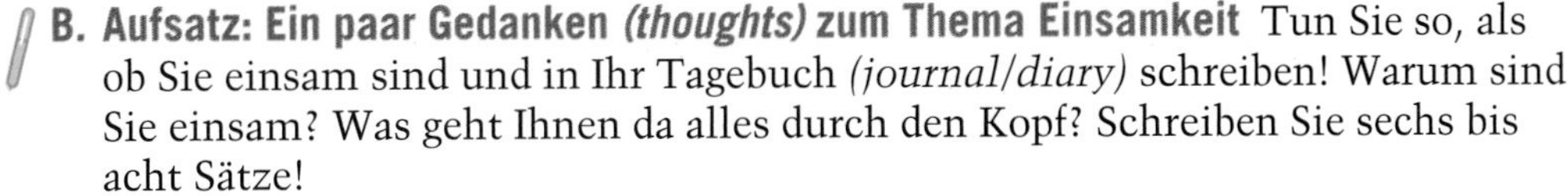

B. Aufsatz: Ein paar Gedanken *(thoughts)* zum Thema Einsamkeit Tun Sie so, als ob Sie einsam sind und in Ihr Tagebuch *(journal/diary)* schreiben! Warum sind Sie einsam? Was geht Ihnen da alles durch den Kopf? Schreiben Sie sechs bis acht Sätze!

Rückschau

Kapitelwortschatz

Hauptwörter

die Abfahrt, -en	*departure*
der Absender, -	*return address*
die Adresse, -n	*address*
die Ankunft, ¨e	*arrival*
die (Ansichts)karte, -n	*(picture) postcard*
der Aufenthalt, -e	*stopover, stay*
die Bahn, -en	*railway, train*
der Bahnsteig, -e	*platform*
der Brief, -e	*letter*
der Briefkasten, ¨	*mailbox*
die Briefmarke, -n	*stamp*
das Dorf, ¨er	*village*
die E-Mail, -s	*e-mail*
die Fahrkarte, -n	*ticket*
der Fahrplan, ¨e	*schedule*
die Fahrt, -en	*trip, drive*
der Flug, ¨e	*flight*
der Flughafen, ¨	*airport*
das Flugzeug, -e	*plane*
die Gegend, -en	*area, region*
die Geschichte, -n	*history; story*
das Gleis, -e	*track*
das Handy, -s	*cell phone*
die (Hin- und) Rückfahrkarte, -n	*round-trip ticket*
das Paket, -e	*package, parcel*
die Post	*post office, mail*
das Postfach, ¨er	*PO box*
die Postleitzahl, -en	*zip code*
die Reise, -n	*trip*
der Schalter, -	*counter, ticket window*
die SMS, -	*text message* (on cell phone)
das Telefon, -e	*(tele)phone*
die Telefonkarte, -n	*telephone card*
die Telefonnummer, -n	*telephone number*
die Vorwahl, -en	*area code*
der Wagen, -	*car; railroad car*
der Zug, ¨e	*train*

Verben

ab·fahren (von)	*to leave, depart* (*from*)
ab·fliegen (von)	*to take off, fly* (*from*)
aus·steigen	*to get off/out*
beschreiben	*to describe*
besuchen	*to visit*
ein·steigen	*to get on/in*
erzählen	*to tell*
fehlen	*to be missing / lacking*
fliegen	*to fly*
hinauf·fahren	*to go / drive up* (*to*)
landen	*to land*
schicken	*to send*
telefonieren	*to call up, phone*
um·steigen	*to change* (*trains,* etc.)
weiter·fahren	*to drive on, keep on driving*

Adjektive

herrlich	*wonderful(ly), great*

Präpositionen

(an)statt (+ gen.)	*instead of*
trotz (+ gen.)	*in spite of*
während (+ gen.)	*during*
wegen (+ gen.)	*because of*

Zeitausdrücke

Abend	*evening* (*6–10* P.M.)
Anfang / Ende der Woche	*at the beginning / end of the week*
diese Woche	*this week*
einen Monat	*for one month*
eines Tages	*one day, some day*
früh, Morgen	*early, morning*
gestern	*yesterday*
heute	*today*
heute Morgen / heute früh	*this morning, today in the morning*
in einer Dreiviertelstunde	*in three-quarters of an hour*
in einer halben Stunde	*in half an hour*
in einer Viertelstunde	*in a quarter of an hour*
jährlich	*yearly, annually*
jeden Tag	*every day; each day*
Mittag	*noon* (*12–2* P.M.)
Mitte des Monats	*in the middle of the month*
monatlich	*monthly*
Montagmorgen	*Monday morning*
montagmorgens	*Monday mornings*
montags	*Mondays*
morgen	*tomorrow*
morgens	*mornings, in the morning* (in general)
morgen früh	*tomorrow morning*
Nachmittag	*afternoon* (*2–6* P.M.)
Nacht	*night* (*after 10* P.M.)
täglich	*daily*
übermorgen	*the day after tomorrow*
vorgestern	*the day before yesterday*
Vormittag	*midmorning* (*9* A.M.*–noon*)
wöchentlich	*weekly*
zwei Wochen	*for two weeks*

Verschiedenes

Ach du meine Güte!	*My goodness!*
Das freut mich (für dich).	*I'm happy (for you).*
Das ist doch egal. / Das macht nichts.	*It's all the same to me.; That doesn't matter.*
Das sieht dir ähnlich.	*That's typical of you.*
Gott sei Dank!	*Thank God!*
mit dem Zug / der Bahn fahren	*to go by train*
Na und?	*So what?*
wessen?	*whose?*

Zum Schluss

1. **Wer ist wer?**
   a. **Ein Foto** Find a picture with a group of people in it: your friends, your family, your classmates. Describe the picture in detail to a classmate. Who is in the picture? What are they wearing? Who is beside (in front of, behind) whom? How do they relate to each other? Remember what you know about two-way prepositions (**vor, neben, zwischen, hinter**) and be sure to use the genitive to describe how the people in the photo are related.
   b. **Eine Fernsehfamilie** Now find a picture of a family from a TV show you like. Explain how the people in the family are related, but don't show the picture. How many relationships can you describe? See if your classmate can guess the family you are talking about!

2. **Meine Reise** You were traveling to a small town, so you used a combination of planes and trains to get there. A few things did not go as planned, but you made the best of it and arrived at your destination. Use the words below as a starting place to tell a story about a trip you took. Be creative!

(an)statt	der Aufenthalt
ab·fahren (von)	die Abfahrt
ab·fliegen (von)	die Ankunft
aus·steigen	der Fahrplan
außerdem	der Flug
ein·steigen	das Gleis
leider	der Schalter
mitten in	der Zug
noch nicht	die Fahrkarte
sogar	die Fahrt
trotz	die Reise
um·steigen	der Bahnsteig
während	der Zug
wegen	die Bahn
weiter·fahren	das Flugzeug

3. **Wann treffen wir uns?**
   a. **Wann genau?** You and your friends are trying to find a time to meet as a study group. Write email exchanges or text messages back and forth as you clear up your schedules. Everyone should explain when he or she is free to meet, then agree on a time you will get together. Here are some details to get you started.

      MARIA: can meet in the afternoon, but not on Wednesdays from 4–6 P.M.

      DIRK: can meet on Monday, Wednesday, or Thursday anytime after 2 P.M.

      ANJA: has to be home in the evenings, and has plans next Thursday afternoon.

      YOU: want to keep Mondays and Fridays free, so you can take weekend trips.

   b. **Noch einmal!** Now write an email to your professor, who asked to be informed about who is working with whom, and tell him/her who is in your study group and when you will be meeting.

iLrn **Onlineaktivitäten** Visit iLrn for online activities related to this chapter. There you will find additional resources, such as a memory game (**Gedächtnisspiel**), a crossword puzzle (**Kreuzworträtsel**), audio flash cards (**Vokabelblitz**), a tutorial quiz (**Mini-Quiz**), and the active vocabulary (**Wortschatz**) for this chapter.

Kapitel 9

Freizeit und Gesundheit

Lernziele In this chapter you will learn about:

Zum Thema

Hobbies, leisure activities, and physical fitness

Fokus

Sports and clubs, telephone customs, idioms, and vacationing

Struktur

- Endings of preceded adjectives
- Reflexive verbs
- Infinitives with **zu**

Einblicke

Lesetext: Freizeit—Lust oder Frust?
Literatur: Johann Wolfgang von Goethe, „Erinnerung" / Tabea Vahlenkamp, „möglichkeiten"

Rückschau

Kapitelwortschatz
Zum Schluss

RESSOURCEN

iLrn

Video
Audio
SAM

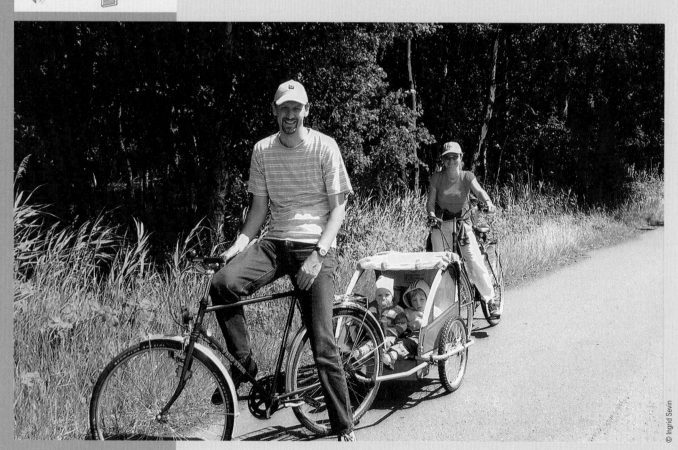

Radtour mit der Familie

Vorschau Sports and Clubs in the German-Speaking Countries

Sports are very popular in Germany, Austria, and Switzerland, not only with spectators (professional sports are big business, as they are everywhere else) but also with amateur athletes. The German Sports Federation **(Deutscher Olympischer Sportbund)** boasts 28 million members in 91,000 affiliated sports clubs **(Sportvereine).** Under the slogan "Sport tut gut—Beweg dich," it sponsors such programs as "Deutsches Sportabzeichen" and "Richtig fit" with competitions in running, swimming, cycling, and skiing. Millions of people participate in these events every year. Soccer **(Fußball)** is as important in Europe as football, baseball, and basketball are in the United States. Germany hosted the 2006 Soccer World Cup; in 2008 Austria and Switzerland co-hosted the European Championships. Other popular sports are **Handball,** ice hockey, roller skating, and inline skating. Golf and tennis are also becoming more popular, but one usually needs to belong to a club in order to play.

High schools and universities are not involved in competitive sports; for that purpose, students usually join a sports club. Such organizations are basically autonomous, but the government provides some support for those with insufficient funds. This applies particularly to the former East Germany, where an effort has been made to set up independent clubs. In the 1970s and 1980s, these clubs did not exist; instead, the East German government spent a great deal of money on making sports accessible to every citizen, seeking out young talents early and training them in special boarding schools—a practice that led to considerable success in the Olympics. In addition to sports clubs, there are associations promoting all kinds of leisure activities, ranging from dog breeding and pigeon racing to gardening, crafts, music, and dancing. Clubs devoted to regional traditions and dress **(Trachtenvereine)** and centuries-old rifle associations **(Schützenvereine)**—with their own emblems, uniforms, and ceremonial meetings—keep old traditions alive and draw thousands to their annual festivals.

You might ask students if they are familiar with any of the great athletes in the German-speaking countries. Also, in the *Zum Schreiben* section of the *Arbeitsbuch* (SAM), there is a report on bike tours. Ask students where they can go biking in their own community and where one could take actual bike trips like the one mentioned in the *Arbeitsbuch*.

Fragen: 1. Wo ist dieser Marathonlauf? 2. Was sehen Sie alles auf dem Bild? 3. Wie ist das Wetter an diesem Tag? 3. Gibt es solche Marathonläufe auch in Ihrer Stadt? Wenn ja, wann und wo? 4. Haben Sie schon einmal an einem Marathon teilgenommen *(participated)*? Warum (nicht)?

Marathonlauf durchs Brandenburger Tor in Berlin

Zum Thema

Gespräche

Am Telefon

Warm-ups: 1. **Was ist das Gegenteil von** aufmachen, einsteigen, sitzen, Abfahrt, Eingang, Tag, geöffnet, weit, leicht, herrlich, immer, ein paar, Glück gehabt? 2. **Antworten Sie mit dem Genitiv!** Was ist der Name Ihrer Eltern / Geschwister? Wie heißen die Tage der Woche? die Monate des Jahres? 3. **Kombinieren Sie Montag mit etwas anderem! (z. B. Montag früh, Montagmorgen . . .)!**

FRAU SCHMIDT Hier Schmidt.
ANNEMARIE Guten Tag, Frau Schmidt. Ich bin's, Annemarie.
FRAU SCHMIDT Tag, Annemarie!
ANNEMARIE Ist Thomas da?
FRAU SCHMIDT Nein, tut mir leid. Er ist gerade zur Post gegangen.
ANNEMARIE Ach so. Können Sie ihm sagen, dass ich heute Abend nicht mit ihm ausgehen kann?
FRAU SCHMIDT Natürlich. Was ist denn los?
ANNEMARIE Ich bin krank. Mir tut der Hals weh und ich habe Kopfschmerzen.
FRAU SCHMIDT Das tut mir leid. Gute Besserung!
ANNEMARIE Danke. Auf Wiederhören!
FRAU SCHMIDT Wiederhören!

As in previous chapters, you could have students act out the dialogues with a partner.

Bis gleich!

YVONNE Bei Mayer.
DANIELA Hallo, Yvonne! Ich bin's, Daniela.
YVONNE Tag, Daniela! Was gibt's?
DANIELA Nichts Besonderes. Hast du Lust, Squash zu spielen oder schwimmen zu gehen?
YVONNE Squash? Nein, danke. Ich habe noch Muskelkater von vorgestern. Mir tut alles weh.
DANIELA Lahme Ente! Wie wär's mit Schach?
YVONNE Okay, das klingt gut. Kommst du zu mir?
DANIELA Ja, bis gleich!

A. Alles verstanden?
1. Annemaries Freund heißt . . . 2. Annemarie spricht mit . . . 3. Thomas ist nicht zu Hause, weil . . . 4. Annemarie kann nicht mit ihm . . . 5. Annemaries Hals . . . 6. Sie hat auch . . . 7. Am Ende eines Telefongesprächs sagt man . . . 8. Danielas Freundin heißt . . . 9. Yvonne will nicht Squash spielen, weil . . . 10. Sie hat aber Lust, . . .

A: 1. Thomas 2. seiner Mutter / Frau Schmidt 3. er zur Post gegangen ist 4. ausgehen 5. tut (ihr) weh 6. Kopfschmerzen 7. (Auf) Wiederhören! / Bis gleich! usw. 8. Yvonne 9. sie Muskelkater hat 10. Schach zu spielen

B. Jetzt sind Sie dran! Diesmal sind Sie am Telefon. Sie rufen Ihren Freund / Ihre Freundin an und fragen, ob er/sie Lust hat, etwas zu tun. Aber Sie haben Pech, denn er/sie hat schon Pläne *(plans)* oder ist krank. Wechseln Sie sich ab!

S1 Hier . . .
S2 Tag, . . . ! Ich bin's, . . . Sag mal, hast du Lust, . . . ?
S1 Nein, ich kann nicht . . .
S2 Warum nicht? Was ist denn los?
S1 Ach, ich bin krank. Mir tut/tun . . . weh.
S2 Hoffentlich . . . Gute Besserung!
S1 . . .

Wortschatz 1

Der Körper, - *(body)*

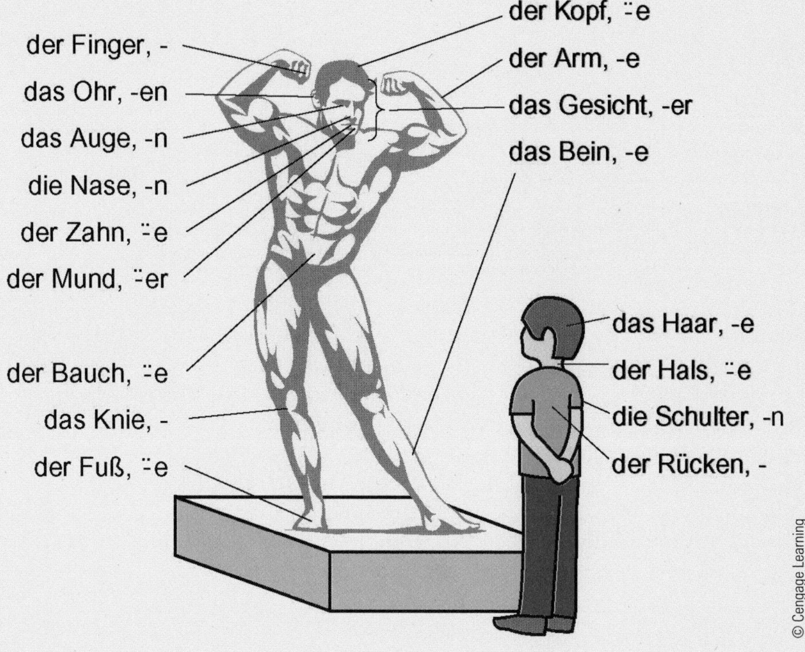

If students ask: *bosom* **der Busen, -;** *bottom / behind* **der Po(po), -s / Hintern, -;** *cheek* **die Backe, -n;** *chest / breast* **die Brust, ¨-e;** *chin* **das Kinn;** *elbow* **der Ell(en)bogen, -;** *eyebrow* **die Augenbraue, -n;** *eyelash* **die Wimper, -n;** *fingernail* **der Fingernagel, ¨-;** *forehead* **die Stirn;** *index finger* **der Zeigefinger, -;** *shoulder* **die Schulter, -n;** *stomach* **der Magen, -;** *thumb* **der Daumen, -;** *toe* **die Zehe, -n;** *toenail* **der Fußnagel, ¨-;** *tongue* **die Zunge, -n**

Haare is usually used in the plural. **Knie** *(sg.)* and **Knie** *(pl.)* are spelled alike but are pronounced differently: [i:] **das Knie,** BUT: [ie:] **die Knie.**

Das Hobby, -s *(hobby)*

angeln	*to fish*
backen (bäckt), gebacken	*to bake*
faulenzen	*to be lazy*
fern·sehen (sieht fern), ferngesehen	*to watch TV*
fotografieren	*to take pictures*
kochen	*to cook*
(Freunde) treffen (trifft), getroffen	*to meet, get together (with friends)*
malen	*to paint*
sammeln	*to collect*
schwimmen, ist geschwommen	*to swim*
wandern, ist gewandert	*to hike*

Verb + *complement*

Schach spielen	*to play chess*
Rad fahren (fährt), ist gefahren	*to bicycle, bike*
Ski laufen (läuft), ist gelaufen	*to ski*
Sport treiben, getrieben	*to engage in sports*

Verb + **gehen**

schwimmen gehen, ist gegangen	*to go swimming*
Ski laufen gehen, ist gegangen	*to go skiing*
spazieren gehen, ist gegangen	*to go for a walk* (lit.: *walking*)

sammeln: ich samm(e)le, du sammelst, er sammelt, wir sammeln, ihr sammelt, sie sammeln. Also like **sammeln: bummeln, angeln, wechseln, tun**

Verb + *complement:* In expressions, such as **Rad fahren, Ski laufen, Schach spielen,** and **Sport treiben,** the verb functions as V1, while the other word (the verb complement) functions as V2. **Ich spiele gern Schach. Sie fährt viel Rad. Er läuft oft Ski. Ihr treibt nie Sport.**

Verb + **gehen:** In these constructions, **gehen** functions as V1 and the other verb or verb + complement as V2, e.g., **Wir gehen gern schwimmen / Ski laufen.** The same holds true for **spazieren gehen,** and could be done with verbs like **angeln, Rad fahren.**

Another way of saying **Ich gehe Ski laufen** is **Ich gehe zum Skilaufen.** In that case, **Skilaufen** is capitalized and one word, since it is used as a noun.

If students ask: *cello* **das Cello, -s;** *coin* **die Münze, -n;** *drum* **die Trommel, -n;** *organ* **die Orgel, -n;** *recorder* **die Blockflöte, -n;** *stein* **der Bierkrug, ¨-e;** *trumpet* **die Trompete, -n;** *violin* **die Geige, -n**

Die Freizeit ***(leisure time)***

der Fußball	*soccer*
Sport	*sport; sports, athletics*
das Klavier, -e	*piano*
Spiel, -e	*game*
die CD, -s	*CD*
DVD, -s	*DVD*
Gitarre, -n	*guitar*
Idee, -n	*idea*
Karte, -n	*card*

NOTE: **Ich habe (keine) Lust, Schach zu spielen.** *I (don't) feel like playing chess.* / **Ich habe Kopfschmerzen.** *I have a headache.* / **Mir tut der Hals weh.** *My throat hurts. I have a sore throat.*

Like **nichts Besonderes: nichts Neues, nichts Schlechtes** OR **etwas Besonderes, etwas Schönes**

Verschiedenes

gesund / krank	*healthy / sick, ill*
fantastisch	*fantastic, great, super*
andere	*others*
die anderen	*the others*
zuerst / danach	*first / after that, then*
Lust haben zu . . .	*to feel like (doing something)*
Schmerzen haben	*to have pain, hurt*
weh·tun (tut weh), wehgetan	*to hurt*
Was ist (denn) los?	*What's the matter?; What's going on?*
nichts Besonderes	*nothing special*
Nein, das geht (heute) nicht.	*No, that won't work (today).*
Ach so.	*Oh, I see.*
Ja, sicher.	*Yes, sure.*
Bis bald!	*See you soon!*
Bis gleich!	*See you in a few minutes!*

Zum Erkennen: Ich bin's. *(It's me.)*; Ich habe Muskelkater. *(My muscles are sore.)*; Lahme Ente! *(someone with no pep,* lit. *lame duck)*; Wie wär's mit . . . ? *(How about . . . ?)*; zu mir *(to my place)*; AUCH: der Dialog, -e; das reflexive Verb, -en; das Reflexivpronomen, -

Fokus Telephone Etiquette

When answering the phone, German speakers usually identify themselves with their last names. If you were answering your own phone, you would say **(Hier) . . .** (plus your own name). If you were answering someone else's phone, say, Ms. Schmidt's, you would say **(Hier) bei Schmidt.** Only afterward do you say **Guten Tag!** or **Hallo!** If you are the one making the call, you usually give your own name before asking for the person you are trying to reach: **Guten Abend, hier spricht . . .** (or **Ich bin's, . . .). Kann ich bitte mit . . . sprechen?** or **Ich möchte gern . . . sprechen.** The answer might be **Einen Moment bitte!** or **. . . ist nicht da. Kann ich ihm/ihr etwas ausrichten** *(take a message for him/her)*? When ending a phone conversation formally, say **Auf Wiederhören!** (lit. *until we hear each other again*). Friends may simply say **Tschüss!, Ciao!, Mach's gut!, Bis bald!,** or **Bis gleich!**

Übungen zum Thema

A. Was tun Sie, wenn . . . ? Beenden Sie *(Complete)* die Sätze mit einer Antwort von der Liste oder mit Ihren eigenen Worten!

_____ 1. Wenn ich Kopfschmerzen habe, . . .

_____ 2. Wenn mir die Füße wehtun, . . .

_____ 3. Wenn mir der Bauch wehtut, . . .

_____ 4. Wenn ich Halsschmerzen habe, . . .

_____ 5. Wenn mir die Augen wehtun, . . .

_____ 6. Wenn ich krank bin, . . .

_____ 7. Wenn ich gestresst bin, . . .

_____ 8. Wenn ich nicht schlafen kann, . . .

a. bleibe ich im Bett.
b. esse ich Nudelsuppe / nichts.
c. gehe ich ins Bett / in die Sauna.
d. gurgele *(gargle)* ich.
e. gehe ich nicht spazieren.
f. mache ich die Augen zu.
g. meditiere ich.
h. nehme ich Aspirin / Vitamin C.
i. sehe ich nicht fern.
j. rufe ich einen Arzt *(doctor)* an.
k. trinke ich Tee.
l. trinke ich heiße Milch / Zitrone mit Honig *(honey)*.
m. . . .

B. Was tust du gern in deiner Freizeit? Lesen Sie mit Ihrem Partner / Ihrer Partnerin die drei Listen und kreuzen Sie an *(check)*, was Sie gern in Ihrer Freizeit tun! Fragen Sie danach andere in der Klasse und finden Sie heraus, was sie angekreuzt haben! Welche fünf Aktivitäten sind besonders populär?

BEISPIEL S1 Ich lese gern. Und du?
S2 Ich auch. Ich spiele aber auch gern Videospiele. Und du?
S1 Ich nicht. Ich spiele lieber *(rather)* . . .

Ich . . . gern

❑ backen
❑ essen
❑ faulenzen
❑ joggen
❑ kochen
❑ lesen
❑ malen
❑ reisen
❑ schwimmen
❑ tanzen
❑ im Internet surfen
❑ . . .

Ich gehe gern . . .

❑ angeln
❑ inlineskaten
❑ Rollschuh laufen *(roller skating)*
❑ Schlittschuh laufen *(ice skating)*
❑ (Wasser)ski laufen
❑ spazieren
❑ wandern
❑ ins Kino
❑ zum Fitnessstudio
❑ . . .

Ich spiele gern . . .

❑ Basketball
❑ Fußball
❑ Golf
❑ Tennis
❑ Tischtennis
❑ Karten
❑ Computerspiele
❑ Videospiele
❑ Gitarre
❑ Klavier
❑ Schach
❑ . . .

In case you are curious: *bowling* **kegeln**, *gliding* **segelfliegen**, *horseback riding* **reiten**, *mountain climbing* **bergsteigen**, *sailing* **segeln**, *windsurfing* **windsurfen**, *badminton* **Federball**, *volleyball* **Volleyball**, *miniature golf* **Minigolf**, *flute* **(die) Flöte**, *the drums* **(das) Schlagzeug**

Germans also say **Ping-Pong** instead of **Tischtennis.** The word **Federball** is generally used for recreation and **Badminton** for competitions. **Rollschuhlaufen** is plain *roller skating; in-line skating is* **Inlineskating** or **Rollerblading.** *To rollerblade =* **inlineskaten** (*I like to go rollerblading.* **Ich gehe gern inlineskaten.**)

© Jonathan Larsen/Shutterstock

Die Europäer lieben ihren Fußball.

C. Interview Fragen Sie einen Nachbarn / eine Nachbarin, . . . !

1. ob er/sie als Kind ein Instrument gelernt hat; wenn ja, welches Instrument und ob er/sie es heute noch spielt
2. ob er/sie gern singt; wenn ja, was und wo (in der Dusche oder Badewanne, im Auto oder Chor)
3. was für Musik er/sie schön findet (klassische oder moderne Musik, Jazz, Hip-Hop-, Rock-, Pop-, Country- oder Volksmusik)
4. ob er/sie viel fernsieht; wenn ja, wann gewöhnlich und was
5. wie lange er/sie jeden Tag vor dem Computer sitzt und warum
6. wie viele SMS er/sie jeden Tag schreibt
7. ob er/sie Twitter benutzt *(uses)*

Aussprache: l, z

A. Laute

For further review, see the Summary of Pronunciation in the front of this book. Study Part III, subsections A.8–10.

1. [l] **l**aut, **l**eicht, **l**ustig, **l**eider, Ha**l**s, Ge**l**d, ma**l**en, spie**l**en, f**l**iegen, ste**ll**en, schne**ll**, Ba**ll**, he**ll**
2. [ts] zählen, zeigen, zwischen, zurück, zuerst, Zug, Zahn, Schmerzen, Kerzen, Einzelzimmer, Pizza, bezahlen, tanzen, jetzt, schmutzig, trotz, kurz, schwarz, Salz, Schweiz, Sitzplatz

B. Wortpaare

Optional tongue twister: **Zehn zahme Ziegen zogen zehn Zentner Zucker zum zehnten Zwickauer Zug.** *(Ten tame goats pulled ten centners [1,000 kilos] of sugar to the tenth train from Zwickau.)*

1. *felt* / Feld
2. *hotel* / Hotel
3. *plots* / Platz
4. Schweiß / Schweiz
5. seit / Zeit
6. so / Zoo

Hörverständnis

Beim Arzt Hören Sie zu, warum Frau Heller zum Arzt *(doctor)* geht und was er ihr sagt! Ergänzen Sie die Aussagen unten!

Zum Erkennen: passieren *(to happen)*; der Ellbogen, - *(elbow)*; hoch·legen *(to put up [high])*; die (Schmerz)tablette, -n *([pain] pill)*

1. Frau Heller geht zum Arzt, weil ihr ___das Knie___ wehtut.
2. Sie ist mit ihrer Freundin im Harz ___Ski laufen___ gegangen.
3. Am letzten Tag ist sie ___gefallen___.
4. Sie darf ein paar Tage nicht ___laufen___.
5. Sie soll das Bein ___hochlegen___.
6. Der Arzt gibt ihr ein paar ___Schmerztabletten___ mit.
7. Wenn Frau Heller in einer Woche immer noch Schmerzen hat, soll sie ___zurückkommen___.
8. Sie kann bald wieder ___schwimmen___ oder ___spazieren gehen___.

Fokus Some Idiomatic Expressions

As in the case of **Lahme Ente!** in the dialogue, names of animals are frequently used in everyday idiomatic expressions to characterize people—often in a derogatory way: **Ich Esel!** *(donkey)* or **Du Affe!** *(monkey)* for someone who made a mistake or behaves in a silly manner; **Du hast einen Vogel!** or **Bei dir piept's!** *(You're cuckoo.)*; **Fauler Hund!** *(dog)* for someone lazy; **Du Brummbär!** *(grumbling bear)* for someone grumpy; **(Das ist) alles für die Katz'!** if everything is useless or in vain; **Du Schwein!** *(pig)* for someone who is messy or a scoundrel. **Schwein haben,** however, has quite a different meaning: *to be lucky*. In addition, names of food are used in special expressions: **Das ist doch Käse!** *(That's nonsense!)*; **Das ist mir Wurst!** *(I don't care!)*; **Es ist alles in Butter!** *(Everything is O.K.!)*; **Das ist doch Sahne!** *(That's O.K.!)*

Schwein muss man haben!

Struktur

For a list of ***der***- and ***ein***-words, see Chapter 7.

You could practice the declension with other examples: **der lange Hals, das lange Bein, die lange Nase; der junge Mann, das junge Mädchen, die junge Frau; der große Fernseher, das große Radio, die große Gitarre**

9.1 Endings of adjectives preceded by *der*- and *ein*-words

1. PREDICATE ADJECTIVES (that is, adjectives that don't precede the noun they refer to) and ADVERBS do not have endings.

Willi ist schnell.	*Willi is quick.*
Willi fährt schnell.	*Willi drives fast.*

2. However, adjectives preceding a noun (ATTRIBUTIVE ADJECTIVES) do have endings that vary according to the type of article that precedes it and according to the noun's case, gender, and number.

Der schnell**e** Fahrer *(m.)* ist mein Bruder.	*The fast driver is my brother.*
Mein Bruder ist ein schnell**er** Fahrer.	*My brother is a fast driver.*
Er hat ein schnell**es** Auto *(n.).*	*He has a fast car.*

   If you look over the two tables below, you will readily see that there are only four different adjective endings: **-e, -er, -es,** and **-en.** Furthermore, the **-en** ending predominates; it is used in the singular masculine accusative and in all datives, genitives, and plurals.

   a. Adjectives preceded by a DEFINITE ARTICLE or **der**-word:

	MASCULINE			NEUTER			FEMININE			PLURAL		
nom.	der	neu**e**	Wagen	das	neu**e**	Auto	die	neu**e**	Farbe	alle	neu**en**	Ideen
acc.	den	neu**en**	Wagen	das	neu**e**	Auto	die	neu**e**	Farbe	alle	neu**en**	Ideen
dat.	dem	neu**en**	Wagen	dem	neu**en**	Auto	der	neu**en**	Farbe	allen	neu**en**	Ideen
gen.	des	neu**en**	Wagens	des	neu**en**	Autos	der	neu**en**	Farbe	aller	neu**en**	Ideen

   b. Adjectives preceded by an INDEFINITE ARTICLE or **ein**-word:

	MASCULINE			NEUTER			FEMININE			PLURAL		
nom.	ein	neu**er**	Wagen	ein	neu**es**	Auto	eine	neu**e**	Farbe	meine	neu**en**	Ideen
acc.	einen	neu**en**	Wagen	ein	neu**es**	Auto	eine	neu**e**	Farbe	meine	neu**en**	Ideen
dat.	einem	neu**en**	Wagen	einem	neu**en**	Auto	einer	neu**en**	Farbe	meinen	neu**en**	Ideen
gen.	eines	neu**en**	Wagens	eines	neu**en**	Autos	einer	neu**en**	Farbe	meiner	neu**en**	Ideen

   If you compare the two preceding tables, you can see:

   - Adjectives preceded by a DEFINITE ARTICLE or any **der**-word have either an **-e** or **-en** ending.
   - Adjectives preceded by an INDEFINITE ARTICLE or any **ein**-word are the same as for the definite article/**der**-word in all cases and genders *except three:* in the masculine nominative, neuter nominative, and neuter accusative. In those three exceptions, the **ein**-word itself has no ending. The adjective ending identifies the gender of the noun by adding an **-er** for masculine nouns and an **-es** for neuter nouns.

The following tables show the adjective endings schematically.

AFTER *der*-WORDS

	MASC.	NEUT.	FEM.	PL.
nom.		-e		
acc.				
dat.		-en		
gen.				

AFTER *ein*-WORDS

	MASC.	NEUT.	FEM.	PL.
nom.	-er	-es	-e	
acc.		-es	-e	
dat.		-en		
gen.				

Or, to put it in another way, the endings are as follows:

- in the NOMINATIVE and ACCUSATIVE SINGULAR

—after **der, das, die,** and **eine** ——————→ **-e**

—after **ein**
- with masc. nouns: → **-er**
- with neut. nouns: → **-es**

- in *all other instances* ——————→ **-en**
  (incl. masc. accusative sg., all datives and genitives, and all plurals)

Der groß**e** Ball, das schön**e** Spiel und die neu**e** CD sind gut.

Das ist ein gut**er** Preis für so ein fantastisch**es** Geschenk.

Das sind keine teu(e)**ren** Geschenke.

NOTE: Adjective endings are not difficult to remember if you understand the basic principle involved: in the nominative and the accusative, one of the words preceding the noun must convey information about its gender, number, and case. If an article does not do so, then the adjective must. For example, **der** is clearly masculine nominative; therefore, the adjective can take the minimal ending **-e. Ein,** however, does not show gender or case; therefore, the adjective must do so.

When adding an ending, some adjectives such as **teuer** and **dunkel** drop the **-e-** in their stem: **Das Geschenk ist teuer. Das sind teu(e)re Geschenke. Das Zimmer ist dunkel. Das ist ein dunkles Zimmer.** In the case of **teuer,** dropping the **-e-** is optional.

3. If two or more adjectives precede a noun, all have the same ending.

Das sind keine groß**en**, teu(e)**ren** Geschenke.

© Ingrid Sevin

Übungen

A. Schlittschuhlaufen vor der Frankfurter Alten Oper Inge erzählt, was man auf diesem Bild sieht.

BEISPIEL Das ist mein **Bruder** Stefan mit seinen vier Kindern. (verrückt)
Das ist mein verrückter Bruder Stefan mit seinen vier Kindern.

A: 1. Alten 2. schnellen 3. große 4. kleines 5. schwarzgelben 6. blauen 7. billiger; ganze 8. schönen

1. Im Dezember gehen sie gern vor der **Oper** Schlittschuh laufen. (Alt)
2. Die zwei **Jungen** können es schon gut. (schnell)
3. Ihre **Schwester** läuft aber noch nicht so gut. (groß)
4. Sein **Mädchen** ist direkt hinter ihm bei der Mutter. (klein)
5. Eva steht auf einem **Pinguin** *(m.)* aus Plastik. (schwarzgelb)
6. Die **Schlittschuhe** haben sie natürlich geliehen *(rented)*. (blau)
7. Es ist wirklich ein **Spaß** *(m.)* für die **Familie.** (billig; ganz)
8. Wegen des **Wetters** sind sie lange da geblieben. (schön)

B: dieser braune Sessel; das lange Sofa; die kleine Lampe, diesen fantastischen Teppich, dieses supermoderne Bild; einem alten Geschäft, das interessante Geschäft; der nächsten Woche, diese schönen Möbel; solche alten Möbel

B. Die neue Wohnung Lesen Sie den Dialog mit den Adjektiven!

BEISPIEL Ist der Schrank neu? (groß)
Ist der große Schrank neu?

S1 Ist dieser Sessel bequem? (braun)
S2 Ja, und das Sofa auch. (lang)
S1 Die Lampe gefällt mir. (klein)
Woher hast du diesen Teppich? (fantastisch)
Und wo hast du dieses Bild gefunden? (supermodern)
S2 In einem Geschäft. (alt)
Wenn du willst, kann ich dir das Geschäft mal zeigen. (interessant)
S1 Während der Woche habe ich aber keine Zeit. (nächst-)
Sind diese Möbel teuer gewesen? (schön)
S2 Natürlich nicht. Für solche Möbel gebe ich nicht viel Geld aus. (alt)

C. Anja zeigt Jens ihr Zimmer. Jens stellt Fragen und kommentiert *(comments)*. Bilden Sie aus zwei Sätzen einen Satz!

BEISPIEL Woher kommt dieses Schachspiel? Es ist interessant.
Woher kommt dieses interessante Schachspiel?

1. Weißt du, was so ein Schachspiel kostet? Es ist chinesisch.
2. Bist du Schachspielerin? Spielst du gut? (*Add **eine!***)
3. Ich bin kein Schachspieler. Ich spiele nicht gut.
4. Woher hast du diese Briefmarkensammlung? Sie ist alt.
5. Mein Vater hat auch eine Sammlung. Sie ist groß.
6. Sammelst du solche Briefmarken auch? Sie sind normal.
7. Was machst du mit so einer Briefmarke? Sie ist doppelt *(double)*.
8. Darf ich diese Briefmarke haben? Sie ist ja doppelt!
9. Hast du diese Bilder gemacht? Sie sind toll.
10. Wer ist der Junge? Er ist klein.
11. Was für ein Gesicht! Es ist fantastisch!
12. Die Augen gefallen mir! Sie sind dunkelbraun.
13. Mit meiner Kamera ist das nicht möglich. Sie ist billig.
14. Und das hier ist ein Tennisspieler, nicht wahr? Er ist bekannt und kommt aus Deutschland.
15. Weißt du, dass wir gestern trotz des Wetters Fußball gespielt haben? Das Wetter ist schlecht gewesen.
16. Leider kann ich wegen meines Knies nicht mehr mitspielen. Das Knie ist kaputt.

C: 1. so ein chinesisches Schachspiel 2. eine gute Schachspielerin 3. kein guter Schachspieler 4. diese alte Briefmarkensammlung 5. eine große Sammlung 6. solche normalen Briefmarken 7. mit so einer doppelten Briefmarke 8. diese doppelte Briefmarke 9. diese tollen Bilder 10. der kleine Junge 11. was für ein fantastisches Gesicht 12. die dunkelbraunen Augen 13. mit meiner billigen Kamera 14. ein bekannter deutscher Tennisspieler 15. trotz des schlechten Wetters 16. wegen meines kaputten Knies.

D. Ist das nicht schön?

1. **Das finde ich auch.** Ihr Partner / Ihre Partnerin findet etwas besonders gut. Sagen Sie ihm/ihr, dass Sie das auch finden und reagieren Sie dann mit einer Frage oder einer Bemerkung *(comment)*!

BEISPIEL S1 Ist der Pullover nicht warm?
S2 Doch, das ist ein warmer Pullover.
Woher hast du den warmen Pullover?

a. Ist das Hemd nicht elegant?
b. Ist die Uhr nicht schön?
c. Ist der Hut *(hat)* nicht verrückt?

BEISPIEL S1 Ist das Hotel nicht gut?
S2 Ja, das ist ein gutes Hotel.
Wo hast du von diesem guten Hotel gehört?

d. Ist die Pension nicht super?
e. Ist der Gasthof nicht billig?
f. Ist das Restaurant nicht gemütlich?

BEISPIEL S1 Ist das alte Schloss nicht wunderbar?
S2 Ja, das ist ein altes, wunderbares Schloss.
Ich gehe gern in alte, herrliche Schlösser.

g. Ist der große Supermarkt nicht modern?
h. Ist das neue Geschäft nicht klein?
i. Ist die alte Kirche nicht interessant?

D.1: a. ein elegantes Hemd; das elegante Hemd b. eine schöne Uhr; die schöne Uhr c. ein verrückter Hut; der verrückte Hut d. eine super Pension; von dieser super Pension e. ein billiger Gasthof; von diesem billigen Gasthof f. ein gemütliches Restaurant; von diesem gemütlichen Restaurant g. ein großer, moderner Supermarkt; große, moderne Supermärkte h. ein neues, kleines Geschäft; neue, kleine Geschäfte i. eine alte, interessante Kirche; alte, interessante Kirchen

D: Alternatively, divide the class into two groups, one giving the first response and the other the second.

2. **Und jetzt sagen Sie etwas, was Sie gut oder nicht so gut finden!** Was sagt Ihr Partner / Ihre Partnerin dazu *(about it)*? Wechseln Sie sich ab!

   BEISPIEL S1 Ist unser Professor nicht gut?
   S2 Doch, er ist ein guter Professor.
   Von einem guten Professor kann man viel lernen.

E. Zwei Beschreibungen *(descriptions)*

Optional activity: Have students bring magazine photos to class. Then, as a group activity, have them describe their photos to classmates, using adjectives.

1. **Brittas Wohnung** Ergänzen Sie die fehlenden *(missing)* Adjektivendungen!
   Britta wohnt in einem toll_en___ Haus im neu_en___ Teil unserer schön_en___ Stadt. Ihre klein_e___ Wohnung liegt im neunt_en___ Stock eines modern_en___ Hochhauses *(high-rise)*. Sie hat eine praktisch_e___ Küche und ein gemütlich_es___ Wohnzimmer. Von dem groß_en___ Wohnzimmerfenster kann sie unsere ganz_e___ Stadt und die viel_en___ Brücken über dem breit_en___ *(wide)* Fluss sehen. Britta liebt ihre Wohnung wegen des schön_en___ Blickes *(view*, m.*)* und der billig_en___ Miete. In ihrem hell_en___ Schlafzimmer stehen ein einfach_es___ Bett und ein klein_er___ Nachttisch mit einer klein_en___ Nachttischlampe. An der Wand steht ein braun_er___ Schreibtisch und über dem braun_en___ Schreibtisch hängt ein lang_es___ Regal mit ihren viel_en___ Büchern. Britta findet ihre Wohnung schön.
2. **Meine Wohnung** Beschreiben Sie jetzt Ihre Wohnung oder Ihr Zimmer! Schreiben Sie 8–10 Sätze mit ein oder zwei Adjektiven in jedem Satz!

9.2 Reflexive verbs

If the subject and one of the objects of a sentence are the same person or thing, a reflexive pronoun is sometimes used for the object. In the English sentence, *I see my self in the picture*, the reflexive pronoun *myself* is the accusative object. *(Whom do I see? —Myself.)* In the sentence, *I am buying myself a CD*, the pronoun *myself* is the dative object. *(For whom am I buying the CD? —For myself.)*

In German, only the third person singular and plural have a special reflexive pronoun: **sich.** *The other persons use the accusative and dative forms of the personal pronouns, which you already know.*

Ich sehe meinen Bruder auf dem Bild.	*I see my brother in the picture.*
Ich sehe **mich** auf dem Bild.	*I see myself in the picture.*
Ich kaufe meinem Bruder eine CD.	*I buy my brother a CD.*
Ich kaufe **mir** eine CD.	*I buy myself a CD.*

nom.	**ich**	**du**	**er/es/sie**	**wir**	**ihr**	**sie**	**Sie**
acc.	mich	dich	sich	uns	euch	sich	sich
dat.	mir	dir					

1. Many verbs you have already learned can be used reflexively, although the English equivalent may not include a reflexive pronoun:

- The reflexive pronoun used as the DIRECT OBJECT (ACCUSATIVE):

sich fragen	*to wonder*	**sich treffen**	*to meet, gather*
sich legen	*to lie down*	usw.	
sich sehen	*to see oneself*		

Ich frage **mich**, ob das richtig ist.	*I wonder (ask myself) whether that's right.*
Ich lege **mich** aufs Sofa.	*I lie down on the sofa.*
Ich sehe **mich** im Spiegel.	*I see myself in the mirror.*

- The reflexive pronoun used as the INDIRECT OBJECT (DATIVE):

sich bestellen	*to order (for oneself)*	**sich nehmen**	*to take (for oneself)*
sich kaufen	*to buy (for oneself)*	**sich wünschen**	*to wish (for oneself)*
sich kochen	*to cook (for oneself)*	usw.	

Ich bestelle **mir** ein Eis.	*I am ordering ice cream (for myself).*
Ich koche **mir** ein Ei.	*I'm cooking myself an egg.*
Ich wünsche **mir** ein Auto.	*I'm wishing for a car (for myself).*

2. Some verbs are always reflexive, or are reflexive when they express a certain meaning. Here are some important verbs that you need to know.

sich an·hören	*to listen to*
sich an·sehen, angesehen	*to look at*
sich an·schauen	*to look at* (colloquial)
sich an·ziehen, angezogen	*to put on (clothing); to get dressed*
sich aus·ziehen, ausgezogen	*to take off (clothing); to get undressed*
sich um·ziehen, umgezogen	*to change (clothing); to get changed*
sich baden	*to take a bath*
sich beeilen	*to hurry*
sich duschen	*to take a shower*
sich erkälten	*to catch a cold*
sich (wohl) fühlen	*to feel (well)*
sich (hin·)legen	*to lie down*
sich kämmen	*to comb one's hair*
sich konzentrieren	*to concentrate*
sich die Zähne / die Nase putzen	*to clean/brush one's teeth / to blow one's nose*
sich rasieren	*to shave*
sich (hin·)setzen	*to sit down*
sich waschen (wäscht), gewaschen	*to wash (oneself)*

Setz dich (hin)!	*Sit down.*
Warum müsst ihr euch beeilen?	*Why do you have to hurry?*
Ich fühle mich nicht wohl.	*I don't feel well.*
Letzte Woche hat sie sich erkältet.	*Last week she caught a cold.*
Wir treffen uns mit Freunden.	*We're meeting with friends.*

Since only the 1st and 2nd person singular distinguish between dative and accusative by form, they are stressed in examples and exercises.

Note that **treffen** *(to meet)* can be used with or without a reflexive pronoun: **Ich *treffe* ein *paar* Freunde.** BUT: **Ich *treffe mich mit* ein paar Freunden.**

Optional practice: Was wünschst du dir zum Geburtstag? z. B. **Ich wünsche mir eine Uhr. Und du?**

It is important for students to realize that reflexive pronouns play exactly the same role as nouns or personal pronouns in a sentence, i.e., they function as accusative (direct) objects, dative (indirect) objects, or objects of prepositions. Remind students not to confuse **sich legen** *(to lie down)* and **liegen** *(to be lying down)*, or **sich setzen** *(to sit down)* and **sitzen** *(to be sitting)*.

Students might find it amusing if you teach them the following verse to the melody from the "Volga Boatman": **Zieht euch warm an, zieht euch warm an, denn die Kälte greift den Darm an** (attacks the intestines)!

- With some of these verbs, the reflexive pronoun may be either the accusative or the dative object. If there are two objects, then the person (the reflexive pronoun) is in the dative and the thing is in the accusative.

Ich wasche **mich.**	*I wash myself.*
Ich wasche **mir** die Haare.	*I wash my hair.*
Ich ziehe **mich** an.	*I'm getting dressed.*
Ich ziehe **mir** einen Pulli an.	*I'm putting on a sweater.*

3. In English, possessive adjectives are used to refer to parts of the body: *I'm washing my hands.* In German, however, the definite article is usually used together with the reflexive pronoun in the dative.

I'm washing ***my*** *hands.*	Ich wasche **mir die** Hände.
She's combing ***her*** *hair.*	Sie kämmt **sich die** Haare.
Brush ***your*** *teeth.*	Putz **dir die** Zähne!

REMEMBER: When there are two object pronouns, the accusative (direct object) pronoun comes before the dative (indirect) pronoun!

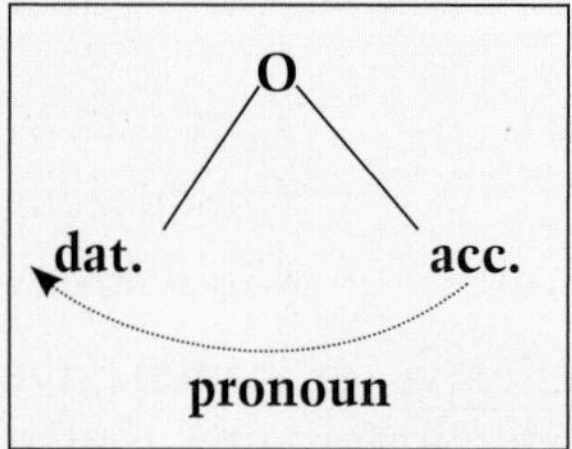

Ich wasche **mir die Hände.**	Du kämmst **dir die Haare.**
Ich wasche **sie mir.**	Du kämmst **sie dir.**

Übungen

F. Antworten Sie mit JA!

F.1: a. Ja, ziehen Sie sich / zieh dich noch um! b. Ja, kämmen Sie sich / kämm dir die Haare! c. Ja, kaufen Sie sich / kauf dir ein Auto! d. Ja, setzen Sie sich / setz dich jetzt! e. Ja, schauen Sie sich / schau dir die Bilder an!

1. **Singular**

BEISPIEL Soll ich mir die Hände waschen?
Ja, waschen Sie sich die Hände!
Ja, wasch dir die Hände!

a. Soll ich mich noch umziehen?
b. Soll ich mir die Haare kämmen?
c. Soll ich mir ein Auto kaufen?
d. Soll ich mich jetzt setzen?
e. Soll ich mir die Bilder anschauen?

F.2: a. Ja, mieten Sie sich / mietet euch ein Zimmer b. Ja, bauen Sie sich / baut euch ein Haus! c. Ja, setzen Sie sich / setzt euch in den Garten! d. Ja, hören Sie sich / hört euch die CDs an! e. Ja, sehen Sie sich / seht euch die Briefmarken an!

2. **Plural**

BEISPIEL Sollen wir uns die Hände waschen?
Ja, waschen Sie sich die Hände!
Ja, wascht euch die Hände!

a. Sollen wir uns ein Zimmer mieten?
b. Sollen wir uns ein Haus bauen?
c. Sollen wir uns in den Garten setzen?
d. Sollen wir uns die CDs anhören?
e. Sollen wir uns die Briefmarken ansehen?

G. Was fehlt? Ergänzen Sie die Reflexivpronomen!

1. Mensch, fühlst du __dich__ nicht wohl?
2. Doch, aber ich muss __mir__ mal schnell die Nase putzen.
3. Du hast __dich__ nicht warm genug angezogen und hast __dich__ mal wieder erkältet.
4. Kommt, Leute, setzt __euch__ !
5. Ich bestelle __mir__ ein Eis, und du?
6. Einen Moment, ich muss __mich__ konzentrieren! Ich will __mir__ erst mal die Speisekarte ansehen.
7. Mensch, schaut __euch__ das an! Max hat __sich__ eine neue Jacke gekauft.
8. So eine Jacke habe ich __mir__ schon lange gewünscht. Nur 400 Euro!
9. Hört __euch__ das an! Super billig!
10. Na und? In der Jacke fühle ich __mich__ wohl.

H. Hoppla, hier fehlt was! Was tun sie morgens? Finden Sie mit Ihrem Partner / Ihrer Partnerin heraus, was die anderen morgens tun! Einer von Ihnen sieht auf die Tabelle unten, der andere auf die Tabelle im Anhang, Teil 11.

S1

	ZUERST	DANN	DANACH
BIRTE	s. duschen s. die Haare waschen	s. kämmen s. die Zähne putzen	s. in die Küche setzen s. ein Ei kochen gemütlich frühstücken s. Musik anhören
OLLI	s. schnell anziehen joggen gehen	s. duschen s. umziehen s. vor den Spiegel stellen	s. die Haare kämmen s. rasieren Joghurt und Müsli essen
VERA	zu lange schlafen schnell aufstehen	s. schnell anziehen s. nicht kämmen	ihre Sachen nicht finden etwas zu essen mitnehmen
INGO	s. das Gesicht waschen s. eine Tasse Kaffee machen s. anziehen	s. an den Computer setzen s. die E-Mails ansehen	s. wieder hinlegen s. nicht beeilen

1. **So ist es bei Birte, Olli, Vera und Ingo.**

   BEISPIEL S1 Was macht Olli morgens?
   S2 Olli zieht sich schnell an und geht joggen. Dann . . .

2. **Und bei Ihnen?**

   BEISPIEL S1 Ich bin wie *(like)* . . . Zuerst . . . Danach . . .
   S2 Wirklich? Ich bin wie . . . Zuerst . . . Danach . . .

 **I. Und du, was machst du den ganzen Tag?** Fragen Sie Ihren Partner / Ihre Partnerin, was er/sie zu einer gewissen *(certain)* Tageszeit tut! Wenn möglich, benutzen Sie in Ihren Fragen und Antworten reflexive Verben! Machen Sie sich Notizen *(take notes)* und erzählen Sie dann der Klasse, was Sie herausgefunden haben!

BEISPIEL S1 Was machst du abends um zehn?
S2 Abends um zehn höre ich mir die Nachrichten an. Und du?
S1 Um diese Zeit lege ich mich ins Bett . . .

9.3 Infinitive with *zu*

English and German use infinitives with **zu** in much the same way.

Es ist interessant **zu reisen.**	*It's interesting to travel.*
Ich habe keine Zeit gehabt **zu essen.**	*I didn't have time to eat.*

Although the spelling reform makes it optional to separate the infinitive phrase from the main clause without a comma, we prefer to stick to the old rule for clarity's sake, i.e., keep the comma.

You might point out again that there is no **zu** after modals: Wir **müssen** jetzt **abfahren.**

1. In German, if the infinitive is combined with other sentence elements, such as a direct object or an adverbial phrase, a comma usually separates the infinitive phrase from the main clause.

   Haben Sie Zeit, eine Reise **zu** machen? — *Do you have time to take a trip?*

   Note that in German the infinitive comes at the end of the phrase.

2. If a separable-prefix verb is used, the **-zu-** is inserted between the prefix and the base verb.

   PREFIX + **zu** + VERB

   Es ist bald Zeit ab**zu**fahren. — *It's soon time to leave.*

3. Infinitive phrases beginning with **um** explain the purpose of the action described in the main clause.

   Ich gehe in die Küche, **um** einen Kuchen **zu** backen. — *(in order to bake a cake)*

   Rudi geht ins Badezimmer, **um** sich **zu** duschen. — *(in order to take a shower)*

Es ist so schön,
mal nichts zu tun
und sich vom Nichtstun
auszuruhen (relax).

© Beatrix Brockman

Übungen

J. Wie geht's weiter?

BEISPIEL Hast du Lust . . . ? (sich ein paar CDs anhören)
Hast du Lust, dir ein paar CDs anzuhören?

1. Dort gibt es viel . . . (sehen, tun, fotografieren, zeigen, essen)
2. Habt ihr Zeit . . . ? (ein Stündchen vorbeikommen, die neuen Nachbarn kennenlernen, ein bisschen faulenzen, euch noch eine DVD anschauen)
3. Es ist wichtig . . . (gut aufpassen, sich konzentrieren, Sprachen lernen, Freunde haben, Sport treiben)
4. Es ist interessant . . . (ihm zuhören, Bücher sammeln, mit der Bahn fahren, mit dem Flugzeug fliegen)
5. Es hat Spaß gemacht . . . (viel reisen, dort wandern, mit ihnen spazieren gehen, mit der Familie aufs Land fahren, Freunde anrufen)

J: 1. zu sehen, zu tun, zu fotografieren, zu zeigen, zu essen 2. vorbeizukommen, kennenzulernen, zu faulenzen, anzuschauen 3. aufzupassen, zu konzentrieren, zu lernen, zu haben, zu treiben 4. zuzuhören, zu sammeln, zu fahren, zu fliegen 5. zu reisen, zu wandern, spazieren zu gehen, zu fahren, anzurufen

J.5: In English, the present perfect isn't used very often in such constructions; the simple past is much more common.

K. So bin ich. Sprechen Sie mit den anderen über Ihre Hobbys und Ihre Freizeit! Benutzen Sie einen Infinitiv mit **zu**!

1. Ich habe keine Lust . . .
2. Ich habe nie Zeit . . .
3. Mir macht es Spaß . . .
4. Ich finde es wichtig . . .
5. Ich finde es langweilig *(boring)* . . .
6. Als *(As)* Kind hat es mir Spaß gemacht . . .
7. Ich brauche das Wochenende gewöhnlich, um . . .
8. Ich lerne Deutsch, um . . .

L. Das tue ich gern. Teilen Sie *(Divide)* die Klasse in zwei Mannschaften *(teams)*. Eine Mannschaft denkt an *(of)* ein Hobby. Die andere Mannschaft versucht *(tries)* dann mit bis zu 10 Fragen herauszufinden, was dieses Hobby ist. Nach 10 Fragen wechselt sich die Mannschaft ab!

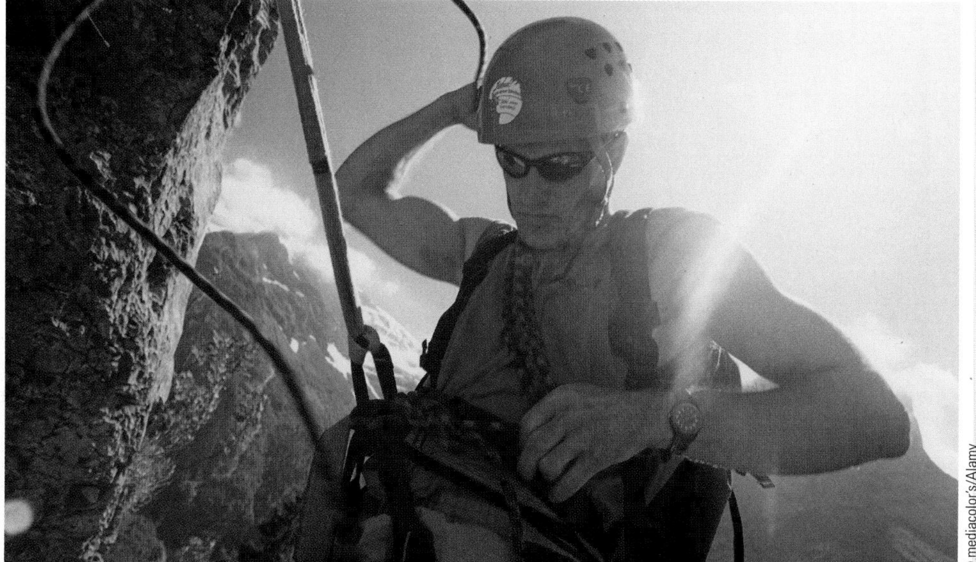

Kletterer (climber) in den Schweizer Alpen.

iLrn

Visit the ***Wie geht's?*** iLrn website for more review and practice of the grammar points you have just learned.

Zusammenfassung

M. Rotkäppchen und der Wolf Was fehlt?

Es hat einmal eine gut_e__ Mutter mit ihrem klein_en__ Mädchen in einem ruhig_en__ Dorf gewohnt. Sie hat zu ihrer klein_en__ Tochter gesagt: „Geh zu deiner alt_en__ Großmutter und bring ihr diese gut_e__ Flasche Wein und diesen frisch_en__ Kuchen! Aber du musst im dunkl_en__ Wald aufpassen, weil dort der groß_e__ bös_e__ *(bad)* Wolf wohnt." Das klein_e__ Mädchen ist mit seiner groß_en__ Tasche in den grün_en__ Wald gegangen. Auf dem dunkl_en__ Weg ist der bös_e__ Wolf gekommen und hat das klein_e__ Mädchen gefragt, wo seine alt_e__ Großmutter wohnt. Er hat dem gut_en__ Kind auch die wunderbar_en__ Blumen am Weg gezeigt. Dann hat der furchtbar_e__ Wolf die arm_e__ *(poor)* Großmutter gefressen *(devoured)* und hat sich in das bequem_e__ Bett der alt_en__ Frau gelegt. Das müd_e__ Rotkäppchen ist in das klein_e__ Haus gekommen und hat gefragt: „Großmutter, warum hast du so groß_e__ Ohren? Warum hast du so groß_e__ Augen? Warum hast du so einen groß_en__ Mund?" Da hat der bös_e__ Wolf geantwortet: „Dass ich dich besser fressen kann!" Nun *(Well)*, Sie kennen ja das Ende dieser bekannt_en__ Geschichte *(story*, f.*)*! Der Jäger *(hunter)* hat den dick_en__ Wolf getötet *(killed)* und dem klein_en__ Mädchen und seiner alt_en__ Großmutter aus dem Bauch des tot_en__ *(dead)* Wolfes geholfen.

Das Rotkäppchen-Haus in Oberammergau

N. Hallo, Max! Auf Deutsch bitte!

1. What have you been doing today?
2. Oh, nothing special. I listened to my old CDs.
3. Do you feel like going swimming (taking a swim)?
4. No, thanks. I don't feel well. I have a headache and my throat hurts. Call Frank.
5. Hello, Frank! Do you have time to go swimming?
6. No, I have to go to town **(in die Stadt)** in order to buy (myself) a new pair of slacks and a warm coat. Do you feel like coming along?
7. No, I already went shopping this morning. I bought (myself) a blue sweater and a white shirt.
8. Too bad. I've got to hurry.
9. Okay, I'm going to put on my swim trunks **(die Badehose)** and go swimming. Bye!

N: 1. Was hast du heute gemacht / getan? 2. Oh, nichts Besonderes. Ich habe mir meine alten CDs angehört. 3. Hast du Lust, schwimmen zu gehen? 4. Nein, danke. Ich fühle mich nicht wohl. Ich habe Kopfschmerzen und der Hals tut mir weh. Ruf (doch) Frank an! 5. Hallo, Frank! Hast du Zeit, schwimmen zu gehen? 6. Nein, ich muss in die Stadt (fahren / gehen), um mir eine neue Hose und einen warmen Mantel zu kaufen. Hast du Lust mitzukommen? 7. Nein, ich bin heute früh / Morgen schon einkaufen gewesen / gegangen. Ich habe mir einen blauen Pullover und ein weißes Hemd gekauft. 8. Schade! Ich muss mich beeilen. 9. Okay, gut, ich ziehe mir die Badehose an und gehe schwimmen. Tschüss! / Auf Wiederhören!

Urlaub an der Ostsee

Fokus Vacationing

In contrast to North Americans, who often prefer to take their vacation days bit by bit and combine them with holidays or a few long weekends, Germans are more likely to view their annual vacation as the year's major event. With relatively high incomes and a minimum of three to four weeks' paid vacation **(der Urlaub)** each year, Germans are among the world's greatest travelers. Many head north to the beaches of the North Sea **(die Nordsee)** or the Baltic Sea **(die Ostsee);** others head south to the warm beaches of southern France, Spain, Italy, Greece, Turkey, and North Africa. Still others opt for educational trips, such as language courses abroad or cultural tours. Favorite destinations include North America, Kenya, and Thailand.

Those who wish to stay closer to home may go swimming in a nearby **Schwimmbad** or lake, take a bike trip, venture out on a canoe or kayak tour, or spend a week on a farm in the countryside. With the pressures of everyday living, more and more people also opt for relaxation in one of the many spa hotels where both body and soul receive special attention.

Einblicke

Lesetext

In German, **Leben** is normally used only in the singular: Sport ist wichtig **in ihrem Leben** *(in her life / in their lives).*

Note the various uses of *other:* Das Leben auf dem Land ist **anders** *(different).* Es ist **ein anderes** *(a different kind of)* **Leben.** In *Wortschatz I*, you also learned two additional forms of *other:* Manche Leute leben gern in der Stadt, **andere** *(others)* gern auf dem Lande. Ich liebe es dort, aber **die anderen** *(the others)* finden es furchtbar.

Wortschatz 2

der Urlaub	*(paid) vacation*
das Leben	*life*
die Musik	*music*
ander-	*other, different*
anders	*different(ly)*
beliebt	*popular*
ganz	*whole, entire(ly), total(ly), all*
etwas (ganz) anderes	*something (totally) different*
(genauso) wie . . .	*(just) like . . .*
aus·geben (gibt aus), ausgegeben	*to spend (money)*
sich entspannen	*to relax*
sich erholen	*to recuperate*
erleben	*to experience*
sich fit halten (hält), gehalten	*to keep in shape*
sich langweilen	*to get / be bored*
vor·ziehen, vorgezogen	*to prefer*

Es kommt nicht darauf an,
dem Leben mehr Jahre
zu geben,
sondern
den Jahren mehr
Leben.

Vor dem Lesen

A: In the United States, people work an average of 230 days a year, in Canada 218 days. Average vacation time: US 13 days; Japan and Korea 25 days; Canada 26 days; England 28 days; Germany 30 days plus national holidays; Brazil 34 days.

A. Allerlei Fragen

1. Wie viele Stunden pro Woche *(per week)* arbeitet man in den USA / in Kanada? 2. Wie viele Wochen Urlaub hat man im Jahr? 3. Was tun die Amerikaner / Kanadier gern in ihrer Freizeit? 4. Was ist der Nationalsport hier? 5. Was sind andere populäre Sportarten? 6. Wohin fahren Sie gern in den Ferien? 7. Sind Ferien für Sie gewöhnlich Lust oder Frust *(frustration)*? Warum?

B. Ferientipps Finden Sie mit ihrem Partner / Ihrer Partnerin heraus, wo diese Kurorte *(health resorts)* sind, was sie zu bieten *(offer)* haben und was das kostet! Wenn Sie wollen, besuchen Sie den Kurort im Internet. Was klingt besonders interessant und warum?

KURORT	WO LIEGT DAS?	WAS BIETEN SIE DORT?	PREIS
BAD NENNDORF			
BAD REICHENHALL			
BAD TÖLZ			
OBERSTDORF			
ROTTACH-EGERN			

BERCHTESGADENER LAND

Gesund bleiben - Gesund werden!

Die sympathische Alpenstadt in Oberbayern bietet Ihnen alle Voraussetzungen: mildes Alpenklima, Sole, Kultur und jede Menge Freizeitvergnügen.

1 Woche Erlebnis-Urlaub:
Bad Reichenhall - Immer ein Gewinn!
ab € 225,–

Bad Reichenhall
Bayerisch Gmain
BAYERISCHES STAATSBAD

ALLGÄU

Oberstdorf Allgäu **im Tal der Täler...**

Heilklimatischer- und Kneippkurort. Allgäuer Alpen. Bergbahnen. 200 km Wanderwege. Freizeit- und Sporteinrichtungen. Kinderferien- und Jugendprogramm...

Wellness pur: "Schönheit und Pflege" - 7 Tage Ü/F pro Person
ab € 395,–

OBERBAYERN

Schön zu jeder Jahreszeit...

50 km südlich von München, am Fuße der bayerischen Alpen gelegen...

Ich weiß was ich will!

BAD TÖLZ
Ich mag dich!

„Schnupperkur"
7 Ü/F im DZ inklusive Massagen, Gymnastik und vielen Extras pro Person **ab € 189,–**

WESERBERGLAND

Hier werden Sie sich erholen...

Bad Nenndorf

Angeschmiegt an den Galenberg präsentiert sich Bad Nenndorf seinen Gästen. Bummeln Sie durch unsere Fußgängerzone oder genießen Sie Momente der Ruhe in unserem gepflegten Kurpark. Wir erwarten Sie!

Entspannung pur
ab € 275,–
7 Ü/F + 9 Anwendungen

OBERBAYERN

ROTTACH EGERN See

Arrangem. vom 20.10.- 02.12.
5 ÜN, 2 Tage

Schönheitsfarm mit Kosmetik, Schönheitsbad, Präsent, **ab € 330,–**

As health insurance companies are covering fewer medical expenses, wellness hotels are flourishing. People enjoy spending a long weekend at any one of those resorts, which offer healthy food and treatments based on the fundamentals of wellness: a balanced lifestyle of movement and relaxation.

C. Das ist leicht zu verstehen! Lesen Sie laut die folgenden Wörter und raten Sie *(guess)*, was sie auf Englisch bedeuten?

der Aktivurlaub, Arbeiter, Boom, Frust, Urlaubstag; das Fernsehen, Gartenhäuschen, Industrieland, Musikfestspiel, Privileg; die Aerobik, Kulturreise, Massage, Schönheitsfarm; mit sich bringen, planen; deutschsprachig, frustriert, überfüllt

Lesetipp

The Importance of Adjectives

Adjectives make a text come alive by providing additional information about people, places, and things with which the reader can form more vivid images. Note the use of adjectives in the following reading passage. How do they make the reading more interesting? What would the reading be like without them? Give specific examples.

Find all the preceded adjectives in the text. In each case, decide why they have that particular ending. How many can you find?

Freizeit—Lust oder Frust?

Vor hundert Jahren war es° das Privileg der Reichen° nicht arbeiten zu müssen. Die Arbeiter in den deutschsprachigen Ländern haben zu der Zeit aber oft noch 75 Stunden pro Woche gearbeitet. Urlaub für Arbeiter gibt es erst seit 1919: zuerst nur drei Tage im Jahr. Heute ist das anders. Die Deutschen arbeiten pro Jahr nur ungefähr 197 Tage, weniger als° die Menschen in fast allen anderen Industrieländern. Außer den vielen Feiertagen haben sehr viele Leute fünf oder sechs Wochen Urlaub im Jahr. So ist die Freizeit ein sehr wichtiger Teil des Lebens und mehr als° nur Zeit, sich vom täglichen Stress zu erholen.

100 years ago, it was / the rich

less than

more than

Was tut man mit der vielen Freizeit? Natürlich ist Fernsehen sehr wichtig. Auch Sport ist sehr populär; nicht nur das Zuschauen°, sondern auch das aktive Mitmachen°, um sich fit zu halten. Beliebt sind nicht nur Schwimmen oder Joggen, sondern auch Aerobik, Yoga, Squash, Tennis oder Golf. Zum Tennisspielen oder Golfen muss man aber gewöhnlich Mitglied° in einem Klub sein, denn öffentliche° Tennisplätze oder Golfplätze gibt es nur wenig. Fußball ist bei den Deutschen und Österreichern, wie überall in Europa, der Nationalsport. Auch Handball und Volleyball sind sehr beliebt.

watching
participation
member
public

Viele Menschen sind gern draußen in der Natur. An Wochenenden fährt man oft mit dem Zug oder mit dem Auto aufs Land und geht spazieren, fährt Rad oder wandert. Danach setzt man sich in ein schönes Restaurant und entspannt sich. Im Sommer geht man auch ins öffentliche Schwimmbad oder fährt an einen schönen See. Man geht auch angeln, segeln oder windsurfen. Manche arbeiten aber auch gern im Garten. Wenn sie in einer Stadtwohnung leben, können sie sich einen Schrebergarten pachten° und dort Blumen und Gemüse ziehen°.

lease / grow

Schrebergärten are small garden colonies on the outskirts of urban areas. The orthopedist Daniel Schreber founded the garden movement in the 19th century as a means for workers to supplement their incomes and defuse urban *Angst*. Today, they provide recreation and give city dwellers a chance to grow their own vegetables, fruit, and flowers.

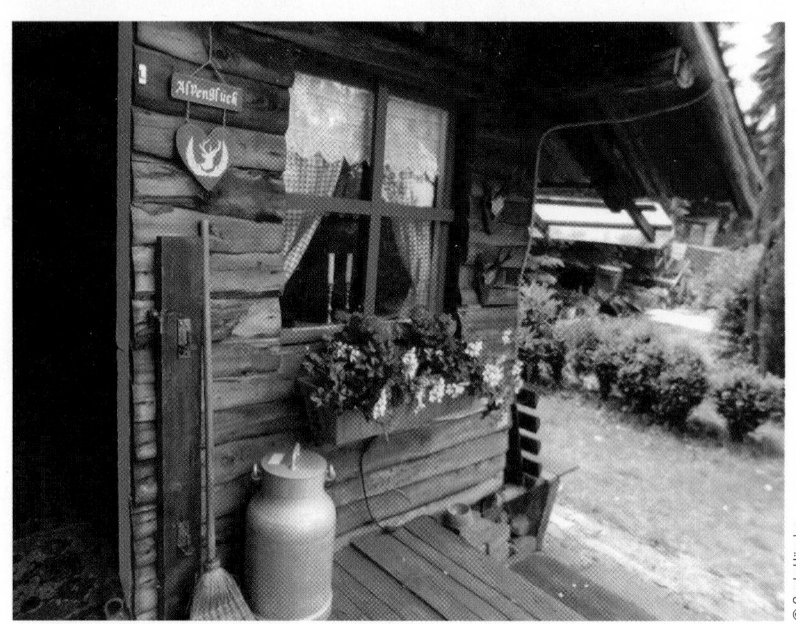

Im Schrebergarten, für Stadtmenschen eine Oase im Grünen

Die Deutschen sind reiselustig°. Immer wieder zieht es sie hinaus in die Ferne, z. B. nach Spanien, Griechenland, Frankreich, aber auch nach Nordamerika, China, Indien oder Thailand. Fast ein Sechstel° des Touristikumsatzes° der ganzen Welt kommt von den deutschen Touristen. Manche machen Kulturreisen, um Land und Leute kennenzulernen, in Museen zu gehen oder sich auf einem der vielen Festspiele Musik anzuhören. Andere reisen, um Sprachen zu lernen oder einmal etwas ganz anderes zu tun, etwas Neues zu erleben. Die Angebote° für Aktivurlaub sind groß, besonders im Internet. Gern fährt man in den warmen Süden, um sich in die Sonne zu legen und schön braun wieder nach Hause zu kommen. Andere ziehen einen Kurort oder eine Schönheitsfarm vor und lassen sich mit Massagen und Hautpflege° verwöhnen°.

eager to travel
one sixth / *here:* travel dollars
offerings
skin care / let themselves be spoiled

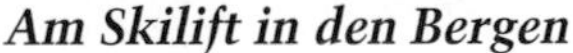
Am Skilift in den Bergen

Hier geht es lang nach Innsbruck

Und die jungen Leute? Außer den oben genannten° Aktivitäten macht es ihnen natürlich Spaß, sich mit Freunden in Kneipen°, Klubs oder Cafés zu treffen.

Dieser ganze Freizeitboom bringt aber auch Probleme mit sich. Manche langweilen sich, weil sie nicht wissen, was sie mit ihrer Freizeit machen sollen. Andere sind frustriert, wenn sie auf der Autobahn in lange Staus° kommen oder die Züge überfüllt sind. Da muss man eben° etwas planen und nicht gerade am ersten oder letzten° Urlaubstag unterwegs sein. Und wenn man seine Ruhe° haben will, darf man auch nicht in der Hauptsaison° zu den bekannten Ferienplätzen fahren. Sonst° wird Freizeitlust zum Freizeitfrust.

above-mentioned
pubs
traffic jams
just
last
peace and quiet / high season
otherwise

Nach dem Lesen

A. Alles verstanden?

1. Wie viele Wochen Urlaub pro Jahr haben die Deutschen heute gewöhnlich?
2. Wie versuchen sie, fit zu bleiben?
3. Was tun sie gern am Wochenende?
4. Warum pachten manche Leute Schrebergärten?
5. Was für Reisen sind beliebt?
6. Wo treffen sich die jungen Leute?
7. Was für Probleme bringt zu viel Freitzeit manchmal mit sich?
8. Wann kann Freizeit zum Frust werden?

A: 1. fünf oder sechs 2. durch Schwimmen, Joggen, Aerobik, Yoga, Squash, Tennis, Golf, Fußball, Handball, Volleyball 3. aufs Land fahren, spazieren gehen, (Fahr)rad fahren, wandern 4. arbeiten gern im Garten, ziehen Blumen und Gemüse 5. Kulturreisen, Aktivurlaub, Kurort, Schönheitsfarm, Spanien, Griechenland, Frankreich, Nordamerika, China, Indien, Thailand 6. in Kneipen, Klubs, Cafés 7. Sie langweilen sich, sind frustriert, wenn es Staus auf der Autobahn gibt oder die Züge überfüllt sind 8. wenn man nicht gut plant oder in der Hauptsaison zu bekannten Ferienplätzen fährt

B. Ich ziehe es vor, . . . Beim Thema Freizeit haben Sie und Ihr Partner / Ihre Partnerin ganz andere Ideen. Folgen Sie *(follow)* dem Beispiel!

BEISPIEL Ich habe Lust, . . . (baden gehen—hier bleiben)
S1 Ich habe Lust, baden zu gehen. Und du?
S2 Ich ziehe es vor, hier zu bleiben.

1. Nach der Vorlesung habe ich Zeit, . . . (Tennis spielen—mein Buch lesen usw.)
2. Ich habe Lust, diesen Sommer . . . (in den Süden fahren—nach Norwegen reisen usw.)
3. Ich finde es schön, . . . (sich Musik anhören—einen Film anschauen)

B: Encourage students to add their own statements and opposing views.

Weiteres

C: 1. in der Provence, 40, 68
2. in Lappland, Langlauf, Motorschlitten-Trip, Sauna
3. in einem italienischen Schloss, im Sommer und Herbst

C. Kreativurlaub Lesen Sie die Ferienangebote mit Ihrem Partner / Ihrer Partnerin und finden Sie heraus, ob das etwas für ihn / sie ist! Erzählen Sie dann den anderen, was ihm / ihr besonders gefällt!

1. Wo gibt es Sprachkurse in Französisch? Wie viele Stunden sind Sie da in der Klasse und wie viele Stunden Praxis *(practice)* bekommen Sie in der Woche?
2. Wo kann man Husky-Safaris und Rentierschlittenfahrten *(trips with a reindeer sled)* erleben? Was gibt's da auch?
3. Wo und wann gibt es Kunstkurse? Ist das etwas für Sie? Warum?

© Ingrid Sevin

© Ingrid Sevin

© Ingrid Sevin

D. Wohin im Urlaub *(vacation)*? Sehen Sie sich die Tabelle *(chart)* an und beantworten Sie dann ein paar Fragen!

■ **der Bundesbürger, -** *German citizen;* **das Bundesland, ⸚er** *German federal state;* **verbringen** *to spend (time);* **der Strand, ⸚e** *beach*

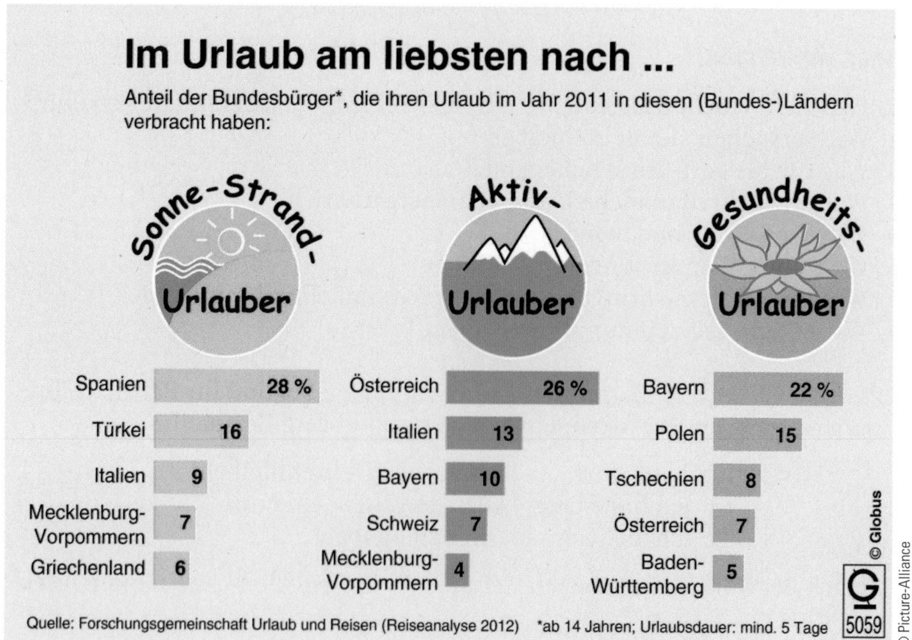

Im Urlaub am liebsten nach ...

Anteil der Bundesbürger*, die ihren Urlaub im Jahr 2011 in diesen (Bundes-)Ländern verbracht haben:

Sonne-Strand-Urlauber		Aktiv-Urlauber		Gesundheits-Urlauber	
Spanien	28 %	Österreich	26 %	Bayern	22 %
Türkei	16	Italien	13	Polen	15
Italien	9	Bayern	10	Tschechien	8
Mecklenburg-Vorpommern	7	Schweiz	7	Österreich	7
Griechenland	6	Mecklenburg-Vorpommern	4	Baden-Württemberg	5

Quelle: Forschungsgemeinschaft Urlaub und Reisen (Reiseanalyse 2012) *ab 14 Jahren; Urlaubsdauer: mind. 5 Tage

© Globus 5059

© Picture-Alliance

1. Wohin fahren viele Deutsche, wenn sie an den Strand *(beach)* wollen? Welches Bundesland ist auch sehr beliebt? Wo liegt es?
2. Welche zwei Länder sind besonders beliebt bei Fitness-Urlaubern?
3. Wohin fahren die Deutschen gern, wenn sie sich einfach entspannen und etwas für die Gesundheit tun wollen?

E. Kurzgespräche Bereiten Sie mit Ihrem Partner / Ihrer Partnerin einen der beiden Dialoge vor und präsentieren Sie ihn danach vor der Klasse!

1. **Ich bin's, Tante Elisabeth!** Your aunt Elisabeth, who lives in Zurich, calls. You answer the phone, greet her, and ask how she and Uncle Hans are doing. She says how they are and asks about you. You tell her you've caught a cold and aren't feeling very well. She expresses her sympathy and asks whether you'd like to visit them during . . . (for example, spring break). Do you want to accept? If so, your aunt says that she's glad, and she reminds you to tell her when you are going to arrive. You both say good-bye.

2. **Hier Reisebüro Eckhardt!** You call a travel agency, Reisebüro Eckhardt. An employee answers the phone and connects you with an agent. You ask the agent about trains to Zurich. He/She wants to know when you want to go. You tell him/her on . . . *(give a date)*. He/She says that you need to reserve a seat **(einen Platz reservieren)**. He/She says it costs . . . *(give a price)*; you tell him/her to reserve a seat. The agent asks when you want the tickets, and you reply that you'll come by on . . . *(give a day)*. You both say good-bye.

As an optional activity, you could have each student pick out one or two pictures in this chapter or book and describe it to their partner. Encourage them to use an adjective in every sentence.

Since you will be departing for Zurich from Stuttgart, the travel agent will use the schedule in Chapter 8 *(Übungen zum Thema*, Exercise C) to tell you about your options, depending on what time of day you would like to travel. You also ask him/her about the return schedule and the cost of a round-trip ticket.

Hörverständnis

Eine tolle Radtour Hören Sie, wo Sabrina mit ihren Freunden gewesen ist! Sind die folgenden Aussagen richtig oder falsch?

Zum Erkennen: im Büro *(at the office)*; das Mietfahrrad, ¨-er *(rent-a-bike)*; ab·holen *(to pick up)*; die Zahnradbahn *(cog railway)*; die Talfahrt *(descent)*; die Fähre, -n *(ferry)*

__f__ 1. Weil Sabrina bei der Post arbeitet, möchte sie in den Ferien etwas ganz anderes tun.
__r__ 2. Im Frühling hat sie eine Radtour um den Bodensee gemacht.
__f__ 3. Sie hat diese Tour mit ihrer Familie gemacht.
__r__ 4. Am ersten Tag sind sie bis nach Heiden gekommen.
__r__ 5. Am zweiten Tag haben sie eine schnelle Talfahrt bis an den See gehabt.
__f__ 6. Am dritten Tag hat sie eine Fähre zurück nach Friedrichshafen gebracht.
__r__ 7. Sie sind in den paar Tagen in drei Ländern gewesen.
__r__ 8. Mit so einer Radtour hält man sich fit.

For further practice, an optional two-part video (**Szenen** and **Interviews**) is available on the ***Wie geht's?*** Premium Website and in iLrn, with corresponding questions and activities in the *Arbeitsbuch* (SAM).

As an optional activity, you could use Google Earth to visit Lake Constance **(Bodensee),** check out the various places around it, and follow Sabrina's bike tour around the lake.

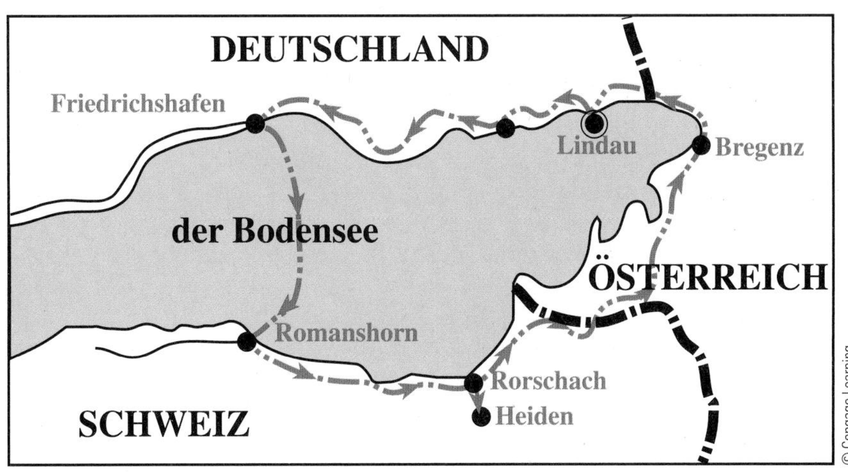

Literatur

Biographisches

Johann Wolfgang von Goethe (1749–1832) was one of Germany's greatest poets, novelists, and playwrights. He was also a leading thinker and scientist. His works include *Faust, Wilhelm Meister*, and *Die Leiden des jungen Werther*, a sensationally successful novel about a sensitive young man alienated from the world around him, which Napoleon is said to have read seven times. Because of his vast scope of knowledge and his comprehensive interest in the world of human experience, Goethe is often referred to as "the last Renaissance Man."

Tabea Vahlenkamp was born in 1965 in the small town of Pößneck in Thüringen, in the former GDR, and grew up in the East German city of Jena. After graduating from high school, she apprenticed and then worked as a photographer. In 1984, she moved to the outskirts of Berlin, married, and started a family. Four children and some years later, she founded her own photo design company in 2001. In 2002, her artistic expression broadened and extended to writing poetry. Since then, Vahlenkamp has published four collections of poems and continues to work as an independent photographer in a Berlin suburb.

Vor dem Lesen

Stilfragen Überfliegen Sie *(Skim through)* die zwei Gedichte und beantworten Sie die Fragen!

1. Wie viele Strophen *(stanzas)* hat das erste Gedicht und wie viele das zweite?
2. Haben die zwei Gedichte Reime *(rhymes)*? Wenn ja, was reimt sich?
3. Welche Anredeform *(form of address)* benutzen sie?
4. In ihrem Gedicht verzichtet *(ignores)* Vahlenkamp auf die Großschreibung *(capitalization)*. Können Sie alle Hauptwörter im Gedicht finden?
5. Das Gedicht von Tabea Vahlenkamp hat kein Komma, keinen Punkt *(period)* und kein Ausrufungszeichen *(exclamation mark)*. Ist das typisch für unsere Zeit oder ist das nur ein besonderes Stilmittel *(stylistic device)*?

Erinnerung

Willst du immer weiter schweifen°?
Sieh, das Gute liegt so nah.
Lerne nur das Glück ergreifen°,
Denn das Glück ist immer da.

Johann Wolfgang von Goethe

continue wandering
take hold of

Source: Johann Wolfgang von Goethe, „Erinnerung", (1827)

möglichkeiten°

du kannst
das leben nicht
aufhalten°

und du
kannst die liebe
nicht hindern
oder den schmerz

doch du kannst
der freude° die
tore° öffnen und
dein wollen
gewöhnen° –

und ausrichten°
auf ein ziel°
deiner wahl°

Tabea Vahlenkamp

possibilities
delay
joy
gates
get used to
direct at
goal
choice

Tabea Vahlenkamp, „möglichkeiten", in *im stillen wohnt ein kleines glück, gedichte und fotos,* (HSLiteraturverlag/Weiden am See, Austria: 2010) p.40

Nach dem Lesen

A. Fragen zu den Gedichten

1. Woran denkt Goethe, wenn er von „weiter schweifen" redet? Was meinen Sie?
2. Was ist der Hauptgedanke *(main idea)* in seinem Gedicht?
3. Glauben Sie, dass er dieses Gedicht früh oder spät in seinem Leben geschrieben hat?
4. Der Titel des Gedichts ist „Erinnerung". Auf Englisch bedeutet Erinnerung entweder *memory* oder *reminder*. Welche Bedeutung von Erinnerung ist hier relevant?
5. Tabea Vahlenkamp weiß, dass wir nicht alles in unserem Leben kontrollieren können. Was will sie uns mit ihrem Gedicht sagen? Was sollen wir tun?
6. Johann Wolfgang von Goethe und Tabea Vahlenkamp haben zu ganz verschiedenen Zeiten gelebt und ihr Leben war *(was)* ganz verschieden. Und doch haben diese zwei Gedichte etwas gemeinsam *(in common)*. Was zum Beispiel?
7. Wie gefallen Ihnen die Gedichte? Erklären Sie Ihre Antwort!

B. Lebensqualität Wie bringt man Qualität in sein Leben? Schreiben Sie ein paar Gedanken auf oder, wenn möglich, schreiben Sie ein Gedicht mit vier bis fünf Zeilen!

In case students ask about the "**s**" in **Lebensqualität,** explain that it is a genitive form of the sort that is sometimes attached to compound nouns.

Rückschau

Kapitelwortschatz

Hauptwörter

der Arm, -e	*arm*
das Auge, -n	*eye*
der Bauch, ¨e	*stomach, belly*
das Bein, -e	*leg*
die CD, -s	*CD*
die DVD, -s	*DVD*
der Finger, -	*finger*
der Fuß, ¨e	*foot*
der Fußball	*soccer*
das Gesicht, -er	*face*
die Gitarre, -n	*guitar*
das Haar, -e	*hair*
der Hals, ¨e	*neck, throat*
das Hobby, -s	*hobby*
die Idee, -n	*idea*
die Karte, -n	*card*
das Klavier, -e	*piano*
das Knie, -	*knee*
der Kopf, ¨e	*head*
der Körper, -	*body*
das Leben	*life*
der Mund, ¨er	*mouth*
die Musik	*music*
die Nase, -n	*nose*
das Ohr, -en	*ear*
der Rücken, -	*back*
die Schulter, -n	*shoulder*
das Spiel, -e	*game*
der Sport	*sport; sports, athletics*
der Urlaub	*(paid) vacation*
der Zahn, ¨e	*tooth*

Verben

angeln	*to fish*
sich an·hören	*to listen to*
sich an·schauen	*to look at* (colloquial)
sich an·sehen	*to look at*
sich an·ziehen	*to put on (clothing); to get dressed*
aus·geben	*to spend (money)*
sich aus·ziehen	*to take off (clothing); to get undressed*
backen	*to bake*
baden	*to take a bath*
sich beeilen	*to hurry*
sich bestellen	*to order (for oneself)*
sich die Nase putzen	*to blow one's nose*
sich die Zähne putzen	*to clean/brush one's teeth*
sich duschen	*to take a shower*
sich entspannen	*to relax*
sich erholen	*to recuperate*
sich erkälten	*to catch a cold*
erleben	*to experience*
faulenzen	*to be lazy*
fern·sehen	*to watch TV*
sich fit halten	*to keep in shape*
fotografieren	*to take pictures*
sich fragen	*to wonder*
sich (wohl) fühlen	*to feel (well)*
sich kämmen	*to comb one's hair*
sich kaufen	*to buy (for oneself)*
kochen	*to cook*
sich kochen	*to cook (for oneself)*
sich konzentrieren	*to concentrate*
sich langweilen	*to get/be bored*
sich (hin·)legen	*to lie down*
malen	*to paint*
sich nehmen	*to take (for oneself)*
Rad fahren	*to bicycle, bike*
sich rasieren	*to shave*
sammeln	*to collect*
Schach spielen	*to play chess*
schwimmen	*to swim*
schwimmen gehen	*to go swimming*
sich sehen	*to see oneself*
sich (hin·)setzen	*to sit down*
Ski laufen	*to ski*
Ski laufen gehen	*to go skiing*
spazieren gehen	*to go for a walk (lit.: walking)*
Sport treiben	*to engage in sports*
(Freunde) treffen	*to meet, get together (with friends)*
sich treffen	*to meet, gather*
sich um·ziehen	*to change (clothing); to get changed*
vor·ziehen	*to prefer*
wandern	*to hike*
sich waschen	*to wash (oneself)*
sich wünschen	*to wish (for oneself)*

Adjektive und Adverbien

ander-	*other, different*
anders	*different(ly)*
beliebt	*popular*
fantastisch	*fantastic, great, super*
ganz	*whole, entire(ly), total(ly), all*
gesund	*healthy, healthily*
krank	*sick, ill*

Verschiedenes

Ach so.	*Oh, I see.*
andere	*others*
die anderen	*the others*
Bis bald!	*See you soon!*
Bis gleich!	*See you in a few minutes!*
danach	*after that, then*
etwas (ganz) anderes	*something (totally) different*
(genauso) wie . . .	*(just) like . . .*
Ja, sicher.	*Yes, sure.*
Lust haben zu . . .	*to feel like (doing something)*
Ich habe (keine) Lust, . . . zu spielen.	*I (don't) feel like playing . . .*
Nein, das geht (heute) nicht.	*No, that won't work (today).*
nichts Besonderes	*nothing special*
Schmerzen haben	*to have pain, hurt*
Ich habe (Kopf)-schmerzen.	*I have a (head)ache.*
Was ist (denn) los?	*What's the matter?; What's going on?*
weh·tun	*to hurt*
Mir tut der Hals weh.	*My throat hurts., I have a sore throat.*
zuerst	*first*

Zum Schluss

1. **Erzählen Sie!**

   a. **Guten Morgen!** Describe your typical weekday morning routine to a classmate. What do you do every morning? Are you usually on time or do you have to hurry? Use as many reflexive verbs as you can. In addition, incorporate at least two phrases using an infinitive with **zu**. Compare your answers!

   b. **Am Wochende** Now, describe your typical weekend routine to a classmate. What do you do differently from what you do during the week? What does your classmate do differently? Again, use as many reflexive verbs as possible, along with at least two phrases using an infinitive with **zu**.

2. **Ganze Sätze**

   a. **Das bin ich!** Using vocabulary from this chapter and earlier chapters, complete the following sentences about yourself.

   Ich habe Lust . . .
   Ich habe nie Zeit . . .
   Ich habe immer Zeit . . .
   Mir macht es Spaß . . .
   Ich finde es interessant . . . / langweilig . . .
   Am Wochenende mache ich . . . , um . . .
   In meiner Freizeit tue ich . . . gern . . . / nicht gern . . .
   Wenn ich gestresst bin, . . .
   Wenn ich eine Prüfung schreibe, . . .
   Wenn ich Schmerzen habe, . . .

   b. **Wer ist das!** Now, complete the previous sentences again to describe a member of your study group or one of your classmates. Then read your sentences aloud. Can your study group guess whom you are describing? How well do their descriptions match your own answers? Remember to pay attention to case and proper word order!

3. **Beschreiben Sie!** Describe your dorm room, your bedroom, or your favorite room. Be as creative and as detailed as possible! Use adjectives from this and earlier chapters. Remember to pay close attention to the rules governing adjectives preceded by **der-**words and **ein-**words. Some ideas are given below, but you may use others.

alt / neu	gut / schlecht	schön / hässlich
ausgezeichnet	hell / dunkel	teuer / billig
fantastisch	lang / kurz	(un)bequem
groß / klein	sauber / schmutzig	(un)praktisch

iLrn **Onlineaktivitäten** Visit iLrn for online activities related to this chapter. There you will find additional resources, such as a memory game (**Gedächtnisspiel**), a crossword puzzle (**Kreuzworträtsel**), audio flash cards (**Vokabelblitz**), a tutorial quiz (**Mini-Quiz**), and the active vocabulary (**Wortschatz**) for this chapter.

Kapitel 10

Unterhaltung

Lernziele In this chapter you will learn about:

Zum Thema

Entertainment, media

Fokus

German film, theater, music, art, and television

Struktur

- Verbs with prepositional objects
- **Da-** and **wo-**compounds
- Endings of unpreceded adjectives

Einblicke

Lesetext: Wer die Wahl hat, hat die Qual.
Literatur: Rainer Maria Rilke, „Du musst das Leben nicht verstehen" / Bertolt Brecht, „Vergnügungen"

Rückschau

Kapitelwortschatz
Zum Schluss

RESSOURCEN

iLrn
Video
Audio
SAM

Szene aus Caroline Links Film Nirgendwo in Afrika

Vorschau German Film

Dates for filmmakers: Staudte (1906–1984), Beyer (1932–2006), Fassbinder (1946–1982), Herzog (1942), v. Trotta (1942), Dörrie (1955), Schlöndorff (1939), Grass (1927), Petersen (1941), Emmerich (1955), Wenders (1945), Szabó (1938), Polanski (1933), Annaud (1943), Becker (1954), Tykwer (1965), Petzold (1960), Link (1964), Ruzowitzky (1961), Donnersmarck (1973), Akin (1973), Wnendt (1977), Bauder (1974)

You could ask students to read the dates above aloud in German.

During the early days of film, the Ufa studios in the Berlin suburb of Potsdam-Babelsberg were second only to Hollywood in churning out world-class productions, including such classics as *Nosferatu, Metropolis, Der blaue Engel*, and *M*. When the National Socialists came to power (1933), movie production continued, although many prominent directors and actors emigrated to the United States and elsewhere. After the war, those studios were taken over by Defa (Deutsche Film AG), whose films were subject to the approval of GDR authorities and have subsequently become a bridge to the past. Among Defa's best-known films are Wolfgang Staudte's *Der Untertan* and Frank Beyer's *Jakob der Lügner*. After the fall of the Berlin Wall, Vivendi Universal took over the studios from Germany's Treuhand privatization agency, bringing real change to the studios, which now belong to two German investors.

Beginning in the 1960s, a new wave of young West German filmmakers seized the world's attention. Directors such as Rainer Werner Fassbinder *(Die Ehe der Maria Braun)*, Werner Herzog *(Stroszek)*, Margarethe von Trotta *(Rosa Luxemburg* and *Das Versprechen)*, Doris Dörrie *(Männer)*, Volker Schlöndorff (*Die Blechtrommel*—based on a Nobel Prize–winning novel by Günter Grass), and Wolfgang Petersen *(Das Boot)* produced critically acclaimed movies. Many German directors continue to work closely with Hollywood. Examples are Roland Emmerich *(Independence Day)* and Wim Wenders (*Wings of Desire*, original title *Der Himmel über Berlin*). While critics lament the domination of American blockbusters (most of which are dubbed), German film has been experiencing a renaissance, characterized by numerous international coproductions, directed by such artists as István Szabó *(Der Fall Furtwängler)*, Roman Polanski *(Der Pianist)*, and Jean-Jacques Annaud *(Stalingrad)*.

Despite internationally renowned achievements such as Wolfgang Becker's *Das Leben ist eine Baustelle* and *Good Bye Lenin!*, Tom Tykwer's *Lola rennt*, Christian Petzold's *Die innere Sicherheit*, Caroline Link's *Nirgendwo in Afrika* and *Im Winter ein Jahr*, Stefan Ruzowitzky's *Die Fälscher*, Florian Henckel von Donnersmarck's *Das Leben der Anderen*, Fatih Akin's *Auf der anderen Seite* and *Müll im Garten Eden*, David Wnendt's *Die Kriegerin*, as well as Marc Bauder's *Das System*, the German film industry is struggling with a relatively small market share. More and more it seems as though film is consumed through the medium of television instead of the big screen. Babelsberg Studio in Potsdam now relies heavily on both television productions and major international movies to make a profit.

M (Eine Stadt sucht einen Mörder), ***von Fritz Lang***

Die Blechtrommel, ***von Volker Schlöndorff***

Das Leben der Anderen, ***von Florian Henckel von Donnersmarck***

Fragen: 1. Haben Sie einen der Filme auf den Fotos oder im Text der *Vorschau* schon mal gesehen? Wenn ja, welchen Film können Sie empfehlen? Warum? 2. Kennen Sie einen Film mit Szenen aus den deutschsprachigen Ländern? Wenn ja, welchen Film? 3. Sehen Sie sich im Kino Filme an, wenn sie Untertitel *(subtitles)* haben? Warum (nicht)?

Zum Thema

Gespräche

Explain that *Gute Zeiten, schlechte Zeiten* is a popular German soap opera taped in the Potsdam-Babelsberg Studios. For a synopsis of *Das Leben der Anderen* ask students to check the Internet.

Warm-ups: 1. **Was kann man in der Freizeit tun?** 2. **Was ist der Artikel?** Wintersportfest, Flugschalter, Klavierlehrerin, Sektglas, Tischtennistisch, Samstagnachmittagfußballspiel, Nachthemd, Bierbauch, Stuhlbein, Zahnfleisch, Haarfarbe, Gitarrenmusik, Handynummer 3. **Welches Verb passt? z. B. Bummler: bummeln** (Anruf, Aufpasser, Bedeutung, Besucher, Gefühl, Gepäck, Langschläfer, Maler, Fotograf, Reise, Sammler, Schwimmer, Skiläufer, Spaziergänger, Wunsch) 4. **Was sind die drei Imperative? z. B. sich setzen: Setzen Sie sich! Setzt euch! Setz dich!** (s. abwechseln, s. beeilen, s. fit halten, s. kämmen, s. die Zähne putzen) 5. **Im Kaufhaus** Was kauft man da?

Blick in die Zeitung

SONJA Du, was gibt's denn heute Abend im Fernsehen?
THEO Keine Ahnung! Sicher nichts Besonderes.
SONJA Mal sehen! *Gute Zeiten, schlechte Zeiten,* einen Dokumentarfilm und einen Krimi.
THEO Ach nee.
SONJA Vielleicht gibt's was im Kino?
THEO Ja, *Das Leben der Anderen* und *Nirgendo in Afrika.*
SONJA *Das Leben der Anderen* habe ich schon zweimal gesehen, außerdem habe ich das auf DVD. Der Film ist echt klasse! Vielleicht können wir ihn mal bei mir zusammen anschauen, aber nicht heute. *Nirgendwo in Afrika* kenne ich auch.
THEO Na gut. . . . He, schau mal! Im Theater gibt's *Der kaukasische Kreidekreis* von Brecht.
SONJA Nicht schlecht. Hast du Lust?
THEO Ja, das klingt gut. Gehen wir!

An der Theaterkasse

THEO Haben Sie noch Karten für heute Abend?
DAME Ja, erste Reihe erster Rang links und Parkett rechts.
THEO Zwei Plätze im Parkett! Hier sind unsere Studentenausweise.
DAME 10 Euro bitte!
SONJA Wann fängt die Vorstellung an?
DAME Um 20.15 Uhr.

Der kaukasische Kreidekreis, *von Bertolt Brecht*

A. Alles verstanden?

1. Was gibt's im Fernsehen? 2. Gefällt das Theo? 3. Hat Sonja Lust, sich *Das Leben der Anderen* im Kino anzuschauen? Warum (nicht)? 4. Wo wollen sie sich den Film einmal anschauen? 5. Was hat Sonja gegen *Nirgendwo in Afrika*? 6. Was gibt's im Theater? 7. Gibt es noch Karten für dieses Stück? 8. Was kosten sie mit Studentenausweis? 9. Wo sind Theos und Sonjas Plätze? 10. Wann fängt die Vorstellung an?

A: 1. *Gute Zeiten, schlechte Zeiten*, einen Dokumentarfilm, einen Krimi 2. nein 3. nein; schon gesehen, DVD 4. bei Sonja / ihr zu Hause 5. schon gesehen 6. Brechts Der kaukasische Kreidekreis 7. ja 8. 10 Euro 9. Im Parkett 10. um 20.15 Uhr

B. Jetzt sind Sie dran! Suchen Sie mit Ihrem Partner / Ihrer Partnerin im Internet, was es heute im Fernsehen, im Kino und im Theater gibt. Vielleicht machen Sie auch Pläne und gehen zur Kino- oder Theaterkasse oder Sie gehen zur Videothek *(video store)* und holen sich *(get)* ein oder zwei DVDs. Wechseln Sie sich ab!

BEISPIEL S1 Was gibt's im Fernsehen / im Kino / im Theater?
S2 Hast du Lust? / Kennst du den Film . . . ?
S1 Das klingt gut, gehen wir! / Nein. Dazu habe ich keine Lust.

Fokus: Again, you could ask students to read the dates aloud in German. In addition, you might initiate classroom discussion on which of these German cultural figures they are already familiar with.

Fokus The Magic of the Theater

Theater plays a central role in the cultural life of Germany, Austria, and Switzerland. Germany has around 300 theaters, the most important ones in major cities such as Berlin, Hamburg, and Munich. But even medium-sized and small cities have their own repertory theaters. Some date back to the 18th century, when—before Germany was united as a country—many local sovereigns founded their own court theaters. By the 19th century, many towns and cities had established theaters as public institutions. Theaters were, after all, a major source of entertainment.

The classic works by Johann Wolfgang von Goethe, Friedrich Schiller, Bertolt Brecht, Max Frisch, Friedrich Dürrenmatt, William Shakespeare, and Molière continue to draw large audiences, as do works by modern playwrights such as Gerlind Reinshagen and the Austrian Elfriede Jelinek, who won the 2004 Nobel Prize for Literature for her controversial novels and plays in which she critiques violence against women and explores sexuality and political extremism in Europe. As in other European countries, the German government has traditionally subsidized the fine arts, but with recent budget cuts, many theater directors are beginning to rely more heavily on corporate sponsorship. States and local governments also subsidize tickets in public venues. Most theaters offer reduced ticket prices for students, seniors, and the unemployed. An active children's theater movement thrives across the country, with marionettes and puppetry drawing delighted crowds.

Municipal theaters in medium-sized cities usually also offer ballet, musicals, and operas. Not only do the traditionally famous German-language operas (for example, Beethoven's *Fidelio*, Mozart's *Die Zauberflöte*, and Richard Strauss's *Der Rosenkavalier*) continue to be popular, but other international and modern operas, such as Puccini's *La Bohème* and Berg's *Wozzeck*, attract large audiences as well. In the summer, many cities entice arts lovers to music, theater, ballet, and open-air film festivals. Broadway musicals have met with notable success in Germany, with special musical theaters being dedicated to the works of British composer Andrew Lloyd Webber, such as *Das Phantom der Oper, Cats, Starlight Express*, and *Die Schöne und das Biest*. Experimental dance has also been well represented in Germany by artists, such as Oskar Schlemmer, Gret Palucca, and the recently deceased Pina Bausch with her world-famous Wuppertal Dance Theater.

Ballettabend im Münchner Opernhaus

Dates for well-known people from the German-speaking countries: Goethe (1749–1832), Schiller (1759–1805), Brecht (1898–1956), Frisch (1911–1991), Dürrenmatt (1921–1990), Reinshagen (1926), Jelinek (1946), Beethoven (1770–1827), Mozart (1756–1791), Strauss (1864–1949), Berg (1885–1935), Schlemmer (1888–1943), Palucca (1902–1993), Bausch (1940-2009).

If students ask: *ballet dancer* **der Balletttänzer, -;** *conductor* **der Dirigent, -en, -en;** *operetta,* **die Operette, -n;** *to whistle* **pfeifen, gepfiffen.**

Note that in Europe whistling in a performance setting is generally a sign of disapproval.

For space reasons, the words *author, composer, painter, actor* are listed only in the masculine form in the chart. The feminine forms are: **die Autorin, -nen; die Komponistin, -nen; die Malerin, -nen; die Schauspielerin, -nen.**

If students ask: *cheesy* (slang) **kitschig;** *disgusting* **ekelhaft;** *tacky* **geschmacklos;** *Damn it!* **Verdammt noch mal!;** *What nonsense!* **So ein Blödsinn!;** *That's the limit!* **Das ist doch die Höhe!**

You might ask students to form other compounds with **Lieblings-**, e.g., **mein Lieblingsfilm, Lieblingsprogramm,** etc.

Like **unheimlich interessant: unheimlich spannend / müde** etc. **Unheimlich** by itself means *tremendous(ly), extreme(ly), uncanny / uncannily,* but it can also mean *frightening, eerie, sinister.*

Wortschatz 1

Die Unterhaltung *(entertainment)*

der Anfang, ¨-e	*beginning, start*
Autor, -en	*author*
Blick (in / auf) (+ *acc.*)	*glance (at); view (of)*
Chor, ¨-e	*choir*
Film, -e	*film, movie*
Komponist, -en, -en	*composer*
Krimi, -s	*detective story*
Maler, -	*painter (artist)*
Roman, -e	*novel*
Schauspieler, -	*actor*
das Ballett, -s	*ballet*
Ende	*end*
Gemälde, -	*painting*
Konzert, -e	*concert*
Orchester, -	*orchestra*
Stück, -e	*piece; (theatrical) play; piece of music or ballet*
die Kunst, ¨-e	*art*
Oper, -n	*opera*
Pause, -n	*intermission, break*
Vorstellung, -en	*performance*
Werbung	*advertising*
Zeitschrift, -en	*magazine*
Zeitung, -en	*newspaper*
dumm	*stupid(ly), silly*
folgend	*following*
komisch	*funny, comical; strange, odd*
langweilig	*boring*
nächst- / letzt-	*next / last*
spannend	*exciting, suspenseful*
traurig / lustig	*sad(ly) / funny, with humor*

Verschiedenes

an·fangen (fängt an), angefangen	*to start, begin*
(sich) entscheiden, entschieden	*to decide*
(sich) holen	*to get, fetch*
klatschen	*to applaud*
lachen / weinen	*to laugh / to cry*
lächeln	*to smile*
vergessen (vergisst), vergessen	*to forget*
am Anfang / am Ende	*in the beginning / at the end*
vor kurzem	*recently*
Was gibt's im Fernsehen?	*What's (playing) on television?*
Keine Ahnung!	*No idea!*
Das ist zu lang (laut, *etc.*).	*That's too long (loud,* etc.*)*
(Das ist) klasse / spitze!	*(That's) great!*
(Das ist doch) unglaublich!	*(That's) unbelievable!, (That's) hard to believe.*
(Das ist) unheimlich interessant!	*(That's) really interesting!*
(Das ist ja) Wahnsinn!	*(That's) crazy / awesome / unbelievable!*
Das ärgert mich.	*That makes me mad.*
Jetzt habe ich aber genug.	*That's enough. I've had it.*
Na gut.	*All right.*

Zum Erkennen: Ach nee. *(I don't think so* [coll.]*)*; die Reihe, -n *(row)*; im Rang *(in the balcony)*; im Parkett *(in the orchestra).* AUCH: die Ausstellung, -en *([art] exhibit / show)*; das **da-/wo-**Kompositum, Komposita *(**da-/wo-**compound)*; das Programm, -e; die Leseratte, -n *(bookworm)*

Übungen zum Thema

© Ingrid Sevin

A. Am Frühstückstisch Beenden Sie die Sätze!

1. Auf diesem Frühstückstisch sieht man ...
2. Ich esse morgens gern ... und trinke ...
3. Wenn ich Zeit habe, lese ich gern ...
4. Diese Woche liest man in den Zeitungen viel über (*about*) ...
5. Es gibt auch viel Werbung in der Zeitung, zum Beispiel für ...

B. Hoppla, hier fehlt was! Was spielt wo und wann? Sehen Sie sich mit Ihrem Partner / Ihrer Partnerin den Spielplan an und finden Sie heraus, was Sie nicht wissen! Einer von Ihnen sieht sich den Spielplan unten an, der andere den Spielplan im Anhang, Teil 11. Entscheiden Sie sich dann, was Sie sehen wollen und warum!

S1:

WO	WAS?	WANN?
Volksbühne	*Nathan der Weise*, Schauspiel von Gotthold Ephraim Lessing	19.30
Urania-Theater	*Die Lustige Witwe*, Operette von Franz Lehár	20.15
Metropol-Theater	*West Side Story*, Musical von Leonard Bernstein	19.00
Im Dom	*Jedermann*, Schauspiel von Hugo von Hofmannsthal	15.00
Philharmonie	*Original Wolga-Kosaken*, Lieder und Tänze	15.30
Konzerthaus	*Flamenco-Festival*, mit Montse Salazar	20.00
Komödie	*Jahre später, gleiche Zeit*, Komödie von Bernhard Slade	16.00
Kammerspiele	*Carmina Burana*, von Carl Orff	17.30
Filmbühne 1	*Das Leben ist eine Baustelle*, von Wolfgang Becker	19.30
Filmbühne 2	*Im Winter ein Jahr*, von Caroline Link	22.00

BEISPIEL S1 Was gibt's heute in der Philharmonie?
S1 Die Wolga-Kosaken.
S2 Und wann?
S1 Um . . . und im Dom gibt's . . .
S2 Oh ja, wann denn?
S1 . . .

BEISPIEL S1 Hast du . . . schon gesehen / gehört? Das ist ein(e) . . . von . . .
S2 Ja / Nein, . . . aber . . .
S1 Hast du Lust . . . ?
S2 . . .
S1 Gut, . . .

C. Allerlei Fragen

1. Sind Sie eine Leseratte (*bookworm*)? Wenn ja, was für Bücher lesen Sie gern? Wie viele Bücher haben Sie in den letzten drei Monaten gelesen? Welche Autoren finden Sie besonders gut? Welche Zeitungen und Zeitschriften lesen Sie gern? Lesen Sie auch Comics?

C: Consult the newspaper or the Internet for current offerings in your area. Also come prepared with names of composers and painters and titles of plays and/or operas.

Fragen zu den Konzerten:
1. Was gibt's am 22. 12. im Nymphenburger Schloss in München? 2. Was für Musik spielen sie am 23. 12.? 3. Was gibt's am 1. 1.? 4. Welches Konzert finden Sie interessant? 5. Welches Musical spielt in ... (z. B. Hamburg, Berlin, Essen, Oberhausen)? 6. Kennen Sie eins von den Musicals? Wenn ja, welches? 7. Mögen Sie Musicals? Warum (nicht)?

2. Wo kann man hier Theaterstücke, Opern oder Musicals sehen? Haben Sie dieses Jahr ein interessantes Stück oder ein gutes Musical / eine gute Oper gesehen? Wenn ja, wo und welche(s)? Wie hat es/sie Ihnen gefallen?
3. Gehen Sie manchmal in ein Rock-, Jazz- oder Popkonzert? Welche Komponisten oder Musikgruppe hören Sie gern?
4. Wer von Ihnen singt gern? Wer von Ihnen spielt ein Instrument? Was denn?
5. Wie gefällt Ihnen abstrakte Kunst? Welche Maler finden Sie gut? Gehen Sie manchmal zu Kunstausstellungen? Wenn ja, wo? Wessen Gemälde gefallen Ihnen (nicht)? Malen Sie auch? Wenn ja, was malen Sie gern?

© Beatrix Brockman

NYMPHENBURGER
SCHLOSSKONZERTE
Hubertussaal
22.12. CANDLE-LIGHT-KLASSIK
Etwas zum Träumen um 19.30 Uhr
23.12. BAROCKE WEIHNACHT
Violinkonzerte von Bach um 19.30 Uhr
28.12. SCHOKOLADEN-ZAUBER
Musikalische Delikatessen um 15.00 Uhr
1. 1. FESTLICHES NEUJAHRSKONZERT
Ein Potpourri der Romantik um 17.00 Uhr

© Ingrid Sevin

Aussprache: r, er

A. Laute

1. [r] **r**ot, **r**osa, **r**uhig, **r**echts, **R**adio, **R**egal, **R**eihe, **R**oman, P**r**og**r**amm, Do**r**f, Konze**r**t, Fah**r**t, Gita**rr**e, t**r**au**r**ig, k**r**ank, He**rr**en
2. [ʌ] Orchest**er**, Theat**er**, Mess**er**, Tell**er**, ab**er**, leid**er**, hint**er**, unt**er**, üb**er**, wied**er**, weit**er**
3. [ʌ/ r] Uh**r** / Uh**r**en; Oh**r** / Oh**r**en; Tü**r** / Tü**r**en; Cho**r** / Chö**r**e; Auto**r** / Auto**r**en; Klavie**r** / Klavie**r**e

You might encourage studens to check out the German website for musicals and possibly report on them!

For further review, see the Summary of Pronunciation in the front of this book. Study Part II, subsection 9, and Part III, subsection 10.

B. Wortpaare

1. *ring* / Ring
2. *Rhine* / Rhein
3. *fry* / frei
4. *brown* / braun
5. *tear* / Tier
6. *tour* / Tour

Fokus Classical Music Yesterday and Today

Composers from the German-speaking countries have played no small role in shaping the world of music. Johann Sebastian Bach is one of the preeminent German composers and was quite prolific: a recent recording of his complete works covers 171 compact discs! His rich work, which includes both religious and secular music, is universally praised for its beauty and perfection. Other important composers of the baroque period are Georg Friederich Händel and Georg Philipp Telemann.

Wolfgang Amadeus Mozart, another musical genius, dominated the classical period, and Ludwig van Beethoven laid the foundations for the Romantic Movement. The final choral movement of Beethoven's Ninth Symphony, known as the "Ode to Joy" (**"Ode an die Freude")**, was chosen as the European anthem. Composers Franz Schubert, Felix Mendelssohn-Bartholdy, Robert Schumann, Carl Maria von Weber, Richard Wagner, and Johannes Brahms all regarded their works as following in the tradition of Beethoven. Through the interpretation of their music, pianists such as Clara Wieck (wife of Robert Schumann) and Elly Ney, violinist Anne-Sophie Mutter, and clarinetist Sabine Meyer have gained international acclaim in a previously male-dominated field.

Great innovators have also influenced the modern era. Gustav Mahler is a link between the lyrical impulse of the Romantic Movement and the more ironic attitudes of the arts in the 20th century. Richard Strauss pioneered musical drama; Paul Hindemith and Carl Orff established new standards in choral music; and Arnold Schönberg introduced the 12-tone system of composition. Contemporary composers Bernd-Alois Zimmermann, Hans Werner Henze, and Karlheinz Stockhausen have all stretched the boundaries of the avant-garde.

Neujahrskonzert im Wiener Musikverein

Hörverständnis

Biedermann und die Brandstifter Hören Sie zu, was Daniel und Christian für den Abend planen! Sind die folgenden Aussagen richtig oder falsch?

Zum Erkennen: mal eben *(just for a minute);* die Inszenierung *(production);* die Hauptrolle, -n *(leading role);* die Einladung, -en *(invitation)*

_f_ 1. Christians Vater hat ihm zwei Theaterkarten gegeben.
_f_ 2. Christian fragt seinen Freund Daniel, ob er mitkommen möchte.
_r_ 3. Die Plätze sind in der 2. Reihe vom 1. Rang.
_f_ 4. Die Vorstellung beginnt um halb sieben.
_f_ 5. Christian muss sich noch die Haare waschen.
_r_ 6. Wenn Daniel sich beeilt, können sie noch schnell zusammen essen.
_f_ 7. Sie treffen sich an der Straßenbahnhaltestelle in der Breslauer Straße.

Fokus: Dates for composers and musicians from the German-speaking countries: Bach (1685–1750), Händel (1685–1759), Telemann (1681–1767), Mozart (1756–1791), Beethoven (1770–1827), Schubert (1797–1828), Mendelssohn-Bartholdy (1809–1847), Schumann (1810–1856), Weber (1786–1826), Wagner (1813–1883), Brahms (1833–1897), Wieck (1819–1896), Ney (1882–1968), Mutter (1963), Meyer (1960), Mahler (1860–1911), Strauss (1864–1949), Hindemith (1895–1963), Orff (1895–1982), Schönberg (1874–1951), Zimmermann (1918–1970), Henze (1926–2012), Stockhausen (1928–2007).

Struktur

10.1 Verbs with prepositional objects

In both English and German, a number of verbs are used together with certain PREPOSITIONS. These combinations often have special idiomatic meanings.

*I'm **thinking of** my vacation. I'm **waiting for** my flight.*

Since the German verb + preposition combinations differ from English, they must be memorized.

Remember that this list as well as all others with a bar on the left are active vocabulary.

denken an (+ ***acc.***)	*to think of, about*
schreiben an (+ ***acc.***)	*to write to*
sich freuen auf (+ ***acc.***)	*to look forward to*
sich vor·bereiten auf (+ ***acc.***)	*to prepare for*
warten auf (+ ***acc.***)	*to wait for*
sich ärgern über (+ ***acc.***)	*to get annoyed / upset about*
lächeln über (+ ***acc.***)	*to smile about*
sich entscheiden für / gegen (+ ***acc.***)	*to decide for / against*
sich informieren über (+ ***acc.***)	*to inform oneself, find out about*
sich interessieren für (+ ***acc.***)	*to be interested in*
erzählen von (+ ***dat.***)	*to tell about*
halten von (+ ***dat.***)	*to think of, be of an opinion about*
sprechen von (+ ***dat.***) **/ über** (+ ***acc.***)	*to talk of / about*

You may need to illustrate the difference between a separable-prefix verb **(aufstehen)** and verbs commonly used in combination with a preposition **(warten auf). Er steht früh auf.** (Nothing follows **auf;** it's a V2, i.e., part of the verb infinitive.) BUT: **Ich warte auf dem Bahnsteig auf den Zug.** (**auf** is followed by an object of the preposition; the infinitive is **warten.**)

CAUTION: The prepositions in these idiomatic combinations (**an, auf, über,** etc.) are not separable prefixes. They function like any other preposition and are followed by nouns or pronouns in the appropriate cases:

Separable-prefix verb	BUT	Verb + preposition
Ich **rufe** dich morgen **an.**		Ich **denke an** dich.
I'll call you tomorrow.		*I'm thinking of you.*

NOTE: In these idiomatic combinations, two-way prepositions most frequently take the accusative.

Er denkt an seine Reise.	*He is thinking about his trip.*
Sie schreibt an ihre Eltern.	*She is writing to her parents.*
Freut ihr euch aufs Wochenende?	*Are you looking forward to the weekend?*
Ich bereite mich auf eine Prüfung vor.	*I'm preparing for an exam.*
Ich warte auf einen Anruf.	*I'm waiting for a phone call.*
Ich ärgere mich über den Brief.	*I'm upset about the letter.*
Über so etwas Dummes kann ich nur lächeln.	*I can only smile about something stupid like that.*
Informier dich über das Programm!	*Find out about the program.*
Interessierst du dich für Sport?	*Are you interested in sports?*
Erzählt uns von eu(e)rem Flug!	*Tell us about your flight.*
Was hältst du denn von dem Film?	*What do you think of the movie?*
Sprecht ihr von *Hotel Ruanda?*	*Are you talking about* Hotel Rwanda?

Remember that the preposition **von** (e.g., after **erzählen** and **halten**) is not a two-way preposition but is always followed by the dative, and that **für** always takes the accusative.

Changing the case can sometimes dramatically change the meaning. Note these two different uses of **auf:**

© Cengage Learning

© Cengage Learning

Ich warte **auf den** Zug. BUT Ich warte **auf dem** Zug.
I'm waiting for the train. *I'm waiting on top of the train.*

Übungen

A. Sagen Sie es noch einmal! Ersetzen Sie das Substantiv!

BEISPIEL Sie warten auf den Zug. (Telefongespräch)
Sie warten auf das Telefongespräch.

1. Wir interessieren uns für Kunst. (Sport, Musik)
2. Er spricht von seinem Urlaub. (Bruder, Hobbys)
3. Sie erzählt von ihrem Flug. (Familie, Geburtstag)
4. Ich denke an seinen Brief. (E-Mail, Name)
5. Wartest du auf deine Familie? (Gäste, Freund)
6. Freut ihr euch auf das Ballett? (Vorstellung, Konzert)
7. Ich habe mich über das Wetter geärgert. (Junge, Leute)
8. Was haltet ihr von der Idee? (Gemälde, Maler)

© Dieter Sevin

A: 1. für Sport, Musik 2. von seinem Bruder, seinen Hobbys 3. von Ihrer Familie, ihrem Geburtstag 4. an seine E-Mail, seinen Namen 5. auf deine Gäste, deinen Freund 6. auf die Vorstellung, das Konzert 7. über den Jungen, die Leute 8. von dem Gemälde, dem Maler

A: These sentences can be used with different objects: 1. **s. interessieren für:** Sprachen, Philosophie, Bücher, Theater . . . 2. **sprechen von:** Geld, Land, Politik, Autos . . . 3. **erzählen von:** Universität, Schweiz, Ferien, Museum . . . 4. **denken an:** Blumen, Prüfung, Werbung, Wochenende . . . 5. **warten auf:** Student, Antwort, Rechnung, Freund . . . 6. **s. freuen auf:** Schiffsreise, Fußballspiel, Postkarte . . . 7. **s. ärgern über:** Konzert, Film, Fernsehprogramm . . . 8. **halten von:** Werbung, Maler, Gemälde, Theaterstück . . .

B. Meine Tante Was fehlt?

Meine Tante hat __an__ mein_en_ Vater geschrieben. Sie will uns __von__ ihr_er_ Reise durch Asien erzählen. Wir freuen uns __auf__ ihr_en_ Besuch *(m.)*. Meine Tante interessiert sich sehr __für__ Asien. Sie spricht hier im Museum __über / von__ ihr_e/en_ Fahrten. Sie malt auch gern und ist __über__ Kunst gut informiert. Ich denke gern __an__ sie. Mein Vater ärgert sich __über__ sie, wenn sie nicht schreibt. Sie hält einfach nicht viel __von__ Briefen und sie hat keinen Computer, aber sie ruft uns manchmal an.

C. Hört euch das an! Erzählen Sie den anderen von drei Situationen, wo Sie sich vor kurzem gefreut oder geärgert haben! Vergessen Sie nicht zu sagen, wie Sie sich fühlen!

BEISPIEL *Wisst ihr, das Autohaus hat mein Auto schon dreimal repariert und es läuft immer noch nicht richtig. Jetzt habe ich aber genug!*

Fokus: Dates for artists from the German-speaking countries: Dürer (1471–1528), Cranach (1472–1553), Holbein the Younger (1497–1543), Friedrich (1774–1840), Klimt (1910–1962), Kokoschka (1866–1980), Klee (1879–1940), Marc (1880–1916), Kollwitz (1867–1945), Beckmann (1884–1950), Dix (1891–1969), Beuys (1921–1986), Richter (1932), Lüpertz (1941), Kiefer (1945), Horn (1944)

D. So beende ich die Sätze. Und du? Beenden Sie die Sätze mit einem Präpositionalobjekt! Fragen Sie dann Ihren Partner / Ihre Partnerin, wie er/sie sie beendet hat!

BEISPIEL Ich lächele nur . . .
S1 Ich lächele nur über solche komischen Fragen. Und du?
S2 Ich lächele nur über meine kleine Schwester.

1. Ich denke oft an . . .
2. Ich warte auf . . .
3. Ich schreibe gern an . . .
4. Ich interessiere mich für . . .
5. Ich freue mich auf . . .
6. Ich ärgere mich manchmal über . . .
7. Ich spreche gern von . . .
8. Ich halte nicht viel von . . .
9. Ich muss mich auf . . . vorbereiten.
10. Es ist schwer, sich für . . . zu entscheiden.

Fokus The Art Scene

As in other parts of Europe, early painting in the German-speaking countries was devoted to religious works, especially altarpieces. In the 16th century, Albrecht Dürer became the first important portrait painter; he also developed landscape painting and is regarded as the inventor of etching. His contemporaries include Lucas Cranach and Hans Holbein. Although painting followed the trends of western European art, it did not reach another zenith until the 19th century. Caspar David Friedrich's landscapes are representative of the Romantic era. Following the Congress of Vienna, the Biedermeier period introduced its idyllic settings. Then, toward the turn of the 20th century, came the Viennese Secession **(der Jugendstil)** with Gustav Klimt.

Early 20th-century artists conveyed the fears and dangers of their times through the style known as expressionism. Two such artists were Oskar Kokoschka, who reflected the anxious, decadent atmosphere of prewar Vienna, and Paul Klee and Franz Marc, who ventured into abstract art. Others, including Käthe Kollwitz, Max Beckmann, and Otto Dix, exercised sharp social criticism through their sculptures and canvasses. The rise of the Nazis, who denounced most modern art as "degenerate," put an abrupt end to this creative period. In the second half of the century, Germany's art scene again came alive with representatives such as Joseph Beuys, who turned visual art into action; Gerhard Richter, whose diversity defies tradition, Markus Lüpertz whose paintings convey a "drunken, rapturous" feeling of life; Anselm Kiefer, who tries to process the past with a new kind of symbolism; and Rebecca Horn, who presents sculptures as performances. Every five years, the **documenta** in Kassel exhibits modern and contemporary art.

Tirol, *von Franz Marc*

In case students ask: 1. After the defeat of Napoleon in 1814, the victorious European monarchs convened at the **Congress of Vienna** (1814–1815) to create a new European order. The mastermind of the diplomatic gathering was Austria's Prince Metternich. 2. **Biedermeier** is a central and eastern European style that flourished between 1815 and 1848. The name comes from a popular cartoon character, "Papa Biedermeier," who symbolized quiet, comfortable bourgeois domesticity. 3. For information about the **Jugendstil**, see the *Fokus* section in Chapter 5.

10.2 *Da-* and *wo-*compounds

1. ***Da***-compounds

In English, pronouns following prepositions can refer to people, things, or ideas:

I'm thinking of him. *I'm thinking of it.*

This is not true for German. Pronouns following prepositions refer only to people: Ich **denke an ihn (an meinen Freund).**

If you wish to refer to a thing or an idea, you must use what's called a **da**-COMPOUND: Ich **denke daran (an die Ferien).**

Most accusative and dative prepositions (except **außer, ohne,** and **seit**) can be made into **da**-compounds. If the preposition begins with a vowel (**an, in,** etc.), it is used with **dar-:**

dafür	*for it/them*	darauf	*on it/them*
dagegen	*against it/them*	darin	*in it/them*
damit	*with it/them*	darüber	*above it/them; about it/them*
danach	*after it/them*	usw.	

Compare with English *thereafter, thereupon, therein, thereby,* etc. Note that the meanings are often slightly different!

—Können Sie mir sagen, wo ein Briefkasten ist?
—Ja, sehen Sie die Kirche dort? **Daneben** ist eine Apotheke, **dahinter** ist die Post und **davor** ist ein Briefkasten mit einem Posthorn **darauf.**

© Beatrix Brockman

2. ***Wo*-compounds**

The interrogative pronouns **wer, wen,** and **wem** refer to people.

Von wem sprichst du?	*About whom are you talking?* *(Who are you talking about?)*
Auf wen wartet ihr?	*For whom are you waiting?* *(Who are you waiting for?)*

In questions about things or ideas, **was** is used. If a preposition is involved, however, a **wo**-COMPOUND is required. Again, if the preposition begins with a vowel, it is combined with **wor-.**

wofür?	*for what?*	worauf?	*on what?*
wogegen?	*against what?*	worüber?	*above what?; about what?*
womit?	*with what?*	usw.	

Compare with English *wherefore, whereby, wherein, whereto,* etc. Note that the meanings are often slightly different!

Wovon sprichst du?	*About what are you talking?* *(What are you talking about?)*
Worauf wartet ihr?	*For what are you waiting?* *(What are you waiting for?)*

REMEMBER: To ask where something is located, use the question word **wo,** regardless of the answer expected: **Wo ist Peter?** To ask where someone is going, use **wohin** (NOT **wo** combined with **nach** or **zu!**): **Wohin ist Peter gegangen?** To ask where a person is coming from, use **woher** (NOT **wo** combined with **aus** or **von!**): **Woher kommt Peter? Wohin** and **woher** are not **wo**-compounds!

To help students figure out when to use **da**- or **wo**-compounds, give them a dozen or so English sentences and have them give you a compound or a pronoun: *I have a pen. I'm writing with it* **(damit).** *With what am I writing* **(womit)***? I'm talking with my friend* **(mit ihm).** *With whom am I talking* **(mit wem)***?*

Übungen

E. Wo ist nur mein Handy? Helfen Sie Ihrem Partner / Ihrer Partnerin, es zu finden! Benutzen Sie dabei immer ein **da**-Kompositum *(**da**-compound)*!

BEISPIEL auf dem Sofa?
S1 Liegt es auf dem Sofa?
S2 Nein, es liegt nicht darauf.

neben dem Bett?	auf dem Esstisch?	zwischen den Zeitungen und Zeitschriften? . . .
vor dem Telefon?	in der Tasche?	
hinter der Lampe?	unter den Fotos?	

E: daneben, davor, dahinter, darauf, darin, darunter, dazwischen

Kombinieren Sie mit da- und wo-! z. B. für: dafür / wofür? (durch, gegen, um, an, auf, hinter, in, neben, über, unter, vor, zwischen, aus, bei, mit, nach, von, zu). Practice the formation of **da**- and **wo**-compounds for several days in one-minute drills.

F: 1. dazu 2. darüber, von ihnen 3. über sie 4. dagegen 5. von ihnen 6. daran 7. Darauf 8. für sie 9. davon, über sie 10. Danach

F. Die Geburtstagsfeier Ersetzen Sie die fettgedruckten Wörter mit einem **da**-Kompositum oder mit einer Präposition + Pronomen!

BEISPIEL Hans steht **neben Christa.** — *Hans steht **neben ihr.***
Mutter steht **neben der Tür.** — *Mutter steht **daneben.***

1. Viele Gäste sind **zu der Feier** gekommen.
2. Sie sprechen **über das Wetter** und erzählen **von ihren Familien.**
3. Nena ärgert sich, wenn Markus **über die Politiker** spricht.
4. „Was hast du eigentlich **gegen Politik**?"
5. „Nichts, aber **von deinen Politikern** halte ich nicht viel."
6. Natürlich denken die Gäste jetzt auch **an das Essen.**
7. **Auf das Essen** müssen sie aber noch ein bisschen warten.
8. Hans hat **für seine Mutter** eine kleine Rede *(speech)* vorbereitet.
9. Er spricht **von seiner Kindheit** und erzählt auch ein paar Geschichten **über seine Mutter.**
10. **Nach der Rede** bringt der Ober das Essen.

G. Das Klassentreffen *(Class reunion)* Ein Freund ist gerade von einem Klassentreffen zurückgekommen. Sie und Ihr Partner / Ihre Partnerin kennen viele der Leute. Mit den verschiedenen Verben links fragen Sie ihn, worüber Horst, Claire und auch Gerd und Elke gesprochen haben, woran sie gedacht haben usw. Wechseln Sie sich nach jeder Frage ab!

BEISPIEL S1 Worüber hat Claire gesprochen?
Sie hat über ihre Arbeit gesprochen.
S2 An wen haben Gerd und Elke gedacht?
Sie haben an ihre Kinder gedacht.

	HORST	CLAIRE	GERD + ELKE
sprechen über	viele Leute	ihre Arbeit	ihre Kinder
denken an	die tollen Partys	ihre Zimmernachbarin	die Schulzeit
schreiben an	die Zeitschriften	ihren Freund	einen Professor
warten auf	eine Antwort	eine SMS	einen Brief
s. freuen auf	die alten Freunde	den Urlaub	das Wiedersehen
s. interessieren für	Theater	Kunst	Musik
s. informieren über	Schauspieler	Kunstkurse	einen Komponisten
s. ärgern über	eine Oper	ihren Boss	das Essen

© Gabi Moisa/Shutterstock

Schau mal, sind das nicht Horst und Inca?

H. Wie bitte? Ihr Partner / Ihre Partnerin sagt Ihnen etwas, aber Sie hören nicht genau hin und gehen ihm/ihr mit Ihren vielen Fragen etwas auf die Nerven. In den Sätzen benutzt er/sie nur Verben von der Liste im Teil 10.1 der *Struktur*. Wechseln Sie sich ab!

BEISPIEL S1 Ich freue mich auf den Besuch im Filmstudio.
S2 Worauf freust du dich?
S1 Auf den Besuch im Filmstudio!
S2 Ach so, darauf!

BEISPIEL S2 Ich freue mich auf meinen Onkel und meine Tante.
S1 Auf wen freust du dich?
S2 Auf meinen Onkel und meine Tante!
S1 Ach so, auf sie!

Wildwestfilm im Filmstudio von Babelsberg

Fokus German Television Productions

Since the invention of TV, the German television landscape has been shaped by many series produced in Germany. The most popular one, called ***Tatort*** *(Scene of the Crime)*, is also the oldest. The publicly-owned ARD network in Germany, the ORF in Austria, and the SF in Switzerland first aired it in 1970. The 90-minute episodes are produced by each of the regional TV channels, which together form the ARD in Germany. The Austrian TV channel ORF, as well as the Swiss channel SF, also produce their own episodes. A distinctive primary detective or team of detectives represents each location. The show airs every Sunday evening at 8:15 p.m., right after the primary news broadcast of the day. Approximately thirty episodes are produced annually among the various channels. On some Sundays, the ARD airs ***Polizeiruf 110***, an adaption of a GDR crime series, now playing in a united Germany.

The second oldest show on television is the ***Traumschiff*** *(Dream Boat)*. Based on the American series *The Love Boat*, it was created in 1981 and has been produced ever since. The episodes initially were sixty minutes long and later were increased to ninety minutes. The show is produced in irregular intervals with two to three episodes usually aired as Christmas specials.

Further long-running and regionally produced TV-shows include ***Großstadtrevier*** (about a small police station in Hamburg, on the air since 1986), ***Rosenheim-Cops*** (about a murder investigation team of detectives in Bavaria, since 2002), and ***Um Himmels Willen*** (a comedy about a group of nuns defending their cloister against the greedy mayor of their little town, since 2002).

Most programming on private German TV-channels is filled with imports from the United States. Since Germans do not appreciate watching English-language productions with subtitles, all foreign productions are dubbed in German. Favorite American shows include *NCIS, CSI, CSI Miami, The Mentalist*, and many others.

10.3 Endings of unpreceded adjectives

In Chapter 9, you learned how to deal with adjectives preceded by either **der-** or **ein-**words. Occasionally, however, adjectives are preceded by neither; they are then called UNPRECEDED ADJECTIVES. The equivalent in English would be adjectives preceded by neither *the* nor *a(n):*

We bought fresh fish and fresh eggs.

1. Unpreceded adjectives take the endings that the definite article would have if it were used.

der frische Fisch	**das** frische Obst	die frische Wurst	**die** frischen Eier
frisch**er** Fisch	frisch**es** Obst	frisch**e** Wurst	frisch**e** Eier

	MASCULINE		NEUTER		FEMININE		PLURAL	
nom.	frisch**er**	Fisch	frisch**es**	Obst	frisch**e**	Wurst	frisch**e**	Eier
acc.	frisch**en**	Fisch	frisch**es**	Obst	frisch**e**	Wurst	frisch**e**	Eier
dat.	frisch**em**	Fisch	frisch**em**	Obst	frisch**er**	Wurst	frisch**en**	Eiern
gen.	(frisch**en**	Fisches)	(frisch**en**	Obstes)	(frisch**er**	Wurst)	frisch**er**	Eier

genitive: The genitive singular forms are relatively rare. Note also that the masculine and neuter forms of the genitive are irregular and the only two that are different from **der**-word endings. (See *Struktur 8.1, The genitive case* to review **der**-word endings in the genitive.)

Heute Abend gibt es heiß**e** Suppe, holländisch**en** Käse, frisch**e** Brötchen und frisch**es** Obst.

- If there are several unpreceded adjectives, all have the same ending.

  Ich wünsche dir schön**e**, interessant**e** Ferien.

2. The following words (sometimes called "quantifiers") are often used as unpreceded adjectives in the plural:

andere	*other*
einige	*some, a few* (pl. only)
mehrere	*several* (pl. only)
viele	*many*
wenige	*few*

Wir haben uns mehrer**e** modern**e** Gemälde angesehen.

Sie haben einig**en** jung**en** Leuten gefallen, aber mir nicht.

- When used in the singular, **viel** *(much, a lot)* and **wenig** *(little, not much)* usually do not have endings in modern German, but they are often used as unpreceded adjectives in the plural.

Viele Studenten haben **wenig** Geld, aber nur **wenige** Studenten haben **viel** Zeit.	*Many students have little money, but only a few students have a lot of time.*

- Numerals, **mehr,** and **ein paar** have no endings. The same holds true for a few of the color words, such as **lila** *(purple)* and **rosa** *(pink),* as well as adjectives of geographic origin, such as **Frankfurter Würstchen, Schweizer Käse,** and so on.

The adjectives **prima, klasse, spitze,** and **super** also never have an ending.

Da sind **drei** junge **Wiener** Studenten mit **ein paar** kurzen Fragen.

Haben Sie noch **mehr** graues oder blaues Papier?

Was mache ich mit diesem alten **rosa** Pullover?

Übungen

I. Ersetzen Sie die Adjektive!

BEISPIEL Das sind nette Leute. (verrückt)
Das sind verrückte Leute.

1. Ich trinke gern schwarzen Kaffee. (heiß, frisch)
2. Sie braucht dünnes Papier. (billig, weiß)
3. Er schreibt tolle Bücher. (spannend, lustig)
4. Heute haben wir wunderbares Wetter. (ausgezeichnet, furchtbar)
5. Dort gibt es gutes Essen. (einfach, gesund)
6. Hier bekommen wir frischen Fisch. (gegrillt, gebacken)
7. Er hat oft komische Ideen. (dumm, fantastisch)

I: 1. heißen, frischen 2. billiges, weißes 3. spannende, lustige 4. ausgezeichnetes, furchtbares 5. einfaches, gesundes 6. gegrillten, gebackenen 7. dumme, fantastische

J. Sagen Sie es anders! Wiederholen Sie die Sätze, aber diesmal ohne die fettgedruckten Wörter!

BEISPIEL **Der** holländische Käse ist ausgezeichnet.
Holländischer Käse ist ausgezeichnet.

1. **Die** deutschen Zeitungen haben auch viel Werbung.
2. Der Mann will mit **dem** falschen Geld bezahlen.
3. Sie hat **das** frische Brot gekauft.
4. Er hat **den** schwarzen Kaffee getrunken.
5. Wir haben **die** braunen Eier genommen.
6. Er ist mit **seinen** alten Tennisschuhen auf die Party gegangen.
7. Sie trinken gern **das** dunkle Bier.
8. Auf der Party haben sie **diese** laute Musik gespielt.
9. Er erzählt gern **solche** traurigen Geschichten.
10. Sie hat Bilder **der** bekannten Schauspieler.

J: 1. Deutsche Zeitungen 2. falschem Geld 3. frisches Brot 4. schwarzen Kaffee 5. braune Eier 6. alten Tennisschuhen 7. dunkles Bier 8. laute Musik 9. traurige Geschichten 10. bekannter Schauspieler

K. Ein Brief an Freunde Was fehlt?

Lieb[e]____ Gudrun, lieb[er]____ Bill! Seit gestern bin ich mit ein paar ander[en]____ Studenten in Dresden. Eine wunderbar[e]____ Stadt mit alt[er]____ Tradition *(f)*! Im Zentrum gibt es viel[e]____ schön[e]____ Gebäude mit barock[en]____ Fassaden *(pl.)*. Die Frauenkirche erinnert an *(reminds of)* furchtbar[e]____ Zeiten. Jetzt hat man sie mit alt[en]____ und neu[en]____ Steinen wieder aufgebaut *(rebuilt)*. Gestern haben wir zwei alt[e]____ Dresdener kennengelernt. Sie haben uns einige interessant[e]____ Geschichten aus alt[er]____ und neu[er]____ Zeit erzählt. Mit ihnen sind wir abends an der Elbe entlang gelaufen, mit herrlich[em]____ Blick *(m.)* auf die Stadt. Danach haben wir im Ballhaus Watzke gegessen. Das ist eine alt[e]____ Brauerei *(brewery)* mit gut[er]____ Atmosphäre *(f.)* und gut[em]____ Bier. Für heute Abend haben wir billig[e]____ Karten für die Oper bekommen. Wie ihr seht, geht es mir gut.

Viele Grüße!

Eure Anne

L. Das mache ich gern. Und du? Beenden Sie die folgenden Sätze mit Substantiven und Adjektiven ohne vorausgehenden *(preceding)* Artikel! Fragen Sie dann die anderen in der Gruppe, wie das bei ihnen ist!

Founded in 1953, **Deutsche Welle (DW)** is Germany's foreign broadcasting network, presenting round-the-clock information from Germany and Europe. **DW-TV,** based in Berlin, broadcasts in German, English, and Spanish. **DW-Radio,** based in Cologne, transmits worldwide in 29 different languages, including Hindi and Swahili. **DW-World** provides a multimedia service that offers analysis and background reports on the Internet (You can find links to **Deutsche Welle** easily on the Web).

BEISPIEL Ich singe gern . . .
S1 Ich höre gern klassische Musik. Und du?
S2 Ich höre gern moderne Musik.
. . .

1. Ich esse gern . . .
2. Ich trinke gern . . .
3. Ich sammle gern . . .
4. Ich lese gern . . .
5. Ich trage gern . . .
6. Ich sehe gern . . .
7. Ich finde . . . prima.
8. Ich möchte . . .
9. Ich besichtige gern . . .
10. Ich ärgere mich über . . .

Fokus German Television

Both public and commercial television are strong in Germany. After World War II, public corporations were created and given regional broadcasting monopolies, independent of state control. This was to prevent any political party or central government from ever again using the airwaves for propaganda, such as was done during the Nazi era. When television was launched in 1954, the regional broadcasters formed a national network known as **ARD,** commonly known as **Das Erste Programm.** Later, in 1961, a second national channel called **ZDF (Zweites Deutsches Fernsehen)** was founded, based in Mainz. In addition, each of the ARD broadcasters operates a third channel **(Drittes Programm),** which focuses on regional affairs, education, and culture. The public networks also participate in the French/German cultural channel **Arte** and a number of satellite television channels. Mandatory fees paid by each household fund this immense bureaucracy. The fees currently amount to some 18 euros a month per household, a total of around 7.5 billion euros per year nationwide. ARD and ZDF are also allowed 20 minutes of advertising per day, restricted to the period before 8 P.M.

It took a constitutional amendment in the mid-1980s to permit private broadcasting in Germany. Now, two major groups dominate what has become a dynamic commercial television market. Market leader **RTL** Group (which operates RTL Television, RTL-2, SuperRTL, Vox, and the all-news channel n-tv) is controlled by publishing and music giant Bertelsmann. The largest group, **ProSiebenSat.1** (which operates SAT 1, Pro 7, Kabel 1, and the news channel N24) was acquired in 2003 by US–Israeli media tycoon Haim Saban. In addition, music channels **MTV** and **Viva,** sports offerings **Eurosport** and **DSF,** and youth-oriented **Tele 5** and **NeunLive** all compete for the remaining viewers. Although some of the commercial channels have over-the-air transmitters in some areas, most Germans watch cable television, which serves about 80 percent of Germany's 33 million TV households. Many of the rest have home satellite dishes that receive both public and commercial channels.

Zusammenfassung

Visit the ***Wie geht's?*** iLrn website for more review and practice of the grammar points you have just learned.

M. Bilden Sie ganze Sätze! In einigen Sätzen müssen Sie die fehlenden Präpositionen ergänzen.

1. wie lange / ihr / warten / schon / — / ich?
2. ihr / sich freuen / auch / — / Reise / morgen / Frankreich?
3. wir / sich ärgern / nur / — / Wetter
4. ob / gut / oder / schlecht / Wetter // wir / sich machen / ein paar / schön / interessant / Tag *(pl.)*
5. ich / sich vorbereiten / gut / und / warm / Kleidung / mitbringen *(pres. perf.)*
6. wo- / ihr / sich interessieren / in Paris?
7. ich / wollen / sich ansehen / ein paar / französisch / Film *(pl.)*
8. ich / möchten / besichtigen / mehrer- / alt / Schloss *(pl.)* und Museum *(pl.)*
9. teuer / Essen / wir / brauchen / nicht
10. frisch / Baguettes / französisch / Käse / und / gut / Wein / immer / schmecken

M: 1. Wie lange wartet ihr schon auf mich? 2. Freut ihr euch auch auf die Reise morgen nach Frankreich? 3. Wir ärgern uns nur über das Wetter. 4. Ob gutes oder schlechtes Wetter, wir machen uns ein paar schöne, interessante Tage. 5. Ich habe mich gut vorbereitet und warme Kleidung mitgebracht. 6. Wofür interessiert ihr euch in Paris? 7. Ich will mir ein paar französische Filme ansehen. 8. Ich möchte mehrere alte Schlösser und Museen besichtigen. 9. Teu(e)res Essen brauchen wir nicht. 10. Frische Baguettes, französischer Käse und guter Wein schmecken immer.

N. Ein guter Film: *Buddenbrooks* Stellen Sie Fragen darüber mit 10 verschiedenen Interrogativpronomen, zum Beispiel mit **wer?, wen?, wem?, wessen?, wann?, wo?, wonach?, wogegen?** usw.!

***Buddenbrooks*, unter der Regie *(direction)* von Heinrich Breloer, spielt in Lübeck in der Mitte des 19. Jahrhunderts. Die alte Familie des Konsuls Buddenbrook hat über Generationen ihr Glück im Getreidehandel *(grain business)* gemacht. Familie und Firma geht es gut. Mit dem Tod des Vaters beginnt ihr guter Stern *(star)* zu sinken und die Dynastie zerbricht *(falls apart)* langsam am Lebenskonflikt zwischen geschäftlichen Interessen und der Suche nach privatem Glück. Der Film basiert *(is based)* auf einem Roman von Thomas Mann. Für den Roman hat Mann 1929 den Nobelpreis für Literatur bekommen.**

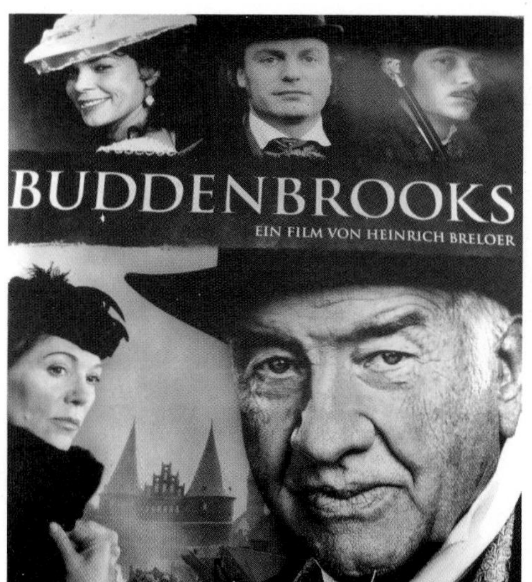

Ein Film mit interessanten, historischen Einblicken

O. Ein Autor zu Gast Auf Deutsch bitte!

1. Two weeks ago an old friend of my father visited us. 2. He is the author of several plays. 3. I'm very interested in the theater. 4. He knows many important people, even some well-known actresses. 5. Our friend knows many other authors. 6. He spoke about them. 7. He told us some exciting stories. 8. He has just been to **(in)** Vienna. 9. He saw several performances of his new play and bought a few expensive books. 10. He's coming back in the summer. 11. We are looking forward to that. 12. We have also bought him some new novels.

O: 1. Vor zwei Wochen hat uns ein alter Freund meines Vaters besucht. 2. Er ist der Autor mehrerer Stücke. 3. Ich interessiere mich sehr fürs Theater. 4. Er kennt viele wichtige Leute, sogar einige bekannte Schauspielerinnen. 5. Unser Freund kennt viele andere Autoren. 6. Er hat über sie gesprochen / von ihnen geredet. 7. Er hat uns einige / ein paar spannende Geschichten erzählt. 8. Er ist gerade in Wien gewesen. 9. Er hat mehrere Vorstellungen seines neuen Stückes gesehen und [er hat] einige / ein paar teu(e)re Bücher gekauft. 10. Er kommt im Sommer zurück. 11. Wir freuen uns darauf. 12. Wir haben ihm auch einige / ein paar neue Romane gekauft.

Einblicke

Lesetext

Note the difference between **die Sendung** and **das Programm** as they refer to TV: **Diese Kultursendung hat mir gut gefallen.** BUT: **Was gibt's im Abendprogramm / im 2. Programm (ZDF)?**

Wortschatz 2

das Fernsehen	*television* (the medium)
Programm, -e	*(general) programming; TV channel*
die Auswahl (an) (+ *dat.*)	*selection, choice (of)*
Nachricht, -en	*news* (on radio and television; usually pl.)
Sendung, -en	*(particular) program*
der Bürger, - / die Bürgerin, -nen	*citizen*
der Zuschauer, - / die Zuschauerin, -nen	*spectator*
etwa	*about, approximately*
öffentlich / privat	*public(ly) / private(ly)*
sowie	*as well as*
vor allem	*mainly, especially, above all*
weder . . . noch	*neither . . . nor*

Lesetipp

Learning Vocabulary *(continued)*

Before reading this text, memorize the vocabulary in *Wortschatz 2*. Make a list of the words that have to do with media. Then scan the reading text and see how many additional media words you recognize that are similar to English and add them to the list. Finally, add any other German words relating to the topic of mass media that you already know to complete the list.

Vor dem Lesen

A. Umfrage *(Survey):* Medien in unserem Leben Beantworten Sie die folgenden Fragen und vergleichen Sie *(compare)* Ihr Resultat mit den anderen! Womit verbringen Sie *(spend)* besonders viel Zeit und womit nicht?

1. Wie viele Stunden pro Tag sehen Sie fern? _____
2. Wie viele Stunden pro Tag sitzen Sie am Computer? _____
3. Wie viele E-Mails pro Tag bekommen Sie? _____
4. Wie viele Minuten pro Tag telefonieren Sie? _____
5. Wie viele Videos sehen Sie pro Woche? _____
6. Wie viele Bücher haben Sie in den letzten drei Monaten gelesen? _____
7. Wie viele Stunden pro Tag hören Sie Musik? _____

B. Gehen wir Wörter angeln *(Let's go fishing for words)*! Überfliegen Sie *(Scan)* schnell den folgenden Text und finden Sie mit Ihrem Partner / Ihrer Partnerin Beispiele für Adjektive mit und ohne vorausgehenden Artikel! Wovon gibt es mehr?

C. Das ist leicht zu verstehen! Lesen Sie laut die folgenden Wörter und raten Sie, was sie auf Englisch bedeuten?

der Aspekt, Dokumentarfilm, Haushalt, Kritiker, Psychologe, Radiohören; das Abendprogramm, Kabarett, Lesen, Magazin, Wissen; die Interessengruppe, Kombination, Kreativität, Produktion, Publikation, Statistik, Wochenzeitung; *(pl.)* die Serien; ausfüllen, finanzieren, produzieren, registrieren; experimentell, finanziell, informativ, kulturell, politisch, staatlich kontrolliert

Wer die Wahl hat, hat die Qual.°

Wie überall spielen die Massenmedien, vor allem das Internet und das Fernsehen, auch in Deutschland eine enorm wichtige Rolle. Mehr als die Hälfte° aller deutschen Haushalte haben heute einen DSL-Internetanschluss° und fast jeder Haushalt hat einen oder zwei Fernseher. Die Auswahl an Sendungen ist groß und wird jedes Jahr größer°. Zu den öffentlichen Sendern° wie ARD (Arbeitsgemeinschaft der öffentlich-rechtlichen Rundfunkanstalten der Bundesrepublik Deutschland) und ZDF (Zweites Deutsches Fernsehen) kommen private Sender sowie Programme aus den Nachbarländern.

Um das öffentliche Fernsehen zu finanzieren, müssen die Deutschen ihre Fernseher und Radios registrieren und monatliche Gebühren° zahlen; die privaten Sender sind ganz auf Werbung angewiesen°. Auch im öffentlichen Fernsehen gibt es Werbung, aber nur relativ wenig—nicht nach acht Uhr abends und nie während der Sendung von Spielfilmen°. Werbung kommt vor allem vor dem Abendprogramm und dauert nur zehn bis zwanzig Minuten.

Das öffentliche Fernsehen ist weder staatlich noch privat kontrolliert, sondern finanziell und politisch unabhängig°. Darum kann es nicht nur die täglichen Nachrichten sowie Serien und Spielfilme produzieren, sondern auch Sendungen für kleine Interessengruppen, z. B. Nachrichten in verschiedenen Sprachen, Sprachunterricht° für Ausländer, experimentelle Musik, politische Diskussionen und lokales Kabarett. Durch die Kombination von öffentlichen und privaten Sendern sowie Sendern aus anderen Ländern bekommen die Zuschauer eine gute Mischung von° Programmen, von aktuellen° Nachrichten, populärem Sport, leichter Unterhaltung, informativen Dokumentarfilmen, internationalen Filmen und kulturellen Sendungen wie Theaterstücken, Opern und Konzerten.

Manche Kritiker halten nicht viel vom Fernsehen. Sie ärgern sich zum Beispiel darüber, dass so viele amerikanische Filme und Serien oder auch Seifenopern° laufen, obwohl die Statistiken zeigen, dass sich die Zuschauer dafür interessieren. Neben diesen und informativen Kultursendungen sind auch spannende Filme mit Sex und Gewalt gefragt°. Aber nicht nur darin sehen die Kritiker Probleme, sondern auch in der passiven Rolle der Zuschauer. Haben die Psychologen vielleicht doch recht°, dass besonders Kinder durch zu viel Fernsehen an Kreativität verlieren°?

Radiohören und Lesen sind weiterhin° sehr populär. Deutschlands Buchproduktion steht international nach den USA auf dem zweiten Platz. Neben den etwa 350 Tageszeitungen gibt es jede Menge° Zeitschriften: gesellschaftspolitische° Magazine und Wochenzeitungen wie *Der Spiegel, Focus* oder *Die Zeit* sowie populäre Society-Publikationen wie *Stern, Bunte* oder *Gala*. Sie alle informieren über moderne Aspekte des gesellschaftlichen° Lebens.

Die Menschen haben heute eine enorme Auswahl an Informationsquellen°. Durchs Internet haben sie Zugang° zum ganzen Wissen der Menschheit° und alle Medien konkurrieren um° die Zeit der Bürger. Für sie ist diese Auswahl aber nicht immer leicht. Ja, wer die Wahl hat, hat die Qual.

Choosing isn't easy (*lit.* it's a pain).
more than half
. . . access
bigger / broadcasters
fees
dependent on
feature films
independent
. . . instruction
mix of / current
soap operas
popular
are right
suffer loss of
still
all sorts of
socio-political
social
. . . sources
access / mankind
compete for

Nach dem Lesen

A. Alles verstanden?

1. Wie viele deutsche Haushalte haben heute einen DSL-Internetanschluss?
2. Was kommt zu den öffentlichen Sendern im Fernsehen noch dazu?
3. Worauf sind die privaten Sender angewiesen?
4. Womit finanzieren die öffentlichen Sender ihr Programm?

A: 1. mehr als die Hälfte 2. private Sender, Programme aus Nachbarländern 3. auf Werbung 4. mit monatlichen Gebühren

A.4: These fees are paid to the GEZ **(die Gebühreneinzugszentrale).**

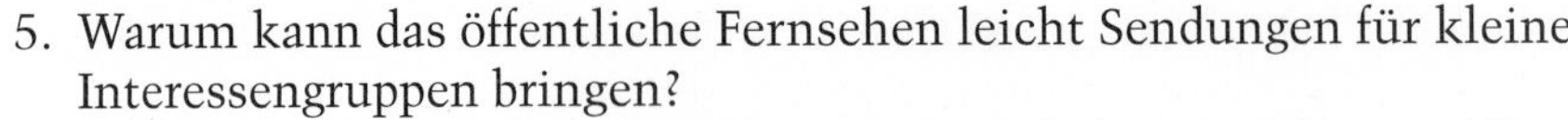

A: 5. finanziell und politisch unabhängig, Gebühren 6. Sprachunterricht, experimentelle Musik, politische Diskussionen, lokales Kabarett 7. viele amerikanische Filme und Serien, Seifenopern 8. Radiohören und Lesen 9. *Der Spiegel, Die Zeit, Stern, Bunte, Gala* 10. das Internet, das Fernsehen, das Radio, Bücher, Zeitungen und Zeitschriften / Magazine

5. Warum kann das öffentliche Fernsehen leicht Sendungen für kleine Interessengruppen bringen?
6. Was für Sendungen bringen sie zum Beispiel? (Nennen Sie zwei!)
7. Worüber ärgern sich manche Fernsehkritiker?
8. Was ist auch weiterhin populär?
9. Wie heißen ein paar deutsche Zeitschriften oder Zeitungen? (Nennen Sie drei!)
10. Was konkurriert um die Zeit der Bürger?

B. Wofür interessieren Sie sich im Fernsehen? Schauen Sie sich die Liste an und bewerten Sie *(rate)* die Programme! Was finden Sie sehr interessant (1), machmal interessant (2) und uninteressant (3)? Wie haben die anderen die Programme bewertet? Vergleichen Sie die Resultate!

❑ Nachrichten	❑ Konzerte	❑ Seifenopern
❑ Politik	❑ Opern	❑ Horrorfilme
❑ Reisen	❑ Krimis	❑ Dokumentarfilme
❑ Hobbys	❑ Western	❑ Geschichtsfilme
❑ Sport	❑ Theaterstücke	❑ Liebesfilme *(love...)*
❑ Sprachen	❑ Fernsehspiele	❑ Science-Fiction-Filme
❑ Ballett	❑ Fernsehquizze	❑ Zeichentrickfilme *(cartoons)*

C. Was fehlt? Ergänzen Sie die fehlenden Präpositionen, **wo**-Komposita oder **da**-Komposita!

Note that one of the assignments in this chapter's Internet activities allows you a closer look at Germany's TV offerings.

Der Lesetext handelt ___von___ Deutschlands Massenmedien. Wenn wir in Nordamerika fernsehen, denken wir nur ___an___ mögliche Kabelgebühren, aber nicht ___an___ Fernsehgebühren. Die Deutschen müssen ___daran___ denken. Sie ärgern sich oft ___über___ diese Gebühren, aber sie können nichts ___dagegen___ *(against it)* tun. Sie haben keine Wahl. Viele interessieren sich nicht nur ___für___ leichte Unterhaltung, sondern auch ___für___ informative Dokumentarfilme. Andere warten jeden Abend ___auf___ die Nachrichten. Sie freuen sich auch hier und da ___auf___ ein Theaterstück oder ein Konzert. Die großen Nachrichtenmagazine sprechen nicht nur ___über___ Politik, sondern auch ___über___ Kultur und Sport. Manche Leute sitzen täglich am Computer, um sich ___über___ alles gut zu informieren. Sie stellen Fragen ___an___ andere Leute im Internet und warten dann ___auf___ ihre Antwort. Ich halte nicht viel ___von / vom___ Fernsehen. Ich bin eine Leseratte und freue mich ___auf___ mein nächstes *(next)* Buch. ___Wofür___ interessieren Sie sich mehr: für Fernsehen, Bücher oder das Internet?

D. Womit? Damit! Stellen Sie Fragen mit einem **wo**-Kompositum oder einer Präposition + **wem** und antworten Sie mit einem **da**-Kompositum oder einer Präposition + Pronomen!

BEISPIEL Das private Fernsehen ist abhängig **von der Werbung.**
Wovon ist es abhängig? —Davon!

Die Werbung ist abhängig **von den Käufern.**
Von wem ist sie abhängig? —Von ihnen!

1. Einige Kritiker halten nicht viel **vom Fernsehen.** 2. Vor allem ärgern sie sich **über die vielen amerikanischen Serien.** 3. Sie sprechen **über die Zuschauer.** 4. Sie warten jede Woche **auf die Fortsetzung** *(continuation)*. 5. Diese Kritiker denken auch **an die Kinder.** 6. **Durch zu viel Fernsehen** verlieren sie an Kreativität. 7. Manche Leute sitzen jede freie Minute **vor dem Computer.** 8. **Für Familie und Freunde** und auch **fürs Hobby** haben sie oft wenig Zeit.

D: 1. Wovon halten sie nicht viel? Davon, vom Fernsehen! 2. Worüber ärgern sie sich? Darüber, über die vielen . . . ! 3. Über wen sprechen sie? Über sie, über die Zuschauer! 4. Worauf warten sie jede Woche? Darauf, auf die Fortsetzung! 5. An wen denken sie auch? An sie, an die Kinder! 6. Wodurch verlieren sie an Kreativität? Dadurch, durch zu viel Fernsehen . . . ! 7. Wovor sitzen manche Leute jede freie Minute? Davor, vorm Computer! 8. Für wen haben sie oft wenig Zeit? Für sie, für Familie und Freunde! Und wofür auch nicht? Dafür, fürs Hobby!

E. Deutsches Fernsehen Ergänzen Sie die Adjektivendungen, wo nötig *(necessary)*!

Das deutsch[e]____ Fernsehen ist eine gut[e]____ Mischung aus kulturell[en]____ Sendungen und leicht[er]____ Unterhaltung. Man bekommt auch viel[e]____ interessant[e]____ Sendungen aus verschieden[en]____ Nachbarländern. Das öffentlich[e]____ Fernsehen finanziert sich durch monatlich[e]____ Gebühren. Öffentlich[e]____ Sender *(pl.)* haben natürlich auch öffentlich[e]____ Aufgaben. Sie können leicht verschieden[e]____ Sendungen für klein[e]____ Interessengruppen bringen, z. B. international[e]____ Nachrichten in verschieden[en]____ Sprachen oder auch lokal[es]____ Kabarett *(n.)*. Privat[es]____ Fernsehen gibt es auch. Kritiker sprechen von schlecht[er]____ Qualität beim privat[en]____ Fernsehen. Viele Deutsche sind groß[e]____ Leseratten. Sie lesen alles, was ihnen in die Hände fällt, von lokal[en]____ Nachrichten und lokal[er]____ Werbung bis zu intellektuell[en]____ Nachrichtenmagazinen. Sie hören aber auch gern Radio, von leicht[er]____ bis zu klassisch[er]____ Musik.

Weiteres

F. Kurzgespräche Bereiten Sie mit Ihrem Partner / Ihrer Partnerin einen der beiden Dialoge vor und präsentieren Sie ihn danach vor der Klasse!

1. **Im Buchladen**
   You are in a bookstore. As the clerk approaches you, tell him/her you need a gift for someone, perhaps a good book about art, music, the theater, or film. He/She shows you several ones that he/she says are very nice, but you don't like any of them. Finally, you find something that's just right, including the price. You take it.

2. **Die Notizen** ***(Notes)***
   You have lent your notebook with class notes to a classmate [give him/her a name] who has failed to return it as promised—again. Not only that, but this classmate has passed the notebook on to a third person who was supposed to return it to you. You have called there and didn't get an answer. You are trying to prepare for a test. Tell your roommate your tale of woe and vent your anger about the situation.

G. Was tun die Deutschen in ihrer Freizeit? Sehen Sie sich die Tabelle an und beantworten Sie ein paar Fragen!

In case you are curious: **der Beruf,-e** *profession*; **erledigen** *to take care of*; **der Heimwerker,-** *handyman*; **die Ausstellung,-en** *exhibition, show*

Kostbare Zeit

Die Top 10 der Freizeitaktivitäten in Deutschland

Aktivität	%
mit Freunden zusammen sein	88 %
gut essen gehen	76
Auto fahren	61
shoppen/bummeln	54
Parties feiern	52
Arbeiten für meinen Beruf erledigen	38
heimwerken	38
Theater, Konzerte besuchen	36
sich beruflich fortbilden	35
Museen, Ausstellungen besuchen	35

Quelle: VA 2008 deutschsprachige Bevölkerung ab 14 Jahren (mache ich besonders gern/gern) © Globus 2509

1. Wie verbringen *(spend)* die Deutschen besonders gern ihre Freizeit?
2. Was besuchen sie gern?
3. Wie viel Prozent (%) interessieren sich für Heimwerken *(doing home improvements)* und extra Arbeit für den Beruf *(profession)*?
4. Wie viel Prozent sind daran interessiert, sich beruflich fortzubilden *(to advance their education)*?
5. Wie viel Prozent der Zeit verbringen Sie womit?

Schreibtipp

Writing an Essay

Before writing an essay, organize your thoughts by making a brief outline. What is your main point? What is the main idea you want to convey? What are the supporting elements of that point? Although your outline may be in English or in German, remember that when you start to write, you need to do so in German only, using the simple vocabulary and structures that you know. Make your writing more interesting in ways that you have learned: by adding adjectives and adverbs, and by varying your sentence structure.

H. Aufsatz: Die Funktion von Medien Lesen Sie den *Lesetext* noch einmal und schreiben Sie dann mit Hilfe der Stichwörter *(cues)* unten einen kleinen Aufsatz (10–12 Sätze) über den Einfluss *(influence)* der Medien auf die Menschen in unserer Zeit!

Radio	Zeitschriften	Zeitungen	Computer
Fernsehen	Filme	Bücher	Internet

Hörverständnis

Pläne für den Abend Wohin will Stefan mit seinen Freunden? Ergänzen Sie die folgenden Aussagen!

Zum Erkennen: ausverkauft *(sold out)*; die Anzeige, -n *(advertisement)*

1. Monika möchte gern __c__ gehen.
   a. ins Kino
   b. in die Bibliothek
   c. ins Theater
2. Felix und Stefan finden das __a__.
   a. eine gute Idee
   b. furchtbar langweilig
   c. komisch
3. Monika ruft an, um __b__.
   a. Karten zu bestellen
   b. zu fragen, ob es noch Karten gibt
   c. zu fragen, wie man zum Theater kommt
4. Sie wollen zur Kabarett-Kneipe KARTOON gehen, weil __b__.
   a. das Programm sehr interessant ist
   b. sie dort auch essen können
   c. Monika Gutes darüber gehört hat
5. Sie wollen um __b__ Uhr essen.
   a. 18.30
   b. 19.30
   c. 21.00
6. Dorthin kommt man __c__ .
   a. zu Fuß
   b. mit der U-Bahn
   c. irgendwie *(somehow)*, aber das wissen wir nicht

The term *cabaret* **(das Kabarett)** describes both a form of theatrical entertainment and the dance halls where the genre emerged in the late 19th century. Performers satirized contemporary culture and politics through skits, pantomimes, poems, and songs. During the Weimar Republic (1919–1933), this type of variety show flourished in Germany, but was then banned by the Nazis for its political nature. After World War II, the cabaret reemerged as a popular form of entertainment.

For further practice, an optional two-part video (**Szenen** and **Interviews**) is available on the ***Wie geht's?*** Premium Website and in iLrn, with corresponding questions and activities in the *Arbeitsbuch* (SAM).

As an optional activity with Google Earth, you could visit any larger city in the German-speaking countries and look for theaters, opera houses, and concert halls.

Literatur

Biographisches

Rainer Maria Rilke (1875–1926) is regarded as one of the greatest 20th-century poets writing in German. Using metaphors and contradictions, his words—both in verse and highly lyrical prose—paint images of intense feelings. A relatively new undertaking, the **Rilke Projekt,** involves contemporary actors and pop artists who interpret Rilke's texts to make them accessible to new generations (on the website of the **Rilke Projekt**, you can find sample tracks and more information).

Bertolt Brecht (1898–1956) is one of Germany's most celebrated 20th-century playwrights. His theory of the "epic theater" has had a considerable influence on modern theories of drama. By using various visual techniques and artificial acting styles—such as having the actors deliver their lines in a deliberately expressionless way—he tried to minimize the audience's rapport with the action while increasing its awareness of the play's moral and political message. Brecht fled Berlin in 1933, seeking refuge in Switzerland, Denmark, Finland, and finally the United States (1941–1947). He returned to East Berlin in 1949 and founded the Berlin Ensemble. Brecht's works include *Die Dreigroschenoper* (1928; first film adaptation in 1931), *Mutter Courage und ihre Kinder* (1939), *Der gute Mensch von Sezuan* (1942), *Das Leben des Galilei* (1938/1939), and *Der kaukasische Kreidekreis* (1945).

Vor dem Lesen

Zwei Gedichte, zwei Stilformen Überfliegen Sie *(Skim through)* die beiden Gedichte und finden Sie heraus, wie sie sich unterscheiden *(differ)*!

1. Wie viele Strophen hat Rilkes Gedicht und wie viele das Gedicht von Brecht?
2. Haben die beiden Gedichte Reime? Wenn ja, was reimt sich? Ist da ein Muster *(pattern)*, z. B. a b a oder . . . ?
3. Sind die Verben konjugiert oder stehen sie nur da als Substantiv?
4. Gibt es in den Gedichten Kommas, Fragezeichen *(question marks)*, Ausrufungszeichen oder Punkte?
5. Welche Anredeform *(form of address)* benutzen sie?

Du musst das Leben nicht verstehen

For a sublime reading of this poem, find the **Rilke-Projekt** on Youtube and look for the German actress Hannelore Elsner.

Du musst das Leben nicht verstehen,
dann wird es werden wie ein Fest.
Und lass dir jeden Tag geschehen° — happen
so wie ein Kind im Weitergehen° — while passing
von jedem Wehen° — blowing of the wind
sich viele Blüten° schenken lässt. — blossoms

Sie aufzusammeln und zu sparen,
das kommt dem Kind nicht in den Sinn°. — wouldn't think of it
Es löst sie leise aus° den Haaren, — quietly takes out
drin sie so gern gefangen° waren, — caught
und hält den lieben jungen Jahren
nach neuen seine Hände hin°. — stretches out

Rainer Maria Rilke

Source: Rainer Maria Rilke, „Du musst das Leben nicht verstehen", (1898)

Vergnügungen

Der erste Blick aus dem Fenster am Morgen
Das wiedergefundene alte Buch
Begeisterte° Gesichter
Schnee, der Wechsel° der Jahreszeiten
Die Zeitung
Der Hund°
Die Dialektik°
Duschen, Schwimmen
Alte Musik
Bequeme Schuhe
Begreifen°
Neue Musik
Schreiben, Pflanzen°
Reisen
Singen
Freundlich sein.

Bertolt Brecht

- enthusiastic
- change
- dog
- conflicting nature
- understanding
- planting

In case students ask: **Das Vergnügen** is a collective noun for *pleasure* or *fun*. **Die Vergnügung, -en** is used less common and more in the sense of *little pleasures*.

Source: Bertolt Brecht, „Vergnügungen" in *Gesammelte Werke,* (Frankfurt/Main: Suhrkamp, 1967)

Nach dem Lesen

A. Fragen zu den Gedichten

1. Was sollen wir laut *(according to)* Rilke im Leben tun oder nicht tun?
2. Was tut das Kind nicht mit den Blüten im Haar?
3. Brecht nimmt auch jeden Tag, wie er kommt. Was für scheinbar *(seemingly)* unwichtige Dinge sind ihm wichtig?
4. Ist sein Gedicht wirklich ein Gedicht oder nur eine Liste? Warum benutzt er diesen Stil? Was denken Sie?
5. Gibt es etwas, was beide verbindet *(connects)*?
6. Welches Gedicht gefällt Ihnen besser? Warum?

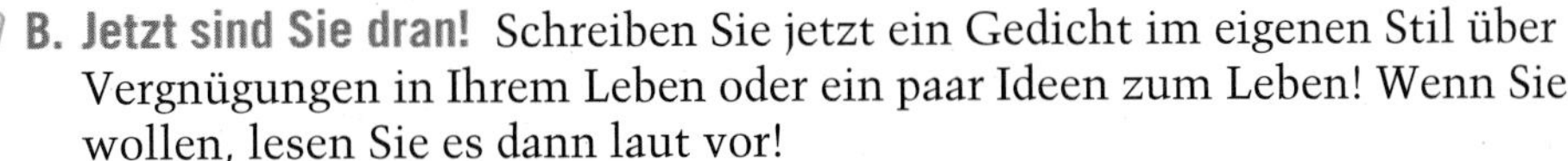

B. Jetzt sind Sie dran! Schreiben Sie jetzt ein Gedicht im eigenen Stil über Vergnügungen in Ihrem Leben oder ein paar Ideen zum Leben! Wenn Sie wollen, lesen Sie es dann laut vor!

Rückschau

Kapitelwortschatz

Hauptwörter

der Anfang, ¨e	*beginning, start*
die Auswahl (an)	*selection, choice (of)*
der Autor, -en	*author* (male)
die Autorin, -nen	*author* (female)
das Ballett, -s	*ballet*
der Blick (in / auf)	*glance (at); view (of)*
der Bürger, -	*citizen* (male)
die Bürgerin, -nen	*citizen* (female)
der Chor, ¨e	*choir*
das Ende	*end*
das Fernsehen	*television* (the medium)
der Film, -e	*film, movie*
das Gemälde, -	*painting*
der Komponist, -en, -en	*composer* (male)
die Komponistin, -nen	*composer* (female)
das Konzert, -e	*concert*
der Krimi, -s	*detective story*
die Kunst, ¨e	*art*
der Maler, -	*painter (artist)* (male)
die Malerin, -nen	*painter (artist)* (female)
die Nachricht, -en	*news* (on radio and television; usually pl.)
die Oper, -n	*opera*
das Orchester, -	*orchestra*
die Pause, -n	*intermission, break*
das Programm, -e	*(general) programming; TV channel*
der Roman, -e	*novel*
der Schauspieler, -	*actor* (male)
die Schauspielerin, -nen	*actor* (female)
die Sendung, -en	*(particular) program*
das Stück, -e	*piece; (theatrical) play; piece of music or ballet)*
die Unterhaltung	*entertainment*
die Vorstellung, -en	*performance*
die Werbung	*advertising*
die Zeitschrift, -en	*magazine*
die Zeitung, -en	*newspaper*
der Zuschauer, -	*spectator* (male)
die Zuschauerin, -nen	*spectator* (female)

Verben

an·fangen	*to start, begin*
sich ärgern über	*to get annoyed / upset about*
denken an	*to think about, of*
(sich) entscheiden (für / gegen)	*to decide (for / against)*
erzählen von	*to tell about*
sich freuen auf	*to look forward to*
halten von	*to think of, be of an opinion about*
(sich) holen	*to get, fetch*
sich informieren über	*to inform oneself, find out about*
sich interessieren für	*to be interested in*
klatschen	*to applaud*
lächeln (über)	*to smile (about)*
lachen	*to laugh*
schreiben an	*to write to*
sprechen von / über	*to talk, speak of / about*
sich vor·bereiten auf	*to prepare for*
vergessen	*to forget*
warten auf	*to wait for*
weinen	*to cry*

Adjektive

andere	*other*
dumm	*stupid(ly); silly*
einige	*some, a few* (pl. only)
folgend-	*following*
komisch	*funny, comical; strange, odd*
langweilig	*boring*
letzt-	*last*
lustig	*funny, with humor*
mehrere	*several* (pl. only)
nächst-	*next*
öffentlich	*public(ly)*
privat	*private(ly)*
spannend	*exciting, suspenseful*
traurig	*sad(ly)*
viele	*many*
wenige	*few*

Da- und *Wo-*Komposita

dafür	*for it/them*
dagegen	*against it/them*
damit	*with it/them*
danach	*after it/them*
darauf	*on it/them*
darin	*in it/them*
darüber	*above it/them; about it/them*
wofür?	*for what?*
wogegen?	*against what?*
womit?	*with what?*
worauf?	*on what?*
worüber?	*above what?; about what?*

Verschiedenes

am Anfang	*in the beginning*
am Ende	*at the end*
Das ärgert mich.	*That makes me mad.*
(Das ist doch) unglaublich!	*(That's) unbelievable!, (That's) hard to believe.*
(Das ist ja) Wahnsinn!	*(That's) crazy / awesome / unbelievable!*
(Das ist) klasse / spitze!	*(That's) great!*
(Das ist) unheimlich interessant!	*(That's) really interesting!*
Das ist zu lang (laut, *etc.*).	*That's too long* (*loud*, etc.).
etwa	*about, approximately*
Jetzt habe ich aber genug.	*That's enough. I've had it.*
Keine Ahnung!	*No idea!*
Na gut.	*All right.*
sowie	*as well as*
vor allem	*mainly, especially, above all*
vor kurzem	*recently*
Was gibt's im Fernsehen?	*What's (playing) on television?*
weder . . . noch	*neither . . . nor*

Zum Schluss

1. **Was sehe ich?**

   a. **Im Zimmer** Look around you. What can you see? Where are you sitting? Who else is there? Can you see out a window? Describe what you see with as many unpreceded adjectives as possible. Vary how you introduce what you see: (**Ich sehe . . .** , **Es gibt . . .** , etc.). Don't forget to use words like **andere**, **einige**, **mehrere**, **viele**, and **wenige**.

   b. **Wo war ich?** Share your description with your classmates. Can they figure out where you were sitting when you wrote it? Can you tell where they were sitting? Describe another place you all know so that your classmates can really recognize it, for example, **die Bibliothek**, **die Mensa**, **das Café**.

2. **Vorfreude ist die schönste Freude** (*Anticipation is the greatest pleasure*). Imagine that last week a performance or lecture was coming to town that you were looking forward to. Write 8–10 sentences using some of the words below about what you were looking forward to, and why. Did you look up information about it? Maybe you told other people about it? What happened when you went? Was it what you hoped for, or were you disappointed?

1	2	3	4	5
sich freuen auf	der Autor	der Anfang	dumm	am Anfang
warten auf	der Film	der Blick	komisch	am Ende
sich ärgern über	der Komponist	das Ende	langweilig	danach
sich interessieren für	der Maler	der Schauspieler	spannend	etwa
halten von	das Ballett	das Programm	traurig	genauso wie
sprechen von	das Konzert	die Pause	lustig	sowie
sich informieren über	das Stück	die Vorstellung	nächst-	vor allem
anschauen	die Oper	der Zuschauer	letzt-	weder . . . noch

3. **Ein Trauminterview**

   a. **Eine Frage, bitte!** Plan an interview with a famous artist, musician, or director. You can interview someone who is famous now, or a historical figure. Be creative! Your questions should use as many **wo-**compounds as possible, but don't forget to use regular question words, too, e.g., **wo**, **wohin**, **woher**, **was**, **warum**, and **wann**.

   b. **Und jetzt die Antwort!** Now pretend you are the famous artist, musician, or director you interviewed. Answer the questions, being sure to use **da-**compounds when appropriate.

iLrn **Onlineaktivitäten** Visit iLrn for online activities related to this chapter. There you will find additional resources, such as a memory game (**Gedächtnisspiel**), a crossword puzzle (**Kreuzworträtsel**), audio flash cards (**Vokabelblitz**), a tutorial quiz (**Mini-Quiz**), and the active vocabulary (**Wortschatz**) for this chapter.

Kapitel 11

Beziehungen

Lernziele In this chapter you will learn about:

Zum Thema

Relationships, friendship, personal characteristics, and pets

Fokus

Family and society, love and marriage, pets, and Liechtenstein

Einblicke

Märchen: Rumpelstilzchen
Literatur: Jutta Strzalka, *Mit zwei Löffeln*

Struktur

- The simple past
- Conjunctions: ***als, wann, wenn***
- The past perfect

Rückschau

Kapitalwortschatz
Zum Schluss

RESSOURCEN

iLrn iLrn | Video
Audio | SAM

Gute Freunde auf bunten Blättern im Herbst

Vorschau Family and Society

In Germany, as in other modern countries, there has been much progress made to achieve equal rights between men and women. Gone is the stereotype of the woman whose life revolves around children, kitchen, and church (**Kinder, Küche, Kirche**), whereby men were expected to be the sole provider. Today, women—self-confident and highly qualified—usually want both: children and a career. Indeed, a reversal of roles, where a man stays at home, is not that unusual any more. Sixty-seven percent of women in Western Germany and seventy-four percent in Eastern Germany work—and more and more in advanced positions. Nevertheless, women are still at a disadvantage when working part-time or in lower positions, thus receiving a lower income.

Until reunification, only half of West German women worked outside the home, compared to more than ninety percent in East Germany, where all men and women were not only entitled but also required to work. To make parenthood possible with full-time employment, state-run day care and other services were readily available. Staying home with a sick child was taken for granted in East Germany, and mothers were able to take as much as one year of maternity leave with full pay.

■ Two main factors contributed to the high employment rate of women in the former GDR: the need for additional income and the law that required all able-bodied men and women to work.

Today, family promotion is playing an increasingly important role. German laws regarding pregnancy and childbirth reflect the conviction that women and men who raise children are performing a task vital to society and, therefore, are granted some tax and social security advantages. Working women are entitled to maternity leave with pay (**der Mutterschutz**) six weeks before and eight weeks after childbirth. After that, the mother or the father is entitled to a subsidy (**das Elterngeld**), limited to the first 12 or 14 months following the child's birth or adoption (up to age 8). The parent who interrupts his or her career to raise children receives sixty-seven percent of his or her last net income, or a minimum of 300 and a maximum of 1,800 euros.

The **Kindergeld** is 184 € for the first two children, 190 € for the third child, and 215 € for the fourth child and any further children.

The legal right to up to three years leave (**die Elternzeit**) from work also makes an important contribution to supporting parents. During this "parental time," parents cannot be fired and can opt to work part time. Moreover, every family receives a monthly child benefit of 184 euros (**das Kindergeld**) for each child until the child is 18 years old. Time spent on raising a child (as well as time spent caring for a sick family member) is counted when calculating a person's social security benefits later in life. This practice aims to assess fairly work within the home as equal to gainful employment. However, the problem of the shortage in child-care facilities in Germany, which is one of the main obstacles to climbing career ladders for women, has yet to be resolved. The government has promised to open more day-care slots for children under the age of three to make it easier for mothers and/or fathers to combine working and raising a family.

■ **Fragen:** 1. Wie heißt das neue Baby? 2. Wann ist es geboren? 3. Wie groß und schwer war Carolin bei der Geburt? Wissen Sie, wie viel das in amerikanischen Maßen *(measures)* ist? 4. Hat Carolin Geschwister? Wenn ja, wie heißt der Bruder / die Schwester? 5. Die Anzeige *(ad)* zeigt das Baby in der Wiege *(cradle)*. Was tut das Brüderchen? 6. Wie heißen die glücklichen Eltern?

ZWISCHEN KIND UND KARRIERE

NILS ist jetzt der große Bruder von

Carolin

3. Juli 2014

3.340 g - 50 cm

Es freuen sich mit ihm seine Eltern

Monika und Arnim Thiemann

Adensen, im Juli 2014

Zum Thema

Warm-ups: 1. **Was finden Sie schön** (furchtbar, langweilig, spannend, leicht, schwer)**?** 2. **Wie viele *da*-Komposita kennen Sie?** Sie haben eine Minute. 3. **Wie geht's weiter?** Bilden Sie Sätze mit: heute Morgen, gestern Nachmittag, vorgestern Abend, am Wochenende, vor einem Jahr, damals, eines Tages! 4. **Kombinieren Sie mit dem Genitiv, z. B. Adresse: Hotel → die Adresse des Hotels!** (a. **der Anfang:** Programm, Vorstellung, Ferien, Flug; b. **das Ende:** Film, Pause, Stück, Nachrichten; c. **die Telefonnummer:** Kino, Flughafen, Kaufhaus, Herr, Studentin, Student, Leute).

You might suggest a personalization activity in which students use the information about the characters presented in the dialogue to write personal ads for Mia, Nicole, and Frank.

Gespräch

Partnersuche

MIA Nicole, hör mal! „Gesucht wird: hübsche, dynamische, zärtliche Eva. Belohnung: gut aussehender Adam mit Herz, Ende 20, mag Antiquitäten, alte Häuser, schnelle Wagen, Tiere, Kinder."

NICOLE Hmm, nicht schlecht, aber nicht für mich. Ich habe Angst in schnellen Autos und gegen Tiere bin ich allergisch.

MIA Dann schau mal hier! „Es gibt, was ich suche. Aber wie finden? Künstler, Anfang 30, charmant, unternehmungslustig, musikalisch, sucht sympathische, gebildete, zuverlässige Frau mit Humor." Ist das was?

Gesucht wird: hübsche, dynamische, zärtliche EVA. Belohnung: gut aussehender ADAM mit Herz, Ende 20, mag Antiquitäten, alte Häuser, schnelle Wagen, Tiere, Kinder.

Es gibt, was ich suche. Aber wie finden? Künstler, Anfang 30, charmant, unternehmungslustig, musikalisch, sucht sympathische, gebildete, zuverlässige Frau mit Humor.

NICOLE Ja, vielleicht. Er sucht jemanden mit Humor. Das gefällt mir; und Musik mag ich auch. Aber ob er Jazz mag?

MIA Vielleicht können wir sie beide kennenlernen?

NICOLE Ich weiß nicht. Mir ist das zu dumm, Leute durch Anzeigen in der Zeitung kennenzulernen.

MIA Quatsch! Versuchen wir's doch! Was haben wir zu verlieren?

NICOLE Was meinst du, Frank?

FRANK Warum versucht ihr's nicht im Internet, wenn ihr's ernst meint? Da habt ihr mehr Auswahl.

NICOLE Ach nee. Das ist mir zu riskant.

FRANK Du bist eben ein Angsthase.

MIA Luca und Emilie haben sich im Internet kennengelernt.

NICOLE Ja, sie haben Glück gehabt.

FRANK Siehst du!

A: Anzeigen in der Zeitung 2. eine hübsche, dynamische zärtliche EVA / Frau 3. für Antiquitäten, alte Häuser, schnelle Wagen, Tiere, Kinder 4. nichts 5. eine sympathische, gebildete, zuverlässige Frau mit Humor 6. nicht schlecht / ganz gut. 7. möchte beide Männer kennenlernen 8. im Internet 9. weil sie nicht nach einem Partner im Internet suchen will 10. Luca und Emilie

A. Alles verstanden?

1. Was sehen sich Nicole und Mia an?
2. Was sucht der erste Mann?
3. Wofür interessiert er sich?
4. Was hält Nicole von dem ersten Mann?
5. Was sucht der zweite Mann?
6. Was hält Nicole von der zweiten Anzeige?
7. Was meint Mia dazu?
8. Wo hat man vielleicht mehr Auswahl?
9. Warum soll Nicole ein Angsthase sein?
10. Wer von den Freunden hat sich im Internet kennengelernt?

B. Jetzt sind Sie dran! Schauen Sie sich mit Ihrem Partner / Ihrer Partnerin Anzeigen im Internet oder in der Zeitung an, wo Leute Lebenspartner, Freunde fürs Hobby oder vielleicht auch ein Tier suchen. Reagieren Sie darauf *(react to it)*! Wechseln Sie sich ab!

Wortschatz 1

Die Beziehung, -en *(relationship)*

der Partner, -	*partner*	ledig	*single*
Wunsch, ¨-e	*wish*	verliebt (in + *acc.*)	*in love (with)*
das Vertrauen	*trust*	verlobt (mit)	*engaged (to)*
die Anzeige, -n	*ad(vertisement)*	(un)verheiratet	*(un)married*
Ehe, -n	*marriage*	geschieden	*divorced*
Freundschaft	*friendship*	sich verlieben (in + *acc.*)	*to fall in love (with)*
Hochzeit, -en	*wedding*	sich verloben (mit)	*to get engaged (to)*
Liebe	*love*	heiraten	*to marry, get married (to)*
Scheidung, -en	*divorce*		

Die Eigenschaft, -en *(attribute, characteristic)*

attraktiv	*attractive*	zärtlich	*affectionate*
charmant	*charming*	(un)ehrlich	*(dis)honest*
ernst / lustig	*serious / funny*	(un)freundlich	*(un)friendly*
fleißig / faul	*industrious / lazy*	(un)gebildet	*(un)educated*
gut aussehend	*good-looking*	(un)geduldig	*(im)patient*
hübsch / hässlich	*pretty / ugly*	(un)glücklich	*(un)happy*
intelligent / dumm	*intelligent / stupid*	(un)kompliziert	*(un)complicated*
jung	*young*	(un)musikalisch	*(un)musical*
lieb	*kind, good*	(un)selbstständig	*(dependent) independent*
nett	*nice*		
reich / arm	*rich, wealthy / poor*	(un)sportlich	*(un)athletic*
schick	*chic, stylish; neat*	(un)sympathisch	*(un)congenial, (un)likable*
schlank	*slim, slender*		
schrecklich	*awful*	(un)talentiert	*(un)talented*
süß	*sweet; cute*	(un)zuverlässig	*(un)reliable*
vielseitig	*versatile*		

Verschiedenes

der Hund, -e	*dog*
Vogel, ¨	*bird*
das Pferd, -e	*horse*
Tier, -e	*animal*
die Katze, -n	*cat*
beid- / beide	*both / both (of them)*
damals	*then, in those days*
eigen-	*own*
jemand	*someone, somebody*
ein·laden (lädt ein), eingeladen	*to invite*
meinen	*to think, be of the opinion*
passieren (ist)	*to happen*
träumen (von)	*to dream (of, about)*
vergleichen, verglichen	*to compare*
verlieren, verloren	*to lose*
versuchen	*to try*
So ein süßes Kätzchen!	*Such a cute kitty!*
Wenn du meinst.	*If you think so.*

Zum Erkennen: gesucht wird *(wanted);* dynamisch *(dynamic);* die Belohnung *(reward);* mit Herz *(kind-hearted);* die Antiquitäten *(antiques);* Angst haben vor *(+ dat.) (to be afraid of);* allergisch gegen *(allergic to);* der Künstler, - *(artist);* unternehmungslustig *(enterprising);* mit Humor *(with a sense of humor);* Ach nee. *(coll: I don't think so.);* riskant *(risky);* der Angsthase *(coll.: scaredy-cat)* AUCH: das Imperfekt *(simple past);* die Konjunktion, -en *(conjunction);* das Perfekt *(present perfect)*

If students ask: *engagement* **die Verlobung, -en,** *honeymoon* **die Flitterwochen *(pl.)*,** *same-sex marriage* **die gleichgeschlechtliche Ehe;** *to separate* **s. trennen,** *to get divorced* **s. scheiden lassen;** *devoted* **anhänglich;** *insecure* **unsicher;** *loving* **liebevoll;** *optimistic* **optimistisch;** *pessimistic* **pessimistisch;** *self-confident* **selbstbewusst;** *shy* **schüchtern;** *stubborn* **stur;** *successful* **erfolgreich**

■ Note: **der Hund = er; das Pferd = es; die Katze = sie.**

■ Note **jemand** in the various cases: **Jemand** ist an der Tür. Er bringt **jemanden** mit. Sie spricht mit **jemandem.**

■ **Kätzchen:** As mentioned in Appendix 1, all nouns with the suffix **-chen** are neuter. This suffix makes diminutives of nouns, that is, it denotes them as being small or (as in the case of people or animals) may indicate affection: **das Herrchen, das Frauchen** *(loving dog owner).* When adding this suffix, other changes might apply: der Hund / **das Hündchen,** der Vogel / **das Vögelchen,** die Katze / **das Kätzchen**

Übungen zum Thema

A: charmant, ernst, freundlich, reich, sportlich; glücklich; attraktiv, gebildet, dumm, ehrlich, faul, geduldig, gemütlich, intelligent, kompliziert, musikalisch, geschieden, selbstständig, sympathisch, zärtlich, zuverlässig; verliebt, verlobt, verheiratet

A. Wie heißt das Adjektiv?

1. der Charme, Ernst, Freund, Reichtum, Sport
2. das Glück
3. die Attraktion, Bildung, Dummheit, Ehrlichkeit, Faulheit, Geduld, Gemütlichkeit, Intelligenz, Komplikation, Musik, Scheidung, Selbstständigkeit, Sympathie, Zärtlichkeit, Zuverlässigkeit
4. sich verlieben, sich verloben, verheiraten

B. Fragen

1. Was machen Sie und Ihre Freunde in der Freizeit? Worüber sprechen Sie?
2. Welche Eigenschaften finden Sie bei Freunden wichtig? Wie dürfen sie nicht sein?
3. Waren Sie schon einmal in einen Schauspieler / eine Schauspielerin oder einen Sänger / eine Sängerin verliebt? Wenn ja, in wen?
4. Was halten Sie vom Zusammenleben vor dem Heiraten? Was halten Sie vom Heiraten? Wie alt sollen Leute mindestens *(at least)* sein, wenn sie heiraten? Finden Sie eine lange Verlobung wichtig? Warum (nicht)?

Fokus Love and Marriage

The practice of advertising for partners on the Internet and in the print media has been commonplace in the German-speaking countries for some time. Television dating shows are popular.

When marrying, women no longer automatically take the name of their husband; instead, they frequently use hyphenated last names or keep their own names. Children can have the name of either partner. Widowed women keep their married name, whereas divorced women are free to use their maiden name **(der Mädchenname)** again. Divorce is granted on the basis of irreconcilable differences—not merely infidelity—and all retirement funds accrued during the marriage are distributed in equal shares.

Same-sex couples in Germany have had the right to marry since 2001, although full equality with traditional marriage—such as tax benefits and survivorship rights—has not yet been realized. For a marriage to be legally recognized, it must be performed at the office of records **(das Standesamt),** usually located in city hall. A church ceremony afterward is still popular. Traditionally, both German men and women wear their wedding bands on the left hand during their engagement. The bands are then switched to the right hand after the wedding. Today, the American custom of a separate engagement ring is becoming more common, but the wedding ring is still worn on the right hand.

Das erste gemeinsame* (joint) *Projekt für die Jungverheirateten

You could mention **Polterabend,** the noisy custom that calls for friends of the couple to go to the bride's house the day before the wedding and smash old plates or pottery outside the door—probably related to the old saying **Scherben bringen Glück.** To help ensure a happy marriage, the couple sweeps up the broken pieces together. The picture above shows the tradition of log sawing. When the newlyweds exit the Church, they have to cut a log situated on sawhorses in half! This is to symbolize how they can accomplish anything in their future, if they work together.

C. Anzeigen über Menschen und Tiere

1. **Adjektivendungen** Ergänzen Sie die fehlenden Adjektivendungen!

a. Millionär bin ich nicht. Will mein Glück auch nicht kaufen. Ich, 28 / 170, suche keine exotische___ Diskoqueen, sondern ein nettes___, natürliches___ Mädchen, darf auch hübsch-___ sein.

b. Tanzen, Segeln und Reisen sind meine große___ Liebe. Welche sympathische___ Frau mit Fantasie will mitmachen? Ich bin Journalist, nicht hässlich-___ und mit unkonventionellen___ Ideen.

c. Sympatischer___ Klarinettenanfänger sucht interessante___ Leute mit Spaß und Freude am Musizieren.

d. Man denkt, man arbeitet, man schläft, man lebt? Ist das alles? Endzwanzigerin, 180, sucht charmanten___, lustigen___ ADAM mit vielseitigen___ Interessen.

e. Neu in Bonn: Attraktive___, dynamische___ Psychotherapeutin, Mutter und kreative___ Frau mit Charme und Esprit sucht Kontakt zu netten___ Leuten für Freizeit und Freundschaft.

f. Verloren: Kleines___, schwarzes___ Hündchen mit rotem___ Halsband und silbernem___ Schild. Hört auf den Namen „Fiffi".

g. Gefunden: Grauweiße___ Katze, ziemlich alt-___, aber sehr lieb-___, hat den Weg nach Hause vergessen. Sind Sie das traurige___ Herrchen oder Frauchen?

For a review of unpreceded adjective endings, see Kapitel 10, Struktur 10.3.

In Europe, the metric system is standard. Is someone who has a height of 180 cm short or tall? Figure it out yourself. Since one inch equals 2.54 cm, divide the height by 2.54 to get the number of inches. How tall are you in metric terms? Multiply your height in inches by 2.54. People generally state their height informally like this: **Ich bin ein Meter achtzig groß.** *I'm 1 meter 80 cm tall.*

2. **Noch einmal!** Lesen Sie die Anzeigen noch einmal und sprechen Sie dann mit den anderen über die folgenden Themen!
   a. Welche Qualitäten suchen die Leute in den Anzeigen? Machen Sie eine Liste!
   b. Wie sehen die Leute sich selbst *(themselves)*? Was sagen sie und was sagen sie nicht? Machen Sie eine Liste!

D. Beziehungen

1. **Freundschaft**
   a. Welche Qualitäten suchen Sie in einem Freund oder einer Freundin?
   b. Sind Freundschaften wichtig? Wenn ja, warum?
   c. Was tun Sie gern mit Ihren Freunden?

2. **Liebe** Lesen Sie die folgende Liste verschiedener Eigenschaften! Welche fünf davon sind Ihnen beim Lebenspartner besonders wichtig? Vergleichen Sie Ihre Auswahl mit den Listen der anderen!

__ häuslich *(domestic)*	__ optimistisch	__ ruhig	__ schick
__ sparsam *(thrifty)*	__ natürlich	__ zuverlässig	__ tolerant
__ sportlich	__ ehrlich	__ zärtlich	__ dynamisch
__ kinderlieb *(loves children)*	__ musikalisch	__ ambitiös	__ lustig
__ tierlieb *(loves animals)*	__ ernst	__ fleißig	__ reich

E. So bin ich. Welche fünf Eigenschaften sind typisch für Sie? Vergleichen Sie Ihre Liste mit der Liste Ihres Nachbarn / Ihrer Nachbarin!

F. Allerlei über Tiere

In case students ask about other pets in German: *ferret* **das Frettchen, -;** *fish* **der Fisch, -e;** *guinea pig* **das Meerschweinchen, -;** *hamster* **der Hamster, -;** *mouse* **die Maus, ¨-e;** *parrot* **der Papagei, -en;** *pig* **das Schwein, -e;** *rabbit* **das Häschen, -;** *snake* **die Schlange, -n;** *pet bird* **der Ziervogel, ¨**

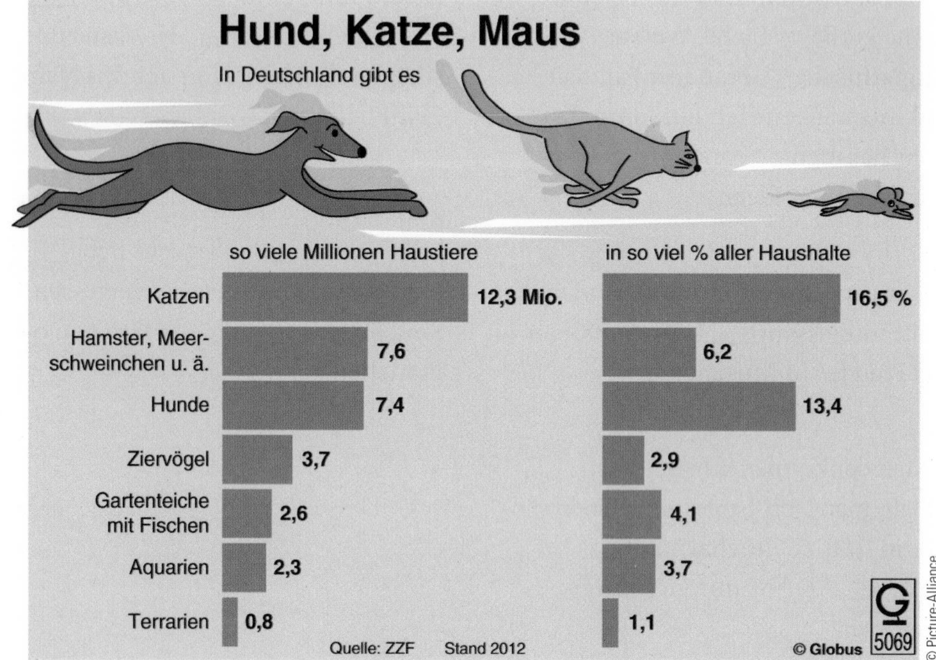

You could also have students bring in a picture of their favorite pet and tell the class about it.

1. Schauen Sie sich die Grafik an und machen Sie ein paar Vergleiche!
2. Was für Tiere haben Sie zu Hause?
3. Was für ein Tier wünschen Sie sich einmal?
4. Was ist Ihnen bei Tieren wichtig und was hassen *(hate)* Sie?

Fokus Beloved Pets

There are approximately 23 million pets **(Haustiere)** in Germany, the majority being cats, dogs, and small animals such as rabbits or guinea pigs, but also birds and fish. Germans are very fond of animals, and over 30 percent of all households own a pet. Usually tenants must have the permission of the landlord before keeping a pet. Dog owners must register with the local tax office **(das Finanzamt)** and pay a dog tax **(die Hundesteuer),** which varies from state to state. Having a personal liability policy is also recommended. Furthermore, certain breeds of dogs that are considered dangerous (pit bulls, Staffordshire bull terriers, etc.) must be kept on leashes, muzzled, and neutered.

Dogs are not allowed in grocery stores, but most cafés and restaurants allow them. Establishments that don't permit dogs inside have a sign on their windows showing a picture of a dog with the following text: **"Wir müssen leider draußen bleiben."** Dogs and cats can be taken on trains and buses; tickets for them are about half the regular fare.

G. Eigene Anzeigen Schreiben Sie Ihre eigene Anzeige auf der Suche nach *(in search of)* Freundschaft, einem Reisepartner / einer Reisepartnerin, nach Liebe oder einem Haustier.

H. Beschreibung Beschreiben Sie sich selbst *(yourself)*, eine andere Person oder ein Tier! Wählen Sie eins der vier Themen und schreiben Sie 8–10 Sätze.

1. So bin ich.
2. Mein(e) . . .
3. Was für ein toller (interessanter, lieber . . .) Mensch!
4. Was für ein komischer (langweiliger, schrecklicher . . .) Mensch!
5. Was für ein süßes (interessantes, liebes . . .) Tier!

© S Kumar/Shutterstock

© Igor Zakowski/Shutterstock

© MisterElements/Shutterstock

Schreibtipp

Describing People or Animals

You have learned enough adjectives to express admiration or dislike for people or animals. When using adjectives in combination with nouns, pay special attention to their endings. Remember that the flavoring particle **aber** can also express admiration (see Chapter 7) and the suffix **-chen** special affection: **Wo ist mein Schätzchen** *(little sweetheart)*?

Many everyday expressions include an animal: **Du hast einen Vogel! / Bei dir piept's!** *(You're crazy!)*; **Fauler Hund!** *(Lazy bum!)*; **Alles für die Katz'!** *(It's all in vain.)* Also, certain animals are associated with certain characteristics: **Schlau wie ein Fuchs** *(sly as a fox)*; **arbeitsam wie ein Pferd** *(hardworking as a horse)*; **geduldig wie ein Lamm** *(patient as a lamb)*.

Aussprache: f, v, ph, w

A. Laute

1. [f] **f**ast, **f**ertig, **f**reundlich, ö**ff**nen, Brie**f**
2. [f] **v**erliebt, **v**erlobt, **v**erheiratet, **v**ersucht, **v**ergessen, **v**erloren, **Ph**iloso**ph**ie
3. [v] **V**ideo, Kla**v**ier, Sil**v**ester, Pullo**v**er, Uni**v**ersität
4. [v] **w**er, **w**en, **w**em, **w**essen, **w**arum, sch**w**arz, sch**w**er, z**w**ischen

B. Wortpaare

1. *wine* / Wein
2. *when* / wenn
3. *oven* / Ofen
4. *veal* / viel
5. Vase / Wasser
6. vier / wir

For further review, see the Summary of Pronunciation in the front of this book. Study Part III, subsections 1, 4–5.

Hörverständnis

Leute sind verschieden. Hören Sie sich an, was man Ihnen über drei Leute erzählt! Welche Adjektive sind typisch für Sie? Schreiben Sie den Anfangsbuchstaben ihrer Namen neben die Adjektive, z. B. **M** = Martin, **O** = Oliver, **S** = Sabine.

Zum Erkennen: das Krankenhaus, ¨er *(hospital)*; während *(while)*; die Katastrophe, -n; nicht einmal *(not even)*

O attraktiv	M musikalisch	S schick
M faul	O nett	S sportlich
O freundlich	O populär	M unsportlich
O intelligent	M reich	
S lustig	O ruhig	

Struktur

11.1 The simple past *(imperfect, narrative past)*

The past tense is often referred to as the SIMPLE PAST because it is a single verb form in contrast to the perfect tenses (or "compound past tenses"), which consist of two parts: an auxiliary and a past participle.

We spoke German. Wir **sprachen** Deutsch.

The present perfect is the preferred tense in spoken German—especially in southern Germany, Austria, and Switzerland. Only the simple past of **haben, sein,** and the modals is common everywhere. The simple past is used primarily in continuous narratives such as novels, short stories, newspaper reports, and letters relating a sequence of events. Therefore, it is often also called the NARRATIVE PAST.

As with other tenses, one German verb form corresponds to several in English.

Sie **sprachen** Deutsch.
- *They **spoke** German.*
- *They **were speaking** German.*
- *They **did speak** German.*
- *They **used to speak** German.*

1. T-VERBS *(weak verbs)*

   T-verbs can be compared to regular English verbs such as *love / loved* and *work / worked*, which form the past tense by adding *-d* or *-ed* to the stem. To form the simple past of t-verbs, add **-te, -test, -te, -ten, -tet, -ten** to the STEM of the verb.

ich	lern**te**	wir	lern**ten**
du	lern**test**	ihr	lern**tet**
er/es/sie	lern**te**	sie	lern**ten**

   Familiar verbs that follow this pattern include: angeln, anschauen, ärgern, benutzen, danken, diskutieren, entspannen, ergänzen, erholen, erleben, erzählen, faulenzen, fehlen, fragen, freuen, glauben, gratulieren, hören, interessieren, kochen, lächeln, lachen, legen, machen, malen, meinen, passieren, reisen, sagen, sammeln, schmecken, setzen, spielen, suchen, stellen, stimmen, träumen, wandern, weinen, wohnen, wünschen.

   a. Verbs with stems ending in **-d, -t,** or certain consonant combinations add an **-e-** before the simple past ending.

ich	arbeit**ete**	wir	arbeit**eten**
du	arbeit**etest**	ihr	arbeit**etet**
er/es/sie	arbeit**ete**	sie	arbeit**eten**

   Familiar verbs that follow this pattern include: antworten, baden, bedeuten, beenden, bilden, heiraten, kosten, landen, mieten, öffnen, übernachten, vorbereiten, warten.

b. Irregular *t*-verbs—sometimes called *mixed verbs*—usually have a stem change. Compare the English *bring* / *brought* with the German **bringen / brachte.**

ich	br**ach**te	wir	br**ach**ten
du	br**ach**test	ihr	br**ach**tet
er/es/sie	br**ach**te	sie	br**ach**ten

Here is a list of the PRINCIPAL PARTS of all the irregular *t*-verbs that you have used thus far. Irregular present-tense forms are also noted. You already know all the forms of these verbs except their simple past. Verbs with prefixes have the same forms as the corresponding simple verbs **(brachte mit).** If you know the principal parts of a verb, you can derive all the verb forms you need!

INFINITIVE	PRESENT	SIMPLE PAST	PAST PARTICIPLE
bringen		**brachte**	gebracht
denken		**dachte**	gedacht
haben	hat	**hatte**	gehabt
kennen		**kannte**	gekannt
nennen		**nannte**	genannt
wissen	weiß	**wusste**	gewusst

Modals also belong to this group. (The past participles of these verbs are rarely used.)

dürfen	darf	**durfte**	(gedurft)
können	kann	**konnte**	(gekonnt)
müssen	muss	**musste**	(gemusst)
sollen	soll	**sollte**	(gesollt)
wollen	will	**wollte**	(gewollt)

NOTE: The simple past of irregular *t*-verbs has the same stem change as the past participle.

2. N-VERBS *(strong verbs)*

N-verbs correspond to such English verbs as *write* / *wrote* / *written* and *speak* / *spoke* / *spoken*. They usually have a stem change in the simple past that is difficult to predict and must therefore be memorized. (Overall they fall into a number of groups with the same changes. For a listing by group, see the Appendix.) To form the simple past, add **-, -st, -, -en, -t, -en** to the IRREGULAR STEM of the verb.

ich	sprach	wir	sprach**en**
du	sprach**st**	ihr	sprach**t**
er/es/sie	sprach	sie	sprach**en**

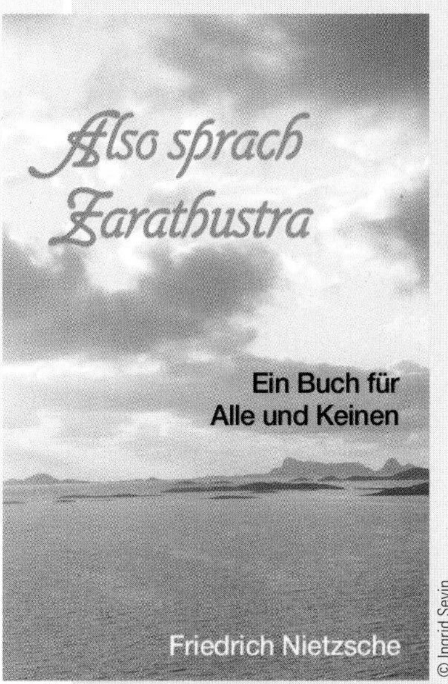

Also sprach
Zarathustra
Ein Buch für
Alle und Keinen
Friedrich Nietzsche

© Ingrid Sevin

Point out that "*n*-verb" refers to the "n" of the past participle (e.g., **gesprochen**) to make the terminology clear.

Have students mark the familiar principal parts in the irregular verb list of the Appendix and consult it from now on. Make them aware that there are two lists: one arranged alphabetically, the other divided into groups with the same stem changes. They should consult the list that best suits their learning style.

Learning the principal parts of *n*-verbs needs to be spread out over several days. Start the reading text early so that many verbs can be seen and learned in context. Stress that all forms but the simple past are already familiar.

Use this opportunity to review the participles while learning the simple past of these common verbs.

Here is a list of the PRINCIPAL PARTS of *n*-verbs that you have used up to now. You already know all the forms except the simple past. Irregular present-tense forms and the auxiliary **sein** are also noted.

INFINITIVE	PRESENT	SIMPLE PAST	PAST PARTICIPLE
an·fangen	fängt an	**fing an**	angefangen
an·ziehen		**zog an**	angezogen
beginnen		**begann**	begonnen
bleiben		**blieb**	ist geblieben
ein·laden	lädt ein	**lud ein**	eingeladen
empfehlen	empfiehlt	**empfahl**	empfohlen
entscheiden		**entschied**	entschieden
essen	isst	**aß**	gegessen
fahren	fährt	**fuhr**	ist gefahren
fallen	fällt	**fiel**	ist gefallen
finden		**fand**	gefunden
fliegen		**flog**	ist geflogen
geben	gibt	**gab**	gegeben
gefallen	gefällt	**gefiel**	gefallen
gehen		**ging**	ist gegangen
halten	hält	**hielt**	gehalten
hängen		**hing**	gehangen
heißen		**hieß**	geheißen
helfen	hilft	**half**	geholfen
kommen		**kam**	ist gekommen
lassen	lässt	**ließ**	gelassen
laufen	läuft	**lief**	ist gelaufen
lesen	liest	**las**	gelesen
liegen		**lag**	gelegen
nehmen	nimmt	**nahm**	genommen
rufen		**rief**	gerufen
schlafen	schläft	**schlief**	geschlafen
schreiben		**schrieb**	geschrieben
schwimmen		**schwamm**	ist geschwommen
sehen	sieht	**sah**	gesehen
sein	ist	**war**	ist gewesen
singen		**sang**	gesungen
sitzen		**saß**	gesessen
sprechen	spricht	**sprach**	gesprochen
stehen		**stand**	gestanden
steigen		**stieg**	ist gestiegen
tragen	trägt	**trug**	getragen
treffen	trifft	**traf**	getroffen
treiben		**trieb**	getrieben
trinken		**trank**	getrunken
tun	tut	**tat**	getan
vergessen	vergisst	**vergaß**	vergessen
vergleichen		**verglich**	verglichen
verlieren		**verlor**	verloren
waschen	wäscht	**wusch**	gewaschen
werden	wird	**wurde**	ist geworden

3. Sentences in the simple past follow familiar word-order patterns.

Der Zug **kam** um acht.
Der Zug **kam** um acht **an.**
Der Zug **sollte** um acht **ankommen.**
V1 V2

Er wusste, dass der Zug um acht **kam.**
Er wusste, dass der Zug um acht **ankam.**
Er wusste, dass der Zug um acht **ankommen sollte.**
V2 V1

Übungen

A. Nennen Sie das Imperfekt *(simple past)*!

BEISPIEL feiern *feierte*

1. fragen, erzählen, klatschen, lächeln, legen, bummeln, ersetzen, wechseln, fotografieren, passieren, erleben, schicken, putzen, benutzen, versuchen, sich kämmen, sich rasieren, sich entspannen, sich ärgern, sich erholen
2. arbeiten, baden, bilden, beenden, bedeuten, kosten, antworten, übernachten, warten, vorbereiten, öffnen
3. haben, müssen, denken, wissen, können, kennen, nennen
4. nehmen, essen, vergessen, sehen, lesen, ausgeben, herausfinden, singen, sitzen, liegen, kommen, wehtun, sein, hängen *(n-verb)*, beschreiben, treiben, heißen, entscheiden, einsteigen, vergleichen, schlafen, fallen, lassen, fahren, tragen, waschen, werden, einladen

A: 1. fragte, erzählte, klatschte, lächelte, legte, bummelte, ersetzte, wechselte, fotografierte, passierte, erlebte, schickte, putzte, benutzte, versuchte, kämmte sich, rasierte sich, entspannte sich, ärgerte sich, erholte sich 2. arbeitete, badete, bildete, beendete, bedeutete, kostete, antwortete, übernachtete, wartete, bereitete vor, öffnete 3. hatte, musste, dachte, wusste, konnte, kannte, nannte 4. nahm, aß, vergaß, sah, las, gab aus, fand heraus, sang, saß, lag, kam, tat weh, war, hing, beschrieb, trieb, hieß, entschied, stieg ein, verglich, schlief, fiel, ließ, fuhr, trug, wusch, wurde, lud ein

B. Ersetzen Sie die Verben!

BEISPIEL Sie schickte das Paket. (mitbringen)
Sie brachte das Paket mit.

1. Sie schickten ein Taxi. (suchen, bestellen, mieten, warten auf)
2. Das hatte ich damals nicht. (wissen, kennen, denken, mitbringen)
3. Wann solltet ihr zurückkommen? (müssen, wollen, dürfen, können)
4. Wir fanden es dort. (sehen, lassen, verlieren, vergessen)
5. Er dankte seiner Mutter. (antworten, zuhören, helfen, schreiben)
6. Du empfahlst den Sauerbraten. (bestellen, nehmen, wollen, bringen)

B: 1. suchten, bestellten, mieteten, warteten . . . auf 2. wusste, kannte, dachte, brachte . . . mit 3. musstet, wolltet, durftet, konntet 4. sahen, ließen, verloren, vergaßen 5. antwortete, hörte . . . zu, half, schrieb 6. bestelltest, nahmst, wolltest, brachtest

C. Wiederholen Sie die Texte im Imperfekt!

1. **Weißt du noch?** Ein Bruder und eine Schwester—Sie und Ihr Partner / Ihre Partnerin—erinnern sich *(remember)*.

BEISPIEL Großvater erzählt stundenlang von seiner Kindheit *(childhood)*.—Wir setzen uns aufs Sofa.
S1 Großvater erzählte stundenlang von seiner Kindheit.
S2 Wir setzten uns aufs Sofa.

a. Ich höre ihm gern zu.—Seine Geschichten interessieren mich auch.
b. Vater arbeitet viel im Garten.—Du telefonierst oder besuchst gern die Nachbarn.
c. Marita und Finn spielen stundenlang Karten.—Mutter kauft ein oder bezahlt Rechnungen.
d. Großmutter legt sich nachmittags ein Stündchen hin.—Sie freut sich danach auf ihre Tasse Kaffee. Richtig?

C.1: a. hörte zu, interessierten b. arbeitete, telefoniertest, besuchtest c. spielten, kaufte ein, bezahlte d. legte sich . . . hin, freute sich

C.2: a. lernte kennen
b. Wusstest, lernte . . . kennen
c. brachte d. feierten, hatte
e. dachte

2. **Haben Sie das nicht gewusst?** Ein paar Nachbarn klatschen *(gossip)* über Lothar und Ute.

BEISPIEL Hat Ute ihren Mann schon lange gekannt?
Kannte Ute ihren Mann schon lange?

a. Wie hat sie ihn kennengelernt?
b. Hast du nichts von ihrer Anzeige gewusst? Sie hat Lothar durch die Zeitung kennengelernt.
c. Der Briefträger *(mail carrier)* hat ihr einen Brief von dem jungen Herrn gebracht.
d. Gestern haben sie Hochzeit gefeiert. Sie hat Glück gehabt.
e. Das habe ich mir auch gedacht.

C.3: a. wollte . . . gehen, konnte
b. durftest c. wollten . . . weggehen d. Musstest bleiben
e. durfte . . . werden, konnte . . . sprechen, wollte . . . sagen, sollte . . . anrufen

3. **Schade!** Anna erzählt ihrer Freundin, warum sie traurig ist.

BEISPIEL Was willst du denn machen?
Was wolltest du denn machen?

a. Ich will mit Thomas ins Kino gehen, aber ich kann nicht.
b. Warum? Darfst du nicht?
c. Doch, aber meine Kopfschmerzen wollen einfach nicht weggehen.
d. Musst du im Bett bleiben?
e. Nein, aber ich darf nicht schon wieder krank werden. Leider kann ich nicht mit Thomas sprechen. Seine Mutter will es ihm sagen. Er soll mich anrufen.

C.4: a. hatten b. hieß
c. schliefen, frühstückten
d. fuhr, ging Ski laufen e. blieb, las, schrieb

4. **Wo wart ihr?** Caroline erzählt von ihrer kurzen Reise in die Schweiz.

BEISPIEL Wir sind eine Woche in Saas-Fee gewesen.
Wir waren eine Woche in Saas-Fee.

a. Von unserem Zimmer haben wir einen Blick auf die Alpen gehabt.
b. Die Pension hat natürlich Alpenblick geheißen.
c. Morgens haben wir lange geschlafen, dann haben wir gemütlich gefrühstückt.
d. Später bin ich mit der Metro-Alpin auf einen Berg gefahren und bin den ganzen Nachmittag Ski laufen gegangen.
e. Wolfgang ist unten geblieben, hat Bücher gelesen und Briefe geschrieben.

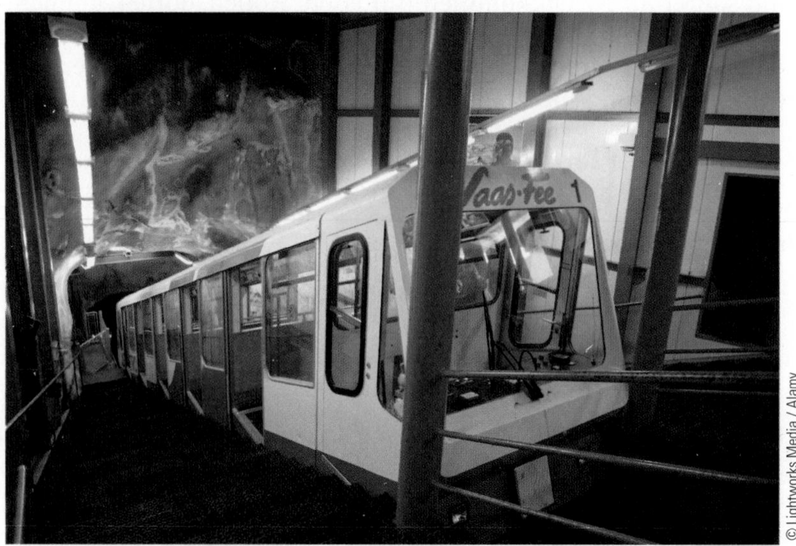

Mit der Metro-Alpin kommt man schnell hoch in die Berge.

Ich koche, wasche, putze und bin gern mit den Kindern zu Hause. Ich bin ein perfekter Hausmann!

D. Eine vielseitige Persönlichkeit Nennen Sie die fehlenden Verbformen im Imperfekt!

Else Lasker-Schüler ist eine vielseitige Persönlichkeit aus der deutschen Kunstszene. Geboren 1868 in Wuppertal, ___gehörte___ (gehören) sie zu einer jüdischen Familie, und man ___ließ___ (lassen) ihr damals viel Freiheit. 1894 ___heiratete___ (heiraten) sie einen Berliner Arzt, ___begann___ (beginnen) zu zeichnen *(draw)* und ihre ersten Gedichte *(poems)* zu schreiben. In Berlin ___brachte___ (bringen) sie 1899 ihren Sohn Paul zur Welt. Bald danach ___stieg___ sie aus dem bürgerlichen *(bourgeois)* Leben ___aus___ (aus·steigen), ___ließ___ (lassen) sich scheiden und ___heiratete___ (heiraten) 1903 Herwarth Walden, den Herausgeber *(editor)* der Zeitschrift *Der Sturm*, und ___kam___ (kommen) dadurch in Kontakt mit vielen Künstlern Berlins. Zwischen 1910 und 1930 ___wurde___ (werden) sie selbst sehr bekannt. Sie ___lebte___ (leben) nicht nur von ihren Gedichten und ihrer Prosa. Sie ___arbeitete___ (arbeiten) auch als Grafikerin. 1933 ___ging___ (gehen) sie ins Exil in die Schweiz, später nach Palästina. Als sie 1939 in Palästina ___ankam___ (an·kommen), ___war___ (sein) sie schockiert. Ihr ganzes Leben lang ___träumte___ (träumen) sie von einem Land, wo verschiedene Kulturen und Religionen harmonisch ___zusammenlebten___ (zusammen·leben). Dieses Palästina ___hatte___ (haben) nichts mit dem Land ihrer Träume zu tun. Sie ___fühlte___ (fühlen) sich dort nicht wohl. So ___schrieb___ (schreiben) sie 1942: „Ich bin keine Zionistin, keine Jüdin, keine Christin, ich glaube aber, ein tieftrauriger Mensch." Lasker-Schüler starb *(died)* 1945 im Alter von 77 Jahren in Jerusalem.

E. So war das damals. Stellen Sie Ihrem Partner / Ihrer Partnerin Fragen über frühere *(earlier)* Zeiten! Wechseln Sie sich ab! Fragen Sie, . . . !

Optional tongue twisters **(Zungenbrecher):** 1. Fischers Fritze fischte frische Fische. Frische Fische fischte Fischers Fritze. 2. Blaukraut bleibt Blaukraut und Brautkleid *(wedding dress)* bleibt Brautkleid.

1. wo er/sie früher wohnte
2. wo er/sie zur Schule ging
3. wie viele Leute zu Hause wohnten
4. was die Familie gewöhnlich am Wochenende machte
5. was sie in den Ferien machten
6. wie eine typische Woche aussah
7. ob er/sie Tiere zu Hause hatte; wenn ja, welche, wie sie waren und wie sie hießen
8. was ihm/ihr damals gefiel und was nicht
9. . . .

Fokus Liechtenstein

The Principality of Liechtenstein **(das Fürstentum Liechtenstein)** lies between Austria and Switzerland. Its territory is about the size of Washington, D.C., and it has about 36,000 inhabitants. The country maintains close relations with Switzerland, sharing customs, currency, postal service, and management of foreign affairs. Although many Liechtensteiners speak Alemannish, a German dialect, standard German is the official language of the country. Thanks to favorable tax policies, a large number of foreign businesses and banks have established nominal headquarters in Liechtenstein, which provides for thirty percent of the country's income. Despite a financial scandal in 2008, Liechtenstein remains with Monaco and Andorra one of the last uncooperative tax havens on the black list of the OECD (Organization for Economic Co-operation and Development).

Blick auf Liechtenstein

The castle in the capital, Vaduz, serves as the residence of Liechtenstein's royal family. According to the 1921 constitution, the country is a constitutional monarchy, hereditary in the male line. In 1989, Prince Hans Adam II succeeded to the throne; he transferred the official duties to his son Prince Alois in 2004. When Prince Alois married Princess Sophie in 1993, the royal family invited all 29,000 subjects to the wedding celebrations.

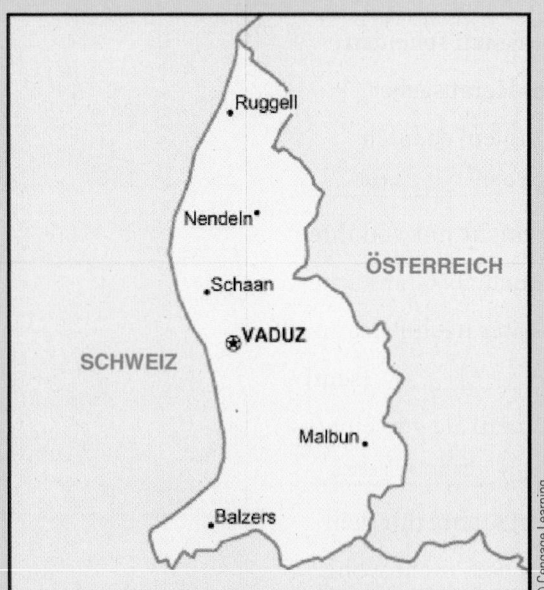

11.2 Conjunctions: *als, wann, wenn*

Care must be taken to distinguish among the conjunctions **als, wann,** and **wenn,** all of which correspond to the English *when.*

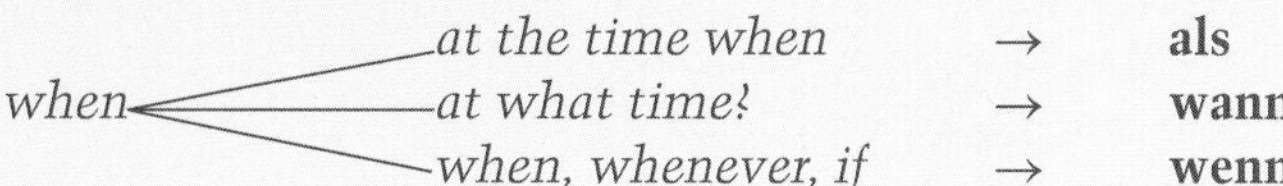

- **Als** refers to *a single (or particular) event in the past.*

  Als ich gestern Abend nach Hause kam, war er noch nicht zurück.
  When I came home last night, he wasn't back yet.

- **Wann** introduces direct or indirect *questions referring to time.*

  Ich frage mich, **wann** er nach Hause kommt.
  I wonder when (or at what time) he'll come home.

- **Wenn** covers all other situations.

  Wenn du ankommst, ruf mich an!
  When you arrive, call me! (referring to a present or future event)

  Wenn er kam, brachte er immer Blumen mit.
  Whenever he came, he brought flowers. (repeated event in the past)

Remember that **wenn** *(if)* can also introduce a conditional clause:

Wenn es nicht regnet, gehen wir spazieren.
If it doesn't rain, we'll take a walk.

Point out to students that the single event can cover an extended period of time, for example, **Als ich jung war, . . .**

Übungen

F. *Als, wann* oder *wenn*?

1. __Wenn__ ihr morgen kommt, zeigen wir euch die Bilder von unserer Reise.
2. Könnt ihr mir sagen, __wann__ euer Zug aus Köln ankommt?
3. __Als__ wir letzte Woche im Theater waren, sahen wir Ute und Lothar.
4. Sie bekommen die Möbel von den Großeltern, __wenn__ sie heiraten; aber wer weiß, __wann__ sie heiraten.
5. __Als__ ich sie das letzte Mal sah, wussten sie es noch nicht.

G. Verbinden Sie die Sätze mit *als, wann* oder *wenn*! Folgen Sie dem Beispiel!

BEISPIEL Emma rief an. Ich duschte mich. *(when)*
Emma rief an, als ich mich duschte.

(when) Ich duschte mich. Sie rief an.
Als ich mich duschte, rief sie an.

1. Wir sahen Emma und Lukas heute früh. Wir gingen einkaufen. *(when)*
2. *(when)* Sie spricht von ihren Freundinnen. Ihr Mann hört nicht zu.
3. Sie möchte (es) wissen. Die Freundin kommt aus Stuttgart an. *(when)*
4. *(when)* Sie las ihre E-Mails. Noch keine Nachricht war von ihr da.
5. *(when)* Diese Freundin besuchte sie. Sie bummelten immer gern durch die Stadt.

G: 1. . . . , als wir einkaufen gingen 2. Wenn sie von ihren Freundinnen spricht, . . . 3. . . . , wann die Freundin aus Stuttgart ankommt 4. Als sie ihre E-Mails las, war . . . 5. Wenn ihre Freundin sie besuchte, . . .

H. Was dann? Stellen Sie den anderen Fragen mit den Konjunktionen **als, wann** oder **wenn!** Benutzen Sie dabei das Präsens *(present tense)*, Perfekt *(present perfect)* oder Imperfekt! Wechseln Sie sich ab!

H: The examples given with **als, wann, wenn** are only suggestions. Students should be free to formulate any questions with these interrogative pronouns.

1. **Wo warst du, als . . . ?**

   BEISPIEL S1 Wo warst du, als am 11. September 2001 die Flugzeuge ins World Trade Center flogen?
   S2 Als das passierte, war ich . . .

2. **Wann warst du . . . ?**

   BEISPIEL S1 Wann warst du in New York?
   S2 Ich war letzten Sommer in New York.

3. **Was tust du gewöhnlich, wenn . . . ?**

   BEISPIEL S1 Was siehst du dir gewöhnlich an, wenn du in New York bist?
   S2 Wenn ich in New York bin, sehe ich mir die Kunst an.

I. Ein Bericht *(report)* oder eine Beschreibung: Damals Schreiben Sie sechs bis acht Sätze über eins der folgenden Themen. Benutzen Sie dabei möglichst viele Verben im Imperfekt und die Konjunktionen **als, wann** oder **wenn**!

1. **Eine schöne Reise** Sagen Sie, wo Sie waren und mit wem, was Sie sahen und erlebten!

2. **Als ich klein war, . . .** Beschreiben Sie etwas aus Ihrer Kindheit *(childhood)* oder Jugend *(youth)*!

   BEISPIEL *Als ich klein war, musste / wollte ich zu Fuß zur Schule gehen . . .*
   Wenn es regnete, fuhr ich mit dem Bus.

11.3 The past perfect

Students often find it difficult to remember to use the past perfect since in English this is often replaced by the simple past: *After we saw the movie, we had dessert.* It might be helpful to study newspaper or magazine articles or literary texts to show proper usage.

1. Like the present perfect, the PAST PERFECT in both English and German is a compound form consisting of an auxiliary and a past participle, with the auxiliary in the simple past.

   Ich **hatte** das gut **gelernt.**
   I had learned that well.

   Er **war** um 10 Uhr nach Hause **gekommen.**
   He had come home at 10 o'clock.

ich	**hatte**	. . . gelernt	**war**	. . . gekommen
du	**hattest**	. . . gelernt	**warst**	. . . gekommen
er/es/sie	**hatte**	. . . gelernt	**war**	. . . gekommen
wir	**hatten**	. . . gelernt	**waren**	. . . gekommen
ihr	**hattet**	. . . gelernt	**wart**	. . . gekommen
sie	**hatten**	. . . gelernt	**waren**	. . . gekommen

2. The past perfect is used to refer to events *preceding other events* in the past.

present

present perfect
or
simple past

past perfect

Er hat mich gestern angerufen. Er rief mich gestern an.	*He called me yesterday.*
Ich **hatte** ihm gerade **geschrieben.**	*I had just written to him.*
Wir sind zu spät am Bahnhof angekommen. Wir kamen zu spät am Bahnhof an.	*We arrived at the station too late.*
Der Zug **war** schon **abgefahren.**	*The train had already left.*

3. The conjunction **nachdem** *(after)* is usually followed by the past perfect in the subordinate clause, whereas the main clause is in the simple past or present perfect.

nachdem *after*

Nachdem er mich **angerufen hatte,** schickte ich den Brief nicht mehr ab.
Nachdem der Zug **abgefahren war,** gingen wir ins Zugrestaurant.

Practicing the past perfect presents an excellent opportunity to review the use of **haben** and **sein** as auxiliaries of the perfect tenses.

Übungen

J. Ersetzen Sie das Subjekt!

BEISPIEL Sie hatten uns besucht. (du)
Du hattest uns besucht.

1. Du hattest den Schlüssel gesucht. (ihr, Sie, sie/*sg.*)
2. Sie hatten das nicht gewusst. (wir, du, ich)
3. Ich war nach Dresden gereist. (sie/*pl.*, ihr, er)
4. Sie waren auch in der Dresdner Oper gewesen. (du, ich, wir)

J: 1. ihr hattet / Sie hatten / sie hat . . . gesucht 2. wir hatten / du hattest / ich hatte . . . gewusst 3. sie war / ihr wart / er war . . . gereist 4. du warst / ich war / wir waren . . . gewesen

K. Nicht schon wieder! Auf Englisch bitte!

1. Meine Schwester wollte den Film sehen.
2. Er war ein großer Erfolg.
3. Ich hatte ihn schon zweimal gesehen.
4. Ich hatte schon lange nicht mehr so gelacht.
5. Aber meine Schwester war nicht mitgekommen.
6. Sie hatte keine Zeit gehabt.
7. So sind wir später noch einmal zusammen ins Kino gegangen.

K: 1. My sister wanted to see the movie. 2. It was a big success. 3. I had seen it twice already. 4. I hadn't laughed that much in a long time. 5. But my sister did not come (along). 6. She didn't have time [*lit.* hadn't had . . .]. 7. So we went later once more together to the movies.

L: You could have students add to this list by telling about other events during the day.

L: a. Nachdem ich aufgestanden war, habe ich mich geduscht. b. Nachdem ich mich geduscht hatte, habe ich mir die Zähne geputzt. c. Nachdem ich mir die Zähne geputzt hatte, habe ich mich angezogen. d. Nachdem ich mich angezogen hatte, habe ich gefrühstückt. e. Nachdem ich gefrühstückt hatte, habe ich Helmut angerufen. f. Nachdem ich Helmut angerufen hatte, habe ich die Zeitung gelesen. g. Nachdem ich die Zeitung gelesen hatte, bin ich zur Arbeit gegangen. i. *(answer varies)*

L. Und dann?

Bei Schneiders Frau/Herr Schneider—Ihr Partner / Ihre Partnerin—erzählt von einem typischen Tag bei sich zu Hause. Fragen Sie immer wieder **Und dann?**, um herauszufinden, was dann passierte! Sehen Sie, wie Frau/Herr Schneider vom Perfekt *(present perfect)* zum Plusquamperfekt *(past perfect)* wechselt? Wechseln Sie sich nach den ersten fünf Sätzen ab!

BEISPIEL S1 Ich bin aufgestanden.
S2 Und dann?
S1 Nachdem ich aufgestanden war, habe ich mir die Zähne geputzt.

a. Ich bin aufgestanden.
b. Ich habe mich geduscht.
c. Ich habe mir die Zähne geputzt.
d. Ich habe mich angezogen.
e. Ich habe gefrühstückt.
f. Ich habe Helmut angerufen.
g. Ich habe die Zeitung gelesen.
h. Ich bin zur Arbeit gegangen.
i. . . .

M. So war's! Beschreiben Sie Ihr Wochenende oder Ihre Ferien. Benutzen Sie dabei die Konjunktion **nachdem**! Schreiben Sie 8–10 Sätze.

At the end of this book, you will find a travel brochure for a trip from fairy-tale town to fairy-tale town in Germany.

Fokus The Brothers Grimm and Their Fairy Tales

The brothers Grimm, Jacob (1785–1863) and Wilhelm (1786–1859), are well remembered for their collection of fairy tales **(Märchen),** including **Hänsel und Gretel, Schneewittchen** *(Snow White),* **Rotkäppchen** *(Little Red Riding Hood),* **Aschenputtel** *(Cinderella),* **Dornröschen** *(Sleeping Beauty),* **Rumpelstilzchen, Rapunzel, König Drosselbart** *(King Thrushbeard),* **Die Bremer Stadtmusikanten,** and many others. Such stories had been transmitted orally from generation to generation and were long considered typically German. Modern research has shown, however, that some of these tales originated in other countries. The story of Rapunzel, for example, had already appeared in an Italian collection in 1634; there the heroine is named "Petrosinella." The next traceable reference is from France, where the girl's name is "Persinette." Researchers assume that the story traveled to Germany and Switzerland with the Huguenots (French Protestants) who left France after Louis XIV lifted the edict that granted them religious freedom. Jacob and Wilhelm Grimm heard many of the stories from women living in and around Kassel in northern Hesse, among them the 16-year-old Dorothea Wild, who later became Wilhelm's wife.

Jacob Grimm also wrote the first historical German grammar **(Deutsche Grammatik),** in which he compared fifteen different Germanic languages and analyzed their stages of development. The brothers' work on the *Deutsches Wörterbuch* was a pioneering effort that served as a model for later lexicographers. In 1840, the brothers became members of the German Academy of Sciences in Berlin.

Zusammenfassung

N. Wiederholen Sie die Sätze im Imperfekt!

1. Lothar denkt an Sabine.
2. Er will ein paar Wochen segeln gehen.
3. Aber sie hat keine Lust dazu.
4. Er spricht mit Holger.
5. Die beiden setzen eine Anzeige in die Zeitung.
6. Ute liest die Anzeige und antwortet darauf.
7. Durch die Anzeige finden sie sich.
8. Danach hat Lothar für Sabine keine Zeit mehr.
9. Er träumt nur noch von Ute.
10. Am 24. Mai heiraten die beiden.
11. Sie laden Holger zur Hochzeit ein.
12. Die Trauung *(ceremony)* ist in der lutherischen Kirche.
13. Ute heißt vorher *(before)* Kaiser.
14. Die Hochzeitsreise verbringen *(spend)* sie auf einem Segelboot.

Wir trauen uns
Lothar Müller
Ute Müller
geb. Kaiser
Vahrenwalder Str. 93
Hannover 1
Wann: Am 24. Mai 2013 um 15:00 Uhr
Wo: in der Ev.-luth. Vahrenwalder Kirche

© Beatrix Brockman

Danke,
dass Du immer
für mich da bist!

© Sheepworld

iLrn

Visit the ***Wie geht's?*** iLrn website for more review and practice of the grammar points you have just learned.

N: 1. dachte 2. wollte segeln gehen 3. hatte 4. sprach 5. setzten 6. las, antwortete 7. fanden 8. hatte 9. träumte 10. heirateten 11. luden . . . ein 12. war 13. hieß 14. verbrachten

You might point out that **Wir trauen uns** actually means *We dare* and that it is a pun on **getraut werden** *(to get married)*.

O: S1 Nachdem Vera die Anzeige gelesen hatte, rief sie den Besitzer an. S2 Nachdem der Besitzer von der Katze erzählt hatte, gab er Vera seine Adresse. S1 Nachdem Vera dorthin gefahren war und sich die Katze angesehen hatte, verliebte sie sich in die Katze. S2 Nachdem Vera die Katze mit nach Hause genommen hatte, zeigte sie Ingo das Kätzchen. S1 Nachdem Ingo ihr etwas Milch gegeben hatte, spielte er mit ihr. S2 Nachdem Ingo die Katze zwei Wochen auf dem Bett gehabt hatte, wurde er richtig krank. S1 Nachdem sie eine lange Diskussion gehabt hatten, setzten sie eine Anzeige in die Zeitung. S2 Nachdem der Besitzer zwei Wochen ohne seine Katze gewesen war, vermisste er sie sehr. S1 Nachdem der Besitzer mit Ingo und Vera gesprochen hatte, nahm er die Katze zurück.

O. Hoppla, was passierte? Ingo und Vera haben durch eine Zeitungsanzeige ein Kätzchen gefunden, aber es ging nicht alles so wie geplant. Erzählen Sie mit Ihrem Partner / Ihrer Partnerin, was passiert ist! Wechseln Sie sich ab! Einer von Ihnen schaut auf die Tabelle unten, der andere auf die Tabelle im Anhang, Teil 11. Benutzen Sie dabei das Plusquamperfek und das Imperfekt!

BEISPIEL S1 Nachdem Vera die Anzeige gelesen hatte, rief sie den Besitzer an.
S2 Nachdem der Besitzer von der Katze erzählt hatte, . . .

S1:

	Nachdem . . .	**Dann . . .**
S1	Vera: die Anzeige lesen	den Besitzer *(owner)* anrufen
S2	Besitzer: von der Katze erzählen	Vera seine Adresse geben
S1	Vera: dorthin fahren und sich die Katze ansehen	sich in die Katze verlieben
S2	Vera: die Katze mit nach Hause nehmen	Ingo das Kätzchen zeigen
S1	Ingo: ihr etwas Milch geben	mit ihr spielen
S2	Ingo: die Katze zwei Wochen auf dem Bett haben	richtig krank werden
S1	Sie *(pl.)*: eine lange Diskussion haben	eine Anzeige in die Zeitung setzen
S2	Besitzer: zwei Wochen ohne seine Katze sein	sie sehr vermissen *(miss)*
S1	Besitzer: mit Ingo und Vera sprechen	die Katze zurücknehmen

P: 1. Arthur hatte an die Hochzeit seiner Tochter gedacht. 2. Als wir Maren im Dezember sahen, war sie in einen charmanten, reichen Mann verliebt. 3. Sie sollten im April heiraten. 4. Ich hatte schon ein schönes Geschenk gekauft. 5. Vor zwei Wochen verlobte sie sich mit einem anderen Mann. 6. Stephan ist ein armer Student an ihrer Universität. 7. Sie sagten nicht, wann sie heiraten wollten. 8. Am Wochenende rief sie ihre Eltern an. 9. Sie und Stephan haben gerade geheiratet. 10. Sie hatten ihre Eltern nicht zur Hochzeit / zur Hochzeit nicht eingeladen. 11. Arthur ärgert sich, wenn er daran denkt. 12. Er kann es einfach nicht glauben.

P. Die Hochzeit Auf Deutsch bitte!

1. Arthur had been thinking of his daughter's wedding.
2. When we saw Maren in December, she was in love with a charming, wealthy man.
3. They were supposed to get married in April.
4. I had already bought a beautiful present.
5. Two weeks ago, on July 9, she got engaged to another man.
6. Stephan is a poor student at (**an**) her university.
7. They didn't say when they wanted to get married.
8. On the weekend, she called her parents.
9. She and Stephan just got married.
10. They hadn't invited the parents to (**zu**) their wedding.
11. Arthur gets annoyed when he thinks about it.
12. He just can't believe it.

Wir haben uns am 9. Juli 2013
in Niendorf an der Ostsee verlobt
Maren Lütje
Stephan Grosser

Einblicke

Märchen

Wortschatz 2

der König, -e	*king*
das Gold	*gold*
Märchen, -	*fairy tale*
die Königin, -nen	*queen*
Welt	*world*
das erste (zweite) Mal	*the first (second) time*
zum ersten (dritten) Mal	*for the first (third) time*
allein	*alone*
froh	*glad, happy*
niemand	*nobody, no one*
nun	*now*
plötzlich	*sudden(ly)*
sofort	*right away, immediately*
voll	*full*
geschehen (geschieht), geschah, ist geschehen	*to happen*
herein·kommen, kam herein, ist hereingekommen	*to enter, come in*
spinnen, spann, gesponnen	*to spin*
springen, sprang, ist gesprungen	*to jump*
sterben (stirbt), starb, ist gestorben	*to die*
versprechen (verspricht), versprach, versprochen	*to promise*

Just like with **jemand**, note the use of **niemand** in the various cases: Da ist **niemand** an der Tür. Er hat **niemanden** mitgebracht. Sie sprach mit **niemandem.** Das sind **niemandes** Schlüssel.

You might point out the word **das Niemandsland** *(no man's land).*

Lesetipp

Recognizing Elements in Fairy Tales

A fairy tale is a story in which strange or unusual events take place. The figures are often out-of-the-ordinary characters, such as kings, princesses, or even nonhuman beings. Magical transformations often play a significant role. The number three is also a recurrent feature of many fairy tales: events often occur three times and things appear in groups of three. As you work with this reading, look for examples of such elements.

Vor dem Lesen

A. Allerlei Fragen

1. Wie beginnen viele Märchen auf Englisch?
2. Wo spielen sie?
3. Welche Personen sind typisch in einem Märchen?
4. Welche Märchen kennen Sie?
5. Haben Sie als Kind gern Märchen gelesen? Warum (nicht)?

B. Gehen wir Wörter angeln! Lesen Sie das Märchen mit Ihrem Partner / Ihrer Partnerin still *(quietly)* durch. Wenn Sie einen Imperfekt finden, lesen Sie diesen laut und nennen Sie den passenden Infinitiv dazu! Das gleiche Verb in der gleichen Verbform brauchen Sie nicht zu wiederholen. Wechseln Sie sich ab!

BEISPIEL S1 war *sein*
S2 hatte *haben*
S1 geschah *geschehen*

C. Das ist leicht zu verstehen! Lesen Sie die folgenden Wörter laut und raten Sie, was sie auf Englisch bedeuten!

der Müller, Ring, Rückweg, Sonnenaufgang; das Feuer, Männchen, Spinnrad; die Nachbarschaft; testen; golden

Rumpelstilzchen

Es war einmal° ein Müller. Er war arm, aber er hatte eine schöne Tochter. Eines Tages geschah es, dass er mit dem König sprach. Weil er dem König gefallen wollte, sagte er ihm: „Ich habe eine hübsche und intelligente Tochter. Sie kann Stroh° zu Gold spinnen." Da sprach der König zum Müller: „Das gefällt mir. Wenn deine Tochter so gut ist, wie du sagst, bring sie morgen in mein Schloss! Ich will sie testen." Am nächsten Tag brachte der Müller seine Tochter aufs Schloss. Der König brachte sie in eine Kammer° mit viel Stroh und sagte: „Jetzt fang an zu arbeiten! Wenn du bis morgen früh nicht das ganze Stroh zu Gold gesponnen hast, musst du sterben." Dann schloss er die Kammer zu° und die Müllerstochter blieb allein darin.

Da saß nun das arme Mädchen und weinte, denn sie wusste nicht, wie man Stroh zu Gold spinnt. Da öffnete sich plötzlich die Tür. Ein kleines Männchen kam herein und sagte: „Guten Abend, schöne Müllerstochter! Warum weinst du denn?" „Ach", antwortete das Mädchen, „weil ich Stroh zu Gold spinnen soll, und ich weiß nicht wie." „Was gibst du mir, wenn ich dir helfe?", fragte das Männchen. „Meine goldene Kette°", antwortete das Mädchen. Das Männchen nahm die Goldkette, setzte sich an das Spinnrad und spann bis zum Morgen das ganze Stroh zu Gold. Bei Sonnenaufgang kam der König. Er freute sich, als er das viele Gold sah, denn das hatte er nicht erwartet°. Dann brachte er sie sofort in eine andere Kammer, wo noch viel mehr° Stroh lag. Er befahl° ihr, auch das Stroh in einer Nacht zu Gold zu spinnen, wenn ihr das Leben lieb war.

Wieder weinte das Mädchen; und wieder öffnete sich die Tür und das Männchen kam herein. „Was gibst du mir, wenn ich dir das Stroh zu Gold spinne?", fragte es. „Meinen Ring vom Finger", antwortete das Mädchen. Wieder setzte sich das Männchen ans Spinnrad und spann das Stroh zu Gold. Der König freute sich sehr, aber er hatte immer noch nicht genug. Nun brachte er die Müllerstochter in eine dritte Kammer, wo noch sehr viel mehr Stroh lag und sprach: „Wenn du mir dieses Stroh auch noch zu Gold spinnst, heirate ich dich morgen." Dabei dachte er sich: Wenn es auch nur eine Müllerstochter ist, so eine reiche Frau finde ich in der ganzen Welt nicht. Als das Mädchen allein war, kam das Männchen zum dritten Mal. Es sagte wieder: „Was gibst du mir, wenn ich dir noch einmal das Stroh spinne?" Die Müllerstochter aber hatte nichts mehr, was sie ihm geben konnte. „Dann versprich mir dein erstes Kind, wenn du Königin bist", sagte das Männchen. Die Müllerstochter wusste nicht, was sie tun sollte, und sagte ja. Am nächsten Morgen heiratete sie den König und wurde Königin.

Nach einem Jahr brachte sie ein schönes Kind zur Welt. Sie hatte aber das Männchen schon lange vergessen. Da stand es aber plötzlich in ihrer Kammer und sagte: „Gib mir das Kind, wie du es mir versprochen hast!" Die Königin bekam Angst° und versprach dem Männchen das ganze Gold im Königreich°, wenn es ihr das Kind lassen wollte. Aber das Männchen sagte: „Nein, etwas Lebendes° ist mir wichtiger als° alles Gold in der Welt." Da fing die Königin an zu weinen, dass das Männchen Mitleid° bekam. „Na gut", sagte es, „du hast drei Tage Zeit. Wenn du bis dann meinen Namen weißt, darfst du das Kind behalten°."

Nun dachte die Königin die ganze Nacht an Namen und sie schickte einen Boten° über Land. Er sollte fragen, was es sonst noch für Namen gab. Am ersten Abend, als das Männchen kam, fing die Königin an mit „Kaspar, Melchior, Balthasar . . . ", aber bei jedem Namen lachte das Männchen und sagte: „Nein, so heiß' ich nicht." Am nächsten Tag fragte man die Leute in der Nachbarschaft nach Namen. Am Abend sagte die Königin dem Männchen viele komische Namen wie „Rippenbiest" und „Hammelbein", aber es antwortete immer: „Nein, so heiß' ich nicht." Am dritten Tag kam der Bote zurück und erzählte: „Ich bin bis an die Grenzen° des Königreichs gegangen und niemand konnte mir

once upon a time there was
straw
chamber
locked
necklace
expected
more / ordered
became afraid / kingdom
living
more important than
pity
keep
messenger
borders

neue Namen nennen. Aber auf dem Rückweg kam ich in einen Wald. Da sah ich ein kleines Häuschen mit einem Feuer davor. Um das Feuer sprang ein komisches Männchen. Es hüpfte° auf einem Bein und schrie°:

> Heute back ich, morgen brau° ich,
> übermorgen hol ich der Königin ihr Kind;
> ach, wie gut, dass niemand weiß,
> dass ich Rumpelstilzchen heiß!

hopped / screamed
brew

Die Königin war natürlich sehr froh, als sie das hörte. Am Abend fragte sie das Männchen zuerst: „Heißt du vielleicht Kunz?" „Nein!" „Heißt du vielleicht Heinz?" „Nein!" „Heißt du vielleicht Rumpelstilzchen?" „Das hat dir der Teufel° gesagt, das hat dir der Teufel gesagt!", schrie das Männchen und stampfte° mit dem rechten Fuß so auf den Boden°, dass es bis zum Körper darin versank°. Dann packte° es den linken Fuß mit beiden Händen und riss° sich selbst in Stücke°.

Märchen der Brüder Grimm (nacherzählt°)

devil
stomped
ground / sank in
grabbed / ripped / to pieces
retold

© Cengage Learning

Optional activity: **Richtig oder falsch?** 1. Die Tochter des Müllers konnte Stroh zu Gold spinnen. (F) 2. Der König sagte: „Wenn du bis morgen nicht das ganze Stroh zu Gold gesponnen hast, musst du wieder zu deinem Vater zurück." (F) 3. Das Männchen spann das Stroh zu Gold, weil die Müllerstochter ihm ihre Goldkette gab. (R) 4. Am nächsten Abend gab das Mädchen ihm ihr erstes Kind. (F) 5. Der König heiratete sie, weil er sie liebte. (F) 6. Nach einem Jahr bekam die Königin ein Kind. (R) 7. Das Männchen sagte: „Gut, ich lasse dir dein Kind, wenn du mir in drei Tagen meinen Namen nennen kannst." (R) 8. Die Königin schickte viele Boten über Land. (R) 9. Als die Königin den Namen „Rumpelstilzchen" nannte, lachte das Männchen und lief aus dem Schloss. (F)

Fairy tales are a great way to show the use of the past tense. They lend themselves to retelling and discussion. Also refer to the special section **Eine Reise durchs Märchenland** at the end of this book.

Nach dem Lesen

A. Alles verstanden?

1. Warum sagte der Müller dem König, dass seine Tochter Stroh zu Gold spinnen könnte *(could)*?
2. Wohin brachte der Vater sie am nächsten Tag?
3. Wohin brachte sie der König und warum weinte sie?
4. Wer half ihr, Stroh zu spinnen, und was musste sie dafür tun?
5. Was gab sie dem Männchen in der zweiten Nacht?
6. Was wollte das Männchen für seine Arbeit in der dritten Nacht haben?
7. Warum heiratete der König die arme Müllerstochter?
8. Was geschah nach einem Jahr, als sie ein Baby bekommen hatte?
9. Was musste sie in drei Tagen herausfinden, um das Baby behalten zu dürfen?
10. Wo hatte der Bote das komische Männchen gesehen?
11. Was schrie es?
12. Wie reagierte *(reacted)* das Männchen, als sie seinen Namen sagte?

A: 1. weil er dem König gefallen wollte 2. aufs Schloss 3. in eine Kammer; sie wusste nicht, wie man Stroh zu Gold spinnt. 4. ein kleines Männchen (Rumpelstilzchen); ihre goldene Kette 5. ihren Ring 6. ihr erstes Kind, wenn sie Königin ist 7. weil sie Stroh zu Gold spinnen konnte / weil sie ihn reich machen konnte 8. Das Männchen kam wieder und wollte ihr Baby. 9. seinen Namen 10. im Wald vor einem Feuer 11. „Ach wie gut, dass niemand weiß, dass ich Rumpelstilzchen heiß!" 12. Es riss sich selbst in Stücke.

B. *Als, wenn* oder *wann*?

1. Als die Müllerstochter das hörte, fing sie an zu weinen.
2. Immer, wenn die Königin nicht wusste, was sie tun sollte, weinte sie.
3. Wenn du mir das Stroh zu Gold spinnst, heirate ich dich morgen.
4. Das Männchen lachte nur, als die Königin fragte, ob es Melchior hieß.
5. Als die Königin den Namen Rumpelstilzchen nannte, ärgerte sich das Männchen furchtbar.
6. Wir wissen nicht genau, wann sie geheiratet haben, aber wenn sie nicht gestorben sind, dann leben sie noch heute.

C. Gespräch zwischen Mutter und Tochter

1. **Wusstest du das?** Lesen Sie, was die Königin ihrer Tochter nach dem Tod *(death)* des Vaters erzählt! Unterstreichen Sie *(underline)* das Plusquamperfekt!

   Jetzt, wo dein Vater gestorben ist, kann ich dir erzählen, wie es dazu kam, dass dein Vater und ich heirateten. Er wollte nie, dass du weißt, dass dein Großvater nur Müller war. Mein Vater brachte mich eines Tages hier aufs Schloss, weil er am Tag davor dem König gesagt hatte, dass ich Stroh zu Gold spinnen kann. Der König brachte mich damals in eine Kammer voll Stroh und ich sollte es zu Gold spinnen. Ich wusste natürlich nicht, wie man das macht. Weil der König gesagt hatte, dass ich sterben sollte, wenn das Stroh nicht am nächsten Morgen Gold geworden war, hatte ich große Angst und fing an zu weinen. Da kam plötzlich ein Männchen in die Kammer. Für meine Halskette wollte es mir helfen. Bevor es Morgen war, hatte es das ganze Stroh zu Gold gesponnen. Aber dein Vater brachte mich in eine andere Kammer voll Stroh. Wieder kam das Männchen und half mir, nachdem ich ihm meinen Ring gegeben hatte. Aber in der dritten Nacht hatte ich nichts mehr, was ich ihm schenken konnte. Da musste ich ihm mein erstes Kind versprechen. Am nächsten Tag heirateten wir und ich wurde Königin. Nach einem Jahr kamst du auf die Welt und plötzlich stand das Männchen vor mir und wollte dich mitnehmen. Ich hatte es aber schon lange vergessen. Um dich behalten zu können, musste ich in drei Tagen seinen Namen wissen. Am letzten Tag kam mein Bote zurück und sagte mir, dass er ein Männchen gesehen hatte, wie es um ein Feuer tanzte und schrie: „Ach, wie gut, dass niemand weiß, dass ich Rumpelstilzchen heiß'!" Nachdem ich dem Männchen seinen Namen gesagte hatte, riss es sich selbst in Stücke und du durftest bei mir bleiben.

2. **Ich muss dir was erzählen!** Spielen Sie jetzt mit Ihrem Partner / Ihrer Partnerin die Rolle von Mutter und Tochter. Die Mutter erzählt die Geschichte noch einmal, aber nach jedem Satz hat die Tochter etwas zu sagen.

   BEISPIEL S1 Jetzt, wo dein Vater gestorben ist, kann ich dir erzählen, wie es dazu kam, dass dein Vater und ich heirateten.
   S2 Dann erzähl mal!

Your students' response to a fairy tale as a reading text will depend on your attitude. You might discuss the genre, typical style, and features. Our students enjoyed occasional telling of familiar tales because they could understand them quite easily.

Erzähltipp

Beginning a Story and Encouraging the Storyteller

As you just saw, many fairy tales start with the phrase **Es war einmal ...** Here are some common expressions to catch a listener's attention when beginning to relate a story: **Weißt du, was mir passiert ist? / Mensch du glaubst nicht, was ... ! / Ich muss dir was erzählen. / Ich vergesse nie ... / Hast du gewusst, dass ... ? / Hast du schon gehört, dass ... ?**

And this is how a listener might reply in order to show interest: **Wirklich? Natürlich! Klar! Und (dann)? Was hast du dann gemacht? Und wo warst du, als ... ? Und wie geht's weiter?**

Weiteres

D. Typisch Märchen

1. Aus welcher Zeit kommen solche Märchen wie *Rumpelstilzchen*?
2. Warum ist *Rumpelstilzchen* ein typisches Märchen? Was ist charakteristisch für Märchen?
3. Was ist die Rolle der Frau in diesem Märchen? Sieht man die Frau auch heute noch so?
4. Warum heiratet der König die Müllerstochter? Gibt es das heute auch noch?
5. Was für Geschichten hören (oder sehen) Kinder heute? Sind sie anders? Wenn ja, wie?

Topics for discussion: a. die Abhängigkeit *(dependence)* der Frau von Vater und Mann b. Frau und Baby als Handelsobjekt *(object for trade)* c. der Materialismus des Königs und Geld als Basis zur Ehe d. Rumpelstilzchens Rolle und seine Perspektive; gibt es positive Eigenschaften? e. gebrochene Versprechen und Versprechen unter Druck *(duress)* f. die soziale Funktion solcher Geschichten

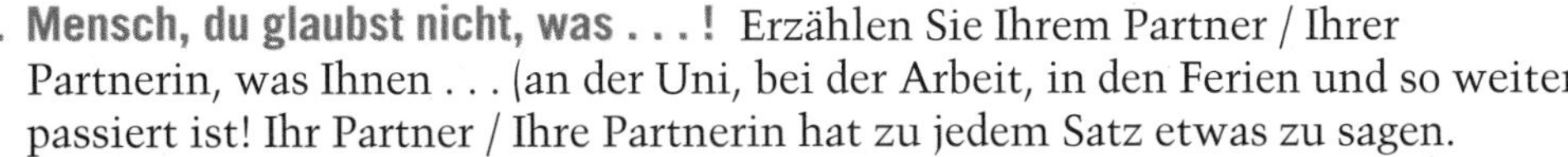

E. Mensch, du glaubst nicht, was . . . ! Erzählen Sie Ihrem Partner / Ihrer Partnerin, was Ihnen . . . (an der Uni, bei der Arbeit, in den Ferien und so weiter) passiert ist! Ihr Partner / Ihre Partnerin hat zu jedem Satz etwas zu sagen.

© lens23/Shutterstock

Schloss Neuschwanstein von Ludwig II. stammt aus **(dates back to)** ***dem 19. Jahrhundert.***

■ Situated near the city of Füssen in southern Germany, the extravagant Neuschwanstein Castle was built between 1869 and 1886 by King Ludwig II of Bavaria. It has come to represent the ultimate fairy-tale castle in the minds of many.

There is an extensive review section following this chapter in the *Arbeitsbuch (Rückblick: Kapitel 8–11)*. The accompanying exercises and answer key will help you prepare for the test.

© Cengage Learning

For further practice, an optional two-part video (**Szenen** and **Interviews**) is available on the ***Wie geht's?*** Premium Website and in iLrn, with corresponding questions and activities in the *Arbeitsbuch* (SAM).

Hörverständnis

Vier berühmte Märchen Welcher Text gehört zu welchem Märchen? Schreiben Sie die Zahl daneben!

Zum Erkennen: brachen ab *(broke off)*; schütteten *(dumped)*; die Linsen *(lentils)*; die Asche; aus·lesen *(to pick out)*; der Turm *(tower)*; das Spinnrad *(spinning wheel)*; die Spindel *(spindle)*; kaum *(hardly)*; erfüllte sich *(was fulfilled)*; der Zauberspruch *(magic spell)*; stach *(pricked)*; schlief ein *(fell asleep)*; also *(thus)*

__2__ *Aschenputtel*	__-__ *Rapunzel*
__3__ *Dornröschen*	__-__ *Rotkäppchen*
__1__ *Hänsel und Gretel*	__4__ *Schneewittchen*

As an optional activity, you could use Google Earth to visit Liechtenstein and get a more complete impression of this small country. You could also check out castles and their surroundings, e.g., Schloss Neuschwanstein, Burg Hohenzollern south of Stuttgart, Burg Stahleck with its youth hostel on the Rhine, the authentic Burg Eltz in the Eifel Mountains, or Liechtenstein Castle in Baden-Württemberg.

Literatur

Biographisches

Jutta Strzalka was born in 1959 in Dortmund. She found her regular day jobs uninteresting, because the writing she had to do seemed dull and routine. To offset such a mundane use of her talents, she began to write stories for her children and thus discovered her love for the short story: thrillers, as well as funny, reflective, or absurd texts, and even fairy tales. When she is not working with pen and paper, she thrives as a freelance music teacher, giving guitar lessons and making music with children and adolescents. Her short stories and thrillers have been published in various anthologies and include **Mörderischer Fußball** (*Murderous Soccer*), **Tatort Internet** (*Crime Scene Internet*), and **Phantastische Morde** (*Fantastic Murders*).

1. Wir wissen nur Erichs Namen. 2. drei 3. Frau 4. Damit Erich weiß, wer sie ist.

Vor dem Lesen

Ein paar Fragen Überfliegen Sie den Text und beantworten Sie die Fragen!

1. Wie heißen die Personen in diesem Text?
2. Wie viele Personen gibt es darin?
3. Ist der Erzähler (nicht der Autor!) ein Mann oder eine Frau?
4. Warum, glauben Sie, will die Frau zwei Löffel in ihrem Eisbecker stecken?

Mit zwei Löffeln

Ich glaube nicht an romantische Abende bei Kerzenlicht. Auch nicht daran, dass meine Träume wahr werden können. Nein, ich bin ein sehr nüchterner° Mensch. Deshalb gehe ich auch nicht zu dem Treffen. Das ist gegen meine Prinzipien. Ich treffe mich nie mit einem unbekannten Mann. Nun, mit mir bekannten Männern treffe ich mich auch nicht. Von den Akzeptablen Männern hat sich noch niemand für mich interessiert und die Unakzeptablen weise ich gleich ab.° Ich meine die, die jeder Frau hinterherlaufen° und einen Blick auf ihre Beine werfen°, sogar wenn sie so unscheinbar° und so alt ist wie ich.

Es ist schon komisch, dass von allen Frauen aus dem Internetkurs ausgerechnet° ich einen Mann kennengelernt habe. Er heißt Erich, ist im Ruhestand° und sein Hobby ist es, an seinem Boot zu basteln.° Er hat den Traum, dieses Boot eines Tages am Baldeneysee zu Wasser zu lassen. Und, das hat er mir einmal geschrieben, er möchte gern diesen Tag zusammen mit mir erleben. Ich antwortete ihm, dass ich Angst vor dem Wasser habe°. Eigentlich hatte ich mehr Angst vor ihm, aber das konnte ich ihm nicht sagen. Er schrieb dann, sein Boot sei nur einen Meter lang und ferngesteuert°. Seitdem chatten wir immer mittwochs zur gleichen Zeit miteinander.

Wir sind uns mittlerweile° recht vertraut°. Es ist fast so, als ob° ich einen Freund hätte°. Und das in meinem Alter. Nur, seit einiger Zeit möchte Erich, dass wir uns richtig kennenlernen. Wir sind nämlich zufällig° beide aus Essen. Aber vor solch einem Treffen fürchte ich mich° und habe ihm gleich geschrieben, dass ich nicht tanzen gehe, weder in einer Disco noch beim Seniorentanz.

Erich hat dann vorgeschlagen°, dass wir uns in einer Eisdiele° im Zentrum treffen. Ich habe ihm geschrieben, dass er mich daran erkennen° kann, dass in meinem Eisbecher° zwei Löffel stecken. Eine verrückte Idee. Wenn ich vielleicht doch komme, bestelle ich einen Kaffee, und dann kann ich unauffällig° sehen, wie er aussieht°. Und danach gehe ich schnell wieder. Oder wenn er mir gefällt, nein, ich bestelle ganz bestimmt kein Eis mit zwei Löffeln. Außerdem will

clear-headed
reject
chase / look at
plain
of all people
retired / tinker
am afraid of the water
remote controlled
by now / familiar / as if
had
coincidentally
am fearful
suggested / ice cream parlor
recognize
ice cream bowl
inconspicuously
looks like

ich gar nicht zu dem Treffen erscheinen. Ich bringe es nur nicht übers Herz°, Erich abzusagen°. Er schreibt immer so schön und wir können uns über alles unterhalten°.

Es ist etwas komisch, inmitten all dieser lauten jungen Leute in der Eisdiele zu sitzen. Ich könnte° ihre Großmutter sein. Sehr wohl fühle ich mich nicht. Wie es wohl dem Kellner geht? Er wirkt recht° sympathisch und er ist ungefähr in meinem Alter. Ich winke ihn heran. „Können Sie mir bitte noch ein Stück Nusstorte bringen?" „Gern, meine Dame." Er lächelt sympathisch. Und er hat mich ein bisschen zu lange angesehen° dabei. Ach, wahrscheinlich° bin ich alte Tante° schon so konfus, dass ich jedes Kellnerlächeln auf mich beziehe°.

Ein großes Stück Nusstorte später bin ich ziemlich ernüchtert°. Schöne Geschichte, sich mit einem Unbekannten zu treffen. Wahrscheinlich heißt er gar nicht Erich, ist auch nicht im Ruhestand und Boote bastelt er auch nicht. Der Kellner muss langsam denken, ich schreibe einen Roman°. Dabei ist es mein Tagebuch,° in das ich hier schreibe. Der einzige Mann, der° in der letzten Viertelstunde hier erschienen ist, steht immer noch bei dem netten älteren Kellner. Es könnte sein Sohn sein, so wie die beiden sich unterhalten°. Der junge Mann lacht plötzlich laut und sagt: „So was Verrücktes°, Vater, kann auch nur von dir stammen°. Das klappt nie!°" Mich interessiert natürlich, was der Kellner sagt. „Du spinnst echt!°", das ist alles, was ich verstehen kann. Dann verlässt° der junge Mann grinsend° die Eisdiele. Schade, ich hätte zu gern gewusst, worum es ging.° Der Kellner sieht nachdenklich° und etwas müde aus. Unsere Blicke treffen sich. Zufällig. Er kommt an meinen Tisch.

„Möchten Sie noch etwas bestellen, vielleicht einen Eisbecher?"

„Ja gern", antworte ich, ohne zu denken. „Mit zwei Löffeln, bitte."

Überrascht sieht er mich an, zieht einen Stuhl heran° und setzt sich. „Würde es Sie sehr wundern°, wenn mich Ihre Bestellung nicht ein bisschen wundert?"

Mein Herz klopft° plötzlich so laut, dass es die jungen Leute am Nachbartisch hören können, und ich werde rot. So rot wie zuletzt° in meiner Backfischzeit°. Dann hole ich tief Luft° und unterbreche° ihn: „Nein, es wundert mich überhaupt nicht, Erich, wenn du es bist." Und dann lachen wir beide, bis uns die Tränen° kommen und wir sie uns vorsichtig wegwischen°, einer dem anderen.

Jutta Strzalka

don't have the heart
cancel
talk about
could
seems rather
looked at / probably
old lady / relate to
disillusioned
novel
diary / who
are talking
crazy
come from / will never work
You're crazy! / leaves
grinning
what it was all about / preoccupied
brings a chair closer
surprise
is pounding
the last time / teenage years
take a deep breath / interrupt
tears
wipe away

Jutta Strzalka, „Mit zwei Löffeln", in *'n paar Schoten Geschichten aus'm Pott,* (Schreiblustverlag, 2008)

Nach dem Lesen

A. Worum geht's? *(What's it all about?)*

1. Worum geht es in dieser Kurzgeschichte (*short story*)?
2. Welche Rolle spielt das Internet?
3. Welchen Beruf hat Erich?
4. Wer ist der junge Mann, mit dem (*with whom*) er spricht?
5. Warum bestellt die Erzählerin einen Eisbecher mit zwei Löffeln?
6. Welche Erkennungszeichen (*identifiers*) kennen Sie von einem Blind Date?
7. Finden Sie die Geschichte lustig? Hat Sie das Ende überrascht?

B. Jetzt sind Sie dran!

1. **Was nun?** Beschreiben Sie das weitere (*further*) Leben der Protagonisten in zwei Absätzen (*paragraphs*).

2. **Was dann?** Stellen Sie sich vor (*imagine*), Erichs Sohn verliebt sich in die Erzählerin. Wie geht die Geschichte dann weiter (*continues*)?

Mein Froschkönig? Jeder sollte mal einen Frosch küssen.

Rückschau

Kapitelwortschatz

Hauptwörter

die Anzeige, -n	*ad(vertisement)*
die Beziehung, -en	*relationship*
die Ehe, -n	*marriage*
die Eigenschaft, -en	*attribute, characteristic*
die Freundschaft	*friendship*
das Gold	*gold*
die Hochzeit, -en	*wedding*
der Hund, -e	*dog*
die Katze, -n	*cat*
der König, -e	*king*
die Königin, -nen	*queen*
die Liebe	*love*
das Märchen, -	*fairy tale*
der Partner, -	*partner* (male)
die Partnerin, -nen	*partner* (female)
das Pferd, -e	*horse*
die Scheidung, -en	*divorce*
das Tier, -e	*animal*
das Vertrauen	*trust*
der Vogel, ¨	*bird*
die Welt, -en	*world*
der Wunsch, ¨e	*wish*

Verben

ein·laden	*to invite*
geschehen	*to happen*
heiraten	*to marry, get married (to)*
herein·kommen	*to enter, come in*
meinen	*to think, be of the opinion*
passieren	*to happen*
spinnen	*to spin*
springen	*to jump*
sterben	*to die*
träumen von	*to dream (of, about)*
vergleichen	*to compare*
sich verlieben (in)	*to fall in love (with)*
verlieren	*to lose*
sich verloben (mit)	*to get engaged (to)*
versprechen	*to promise*
versuchen	*to try*

Adjektive

allein	*alone*
arm	*poor*
attraktiv	*attractive*
charmant	*charming*
dumm	*stupid*
(un)ehrlich	*(dis)honest*
ernst	*serious*
faul	*lazy*
fleißig	*industrious*
(un)freundlich	*(un)friendly*
froh	*glad, happy*
(un)gebildet	*(un)educated*
(un)geduldig	*(im)patient*
geschieden	*divorced*
(un)glücklich	*(un)happy*
gut aussehend	*good-looking*
hässlich	*ugly*
hübsch	*pretty*
intelligent	*intelligent*
jung	*young*
(un)kompliziert	*(un)complicated*
ledig	*single*
lieb	*kind, good*
lustig	*funny*
(un)musikalisch	*(non)musical*
nett	*nice*
reich	*rich, wealthy*
schick	*chic, stylish; neat*
schlank	*slim, slender*
schrecklich	*awful*
selbstständig	*independent*
(un)sportlich	*(un)athletic*
süß	*sweet; cute*
unselbstständig	*dependent*
(un)sympathisch	*(un)congenial, (un)likable*
(un)talentiert	*(un)talented*
(un)verheiratet	*(un)married*
verliebt (in)	*in love (with)*
verlobt (mit)	*engaged (to)*
vielseitig	*versatile*
voll	*full*
zärtlich	*affectionate*
(un)zuverlässig	*(un)reliable*

Verschiedenes

als	*when, at the time when*
beid- / beide	*both / both (of them)*
damals	*then, in those days*
das erste (zweite) Mal	*the first (second) time*
eigen-	*own*
jemand	*someone, somebody*
nachdem	*after*
niemand	*nobody, no one*
nun	*now*
plötzlich	*sudden(ly)*
So ein süßes Kätzchen!	*Such a cute kitty!*
sofort	*right away, immediately*
wann	*when, at what time?*
wenn	*when, whenever; if*
Wenn du meinst.	*If you think so.*
zum ersten (dritten) Mal	*for the first (third) time*

Zum Schluss

1. **Partnersuche**
   a. **Was suchen Sie?** Pretend you are a historical or fictional figure. Write a personal ad that describes what you are looking for in a partner. Use adjectives from this chapter and earlier chapters to write an ad that is as detailed as possible. Make sure to pay attention to adjective endings. Be creative!
   b. **Wer ist wer?** Share your personal ad with your study group or classmates. Can they guess who you are? Can you guess who they are?
   c. **Nachdem . . .** Now pretend that, thanks to the personal ad, the historical or fictional figure you described above has found an ideal partner. Describe what happened on their first date. Write a few sentences in the simple past and past perfect, using **nachdem.**

2. **Beschreiben Sie!**
   a. **Was dann?** Complete the following questions. Add a few more questions of your own, and write out your own answers. Pay attention to case and word order!

      Wo warst du, als . . . ?
      Wann warst du . . . ?
      Was tust du gewöhnlich, wenn . . . ?
      Als du klein warst, . . . ?
      Wenn du keine Zeit hast, . . . ?
      Wann . . . ?
      . . . .
      . . . .
      . . . .

   b. **Fragen Sie!** Ask your study partner to respond to your questions. Are you surprised by the answers? Next, answer your study partner's questions. How do your answers compare?

3. **Es war einmal . . .** In this chapter, you read the story of *Rumpelstilzchen.* Now, write your own fairy tale. What happens? Where does the story take place? Who are the main characters? Use vocabulary from this chapter and earlier chapters to create a detailed story, including plenty of adjectives and verbs. Write 7–10 sentences using the simple past and, where appropriate, the past perfect. Remember to use conjunctions such as **als, wenn, wann,** and **nachdem**. Be creative!

iLrn **Onlineaktivitäten** Visit iLrn for online activities related to this chapter. There you will find additional resources, such as a memory game (**Gedächtnisspiel**), a crossword puzzle (**Kreuzworträtsel**), audio flash cards (**Vokabelblitz**), a tutorial quiz (**Mini-Quiz**), and the active vocabulary (**Wortschatz**) for this chapter.

Kapitel 12

Wege zum Beruf

Lernziele In this chapter you will learn about:

Zum Thema

Professions, education, and employment

Fokus

German school system, gender bias and language, women in business and industry, foreign workers, and social policy after unification

Einblicke

Diskussion: Die Berufswahl
Literatur: Jörg Zschocke, *Die zwei Chefs*

Struktur

- Comparison of adjectives and adverbs
- The future tense
- Predicate nouns and adjectival nouns

Rückschau

Kapitelwortschatz
Zum Schluss

RESSOURCEN

iLrn | Video | Audio | SAM

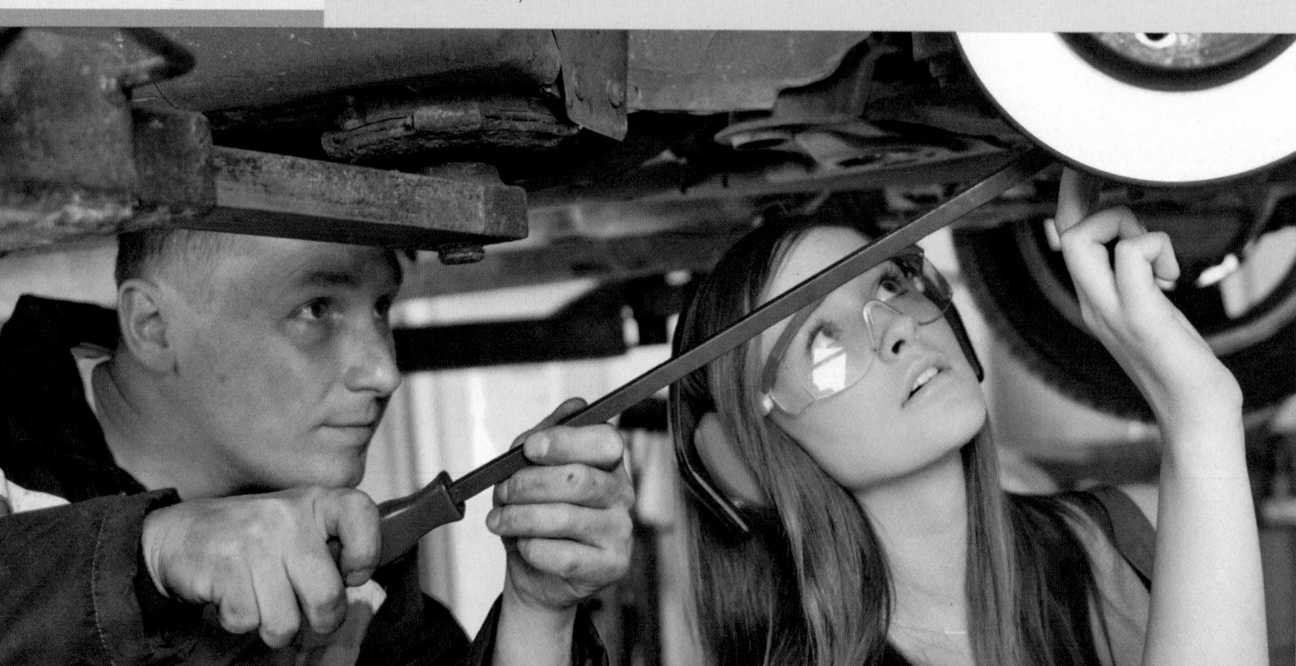

© Jörn buchheim/Fotolia

Eine Auszubildende* (apprentice) *in der Autowerkstatt

Vorschau German Schools and Vocational Training

In Germany, education falls under the authority of the individual states. Every child attends the elementary school **(die Grundschule)** for the first four years of schooling (six years in Berlin and Brandenburg). After that, teachers, parents, and students choose one of three possible educational tracks, dependent on which track best suits a child's interests and abilities. About one third of German students go to a college preparatory school **(das Gymnasium, die Oberschule)**, which in most of the states now runs from grades 5 through 12. During their final two years, students must pass a series of rigorous exams to earn their diploma **(das Abitur** or **Reifezeugnis),** a prerequisite for university admission. Students who do not aim to go to a university attend either a **Hauptschule** or **Realschule.** The **Hauptschule** runs through grade 9 and usually leads to some form of vocational training. The **Realschule,** a six-year intermediate school covering grades 5 through 10, offers business subjects in addition to a regular academic curriculum, but one less demanding than that of a **Gymnasium.** Its diploma **(die Mittlere Reife)** qualifies students to enter a business or technical college **(die Fachschule** or **Fachoberschule).**

This three-tiered school system has often been criticized for forcing decisions about a child's future too early. As a result, an orientation phase **(die Orientierungsstufe)** was introduced for grades 5 and 6 in some German states and later abolished in some. The purpose of this 2-year phase was to give parents more time to decide which type of school their child should attend. In another effort to increase flexibility, comprehensive schools **(Gesamtschulen)** have been established that combine the three different types of schools into one and offer a wide range of courses at various degrees of difficulty.

Since school attendance is compulsory for ages 6 to 18, most of those who end their general schooling at age 15 or 16 must continue in a three-year program of practical, on-the-job training that combines an apprenticeship **(die Lehre)** with 8 to 10 hours per week of theoretical instruction in a vocational school **(die Berufsschule).** Apprentices are called **Lehrlinge** or **Auszubildende** (shortened to **der/die Azubi, -s**). At the end of their training **(die Ausbildung)** and after passing exams at school and at the training site, they become journeymen/journeywomen **(Gesellen/Gesellinnen).** Five years later, after further practical and theoretical training and after passing another rigorous exam **(die Meisterprüfung)**, qualified professionals can attain the status of masters **(Meister/Meisterinnen),** a certification that allows them to become independent and train the new generation of apprentices, who are considered invaluable by German business and industry.

Apprenticeships date back to the Middle Ages, when apprentices served for approximately three years under one or several masters in order to learn a trade. This principle extends today to all nonacademic job training. Very few young Germans enter the job market **(der Arbeitsmarkt)** without such preparation. Apprenticeship training is carefully regulated in order to ensure a highly skilled workforce.

Fragen zum Schulsystem: 1. Von wann bis wann gehen die Kinder in den Kindergarten? 2. Wie lange gehen sie in die Grundschule? 3. Welche drei Möglichkeiten haben sie danach? 4. Wie viele Jahre geht man gewöhnlich zur Hauptschule oder zur Realschule? 5. Wie viele Schuljahre haben die Gesamtschule und das Gymnasium? 6. Wie alt sind die Schüler meistens, wenn sie mit der Gesamtschule oder dem Gymnasium fertig sind? 7. Wie alt waren Sie, als Sie mit der High School fertig waren?

To be precise, the term **Lehrling** is still used strictly for the trades **(das Handwerk)**, whereas the term **Azubi** refers to young people being trained for nonacademic professions in general.

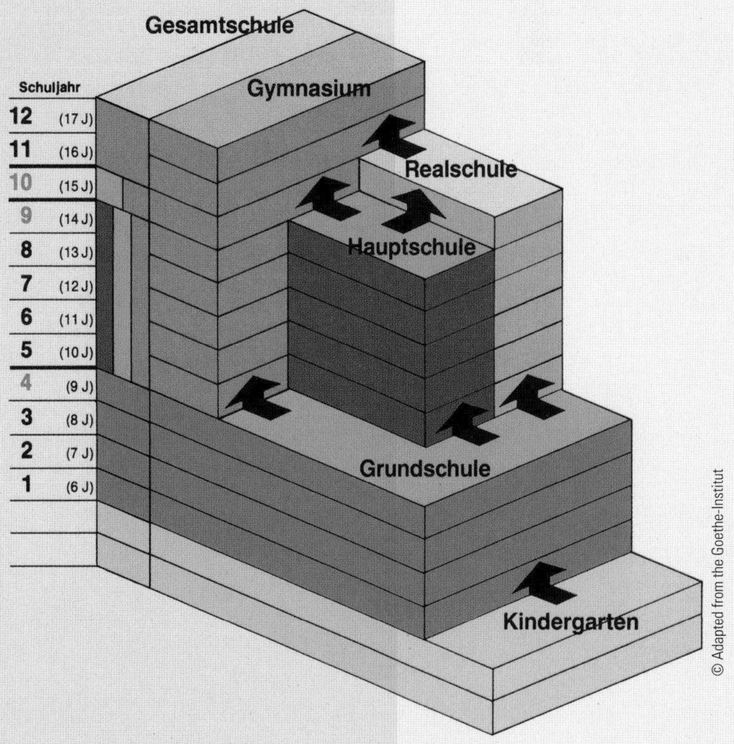

Zum Thema

Gespräch

Warm-ups: 1. **Nennen Sie die Verbformen, z. B. sein, war, ist gewesen** (annehmen, arbeiten, bleiben, bringen, denken, erzählen, essen, feiern, finden, geben, geschehen, haben, heißen, hereinkommen, kennen, können, laufen, lesen, müssen, nennen, öffnen, reagieren, sterben, umtauschen, vergessen, verlieren, versprechen, warten, wehtun, werden, wissen)! 2. **Was nehmen Sie mit, wenn Sie zur Uni gehen?**

You could ask students why Elke wants to become a cabinetmaker and Katja a dentist, and what they think of their arguments. What are the advantages and disadvantages **(Vorteile und Nachteile)** of these two professions?

Weißt du, was du einmal werden willst?

KATJA Sag mal, Elke, weißt du schon, was du einmal werden willst?
ELKE Ja, ich will Tischlerin werden.
KATJA Ist das nicht viel Schwerarbeit?
ELKE Ach, daran gewöhnt man sich. Ich möchte mich vielleicht mal selbstständig machen.
KATJA Das sind aber große Pläne!
ELKE Warum nicht? Ich habe keine Lust, immer nur im Büro zu sitzen und für andere Leute zu arbeiten.
KATJA Und wo willst du dich um eine Lehrstelle bewerben?
ELKE Überhaupt kein Problem. Meine Tante hat ihre eigene Firma und hat mir schon einen Platz angeboten.
KATJA Da hast du aber Glück.
ELKE Und wie ist es denn mit dir? Weißt du, was du machen willst?
KATJA Vielleicht werde ich Zahnärztin. Gute Zahnärzte braucht man immer und außerdem verdient man sehr gut.
ELKE Das stimmt, aber das dauert doch so lange.
KATJA Ich weiß, aber ich freue mich trotzdem schon darauf.

A. Was stimmt?

The most popular jobs requiring apprenticeships are auto mechanic, painter, electrician, carpenter, hairdresser, administrative assistant, physician's assistant, and dental assistant.

1. Elke will __c__ werden.
   a. Lehrerin b. Sekretärin c. Tischlerin
2. Sie möchte später gern __a__.
   a. selbstständig sein b. im Büro sitzen c. für andere Leute arbeiten
3. Elkes Tante hat __b__ für sie.
   a. eine Lehrerstelle b. eine Lehrstelle c. ein Möbelgeschäft
4. Katja will __c__ werden.
   a. Augenärztin b. Kinderärztin c. Zahnärztin
5. Zahnärzte sollen gut __b__.
   a. dienen b. verdienen c. bedienen

B. Jetzt sind Sie dran! Sprechen Sie mit Ihrem Partner / Ihrer Partnerin über Ihre Berufspläne. Bereiten Sie ein kleines Gespräch vor; es darf auch länger *(longer)* sein. Präsentieren Sie es dann vor der Klasse!

S1 Weißt du schon, was du mal werden willst?
S2 Ich werde . . .
S1 Und warum?
S2 . . . Und wie ist es denn mit dir? Weißt du, was du machen willst?
S1 . . .
S2 Ist das nicht sehr . . . ?
S1 . . .

Wortschatz 1

The feminine form of a noun can usually be derived by adding **-in** to the masculine form: **Architekt/Architektin.** Some also require an umlaut in the feminine form (**Arzt/Ärztin**) and/or other minor spelling changes (**Franzose/Französin**). In help wanted ads, forms are often listed with slashes, with the feminine ending in parentheses, or with the **I** of **-in** capitalized: **Journalist/Journalistin, Journalist/in, Journalist(in),** or **JournalistIn.** To save space, this chapter lists only the masculine forms, unless irregular changes are required for the feminine version.

Have students give you the feminine version of all the professions listed in *Wortschatz 1*.

Der Beruf, -e *(profession, career)*

der Architekt, -en, -en	*architect*
Arzt, ¨-e	*physician, doctor*
Betriebswirt, -e	*graduate in business management*
Geschäftsmann, ¨-er	*businessman*
Hausmann, ¨-er	*househusband*
Ingenieur, -e	*engineer*
Journalist, -en, -en	*journalist*
Krankenpfleger, -	*(male) nurse*
Künstler, -	*artist*
Lehrer, -	*teacher*
Polizist, -en, -en	*policeman*
der Rechtsanwalt, ¨-e	*lawyer*
Reiseleiter, -	*travel agent*
Sekretär, -e	*secretary*
Wissenschaftler, -	*scientist*
Zahnarzt, ¨-e	*dentist*
die Ärztin, -nen	*physician, doctor*
Geschäftsfrau, -en	*business woman*
Hausfrau, -en	*housewife*
Krankenschwester, -n	*(female) nurse*
Rechtsanwältin, -nen	*lawyer*
Zahnärztin, -nen	*dentist*

Note, **Geschäftsmann / Geschäftsfrau, Hausmann / Hausfrau.** When referring to *business people*, the plural **Geschäftsleute** is common.

When talking about elementary or secondary school, German refers to **die Schule.** At the postsecondary level, it becomes **die Hochschule** or **die Universität.** To indicate what university you attend, you can say: **Ich studiere an der Uni** [*or actual institution name*] **in** [*city, location, etc.*], for example: **Ich studiere an der Uni in Tübingen.**

Die Ausbildung *(training, education)*

Die Schule, -n *(school)*

der Kurs, -e	*course*
Plan, ¨-e	*plan*
das Büro, -s	*office*
Einkommen, -	*income*
Geschäft, -e	*business; store*
die Erfahrung, -en	*experience*
Firma, Firmen	*company; business*
Klasse, -n	*class*
Sicherheit	*safety, security*
Stelle, -n	*position, job*
Stunde, -n	*hour*
Verantwortung	*responsibility*
Zukunft	*future;* also: *future tense auxiliary*

The word **Kurs** is a rather general term for *class*, e.g., **Sie sind in meinem Deutschkurs.** The word **Klasse** is commonly used for a group of students or classmates, but also for a specific grade (level): **Sabine ist in der fünften Klasse.** *Sabine is in the fifth grade.*

When talking about an instructional period in elementary or secondary school, German refers to **die Stunde.** At the university level, terminology becomes more specific, e.g., **die Vorlesung** *(lecture)* versus **das Seminar. Stunde** also refers to work hours at a job: **Wie viele Stunden arbeitest du?**

Verschiedenes

anstrengend	*strenuous*
arbeitslos	*unemployed*
früher	*earlier; once; former(ly)*

hoch is the predicate adjective and adverb; **hoh-** is the attributive adjective: **Die Berge sind hoch.** BUT: **die hohen Berge.**

Note: **Was willst du (ein)mal werden?** *What do you want to be one day?*—**Ich will . . . werden.** *I want to be a(n) . . .*

gleich	*equal, same*
hoch (hoh-)	*high*
(un)sicher	*(un)safe, (in)secure*
(an·)bieten, bot (an), (an)geboten	*to offer*
sich bewerben (bewirbt), bewarb, beworben (um)	*to apply (for)*
erklären	*to explain*
sich gewöhnen an (+ *acc.*)	*to get used to*
glauben (an + *acc.*)	*to believe (in)*
recht haben (hat), hatte, gehabt	*to be right*
Du hast recht.	*You're right.*
verdienen	*to earn, make money*
werden (wird), wurde, ist geworden	*to become*
Ach was!	*Oh, come on!*
Nun / Also / Na ja / Tja, . . .	*Well, . . .*

Zum Erkennen: der Tischler, - *(cabinetmaker);* die Schwerarbeit *(hard / menial work);* Überhaupt kein Problem! *(No problem at all!);* AUCH: das Adverb, -ien; die Aussage, -n *(statement);* der Komparativ, -e *(comparative);* der Superlativ, -e *(superlative);* vergleichen *(to compare)*

Übungen zum Thema

A. Kurze Fragen

1. Was ist die weibliche *(fem.)* Form von Ingenieur? Betriebswirt? Reiseleiter? Künstler? Arzt? Rechtsanwalt?
2. Was ist die männliche *(masc.)* Form von Architektin? Lehrerin? Krankenschwester? Geschäftsfrau? Hausfrau?
3. Wo arbeitet die Apothekerin? der Bäcker? die Sekretärin? die Hausfrau? der Pfarrer *(pastor)*? der Lehrer? die Professorin? der Verkäufer?

If students ask: **der Angestellte, -n, -n** *employee;* **der Buchhalter, -** *bookkeeper;* **der Fernfahrer, -** *truck driver;* **der Fonotypist, -en, -en** *audio typist* (rare today); **der Freiberufler, -** *freelancer;* **der Friseur, -e** *barber;* **die Friseurin, -nen** *hairdresser;* **der Kassierer, -** *cashier;* **der Kaufmann, -leute** *trained employee in some branch of business;* **der Koch, ¨-e / die Köchin, -nen** *cook;* **der Krankengymnast, -en, -en** *physical therapist;* **der Psychiater, -** *psychiatrist;* **der Systemberater, -** *computer consultant;* **der Telefonist, -en, -en** *switchboard operator;* **der Webdesigner, - ;** **der Zahntechniker, -** *dental technician.*

B. Was sind das für Berufe?

Sagen Sie die Berufe auf Englisch und erklären Sie dann auf Deutsch, was die Leute tun!

Zahntechniker/in
Uhrmacher (Meister)
Gebrauchtwagenverkäufer
Putzfrau
Fernfahrer
Koch
Chemie-Laboranten(innen)
Bankangestellter
Damen- und Herrenfriseur
Telefonistin
Sozialpädagogin
Fonotypistinnen
Arztsekretärin
Industriekaufmann
Rechtsanwaltsgehilfin
Diplom-Ingenieur
Krankengymnast(in)
REISELEITER/-INNEN
Systemberater(in)
Repräsentanten
Bäcker
Haushälterin
Zahnarzthelferin
Buchhalter/in
PSYCHOLOGE/IN
Kassiererin
Fremdsprachenkorrespondentin
Hausmeister

C. Zu welchem Arzt / welcher Ärztin geht man?

1. Wenn man Zahnschmerzen hat, geht man zum/zur . . .
2. Wenn man schlechte Augen hat, geht man zum/zur . . .
3. Mit einem kranken Kind geht man zum/zur . . .
4. Wenn man Hals-, Nasen- oder Ohrenprobleme hat, geht man zum/zur . . .
5. Frauen gehen zum/zur. . .

C.1: Zahnarzt /-ärztin
2. Augenarzt /-ärztin
3. Kinderarzt /-ärztin
4. Hals-Nasen-Ohrenarzt /-ärztin
5. Frauenarzt /-ärztin

Fokus Gender Bias and Language

The traditional use of the masculine German plural to refer collectively to both men and women serves to reinforce outmoded notions that certain professions are only for men (for example, **Ärzte, Wissenschaftler,** and so on). Women appear to be left out of the picture and out of speech. In current-day usage, official documents and journalistic writing often use both masculine and feminine forms in an effort to break out of this pattern of gender exclusivity and be overtly gender inclusive, for example, **Ärzte und Ärztinnen, Wissenschaftler und Wissenschaftlerinnen.** Some publications have opted for a new formation that combines the masculine and feminine into one word: **ÄrztInnen, WissenschaftlerInnen.**

D. Damals und heute

Was waren früher typische Männer- und Frauenberufe? Machen Sie mit den anderen eine Liste und besprechen Sie *(discuss)* dann, wie das heute ist!

E. Ein interessanter Beruf

1. **Das ist mir wichtig.** Fragen Sie Ihren Partner / Ihre Partnerin, was ihm/ihr am Beruf wichtig ist und in welcher Reihenfolge *(sequence)*! Vergleichen Sie dann Ihre Antworten mit den Resultaten der anderen!

- ❑ Reisen
- ❑ freies Wochenende
- ❑ lange Sommerferien
- ❑ saubere Arbeit
- ❑ interessante Arbeit
- ❑ Kreativität
- ❑ elegante Kleidung
- ❑ flexible Arbeitszeit
- ❑ Prestige
- ❑ Sicherheit
- ❑ Erfahrung
- ❑ wenig Stress
- ❑ wenig Papierkrieg *(paperwork)*
- ❑ Arbeit in der freien Natur
- ❑ Abenteuer *(adventure)*
- ❑ Abwechslung *(variety)*
- ❑ Aussichten *(prospects)* für die Zukunft
- ❑ eigener Firmenwagen
- ❑ Verantwortung
- ❑ Kontakt zu Menschen
- ❑ Selbstständigkeit
- ❑ hohes Einkommen

If students ask: *accountant* **der Wirtschaftsprüfer, -;** *banker* **der Bankier, -s;** *conductor* **der Dirigent, -en, -en;** *electrician* **der Elektriker, -;** *insurance agent* **der Versicherungsagent, -en, -en;** *kindergarten teacher* **der Kindergärtner, -;** *mechanic* **der Mechaniker, -;** *(house) painter* **der Maler, -;** *pilot* **der Pilot, -en, -en;** *plumber* **der Klempner, -;** *real estate broker* **der Grundstücksmakler, -;** *stockbroker* **der Börsenmakler, -;** *tax consultant* **der Steuerberater, -.**

2. **In welchen Berufen findet man das?** Schauen Sie sich mit Ihrem Partner / Ihrer Partnerin Ihre Listen noch einmal an und sagen Sie dann, in welchen Berufen man diese Kriterien *(criteria)* findet!

Aussprache: b, d, g

Laute

For further review, see the Summary of Pronunciation in the front of this book. Study Part III, subsection 3.

1. [p] **Obst, Herbst, Erbse, hübsch, ob, halb, gelb**
   BUT [p / b] verlie**b**t / verlie**b**en; blei**b**t / blei**b**en; ha**b**t / ha**b**en
2. [t] **und, gesund, anstrengend, Geld, Hand, sind**
   BUT [t / d] Freun**d** / Freun**d**e; Ba**d** / Bä**d**er; Kin**d** / Kin**d**er; wir**d** / wer**d**en
3. [k] **Tag, Zug, Weg, Bahnsteig, Flugzeug, Berg**
   BUT [k / g] fra**g**st / fra**g**en; flie**g**st / flie**g**en; trä**g**st / tra**g**en; le**g**st / le**g**en

Hörverständnis

Was bin ich? Welcher Sprecher ist was auf dieser Liste? Schreiben Sie die Nummer des Sprechers links neben den richtigen Beruf!

Zum Erkennen: unterwegs *(on the go)*; die Politiker *(politicians)*; weg *(gone)*

__–__ Architekt/in	__3__ Journalist/in	__–__ Rechtsanwalt/-anwältin
__–__ Reiseleiter/in	__–__ Künstler/in	__–__ Sekretär/in
__1__ Hausmann/-frau	__2__ Lehrer/in	__4__ Zahnarzt/-ärztin
__–__ Ingenieur/in	__–__ Polizist/in	__–__ Zeitungsverkäufer/in

Fokus Women in Business and Industry

In Germany as in North America, many jobs were considered for a long time exclusively "men's work." There has been quite a shift in attitude, and more professions are now open to both sexes. For instance, the percentage of female apprentices in Germany has continuously risen since the 1950s to reach 42 percent today. The percentage of professionally trained working women increased from 38 percent in 1970 to 72 percent in 2013. In technical and scientific professions, however, women still make for a rather low showing in the statistics. As a matter of fact, at the university level women account for only 20 percent of those studying technical and engineering subjects. They are well represented, however, in the arts and humanities, and an increasing number of female students are pursuing degrees in economics, law, and business administration. This relatively new trend is not yet reflected by the composition of leadership positions at the top of the professional ladder. The total number of female professors has risen to 25 percent, yet only 15 percent of them are full professors, a percentage that holds true also for the top positions in business and industry. The situation should continue to improve as more highly trained women enter the workforce.

Frauen haben heute viel bessere Berufschancen als früher.

Struktur

12.1 Comparison of adjectives and adverbs

In English and German, adjectives have three degrees:

POSITIVE	COMPARATIVE	SUPERLATIVE
cheap	*cheaper*	*cheapest*
expensive	*more expensive*	*most expensive*

Whereas there are two ways to form the comparative and the superlative in English, there is only *one way* in German; it corresponds to the forms of *cheap* above. In German there is no equivalent to such forms as *more expensive* and *most expensive.*

1. To form the COMPARATIVE, add **-er;** to form the SUPERLATIVE, add **-(e)st.**

   billig   billig**er**   billig**st-**

   a. Many one-syllable adjectives with the stem vowel **a, o,** or **u** have an umlaut in the comparative and superlative, which is shown in the end vocabulary as follows: warm **(ä)**, groß **(ö)**, jung **(ü).**

warm	w**ä**rmer	w**ä**rmst-
groß	gr**ö**ßer	gr**ö**ßt-
jung	j**ü**nger	j**ü**ngst-

   Other adjectives that take an umlaut include: alt, arm, dumm, gesund, kalt, krank, kurz, lang, nah, rot, schwarz.

   b. Most adjectives ending in **-d** or **-t,** in an **s**-sound, or in vowels add **-est** in the superlative.

gesund	gesünder	gesünd**est-**
kalt	kälter	kält**est-**
heiß	heißer	heiß**est-**
kurz	kürzer	kürz**est-**
neu	neuer	neu**est-**

   Note that with the spelling reform, the extra **-e-** after words ending in vowels is optional, e.g., **neu(e)st-, frei(e)st-.**

   Adjectives and adverbs that follow this pattern include: alt (ä), bekannt, beliebt, charmant, ernst, intelligent, interessant, kompliziert, laut, leicht, nett, oft (ö), rot (ö), schlecht, talentiert, verrückt; hübsch, weiß, süß, schwarz (ä), stolz; frei, schlau.

   c. A few adjectives and adverbs have irregular forms in the comparative and/or superlative.

gern	**lieber**	**liebst-**
groß	**größer**	**größt-**
gut	**besser**	**best-**
hoch (hoh-)	**höher**	**höchst-**
nah	**näher**	**nächst-**
viel	**mehr**	**meist-**

A few adjectives ending in **-el** or **-er** (e.g., **dunkel, teuer**) drop the **-e-** in the comparative: **dunkler, teurer.**

2. The comparative of PREDICATE ADJECTIVES (after **sein, werden,** and **bleiben**) and of ADVERBS is formed as described above. The superlative, however, is preceded by **am** and ends in **-sten.**

billig billig**er** **am** billig**sten**

Die Wurst ist billig.	*The sausage is cheap.*
Der Käse ist billig**er.**	*The cheese is cheaper.*
Das Brot ist **am** billig**sten.**	*The bread is cheapest.*
Ich fahre **gern** mit dem Bus.	*I like to go by bus.*
Ich fahre **lieber** mit dem Fahrrad.	*I prefer to (I'd rather) go by bike.*
Ich gehe **am liebsten** zu Fuß.	*Best of all I like (I like best) to walk.*
Ich laufe **viel.**	*I walk a lot.*
Theo läuft **mehr.**	*Theo walks more.*
Katrin läuft **am meisten.**	*Katrin walks the most (i.e., more than Theo and I).*

CAUTION: Meisten in **die meisten Leute** is an adjective; **am meisten** is an adverb of manner; and **meistens** is an adverb of time.

Die **meisten** Leute gehen gern spazieren.	*Most people love to walk.*
Mein Vater geht **am meisten** spazieren.	*My father walks the most.*
Mein Vater geht **meistens** in den Park.	*My father goes mostly to the park.*

3. Adjectives preceding nouns are called ATTRIBUTIVE ADJECTIVES. In the comparative and superlative, attributive adjectives have not only the appropriate comparative or superlative markers but also the adjective endings just as in the positive degree (see Chapters 9 and 10).

der gut**e** Käse	der besser**e** Käse	der best**e** Käse
Ihr gut**er** Käse	Ihr besser**er** Käse	Ihr best**er** Käse
gut**er** Käse	besser**er** Käse	best**er** Käse

Haben Sie keinen besser**en** Käse? Doch, aber besser**er** Käse ist teu(e)**rer.**

4. There are four special phrases frequently used in comparisons:
   a. When you want to say that one thing is like another or not quite like another, use the following:

   (genau)so . . . wie or **nicht so . . . wie**

Ich bin **(genau)so alt wie** er.	*I'm (just, exactly) as old as he is.*
Er ist **nicht so fit wie** ich.	*He is not as fit as I am.*

   NOTE: Ich bin **so alt wie** er (nominative). Ich bin **älter als** er (nominative).

   b. If you want to express a difference, use the following:

   comparative + **als**

Ich bin **älter als** Maya.	*I'm older than Maya.*
Sie ist **jünger als** Leon.	*She is younger than Leon (is).*

c. If you want to express the idea that something is increasingly more so, use the following:

immer + comparative

Die Tage werden **immer länger.**	*The days are getting longer and longer.*
Ich gehe **immer später** ins Bett.	*I'm going to bed later and later.*
Wir schlafen **immer weniger.**	*We sleep less and less*

d. If you are dealing with a pair of comparatives, use the following:

je + comparative . . . **desto** + comparative

Je länger, **desto** besser.	*The longer, the better.*
Je länger ich arbeite, **desto** müder bin ich.	*The longer I work, the more tired I am.*
Je früher ich ins Bett gehe, **desto** früher stehe ich morgens auf.	*The earlier I go to bed, the earlier I get up in the morning.*

Note that **je** introduces a dependent clause. The **desto** + comparative phrase is followed by a main clause in inverted word order.

If you prefer, **je . . . desto = je . . . umso.**

Übungen

A. Komparativ und Superlativ Nennen Sie den Komparativ und den Superlativ, und dann die Formen des Gegenteils!

BEISPIEL schnell *schneller, am schnellsten*
langsam *langsamer, am langsamsten*

billig, gesund, groß, gut, hübsch, intelligent, jung, kalt, kurz, laut, nah, sauber, schwer, viel

A: billiger, am billigsten / teu(e)rer, am teuersten; (un)gesünder, am (un)gesündesten; größer, am größten / kleiner, am kleinsten; besser, am besten / schlechter, am schlechtesten; hübscher, am hübschesten / hässlicher, am hässlichsten; intelligenter, am intelligentesten / dümmer, am dümmsten; jünger, am jüngsten / älter, am ältesten; kälter, am kältesten / wärmer, am wärmsten (heißer, am heißesten); kürzer, am kürzesten / länger, am längsten; lauter, am lautesten / ruhiger, am ruhigsten (leiser, am leisesten); näher, am nächsten; weiter, am weitesten (ferner, am fernsten); sauberer, am saubersten / schmutziger, am schmutzigsten; schwerer, am schwersten / leichter, am leichtesten; mehr, am meisten / weniger, am wenigsten

B. Ersetzen Sie die Adjektive!

BEISPIEL Diese Zeitung ist so langweilig wie die andere Zeitung. (interessant)
Diese Zeitung ist so interessant wie die andere Zeitung.

1. Axel ist so groß wie Tim. (alt, nett)
2. Hier ist es kühler als bei euch. (kalt, heiß)
3. Fernsehsendungen werden immer langweiliger. (verrückt, dumm)
4. Je länger das Buch ist, desto besser. (spannend / interessant; komisch / populär)

B: 1. so alt / nett wie 2. kälter / heißer als 3. verrückter / dümmer 4. spannender, interessanter / komischer, populärer

C. Antworten Sie mit NEIN! Benutzen Sie das Gegenteil des Adjektivs oder Adverbs für den Komparativ!

BEISPIEL Ist dein Bruder auch so alt wie du?
Nein, er ist jünger als ich.

1. Sind deine Schuhe auch so schmutzig wie meine?
2. Verdient Jutta auch so wenig wie du?
3. Sind die Verkäufer bei Edeka auch so unfreundlich?
4. Ist es bei euch im Studentenwohnheim auch so laut?
5. Ist deine Wohnung auch so weit weg wie meine?
6. Sind deine Kurse auch so anstrengend?

C: 1. Nein, sie sind sauberer als deine. 2. Nein, sie verdient mehr als ich. 3. Nein, sie sind freundlicher. 4. Nein, es ist ruhiger. 5. Nein, sie ist näher als deine. 6. Nein, sie sind leichter.

D: 1. am längsten 2. am besten 3. am liebsten 4. am meisten 5. am schönsten

D. In der Wohngemeinschaft Ergänzen Sie die Superlative!

BEISPIEL Pia spricht schnell, Boris spricht schneller, aber Jonas spricht . . .
Pia spricht schnell, Boris spricht schneller, aber Jonas spricht am schnellsten.

1. Pia hat lange geschlafen, Boris hat länger geschlafen, aber Jonas hat . . . geschlafen.
2. Müsli zum Frühstück schmeckt Pia gut, Brot mit Marmelade schmeckt ihr besser, aber Brötchen mit Käse oder Wurst schmeckt ihr . . .
3. Boris sieht gern fern, Jonas arbeitet lieber am Computer, aber Pia liest . . . ein Buch.
4. Pia spricht viel am Telefon, Jonas telefoniert mehr als sie, aber Boris telefoniert . . .
5. Jonas findet es in den Bergen schön, Pia findet es an der See schöner, aber Boris findet es zu Hause . . .

E. Eine bessere Stelle Was fehlt?

1. Möchtest du nicht __lieber__ Beamtin *(civil servant)* werden? *(rather)*
2. Der Staat bezahlt __besser als__ deine Firma. *(better than)*
3. Da hast du __die größte__ Sicherheit. *(the greatest)*
4. Beim Staat hast du __(genau)so viel__ Freizeit __wie__ bei deiner Firma. *([just] as much . . . as)*
5. Vielleicht hast du dann __mehr__ Zeit __als__ jetzt. *(more . . . than)*
6. Es ist auch nicht __so__ anstrengend __wie__ jetzt. *(as . . . as)*
7. __Immer mehr__ Leute arbeiten für den Staat. *(more and more)*
8. Den __meisten__ Leuten gefällt es. *(most)*
9. Ich finde es beim Staat __am interessantesten__ und __am sichersten__ *(the most interesting, the most secure)*
10. Eine __schönere__ Stelle gibt es nicht. *(nicer)*
11. __Je älter__ du wirst, __desto schwerer__ ist es zu wechseln. *(the older . . . the harder)*
12. Vielleicht verdienst du etwas __weniger__, aber dafür hast du __meistens__ keine Probleme. *(less, mostly)*

F. Was ist im Leben am wichtigsten?

1. **Umfrage *(Survey)* bei jungen Deutschen** Die folgende Tabelle zeigt, was ihnen im Leben am wichtigsten ist. Sehen Sie sich die Tabelle an und machen Sie so viele Vergleiche *(comparisons)* wie möglich!

Freizeit	93%
Liebe	83%
Freundschaft	82%
Familie	78%
Gesundheit	65%

Beruf und Karriere	59%
Materielle Sicherheit	58%
Musik und Kultur	40%
Sport	40%
Idealismus	19%

BEISPIEL *Sport ist wichtiger als Idealismus und genauso wichtig wie Musik und Kultur.*

2. **Was ist dir am wichtigsten?** Wie sehen die eigenen Prioritäten *(own priorities)* aus im Vergleich zu den Prioritäten der anderen? Fragen Sie Ihren Partner / Ihre Partnerin!

   BEISPIEL S1 Was ist dir am wichtigsten? am unwichtigsten?
   S2 Die Familie ist mir am wichtigsten. Geld ist mir am unwichtigsten.

Optional activity: You could also have students make comparative statements about various realia in this book, e.g., a weather map *(Schritt 4)*, a menu (Ch. 3), a train schedule (Ch. 8), and charts (ch. 2, 9, 10-11).

G. Interview Fragen Sie einen Nachbarn / eine Nachbarin, . . . !

1. ob er/sie jüngere Geschwister hat; wer am jüngsten und am ältesten ist
2. welche Fernsehsendung ihm/ihr am besten gefällt; was er/sie am meisten sieht
3. was er/sie am liebsten in der Freizeit macht; was er/sie am nächsten Wochenende tut
4. welche amerikanische oder kanadische Stadt er/sie am schönsten und am hässlichsten findet und warum
5. welche drei Eigenschaften ihm/ihr bei einem Freund / einer Freundin oder Partner / Partnerin am wichtigsten sind

Friedrich Nietzsche (1844–1900)

12.2 The future tense

If students ask: **Ereignisse** *events;* **stillsten** *quietest.*

Future events are often referred to using the PRESENT TENSE in both English and German, particularly when a time expression points to the future.

Wir **sehen** uns heute Abend eine DVD **an**. { *We're watching a DVD tonight.* / *We will watch a DVD tonight.* }

We omitted *shall*, since US English does not use it in everyday speech.

In German conversation, the present tense is the preferred form. German does have a FUTURE TENSE, however. It is used when there is no time expression and the circumstances are somewhat more formal.

werden . . . + infinitive

ich **werde** . . . gehen	wir **werden** . . . gehen
du **wirst** . . . gehen	ihr **werdet** . . . gehen
er **wird** . . . gehen	sie **werden** . . . gehen

It is more important for students to *recognize* the future tense than to be able to *use* it actively. Understanding the future tense is an important foundation for learning the subjunctive.

1. The future tense consists of **werden** as the auxiliary and the infinitive of the main verb.

   Ich **werde** ins Büro **gehen.** *I'll go to the office.*
   Wirst du mich **anrufen?** *Will you call me?*

2. If the future tense sentence also contains a modal, the modal appears as an infinitive at the very end.

   werden . . . + verb infinitive + modal infinitive

   Ich **werde** ins Büro **gehen müssen.** *I'll have to go to the office.*
   Wirst du mich **anrufen können?** *Will you be able to call me?*

Please note that we are not using the DOUBLE INFINITIVE in dependent clauses in this text.

You might want to remind students not to confuse the modal **wollen** with the future auxiliary **werden:** Er **will** mitkommen. *He wants to (intends to) come along.* BUT: Er **wird** mitkommen. *He will come along.*

You may wish to ask questions about the statistics below, and then have students ask each other in German for more specific comparisons: 1. Wo gibt es die meisten Kindertagesstätten oder Kitas *(daycare centers)* mit Kleinkindern aus Ausländerfamilien mit Migrationshintergrund *(background of migration)*! Machen Sie ein paar Vergleiche! 2. In wie vielen Familien davon spricht man Deutsch oder eine andere Sprache im Elternhaus? Geben Sie Statistiken in Prozentzahlen!

3. Sentences in the future follow familiar word order rules.

   Er **wird** auch **kommen.**
   Er **wird** auch **mitkommen.**
   Er **wird** (V1) auch **mitkommen wollen.** (V2)

   Ich weiß, dass er auch **kommen wird.**
   Ich weiß, dass er auch **mitkommen** (V1) **wird.** (V2)

4. The future form can also express PRESENT PROBABILITY, especially when used with the word **wohl.**

   Er wird **wohl** auf dem Weg sein. *He is probably on the way (now).*

5. Remember that **werden** is also a full verb meaning *to get, to become.*

   present tense: Wir **werden** müde. *We're getting tired.*
   future tense: Wir **werden** müde **werden.** *We will get tired.*

Fokus Foreign Workers in Germany

In the 1950s, the West German and Turkish governments signed a contract that allowed Turkish nationals to be recruited as guest workers (**Gastarbeiter**) in Germany. In 1961, 2,500 Turks were living in Germany; today there are almost 3 million residents of Turkish origin in Germany, approximately 50 percent of whom have German citizenship. In the 1960s and 1970s, Turks were mainly employed in mining and in the steel and auto industries. Today they are by far the biggest ethnic group in Germany (Italians and Poles are the second-largest group, see chart), and they are becoming more involved in domestic politics and service organizations. In addition to foreign guest workers from around the Mediterranean and asylum-seekers from all over the world, Germany also has received many other ethnic immigrants of German heritage **(Aussiedler),** most of them from the successor states to the Soviet Union, who are granted citizenship immediately.

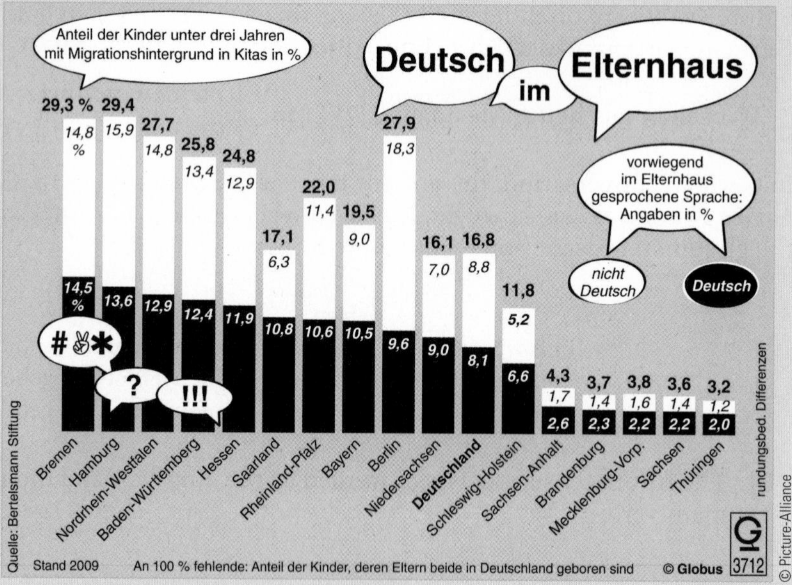

© Picture-Alliance

Since the year 2000, children born in Germany to non-German parents also obtain German citizenship automatically, on the condition that one of the parents has been a resident for at least eight years and is in possession of an unlimited residence permit for at least three years. As of January 2005, the new Immigration Act **(das Einwanderungsgesetz)** regulates immigration and the integration of foreigners in Germany. This law simplifies the granting of residence permits, prompts the integration of non-EU foreigners through compulsory language courses, and speeds up the procedures for asylum seekers. Another important aspect of the law is the opening of the employment market to highly skilled foreigners and foreign graduates of German universities. In 2007, the law was revised yet again in order to bring it line with the European Union's legal guidelines concerning asylum. Furthermore, the law includes an integration-oriented change regarding the immigration of spouses of residents. That change requires a minimum age as well as a minimum knowledge of German.

Übungen

H. Sagen Sie die Sätze in der Zukunft!

BEISPIEL Gute Zahnärzte braucht man immer.
Gute Zahnärzte wird man immer brauchen.

1. Dabei verdiene ich auch gut. 2. Aber du studierst einige Jahre an der Universität. 3. Ich gehe nicht zur Uni. 4. Meine Tischlerarbeit ist anstrengend. 5. Aber daran gewöhnt man sich. 6. Dieser Beruf hat bestimmt Zukunft. 7. Ihr seht das schon. 8. Eines Tages mache ich mich selbstständig. 9. Als Chefin *(boss)* in einem Männerberuf muss ich besonders gut sein.

H: 1. Dabei werde ich auch gut verdienen. 2. Aber du wirst einige Jahre an der Universität studieren. 3. Ich werde nicht zur Uni gehen. 4. Meine Tischlerarbeit wird anstrengend sein. 5. Aber daran wird man sich gewöhnen. 6. Dieser Beruf wird bestimmt Zukunft haben. 7. Ihr werdet das schon sehen. 8. Eines Tages werde ich mich selbsständig machen. 9. Als Chefin in einem Männerberuf werde ich besonders gut sein müssen.

I. Kampf im Alltag *(Struggle in everyday life)*

Schauen Sie sich die Illustration an und wiederholen Sie dann die Sätze in der Zukunft!

1. Meine Freundin **heiratet** einen Mann mit vier Kindern. 2. Das **ist** nicht leicht. 3. Sie **hat** dann keine ruhige Minute mehr. 4. Morgens **darf** sie erst einmal alle **wecken.** 5. Dann **muss** sie allen Frühstück **machen.** 6. Beim Einkaufen und Kochen **muss** sie **sich beeilen,** denn bald **sind** sie alle wieder zu Hause. 7. Sie **sitzen** sicher auch lieber vorm Computer oder vorm Fernseher, als Hausaufgaben zu machen. 8. Beim Kochen **hilft** ihr niemand. 9. Wenn sie dann abends alle im Bett sind, **ist** sie auch müde. 10. Ich **warne** sie, aber sie **tut** es trotzdem.

Der moderne MÜTTERZWÖLFKAMPF

- Weckdienst
- Frühstück für alle
- Haushalt
- Einkaufen
- Kochen
- Hausaufgabenstress
- Kampf dem Computer
- Kampf dem Handy
- Kampf dem Fernseher
- wieder Kochen
- wieder Haushalt
- Bettgehstress

und das ohne NERVENZUSAMMENBRUCH!

I: 1. wird . . . heiraten 2. wird . . . sein 3. wird . . . haben 4. wird . . . wecken dürfen 5. wird . . . machen müssen 6. wird . . . sich beeilen müssen, werden . . . sein 7. werden . . . sitzen 8. wird . . . helfen 9. wird . . . sein 10. werde . . . warnen, wird . . . tun

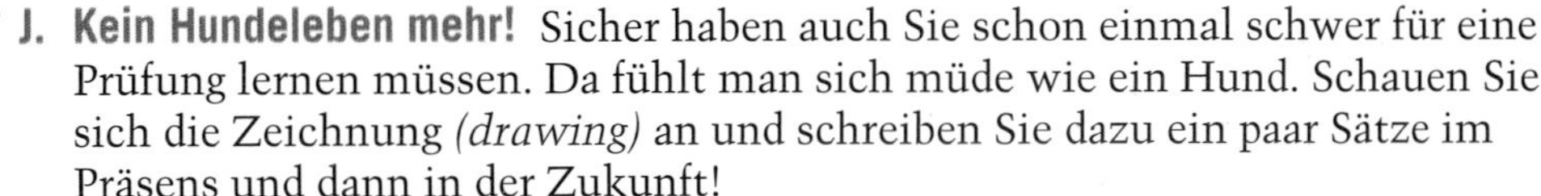

J. Kein Hundeleben mehr!

Sicher haben auch Sie schon einmal schwer für eine Prüfung lernen müssen. Da fühlt man sich müde wie ein Hund. Schauen Sie sich die Zeichnung *(drawing)* an und schreiben Sie dazu ein paar Sätze im Präsens und dann in der Zukunft!

1. Im Präsens: Wenn die nächste Prüfung vorbei ist, . . .
2. In der Zukunft: Wenn ich mit meinem Studium *(course of studies)* fertig bin, . . .

Das "Hundeleben" ist vorbei.
der Prüfungsstress nun einerlei!

Drawing: **Das ist nun einerlei.** *That doesn't matter anymore.* **Es ist mir einerlei.** *I don't care.*

12.3 Predicate nouns and adjectival nouns

1. Certain predicate nouns

As you already know, German—unlike English—does *not* use the indefinite article before PREDICATE NOUNS denoting professions, nationalities, religious affiliation, or political adherence (see Chapter 1, **Übungen zum Thema**).

Er ist **Amerikaner.**	*He is an American.*
Sie ist **Ingenieurin.**	*She's an engineer.*

However, when a predicate noun is used in the singular and preceded by an adjective, the definite article **ein** is used. In the plural, that does not apply.

Er ist **ein** typischer Amerikaner.	*He's a typical American.*
Sie ist **eine** gute Ingenieurin.	*She's a good engineer.*
Das sind interessante Leute.	*They are interesting people.*

2. Adjectival nouns

ADJECTIVAL NOUNS are nouns derived from adjectives; that is, the original noun is dropped and the adjective itself becomes the noun. Adjectival nouns are used in English, but not very often. Plural forms usually refer to people, singular nouns to abstract concepts.

Give me your ***tired*** *(people), your* ***poor.***

The ***best*** *is yet to come.*

German uses adjectival nouns quite frequently. They are capitalized to show that they are nouns, and they have the endings they would have had as attributive adjectives, depending on the preceding article, case, number, and gender. Use the same system you have already learned for adjectives to put the correct endings on adjectival nouns (see below and Chapters 9 and 10). Masculine forms refer to males, feminine forms to females, and neuter forms to abstract concepts.

Das berühmteste Antikriegsbuch von Erich Maria Remarque

der Alte	*the old man*	mein Alter	*my old man, my husband*
die Alte	*the old woman*	meine Alte	*my old woman, my wife*
die Alten	*the old people*	meine Alten	*my old people, my parents*

das Alte	*the old, that which is old, old things*
das Beste	*the best thing(s)*

After **etwas** and **nichts, viel** and **wenig,** the adjectival noun will always be NEUTER.

etwas Interessantes	*something interesting*
nichts Neues	*nothing new*
viel Hässliches	*a lot of ugly things*
wenig Schönes	*not much that's beautiful*

Here are examples of common adjectival nouns:

der/die Angestellte	*employee*	**der/die Kranke**	*sick person*
der/die Bekannte	*acquaintance*	**der/die Verlobte**	*fiancé / fiancée*
der/die Deutsche	*German person*	Also: **der Beamte**	*civil servant*

These adjectival nouns are sometimes listed as follows: **der Angestellte (ein Angestellter), der Deutsche (ein Deutscher)**; the rest of the forms can be deduced.

der Beamte, BUT: die Beam**tin**! Also: der/die **Schwerbehinderte** *(disabled person)*, **Verwandte** *(relative)* (see exercise L).

	SINGULAR MASC.	SINGULAR FEM.	PLURAL
nom.	der Deutsche ein Deutscher	die Deutsche eine Deutsche	die Deutschen keine Deutschen
acc.	den Deutschen einen Deutschen	die Deutsche eine Deutsche	die Deutschen keine Deutschen
dat.	dem Deutschen einem Deutschen	der Deutschen einer Deutschen	den Deutschen keinen Deutschen
gen.	des Deutschen eines Deutschen	der Deutschen einer Deutschen	der Deutschen keiner Deutschen

Students could practice converting adjectives such as **verliebt, verheiratet, verrückt,** etc. into nouns **(Verliebte, Verheiratete, Verrückte)**; also superlatives such as **billigst-, teuerst-liebst-, größt-, höchst-, nächst-,** etc. (**das Billigste, Teuerste, Liebste,** etc.).

Have students express these examples in English.

Karl ist Angestellt**er** bei uns und seine Frau Angestellt**e** bei VW.
Ein Angestellt**er** wollte dich sprechen. Wie heißt der Angestellt**e?**
Siehst du den Angestellt**en** da drüben? Nein, ich sehe keinen Angestellt**en.**

Übungen

K. Artikel oder nicht? Entscheiden Sie in den folgenden Sätzen, ob man einen Artikel braucht oder nicht! Wenn ja, welchen Artikel? Wiederholen Sie dann den Satz auf Englisch!

BEISPIEL sie / sein / Mutter / von / zwei Kinder
Sie ist Mutter von zwei Kindern.

1. sie / sein / aber auch / Wissenschaftlerin
2. sie / sein / sehr gut / Biologin
3. er / werden / Hausmann
4. er / sein *(simple past)* / dynamisch / Lehrer / und / er / sein *(future)* / geduldig / Vater
5. sie / sein /charmant / Österreicherin
6. er / sein / gemütlich / Schweizer

K: 1. Sie ist aber auch Wissenschaftlerin. *She's also a scientist.* 2. Sie ist eine sehr gute Biologin. *She's a very good biologist.* 3. Er wird Hausmann. *He's becoming a househusband.* 4. Er war ein dynamischer Lehrer und er wird ein geduldiger Vater sein. *He was a dynamic teacher, and he'll be a patient dad.* 5. Sie ist eine charmante Österreicherin. *She is a charming Austrian.* 6. Er ist ein gemütlicher Schweizer. *He's a congenial Swiss.*

L. Substantivierte Adjektive *(Adjectival nouns)* Welches substantivierte Adjektiv passt?

BEISPIEL Bist du mit diesem Herrn **verwandt** *(related to)*?
*Nein, das ist kein **Verwandter** (relative) von mir.*

1. Herr Schneider war lange bei uns **angestellt.** Geben Sie dem __Angestellten__ die Papiere!
2. Er ist uns allen gut **bekannt.** Er ist ein guter __Bekannter__ von uns allen.
3. Jetzt hat er seine Arbeit verloren und sucht, wie viele **deutsche** Kollegen, eine andere Stelle. Wie ihm geht es vielen __Deutschen__.
4. Herr Schneider ist noch jung, aber **schwerbehindert** *(disabled)*. Als __Schwerbehinderter__ wird er sicher Hilfe vom Arbeitsamt *(unemployment agency)* bekommen.
5. Er ist mit einer Schweizerin **verlobt.** Seine __Verlobte__ ist Krankenpflegerin.
6. Sie pflegt *(takes care of)* **kranke** Menschen. Alle ihre __Kranken__ lieben sie.
7. Herr Schneider träumt von einer **Beamten**stelle. Als __Beamter__ verdient man ganz gut.
8. Wenn er damit kein Glück hat, will er sich **selbstständig** machen. __Selbstständige__ müssen viel arbeiten.
9. Das wird für ihn kein Problem sein, denn er ist sehr **fleißig.** Er ist wirklich ein __Fleißiger__.
10. Er ist auch **unternehmungslustig.** __Unternehmungslustige__ finden immer einen Weg.

M. Das ist nichts Neues. Lesen Sie die folgende Adjektivliste und reagieren Sie dann auf die Aussagen Ihres Partners / Ihrer Partnerin mit einem substantivierten Adjektiv!

BEISPIEL S1 Er hat wieder mal kein Geld.
S2 Das ist nichts Neues!

besonder-, besser, billig, dumm, furchtbar, interessant, schön, toll, traurig, verrückt . . .

S1 In diesem Geschäft ist nichts, was mir gefällt.
S2 Ich finde auch nichts . . .
S1 Gehen wir zu dem Laden da drüben!
S2 Wenn du meinst. Vielleicht gibt's da etwas . . .
S1 Carlos sagt, dass sein Vater ihm einen Porsche kaufen wird.
S2 Und so etwas . . . soll ich glauben?
S1 Hast du von der Katastrophe in Asien (in . . .) gehört?
S2 Ja, es gibt doch viel . . . auf dieser Welt.
S1 Und doch gibt es auch viel . . . , worüber man sich freuen kann.

N. Kurzgespräch mit den Eltern Bereiten Sie ein Gespräch mit dem Vater oder der Mutter (Ihrem Partner / Ihrer Partnerin) vor und präsentieren Sie den Dialog danach vor der Klasse!

N: As preparation for the talk with the parents, you might ask students to have a look at the chart in the *Zum Schreiben* section of the *Arbeitsbuch* (SAM).

You are discussing your career choice (**Autoverkäufer, Beamter, Krankenpfleger/in,** etc.) with your parents. They are not happy with your decision and express their disagreement. You agree or disagree with their objections.

Zusammenfassung

O. Wie viel Ansehen *(prestige)* haben die verschiedenen Berufe bei den Deutschen? Sehen Sie sich die Tabelle an und sprechen Sie mit den anderen darüber! Wie vergleicht sich das mit dem Ansehen dieser Berufe in Ihrem Land?

In case you are curious: **der Spitzensportler, -** *top athlete;* **der Botschafter, -** *ambassador;* **der Polizist, -en, -en** *police officer;* **der Unternehmer, -** *entrepreneur, businessman;* **der Geistliche, - n (ein Geistlicher)** *clergyperson;* **der Pfarrer,-** *Protestant minister;* **der Hochschulprofessor, -en,** *university professor*

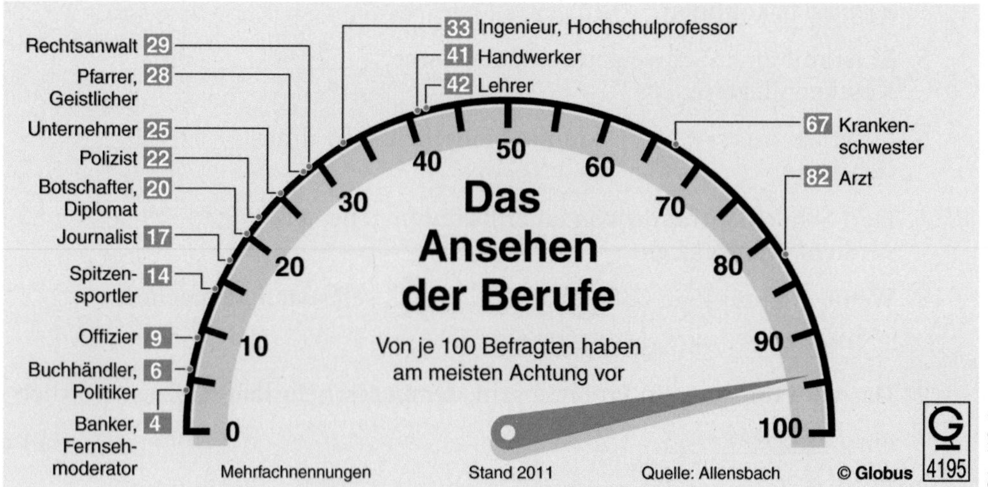

P. Zukunftspläne Auf Deutsch bitte!

1. Did you (*pl.* fam.) know that Alex wants to become a journalist? 2. He doesn't want to be a teacher. 3. There are only a few positions. 4. I've gotten used to it. 5. Nina is as enterprising as he is. 6. She was my most talented student. 7. If she wants to become a doctor, she will become a doctor. 8. She's smarter, more independent, and nicer than her brother. 9. She says that she will work hard. 10. I know that she'll be self-employed one day. 11. I'll go to her rather than to another doctor (I'll rather go to her than . . .). 12. The more I think of it, the better I like the idea.

ARZT-AUSFAHRT
TAG UND NACHT
FREIHALTEN

iLrn

Visit the ***Wie geht's?*** iLrn website for more review and practice of the grammar points you have just learned.

P: 1. Habt ihr gewusst (wusstet ihr), dass Alex Journalist werden will? 2. Er will kein / nicht Lehrer werden. 3. Es gibt nur wenige Stellen. 4. Ich habe mich daran gewöhnt. 5. Nina ist (genau)so unternehmungslustig wie er. 6. Sie war meine talentierteste Schülerin. 7. Wenn sie Ärztin werden will, wird sie Ärztin. 8. Sie ist klüger, unabhängiger und netter als ihr Bruder. 9. Sie sagt, dass sie fleißig / schwer arbeiten wird. 10. Ich weiß, dass sie eines Tages selbstständig sein wird (sich selbstständig machen wird). 11. Ich werde lieber zu ihr als zu einem anderen Arzt gehen. 12. Je mehr ich daran denke (darüber nachdenke), desto besser gefällt mir die Idee.

Fokus Hard Times and Social Policy

The worldwide trend toward greater industrial efficiency, higher productivity, and lower labor costs, coupled with the enormous expense of reunification, have led to high unemployment **(die Arbeitslosigkeit).** Rebuilding and privatizing the uncompetitive, formerly state-run East German industries during an era of increased international competition and slow growth in Europe turned out to be much more difficult than anticipated. The extensive modernization necessitated costly, federally financed training and retraining programs, large-scale early retirements, and a huge transfer of funds to the new eastern states.

To deal with additional challenges (i.e., a longer life expectancy, low birthrates, and high unemployment), the government passed a series of social reforms, including the encouragement of private pensions, raising the mandatory age of retirement to age 67, as well as a cost-cutting health insurance reform. Despite some cutbacks in social benefits, the fundamental principles of a social policy aimed at achieving a high degree of social justice have not changed. All sorts of government assistance programs continue to be provided, including social security **(die Rentenversicherung),** public welfare **(die Sozialhilfe),** and a mandatory health insurance **(die Krankenversicherung).** An important addition is the long-term care insurance **(die Pflegeversicherung),** which was put into law in the early 1990s.

Labor unions **(Gewerkschaften)** have always been very important in Germany. However, with the onset of a recessionary time since reunification, they have been forced to compromise on their long-standing goals of job security with ever higher pay and more benefits. Nevertheless, labor unions remain quite strong. As they participate in the decision-making process of many companies, their relationship with management has been—with a few exceptions—a flexible, cooperative, non-confrontational partnership that has contributed to industrial peace and to one of the highest standards of living in the world. Germany's extensive social benefits net helped alleviate the impact of unemployment during the worldwide economic downturn, which began in 2008 and which has been impacting export-dependent Germany especially hard. As the crisis has caused many member-nations of the Euro-currency to flounder due to high national debts, the European Union has had to draw heavily on Germany for bailout funding since 2011.

Besuch bei der Ärztin

Einblicke

Diskussion

Wortschatz 2

der Arbeiter, -	*(blue-collar) worker*
Bereich, -e	*area, field*
Handel	*trade*
Rat	*advice, counsel*
das Praktikum, Praktika	*internship*
Unternehmen, -	*large company*
die Arbeiterin, -nen	*(blue-collar) worker*
Arbeitslosigkeit	*unemployment*
Berufswahl	*choice of profession*
Entscheidung, -en	*decision*
(Fach)kenntnis, -se	*(special) knowledge, skill*
darum	*therefore*
ins/im Ausland	*abroad*
jedoch	*however*
momentan	*at the moment, right now*
unbedingt	*definitely, absolutely*
unter (+ *dat.*)	*among*
aus•sehen (sieht aus), sah aus, ausgesehen (wie + *nom.*)	*to look (like)*
bitten, bat, gebeten (um)	*to ask (for), request*
hoffen	*to hope*
sich *(dat.)* Sorgen machen (um)	*to be concerned / worried (about)*
sich *(dat.)* vor•stellen	*to imagine*
Ich stelle mir vor, dass . . .	*I imagine that . . .*

Vor dem Lesen

Lesetipp

Identifying a Speaker's Main Point

Just as speakers typically introduce the topic of their discourse in the first sentence of a paragraph, they often encapsulate the main idea in the final sentence. Find examples in this reading where speakers summarize their ideas in their last sentence.

A. Was denken Sie?

1. Ist es momentan schwer, in Ihrem Land Arbeit zu finden?
2. Was für Stellen findet man leicht?
3. Welche Jobs sind schwerer zu finden?
4. Welche Berufe haben eine gute Zukunft?

B. Gehen wir Wörter angeln! Lesen Sie mit Ihrem Partner / Ihrer Partnerin den folgenden Text gemeinsam durch. Welche Berufe sowie *(as well as)* Komparative und Superlative finden Sie darin?

C. Das ist leicht zu verstehen! Lesen Sie laut die folgenden Wörter und raten Sie, was sie auf Englisch bedeuten?
der Akademiker, Auslandsaufenthalt, Computerkünstler, Experte, Job, Telekommunikationsspezialist, Tourismus; das Filmstudio, Industrieunternehmen, Risiko, Studium, Team; die Berufsmöglichkeit, Flexibilität, Geduld, Generation, Lebenskrise, Mobilität, Perspektive, Suche (nach); in der Zwischenzeit; beruflich, flexibel, praktisch, relativ, qualifiziert, spontan; jobben, organisieren

Zwei Schüler* (pupils) *eines Gymnasiums am Computer in ihrer Schulbibliothek

Die Berufswahl

(Eine öffentliche Diskussion an der Universität Göttingen)

Wie viele andere Studenten und Studentinnen macht Lore Weber sich Sorgen um ihre berufliche Zukunft. Sie hat darum eine Diskussionsgruppe organisiert und eine Professorin und andere Studenten gebeten, Ideen beizutragen°.

beizutragen: to contribute

LORE WEBER: Eine der wichtigsten Entscheidungen im Leben ist die Frage der Berufswahl. Momentan ist die Arbeitslosigkeit relativ hoch, nicht nur unter den Arbeitern, sondern auch unter uns Akademikern. Viele Industrieunternehmen werden in den nächsten Jahren weitere° Arbeitsplätze abbauen° und im öffentlichen Dienst° wird es nicht besser aussehen. Einige meiner Freunde mit abgeschlossener° Ausbildung suchen seit Monaten Arbeit und jobben in der Zwischenzeit als Bedienung, Verkäufer, Taxifahrer usw.°. Wir fragen uns alle, wie unsere Zukunft aussehen wird, und hoffen, dass wir durch unsere Diskussion eine bessere Vorstellung° davon bekommen. Ich möchte jetzt Frau Professor Weigel bitten, ihre Perspektive über das Problem zusammenzufassen. Frau Professor Weigel!

additional / cut back
civil service
completed
etc.
idea

PROFESSOR WEIGEL: Vielen Dank, Frau Weber! Auf die Frage nach sicheren Berufen kann man nur schwer eine Antwort geben. Ich stelle mir vor, dass die Berufswahl immer komplizierter wird. Zu den Berufen mit Zukunft zählen aber bestimmt Umweltexperten° und Biochemiker, Telekommunikations- und Computerspezialisten, Betriebswirte und Mathematiker. Selbstständige in den verschiedenen Bereichen, vor allem auch im Tourismus, werden sicher genug Arbeit finden. Auch für Lehrer wird es weiter eine größere Nachfrage° geben. Jedoch sinkt der Bedarf° für Rechtsanwälte und Architekten. Den Geisteswissenschaftlern° unter Ihnen empfehle ich, flexibel zu bleiben und auch außerhalb° Ihres Studiums praktische Erfahrungen zu sammeln, zum Beispiel bei Verlagen° und anderen Firmen und auch durch Auslandsaufenthalte. Neben guten Sprach- und Fachkenntnissen wird man besondere Eigenschaften suchen, wie zum Beispiel Flexibilität, Mobilität und die Fähigkeit°, immer wieder Neues zu lernen und kreativ zu denken, im Team zu arbeiten und Umbrüche° als Chance statt als Risiko zu sehen. Es ist heute keine Lebenskrise mehr, wenn man den Job wechselt. Eins ist jedoch klar: Eine gute und breite° Ausbildung ist und bleibt die beste Sicherheit.

environmental . . .
demand
need
humanities scholars
outside
publishing houses
ability
radical changes
broad

Christl Meininger: Ich leite° seit drei Jahren ein Wellness-Hotel. Ich liebe meine Arbeit, aber die Suche nach qualifizierten Arbeitskräften° habe ich mir leichter vorgestellt. Ich glaube, dass Bereiche wie Wellness, Freizeit und Beratung° immer beliebter werden. Wir leben heute unter größerem Stress als früher und sind viel gesundheitsbewusster° geworden. Man wird also mehr und mehr Geld für sein eigenes Wohlbefinden° ausgeben. Mein Rat: Lernen Sie das, was Ihnen Spaß macht, und lernen Sie viel! Fit machen für den Job muss sich jeder selbst°. Je mehr man in seinem Fach° weiß, desto besser.

direct
workers
counseling
more health-conscious
well-being
himself, herself
field, subject

Jonas Wendland: Ich bin Lehrer für Geschichte und Englisch an einem Gymnasium. Das finde ich unheimlich interessant und man lernt immer etwas Neues dazu. Vor allem hat man aber einen Einfluss° auf die junge Generation. Als Lehrer muss man nicht nur gute Fachkenntnisse mitbringen und sich immer gut vorbereiten, sondern auch spontan sein. Natürlich muss man Geduld haben und auch mal streng sein können. Es gibt viel Papierkrieg°, aber dafür hat man auch ein sicheres Einkommen und viele Ferien. Ich habe meine Entscheidung nie bereut°.

influence
paper work
regretted

Brigitte Schindler: Ich studiere Kunst und Informatik. Ich hoffe, dass ich eines Tages als Computerkünstlerin für ein Filmstudio oder beim Fernsehen arbeiten werde. Ich versuche gerade, einen Platz für ein Praktikum in Amerika zu finden. Je mehr man gemacht hat, desto besser die Chancen. Auslandserfahrung ist wichtig. Mit der wachsenden Bedeutung° der EU—wo wir mit unserer Ausbildung überall arbeiten können—und Deutschlands Handelsbeziehungen mit der ganzen Welt werden unsere Berufsmöglichkeiten immer interessanter. Die Konkurrenz° wird natürlich auch größer. Ich stelle mir vor, dass jedes bisschen Erfahrung hilft. Die besten Jobs werden immer die Besten bekommen.

growing importance
competition

Es ist nicht gut genug, klug zu sein. Es ist besser, gut zu sein.

Nach dem Lesen

A. Alles verstanden?

1. Was ist momentan relativ hoch?
2. Wo jobben viele, sogar mit abgeschlossener Ausbildung?
3. Was wird immer komplizierter?
4. Welche Berufe versprechen eine gute Zukunft?
5. Was hilft außer dem Studium auch?
6. Welche besonderen Eigenschaften suchen Arbeitgeber *(employers)* bei ihren Angestellten?
7. Warum glaubt Christl Meininger, dass Bereiche wie Wellness, Freizeit und Beratung beliebt bleiben?
8. Was gefällt Jonas Wendland am Lehrerberuf?
9. Was möchte Brigitte Schindler eines Tages tun?
10. Wovon ist sie überzeugt *(convinced)*?

A: 1. die Arbeitslosigkeit 2. als Bedienung, Verkäufer oder Taxifahrer 3. die Berufswahl 4. Umweltexperten, Biochemiker, Telekommunikations- und Computerspezialisten, Betriebswirte, Mathematiker, Lehrer 5. praktische Erfahrung, Auslandsaufenthalte 6. Sprach- und Fachkenntnisse, Flexibilität, Mobilität, Lernfähigkeit, Kreativität, Teamarbeit 7. mehr Stress, gesundheitsbewusster 8. interessant, immer etwas Neues, Einfluss auf die junge Generation, sicheres Einkommen, viele Ferien 9. Computerkünstlerin bei einem Filmstudio / beim Fernsehen 10. Die besten Jobs werden immer die Besten bekommen.

B. Blick auf den Arbeitsmarkt Wiederholen Sie die Sätze in der Zukunft!

1. Die Berufswahl bleibt eine der wichtigsten Entscheidungen. 2. So fragen wir uns alle, wie unsere Zukunft aussieht. 3. Habe ich mit meiner Ausbildung gute Berufsmöglichkeiten oder sitze ich eines Tages auf der Straße? 4. Absolute Sicherheit gibt es in keinem Beruf. 5. Man muss flexibel bleiben. 6. Praktische Erfahrung im Ausland und Sprachkenntnisse helfen auch. 7. Die Konkurrenz wird immer größer. 8. Mit einer guten Ausbildung können die Deutschen in Zukunft überall in der EU arbeiten.

B: 1. wird . . . bleiben 2. werden . . . fragen, aussehen . . . wird 3. Werde . . . haben, werde . . . sitzen 4. wird . . . geben 5. wird . . . bleiben müssen 6. werden . . . helfen 7. wird . . . werden 8. werden . . . arbeiten können

C. So wird's werden. Was fehlt?

1. ___Die meisten___ Leute müssen mindestens *(at least)* einmal ihren Beruf wechseln. *(most)*
2. Gute theoretische Kenntnisse werden ___genauso___ wichtig sein ___wie___ praktische Erfahrungen. *(just as . . . as)*
3. ___Je mehr___ praktische Erfahrung man hat, ___desto besser___ sind die Berufschancen. *(the more . . . the better)*
4. Man wird auch ___immer mehr___ Zusatzqualifikationen suchen. *(more and more)*
5. ___Sobald___ man seine Prüfungen hinter sich hat, muss man bereit *(willing)* sein, dorthin zu ziehen, wo es Arbeit gibt. *(as soon as)*
6. Wer nicht flexibel ist, wird ___weniger___ Chancen auf dem Arbeitsmarkt haben und vielleicht auch ___weniger___ verdienen. *(fewer; less)*

Weiteres

D. Wunschprofil von Arbeitgebern Sehen Sie sich die beiden Illlustrationen an und finden Sie heraus, wonach Arbeitgeber suchen und wonach nicht. Machen Sie Aussagen darüber, wenn möglich mit Komparativen und Superlativen!

BEISPIEL *Flexibilität ist den Arbeitgebern am wichtigsten.*
Perfekte Leute suchen sie nicht.

D: You might ask students to provide their own ranking. Have them tabulate on the board.

Ingenieurbüro sucht Nachfolger/in

Sind Sie perfekt? Schön für Sie. Aber leider suchen wir nicht jemanden, der perfekt ist. Im Gegenteil: Wir suchen Menschen, die gern neue Lösungen finden und innovative Ideen haben. Und wenn Ihnen mal etwas nicht gut gelingt, ist das auch nicht so schlimm!

Engineering aus Deutschland

Bewerben Sie sich noch heute!

© Beatrix Brockman

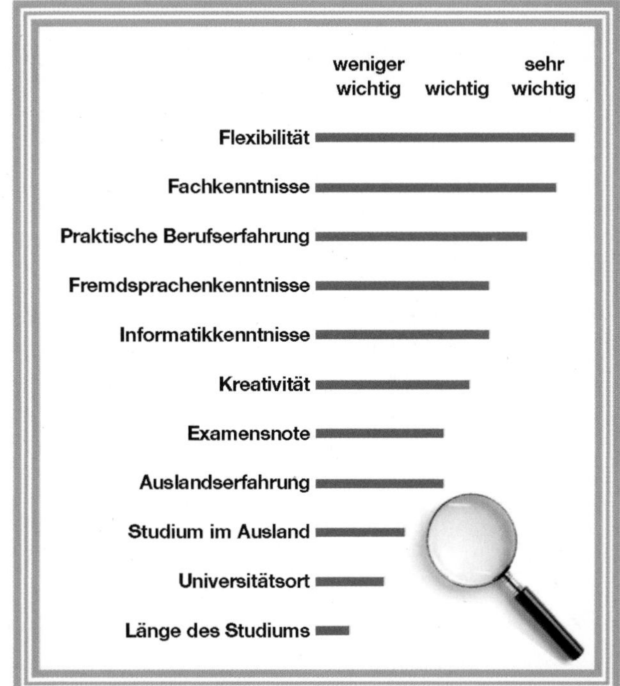

© Ingrid Sevin

E. Was bin ich? Nehmen Sie die *Hörverständnis*-Übung auf Seite 344 als Muster *(model)* und schreiben Sie ein paar Sätze! Lesen Sie laut, was Sie geschrieben haben! Die anderen versuchen dann zu raten *(guess)*, was Sie sind.

BEISPIEL *Viele Leute kommen zu mir nur, wenn ihnen etwas wehtut. Sie kommen mit Schmerzen, setzen sich in meinen gemütlichen Stuhl und bald sind die Schmerzen weg. Was bin ich?*

F. Aufsatz: Etwas über mich Schreiben Sie sechs bis acht Sätze über eins der folgenden Themen!

1. Was ich einmal werden möchte/wollte und warum
2. Mein Leben in . . . Jahren. So stelle ich mir mein Leben in zehn, zwanzig oder dreißig Jahren vor.

G. Mein Lebenslauf *(résumé)* Lesen Sie den folgenden Lebenslauf und schreiben Sie dann Ihren eigenen! Vergleichen Sie ihn mit dem der *(that of)* anderen!

Schreibtipp

Writing a Résumé

A résumé provides general information about your life and describes the development of your professional career beginning with your education. The traditional **Lebenslauf** was handwritten and in narrative form; however, the modern version is typed, brief, and to the point. Limit yourself to just one page. **In der Kürze liegt die Würze** *(Clarity is in brevity*, lit. *In brevity lies the spiciness)*. The sample shown here shows just one way to prepare a German-style résumé. A photograph is common and usually required in the job application process. Don't forget to sign your résumé at the bottom. Do remember to provide a professional-sounding e-mail address.

Lebenslauf

Persönliche Daten:

Susan Gerber
512 Rainer Blvd.
Maple Valley, Wa 98038
Tel.: 001 (425) 555-5583
Email: sgerber@muster.com

Geboren am 21.12.1992 in Palo Alto, Kalifornien; US-Amerikanerin

Schulbildung: 20 Mai 2007	Nathan Hale High School, Seattle, Washington High School Abschluss
Studium: 09/2007-05/2011	University of Washington, Seattle, Washington Studienfächer: Betriebswirtschaft und Deutsch Studienschwerpunkte: Buchhaltung, Finanzwesen, Deutsche Kultur und Sprache
16. Mai 2011	BA in Business Administration Studienabschluss: Betriebswirtschaft
Berufserfahrung: Seit 07/2011	Boeing Company, Seattle, Washington Buchhaltungsassistentin, Mitarbeit im Export-Team
Kenntnisse und Interessen:	Computer Microsoft Office, Account Geek, SAP Präsidentin des Businessclubs meiner Universität
Sprachkenntnisse:	Englisch (Muttersprache) Deutsch (fließend)
	13. März 2013 *Susan Gerber*

Hörverständnis

Zwei Lebensläufe Hören Sie sich an, was die zwei jungen Deutschen über sich zu erzählen haben! Bevor Sie aber die folgenden Sätze als richtig oder falsch markieren, lesen Sie noch einmal kurz die *Vorschau* am Anfang des Kapitels!

Zum Erkennen: der Vorarbeiter *(foreman)*; zum Militär *(to the army)*; der Autounfall *(accident)*

__f__ 1. Wolf Wicke ist in Dresden geboren.

__r__ 2. Wolf macht eine Lehre als Automechaniker und geht zur Berufsschule.

__f__ 3. Wolf war schon beim Militär.

__f__ 4. Kristinas Mutter lebt nicht mehr.

__r__ 5. Kristinas Bruder ist fünf Jahre älter als sie.

__f__ 6. Nach dem Abitur hat sie zuerst ein Jahr gearbeitet.

__r__ 7. Jetzt ist sie Medizinstudentin in Heidelberg.

For further practice, an optional two-part video **(Szenen** and **Interviews)** is available on the ***Wie geht's?*** Premium Website and in iLrn, with corresponding questions and activities in the *Arbeitsbuch* (SAM).

As an optional activity, you could use Google Earth to visit any city in the German-speaking countries and check out some schools in that town.

Literatur

Biographisches

Jörg Zschocke (born in 1944) is an engineer, but writes, often humorously, as a vocation. He often brags in his stories about his "most amazing" Canadian wife and their three "fantastic" children, but he always tries to be graciously humble when it comes to himself. A passionate traveler, he loves to tell stories about his adventures all over the world, including in his blog about touring South America together with his wife in their Toyota Landcruiser. His role models include theoretical physicist Max Planck, Don Quixote (the fictional character in the Cervantes novel), and 20th-century theologian Dietrich Bonhoeffer. His life's motto is a quote from the late tennis champion Arthur Ashe: "Start where you are. Use what you have. Do what you can."

Vor dem Lesen

Allgemeine Fragen

1. Kennen Sie Ausländer in Ihrer Umgebung *(environment)*? Woher kommen sie?
2. Warum sind sie wohl gekommen?
3. Welche Probleme haben viele von ihnen?
4. Kann man ihnen helfen? Was sollten sie tun?
5. Warum bekommen manche Ausländer Heimweh *(homesickness)*? Was ist anders in Ihrem Land als in der Heimat *(home)* der Ausländer?

Die zwei Chefs

(Eine Geschichte aus Deutschland)

Sie hieß Simaida Keller. Gekannt hatte ich sie schon lange. Wer sie wirklich war, erfuhr° ich erst später. Dienstlich° hatte ich nichts mit ihr zu tun. Außer wenn sie zaghaft an die Tür klopfte,° weil sie mein Zimmer putzen wollte. Während der Zeit, die° sie zum Saubermachen brauchte, ging ich meist ins Labor oder in einen Hörsaal°, die nachmittags oft leer° waren. Zwischen ihr und mir waren noch ein paar Leiter°, die ihr Anordnungen° gaben. Wegen der Lautstärke°, insbesondere° des einen Leiters, habe ich das manchmal mitbekommen°. Gedacht habe ich mir nichts dabei°. Ich grüßte sie freundlich. Und sie mich. Aber ihr Blick kam mir immer so unterwürfig° vor. Hierarchie schien ihr wichtig. All dem schenkte ich keine Beachtung°.

Bis zu diesem grauen Novembertag, als ich sie kennenlernte. Ich suchte meine Unterlagen°, die ich im Hörsaal IV nach der letzten Mathematik-Vorlesung wohl vergessen hatte. Als ich die Tür öffnete, stand sie an der Tafel und war gerade dabei°, die Kreide in die Ablage° zurückzulegen. Ich starrte erst an die Tafel, dann auf sie, dann wieder zurück an die Tafel. „Ich glaube, Ihnen ist da ein kleiner Fehler° unterlaufen", sagte sie leise und ein spitzbübisches Schmunzeln° huschte° über ihr Gesicht. „Ich habe es geändert°."

Und wieder war da dieses Lächeln. Ein Lächeln, das° ich noch nie° bei ihr gesehen hatte. Noch immer stand ich in der Tür und begriff° nicht. In der Vorlesung am Morgen hatte mich das Pausenzeichen° überrascht. Schnell hatte ich noch einen Lösungsansatz° an die Tafel geschrieben und eine Hausaufgabe für die Studenten daraus gemacht. Und jetzt stand alles richtig an der Tafel. Der kleine Fehler in meinem Lösungsansatz war verbessert° und ein kurzer und eleganter Lösungsweg° war direkt darunter skizziert°.

Bei meiner dritten Einladung zu einer Tasse Kaffee sagte sie dann zu. Das Gespräch begann zögerlich°, wurde dann aber sehr interessant. Sie war Deutsche, in Kasachstan geboren und aufgewachsen°, genau zwanzig Tage jünger als ich. Ihr Mathematikexamen in Moskau hatte sie mit Auszeichnung gemacht. War dann zurück nach Kasachstan gegangen und Lehrerin geworden. 1994 war sie mit ihrer Familie nach Deutschland gekommen. Um die Anerkennung° ihrer Diplome hatte sie lange gekämpft°. Es war vergeblich° gewesen. Heute ist sie Putzfrau, pardon, Raumpflegerin° in unserem Betrieb°.

Nach diesem Tag lud ich sie ab und an° zu einer Tasse Kaffee ein. Wir sprachen über Deutschland und über Kasachstan, über das Reisen und über die Mathematik. Weil ich ihr Lächeln mochte, versuchte ich manchmal sie zu necken°. Meist wurde ihr Blick dann aber noch strenger°.

Vor einem Jahr habe ich sie in der Stadt getroffen. Wie krank sie da schon war, habe ich nicht bemerkt°. Ganz offensichtlich° freute auch sie sich über diese zufällige Begegnung. Begeistert° erzählte ich ihr von meiner letzten Reise durch Mittelamerika. Sie hörte aufmerksam° zu. Auf ihre Frage, ob denn das Reisen in diesen Ländern nicht gefährlich sei° und ob ich denn nicht manchmal Angst hätte°, antwortete ich ihr mit einem Lächeln: „Nein. ich habe nämlich zwei Chefs° und die passen gut auf mich auf." Das Fragezeichen° in ihrem Gesicht löste sich in° ein helles, herzliches° Lachen, als sie mich sagen hörte: „Meine Frau ist der eine Chef. Der andere ist der da oben°." Mit der Hand wies ich dabei in den blauen Sommerhimmel° über uns. „Meine zwei Chefs sind manchmal ganz schön nervig°. Aber ich weiß, mich zu wehren°. Ich kenne da ein paar Tricks."

Noch immer war ihr Lächeln freundlich, aber ihre Augen wurden sehr ernst, als sie mir sagte: „Den Chef da oben kann man nicht austricksen°. Aber machen Sie sich keine Sorgen, der ist ein guter Chef." Noch einmal schenkte sie mir ihr Lächeln. Dann war sie in der Menge° verschwunden°.

Ich habe sie nie wieder gesehen. Aber diese Geschichte fiel mir ein°, als ich heute auf ihrer Beerdigung° war.

Jörg Zschocke, Erstveröffentlichung

found out / Officially
knocked
which / lecture hall
empty / supervisors
instructions / volume / especially
heard / of it
submissive
attention
documents
was about to / chalk tray
error / mischievous smile
flitted / changed
which / never until now
understood
bell
method of resolution
corrected
solution / sketched
haltingly
grown up
recognition
fought for / in vain
custodian / offices
off and on
tease / more serious
realized / obviously
Excited
attentively
might be
was afraid
bosses / question mark
turned into / hearty
up there
summer sky
annoying / how to defend myself
outsmart
crowd / disappeared
came back to me
funeral

Nach dem Lesen

A. Alles verstanden?

1. Welches Thema hat diese Geschichte?
2. Welchen Vorteil *(advantage)* hat Deutschland der Putzfrau gebracht?
3. Warum kann sie sich nicht so richtig freuen, in Deutschland zu arbeiten?
4. Was und wo hat sie studiert?
5. Warum arbeitet sie als Raumpflegerin?
6. Wer sind die zwei Chefs des Erzählers?
7. Wie reagiert sie darauf?
8. Wo arbeitet der Erzähler und was ist er?
9. Warum werden der Erzähler und die Putzfrau keine Freunde?

Raumpflegerin beim Staubsaugen **(vacuuming)**

B. Leben in einem anderen Land

1. In welchen deutschen Bundesländern gibt es viele ausländische Mitbürger *(fellow citizens)*? (Siehe *Fokus: Deutsch im Elternhaus.*) Vergleichen Sie die Statistiken!
2. Warum gibt es manchmal Ausländerhass *(xenophobia)*? Was kann man dagegen tun?
3. Welche Ausländer dürfen in Deutschland arbeiten. Wo arbeiten sie oft? Wer hat es schwerer Arbeit zu finden?
4. Möchten Sie gern einmal in Europa arbeiten? Wenn ja, wo und als was? Wenn nein, warum nicht?

Rückschau

Kapitelwortschatz

Hauptwörter

der/die Angestellte, -n	*employee*
der Arbeiter, -	*(blue-collar) worker* (male)
die Arbeiterin, -nen	*(blue-collar) worker* (female)
die Arbeitslosigkeit	*unemployment*
der Architekt, -en, -en	*architect* (male)
die Architektin, -nen	*architect* (female)
der Arzt, ¨-e	*physician, doctor* (male)
die Ärztin, -nen	*physician, doctor* (female)
die Ausbildung	*training, education*
der Beamte, -n	*civil servant* (male)
die Beamtin, -nen	*civil servant* (female)
der/die Bekannte, -n	*acquaintance*
der Bereich, -e	*area, field*
der Beruf, -e	*profession, career*
die Berufswahl	*choice of profession*
der Betriebswirt, -e	*graduate in business management* (male)
die Betriebswirtin, -nen	*graduate in business management* (female)
das Büro, -s	*office*
der/die Deutsche, -n	*German person*
das Einkommen, -	*income*
die Entscheidung, -en	*decision*
die Erfahrung, -en	*experience*
die (Fach)kenntnis, -se	*(special) knowledge, skill*
die Firma, Firmen	*company; business*
das Geschäft, -e	*business; store*
die Geschäftsfrau, -en	*businesswoman*
der Geschäftsmann, ¨-er	*businessman*
die Geschäftsleute (*pl.*)	*businesspeople*
der Handel	*trade*
die Hausfrau, -en	*housewife*
der Hausmann, ¨-er	*househusband*
der Ingenieur, -e	*engineer* (male)
die Ingenieurin, -nen	*engineer* (female)
der Journalist, -en, -en	*journalist* (male)
die Journalistin, -nen	*journalist* (female)
die Klasse, -n	*class*
der/die Kranke, -n	*sick person*
der Krankenpfleger, -	*nurse* (male)
die Krankenschwester, -n	*nurse* (female)
der Künstler, -	*artist* (male)
die Künstlerin, -nen	*artist* (female)
der Kurs, -e	*course*
der Lehrer, -	*teacher* (male)
die Lehrerin, -nen	*teacher* (female)
der Plan, ¨-e	*plan*
der Polizist, -en, -en	*policeman*
die Polizistin, -nen	*policewoman*
das Praktikum, Praktika	*internship*
der Rat	*advice, counsel*
der Rechtsanwalt, ¨-e	*lawyer* (male)
die Rechtsanwältin, -nen	*lawyer* (female)
der Reiseleiter, -	*travel agent* (male)
die Reiseleiterin, -nen	*travel agent* (female)
die Schule, -n	*school*
der/die Schwerbehinderte, -n	*disabled person*
der Sekretär, -e	*secretary* (male)
die Sekretärin, -nen	*secretary* (female)
die Sicherheit	*safety, security*
die Stelle, -n	*position, job*
die Stunde, -n	*hour*
das Unternehmen, -	*large company*
die Verantwortung	*responsibility*
der/die Verlobte, -n	*fiancé / fiancée*
der/die Verwandte, -n	*relative*
der Wissenschaftler, -	*scientist* (male)
die Wissenschaftlerin, -nen	*scientist* (female)
der Zahnarzt, ¨-e	*dentist* (male)
die Zahnärztin, -nen	*dentist* (female)
die Zukunft	*future*

Verben

(an·)bieten	*to offer*
aus·sehen (wie)	*to look (like)*
sich bewerben (um)	*to apply (for)*
bitten	*to ask (for), request*
erklären	*to explain*
sich gewöhnen an	*to get used to*
glauben (an)	*to believe (in)*
hoffen	*to hope*
recht haben	*to be right*
sich Sorgen machen (um)	*to be concerned / worried (about)*
verdienen	*to earn, make money*
sich vor·stellen	*to imagine*
werden	*to become; to be* (a profession when you grow up)

Adjektive und Adverbien

anstrengend	*strenuous*
arbeitslos	*unemployed*
besser / best-	*better / best*
früher	*earlier; once; former(ly)*
gleich	*equal, same*
größer / größt-	*bigger / biggest*
hoch (hoh-)	*high*
höher / höchst-	*higher / highest*
lieber / liebst-	*rather / favorite*
mehr / meist-	*more / most*
näher / nächst-	*closer / closest*
(un)sicher	*(un)safe, (in)secure*
unbedingt	*definitely, absolutely*

Verschiedenes

Ach was!	*Oh, come on!*
. . . als	*. . . than*
darum	*therefore*
Du hast recht.	*You're right.*
(genau)so . . . wie	*just (exactly) as*
Ich stelle mir vor, dass . . .	*I imagine that . . .*
Ich will . . . werden.	*I want to be a(n) . . .*
ins/im Ausland	*abroad*
immer (+ *comparative*)	*more and more . . . , increasingly more . . .*
je (früher) . . . desto (besser)	*the (earlier) . . . , the (better)*
jedoch	*however*
momentan	*at the moment, right now*
nicht so . . . wie	*not as . . . as*
Nun, . . . / Also, . . . / Na ja, . . . / Tja, . . .	*Well, . . .*
unter *(+ acc. / dat.)*	*among*
Was willst du (ein)mal werden?	*What do you want to be one day?*

Zum Schluss

1. **Wer bin ich?**
   a. **Kann ich Ihnen helfen?** Look over the occupations listed on the previous page. Write a two-line dialogue in which a customer or patient asks a question or identifies a problem and the person with that occupation offers some kind of assistance.

   BEISPIEL A: Ich habe furchtbare Zahnschmerzen, Frau Doktor.
   B: Nun, der Zahn muss leider raus.

   b. **Wer bin ich?** Share your dialogue with your classmates. Can they tell what career corresponds to your dialogue? How many different dialogues can you come up with as a group?

2. **Ein komplizierter Plan** What is involved in choosing a career? What must you consider? What experience do you have looking for jobs? What will be different when you are done with your studies? Use as many of the words as you can from the table below to write 8–10 sentences that discuss what is important when deciding what career to pursue.

1	2	3	4	5
anbieten	der Beruf	die Ausbildung	anstrengend	darum
sich bewerben um	der Plan	die Erfahrung	arbeitslos	jedoch
erklären	der Bereich	die Firma	früher	momentan
sich gewöhnen an	der Ort	die Schule	gleich	Nun/Also
glauben an	das Rat	die Sicherheit	hoch	je . . . desto . . .
recht haben	das Praktikum	die Stelle	sicher	genauso . . . wie
aussehen (wie)	das Unternehmen	die Verantwortung	unbedingt	. . . als
sich vorstellen	das Einkommen	die Entscheidung	vielseitig	immer . . .

3. **Angst vor der Zukunft** *(Fear of the future)*
   a. **Ja, aber . . .** Write an essay imagining you are someone worried about the future. Whatever future career you imagine for yourself, you think someone else is going to be better, faster, or smarter than you are. Use the future tense and comparative adjectives.

   b. **Ich hatte Erfolg!** Now rewrite the essay, this time from five years in the future, after you have achieved the goal you set for yourself. You were the best, fastest, or smartest person, and now you have the job and are successful. Use the simple past to explain how you got to where you are.

iLrn **Onlineaktivitäten** Visit iLrn for online activities related to this chapter. There you will find additional resources, such as a memory game (**Gedächtnisspiel**), a crossword puzzle (**Kreuzworträtsel**), audio flash cards (**Vokabelblitz**), a tutorial quiz (**Mini-Quiz**), and the active vocabulary (**Wortschatz**) for this chapter.

Kapitel 13

Das Studium

Lernziele In this chapter you will learn about:

Zum Thema

University studies and student life

Fokus

The German university system, studying in Germany, German bureaucracy, US and German companies abroad

Struktur

- The subjunctive mood
- The present-time general subjunctive (Subjunctive II)
- The past-time general subjunctive

Einblicke

Dialog: Ein Jahr drüben wäre super!
Literatur: Evelyne Weissenbach, *Von der Zufriedenheit*

Rückschau

Kapitelwortschatz
Zum Schluss

RESSOURCEN

iLrn | Video
Audio | SAM

Zwei Studentinnen beim Besprechen des Kursmaterials in der Bibliothek der Jacobs Universität in Bremen

Vorschau German Universities

The first German universities were founded in the Middle Ages: Heidelberg in 1386, Cologne in 1388, Erfurt in 1392, Leipzig in 1409, and Rostock in 1419. At the beginning of the 19th century, Wilhelm von Humboldt redefined the purpose and mission of universities, viewing them as institutions for pure research and independent study by the nation's preeminent minds. In time, however, it became obvious that this ideal conflicted with modern education. While the universities continue to be purely academic in orientation, the **Fachhochschulen,** first established in the 1960s, prepare students for specific careers in such fields as business and engineering. Courses of study are shorter, although curriculum choices are more limited.

Eingang zur Berliner Humboldt-Universität in der Straße Unter den Linden

There is no tradition of private higher education as in North America, though a few small and expensive private institutions of higher learning have recently been established, most of them with a strong business focus. So far, practically all universities have been fully state supported; students pay only registration fees, which include public transportation and health insurance. However, as record numbers of young people have chosen the academic track, universities have come under extreme pressure to keep up with the influx of students, and so many states have introduced modest tuition fees **(Studiengebühren).** Under the Federal Education Promotion Act **(Bundesausbildungsförderungsgesetz = BAföG),** students can obtain financial assistance, receiving one part in the form of a grant and the other part as an interest-free loan to be repaid in relatively small portions over several years after the student has finished his or her education.

Fragen: 1. Von welcher Universität sehen wir oben ein Bild? 2. In welcher bekannten Straße Berlins ist diese Universität? 3. Was sieht man außer dem Büchermarkt vor dem Eingang dieser Uni? 4. Sieht diese Uni modern oder alt aus? 5. Beschreiben Sie das Bild auf der linken Seite?

Generally speaking, a student can choose to enter most programs of study at the university upon completion of the **Gymnasium** (college-preparatory high school) and upon passing the **Abitur,** a state comprehensive exam. Openings **(Studienplätze)** in certain academic programs, however, are limited and are filled on the basis of the average grade received in the **Abitur;** admission restrictions **(Numerus Clausus)** for certain subjects also apply. Spots are allocated by a central office in Dortmund, with a certain percentage of places reserved for foreign applicants. In the past, young German people took it for granted that they could study at minimal cost for as long as they wanted. Today, there are time limits attached.

Following a series of reforms, in Europe and in Germany, aiming to adapt the European university system to new international standards, there is a push for greater competition among universities and their faculties. It is hoped that this will make German universities more attractive internationally. The recent introduction of internationally recognized bachelor's and master's degrees is contributing to shorter stays at the university for young people and earlier starts in the job market. These degree programs have become rather popular as graduates increasingly seek jobs outside Germany.

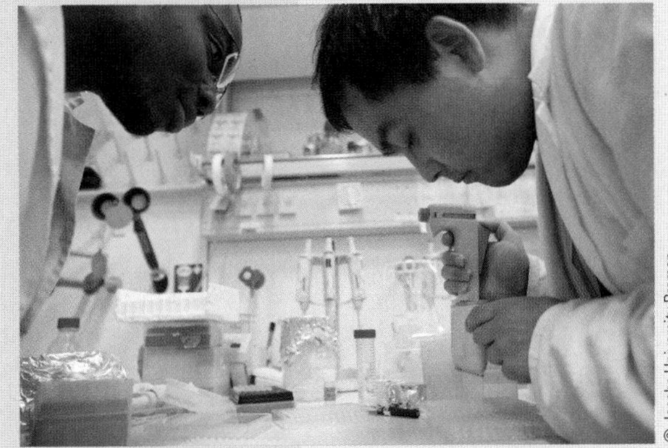

Studenten im Labor der Jacobs Universität in Bremen

Zum Thema

Gespräche

Bei der Immatrikulation

Warm-ups: 1. **Welche Adjektive beginnen mit** a, b, c, f, g, h, k, l, n, r, s, v? **Was ist der Komparativ und der Superlativ dazu?** z. B. neu: neuer, am neu(e)sten 2. **Wofür geben Sie viel Geld aus?** Was ist billig / teuer? 3. **Was tun Sie,** wenn Sie keine Lust haben zu lernen, d. h., wenn Sie faul sind? wenn Sie sich erkältet haben? wenn es regnet? wenn es sehr heiß ist? . . . 4. **Welche Berufe kennen Sie?**

PETRA Hallo, John! Wie geht's?
JOHN Ganz gut. Und dir?
PETRA Ach, ich kann nicht klagen. Was machst du denn da?
JOHN Ich muss noch Immatrikulationsformulare ausfüllen.
PETRA Soll ich dir helfen?
JOHN Wenn du Zeit hast. Ich kämpfe immer mit der Bürokratie.
PETRA Hast du deinen Pass dabei?
JOHN Nein, wieso?
PETRA Darin ist deine Aufenthaltserlaubnis; die brauchst du unbedingt.
JOHN Ich kann ihn ja schnell holen.
PETRA Tu das! Ich warte hier so lange auf dich.

Etwas später

Optional activity: Have students spell some of the new words in the dialogue to each other and see how long it takes the partner to recognize the word. While one spells something, the other should not look at the dialogue!

JOHN Hier ist mein Pass. Ich muss mich jetzt auch bald entscheiden, welche Seminare ich belegen will. Kannst du mir da auch helfen?
PETRA Na klar. Was studierst du denn?
JOHN Mein Hauptfach ist moderne Geschichte. Ich möchte Seminare über deutsche Geschichte und Literatur belegen.
PETRA Hier ist mein Vorlesungsverzeichnis. Mal sehen, was sie dieses Semester anbieten.

A. Was fehlt?

1. John füllt gerade ein __Immatrikulationsformular__ aus.
2. Leider hat er seinen __Pass__ nicht dabei.
3. Er muss ihn erst __holen__.
4. Im Pass ist seine __Aufenthaltserlaubnis__.
5. John weiß noch nicht, was er __belegen__ will.
6. Petra fragt ihn, was er __studiert__.
7. Sein Hauptfach ist __moderne Geschichte__.
8. Petra kann ihm helfen, weil sie ihr __Vorlesungsverzeichnis__ dabei hat.

B. Jetzt sind Sie dran! Beraten Sie *(Advise)* einen Studenten oder eine Studentin aus Deutschland an Ihrer Uni. Hören Sie zu, was sie/ihn interessiert und schlagen Sie ein paar Kurse und vielleicht auch Professoren vor! Wechseln Sie sich ab!

Wortschatz 1

Das Studium *([course of] study)*

der Abschluss, ⸚e	*degree; diploma*
Hörsaal, Hörsäle	*lecture hall*
Mitbewohner, -	*housemate; roommate*
Professor, -en	*professor*
Student, -en, -en	*(college) student*
das Fach, ⸚er	*subject*
Hauptfach, ⸚er	*major (field)*
Nebenfach, ⸚er	*minor (field)*
Labor, -s	*lab(oratory)*
Quartal, -e	*quarter*
Referat, -e	*oral presentation*
Semester, -	*semester*
Seminar,-e	*seminar*
Stipendium, Stipendien	*scholarship*
System, -e	*system*
die Fachrichtung, -en	*field of study*
Mitbewohnerin, -nen	*housemate; roommate*
(Natur)wissenschaft, -en	*(natural) science*
Note, -n	*grade*
Professorin, -nen	*professor*
(Seminar)arbeit, -en	here: *term paper*
Studentin, -nen	*(college) student*
aus·füllen	*to fill out*
belegen	*to sign up for, take (a course)*
etwas dagegen haben	*to mind s.th* (lit. *to have s.th. against s.th.)*

Verschiedenes

Hast du etwas dagegen, wenn . . . ?	*Do you mind, if . . . ?*
lehren	*to teach*
das Studium ab·schließen, schloss ab, abgeschlossen	*to finish one's degree, graduate*
eine Prüfung machen	*to take an exam*
(eine Prüfung) bestehen, bestand, bestanden	*to pass (a test)*
(bei einer Prüfung) durch·fallen (fällt durch), fiel durch, ist durchgefallen	*to flunk, fail (a test)*
ein Referat halten (hält), hielt, gehalten	*to give an oral presentation*
teil·nehmen (nimmt teil), nahm teil, teilgenommen (an + *dat.*)	*to participate (in)*
schwierig	*difficult, with difficulty*
Wieso?	*Why?, How come?*

Zum Erkennen: klagen *(to complain);* das Immatrikulationsformular, -e *(enrollment form);* kämpfen *(to struggle, fight);* die Bürokratie (here*: red tape*); dabei haben *(to bring along);* das Vorlesungsverzeichnis, -se *(course catalog);* AUCH: der Indikativ; der Konjunktiv *(subjunctive)*

The German word **Studenten** generally refers to university students or students at other institutions of higher learning, but not to high school students **(Schüler)**.

If students ask: *to cram* **pauken;** *to skip class* **schwänzen.**

Fokus German Bureaucracy

Everyone living in Germany must register with the local registration office **(das Einwohnermeldeamt)** within 7 to 14 days of changing address. Likewise, when moving again, residents give the registration office notice with an **Abmeldung.** Non-Germans who wish to stay in Germany longer than three months must go to the **Ausländeramt** and request a residence permit **(die Aufenthaltserlaubnis).** They will need to prove that they can support themselves financially. Non-EU citizens who wish to work in Germany have to show an employment contract before obtaining a work permit **(die Arbeitserlaubnis).** Exceptions are made for students and participants in training programs.

Übungen zum Thema

A. Ausländische Studenten an Deutschlands Universitäten Stellen Sie Ihrem Partner / Ihrer Partnerin Fragen über die folgende Grafik! Benutzen Sie darin so viele Komparative, Superlative und andere Vergleiche wie möglich! Wechseln Sie sich dabei ab!

Find out whether there are any foreign students in your class. Where do they come from and why are they here? Ask the class where some of the foreign students at your entire university come from, and have them make comparative statements.

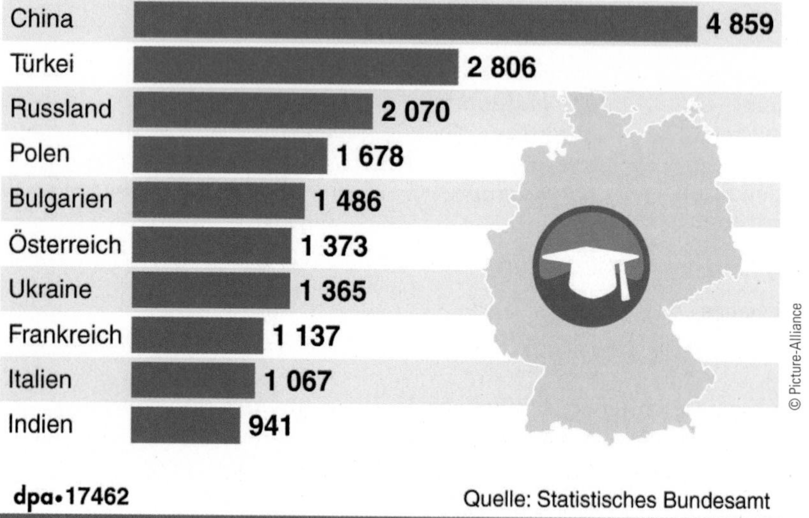

Point out that the fields listed here are not active vocabulary but should help make this exercise more meaningful to the students because they probably want to know the German word for their major or minor.

■ Accounting is part of **Betriebswirtschaft**; *the accountant* = **der Wirtschaftsprüfer, -**.

B. Sag mal, was studierst du? Finden Sie Ihr Hauptfach auf der Liste; wenn es nicht dabei ist, fügen Sie es hinzu *(add)*! Fragen Sie dann herum *(around)*, wer das auch noch studiert!

BEISPIEL S1 Sag mal, was studierst du?
S2 Ich studiere Psychologie. Und du?
S1 Ich studiere Wirtschaftswissenschaft.

Anglistik°
Archäologie
Architektur
Astronomie
Betriebswirtschaft°
Biochemie
Biologie
Chemie
Elektrotechnik
Finanzwesen
Forstwirtschaft°
Geographie
Geologie
Germanistik
Geschichte
Gesundheitswissenschaft
Hauswirtschaft°
Informatik°
Ingenieurwesen°
Jura°
Kommunikationswissenschaft
Krankenpflege°
Kunst
Landwirtschaft°
Lebensmittelchemie
Lehramt°
Maschinenbau°
Linguistik
Mathematik
Medizin
Musik
Naturwissenschaft
Pädagogik
Pharmazie
Philosophie
Physik
Politologie°
Psychologie
Romanistik°
Soziologie
Sport
Theologie
Tiermedizin°
Wirtschaftswissenschaft°
Zahnmedizin°

English studies
home economics
computer science
engineering
business administration / law
nursing / political science
agriculture / Romance languages
dentistry
forestry / education
mechanical engineering
veterinary science
economics

C. Fragen zum Studium Fragen Sie einen Nachbarn / eine Nachbarin, . . . !

1. wie viele Kurse er/sie dieses Semester / Quartal belegt hat und welche
2. welche Kurse er/sie besonders gut findet, und worin er/sie die besten Noten hat
3. ob er/sie viele Arbeiten schreiben muss; wenn ja, in welchen Fächern
4. ob er/sie schon Referate gehalten hat; wenn ja, in welchen Fächern und worüber
5. ob er/sie außer Deutsch noch andere Sprachen spricht oder lernt
6. wie lange er/sie noch studieren muss
7. was er/sie danach macht
8. wie die Chancen sind, in seinem/ihrem Beruf eine gute Stelle zu bekommen

C: This could also be a written exercise.

Optional practice: Wohnen Sie im Studentenwohnheim? Haben Sie Ihr eigenes Zimmer oder haben Sie einen Mitbewohner/ eine Mitbewohnerin? Wie heißt er/sie? Ist er/sie nett? Haben Sie im Studentenwohnheim einen Kühlschrank? Kann man dort kochen? Wie ist das Essen in der Mensa? Wo essen Sie meistens? Wo essen Sie am liebsten?

Aussprache: s, ss, ß, st, sp

Laute

1. [z] **s**auber, **s**icher, **S**eme**s**ter, **S**eminar, Pau**s**e
2. [s] Auswei**s**, Kur**s**, Profe**ss**or, wi**ss**en, la**ss**en, flei**ß**ig, Fu**ß**, Grü**ß**e
3. [št] **St**udium, **St**ipendium, **St**elle, **st**udieren, be**st**ehen, an**st**rengend
4. [st] zuer**st**, mei**st**ens, de**st**o, Komponi**st**, Kün**st**ler
5. [šp] **Sp**iel, **Sp**ort, **Sp**aß, **Sp**rache, Bei**sp**iel, **sp**ät

For further review, see the Summary of Pronunciation in the front of this book. Study Part III, subsections 6 and 12.

Hörverständnis

Ein guter Start Hören Sie, warum und wo verschiedene Studenten in Deutschland an ihrem MBA arbeiten. Ergänzen Sie die folgenden Aussagen!

Zum Erkennen: das Privileg; wissenschaftlich *(scientific)*; verbessern *(to improve)*; Vollzeitstudenten; die Abschlussarbeit *(thesis)*; die Karriere *(career)*

1. Den MBA __c__.
   a. gibt es nur in Amerika
   b. wird es bald auch in Deutschland geben
   c. gibt es jetzt auch in Deutschland
2. Die Studenten am Europa-Institut kommen __b__.
   a. nur aus Deutschland
   b. aus vielen verschiedenen Ländern
   c. alle aus Europa
3. Der Franzose Dominique Laurent ist __b__ und verspricht sich vom MBA bessere Berufschancen.
   a. Rechtsanwalt
   b. Ingenieur
   c. Geschäftsmann
4. Am Ende des MBAs steht __a__ mit einer Abschlussarbeit.
   a. ein Praktikum
   b. eine Lehre
   c. eine Auslandsreise
5. Die Wissenschaftliche Hochschule in Koblenz ist __b__.
   a. schon alt
   b. privat
   c. öffentlich

Struktur

13.1 The subjunctive mood

Assure students that there is nothing extraordinary about the subjunctive. It is used all the time in everyday speech.

Until now, almost all sentences in this book have been in the INDICATIVE MOOD. Sentences in the indicative mood generally reflect a direct, factual reality. Sometimes, however, we want to speculate on matters that are unreal, uncertain, or unlikely; or we wish for something that cannot be; or we want to approach other people less directly, more discretely and politely. For that purpose we use the SUBJUNCTIVE MOOD.

1. Polite requests or questions — *Would you like a cup of coffee?* *Could you help me for a moment?*
2. Hypothetical statements and questions — *What would you do?* *You should have been there.*
3. Wishes — *If only I had more time.* *I wish you would hurry up.*
4. Unreal conditions

If I had time, I'd go to the movies. (But since I don't have time, I'm not going.)
If the weather were good, we'd go for a walk. (But since it's raining, we won't go.)
If you had told me, I could have helped you. (But since you didn't tell me, I couldn't help you.)

Contrast the sentences above with real conditions:

If I have time, I'll go to the movies.
If the weather is good, we'll go for a walk.

In real conditions, the possibility exists that the events will take place. In unreal conditions, this possibility does not exist or is highly unlikely.

- The forms of the PRESENT-TIME SUBJUNCTIVE are derived from the simple past: *If I told you (now) . . .*
- Those of the PAST-TIME SUBJUNCTIVE are derived from the past perfect: *If you had told me (earlier) . . .*
- Another very common way to express the subjunctive mood is with the form *would: I'd go; I would not stay home.*

A: This exercise is intended to give students a feeling for the subjunctive vs. the indicative. You might ask them to look for such sentences in conversation or in assignments for other subjects. You also can bring similar sentences to class until the students are confident about the subjunctive. They must become aware of this difference in English before trying to cope with it in German.

A. 1. indicative, now or later
2. subjunctive, earlier
3. subjunctive, now
4. indicative, later
5. subjunctive, now
6. indicative, earlier
7. subjunctive, now
8. subjunctive, earlier
9. subjunctive, now or later
10. subjunctive, earlier

Übung

A. Indikativ oder Konjunktiv *(subjunctive)*? Analysieren Sie *(Analyze)* die Sätze und sagen Sie, ob sie im Indikativ oder Konjunktiv sind. Entscheiden Sie auch, ob sie sich auf jetzt, früher oder später beziehen *(refer to)*!

BEISPIEL If you don't ask, you won't know. — *indicative: now or later*
What would you have done? — *subjunctive: earlier*

1. If she can, she'll write. 2. If I had only known that. 3. They could be here any minute. 4. Will you take the bike along? 5. Would you please hold this? 6. I had known that a long time. 7. We should really be going. 8. I wish he had told me. 9. If you could stay until Sunday, you could fly for a lower fare. 10. What would he have done if you hadn't come along?

13.2 The present-time general subjunctive

German has two subjunctives. The one most commonly used is often referred to in grammar books as the GENERAL SUBJUNCTIVE or SUBJUNCTIVE II. (The SPECIAL SUBJUNCTIVE or SUBJUNCTIVE I is explained in Chapter 15.)

1. Forms

The PRESENT-TIME SUBJUNCTIVE refers to the present *(now)* or the future *(later)*. As in English, its forms are derived from the forms of the simple past. You already know the verb endings from having used the **möchte**-forms of **mögen,** which are actually subjunctive forms. All verbs in the subjunctive have these endings:

INFINITIVE	SIMPLE PAST, INDICATIVE		PRESENT-TIME SUBJUNCTIVE
mögen	ich	mochte	möch**te**
	du	mochtest	möch**test**
	er	mochte	möch**te**
	wir	mochten	möch**ten**
	ihr	mochtet	möch**tet**
	sie	mochten	möch**ten**

Point out that in many verbs, the umlaut constitutes the difference between indicative and subjunctive. Omitting the umlaut is not just a misspelling or a minor error. In quizzes and tests, students should lose full points for incorrect use of it.

a. *T*-verbs *(weak verbs)*

The present-time subjunctive forms of regular *t*-verbs are identical to those of the simple past. Their use usually becomes clear from context.

INFINITIVE	SIMPLE PAST, INDICATIVE	PRESENT-TIME SUBJUNCTIVE
glauben	glaubte	**glaubte**
antworten	antwortete	**antwortete**

Wenn Sie mir nur **glaubten!** — *If you only believed me!*
Wenn er mir nur **antwortete!** — *If he would only answer me!*

b. Irregular *t*-verbs *(mixed verbs)*

Most of the irregular *t*-verbs, which include the modals, have an umlaut in the present-time subjunctive. Exceptions are **sollen** and **wollen.**

Modals with an umlaut in the infinitive also have one in the subjunctive **(dürfte, könnte, möchte, müsste),** whereas those without an umlaut do not have one in the subjunctive **(sollte, wollte).**

INFINITIVE	SIMPLE PAST, INDICATIVE	PRESENT-TIME SUBJUNCTIVE
haben	hatte	**hätte**
bringen	brachte	**brächte**
denken	dachte	**dächte**
wissen	wusste	**wüsste**
dürfen	durfte	**dürfte**
müssen	musste	**müsste**
können	konnte	**könnte**
mögen	mochte	**möchte**
sollen	sollte	**sollte**
wollen	wollte	**wollte**

haben		wissen	
ich hätte	wir hätt**en**	ich wüsste	wir wüsst**en**
du hätt**est**	ihr hätt**et**	du wüsst**est**	ihr wüsst**et**
er hätte	sie hätt**en**	er wüsste	sie wüsst**en**

Hättest du Zeit? — *Would you have time?*
Könntest du kommen? — *Could you come?*

Refer students to part 7a or b in the Appendix.

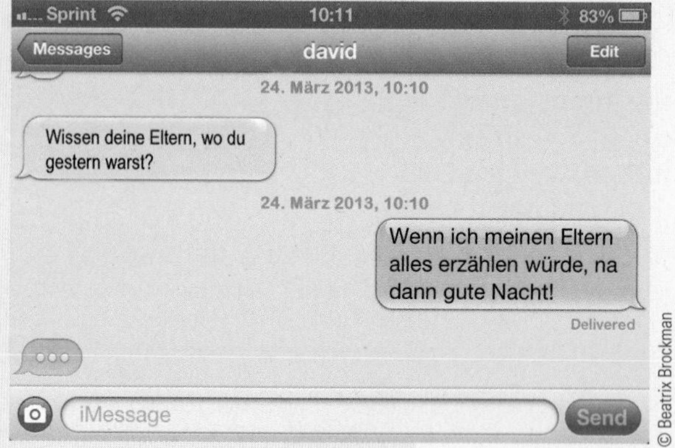

© Beatrix Brockman

c. *N*-verbs *(strong verbs)*

The present-time subjunctive forms of *n*-verbs add subjunctive endings to the simple past stem. If the simple past stem vowel is an **a, o,** or **u,** the subjunctive forms have an umlaut.

INFINITIVE	SIMPLE PAST, INDICATIVE	PRESENT-TIME SUBJUNCTIVE
sein	war	**wäre**
werden	wurde	**würde**
bleiben	blieb	**bliebe**
fahren	fuhr	**führe**
finden	fand	**fände**
fliegen	flog	**flöge**
geben	gab	**gäbe**
gehen	ging	**ginge**
laufen	lief	**liefe**
sehen	sah	**sähe**
tun	tat	**täte**

sein		gehen	
ich wäre	wir wär**en**	ich ginge	wir ging**en**
du wär**est**	ihr wär**et**	du ging**est**	ihr ging**et**
er wäre	sie wär**en**	er ginge	sie ging**en**

Wenn ich du **wäre, ginge** ich nicht. — *If I were you, I wouldn't go.*

Wenn er **flöge, könnte** er morgen hier sein. — *If he were to fly, he could be here tomorrow.*

Because of its simplicity, the **würde**-form is very common in everyday speech. It is preferred especially where there are irregular subjunctive forms (**kennte, nennte; begönne, hülfe, stünde**, etc.), which we avoid in this text.

d. The **würde**-form

In conversation, speakers of German commonly use the subjunctive forms of **haben, sein, werden, wissen,** and the modals.

Hättest du Zeit? — *Would you have time?*

Das **wäre** schön. — *That would be nice.*

Was **möchtest** du tun? — *What would you like to do?*

Wenn ich das nur **wüsste!** — *If only I knew that!*

For the subjunctive forms of other verbs, however, German speakers frequently substitute a simpler verb phrase that closely corresponds to the English *would + infinitive*. It is preferred when the subjunctive form is identical to the indicative form, as is the case with *t*-verbs and with the plural forms of *n*-verbs whose subjunctive forms don't have an umlaut (e.g., **gingen**). It is also frequently used in the conclusion clause of contrary-to-fact conditions.

Das täte ich nicht.
Das **würde** ich nicht **tun.** } *I wouldn't do that.*

Wenn er mir nur glaubte!
Wenn er mir nur **glauben würde!** } *If he would only believe me!*

Wir gingen lieber ins Kino.
Wir **würden** lieber ins Kino **gehen.** } *We would rather go to the movies.*

Wenn sie Zeit hätte, käme sie mit.
Wenn sie Zeit hätte, **würde** sie **mitkommen.** } *If she had time, she would come along.*

2. Uses

You are already familiar with the most common uses of the subjunctive in English. Here are examples of these uses in German.

a. Polite requests or questions

Möchtest du eine Tasse Kaffee?	*Would you like a cup of coffee?*
Würdest du mir die Butter geben?	*Would you pass me the butter?*
Dürfte ich etwas Käse haben?	*Could I have some cheese?*
Könntest du mir einen Moment helfen?	*Could you help me for a minute?*

b. Hypothetical statements and questions

Er **sollte** jeden Moment hier sein.	*He should be here any minute.*
Das **wäre** schön.	*That would be nice.*
Es **wäre** mir lieber, wenn er hier **wäre**.	*I'd rather he be here.* (lit. *I'd prefer it if he would be here.*)
Was **würdest** du tun?	*What would you do?*
Ich **würde** ihm alles erzählen.	*I'd tell him everything.*

c. Wishes

- Wishes starting with **Wenn . . .** usually add **nur** after the subject or any pronoun object.

Wenn ich **nur** mehr Zeit **hätte**!	*If I only had more time!*
Wenn er mir **nur** glauben **würde**!	*If he'd only believe me!*

- Wishes starting with **Ich wünschte, . . .** have both clauses in the subjunctive.

Ich **wünschte**, ich **hätte** mehr Zeit.	*I wish I had more time.*
Ich **wünschte**, du **würdest** dich beeilen.	*I wish you'd hurry.*

d. Unreal conditions

Wenn ich morgen Zeit **hätte, würde** ich mit dir ins Kino gehen.	*If I had time tomorrow, I'd go to the movies with you.*
Wenn das Wetter schöner **wäre, würden** wir draußen essen.	*If the weather were nicer, we'd eat outside.*
Wenn wir euch helfen **könnten, würden** wir das tun.	*If we could help you, we would do it.*

Contrast the preceding sentences with real conditions.

Wenn ich morgen Zeit **habe, gehe** ich mit dir ins Kino.	*If I have time tomorrow, I'll go to the movies with you.*
Wenn das Wetter schön **ist, essen** wir draußen.	*If the weather is nice, we'll eat outside.*
Wenn wir euch helfen **können, tun** wir es.	*If we can help you, we'll do it.*

Wenn ich ein Vöglein° wär'
und auch zwei Flügel° hätt',
flög' ich zu dir.
Weil's aber nicht kann sein,
weil's aber nicht kann sein,
bleib' ich allhier°.

Mein Hut, der hat drei Ecken.
Drei Ecken hat mein Hut.
Und hätt' er nicht drei Ecken,
dann wär' er nicht mein Hut.

Heu — Mäuse — Moneten — Penunze — Pinke Pinke — Schotter — Zaster — Lappen — Flöhe — Eier — Kies — Kröten — Moneten — Moos — Kohle — Knete

Wenn das Wörtchen „wenn" nicht wär, wär mein Vater Millionär!

Translating the old songs might help clarify the difference between the indicative and the subjunctive. You could sing them, too. **"Mein Hut . . ."** can be a lot of fun as you leave out one word in each round and replace it with a gesture.

You can find different versions of these old German folk songs on YouTube.

little bird
wings

right here

■ Do you understand this saying? **Wenn mancher Mann wüsste, wer mancher Mann wär', gäb' mancher Mann manchem Mann manchmal mehr Ehr'** *(respect, honor).*

B: 1. Where would you like to go? 2. We could see a movie. 3. We ought to / should get a newspaper. 4. I'd like to go to the movies 5. I wish(ed) I weren't so tired. 6. I would rather stay at home. 7. Would you mind if I brought a couple of friends along? 8. I would prefer that we'd go alone / on our own. 9. Would you have time tomorrow evening? 10. I'd rather / prefer to go to bed early today. 11. Tomorrow I could sleep longer. 12. Then I wouldn't be so tired. 13. Then you could also bring your friends along. 14. Wouldn't this be a better idea?

C: 1. fragte, fragte; machte, machte; hoffte, hoffte; belegte, belegte; lächelte, lächelte; studierte, studierte; versuchte, versuchte 2. arbeitetest, arbeitetest; antwortetest, antwortetest; beendetest, beendetest; öffnetest, öffnetest; heiratetest, heiratetest 3. musste, müsste; konnte, könnte; durfte, dürfte; sollte, sollte; mochte, möchte 4. brachten, brächten; dachten, dächten; wussten, wüssten; hatten, hätten 5. bliebt, bliebet; schlieft, schliefet; flogt, flöget; wart, wäret; gabt, gäbet; aßt, äßet; sangt, sänget; saßt, säßet; tatet, tätet; saht, sähet; verspracht, verspräch et; wurdet, würdet; fuhrt, führet

Übungen

B. Was tun? Auf Englisch bitte!

1. Wohin möchtest du gehen?
2. Wir könnten uns einen Film ansehen.
3. Wir sollten uns eine Zeitung holen.
4. Ich würde gern ins Kino gehen.
5. Ich wünschte, ich wäre nicht so müde.
6. Ich würde lieber zu Hause bleiben.
7. Hättest du etwas dagegen, wenn ich ein paar Freunde mitbringen würde?
8. Es wäre mir lieber, wenn wir allein gehen würden.
9. Hättest du morgen Abend Zeit?
10. Ich ginge heute lieber früh ins Bett.
11. Morgen könnte ich länger schlafen.
12. Dann wäre ich nicht so müde.
13. Du könntest dann auch deine Freunde mitbringen.
14. Wäre das nicht eine bessere Idee?

C. Nennen Sie das Imperfekt und die Konjunktivform!

BEISPIEL		
ich hole	*ich holte*	*ich holte*
du bringst	*du brachtest*	*du brächtest*
er kommt	*er kam*	*er käme*

1. ich frage, mache, hoffe, belege, lächele, studiere, versuche
2. du arbeitest, antwortest, beendest, öffnest, heiratest
3. er muss, kann, darf, soll, mag
4. wir bringen, denken, wissen, haben
5. ihr bleibt, schlaft, fliegt, seid, gebt, esst, singt, sitzt, tut, seht, versprecht, werdet, fahrt

D. Reisepläne

1. **In Wien** Was fehlt? Ergänzen Sie die richtige Form von **würde**!

   BEISPIEL Bauers *würden* nach Wien fahren.

   a. Dort ___würden___ wir erst eine Stadtrundfahrt machen.
   b. Dann ___würde___ Dieter sicher den Stephansdom ansehen. Und du ___würdest___ dann durch die Kärntner Straße bummeln. Natürlich ___würdet___ ihr auch in die Hofburg gehen.
   c. Ja, und einen Abend ___würden___ wir in Grinzing feiern.
   d. Das ___würde___ euch gefallen.

2. **In der Schweiz** Ergänzen Sie die richtige Form vom Konjunktiv II!

   BEISPIEL Ute *führe* in die Schweiz. (fahren)

   a. Ich ___könnte___ mit ein paar Freunden in die Schweiz fahren. (können)
   b. Erst ___führen___ wir an den Bodensee. (fahren)
   c. Von dort ___ginge___ es weiter nach Zürich und Bern. (gehen)
   d. In Zürich ___sähe___ ich mir gern das Thomas-Mann-Archiv *(archives)* ___an___. (ansehen)
   e. Ihr ___solltet___ auch nach Genf fahren. (sollen)
   f. Dort ___müsstest___ du Französisch sprechen. (müssen)
   g. Das ___wäre___ keine schlechte Idee! (sein)

E. Und noch einmal ganz höflich *(politely)*! Welche Aussage ist am höflichsten?

E: 1a, 2b, 3c, 4a

1. Der Student sagt:
   a. „Hättest du vielleicht ein Stück Papier?"
   b. „Wenn ich doch nur ein Stück Papier hätte!"
   c. „Ein Stück Papier, aber schnell bitte!"
2. Die Studentin sagt:
   a. „Ich brauche unbedingt ein Vorlesungsverzeichnis."
   b. „Würdest du mir bitte mal das Vorlesungsverzeichnis geben?"
   c. „Gibst du mir jetzt das Vorlesungsverzeichnis oder nicht?"
3. Der Beamte sagt:
   a. „Geben Sie mir Ihr Immatrikulationsformular!"
   b. „Ich will jetzt aber Ihr Immatrikulationsformular sehen."
   c. „Dürfte ich bitte Ihr Immatrikulationsformular sehen?"
4. Die Studenten sagen:
   a. „Wären Sie wohl so nett, uns die Noten zu sagen?"
   b. „Unsere Noten!"
   c. „Wenn Sie uns nicht die Noten sagen, dann gehen wir."

F. Sagen Sie's höflicher!

1. **Ein paar Fragen**

BEISPIEL Darf ich dich kurz etwas fragen?
Dürfte ich dich kurz etwas fragen?

a. Kannst du mir etwas über die letzte Vorlesung erzählen?
b. Hast du ein paar Notizen *(notes)* darüber?
c. Kann ich sie mir mal durchlesen?
d. Hast du etwas dagegen, wenn ich sie mir kopiere?

F.1: a. Könntest du . . . erzählen? b. Hättest du . . . ? c. Könnte ich . . . durchlesen? d. Hättest du . . . , wenn ich . . . kopiere / kopieren würde?

2. **Ein paar Bitten *(requests)***

BEISPIEL Nein, aber bring sie mir morgen bitte wieder mit!
Nein, aber würdest / könntest du sie mir morgen bitte wieder mitbringen?

a. Erzähl mir etwas über den Expressionismus!
b. Nenne mir bitte ein paar Namen von expressionistischen Malern!
c. Zeig mir ein paar Bilder von ihnen!
d. Gib mir bitte mal das Kunstbuch!

F.2: a. Würdest / Könntest du . . . erzählen? b. Würdest / Könntest du . . . nennen? c. Würdest / Könntest du . . . zeigen? d. Würdest / Könntest du . . . geben?

G. Allerlei Wünsche

BEISPIEL Das Seminar ist schwer.
Ich wünschte, das Seminar wäre nicht so schwer.

1. Ich muss viel lesen.
2. Das kostet viel Zeit.
3. Ich bin müde.
4. Ihr seid faul.

G.1–4: When converting these German statements into wishes, **nicht so** is added immediately *after* the verb. If this switch from statement to wish creates a problem, have students give the equivalent in English first. 1. ich müsste nicht so viel lesen 2. das kostete nicht so viel Zeit 3. ich wäre nicht so müde 4. ihr wäret nicht so faul

BEISPIEL Ich wünschte, ich könnte schlafen.
Wenn ich nur schlafen könnte!

5. Ich wünschte, wir hätten keine Referate.
6. Ich wünschte, ich wüsste mehr über das Thema Wirtschaft.
7. Ich wünschte, du könntest mir helfen.
8. Ich wünschte, diese Woche wäre schon vorbei.

G.5–8: When converting these wishes into the **wenn**-form, **nur** is added *after* the subject and any pronoun object. Again, you might have students give the English equivalents first. 5. Wenn wir nur keine Referate hätten! 6. Wenn ich nur mehr über das Thema Wirtschaft wüsste! 7. Wenn du mir nur helfen könntest! 8. Wenn diese Woche nur schon vorbei wäre!

H: 1. Wenn . . . wäre, würde . . . zeigen. 2. Wenn . . . sehen wolltest, müsstest . . . beeilen. 3. Wenn . . . kämet / kommen würdet, würdet . . . ärgern. 4. Wenn . . . zu wäre, könnten . . . gehen. 5. Wenn . . . sehen wolltet, müsstet . . . bleiben

H. Wiederholen Sie die Sätze im Konjunktiv!

BEISPIEL Wenn das Wetter schön ist, kann man die Berge sehen.
Wenn das Wetter schön wäre, könnte man die Berge sehen.

1. Wenn es möglich ist, zeige ich euch das Schloss.
2. Wenn du das Schloss sehen willst, musst du dich beeilen.
3. Wenn ihr zu spät kommt, ärgert ihr euch.
4. Wenn das Schloss zu ist, können wir in den Schlosspark gehen.
5. Wenn ihr mehr sehen wollt, müsst ihr länger hier bleiben.

Optional activity: Have students prepare five or six **Wenn ich . . .** -statements at home, each on a card or small piece of paper that can be exchanged. The next day, students should complete somebody else's wish (e.g., **Wenn ich Millionär wäre, . . .**) with their own response (e.g., **dann könntest du ein Schloss kaufen**). Have each card or paper returned to the student who expressed the wish and let him/her read the answer aloud, changing the subject accordingly **(Wenn ich Millionär ware, [dann] könnte ich mir ein Schloss kaufen).**

I. Studium an der Europa-Akademie in Köln

Lesen Sie, was der Vater seinem Sohn erzählt! Was fehlt?

Für einen B.A. in Management, Wirtschaft und Sprachen ___müsstest___ du zwei Jahre an dieser Akademie und dann ein Jahr in England ___studieren___. *(would have to study)* Dazu ___käme___ noch ein Praktikum. *(would come)* Wenn du ___wolltest___, ___könntest___ du dort auch deinen Magister (M.A.) ___machen___. *(wanted, could make)* Weil du über 25 Jahre alt bist, ___bräuchtest___ du kein Abitur. *(would need)* Mensch, ___wäre___ das nicht was für dich? *(would be)* Das ganze Studium ___dürfte/sollte___ nicht länger als vier Jahre ___dauern___. *(ought to take)* Dann ___hättest___ du deinen Abschluss in der Tasche. *(would have)* Du ___könntest___ entweder im August oder im Februar ___anfangen/beginnen___. *(could start)* Ich ___wünschte___, ich ___wäre___ noch einmal so jung wie du! *(wish, were)* Ich ___täte/würde___ das ___- / tun___. *(would do)*

J. Wie geht's weiter?

BEISPIEL Ich wäre glücklich, wenn . . .
Ich wäre glücklich, wenn ich gut Deutsch sprechen könnte. Und du?

1. Ich wäre froh, wenn . . .
2. Ich fände es prima, wenn . . .
3. Es wäre furchtbar, wenn . . .
4. Ich würde mich ärgern, wenn . . .
5. Ich würde sparen, wenn . . .
6. Ich wüsste, was ich täte, wenn . . .

The song "Es ist nicht immer leicht, ich zu sein" by the Wise Guys playfully demonstrates the everyday usage of the subjunctive. You can find it with lyrics on YouTube.

Fantasie ist wichtiger als alles Wissen, denn Wissen ist begrenzt.
E=mc²
Albert Einstein

K. Zwei wichtige Fragen für junge Deutsche und für Sie

1. **Das würden junge Deutsche tun.** Schauen Sie sich die folgenden Tabellen an und stellen Sie den anderen in Ihrer Gruppe Fragen dazu!

BEISPIEL S1 Was würden 20 Prozent der jungen Deutschen tun?
S2 20 Prozent würden als Single in einer Penthouse-Wohnung wohnen.

Was wäre, wenn Sie so leben könnten, wie Sie wollten?	
als Globetrotter um die Welt ziehen	25%
als Single in einer Penthouse-Wohnung wohnen	20%
als Handwerker/in in einer Kleinstadt leben	14%
als Chirurg/in mit Familie in einer Villa wohnen	13%
als Künstler/in in einem alten Haus leben	12%
als Playboy / Model immer da sein, wo etwas los ist	8%
Aktivist/in für Greenpeace sein	4%
als Bundespräsident/in im Schloss Bellevue wohnen	4%

Was wäre, wenn Ihre Oma Ihnen 5 000 Euro hinterlassen würde?	
das Geld zur Bank bringen	25%
verreisen	22%
sich Kleidung kaufen	18%
etwas Größeres kaufen	13%
sich fragen, wo die restlichen 45 000 Euro sind	8%
mit Freunden feiern und alles zahlen	6%
Aktien *(stocks)* kaufen	5%
den Armen etwas geben	3%

2. **Das würde ich tun.** Beschreiben Sie nun, wie das bei Ihnen aussähe, was Ihnen wichtig und weniger wichtig wäre! Wenn Sie wollen, können Sie auch eigene Aussagen hinzufügen.

BEISPIEL S1 Wie wäre es, wenn du so leben könntest, wie du wolltest?
S2 Wenn ich leben könnte, wie ich wollte, zöge ich . . .

Fokus US and German Companies Doing Business Abroad

Germany is an essential trade partner of the United States and vice versa. The European Union is the second-largest trading partner of the United States, and Germany alone ranks number five. The 3,000 German companies in the United States account for approximately 700,000 jobs, and American companies account for about 800,000 jobs in Germany. Many major US companies in Germany include UPS, FedEx, IBM, Canon, Hewlett Packard, Proctor & Gamble, and GE. In turn, the names of many German companies are familiar in the United States: car makers Volkswagen, Audi, BMW, and Porsche; shoe and sporting goods companies Birkenstock, Adidas, and Puma; the electronic innovator Siemens; the software company SAP; the telecom group Deutsche Telekom; and the chemical giant BASF.

Dieser VW bringt Fahrvergnügen!

If students are not comfortable with English sentences in the past-time subjunctive, set aside a few minutes to make up some sample sentences.

13.3 The past-time general subjunctive

You already know that a simple-past form in English can express the present-time subjunctive (referring to now or later). The past-perfect form, or *would have* + participle, expresses the same thought in the PAST-TIME SUBJUNCTIVE (referring to an *earlier* point of time).

NOW OR LATER: If I *had* time, I *would go* with you.
EARLIER: If I *had had* time, I *would have gone* with you.

Note that the same verbs that use **haben** or **sein** for the present perfect use **hätte** or **wäre** for the past perfect forms of the past-time subjunctive.

1. Forms

a. In German, the forms of the past-time subjunctive are based on the forms of the past perfect. The past-time subjunctive is very easy to learn because it consists simply of a form of **hätte** or **wäre** plus the past participle:

hätte . . . } + participle
wäre . . .

Hättest du das **getan?**	*Would you have done that?*
Das **hätte** ich nicht **getan.**	*I wouldn't have done that.*
Wärest du nicht lieber ins Kino **gegangen?**	*Wouldn't you have rather gone to the movies?*
Ich wünschte, du **hättest** mir das **gesagt!**	*I wish you had told me that!*
Wenn ich das **gewusst hätte, wären** wir ins Kino **gegangen.**	*If I had known that, we would have gone to the movies.*

This double construction of *verb infinitive + modal infinitive* is also called the DOUBLE INFINITIVE CONSTRUCTION. You may wish to introduce that term.

b. All modals follow this pattern in the past-time subjunctive:

hätte . . . + verb infinitive + modal infinitive

Du **hättest** mir das **sagen sollen.**	*You should have told me that.*
Wir **hätten** noch ins Kino **gehen können.**	*We still could have gone to the movies.*

For now, avoid using these forms in dependent clauses.

2. Uses

The past-time subjunctive is used for the same purposes as the present-time subjunctive. Note that there are no polite requests in the past.

a. Hypothetical statements and questions

Ich wäre zu Hause geblieben.	*I would have stayed home.*
Was hättet ihr gemacht?	*What would you have done?*

b. Wishes

Wenn ich das nur gewusst hätte!	*If I had only known that!*
Ich wünschte, du wärest da gewesen.	*I wish you had been there.*

c. Unreal conditions

Wenn du mich gefragt hättest, hätte ich es dir gesagt.	*If you had asked me, I would have told you.*
Wenn du da gewesen wärest, hättest du alles gehört.	*If you had been there, you would have heard everything.*

Übungen

L. Sagen Sie die Sätze in der Vergangenheit!

1. **Ohne Modalverb**

BEISPIEL Sie würde das tun.
Sie hätte das getan.

a. Sie würde euch anrufen.
b. Ihr würdet ihr helfen.
c. Ihr würdet schnell kommen.
d. Du würdest alles für sie tun.

L.1: Again, you might have students give the English first.
a. hätte . . . angerufen
b. hättet . . . geholfen
c. wäret . . . gekommen
d. hättest . . . getan

2. **Mit Modalverb**

BEISPIEL Hannes sollte nicht so viel Schokolade essen.
Hannes hätte nicht so viel Schokolade essen sollen.

a. Wir dürften ihm keine Schokolade geben.
b. Das sollten wir wissen.
c. Er könnte auch Obst essen.
d. Wir müssten besser aufpassen.

L.2: a. hätten . . . geben dürfen
b. hätten . . . wissen sollen
c. hätte . . . essen können
d. hätten . . . aufpassen müssen

M. Was wäre gewesen, wenn . . . ?

1. **Wiederholen Sie die Sätze in der Vergangenheit!**

BEISPIEL Wenn ich es wüsste, würde ich nicht fragen.
Wenn ich es gewusst hätte, hätte ich nicht gefragt.

a. Wenn wir eine Theatergruppe hätten, würde ich mitmachen.
b. Wenn der Computer billiger wäre, würden wir ihn kaufen.
c. Wenn ich Hunger hätte, würde ich mir etwas kochen.
d. Wenn sie mehr arbeitete, würde es ihr besser gehen.

M.1: a. gehabt hätten, hätte . . . mitgemacht
b. gewesen wäre, hätten . . . gekauft
c. gehabt hätte, hätte . . . gekocht
d. gearbeitet hätte, wäre . . . gegangen

2. **Und dann?** Was würden Sie tun oder hätten Sie getan? Wechseln Sie sich ab!

M.2: Student 2 follows up with at least two **Und dann?**-questions.

BEISPIEL Ich hatte keinen Hunger. Wenn ich Hunger gehabt hätte, . . .
S1 Ich hatte keinen Hunger. Wenn ich Hunger gehabt hätte, wäre ich in die Küche gegangen.
S2 Und dann?
S1 Dann hätte ich mir ein Wurstbrot gemacht.
S2 Und dann?
S1 . . .

a. Gestern hat es geregnet. Wenn das Wetter schön gewesen wäre, . . .
b. Ich bin nicht lange auf der Party geblieben. Wenn ich zu lange gefeiert hätte, . . .
c. Natürlich hatten wir letzte Woche Vorlesungen. Wenn wir keine Vorlesungen gehabt hätten, . . .

HÄTTE ICH DIE
KRAFT NICHTS ZU
TUN, TÄTE ICH
NICHTS!

N. Hoppla, hier fehlt was: Wie war das bei deinen Großeltern?

1. **Imaginäre *(Imaginary)* Großeltern** Hören Sie, was Ihnen Ihr Partner / Ihre Partnerin mit Hilfe der Information im Anhang über seinen/ihren imaginären Großvater vorliest *(reads to you)*! Schauen Sie dabei auf die Tabelle unten und markieren Sie **Ja** oder **Nein,** je nachdem *(depending on)*, was der Großvater getan oder nicht getan hat. Wechseln Sie sich dann ab! Während Sie den unteren Text (S1) über Ihre imaginäre Großmutter vorlesen, markiert Ihr Partner / Ihre Partnerin seine/ihre Tabelle im Anhang. Vergleichen Sie am Ende, ob die Tabellen stimmen!

   S1: Meine Oma ist gern zur Schule gegangen. Sie war besonders gut in Mathe. Wenn ihre Familie Geld gehabt hätte, hätte sie gern studiert. Sie wäre furchtbar gern Lehrerin geworden. Aber sie musste als Kindermädchen *(nanny)* bei einer reichen Familie arbeiten. Dann hat sie meinen Großvater kennengelernt und geheiratet. Meine Oma liebt Kinder und sie hätte gern eine große Familie gehabt. Sie hatten aber nur ein Kind. Sie ist immer gern gereist. Wenn mein Großvater länger gelebt hätte, hätten sie zusammen eine große Weltreise gemacht.

Mathe *(coll.)* = **Mathematik**

Und was sagt Ihnen Ihr Partner / Ihre Partnerin?

	Ja	Nein
Der Opa ist aus Deutschland gekommen.	x	
Die Familie ist mit dem Schiff gefahren.		
Der Opa ist gern nach Amerika gekommen.		
Die Familie hat in New York gewohnt.		
Er ist Polizist geworden.		
Er konnte gut singen.		
Er hat gelernt, Klavier zu spielen.		
Er ist dieses Jahr nach Deutschland gefahren.		

2. **Meine Großeltern** Erzählen Sie den anderen von Ihren wirklichen Großeltern!

N.2: This could also be a written exercise.

Zusammenfassung

O. Indikativ oder Konjunktiv? Was bedeutet das auf Englisch?

1. Wenn er uns besuchte, brachte er immer Blumen mit.
2. Können Sie mir Dominiks Telefonnummer geben?
3. Wenn du früher ins Bett gegangen wärest, wärest du jetzt nicht so müde.
4. Gestern konnten sie nicht kommen, aber sie könnten uns morgen besuchen.
5. Er sollte gestern anrufen.
6. Ich möchte Architektur studieren.
7. Sie waren schon um 6 Uhr aufgestanden.

iLrn

Visit the ***Wie geht's?*** iLrn website for more review and practice of the grammar points you have just learned.

O: 1. Whenever he visited us, he always brought flowers. (I) 2. Can you give me Horst's telephone number? (I) 3. If you had gone to bed earlier, you wouldn't be so tired now. (K) 4. Yesterday they couldn't come, but they could visit us tomorrow. (I / K) 5. He was supposed to call yesterday. (I) 6. I would like to study architecture. (K) 7. They had already gotten up at 6 A.M. (I)

P. Guter Rat ist teuer *(hard to come by).*

1. **Was soll ich tun?** Jemand in Ihrer Gruppe erwähnt *(mentions)* ein Problem, echt *(real)* oder nicht echt (zum Beispiel: er/sie hat kein Geld oder keine Energie / Hunger oder Durst / etwas verloren . . .) und die anderen geben Rat.

   BEISPIEL S1 Ich bin immer so müde.
   S2 Wenn ich du wäre, würde ich früher ins Bett gehen.

2. **Was hätte ich tun sollen?** Geben Sie Rat, was man (nicht) hätte tun sollen!

   BEISPIEL S1 Ich habe meine Schlüssel verloren.
   S2 Du hättest besser aufpassen sollen.

Q. Der Weg ist frei. Auf Deutsch bitte!

1. My friends told me about Germany's immigration law **(das Zuwanderungsgesetz).** 2. That is supposed to make Germany interesting for foreign experts **(der ausländische Experte).** 3. Sibi is from India and just graduated from the University of Tübingen. 4. As a computer expert, he would not have to return to India. 5. He could stay here and work. 6. Irina Burlakov is becoming a doctor. 7. She is from Russia and speaks German very well. 8. Without the language, everything would have been much more difficult. 9. She also would not have found friends so quickly. 10. Irina will stay in Germany.

Q: 1. Meine Freunde haben mir von Deutschlands Zuwanderungsgesetz erzählt. 2. Das soll Deutschland für ausländische Experten interessant machen. 3. Sibi ist aus Indien und hat gerade sein Studium an der Universität Tübingen abgeschlossen. 4. Als Computerexperte müsste er nicht nach Indien zurückgehen. 5. Er könnte hier bleiben und arbeiten. 6. Irina Burlakov wird Ärztin. 7. Sie ist (kommt) aus Russland und spricht sehr gut Deutsch. 8. Ohne die Sprache wäre alles viel schwieriger / schwerer gewesen. 9. Sie hätte auch nicht so schnell Freunde gefunden. 10. Irina wird in Deutschland bleiben.

Fokus Studying in Germany

Studying in Germany is considerably different from studying in North America. Students enter the university with a broad general education received during their years at the Gymnasium and can therefore immediately focus on their major **(das Hauptfach),** with few courses required in unrelated fields.

More than 2 million students are enrolled in German universities. Approx. 10% of them come from different countries. For European students it has become easier than ever to study in Germany. In 1999, Germany and 31 other European states signed the so-called "Bologna Accords," which provides for a unified European Education System.

The greatest common goal of the 40 countries that have by now joined the Bologna-Process, is the award of uniform degrees for Bachelors, Masters, and PhDs. Germany differentiates between the BA, BS and BE (Bachelor of Engineering). The German **Diplom, Magister,** and some **Staatsexamen** (*comprehensive state exam*) have been replaced by these new degrees. Remaining **Staatsexamen** are administered for degrees in Medicine, Pharmacy, Law, Food Chemistry, and some Education degrees. The new system, which has not been completely implemented yet, has created many new majors, which are of interest to foreign students, and some of which were especially developed for them.

Germany has more than 400 universities. Since the winter semester 2006/2007, some of them have been charging tuition amounting to 500€ per semester. This is considerably less than tuition costs in the USA, Great Britain, or France. Nevertheless, many students and some politicians consider the practice of charging tuition in Germany questionable.

The academic calendar is officially divided into a winter semester (from mid-October to mid-February) and a summer semester (from about mid-April to mid-July), varying somewhat from state to state. The vacation period **(die vorlesungsfreie Zeit;** literally: a period without lectures)—two months in spring and three months in summer—is intended to allow students to catch up on work, to take a job, or to go on vacation. German universities are academically self-governing and are headed by a president **(der Rektor),** elected for several years. Purely administrative matters are handled by a permanent staff of civil servants under the direction of a chancellor **(der Kanzler).**

While some foreign students study in Germany for one or two semesters through one of the many study-abroad programs, a large number of students from a wide variety of different countries get their degrees in Germany from start to finish. (Your university's International Studies Office will be able to supply you with more information about studying in Germany, Austria, or Switzerland).

Einblicke

Dialog

Extra practice with *in your shoes*, e.g., **ich: an meiner Stelle** (du, er, sie / *sg.*, wir, ihr, sie / *pl.*, Bernd, Margaret, Margaret und Tina, Frau Meier)

Wortschatz 2

an deiner/seiner Stelle	*in your/his shoes; if I were you/he*
auf diese Weise	*(in) this way*
ausländisch	*foreign*
bestimmt	*surely, for sure; certain(ly)*
deshalb	*therefore*
jedenfalls	*in any case*
so dass	*so that*
wahrscheinlich	*probably*
Angst haben (vor + *dat.*)	*to fear, be afraid (of)*
an·nehmen (nimmt an), nahm an, angenommen	*to suppose; to accept*
auf·hören	*to end; to stop doing something*
teilen	*to share;* also: *to divide*

Lesetipp

Brainstorming Contextual Knowledge

You have learned quite a bit about the German university system in this chapter. With a partner, make a list of at least five ways in which the system in your country is different from the German system. With these differences in mind, you will be more prepared to read the conversation on the next page, which deals with this subject.

Vor dem Lesen

A. Allerlei Fragen

1. Würden Sie gern in Europa studieren? Wo, wann und wie lange?
2. Hat Ihre Uni ein Austauschprogramm? Wenn ja, wo?
3. Haben Sie Freunde, die *(who)* drüben studiert haben? Wenn ja, wo und wie hat es ihnen gefallen?

B. Das ist leicht zu verstehen! Lesen Sie laut die folgenden Wörter und raten Sie, was sie auf Englisch bedeuten.

der Grammatikkurs, Intensivkurs, Lesesaal; das Archiv, Auslandsprogramm; die Sprachprüfung; teilmöbliert

C. Gehen wir Wörter angeln! Lesen Sie still *(quietly)* das folgende Gespräch mit Ihrem Partner / Ihrer Partnerin! Welche Konjunktive finden Sie darin? Wie würde man das auf Englisch sagen?

© Ingrid Sevin

Studenten im Bus zur Fachhochschule

Ein Jahr drüben wäre super!

(Gespräch an einer amerikanischen Universität)

TINA Hallo, Margaret!

MARGARET Tag, Tina! Kennst du Bernd? Er ist aus Heidelberg und studiert ein Jahr bei uns.

TINA Guten Tag! Na, wie gefällt's dir hier?

BERND Sehr gut. Meine Vorlesungen und die Professoren sind ausgezeichnet. Ich wünschte nur, es gäbe nicht so viele Prüfungen!

TINA Habt ihr keine Prüfungen in Deutschland?

BERND Doch, aber weniger. Dafür° haben wir nach ungefähr vier Semestern eine große Zwischenprüfung und dann am Ende des Studiums das Examen.

Instead

TINA Ich würde gern einmal in Europa studieren.

MARGARET Ja, das solltest du unbedingt.

TINA Es ist bestimmt sehr teuer.

MARGARET Ach was, so teuer ist es gar nicht. Mein Jahr in München hat auch nicht mehr gekostet als ein Jahr hier.

TINA Wirklich?

BERND Ja, unsere Studentenwohnheime und die Mensa sind etwas billiger als bei euch und wir haben nur geringe° Studiengebühren°. Ohne mein Stipendium könnte ich nicht in den USA studieren.

minimal / tuition

TINA Ist es schwer, dort drüben einen Studienplatz zu bekommen?

BERND Wenn du Deutsche wärest, wäre es wahrscheinlich nicht so einfach—je nachdem°, was du studieren willst. Aber als Ausländerin in einem Auslandsprogramm hättest du gar kein Problem.

depending on

TINA Ich muss noch mal mit meinen Eltern sprechen. Sie haben Angst, dass ich ein Jahr verlieren würde.

MARGARET Wieso denn? Wenn du mit einem Auslandsprogramm nach Deutschland gingest, würde das doch wie ein Jahr hier zählen.

TINA Ich weiß nicht, ob ich genug Deutsch kann.

MARGARET Keine Angst! Viele Studenten können weniger Deutsch als du. Du lernst es ja schon seit vier Jahren. Außerdem bieten die meisten Programme vor Semesteranfang einen Intensivkurs für ausländische Studenten an. Du kannst auch Kurse in „Deutsch als Fremdsprache" belegen.

TINA Vielleicht kann ich dann doch ein Semester nach Deutschland.

BERND Bei uns gibt es ein Wintersemester und ein Sommersemester. Ein ganzes Jahr wäre natürlich besser, denn dann hättest du auch Zeit zu reisen.

TINA Super! Was für Vorlesungen soll ich belegen?

BERND Im ersten Semester würde ich nur Vorlesungen belegen. Da hört man nur zu und schreibt mit°. Im zweiten Semester solltest du dann aber auch ein Seminar belegen. Bis dann ist dein Deutsch jedenfalls gut genug, so dass du auch eine längere Seminararbeit schreiben oder ein Referat halten könntest.

takes notes

TINA Seminararbeiten und Referate auf Deutsch?

MARGARET Am Anfang geht's langsam, aber man lernt's.

BERND Ich mach's ja auch auf Englisch.

TINA Und wie ist das mit Studentenwohnheimen?

MARGARET Wenn du an einem Auslandsprogramm teilnimmst, hast du keine Probleme.

Bernd An deiner Stelle würde ich versuchen, ein Zimmer im Studentenwohnheim zu bekommen. Auf diese Weise könntest du leichter andere Studenten kennenlernen. Die Zimmer sind nicht schlecht, teilmöbliert und mit Bad. Die Küche müsstest du aber mit anderen Studenten teilen.

Tina Da habe ich nichts dagegen. Findet ihr, Heidelberg wäre besser als Berlin oder München?

Bernd Ach, das ist schwer zu sagen.

Margaret Ich glaube, wenn ich Berlin gekannt hätte, hätte ich bestimmt dort studiert. Mir hat es da sehr gut gefallen. Aber erst musst du dich entscheiden, ob du wirklich nach Deutschland willst. Wenn du das weißt, dann kann ich dir weiterhelfen.

Tina Danke! Macht's gut! Ich muss zur Vorlesung.

■ A good organization to obtain stipends for studying in Germany is the German Academic Exchange Service (DAAD), a publicly funded independent organization of higher-education institutions in Germany, which promotes cooperative academic and scientific exchange for students and faculty.

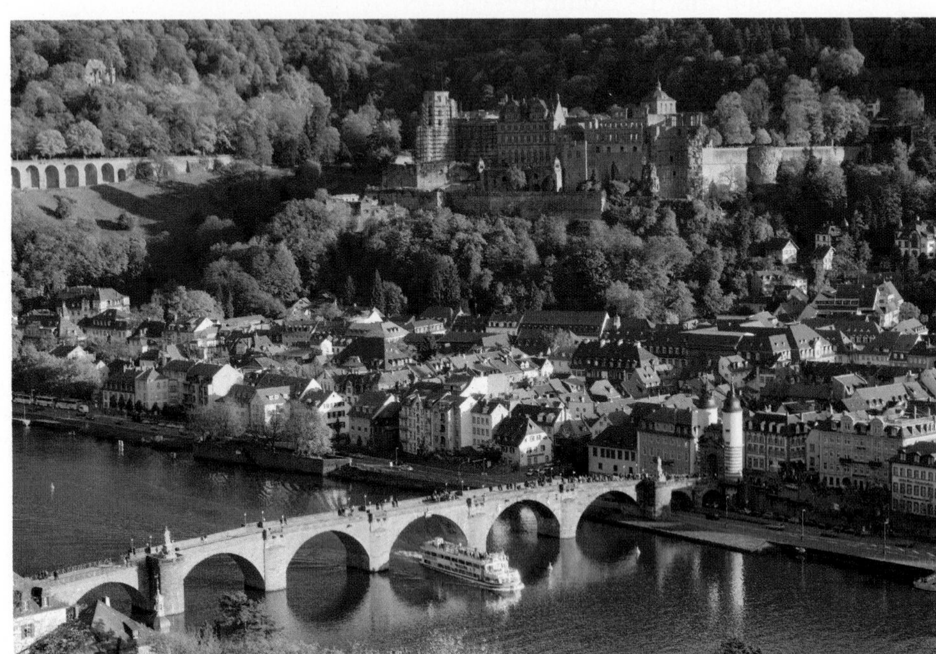

Heidelberg am Neckar mit Blick auf die Altstadt und das Schloss

Nach dem Lesen

A. Alles verstanden?

A: 1. aus Heidelberg, ausgezeichnet 2. zu viele 3. Tina 4. Margaret, München 5. in Deutschland 6. an einem Auslandsprogramm 7. Intensivkurse für ausländische Studenten, Deutsch als Fremdsprache 8. reisen 9. Vorlesungen; da hört man nur zu, keine Seminarbeiten, keine Referate 10. leichter, andere Studenten kennenzulernen

1. Woher kommt Bernd und wie findet er die Vorlesungen und Professoren an der Uni?
2. Was sagt er über die Prüfungen?
3. Wer würde auch gern einmal in Deutschland studieren?
4. Wer hat das schon mal gemacht und wo?
5. Wo sind die Studentenheime billiger, in Deutschland oder in den USA?
6. Woran sollte Tina teilnehmen, wenn sie ein Jahr in Deutschland studieren wollte?
7. Was bieten die meisten Unis den ausländischen Studenten an?
8. Was könnte Tina in den Semesterferien tun?
9. Was sollte sie im ersten Semester belegen und warum?
10. Warum wäre es gut, wenn sie in einem Studentenheim wohnen würde?

B. An der Uni Was fehlt?

1. Bernd <u>wünschte</u>, es <u>gäbe</u> nicht so viele Prüfungen. *(wished, [there] were)*
2. Wenn Bernd kein Stipendium <u>bekommen hätte</u>, <u>hätte</u> er hier nicht <u>studieren können</u>. *(had gotten, could have studied)*
3. Wenn Tina mit einem Austauschprogramm nach Deutschland <u>ginge / gehen würde</u>, <u>würde</u> das wie ein Jahr hier <u>zählen</u>. *(would go, would count)*
4. Ein ganzes Jahr drüben <u>wäre</u> besser. *(would be)*
5. Dann <u>hätte</u> Tina Zeit, in den Semesterferien zu reisen. *(would have)*
6. In einem Studentenwohnheim <u>würde</u> Tina leichter deutsche Studenten <u>kennenlernen</u>. *(would get to know)*
7. Wenn Margaret nicht an einer deutschen Uni <u>studiert hätte</u>, <u>könnte</u> sie nicht so gut Deutsch <u>sprechen</u>. *(had studied, could speak)*
8. Tina <u>hat Angst</u>, dass ihr Deutsch nicht gut genug ist. Aber das <u>sollte</u> kein Problem <u>sein</u>. *(is afraid, shouldn't be)*

Optional tongue twister: **Wir würden weiße Wäsche waschen, wenn wir wüssten, wo warmes Wasser ist.**

C. Am liebsten würde ich . . . Beenden Sie die Sätze und vergleichen Sie sie dann mit den Sätzen der anderen!

1. Wenn ich könnte, würde ich einmal in . . . studieren.
2. Am liebsten würde ich in . . . wohnen, weil . . .
3. Am Anfang des Semesters . . .
4. An Wochenenden und während der Ferien . . .
5. Wenn ich in Deutschland arbeiten könnte, würde ich bei . . . arbeiten.
6. Ein Praktikum bei . . . wäre auch nicht schlecht.

Tübingen, eine schöne, alte Universitätsstadt am Neckar

Weiteres

 **D. Selbstständige in freien Berufen** Sehen Sie sich die Grafik an und sprechen Sie mit den anderen darüber!

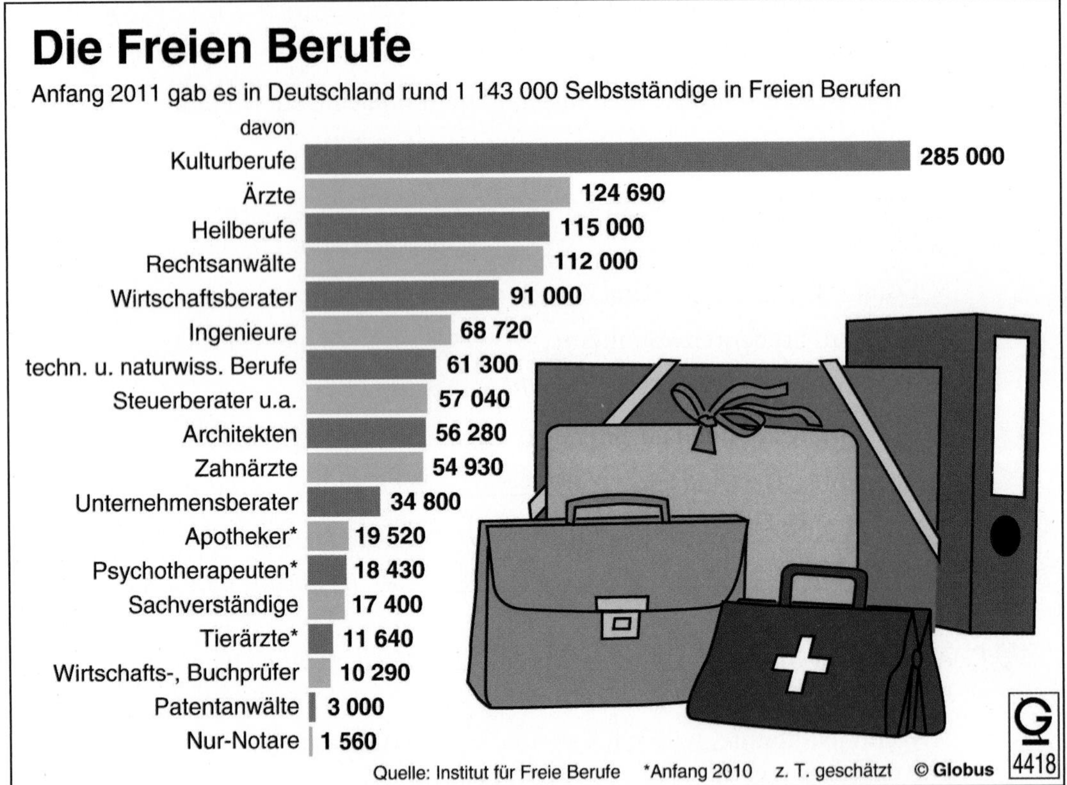

■ In case you are curious: **der Heilberuf, -e** *health-care profession*; **der Wirtschaftsberater, -** *financial advisor*; **der Steuerberater, -** *tax advisor*; **der Unternehmensberater, -** *management consultant*; **der Psychotherapeut, -en, -en** *psychotherapist*; **der Sachverständige, -n, -n** *expert*; **der Wirtschaftsprüfer, -** *certified public accountant*; **der Buchprüfer, -** *book-keeper*; **der Nur-Notar, -e** *certified notary*

1. Wer gehört zu den Freiberuflern?
2. In welchen Berufen gibt es die meisten Freiberufler in Deutschland? Wie viele gibt es von ihnen?
3. Wie vergleichen sich die Berufe in der Grafik? Wovon gibt es mehr oder weniger? Benutzen Sie den Komparativ in 3–4 Sätzen!
4. Was ist besonders gut und weniger gut, wenn man selbstständig ist?
5. Für welchen dieser freien Berufe würden Sie sich interessieren und wofür nicht? Warum (nicht)?

 **E. Ein Kurzgespräch mit Margaret** Bereiten Sie mit Ihrem Partner / Ihrer Partnerin den folgenden Dialog vor und präsentieren Sie ihn danach vor der Klasse!

You call Margaret, who has been to Germany. You introduce yourself and inquire whether you might ask her some questions. She says to go ahead, and you ask all sorts of questions to which she replies. You ask whether you could have lunch together the next day. She says she would prefer it if you could have dinner. You agree and say good-bye.

 **F. Das wäre schön!** Schreiben Sie sechs bis acht Sätze über eines der folgenden Themen! Benutzen Sie dabei mindestens *(at least)* fünf Konjunktivformen!

1. Ein Jahr drüben wäre super!
2. Mein Traumhaus
3. Meine Traumfamilie
4. Das würde mir gefallen.
5. Das hätte mir gefallen.
6. Das wäre schrecklich!

G. Bewerbung *(Application)*: Meine Antwort Lesen Sie die Anzeige und Bewerbung und schreiben Sie dann Ihre eigene Bewerbung!

Benjamin Bode
Mainstraße 26
64625 Bensheim
Tel.: 06251/69222

Bensheim, den 11.4.2014

Traumreisen GmbH
Leopoldstraße 65
D-81925 München 81

Bewerbung als Service-Manager auf dem Traumschiff Verdi

Sehr geehrte Damen und Herren,

Ich bin teamfähig, flexibel und arbeite selbstständig. Der freundliche Umgang mit dem Gast ist mir ebenso wichtig wie sauberes und sorgfältiges Arbeiten. Darum bin ich der beste Kandidat für Ihr Team.

Meine Ausbildung zum Hotelfachmann habe ich am 8. August 2010 im Hotel ***Zum Kurfürsten*** in Würzburg abgeschlossen. Seitdem habe ich dort als Chef de Rang gearbeitet. Ich bin sicher, dass ich meine Erfahrung auch sehr gut auf dem Traumschiff einbringen kann.

Ich würde mich sehr über einen Termin zu einem persönlichen Vorstellungsgespräch mit Ihnen freuen.

Mit freundlichem Gruß

Benjamin Bode

TRAUMSCHIFF VERDI sucht: Reiselustige Studenten

Alter:	**18-30**
Sprachen:	**Deutsch und Englisch oder Spanisch**
Sport:	**Segeln, Tennis oder Volleyball**
Unterhaltung:	**Musik, Tanzen**
Service:	**Restaurant, Boutique, Rezeption**

Bewerbung mit Foto an: Traumreisen GmbH
Leopoldstraße 65 D-81925 München 81
Tel.: (089) 348 55 52 E-Mail: traumreisen@verdi-web.de

Schreibtipp

Applying for a Job

When applying for a job, introduce yourself briefly, state why that position is of interest to you, and state why your particular background should be of interest to the employer. Note that here the use of the subjunctive comes in handy and adds politeness to your letter. Even though your letter should be typed, be sure to sign it by hand. Note that in Germany it is customary, even expected, that you include a photo with your job application.

This might help: **der Umgang** *dealing(s) with*; **der Gast, ¨-e** *guest*; **sorgfältig** *careful*; **der Fachmann, -leute** *specialist*; **der Hotelfachmann, -leute** *hotel manager*; **ab·schließen** *to finish*; **seitdem** *since then*; **der Chef, -s de Rang** *dining room supervisor*; **der Temin, -e** *appointment*; **das Vorstellungsgespräch, -e** *interview*

Hörverständnis

Zwei Briefe Hören Sie, an wen Dagmar Schröder und Joe Jackson einen Brief schreiben und warum! Sind die folgenden Aussagen richtig oder falsch?

Zum Erkennen: das Stellenangebot *(job opening)*; erfüllen *(to fulfill)*; der ADAC *(AAA)*; beigelegt *(enclosed)*; sich vorstellen *(to introduce or present oneself)*; absolvieren *(to complete)*; vermitteln *(to help find)*

__f__ 1. Dagmar Schröder hat Touristik studiert.
__r__ a. Sie würde gern als Reiseleiterin arbeiten.
__r__ b. Sie spricht gut Italienisch.

__f__ 2. Joe Jackson studiert Betriebswirtschaft in Seattle, Washington.
__r__ a. Er würde gern noch etwas mehr Geschäftsdeutsch lernen.
__r__ b. Er würde sich freuen, wenn ihm die Carl-Duisberg-Gesellschaft in Köln Informationen und Formulare dazu schicken könnte.

For further practice, an optional two-part video (**Szenen** and **Interviews**) is available on the ***Wie geht's?*** Premium Website and in iLrn, with corresponding questions and activities in the *Arbeitsbuch* (SAM).

As an optional activity, you could use Google Earth to visit any major city in the German-speaking countries and look for universities and technical schools.

Literatur

Biographisches

Evelyne Weissenbach, born in Vienna in 1948, has been writing for more than twenty-five years about the topic of love. She is concerned not with the notion of romantic love, but rather with love as the most human of qualities. She applies her findings about love, described in her non-fiction book *Das Phänomen der Liebe*, not only to her works of fiction but also to her own life.

Weissenbach has written novels, poems, satirical meditations, and reflections on everyday topics. Her works reflect on love as a human quality and always offer options for self-help. She garnered special attention with her publication on the concentration camp Flossenbürg, where theologian and anti-Nazi conspirator Dietrich Bonhoeffer was executed (*Flossenbürg 2011: Ein Spürbericht*), and again for her book *In der Umarmung des Vergessens: Dementielles*. She is one of the first authors to write short stories and poems for people with dementia.

Vor dem Lesen

Allgemeine Fragen

1. Was verstehen Sie unter Sorgen?
2. Wie wichtig ist die Gesundheit für Sie? Wie sähe Ihr Leben ohne sie aus? (*What would your life look like without it?*)
3. Wie behandeln (*treat*) Sie kranke oder schwerbehinderte Menschen?
4. Mögen Sie alte Menschen? Warum (nicht)? Würden Sie mit ihnen arbeiten?

contentment

Von der Zufriedenheit°

talk

„Du kannst leicht reden"°, sagt sie. „Du bist gesund und gut verheiratet. Hast keine Sorgen. Da kann man gut alt sein."
Kann man das?
Ja, das kann man. Ich weiß es.
Aber wieso machen es dennoch° so wenig andere?

nonetheless

„Gesundheit ist das Wichtigste", sagt sie.
Aha, denke ich. Da scheiden sich schon unsere Geister.°
„Zufriedenheit", sage ich. "Zufriedenheit ist das Wichtigste."
Sie schüttelt° den Kopf. „Ohne Gesundheit ist alles nichts."

That's were we differ.

shakes

„Faschistoid"°, sage ich. „ist dieser Gedanke°." Und spüre°, wie die Jugend in mir hochdrängt°. Als Kämpfergeist° für all die Kranken. Deren° Leben dadurch pauschal abgewertet wird°.

Fascistic / idea / (I) feel
my youth swells / fighting spirit /
Whose / is globally devalued

„Und dein Mann. So einen findet man selten. Da hast du viel Glück gehabt", sagt sie.
Gehabt? Frage ich mich. Und bin glücklich.
„Zufriedenheit", sage ich. „Zufriedenheit macht glücklich."
Sie schüttelt den Kopf. „Aber wenn man keinen solchen Mann hat."

„Nicht jede war mit ihm glücklich", sage ich. Und spüre wie die Jugend in mir hochdrängt. Als Egoismus. Diesen Mann lieben zu wollen. So wie er ist.

„Hast keine Sorgen", wiederholt sie.
Nicht? Denke ich. Und an meinen Alltag° voller Ansprüche°. An mich.
„Zufriedenheit", sage ich. „Zufriedenheit schafft viele Sorgen aus der Welt."°
Sie schüttelt den Kopf. „Aber wenn man kein Geld hat."

everyday life / demands
gets rid of many problems

"Geld bringt Sorgen in die Welt", sage ich. Und spüre wie die Jugend in mir hochdrängt. Als ich mit sehr viel weniger genauso glücklich war, wie ich es heute wieder bin.

Demut breitet sich in mir aus.° Weil ich nach all den Jahren auf der Jagd nach° Gesundheit, Partnerschaft und Geld zu der Erfahrung fand°:
Zufriedenheit ist das Wichtigste.

Humility spreads through me. / hunt for / realized

Und [dass ich] glücklich alt werden kann.

Evelyne Weissenbach, *Erstveröffentlichung*

Nach dem Lesen

A. Allerlei Fragen

1. Die Autorin benutzt viele Punkte (*periods*) und wenig Kommas. Was passiert dadurch mit dem Text?
2. Wer unterhält sich hier mit wem?
3. Was ist das Thema von diesem Text?
4. Welchen Standpunkt (*point of view*) hat die Erzählerin? Welchen hat ihre Dialogpartnerin?
5. Warum denken viele heutzutage (*nowadays*), dass „alt" und „krank" identisch sind?
6. Kann man krank und zufrieden sein? Begründen (*Justify*) Sie Ihre Antwort!
7. Wie alt könnte die Erzählerin wohl sein? Glauben Sie, das sie auf ein glückliches Leben zurückschaut? Warum (nicht)?
8. Finden Sie, dass die Einstellung (*attitude*) der Erzählerin zu Krankheit und Alter anders ist als bei vielen Menschen?
9. Glauben Sie, dass eines Tages mehr Menschen ihre Meinung teilen werden *(will share her opinions)*?

B. Nacherzählung Erzählen Sie die Geschichte noch einmal mit Ihren eigenen Worten! Benutzen Sie dabei so viele Konjunktive wie möglich.

Man muss nicht immer einer Meinung sein **(agree).**

Rückschau

Kapitelwortschatz

Hauptwörter

der Abschluss, ¨-e	*degree; diploma*
die (Seminar)arbeit, -en	here: *term paper*
das Fach, ¨-er	*subject*
die Fachrichtung, -en	*field of study*
das Hauptfach, ¨-er	*major (field)*
der Hörsaal, Hörsäle	*lecture hall*
das Labor, -s	*lab(oratory)*
der Mitbewohner, -	*housemate, roommate* (male)
die Mitbewohnerin, -nen	*housemate, roommate* (female)
das Nebenfach, ¨-er	*minor (field)*
die Note, -n	*grade*
der Professor, -en	*professor* (male)
die Professorin, -nen	*professor* (female)
das Quartal, -e	*quarter*
das Referat, -e	*oral presentation*
das Semester, -	*semester*
das Seminar,-e	*seminar*
das Stipendium, Stipendien	*scholarship*
der Student, -en, -en	*(college) student* (male)
die Studentin, -nen	*(college) student* (female)
das Studium	*(course of) study*
das System, -e	*system*
die (Natur)wissenschaft, -en	*(natural) science*

Verben

das Studium ab·schließen	*to finish one's degree, graduate*
Angst haben (vor + *dat.*)	*to fear, be afraid (of)*
an·nehmen	*to suppose; to accept*
auf·hören	*to end; to stop doing something*
aus·füllen	*to fill out*
belegen	*to sign up for, take (a course)*
etwas dagegen haben	*to mind sth.* (lit. *to have sth. against sth.)*
lehren	*to teach*
eine Prüfung machen	*to take an exam*
(eine Prüfung) bestehen	*to pass (a test)*
(bei einer Prüfung) durch·fallen	*to flunk, fail (a test)*
ein Referat halten	*to give an oral presentation*
teilen	*to share; to divide*
teil·nehmen (an + *dat.*)	*to participate (in)*

Adjektive und Adverbien

ausländisch	*foreign*
bestimmt	*surely, for sure; certain(ly)*
schwierig	*difficult, with difficulty*

Verschiedenes

an deiner/seiner Stelle	*in your/his shoes; if I were you/he*
auf diese Weise	*(in) this way*
deshalb	*therefore*
Hast du etwas dagegen, wenn . . . ?	*Do you mind, if . . . ?*
jedenfalls	*in any case*
so dass	*so that*
wahrscheinlich	*probably*
Wieso?	*Why?, How come?*

Zum Schluss

1. **Wie wäre es, wenn . . . ?** Complete the following sentences, and write a couple of your own at the end. Use the subjunctive mood and pay attention to tense!

   a. Ich wünschte, . . .
   b. Wenn ich mehr Geld hätte, . . .
   c. Wenn ich mehr Zeit hätte, . . .
   d. Ich ginge . . .
   e. Gestern hätte/wäre ich . . .
   f. Am Wochenende hätte ich . . . sollen/können/wollen.
   g. Was hättest du . . . ?
   h. Wenn ich gewusst hätte, dass . . ., hätte/wäre . . .
   i. . . .
   j. . . .

2. **Stell dir vor!** Ask your partner or classmate about a hypothetical situation, a wish, or an unreal condition. Use the subjunctive mood. Trade questions and compare your answers!

   BEISPIEL: Was würdest du machen, wenn du Professor/Professorin wärest?

3. **Rat geben.** You've already practiced getting and giving advice. This time, pretend you are a historical or fictional figure. With your study group or classmates, ask for and give advice in character. Use the subjunctive mood and pay attention to tense! Can your classmates guess who you are?

4. **Was hätten Sie gemacht?** What would be different, if you had decided to study in Germany, Austria, or Switzerland this year? Write 5–7 sentences in the subjunctive mood, describing a hypothetical year abroad at a university. Use the verbs below to get started. Don't forget to use the correct tense!

(das Studium) abschließen	belegen	ein Referat halten
Angst haben vor	lehren	teilen
annehmen	eine Prüfung machen	teilnehmen (an)
aufhören	eine Prüfung bestehen	
ausfüllen	(bei einer Prüfung) durchfallen	

iLrn **Onlineaktivitäten** Visit iLrn for online activities related to this chapter. There you will find additional resources, such as a memory game (**Gedächtnisspiel**), a crossword puzzle (**Kreuzworträtsel**), audio flash cards (**Vokabelblitz**), a tutorial quiz (**Mini-Quiz**), and the active vocabulary (**Wortschatz**) for this chapter.

Kapitel 14

Berlin: Damals und heute

Lernziele In this chapter you will learn about:

Zum Thema

Life in Berlin

Fokus

German history since WWII, history of Berlin, multiculturalism

Struktur

- Relative clauses
- Indirect speech

Einblicke

Lesetext: Berlin, ein Tor zur Welt
Literatur: Gisela Reuter, *Café LebensArt*

Rückschau

Kapitelwortschatz
Zum Schluss

RESSOURCEN

iLrn | Video
Audio | SAM

Vor der Kuppel des Berliner Reichstagsgebäudes

Vorschau Chronicle of German History since World War II

1945 Unconditional surrender of Germany (May 9). The Allies assume supreme power, dividing Germany into four zones and Berlin (in the middle of the Russian zone) into four sectors. Potsdam Conference determines Germany's new borders.

1947 American Marshall Plan provides comprehensive aid for the rebuilding of Europe, including West Germany. Plan is rejected by the Soviet Union and its Eastern European satellites.

1948 Introduction of the D-Mark *(Deutsche Mark)* in the Western Zone leads to the Soviet blockade of West Berlin. Allies respond with Berlin Airlift (June 1948–May 1949).

1949 Founding of the Federal Republic of Germany in the West (May 23) and the German Democratic Republic (October 7) in the East.

1952 East Germany begins to seal the border with West Germany (May 27).

1953 Workers' uprising in East Berlin (June 17) is crushed by Soviet tanks.

1954 West Germany becomes a NATO member.

1955 East Germany joins the Warsaw Pact. West Germany becomes a sovereign nation; the occupation is ended.

1961 East Germany constructs the Berlin Wall and extensive fortifications along the border with West Germany to prevent East Germans from fleeing to the West.

1971 Four-Power Agreement on Berlin guarantees unhindered traffic between West Berlin and West Germany. De facto recognition of East Germany.

1973 Bundestag approves treaty of mutual recognition with East Germany. Brandt's opponents accuse him of forsaking the goal of unification.

1989 Opening of Hungarian border to Austria (September 10) brings streams of refugees from East to West Germany. Protest rallies take place all across East Germany. Berlin Wall opens on November 9.

1990 Economic union of both German states (July 2) is followed by German reunification (October 3). First all-German elections are held (December 2).

1994 Last Allied troops withdraw from Berlin.

1999 Reopening of the renovated Reichstag building.

2000 Relocation of the federal government to Berlin complete.

2002 The **Euro** replaces the *Deutsche Mark*.

2005 Introduction of a new immigration law to regulate the entry and integration of immigrants.

2005 Angela Merkel succeeds Gerhard Schröder as first woman chancellor of Germany.

2008 Germany hit by world economic crisis.

2010 German President Horst Koehler steps down over criticism regarding the German military.

2011 German government plans to phase out all nuclear power plants by 2022.

2012 German President Christian Wulff resigns following a financial scandal. He is succeeded by Joachim Gauck, best known as an anti-communist activist in East Germany and head of the Gauck-Behörde *(Office Investigating Stasi Files)* after the fall of the Berlin Wall.

Fragen: 1. Auf welchem Gebäude ist die Kuppel auf der linken Seite? 2. Man sieht darauf viel Glas und Spiegel, aber was noch? Beschreiben Sie das Bild! 3. Kennen Sie ein anderes Parlamentsgebäude, wo man von oben auf die Politiker hinunterschauen (look down) kann? 4. Wie sieht das Parlamentsgebäude in Ihrem Bundestaat (federal state) und Ihrem Land aus? 5. Haben Sie es schon einmal besichtigt.

Ronald Reagan: "Mr. Gorbachev, tear down this wall!"

Zum Thema

Gespräch

In Berlin ist immer etwas los.

(Heike zeigt Martin Berlin.)

HEIKE Und das hier ist die Gedächtniskirche mit ihren drei Gebäuden. Wir nennen sie den „Hohlen Zahn", den „Lippenstift" und die „Puderdose".
MARTIN Berliner haben doch für alles einen Spitznamen.
HEIKE Der alte Turm der Gedächtniskirche soll als Mahnmal so bleiben, wie er ist; die neue Gedächtniskirche mit dem neuen Turm ist aber modern—wie so manches in Berlin: jede Menge Altes und jede Menge Neues.
MARTIN Sag mal, wohnst du gern hier in Berlin?
HEIKE Na klar! Berlin ist unheimlich lebendig und hat so viel zu bieten, nicht nur historisch, sondern auch kulturell. Hier ist immer was los. Außerdem ist die Umgebung wunderschön.
MARTIN Ich hab' irgendwo gelesen, dass 24 Prozent der Stadtfläche Wälder und Seen sind, mit 800 Kilometern Fahrradwegen.
HEIKE Ist doch toll, oder?
MARTIN Wahnsinn! Sag mal, warst du dabei, als sie die Mauer durchbrochen haben?
HEIKE Und ob! Meine Eltern und ich, wir haben die ganze Nacht gewartet, obwohl es ganz schön kalt war. Als das erste Stück Mauer kippte, haben wir alle laut gesungen: „So ein Tag, so wunderschön wie heute, so ein Tag, der dürfte nie vergeh'n."
MARTIN Ja, das war schon einmalig. Und jetzt ist das alles schon wieder so lange her.
HEIKE Seitdem hat sich in Berlin enorm viel verändert. Die Spuren der Mauer sind fast verschwunden.
MARTIN Wer hätte das je gedacht!
HEIKE Hier gibt's heute wirklich alles, ein buntes Gemisch an Leuten und Sprachen.
MARTIN Bist du froh, dass Berlin wieder Hauptstadt ist?
HEIKE Nun, ich könnte mir's gar nicht mehr anders vorstellen.

Also check YouTube.

Warm-ups: 1. **Was könnte man an der Uni studieren?** Welche Fächer oder Fachbereiche gibt es? Sie haben eine Minute. 2. **Was möchten Sie einmal werden?** Warum? 3. **Wie geht's weiter?** Wenn das Wetter heute besser wäre, . . . Wenn ich könnte, . . . Wenn ich Geld bräuchte, . . . Wenn ich heute nicht hier sein müsste, . . .

A. Richtig oder falsch?

__f__ 1. Martin ist Berliner.
__r__ 2. Der „Hohle Zahn" ist ein Teil der Gedächtniskirche.
__r__ 3. Heike gefällt's unheimlich gut in Berlin.
__r__ 4. Heike war dabei, als sie die Mauer durchbrochen haben.
__f__ 5. Martin hat dort auch mitgefeiert.
__f__ 6. Das Ganze geschah an einem schönen, warmen Nachmittag.
__r__ 7. Manche haben laut gesungen.
__f__ 8. Seitdem hat sich in Berlin nicht viel verändert.
__r__ 9. Berlin ist heute international und dort gibt es ein buntes Gemisch an Menschen.

B. Jetzt sind Sie dran! Was würden Sie einem ausländischen Besucher (Ihrem Partner / Ihrer Partnerin) sagen, dem *(to whom)* Sie Ihre eigene Stadt zeigen? Machen Sie es so interessant wie möglich!

S1 Und das ist . . .
S2 . . .
S1 Ja, wir finden das auch . . .
S2 Wie ist das Leben . . . ?
S1 . . .
S2 Ist hier kulturell viel los?
S1 . . .
S2 Die Umgebung ist . . .
S1 Wie findest du / finden Sie . . . ?
S2 . . .

Wortschatz 1

Damals und heute *(then and today)*

der Frieden	*peace*
Krieg, -e	*war*
Spitzname, -ns, -n	*nickname*
Turm, ¨-e	*tower*
das Gebäude, -	*building*
Volk, ¨-er	*people* (as a whole or nation)
die Kneipe,-n	*pub*
Mauer, -n	*wall*
Umgebung	*surrounding(s)*

■ Note the difference between **Wand** and **Mauer:** A **Wand** is usually thinner and part of the inside of a house. A **Mauer** is much thicker—like an outside wall of a fortress—and usually freestanding.

Verschiedenes

einmalig	*unique; incredible*
historisch	*historical(ly)*
wunderschön	*very beautiful*
berichten	*to report*
erinnern (an + *acc.*)	*to remind (of)*
sich erinnern (an + *acc.*)	*to remember*
führen	*to lead*
(sich) verändern	*to change*
verschwinden, verschwand, ist verschwunden	*to disappear*
vorbei·führen (an + *dat.*)	*to pass by (s.th.); to guide (s.o.) along (s.th.)*
irgendwo	*somewhere*
jede Menge *(+ nom.)*	*all sorts of*
kaum	*hardly, barely, scarcely*
oder?	*isn't it?, don't you think so?*
Und ob!	*You bet!, You better believe it!*
seitdem	*since then*

■ **(sich) erinnern:** Ich werde dich **an** die Karten **erinnern.** *(I'll remind you of the tickets.)* BUT: Ich kann **mich an** nichts **erinnern.** *(I can't remember anything.)*

■ Like **irgendwo: irgendwann, irgendwie, irgendwer,** etc.

Zum Erkennen: hohl *(hollow);* der Lippenstift, -e *(lipstick);* die Puderdose, -n *(compact);* als Mahnmal *(as a memorial of admonishment);* lebendig *(lively);* die Fläche, -n *(area);* durchbrochen *(broken through);* (um·)kippen *(to tip over);* vergehen *(to pass);* das ist schon lange her *(that's a long time ago);* die Spur, -en *(trace, track);* je *(ever);* ein buntes Gemisch an *(+ dat.) (a diverse, colorful mixture of);* AUCH: das Relativpronomen, - *(relative pronoun);* der Relativsatz, ¨-e *(relative clause);* die indirekte Rede *(indirect speech)*

You may want to point out how easy it is to form adjectives from the names of cities (e.g., Berlin**er**, Brandenburg**er**, Potsdam**er**) and to mention that these adjectives don't have the usual endings: das alte Tor BUT das Brandenburger Tor.

Übungen zum Thema

Stadtplan von Berlin Sehen Sie auf den Stadtplan und beenden Sie dann die Sätze mit einem Wort aus der Liste!

Brandenburger	Juni	Spree
Dom	Kulturen der Welt	Stadtplan
Fernsehturm	Philharmonie	Unter den Linden
Gedächtniskirche	Reichstagsgebäude	Zoo(logische Garten)

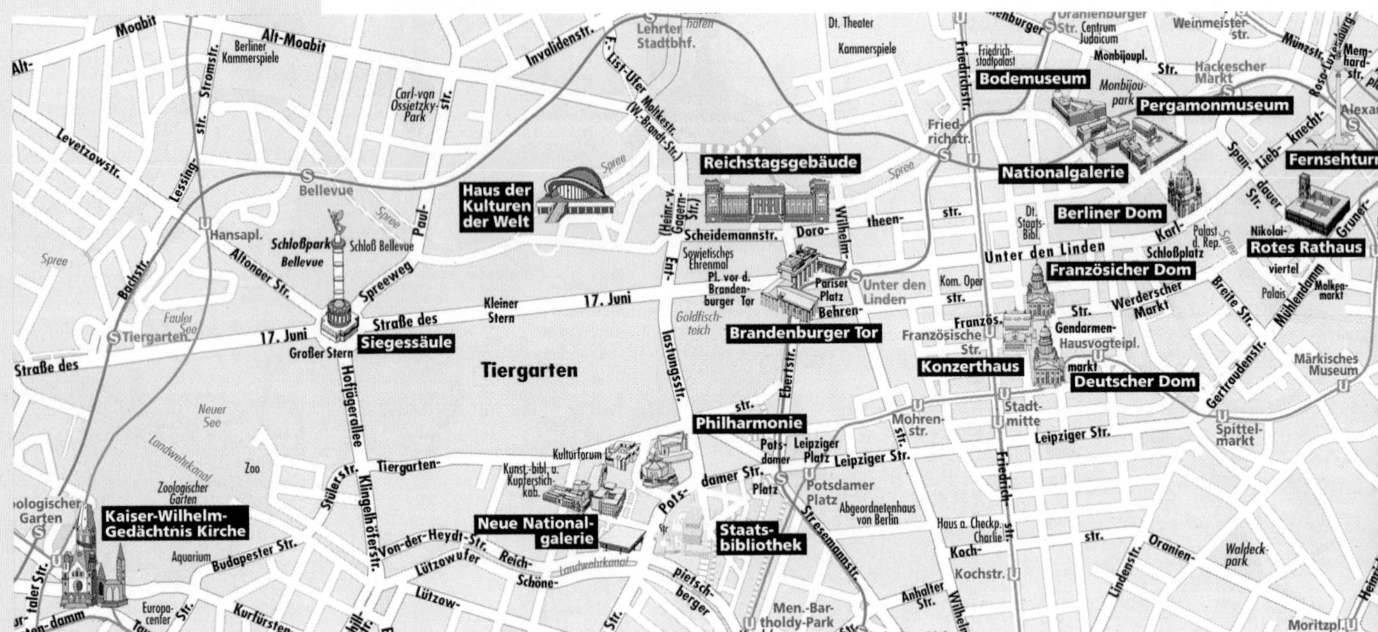

Dieser Stadtplan von Berlin zeigt Ihnen, wo die verschiedenen Straßen und wichtigsten Gebäude sind. Im Südwesten ist der Kurfürstendamm oder Ku'damm. Er führt zur Gedächtniskirche. In der Nähe ist auch der Zoo(logische Garten). Quer durch den großen Park läuft eine lange Straße. Sie erinnert an den 17. Juni 1953, als die Ostberliner und die Deutschen in Ostdeutschland gegen die Sowjetunion rebellierten. Sie führt vorbei am Großen Stern mit der Siegessäule *(Victory Column)* und weiter bis zum Brandenburger Tor. Östlich vom Brandenburger Tor heißt sie Unter den Linden. Südlich vom Brandenburger Tor ist der Potsdamer Platz und an der Potsdamer Straße sind die Staatsbibliothek und die Philharmonie. Ganz in der Nähe vom Brandenburger Tor ist auch das renovierte Reichstagsgebäude mit der neuen Glaskuppel, die *(which)* nachts den Himmel von Berlin erhellt *(brightens up)*. Nicht weit davon ist das Haus der Kulturen der Welt, die frühere Kongresshalle mit dem Spitznamen „Schwangere Auster" *(pregnant oyster)*. Unter den Linden führt ins alte Zentrum von Berlin und auf eine Insel mit dem Pergamonmuseum und dem Berliner Dom. Auf beiden Seiten der Insel fließt *(flows)* die Spree. Beim Dom bekommt die Straße wieder einen neuen Namen und geht weiter bis zum Alexanderplatz mit dem modernen Fernsehturm.

Fokus The Colorful Names of Berlin's Landmarks

Berliners are known for their self-assured manner, their humor, and their "big mouth" **(die Berliner Schnauze).** They always manage to find the right words at the right time, especially when it comes to choosing amusing names for places around their city. Besides the nicknames for parts of the Memorial Church **(Hohler Zahn, Lippenstift,** and **Puderdose),** places already mentioned in the dialogue, Berliners talk about the **Schwangere Auster** *(pregnant oyster)*, a cultural center; the **Hungerkralle** *(hunger claw)*, the monument to the Berlin Airlift; the **Telespargel** *(television-asparagus)*, the television tower; the **Mauerspechte** *(wall woodpeckers)*, the souvenir hunters who chipped away at the Berlin Wall after it was opened; and for the new chancellor's office, the **Waschmaschine** *(washing machine)*, a reference to its architectural style.

Die Gedächtniskirche bei Nacht

Aussprache: qu, pf, ps

For further review, see the Summary of Pronunciation in the front of this book. Study Part III, subsections 19, 21–22

Laute

1. [kv] **Qu**atsch, **Qu**alität, **Qu**antität, **Qu**artal, be**qu**em
2. [pf] **Pf**arrer, **Pf**effer, **Pf**lanze, **Pf**und, A**pf**el, Ko**pf**, em**pf**ehlen
3. [ps] **Ps**ychologe, **Ps**ychologie, **ps**ychologisch, **Ps**alm, **Ps**eudonym, Ka**ps**el

Hörverständnis

Mit dem Fahrrad durch Berlin Hören Sie zu, wie man Berlin auch kennenlernen kann! Was fehlt in den folgenden Aussagen?

Zum Erkennen: der Doppeldeckerbus, -se *(double-decker bus)*; in Ruhe *(quietly, without being rushed)*; der Stadtbummel *(stroll through the city)*; völlig *(totally)*; radeln (ist) *(to bike)*; der Zauber *(magic)*

1. Der Sprecher erzählt von Möglichkeiten, Berlin __kennenzulernen__. 2. Man könnte zum Beispiel eine __(Stadt)Rundfahrt__ mit dem Tourbus machen. 3. Von oben im Doppeldeckerbus hätte man einen guten __Blick__. 4. Eine ganz andere Perspektive gäbe eine kleine Fahrt mit dem __Boot__. 5. Dem Erzähler würde aber der Stadtbummel __zu Fuß__ und mit der U-Bahn besser gefallen. 6. Was ihm das letzte Mal besonders gut gefallen hat, war eine Stadttour mit dem __Fahrrad__. 7. Die Gruppe wäre ungefähr __vier__ Stunden unterwegs *(on the go)* gewesen. 8. Das nächste Mal hätte er Lust, an einer Nightseeing-Tour teilzunehmen, denn nachts hätte Berlin eine ganz andere __Atmosphäre__.

Struktur

Point out that syntax of relative clauses in German is basically the same as in formal English except for verb position.

If students ask about it, you can tell them that German does not have different relative pronouns to distinguish between restrictive and nonrestrictive relative clauses as English does, for example: "The car that belongs to me is the blue one." (restrictive, *that*) versus "The car, which belongs to me, gets really good gas mileage." (nonrestrictive, *which*). In both instances the German would be: **Das Auto, das mir gehört . . . .**

To be more precise, relative pronouns in English are omitted only if they are objects or objects of prepositions.

14.1 Relative clauses

RELATIVE CLAUSES supply additional information about a noun in a sentence.

There's the professor **who** *teaches the course.*

He taught the course **(that)** *I enjoyed so much.*

He teaches a subject **in which** *I'm very interested* (. . . **that** *I'm very interested* **in**).

He's the professor **whose** *course I took last semester.*

English relative clauses may be introduced by the RELATIVE PRONOUNS *who, whom, whose, which,* or *that*. The noun to which the relative pronoun "relates" is called the ANTECEDENT. The choice of the relative pronoun depends on the antecedent (is it a person or a thing?) and on its function in the relative clause. The relative pronoun may be the subject *(who, which, that)*, an object, or an object of a preposition *(whom, which, that)*, or it may indicate possession *(whose)*. German relative clauses work essentially the same way. However, whereas in English the relative pronouns are frequently omitted (especially in conversation), in German they must always be used.

Ist das der Roman, **den** ihr gelesen habt? *Is that the novel you read?*

1. Forms and use

The German relative pronouns have the same forms as the definite article, except for the genitive forms and the dative plural.

	MASC.	NEUT.	FEM.	PL.
nom.	der	das	die	die
acc.	den	das	die	die
dat.	dem	dem	der	**denen**
gen.	**dessen**	**dessen**	**deren**	**deren**

The form of the relative pronoun is determined by two factors:

- Its ANTECEDENT: is the antecedent masculine, neuter, feminine, or in the plural?

  Das ist **der Fluss, der** auf der Karte ist.
  Das ist **das Gebäude, das** auf der Karte ist.
  Das ist **die Kirche, die** auf der Karte ist.
  Das sind **die Plätze, die** auf der Karte sind.

- Its FUNCTION in the relative clause: is the relative pronoun the subject, an accusative or dative object, an object of a preposition, or does it indicate possession?

  Ist das der Mann, **der** in Berlin wohnt? = SUBJECT
  Ist das der Mann, **den** du meinst? = ACCUSATIVE OBJECT
  Ist das der Mann, **dem** du geschrieben hast? = DATIVE OBJECT
  Ist das der Mann, **mit dem** du gesprochen hast? = OBJECT OF A PREPOSITION
  Ist das der Mann, **dessen** Tochter hier studiert? = GENITIVE

The following examples indicate the antecedent and state the function of the relative pronoun (RP) in each relative clause.

. . . ANTECEDENT, (preposition +) RP ______________ V1.

Das ist der Professor. Er lehrt an meiner Universität.
Das ist **der Professor, der** an meiner Universität lehrt.
*That's **the professor who** teaches at my university.*

ANTECEDENT: der Professor = sg. / masc.
PRONOUN FUNCTION: subject → nom.

Wie heißt der Kurs? Du findest ihn so interessant.
Wie heißt **der Kurs, den** du so interessant findest?
*What's the name of **the course (that)** you find so interesting?*

ANTECEDENT: der Kurs = sg. / masc.
PRONOUN FUNCTION: object of **finden** → acc.

Da ist der Student. Ich habe ihm mein Buch gegeben.
Da ist **der Student, dem** ich mein Buch gegeben habe.
*There's **the student to whom** I gave my book (. . . I gave my book to).*

ANTECEDENT: der Student = sg. / masc.
PRONOUN FUNCTION: object of **geben** → dat.

Kennst du die Professorin? Erik hat ihr Seminar belegt.
Kennst du **die Professorin, deren Seminar** Erik belegt hat?
*Do you know **the professor whose seminar** Erik took?*

ANTECEDENT: die Professorin = sg. / fem.
PRONOUN FUNCTION: related possessively to **Seminar** → gen.

Das Buch ist von einem Autor. Ich interessiere mich sehr für ihn.
Das Buch ist von **einem Autor, für den** ich mich sehr interessiere.
*The book is by **an author in whom** I'm very interested.*

ANTECEDENT: der Autor = sg. / masc.
PRONOUN FUNCTION: object of **für** → acc.

Die Autoren sind aus Leipzig. Der Professor hat von ihnen gesprochen.
Die Autoren, von denen der Professor gesprochen hat, sind aus Leipzig.
***The authors of whom** the professor spoke are from Leipzig.*

ANTECEDENT: die Autoren = pl.
PRONOUN FUNCTION: object of **von** → dat.

CAUTION: Don't use the interrogative pronoun in place of the relative pronoun!

Wer hat das Seminar gegeben?
Das ist der Professor, **der** das Seminar gegeben hat.

***Who** gave the seminar?*
*That's the professor **who** gave the seminar.*

2. Word order

   a. Relative pronouns can be the objects of prepositions. If that is the case, the preposition will always precede the relative pronoun.

   Das Buch ist von einem Autor, **für den** ich mich sehr interessiere.

   The book is by an author ***in whom*** *I'm very interested.*

   b. The word order in the RELATIVE CLAUSE is like that of all subordinate clauses: the inflected part of the verb (V1) comes last. Always separate the relative clause from the main clause by a comma. If the relative clause is imbedded in the main clause, then place a comma before and after the relative clause.

. . . , RP __________ V1, . . .

   Der Professor, **der** den Prosakurs **lehrt,** ist sehr nett.

   RP V1

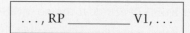

   The professor ***who teaches*** *the prose course is very nice.*

   c. Relative clauses immediately follow the antecedent unless the antecedent is followed by a prepositional phrase that modifies it, by a genitive, or by a verb complement (V2).

   Das Buch von Dürrenmatt, **das wir gelesen haben,** ist prima.

   Das andere Buch des Autors, **das wir auch lesen sollen,** ist teuer.

   Ich kann **das Buch** nicht bekommen, **das wir lesen sollen.**

Relative clauses require regular practice. Give students two simple German sentences to connect with a relative pronoun, or a few easy English sentences or phrases to express in German: 1. **Das ist das Restaurant:** Es ist so teuer. Wir haben in dem Restaurant gegessen. Seine Weine sind bekannt. Wir möchten in dem Restaurant meinen Geburtstag feiern. 2. **Ich habe das Buch gekauft:** Ich habe viel von dem Buch gehört. Du hast über das Buch gesprochen. Erika hat es mir empfohlen. Sein Titel ist *Krieg und Frieden*. Die Geschichte spielt in Russland.

Übungen

A. Analysieren Sie die Sätze! Finden Sie das vorhergehende Wort *(antecedent)*, beschreiben Sie es und nennen Sie die Funktion des Relativpronomens im Relativsatz!

A: Do this exercise in class. A close analysis of each sentence will help students understand relative clauses.

BEISPIEL Renate Berger ist eine Frau, die für gleiche Arbeit gleiches Einkommen möchte.

ANTECEDENT: eine Frau = sg. / fem.

PRONOUN FUNCTION: subject → nom.

1. Der Mann, der neben ihr arbeitet, verdient mehr.
2. Es gibt leider noch viele Frauen, deren Kollegen ein höheres Gehalt *(salary)* bekommen.
3. Und es gibt Frauen, denen schlecht bezahlte Arbeit lieber ist als keine Arbeit.
4. Was denken die Männer, deren Frauen weniger Geld bekommen als ihre Kollegen?
5. Der Mann, mit dem Renate Berger verheiratet ist, findet das nicht so schlecht.
6. Frau M. in Christine Nöstlingers Geschichte war eine Frau, die sich darüber geärgert hat, aber sich nicht beklagte.
7. Den besseren Job, von dem sie träumte, bekamen aber immer andere.
8. Der Chef, den sie hatte, war ein Mensch mit großen Vorurteilen gegen Frauen.
9. Chefs, die so denken wie Frau M.s Chef, gibt es überall.
10. Das ist ein Problem, das andere Firmen auch haben.
11. Die Berufe, in denen fast nur Frauen arbeiten, sind am schlechtesten bezahlt.
12. Wir leben in einer Welt, in der Gleichberechtigung noch nicht überall Realität ist.

A: 1. der Mann = sg. / masc.; subject → nom. 2. viele Frauen = pl.; related poss. to **Kollegen** → gen. 3. Frauen = pl.; indirect object → dat. 4. die Männer = pl.; related poss. to **Frauen** → gen. 5. der Mann = sg. / masc.; object of **mit** → dat. 6. eine Frau = sg. / fem.; subject → nom. 7. Job = sg. / masc.; object of preposition → dat. 8. der Chef = sg. / masc.; direct object → acc. 9. Chefs = pl.; subject → nom. 10. ein Problem = sg. / neut.; direct object → acc. 11. die Berufe = pl.; object of preposition → dat. 12. einer Welt = sg. / fem.; object of preposition → dat.

B. Stadtrundfahrt Während Sepp Bilder von seinem Besuch in Berlin zeigt, stellen seine österreichischen Freunde Fragen zu den Bildern. Antworten Sie wie im Beispiel und benutzen Sie dabei Relativpronomen!

BEISPIEL Ist das der Alexanderplatz?
Ja, das ist der Alexanderplatz, der so bekannt ist.

1. Ist das der Fernsehturm? 2. Ist das das Rote Rathaus? 3. Ist das der Berliner Dom? 4. Ist das das Hotel Adlon? 5. Sind das die Museen?

BEISPIEL Ist das das Pergamonmuseum?
Ja, das ist das Pergamonmuseum, das du da siehst.

6. Ist das die Konzerthalle? 7. Ist das das Nikolaiviertel? 8. Ist das der Gendarmenmarkt? 9. Ist das die Spree? 10. Ist das der Berliner Antikmarkt?

BEISPIEL Ist das die Hochschule für Musik?
Ja, das ist die Hochschule für Musik, zu der wir jetzt kommen.

11. Ist das der Zoo? 12. Ist das die Siegessäule? 13. Ist das die alte Kongresshalle? 14. Ist das das Reichstagsgebäude? 15. Sind das die Universitätsgebäude?

BEISPIEL Wo ist der Student? Sein Vater lehrt an der Universität.
Da ist der Student, dessen Vater an der Universität lehrt.

16. Wo ist die Studentin? Ihre Eltern wohnten früher *(formerly)* in Berlin. 17. Wo ist das Mädchen? Ihr Bruder war so lustig. 18. Wo ist der Herr? Seine Frau sprach so gut Englisch. 19. Wo sind die alten Leute? Ihr Sohn lebt jetzt in den USA.

B: **Nominative:** 1. der Fernsehturm, der 2. das Rote Rathaus, das 3. der Berliner Dom, der 4. das Hotel Adlon, das 5. die Museen, die

Accusative: 6. die Konzerthalle, die 7. das Nikolaiviertel, das 8. der Gendarmenmarkt, den 9. die Spree, die 10. der Berliner Antikmarkt, den

Dative: 11. der Zoo, zu dem 12. die Siegessäule, zu der 13. die alte Kongresshalle, zu der 14. das Reichstagsgebäude, zu dem 15. die Universitätsgebäude, zu denen

Genitive: 16. die Studentin, deren Eltern 17. das Mädchen, dessen Bruder 18. der Herr, dessen Frau 19. die alten Leute, deren Sohn

C. Kein Wiedersehen Ergänzen Sie die fehlenden Relativpronomen!

1. Der junge Mann, ___der___ da steht, heißt David.
2. Das Mädchen, mit ___dem___ er spricht, heißt Tina.
3. Der Film, über ___den___ sie sprechen, spielte in Berlin.
4. Die Geschichte spielte kurz vor dem Bau der Mauer, ___die___ Berlin von 1961 bis 1989 geteilt hat.
5. In den fünfziger Jahren sind viele mit der S-Bahn, ___die___ ja quer durch *(right through)* die Stadt fuhr, geflohen.
6. Ein junger Mann, ___dessen___ Freundin nicht wusste, ob sie in den Westen wollte, fuhr mit der S-Bahn nach West-Berlin und blieb dort.
7. Die Freundin, ___deren___ Arbeit in Halle war, ging in den Osten zurück.
8. Das war kurz vor dem Tag, an ___dem___ man die Mauer baute.
9. Es war ein Ereignis *(m., event)*, ___das___ ihr Leben total verändern sollte.
10. Den Freund, ___den___ sie in West-Berlin zurückgelassen hatte, würde sie nie wiedersehen.
11. So wie ihnen ging es vielen Menschen, durch ___deren___ Privatleben plötzlich diese schreckliche Mauer ging.
12. Heute ist von der Mauer, ___die___ so viel Leid *(suffering)* brachte, fast nichts mehr zu sehen.

C: Assign this as homework or give students a few minutes in class to complete it. Each student should work with it individually.

By the way, the film discussed is *Der geteilte Himmel* by Konrad Wolf, based on the novel by Christa Wolf.

D. Wer oder was ist das genau? Lesen Sie mit den anderen durch die folgenden Kategorien und nennen Sie dann eigene Beispiele dazu mit Relativpronomen!

BEISPIEL ein Restaurant *Das Taj Mahal ist ein Restaurant, das mir gefällt.*
ein Film *Der Film, über den wir sprachen, heißt* Good Bye Lenin!

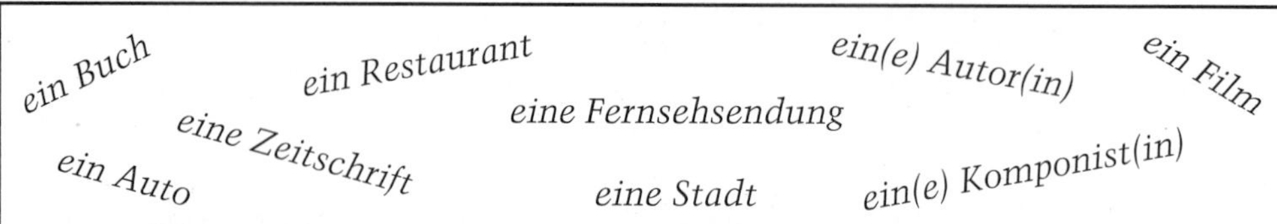

ein Buch
ein Restaurant
ein(e) Autor(in)
ein Film
eine Fernsehsendung
eine Zeitschrift
ein Auto
eine Stadt
ein(e) Komponist(in)

E. Verbinden Sie die Sätze! Verbinden Sie sie mit Hilfe von Relativpronomen! Wenn nötig, übersetzen Sie *(translate)* den Satz zuerst!

E: 1. Die Gedächtniskirche, von der . . . gehört habt, gefällt mir. 2. Der alte Turm, den . . . nennen, soll kaputt bleiben. 3. Der Ku'damm, an dem es . . . , beginnt bei der Gedächtniskirche. 4. Mittags gingen wir ins Nikolaiviertel, das . . . hat. 5. Da gibt's auch kleine Restaurants, in denen man . . . sitzen kann. 6. Mein Freund, dessen Familie . . . wohnt, hat mir wirklich alles gezeigt. 7. Seine Schwester, mit der ich . . . gegangen bin, war auch sehr nett. 8. Dieser Klub, dessen Atmosphäre . . . war, war in der Nähe der neuen Synagoge. 9. Die Synagoge, in der Albert Einstein . . . gegeben hatte, ist im maurischen Stil gebaut.

BEISPIEL Der Ku'damm ist eine bekannte Berliner Straße. Jeder kennt sie.
(The Ku'damm is a famous Berlin street [that] everyone knows.)
Der Ku'damm ist eine bekannte Berliner Straße, die jeder kennt.

1. Die Gedächtniskirche gefällt mir. Ihr habt schon von der Gedächtniskirche gehört.
2. Der alte Turm soll kaputt bleiben. Die Berliner nennen ihn den „Hohlen Zahn".
3. Der Ku'damm beginnt bei der Gedächtniskirche. Am Ku'damm gibt es viele schöne Geschäfte.
4. Mittags gingen wir ins Nikolaiviertel. Es hat schöne alte Gebäude und die älteste Kirche Berlins.
5. Da gibt's auch kleine Restaurants. Man kann in den Restaurants gemütlich sitzen.
6. Mein Freund hat mir wirklich alles gezeigt. Seine Familie wohnt in Berlin-Mitte.
7. Seine Schwester war auch sehr nett. Ich bin mit ihr am Abend in einen Klub in den Hackeschen Höfen gegangen.
8. Dieser Klub war in der Nähe der neuen Synagoge. Die Atmosphäre des Klubs war einmalig.
9. Die Synagoge ist im maurischen Stil *(Moorish style)* gebaut. In dieser Synagoge hatte Albert Einstein am 29.1.1930 ein Violinkonzert gegeben.

In Berlins Hackeschen Höfen kann man sich gemütlich mit Freunden treffen.

F. Woran denke ich? Erklären Sie Ihrem Partner / Ihrer Partnerin verschiedene Wörter mit Relativsätzen, die er/sie dann versucht zu erkennen. Wechseln Sie sich ab!

BEISPIEL S1 Ich denke an ein Tier mit zwei Beinen, das klein ist und fliegen kann.
S2 Ist es ein Vogel? . . .
S2 Ich denke an jemanden in der Klasse, der immer zu spät kommt.
S1 Ist es . . . ?

Fokus A Multicultural Melting Pot

Berlin is one of Europe's most cosmopolitan urban centers, with more than 400,000 foreign nationals from more than 180 countries living within the city limits. In addition to the influx of Jews from the former Soviet Union since the fall of the Berlin Wall in 1989, Germany's liberal asylum laws and the need for manual laborers have drawn people to Berlin from around the globe. Despite signs of cultural tensions in some neighborhoods, the presence and the continuing influx of foreigners add to the cosmopolitan flair of Berlin. The traditionally homogeneous German society is thus changing rapidly in the capital of a reunited Germany. The annual **Karneval der Kulturen,** a three-day music and dance festival with a street parade organized by the various cultural and ethnic associations of Berlin, is testament to the active multicultural scene in the city.

14.2 Indirect speech

If you feel that indirect speech is not necessary in the first year, or that your students can't handle it at this time, omit this section. Skip Exercises G–J and L–M in the *Zusammenfassung*, as well as Exercises B and D in *Nach dem Lesen*.

When reporting what someone else has said, you can use DIRECT SPEECH with quotation marks, or INDIRECT SPEECH without quotation marks.

Heike said, "Berlin has a lot to offer."
Heike said (that) Berlin has a lot to offer.

An utterance in indirect speech may well require different personal pronouns and possessive adjectives from the ones used in the direct speech sentence, depending on who reports the conversation.

- If Heike says to Martin "I'll bring my map," and she reports the conversation to someone else later, she will say: *I told him I would bring my map.*
- If Martin reported the conversation, he would say: *She told me she would bring her map.*
- If a third person reported the same conversation, he or she would say: *She told him she would bring her map.*

In spoken German such indirect speech is generally in the INDICATIVE when the opening verb is in the PRESENT **(Sie sagt, . . .).** However, when the opening verb is in the PAST **(Sie sagte, . . .),** the SUBJUNCTIVE usually follows. This section focuses on the latter.

Direct speech:	„Ich **bringe** meinen Stadtplan mit."
Indirect speech:	
Indicative	Sie sagt, sie **bringt** ihren Stadtplan mit.
Subjunctive	Sie sagte, sie **würde** ihren Stadtplan **mitbringen.**

NOTE: In German, opening quotation marks are placed at the bottom of the line, especially in handwriting. Many publishers use an alternative form of quotation mark: »**Ich bringe meinen Stadtplan mit.**« With the increased use of the Internet, English style quotation marks are becoming more common.

1. Statements

   The tense of the indirect statement is determined by the tense of the direct statement.

   a. Direct statements in the present or the future are reported indirectly in the present-time subjunctive or the **würde**-form.

present tense / future tense	present-time subjunctive or **würde**-form

   „Ich komme später." — Sie sagte, sie käme später.
   „Ich werde später kommen." — Sie sagte, sie würde später kommen.

   b. Direct statements in *any past tense* are reported indirectly in the past-time subjunctive.

simple past tense / present perfect tense / past perfect tense	past-time subjunctive

   „Ich hatte keine Zeit."
   „Ich habe keine Zeit gehabt."
   „Ich hatte keine Zeit gehabt."
   } Sie sagte, sie hätte keine Zeit gehabt.

   c. The conjunction **dass** may or may not be used. If it is not used, the clause retains the original word order. If **dass** is used, the inflected part of the verb comes last.

   Sie sagte, sie käme morgen. — Sie sagte, sie hätte andere Pläne gehabt.
   Sie sagte, **dass** sie morgen **käme.** — Sie sagte, **dass** sie andere Pläne gehabt **hätte.**

2. Questions

   The tense of the indirect question is also determined by the tense of the direct question. Indirect YES/NO QUESTIONS are introduced by **ob,** and indirect INFORMATION QUESTIONS by a question word.

   Er fragte: „Hast du jetzt Zeit?" — *He asked, "Do you have time now?"*
   Er fragte, **ob** sie jetzt Zeit hätte. — *He asked whether she had time now.*

   Er fragte: „Wo warst du?" — *He asked, "Where were you?"*
   Er fragte, **wo** sie gewesen wäre. — *He asked where she had been.*

3. Imperatives

   Direct requests in the imperative are expressed indirectly with the auxiliary **sollen.**

   Sie sagte: „Frag nicht so viel!" — *She said, "Don't ask so many questions."*

   Sie sagte, er **sollte** nicht so viel **fragen.** — *She said he shouldn't ask so many questions.*

Fokus Berlin Today

Since becoming the capital of the reunified Germany, Berlin has seen tremendous changes, especially as a new government and business district was constructed where the wall once stood. The historic Reichstag building has been transformed by the British architect Sir Norman Foster into a modern seat of parliament, with a glass dome atop the roof to represent a link between past and present. Numerous embassies and organizations are located in Berlin, and several prominent German and foreign firms have chosen Berlin as their headquarters.

Berlin now boasts some thirty museums, two important symphony orchestras, three opera houses, numerous theaters and cabarets, and three major universities. Young people from all over Europe have come to appreciate Berlin's groundbreaking film, theater, art, and music scenes. Tourism has experienced a major boom since reunification.

More than any other city in Europe, Berlin embodies both the confrontational division of the Cold War and the subsequent coming together of the continent's nations. Germany's unique modern history enhances its role as a mediator between East and West. The eastward expansion of the EU will profit Berlin politically as well as economically, making it the new center of Europe

Im Pergamonmuseum

Übungen

G. Wie war das noch mal? Bestätigen Sie *(Confirm)*, dass die Leute in Phillips Familie das wirklich gesagt haben! Beginnen Sie die indirekte Rede mit **dass!**

BEISPIEL Hat Phillip Sanders gesagt, er hätte vorher in Bonn gewohnt?
Ja, er hat gesagt, dass er vorher in Bonn gewohnt hätte.

1. Hat Phillip gesagt, seine Familie wäre nicht gern nach Berlin gezogen *(moved)*?
2. Hat seine Mutter gesagt, sie wäre lieber in Bonn geblieben?
3. Hat seine Mutter gesagt, sie hätten dort ein wunderschönes Haus mit Garten gehabt?
4. Hat sein Bruder gesagt, er wollte nicht die Schule wechseln?
5. Hat sein Bruder gesagt, er würde lieber in Bonn sein Abitur machen?
6. Hat Phillip gesagt, er würde Berlin eine Chance geben?

G: 1. Ja, er hat gesagt, dass seine Familie nicht gern nach Berlin gezogen wäre. 2. Ja, sie hat gesagt, dass sie lieber in Bonn geblieben wäre. 3. Ja, sie hat gesagt, dass sie dort ein wunderschönes Haus mit Garten gehabt hätten. 4. Ja, er hat gesagt, dass er nicht die Schule wechseln wollte. 5. Ja, er hat gesagt, dass er lieber in Bonn sein Abitur machen würde. 6. Ja, er hat gesagt, dass er Berlin eine Chance geben würde.

H. Verschiedene Leute im Gespräch Wiederholen Sie auf Englisch die Beispiele von indirekter Rede!

1. **Elke erzählt von Trudi.**

   Trudi sagte, . . .
   a. sie wollte Zahnärztin werden.
   b. gute Zahnärzte würde man immer brauchen.
   c. als Zahnarzt würde man gut verdienen.
   d. man müsste natürlich lange studieren, aber darauf würde sie sich schon freuen.

H: As additional practice, have students repeat parts 1–2 with the conjunction **dass.** You could also have them convert these sentences into direct speech.

H.1 = *present-time subjunctive:* Trudi said (that) . . . a. she wanted to become a dentist. b. they would always need good dentists. c. as a dentist you would earn well. d. you would, of course, have to study for a long time, but she'd look forward to that. (Note that translations may vary.)

H.2 = *past-time subjunctive:* Carolyn said (that) . . . a. last year she studied in Germany. b. she really liked it a lot. c. during the summer vacation she went / drove to Switzerland. d. she came back only three weeks ago.

H.3: He asked her . . . a. how long she had been (living) in Berlin. b. where the Brandenburg Gate was. c. how one would get there.

She told him . . . d. he should / ought to visit the museums. e. he should go to a concert. f. he should visit the film festivals.

H.4: a. Leonie told (us) that she was in / had been to Berlin last summer. b. She did an internship at a hospital there. c. She met many nice people. d. When Leonie said that she'd probably go back to Berlin this summer, her sister Simone wanted to know whether she could come along.

I: 1. Claire sagte, in den S-Bahnbögen gäbe es etwa 40 Antikhändler (würde . . . geben). Da fände man vieles (würde . . . finden). Man müsste nur Zeit haben. Sie hätte sich einen Ring gekauft. 2. Tom sagte, er interessierte sich (würde . . . interessieren) für alte Bücher und Bilder von Berlin. Da könnte man wirklich gut herumschnuppern. Das hätte ihm Spaß gemacht. Er hätte aber nichts gekauft.

2. **Bernd erzählt von Carolyn.**

   Carolyn sagte, . . .
   a. sie hätte letztes Jahr in Deutschland studiert.
   b. es hätte ihr unheimlich gut gefallen.
   c. während der Semesterferien wäre sie in die Schweiz gefahren.
   d. sie wäre erst vor drei Wochen zurückgekommen.

3. **Martin und Heike**

   Er hat sie gefragt, . . .
   a. wie lange sie schon in Berlin wäre.
   b. wo das Brandenburger Tor wäre.
   c. wie man dorthin käme.

   Sie hat ihm gesagt, . . .
   d. er sollte sich die Museen ansehen.
   e. er sollte in ein Konzert gehen.
   f. er sollte die Filmfestspiele besuchen.

4. **Leonie und Simone**

   a. Leonie erzählte, dass sie letzten Sommer in Berlin gewesen wäre.
   b. Sie hätte dort ein Praktikum an einem Krankenhaus gemacht.
   c. Sie hätte viele nette Leute kennengelernt.
   d. Als Leonie sagte, dass sie diesen Sommer wahrscheinlich wieder nach Berlin gehen würde, wollte ihre Schwester Simone wissen, ob sie mitkommen könnte.

I. Der Berliner Antik- und Flohmarkt Wiederholen Sie in indirekter Rede, was Ihnen Freunde darüber erzählt haben!

BEISPIEL Erika: „Der Antikmarkt liegt mitten in Berlins historischem Zentrum."
Erika sagte, dass der Antikmarkt mitten in Berlins historischem Zentrum läge.

1. Claire: „In den 13 ausgebauten S-Bahnbögen *(. . . arches)* am Bahnhof Friedrichstraße gibt es etwa 40 Antikhändler *(merchants)*. Da findet man vieles. Man muss nur Zeit haben. Ich habe mir einen Ring gekauft."

2. Tom: „Ich interessiere mich für alte Bücher und Bilder von Berlin. Da kann man wirklich gut herumschnuppern *(snoop around)*. Das hat mir Spaß gemacht. Ich habe aber nichts gekauft."

J. Was hat er/sie gesagt? Stellen Sie Ihrem Nachbarn / Ihrer Nachbarin ein paar persönliche Fragen. Berichten Sie dann den anderen in indirekter Rede!

BEISPIEL *Er/Sie hat mir erzählt, er/sie wäre aus Chicago, er/sie hätte zwei Brüder . . .*

Fokus Berlin's Past

Today it is nearly impossible to pass through Berlin without uncovering reminders of the city's long history. Founded more than 750 years ago, Berlin became the seat of the Prussian kings in 1701. The Brandenburg Gate, constructed at the end of the 18th century, was intended as a "Gate of Peace." Instead, it would witness two centuries of war and revolution.

Unter den Linden, the city's most prominent boulevard, led up to the famous gate. Here Napoleon's victorious army paraded through Berlin; revolutionaries erected barricades in 1848 and 1918; and the Nazis staged their book burnings in 1933. After World War II, the devastated capital was divided into Allied and Soviet sectors. At first it was relatively easy to cross from one zone to the other, but Berlin soon became the first battlefield in the Cold War. The Soviet blockade of the Allied zones in 1948–1949 triggered the Berlin Airlift, a humanitarian effort that won over the hearts of West Berliners. Later, as increasing numbers of East Berliners fled to the West, the East German regime constructed the Berlin Wall in 1961. The Wall, which cut through the heart of the city, was reinforced with minefields, self-firing machine guns, and steel fences to prevent East Germans from escaping. The Brandenburg Gate stood right next to the Wall, just inside East Berlin.

For almost 30 years, West Berlin remained an island of capitalism in Communist East Germany—until Mikhail Gorbachev's spirit of reform in the Soviet Union swept across Eastern Europe. Again, thousands of East Germans tried to flee to West Germany, and in the confusion that ensued, a Communist Party official mistakenly announced an easing of travel restrictions. Almost by accident, the Wall was opened on November 9, 1989. Reunification followed almost a year later on October 3, 1990, and the Brandenburg Gate once more became the focal point of the city.

Bild der Mauer auf der Mauer

Zusammenfassung

K. Ein toller Tag! Ergänzen Sie das fehlende Relativpronomen!

Christa Grauer ist eine Frau, ___die___ mit einem Computer die Anzeigetafeln *(scoreboards)* in einem Kölner Fußballstadion bedient *(operates)*. Sie erzählt von einem Tag, ___den___ sie nie vergessen wird. Eine Woche nach dem 9. November 1989, einem Tag, ___der___ Geschichte gemacht hat, spielte die deutsche Fußballnationalmannschaft *(. . . team)* gegen Wales. Vor dem Spiel, zu ___dem___ 60 000 Menschen gekommen waren, schrieb Christa wie immer die dritte Strophe *(stanza)* des Deutschlandliedes auf die Anzeigetafeln. Das hatte sie schon Jahre lang getan. Aber es gab wenige Spiele, bei ___denen___ die Leute wirklich mitsangen. Aber diesmal sangen Tausende mit, denn die Strophe, ___deren___ Text ihnen bisher nicht viel bedeutet hatte, bewegte sie *(moved them)* plötzlich sehr.

Einigkeit und Recht und Freiheit für das deutsche Vaterland!
Danach lasst uns alle streben, brüderlich mit Herz und Hand!
Einigkeit und Recht und Freiheit sind des Glückes Unterpfand;
Blüh' im Glanze dieses Glückes, blühe, deutsches Vaterland!
Hoffmann von Fallersleben
1798—1874

iLrn

Visit the ***Wie geht's?*** iLrn website for more review and practice of the grammar points you have just learned.

This is the official text of Germany's national anthem and the third stanza of the original hymn written by Hoffmann von Fallersleben in 1841: *Unity and justice and freedom for the German fatherland. For that let us all strive as brothers with our hearts and hands. Unity and justice and freedom are the foundation for happiness. May you flourish in this happiness, may you flourish, German Fatherland!*

L.1: Hiroko sagte: a. „Ich bin . . . und arbeite . . . b. Mein Mann ist . . . c. Mir hat Berlin . . . gefallen, aber jetzt ist es . . . geworden d. Ich habe nie gedacht, dass ich . . . hier bleibe."

L.2: Moha sagte: a. „Ich bin . . . b. Meine Eltern sind . . . gekommen, weil mein Onkel . . . gehabt hat / hatte c. Meine Schwester und ich sind . . . geboren . . . groß geworden d. Wir sind . . . gewesen und kennen . . .

M: 1. Käthe Kollwitz war eine Künstlerin, die in Berlin zu Hause war. 2. Ihre Bilder und Skulpturen waren voller Mitgefühl für arme Leute, deren Leid sie zeigen wollte. 3. Sie erinnern uns an Hunger und Krieg, die das Leben der Menschen furchtbar machen. 4. Kaiser Wilhelm II. war kein Freund ihrer Kunst, die für ihn „Kunst der Gosse" war. 5. (Im Jahre) 1918 wurde sie Professorin an der Kunstakademie in Berlin, an der sie bis 1933 lehrte. 6. Dann kamen die Nazis, denen ihre Kunst auch nicht gefiel (die ihre Kunst auch nicht mochten), und sie verlor ihre Stelle. 7. Sie starb 1945, kurz vor (dem) Ende des Krieges / Kriegsende.

L. Stimmen der Zeit Berichten Sie in direkter Rede, was die zwei Sprecher gesagt haben!

1. **Hiroko Hashimoto, Journalistin**

   a. Hiroko sagte, sie wäre Journalistin und arbeitete freiberuflich *(freelance)* für eine japanische Firma. b. Ihr Mann wäre Deutscher und Wissenschaftler an der Technischen Universität. c. Ihr hätte Berlin schon immer gefallen, aber jetzt wäre es noch viel interessanter geworden. d. Sie hätte nie gedacht, dass sie so lange hier bleiben würde.

2. **Moha Rezaian, Schüler**

   a. Moha sagte, er wäre Schüler an einem Gymnasium. b. Seine Eltern wären vor Jahren aus dem Iran gekommen, weil sein Onkel in Kreuzberg einen Teppichladen gehabt hätte. c. Seine Schwester und er wären aber in Berlin geboren und hier groß geworden. d. Sie wären noch nie im Iran gewesen und würden den Rest der Familie nur von Besuchen kennen.

M. Eine bekannte Berlinerin: Käthe Kollwitz Auf Deutsch bitte!

1. Käthe Kollwitz was an artist who was at home in Berlin.
2. Her pictures and sculptures (**Skulpturen**) were full of compassion (**voller Mitgefühl**) for poor people, whose suffering (**das Leid**) she wanted to show.
3. They remind us of hunger and war, which make the life of people terrible.
4. Kaiser Wilhelm II was no friend of her art, which for him was "gutter art" (**Kunst der Gosse**).
5. In 1918 she became a professor at the Art Academy (**die Kunstakademie**) in Berlin, at which she taught until 1933.
6. Then came the Nazis, who also didn't like / care for her art, and she lost her position.
7. She died (**starb**) in 1945, shortly before the end of the war.

Große Freude am Brandenburger Tor nach dem Mauerdurchbruch

N. Hoppla, hier fehlt was: Reaktionen auf den Durchbruch der Mauer Hier sind Aussagen, die verschiedene Leute damals über den Mauerdurchbruch gemacht haben. Manche Aussagen zeigen, von wem sie sind, und andere nicht. Lesen Sie durch die Liste von Leuten und fragen Sie dann Ihren Partner / Ihre Partnerin, dessen/deren Tabelle und Liste im Anhang sind, wer die verschiedenen Aussagen gemacht haben könnte! Wechseln Sie sich ab!

Liste von Leuten:
ein Ostberliner Taxifahrer
ein kanadischer Fußballspieler
die Autorin Christa Wolf
der Autor Günter Grass
Michail Gorbatschow
der Autor Stephan Heym
Ronald Reagan

BEISPIEL S1 Wer hat gesagt, so viel Fernsehen hätte er noch nie gesehen? War das Ronald Reagan?
S2 Nein, das war nicht Ronald Reagan, sondern ein Ostberliner Taxifahrer. Und wer hat gesagt, . . . ? War das . . . ?

S1:

WER?	AUSSAGEN
NBC-Korrespondent:	„Vor meinen Augen tanzte die Freiheit."
Ostberliner Taxifahrer:	„So viel Fernsehen habe ich noch nie gesehen."
Sänger Wolf Biermann:	„Ich muss weinen vor Freude, dass es so schnell und einfach ging. Und ich muss weinen vor Zorn *(anger)*, dass es so elend *(terribly)* lange dauerte."
Autor Günter Grass:	„Jetzt wird sich zeigen, ob der jahrzehntelangen Rhetorik von den ‚Brüdern und Schwestern' auch entsprechendes *(corresponding)* politisches Handeln *(action)* folgen wird."
Autor Stephan Heym:	„Die einzige Chance, die wir haben, den Sozialismus zu retten *(save)*, ist richtiger Sozialismus."
Ex-Bundeskanzler Willy Brandt:	„Ich bin Gott dankbar, dass ich das noch erleben darf."
Amerikanischer Präsident Ronald Reagan:	„Auf beiden Seiten sind Deutsche. Der Kommunismus hat seine Chance gehabt. Er funktioniert nicht."
Tschechischer Reformpräsident Alexander Dubček:	„Wir haben zu lange im Dunkeln gelebt. Treten wir *(Let's step)* ins Licht!"

Einblicke

Lesetext

Wortschatz 2

der Gedanke, -ns, -n	*thought*
das Tor, -e	*gate; gateway*
die Grenze, -n	*border*
Heimat	*homeland, home*
Insel, -n	*island*
Jugend	*youth*
Luft	*air*
Macht, ¨-e	*power*
Mitte	*middle*
(Wieder)vereinigung	*(re)unification*
berühmt	*famous*
einst	*once*
leer	*empty*
vereint	*united*
aus·tauschen	*to exchange*
erkennen, erkannte, erkannt	*to recognize*
verlassen (verlässt), verließ, verlassen	*to leave (a place)*

Vor dem Lesen

A: 1. *(answer varies)* 2. an der Spree 3. 1939–1945 4. vier 5. 1989 6. Hauptstadt der DDR 7. 1990 8. *(answer varies)*

A. Allerlei Fragen

1. Wo liegt Berlin?
2. An welchem Fluss liegt es?
3. Was sind die Daten des Zweiten Weltkrieges?
4. In wie viele Teile war Berlin geteilt?
5. Wann fiel die Berliner Mauer?
6. Was war Ost-Berlin bis dahin *(then)*?
7. Seit wann ist Berlin wieder die Hauptstadt / der Regierungssitz *(seat of parliament)* von Deutschland?
8. Was wissen Sie noch über Berlin?

B. Das ist leicht zu verstehen! Lesen Sie laut die folgenden Wörter und raten Sie, was sie auf Englisch bedeuten?

der Bomber, Einmarsch, Ökologe, Sonderstatus, Städteplaner; das Angebot, Turmcafé; die Blockade, Demokratie, Funktion, Luftbrücke, Metropole, Olympiade, Orientierung, Passkontrolle, Rampe, Rote Armee; *(pl.)* die Medikamente, Westmächte, zwanziger Jahre; aus aller Welt; grenzenlos, kapitalistisch, sowjetisch, sozialistisch, symbolisch, teils, total blockiert, ummauert, unfreiwillig

C. Gehen wir Wörter angeln! Unterstreichen Sie zusammen mit Ihrem Partner / Ihrer Partnerin alle Relativpronomen und vorhergehenden Wörter im Lesetext! Wie viele Beispiele haben Sie gefunden?

Lesetipp

Anticipating Content

You have learned a lot about Berlin and its people. This reading also deals with the city. Look at the title of the reading and at the subheadings in the reading. Based on them and your knowledge thus far about the city, what sorts of topics and themes do you expect might come up? Anticipating content of a reading helps you prepare the vocabulary and think about the ideas you will need to understand the reading successfully.

Berlin, ein Tor zur Welt

Antje Dirks, eine Amerikanerin, erinnert sich an den Besuch mit ihrem Vater in Berlin und berichtet über ihren Eindruck° von Berlin heute.

Besuch im Jahre 1985

Da saßen wir nun, Vater und Tochter, im Flugzeug auf dem Weg zu der Stadt, die er eigentlich nie vergessen konnte: Berlin. „Ich bin schon lange in Amerika, aber Berlin . . . Nun, Berlin ist eben meine Heimat. Da bin ich geboren und aufgewachsen°." Und dann wanderten seine Gedanken zurück zu den zwanziger bis vierziger Jahren, zu der Zeit, als er dort gelebt hatte. Die Viereinhalbmillionenstadt, von deren Charme und Esprit er immer noch schwärmte°, hatte seine Jugend geprägt°. Und er erzählte mir von dem, was er dort so geliebt hatte: von den Wäldern und Seen in der Umgebung und von der berühmten Berliner Luft; von den Museen, der Oper und den Theatern, deren Angebot damals einmalig gewesen wäre; vom Kabarett mit seiner typischen „Berliner Schnauze" und den Kaffeehäusern, in denen immer etwas los war. „In Berlin liefen alle Fäden° zusammen, nicht nur kulturell, sondern auch politisch und wirtschaftlich. Es war einst die größte Industriestadt Europas. Die Zentralverwaltung° fast aller wichtigen Industriefirmen war in Berlin. Und man kannte sich, tauschte Gedanken aus, auch mit Wissenschaftlern an der Universität. Einfach fantastisch!"

„Und dann kam 1933. Viele verließen Berlin, teils freiwillig, teils unfreiwillig. Die Nazis beherrschten° das Straßenbild°. Bei der Olympiade 1936 sah die ganze Welt nicht nur Berlins moderne S-Bahn und schöne Straßen, sondern auch Hitler. Und drei Jahre später war Krieg!" Nun sprach er von den schweren Luftangriffen° und den Trümmern°, die diese hinterlassen° hatten, vom Einmarsch der Roten Armee, der Teilung Deutschlands unter den vier Siegermächten° (1945) und auch von der Luftbrücke, mit der die Westmächte auf die sowjetische Blockade reagiert hatten. „Plötzlich waren wir total blockiert, eine Insel. Es gab nichts zu essen, keine Kleidung, kein Heizmaterial°, keine Medikamente, kaum° Wasser und Strom°. An guten Tagen landeten in den nächsten 10 Monaten alle paar Minuten britische und amerikanische Transportflugzeuge—wir nannten sie die Rosinenbomber°—und brachten uns, was wir brauchten. Ohne die Westmächte hätten wir es nie geschafft°!" . . .

impression
have grown up
raved / shaped
threads
headquarters
dominated / . . . scene
air raids
rubble / left behind
victorious Allies
heating fuel / hardly any
electricity
raisin bombers
accomplished

Related to the reading material of this chapter is the 1955 Pete Seeger folk song, "Where have all the flowers gone?" Owing to its universal message, it was translated into many languages, and its German title is "Sag mir wo die Blumen sind." In 1962, the popular German-born singer and actress Marlene Dietrich performed it first in French and soon after in German. Find versions sung by Marlene Dietrich and Juliane Werding on YouTube.

Ein „Rosinenbomber" während der Blockade

Dann kamen wir in West-Berlin an. Erst machten wir eine Stadtrundfahrt. „Es ist wieder schön hier; und doch, die Weite° ist weg. Berlin schien früher grenzenlos, und jetzt . . . überall diese Grenze." Immer wieder stand man vor der Mauer, die seit 1961 mitten durch Berlin lief. Besonders traurig machte ihn der Blick auf das Brandenburger Tor, das auf der anderen Seite der Mauer stand. Und doch gefiel mir diese ummauerte Insel. West-Berlin war wieder eine lebendige Metropole, die unheimlich viel zu bieten hatte.

wide-open space

Der Besuch in Ost-Berlin, der damaligen Hauptstadt von Ostdeutschland, war wirklich ein Erlebnis°, wie eine Reise in eine andere Welt. Allein schon die Gesichter der Vopos° am Checkpoint Charlie und das komische Gefühl, das man bei der Passkontrolle hatte! Berlin-Mitte war für meinen Vater schwer wiederzuerkennen. Der Potsdamer Platz, der früher voller Leben gewesen war, war leer. Leichter zu erkennen waren die historischen Gebäude entlang Unter den Linden: die Staatsbibliothek, die Humboldt-Universität und die Staatsoper. Interessant waren auch das Pergamonmuseum, der Dom und gegenüber davon der Palast der Republik, den die Berliner „Palazzo Prozzo" nannten und in dem die Volkskammer° saß. Dann über allem der Fernsehturm, dessen Turmcafé sich dreht°. Wir sahen auch einen britischen Jeep, der Unter den Linden Streife fuhr°, was uns an den Sonderstatus Berlins erinnerte. Hier trafen die kapitalistische und die sozialistische Welt aufeinander°; und für beide Welten waren Ost- und West-Berlin Schaufenster° zweier gegensätzlicher° Systeme.

experience
GDR police (Volkspolizei)
GDR house of representatives
turns / patrolled
came together
display windows / opposing

Heute

Heute ist das alles Geschichte. Die Berliner können wieder reisen, wohin sie wollen. Berlin ist keine Insel mehr. Ich erinnere mich noch gut an die Reaktion meines Vaters, als wir den Mauerdurchbruch im amerikanischen Fernsehen sahen. Immer wieder sagte er „Wahnsinn! Dass ich das noch erleben durfte!" und ihm standen Tränen° in den Augen. Unsere Gedanken gingen damals zurück zu Präsident Kennedys Worten 1963 an der Mauer: „Alle freien Menschen sind Bürger Berlins . . . Ich bin ein Berliner!"

tears

26. Juni 2013: John F. Kennedy und Ronald Reagan auf der Berliner Mauer—50. Jahrestag von Kennedys Rede

Seit der Wiedervereinigung hat sich in Berlin sehr viel verändert. Politiker, Städteplaner, Architekten und Ökologen haben enorme Arbeit geleistet°. Da, wo einst die Mauer stand, stehen jetzt moderne Gebäude und die alte Mitte Berlins ist wieder Stadtmitte geworden. Hier findet man Menschen aus aller Welt, die überall ihre Spuren hinterlassen°. Die moderne Kuppel° des Reichstagsgebäudes hat eine neue, symbolische Funktion. Einerseits° strahlt° sie in der Nacht wie eine Laterne°, wie eine Erhellung der Vernunft°. Andererseits° haben die Leute, die auf der Rampe nach oben zur Aussichtsplattform° laufen, die Möglichkeit, auf ihre Politiker herabzuschauen°. Hier diskutiert man nicht mehr hinter verschlossenen° Türen, sondern die Demokratie ist offener geworden. Als Hauptstadt des vereinten Deutschlands in einem neuen, erweiterten° Europa hat Berlin neue Aufgaben bekommen und durch seine Lage—nur knapp 100 km von Polen entfernt°—erlebt es jetzt auch eine größere Orientierung zum Osten. Berlin ist wieder ein Tor zur Welt.

achieved
leave their traces / dome
on the one hand / shines
lantern / enlightenment / on the other hand / observation deck
look down
closed
expanded
barely away

Nach dem Lesen

A. Alles verstanden?

1. Wohin wanderten die Gedanken des Vaters, als er 1985 zum ersten Mal Berlin wiedersah?
2. Warum verließen 1933 viele Leute Berlin?
3. Wann war die Olympiade und was begann drei Jahre danach?
4. Wer blockierte 1948 Berlin und wie beschreibt der Vater die zehn Monate während der Luftbrücke?
5. Wie nannten die Berliner die Flugzeuge, die ihnen alles zum Überleben *(survival) brachten*?
6. Seit wann lief eine Mauer mitten durch Berlin und womit verglich der Vater West-Berlin?
7. Wie fanden sie die Reise nach Ost-Berlin?
8. Wie reagierte *(reacted)* der Vater, als er den Mauerdurchbruch im amerikanischen Fernsehen sah?
9. Was waren Präsident Kennedys berühmte Worte 1963 an der Mauer?
10. Was strahlt heute in der Nacht wie eine Laterne über der Stadt?
11. Auf wen kann man von der Reichtstagskuppel herabschauen?
12. Wie weit entfernt ist Berlin von Polen und warum sieht der Autor es als ein Tor zur Welt?

A: 1. zurück zu den 20er bis 40er Jahren, als er dort gelebt hatte 2. wegen der Nazis 3. 1936; der Krieg 4. die Sowjets; nichts zu essen, keine Kleidung / Heizung / Medizin, kaum Wasser und Strom 5. Rosinenbomber 6. seit 1961; mit einer ummauerten Insel 7. wie eine Reise in eine andere Welt 8. Wahnsinn!, weinte 9. „Alle freien Menschen sind Bürger Berlins. Ich bin ein Berliner." 10. die Kuppel des Reichstagsgebäudes 11. Auf die Politiker / Abgeordneten 12. knapp 100 km; neue Aufgaben, größere Orientierung auch zum Osten

Optional tongue twister **(der Zungenbrecher):** Der Mondschein *(moonlight)* schien schon schön.

B. Gespräch zwischen Vater und Tochter

Lesen Sie das Gespräch und berichten Sie indirekt zusammen mit einem Partner / einer Partnerin, was die beiden gesagt haben!

BEISPIEL S1 Die Tochter fragte, wie lange er dort gewohnt hätte.
S2 Er sagte, dass er ungefähr 25 Jahre dort gewohnt hätte.

TOCHTER Wie lange hast du dort gewohnt?
VATER Ungefähr 25 Jahre.
TOCHTER Wohnten deine Eltern damals auch in Berlin?
VATER Nein, aber sie sind 1938 nachgekommen.
TOCHTER Hast du dort Mutti kennengelernt?
VATER Ja, das waren schöne Jahre.
TOCHTER Und wann seid ihr von dort weggegangen?
VATER Ach, das ist eine lange Geschichte. Setzen wir uns in ein Café! Dann werde ich dir davon erzählen.

B: Sie fragte, ob seine Eltern damals auch in Berlin gewohnt hätten. Er sagte, dass sie erst 1938 nachgekommen wären. —Sie fragte, ob er dort ihre Mutter (Mutti) kennengelernt hätte. Er sagte ja, und dass das schöne Jahre gewesen wären. —Sie fragte, wann sie von dort weggegangen wären. Er sagte, dass das eine lange Geschichte wäre. Sie sollten sich in ein Café setzen. Dann würde er ihr davon erzählen.

Weiteres

C. Hier gibt's so viel zu sehen!

1. Mir gefällt diese Stadt, in _der_ mehr als drei Millionen Menschen wohnen.
2. Berlin ist ein Kulturzentrum *(n.)*, _das_ unheimlich viel zu bieten hat.

3. Gestern waren wir im Pergamonmuseum, _das_ für seine ägyptische Sammlung und seinen Altar berühmt ist. 4. Darin gibt es auch einen islamischen Teil, _der_ eine große Fassade von einem Palast aus dem 8. Jahrhundert zeigt. 5. Danach gingen wir ins Deutsche Historische Museum, _dessen_ Angebot einmalig ist. 6. Abends hatten wir Karten für Beethovens Oper *Fidelio*, _die_ in der Staatsoper spielte. 7. Es war ein Tag, _den_ ich so schnell nicht vergessen werde. 8. Heute früh waren wir am Gendarmenmarkt, _den_ viele als den schönsten Platz Berlins ansehen. 9. Am Nachmittag werden wir zum Wannsee fahren, auf _dem_ wir eine Bootsfahrt machen wollen. 10. Morgen geht's nach Potsdam und Schloss Sanssouci, _das_ zum Weltkulturerbe *(World Heritage Site)* der UNESCO gehört.

Am Gendarmenmarkt

Schreibtipp

Interview Synopsis

An interview is typically a formal situation, taking place between strangers. Therefore, you can expect to use the **Sie**-form. However, if you are interviewing another student for a student publication, then your conversation might be conducted using the **du**-form. In either case, plan your questions using the correct level of language. If you are the one conducting the interview, be sure to write out your questions ahead of time. Leave space between questions to jot down notes about your subject's answers. You will need written notes in order to write up your interview synopsis; don't trust your memory! Be sure to indicate exact quotations from your subject by using quotation marks.

D. Menschen in Berlin

1. **Interview** Stellen Sie Fragen an jemanden (Ihren Partner / Ihre Partnerin), den Sie in Berlin kennengelernt haben! Vielleicht ist dieser Jemand jung oder alt, Student/in oder Geschäftsmann/frau, Künstler/in oder Politiker/in, Berliner oder Ausländer. Entscheiden Sie zuerst, welche Rolle dieser Jemand spielt und bereiten Sie dann sechs bis acht Fragen vor!
2. **Bericht** Erzählen Sie nun, was er/sie Ihnen gesagt hat!

BEISPIEL *Er/Sie sagt, er/sie wäre Student an der Humboldt Universität. Dort studierte er . . .*

Hörverständnis

Realität und Hoffnung Hören Sie zu, was der Sprecher über die Situation in den neuen Bundesländern zu sagen hat! Sind die folgenden Aussagen richtig oder falsch?

Zum Erkennen: blühende Landschaften *(flourishing areas)*; restaurieren *(to restore)*; die Sächsische Schweiz *(part of the* ***Elbsandsteingebirge*** *south of Dresden)*; sind neu entstanden *(have reemerged)*; liefern *(to distribute)*; die Fabrik, -en *(factory)*; konkurrieren *(to compete)*; der Verlag, -e *(publisher)*; die Entwicklung *(development)*; der Zusammenbruch *(collapse)*; verschwand *(disappeared)*; die Personalkosten (pl., *staffing costs)*; vermeiden *(to avoid)*; die Forschung *(research)*; investieren *(to invest)*

__r__ 1. Helmut Kohl meinte, dass sich die neuen Bundesländer nach dem Mauerfall in blühende Landschaften verwandeln *(transform)* würden.

__r__ 2. Er hat nur teilweise *(partially)* recht gehabt.

__f__ 3. Nur wenige Touristen fahren in den Ferien an die Ostsee.

__r__ 4. In der Sächsischen Schweiz gibt es schöne Schlösser.

__r__ 5. In Dresden macht die amerikanische Firma AMD *(Advanced Micro Devices)* Computerchips.

__f__ 6. BMW hat eine Fabrik in Mecklenburg-Vorpommern.

__f__ 7. Die neuen Bundesländer haben viel Geld in die alten Bundesländer gepumpt.

__r__ 8. Um für junge qualifizierte Leute attraktiv zu bleiben, investiert man im Osten viel Geld in Forschung und Wissenschaft.

__r__ 9. Diese wissenschaftlichen Zentren, oder Clusters, kooperieren mit den Hochschulen und der Geschäftswelt.

You might ask students to correct the statements that are wrong.

For further practice, an optional two-part video (**Szenen** and **Interviews**) is available on the ***Wie geht's?*** Premium Website and in iLrn, with corresponding questions and activities in the *Arbeitsbuch* (SAM).

As an optional activity, you could use Google Earth to visit Berlin to get an impression of the city and its surroundings. Try to find some of the sights mentioned in this chapter.

Blick von der Festung Königstein in der Sächsischen Schweiz (im Osten von Deutschland)

Literatur

Biographisches

Gisela Reuter was born in 1957 in the town of Siegburg in the German Rhineland. She obtained professional training as a pharmaceutical wholesale and export trade specialist. Later she married and had two children. A woman of many interests, she became a licensed massage therapist in 2004. Reuter has always managed to find time for her hobbies, which include guitar, African drumming, painting, reading, antique furniture, and writing short stories. Since March 2012, she has been living and working on the North Sea Island of Juist.

Vor dem Lesen

Allgemeine Fragen

1. Was wissen Sie über den Zweiten Weltkrieg *(WWII)*?
2. Was wissen Sie über die Zeit nach dem Krieg in Deutschland und die Teilung Deutschlands *(division of Germany)*?
3. Kennen Sie Kriegsveteranen in Ihrer Familie oder in Ihrer Stadt?
4. Wenn Sie alte Menschen treffen, sprechen Sie manchmal mit ihnen über ihre Jugend und ihr Leben? Warum (nicht)?
5. Haben Sie Soldaten in Ihrer Familie? Wenn ja, sprechen diese mit Ihnen über ihren Beruf? Wenn nein, welche Fragen würden Sie ihnen gern stellen?

Café LebensArt, Pariser Platz, Berlin

looked around / went away / a little
looked around again
describe
gait / stooped / marked by experiences
after a while
wondered
by chance / have a view of
leaned back
nodded
pensively
darn
closely
remained silent
turned out to be
twin brother
devoutly / reached for / hesitated
almost imperceptibly
feels like
continued
drafted / expression
shouted the slogans together /
homesickness / murdered

Er sah sich um°, als würde er auf jemanden warten. Er entfernte sich° ein wenig° von dem Café, kam jedoch gleich zurück und hielt wieder Ausschau°. Mich faszinierten seine Augen und sein Blick, in dem etwas lag, das ich nicht genau benennen° konnte. Er erinnerte mich an meinen Großvater. Das weiße Haar akkurat nach hinten gekämmt. Der Gang° leicht gebeugt°. Das Gesicht von Alter und Erlebtem gezeichnet°.

Ob er sich zu mir setzen könnte, fragte er nach einer Weile°. „Ja, sicher, gerne." Ich lächelte und wunderte mich°. Später verstand ich, dass er einfach genau an diesem Tag und genau in diesem Moment reden musste. Und ich saß eben zufällig° da. Er stellte den Stuhl so, dass er den Pariser Platz überblicken° konnte. Dann lehnte er sich zurück° und lächelte. Der Kellner schien ihn zu kennen und fragte nur: „Wie immer?" „Ja, wie immer." Er nickte° freundlich. Ich fragte mich, was wohl ‚wie immer' sein würde, und bestellte mir Apfelkuchen und Kaffee. „Sie sind also öfter hier", sagte ich nach einer Weile. „Ja." Er nickte. „An jedem ersten Sonntag im Monat." Sein Blick wanderte versonnen° über den Platz. „Seit sechzig Jahren." Sechzig Jahre. Das ist eine verdammt° lange Zeit. Ich dachte sofort an den Krieg und sah ihn prüfend° an. Und er schien zu wissen, was ich dachte. Wir schwiegen°, bis der Kellner mit unserer Bestellung kam. ‚Wie immer' stellte sich als Käsekuchen und Kakao heraus.°

Und dann begann er zu erzählen. Und ich vergaß darüber meinen Kuchen und meinen Kaffee. „Wilhelm heißt er", sagte er leise, „ich habe einen Zwillingsbruder°. Er zeigte auf seinen Teller. „Wilhelm mag Käsekuchen am liebsten." Fast andächtig° griff er nach° der Kuchengabel. Er zögerte°, bevor er zu essen begann, und sah mich an. „Wir waren in derselben Kompanie." Ich nickte kaum merklich°. Ja, meine Generation weiß es aus Büchern, Zeitungsartikeln und Erzählungen. Aber seine Generation hat es erlebt und weiß, wie sich Krieg anfühlt°.

„Wilhelm und ich", fuhr er fort°, „waren immer zusammen. Immer. Wir schliefen in einem Zimmer, weil wir zu Hause wenig Platz hatten. Mit siebzehn wurden wir einberufen°," Seine Miene° wurde wieder ernst. „Wir haben gemeinsam die Parolen gebrüllt.° Wir haben gemeinsam vor Heimweh° geweint. Und wir haben gemeinsam gemordet°."

Er sprach klar und mit fester Stimme°. Seine Augen wanderten immer wieder über den Platz und ich hörte ihm wortlos zu. Ich glaube, zu diesem Zeitpunkt° sprach er schon gar nicht mehr zu mir, sondern mehr zu sich selber°. „Ich weiß nicht, wie viele wir erschossen° haben. Waren es zehn? Zwanzig? Was sollten wir machen entweder sie oder wir. Ich habe gebetet°, Gott möge mir verzeihen°."

Um uns herum war es laut. Ich rückte° etwas näher, um ihn besser verstehen zu können. Menschen lachten. Kinder schrien°. Eine Dame beschwerte sich° laut, dass sie schon vor einer halben Stunde ein Schokoladeneis mit Sahne bestellt hätte. Ich sah Soldaten. Soldaten, ohnmächtig vor Angst°. Verzweifelt vor Wut° über diese Sinnlosigkeit°. Ich sah Brüder, die nicht wussten, ob sie die nächste Stunde noch gemeinsam erleben würden.

„Es war der erste Sonntag im August", sprach er nach einer kleinen Pause weiter. „Am nächsten Morgen sollten wir uns bei der Kompanie melden°. Wir standen ungefähr hier, wo heute das Café ist, und haben uns geschworen°, falls wir getrennt würden°, uns genau hier an einem ersten Sonntag im Monat wieder zu sehen. Es gab keine andere Möglichkeit. Berlin brannte°. Unser Elternhaus war zerstört°. Irgendeinen Treffpunkt° mussten wir haben. Ein Versprechen, ein Händedruck°. Ich fragte ihn nicht, ob Wilhelm jemals° hierher gekommen war.

Er erzählte von der letzten gemeinsamen Stunde. Von dem überraschenden Angriff°. Von Sanitätern°, die Wilhelm abgeholt haben°. Von dem verzweifelten Versuch°, Wilhelm ins Lazarett° zu folgen. Von einer Spur°, die sich verlor, und von der Hoffnung, dem einzigen Lebensziel°, den Bruder wieder zu finden. Und von der neuen Chance, nachdem die Mauer° gefallen war.

Ich weiß nicht, weshalb er sich zu mir gesetzt hat, und eigentlich ist es auch egal. Ich weiß auch nicht, ob es im Leben Zufälle° gibt. Aber ich bin froh, dass ich gerade° an diesem ersten Sonntag im Monat draußen vor dem Café saß und Zeit hatte, Zeit zum Zuhören. Und wer weiß, vielleicht werde ich öfter an einem ersten Sonntag im Monat auf dem Pariser Platz vor diesem Café sitzen.

Gisela Reuter, *Erstveröffentlichung*

firm voice
point (in time)
himself
shot
prayed / would forgive me
moved
screamed / complained
powerless with fear / desperate with anger / senselessness
report back
swore
in case we were separated
was burning
destroyed / meeting place
handshake / ever
attack / medics / picked up
attempt / military hospital / trace
life's goal
wall
coincidences
just

Nach dem Lesen

A. Inhaltsfragen

1. Die Geschichte beginnt mit „er" und nennt den Gesprächspartner der Erzählerin nie mit Namen. Mit wem trinkt die Erzählerin Kaffee?
2. Die beiden haben sich nicht im Café verabredet *(arranged to meet)*. Wie treffen sie aufeinander?
3. Was bestellen die beiden?
4. Wie lange kommt „er" schon in das Café?
5. Wer ist Wilhelm?
6. Warum ist Wilhelm so wichtig für den alten Mann?
7. Was sagt die Erzählerin über ihre Generation?
8. Was bereut *(regrets)* der alte Mann? Welches Wort zeigt, dass er etwas bereut?
9. Warum kommt der alte Mann einmal im Monat ins Café LebensArt?
10. Welche Mauer wird im Text erwähnt *(mentioned)* und warum ist sie wichtig?
11. Was nimmt sich die Erzählerin vor *(resolves to do)*?
12. Warum der Titel *Café LebensArt*? Wie könnte man diesen interpretieren? Sagt er vielleicht etwas über den Lebensstil oder die Einstellung *(attitude)* der beiden Menschen zum Leben aus?

B. Wenn es wahr werden würde!

1. Schreiben Sie einen kurzen Dialog, in dem Wilhelm und der alte Mann sich doch endlich treffen.
2. Berichten Sie über den Tag, als Sie überraschenderweise Zeuge *(witness)* wurden beim Wiedersehen der beiden Brüder.

Rückschau

Kapitelwortschatz

Hauptwörter

der Frieden — *peace*
das Gebäude, - — *building*
der Gedanke, -ns, -n — *thought*
die Grenze, -n — *border*
die Heimat — *homeland, home*
die Insel, -n — *island*
die Jugend — *youth*
die Kneipe,-n — *pub*
der Krieg, -e — *war*
die Luft — *air*
die Macht, ¨-e — *power*
die Mauer, -n — *wall*
die Mitte — *middle*
der Spitzname, -ns, -n — *nickname*
das Tor, -e — *gate; gateway*
der Turm, ¨-e — *tower*
die Umgebung — *surrounding(s)*
das Volk, ¨-er — *people* (as a whole or nation)
die (Wieder)vereinigung — *(re)unification*

Verben

aus·tauschen — *to exchange*
berichten — *to report*
erinnern (an) *(+ acc.)* — *to remind (of)*
sich erinnern (an) *(+ acc.)* — *to remember*
erkennen — *to recognize*
führen — *to lead*
(sich) verändern — *to change*
verlassen — *to leave (a place)*
verschwinden — *to disappear*
vorbei·führen (an) *(+ dat.)* — *to pass by (s.th.); to guide (s.o.) along (s.th.)*

Adjektive und Adverbien

berühmt — *famous*
einmalig — *unique; incredible*
einst — *once*
historisch — *historical(ly)*
leer — *empty*
vereint — *united*
wunderschön — *very beautiful(ly)*

Verschiedenes

damals — *then*
irgendwo — *somewhere*
jede Menge — *all sorts of*
kaum — *hardly, barely, scarcely*
oder? — *isn't it?, don't you think so?*
seitdem — *since then*
Und ob! — *You bet!, You better believe it!*

Zum Schluss

1. **Was sehe ich?**
   a. **Zu Hause** Write a description of your house or a room at home. Use relative clauses to describe every object or person you mention.

      BEISPIEL: *Ich sehe meine Mutter, deren Tochter ich bin. Sie sitzt auf dem Sofa, auf dem mein Hund gern schläft.*

   b. **Wie sieht es bei dir aus?** Share your description with your classmates and listen to theirs. What differences did you notice in the various descriptions? What do they have in common? As a group, write a similar description of the room you are in now.
2. **Vergleich zwischen Berlin und der Hauptstadt meines Landes** Use what you have learned about Berlin in this chapter to make a comparison with the capital city of your home country. Have you ever been to your national capital? What about the capital of your state? Do your capital and Berlin share common histories? What is the biggest difference between them? How would you describe your capital to someone in Berlin?
3. **Was wurde gesagt?** Go back through your book and find a story or article about Germany that you thought was particularly interesting. Summarize it in 8–10 sentences, being sure to use indirect speech (**indirekte Rede**) when you repeat what a person said. Share your opinion on why you chose that text as interesting!

iLrn **Onlineaktivitäten** Visit iLrn for online activities related to this chapter. There you will find additional resources, such as a memory game (**Gedächtnisspiel**), a crossword puzzle (**Kreuzworträtsel**), audio flash cards (**Vokabelblitz**), a tutorial quiz (**Mini-Quiz**), and the active vocabulary (**Wortschatz**) for this chapter.

Berlin gefällt mir!

Kapitel 15

Deutschland, Europa und die Umwelt

Lernziele In this chapter you will learn about:

Zum Thema

Landscape and the environment

Fokus

A united Europe, European cultural capital Weimar, German identity

Struktur

- The passive voice
- Review of the uses of **werden**
- The special subjunctive (Subjunctive I)

Einblicke

Lesetext: Der Wind kennt keine Grenzen.
Literatur: Franz Kafka, „Der Aufbruch" / Erich Kästner, „Das Eisenbahngleichnis"

Rückschau

Kapitelwortschatz
Zum Schluss

RESSOURCEN

iLrn | Video
Audio | SAM

© Otmar Smit/Shutterstock

Windräder mit Schafen **(sheep)** ***in der Nähe der Nordsee***

Vorschau The Path to a United Europe

1945 World War II leaves Europe devastated and hungry.

1949 The North Atlantic Treaty Organization (NATO) and the Council of Europe are established.

1950 France launches the Schuman Plan, which proposes putting French and West German coal and steel production under a single authority.

1951 Germany, France, Italy, Belgium, the Netherlands, and Luxembourg found the European Coal and Steel Community (ECSC), known as *Montanunion*.

1957 France, Germany, Italy, Belgium, the Netherlands, and Luxembourg establish the European Economic Community (EEC) and the European Atomic Energy Commission (EURATOM), known collectively as the Treaties of Rome. The EEC, EURATOM, and ECSC are called the "European Communities," or EC.

1960 Great Britain, Austria, Switzerland, Portugal, and the Scandinavian countries form the European Free Trade Association (EFTA), an alternative to the EC.

1973 Denmark, Ireland, and Great Britain join the EC.

1979 First direct elections to the European Parliament are held.

1981 Greece joins the EC.

1986 Spain and Portugal become members of the EC.

1989 With the fall of the Berlin Wall, Europe's division is ended.

1990 German unification extends EC membership to the former East Germany.

1993 Signed in 1991, the Maastricht Treaty now goes into effect, paving the way to economic and monetary union and increasing political unity. The "European Communities" are now called the European Union (EU).

1995 The entry of Austria, Finland, and Sweden into the EU brings the number of member states to 15. The Schengen Agreement, an EU treaty that makes passport-free travel possible between signatory states, goes into effect.

1997 The heads of the member states draw up the Amsterdam Treaty, which lays out internal reform and expansion eastward.

1999 The euro is introduced as common currency for financial transactions in 11 member states.

2002 The euro replaces national currencies such as the deutsche mark and schilling for all daily transactions in 12 EU nations.

2004 Expansion of the EU to 25 member countries with the accession of Poland, Hungary, the Czech Republic, Slovenia, Slovakia, Latvia, Lithuania, Estonia, Cyprus (represented by the Greek Cypriot government), and Malta.

2007 Bulgaria and Romania enter the EU; Slovenia adopts the euro (followed by Slovakia in 2009, Estonia in 2011, and Latvia in 2014).

2008 The Treaty of Lisbon provides EU citizens with a stronger voice in the decision-making process, modernizes the institutions that run the EU, and equips it to address issues, such as globalization, climate and demographic changes, security, and energy. The Eurozone enters its first recession.

2010 Extension of the EU's role in military defense and its supervision.

2013 Croatia becomes the 28th member state of the European Union.

2013 The Treaty on Stability, Coordination and Governance in the Economic and Monetary Union (popularly known as the "Fiscal Compact") enters into force. It aims to strengthen fiscal discipline in the euro area through the "balanced budget rule" and a correction mechanism.

Fragen: 1. Wie finden Sie das linke Bild mit den Windrädern und Schafen? 2. Wo gibt es so etwas in Ihrem Land? 3. Wer hat seinen Sitz in dem Gebäude unten? 4. In welcher Stadt ist das? 5. Welche Flaggen erkennen Sie?

Vor dem Europaparlament in Straßburg

Zum Thema

Gespräche

Warm-ups: 1. **Definieren Sie!** z. B. Sekretärin: Eine Sekretärin ist eine Frau, die in einem Büro arbeitet. (Verkäufer, Hausfrau, Geburtstag, Silvester, Ferien, Bibliothek, Kaufhaus, Jugendherberge, Ausweis, Bekannte, Arbeitsplatz)
2. **Nennen Sie die Verbformen!** z. B. aussehen, sah aus, ausgesehen (annehmen, bestehen, erkennen, haben, nennen, scheinen, teilnehmen, verlassen, vorbereiten, werden)
3. **Nennen Sie den Konjunktiv!** Das sieht schön aus. Was habt ihr zu bieten? Erinnerst du dich daran? Das erkenne ich sofort. Das habe ich nicht versprochen. Ich bin nicht geblieben.

Zu Besuch in Weimar

TOM Komisch, dieses Denkmal von Goethe und Schiller kenne ich doch! Ich glaube, ich habe es schon irgendwo gesehen.
DANIELA Warst du schon mal in San Francisco?
TOM Na klar!
DANIELA Warst du auch im Golden Gate Park?
TOM Ach ja, da steht genau das gleiche Denkmal! Das haben, glaub' ich, die Deutsch-Amerikaner in Kalifornien einmal bauen lassen.
DANIELA Richtig! Im 18. Jahrhundert haben hier viele berühmte Leute gelebt und die Weimarer Republik ist auch danach benannt.
TOM Ja ja, aber heute früh, als ich am Mahnmal vom Konzentrationslager Buchenwald auf die Stadt herabblickte, hatte ich sehr gemischte Gefühle.
DANIELA Ja, da hast du natürlich recht.

Das Goethe-Schiller-Denkmal vor dem Nationaltheater

In der Altstadt

DANIELA Schau mal, die alten Häuser hier sind doch echt schön.
TOM Ja, sie sind gut restauriert worden. Ich finde es vor allem schön, dass hier keine Autos fahren dürfen.
DANIELA Gott sei Dank!
TOM Bei uns gibt es jetzt auch eine Bürgerinitiative, alle Autos in der Altstadt zu verbieten, um die alten Gebäude zu retten.
DANIELA Das finde ich gut.
TOM Sind die Container da drüben für die Mülltrennung?
DANIELA Ja, habt ihr auch Mülltrennung?
TOM Ja, freiwillig. Da könnte man ganz bestimmt noch viel mehr tun. Zum Beispiel weiß ich nie, wohin mit alten Batterien oder Medikamenten.
DANIELA Die alten Batterien kann man in jedem Supermarkt in spezielle Sammelbehälter werfen und die alten Medikamente, die bringst du zur Apotheke.
TOM Das geht bei uns nicht und so landet schließlich vieles in der Mülltonne.
DANIELA Das ist bei uns verboten.
TOM Das sollte es auch sein. Ihr seid da eben weiter als wir.

A. Alles verstanden?

1. Über welches Denkmal sprechen Tom und Daniela? Wo steht eine Kopie?
2. Wofür ist Weimar bekannt?
3. Was war aber auch ganz in der Nähe?
4. Was gefällt Tom an Weimars Innenstadt?
5. Wofür gibt es in Weimar überall besondere Container?
6. Wohin bringen die Deutschen ihre alten Batterien und Medikamente?

B. Jetzt sind Sie dran! Sprechen Sie mit Ihrem Partner / Ihrer Partnerin über das Thema „Autos in der Altstadt". Finden Sie heraus, was er/sie davon hält, dort alle Autos zu verbieten! Welche Konsequenzen *(consequences)* hätte das?

A: 1. das Goethe-Schiller-Denkmal; im Golden Gate Park von San Francisco 2. Da haben viele berühmte Leute gelebt, die Weimarer Republik 3. das Konzentrationslager Buchenwald 4. schöne alte, restaurierte Häuser; keine Autos 5. für die Mülltrennung 6. zu Sammelbehältern im Supermarkt; zur Apotheke

Students could also make a list of cars that are gas guzzlers **(der Benzinschlucker, -)** and thereby put special demands on the environment. Should those cars be forbidden, or should people who drive them pay higher taxes **(Steuern)?**

Wortschatz 1

Die Landschaft *(landscape, scenery)*

Die Umwelt *(environment)*

der Abfall, ¨-e	*trash*
Bau, -ten	*building; structure*
Behälter, -	*container*
Müll	*garbage; waste*
(Umwelt)schutz	*(environmental) protection*
das Denkmal, ¨-er	*monument*
Gebiet, -e	*area, region*
Naturschutzgebiet,- e	*nature preserve*
die Erhaltung	*preservation*
Küste, -n	*coast*
Mülltonne, -n	*garbage can*
Natur	*nature*
Rede, -n	*speech*
Sammelstelle, -n	*collection site*
Verschmutzung	*pollution*

Verschiedenes

allerdings	*however*
schließlich	*after all, in the end*
übrigens	*by the way*
umweltbewusst	*environmentally aware*
ab·reißen, riss ab, abgerissen	*to tear down*
(wieder) auf·bauen	*to (re)build*
finanzieren	*to finance*
garantieren	*to guarantee*
planen	*to plan*
reden (mit + *dat.* / über + *acc.*)	*to talk (to/about)*
renovieren	*to renovate*
restaurieren	*to restore*
retten	*to save, rescue*
schaden	*to hurt; to damage*
schonen	*to go easy on, protect*
schützen	*to protect*
trennen	*to separate*
verbieten, verbot, verboten	*to forbid*
verwenden	*to use, utilize*
werfen (wirft), warf, geworfen	*to throw*
weg·werfen (wirft weg), warf weg, weggeworfen	*to throw away, discard*
zerstören	*to destroy*

Don't confuse **retten** *(to save in the sense of to rescue)* with **sparen** *(to save in the sense of saving money or time).*

Note that **wegwerfen** means the same as **fortwerfen** (used in the illustration on page 427), but in everyday speech **wegwerfen** might be more common.

Zum Erkennen: bauen lassen *(to have built)*; benennen nach *(to name after)*; das Konzentrationslager, - *(concentration camp)*; herab·blicken auf *(+ acc.)(to look down on)*; gemischte Gefühle *(mixed feelings)*; die Fassade, -n; die Abgase *(exhaust fumes)*; überleben *(to survive)*; die Bürgerinitiative, -n *(citizens' initiative)*; der Container, -; die Mülltrennung *(waste separation)*; freiwillig *(voluntary)*; die Batterie, -n; die Medikamente (pl., *medicine*); ihr seid da eben weiter *(in that regard, you are just more progressive)*; AUCH: das Aktiv *(active voice)*; das Passiv *(passive voice)*; die Zeitform, -en *(tense)*; die Konsequenz, -en; erfahren *(to find out)*

Fokus Weimar, a European Cultural Capital

Weimar boasts a proud cultural history. Johann Sebastian Bach was court organist there in the early 18th century. Goethe, who lived and worked in Weimar from 1775 until his death in 1832, drew Schiller, Gottfried Herder, and many others to the town, which, nourished by genius, gave birth to "Weimar Classicism." Franz Liszt was musical director in Weimar in the mid-19th century, and the philosopher and author Friedrich Nietzsche lived there during his final years as well. In 1919, following World War I, the National Assembly met in Weimar to draft a constitution for the new republic—henceforth known as the Weimar Republic. The assembly chose this site because of its popular associations with Germany's classical tradition. The new republic lasted only 14 years, dissolved by Hitler soon after he was appointed chancellor in 1933. During the Nazi period, Weimar and its traditions were used selectively to promote Nazi ideology, and some of Goethe's works were even banned from schools. On the Ettersberg, a hill above the town, a memorial recalls the nearby Nazi concentration camp of Buchenwald. Since the fall of East Germany, tourists from across Europe are again flocking to Weimar's historical and cultural landmarks. In September 2004, a fire swept through the 17th-century Anna Amalia Library, which housed around one million books. Many were damaged, including the world's largest collection of works on Goethe's *Faust*.

Die Anna-Amalia-Bibliothek in Weimar

Übungen zum Thema

A. Im Rathaus Als Radioreporter hören Sie sich die Rede eines Städteplaners an. Berichten Sie Ihren Zuhörern *(listeners)*, was Sie gehört haben!

BEISPIEL *Der Städteplaner hat gesagt, wir sollten nicht auf die Bürger hören, die immer . . .*

„Hören Sie nicht auf die Bürger, die immer wieder alles, ja die ganze Altstadt, retten wollen. Viele alte Innenhöfe *(inner courts)* sind dunkel und hässlich. Abreißen ist viel billiger und einfacher als zu renovieren. Wenn man die alten Gebäude abreißt und die Innenstadt schön modern aufbaut, dann kommt bestimmt wieder Leben in unser Zentrum. Auf diese Weise kann man auch die Straßen verbreitern *(widen)* und alles besser planen. Fußgängerzonen sind sicher schön und gut, aber nicht im Zentrum, denn alle wollen ihr Auto in der Nähe haben. Das ist doch klar, weil's viel bequemer und sicherer ist! Ich kann Ihnen garantieren, wenn Sie aus dem Zentrum eine Einkaufszone machen, zu deren Geschäften man nur zu Fuß hinkommt *(gets to)*, dann verlieren Sie alle, meine Damen und Herren, viel Geld!"

B. Schützt unsere Umwelt!

1. **Etwas für uns alle** Lesen Sie die folgenden Illustrationen und wiederholen Sie dann mit eigenen Worten, was man tun und nicht tun sollte!

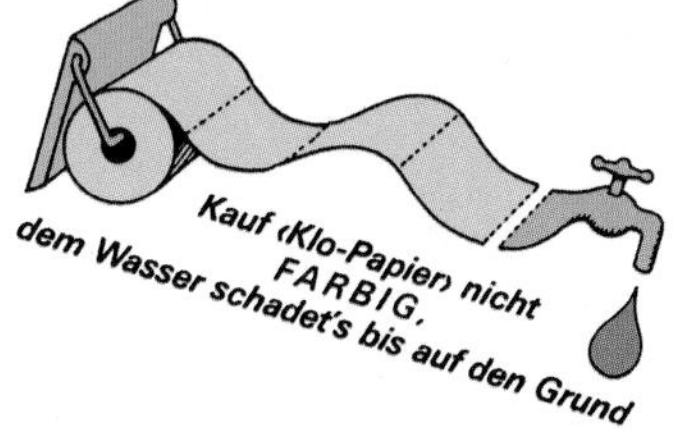

2. **Wie sieht das bei dir aus?** Fragen Sie einen Nachbarn / eine Nachbarin, . . . !

   a. was er/sie mit Altglas, Altpapier, alten Batterien, Medikamenten, Plastikflaschen, Plastiktüten (*. . . bags*), CDs und DVDs macht
   b. wofür er/sie Chemikalien benutzt und wie oft
   c. ob er/sie einen Hund hat; wenn ja, ob er/sie beim „Gassi gehen" seine „Geschäfte" aufsammelt

If you are curious: **s. erbauen an** *to enjoy;* **der Abfall-Wurf** *littering;* **das Waschmittel, -** *laundry detergent;* **in kleinen Gaben** *in small amounts;* **üblich** *customary;* **entgegen·nehmen** *to accept;* **der Verstand** *common sense;* **der Ölwechsel** *oil change;* **sei helle** *be smart;* **Gassi gehen** *to walk the doggie*

Auch Sonnenkollektoren auf dem Dach helfen der Umwelt.

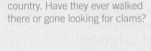

Aussprache

For further review, see the Summary of Pronunciation in the front of this book. Study Part II, subsection F.

Knacklaute *(Glottal stops)*

1. +Erich +arbeitet +am +alten Schloss.
2. Die +Abgase der +Autos machen +einfach +überall +alles kaputt.
3. +Ulf +erinnert sich +an +ein +einmaliges +Abendkonzert +im +Ulmer Dom.
4. +Otto sieht +aus wie +ein +alter +Opa.
5. +Anneliese +ist +attraktiv +und +elegant.

Ask students if they know of any such mudflats in their own country. Have they ever walked there or gone looking for clams?

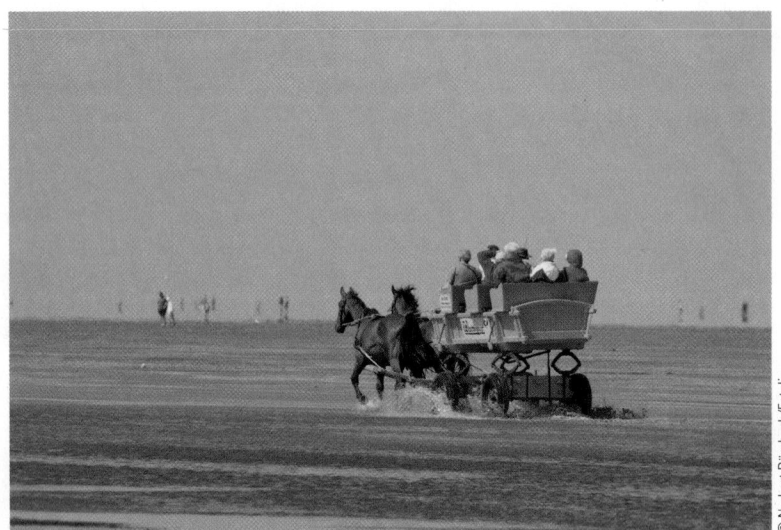

Mit dem Pferdewagen durchs Wattenmeer oder Watt bei Cuxhaven

Hörverständnis

Habitat Wattenmeer Hören Sie zu, was man Ihnen über das Wattenmeer erzählt! Sind die folgenden Aussagen richtig oder falsch?

Zum Erkennen: das flache Vorland *(tidal flats)*; grenzen an *(to border on)*; die Ebbe *(low tide)*; die Flut *(high tide)*; die Muschel, -n *(clam)*; das Paradies; die Krabbe, -n *(crab)*; knabbern *(to nibble)*; der Seehund, -e *(seal)*; das empfindliche Ökosystem *(delicate ecosystem)*; das Düngemittel, - *(fertilizer)*; der Kompromiss, -e; das Reservat, -e *(reservation)*; der Fischfang *(fishing)*; begrenzt *(limited)*; der/die Gehfaule (ein Gehfauler) *(a person too lazy to walk)*

__f__ 1. Das Wattenmeer liegt vor der Ostseeküste.

__f__ 2. Alle 12 Stunden wechselt es von Ebbe zu Flut.

__r__ 3. Bei Ebbe kann man weit ins Watt hinauslaufen.

__r__ 4. Dabei kann man alle möglichen *(all sorts of)* Tiere beobachten.

__r__ 5. Gehfaule können auch mit dem Pferdewagen ins Watt fahren.

__r__ 6. Wegen seines empfindlichen Ökosystems haben die Deutschen dieses Gebiet zum Naturschutzgebiet erklärt.

__r__ 7. Auch die Dänen und Niederländer sind am Schutz dieser Landschaft interessiert.

Struktur

15.1 The passive voice

English and German sentences are in one of two voices: the active or the passive. In the ACTIVE VOICE, the subject of the sentence is doing something; it's "active."

The students ask the professor.

In the PASSIVE VOICE, the subject is not doing anything, rather, something is being done to it; it's "passive."

The professor is asked by the students.

Note what happens when a sentence in the active voice is changed into the passive voice: The direct object of the active becomes the subject of the passive.

subj. obj.
*The students ask **the professor.***

***The professor** is asked by the students.*
subj. obj. of prep.

In both languages, the active voice is used much more frequently than the passive voice, especially in everyday speech. The passive voice is used when the focus is on the action itself or on the person or thing at whom the action is directed, rather than on the agent who is acting.

Active Voice	**Die Studenten** fragen den Professor.
Passive Voice	**Der Professor** wird von den Studenten gefragt.

The passive voice is treated only briefly because by now many students will be saturated with verb forms. If you want your students to use the passive, elaborate on the explanations; there are plenty of exercises for active mastery of the passive. Otherwise, teach the passive for recognition only. In that case, use Exercises C and D for translation into English and omit Exercises E–G.

1. Forms
   a. In English, the passive voice is formed with the auxiliary *to be* and the past participle of the verb. In German, it is formed with the auxiliary **werden** and the past participle of the verb.

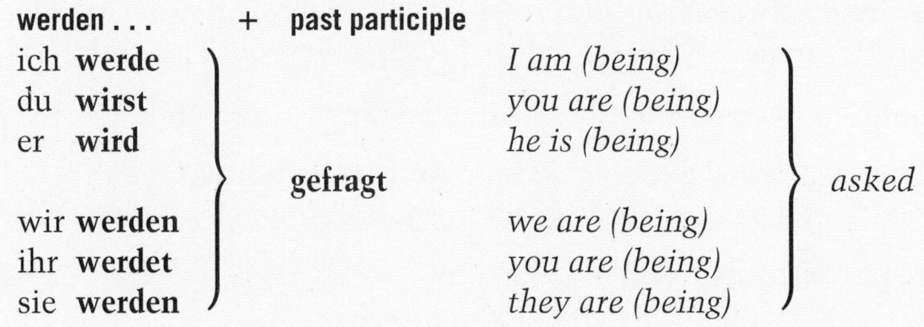

werden . . .	+ **past participle**		
ich **werde**		*I am (being)*	
du **wirst**		*you are (being)*	
er **wird**		*he is (being)*	
	gefragt		*asked*
wir **werden**		*we are (being)*	
ihr **werdet**		*you are (being)*	
sie **werden**		*they are (being)*	

Der Professor **wird** von den Studenten **gefragt.**
Die Professoren **werden** von den Studenten **gefragt.**

Wissen
was gespielt
wird
der neue kalender ist da!
semperoper.2013
www.semperoper.de/2013

© Beatrix Brockman

b. The passive voice has the same tenses as the active voice. They are formed with the various tenses of **werden** + the past participle of the verb. Note, however, that in the perfect tenses of the passive voice, the past participle of **werden** is **worden!** When you see or hear **worden,** you know immediately that you are dealing with a sentence in the passive voice.

PRESENT	Er **wird**	. . . gefragt.	*He is being asked . . .*
SIMPLE PAST	Er **wurde**	. . . gefragt.	*He was asked . . .*
FUTURE	Er **wird**	. . . gefragt **werden.**	*He will be asked . . .*
PRES. PERF.	Er **ist**	. . . gefragt **worden.**	*He has been asked . . .*
PAST PERF.	Er **war**	. . . gefragt **worden.**	*He had been asked . . .*

Die Altstadt wird renoviert. — *The old part of town is being renovated.*
Die Pläne wurden letztes Jahr gemacht. — *The plans were made last year.*
Alles wird finanziert werden. — *Everything will be financed.*
Das ist entschieden worden. — *That has been decided.*
Viele Gebäude waren im Krieg zerstört worden. — *Many buildings had been destroyed during the war.*

In subordinate clauses, the pattern is this:

Ich weiß, dass die Altstadt renoviert wird.
, dass die Pläne letztes Jahr gemacht wurden.
, dass alles finanziert werden wird.
, dass das schon entschieden worden ist.
, dass viele Gebäude im Krieg zerstört worden waren.

c. Modals themselves are not put into the passive voice. Rather, they follow this pattern:

modal . . . + past participle + **werden**

In this book, only the present tense and the simple past tense of the modals are used in the passive.

PRESENT	Er **muss**	. . . gefragt **werden.**	*He must (has to) be asked.*
SIMPLE PAST	Er **musste**	. . . gefragt **werden.**	*He had to be asked.*

Because of student burnout by the end of the book, we have chosen to omit certain points of structure, such as the present perfect and past perfect tenses of the modals in the passive, and the agent **durch.** Feel free to introduce them, however.

Das Gebäude muss renoviert werden. — *The building must be renovated.*
Das Gebäude sollte letztes Jahr renoviert werden. — *The building was supposed to be renovated last year.*

In subordinate clauses the inflected verb stands at the end.

Ich weiß, dass das Gebäude renoviert werden **muss.**
, dass das Gebäude letztes Jahr renoviert werden **sollte.**

2. Expression of the agent

If the agent who performs the act is expressed, the preposition **von** is used.

Der Professor wird **von den Studenten** gefragt. — *The professor is asked by the students.*
Alles ist **vom Staat** finanziert worden. — *Everything was financed by the state.*

3. Impersonal use

In German, the passive voice is frequently used without a subject or with **es** functioning as the subject.

Hier darf nicht gebaut werden.	*You can't build here.*
Es darf hier nicht gebaut werden.	*Building is not permitted here.*

4. Alternative to the passive voice

One common substitute for the passive voice is a sentence in the active voice with **man** as the subject.

Hier darf nicht gebaut werden.
Es darf hier nicht gebaut werden.
Man darf hier nicht bauen.

There are three other substitutes for the passive that are not included here: a. the reflexive; b. **sein . . . zu** + infinitive; c. **sich lassen** + infinitive. (**Hier verändert sich nichts.** *Nothing changes here* / **Hier ist nichts zu verändern.** *Nothing is to be changed here* / **Hier lässt sich nichts verändern.** *Nothing can be changed here.*)

Übungen

A. Trier Aktiv oder Passiv?

1. Trier was founded by the Romans in 15 B.C.E.
2. Its original name was *Augusta Treverorum.*
3. Under Roman occupation, Germania along the Rhine and Danube had been transformed into a series of Roman provinces.
4. The names of many towns derive from Latin.
5. Remnants from Roman times can still be seen today.
6. New discoveries are made from time to time.
7. Beautiful Roman museums have been built.
8. One of them is located in the former *Colonia Agrippina* (Cologne).

A: 1P, 2A, 3P, 4A, 5P, 6P, 7P, 8A

B. Köln Was bedeutet das auf Englisch?

1. a. Köln wurde während des Krieges schwer zerbombt *(destroyed by bombs).*
   b. Achtzig Prozent der Häuser in der Innenstadt waren zerbombt worden.
   c. Inzwischen *(in the meantime)* ist Köln wieder schön aufgebaut und restauriert worden.
   d. Zur Karnevalszeit wird hier schwer gefeiert.
   e. Es ist eine Stadt, in der jedes Jahr verschiedene Messen *(fairs)* gehalten werden.
   f. Die Popkomm, Kölns Messe für Popmusik und Unterhaltung, wird von einem großen Musikfestival begleitet *(accompanied)*, das in der ganzen Stadt gefeiert wird.
2. a. Erst mussten neue Wohnungen gebaut werden.
   b. Manche alten Gebäude konnten gerettet werden.
   c. Der Dom musste restauriert werden.
   d. Die alten Kirchen aus dem 12. Jahrhundert dürfen auch nicht vergessen werden.
   e. Das kann natürlich nicht ohne Geld gemacht werden.
   f. Durch Bürgerinitiativen wurde genug Geld für die Restaurierung gesammelt.
3. a. In der Altstadt wird in Parkgaragen geparkt.
   b. Es wird viel mit dem Bus gefahren.
   c. In der „Hohen Straße" wird nicht Auto gefahren.
   d. Dort wird zu Fuß gegangen.
   e. Dort wird gern eingekauft.
   f. In der Vorweihnachtszeit wird die Fußgängerzone mit vielen Lichtern dekoriert.

B.1: a. Cologne was heavily destroyed by bombs during the war. b. Eighty percent of the houses in the inner city had been destroyed by bombs. c. In the meantime, Cologne has been nicely rebuilt and restored. d. During the carnival season, there is lots of celebrating going on / they celebrate a lot. e. It is a city in which different fairs are held every year. f. The Popkomm, Cologne's fair for pop music and entertainment, is accompanied by a big music festival that's celebrated all over town.

B.2: a. First of all, new apartments had to be built. b. Some old buildings could be saved. c. The cathedral had to be restored. d. The old churches from the 12th century should / must also not be forgotten. e. That can't be done, of course, without money. f. Through citizens' initiatives, enough money for the restoration was collected.

B.3: a. In the old part of town, there are parking garages / people park in parking garages. b. Many take the bus. c. You can't drive / there's no driving in the "Hohe Straße." d. There you walk. e. There's lots of shopping / people like to shop there. f. In the pre-Christmas season, the pedestrian area is decorated with many lights.

C. Ein schönes Haus Sagen Sie die Sätze im Aktiv!

BEISPIEL Nicht alle Gebäude waren vom Krieg zerstört worden.
Der Krieg hatte nicht alle Gebäude zerstört.

C: 1. Planierraupen haben . . . zerstört. 2. Die Bürger retteten . . . (haben . . . gerettet). 3. Die Studenten sammelten . . . (haben . . . gesammelt). 4. Die Uni hat . . . gekauft.

1. Viele Gebäude sind von Planierraupen *(bulldozers)* zerstört worden.
2. Dieses Haus wurde von den Bürgern gerettet.
3. Viele Unterschriften *(signatures)* wurden von Studenten gesammelt.
4. Das Haus ist von der Uni gekauft worden.

BEISPIEL Die Fassade darf von den Architekten nicht sehr verändert werden.
Die Architekten dürfen die Fassade nicht sehr verändern.

C: 5. Die Stadt soll . . . finanzieren. 6. Die Universität muss . . . bezahlen. 7. Die Uni konnte . . . ausbauen. 8. Die Studenten dürfen . . . benutzen.

5. Ein Teil soll von der Stadt finanziert werden.
6. Der Rest muss von der Universität bezahlt werden.
7. Das Haus konnte von der Uni als Gästehaus ausgebaut werden.
8. Der große Raum im Parterre darf von den Studenten als Treffpunkt *(meeting place)* benutzt werden.

BEISPIEL Das Gästehaus wird viel besucht.
Man besucht das Gästehaus viel.

C: 9. Man spricht . . . 10. Heute Abend gibt man . . . 11. Letzte Woche hat man . . . gezeigt (zeigte man . . .). 12. Hier wird man . . . halten.

9. Es wird dort auch Englisch und Italienisch gesprochen.
10. Heute Abend wird ein Jazzkonzert gegeben.
11. Letzte Woche wurde ein Film gezeigt.
12. Hier werden auch Seminare gehalten werden.

D. Ein alter Film Wiederholen Sie die Sätze im Passiv, aber in einer anderen Zeitform *(tense)*!

BEISPIEL Ein alter Film wird gespielt. *(simple past)*
Ein alter Film wurde gespielt.

D: 1. ist . . . empfohlen worden 2. wurde . . . gezeigt 3. war verboten worden 4. wird . . . geredet werden 5. konnte . . . gelernt werden 6. sollte . . . wiederholt werden

1. Er wird von den Studenten sehr empfohlen. *(present perfect)*
2. Zu DDR-Zeiten wird er nicht gezeigt. *(simple past)*
3. Er wird verboten. *(past perfect)*
4. Es wird viel darüber geredet. *(future)*
5. Daraus kann viel gelernt werden. *(simple past)*
6. Er soll übrigens wiederholt werden. *(simple past)*

E. Post und Geld Wiederholen Sie die Sätze im Passiv, aber mit einem Modalverb! Wie heißt das auf Englisch?

BEISPIEL Das Paket wird zur Post gebracht. (sollen)
Das Paket soll zur Post gebracht werden.
The package is supposed to be taken to the post office.

E: 1. Ein Formular muss noch ausgefüllt werden. *A form still has to be filled out.* 2. Dann kann es abgegeben werden. *Then it can be turned in.* 3. Auf der Post dürfen auch Telefongespräche gemacht werden. *You are also allowed to make phone calls at the post office.* 4. Dollar sollen am Geldautomaten umgetauscht werden. *Dollars should / ought to be exchanged at the ATM machine.* 5. Nicht überall kann mit Kreditkarte bezahlt werden. *Not everywhere can you pay with credit card. / You can't pay with credit card everywhere.* 6. Buskarten wollen mit Bargeld . . . bezahlt werden. *Bus tickets must be paid in cash . . .*

1. Ein Formular wird noch ausgefüllt. (müssen)
2. Dann wird es abgegeben. (können)
3. Auf der Post werden auch Telefongespräche gemacht. (dürfen)
4. Dollar werden am Geldautomaten umgetauscht. (sollen)
5. Nicht überall wird mit Kreditkarte bezahlt. (können)
6. Buskarten werden mit Bargeld oder Kreditkarte bezahlt. (wollen)

F. Im Restaurant Sagen Sie die Sätze im Passiv!

BEISPIEL Hier spricht man Deutsch.
Hier wird Deutsch gesprochen.

1. Am anderen Tisch spricht man Französisch.
2. Mittags isst man warm.
3. Dabei redet man gemütlich.
4. Natürlich redet man nicht mit vollem Mund.
5. Übrigens hält man die Gabel normalerweise *(normally)* in der linken Hand.
6. Und vor dem Essen sagt man „Guten Appetit!"

F: Remind students not to express the agent!
1. Am anderen Tisch wird Französisch gesprochen.
2. Mittags wird warm gegessen.
3. Dabei wird gemütlich geredet.
4. Natürlich wird nicht mit vollem Mund geredet. 5. Übrigens wird die Gabel normalerweise in der linken Hand gehalten.
6. Und vor dem Essen wird „Guten Appetit!" gesagt.

G. Die Party: Was muss noch gemacht werden? Sagen Sie im Passiv, dass alles schon gemacht (worden) ist!

BEISPIEL Fritz und Lisa müssen noch angerufen werden.
Fritz und Lisa sind schon angerufen worden.

1. Die Wohnung muss noch geputzt werden.
2. Der Tisch muss noch in die Ecke gestellt werden.
3. Die Gläser müssen noch gewaschen werden.
4. Das Bier muss noch kalt gestellt werden.
5. Die Kartoffelchips müssen noch in die Schüssel *(bowl)* getan werden.
6. . . .

G: 1. Die Wohnung ist schon geputzt worden. 2. Der Tisch ist schon in die Ecke gestellt worden. 3. Die Gläser sind schon gewaschen worden.
4. Das Bier ist schon kalt gestellt worden. 5. Die Kartoffelchips sind schon in die Schüssel getan worden. 6. *(add one or two sentences)*

15.2 Review of the uses of *werden*

Distinguish carefully among the various uses of **werden.**

1. **werden** + predicate noun / adjective = a FULL VERB

Er wird Arzt.	*He's going to be a doctor.*
Es wird dunkel.	*It's getting dark.*

2. **werden** + infinitive = auxiliary of the FUTURE TENSE

Ich werde ihn fragen.	*I'll ask him.*

3. **würde** + infinitive = auxiliary in the PRESENT-TIME SUBJUNCTIVE

Ich würde ihn fragen.	*I would ask him.*

4. **werden** + past participle = auxiliary in the PASSIVE VOICE

Er wird von uns gefragt.	*He's (being) asked by us.*
Goethe wurde 1749 geboren.	*Goethe was born in 1749.*

„Je weniger die Leute darüber wissen, wie Würste und Gesetze gemacht werden, desto besser schlafen sie nachts!"

Otto von Bismarck

NOTE: To express *I was born . . .*, either **ich bin . . . geboren** or **ich wurde . . . geboren** are used. The simple past of the passive form must be used for people who are no longer living.

Übungen

H. Was ist was? Lesen Sie die folgenden Sätze und analysieren Sie sie mit Ihrem Partner / Ihrer Partnerin! Sagen Sie, wie **werden** benutzt wird und wie Sie das auf Englisch sagen würden! Wechseln Sie sich ab!

BEISPIEL Leonie ist nach Amerika eingeladen worden.
ist eingeladen worden = pres. perfect = passive voice
Leonie was invited to America.

1. Leonie möchte Englischlehrerin werden.
2. Das Studium dort musste von ihr bezahlt werden.
3. Es ist allerdings teurer geworden, als sie dachte.
4. Das wurde ihr nie erklärt.
5. Was würdest du an ihrer Stelle tun?
6. Ich würde ein Semester arbeiten.
7. Das wird nicht erlaubt werden.
8. Übrigens wird ihr Englisch schon viel besser.
9. Der USA-Aufenthalt wird ihr später helfen.

H: 1. möchte werden = present tense with modal = full verb; *wants to become* 2. musste bezahlt werden = simple past with modal = passive voice; *had to be paid* 3. ist geworden = pres. perfect = full verb; *became* 4. wurde erklärt = simple past = passive voice; *was explained* 5. würdest tun = present tense = subjunctive; *would do* 6. würde arbeiten = present tense = subjunctive; *would work* 7. wird erlaubt werden = future tense = passive voice; *won't be allowed* 8. wird = present tense = full verb; *is getting* 9. wird helfen = future tense = full verb; *will help*

I. Die Energie der Zukunft

1. **Was ist schon getan worden und was wird noch getan werden müssen?** Lesen Sie den folgenden Text und entscheiden Sie, wie **werden** benutzt wird! Wie würde man das auf Englisch sagen?

BEISPIEL Über die Umwelt wird viel geschrieben.
present tense = passive voice; is (being) written

Die Frage ist, wird man etwas dafür tun?
future tense = indicative; will do

a. Seit der Ölkrise 1973 wurde in Deutschland viel Geld in die Forschung von alternativen Energien investiert.
b. Ein Resultat sind moderne „Windräder", durch die Strom *(electricity)* gewonnen wird.
c. Investoren wissen, dass sie damit gut verdienen werden.
d. Die Windräder werden vom Staat subventioniert *(subsidized)*.
e. Wenn man heute durch Deutschlands Norden fährt, wird man immer wieder Windparks sehen.
f. Viele sprechen von einer „brutalen Zerstörung" der Landschaft. Häuser, die in der Nähe von solchen „Monstern" stehen, werden schlecht zu verkaufen sein.
g. Viele Leute haben dagegen protestiert. Sie sagen, man könnte diese „Windtürme" hören und ihre roten Warnlichter würden nachts einen Disko-Effekt geben.
h. Ein Politiker, der dagegen ist, wurde von der Windlobby als „Don Quichotte" verlacht *(made fun of)*.
i. So wie es aussieht, wird der Strom der Zukunft von einem Mix aus traditionellen und erneuerbaren *(renewable)* Energien kommen müssen.
j. Dabei werden die erneuerbaren Energien eine immer größere Rolle spielen.

I. 1: a. simple past = passive voice; *was invested* b. present tense = passive voice; *is (being) won* c. future tense = indicative; *will earn* d. present tense = passive voice; *are (being) subsidized* e. future tense = indicative; *will see* f. future tense = indicative; *will be hard (to sell)* g. present tense = subjunctive; *would cast / produce* h. simple past = passive voice; *was made fun of* i. present tense = indicative; *will have to come* j. future tense = indicative; *will play*

2. **Der Energieverbrauch *(energy consumption)* weltweit** Sehen Sie sich die Grafik an und beantworten Sie ein paar Fragen!

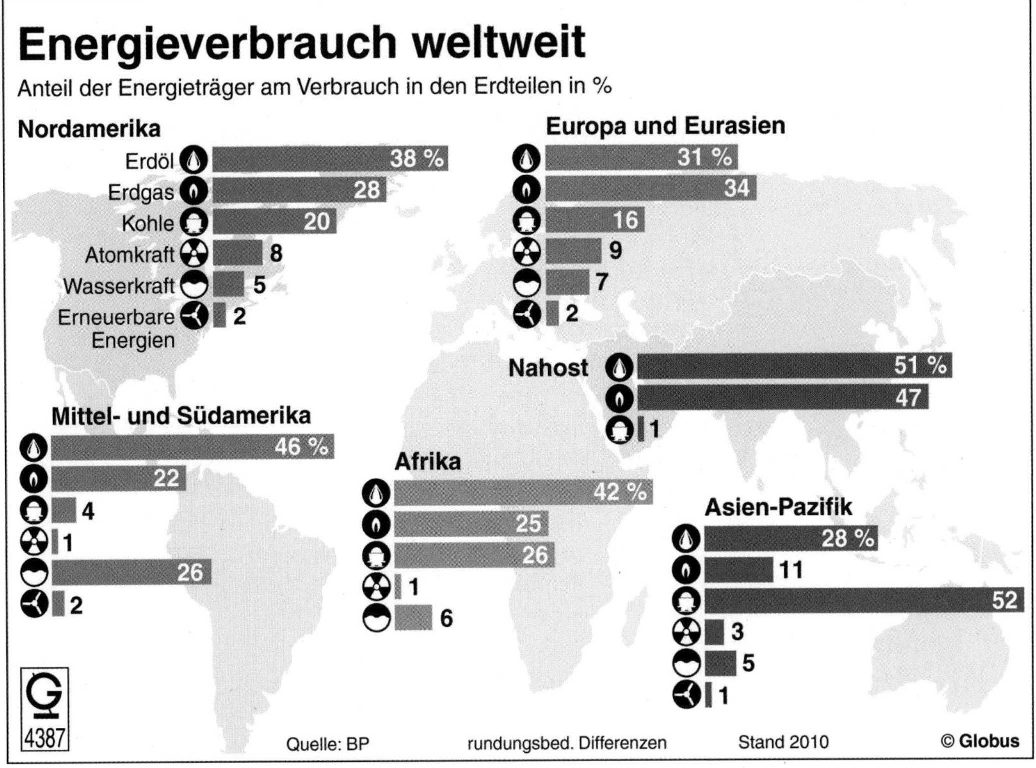

a. Wer verbraucht *(uses)* das meiste Erdöl und wer das wenigste *(the least)*?
b. Wo wird am wenigsten Erdgas verbraucht und wo am meisten?
c. Wie viel Atomkraft benutzen die verschiedenen Kontinente?
d. Wo werden erneuerbare Energien besonders verbraucht?

In case you are curious: **der Anteil, -e** *share*; **der Energieträger, -** *source of energy;* **das Erdöl** *oil;* **die Kohle** *coal;* **die Atomkraft** *nuclear power;* **die Wasserkraft** *hydro (water) power;* **die erneuerbare Energie, -n** *renewable energy*

15.3 The special subjunctive

German has another type of subjunctive, often called the SPECIAL SUBJUNCTIVE or SUBJUNCTIVE I. English has only a few remnants of this subjunctive.

Thanks be to God! / Long live Freedom! / Be that as it may.

In German, the special subjunctive is used in similar expressions.

Gott sei Dank! / Es lebe die Freiheit! / Wie dem auch sei.

Other than in such phrases, the Subjunctive I is rarely heard in conversation. It is primarily used in formal writing and indirect speech, often to summarize another person's findings or opinion. It is most frequently encountered in critical literary or scientific essays, in literature, and in news articles, where it distances the author from his or her report and preserves a sense of objectivity.

In general, the forms of the third person singular are the ones used most often because they clearly differ from those of the indicative. When the forms of the special subjunctive are identical with those of the indicative, the general subjunctive is used instead. At this point, you need only to be able to recognize the forms of the special subjunctive and know why they are used.

The section on the special subjunctive may be omitted if desired. At any rate, it is designed for recognition only.

1. PRESENT-TIME forms

   The PRESENT-TIME forms of the special subjunctive have the same endings as the general subjunctive and are added to the stem of the infinitive:

glauben

ich glaub**e**	wir glaub**en**
du glaub**est**	ihr glaub**et**
er glaub**e**	sie glaub**en**

Note, however, that verbs having a vowel change in the second and third person singular of the indicative *do not* have that vowel change in the special subjunctive. Note also that the first and third person singular forms of **sein** are irregular in that they do not have an **-e** ending.

INFINITIVE	SPECIAL SUBJ. er / es / sie	INDICATIVE er / es / sie
haben	**habe**	hat
sein	**sei**	ist
tun	**tue**	tut
denken	**denke**	denkt
fahren	**fahre**	fährt
sehen	**sehe**	sieht
werden	**werde**	wird
wissen	**wisse**	weiß
dürfen	**dürfe**	darf
können	**könne**	kann
mögen	**möge**	mag
müssen	**müsse**	muss
wollen	**wolle**	will

ich hab**e**	wir hab**en**
du hab**est**	ihr hab**et**
er hab**e**	sie hab**en**

ich müss**e**	wir müss**en**
du müss**est**	ihr müss**et**
er müss**e**	sie müss**en**

ich sei	wir sei**en**
du sei**est**	ihr sei**et**
er sei	sie sei**en**

Er sagte, er **habe** keine Zeit. — *He said he had no time.*
Er sagte, sie **sei** nicht zu Hause. — *He said she wasn't home.*

2. To refer to the FUTURE *(to later)*, combine the special subjunctive of **werden** with an infinitive.

   werde . . . + infinitive

   Er sagte, er **werde** bald fertig **sein.** — *He said he'd be finished soon.*

3. To form the PAST-TIME special subjunctive, use the special subjunctive of **haben** or **sein** with a past participle.

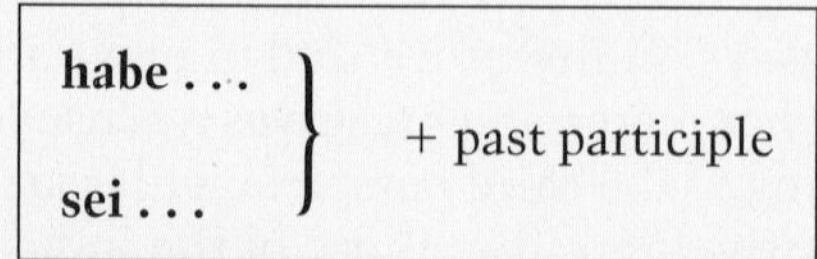

Er sagt, er **habe** keine Zeit **gehabt.** — *He says he didn't have time.*
Er sagte, sie **sei** nicht zu Hause **gewesen.** — *He said she hadn't been home.*

Übungen

J: As a review, you might ask students to spell in German the names of cities and celebrities mentioned here.

Goethe (1749–1832), Schiller (1759–1805), Bach (1685–1750), Händel (1685–1759), Luther (1483–1546)

J. Finden Sie den Konjunktiv und unterstreichen Sie *(underline)* ihn!

1. **Städte deutscher Kultur**

Mein Onkel sagte, dass Weimar, Leipzig, Halle, Wittenberg und Eisenach wichtige deutsche Kulturstädte seien. In Weimar sei Johann Wolfgang von Goethe Theaterdirektor und Staatsminister gewesen und dort habe Friedrich von Schiller seine wichtigsten Dramen geschrieben. In Leipzig habe Johann Sebastian Bach 27 Jahre lang Kantaten und Oratorien für den Thomanerchor komponiert. Dieser Knabenchor *(boys' choir)* sei heute noch sehr berühmt. Nicht weit von Leipzig liege Halle, wo Georg Friedrich Händel geboren worden sei. In Wittenberg, das man heute die Lutherstadt nennt, habe Martin Luther mit seinen 95 Thesen die Reformation begonnen. Sein Zimmer auf der Wartburg bei Eisenach, wo er die Bibel ins Deutsche übersetzt hat, sei heute noch zu besichtigen. Man könne auch heute noch sehen, wo er dem Teufel ein Tintenfass nachgeworfen habe *(had thrown an inkwell at the devil)*. Er wisse allerdings nicht, woher diese Geschichte komme. Er glaube sie nicht.

Die Wartburg bei Eisenach

2. **Gedanken zur Umwelt**

Die Wissenschaftler sagten, dass man mit mehr Wohlstand *(affluence)* mehr Energie brauchen werde. Mehr Energie bedeute aber mehr Kohlendioxid-Emissionen *(carbon dioxide . . .)*. Kohlendioxid sei mitverantwortlich für den so genannten Treibhauseffekt *(greenhouse effect)*. Damit man die Umwelt nicht noch mehr verschmutze und ihr auf diese Weise noch mehr schade, müsse man alles tun, um sie zu schützen. Es müsse mehr in die Umwelttechnologie investiert werden. Die Nordamerikaner und Europäer tragen dabei eine besondere Verantwortung, denn sie, mit nur 10 Prozent der Weltbevölkerung, verbrauchen *(consume)* fast die Hälfte der Energie. In Asien liege der Verbrauch bei etwas über einem Viertel der Weltenergie, obwohl allein in China 20 Prozent der Menschheit *(mankind)* lebe. Darüber solle man sich echt einmal Gedanken machen. Die Gefahr *(danger)* der Klimaveränderung und seiner Konsequenzen sei für viele Wissenschaftler die wichtigste Herausforderung *(challenge)* des 21. Jahrhunderts.

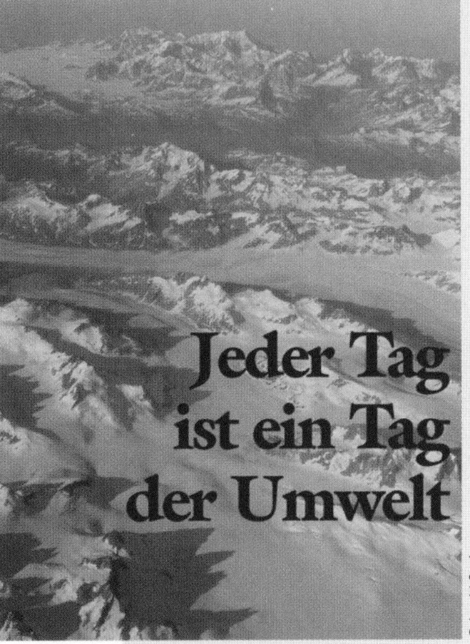
Jeder Tag
ist ein Tag
der Umwelt

Fokus In Search of an Identity

The unification of Germany and the progressive emergence of an ever more integrated Europe have contributed to a new assessment of what it means to be German. This search for a national identity goes back to a time well before Bismarck united the country in 1871. For centuries, Germany had been divided into numerous small, autocratically ruled principalities. This fragmentation contributed to the significant diversity among various parts of Germany, yet also inhibited the development of a broadly based democratic consciousness. Altough most Germans continue to reject nationalism and embrace the idea of a united Europe enthusiastically, a new pride in their own localities is noticeable at the same time. A new interest in local dialects, history, and the restoration and rebuilding of destroyed historical sites is symptomatic of this trend. As more people of other ethnic and religious heritages become German citizens, and the corresponding new customs and ways of living make for an increasingly diverse culture, the question of what it means to be German takes on new dimensions and continues to be as relevant as ever.

iLrn

Visit the ***Wie geht's?*** iLrn website for more review and practice of the grammar points you have just learned.

K: 1. *was opened* 2. *was planned* 3. *had to be rerouted, was built* 4. *were connected to* 5. *are visited* 6. *can be played*

Zusammenfassung

K. Der Berliner Hauptbahnhof Übersetzen Sie die verschiedenen unterstrichenen Verbformen!

1. Im Mai 2006 wurde der neue Berliner Hauptbahnhof eröffnet.
2. An dem Projekt ist lange geplant worden.
3. Die Spree musste eine Weile umgeleitet *(rerouted)* werden, weil ein neuer Tunnel gebaut wurde.
4. Heute kreuzen sich *(cross)* hier die Ost-West- und Nord-Süd-Verbindungen, denen die Regionalzüge und S-Bahnen angeschlossen *(connected to)* worden sind.
5. Dieses moderne Glasgebäude im Herzen der Stadt—nicht weit von dem Regierungsgebäude und dem Reichstag—hat viele Geschäfte und Restaurants, die täglich von 8.00 bis 22.00 Uhr geöffnet sind und immer gut besucht werden.
6. Der unkonventionelle Bahnhof liegt direkt an der Spree, an deren Strand *(beach)* auch gegrillt, gefaulenzt, getanzt oder Volleyball gespielt werden kann.

Im modernen Berliner Hauptbahnhof

L: 1. *put* (simple past) 2. *was made* (simple past); *had participated in* (lit. also *flown*) (past perf.) 3. had *died* (past perf.) 4. *said* (simple past); *were* (simple past); *had brought together* (past subj.) 5. *appealed* (simple past); *to forget* (infinitive) 6. is (present) 7. *have played* (pres. perf.)

L. Dresdens Frauenkirche Lesen Sie den folgenden Text und übersetzen Sie die verschiedenen Verbformen; nur eine davon ist im Passiv! Welche Zeitformen werden dabei benutzt?

BEISPIEL Die Frauenkirche zeigt sich wieder in voller Pracht *(full splendor)*.
presents itself (present)

1. Im Juni 2004 setzte ein Spezialkran° die kupferne Turmhaube° wieder auf die Kuppel° der Dresdner Frauenkirche.
2. Das neue goldene Kreuz° wurde in England unter Leitung° eines Silberschmiedes° hergestellt°, dessen Vater 1945 als Pilot den Luftangriff° auf Dresden mitgeflogen hatte.
3. Rund 35,000 Menschen waren dabei ums Leben gekommen°.
4. Der Herzog° von Kent, Präsident des „Dresden Trust", sagte bei der Feier im Juni, dass das Projekt Menschen, die einst Feinde° waren, in Freundschaft zusammengebracht hätte.
5. Er appellierte°, beim Aufbau° eines vereinten Europas die traurige Vergangenheit nicht zu vergessen.
6. Seit Oktober 2004 ist der Wiederaufbau der Frauenkirche abgeschlossen.
7. In der Festwoche haben die New Yorker Philharmoniker in dem wieder aufgebauten Wahrzeichen° Dresdens gespielt.

. . . crane / copper hood
dome
cross / direction
silversmith / made / air raid
died
duke
enemies
appealed / building
landmark

Die Frauenkirche, das Wahrzeichen von Dresden

Einblicke

Lesetext

Wortschatz 2

die Bevölkerung	*population*
einzeln	*individual(ly)*
endlich	*finally*
gefährlich	*dangerous (ly)*
gemeinsam	*(in) common, together, jointly*
inzwischen	*in the meantime*
stolz (auf + *acc.*)	*proud (of), proudly*
typisch	*typical (ly)*
verbinden, verband, verbunden	*to connect, tie together, link*
wachsen (wächst), wuchs, ist gewachsen	*to grow*
zusammen·wachsen (wächst zusammen), wuchs zusammen, ist zusammengewachsen	*to grow together*

Vor dem Lesen

A. Unterwegs in der EU und im eigenen Land Fragen Sie die anderen, . . . !

© gcpics/Shutterstock

© Gina Sanders/Fotolia

1. Mit ihrem Pass können die Deutschen überall in der EU herumreisen. Wie ist das bei Ihnen? Haben Sie einen Pass? Warum (nicht)? Wozu bräuchten Sie einen?
2. Der deutsche Führerschein *(driver's license)* ist überall in der EU gültig *(valid)* und muss nicht erneuert werden. Wie ist das bei Ihnen? Wann und wie oft müssen Sie ihn erneuern?
3. Viele Europäer haben keinen Führerschein, weil er teuer ist und man nicht unbedingt ein Auto braucht. Wie ist das bei Ihnen? Wozu braucht man ihn auch?
4. Die Deutschen können überall in der EU arbeiten. Wie ist das bei Ihnen? Wird Ihre Ausbildung im ganzen Land anerkannt *(recognized)*?

> **Lesetipp**
>
> **Anticipating Content**
>
> Anticipating the content of a text can help you prepare not only the vocabulary you need to understand the reading but also the ideas that will be explored in the reading. This reading deals with issues of loss of national identity associated with the European Union. Brainstorm with a small group what you think the word **Europäisierung** could mean. What do you think some member states might be fearful of giving up? Make a list.

B. Das ist leicht zu verstehen! Lesen Sie laut die folgenden Wörter und raten Sie, was sie auf Englisch bedeuten?

der Dialekt, Kontakt, Lebensstandard; das Ausländische; die Armee, Identität, Kooperation, Kriminalität, Lebensqualität, Luftverschmutzung, Solidarität, Zusammengehörigkeit; aufwachsen; arrogant, europaweit, geteilt, kritisch, offiziell, regional, weltoffen, weltweit; im Prinzip, teilweise, zu Beginn

Der Wind kennt keine Grenzen.

Europa ist größer geworden. Seine Mitgliedstaaten° haben einen gemeinsamen Pass, ein gemeinsames Parlament, einen gemeinsamen Gerichtshof° und sogar eine kleine gemeinsame Armee. Allerdings haben sie nicht in allem eine gemeinsame Meinung, wie zum Beispiel in der Außenpolitik°. Und doch macht man Fortschritte°; Europa scheint enger° zusammenzuwachsen. Jeder Europäer kann jetzt in jedem europäischen Land arbeiten; seine Ausbildung soll europaweit anerkannt° werden. Durch persönliche Kontakte wird sich allmählich° ein Gefühl der Zusammengehörigkeit und Solidarität entwickeln°. Auf eine europäische Hauptsprache hat man sich nicht einigen° können.

Was bedeutet es für Deutschland, dass es jetzt nicht mehr am Rande°, sondern in der Mitte Europas liegt? Natürlich fühlen sich die Deutschen als Europäer, aber sie wollen auch Deutsche bleiben. Vor allem aber muss Deutschland selbst erst einmal° zusammenwachsen, denn es war ja bis 1990 offiziell ein geteiltes Land. Als die Mauer dann endlich fiel, existierte sie weiter in den Köpfen: Plötzlich gab es „Ossis" und „Wessis"°. Viele Westdeutsche meinten, dass die „Ossis" unselbstständige und ehrgeizlose arme Teufel° seien. Auf der anderen Seite meinten viele Ostdeutsche, dass die „Wessis" arrogant seien und dächten, ihnen gehöre die Welt. Sie würden immer alles besser wissen—daher° der Spitzname „Besserwessis".

Was verbindet nun eigentlich alle Deutschen? Natürlich die Sprache, Kultur und Geschichte, aber im Prinzip gibt es eigentlich wenig, was typisch für alle Deutschen wäre. Vielleicht sind es die kleineren Dinge im Leben. So könnte man zum Beispiel sagen, dass die meisten gesellig° sind und gern in Straßencafés oder Gartenrestaurants sitzen, dass sie Fußball lieben und sich in Vereinen organisieren. Die Familie und die Freizeit bedeutet ihnen oft mehr als der Staat. Sicherlich sind viele Deutsche reiselustig, aber sie lieben auch ihre Heimat: die Landschaft, in der sie aufgewachsen sind, die Stadt oder das Dorf. Viele sind wieder stolz auf ihre Herkunft°; regionale Dialekte werden wieder mehr gesprochen und auch im Radio und im Theater gepflegt°. Das mag teilweise historische Gründe° haben, denn die Bevölkerung bestand schon immer aus° verschiedenen Volksstämmen° und sie waren nur kurze Zeit *ein* Staat, nämlich von Bismarcks Reichsgründung° 1871 bis zum Ende des 2. Weltkrieges 1945. Mit der zunehmenden° Europäisierung möchten viele gerade heute ihre regionale Identität nicht verlieren.

Wenn es schon schwer zu sagen ist, wie die Deutschen sind, so kann man doch sehen, dass sie europäischer geworden sind, das heißt weltoffener und informierter. Auch ist die Bevölkerung mit einem größeren Anteil° von Ausländern multikultureller geworden. Die Deutschen sind heute kritischer und nicht mehr so autoritätsgläubig° wie zu Beginn des 20. Jahrhunderts. Das so genannte Typisch-Deutsche ist nicht mehr so wichtig; das Ausländische ist interessanter geworden. Die Musik in Deutschland ist international. Man isst besonders gern Italienisch und französischer Wein wird genauso gern getrunken wie deutsches Bier.

member . . .
court
foreign policy
progress / closer
recognized / gradually
develop
agree on
at the outskirts
first of all
East and West Germans *(derogatory)*
poor devils without ambition
hence
sociable
origin
cultivated
reasons / consisted of
ethnic groups
founding of the empire
increasing
share
believing in authority

struggle for
necessary
it's a matter of
combatting

. . . consumption
taken seriously
overcome

Der Kampf um° Umweltschutz und um eine bessere Lebensqualität ist auch sehr wichtig geworden. Man weiß, wie notwendig° die Kooperation der Nachbarländer ist, wenn es darum geht°, Probleme wie Kriminalität und Terrorismus zu bekämpfen°. Natürlich wollen die Deutschen ihren hohen Lebensstandard erhalten, aber sie glauben, das dürfte auch mit weniger Energieverbrauch° und weniger Chemie möglich sein. Mülltrennung wird zum Beispiel in weiten Kreisen der Bevölkerung sehr ernst genommen°. Auch wissen sie, dass zum Beispiel die Luftverschmutzung nur europaweit bewältigt° werden kann, denn der Wind kennt keine Grenzen.

Nach dem Lesen

A: 1. ein Parlament, einen Gerichtshof, eine kleine Armee 2. oder eine gemeinsame Sprache 3. soll europaweit anerkannt werden 4. in den Köpfen 5. Die Ossis seien / wären unselbstständige, ehrgeizlose arme Teufel. Die Wessis seien / wären arrogant und dächten, ihnen gehöre / gehörte die Welt; sie wissen / wüssten alles besser. 6. die Bevölkerung, die Musik, Essen und Trinken 7. die Mülltrennung 8. gemeinsam mit den anderen europäischen Staaten / europaweit

A. Alles verstanden?

1. Was haben die EU-Mitgliedstaaten gemeinsam?
2. Was haben sie aber nicht alle?
3. Was soll mit der Ausbildung geschehen?
4. Wo existierte nach der Wiedervereinigung weiter eine Mauer?
5. Was hielten die „Wessis" von den „Ossis"? die „Ossis" von den „Wessis"?
6. Was ist internationaler geworden in Deutschland?
7. Was wird in weiten Kreisen der Bevölkerung sehr ernst genommen?
8. Wie müssen Probleme wie Kriminalität, Terror und Luftverschmutzung bekämpft werden?

B. Typisch Deutsch! Machen Sie mit den anderen eine Liste mit all den Eigenschaften, die der Autor im Text über die Deutschen erwähnt! Wie sehen diese *(these)* im Vergleich zu Ihrem Bild der Deutschen aus?

C. Meinungsumfrage: Bei den Deutschen und bei uns

1. **Bei den Deutschen** Was erfahren Sie *(learn)* durch diese Umfrage? Stellen Sie ein paar Vergleiche auf!

BEISPIEL *Die Sorge um die Ausbildung ist ihnen wichtiger als die Sorge um die Gesundheit.*
Bei dem Wort EUROPA denken sie mehr an Kultur als an Geschichte.

Worüber machen sich die Deutschen Sorgen?	
Wirtschaft, Arbeitslosigkeit	24%
Ausbildung, Prüfungen	16%
Gesundheit	15%
Familie, Kinder, Jugend	12%
Umweltkatastrophen	10%
Kriminalität	9%
Einsamkeit	8%
Terrorismus	6%

Beim Wort EUROPA denke ich an ...	
Kultur	25%
Geschichte	21%
Geographie und Reisen	21%
Sprachen	18%
Bürokratie	15%

Ich fühle mich vor allem als ...	
Deutscher	35%
Kölner, Leipziger ...	20%
Weltbürger	18%
Hesse, Thüringer ...	15%
Europäer	12%

2. **Bei uns** Worüber machen Sie sich Sorgen? Machen Sie eine Umfrage in Ihrer Klasse und listen Sie die Punkte nach Wichtigkeit!

BEISPIEL 1 Umweltkatastrophen
2 Wirtschaft, Arbeitslosigkeit
3 . . .

You may wish to ask students whether they like to go to the beach (**der Strand, ⸚e**). Why, where, and when? What kind of life can one observe along the beach or in the water? Are beaches always very clean? If not, what might one find there that doesn't belong? What kind of protection do beaches need?

© Neftali/Shutterstock

In case you are curious: *clam* **die Muschel, -n**; *crab* **die Krabbe, -n**; *dolphin* **der Delfin, -e**; *fish* **der Fisch, -e**; *jellyfish* **die Qualle, -n**; *lobster* **der Hummer, -**; *pelican der* **Pelikan, -e**; *sandpiper* **der Strandläufer, -**; *seagull* **die Möwe, -n**; *seal* **der Seehund, -e**; *shark* **der Hai, -e**; *starfish* **der Seestern, -e**

D. Hoppla, hier fehlt was: So sind sie. Schauen Sie sich die folgende Collage mit den verschiedenen nationalen Eigenschaften an! Eine zweite Collage ist im Anhang. Finden Sie mit Ihrem Nachbarn / Ihrer Nachbarin heraus, was die Leute aus diesen 12 Ländern charakterisiert. Sie brauchen nicht alles über sie aufzuschreiben, nur ein paar Wörter.

Die Iren: sehr sportlich, . . .
Die Luxemburger: . . .
Die Portugiesen: . . .
Die Italiener: . . .
Die Holländer: . . .
Die Spanier: . . .

BEISPIEL S1 Wie sind die Iren?
S2 Die Iren lieben den Sport. Jeder zweite . . . Und wie sind die Belgier?
S1 Sie haben . . .

Versorgte Belgier

Belgien ist mit Medikamenten super versorgt, hat die meisten Apotheken je Einwohner.

Patente Deutsche

Die Deutschen sind in Europa die größten Erfinder – sie melden jährlich über 260 000 Patente an.

Gesunde Griechen

Die Griechen essen die meisten Vitamine. Je Einwohner und Jahr 195 Kilo Gemüse und 76 Kilo Obst.

Gesellige Dänen

Die Dänen sind die geselligsten Europäer. 83 Prozent der Bevölkerung sind Mitglieder in Vereinen.

Lebensfrohe Franzosen

In Frankreich leben die Europäer am längsten, besonders Frauen. Sie werden im Schnitt älter als 80.

Belesene Briten

Die Briten sind zeitungsgierig. Auf jeden kommen 3 Zeitungen – Europa-Rekord im Zeitungslesen.

© Ingrid Sevin

Hörverständnis

Europa-Schulen Hören Sie, was an diesen Schulen so besonders ist! Ergänzen Sie dann die folgenden Aussagen!

Zum Erkennen: erziehen *(to educate, raise)*; die Klassenkameradin *(classmate)*; das Lehrbuch, ¨er *(textbook)*; chauvinistisch; die Flotte *(fleet)*; sich konzentrieren auf *(to concentrate on)*

1. Europa-Schulen gibt es __b__.
   a. in jedem Land der EU
   b. in mehreren europäischen Ländern
   c. auf der ganzen Welt
2. Die Schüler haben __b__.
   a. keine Fächer in ihrer Muttersprache
   b. manche Fächer in ihrer Muttersprache
   c. nicht mehr als zwei Sprachen
3. Sie lernen Geschichte __c__.
   a. immer in ihrer Muttersprache
   b. aus internationalen Lehrbüchern
   c. nie in ihrer Muttersprache
4. In französischen Lehrbüchern liest man __a__.
   a. nicht viel über solche Länder wie Belgien oder Luxemburg
   b. interessante Informationen über englische Kultur
   c. stolz, wie Nelson die spanische Flotte bei Trafalgar zerstört hat
5. Die Schüler lernen im Geschichtsunterricht, __b__.
   a. chauvinistischer zu werden
   b. die Geschichte ihres eigenen Landes objektiver zu sehen
   c. gutes Deutsch

There is an extensive review section following this chapter in the *Arbeitsbuch* (SAM) *(Rückblick: Kapitel 12–15)*. The accompanying exercises and answer key will help you prepare for the test.

For further practice, an optional two-part video (**Szenen** and **Interviews**) is available on the ***Wie geht's?*** Premium Website and in iLrn, with corresponding questions and activities in the *Arbeitsbuch* (SAM).

As an optional activity, you could use Google Earth to visit Weimar and some of the other cities mentioned in this chapter, or you could visit islands in the North Sea and the Baltic Sea.

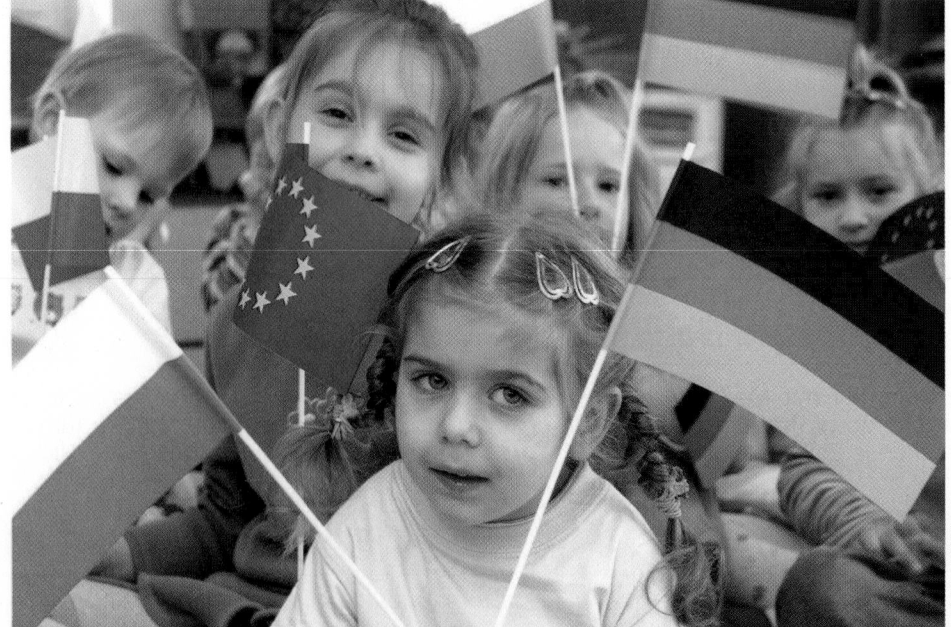

Kindergartenkinder mit deutschen und polnischen Flaggen sowie einer für Europa

Literatur

Biographisches

Franz Kafka (1883–1924) was a German-speaking Jewish writer, born in Prague, who gained international fame after World War II. His works depict modern man's anxiety and alienation in a hostile and indifferent world. Typical for his work are characters who are frustrated in their attempts to gain knowledge, social acceptance, or salvation; their alienation is rooted in a feeling of personal guilt and an inescapable destiny. In his novel *Der Prozeß* (1925), a man is arrested, convicted, and executed by a mysterious court without ever learning the nature of his crime. *Das Schloß* (1930) portrays the futile struggle of a newcomer to gain acceptance in a village that is ruled by an unknown authority in the castle. *Amerika* (1927) describes the inconclusive struggle of a young immigrant trying to gain a foothold in an alien, incomprehensible country. Kafka's best-known short stories include: "Das Urteil," the story of a rebellious son condemned to suicide by his father; "Die Verwandlung," a detailed description of a son who suffers the literal and symbolic transformation into an ugly, fatally wounded beetle; and "Ein Hungerkünstler," an exploration of the community where Kafka was born and the solitary life of an artist. For financial support Kafka worked most of his life as an insurance lawyer. He died of tuberculosis.

Erich Kästner (1899–1974) was a German writer known for his sarcastic poems—often directed against narrow-mindedness and militarism—and his witty novels and children's books. In 1933, the Nazis burned those books by Kästner that they considered disrespectful. Yet when officials noticed how well received his books were abroad, they relaxed their prohibition and allowed him to write apolitical and humorous stories and publish them through a Swiss publishing house. Kästner's works include the poetry anthology *Bei Durchsicht meiner Bücher* (1946) and the stories *Emil und die Detektive* (1929), *Das fliegende Klassenzimmer* (1933), *Das doppelte Lottchen* (1949), and *Konferenz der Tiere* (1949), in which he denounced the madness of armament. All his best-known works have become movies. His satirical comedy *Die Schule der Diktatoren* appeared in 1957, the year in which he was awarded the renowned Büchner Prize.

Vor dem Lesen

Stilfragen zu Kafkas Parabel und Kästners Gedicht

1. a. Welches Pronomen benutzt der Erzähler immer wieder für sich?
   b. Wie spricht der Diener *(servant)* seinen Herrn an *(addresses)*, mit **Sie** oder mit **du**?
   c. Hat der Diener oder der Herr einen Namen?

2. a. Gibt es Reime in diesem Gedicht? Wenn ja, folgen sie einem bestimmten Muster *(pattern)*, z. B. ababa, abbab oder abaab?
   b. Welches Pronomen wird immer wieder wiederholt?
   c. In der ersten und letzten Strophe ist ein Satz zweimal in der Vergangenheit. Wie heißt dieser Satz?

Der Aufbruch°

Ich befahl° mein Pferd aus dem Stall° zu holen°. Der Diener° verstand mich nicht. Ich ging selbst in den Stall, sattelte° mein Pferd und bestieg° es. In der Ferne° hörte ich eine Trompete blasen°, ich fragte ihn, was das bedeute. Er wusste nichts und hatte nichts gehört. Beim Tore hielt er mich auf und fragte: „Wohin reitest du, Herr?" „Ich weiß es nicht", sagte ich, „nur weg von hier, nur weg von hier. Immerfort° weg von hier, nur so kann ich mein Ziel° erreichen°." „Du kennst also dein Ziel?" fragte er. „Ja" antwortete ich, „ich sagte es doch: ‚Weg-von-hier', das ist mein Ziel." „Du hast keinen Essvorrat° mit", sagte er. „Ich brauche keinen", sagte ich, „die Reise ist so lang, dass ich verhungern° muss, wenn ich auf dem Weg nichts bekomme. Kein Essvorrat kann mich retten. Es ist ja zum Glück° eine wahrhaft ungeheuere° Reise."

Franz Kafka

departure
ordered / stable / get / servant
saddled / climbed on
In the distance / sound of a trumpet
Always / destination / reach
provisions
starve
luckily / truly big

Source: Franz Kafka, "Der Aufbruch" in *Das Franz Kafka Buch*, ed. Knut Beck (Frankfurt/Main: S. Fischer Verlag GmbH, 1949).

Das Eisenbahngleichnis°

Wir sitzen alle im gleichen Zug
und reisen quer durch° die Zeit.
Wir sehen hinaus. Wir sahen genug.
Wir fahren alle im gleichen Zug
und keiner weiß wie weit.

Ein Nachbar schläft, ein anderer klagt°,
ein dritter redet viel.
Stationen° werden angesagt°.
Der Zug, der durch die Jahre jagt,°
kommt niemals an sein Ziel.

Wir packen aus. Wir packen ein.
Wir finden keinen Sinn°.
Wo werden wir wohl morgen sein?
Der Schaffner° schaut zur Tür herein
und lächelt vor sich hin°.

Auch er weiß nicht, wohin er will.
Er schweigt° und geht hinaus.
Da heult° die Zugsirene schrill!
Der Zug fährt langsam und hält still.
Die Toten° steigen aus.

Ein Kind steigt aus. Die Mutter schreit.
Die Toten stehen stumm°
am Bahnsteig der Vergangenheit.
Der Zug fährt, er jagt durch die Zeit,
und niemand weiß, warum.

Die 1. Klasse ist fast leer.
Ein feister° Herr sitzt stolz
im roten Plüsch° und atmet° schwer.
Er ist allein und spürt° das sehr.
Die Mehrheit° sitzt auf Holz°.

Wir reisen alle im gleichen Zug
zur Gegenwart in spe°.
Wir sehen hinaus. Wir sahen genug.
Wir sitzen alle im gleichen Zug
und viele im falschen Coupé°.

Erich Kästner

. . . parable
all across
complains
stops / announced
races
purpose
conductor
to himself
keeps quiet
howls
dead
silently
fat
plush upholstery / breathes
senses
majority / wood(en benches)
full of hope
compartment

Source: Erich Kästner, "Das Eisenbahngleichnis" from *Doktor Erich Kästners Lyrische Hausapotheke* (Zurich: Atrium, 1936).

Nach dem Lesen

A. Inhaltsfragen zu Kafkas Parabel und Kästners Gedicht

1. a Was befiehlt *(orders)* der Herr dem Diener in Kafkas Parabel?
   b. Tut der Diener das? Warum (nicht)?
   c. Was hört der Herr in der Ferne?
   d. Warum will der Herr weg?
   e. Was nimmt er mit?

2. a Wohin fährt der Zug in Kästners Gedicht?
   b. Fährt er langsam oder schnell?
   c. Wohin fahren die Leute und was tun sie während der Fahrt?
   d. Wer sitzt allein? Wo sitzen die meisten Leute?
   e. Was meint Kästner damit, wenn er sagt, dass wir alle im gleichen Zug sitzen?

A.1: a. Er soll das Pferd aus dem Stall holen. b. Nein. Er versteht / verstand ihn nicht. c. Er hört eine Trompete. d. Das weiß er nicht. Er sucht ein Ziel. e. Er nimmt nichts (zu essen) mit.

A.2: a. Das weiß man nicht. b. Er fährt schnell c. Sie wissen es nicht. Sie schlafen, klagen oder reden viel. d. Ein dicker Herr in der 1. Klasse sitzt allein. Die meisten sitzen auf Holz (in der 2. oder 3. Klasse). e. *(answers may vary)*

B. Ein Vergleich der beiden Parabeln

1. In Kafkas Geschichte beginnt die Reise gerade erst *(only just)*. Der Herr geht allein auf diese Reise. Er ergreift *(takes)* selbst die Initiative und sattelt sein Pferd. Was motiviert ihn? Wie bereitet er sich vor? Warum kann ihm niemand dabei helfen? Warum nimmt er nichts mit? Was ist sein Ziel? Wie interpretieren Sie das? Was will Kafka uns über den Sinn des Lebens sagen?
2. In Kästners Gedicht hat die Reise schon begonnen. Die Menschen sitzen gemeinsam im Zug. Gibt es Zeichen *(indications)* von Initiative oder Resignation? Was ist das Ziel der Leute? Warum lächelt der Schaffner? Wer könnte das sein? Was will Kästner uns über den Sinn des Lebens sagen?

You might expand on Kafka's topic to new beginnings, the importance of taking the initiative for change, of taking one step at a time, and of growth in the process. Is the **Weg** in itself the true destination?

You could ask students to write a small composition expressing their own thoughts on one of these parables.

„Wir sitzen alle im gleichen Zug und reisen quer durch die Zeit" (Erich Kästner).

Rückschau

Kapitelwortschatz

Hauptwörter

der Abfall, ¨-e	*trash*
der Bau, -ten	*building; structure*
der Behälter, -	*container*
die Bevölkerung	*population*
das Denkmal, ¨-er	*monument*
die Erhaltung	*preservation*
das Gebiet, -e	*area, region*
die Küste, -n	*coast*
die Landschaft	*landscape, scenery*
der Müll	*garbage; waste*
die Mülltonne, -n	*garbage can*
die Natur	*nature*
das Naturschutzgebiet, -e	*nature preserve*
die Rede, -n	*speech*
die Sammelstelle, -n	*collection site*
der Schutz	*protection*
die Umwelt	*environment*
der Umweltschutz	*environmental protection*
die Verschmutzung	*pollution*

Verben

ab·reißen	*to tear down*
(wieder) auf·bauen	*to (re)build*
finanzieren	*to finance*
garantieren	*to guarantee*
planen	*to plan*
reden (mit + *dat.* / über + *acc.*)	*to talk (to / about)*
renovieren	*to renovate*
restaurieren	*to restore*
retten	*to save, rescue*
schaden	*to hurt; to damage*
schonen	*to go easy on, protect*
schützen	*to protect*
trennen	*to separate*
verbieten	*to forbid*
verbinden	*to connect, tie together, link*
verwenden	*to use, utilize*
wachsen	*to grow*
weg·werfen	*to throw away, discard*
werfen	*to throw*
zerstören	*to destroy*
zusammen·wachsen	*to grow together*

Adjektive und Adverbien

einzeln	*individual(ly)*
gefährlich	*dangerous(ly)*
gemeinsam	*(in) common; together, jointly*
stolz (auf + *acc.*)	*proud (of), proudly*
typisch	*typical(ly)*
umweltbewusst	*environmentally aware*

Verschiedenes

allerdings	*however*
endlich	*finally*
inzwischen	*in the meantime*
schließlich	*after all, in the end*
übrigens	*by the way*

Zum Schluss

1. **Gleiches Verb, verschiedene Bedeutungen** You have learned four different uses of **werden** as you have studied ***Wie geht's?***. Work with a partner first to identify the four different ways to use **werden**, and then together write 3–5 sentences that demonstrate each one. When you are finished, share your sentences with another pair of students.

2. **So bin ich, so sind wir.**
   a. **Bei mir** Where are you from? What kind of stereotypes do you think others have about your nationality? About your region? Or about your university? How would you describe yourself? Do you think you are "typical" for your nationality, your region, or your university? Using vocabulary and structures from this chapter, write 5–7 sentences about your identity. Compare your response with those in your group. What kinds of differences do you find?
   b. **Bei uns** What do you see as some of the major problems facing young people in your country? How about in your region? Or at your university? Make a list and share it with your group. Why do you think certain things are problems? What do your classmates think? How do your lists compare?
3. **Meine Parabel** In this chapter, you read a parable by Kafka and a thought-provoking poem by Kästner. Now it's your turn. Drawing on the concerns you discussed with your study group in the activity above, write a parable—in whatever form you prefer—using vocabulary from this and earlier chapters. Write at least 10 sentences and make sure to include at least three sentences in the passive voice.

iLrn **Onlineaktivitäten** Visit iLrn for online activities related to this chapter. There you will find additional resources, such as a memory game (**Gedächtnisspiel**), a crossword puzzle (**Kreuzworträtsel**), audio flash cards (**Vokabelblitz**), a tutorial quiz (**Mini-Quiz**), and the active vocabulary (**Wortschatz**) for this chapter.

On the website of the *Deutsche ...rchenstraße* you can find this ...p and a much larger version of ...ith a legend for your perusal.

All images in this section: Courtesy of the Deutsche Märchenstraße GmbH

Eine Reise ins Märchenland

Vorschau

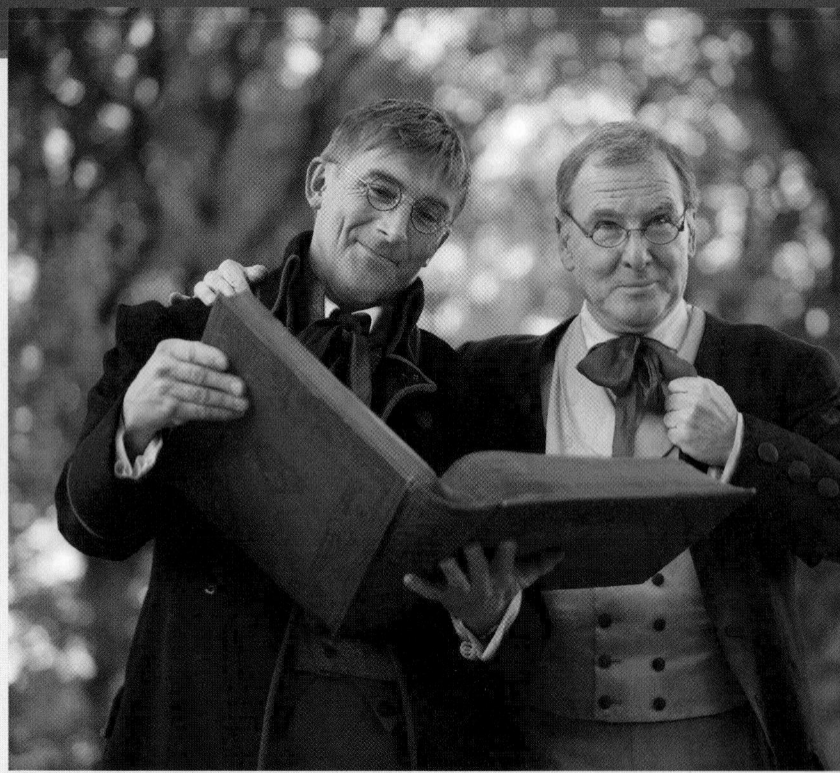

Die Märchen der Gebrüder Grimm leben immer weiter.

You probably know a few fairy tales . . . maybe not the originals . . . , but think about it. Which ones are you familiar with? Do you know how ubiquitous fairy tales have become in the pop culture of the 21st century? In 2011 alone, two TV series (*Once Upon a Time* and *Grimm*) were launched, while in recent years many movies loosely based on fairy tales (among them *Red Riding Hood, Mirror Mirror, Snow White and the Huntsman, Hansel & Gretel, Jack and the Beanstalk*) hit the big screen.

There is, of course, no real fairytale land. But what if there were? Or what if you could at least trace the imagined footsteps of some of the fairytale characters from the collected stories of the Brothers Grimm? Yes, what if you could go back to the origins of some of those stories you only know from the big or little screen, as presented through the eyes of Walt Disney's gifted animators or the writers of recent television shows and films?

The German Fairytale Route *(Deutsche Märchenstraße)* gives you exactly this opportunity. In 1973, a trip to Russia—where then state representative Dr. Herbert Günther was shown a well-thumbed edition of the *Kinder- und Hausmärchen (Children's and Household Tales)* by the Brothers Grimm—sparked the idea of developing the *Deutsche Märchenstraße*. By 1975, forty German cities joined the consortium in addition to the City State of Bremen and some counties.

Together, they developed a concept in which, first of all, the *Märchenstraße* was to be mostly dedicated to the brothers Jacob and Wilhelm Grimm, connecting some geographic points in Germany where the two philologists spent important periods of their lives. These include Hanau, where they were born; Steinau, the city of their youth; Marburg, the city of their academic studies and cradle of the German Romantic Movement; Kassel, the central location where they collected fairy tales and had their first scholarly

Die Schwalm-Region, Heimat von König Drosselbart

triumphs; and Göttingen, where they worked as professors and political activists. As deemed appropriate, other locations of men and women were included who had supported the Brothers Grimm in their endeavors, for example, the birthplace of Dorothea Viehmann, the „Märchenfrau" *(woman who told fairy tales)*.

Although fairy tales truly are not set at specific locations, the people of the Romantic Age in general attributed them to certain locales. The *Märchenstraße* had to lead to sites or landscapes that proved to be the origin of some of the Grimm's tales. Those include the Kinzig River Valley as the home of the Grimms; the Hessian Schwalm region, where *Rotkäppchen (Little Red Riding Hood)* met the wolf; the Werra River region, where *Frau Holle (Mother Holle)* shook out her feather beds; and, of course, Bremen for the *Bremer Stadtmusikanten*, to mention only a few rich hunting grounds for people who love fairy tales. Next to fairy tales, however, the Grimms also collected German legends from all kinds of German regions, which also were included as part of the attractions of the *Märchenstraße,* like the *Rattenfänger von Hameln (Pied Piper of Hamlin)* or *Baron von Münchhausen*, the champion of tall tales.

The fairytale atmosphere in the region stretching from the Main River to the North Sea is grounded in many half-timbered settlements throughout Hesse, Lower Saxony, and finally in Bremen, richly embroidered by castles, fortresses, and people celebrating events related to the fairy tales and legends of their land.

Baron von Münchhausen in Bodenwerder, südlich von Hameln

Eingang zur Aschenputtel Burgruine in Polle, südlich von Bodenwerder

The following activities have purposely not been glossed. While a majority of Germans you meet will have at least a rudimentary knowledge of English and many materials by tourist information agencies might be bilingual, you may likely encounter situations where neither is the case. Trust in what you have learned from working with ***Wie geht's?***, and trust your instincts! You will be able to figure out much, much more than you might think. Enjoy your trip through the *Märchenland*!

Encourage your students to ask you questions but not to cling to wanting to know every single word.

Beginnen wir die Reise ins Märchenland!

Sie können Ihre gesamte Reise in Einzelschritten oder einfacher über das Internet-Portal der *Deutschen Märchenstraße* planen.

Sie planen, mit dem Flugzeug von Ihrem Heimatland nach Frankfurt am Main zu fliegen. Frankfurt ist Deutschlands größter internationaler Flughafen und liegt gar nicht weit von Hanau, dem Geburtsort der Gebrüder Grimm. Anstatt sich ein Auto zu mieten, fahren sie lieber mit dem Zug von Frankfurt nach Hanau!

Märchen-Freilichtbühne in Gudensberg, südlich von Kassel

Reiseplanung

Hanau

Aufgabe 1. Suchen Sie im Internet eine Zugverbindung vom Frankfurter Flughafen nach Hanau heraus! Gehen Sie dazu auf die Website der Deutschen Bundesbahn!

Aufgabe 1.1: Zugverbindungen und Preise suchen und Fahrkarten kaufen.

1. Finden Sie die Website der Deutschen Bundesbahn. Was kann man dort alles machen?
2. Sie kommen um 13 Uhr in Frankfurt an. Wann fährt der nächste Zug nach Hanau? Berichten Sie!
3. Können Sie direkt nach Hanau fahren oder müssen Sie umsteigen?
4. Was kostet die Fahrkarte? Ist das erster oder zweiter Klasse?

Alle großen deutschen Städte haben ihre eigene Website. Diese finden Sie entweder über eine Suchmaschine wie Google oder Bing oder fast immer durch die Kombination von **www.Name der Stadt.de**. Versuchen Sie es einmal mit Hamburg oder München! Umlaute müssen Sie dabei mit **ae**, **oe** oder **ue** ersetzen.

Aufgabe 2. Wo werden Sie in Hanau übernachten? Suchen Sie drei Unterkunftsmöglichkeiten heraus! Sie finden alle nötigen Informationen auf der Website der Stadt Hanau und auf Webseiten, die sich auf Pensionen und Jugendherbergen in Hanau beziehen.

1. Gibt es in Hanau eine Jugendherberge? Nein.
2. Können Sie eine günstige *(bargain)* Pension finden? z. B. Pension Villa Sonnenstrahl
3. Was ist eine Pension?
4. Geben Sie den Namen eines billigen Hotels in Hanau und die Einzelzimmer- und Doppelzimmerkosten dort! z. B. Hotel Domino: EZ ab 44 €, DZ ab 68 €
5. Was kostet eine Nacht in einem Drei-Sterne-Hotel in Hanau? z.B. Hotel zur Linde: EZ ab 78 €, DZ ab 110 €

Aufgabe 3. Suchen Sie eine kulturelle Veranstaltung *(event)*, die mit den Brüdern Grimm zu tun hat! Besuchen Sie dazu die Website der Brüder-Grimm-Märchenfestspiele. Wo und wann finden sie statt? Was kostet die Eintrittskarte?

Denkmal der Gebrüder Grimm in Hanau

Am nächsten Tag reisen Sie weiter nach . . .

Marburg

Marburg an der Lahn

Aufgabe 1. Wie für Hanau, suchen Sie jetzt eine günstige Zugverbindung für Marburg heraus und notieren Sie die Kosten! Welches ist die günstigste Übernachtungsmöglichkeit? Suchen Sie danach auf der Website der Stadt Marburg!

Aufgabe 2. Sie haben nun alle Proteinriegel aufgegessen, die Sie im Koffer hatten. Für das Frühstück haben Sie nur 5 €, für das Abendessen 15 €. Wo wollen Sie in Marburg frühstücken und wo zu Abend essen?

Aufgabe 3. In Marburg gibt es einen Grimm-Dich-Pfad. Erzählen Sie Ihren Mitstudenten, was das ist! In dem Namen des Grimm-Dich-Pfads steckt auch ein Wortspiel. Können Sie herausfinden, worauf sich das Wortspiel bezieht und es erklären? Welche anderen Angebote zum Thema Grimm hat die Stadt Marburg unter Tourismus und Kultur?

Ihre dritte Station ist . . .

Kassel

Aufgabe 1. Informieren Sie sich wie immer zuerst über Möglichkeiten zum Fahren, Essen und Trinken sowie zum Schlafen! Wie kommen Sie am besten von Marburg nach Kassel? Wo schlafen Sie am billigsten? Wo kann man als Student günstig essen? Sie finden alle nötigen Informationen auf der Website der Stadt Kassel.

Aufgabe 2. Jacob und Wilhelm Grimm haben auch ein *Deutsches Wörterbuch* und eine *Deutsche Grammatik* geschrieben. Recherchieren Sie die Bedeutung dieser Werke! Was können Sie herausfinden? Wie lange haben die Grimms in Kassel gelebt? Welchen Beruf hatten sie?

Aufgabe 3. Besuchen Sie die Website des Brüder-Grimm-Festivals in Kassel! Benutzen Sie eine Suchmaschine, um sie zu finden! Welche Angebote finden Sie dort? Welchen Event würden Sie gern besuchen? Erkunden Sie die Umgebung von Kassel in den Fußstapfen der Grimms! Was erleben Sie im Internet auf der Website von der Grimm-Heimat? Berichten Sie!

Bergpark Kassel-Wilhelmshöhe

Jetzt geht die Reise weiter nach . . .

Hameln

Aufgabe 1. Machen Sie Ihre Reiseplanung: Bahn, Unterkunft, Verpflegung! Stellen Sie sich vor, Sie haben Karriere gemacht und können sich ein bisschen mehr Luxus leisten. Welches Hotel wählen Sie? Wo werden Sie dinieren?

Der Rattenfänger von Hameln

Aufgabe 2. Für welche Figur ist Hameln bekannt? Ist das eine Märchenfigur oder eine Figur aus einer Sage? Was geschieht in der Geschichte vom Rattenfänger? Was hat sie mit dem englischen Idiom *„pay the piper"* zu tun?

Rats, Theaterstück zum Rattenfänger

Aufgabe 3. Welche kulturellen Ereignisse rund um den *Rattenfänger von Hameln* können Sie finden? Woran erinnert Sie der Name des Musicals? Wie lang ist die Aufführung und wo findet sie statt? Besuchen Sie die Website des Grimm-Jubiläums und suchen Sie dort nach dem Rattenfänger! Was können Sie berichten?

Und nun zu unserer letzten Station der Reise auf der *Deutschen Märchenstraße* . . .

Bremen

Aufgabe 1. Jetzt wissen Sie, was Sie tun müssen, oder?

Aufgabe 2. Die Websites vom Bremen-Tourismus, vom Stadtmusikantenarchiv und von der Stadt Bremen laden dazu ein, sich mit Bremen und den *Bremer Stadtmusikanten* zu beschäftigen. Besuchen Sie sie und finden Sie so viel wie möglich über Bremen und die *Stadtmusikanten* heraus! Bereiten Sie eine Präsentation darüber vor!

Aufgabe 3. Bremen ist nicht nur für seine *Stadtmusikanten* bekannt. Bremen ist wie Niedersachsen oder Hessen auch ein Bundesland, ein sogenannter Stadtstaat (wie auch Berlin und Hamburg) mit den gleichen Rechten wie ein Bundesland. Recherchieren Sie! Warum ist das so; was bedeutet das? Warum ist das Autokennenzeichen für Bremen HB?

Das Denkmal der Bremer Stadtmusikanten

Und zum Schluss

Schnitzeljagd

Dornröschenschloss Sababurg, westlich von Göttingen

Viele Märchenorte, die Sie auf der Karte der *Deutschen Märchenstraße* sehen, haben wir noch gar nicht erwähnt.

Wo finden Sie . . .

1. das Dornröschenschloss?
2. das Münchhausen-Spiel und -Musical?
3. das Nationaldenkmal der Brüder Grimm?
4. das Tor zum Rotkäppchenland?
5. den Frau Holle-Park?
6. den gestiefelten Kater und Schneewittchen?
7. den Märchen-Laternenpfad?
8. die Aschenputtelspiele?
9. die Hauptstadt der Märchenspiele?
10. Esel, Hund, Katze und Hahn?
11. Max und Moritz?
12. Rapunzels Turm?

Welchen dieser Orte würden Sie am liebsten einmal besuchen? Warum? Können Sie im Internet ein Bild davon finden?

Für diese Aktivität brauchen Sie die komplette Karte der Märchenstraße mit Legende, die Sie auf dem Portal der Märchenstraße und auf der **Wie geht's?** Premium Website oder iLrn finden können.

Zeigen Sie jetzt Ihre Kreativität!

A. Schreiben Sie einen imaginären Reisebericht! Was haben Sie auf der virtuellen Reise entlang der *Deutschen Märchenstraße* erlebt?
B. Sie haben ein Reisebüro und empfehlen Kunden, die zum ersten Mal nach Deutschland reisen, die *Deutsche Märchenstraße*. Was haben Sie Gutes darüber zu erzählen?
C. Zu welchen bekanntesten Märchen können Sie auf der großen Märchenkarte etwas finden? Recherchieren Sie weitere Orte, die auf der Karte erwähnt werden, und berichten Sie!
D. Erzählen Sie Ihre eigene (echte oder virtuelle) Reise auf der *Märchenstraße* in Form eines Märchens: *„Es war einmal ein(e) Student(in) . . .“*

Der Rumpelstilzchen-Brunnen in Helsa, östlich von Kassel

Der Wolf und das Geislein-Brunnen in Wolfhagen, westlich von Kassel

Weitere Möglichkeiten

Alte Märchenbücher der Gebrüder Grimm

Nutzen Sie Ihr Smartphone für eine Reise in Deutschland!

Wenn Sie ein Smartphone haben, suchen Sie sich eine *App*, mit der Sie kostenlos Landkarten schon vor Ihrer Reise herunterladen können! So sparen Sie Kosten für das *Roaming* in Deutschland. Zum Beispiel gibt es eine „Germany - Offline map with directU - (free)" für das iPhone. Die Stadt Göttingen hat sogar ihre eigene *App* für Veranstaltungen, die Sie für iPhone oder Android herunterladen können (GOE EVENTS). Suchen Sie im Internet nach anderen Möglichkeiten, wie Ihnen Ihr *Smartphone* in Deutschland weiterhelfen kann!

Die Märchen

A. Welche Märchen kennen Sie? Erzählen Sie Ihren Mitstudenten, wo Sie sie zum ersten Mal gelesen/gehört/gesehen haben!

B. Welche Geschichten gehören zur Ihren schönsten Kindheitserinnerungen? Es muss kein Märchen von Grimm sein!

C. Lesen Sie eins der Märchen auf der Website von Gutenberg.Spiegel. Zum Beispiel *Schneewittchen*! Besonders wenn Sie ein Märchen schon gut kennen, versuchen Sie einfach, den Text auf Deutsch zu lesen und so viel wie möglich zu verstehen, ohne jedes Wort nachzuschlagen. Sie werden überrascht sein, wie viel Sie sofort verstehen werden.
   1. Können Sie das Meiste ohne die Hilfe eines Wörterbuches verstehen? Was macht Ihnen die größten Probleme?
   2. Verlassen Sie sich auf Ihre Erinnerung, wenn Sie die Geschichte von *Schneewittchen* kennen!
   3. Ist die deutsche Version anders als die von Walt Disney? Sicher gibt es Unterschiede. Wie sehen die aus?
   4. Welche Märchen- oder Sagenfiguren erkennen Sie auf dem Bild unten?

Rapunzel, Frau Holle mit Pechmarie und Goldmarie, Rotkäppchen, Baron von Münchhausen, Der gestiefelte Kater

D. Auf der deutschen Internetseite von Gutenberg.Spiegel finden Sie die komplette Sammlung von Grimms *Kinder- und Hausmärchen*. Links zu den bekanntesten von ihnen (wie z. B. zu *Schneewittchen, Dornröschen, Aschenputtel* und mehr) finden Sie auf iLrn / oder der Premium Website von ***Wie geht's?***

Verschiedene Märchenfiguren auf der Trendelburg, nördlich von Kassel

End Matter

Appendix

Vocabulary:

Index

Appendix

1. Predicting the Gender of Certain Nouns

As a rule, nouns must be learned with their articles because their genders are not readily predictable. However, here are a few hints to help you determine the gender of some nouns in order to eliminate unnecessary memorizing.

a. Most nouns referring to males are MASCULINE.

der Vater, der Bruder, der Junge

- Days, months, and seasons are masculine.

  der Montag, der Juni, der Winter

b. Most nouns referring to females are FEMININE.

die Mutter, die Schwester, die Frau BUT das Mädchen, das Fräulein (*Miss*, seldom used today)

- Many feminine nouns can be derived from masculine nouns by adding **-in.** Their plurals always end in **-nen.**

  sg.: der Schweizer / die Schweizerin; der Österreicher / die Österreicherin

  pl.: die Schweizerinnen, Österreicherinnen

- Most nouns ending in **-heit, -keit, -ie, -ik, -ion, -schaft, -tät,** and **-ung** are feminine. Their plurals end in **-en.**

  sg.: die Schönheit, Richtigkeit, Geographie, Musik, Religion, Nachbarschaft, Qualität, Rechnung

  pl.: die Qualitäten, Rechnungen usw.

- Most nouns ending in **-e** are feminine. Their plurals end in **-n.**

  sg.: die Sprache, Woche, Hose, Kreide, Farbe, Seite

  pl.: die Sprachen, Wochen usw.

There are exceptions, e.g., **der Käse, der Affe, der Löwe, der Neffe, der Name; das Ende, das Schöne**, etc.

c. All nouns ending in **-chen** or **-lein** are NEUTER. These two suffixes make diminutives of nouns, that is, they denote them as being small. In the case of people, the diminutive may indicate affection, or even belittlement. Such nouns often have an umlaut, but there is no plural ending.

  sg.: der Bruder → das Brüderchen; die Schwester → das Schwesterlein

  pl.: die Brüderchen, Schwesterlein

- Because of these suffixes, two nouns referring to females are neuter.

  das Mädchen, das Fräulein *(see b. above)*

- Most cities and countries are neuter.

  (das) Berlin, (das) Deutschland BUT die Schweiz, die Türkei, der Irak

2. Summary Chart of the Four Cases

<table>
<tr><th></th><th>use</th><th>follows . . .</th><th>masc.</th><th>neut.</th><th>fem.</th><th>pl.</th></tr>
<tr><td>nom.</td><td>Subject, predicate noun
wer?
was?</td><td>heißen, sein, werden</td><td>der
dieser[1]
ein
mein[2]</td><td rowspan="3">das
dieses
ein
mein</td><td rowspan="3">die
diese
eine
meine</td><td rowspan="3">die
diese
keine
meine</td></tr>
<tr><td rowspan="2">acc.</td><td rowspan="2">Direct object
wen?
was?</td><td>durch, für, gegen, ohne, um</td><td rowspan="2">den
diesen
einen
meinen</td></tr>
<tr><td>an, auf, hinter, in, neben, über, unter, vor, zwischen</td></tr>
<tr><td>dat.</td><td>Indirect object
wem?</td><td>aus, außer, bei, mit, nach, seit, von, zu

antworten, danken, gefallen, gehören, glauben,[3] helfen, zuhören usw.</td><td>dem
diesem
einem
meinem</td><td>dem
diesem
einem
meinem</td><td rowspan="2">der
dieser
einer
meiner</td><td>den
diesen
keinen
meinen</td></tr>
<tr><td>gen.</td><td>Possessive
wessen?</td><td>(an)statt, trotz, während, wegen</td><td>des
dieses
eines
meines</td><td>des
dieses
eines
meines</td><td>der
dieser
keiner
meiner</td></tr>
</table>

NOTE: [1] The **der**-words are **dieser, jeder, welcher, alle, manche, solche.**

[2] The **ein**-words are **kein, mein, dein, sein, ihr, unser, euer, ihr, Ihr.**

[3] Ich glaube **ihm.** BUT Ich glaube **es.**

3. Adjective Endings

a. **Preceded adjectives**

	MASCULINE	NEUTER	FEMININE	PLURAL
nom.	der neue Krimi	das neue Stück	die neue Oper	die neu**en** Filme
acc.	den neu**en** Krimi	das neue Stück	die neue Oper	die neu**en** Filme
dat.	dem neu**en** Krimi	dem neu**en** Stück	der neu**en** Oper	den neu**en** Filmen
gen.	des neu**en** Krimis	des neu**en** Stückes	der neu**en** Oper	der neu**en** Filme

	MASCULINE	NEUTER	FEMININE	PLURAL
nom.	ein neu**er** Krimi	ein neu**es** Stück	eine neue Oper	keine neu**en** Filme
acc.	einen neu**en** Krimi	ein neu**es** Stück	eine neue Oper	keine neu**en** Filme
dat.	einem neu**en** Krimi	einem neu**en** Stück	einer neu**en** Oper	keinen neu**en** Filmen
gen.	eines neu**en** Krimis	eines neu**en** Stückes	einer neu**en** Oper	keiner neu**en** Filme

When you compare the two tables on the previous page, you can see:

- Adjectives preceded by the definite article or any **der**-word have either an **-e** or **-en** ending.
- Adjectives preceded by the indefinite article or any **ein**-word have two different adjective endings WHENEVER **ein** HAS NO ENDING: **-er** for masculine nouns and **-es** for neuter nouns. Otherwise, the **-en** ending predominates and is used in the masculine accusative singular, all datives and genitives, and in all plurals.

after **der-**words

	masc.	neut.	fem.	pl.
nom.		-e		
acc.				
dat.				
		-en		
gen.				

after **ein-**words

	masc.	neut.	fem.	pl.
nom.	**-er**	**-es**	-e	
acc.		**-es**	-e	
dat.				
		-en		
gen.				

Or, to put it in another way, the endings are as follows:

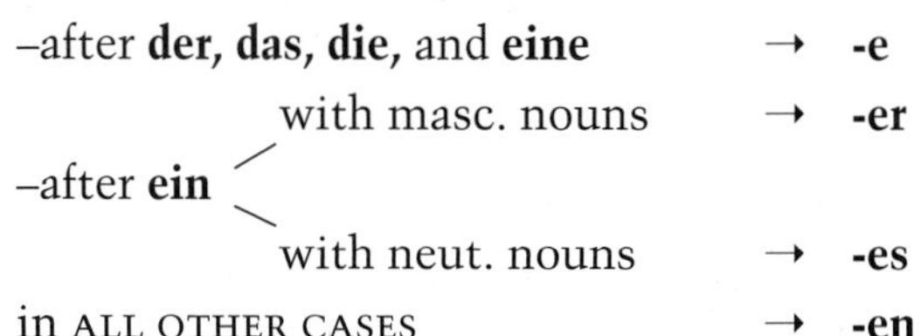

- in the NOMINATIVE AND ACCUSATIVE SINGULAR
  - –after **der, das, die,** and **eine** → **-e**
  - –after **ein** with masc. nouns → **-er**
  - –after **ein** with neut. nouns → **-es**
- in ALL OTHER CASES → **-en**

b. **Unpreceded adjectives**

Unpreceded adjectives take the endings that the definite article would have, if it were used.

der frische Fisch	**das** frische Obst	**die** frische Wurst	**die** frischen Eier
frische**r** Fisch	frische**s** Obst	frisch**e** Wurst	frisch**e** Eier

	MASCULINE	NEUTER	FEMININE	PLURAL
nom.	frisch**er** Fisch	frisch**es** Obst	frisch**e** Wurst	frisch**e** Eier
acc.	frisch**en** Fisch	frisch**es** Obst	frisch**e** Wurst	frisch**e** Eier
dat.	frisch**em** Fisch	frisch**em** Obst	frisch**er** Wurst	frisch**en** Eiern
gen.	(frisch**en** Fisches)	(frisch**en** Obstes)	(frisch**er** Wurst)	frisch**er** Eier

Several important words are often used as unpreceded adjectives in the plural: **andere, einige, mehrere, viele, wenige.**

4. Endings of Nouns

a. ***N*-nouns**

	SINGULAR	PLURAL
nom.	der Student	die Studenten
acc.	den Student**en**	die Studenten
dat.	dem Student**en**	den Studenten
gen.	des Student**en**	der Studenten

Other *n*-nouns are **Herr (-n, -en), Franzose, Gedanke (-ns, -n), Geldautomat, Journalist, Junge, Komponist, Mensch, Nachbar, Name (-ns, -n), Polizist, Tourist.**

b. Adjectival nouns

	SINGULAR		PLURAL
	masc.	fem.	
nom.	der Deutsche ein Deutscher	die Deutsche eine Deutsche	die Deutschen keine Deutschen
acc.	den Deutschen einen Deutschen	die Deutsche eine Deutsche	die Deutschen keine Deutschen
dat.	dem Deutschen einem Deutschen	der Deutschen einer Deutschen	den Deutschen keinen Deutschen
gen.	des Deutschen eines Deutschen	der Deutschen einer Deutschen	der Deutschen keiner Deutschen

Other adjectival nouns are as follows: **der/die Angestellte, Bekannte, Kranke, Verlobte; der Beamte** (BUT **die Beamtin**).

5. Pronouns

a. **Personal pronouns**

nom.	ich	du	er	es	sie	wir	ihr	sie	Sie
acc.	mich	dich	ihn	es	sie	uns	euch	sie	Sie
dat.	mir	dir	ihm	ihm	ihr	uns	euch	ihnen	Ihnen

b. **Reflexive pronouns**

nom.	ich	du	er/es/sie	wir	ihr	sie	Sie
acc.	mich	dich	sich	uns	euch	sich	sich
dat.	mir	dir	sich	uns	euch	sich	sich

c. **Relative pronouns**

	masc.	neut.	fem.	pl.
nom.	der	das	die	die
acc.	den	das	die	die
dat.	dem	dem	der	denen
gen.	dessen	dessen	deren	deren

6. Comparison of Irregular Adverbs and Adjectives

	gern	groß	gut	hoch	nah	viel
comparative	lieber	größer	besser	höher	näher	mehr
superlative	liebst-	größt-	best-	höchst-	nächst-	meist-

7. *N*-verbs ("Strong Verbs") and Irregular *T*-verbs ("Weak Verbs")

a. **Principal parts listed alphabetically**

This list is limited to the active *n*-verbs and irregular *t*-verbs used in this text. Compound verbs such as **ankommen** and **abfliegen** are not included, since their principal parts are the same as those of the basic verbs **kommen** and **fliegen.**

INFINITIVE	PRESENT	SIMPLE PAST	PAST PARTICIPLE	MEANING
anfangen	fängt an	fing an	angefangen	*to begin*
backen	bäckt	buk (backte)	gebacken	*to bake*
beginnen		begann	begonnen	*to begin*
bekommen		bekam	bekommen	*to receive, get*
bewerben	bewirbt	bewarb	beworben	*to apply*
bieten		bot	geboten	*to offer*
binden		band	gebunden	*to bind, tie*
bitten		bat	gebeten	*to ask, request*
bleiben		blieb	ist geblieben	*to remain*
bringen		brachte	gebracht	*to bring*
denken		dachte	gedacht	*to think*
einladen	lädt ein	lud ein	eingeladen	*to invite*
empfehlen	empfiehlt	empfahl	empfohlen	*to recommend*
entscheiden		entschied	entschieden	*to decide*
essen	isst	aß	gegessen	*to eat*
fahren	fährt	fuhr	ist gefahren	*to drive, go*
fallen	fällt	fiel	ist gefallen	*to fall*
finden		fand	gefunden	*to find*
fliegen		flog	ist geflogen	*to fly*
geben	gibt	gab	gegeben	*to give*
gefallen	gefällt	gefiel	gefallen	*to please*
gehen		ging	ist gegangen	*to go*
geschehen	geschieht	geschah	ist geschehen	*to happen*
haben	hat	hatte	gehabt	*to have*
halten	hält	hielt	gehalten	*to hold; stop*
hängen		hing	gehangen	*to be hanging*
heißen	heißt	hieß	geheißen	*to be called / named*
helfen	hilft	half	geholfen	*to help*
kennen		kannte	gekannt	*to know*
klingen		klang	geklungen	*to sound*
kommen		kam	ist gekommen	*to come*
lassen	lässt	ließ	gelassen	*to let; leave (behind)*
laufen	läuft	lief	ist gelaufen	*to run; walk*
lesen	liest	las	gelesen	*to read*
liegen		lag	gelegen	*to lie*
nehmen	nimmt	nahm	genommen	*to take*
nennen		nannte	genannt	*to name, call*
reißen	reißt	riss	gerissen	*to tear*
rufen		rief	gerufen	*to call*
scheinen		schien	geschienen	*to shine; seem*
schlafen	schläft	schlief	geschlafen	*to sleep*
schreiben		schrieb	geschrieben	*to write*
schwimmen		schwamm	ist geschwommen	*to swim*
sehen	sieht	sah	gesehen	*to see*

INFINITIVE	PRESENT	SIMPLE PAST	PAST PARTICIPLE	MEANING
sein	ist	war	ist gewesen	*to be*
singen		sang	gesungen	*to sing*
sitzen		saß	gesessen	*to sit*
spinnen		spann	gesponnen	*to spin*
sprechen	spricht	sprach	gesprochen	*to speak*
springen		sprang	ist gesprungen	*to jump*
stehen		stand	gestanden	*to stand*
steigen		stieg	ist gestiegen	*to climb*
sterben	stirbt	starb	ist gestorben	*to die*
tragen	trägt	trug	getragen	*to carry; wear*
treffen	trifft	traf	getroffen	*to meet*
treiben		trieb	getrieben	*to engage in (sports)*
trinken		trank	getrunken	*to drink*
tun	tut	tat	getan	*to do*
vergessen	vergisst	vergaß	vergessen	*to forget*
vergleichen		verglich	verglichen	*to compare*
verlieren		verlor	verloren	*to lose*
verschwinden		verschwand	ist verschwunden	*to disappear*
wachsen	wächst	wuchs	ist gewachsen	*to grow*
waschen	wäscht	wusch	gewaschen	*to wash*
werden	wird	wurde	ist geworden	*to become; get*
werfen	wirft	warf	geworfen	*to throw*
wissen	weiß	wusste	gewusst	*to know*
ziehen		zog	(ist) gezogen	*to pull; (move)*

b. **Principal parts listed by stem-changing groups**

This is the same list as the previous one, but this time it is divided into groups with the same stem changes.

I.	essen	(isst)	aß	gegessen
	vergessen	(vergisst)	vergaß	vergessen
	geben	(gibt)	gab	gegeben
	geschehen	(geschieht)	geschah	ist geschehen
	lesen	(liest)	las	gelesen
	sehen	(sieht)	sah	gesehen
	bitten		bat	gebeten
	liegen		lag	gelegen
	sitzen		saß	gesessen
II.	bewerben	(bewirbt)	bewarb	beworben
	empfehlen	(empfiehlt)	empfahl	empfohlen
	helfen	(hilft)	half	geholfen
	nehmen	(nimmt)	nahm	genommen
	sprechen	(spricht)	sprach	gesprochen
	sterben	(stirbt)	starb	ist gestorben
	treffen	(trifft)	traf	getroffen
	werfen	(wirft)	warf	geworfen
	beginnen		begann	begonnen
	schwimmen		schwamm	ist geschwommen
	spinnen		spann	gesponnen
	bekommen		bekam	bekommen
	kommen		kam	ist gekommen

III.	binden		b**a**nd		geb**u**nden
	finden		f**a**nd		gef**u**nden
	klingen		kl**a**ng		gekl**u**ngen
	singen		s**a**ng		ges**u**ngen
	springen		spr**a**ng	ist	gespr**u**ngen
	trinken		tr**a**nk		getr**u**nken
	verschwinden		verschw**a**nd	ist	verschw**u**nden
IV.	bleiben		bl**ie**b	ist	gebl**ie**ben
	entscheiden		entsch**ie**d		entsch**ie**den
	scheinen		sch**ie**n		gesch**ie**nen
	schreiben		schr**ie**b		geschr**ie**ben
	steigen		st**ie**g	ist	gest**ie**gen
	treiben		tr**ie**b		getr**ie**ben
	reißen	(reißt)	r**i**ss		ger**i**ssen
V.	bieten		b**o**t		geb**o**ten
	fliegen		fl**o**g	ist	gefl**o**gen
	verlieren		verl**o**r		verl**o**ren
	ziehen		z**o**g	ist	gez**o**gen
VI.	einladen	(lädt ein)	l**u**d ein		eingel**a**den
	fahren	(fährt)	f**u**hr	ist	gef**a**hren
	tragen	(trägt)	tr**u**g		getr**a**gen
	wachsen	(wächst)	w**u**chs	ist	gew**a**chsen
	waschen	(wäscht)	w**u**sch		gew**a**schen
VII.	fallen	(fällt)	f**ie**l	ist	gef**a**llen
	gefallen	(gefällt)	gef**ie**l		gef**a**llen
	halten	(hält)	h**ie**lt		geh**a**lten
	lassen	(lässt)	l**ie**ß		gel**a**ssen
	schlafen	(schläft)	schl**ie**f		geschl**a**fen
	laufen	(läuft)	l**ie**f	ist	gel**au**fen
	heißen	(heißt)	h**ie**ß		geh**ei**ßen
	rufen		r**ie**f		ger**u**fen
VIII.	*N*-verbs that do not belong to any of the groups above:				
	anfangen	(fängt an)	fing an		angefangen
	backen	(bäckt)	buk (backte)		gebacken
	gehen		ging	ist	gegangen
	hängen		hing		gehangen
	sein	(ist)	war	ist	gewesen
	stehen		stand		gestanden
	tun	(tut)	tat		getan
	werden	(wird)	wurde	ist	geworden
IX.	Irregular *T*-verbs:				
	bringen		br**a**chte		gebr**a**cht
	denken		d**a**chte		ged**a**cht
	haben	(hat)	h**a**tte		geh**a**bt
	kennen		k**a**nnte		gek**a**nnt
	nennen		n**a**nnte		gen**a**nnt
	wissen	(weiß)	w**u**sste		gew**u**sst

8. Sample Forms of the Subjunctive

a. **General subjunctive (Subjunctive II)**

	können	haben	sein	werden	lernen	bringen	gehen
ich	könnte	hätte	wäre	würde	lernte	brächte	ginge
du	könntest	hättest	wärest	würdest	lerntest	brächtest	gingest
er	könnte	hätte	wäre	würde	lernte	brächte	ginge
wir	könnten	hätten	wären	würden	lernten	brächten	gingen
ihr	könntet	hättet	wäret	würdet	lerntet	brächtet	ginget
sie	könnten	hätten	wären	würden	lernten	brächten	gingen

b. **Special subjunctive (Subjunctive I)**

	können	haben	sein	werden	lernen	bringen	gehen
ich	könne	habe	sei	werde	lerne	bringe	gehe
du	könnest	habest	seiest	werdest	lernest	bringest	gehest
er	könne	habe	seie	werde	lerne	bringe	gehe
wir	können	haben	seien	werden	lernen	bringen	gehen
ihr	könnet	habet	seiet	werdet	lernet	bringet	gehet
sie	können	haben	seien	werden	lernen	bringen	gehen

9. Verb Forms in Different Tenses

a. **Indicative**

	present		simple past		future	
ich	frage	fahre	fragte	fuhr	werde	fragen / fahren
du	fragst	fährst	fragtest	fuhrst	wirst	
er	fragt	fährt	fragte	fuhr	wird	
wir	fragen	fahren	fragten	fuhren	werden	
ihr	fragt	fahrt	fragtet	fuhrt	werdet	
sie	fragen	fahren	fragten	fuhren	werden	

	pres. perf.				past perf.			
ich	habe	gefragt	bin	gefahren	hatte	gefragt	war	gefahren
du	hast		bist		hattest		warst	
er	hat		ist		hatte		war	
wir	haben		sind		hatten		waren	
ihr	habt		seid		hattet		wart	
sie	haben		sind		hatten		waren	

b. **Subjunctive**

PRESENT-TIME

	general subj.				special subj.	
ich	fragte	führe	würde	fragen / fahren	frage	fahre
du	fragtest	führest	würdest		fragest	fahrest
er	fragte	führe	würde		frage	fahre
wir	fragten	führen	würden		fragen	fahren
ihr	fragtet	führet	würdet		fraget	fahret
sie	fragten	führen	würden		fragen	fahren

PAST-TIME

	general subj.				special subj.			
ich	hätte	gefragt	wäre	gefahren	habe	gefragt	sei	gefahren
du	hättest		wärest		habest		seiest	
er	hätte		wäre		habe		sei	
wir	hätten		wären		haben		seien	
ihr	hättet		wäret		habet		seiet	
sie	hätten		wären		haben		seien	

c. **Passive voice**

	present		simple past		future	
ich	werde	gefragt	wurde	gefragt	werde	gefragt werden
du	wirst		wurdest		wirst	
er	wird		wurde		wird	
wir	werden		wurden		werden	
ihr	werdet		wurdet		werdet	
sie	werden		wurden		werden	

	pres. perf.		past perf.	
ich	bin	gefragt worden	war	gefragt worden
du	bist		warst	
er	ist		war	
wir	sind		waren	
ihr	seid		wart	
sie	sind		waren	

10. Translation of the *Gespräche*

p. 4 **Schritt 1**

Hello! MR. SANDERS: Hello. MS. LEHMANN: Hello. MR. SANDERS: My name is Sanders, Willi Sanders. And what's your name? MS. LEHMANN: My name is Erika Lehmann. MR. SANDERS: Pleased to meet you. How are you? MS. LEHMANN: Fine, thank you. And you? MR. SANDERS: I'm fine, too. Thank you.

LUCA SEIBEL: Hello! EVA BACH: Hi! LUCA SEIBEL: My name is Luca Seibel. And what's your name? EVA BACH: My name is Eva Bach. LUCA SEIBEL: Pleased to meet you. And how are you? EVA BACH: Oh, pretty good (*lit.*: not bad).

HEIDI: Hi, Ute! How are you? UTE: Hi, Heidi! Oh, I'm tired. HEIDI: So am I. Too much stress. See you later! UTE: Bye! Take care!

p. 8 **Schritt 2**

What's that? GERMAN PROFESSOR: Listen carefully and answer in German. What is that? JIM MILLER: That's the pencil. GERMAN PROFESSOR: What color is the pencil? SUSAN SMITH: Yellow. GERMAN PROFESSOR: Make a sentence, please. SUSAN SMITH: The pencil is yellow. GERMAN PROFESSOR: Is the notebook yellow, too? DAVID JENKINS: No, the notebook isn't yellow. The notebook is light blue. GERMAN PROFESSOR: Good. SUSAN SMITH: What does *hellblau* mean? GERMAN PROFESSOR: *Hellblau* means *light blue* in English. SUSAN SMITH: And how does one say *dark blue*? GERMAN PROFESSOR: *Dunkelblau*. SUSAN SMITH: Oh, the pen is dark blue. GERMAN PROFESSOR: Correct. That's all for today. For tomorrow, please read the dialogue again and learn the vocabulary, too.

p. 12 **Schritt 3**

In the department store SALESCLERK: Well, how are the pants? CHRISTIAN: Too big and too long. SALESCLERK: And the sweater? MEIKE: Too expensive. CHRISTIAN: But the colors are great. Too bad!

SALESCLERK: Hello. May I help you? SILVIA: I need some pencils and paper. How much are the pencils? SALESCLERK: 55 cents. SILVIA: And the paper? SALESCLERK: 2 euros 40 cents. SILVIA: Fine. I'll take six pencils and the paper. SALESCLERK: Is that all? SILVIA: Yes, thank you. SALESCLERK: 5 euros 70 cents.

p. 17 **Schritt 4**

The weather in April NORBERT: It's nice today, isn't it? JULIA: Yes, that's for sure. The sun is shining again. RUDI: Only the wind is cool. JULIA: Oh, that doesn't matter. NORBERT: I think it's great.

HANNES: Man, what lousy weather! It's already snowing again. MARTIN: So what? HANNES: In Mallorca it's nice and beautiful. MARTIN: But we're here, and not in Mallorca. HANNES: Too bad.

LEA: The weather is awful, isn't it? HEIKO: I think so, too. It's raining and raining. SARA: And it's so cold again. Only 7 degrees! HEIKO: Yes, typical April.

p. 22 **Schritt 5**

What time is it? RITA: Hi, Axel! What time is it? AXEL: Hi, Rita! It's ten to eight. RITA: Oh no, in ten minutes I have philosophy. AXEL: Take care, then. Bye! RITA: Yes, bye!

PHILLIP: Hi, Steffi! What time is it? STEFFI: Hi, Phillip! It's eleven thirty. PHILLIP: Shall we eat now? STEFFI: OK, the lecture doesn't start till a quarter past one.

ANTON: When are you finished today? PAUL: At two o'clock. Why? ANTON: Are we going to play tennis today? PAUL: Yes, great! It's now twelve thirty. How about at quarter to three? ANTON: Fine! See you later!

Kapitel 1

p. 32

At the Goethe Institute SHARON: Roberto, where are you from? ROBERTO: I'm from Rome. And you? SHARON: I'm from Sacramento, but now my family lives in Seattle. ROBERTO: Do you have (any) brothers or sisters? SHARON: Yes, I have two sisters and two brothers. How about you? ROBERTO: I have only one sister. She lives in Montreal, in Canada. SHARON: Really? What a coincidence! My uncle lives there, too.

Later ROBERTO: Sharon, when is the test? SHARON: In ten minutes. Say, what are the names of some rivers in Germany? ROBERTO: In the north is the Elbe, in the east the Oder, in the south . . . SHARON: . . . the Danube? ROBERTO: Right! And in the west the Rhine. Where is Düsseldorf? SHARON: Düsseldorf? Hm. Where's a map? ROBERTO: Oh, here. In the west of Germany, north of Bonn, on the Rhine. SHARON: Oh yes, right! Well, good luck!

Kapitel 2

p. 58

At the grocery store CLERK: Hello. May I help you? OLIVER: I'd like some fruit. Don't you have any bananas? CLERK: Yes, over there. OLIVER: How much are they? CLERK: 90 cents a pound. OLIVER: And the oranges? CLERK: 45 cents each. OLIVER: Fine, two pounds of bananas and six oranges, please. CLERK: Anything else? OLIVER: Yes, two kilos of apples, please. CLERK: 8 euros 10 cents, please. Thank you. Good-bye.

In the bakery CLERK: Good morning. May I help you? SIMONE: Good morning. One rye bread and six rolls, please. CLERK: Anything else? SIMONE: Yes, I need some cake. Is the apple strudel fresh? CLERK: Of course, very fresh. SIMONE: Fine, then I'll take four pieces. CLERK: Is that all? SIMONE: I'd also like some cookies. What kind of cookies do you have today? CLERK: Lemon cookies, chocolate cookies, butter cookies . . . SIMONE: Hm . . . I'll take 300 grams of chocolate cookies. CLERK: Anything else? SIMONE: No, thank you. That's all. CLERK: Then that comes to 9 euros 55 cents, please.

Kapitel 3

p. 84

In the restaurant AXEL: Waiter, the menu, please. WAITER: Here you are. AXEL: What do you recommend today? WAITER: All of today's specials are very good. AXEL: Gabi, what are you having? GABI: I don't know. What are you going to have? AXEL: I think I'll take menu number one: veal cutlet and potato salad. GABI: And I will take menu number two: stuffed beef rolls with potato dumplings. WAITER: Would you like something to drink? GABI: A glass of apple juice. And what about you? AXEL: Mineral water. *(The waiter comes with the food.)* Enjoy your meal! GABI: Thanks, you too . . . Mm, that tastes good. AXEL: The veal cutlet, too.

Later GABI: We'd like to pay, please. WAITER: All right. All together? GABI: Yes. Please give me the bill. AXEL: No, no, no. GABI: Yes, Axel. Today I'm paying. WAITER: Well, one menu number one, one menu number two, one apple juice, one mineral water, two cups of coffee. Anything else? AXEL: Yes, one roll. WAITER: That comes to 30 euros 30 cents, please. GABI: *(She gives the waiter 40 euros)* Make it 32 euros, please. WAITER: And eight euros change (back). Thank you very much.

Kapitel 4

p. 110

On the telephone NADJA: Hi, Simon! SIMON: Hi, Nadja! How are you? NADJA: Not bad, thanks. What are you doing on the weekend? SIMON: Nothing special. Why? NADJA: It's Erik's birthday the day after tomorrow, and we're giving a party. SIMON: Great! But are you sure that Erik's birthday is the day after tomorrow? I think his birthday is on May 7. NADJA: Nonsense. Erik's birthday is on May 3. And Saturday is the third. SIMON: OK. When and where is the party? NADJA: Saturday at seven at my place. But don't say anything. It's a surprise. SIMON: OK. Well, see you then. NADJA: Bye. Take care!

Klaus rings Christa's doorbell. NADJA: Hi, Erik! Happy birthday! ERIK: What? SIMON: All the best on your birthday! ERIK: Hello, Simon! . . . Hello, Silke! Tobias and Sabine, you too?

ALL: We wish you a happy birthday! ERIK: Thanks! What a surprise! But my birthday isn't today; my birthday is on the seventh. NADJA: Really?—Well, then Simon was right. Oh well, it doesn't matter. We'll celebrate today.

p. 140
Kapitel 5

Excuse me! Where is . . . ? TOURIST: Excuse me! Can you tell me where the Hotel Sacher is? VIENNESE PASSERBY: First street on the left behind the opera. TOURIST: And how do I get from there to St. Stephen's Cathedral? VIENNESE PASSERBY: Straight ahead along Kärtner Straße. TOURIST: How far is it to the cathedral? VIENNESE PASSERBY: Not far. You can walk (there). TOURIST: Thank you. VIENNESE PASSERBY: You're welcome.

Over there TOURIST: Excuse me. Where is the Burgtheater? MAN: I'm sorry. I'm not from Vienna. TOURIST: Pardon me. Is that the Burgtheater? WOMAN: No, that's not the Burgtheater, but the opera house. Take the streetcar to city hall. The Burgtheater is across from city hall. TOURIST: And where does the streetcar stop? WOMAN: Over there on your left. TOURIST: Thank you very much. WOMAN: You're most welcome.

p. 168
Kapitel 6

Apartment for rent ANNA: Hello, my name is Anna Moser. I've heard that you have a two-room apartment for rent. Is that right? LANDLORD: Yes, near the cathedral, with a view of the market square. ANNA: How old is the apartment? LANDLORD: Fairly old, but it's been renovated and it's quite big and light. It even has a balcony. ANNA: A balcony? That's super. I have a lot of plants. What floor is it on? LANDLORD: On the fourth floor. ANNA: Is it furnished or unfurnished? LANDLORD: Unfurnished. ANNA: And how much is the rent? LANDLORD: 550 euros. ANNA: Is that without or with heat? LANDLORD: Without heat. ANNA: Oh, that's a little too expensive. Well, thank you very much. Good-bye! LANDLORD: Good-bye!

In the co-op ANNA: I like your house. JÖRG: We still have room for you. Come, I'll show you everything . . . Here on the left is our kitchen. It's small, but practical. ANNA: Who does the cooking? JÖRG: We all (do): Benno, Verena, and I. ANNA: And that's the living room? JÖRG: Yes. It's a bit dark, but that's all right. ANNA: I like your chairs. JÖRG: They're old, but really comfortable . . . Well, and up here are four bedrooms and the bathroom. ANNA: Mm, the bedroom is very cozy, but only one bath? JÖRG: Yes, unfortunately! But downstairs is another toilet. ANNA: How much do you pay per month? JÖRG: 200 euros each. ANNA: Not bad. And how do you get to the university? JÖRG: No problem. I walk. ANNA: (That) sounds good!

p. 196
Kapitel 7

At the bank TOURIST: Hello. Where can I exchange dollars here? TELLER: Do you have a credit card? TOURIST: Yes, a credit card and a debit card from Canada. TELLER: Well, then the best thing is you go to the ATM machine over there or outside at the entrance. With the debit card, the exchange rate is a little better. TOURIST: Thank you very much. TELLER: You are welcome.

At the hotel reception desk RECEPTIONIST: Good evening. GUEST: Good evening. Do you have a single room available? RECEPTIONIST: For how long? GUEST: For two or three nights; if possible, quiet and with a bath. RECEPTIONIST: Unfortunately today we have only one double room, and that for only one night. But tomorrow there will be a single room available. Would you like to see the double room? GUEST: Yes, I would. RECEPTIONIST: Room number 12, on the second floor to the right. Here's the key. GUEST: Say, can I leave my suitcase here for a minute? RECEPTIONIST: Yes, of course. Put it over there in the corner. GUEST: Thank you. One more thing, when do you close at night? RECEPTIONIST: At midnight. If you come later, you'll have to ring the doorbell.

p. 222
Kapitel 8

At the post office in the train station CLERK: Hi! UTA: Hi! UTA: I'd like to send this package to the United States. CLERK: By surface mail or by airmail? UTA: By airmail. How long will it take? CLERK: About one week. Please fill out this parcel form! . . . Just a minute. Your return address is missing here. UTA: Oh yes . . . One more thing. I need a telephone card. CLERK: For five, ten, twenty, or fifty francs? UTA: For twenty francs. Thank you!

At the ticket counter in Zurich Anne: When does the next train for Interlaken leave? Clerk: In five minutes. Departure at 11:28 a.m., track 2. Anne: Good grief! And when does it arrive there? Clerk: Arrival in Interlaken at 2:16 p.m. Anne: Do I have to change trains? Clerk: Yes, in Bern, but you have a connection to the InterCity Express with only a 24-minute stopover. Anne: Fine. Give me a round-trip ticket to Interlaken, please. Clerk: First or second class? Anne: Second class.

Kapitel 9 p. 252

On the telephone Mrs. Schmidt: This is Mrs. Schmidt. Annemarie: Hello, Mrs. Schmidt. It's me, Annemarie. Mrs. Schmidt: Hi, Annemarie! Annemarie: Is Thomas there? Mrs. Schmidt: No, I'm sorry. He just went to the post office. Annemarie: I see. Can you tell him that I can't go out with him tonight? Mrs. Schmidt: Naturally. What's the matter? Annemarie: I'm sick. My throat hurts and I have a headache. Mrs. Schmidt: I'm sorry. I hope you get better soon. Annemarie: Thank you. Good-bye. Mrs. Schmidt: Good-bye.

See you in a few minutes! Yvonne: Mayer residence. Daniela: Hi, Yvonne! It's me, Daniela. Yvonne: Hi, Daniela! What's up? Daniela: Nothing special. Do you feel like playing squash or going swimming? Yvonne: Squash? No thanks. I'm still sore from the day before yesterday. I am hurting all over. Daniela: Poor baby (*lit.* lame duck)! How about chess? Yvonne: OK, that sounds fine. Are you coming to my place? Daniela: Yes, see you in a few minutes.

Kapitel 10 p. 282

A glance at the newspaper Sonja: Hey, what's on TV tonight? Theo: I have no idea. Nothing special for sure. Sonja: Let me see. *Good Times, Bad Times*, a documentary, and a detective story. Theo: Oh no. Sonja: Maybe there's something at the movies? Theo: Yes, *Das Leben der Anderen* and *Nirgendo in Afrika*. Sonja: *Das Leben der Anderen* I've seen twice already; besides, I also have that on DVD. The movie is really great! Maybe one day we can watch it together at my place, but not today. I also know *Nirgendwo in Afrika*. Theo: All right . . . Hey, look! At the theater, they're playing *The Caucasian Chalk Circle*, by Brecht. Sonja: Not bad. Do you feel like going? Theo: Yes, that sounds good. Let's go.

At the ticket window Theo: Do you still have tickets for tonight? Woman: Yes, in the first row of the first balcony on the left, and on the right in the orchestra. Theo: Two seats in the orchestra. Here are our student IDs. Woman: 10 euros, please. Sonja: When does the performance start? Woman: At 8:15 p.m.

Kapitel 11 p. 310

Looking for a partner Mia: Nicole, listen! "Wanted: pretty, dynamic, affectionate Eva. Reward: good-looking Adam with a big heart, late 20s, likes antiques, old houses, fast cars, animals, (and) kids. Nicole: Hmm, not bad, but not for me. I'm afraid of fast cars, and I'm allergic to animals. Mia: Then have a look at this! "What I'm looking for exists. But how to find it? Artist, early 30s, charming, enterprising, musical is looking for a congenial, well-educated, reliable woman with a sense of humor." Does that sound interesting? Nicole: Yes, perhaps. Mia: He's looking for someone with a sense of humor. I like that; and I also like music. But whether he likes jazz? Mia: Perhaps we could meet them both. Nicole: I don't know. I think it's sort of stupid to meet people through ads in the newspaper. Mia: Nonsense! Let's try it! What do we have to lose? Nicole: What do you think, Frank? Frank: Why don't you try the Internet if you are serious? There you have more choice. Nicole: Oh no, that's too risky for me. Frank: You're such a scaredy-cat. Mia: Luca and Emilie met through the Internet. Nicole: Yes, they were lucky. Frank: You see!

Kapitel 12 p. 340

Do you know what you want to be? Katja: Say, Elke, do you already know what you want to be? Elke: Yes, I'd like to become a cabinetmaker. Katja: Isn't that very strenuous? Elke: Oh, you get used to it. Perhaps someday I'll open my own business. Katja: Those are big plans. Elke: Why not? I don't feel like always sitting in an office and working for other people. Katja: And where do you want to apply for an apprenticeship? Elke: No problem at all. My aunt has her own business and has already offered me a position. Katja: You're lucky. Elke: And how about you? Do you know what you want to do? KATJA: Perhaps I'll be a dentist. Good dentists are always needed, and besides, it pays very well. ELKE: That's true, but that takes so long. KATJA: I know, but I'm looking forward to it anyway.

p. 338 Kapitel 13

During registration PETRA: Hi, John. How are you? JOHN: Pretty well, and you? PETRA: Well, I can't complain. What are you doing there? JOHN: I've still got to fill out these registration forms. PETRA: Shall I help you? JOHN: If you have time. I'm always struggling with red tape. PETRA: Do you have your passport with you? JOHN: No, why? PETRA: Your residence permit is in it; you really need it. JOHN: I can get it quickly. PETRA: Do that. I'll wait for you here.

A little later JOHN: Here's my passport. I'll also have to decide soon what seminars I want to take. Can you help me with that, too? PETRA: Sure. What's your major? JOHN: My major is modern history. I'd like to take some seminars in German history and literature. PETRA: Here's my course catalog. Let's see what they're offering this semester.

p. 396 Kapitel 14

There's always something going on in Berlin. HEIKE: And that's the Memorial Church with its three buildings. We call them the "Hollow Tooth," the "Lipstick," and the "Compact." MARTIN: Berliners have nicknames for everything, you know. HEIKE: The old tower of the Memorial Church is to stay the way it is, as a memorial (to the war). The new Memorial Church with the new tower, however, is modern. Like so many things in Berlin: a lot of old things and a lot of new things. MARTIN: Tell me, do you like living here in Berlin? HEIKE: Of course! Berlin is really alive and has so much to offer, not only historically but also culturally. There's always something going on here. Besides, the surroundings are beautiful. MARTIN: Somewhere I read that 24 percent of Berlin's total area consists of forests and lakes, with 800 kilometers of biking trails. HEIKE: That's great, isn't it? MARTIN: Awesome! Say, were you there when they broke through the Wall? HEIKE: You bet! My parents and I waited all night, even though it was really cold. When the first piece of Wall tipped over, we all sang loudly: "Such a beautiful day like today, a day like this should never end." MARTIN: Yes, that was really incredible (*lit.* a unique experience). And now that's already a long time ago. HEIKE: Since then, a lot of things have changed in Berlin. The traces of the Wall are almost gone. MARTIN: Who would have ever thought that! HEIKE: Today, you really find everything here, a diverse (*lit.* colorful) mix of people and languages. MARTIN: Are you glad that Berlin is again the capital (of Germany)? HEIKE: Well, I couldn't imagine it any other way.

p. 424 Kapitel 15

A visit to Weimar TOM: It's funny, but this monument of Goethe and Schiller seems so familiar to me. I think I've seen it somewhere before. DANIELA: Have you (ever) been to San Francisco? TOM: Of course! DANIELA: Were you in Golden Gate Park, too? TOM: I see, there's exactly the same monument! I think the German-Americans in California had it built. DANIELA: Right! In the 18th century, a lot of famous people lived here, and the Weimar Republic is also named for it. TOM: Yes, that's true. But this morning, when I looked down at the town from the memorial of the Buchenwald concentration camp, I had very mixed feelings. DANIELA: Yes, there you have a point (*lit.* you're right).

In the old part of town DANIELA: Look, the old houses here are really pretty, aren't they? TOM: Yes, they've been wonderfully restored. I find it especially nice that no cars are allowed here. DANIELA: Thank God! TOM: In our city, there's now also a citizens' initiative to ban all cars from the old part of town in order to save the old buildings. DANIELA: I think that's good. TOM: Are the containers over there for recycling (*lit.* waste separation)? DANIELA: Yes, do you also have recycling? TOM: Yes, on a voluntary basis. In that respect, certainly much more could be done. For example, I never know how to get rid of my old batteries or medicine. DANIELA: Old batteries you can throw into special containers at every supermarket, and the old medications you bring to the pharmacy. TOM: We can't do that, and therefore a lot of things finally end up in the garbage can. DANIELA: With us [in Germany], that's forbidden. TOM: And that's the way it should be. In that regard, you're just more progressive than we are.

11. Supplementary Charts for *Hoppla, hier fehlt was!*

Kapitel 1

p. 46

S2:

NAME	NATIONALITÄT	WOHNORT	ALTER
Toni	Schweizer		32
Katja		Ulm	
	Österreicherin		61
	Französin	Lyon	
Pierre	Franzose		
	Italianer		25
Maria		Madrid	
	Kanadier		28
Amy		Miami	

Kapitel 3

p. 96

S2:

	BRUDER	SCHWESTER	MUTTER	VATER	GROSSELTERN
Bild					
Bücher					x
Tennishose					
Hausschuhe				x	
Pulli					
Ringe *(pl.)*					
T-Shirts		x			
Mantel			x		
Messer *(sg.)*	x				
Gläser					

Kapitel 4

p. 123

S2:

	KAI	EVA	MAX	SVEN	ICH	PARTNER/IN
an alles denken						
mit dem Essen helfen	x					
Getränke bringen			x		x	
den Sekt öffnen						
viel essen			x		x	
viel trinken			x			
schön singen						
etwas tanzen	x					
mit allen sprechen						
nichts tun						
nicht lange bleiben					x	

p. 151 **Kapitel 5**

S2:

WER?	WAS?	WARUM?	WANN?
Dieter	bei den Wiener Festwochen in Wien sein	Er sieht nicht genug Opern und Theaterstücke. (können)	
	Silvester in Wien feiern		31.12–1.1.
Sonja	das Museum moderner Kunst besichtigen	Es hat alles, von Pablo Picasso bis Andy Warhol. (sollen)	
	zum Christkindlmarkt am Rathausplatz		17.11–24.12.
Karen + Charlie	zum Wiener Eistraum gehen	Da tanzen die Leute auf dem Eis vor dem Rathaus. (dürfen)	

p. 184 **Kapitel 6**

S2:

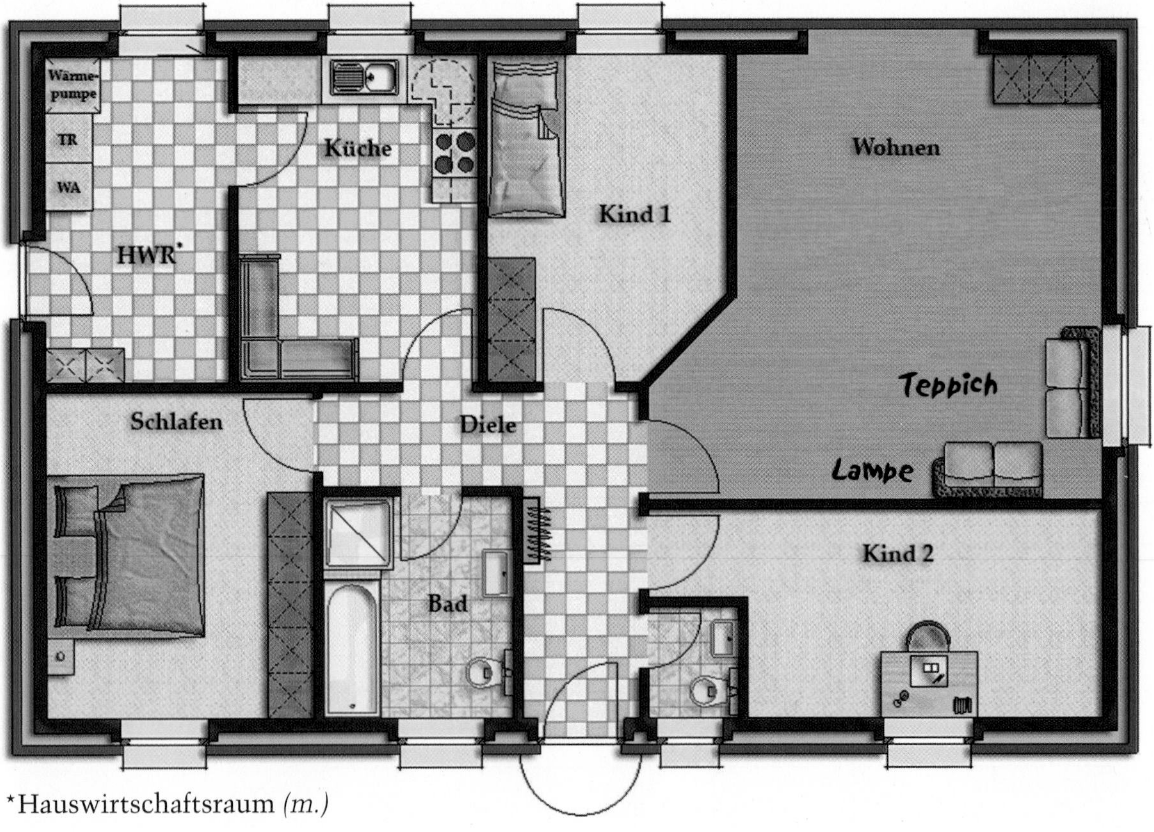

*Hauswirtschaftsraum *(m.)*

Kapitel 7

p. 208

S2:

WER?	WAS TUN?	JA. / NEIN.
Vater	bei der Bank vorbeigehen	Ja, gestern.
Vater	Geld umtauschen	Ja.
Mutter	die Kamera mitnehmen	
Mutter	die Nachbarn anrufen	
Thomas	die Telefonnummer aufschreiben	
Thomas	die Garagentür zumachen	Nein, noch nicht.
Carla	bei der Post vorbeigehen	Ja, gestern.
Carla	die Fenster zumachen	
Kinder	den Fernseher ausmachen (*turn off*)	
Kinder	die Lichter (*lights*) ausmachen	Nein, noch nicht.
Du	ein paar Bücher mitnehmen	

Kapitel 8

p. 239

S2:

WER	WANN / WIE LANGE	WIE / OBJ. + PRÄPOSITION	WO UND WAS
Lucian	ein paar Wochen		
Christl		bei ein- Gastfamilie	in Amerika sein
Steffi		wegen ihr- Prüfung	
Nina + Kim	während d- Ferien		von Passau bis Wien fahren
Ben + Michi			in ein- Pizzeria arbeiten
Günther		trotz d- Wetter	auf der Insel Rügen campen
Jutta	vom 1. bis 31. Juli		
Nicole		wieder	von Griechenland zurückkommen
Yvonne	morgens		
Jochen	mittags	gewöhnlich	

p. 265 **Kapitel 9**

S2:

	ZUERST	DANN	DANACH
BIRTE			
OLLI	s. schnell anziehen joggen gehen	s. duschen s. umziehen s. vor den Spiegel stellen	s. die Haare kämmen s. rasieren Joghurt und Müsli essen
VERA			
INGO	s. das Gesicht waschen s. eine Tasse Kaffee machen s. anziehen	s. an den Computer setzen s. die E-Mails ansehen	s. wieder hinlegen s. nicht beeilen

p. 285 **Kapitel 10**

S2:

WO?	WAS?	WANN?
Volksbühne	*Nathan der Weise,* Schauspiel von Gotthold Ephraim Lessing	19.30
Urania-Theater		
Metropol-Theater	*West Side Story,* Musical von Leonard Bernstein	19.00
Im Dom		
Philharmonie		
Konzerthaus	*Flamenco-Festival,* mit Montse Salazar	20.00
Komödie		
Kammerspiele		
Filmbühne 1	*Das Leben ist eine Baustelle,* von Wolfgang Becker	
Filmbühne 2	*In Winter ein Jahr,* von Caroline Link	

p. 328 **Kapitel 11**

S2:

	NACHDEM . . .	DANN . . .
S1	Vera: die Anzeige lesen	den Besitzer *(owner)* anrufen
S2	Besitzer: von der Katze erzählen	Vera seine Adresse geben
S1	Vera: dorthin fahren und sich die Katze ansehen	
S2	Vera: die Katze mit nach Hause nehmen	Ingo das Kätzchen zeigen
S1	Ingo: ihr etwas Milch geben	
S2	Ingo: die Katze zwei Wochen auf dem Bett haben	richtig krank werden
S1	Sie *(sg.)*: eine lange Diskussion haben	
S2	Besitzer: zwei Wochen ohne seine Katze sein	sie sehr vermissen *(miss)*
S1	Besitzer: mit Ingo und Vera sprechen	

Kapitel 13

p. 382

Und was sagt Ihnen Ihr Partner / Ihre Partnerin?

	JA	NEIN
Die Oma ist gern zur Schule gegangen.	x	
Sie war gut in Mathe.		
Sie hat an der Uni studiert.		
Sie ist Lehrerin geworden.		
Sie hat bei einer reichen Familie gearbeitet.		
Sie hat geheiratet.		
Sie hatte viele Kinder.		
Sie hat mit ihrem Mann eine große Weltreise gemacht.		

S2:

Erzählen Sie Ihrem Partner / Ihrer Partnerin:

Mein Opa ist aus Deutschland gekommen. Seine Familie ist mit dem Schiff nach Amerika gefahren. Opa konnte kein Englisch und er wäre lieber in Deutschland geblieben. Seine Familie hat in New York gewohnt. Er ist Polizist geworden. Er hat sich immer für Musik interessiert. Er konnte gut singen, und ich habe viele deutsche Lieder von ihm gelernt. Wenn er Zeit gehabt hätte, hätte er gelernt, Klavier zu spielen. Er hat seine Verwandten in Deutschland oft besucht. Dieses Jahr wäre er auch nach Deutschland gefahren, wenn er nicht krank geworden wäre.

p. 411 **Kapitel 14**

Liste von Leuten:

ein NBC-Korrespondent
Lyndon Johnson
Westberliner Polizist
Ronald Reagan
der Sänger Wolf Biermann
eine amerikanische Studentin
Willy Brandt
Alexander Dubček
Leonard Bernstein

S2:

WER?	AUSSAGEN
	„Vor meinen Augen tanzte die Freiheit."
Ostberliner Taxifahrer:	„So viel Fernsehen habe ich noch nie gesehen."
	„Ich muss weinen vor Freude, dass es so schnell und einfach ging. Und ich muss weinen vor Zorn *(anger)*, dass es so elend *(terribly)* lange dauerte."
Autor Günter Grass:	„Jetzt wird sich zeigen, ob der jahrzehntelangen Rhetorik von den ‚Brüdern und Schwestern' auch entsprechendes *(corresponding)* politisches Handeln *(action)* folgen wird."
Autor Stephan Heym:	„Die einzige Chance, die wir haben, den Sozialismus zu retten *(save)*, ist richtiger Sozialismus."
	„Ich bin Gott dankbar, dass ich das noch erleben *(experience)* darf."
Amerikanischer Präsident Ronald Reagan:	„Auf beiden Seiten sind Deutsche. Der Kommunismus hat seine Chance gehabt. Er funktioniert nicht."
	„Wir haben zu lange im Dunkeln gelebt. Treten wir *(Let's step)* ins Licht!"

p. 443 **Kapitel 15**

Die Belgier: . . .
Die Deutschen: . . .
Die Briten: . . .
Die Dänen: . . .
Die Franzosen: . . .
Die Griechen: . . .

S2:

Sportliche Iren

Die Iren lieben den Sport mehr als alle anderen Europäer. Jeder zweite ist verrückt danach.

Offene Luxemburger

Luxemburg hat europaweit die meisten Ausländer—29%. Die meisten Beamte der EU.

Fleißige Portugiesen

Die Portugiesen sind das fleißigste Völkchen Europas, höchste Jahresarbeitszeit—2025 Stunden.

Schnelle Italiener

Jedes Jahr kommen die Hälfte aller europäischen Telegramme allein aus ihrem Land.

Maritime Holländer

Die Holländer sind die größten Seefahrer Europas. Das Land besitzt fast 4000 Schiffe.

Sehfreudige Spanier

Die Spanier sitzen am häufigsten unter den Europäern vor dem Fernseher—vier Stunden am Tag.

German–English Vocabulary

The German–English Vocabulary includes all the ACTIVE and PASSIVE vocabulary used in ***Wie geht's?*** The English definitions of the words are limited to their use in the text. Each active vocabulary item is followed by a number and a letter indicating the chapter and section where it first occurs.

Nouns Nouns are followed by their plural endings unless the plural is rare or nonexistent. In the case of n-nouns, the singular genitive ending is also given: **der Herr, -n, -en.** Nouns that require adjective endings appear with two endings: **der Angestellte (ein Angestellter).** Female forms of masculine nouns are usually not listed if only **-in** needs to be added: **der Apotheker.**

Verbs For regular t-verbs ("weak verbs"), only the infinitive is listed. All irregular t-verbs ("irregular weak verbs") and basic n-verbs ("strong verbs") are given with their principal parts: **bringen, brachte, gebracht; schreiben, schrieb, geschrieben.** Separable-prefix verbs are identified by a dot between the prefix and the verb: **mit·bringen.** Compound mixed and n-verbs are printed with an asterisk to indicate that the principal parts can be found under the listing of the basic verb: **mit·bringen*, beschreiben*.** When **sein** is used as the auxiliary of the perfect tenses, the form **ist** is given: **wandern (ist); kommen, kam, ist gekommen.**

Adjectives and Adverbs Adjectives and adverbs that have an umlaut in the comparative and superlative are identified by an umlauted vowel in parentheses: **arm (ä) = arm, ärmer, am ärmsten.**

Accentuation Stress marks are provided for all words that do not follow the typical stress pattern. The accent follows the stressed syllable: **Balkon', Amerika'ner, wiederho'len.** The stress is not indicated when the word begins with an unstressed prefix, such as **be-, er-, ge-.**

Abbreviations

~	repetition of the key word	*nom.*	nominative
abbrev.	abbreviation	*o.s.*	oneself
acc.	accusative	*pl.*	plural
adj.	adjective	*refl. pron.*	reflexive pronoun
adv.	adverb	*rel. pron.*	relative pronoun
coll.	colloquial	*sb.*	somebody
comp.	comparative	*sg.*	singular
conj.	subordinate conjunction	*s.th.*	something
dat.	dative		
fam.	familiar	*S*	Schritt
gen.	genitive	*1.1*	Chapter 1.Wortschatz 1
inf.	infinitive	*1.G*	Chapter 1.Grammatik
lit.	literally	*1.2*	Chapter 1.Wortschatz 2
n.	noun		

A

der **Aal, -e** eel
ab- away, off (7.G)
ab starting, as of
ab und zu once in a while
ab·bauen to reduce, cut back; take down
ab·brechen* to break off
ab·brennen* to burn down
der **Abend, -e** evening; **(Guten) ~!** (Good) evening. (S1); **am ~** in the evening (6.2); **gestern ~** yesterday evening (8.G); **heute ~** this evening (8.G)
das **Abendbrot** evening meal
das **Abendessen, -** supper, evening meal (3.1); **zum ~** for supper (3.1)
abends in the evening, every evening (S5); **donnerstag ~** Thursday evenings (8.G)
das **Abenteuer, -** adventure
abenteuerlich adventurous
aber but, however (S3, 2.G, 5.G); *flavoring particle expressing admiration* (7.G)
ab·fahren* (von) to depart, leave (from) (8.1)
die **Abfahrt, -en** departure (8.1); descent
der **Abfall, ¨e** waste, garbage (15.1)
ab·fliegen* (von) to take off, fly (from) (8.1)
die **Abgase** (*pl.*) exhaust fumes
ab·geben* to give away, hand in
der **Abgeordnete (ein Abgeordneter) / die Abgeordnete, -n, -n** member of parliament
abgeschlossen finished
abhängig (von) dependent (on)
die **Abhängigkeit** dependence
ab·holen to pick up
das **Abitur, -e** = **Abi** *(coll.)* final comprehensive exam at the end of the *Gymnasium*
die **Abmeldung** report that one is leaving or moving
ab·nehmen* to take s.th. from, take away
abonnie'ren to subscribe
ab·pflücken to pick, break off
ab·reißen* to tear down (15.1)
der **Absatz, ¨e** paragraph
ab·schießen* to shoot down
ab·schließen, schloss ab, abgeschlossen to conclude, finish; **das Studium / die Ausbildung ~** to graduate, finish one's degree / education (13.1)
der **Abschluss, ¨e** degree, diploma (13.1)
die **Abschlussparty, -s** graduation party
die **Abschlussprüfung, -en** final exam
ab·schneiden* to cut off
der **Absender, - (Abs.)** return address (8.1)
absichtlich intentional(ly)
absolut' absolute(ly)
absolvie'ren to complete
ab·stellen to turn off
sich **ab·wechseln** to take turns
die **Abwechslung, -en** distraction, variety
ach oh; **~ so!** Oh, I see! (9.1); **~ was!** Oh, come on! (12.1)
achten auf *(+ acc.)* to pay attention to, watch out for
die **Achtung** respect; **~!** Watch out! Be careful!
der **ADAC** = **Allgemeiner Deutscher Automobil-Club** a German automobile association
ade (*or* **adé**) good-bye, farewell
addie'ren to add
das **Adjektiv, -e** adjective; **substantivier'te ~** adjectival noun
der **Adler, -** eagle
die **Adres'se, -n** address (8.1)
der **Advents'kranz, ¨e** Advent wreath
die **Advents'zeit** Advent season
das **Adverb', -ien** adverb
die **Aero'bik** aerobics
der **Affe, -n, -n** monkey; **Du ~!** You nut!
die **Agentur', -en** agency; **Werbe~** advertising agency
(das) **Ägyp'ten** Egypt
der **Ägyp'ter, -** the Egyptian
ägyp'tisch Egyptian
Aha'! There, you see. Oh, I see.
ähnlich similar; **Das sieht dir ~.** That's typical of you. (8.1)
die **Ahnung: Keine ~!** (I have) no idea. (10.1)
die **Akademie', -n** academy
der **Akade'miker, -** (university) graduate
akade'misch academic
der **Akku'sativ, -e** accusative
der **Akt, -e** act (play)
das **Aktiv** active voice
aktiv' active
die **Aktivität', -en** activity
aktuell' up-to-date, current
der **Akzent', -e** accent
akzeptie'ren to accept
das **All** space, universe; **aus dem ~** from out of space
all- all (7.G); **vor ~em** above all, mainly (10.2); **~e drei Jahre** every three years
allein' alone (11.2)
allerdings however (15.1)
die **Allergie', -n** allergy
aller'gisch gegen allergic to
allerlei all sorts of (2.1)
alles everything, all (2.1); **Das ist ~.** That's all. (2.1)
allgemein' (in) general; **im ~en** in general
allmäh'lich gradual(ly)
der **Alltag** everyday life
alltäglich everyday
die **Alpen** (*pl.*) Alps
die **Alpenblume, -n** Alpine flower
das **Alphabet'** alphabet
als as; (*conj.*) (at the time) when (11.G); (*after comp.*) than (12.G)
also therefore, thus, so; in other words; well (12.1)
alt (ä) old (S3); **stein~** very old; **ur~** ancient
der **Alte (ein Alter)** old man (12.G); **die ~, -n, -n** old lady (12.G); **das ~** old things (12.G)
das **Alter** age
die **Altstadt, ¨e** old part of town
der **Amateur', -e** amateur
ambitiös' ambitious
die **Ameise, -n** ant
(das) **Ame'rika** America (1.1)
der **Amerika'ner, -** the American (1.1)
amerika'nisch American (1.1)
die **Ampel, -n** traffic light
sich **amüsie'ren** to have fun
an- to, up to (7.G)
an (+ *acc. / dat.*) to, at (the side of), on (vertical surface) (6.G)
die **Analy'se, -n** analysis
analysie'ren to analyze
die **Ananas, -** pineapple
an·bieten* to offer (12.1)
(an)dauernd constantly, all the time
ander- other (9.2); **~e** others (9.1); **der / die ~e** the other one; **die ~en** the others (9.1); **etwas (ganz) ~es** s.th. (quite) different (9.2)

andererseits on the other hand
ändern to change
anders different(ly), in other ways (9.2); **Sagen Sie es ~!** Say it differently!
anerkannt recognized, accredited
an·erkennen* to recognize; acknowledge
die **Anerkennung, -en** recognition
der **Anfang, ¨-e** beginning, start (10.1); **~ der Woche** at the beginning of the week (8.G); **am ~** in the beginning (10.1)
an·fangen* to begin, start (10.1)
der **Anfänger, -** beginner
an·feuern to cheer for
die **Angabe, -n** information
das **Angebot, -e** offering, offer; **im ~** on special
die **Angelegenheit, -en** matter; thing
angeln to fish (9.1); **~ gehen*** to go fishing (9.1)
angepasst geared / adjusted to
angeschlagen posted
der **Angestellte (ein Angestellter) / die Angestellte, -n, -n** employee, clerk (12.G)
angewiesen sein* auf *(+ acc.)* to be dependent on
die **Anglis'tik** English studies
der **Angriff, -e** attack; raid
die **Angst, ¨-e** fear, anxiety; **~ haben*** **(vor** + *dat.*) to fear, be afraid (of) (13.2); **Keine ~!** Don't worry!; **~ bekommen*** to become afraid, get scared
an·halten* to continue
der **Anhang** appendix
anhänglich devoted, attached
sich **an·hören** to listen to (9.G); **Hör dir das an!** Listen to that.; to sound
an·kommen* **(in** + *dat.*) to arrive (in) (7.2); **Das kommt darauf an.** That depends. (7.2)
an·kreuzen to mark with an X
die **Ankunft** arrival (8.1)
an·machen to turn on (a radio, etc.)
die **Anmeldung** reception desk; registration
die **Annahme, -n** hypothetical statement or question; supposition
an·nehmen* to accept (7.2); to suppose (13.2)
der **Anorak, -s** parka
anpassungsfähig adaptable
an·probie'ren to try on
die **Anrede** address; **~form** form of address
an·reden to address
an·richten to do (damage)
der **Anruf, -e** (phone) call
der **Anrufbeant'worter, -** answering machine
an·rufen* to call up, phone (7.G)
an·sagen to announce
sich **an·schauen** to look at; to watch (9.G)
an·schlagen* to post
anschließend afterwards
der **Anschluss, ¨-e** connection
die **Anschrift, -en** address
(sich) **an·sehen*** to look at (9.G); to watch
die **Ansicht, -en** opinion, attitude; view
die **Ansichtskarte, -n** (picture) postcard (8.1)
ansonsten otherwise
an·sprechen* to address, speak to
(an)statt (+ *gen.*) instead of (8.G)
anstrengend strenuous (12.1)
der **Anteil, -e** share; proportion
der **Antikmarkt, ¨-e** antique mall
die **Antiquität', -en** antique
der **Antrag, ¨-e** application
die **Antwort, -en** answer
antworten to answer (S2)
an·wachsen* to increase
die **Anwaltsfirma, -firmen** law firm
die **Anzahl** number, amount
die **Anzeige, -n** ad(vertisement) (11.1)
die **Anzeigetafel, -n** scoreboard
(sich) **an·ziehen*** to put on (clothing), get dressed (9.G)
der **Anzug, ¨-e** men's suit
an·zünden to light
der **Apfel, ¨** apple (2.1)
die **Apfelschorle** apple juice with mineral water
der **Apfelstrudel, -** apple strudel
die **Apothe'ke, -n** pharmacy (2.2)
der **Apothe'ker, -** pharmacist
appellie'ren to appeal
der **Appetit'** appetite; **Guten ~!** Enjoy your meal. (3.1)
die **Apriko'se, -n** apricot
der **April'** April (S4); **im ~** in April (S4)
der **Äqua'tor** equator
das **Äquivalent'** equivalent
der **Araber, -** Arab
ara'bisch Arabic
die **Arbeit, -en** work (6.2); (term) paper (13.1); **bei der ~** at work; **Tag der ~** Labor Day
arbeiten to work (1.2)
der **Arbeiter, -** (blue-collar) worker (12.1); **Vor~** foreman
der **Arbeitgeber, -** employer
der **Arbeitnehmer, -** employee
arbeitsam hardworking; **~ wie ein Pferd** extremely hardworking
das **Arbeitsbuch, ¨-er** workbook
die **Arbeitserlaubnis** work permit
das **Arbeitsklima** work climate
die **Arbeitskraft, ¨-e** worker
die **Arbeitsleistung** output; performance
arbeitslos unemployed (12.1)
der **Arbeitslose (ein Arbeitsloser) / die Arbeitslose, -n, -n** unemployed person
die **Arbeitslosigkeit** unemployment (12.2)
der **Arbeitsmarkt, ¨-e** job market
der **Arbeitsplatz, ¨-e** job; place of employment
das **Arbeitszimmer, -** study (6.1)
archa'isch archaic
die **Archäologie'** archeology
der **Architekt', -en, -en** architect (12.1)
architekto'nisch architectural(ly)
die **Architektur'** architecture
das **Archiv', -e** archive
ärgerlich annoying
sich **ärgern über** (+ *acc.*) to get annoyed / upset about (10.G); **Das ärgert mich.** That makes me angry / mad. (10.1)
die **Arka'de, -n** arcade
arm (ä) poor (11.1)
der **Arm, -e** arm (9.1)
die **Armbanduhr, -en** wristwatch
die **Armee', -n** army
die **Armut** poverty
arrogant' arrogant
die **Art, -en (von)** kind, type (of)
der **Arti'kel, - (von)** article (of)
der **Arzt, ¨-e / die Ärztin, -nen** physician, doctor (12.1)
die **Asche** ashes
der **Asiate, -n, -n / die Asiatin, -nen** person from Asia
assoziie'ren to associate
ästhe'tisch aesthetic

die **Assisten'tin, -nen** assistant
die **Astronomie'** astronomy
der **Asylant', -en, -en** asylum seeker
der **Atem** breath
atmen to breathe
die **Atmosphä're** atmosphere
die **Attraktion', -en** attraction
attraktiv' attractive (11.1)
auch also, too (S1); **ich ~** me too
das **Audimax** main (university) auditorium
auf (+ *acc.* / *dat.*) on (top of) (6.G); open (7.1)
auf- up, open (7.G)
auf·atmen to breathe a sigh of relief
auf·bauen to build, put up (15.1); **wieder ~** to rebuild (15.1)
aufeinan'der treffen* (ist) to come together
der **Aufenthalt, -e** stay, stopover (8.1); **Auslands~** stay abroad
die **Aufenthaltserlaubnis** residence permit
auf·essen* to eat up
auf·fassen to consider (to be)
die **Aufgabe, -n** assignment; task, challenge
auf·geben* to give up
auf·gehen* to rise (sun)
auf·halten* to hold open; to stay
auf·holen to catch up
auf·hören (zu + *inf.*) to stop (doing s.th.) (13.2)
die **Aufklärung** enlightenment
der **Aufkleber, -** sticker
die **Auflage, -n** edition
auf·machen to open (7.G)
die **Aufnahme** acceptance, reception
auf·nehmen* to take (a picture)
auf·passen to pay attention, watch out (7.1)
der **Aufsatz, ¨-e** essay, composition, paper
der **Aufschnitt** (*sg.*) assorted meats / cheeses, cold cuts
auf·schreiben* to write down (7.G)
auf·stehen* to get up (7.G)
auf·stellen to put up, set up
die **Aufteilung** sharing
auf·wachen (ist) to wake up
auf·wachsen* to grow up
der **Aufzug, ¨-e** elevator
das **Auge, -n** eye (9.1)
der **Augenblick, -e** moment; **(Einen) ~!** Just a minute!
die **Augenbraue, -n** eyebrow
der **August'** August (S4); **im ~** in August (S4)
aus (+ *dat.*) out of, from (a place of origin) (3.G); **Ich bin ~ . . .** I'm from (a native of) . . . (1.1); **aus sein*** to be over
aus- out, out of (7.G)
aus·arbeiten to work out
aus·(be)zahlen to pay out
aus·bilden to train, educate
die **Ausbildung** training, education (12.1)
der **Ausdruck, ¨-e** expression
sich **auseinan'der entwickeln** to develop apart
der **Ausflug, ¨-e** excursion; **~ ins Grüne** excursion into nature
die **Ausfuhr** export
aus·füllen to fill out (13.1)
der **Ausgang, ¨-e** exit (7.1)
aus·geben* to spend (money) (9.2)
aus·bilden to train, educate
ausgebildet (als) trained (as); **gut ~** well-trained
ausgefallen extravagant, unusual
aus·gehen* to go out (7.G)
ausgezeichnet excellent (6.2)
aus·helfen* to help out
die **Aushilfskraft, ¨-e** temporary help
sich **aus·kennen* mit** to be familiar with
das **Ausland** foreign country; **im/ins ~** abroad (12.2)
der **Ausländer, -** foreigner (1.2); **~hass** xenophobia
ausländisch foreign (13.2)
der **Auslandsaufenthalt, -e** stay abroad
das **Auslandsprogramm, -e** foreign-study program
aus·leihen* to loan, lend out
aus·lesen* to pick out
aus·machen turn off (a radio, etc.)
aus·packen to unpack
die **Ausrede, -n** excuse
aus·reichen to suffice
ausreichend sufficient; approx. grade D
aus·richten to tell; **Kann ich etwas ~?** Can I take a message?
das **Ausrufungszeichen, -** exclamation mark
die **Aussage, -n** statement
aus·sehen* (wie + *nom.*) to look (like) (12.2)
außer (+ *dat.*) besides, except for (3.G)
äußer- outer
außerdem (*adv.*) besides, in addition (6.2)
außerhalb (+ *gen.*) outside (of)
die **Aussicht, -en (auf** + *acc.*) prospect (for); view (of)
die **Aussichtsplattform, -en** observation deck
der **Aussiedler, -** emigrant; ethnic immigrant
die **Aussprache** pronunciation
aus·steigen* to get off (8.1)
aus·stellen to issue; to exhibit
die **Ausstellung, -en** exhibition, show
aus·sterben* to become extinct
der **Ausstoß, ¨-e** exhaust
der **Austausch** exchange; **das ~programm, -e** exchange program
aus·tauschen to exchange (14.2)
ausverkauft sold out
die **Auswahl (an** + *dat.*) choice, selection (of) (10.2)
der **Ausweis, -e** ID, identification (7.1)
auswendig by heart
aus·werten to evaluate, assess
sich **aus·wirken auf** (+ *acc.*) to affect
aus·zahlen to pay out
die **Auszeit, -en** time-out
(sich) **aus·ziehen*** to get undressed (9.G)
der **Auszubildende (ein Auszubildender) / die Auszubildende, -n, -n = Azu'bi, -s** *(coll.)* trainee
authen'tisch authentic
das **Auto, -s** car (5.1)
die **Autobahn, -en** freeway
das **Autobahnkreuz, -e** freeway intersection
autofrei free of cars
der **Automat', -en, -en** machine
automatisiert' automated
die **Automobil'branche** car industry
der **Autor', -en** author (10.1)
autoritäts'gläubig believing in authority

B

die **Backe, -n** cheek
backen (bäckt), buk (backte), gebacken to bake (9.1)
der **Bäcker, -** baker
die **Bäckerei', -en** bakery (2.1)
das **Bad, ¨-er** bath(room) (6.1)
der **Badeanzug, ¨-e** swimsuit
die **Badehose, -n** swimming trunks
baden to bathe, swim (6.1); **sich ~** to take a bath (9.G)
die **Badewanne, -n** bathtub
das **Badezimmer, -** bathroom
die **Bahn, -en** railway, train (8.1)
der **Bahnübergang, ¨-e** railroad crossing
bahnen to clear / prepare the way
der **Bahnhof, ¨-e** train station (5.1)
der **Bahnsteig, -e** platform (8.1)
bald soon (7.1); **Bis ~!** See you soon! (9.1); **so~'** (*conj.*) as soon as (12.2)
baldig soon-to-come
der **Balkon', -s/-e** balcony (6.1)
der **Ball, ¨-e** ball
das **Ballett'** ballet (10.1)
der **Ballett'tänzer, -** ballet dancer
die **Bana'ne, -n** banana (2.1); **Alles ~!** Everything's nuts / crazy.
bange worried
die **Bank, -en** bank (7.1)
die **Bank, ¨-e** bench
der **Bankier', -s** banker
der **Bann** ban
die **Bar, -s** bar, pub
der **Bär, -en, -en** bear; **Du bist ein Brumm~.** You're a grouch.
barfuß barefoot
das **Bargeld** cash (7.1)
der **Bart, ¨-e** beard
basteln to do crafts
die **Batterie', -n** battery
der **Bau, -ten** building construction (15.1)
der **Bauch, ¨-e** stomach, belly (9.1)
bauen to build (6.2); **~ lassen*** to have built
der **Bauer, -n, -n** farmer
der **Bauernhof, ¨-e** farm
das **Baugesetz, -e** building code
der **Bauingenieur, -e** structural engineer
das **Bauland** building lots
der **Baum, ¨-e** tree (6.1)
die **Baumwolle** cotton
die **Baustelle, -n** construction site
der **Baustoff, -e** building material
der **Bayer, -n, -n** the Bavarian
(das) **Bayern** Bavaria (in south-east Germany)
bay(e)risch Bavarian
der **Beamte (ein Beamter) / die Beamtin, -nen** civil servant (12.G)
beantworten to answer
der **Bedarf (für)** need (for)
bedeuten to mean, signify (S2)
die **Bedeutung, -en** meaning; significance, importance
bedienen to take care of, serve; **Bedient euch!** Help yourself.
die **Bedienung** server, service (3.1); **~!** Waiter! / Waitress! (3.1); service charge
bedingt on a limited scale
bedroht threatened; **sich ~ fühlen** to feel threatened
sich **beeilen** to hurry (9.G)
beeindrucken to impress
beeinflussen to influence
beenden to finish, complete
der **Befehl, -e** instruction, request, command
befehlen (befiehlt), befahl, befohlen to order, command
befriedigend satisfactory; approx. grade C
befürchten to fear
begegnen (ist) to encounter
begehrt desired
begeistert enthusiastic(ally)
der **Beginn** beginning; **zu ~** in the beginning
beginnen, begann, begonnen to begin (S5)
die **Begleitung** accompaniment
begreifen* to understand, grasp
begrenzt limited
die **Begrenzung, -en** limit(ation), restriction
begrüßen to greet, welcome
die **Begrüßung, -en** greeting; **zur ~** as a greeting
behalten* to keep
der **Behälter, -** container (15.1)
behandeln (wie) to treat like
die **Behandlung, -en** treatment
beherrschen to dominate, rule
bei (+ *dat.*) at, near, at the home of (3.G); **Hier ~ ___.** This is ___'s office / residence.
beide both (11.1)
beige beige
bei·legen to enclose
das **Bein, -e** leg (9.1); **auf den ~en** on the go
das **Beispiel, -e** example; **zum ~ (z. B.)** for example (e.g.)
bei·tragen* (zu) to contribute (to)
bekämpfen to combat
bekannt well-known (5.2); **Das kommt mir ~ vor.** That seems familiar to me.
der **Bekannte (ein Bekannter) / die Bekannte, -n, -n** acquaintance (12.G)
bekommen* (hat) to get, receive (4.1)
bekümmert sad
belasten to burden; pollute
belegen to sign up for, take (a course) (13.1)
belgisch Belgian
beliebt popular (9.2)
die **Belohnung, -en** reward
bemerken to notice
sich **bemühen** to try (hard)
benennen* nach to name after
benutzen to use
das **Benzin'** gas(oline)
der **Benzin'kanis'ter, -** gasoline can
der **Benzin'schlucker, -** gas guzzler
beo'bachten to watch, observe
die **Beo'bachtung, -en** observation
bequem' comfortable, convenient (6.1)
der **Berater, -** counselor, adviser, consultant
die **Beratung** counseling
berauben to rob
der **Bereich, -e** area, field (12.2)
die **Berei'cherung** enrichment
der **Berg, -e** mountain (1.1)
bergab' downhill
bergauf' uphill
die **Bergbahn, -en** mountain train
der **Bergbau** mining
berghoch' uphill
bergsteigen gehen* to go mountain climbing
der **Bericht, -e** report
berichten to report (14.1)
berieseln *here:* to shower with
der **Beruf, -e** profession (12.1)

beruflich professional(ly); ~ **engagiert'** professionally active
die **Berufsschule, -n** vocational school
berufstätig working (professionally)
der **Berufstätige (ein Berufstätiger) / die Berufstätige, -n, -n** s.b. working in a profession
die **Berufswahl** choice of profession (12.2)
berühmt famous (14.2)
sich **beschäftigen mit** to be occupied with
die **Beschäftigung** activity; occupation
beschämend embarrassing
bescheinigen to verify, to document
beschreiben* to describe (8.2)
die **Beschreibung, -en** description
beschriftet labeled
beschuldigen to accuse
die **Beschwerde, -n** complaint; **~n machen** to give trouble
besetzen to fill, occupy
besichtigen to visit (an attraction), tour (5.1)
der **Besitz** property, possession
besitzen* to own
der **Besitzer, -** owner
besonders especially (3.2); **nichts Besonderes** nothing special (9.1)
besprechen* to discuss, talk about
besser better (12.G)
die **Besserung** improvement; **Gute ~!** Get well soon. (4.1)
best- best (12.G); **am ~en** it's best (12.G)
bestätigen to confirm
bestehen* to pass (an exam) (13.1); ~ **aus** (+ *dat.*) to consist of; **es besteht** there is; ~ **auf** *(+ dat.)* to insist on
besteigen* to climb on
bestellen to order (3.1)
die **Bestellung, -en** order
bestimmt surely, for sure, certain(ly) (13.2)
der **Besuch, -e** visit; visitor(s)
besuchen to visit (8.1); attend
der **Besucher, -** visitor
beten to pray
der **Beton'** concrete
betonen to stress, emphasize
Betr(eff) concerning

betreffen* to concern
betreiben* to (sports, a hobby)
betreten* to enter, step on
der **Betriebswirt, -e** graduate in business management (12.1)
die **Betriebswirtschaft** business administration
das **Bett, -en** bed (6.1); **ins ~** to bed
beugen to bend; **sich ~ über** *(+ acc.)* to bend over
die **Beute** booty, loot
die **Bevölkerung** population (15.2)
bevor (*conj.*) before (4.G)
bewachen to guard, watch over
bewältigen to overcome, cope with; finish
sich **bewegen** to move
die **Bewegung, -en** movement
der **Beweis, -e** proof; **das ~stück** (piece of) evidence
sich **bewerben (um)** to apply (for) (12.1)
die **Bewerbung, -en (um** + *acc.*) application (for)
das **Bewerbungsgespräch, -e** job interview
bewerten to rate
die **Bewertung, -en** evaluation, grading
der **Bewohner, -** inhabitant; resident
bewölkt cloudy
bewusst conscious(ly)
das **Bewusstsein** awareness
bezahlen to pay (for) (3.1)
sich **beziehen* auf** (+ *acc.*) to refer to, relate to
die **Beziehung, -en** relationship (11.1)
der **Bezirk, -e** district
die **Bibel, -n** Bible
die **Bibliothek', -en** library (5.1)
die **Biene, -n** bee
das **Bier, -e** beer (2.1); ~ **vom Fass** draught beer
der **Biergarten, ⸚** beer garden
der **Bierkrug, ⸚e** stein
bieten, bot, geboten to offer
der **Biki'ni, -s** bikini
die **Bilanz', -en: eine ~ auf·stellen** to make an evaluation
das **Bild, -er** picture (S2)
bilden to form; ~ **Sie einen Satz!** Make / Form a sentence.
die **Bildung** education
das **Billard** billiards
billig cheap(ly), inexpensive(ly) (S3)

binden, band, gebunden to bind
die **Biochemie'** biochemistry
der **Bioche'miker, -** biochemist
Biogra'phisches biographical data
der **Bio-Laden, ⸚** health-food store
der **Biolo'ge, -n, -n / die Biolo'gin, -nen** biologist
die **Biologie'** biology
die **Birne, -n** pear
bis to, until; ~ **später!** See you later! So long! (S1); ~ **bald!** See you soon! (9.1); ~ **gleich!** See you in a few minutes! (9.1)
bisher' until now
bishe'rig previous
bisschen: ein ~ some, a little bit (of) (4.2)
bitte please (S1); **~! / ~ bitte!** You're welcome. (S1, S5, 2.2); ~ **schön!** You're welcome. (4.1); **Hier ~!** Here you are.; ~ **schön?** May I help you?; **Wie ~?** What did you say? Could you say that again? (S5)
die **Bitte, -n** request
bitten, bat, gebeten (um) to ask (for), request (12.2)
das **Blatt, ⸚er** leaf; sheet
blau blue (S2)
der **Blazer, -** blazer
das **Blei** lead
bleiben, blieb, ist geblieben to stay, remain (3.1)
der **Bleistift, -e** pencil (S2)
der **Blick (in / auf** + *acc.*) view (of) (7.1); glance at (10.1)
der **Blickpunkt, -e** focus
blind blind
der **Blitz, -e** flash of lightning
blitzen to sparkle; **es blitzt** there's lightning
die **Blitzreaktion', -en** quick reaction
der **Block, ⸚e** block
die **Blocka'de, -n** blockade
die **Blockflöte, -n** recorder (*musical instrument*)
blockie'ren to block
blöd stupid
der **Blödsinn** nonsense; **So ein ~!** What nonsense!
blond blond
bloß only; **was . . . ~?** what on earth . . . ?; **wie . . . ~?** how on earth . . . ?

blühen to flourish; to bloom, blossom; ~**d** flourishing
die **Blume, -n** flower (2.2)
der **Blumenkohl** cauliflower
die **Bluse, -n** blouse (S3)
die **Blüte, -n** blossom
der **Boden, ¨** ground, floor
der **Bogen, ¨** bow; arch
die **Bohne, -n** bean (2.1)
der **Bomber, -** bomber
das **Bonbon, -s** (piece of) candy
der **Bonus, -se** bonus
das **Boot, -e** boat; **Tret~** pedal boat
borgen to borrow
die **Börse, -n** stockmarket
der **Börsenmakler, -** stockbroker
böse angry, mad, upset
der **Bote, -n, -n / die Botin, -nen** messenger
die **Bouti'que, -n** boutique
die **Bowle, -n** alcoholic punch
boxen to box
die **Branche, -n** branch
der **Brasilia'ner, -** Brasilian
brasilia'nisch Brasilian
braten (brät), briet, gebraten to fry
der **Braten, -** roast; **Schweine~** pork roast; **Rinder~** beef roast; **Sauer~** marinated pot roast
die **Bratkartoffeln** (*pl.*) fried potatoes
die **Bratwurst, ¨e** fried sausage
der **Brauch, ¨e** custom
brauchen to need (S3)
brauen to brew
die **Brauerei, -en** brewery
braun brown (S2); ~**gebrannt** tanned
die **Braut, ¨e** bride
der **Bräutigam, -e** bridegroom
das **Brautkleid, -er** wedding dress
die **BRD (Bundesrepublik Deutschland)** FRG (Federal Republic of Germany)
brechen (bricht), brach, gebrochen to break
der **Brei, -e** porridge; **Kartoffel~** (*sg.*) mashed potatoes
breit broad, wide
das **Brett, -er** board; das **Schwarze ~** bulletin board
die **Brezel, -n** pretzel
der **Brief, -e** letter (8.1)
der **Briefkasten, ¨** mailbox (8.1)
brieflich by letter
die **Briefmarke, -n** stamp (8.1)
der **Briefträger, -** mailman
die **Brille, -n** glasses
bringen, brachte, gebracht to bring (3.1); **mit sich ~** to bring with itself / o.s.
die **Brokkoli** (*pl.*) broccoli
die **Broschü're, -n** brochure
das **Brot, -e** bread (2.1); **Toast~** piece of toast; **Grau~** bread with wheat and rye; **Vollkorn~** bread with cracked rye and wheat grains; **Leinsamen~** bread with linseed; **Sonnenblumenkern~** bread with sunflower seeds
das **Brötchen, -** roll (2.1); **belegte ~** sandwich
der **Brotkrümel, -** bread crumb
der **Brotwürfel, -** small piece of bread, cube
die **Brücke, -n** bridge (5.1)
der **Bruder, ¨** brother (1.1)
das **Brüderchen, -** little brother
brüderlich brotherly
brüllen to scream
brummig grouchy
der **Brunnen, -** fountain
die **Brust, ¨e** chest, breast
das **Buch, ¨er** book (S2)
der **Bücherwurm, ¨er** bookworm
die **Buchführung** bookkeeping
der **Buchhalter, -** bookkeeper
die **Buchhandlung, -en** bookstore (2.1)
das **Büchlein, -** booklet, little book
der **Buchstabe, -n, -n** letter (of the alphabet)
buchstabie'ren to spell; **~ Sie auf Deutsch!** Spell in German!
die **Bude, -n** booth, stand; **Schieß~** shooting gallery
das **Büfett', -s** dining room cabinet; buffet
das **Bügeleisen, -** (clothing) iron
die **Bühne, -n** stage; **auf der ~** on stage
der **Bummel** stroll
bummeln (ist) to stroll (5.2)
der **Bund, ¨e** confederation; federal government
die **Bundesbank** central bank
der **Bundesbürger, -** citizen of the Federal Republic
die **Bundesfeier, -n** Swiss national holiday
das **Bundesland, ¨er** state, province
die **Bundespost** federal postal service
die **Bundesrepublik Deuthschland (BRD)** Federal Republic of Germany (FRG)
der **Bundesstaat, -en** federal state
der **Bundestag** German federal parliament
bunt colorful; multicolored; diverse
die **Burg, -en** castle, fortress
der **Bürger, -** citizen (10.2); **Mit~** fellow citizen
bürgerlich bourgeois, middle-class
der **Bürgersteig, -e** sidewalk
das **Bürgertum** citizenry
das **Büro', -s** office (12.1)
die **Bürokratie'** bureaucracy, red tape
die **Bürste, -n** brush
der **Bus, -se** bus (5.1); **mit dem ~ fahren*** to take the bus (5.1)
der **Busbahnhof, ¨e** bus depot
der **Busch, ¨e** bush
der **Busen, -** bosom
die **Butter** butter (2.1); **(Es ist) alles in ~.** Everything is all right.

C

das **Café', -s** café (3.1)
die **Cafeteri'a, -s=Cafe'te** (*coll.*) cafeteria
campen to camp; **~ gehen*** to go camping
der **Campingplatz, ¨e** campground
der **Cappucci'no, -s** cappuccino
die **CD, -s** CD (9.1)
der **Cellist', -en, -en** cello player
das **Cello, -s** cello
der **Cent, -s** cent (S3); **fünf ~** five cents (S3)
CH = Confoederatio Helvetica Helvetic Confederation (Switzerland)
das **Chaos** chaos
chao'tisch chaotic
die **Charakterisie'rung, -en** characterization
charakteris'tisch characteristic
charmant' charming (11.1)
der **Charme** charm
der **Chauffeur', -e** chauffeur
chauvinis'tisch chauvinist
der **Chef, -s** boss

die **Chemie'** chemistry
die **Chemika'lie, -n** chemical
chemisch chemical(ly)
der **Chine'se, -n, -n / die Chine'sin, -nen** Chinese
chine'sisch Chinese
der **Chor, ¨-e** choir (10.1)
der **Christbaum, ¨-e** Christmas tree
der **Christkindlmarkt, ¨-e** Christmas fair
chronolo'gisch chronological
Ciao! *(coll.)* Bye!
der **Clown, -s** clown
der **Cockerspaniel, -** Cocker spaniel
die **Cola** cola drink, soft drink (2.1)
das **College, -s** college
der **Collie, -s** Collie; Sheltie
die **Combo, -s** (musical) band
der **Compu'ter, -** computer; **~künstler, -** graphic designer
computerisiert' computerized
der **Contai'ner, -** container
die **Cornflakes** *(pl.)* cornflakes, cereal
das **Coupé, -s** compartment
der **Cousin', -s / Cousi'ne, -n** cousin
cremig creamy, smooth

D

da there (S2); ~ **drüben** over there (5.1)
dabei' along; there; yet; ~ **haben*** to have with o.s.; ~ **sein*** to come along
das **Dach, ¨-er** roof
der **Dachboden, ¨-** attic
der **Dachdecker, -** roofer
das **Dachgeschoss** attic floor; **im ~** on the attic floor
die **Dachrinne, -n** gutter
der **Dackel, -** dachshund
dadurch, dass because
dage'gen against it (10.G); **Hast du etwas ~, wenn . . . ?** Do you mind, if . . . ? (13.1)
daheim' at home
daher therefore, hence; from there
dahin: bis ~ until then
dahin'ten back there
die **Dahlie, -n** dahlia
das ***da*-Kompo'situm, Kompo'sita** *da*-compound
damalig *(adj.)* then
damals then, in those days (11.1)
die **Dame, -n** lady (5.1); **Sehr geehrte ~n und Herren!** Ladies and gentlemen!; ~ **spielen** to play checkers (9.1)
danach' later, after that (9.1)
der **Däne, -n, -n / die Dänin, -nen** the Dane
(das) **Dänemark** Denmark
dänisch Danish
der **Dank: Vielen / Herzlichen ~!** Thank you very much. (4.1); **Gott sei ~!** Thank God! (8.1)
dankbar grateful, thankful
danke thank you (S1); ~ **schön!** Thank you very much! (4.1); ~ **gleichfalls!** Thanks, the same to you. (3.1)
danken (+ *dat.*) to thank (3.G); **Nichts zu ~!** You're welcome. My pleasure. (4.1)
dann then (2.1)
dar·stellen to portray
der **Darsteller, -** actor
darü'ber above; ~ **hinaus** beyond that
darum therefore (12.2); **eben ~** that's why
das that (S2)
dass *(conj.)* that (4.G); **so~** *(conj.)* so that (13.2)
der **Dativ, -e** dative
das **Datum, Daten** *(calendar)* date (4.1); **Welches ~ ist heute?** What date is today? (4.1)
die **Dauer** length, duration
dauern to last (duration) (4.1); **Wie lange dauert das?** How long does that take? (4.1)
dauernd constantly, all the time
der **Daumen, -** thumb
die **DDR (Deutsche Demokratische Republik)** (German Democratic Republic)
die **Decke, -n** blanket; tablecloth
definie'ren to define
dein *(sg. fam.)* your (1.1)
die **Dekoration', -en** decoration
dekorie'ren to decorate
demnächst' before long, soon
der **Demokrat', -en, -en** democrat
die **Demokratie'** democracy
demokra'tisch democratic
der **Demonstrant', -en, -en** demonstrator
die **Demonstration', -en** demonstration
demonstrie'ren to demonstrate
denken, dachte, gedacht to think (4.1); ~ **an** (+ *acc.*) to think of / about (10.G)
der **Denker, -** thinker
das **Denkmal, ¨-er** monument (15.1)
denn because, for (2.G); *flavoring particle expressing curiosity, interest* (7.G)
der **Deo-Stift, -e** deodorant stick
die **Depression', -en** (mental) depression
deshalb therefore (13.2)
deskriptiv' descriptive
deswegen therefore
deutsch German
(das) **Deutsch: auf ~** in German (S2); **Sprechen Sie ~?** Do you speak German? (1.1); **Hoch~** (standard) High German; **Platt~** Low German (*northern German dialect*)
der **Deutsche (ein Deutscher) / die Deutsche, -n, -n** the German (1.1,12.G)
die **Deutsche Demokratische Republik (DDR)** German Democratic Republic (GDR)
(das) **Deutschland** Germany (1.1)
deutschsprachig German-speaking
die **Devi'se** motto
der **Dezem'ber** December (S4); **im ~** in December (S4)
sich **drehen** to turn
d. h. (das heißt) that is (i.e.)
das **Dia, -s** slide (photograph)
der **Dialekt', -e** dialect
die **Dialek'tik** conflicting nature, dialectics
der **Dialog', -e** dialogue
der **Diamant', -en, -en** diamond
dick thick, fat (S3); ~ **machen** to be fattening (3.2)
dickköpfig stubborn
der **Dieb, -e** thief
die **Diele, -n** (entrance) foyer
dienen to serve
der **Diener, -** servant
der **Dienst, -e** service; **öffentliche ~** civil service
der **Dienstag** Tuesday (S4); **am ~** on Tuesday (S4)
dienstags on Tuesdays (2.2)
dies- this, these (7.G)

diesig misty
diesmal this time (10.1)
das **Diktat', -e** dictation
die **Dimension', -en** dimension
das **Ding, -e** thing; **vor allen ~en** mainly
das **Diplom', -e** diploma (*e.g., in natural and social sciences, engineering*), M.A
der **Diplomat', -en, -en** diplomat
direkt' direct(ly)
der **Direk'tor, -en, -en** (school) principal, manager
der **Dirigent', -en, -en** (music) conductor
die **Diskothek', -en = Disko, -s** discotheque
die **Diskussion', -en** discussion
diskutie'ren to discuss
sich **distanzie'ren** to keep apart
die **Disziplin'** discipline
die **DM (Deutsche Mark)** German mark
der **Dobermann, ¨er** Doberman
doch yes (I do), indeed, sure (2.1); yet, however, but; on the contrary; *flavoring particle expressing concern, impatience, assurance* (7.G)
der **Dokumentar'film, -e** documentary
der **Dollar, -(s)** dollar (7.1)
der **Dolmetscher, -** interpreter
der **Dom, -e** cathedral (5.1)
dominie'ren to dominate
donnern to thunder; **es donnert** it's thundering
donnernd rumbling
der **Donnerstag** Thursday (S4); **am ~** on Thursday (S4)
donnerstags on Thursdays (2.2)
der **Doppelpunkt, -e** colon
doppelt double
das **Doppelzimmer, -** double room (7.1)
das **Dorf, ¨er** village (8.2)
dort (over) there (4.2)
dorthin to there (5.1)
der **Drachenflieger, -** hangglider
dran at it; **Jetzt sind Sie ~!** Now it's your turn.
draußen outside, outdoors; **hier ~** out here; **weit ~** far out
die **Dreißigerin, -nen** woman in her 30s
dringend urgent(ly)
die **Droge, -n** drug
die **Drogerie', -n** drugstore (2.2)
der **Drogist', -en, -en** druggist
drohen to threaten
der **Dschungel** jungle
duften to smell good; **~d** fragrant
dumm (ü) stupid, silly (10.1, 11.1); **Das ist (wirklich) zu ~.** That's (really) too bad.
die **Dummheit, -en** stupidity
der **Dummkopf, ¨e** dummy
die **Düne, -n** dune
das **Düngemittel, -** fertilizer
dunkel dark (6.1); **~haarig** dark-haired; **im Dunkeln** in the dark(ness)
die **Dunkelheit** darkness
dünn thin, skinny (S3)
durch (+ *acc.*) through (2.G); **mitten~** right through; by (*agent*)
durchbre'chen* to break through, penetrate
der **Durchbruch** breakthrough
durcheinan'der mixed up, confused
durch·fallen* to flunk (an exam) (13.1)
der **Durchschnitt** average; **im ~** on the average
dürfen (darf), durfte, gedurft to be allowed to, may (5.1); **Was darf's sein?** May I help you?
der **Durst** thirst (2.2); **Ich habe ~.** I'm thirsty. (2.2)
die **Dusche, -n** shower
(sich) **duschen** to take a shower (6W; 9.G)
der **Duschvorhang, ¨e** shower curtain
das **Dutzend, -e** dozen
sich **duzen** to call each other "*du*"
die **DVD, -s** DVD (9.1)
die **Dyna'mik** dynamics
dyna'misch dynamic

E

die **Ebbe** ebb tide, low tide
eben after all, just (*flavoring particle*); just now; **mal ~** just for a minute; **~!** That's it!
die **Ebene, -n** plain, level
ebenfalls also, likewise
ebenso just as, just the same
der **EC, -s** EuroCity (train)
echt real, authentic, genuine; **~?** Really? (4.1); **un~** fake
die **Ecke, -n** corner (6.1)
der **Effekt', -e** effect
egal' the same; **Das ist doch ~.** That doesn't matter. (8.1); **Es ist mir ~.** It's all the same to me. I don't care.; **~ wie/wo** no matter how/where
die **Ehe, -n** marriage (11.1)
ehemalig former
das **Ehepaar, -e** married couple
eher rather
die **Ehre, -n** honor
ehrgeizig ambitious
ehrgeizlos without ambition
ehrlich honest (11.1)
die **Ehrlichkeit** honesty
das **Ei, -er** egg (2.1); **ein gekochtes ~** boiled egg; **Rühr~** scrambled egg; **Spiegel~** fried egg; **verlorene ~er** poached eggs
die **Eidgenossenschaft** Swiss Confederation
das **Eigelb** egg yolk
eigen- own (11.1)
eigenartig strange
die **Eigenschaft, -en** characteristic (11.1)
eigentlich actual(ly) (4.2); **~ schon** actually, yes
der **Eigentümer, -** owner
die **Eigentumswohnung, -en** condo(minium) (6.2)
eilig hurried; **es ~ haben*** to be in a hurry
ein a, an (16.17.G); **die ~en** the ones
einan'der each other
die **Einbahnstraße, -n** one-way street
der **Einbau** installation
der **Einblick, -e** insight
der **Eindruck, ¨e** impression
eindrucksvoll impressive
eine(r) von Ihnen one of you
einerlei: Das ist nun ~. That doesn't matter anymore; **Es ist mir ~.** I don't care.
einerseits . . . andererseits on the one hand . . . on the other hand
einfach simple, simply (7.2)
die **Einfahrt, -en** driveway; **Keine ~!** Do not enter.
einfarbig all one color
der **Einfluss, ¨e** influence
die **Einfuhr** import
ein·führen to introduce
die **Einführung, -en** introduction

der **Eingang, ¨-e** entrance (7.1)
ein·halten* to keep, abide by
die **Einheit** unity, unification
einher'·stolzie'ren (ist) to strut around
das **Einhorn, ¨-er** unicorn
einig- (*pl. only*) some, a few (10.G); **so ~es** all sorts of things
einigen to unite; **sich ~** (+ *acc.*) to agree (on)
die **Einigkeit** unity
ein·kaufen to shop; **~ gehen*** to go shopping (2.2, 7.G)
die **Einkaufsliste, -n** shopping list
die **Einkaufstasche, -n** shopping bag
das **Einkaufszentrum, -zentren** shopping center
das **Einkommen, -** income (12.1)
ein·laden (lädt ein), lud ein, eingeladen (zu) to invite (to) (11.1)
die **Einladung, -en** invitation
sich **ein·leben** to settle down
ein·lösen to cash (in) (7.G); **einen Scheck ~** to cash a check
(ein)mal once, (at) one time / day (5.2); **noch ~** once more, again (S3); one order of; **auch ~** for once; **erst ~** first of all; **nicht ~** not even; **es war ~** once upon a time
einmalig unique, incredible (14.1)
der **Einmarsch, ¨-e** entry, invasion
ein·packen to pack (in a suitcase)
ein·richten to furnish
die **Einrichtung, -en** furnishings and appliances
einsam lonely
die **Einsamkeit** loneliness
ein·schlafen* (ist) to fall asleep
ein·schließen* to lock up
sich **ein·schreiben*** to register
das **Einschreibungsformular', -e** application for university registration
sich **ein·seifen** to put on soap
sich **ein·setzen (für)** to support actively
einst once (14.2)
ein·steigen* to get on / in (8.1)
ein·stimmen to join in the applause
die **Einteilung** division
der **Eintopf** stew
der **Eintritt** entrance fee
Einverstanden? Okay?
die **Einwanderung** immigration
der **Einwohner, -** inhabitant
das **Einwohnermeldeamt, ¨-er** resident registration office
einzeln individual(ly) (15.2)
das **Einzelzimmer, -** single room (7.1)
einzig- only; **ein ~er** just one
das **Eis** ice, ice cream (3.1)
das **Eisbein** pork knuckle
die **Eisenbahn, -en** train
eisern (made of) iron
eisig icy
eiskalt ice-cold
eitel vain
ekelhaft disgusting
sich **ekeln** to be digusted
der **Elefant', -en, -en** elephant
elegant' elegant
der **Elek'triker, -** electrician
elek'trisch electric
die **Elektrizität'** electricity
der **Elek'tromecha'niker, -** electrical mechanic / technician
elektro'nisch electronic
die **Elek'trotech'nik** electrical engineering
das **Element', -e** element
der **Ell(en)bogen, -** elbow
die **Eltern** (*pl.*) parents (1.1); **Groß~** grandparents (1 .1); **Schwieger~** parents-in-law; **Stief~** step-parents; **Urgroß~** great-grandparents
die **E-Mail, -s** e-mail (8.1); **~-Adresse, -n** e-mail address
die **Emanzipation'** emancipation
emanzipiert' emancipated
emotional' emotional(ly)
empfangen* to receive
die **Empfangsdame, -n** receptionist
empfehlen (empfiehlt), empfahl, empfohlen to recommend (3.1)
die **Empfehlung, -en** recommendation
empfindlich delicate; sensitive
das **Ende** end (10.1); **~ der Woche** at the end of the week (8.G); **am ~** in the end (10.1); **zu ~ sein*** to be finished
enden to end
endlich finally (15.2)
die **Endung, -en** ending
die **Energie', -n** energy
eng narrow
sich **engagie'ren (in** + *dat.*) to get involved (in)
der **Engel, -** angel
(das) **England** England (1.1)
der **Engländer, -** the Englishman (1.1)
englisch English
(das) **Englisch: auf ~** in English (S2); **Sprechen Sie ~?** Do you speak English? (1.1)
der **Enkel, -** grandchild
das **Enkelkind, -er** grandchild
die **Enkeltochter, ¨-** granddaughter
der **Enkelsohn, ¨-e** grandson
enorm' enormous; **~ viel** an awful lot
die **Ente, -n** duck; **Lahme ~!** Poor baby! Lame duck!
entfernt' away
die **Entfernung, -en** distance
entgegen·nehmen* to accept
enthalten* to contain
der **Enthusias'mus** enthusiasm
entlang' along (5.1)
sich **entscheiden, entschied, entschieden** to decide (10.1); **~ (für / gegen)** to decide for / against (10.G)
die **Entscheidung, -en** decision (12.2); **eine ~ treffen*** to make a decision
entschuldigen to excuse; **~ Sie bitte!** Excuse me, please. (5.1)
die **Entschuldigung, -en** excuse; **~!** Excuse me! Pardon me! (5.1)
sich **entspannen** to relax (9.2)
entspannt relaxed
entsprechen* to correspond to; **~d** corresponding
entstehen* (ist) to develop, emerge, be built; **neu ~** to reemerge
entweder . . . oder either . . . or
entwerten to cancel (ticket); devalue (currency)
(sich) **entwickeln** to develop; **sich auseinan'der·~** to develop apart
die **Entwicklung, -en** development
entzwei'·brechen* to break apart
(sich) **entzwei'·reißen*** to tear (o.s.) apart
sich **erbauen an** (+ *dat.*) to be delighted about, enjoy
die **Erbse, -n** pea (2.1)

das **Erdbeben, -** earthquake
die **Erdbeere, -n** strawberry (2.1)
die **Erde** earth (12.2); **unter der ~** underground; **zur ~ fallen*** to fall down
die **Erderwärmung** global warming
das **Erdgeschoss, -e** ground level (6.1); **im ~** on the ground level
die **Erdnuss, ¨-e** peanut; **~ butter** peanut butter
das **Ereignis, -se** event
erfahren* to find out, learn
die **Erfahrung, -en** experience (12.1); **Lebens~** life experience
erfinden* to invent
der **Erfolg, -e** success
erfolgreich successful
erforderlich necessary; **zwingend ~** absolutely necesssary
erfrieren* (ist) to freeze to death
erfüllen to fulfill; **sich ~** to be fulfilled, come true
die **Erfüllung** fulfillment
ergänzen to supply, add to
ergreifen* to take (hold of)
erhalten* to keep up, preserve, maintain; get, receive
die **Erhaltung** preservation (15.1)
die **Erhellung** illumination
sich **erholen** to recuperate (9.2)
die **Erholung** recuperation, relaxation
erinnern (an + *acc.*) to remind (of) (14.1); **sich ~ (an** + *acc.*) to remember (14.1)
die **Erinnerung, -en (an** + *acc.*) reminder, memory (of)
erkalten (ist) to grow cold; (*poetic*) to become insensitive
sich **erkälten** to catch a cold (9.G)
die **Erkältung, -en** cold
erkennen* to recognize (14.2); **Zum Erkennen** for recognition
erklären to explain (12.1)
die **Erklärung, -en** explanation
erlauben to permit, allow
die **Erlaubnis** permit, permission; **Arbeits~** work permit; **Aufenthalts~** residence permit
erleben to experience (9.2)

das **Erlebnis, -se** experience
erlesen exquisite, high-quality
die **Ermäßigung, -en** discount
die **Ernährung** nutrition
erneuerbar renewable
ernst serious(ly)
die **Ernsthaftigkeit** seriousness
die **Ernte, -n** harvest
das **Erntedank'fest** (Harvest) Thanksgiving
eröffnen to open up, establish
erreichen to reach
erscheinen* (ist) to appear, seem (4.G)
erschrecken (erschrickt), erschrak, ist erschrocken to be frightened
ersetzen to replace
erst- first
erst only, not until
ertragen* to tolerate, stand
erwachsen grown-up, adult
der **Erwachsene (ein Erwachsener) / die Erwachsene, -n, -n** adult
erwähnen to mention
erwärmen to heat (up)
erwarten to expect
erweitern to expand; **erweitert** expanded
erzählen to tell (8.1); **~ (von** + *dat.*) to tell (about) (10.G); **nach·~** to retell
erzeugen to produce
erziehen* to educate, raise
die **Erziehung** education
das **Erziehungsgeld** monthly child-raising benefit
der **Esel, -** donkey, ass; **Du ~!** You dummy!
der **Espres'so, -s** espresso
der **Esprit'** esprit
essbar edible
essen (isst), aß, gegessen to eat (S5)
das **Essen, -** food, meal (2.1); **beim ~** while eating
der **Essig** vinegar
der **Essvorrat, ¨-e** provision
das **Esszimmer, -** dining room (5.1)
der **Este, -n, -n / die Estin, -nen** Estonian
(das) **Estland** Estonia
estnisch Estonian
die **Eta'ge, -n** floor
ethnisch ethnic
etliche many
etwa about, approximately (10.2)

etwas some, a little (2.1); something (3.1); **so ~ wie** s.th. like; **noch ~** one more thing, s.th. else; **Sonst noch ~?** Anything else?; **so ~** s.th. like that
euer (*pl. fam.*) your (7.G)
der **Euro, -s** euro (S3); **zehn ~** ten euros
(das) **Euro'pa** Europe
der **Europä'er, -** the European
europä'isch European
die **Europäische Union (EU)** European Union (1.1); **in der Europäischen Union** in the EU (1.2)
das **Euroland** euro region
die **Europäisie'rung** Europeanization
euro'paweit all over Europe
der **Evangelist', -en, -en** evangelist
eventuell' perhaps, possibly
ewig eternal(ly); **für ~** forever
exakt' exact(ly)
das **Exa'men, -** exam; **Staats~** comprehensive state exam
das **Exemplar', -e** sample, copy
das **Exil', -e** exile
existie'ren to exist
experimentell' experimental(ly)
der **Exper'te, -n, -n / die Expertin, -nen** expert
extra extra
das **Extrablatt, ¨-er** special publication
exzen'trisch excentric

F

die **Fabel, -n** fable
fabelhaft fabulous
die **Fabrik', -en** factory
das **Fach, ¨-er** subject (13.1); **Haupt~** major (field) (13.1); **Neben~** minor (field) (13.1); **Schwerpunkt~** major (field)
das **Fach, ¨-er** special field
der **Fachbereich, -e** field (of study)
die **Fachhochschule, -n** university of applied sciences
die **Fachkenntnis, -se** special skill
die **Fach(ober)schule, -n** business or technical school
die **Fachrichtung, -en** field of study, specialization (13.1)
das **Fachwerkhaus, ¨-er** half-timbered house
der **Faden, ¨-** thread

die **Fähigkeit, -en** ability
die **Fahne,-n** flag; **getreu zur ~ halten*** to remain faithful
die **Fähre, -n** ferry
fahren (fährt), fuhr, ist gefahren to drive, go (by car, etc.) (3.G)
die **Fahrerei'** (incessant) driving
die **Fahrkarte, -n** ticket (8.1)
der **Fahrplan, ¨-e** schedule (of trains, etc.) (8.1)
das **(Fahr)rad, ¨-er** bicycle (5.1); **mit dem ~ fahren*** to bicycle
der **(Fahr)radweg, -e** bike path
der **Fahrstuhl, ¨-e** elevator
die **Fahrt, -en** trip, drive (8.1)
fair fair(ly)
der **Fall, ¨-e** case; **auf jeden ~** in any case; definitely; **für alle Fälle** just in case
fallen (fällt), fiel, ist gefallen to fall (4.2); **~ lassen*** to drop
falsch wrong, false (S2)
die **Fami'lie, -n** family (1.1)
der **Fami'lienstand** marital status
fangen (fängt), fing, gefangen to catch
die **Fantasie', -n** fantasy, imagination
fantas'tisch fantastic(ally) (9.1)
die **Farbe, -n** color (S2); **Welche ~ hat . . . ?** What color is . . . ? (S2)
der **Farbstoff, -e** dye, (artificial) color
der **Fasching** carnival; **zum ~** for carnival (Mardi Gras)
das **Fass, ¨-er** barrel; **Bier vom ~** beer on tap
die **Fassa'de, -n** façade
fast almost (6.2)
die **Fastenzeit** Lent
die **Faszination'** fascination
faszinie'ren to fascinate
faul lazy (11.1)
faulenzen to be lazy (9.1)
die **Faulheit** laziness
das **Fax, -e** fax
das **Faxgerät, ¨-e** fax machine
der **Februar** February (S4); **im ~** in February (S4)
fechten (ficht), focht, gefochten to fence
der **Federball, ¨-e** badminton (ball)
fehlen to be missing, lacking (8.1); **hier fehlt was** s.th. is missing (here); **Was fehlt?** What's missing?
fehlend missing
der **Fehler, -** mistake
die **Feier, -n** celebration, party (4.1)
feierlich festive
feiern to celebrate (4.1)
der **Feiertag, -e** holiday (4.1)
feige cowardly; **er ist ~** he's a coward
fein fine
die **Feind, -e** enemy
feindlich hostile
das **Feld, -er** field
das **Fenster, -** window (S2)
die **Ferien** *(pl.)* vacation (4.1)
der **Ferienplatz, ¨-e** vacation spot
fern far, distant
die **Ferne** distance
der **Fernfahrer, -** truck driver
das **Ferngespräch, -e** long-distance call
fern·sehen* to watch TV (9.1)
das **Fernsehen** TV (the medium) (10.2); **im ~** on TV (10.1)
der **Fernseher, -** TV set (6.1)
das **Fernweh** nostalgia; **von ~ krank** sick with wanderlust
fertig finished, done (S5); worn-out; **~·machen** to finish
das **Fest, -e** celebration (4.1)
festgesetzt fixed
festlich festive(ly)
das **Festspiel, -e** festival; **~haus ¨-er** festival hall
die **Fete, -n** *(coll.)* party
fettfrei fat-free
fettig greasy
das **Feuer, -** fire
das **Feuerwerk, -e** firework(s)
die **Figur', -en** figure
der **Film, -e** film (10.1)
filmen to shoot a film
die **Finan'zen** *(pl.)* finances
finanziell' financial(ly)
finanzie'ren to finance (15.1)
die **Finanzie'rung** financing
finden, fand, gefunden to find (S4); **Ich finde es . . .** I think it's . . . (S4); **Das finde ich auch.** I think so, too. (S4)
der **Finger, -** finger (9.1); **Zeige~** index finger
der **Fingernagel, ¨** fingernail
der **Finne, -n, -n / die Finnin, -nen** the Finn
finnisch Finnish
(das) **Finnland** Finland
die **Firma, Firmen** company, business (12.1)
der **Fisch, -e** fish (2.1); Pisces; **ein kalter ~** a cold-hearted person
der **Fischfang** fishing
fit in shape; **sich ~ halten*** to keep in shape (9.2)
flach flat
die **Fläche, -n** area
der **Flachs** flax
die **Flagge, -n** flag
die **Flamme, -n** flame
die **Flasche, -n** bottle (3.2); **eine ~ Wein** a bottle of wine (3.2); **Mehrweg~** bottle with a deposit
das **Fleisch** *(sg.)* meat (2.1)
der **Fleischer, -** butcher
die **Fleischerei', -en** butcher shop
fleißig industrious(ly), hardworking (11.1)
flexi'bel flexible, flexibly
die **Flexibilität'** flexibility
flicken to patch, repair
die **Fliege, -n** fly
fliegen, flog, ist geflogen to fly (8.1); **mit dem Flugzeug ~** to go by plane (8.1)
fliehen, floh, ist geflohen to flee, escape
der **Flieger, -** airplane; **der Düsen~** fighter jet; **die ~staffel, -n** flying squadron
die **Fliese, -n** tile
fließen, floss, ist geflossen to flow
fließend fluent(ly)
die **Flitterwochen** *(pl.)* honeymoon
flitzen (ist) to dash
der **Flohmarkt, ¨-e** flea market
das **Floß, ¨-e** raft
die **Flöte, -n** flute; **(Block)~** recorder, wooden flute
die **Flotte, -n** fleet
die **Flucht** escape
der **Flüchtling, -e** refugee
der **Flug, ¨-e** flight (8.1)
der **Flügel, -** wing
die **Fluggesellschaft, -en** airline company
der **Flughafen, ¨** airport (8.1)
die **Flugkarte, -n** plane ticket
der **Flugsteig, -e** gate
das **Flugzeug, -e** airplane (8.1)
der **Flur** hallway (6.1)
der **Fluss, ¨-e** river (1.1)
flüstern to whisper
die **Flut** high tide

der **Fokus** focus
folgen (ist) (+ *dat.*) to follow
folgend following (10.1)
der **Fön, -e** hair dryer
das **Fondue', -s** fondue
die **Fonotypist', -en, -en** audio/dictaphone-typist
fördern to encourage
die **Forel'le, -n** trout
die **Form, -en** form, shape
das **Format** shape, size
das **Formular', -e** form
formulie'ren to formulate
die **Forschung** research; **der ~szweig, -e** field of research
der **Förster,-** forest ranger
die **Forstwirtschaft** forestry
fort- away
fort·fahren* to drive away; to continue
der **Fortschritt, -e** progress
fort·werfen* to throw away
die **Fotografie'** photo(graph); photography
fotografie'ren to take pictures (9.1)
die **Frage, -n** question (1.1); **Ich habe eine ~.** I have a question. (S5); **jemandem eine ~ stellen** to ask sb. a question
fragen to ask (S2); **sich ~** to wonder (9.G)
das **Fragezeichen, -** question mark
fraglich questionable
der **(Schweizer) Franken, -** (Swiss) franc
(der) **Frankfurter Kranz** rich cake ring with whipped cream and nuts
fränkisch Franconian
(das) **Frankreich** France (1.1)
der **Franzo'se, -n, -n / die Franzö'sin, -nen** French person (1.1, 2.G)
franzö'sisch French (1.1)
(das) **Franzö'sisch; auf ~** in French (1.1); **Ich spreche ~.** I speak French. (1.1)
die **Frau, -en** Mrs., Ms. (S1); woman; wife (1.1)
das **Frauchen, -** *(coll.)* (female) owner of a pet
die **Frauenbewegung** women's movement
das **Fräulein, -** *(old fashioned)* Miss; young lady
frech impudent(ly), sassy, fresh
die **Frechheit** impertinence
frei free, available (7.1)
freiberuf'lich self-employed, freelance
freigiebig generous(ly)
die **Freiheit** freedom
das **Freilichtspiel, -e** outdoor performance
frei·nehmen* to take time off
der **Freitag** Friday (S4); **am ~** on Friday (S4); **Kar~** Good Friday
freitags on Fridays (2.2)
freiwillig voluntary; voluntarily
die **Freizeit** leisure time (9.1)
fremd foreign, strange
das **Fremdenzimmer, -** guestroom
die **Fremdsprache, -n** foreign language
der **Fremdsprachenkorrespondent', -en, -en** bilingual secretary
fressen (frisst), fraß, gefressen to eat (like a glutton or an animal); **auf·~** to devour
das **Frettchen, -** ferret
die **Freude, -n** joy; **~ machen** to be fun
sich **freuen auf** (+ *acc.*) to look forward to (10.G); **Freut mich.** I'm pleased to meet you. (S1); **(Es) freut mich auch.** Likewise, pleased to meet you, too; **Das freut mich für dich.** I'm happy for you. (8.1)
der **Freund, -e** (boy) friend (3.2)
die **Freundin, -nen** (girl)friend (3.2)
freundlich friendly (11.1)
die **Freundlichkeit** friendliness
die **Freundschaft, -en** friendship (11.1)
der **Frieden** peace (14.1)
der **Friedhof, ¨-e** cemetery
friedlich peaceful(ly)
frieren, fror, gefroren to freeze, be freezing
frisch fresh(ly) (2.1)
der **Friseur', -e** barber, hairdresser
die **Friseu'se, -n** = **Friseu'rin, -nen** beautician, hairdresser
friesisch Frisian
froh glad(ly), happy, happily (11.2); **Frohe Weihnachten!** Merry Christmas (4.1)
fröhlich cheerful(ly), merry, merrily; **Fröhliche Weihnachten!** Merry Christmas! (4.1)
der **Fronleich'nam(stag)** Corpus Christi (holiday)
der **Frosch, ¨-e** frog
früh early, morning (8.G)
früher earlier, once, former(ly) (12.2)
der **Frühling, -e** spring (S4)
das **Frühjahrssemes'ter, -** spring semester
das **Frühstück** breakfast (2.2); **Was gibt's zum ~?** What's for breakfast? (3.1)
frühstücken to eat breakfast (3.1)
der **Frust** frustration
frustriert' frustrated
die **Frustrie'rung** frustration
der **Fuchs, ¨-e** fox; **schlau wie ein ~** clever as a fox; **ein alter ~** a sly person
sich **fühlen** to feel (a certain way) (9.1)
führen to lead (14.1)
der **Führerschein, -e** driver's license
die **Führung, -en** guided tour
die **Fülle** abundance; **in ganzer ~** to the fullest
füllen to fill
die **Funktion', -en** function
für (+ *acc.*) for (S2,2.G); **was ~ ein . . . ?** what kind of a . . . ? (2.1)
die **Furcht** fear, awe
furchtbar terrible, terribly, awful(ly) (S4)
sich **fürchten** (**vor** + *dat.*) to be afraid (of)
der **Fürst, -en, -en** sovereign, prince
das **Fürstentum, ¨-er** principality
der **Fuß, ¨-e** foot (9.1); **zu ~ gehen*** to walk (5.1)
der **Fußball, ¨-e** soccer (ball) (9.1)
der **Fußgänger, -** pedestrian; **~weg, -e** pedestrian sidewalk; **~überweg, -e** pedestrian crossing; **~zone, -n** pedestrian area
der **Fußnagel, ¨** toenail
die **Fußstapfe, -n** footstep

G

die **Gabe, -n** gift; **in kleinen ~n** in small doses
die **Gabel, -n** fork (3.1)
gähnen to yawn

die **Galerie', -n** gallery
die **Gämse, -n** mountain goat
die **Gans, ¨-e** goose; **eine dumme ~** a silly person *(fem.)*
ganz whole, entire(ly), total(ly), all (9.2); very; **~ meinerseits.** The pleasure is all mine; **~ schön** quite (nice); **~tags** full-time
das **Ganze** the whole thing; **im Großen und ~n** on the whole
die **Gara'ge, -n** garage (6.1)
garantie'ren to guarantee (15.1)
die **Gardi'ne, -n** curtain
gar nicht not at all (13.2)
der **Garten, ¨** garden (6.1); **Bier~** beer garden
das **Gartenstück, -e** garden plot
die **Gasse, -n** narrow street
Gassi gehen* to take a dog on a walk
der **Gast, ¨-e** guest (7.1)
der **Gastarbeiter, -** foreign (guest) worker
das **Gästezimmer, -** guest room
das **Gasthaus, ¨-er** restaurant, inn
der **Gasthof, ¨-e** small hotel (7.2)
die **Gaststätte, -n** restaurant, inn
die **Gastwirtschaft, -en** restaurant, inn
das **Gebäck** pastry
das **Gebäude, -** building (14.1)
geben (gibt), gab, gegeben to give (3.G); **es gibt** there is, there are (2.1); **Was / Wo gibt's . . . ?** What / Where do you (they) have . . . ? (1.1); **Was gibt's zu essen / trinken?** What's there to eat / drink? (3.1); **Was gibt's?** What's up?; **Was gibt's Neues?** What's new? (9.1); **Was gibt's im . . . ?** What's (playing) on . . . ? (10.1); **Das gibt's doch nicht!** I don't believe it! That's impossible! (4.1)
das **Gebiet, -e** area, region (15.1)
gebildet well educated (11.1)
geboren: Ich bin . . . ~. I was born . . . (S4); **Wann sind Sie ~?** When were you born? (S4); **Wann wurde . . . ~?** When was . . . born?
die **Geborgenheit** security
gebrauchen to use, utilize
der **Gebrauchtwagen, -** used car
die **Gebühr, -en** fee
gebunden tied down; **orts~** tied to a certain town or place
die **Geburt, -en** birth; **Wieder~** rebirth
der **Geburtstag, -e** birthday (4.1); **Wann haben Sie ~?** When is your birthday? (4.1); **Ich habe am . . .-(s)ten ~.** My birthday is on the . . . (date) (4.1); **Ich habe im . . . ~.** My birthday is in . . . (month). (4.1); **Alles Gute / Herzlichen Glückwunsch zum ~!** Happy birthday! (4.1); **zum ~** at the / for the birthday (4.1)
der **Geburtsort, -e** place of birth
das **Gedächtnis** memory
der **Gedanke, -ns, -n** thought (14.2)
das **Gedeck, -e** complete dinner
das **Gedicht, -e** poem
die **Geduld** patience
geduldig patient (11.1); **~ wie ein Lamm** really patient
die **Gefahr, -en** danger (12.2)
gefährlich dangerous (15.2)
das **Gefälle, -** decline
gefallen (gefällt), gefiel, gefallen (+ *dat.*) to like, be pleasing to (3.G); **Es gefällt mir.** I like it. (3.G)
gefangen halten* to keep prisoner
gefangen sein* (in + *dat.***)** to be caught (in)
das **Gefängnis, -se** prison
gefettet greased
der **Gefrierschrank, ¨-e** freezer
das **Gefühl, -e** feeling; **Mit~** compassion
gegen (+ *acc.*) against (2.G); toward (time), around
die **Gegend, -en** area, region (8.2)
der **Gegensatz, ¨-e** contrast, opposite
gegensätzlich opposing
das **Gegenteil, -e** opposite (S3); **im ~** on the contrary
gegenüber (von + *dat.***)** across (from) (5.1)
die **Gegenwart** present (tense)
der **Gegner, -** opponent
das **Gehalt, ¨-er** salary
geheim secret
gehen, ging, ist gegangen to go, walk (S5); **Es geht mir . . .** I am (feeling) . . . (S1); **Wie geht's? Wie geht es dir? Wie geht es Ihnen?** How are you? (S1); **zu Fuß ~** to walk (5.1); **Das geht.** That's OK. (13.2); **Das geht (heute) nicht.** That won't work (today). (9.1); **So geht's.** That's the way it goes.; **wenn es darum geht** when it's a matter of
gehorchen to obey
gehören (+ *dat.*) to belong to (3.G)
die **Geige, -n** violin
der **Geisteswissenschaftler, -** humanities scholar
geistig mental(ly), intellectual(ly)
geizig stingy
das **Gelände, -** lot, tract of land; ground
das **Geländer, -** railing, banister
gelaunt: gut / schlecht ~ in a good / bad mood
gelb yellow (S2)
das **Geld** money (7.1); **Bar~** cash (7.1); **Klein~** change (7.1); **Erziehungs~** government stipend for child care; **~ aus·geben*** to spend money (9.2)
der **Geldautomat', -en, -en** ATM machine (7.1)
der **Geldbeutel, -** pocket book
der **Geldschein, -e** banknote (15.2)
die **Gelegenheit, -en** opportunity, chance
der **Gelieb'te (ein Geliebter) / die Geliebte, -n, -n** darling; lover
gelingen, gelang, ist gelungen to succeed; **Es gelingt mir nicht.** I can't (do it).
gelungen successful
gelten (gilt), galt, gegolten to apply to, be valid for, be true
das **Gemälde, -** painting (10.1)
die **Gemeinde, -n** community
gemeinsam together, shared, joint(ly); (in) common (15.2)
die **Gemeinschaft, -en** community
das **Gemisch** mixture; **ein buntes ~ an** *(+ dat.)* a great diversity in
gemischt mixed
das **Gemüse, -** vegetable(s) (2.1)
gemütlich cozy, pleasant, comfortable, convivial (5.2)

die **Gemütlichkeit** nice atmosphere, coziness
genau exact(ly), precise(ly); **~so** the same; **~so ___ wie** just as ___ as; **~ wie** (+ *nom.*) just like (9.2)
die **Generation', -en** generation
generös' generous(ly)
sich **genieren** to be embarrassed
genießen, genoss, genossen to enjoy
der **Genitiv, -e** genitive
genug enough (5.2); **Jetzt habe ich aber ~.** That's enough. I've had it. (10.1)
geöffnet open (7.1)
die **Geographie'** geography
geolo'gisch geological
die **Geologie'** geology
das **Gepäck** baggage, luggage (7.1)
die **Gepäckaufgabe, -n** checked luggage room
gepunktet dotted
gerade just, right now (4.1); straight (forward); **~ als** just when; **(immer) ~aus'** (keep) straight ahead (5.1)
das **Gerät, -e** tool, equipment
die **Gerechtigkeit** justice
das **Gericht, -e** dish; **Haupt~** main dish
der **Gerichtshof, ¨-e** court
gering' little, small; **~er** less
germa'nisch Germanic
die **Germanis'tik** study of German language and literature
gern (lieber, liebst-) gladly (2.1); **furchtbar ~** very much; **~ geschehen!** Glad to . . . ; **Ich hätte ~.** I'd like to have . . . (2.1)
die **Gesamtschule, -n** comprehensive high school
das **Geschäft, -e** store (2.1); business (12.1)
geschäftlich concerning business
die **Geschäftsfrau, -en** businesswoman / **Geschäftsmann, ¨-er** businessman / **Geschäftsleute** *(pl.)* business people (12.1)
geschehen (geschieht), geschah, ist geschehen to happen (11.2); **Das geschieht dir recht.** That serves you right.

das **Geschenk, -e** present (4.1)
die **Geschichte, -n** story, history (8.2)
geschickt talented, skillful
geschieden divorced (11.1)
das **Geschlecht, -er** gender, sex
geschlossen closed (7.1)
der **Geschmack, ¨-er** taste
geschmacklos tacky
das **Geschrei** screaming
gechwind quickly
die **Geschwindigkeit, -en** speed; **~sbegrenzung** speed limit; **Richt~** recommended speed
die **Geschwister** *(pl.)* brothers and/or sisters, siblings (1.1)
der **Geselle, -n, -n / die Gesellin, -nen** journeyman / journey woman
gesellig sociable
die **Gesell'schaft, -en** society
gesellschaftlich' societal, social(ly)
gesell'schaftspoli'tisch sociopolitical
das **Gesetz, -e** law
gesetzlich legal(ly)
gesichert secure
das **Gesicht, -er** face (9.1)
das **Gespräch, -e** conversation, dialogue
die **Gestal'tung** style, shape
das **Geständnis, -se** confession
gestern yesterday (4.1,8.G); **vor~** the day before yesterday (4.1)
gestreift striped
gesucht wird wanted
gesund (ü) healthy (9.1)
die **Gesundheit** health
das **Gesundheitsamt** health department
gesundheitsbewusst health conscious
der **Gesundheitsfana'tiker, -** health nut
geteilt divided; shared
das **Getränk, -e** beverage
getrennt separated, separate(ly)
die **Gewalt** violence
die **Gewerkschaft, -en** trade / labor union
der **Gewinn, -e** profit, benefit
gewinnen, gewann, gewonnen to win (12.2)
gewiss for sure
die **Gewissenhaftigkeit** conscientiousness
das **Gewitter, -** thunderstorm

sich **gewöhnen an** (+ *acc.*) to get used to (12.1)
gewöhnlich usual(ly) (3.2)
gezwungen obligated
gierig greedy
gießen, goss, gegossen to pour; **es gießt** it's pouring
das **Gift, -e** poison
der **Giftstoff, -e** toxic waste (15.1)
die **Giraf'fe, -n** giraffe
die **Gitar're, -n** guitar (9.1)
die **Gladio'le, -n** gladiola
der **Glanz** brilliance, splendor
glänzend shiny
das **Glas, ¨-er** glass (2.2); **ein ~** a glass of (2.2)
glauben to believe, think (2.1;3.G); **Ich glaube es/ihr.** I believe it / her.; **~ an** (+ *acc.*) to believe in (12.1)
glaubhaft convincing(ly)
gleich equal(ly), same (12.1); right away; **Bis ~!** See you in a few minutes! (9.1)
gleichberechtigt with equal rights
die **Gleichberechtigung** equality, equal rights
gleichfalls: Danke ~! Thank you, the same to you. (3.1)
gleichgeschlechtlich same-sex
gleichmäßig regularl(ly)
das **Gleichnis, -se** parable
gleichzeitig at the same time
das **Gleis, -e** track (8.1)
der **Gletscher, -** glacier
glitzernd glittering
die **Glocke, -n** bell
glorreich glorious
das **Glück** luck, happiness; **~ haben*** to be lucky (4.2); **~ gehabt!** I was (you were, etc.) lucky! (4.2); **Viel ~!** Good luck! (4.1); **Du ~spilz!** You lucky thing!; **zum ~** luckily
glücklich happy, happily (11.1); **~erweise** luckily
der **Glücksstern** lucky star
der **Glückwunsch, ¨-e** congratulation; **Herzlichen ~ (zum Geburtstag)!** Congratulations (on your birthday)! (4.1); **Herzliche Glückwünsche!** Congratulations! Best wishes! (4.1)
der **Glühwein** mulled wine
der **Gnom, -e** gnome, goblin
das **Gold** gold (11.2)
golden golden

der **Goldfisch, -e** goldfish
(das) **Golf** golf; **Mini~** miniature golf
der **Gott** God; **~ sei Dank!** Thank God! (8.1); **Um ~es willen!** For Heaven's sake! My goodness!
der **Gott, ¨er** god
das **Grab, ¨er** grave
der **Graben, ¨** ditch, drench
der **Grad, -e** degree
die **Gramma'tik** grammar
gramma'tisch grammatical(ly)
die **Grapefruit, -s** grapefruit
das **Gras** grass
gratulie'ren (+ *dat.*) to congratulate (4.1); **Wir ~! / Ich gratuliere!** Congratulations!
grau gray (S2)
greifen, griff, gegriffen to grab, seize; **~ nach** to reach for
die **Grenze, -n** border (14.2)
grenzen (**an** + *acc.*) to border
grenzenlos unlimited, endless(ly)
der **Grieche, -n, -n / die Griechin, -nen** the Greek
(das) **Griechenland** Greece
griechisch Greek
die **Grippe** flu, influenza
grob (ö) rough; **das Gröbere draußen** dirty stuff outside
groß (größer, größt-) large, big, tall (S3); **im Großen und Ganzen** on the whole, by and large
die **Größe, -n** size, height
die **Großeltern** (*pl.*) grandparents (1.1); **Ur~** great-grandparents
das **Großmaul, ¨er** big mouth
die **Großmutter, ¨** grandmother (1.1); **Ur~** great-grandmother
der **Großteil** major part / portion
der **Großvater, ¨** grandfather (1.1); **Ur~** greatgrandfather
Grüezi! Hi! *(in Switzerland)*
grün green (S2); **ins Grüne / im Grünen** out in(to) nature
der **Grund, ¨e** reason; **aus diesem ~** for that reason; **im ~e genommen** basically
gründen to found
das **Grundgesetz** Constitution, Basic Law
grundsätzlich basically
die **Grundschule, -n** elementary school, grades 1–4
das **Grundstück, -e** building lot
der **Grundstücksmakler, -** real estate broker
die **Gründung, -en** founding
die **Grünfläche, -n** green area
die **Gruppe, -n** group
der **Gruß, ¨e** greeting; **Viele Grüße (an** [+ *acc.*] . . . **)!** Greetings (to . . .)!
grüßen to greet; **Grüß dich!** Hi!; **Grüß Gott!** Hello! Hi! (*in southern Germany*)
gucken *(coll.)* to look; **hin·~** to look at
der **Gummi** rubber
gurgeln to gargle
die **Gurke, -n** cucumber (2.1); **saure ~** pickle
der **Gürtel, -** belt
gut (besser, best-) good, fine, well (S1); **~ aussehend** good-looking (11.1); **Das ist noch mal ~ gegangen.** Things worked out all right (again); **na ~** well, all right (10.1); **Mach's ~!** Take care. (S1); ~ approx. grade B; **schon ~** okay; **sehr ~** approx. grade A
das **Gute: Alles ~!** All the best! (4.1); **Alles ~ zum Geburtstag!** Happy birthday! (4.1)
die **Güte** goodness; **Ach du meine ~!** My goodness! (8.1)
gütig kind(ly)
das **Gymna'sium, Gymna'sien** academic high school (grades 5–12)

H

das **Haar, -e** hair (9.1)
haben (hat), hatte, gehabt to have (S5,2.G); **Ich hätte gern . . .** I'd like (to have) . . . (2.1)
das **Habitat, -e** habitat
der **Hafen, ¨** port; **~schlepper, -** tugboat
die **Haferflocken** *(pl.)* oatmeal
das **Hähnchen, -** grilled chicken
der **Haken, -** hook
halb half (to the next hour) (S5); **~tags** part-time; **in einer ~en Stunde** in half an hour (8.1)
die **Hälfte, -n** half
die **Halle, -n** large room for work, recreation, or assembly
Hallo! Hello! Hi!
der **Hals, ¨e** neck, throat (9.1)
das **Halsband, ¨er** collar
Halt! Stop! (7.1)
halten (hält), hielt, gehalten to hold; stop (a vehicle) (5.1); **~ von** to think of, be of an opinion about (10.G)
die **Haltestelle, -n** (bus, etc.) stop (5.1)
das **Halteverbot, -e** no stopping or parking
der **Matjes** white herring; **Hamburger ~topf** pickled herring with sliced apples and onion rings in a sour-cream sauce
der **Hamster, -** hamster
die **Hand, ¨e** hand (3.2, 9.1)
die **Handarbeit, -en** needlework
der **Handball, ¨e** handball
der **Handel** trade
das **Handeln** action
die **Handelsbeziehung, -en** trade relation(s)
die **Handelsnation', -en** trading nation
der **Handelspartner, -** trading partner
der **Händler, -** merchant, dealer
der **Handschuh, -e** glove
das **Handtuch, ¨er** towel
der **Handwerker, -** craftsman
das **Handy, -s** cell phone (8.1)
hängen to hang (up) (6.1)
hängen, hing, gehangen to hang (be hanging) (6.1)
harmlos harmless
harmo'nisch harmonious
hart (ä) hard; tough
das **Häschen, -** rabbit, bunny
der **Hass** hate
hassen to hate
hässlich ugly (11.1)
die **Haube, -n** hood
das **Hauptfach, ¨er** major (field of study) (13.1)
der **Hauptmann, ¨er** captain
die **Hauptrolle, -n** leading role
die **Hauptsache, -n** main thing
hauptsächlich mainly
die **Hauptsaison** (high) season
die **Hauptschule, -n** basic high school (grades 5–9)
die **Hauptstadt, ¨e** capital (1.1)
das **Hauptwort, ¨er** noun
das **Haus, ¨er** house (6.1); **nach ~e** (toward) home (3.1); **zu ~e** at home (3.1)
der **Hausbesetzer, -** squatter
das **Häuschen, -** little house

die **Hausfrau, -en** housewife (12.1)
der **Haushalt, -e** household
der **Haushälter, -** housekeeper
häuslich home-loving, domestic
das **Haustier, -e** pet
die **Hauswirtschaft** home economics
die **Haut** skin
die **Hautpflege** skin care
das **Heft, -e** notebook (S2)
heilig holy; **Aller ~en** All Saints' Day; **~e Drei Könige** Epiphany
der **Heiligabend** Christmas Eve; **am ~** on Christmas Eve
die **Heimat** homeland, home (14.2)
der **Heimcompu'ter, -** home computer
die **Heimreise, -n** trip home
der **Heimtrainer, -** (at home) exercise machine
Heimweh haben* to be homesick
heiraten to marry, get married (11.1)
heiratslustig eager to marry
heiß hot(ly) (S4)
heißen, hieß, geheißen to be called; **Ich heiße . . .** My name is . . . (S1); **Wie ~ Sie? / Wie heißt du?** What's your name? (S1)
die **Heizung** heating (system)
das **Heizmaterial'** heating material, fuel
helfen (hilft), half, geholfen (+ *dat.*) to help (3.G)
hell light, bright (6.1); **Sei ~e!** Be smart!
das **Hemd, -en** shirt (S3); **Nacht~** nightgown
die **Henne, -n** hen
her- toward (the speaker) (7.G)
herab'·blicken (**auf** + *acc.*) to look down (on)
herab'·schauen (**auf** + *acc.*) to look down (on)
heran'- up to
sich **heran'·machen an** (+ *acc.*) to pursue
heraus'·finden* to find out
die **Heraus'forderung, -en** challenge
der **Herbst, -e** fall, autumn (S4)
der **Herd, -e** (kitchen) range
herein'- in(to)
herein'·kommen* to come in, enter (11.2)
herein'·lassen* to let in
der **Hering, -e** herring
die **Herkunft** origin
der **Herr, -n, -en** Mr., gentleman (S1,2.G); Lord; **Sehr geehrte Damen und ~en!** Ladies and gentlemen!
das **Herrchen, -** (*coll.*) (male) owner of a pet
Herrschaft: Meine ~en! Ladies and gentlemen!
herrlich wonderful(ly), great(ly), splendid(ly) (8.2)
her'·stellen to manufacture, produce
herum'- around
herum'·fragen to ask around
herum'·laufen* to run around
herum'·reisen (ist) to travel around
herum'·schnuppern to snoop around
(he)run'ter down; **~·fallen*** to fall down; **~·kommen*** to come down
hervor'·bringen* to produce
das **Herz, -ens, -en** heart; **mit ~** with feelings
herzförmig heart-shaped
der **Herzog, ¨-e** duke
heulen to cry; howl
der **Heurige, -n** (*sg.*) new wine
die **Heurigenschänke, -n** Viennese wine-tasting inn
heute today (S4); **für ~** for today (S2)
heutig- of today
heutzutage nowadays
hier here (S2)
die **Hilfe, -n** help (15.2)
hilfsbereit helpful
das **Hilfsverb, -en** auxiliary verb
der **Himmel** sky; heaven; **~fahrt(stag)** Ascension (Day)
himmlisch heavenly
der **Himmlische (ein Himmlischer) / die Himmlische, -n, -n** Heavenly one
hin- toward (the speaker) (7.G)
hin und her back and forth
hinauf'·fahren* to go or drive up (to) (8.2)
hinaus' out; **darü'ber ~** beyond that
hinein'·gehen* to go in(to), enter
hin·kommen* to get / come to
hin·legen to lay or put down; **sich ~** to lie down (9.G)
hin·nehmen* to accept
sich **(hin·)setzen** to sit down (9.G)
hinten in the back; **da~** back there
hinter (+ *acc. / dat.*) behind (6.G)
der **Hinterblie'bene (ein Hinterbliebener) / die Hinterbliebene, -n, -n** survivor
hinterlas'sen* to leave behind
der **Hintern, -** behind
die **(Hin- und) Rückfahrkarte, -n** round-trip ticket (8.1)
hinun'ter·fahren* to drive down
hinzu'- added to
hinzu'·fügen to add
das **Hirn** brain
der **Hirsch, -e** red deer
histo'risch historical(ly) (14.1)
das **Hobby, -s** hobby (9.1)
hoch (hoh-) (höher, höchst-) high(ly) (12.1); **~ im Kurs** high in demand
das **Hochdeutsch** standard High German
das **Hochhaus, ¨-er** high-rise building
hoch·kriechen* (**an** + *dat.*) to creep up (on)
hoch·legen to put up (high)
die **Hochschule, -n** university, college; **Fach~** university of applied sciences
die **Hochzeit, -en** wedding (11.1); **der ~stag, -e** wedding day / anniversary
(das) **Hockey** hockey
der **Hof, ¨-e** court, courtyard
hoffen to hope (12.2)
hoffentlich hopefully, I hope (5.2)
die **Hoffnung, -en** hope
höflich polite(ly)
die **Höhe, -n** height, altitude; **in die ~** up high; **Das ist doch die ~!** That's the limit!
der **Höhepunkt, -e** climax
hohl hollow
die **Höhle, -n** cave
(sich) **holen** to (go and) get, pick up, fetch (10.1)
der **Holländer, -** the Dutchman
holländisch Dutch
die **Hölle** hell

das **Holz** wood; **die ~terrasse, -n** wooden terrace
hölzern wooden
der **Honig** honey
hoppla oops, whoops
hörbar audible, audibly
horchen (nach) to listen (for)
hören to hear (S2)
der **Hörer, -** listener; receiver
der **Hörsaal, -säle** lecture hall (13.1)
das **Hörspiel, -e** radio play
das **Hörverständnis** listening comprehension (activity)
die **Hose, -n** slacks, pants (S3); **die ~n an·haben*** to be the boss
der **Hosenanzug, ¨-e** pantsuit
das **Hotel', -s** hotel (5.17.1)
hübsch pretty (11.1)
der **Hügel, -** hill
das **Huhn, ¨-er** chicken
das **Hühnchen, -** (little) chicken
der **Humor'** (sense of) humor
der **Hund, -e** dog (11.1); **Fauler ~!** Lazy bum!
hundert hundred; **Hunderte von** hundreds of
der **Hunger** hunger (2.2); **Ich habe ~.** I'm hungry. (2.2)
hungrig hungry, hungrily
hüpfen (ist) to hop
der **Hut, ¨-e** hat
hüten to watch (over)
die **Hütte, -n** hut, cottage
die **Hymne, -n** hymn, anthem

I

der **ICE, -s** InterCityExpress (train)
ideal' ideal(ly)
das **Ideal', -e** ideal
der **Idealis'mus** idealism
die **Idee', -n** idea (9.1); **Gute ~!** That's a good idea!
sich **identifizie'ren** to identify o.s.
iden'tisch identical(ly)
die **Identität', -en** identity; **der ~sschwund** loss of identity
idyl'lisch idyllic(ally)
ignorie'ren to ignore
ihr her, its, their (7.G)
Ihr (*formal*) your (1.17.G)
imaginär' imaginary
die **Imbissbude, -n** snack bar, fast-food stand
die **Immatrikulation'** enrollment (at university)
immer always (4.2); **~ geradeaus** always straight ahead (5.1); **~ länger** longer and longer (12.G); **~ noch** still; **~ wieder** again and again (12.G)
der **Imperativ, -e** imperative
das **Imperfekt** imperfect, simple past
in (+ *acc. / dat.*) in, into, inside of (6.G)
indem' by
inbegriffen (in + *dat.*) included (in)
der **Inder, -** person from India
der **India'ner, -** the Native American
der **In'dikativ** indicative
in'direkt indirect(ly)
die **Individualität'** individuality
individuell' individual(ly)
die **Industrie', -n** industry
der **Industrie'kaufmann / die ~kauffrau / die ~kaufleute** industrial manager
industriell' industrial
das **Industrie'unternehmen, -** large industrial company
der **Infinitiv, -e** infinitive
die **Informa'tik** computer science
die **Information', -en** information
die **Informations'suche** search for information
informativ' informative
(sich) **informie'ren (über** + *acc.*) to inform o.s., find out (about) (10.G)
der **Ingenieur', -e** engineer (12.1)
der **Inhalt** content
die **Initiati've, -n** initiative
inlineskaten to rollerblade; **~ gehen*** to go rollerblading
innen (*adv.*) inside
der **Innenhof, ¨-e** inner court
die **Innenstadt, ¨-e** center (of town), downtown
inner- inner
innerhalb within
die **Insel, -n** island (14.2)
insgesamt' altogether
das **Institut', -e** institute
das **Instrument', -e** instrument; **Musik'~** musical instrument
die **Inszenie'rung, -en** production
intellektuell' intellectual(ly)
intelligent' intelligent(ly) (11.1)
die **Intelligenz'** intelligence
der **Intendant', -en, -en** artistic director
intensiv' intensive(ly)
interessant' interesting (5.2); **etwas Interessantes** s.th. interesting; **unheimlich ~** really interesting (10.1)
das **Interes'se, -n (an** + *dat.*) interest (in)
sich **interessie'ren für** to be interested in (10.G)
international' international(ly)
das **Internet** Internet
interpretie'ren to interpret
das **Interview, -s** interview
interviewen to interview
in'tolerant intolerant
das **Inventar', -e** inventory
investie'ren to invest
der **Inves'tor, Investo'ren** investor
inzwi'schen in the meantime
irden (*poet.*) earthen
irgend: ~wie somehow; **~wo** somewhere (14.1)
(das) **Ita'lien** Italy (1.1)
der **Italie'ner, -** the Italian (1.1)
italie'nisch Italian (1.1)

J

ja yes (S1); *flavoring particle expressing emphasis* (7.G)
die **Jacke, -n** jacket (S3); **Strick~** cardigan
das Jackett, -s (man's) jacket
jagen (ist) to race
der **Jäger, -** hunter
das **Jahr, -e** year (S4); **Ein gutes neues ~!** Have a good New Year! (4.1)
jahrelang for years
die **Jahreszeit, -en** season
das **Jahrhun'dert, -e** century
-jährig years old; years long
jährlich yearly
das **Jahrtau'send, -e** millennium (15.2); **die ~wende** turn of the millennium
jammern to complain, grieve
der **Januar** January (S4); **im ~** in January (S4)
der **Japa'ner, -** Japanese
japa'nisch Japanese
je (+ comp.) . . . desto (+ comp.) . . . the . . . the . . . (12.G); **~ nachdem'** depending on
die **Jeans** (*pl.*) jeans (S3)

jed- *(sg.)* each, every (7.G)
jedenfalls in any case (13.2)
jeder each one, everyone, everybody
jederzeit any time
jedoch' however (12.2)
der **Jeep, -s** jeep
jeglich- every; **jegliches** everything
jemand someone, somebody (11.1)
jetzt now (S5)
der **Job, -s** job
jobben to have a job that is not one's career
joggen to jog; ~ **gehen*** to go jogging
der **Jog(h)urt** yogurt (*frequently also used with* **das**) (2.1)
der **Journalist', -en, -en** journalist (12.1)
das **Jubilä'um, Jubilä'en** anniversary
der **Jude, -n, -n / die Jüdin, -nen** Jew
das **Judentum** Jewry
jüdisch Jewish
(das) **Judo:** ~ **kämpfen** to do judo
die **Jugend** youth (14.2)
die **Jugendherberge, -n** youth hostel (7.2)
der **Juli** July (S4); **im** ~ in July (S4)
jung (ü) young (11.1)
der **Junge, -n, -n** boy (1.12.G)
die **Jungfrau, -en** virgin; Virgo
der **Junggeselle, -n, -n** bachelor
der **Juni** June (S4); **im** ~ in June (S4)
Jura: Er studiert ~. He's studying law.
der **Juwelier'laden, ¨** jewelry store

K

das **Kabarett', -e** (*or* **-s**) cabaret
das **Kabelfernsehen** cable TV
der **Kaffee** coffee (2.1); ~ **mit Schlag** coffee with whipped cream; **Das ist alles kalter ~.** That's for the birds.
der **Kaffeeklatsch** coffee klatsch, chatting over coffee (and cake)
der **Kaiser, -** emperor
der **Kaiserschmarren** pancakes pulled to pieces and sprinkled with powdered sugar and raisins
der **Kaka'o** hot chocolate
das **Kalb, ¨er** calf; **die ~sleber** calves' liver
der **Kalen'der, -** calendar
kalt (ä) cold (S4); ~ **oder warm?** with or without heat?
die **Kälte** cold(ness)
die **Kamera, -s** camera
der **Kamin', -e** fireplace
der **Kamm, ¨e** comb
(sich) **kämmen** to comb (o.s.) (9.G)
die **Kammer, -n** chamber
der **Kampf, ¨e (um)** fight, struggle (for)
kämpfen (um + *acc.*) to fight, struggle (for)
(das) **Kanada** Canada (1.1)
der **Kana'dier, -** the Canadian (1.1)
kana'disch Canadian (1.1)
der **Kanal', ¨e** channel
das **Känguru, -s** kangaroo
die **Kanti'ne, -n** cafeteria (at work)
der **Kanton', -e** canton
das **Kanu, -s** canoe
der **Kanzler, -** chancellor
kapie'ren *(coll.)* to understand, get
kapitalis'tisch capitalist
das **Kapi'tel, -** chapter
das **Käppi, -s** *(coll.)* cap
kaputt' broken; ~**•gehen*** to break, get broken; **sich ~•lachen** to crack up laughing
das **Karenz'jahr, -e** year's leave
der **Karfreitag** Good Friday
kariert' checkered
der **Karneval** carnival
die **Karot'te, -n** carrot (2.1)
die **Karrie're, -n** career
die **Karte, -n** ticket (8.1); card (9.1); **~n spielen** to play cards (9.1)
die **Kartof'fel, -n** potato (3.1); **der ~brei** *(sg.)* mashed potatoes; **die ~chips** *(pl.)* potato chips; **das ~mehl** potato flour, starch; **der ~salat** potato salad
der **Käse** cheese (2.1); **Das ist (doch) ~!** That's nonsense!; **Kräuter~** herbed cheese
die **Kaser'ne, -n** army barrack
die **Kasse, -n** cash register, cashier's window (7.1)
das **Kasseler Rippchen, -** smoked loin of pork
die **Kassie'rer, -** cashier; clerk, teller
der **Kasten, ¨** box
die **Katastro'phe, -n** catastrophe
die **Katze, -n** cat (11.1); **(Das ist) alles für die Katz'!** (That's) all for nothing!
kauen to chew
der **Kauf** purchase
kaufen to buy (2.1)
das **Kaufhaus, ¨er** department store (2.1)
käuflich can be bought
der **Kaufmann / die -frau / die -leute** trained employee in some branch of business
kaum hardly, barely, scarcely (14.1); **wohl** ~ probably not
kegeln to bowl
kein no, not a, not any (1.G)
der **Keller, -** basement, cellar (6.1)
der **Kellner, -** waiter / die **Kellnerin, -nen** waitress (3.1)
kennen, kannte, gekannt to know, be acquainted with (6.G)
kennen•lernen to get to know, meet (7.2)
der **Kenner, -** connoisseur
die **Kenntnis, -se** knowledge, skill (12.2)
der **Kerl, -e** guy
der **Kern, -e** core
die **Kern'energie'** nuclear energy
kernlos seedless
die **Kerze, -n** candle (4.2)
die **Kette, -n** chain, necklace
die **Ket'tenreaktion', -en** chain reaction
khaki khaki
das **Kilo, -s (kg)** kilogram
der **Kilome'ter, - (km)** kilometer
das **Kind, -er** child (1.1)
der **Kindergarten, ¨** kindergarten
der **Kindergärtner, -** kindergarten teacher
kinderlieb fond of children; **sie ist** ~ she loves children
das **Kinn, -e** chin
das **Kino, -s** movie theater (5.1)
kippen von (ist) to fall off
die **Kirche, -n** church (5.1)
die **Kirsche, -n** cherry
kitschig cheesy, kitschy
die **Kiwi, -s** kiwi
klagen (über + *acc.*) to complain (about) (14.1)
die **Klammer, -n** parenthesis
die **Klamotten** *(pl.) (coll.)* clothes
klappen to work out

klappern to rattle
klar clear; **(Na) ~!** Sure! Of course! (2.2); **eins ist ~** one thing is for sure
klasse *(adj.)* great, superb (10.1)
die **Klasse, -n** class (12.1)
der **Klas'senkamerad', -en, -en** classmate
das **Klassentreffen, -** class reunion
das **Klassenzimmer, -** classroom
klassisch classical(ly)
die **Klausur', -en** big test
klatschen to clap (10.1); to gossip
klauen *(coll.)* to steal
das **Klavier', -e** piano (9.1)
das **Kleid, -er** dress (S3)
der **(Kleider) bügel, -** clothes hanger
der **Kleiderschrank, ¨-e** closet
die **Kleidung** clothing (S3)
der **Kleidungsarti'kel, -** article of clothing
klein small, little, short (S3)
die **Kleinbürgerlichkeit** narrow-mindedness
das **Kleingeld** change (7.1)
der **Klempner, -** plumber
klettern (ist) to climb; **hoch·~** to climb up
das **Klima, -s** climate
die **Klimaanlage, -n** air-conditioning
der **Klimawandel** climate change
klingeln to ring a (door) bell
klingen, klang, geklungen to sound; **(Das) klingt gut.** (That) sounds good. (6.1)
das **Klo, -s** *(coll.)* toilet
klopfen to knock
der **Klops, -e** meat ball
der **Kloß, ¨-e** dumpling
das **Kloster, ¨** monastery; convent
der **Klotz, ¨-e** block
der **Klub, -s** club
klug (ü) smart, clever(ly)
knabbern to nibble
der **Knabe, -n, -n** boy
die **Knappheit** shortage
die **Kneipe, -n** pub (14.1)
das **Knie, -** knee (9.1)
der **Knirps, -e** little fellow, dwarf
der **Knoblauch** garlic
der **Knöd(e)l, -** dumpling (in southern Germany)
der **Knopf, ¨-e** button
der **Knoten, -** knot
knuspern to nibble
k.o. knocked-out; **ich bin ~** I am exhausted

der **Koch, ¨-e / die Köchin, -nen** cook
kochen to cook (9.1)
der **Koffer, -** suitcase (7.1)
die **Kohle** coal; ~ *(coll.)* money, dough
das **Kohlendioxid', -e** carbon dioxide
der **Kolle'ge, -n, -n / die Kolle'- gin, -nen** colleague
die **Kolonialisie'rung** colonization
kombinie'ren to combine
der **Komfort'** comfort
komisch funny, strange(ly), comical(ly) (10.1)
das **Komitee, -s** committee
das **Komma, -s** comma
kommen, kam, ist gekommen to come (1.1); **Komm rüber!** Come on over!
der **Kommentar', -e** commentary
kommentie'ren to comment
kommerziell' commercial(ly)
die **Kommo'de, -n** dresser (6.1)
die **Kommunikation** communication; **~swissenschaft** communication science
kommunis'tisch communist
der **Kom'parativ, -e** comparative
die **Komplikation', -en** complication
kompliziert' complicated (11.1)
komponie'ren to compose
der **Komponist', -en, -en** composer (10.1)
das **Kompott', -e** stewed fruit
der **Kompromiss', -e** compromise
die **Konditorei', -en** pastry shop
die **Konferenz', -en** conference
der **Konflikt', -e** conflict
der **Kongress', -e** conference
der **König, -e** king (11.2); **Heilige Drei ~e** Epiphany (Jan. 6)
die **Königin, -nen** queen (11.2)
das **Königreich, -e** kingdom
konjugie'ren to conjugate
die **Konjunktion', -en** conjunction
der **Kon'junktiv** subjunctive
die **Konkurrenz'** competition
konkurrie'ren to compete
können (kann), konnte, gekonnt to be able to, can (5.G)
die **Konsequenz', -en** consequence
konservativ conservative

das **Konservie'rungsmittel, -** preservative
das **Konsulat', -e** consulate
die **Kontakt'linse, -n** contact lense
das **Konto, -s (*or* Konten)** account
der **Kontrast', -e** contrast
die **Kontrol'le, -n** control
kontrollie'ren to control, check
die **Konversation', -en** conversation; **~sstunde, -n** conversation lesson
das **Konzentrations'lager, -** concentration camp
sich **konzentrie'ren (auf** + *acc.*) to concentrate (on)
das **Konzert', -e** concert (10.1)
die **Kooperation'** cooperation
der **Kopf, ¨-e** head (9.1); **pro ~** per person; **~ stehen*** to stand on one's head
das **Kopftuch, ¨-er** head scarf
die **Kopie', -n** copy
der **Kopie'rer, -** copy machine
der **Korb, ¨-e** basket
der **Korbball, ¨-e** basketball
der **Körper, -** body (9.1)
körperlich physical(ly)
die **Korrektur', -en** correction
der **Korrespondent', -en, -en** correspondent
korrigie'ren to correct
kosten to cost; **Was ~. . . ?** How much are . . . ? (S3); **Das kostet (zusammen) . . .** That comes to . . . (S3)
die **Kosten** *(pl.)* cost
kostenlos free (of charge)
das **Kostüm', -e** costume; lady's suit
die **Krabbe, -n** crab
der **Kracher, -** firecracker
die **Kraft, ¨-e** strength, power
der **Kragen, -** collar
die **Kralle, -n** claw
der **Kran, ¨-e** crane
krank (ä) sick, ill (9.1)
der **Kranke (ein Kranker) / die Kranke, -n, -n** sick person (12.G)
der **Krankenbesuch, -e** sick visit
die **Krankengymnast', -en, -en** physical therapist
das **Krankenhaus, ¨-er** hospital
die **Krankenkasse, -n** health insurance agency
die **Krankenpflege** nursing

der **Krankenpfleger, -** male nurse (12.1)
die **Krankenschwester, -n** female nurse (12.1)
die **Krankenversicherung, -en** health insurance
die **Krankheit, -en** sickness, illness, disease
der **Kranz, ¨-e** wreath; **Advents'~** Advent wreath
der **Krapfen, -** doughnut
der **Kratzer, -** scratch
das **Kraut** cabbage
die **Krawat'te, -n** tie
kreativ' creative(ly)
die **Kreativität'** creativity
der **Krebs, -e** crab; cancer; Cancer
die **Kredit'karte, -n** credit card (7.1)
die **Kreide** chalk (S2)
der **Kreis, -e** circle; county; **im ~** in a circle
das **Kreuz, -e** cross, mark
die **Kreuzung, -en** intersection
das **Kreuzworträtsel, -** crossword puzzle
kriechen, kroch, ist gekrochen to creep, crawl
der **Krieg, -e** war (14.1); **die Nach~szeit** postwar period
kriegen *(coll.)* to get; **Das ~ wir wieder hin.** We'll fix it.
der **Krieger, -** warrior
der **Krimi, -s** detective story (10.1)
die **Kriminalität'** crime
der **Krimskrams** old junk
die **Krise, -n** crisis
das **Krite'rium, Krite'rien** criterion
der **Kritiker, -** critic
kritisch critical(ly)
kritisie'ren to criticize
die **Krone, -n** crown
krönen to crown
krumm crooked
die **Küche, -n** kitchen (6.1); cuisine
der **Kuchen, -** cake (2.1)
der **Küchenschrank, ¨-e** kitchen cabinet
die **Kugel, -n** ball
die **Kuh, ¨-e** cow
kühl cool (S4)
der **Kühlschrank, ¨-e** refrigerator (6.1)
der **Kuli, -s** pen (S2)
die **Kultur', -en** culture
kulturell' cultural(ly) (14.1)
sich **kümmern (um)** to take care (of)
der **Kunde, -n, -n / die Kundin, -nen** client
die **Kunst, ¨-e** art (10.1)
der **Künstler, -** artist (12.1); **Compu'ter~** graphic designer
das **Kupfer** copper
kupfern *(adj.)* (made of) copper
die **Kuppel, -n** cupola, dome
der **Kurfürst, -en, -en** elector (prince)
der **Kurort, -e** health resort, spa
der **Kurs, -e** course (S5)
kurz (ü) short(ly), brief(ly) (S3); **~ vor** shortly before; **vor ~em** recently (10.1)
die **Kürze** shortness, brevity; **In der ~ liegt die Würze.** Brevity is the soul of wit.
das **Kurzgespräch, -e** brief conversation
die **Kusi'ne, -n** *(fem.)* cousin (1.1)
küssen to kiss
die **Küste, -n** coast (15.1)

L

das **Labor', -s** (*or* **-e**) lab(oratory) (13.1)
der **Laborant', -en, -en** lab assistant
der **Labrador, -s** Labrador (dog)
lachen to laugh (10.1); **sich kaputt-~** to crack up laughing
lächeln to smile (10.1); **~ über** *(+ acc.)* to smile about (10.G)
lächerlich ridiculous
laden (lädt), lud, geladen to load
der **Laden, ¨** store (2.2); **Bio-~ / grüne ~** environmental store; **Tante-Emma-~** small grocery store
die **Lage, -n** location (7.1)
lahm lame; lacking enthusiasm; **~e Ente!** Poor baby!
das **Lamm, ¨-er** lamb; **~kotelett, -s** lamb chop; **geduldig wie ein ~** really patient
die **Lampe, -n** lamp (6.1); **Hänge~** hanging lamp; **Steh~** floor lamp
das **Land, ¨-er** country, state (1.1); **auf dem ~(e)** in the country (6.2); **aufs ~** in(to) the country(side) (6.2)
landen (ist) to land (8.1)
die **Landeskunde** cultural and geographical study of a country
die **Landkarte, -n** map (1.1)
die **Landschaft, -en** landscape, scenery (15.1)
die **Landung, -en** landing; **~sbrücke** pier
der **Landwirt, -e** farmer
die **Landwirtschaft** agriculture
landwirtschaftlich agricultural
lang (ä) *(adj.)* long (S3)
lange long, for a long time; **noch ~ nicht** not by far; **schon ~ (nicht mehr)** (not) for a long time; **wie ~?** how long? (4.1)
langsam slow(ly) (S3)
sich **langweilen** to get / be bored (9.2)
langweilig boring, dull (10.1)
lassen (lässt), ließ, gelassen to leave (behind) (7.1)
lässig casual(ly)
die **Last, -en** burden
(das) **Latein'** Latin
die **Later'ne, -n** lantern
der **Lauch** leek
laufen (läuft), lief, ist gelaufen to run, walk (3.G)
der Laut, -e sound
laut loud(ly), noisy (4.2;7.1); **Lesen Sie ~!** Read aloud.; **Sprechen Sie ~er!** Speak up. (S3)
läuten to ring
der **Lautsprecher, -** loudspeaker
leben to live (6.2)
das **Leben** life (9.2); **ums ~ kommen*** to die, perish
lebend living; **etwas Lebendes** s.th. living
leben'dig alive; lively
die **Lebensfreude** zest for life
lebensfroh cheerful, full of life
der **Lebenslauf, ¨-e** résumé
die **Lebensmittel** *(pl.)* groceries (2.1)
der **Lebensstandard** standard of living
die **Leber, -n** liver; **Kalbs~** calves' liver
der **Leberkäs(e)** (Bavarian) meat-loaf made from minced pork
die **Leberwurst** liver sausage
der **Lebkuchen, -** gingerbread
lecker delicious
das **Leder** leather
die **Lederhose, -n** leather pants
ledig single (11.1)
leer empty (14.2)

legen to lay, put (flat) (6.1); **sich (hin·)~** to lie down (9.G)
leger casual
das **Lehrbuch, ¨er** textbook
die **Lehre, -n** apprenticeship
lehren to teach (13.1)
der **Lehrer, -** teacher (12.1)
der **Lehrling, -e** apprentice
die **Lehrstelle, -n** apprenticeship (position)
leicht light, easy, easily (6.2); **Das ist ~ zu verstehen!** That's easy to understand.
das **Leid** misery.1)
leid: Es tut mir ~. I'm sorry. (5.1)
die **Leidenschaft, -en** passion
leider unfortunately (5.2)
leihen, lieh, geliehen to lend; borrow
die **Leine, -n** leash
leise quiet(ly), soft(ly)
leisten to achieve
leiten to direct
der **Leiter, -** director
die **Leiter, -n** ladder
die **Leitung** leadership, direction
das **Leitungswasser** tap water
lenken to direct
lernen to learn, study (S2)
der **Lerntipp, -s** study tip
das **Lernziel, -e** learning objective
lesbar legible, legibly
lesen (liest), las, gelesen to read (S2); **~ Sie laut!** / **~ Sie es vor!** Read it aloud.
der **Leser, -** reader
die **Leseratte, -n** bookworm
der **Lesesaal, -säle** reading room
der **Lesetext, -e** reading text
(das) **Lettland** Latvia
der **Lette, -n, -n / die Lettin, -nen** Latvian
lettisch Latvian
letzt- last (10.1)
(das) **Letzeburgisch** Luxembourg dialect
die **Leute** (*pl.*) people (1.1)
licht *(poetic)* light
das **Licht, -er** light; **ins ~ treten*** to step out into the light
die **Lichterkette, -n** candlelight march
der **Lichtschalter, -** light switch
lieb- dear (5.2, 11.1)
die **Liebe** love (11.1); **~ auf den ersten Blick** love at first sight
lieben to love (6.2)
lieber rather (12.G); **Es wäre mir ~, wenn . . .** I would prefer it, if . . .
liebevoll loving
der **Liebling, -e** darling
Lieblings . . . favorite . . .
liebst-: am ~en best of all (12.G)
das **Lied, -er** song (4.2); **Volks~** folk song
liefern to distribute, deliver
liegen, lag, gelegen to lie, be (located) (1.1); be lying (flat) (6.1)
der **Liegestuhl, ¨e** lounge chair
lila purple
die **Lilie, -n** lily, iris
die **Limona'de, -n = Limo, -s** soft drink (2.1); **die Zitro'nen~** carbonated lemonade
die **Linguis'tik** linguistics
die **Linie, -n** line
link- left; **auf der ~en Seite** on the left
links left (5.1); **erste Straße ~** first street on the left (5.1)
die **Linse, -n** lentil; lense
die **Lippe, -n** lip
der **Lippenstift, -e** lipstick
die **Liste, -n** list; **eine ~ auf·stellen** to make a list
der **Litaue, -n, -n / die Litauin, -nen** Lithuanian
(das) **Litauen** Lithuania
litauisch Lithuanian
der **Liter, -** liter
die **Literatur'** literature
das **Loch, ¨er** hole
locken to lure, attract
der **Löffel, -** spoon (3.1); **Ess~** tablespoon (of); **Tee~** teaspoon (of)
logisch logical(ly)
der **Lohn** pay; reward
sich **lohnen** to be worthwhile
lokal' local(ly)
das **Lokal', -e** restaurant
los: ~·gehen* to start; **~·werden*** to get rid of; **etwas ~ sein*** to be happening, going on; **Was ist (denn) ~?** What's the matter? (9.1); **Jetzt aber ~!** Let's go!; **Ich muss ~.** I have to go.
lose loose
lösen to solve; **sich ~ von** to free o.s. of
die **Lösung, -en** solution
die **Lotterie'** lottery
der **Löwe, -n, -n / die Löwin, -nen** lion; Leo
die **Luft** air (14.2)
der **Luftangriff, -e** air raid
der **Luftballon,-s** balloon
die **Luftbrücke** airlift
die **Luftpost** airmail; **per ~** by airmail
die **Luftverschmutzung** air pollution
die **Lüge, -n** lie
lügen to lie
die **Lust** inclination, desire, fun; **Ich habe (keine) ~ (zu) . . .** I (don't) feel like (doing s.th.) . . . (9.1)
lustig funny (4.2); **reise~ sein*** to love to travel; **sich ~ machen (über** + *acc.*) to make fun of (14.1)
luxemburgisch Luxembourgish
luxuriös' luxurious(ly)
der **Luxus** luxury

M

machen to make, do (2.1); **Spaß ~** to be fun (4.2); **Mach's gut!** Take care! (S1); **Was machst du Schönes?** What are you doing?; **(Das) macht nichts.** (That) doesn't matter. That's okay. (8.1); **Das macht zusammen . . .** That comes to . . .
die **Macht, ¨e** power (14.2); **die Westmächte** (*pl.*) Western Allies
mächtig powerful
das **Mädchen, -** girl (1.1); **der ~name** maiden name
das **Magazin', -e** magazine; feature (e.g., on TV)
die **Magd, ¨e** (*archaic*) maid
der **Magen, ¨ / -** stomach
der **Magis'ter, -** master's degree, M.A.
der **Magnet', -en, -en** magnet
die **Mahlzeit, -en** meal; **~!** Enjoy your meal (food)!
das **Mahnmal, -e** memorial (of admonishment)
der **Mai** May (S4); **im ~** in May (S4)
der **Mais** corn
mal times, multiplied by; **~ sehen!** Let's see.; **~ eben** just for a minute

das **Mal, -e: das erste ~** the first time (11.2); **zum ersten ~** for the first time (11.2)
malen to paint (9.1)
der **Maler, -** painter(-artist) (10.1); house painter
malerisch picturesque
man one (they, people, you) (3.2)
man *(adv.; north German coll.)*: **Komm ~!** Come on!; **Lass ~ gut sein!** Forget it!
das **Management** management
manch- many a, several, some (7.G)
manchmal sometimes (3.2)
der **Mangel (an** + *dat.*) lack (of)
mangelhaft poor; approx. grade D
die **Mango, -s** mango
manipuliert' manipulated
der **Mann, ¨er** man; husband (1.1)
das **Männchen, -** little guy
männlich masculine, male
die **Mannschaft, -en** team
der **Mantel, ¨** coat (S3)
das **Manuskript', -e** manuscript
das **Märchen, -** fairy tale (11.2)
die **Margari'ne, -n** margarine
die **Mari'ne, -n** navy
markie'ren to mark
der **Markt, ¨e** market (2.1); **Super~** supermarket (2.1); **Wachstums~** growth market
die **Marmela'de, -n** marmalade, jam (2.1)
der **März** March (S4); **im ~** in March (S4)
die **Maschi'ne, -n** machine
der **Maschi'nenbau** mechanical engineering
die **Maske, -n** mask
die **Massa'ge, -n** massage
die **Maß** large glass holding about 1 liter of beer
die **Masse, -n** mass
die **Massenmedien** (*pl.*) mass media
die **Maßnahme, -n** step, measure
das **Material'** material
die **Mathematik'** mathematics
die **Mauer, -n** (thick) wall (14.1)
das **Maul, ¨er** big mouth (of animal)
der **Maurer, -** bricklayer
maurisch Moorish
die **Maus, ¨e** mouse; **~efalle, -n** mousetrap
der **Mecha'niker, -** mechanic

die **Medien** (*pl.*) media; **~wissenschaft** media science
das **Medikament', -e** medicine, medication
die **Medizin'** (the field of) medicine
das **Meer, -e** ocean, sea
das **Meerschweinchen, -** guinea pig
das **Mehl** flour
mehr more (12.G); **immer ~** more and more (12.G); **~ als** more than
mehrer- (*pl.*) several (10.G)
die **Mehrheit** majority
die **Mehrwertsteuer, -n** value-added tax
meiden, mied, gemieden to avoid
mein my (1.17.G)
meinen to mean, think (be of the opinion) (11.1); **Wenn du meinst.** If you think so. (11.1)
die **Meinung, -en** opinion; **meiner ~ nach** in my opinion
die **Meinungsumfrage, -n** opinion poll
meist-: am ~en most (12.G)
meistens mostly, usually (7.2)
der **Meister, -** master; champion
meistern to master
die **Meisterschaft, -en** championship
die **Melo'ne, -n** melon
die **Menge, -n** crowd; **jede ~** all sorts of (14.1)
die **Mensa** student cafeteria (3.1)
der **Mensch, -en, -en** human being, person; people (*pl.*) (1.2, 2.G); **~!** Man! Boy! Hey!; **Mit~** fellow human being
die **Menschheit** humankind
das **Menü', -s** complete meal (usually including soup and dessert); **Tages~** daily special
merken to notice, find out
die **Messe, -n** (trade) fair
das **Messegelände, -** fairgrounds
das **Messer, -** knife (3.2); **Taschen~** pocket knife
das **Metall', -e** metal
der **Meter, -** meter
die **Metropo'le, -n** metropolis
der **Metzger, -** butcher
mies miserable
die **Miete, -n** rent
mieten to rent (6.1)

der **Mieter, -** renter, tenant
die **Mietwohnung, -en** apartment
die **Migrä'ne** migraine headache
der **Mikrowellenherd, -e** = **die Mikrowelle, -n** microwave oven
die **Milch** milk (2.1)
das **Militär'** military, army
militä'risch military
der **Million', -en** million
der **Millionär', -e** millionaire
der **Mindestbestellwert** minimum order
mindestens at least
die **Mineralogie'** mineralogy
das **Mineral'wasser** mineral water
der **Minimumbestellwert** minimum order
minus minus
die **Minu'te, -n** minute (S5)
mischen to mix; **darun'ter·~** to blend in
der **Mischmasch** mishmash, hodgepodge
die **Mischung, -en (aus** + *dat.*) mixture (of)
misera'bel miserable, miserably
die **Mission', -en** mission
der **Mist** junk; manure; **~!** Darn it!
mit- together, with, along (7.G)
mit (+ *dat.*) with (3.G); along
miteinander together
das **Mitbestimmungsrecht** right to participate in the decision-making process
der **Mitbewoh'ner, -** housemate, roommate (13.1)
mit·bringen* to bring along (7.G)
mit·fahren* to drive along
mit·feiern to join in the celebration
das **Mitgefühl** compassion
mit·gehen* to go along (7.G)
das **Mitglied, -er** member
mit·kommen* to come along (7.G)
das **Mitleid** pity
mit·machen to participate
mit·nehmen* to take along (7.G)
mit·schicken to send along
mit·singen* to sing along
der **Mittag, -e** noon; **heute ~** at noon today (8.G)

das **Mittagessen, -** lunch, midday meal (3.1); **beim ~** at lunch; **zum ~** for lunch (3.1)
mittags at noon (S5); **dienstag~** Tuesdays at noon (8.G)
die **Mitte** middle, center (14.2); **~ des Monats** in the middle of the month (8.G); mid
das **Mittel, -** means (of)
das **Mittelalter** Middle Ages; **im ~** in the Middle Ages (14.1)
mittelalterlich medieval
(das) **Mitteleuro'pa** Central Europe
mittelgroß average size
mitten: ~durch right through the middle of (6.2); **~drin** right in the middle of it
die **Mitternacht: um ~** at midnight
der **Mittwoch** Wednesday (S4); **am ~** on Wednesday (S4); **Ascher~** Ash Wednesday
mittwochs on Wednesdays (2.2)
der **Mix** mixture
die **Möbel** (*pl.*) furniture (6.1)
die **Mobilität'** mobility
möbliert' furnished
möchten (*subj. of* **mögen**) would like (2W;5.G); **Ich möchte . . .** I would like (to have) . . . (2.1)
das **Modal'verb, -en** modal auxiliary
die **Mode** fashion; custom; **in ~** in(to) vogue
modern' modern
mögen (mag), mochte, gemocht to like (5.G); **Ich mag kein(e/en) . . .** I don't like (any) . . . (+ *acc. noun*) (3.1)
möglich possible (7.1); **Das ist doch nicht ~!** That's impossible. (7.1); **alle ~en** all sorts of
die **Möglichkeit, -en** possibility
der **Mohnkuchen** poppy seed cake
der **Moment', -e** moment; **(Einen) ~!** One moment! Just a minute! (2.17.1)
momentan' at the moment, right now (12.2)
der **Monat, -e** month (S4); **im ~** a month, per month (6.1); **einen ~** for one month (8.G)
monatelang for months
monatlich monthly (8.G)
der **Mond, -e** moon
der **Mondschein** moonlight
das **Monster, -** monster
der **Montag** Monday (S4); **am ~** on Monday (S4)
montags on Mondays (2.2)
die **Moral'** moral
der **Mörder, -** murderer
morgen tomorrow (S4,4.1); **Bis ~!** See you tomorrow; **für ~** for tomorrow (S2); **über~** the day after tomorrow (4.1)
der **Morgen** morning: **Guten ~!** Good morning. (S1); **heute ~** this morning (8.G)
morgens in the morning (S5), every morning; **montag~** Monday mornings (8.G)
das **Mosaik', -e** mosaic
der **Moslem, -s / die Moslime, -n** Muslim man / woman
mosle'misch Muslim
der **MP3-Spieler,-** MP3 player
müde tired (S1); **tod~** dead tired
die **Müdigkeit** fatigue
der **Müll** garbage, waste (15.1)
der **Müller, -** miller
der **Müllschlucker, -** garbage disposal
die **Mülltonne, -n** garbage can (15.1)
die **Mülltrennung** garbage sorting (15.1)
der **Mund, ¨er** mouth (9.1)
münden (ist) (**in** + *acc.*) to flow into
die **Mundharmonika, -s** harmonica
mündlich oral(ly)
das **Münster, -** Protestant cathedral
die **Münze, -n** coin
die **Muschel, -n** clam; shell
das **Muse'um, Muse'en** museum (5.1)
die **Musik'** music (9.2)
der **Musikant', -en, -en** musician
musika'lisch musical(ly) (11.1)
der **Musiker, -** musician
die **Musik'wissenschaft** musicology
(der) **Muskat'** nutmeg
der **Muskelkater** sore muscle(s); **Ich habe ~.** My muscles are sore.
das **Müsli** whole-grain granola
müssen (muss), musste, gemusst to have to, must (5.G)
das **Muster, -** example, model; pattern
der **Mustersatz, ¨e** sample sentence
der **Mut** courage
die **Mutter, ¨** mother (1.1); **Groß~** grandmother (1.1); **Schwieger~** mother-in-law; **Urgroß~** great-grandmother
mütterlich motherly
der **Mutterschaftsurlaub** maternity leave
die **Muttersprache** mother tongue
die **Mutti, -s** Mom

N

na well; **~ also** well; **~ gut** well, all right (10.1); **~ ja** well (12.1); **~ klar** of course (2.2); **~ und?** So what? (8.1); **~ los!** Do it!
nach- after, behind (7.G); **~ wie vor** still
nach (+ *dat.*) after (time), to (cities, countries, continents) (3.G); **je ~** depending on
der **Nachbar, -n, -n** neighbor (1E,2.G)
die **Nachbarschaft, -en** neighborhood; neighborly relations
nachdem' *(conj.)* after (11.G); **je ~** depending on
nach·denken* über *(+ acc.)* to think about
nacherzählt retold, adapted
die **Nachfrage** demand
nachher afterwards
nach·kommen* to follow
nach·laufen* to run after
nach·machen to imitate
der **Nachmittag, -e** afternoon; **am ~** in the afternoon; **heute ~** this afternoon (8.G)
nachmittags in the afternoon (S5), every afternoon
der **Nachname, -ns, -n** last name
die **Nachricht, -en** news (10.2)
nächst- next (11.2)
die **Nacht, ¨e** night (7.1); **Gute ~!** Good night!; **heute ~** tonight; last night (8.G)
der **Nachteil, -e** disadvantage
die **Nachteule, -n** night owl
das **Nachthemd, -en** nightgown
der **Nachtisch** dessert (3.1); **zum ~** for dessert (3.1)
der **Nachtmensch, -en, -en** night person
nachts during the night, every night (8.G); **sonntag~** Sunday nights (8.G)

der **Nachttisch, -e** nightstand
nach·werfen* to throw after
nackt naked
die **Nadel, -n** needle
nah (näher, nächst-) near, nearby, close (5.112.G)
die **Nähe** nearness, vicinity; **in der ~** nearby; **in der ~ von** (+ *dat.*) near (5.1)
nähen to sew
der **Name, -ns, -n** name (8.G); **Mein ~ ist . . .** My name is . . . (S1); **Mädchen~** maiden name; **Vor~** first name; **Nach~** last name; **Spitz~** nickname (14.1)
nämlich namely, you know
die **Nase, -n** nose (9.1); **Ich habe die ~ voll.** I'm fed up (with it).
nass wet
die **Nation', -en** nation, state
national' national(ly)
der **Nationalis'mus** nationalism
die **Nationalität', -en** nationality
die **Natur'** nature (15.1)
das **Natur'kind, -er** child of nature
natür'lich natural(ly), of course (2.1)
das **Natur'schutzgebiet, -e** nature preserve (15.1)
die **Natur'wissenschaft, -en** natural science (13.1)
natur'wissenschaftlich scientific(ally)
der **Nebel** fog
neben (+ *acc.* / *dat.*) beside, next to (6.G)
nebeneinander next to each other
das **Nebenfach, ¨er** minor (field of study) (14.1)
nebensächlich unimportant
der **Nebensatz, ¨e** subordinate clause
neblig foggy
nee *(coll.)* no
der **Neffe, -n, -n** nephew
negativ negative(ly)
nehmen (nimmt), nahm, genommen to take (S3); to have (food) (3.G)
nein no (S1)
die **Nelke, -n** carnation
nennen, nannte, genannt to name, call (4.1; 11.G); **Ich nenne das . . .** That's what I call . . .

nett nice (11.1)
neu new(ly) (S3); **Was gibt's Neues . . . ?** What's new? (9.1)
neugierig curious(ly)
der **Neujahrstag** New Year's Day
nicht not (S1); **~ wahr?** isn't it? (S4); **gar ~** not at all (13.2); **~ nur . . . sondern auch** not only . . . but also (3.2); **~ einmal** not even
die **Nichte, -n** niece
nichts nothing (3.1); **~ Besonderes / Neues** nothing special / new (9.1)
nicken to nod
nie never (4.2); **noch ~** never before, not ever (4.2)
sich **nieder·legen** to lie down
niedrig low
niemals never
niemand nobody, no one (11.2)
das **Niemandsland** no man's land
nimmermehr *(poetic)* nevermore, never again
nirgends nowhere; **ins Nirgends** into nowhere
nobel noble, nobly
noch still (4.1); **~ (ein)mal** once more, again (S2); **~ ein** another (3.1); **~ kein(e)** still no; **~ etwas** s.th. else; **~ lange nicht** not by far; **~ nie** never (before), not ever (4.2); **~ nicht** not yet (6.2); **Sonst ~ etwas?** Anything else?; **was ~?** what else?; **weder . . . ~** neither . . . nor (10.2); **immer ~** still
der **Nominativ, -e** nominative
der **Norden: im ~** in the north (1.1)
nördlich (von) to the north, north (of) (1.1)
normal' normal; by regular (surface) mail
norma'lerweise normally
(das) **Nor'wegen** Norway
der **Nor'weger, -** the Norwegian
nor'wegisch Norwegian
die **Note, -n** grade (13.1)
nötig necessary, needed
die **Notiz', -en** note; **~en machen** to take notes
notwendig necessary
der **Novem'ber** November (S4); **im ~** in November (S4)
nüchtern sober

die **Nudel, -n** noodle (3.1)
null zero (S3)
der **Numerus clausus** admissions restriction at a university
die **Nummer, -n** number (7.1)
nun now (11.2); **~, . . .** well, . . . (12.1)
nur only (S4)
die **Nuss, ¨e** nut
der **Nussknacker, -** nutcracker
nutzen to use
nützlich useful

O

ob (*conj.*) if, whether (4.G); **Und ~!** You bet. You better believe it. (14.1)
oben upstairs (6.1); up; **~ genannt** above-mentioned
der **Ober, -** waiter (3.1); **Herr ~!** Waiter! (3.1)
das **Oberteil, -e** top
die **Oberin, -nen** mother superior
die **Oberschule, -n** college preparatory school (*see* **Gymnasium**)
die **Oberstufe, -n** upper level
das **Objekt', -e** object
objektiv' objective(ly)
das **Obst** (*sg.*) fruit (2.1)
obwohl (*conj.*) although (4.G)
oder or (S3,2.G); **~?** Isn't it? Don't you think so? (14.1)
der **Ofen, ¨** oven
offen open (2.2)
offiziell' official(ly)
öffnen to open; **~ Sie das Buch auf Seite . . . !** (S5) Open the book on / to page . . . !
öffentlich public(ly) (10.2)
oft often (2.2)
ohne (+ *acc.*) without (2.G)
das **Ohr, -en** ear (9.1)
Oje'! Oops! Oh no!
der **Ökolo'ge, -n, -n / die Ökolo'gin, -nen** ecologist
die **Ökologie'** ecology
ökolo'gisch ecological(ly)
das **Ökosystem', -e** ecological system
der **Okto'ber** October (S4); **im ~** in October (S4)
das **Öl, -e** oil; lotion
oliv' olive-colored
der **Ölwechsel** oil change
die **Olympia'de, -n** Olympics
die **Oma, -s** grandma

das **Omelett', -s** omelet(te)
der **Onkel, -** uncle (1.1)
der **Opa, -s** grandpa
die **Oper, -n** opera (10.1); **Seifen~** soap opera
die **Operet'te, -n** operetta
das **Opfer, -** victim
optimal' optimal(ly)
optimis'tisch optimistic(ally)
oran'ge (color) orange (S2)
die **Oran'ge, -n** orange (2.1)
das **Orches'ter, -** orchestra (10.1)
ordentlich orderly; regular(ly)
die **Ordinal'zahl, -en** ordinal number (4.1)
die **Ordnung** order; **In ~ !** Okay!
die **Ordnungszahl, -en** ordinal number
die **Organisation', -en** organization
(sich) **organisie'ren** to organize
die **Orgel, -n** organ
die **Orientie'rung** orientation
das **Original', -e** original
der **Ort, -e** place, location; town
der **Ossi, -s** *(derogatory nickname)* East German
der **Osten: im ~** in the east (1.1)
(das) **Ostern: zu ~** at / for Easter (4.1); **Frohe ~!** Happy Easter!
(das) **Österreich** Austria (1.1)
der **Österreicher, -** the Austrian (1.1)
österreichisch Austrian
östlich (von) east (of), to the east (of) (1.1)
der **Ozean, -e** ocean

P

paar: ein ~ a couple of, some (2.2)
das **Paar, -e** couple, pair
die **Pacht** lease; **der ~vertrag, ¨-e** lease agreement / contract
pachten to lease
packen to pack (7.2); to grab
die **Pädago'gik** education
das **Paddelboot, -e** canoe
paddeln to paddle
das **Paket', -e** package, parcel (8.1)
die **Paket'karte, -n** parcel form
die **Palatschinken** *(pl.)* crêpes
das **Panora'ma** panorama
die **Panne, -n** mishap
der **Panzer, -** tank
der **Papagei', -en** parrot
das **Papier', -e** paper (S2)
der **Papier'krieg** paperwork, red tape
das **Papier'warengeschäft, -e** office supply store
die **Pappe** cardboard
die **Para'bel, -n** parable
das **Paradies'** paradise
der **Paragraph', -en, -en** paragraph
das **Parfüm', -s** perfume
parie'ren to obey
der **Park, -s** park (5.1)
die **Parkanlage, -n** park
parken to park (15.1)
das **Parkett': im ~** (seating) in the orchestra
der **Parkplatz, ¨-e** parking lot (7.1)
parlamenta'risch parliamentary
die **Partei', -en** (political) party
das **Parter're: im ~** on the first / ground floor (6.1)
das **Partizip', -ien** participle
der **Partner, -** partner (11.1)
die **Partnerschaft, -en** partnership
die **Party, -s** party (4.1)
der **Pass, ¨-e** passport (7.1)
passen to fit; **Was passt?** What fits?; **Das passt mir nicht.** That doesn't suit me.
passend appropriate(ly), suitable, suitably
passie'ren (ist) to happen (11.1)
passiv passive(ly)
das **Passiv** passive voice
pauken to cram
die **Pause, -n** intermission, break; **eine ~ machen** to take a break
das **Pech** tough luck; **~ haben*** to be unlucky (4.2); **~ gehabt!** Tough luck!; **Du ~vogel!** You unlucky thing!
der **Pekine'se, -n, -n** Pekinese
pendeln (ist) to commute; **hin- und her-~** to commute back and forth
die **Pension', -en** boarding house; hotel (7.2)
die **Pensionie'rung** retirement
das **Perfekt** present perfect
permanent' permanent(ly)
perplex' baffled
die **Person', -en** person; **pro ~** per person
das **Personal'** personnel, staff; **die ~kosten** *(pl.)* staffing cost
persön'lich personal(ly)
der **persön'liche digita'le Assistent', -en, -en (PDA)** personal digital assistant
die **Persön'lichkeit, -en** personality
die **Perspekti've, -n** perspective
pessimis'tisch pessimistic(ally)
das **Pfand, ¨-er** deposit; security; **die ~dose, -n** returnable can; **die ~flasche, -n** returnable bottle
die **Pfanne, -n** pan
der **Pfannkuchen, -** pancake
der **Pfarrer, -** (Protestant) minister; cleric
der **Pfeffer** pepper (3.1)
die **Pfeffermin'ze** peppermint
die **Pfeife, -n** pipe
pfeifen, pfiff, gepfiffen to whistle; boo
der **Pfeil, -e** arrow
das **Pferd, -e** horse (11.1); **arbeitsam wie ein ~** really hardworking; **Schaukel~** rocking horse
der **Pferdewagen, -** horse-drawn wagon
(das) **Pfingsten** Pentecost
der **Pfirsich, -e** peach
die **Pflanze, -n** plant
pflanzen to plant
das **Pflaster, -** adhesive bandage
pflaume plum-colored
die **Pflaume, -n** plum
die **Pflegemutter, ¨-** foster mother
pflegen to take care of, cultivate; **er pflegt, das zu tun** he usually does that
die **Pflegeversicherung, -en** longterm care insurance
die **Pflicht, -en** duty, obligation
das **Pflichtfach, ¨-er** required subject
pflücken to pick (flowers)
das **Pfund, -e** pound (2.1); **zwei ~** two pounds (of) (2.1)
die **Pharmazie'** pharmaceutics; pharmacy (study)
die **Philologie'** philology
der **Philosoph', -en, -en** philosopher
die **Philosophie'** philosophy
die **Physik'** physics
der **Physiker, -** physicist
physisch physical(ly)
das **Picknick, -s** picnic
picknicken to (have a) picnic; **~ gehen*** to go picnicing
piepen to peep, chirp; **Bei dir piept's!** You're cuckoo. You must be kidding.

richtig right, correct (S2); **Das ist genau das Richtige.** That's exactly the right thing.
die **Richtigkeit** correctness
die **Richtung, -en** direction; **in ~** in the direction of
riechen, roch, gerochen to smell; **angebrannt ~** to smell burnt
das **Riesenrad, ⸚er** ferris wheel
riesig huge, enormous(ly)
die **Rindsroulade, -n** stuffed beef roll
der **Ring, -e** ring
rings um *(+ acc.)* all around
das **Risiko, Risiken** risk
der **Ritter, -** knight
der **Rock, ⸚e** skirt (S3)
der **Rolladen, ⸚** (roller) shudder
die **Rolle, -n** role; **Haupt~** leading role; **Das spielt (überhaupt) keine ~.** That doesn't matter (at all).
das **Rollo', -s** (roller) shudder
der **Rollschuh, -e** roller skate; **~ laufen*** to rollerskate; **~laufen gehen*** to go roller skating
der **Roman', -e** novel (10.1)
die **Romanis'tik** study of Romance languages
die **Roman'tik** romanticism
roman'tisch romantic(ally)
der **Römer, -** Roman
römisch Roman
rosa pink (S2)
die **Rös(ch)ti** *(pl.)* fried potatoes with bacon cubes
die **Rose, -n** rose
der **Rosenkohl** Brussels sprout
die **Rosi'ne, -n** raisin
rost rust-colored
rot (ö) red (S2); **bei Rot** at a red light
die **Rote Grütze** berry sauce thickened with cornstarch
(das) **Rotkäppchen** Little Red Riding Hood
das **Rotkraut** red cabbage
rötlich reddish
rot werden* to blush
die **Roula'de, -n** stuffed beef roll
die **Routi'ne, -n** routine
der **Rückblick, -e** review
der **Rücken, -** back
die **(Hin- und) Rückfahrkarte, -n** round-trip ticket (8.1)
das **Rückgrat,-e** backbone
die **Rückreise, -n** return trip
der **Rückgang, ⸚e** decline
das **Rückgrat** backbone
der **Rucksack, ⸚e** backpack
die **Rückschau** review
der **Rückweg, -e** return trip, way back
ruck, zuck quickly, in a jiffy
das **Ruderboot, -e** rowboat
rudern to row
der **Ruf** reputation
rufen, rief, gerufen to call
die **Ruhe** peace and quiet; **in ~** quietly, without being rushed; **ohne Rast und Ruh** restless
der **Ruhetag, -e** holiday, day off
ruhig quiet (7.1)
der **Ruhm** fame
der **Rumä'ne, -n, -n / die Rumä'nin, -nen** Rumanian
rumä'nisch Rumanian
rühren to stir; **sich ~** to move; **Ich kann mich kaum ~.** I can hardly move.
der **Rum** rum
rund round
die **Rundfahrt, -en** sightseeing trip
der **Rundfunk** radio, broadcasting
runter·kommen* to come down
runter·schalten to turn down
der **Russe, -n, -n / die Russin, -nen** the Russian
russisch Russian
(das) **Russland** Russia

S

der **Saal, Säle** large room, hall
die **Sache, -n** thing, matter; **Haupt~** main thing
sächsisch Saxonian
der **Saft, ⸚e** juice (2.1)
die **Sage, -n** legend
sagen to say, tell (S2); **Wie sagt man . . . ?** How does one say. . . ? (S2); **Sag mal!** Say. Tell me (us, etc.).; **wie gesagt** as I (you, etc.) said
die **Sahne** cream; **Alles ist ~.** Everything is fine.
die **Saison', -s** season
der **Salat', -e** salad, lettuce (2.1)
die **Salbe, -n** ointment
das **Salz** salt (3.1)
salzig salty
die **Salzstange, -n** pretzel stick
sammeln to collect (9.1)
die **Sammelstelle, -n** collection site (15.1)
der **Sammler, -** collector
der **Samstag** Saturday (S4); **am ~** on Saturday (S4)
samstags on Saturdays (2.2)
der **Samt** velvet
der **Sand** sand
die **Sanda'le, -n** sandal
sanft gentle, gently
der **Sängerknabe, -n, -n** choir boy
der **Sarg, ⸚e** coffin
der **Satellit', -en, -en** satellite
der **Satelli'tenteller, -** satellite dish
satt: ich bin ~. I'm full, I've enough; **es macht ~** it's filling
satteln to saddle
der **Satz, ⸚e** sentence (1.1); **Bilden Sie einen ~!** Make a sentence.
die **Sau, ⸚e** dirty pig, *lit.* sow; **Mensch, so ein ~wetter!** Man, what lousy weather!
sauber clean, neat (S3)
die **Sauberkeit** cleanliness
sauber·machen to clean
sauer sour; acid
das **Sauerkraut** sauerkraut
die **Säule, -n** column
säumen to delay
sauschwer *(coll.)* darn hard
die **S-Bahn, -en = Schnellbahn** commuter train
das **Schach: ~ spielen** to play chess (9.1)
schade too bad (S4)
schaden to hurt, damage (15.1)
der **Schaden, ⸚** damage; **Total'~** total loss
der **Schadstoff, -e** harmful chemical
das **Schaf, -e** sheep
der **Schäferhund, -e** German shepherd
schaffen to work hard, accomplish; **das kann ich nicht ~.** I can't do it.
schaffen, schuf, geschaffen to create; **Das ~ wir.** We'll make it (in time).
der **Schaffner, -** conductor
die **Schale, -n** shell, peel
die **(Schall)platte, -n** record
der **Schalter, -** ticket window, counter (8.1)
sich **schämen** to be embarrassed
scharf (ä) sharp

der **Schaschlik, -s** shish kebab
der **Schatten, -** shadow
schätzen to appreciate
schauen to look; **Schau mal!** Look!; **an·~** to look at, watch; **heraus·~** to look out; **nach vorne ~** to look ahead
das **Schaufenster, -** display window
das **Schaukelpferd,-e** rocking horse
das **Schaumbad, ¨-er** bubble bath
der **Schauspieler, -** actor (10.1)
der **Scheck, -s** check (7.1)
die **Scheibe, -n** slice; **eine ~ Brot** a slice of bread
sich **scheiden lassen*** to get divorced
die **Scheidung, -en** divorce (11.1)
der **Schein, -e** certificate; shine; **Geld~** banknote (15.2)
scheinen, schien, geschienen to shine (S4); to seem (like), appear (to be) (14.2)
schenken to give (as a present) (4.1)
die **Schere, -n** scissors
die **Schicht, -en** level; **die obere ~** upper level (of society)
schick chic(ly), neat(ly) (11.1)
schicken to send (8.1)
schief crooked, not straight; **~ gehen*** to go wrong
die **Schießbude, -n** shooting gallery
schießen, schoss, geschossen to shoot; **ab·~** to shoot down
das **Schiff, -e** ship, boat; **mit dem ~ fahren*** to go by boat
das **Schild, -er** sign
die **Schildkröte, -n** turtle
der **Schinken, -** ham
der **Schirm, -e** umbrella
der **Schlachter, -** butcher
der **Schlafanzug, ¨-e** pyjama
schlafen (schläft), schlief, geschlafen to sleep (3.2)
schlaflos sleepless
der **Schlafsack, ¨-e** sleeping bag
die **Schlafstadt, ¨-e** bedroom community
das **Schlafzimmer, -** bedroom (6.1)
schlagen (schlägt), schlug, geschlagen to hit, beat
der **Schlager, -** popular song, hit
der **Schlagersänger, -** pop singer
die **Schlagsahne** whipped cream, whipping cream
das **Schlagzeug** drums

die **Schlange, -n** snake; **~ stehen* (hat)** to stand in line
schlank slim, slender (11.1)
schlapp weak
schlau clever(ly), sly(ly); **~ wie ein Fuchs** clever as a fox
das **Schlauchboot, -e** rubber boat
schlecht bad(ly) (S1); **Mir wird ~.** I'm getting sick.
der **Schlemmer, -** gourmet
schließen, schloss, geschlossen to lock, close
das **Schließfach, ¨-er** locker
schließlich after all, in the end, finally (15.1)
schlimm bad, awful
der **Schlips, -e** tie
der **Schlitten, -** sled
das **Schloss, ¨-er** palace (5.1)
der **Schluck** zip; **ein / zwei ~** one / two zip(s) of
der **Schlüssel, -** key (7.1)
der **Schlüsseldienst** locksmith service
das **Schlüsselkind, -er** latchkey child
schmecken to taste (good); **Das schmeckt (gut).** That tastes good. (3.1)
schmelzen (schmilzt), schmolz, ist geschmolzen to melt
der **Schmerz, -en** pain, ache; **~en haben** to have pain (9.1); **Ich habe (Kopf)schmerzen.** I have a (head)ache. (9.1)
schmerzhaft painful
der **Schmetterling, -e** butterfly
der **Schmied, -e** blacksmith
der **Schmutz** dirt
der **Schmutzfink, -en** (dirty) pig
schmutzig dirty (S3)
das **Schnäppchen, -** bargain
der **Schnee** snow
schneiden, schnitt, geschnitten to cut
schneien to snow; **es schneit** it's snowing (S4)
schnell quick(ly), fast (S3)
der **Schnellweg, -e** express route
das **Schnitzel, -** veal cutlet
die **Schnitzeljagd** treasure hunt (*lit.* paper chase)
der **Schock, -s** shock
die **Schokola'de** chocolate
schon already (1.2); **das ~** that's true, sure; **~ gut** okay
schön fine, nice(ly), beautiful(ly) (S4)
schonen to protect (15.1)

die **Schönheit** beauty
die **Schrammelmusik** *(Viennese)* music with violins, guitars, and accordions
der **Schrank, ¨-e** closet, cupboard (6.1); **Gefrier~** freezer; **Kleider~** closet; **Küchen~** kitchen cabinet; **Kühl~** refrigerator
der **Schrebergarten, ¨-** leased garden
der **Schreck** shock; **Auch du ~!** My goodness!
schrecklich terrible, terribly (11.1)
schreiben, schrieb, geschrieben to write (S3); **~ Sie bitte!** Please write! (S5); **Wie schreibt man das?** How do you write that?; **~ an** (+ *acc.*) to write to (10.G)
die **Schreibmaschine, -n** typewriter
der **Schreibtisch, -e** desk (6.1)
schreien, schrie, geschrien to scream
die **Schrift, -en** script; (hand)writing
schriftlich written; in writing
der **Schriftsteller, -** writer, author
der **Schritt, -e** step; pre-unit
schubsen to shove
schüchtern shy
der **Schuh, -e** shoe (S3); **Sport~** gym shoe, sneaker
die **Schule, -n** school (5.1)
der **Schüler, -** pupil, student
die **Schulter, -n** shoulder
die **Schüssel, -n** bowl
schütteln to shake
schütten (in + *acc.*) to dump, pour (into), spill
der **Schutz** protection (15.1); **Umwelt~** environmental protection (15.1)
der **Schütze, -n, -n** rifleman, marksman; Sagittarius
schützen to protect (15.1)
der **Schwabe, -n, -n / die Schwäbin, -nen** the Swabian
(das) **Schwaben(land)** Swabia
schwäbisch (*adj.*) Swabian
schwach (ä) weak
die **Schwäche, -n** weakness
der **Schwager, -** brother-in-law
die **Schwägerin, -nen** sister-in-law
schwanger pregnant
schwänzen to skip class
schwärmen (von + *dat.*) to rave (about)

schwarz (ä) black (S2); **~·fahren*** to ride (a bus, subway, etc.) without paying
das **Schwarzbrot, -e** rye bread
schwatzen *(coll.)* to chat
der **Schwede, -n, -n / die Schwedin, -nen** the Swede
(das) **Schweden** Sweden
schwedisch Swedish
schweifen (ist) to wander, roam; **immer weiter·~** to continue wanderinglion
schweigen, schwieg, geschwiegen to be/remain silent
das **Schwein, -e** pig, pork; scoundrel; **~ gehabt!** I was (you were, etc.) lucky!
der **Schweinebraten** pork roast
die **Schweinshaxe, -n** pigs' knuckles
der **Schweiß** sweat
die **Schweiz** Switzerland (1.1)
der **Schweizer, -** the Swiss (1.1)
Schweizer / schweizerisch Swiss
schwer heavy, heavily, hard, difficult (6.2)
die **Schwerarbeit** hard / menial work
der **Schwerbehinderte (ein Schwerbehinderter) / die Schwerbehinderte, -n, -n** handicapped person
die **Schwester, -n** sister (1.1)
das **Schwesterchen, -** little sister
Schwieger- in-law; **der ~vater** father-in-law; **die ~mutter** mother-in-law; **die ~eltern** parents-in-law
schwierig difficult (13.1)
die **Schwierigkeit, -en** difficulty
das **Schwimmbad, ¨er** (large) swimming pool
schwimmen, schwamm, ist geschwommen to swim (9.1); **~ gehen*** to go swimming (9.1)
der **Schwimmer, -** swimmer
schwühl humid
der **Schwund** loss
(das) **Schwyzerdütsch** Swiss-German
ein **Sechstel** one sixth
der **See, -n** lake (1.1)
die **See** sea, ocean
der **Seehund, -e** seal
die **Seele, -n** soul
das **Segelboot, -e** sailboat
segelfliegen gehen* to go gliding
segeln to sail; **~ gehen*** to go sailing
sehen (sieht), sah, gesehen to see, look (3.G); **Mal ~!** Let's see! (13.1)
die **Sehenswürdigkeit, -en** sight (worth seeing), attraction
sehr very (S4)
die **Seide, -n** silk
die **Seife, -n** soap
die **Seifenoper, -n** soap opera
die **Seilbahn, -en** cable car
sein his, its (7.G)
sein (ist), war, ist gewesen to be (S1, S2, 2.G); **Ich bin's.** It's me.; **So bin ich.** That's the way I am.; **Wie wär's mit . . . ?** How about . . . ?
seit (+ *dat.*) since, for (time) (3.G)
seitdem since then (14.1)
die **Seite, -n** page; **auf ~** on page, to page (S5); **auf der einen / anderen ~** on the one / other hand
die **Sekretär', -e** secretary (12.1)
der **Sekt** champagne (4.1)
die **Sekun'de, -n** second (S5)
selbst -self; **~ wenn** even if
selbstbewusst self-confident
das **Selbstbewusstsein** self-confidence
selbstständig self-employed, independent (11.1)
die **Selbstständigkeit** inde-pendence
selten seldom
seltsam strange, weird
das **Semes'ter, -** semester (13.1)
das **Seminar', -e** seminar paper (13.1)
die **(Seminar')arbeit, -en** term paper
der **Sender, -** (radio or TV) station
die **Sendung, -en** (part of) TV or radio program (10.2)
der **Senf** mustard
der **Septem'ber** September (S4); **im ~** in September (S4)
die **Serie, -n** series
servie'ren to serve (food)
die **Serviet'te, -n** napkin (3.1)
Servus! Hi! / Bye! *(in Bavaria and Austria)*
der **Sessel, -** armchair (6.1)
der **Sessellift, -e** chairlift
setzen to set (down), put (6.1); **sich ~** to sit down (9.G); **sich dazu ~** to join sb. at a table
seufzen to sigh
das **Shampoo', -s** shampoo
die **Show, -s** show
sicher sure, certain (4.1); safe, secure (12.1); **Ja, ~.** Yes, sure. (9.1); **Es geht ~.** It's probably all right.
die **Sicherheit** safety, security (12.1)
sicherlich surely, certainly, undoubtedly (15.1)
sichern to secure
sichtbar visible, visibly
die **Siedlung, -en** settlement, subdivision
der **Sieg, -e** victory
der **Sieger, -** victor, winner; **die ~mächte** (*pl.*) victorious Allies
die **Siegesgöttin** goddess of victory
siezen to call each other *"Sie"*
die **Silbe, -n** syllable
das **Silber** silver; **der ~schmied, -e** silver smith
silbern (*adj.*) silver
(das) **Silves'ter: zu ~** at / for New Year's Eve (4.1)
singen, sang, gesungen to sing (4.1)
sinken, sank, ist gesunken to sink
der **Sinn, -e** mind, sense, meaning, purpose; **in den ~ kommen*** to come to mind
sinnvoll meaningful; **es ist ~** it makes sense
die **Situation', -en** situation
der **Sitz, -e** seat; headquarters
die **Sitzecke, -n** corner bench (seating arrangement)
sitzen, saß, gesessen to sit (be sitting) (6.1)
der **Ski, -er** ski; **~ laufen*** to ski (9.1); **~laufen gehen*** to go skiing (9.1)
der **Skilanglauf** cross-country skiing
der **Skiläufer, -** skier
der **Skilift, -e** skilift
der **Skorpion', -e** scorpion; Scorpio
skrupellos unscrupulous(ly)
die **Skulptur', -en** sculpture
die **Slawis'tik** study of Slavic language and literature
der **Slowa'ke, -n, -n / die Slowa'kin, -nen** the Slovak
slowa'kisch Slovakian

die **Slowa'kische Republik'** = **Slowakei'** Slovak Republic = Slovakia
der **Slowe'ne, -n, -n / die Slowe'nin, -nen** the Slovene
(das) **Slowe'nien** Slovenia
slowe'nisch Slovenian
die **SMS, -** text message (8.1)
so so, like that; in this way; ~ **lala** so so; ~**dass** (*conj.*) so that (13.2); ~ **ein** such a (7.G); ~ **so** fair; ~ **. . . wie** as . . . as (12.G)
sobald' as soon as
die **Socke, -n** sock
das **Sofa, -s** sofa, couch (6.1)
sofort' immediately, right away (11.2)
sogar' even (6.1)
sogenannt so-called
der **Sohn, ¨-e** son (1.1)
die **Solar'zelle, -n** solar cell
solch- such (7.G)
der **Soldat', -en, -en** soldier
sollen (soll), sollte, gesollt to be supposed to (5.G)
der **Sommer, -** summer (S4); **im ~** in the summer (S4)
das **Sonderangebot, -e: im ~** on sale, special
sondern but, on the contrary, rather (5.15.G); **nicht nur . . . , ~ auch** not only . . . but also (3.2)
der **Sonderstatus** special status
der **Sonnabend** Saturday *(in northern and central Germany)*
die **Sonne** sun; **Die ~ scheint.** The sun is shining. (S4)
der **Sonnenaufgang, ¨-e** sunrise
die **Sonnenblume, -n** sunflower
die **Sonnenbrille, -n** sunglasses
die **Sonnencreme, -s** suntan lotion
das **Sonnenöl** suntan lotion
der **Sonnenuntergang, ¨-e** sunset
sonnig sunny
der **Sonntag** Sunday (S4); **am ~** on Sunday (S4); **Toten~** Memorial Day
sonntags on Sundays (2.2)
sonst otherwise, normally; **~ noch etwas?** Anything else?; ~ **wer** just anybody
die **Sorge, -n** worry, concern; **sich** *(dat.)* **~n machen (um)** to be concerned, worried (about) (12.2)
die **Sorte, -n** type, variety
sortie'ren to sort
die **Soße, -n** sauce, gravy
die **Souveränität'** sovereignty
soviel' as much as; **~ ich weiß** as much as I know
sowie' as well as (12.2)
sowieso' anyway, anyhow (10.2)
sowje'tisch Soviet
sowohl . . . als auch as well as
die **Sozial'hilfe** social welfare
der **Sozialis'mus** socialism
sozialis'tisch socialist
die **Sozial'kunde** social studies
der **Sozial'pädagoge, -n, - n / die Sozial'pädago'gin, -nen** social worker
die **Soziologie'** social studies, sociology
das **Spanferkel, -** suckling pig
(das) **Spanien** Spain (1.1)
der **Spanier, -** the Spaniard (1.1)
spanisch Spanish (1.1)
spannend exciting, suspenseful (10.1)
sparen to save (money or time) (6.2)
der **Spargel** asparagus
die **Sparkasse, -n** savings bank
sparsam thrifty
sparta'nisch Spartan, frugal(ly)
der **Spaß** fun; ~ **machen** to be fun (4.2); **Das macht (mir) ~.** That's fun. I love it.
spät late; **Wie ~ ist es?** How late is it? What time is it? (S5)
später later; **Bis ~!** See you later! (S1)
der **Spatz, -en** sparrow
die **Spätzle** (*pl.*) tiny Swabian dumplings
spazie'ren gehen* to go for a walk (9.1)
der **Spazier'gang, ¨-e** walk
der **Speck** bacon
die **Speise, -n** food, dish; **Vor~** appetizer; **Nach~** dessert
die **Speisekarte, -n** menu (3.1)
der **Speisewagen, -** dining car
die **Spekulation', -en** speculation
das **Spezial'geschäft, -e** specialty shop
die **Spezialisie'rung** special- ization
der **Spezialist', -en, -en** specialist
die **Spezialität', -en** specialty
spezi'fisch specific(ally)
der **Spiegel, -** mirror
das **Spiel, -e** game, play (9.1)
das **Spielzeug** toy(s)
spielen to play; **Tennis ~** to play tennis (S5); **Ball ~** to play ball; **Dame ~** to play checkers; **Federball ~** to play badminton; **Fußball ~** to play soccer; **Schach ~** to play chess (9.1)
der **Spielplan, ¨-e** program, performance schedule
der **Spielplatz, ¨-e** playground
der **Spieß, -e** spit; spear
der **Spinat'** spinach
die **Spindel, -n** spindle
die **Spinne, -n** spider
spinnen, spann, gesponnen to spin (yarn) (11.2); **Du spinnst wohl!** You're crazy!
das **Spinnrad, ¨-er** spinningwheel
der **Spitz, -e** pomeranian
spitze *(adj.)* great, super (10.1)
die **Spitze, -n** top
der **Spitzname, -ns, -n** nickname (14.1)
spontan' spontaneous(ly)
der **Sport** sport(s) (9.1); ~ **treiben*** to engage in sports (9.1)
der **Sportler, -** athlete
sportlich athletic(ally), sporty (11.1)
der **Sportverein, -e** sports club
die **Sprache, -n** language (1.1)
-sprachig -speaking
sprechen (spricht), sprach, gesprochen to speak (S3); **~ Sie langsam bitte!** Speak slowly, please.; **~ Sie lauter!** Speak louder. (S3); **Man spricht . . .** They (people) speak . . . ; **~ von** (+ *dat.*) / **über** (+ *acc.*) to speak of / about (10.G); **Ist . . . zu ~?** May I speak to . . . ?
der **Sprecher, -** speaker
die **Sprechstunde, -n** office hour
das **Sprichwort, ¨-er** saying, proverb
springen, sprang, ist gesprungen to jump (11.2); **raus·~** to jump out
das **Spritzgebäck** cookies shaped with a cookie press
der **Spruch, ¨-e** saying
der **Sprung, ¨-e** jump
spülen to wash dishes
die **Spülmaschine, -n** dishwasher
das **Spülmittel, -** dishwashing liquid; detergent

die **Spur, -en** trace
spüren to feel; sense
der **Staat, -en** state, nation (1.2)
der **Staatenbund** confederation
staatlich public; ~ **kontrolliert'** state-controlled
die **Staatsangehörigkeit** citizenship
der **Staatsbürger, -** citizen
der **Staatssicherheitsdienst** = **die Stasi** GDR secret police
das **Stadion, -s** stadium
das **Stadium, Stadien** stage
die **Stadt, ⸚e** city, town (1.1)
das **Stadtbild, -er** overall appearance of a city
das **Städtchen, -** small town
der **Stadtführer, -** city guide
der **Stadtplan, ⸚e** city map (5.1)
der **Stadtrand** outskirts (of town)
der **Stall, ⸚e** stable
der **Stamm, ⸚e** tribe
der **Stammbaum, ⸚e** family tree
der **Stammtisch, -e** regular table
stammen (**aus** + *dat.*) to stem (from), originate (in)
stampfen to stomp
der **Standard, -s** standard
das **Standesamt, ⸚er** marriage registrar
die **Stange, -n** pole
stark (ä) strong(ly); **echt** ~ *(coll.)* really super
starren to stare
die **Stärke, -n** strength
die **Station', -en** (bus) stop
die **Statis'tik, -en** statistic
statt (+ *gen.*) instead of (8.G); **~dessen** instead of that
stattlich considerable, impressive
der **Stau, -s** traffic jam
der **Staub** dust
der **Staubsauger, -** vacuum cleaner
staunen to be amazed
stechen (sticht), stach, gestochen to prick, sting
stecken (**in** + *acc.*) to stick / put (into)
stehen, stand, gestanden to stand (or be standing) (6.1); **Das steht dir gut.** That looks good on you.
stehen bleiben* to come to a stop, remain standing
stehlen (stiehlt), stahl, gestohlen to steal
steif stiff(ly)
steigen, stieg, ist gestiegen to go up, rise, climb, increase
steigern to increase
steil steep(ly)
der **Stein, -e** stone
der **Steinbock, ⸚e** ibex; Capricorn
die **Stelle, -n** job, position, place (12.1); **an deiner** ~ in your shoes, if I were you (13.2)
stellen to stand (upright), put (6.1); **eine Frage** ~ to ask a question
das **Stellenangebot, -e** job opening / offer
sterben (stirbt), starb, ist gestorben to die (11.2)
die **Stereoanlage, -n** stereo system
das **Sternzeichen, -** sign of the zodiac
die **Steuer, -n** tax; **Mehrwert~** value-added tax
der **Steuerberater, -** tax consultant
das **Stichwort, ⸚er** key word
Stief-: die ~eltern stepparents; **die ~mutter** stepmother; **der ~vater** stepfather
der **Stiefel, -** boot
der **Stier, -e** bull; Taurus
der **Stil, -e** style
still quiet(ly)
still·stehen* *(hat)* to stand still
die **Stimme, -n** voice
stimmen to be right / true; **(Das) stimmt.** (That's) true. (That's) right. (6.1)
die **Stimmung, -en** mood
das **Stipen'dium, Stipen'dien** scholarship (13.1)
die **Stirn** forehead
der **Stock, ⸚e** stick, pole
der **Stock, -werke: im ersten** ~ on the second floor (6.1)
stöhnen to complain, moan
der **Stollen, -** Christmas cake / bread with almonds, raisins, and candied peel
stolz (**auf** + *acc.*) proud (of) (15.2)
der **Stopp, -s** stop
das **Stoppschild, -er** stop sign
der **Storch, ⸚e** stork
stören to bother, disturb
der **Strafzettel, -** (traffic violation) ticket
strahlen to shine
der **Strand, ⸚e** beach; **~korb, ⸚e** beach basket (chair)
die **Straße, -n** street (5.1)
die **Straßenbahn, -en** streetcar (5.1)
das **Straßenbild** scene
die **Strategie', -n** strategy
strate'gisch strategic(ally)
der **Strauch, ⸚er** bush
der **Strauß, ⸚e** bouquet (of flowers)
streben (nach) to strive (for)
der **Streber, -** one who studies excessively, grind
strebsam ambitious(ly)
das **Streichholz, ⸚er** match
die **Streife, -n** patrol; ~ **fahren** to patrol
der **Streifen, -** strip of land
der **Streit** fight, dispute
streiten, stritt, gestritten to fight, argue
streng strict(ly)
der **Stress** stress; **zu viel** ~ too much stress
das **Stroh** straw
der **Strom** electricity
die **Strophe, -n** stanza
die **Struktur', -en** structure; *here:* grammar
der **Strumpf, ⸚e** stocking
das **Stück, -e** piece; (theatrical) play; piece of music or ballet (10.1); **ein** ~ a piece of (2.1); **zwei** ~ two pieces of (2.1)
der **Student', -en, -en** (college) student (S5, 13.1)
das **Studen'tenwohnheim, -e** dorm(itory) (6.1)
die **Studiengebühr, -en** tuition
der **Studiengang, ⸚e** course of study
der **Studienplatz, ⸚e** opening to study at the university
studie'ren to study a particular field, be a student at a university (4.2); ~ (**an** + *dat.*) to be a student (at) (4.2)
der **Studie'rende (ein Studierender) / die Studierende, -n, -n** student
das **Studio, -s** studio
das **Studium, Studien** course of study (13.1)
der **Stuhl, ⸚e** chair (S2,5.1)
stumm silent(ly)
die **Stunde, -n** hour, class lesson (S5, 12.1); **in einer halben** ~ in half an hour (8.1); **in einer Viertel~** in 15 minutes (8.1); **in einer Dreiviertel~** in 45 minutes (8.1)

stundenlang for hours (5.2)
der **Stundenplan, ¨-e** schedule (of classes)
stur stubborn(ly)
stürmisch stormy
das **Subjekt', -e** subject
subventioni'eren to subsidize
die **Suche** search; **auf der ~ nach** in search for
suchen to look for (2.1); **gesucht wird** wanted
süchtig werden* to become addicted
der **Süden: im ~** in the south (1.1)
südlich (von) south (of), to the south (of) (1.1)
super superb(ly), terrific(ally) (S4)
der **Superlativ, -e** superlative
der **Supermarkt, ¨-e** supermarket (2.1)
su'permodern' very modern
die **Suppe, -n** soup (3.1)
das **Suppengrün** greens for making soup
surfen to surf; **wind~ gehen** to go windsurfing
süß sweet, cute (11.1)
das **Sweatshirt, -s** sweatshirt (S3)
der **Swimmingpool, -s** pool
das **Symbol', -e** symbol
symbolisie'ren to symbolize
die **Sympathie'** congeniality
sympa'thisch congenial, likable (11.1); **sie sind mir ~** I like them
die **Symphonie', -n** symphony
die **Synago'ge, -n** synagogue
synchronisiert' dubbed
die **Synthe'tik** synthetics
das **System', -e** system (13.1)
der **System'berater, -** computer consultant
die **Szene, -n** scene

T

die **Tabel'le, -n** chart
die **Tablet'te, -n** pill
die **Tafel, -n** (black)board (S2); **Gehen Sie an die ~!** Go to the (black)board.
der **Tag, -e** day (S4); **Guten ~!** Hello! (S1); **am ~** during the day (6.2); **eines Tages** one day (8.G); **jeden ~** every day (8.G); **~ der Arbeit** Labor Day
das **Tagebuch, ¨-er** journal, diary
tagelang for days
der **Tagesablauf** daily routine
-tägig days long
täglich daily (8.G)
das **Tal, ¨-er** valley
das **Talent', -e** talent
talentiert' talented (11.1)
die **Tankstelle, -n** gas station
die **Tante, -n** aunt (1.1)
der **Tanz, ¨-e** dance
tanzen to dance (4.1)
tappen (ist) to tiptoe
die **Tasche, -n** bag, pocket (7.1); **Hand~** handbag; **Umhänge~** shoulder bag
die **Taschenlampe, -n** flashlight
das **Taschenmesser, -** pocket knife
die **Tasse, -n** cup (2.2); **eine ~** a cup of (2.2)
die **Tatsache, -n** fact
taub deaf
die **Taube, -n** dove; pigeon
tauchen (in + *acc.*) to dip (into)
tauschen to trade
das **Taxi, -s** taxi (5.1)
die **Technik** technic
der **Techniker, -** technician
das **Technikum, -s** technical college
technisch technical(ly)
die **Technologie', -n** technology
der **Tee, -s** tea (2.1)
der **Teenager, -** teenager
der **Teil, -e** part (1.2)
teilen to share, divide (13.2)
teilmöbliert partly furnished
die **Teilnahme** participation
teil·nehmen* (**an** + *dat.*) to participate, take part (in) (13.1)
teils partly
die **Teilung, -en** division
teilweise partly
das **Telefon', -e** telephone (6.1)
telefonie'ren to call up, phone (8.1)
der **Telefonist', -en, -en** switchboard operator
die **Telefon'karte, -n** telephone card (8.1)
die **Telefon'nummer, -n** telephone number (8.1)
die **Telefon'zelle, -n** telephone booth
die **Telekommunikation'** telecommunications
der **Teller, -** plate (3.1)
das **Temperament', -e** temperament
temperament'voll dynamic (11.1)
die **Temperatur', -en** temperature
das **Tempo, -s** speed;
das **Tempolimit, -s** speed limit
das **Tennis: ~ spielen** to play tennis (S5)
der **Teppich, -e** carpet (6.1)
der **Termin', -e** (business) appointment
die **Terras'se, -n** terrace
der **Terrier, -** Terrier
der **Terroris'mus** terrorism
testen to test
teuer expensive (S3)
der **Teufel, -** devil
der **Text, -e** text
das **Textil'geschäft, -e** clothing store
das **Thea'ter, -** theater (5.1)
das **Thema, Themen** topic
der **Theolo'ge, -n, -n / die Theolo'gin, -nen** theologian
die **Theologie'** theology
die **Theorie', -n** theory
die **Therapie', -n** therapy
das **Thermal'bad, ¨-er** thermal bath / spa
das **Thermome'ter, -** thermometer
der **Thron** throne
thüringisch Thuringian
tief deep
der **Tiefbau** civil engineering
der **Tiefbauingenieur', -e** civil engineer
tiefgefroren frozen
die **Tiefkühlkost** frozen foods
das **Tier, -e** animal (11.1); **Haus~** pet
die **Tierart, -en** animal species
tierlieb fond of animals
das **Tierkreiszeichen, -** sign of the zodiac
die **Tiermedizin'** veterinary science
der **Tiger, -** tiger
die **Tinte** ink
das **Tintenfass, ¨-er** inkwell
der **Tipp, -s** hint
der **Tisch, -e** table (S2,5.1); **Nacht~** nightstand
die **Tischdecke, -n** tablecloth
der **Tischler, -** cabinetmaker
das **Tischtennis: ~ spielen** to play ping-pong
das **Tischtuch, ¨-er** tablecloth
der **Titel, -** title

tja well (12.1)
der **Toast, -s** (piece of) toast
das **Toastbrot, -e** (piece of) toast
der **Toaster, -** toaster
die **Tochter, ¨** daughter (1.1)
der **Tod** death
todmüde dead-tired
Toi, toi, toi! Good luck!
die **Toilet'te, -n** toilet (6.1)
tolerant' tolerant
toll great, terrific (S4)
die **Toma'te, -n** tomato (2.1)
der **Ton, ¨e** tone, note, pitch
der **Topf, ¨e** pot
das **Tor, -e** gate, gateway (14.2)
die **Torte, -n** (fancy) cake
tot dead
total' total(ly)
der **Total'schaden, ¨** total wreck
der **Tote (ein Toter) / die Tote, -n, -n** dead person
töten to kill
die **Tour, -en** tour
der **Touris'mus** tourism
der **Tourist', -en, -en** tourist (5.1)
der **Touris'tikumsatz** spending on travel
das **Tournier', -e** tournament
die **Tracht, -en** traditional folk costume / garb
der **Trachtenzug, ¨e** parade with people dressed in traditional dress / garb
die **Tradition', en** tradition
traditionell' traditional(ly)
tragen (trägt), trug, getragen to carry (3.G); to wear (3.G)
die **Tragetasche, -n** tote bag
der **Trainer, -** coach
das **Training** training
die **Träne, -n** tear
das **Transport'flugzeug, -e** transport plane
transportie'ren to transport
die **Traube, -n** grape
trauen to trust; **sich ~** to dare
der **Traum, ¨e** dream; **selige Träume** sweet dreams
träumen (von) to dream (of, about) (11.1)
der **Träumer, -** dreamer
traurig sad(ly) (10.1)
die **Traurigkeit** sadness
die **Trauung, -en** wedding ceremony
(sich) **treffen (trifft), traf, getroffen** to meet (with) (9.1); **Freunde ~** to meet / get together with friends (9.1)
das **Treffen, -** meeting, reunion
der **Treffpunkt, -e** meeting place
treiben, trieb, getrieben to push; **Sport ~** to engage in sports (9.1)
das **Treiben** hubbub, activities
der **Treib'hauseffekt'** greenhouse effect
(sich) **trennen** to separate (15.1)
die **Treppe, -n** stairs, stairway
das **Treppenhaus, ¨er** stairwell
treten (tritt), trat, ist getreten (auf + acc.) to step (on)
treu faithful(ly), true, loyal(ly)
sich **trimmen** to keep fit
trinken, trank, getrunken to drink (2.1)
das **Trinkgeld, -er** tip
der **Trockner, -** dryer
die **Trommel, -n** drum
die **Trompe'te, -n** trumpet
trompe'ten to trumpet
der **Trost** consolation
trotz (+ *gen.* / [+ *dat.*]) in spite of (8.G)
trotzdem nevertheless, in spite of that (6.2); still
trüb(e) dim(ly)
die **Trümmer** *(pl.)* rubble, ruins
der **Trümmerhaufen, -** pile of rubble
der **Tscheche, -n, -n / die Tschechin, -nen** the Czech
tschechisch Czech
(das) **Tschechien** = **die Tschechische Republik'** Czech Republic
die **Tschechoslowakei'** (former) Czechoslovakia
Tschüss! So long; (Good-) bye! (S1)
das **T-Shirt, -s** T-shirt (S3)
tüchtig (very) capable
tun (tut), tat, getan to do (4.1); **es tut sich was** things are happening
tünchen to whitewash
der **Tunnel, -** tunnel
die **Tür, -en** door (S2)
der **Türke, -n, -n/die Türkin, -nen** the Turk
die **Türkei'** Turkey
türkis' turquoise
türkisch Turkish
der **Turm, ¨e** tower (14.1); steeple
turnen to do sports or gymnastics
die **Turnhalle, -n** gym
der **Turnschuh, -e** gym shoe; tennis shoe
der **Turnverein, -e** athletic club
die **Tüte, -n** bag
typisch typical(ly) (15.2)

U

die **U-Bahn, -en** = **Untergrundbahn** subway (5.1)
über (+ *acc.* / *dat.*) over, above (6.G); about (10.G)
überall everywhere (3.2)
der **Überblick** overview
überein'·stimmen to agree
überflie'gen* (hat) to skim through
überfüllt' (over)crowded
überhaupt' at all; **~ nicht** not at all; **~ kein Problem** no problem at all
das **Überhol'verbot, -e** no passing restriction
überle'ben to survive
überle'gen to wonder, ponder
überneh'men* to take over
übermorgen the day after tomorrow (4.1)
übernach'ten to spend the night (7.2)
die **Übernach'tung, -en** (overnight) stay / accommodations
überprü'fen to check
überra'schen to surprise (4.1)
die **Überra'schung, -en** surprise (4.1); **So eine ~!** What a surprise! (4.1)
überset'zen to translate
die **Überset'zung, -en** translation
überste'hen* (hat) to survive
die **Überstunde, -n** overtime
üblich usual, customary
übrig bleiben* to be left, remain
übrigens by the way (15.1)
die **Übrigen** the rest
die **Übung, -en** exercise, practice
das **Ufer, -** riverbank
das **Ufo, -s** flying saucer
die **Uhr, -en** watch, clock; o'clock (S5); **Wie viel ~ ist es?** What time is it? (S5); **~zeit** time of the day (7.1)
der **Uhrmacher, -** watchmaker
der **Ukrai'ner, -** Ukrainian
ukrai'nisch Ukrainian
um- around, over, from one to the other (7.G)

um *(+ acc.)* around (the circumference) (2.G); at . . . o'clock (S5); ~ **. . . zu** in order to (9.G); **fast ~** almost over
um sein* to be over / up; **die Zeit ist ~** the time is up
sich **um·blicken** to look around
der **Umbruch, ¨-e** radial change
umfas'sen* to include
die **Umfrage, -n** survey; **Meinungs~** opinion poll
die **Umgangsform, -en** manners
die **Umgangssprache** colloquial speech
umge'ben (von) surrounded by
die **Umge'bung** *(sg.)* surroundings (14.1)
umgekehrt vice versa
umher'·sehen* to look around
(um·)kippen (ist) to tip over
um·leiten to detour
umliegend surrounding
ummau'ern to surround by a wall
der **Umsatz** sales, spending
umso the (more)
sich **um·sehen*** to look around
um·setzen to implement
der **Umstand, ¨-e** circumstance
um·steigen* (ist) to change (trains, etc.) (8.1)
der **Umtausch** exchange
um·tauschen to exchange (7.G)
die **Umwelt** environment, surroundings (15.1)
umweltbewusst environmentally aware (15.1)
sich **um·ziehen*** to change (clothing), get changed (9.G)
der **Umzug, ¨-e** parade; move, moving
unabhängig (von) independent (of)
un'attraktiv' unattractive(ly)
unbebaut vacant, empty
unbedingt definitely (12.2)
unbegehrt undesired
unbegrenzt unlimited
die **Begrenzung** restriction
unbequem uncomfortable, inconvenient (6.1)
und and (S1,2.G)
und so weiter = usw. and so on, etc. (5.2)
unecht fake
unehrlich dishonest(ly) (11.1)

unentrinn'bar inescapable
unerfahren inexperienced
unerwartet unexpected(ly) (14.1)
der **Unfall, ¨-e** accident
unflexibel inflexible
unfreiwillig involuntary, involuntarily
unfreundlich unfriendly (11.1)
der **Ungar, -n, -n** the Hungarian
ungarisch Hungarian
(das) **Ungarn** Hungary
ungebildet uneducated (11.1)
ungeduldig impatient(ly) (11.1)
ungefähr approximately, about (1.2)
ungemütlich unpleasant, uncomfortable
ungenügend insufficient; approx. grade F
ungestört unhindered
unglaublich unbelievable, unbelievably, incredible, incredibly; **(Das ist doch) ~!** That's unbelievable / hard to believe! (10.1)
das **Unglück** bad luck
unglücklich unhappy, unhappily (11.1)
unheimlich tremendous(ly), extreme(ly) (14.1); **(Das ist) ~ interessant'.** (That's) really interesting. (10.1)
die **Universität', -en = Uni, -s** *(coll.)* university (5.1)
unkompliziert' uncomplicated (11.1)
unmittelbar right, directly
unmöbliert unfurnished
unmög'lich impossible, impossibly
unmusikalisch unmusical (11.1)
unrecht haben* to be wrong (12.1)
uns us, to us (5.G); **bei ~** at our place (3.G); in our city / country
unselbstständig dependent (11.1)
unser our (7.G)
unsicher insecure, unsafe (12.1)
der **Unsinn** nonsense
unsportlich unathletic (11.1)
unsympathisch uncongenial, unlikable (11.1)
untalentiert untalented (11.1)
unten downstairs (6.1)

unter (+ *acc.* / *dat.*) under, below (6.G); among (12.2); **~ einander** among each other
unterbrochen interrupted
die **Unterdrü'ckung** oppression
der **Untergang** fall, downfall
unter·gehen* to set (sun)
sich **unterhalten*** to talk, converse
unterhal'tend entertaining
die **Unterhal'tung** entertainment (10.1)
das **Unterneh'men, -** company (12.2)
unterneh'mungslustig enterprising
das **Unterpfand** pledge (for)
der **Unterricht** instruction, lesson, class
unterscheiden, unterschied, unterschieden to differentiate; **sich ~** to differ
der **Unterschied, -e** difference
unterschiedlich different
unterschrei'ben* to sign (7.1)
die **Unterschrift, -en** signature
unterstrei'chen, unterstrich, unterstrichen to underline
unterstüt'zen to support
unterwegs' on the go, on the road
untreu unfaithful
unverheiratet unmarried, single (11.1)
unverschämt impertinent
unvollständig incomplete, incompletely
die **Unwahrscheinlichkeit** *here:* unreal condition
unwiderstehlich irresistable
unwillig reluctant(ly)
unzerstört intact
unzufrieden discontent
unzuverlässig unreliable, unreliably (11.1)
Urgroß-: die ~eltern greatgrandparents; **die ~mutter** great-grandmother; **der ~vater** great-grandfather
der **Urlaub** paid vacation (9.2); **der Mutterschafts~** maternity leave
der **Urlaubstag, -e** (paid) vacation day
ursprünglich original(ly)
die **USA = Vereinigten Staaten von Amerika** *(pl.)* USA
usw. (und so weiter) etc. (and so on)

V

der **Valentinstag** Valentine's Day
der **Vampir', -e** vampire
die **Vanil'le** vanilla
die **Varian'te, -n** variation
die **Variation', -en** variation
variie'ren to vary
die **Vase, -n** vase
der **Vater, ¨** father (1.1); **Groß~** grandfather (1.1); **Urgroß~** great-grandfather; **Stief~** stepfather
der **Vati, -s** Dad
der **Vegeta'rier, -** vegetarian
verallgemei'nern to generalize
die **Verallgemei'nerung, -en** generalization
(sich) **verändern** to change (14.1)
verantwortlich responsible
die **Verantwortung, -en** responsibility (12.1)
verantwortungsvoll responsible, responsibly
das **Verb, -en** verb; **Hilfs~** auxiliary verb; **Modal~** modal auxiliary; **reflexive ~** reflexive verb
verbannen to ban
verbessern to improve
verbieten, verbot, verboten to forbid, prohibit (15.1)
verbinden, verband, verbunden to connect, tie together, link (15.2); blindfold
verbittert bitter
das **Verbot, -e** restriction
verboten forbidden (15.1)
der **Verbrauch** consumption
verbrauchen to consume
der **Verbraucher, -** consumer
verbreiten to distribute, spread
verbreitern to widen
die **Verbreitung, -en** distribution
verbrennen, verbrannte, verbrannt to burn
verbringen* to spend (time)
verbunden in touch, close
die **Verbundenheit** closeness
verdammen to curse; **Verdammt noch mal!** Darn it!
verderben (verdirbt), verdarb, verdorben to spoil
verdienen to earn, make money (12.1); to deserve
verdorben rotten
der **Verein, -e** club, association; **Turn~** athletic club
vereinigen to unite; **wieder~** to reunite
die **Vereinigten Staaten (USA)** *(pl.)* United States (US)
die **Vereinigung** unification (15.2)
vereint united (15.2)
die **Verfassung, -en** constitution; **das ~sgericht** Constitutional Court
Verflixt (noch mal)! Darn it!
verfolgen to pursue
vergangen past
die **Vergangenheit** past; past tense; simple past
vergeben* to forgive
vergehen* (ist) to pass (time); end
vergessen (vergisst), vergaß, vergessen to forget (10.1)
der **Vergleich, -e** comparison; **im ~ zu** in comparison to
vergleichen, verglich, verglichen to compare (11.1)
das **Vergnügen** pleasure
die **Vergnügung, -en** leisure time, entertainment; little pleasure, pastime
das **Verhalten (gegenüber** + *dat.*) behavior (toward)
das **Verhältnis, -se** relationship, condition
verheiratet married (11.1)
verhindern to prevent
verhungern (ist) to starve (to death)
die **Verkabelung** connection by cable
verkaufen to sell (2.1)
der **Verkehr (von)** sale (of)
der **Verkehr** traffic
der **Verkäufer, -** salesman, salesperson, salesclerk (2.1)
das **Verkehrsmittel, -** means of transportation
verklagen to sue
verkrampft tense
verlachen: jemanden ~ to make fun of sb.
der **Verlag, -e** publishing house
verlangen to demand
verlassen (verlässt), verließ, verlassen to leave (14.2)
sich **verlassen auf** *(+ acc.)* to rely on
sich **verlaufen*** to get lost
verlegen to transfer, relocate
die **Verlegenheit** embarrassment; **jemanden in ~ bringen*** to embarrass sb.
sich **verlieben (in** + *acc.*) to fall in love (with) (11.1)
verliebt (in + *acc.*) in love (with) (11.1)
verlieren, verlor, verloren to lose (11.1)
sich **verloben (mit)** to get engaged (to)
verlobt (mit) engaged (to) (11.1)
der **Verlobte (ein Verlobter) / die Verlobte, -n, -n** fiancé(e) (12.G)
die **Verlobung, -en** engagement
verlockend tempting
vermeiden, vermied, vermieden to avoid
vermieten to rent out (6.1)
der **Vermieter, -** landlord
vermissen to miss
vermitteln to help find
verneinen to negate
die **Vernichtung** destruction
die **Vernunft** reason; common sense
verpassen to miss (by delay)
verrückt crazy (4.2)
verschenken to give away
verschieden various, different (kinds of) (10.2); **Verschiedenes** *here:* Different words and phrases (S1)
verschlechtern to deteriorate
verschlingen, verschlang, verschlungen to gulp down, devour
verschlossen closed, locked
die **Verschmutzung** pollution (15.1)
verschönern to beautify
die **Verschwendung** waste
verschwiegen discreet
verschwinden, verschwand, ist verschwunden to disappear
versichern to insure; **jemandem etwas ~** to assure sb. sth.
die **Versicherung, -en** insurance
der **Versicherungsagent', -en, -en** insurance agent
versinken* to sink (in)
die **Version', -en** version
versorgen to take care of
die **Verspätung** delay; **Der Zug hat ~.** The train is late.
versprechen* to promise (11.2)
der **Verstand** reasoning, logic; common sense; **jemandem den ~ nehmen*** to drive s.b. out of one's mind

verständlich understandable
verständnislos lacking empathy
verständnisvoll with understanding
verstecken to hide
verstehen* to understand (S3); **Das verstehe ich nicht.** I don't understand (that). (S5)
verstär'ken to strengthen
versuchen to try (11.1)
die **Verteidigung** defense
der **Vertrag, ¨-e** contract
vertragen* to stand, tolerate
das **Vertrauen** trust
vertreiben, vertrieb, vertrieben to chase away
die **Verwaltung, -en** administration
verwandeln to change, transform
verwandt related
der **Verwandte (ein Verwandter) / die Verwandte, -n, -n** relative
verweigern to refuse
verwenden to use, utilize (15.1)
der **Verwendung** use
verwitwet widowed
verwöhnen to indulge, spoil; **sich ~ lassen*** to let o.s. be spoiled
das **Verzeichnis, -se** index, catalog
verzeihen, verzieh, verziehen to forgive; **~ Sie (mir)!** Forgive me. Pardon (me)!
die **Verzeihung** pardon; **~!** Excuse me! Pardon me! (5.1)
der **Vetter, -n** alternate form for **der Cousin, -s**
das **Video, -s** video
der **Videorecorder, -** VCR
die **Videothek, -en** video store
viel (mehr, meist-) much, many (3.1, 10.G, 12.G); **ganz schön ~** quite a bit; **so ~' ich weiß** as far as I know
die Vielfalt versatility
vielfältig versatile, diverse
vielleicht' perhaps (3.2)
vielseitig versatile (11.1)
vielsprachig multilingual
viereckig square
das **Viergespann, -e** quadriga, four-(horses-)in-hand
die **Viersprachigkeit** quadrilingualism, speaking four languages

das **Viertel, -** quarter; **(um) ~ nach** (at) a quarter past (S5); **(um) ~ vor** (at) a quarter to (S5); **in einer ~stunde** in a quarter of an hour (8.1); **in einer Dreiviertelstunde** in three quarters of an hour (45 minutes) (8.1)
die **Vision', -en** vision
vital' energetic, vital
das **Vitamin', -e** vitamine
der **Vogel, ¨-** bird (11.1); **Du hast einen ~.** You're crazy.
die **Voka'bel, -n** (vocabulary) word
das **Vokabular'** vocabulary
das **Volk, ¨-er** folk; people, nation (14.1)
die **Völkerkunde** ethnology
die **Volksherrschaft** *here:* rule by the people
die **Volkskammer** (GDR) house of representatives
das **Volkslied, -er** folk song
der **Volksmarsch, ¨-e** group-hiking event
die **Volkspolizei** (GDR) People's Police
der **Volkspolizist, -en, -en** = **Vopo, -s** member of the GDR People's Police
der **Volksstamm, ¨-e** ethnic group
der **Volkswagen, -** VW
die **Volkswirtschaft** (macro) economics
voll full(y) (11.2)
der **Volleyball, ¨-e** volleyball
völlig total(ly)
vollkommen total(ly)
der **Vollzeitstudent, -en, -en** full-time student
von (+ *dat.*) of, from, by (3.G); **~ . . . bis** from . . . until; **vom . . . bis zum/zur** from the . . . to the (4.1)
vor- ahead, before (7.G)
vor (+ *acc. / dat.*) in front of, before (6.G); **~ einer Woche** a week ago (4.1); **~ allem** above all, mainly (10.2)
voran'·kommen* to advance, progress
der **Vorarbeiter, -** foreman
voraus'gehend preceding
voraus'·sehen* to foresee
vorbei'- past, by (7.G); over
vorbei'·bringen* to bring over
vorbei'·fahren* to drive by, pass

vorbei'·führen (an + *dat.***)** to pass (by), guide along (14.1)
vorbei·'gehen* (bei + *dat.***)** to pass by (7.G)
vorbei'·kommen* to come by, pass by
vorbei' sein* to be over, finished
(sich) **vor·bereiten (auf** + *acc.***)** to prepare (for) (13.2)
die **Vorbereitung, -en** preparation
die **Vorbeugung, -en** prevention
die **Vorfahrt** right of way
vor·gehen* to proceed; **der Reihe nach ~** to proceed one after the other
vorgestern the day before yesterday (4.1)
vor·haben* to plan (to), intend (to)
der **Vorhang, ¨-e** curtain (6.1)
vorher ahead (of time), in advance; before, previously
vorher'gehend preceding; **das ~e Wort** antecedent
vor·herrschen to prevail
vor·kommen* (in + *dat.***)** to appear (in); **Das kommt mir . . . vor.** That seems . . . to me.
das **(flache) Vorland** *here:* tidal flats
die **Vorlesung, -en** lecture, class (university) (S5); **der ~ssaal, -säle** (lecture hall); **das ~sverzeichnis** course catalog
der **Vormittag, -e** (mid)morning; **heute ~** this (mid)morning (8.G)
der **Vorname, -ns, -n** first name
die **Vorschau** preview
der **Vorschlag, ¨-e** suggestion, proposal
die **Vorsicht: ~!** Careful! (7.1)
die **Vorspeise, -n** appetizer, hors d'oeuvre
vor·stellen to introduce; **Darf ich ~?** May I introduce?
sich **vor·stellen** to imagine (12.2); **Ich stelle mir vor, dass . . .** I imagine that . . . (12.2)
die **Vorstellung, -en** performance (10.1); idea
der **Vorteil, -e** advantage
der **Vortrag, ¨-e** talk, speech, lecture
vor·tragen* to recite

vorü'bergehend temporary, temporarily
das **Vorurteil, -e** prejudice
die **Vorwahl, -en** area code (8.1)
vor·wärmen to preheat
vor·ziehen* to prefer (9.2)

W

die **Waage, -n** scale, Libra
wach awake
das **Wachs** wax
wachsen (wächst), wuchs, ist gewachsen to grow (15.2); **zusam'men·wachsen*** to grow together (15.2)
die **Waffe, -n** weapon
die **Waffel, -n** waffel
wagen to dare
der **Wagen, -** car (8.1); railroad car (8.1)
die **Wahl** choice, selection
wählen to choose; elect; select
das **Wahlfach, ¨er** elective (subject)
der **Wahnsinn** insanity; **(Das ist ja) ~!** (That's) crazy / awesome / unbelievable! (10.1)
wahnsinnig crazy, crazily
während (+ *gen.*) during (8.G); while *(conj.)*
wahr true; **nicht ~?** isn't it? (S4); **Das kann doch nicht ~ sein!** That can't be true! (7.1); **~ werden*** to come true
die **Wahrheit** truth
wahrlich *(poetic)* truly
wahrschein'lich probable, probably (13.2)
die **Währung, -en** currency; **die ~sunion** currency union
das **Wahrzeichen, -** landmark
der **Wald, ¨er** forest, woods (7.2); **das ~sterben** dying of the forests
der **Walzer, -** waltz
die **Wand, ¨e** wall (S2)
der **Wandel** change; **Klima~** climate change
der **Wanderer, -** hiker
wandern (ist) to hike (9.1)
der **Wanderweg, -e** (hiking) trail
wann? when?, at what time? (S4,11.G)
wäre: Wie wär's mit . . . ? How about . . . ?
die **Ware, -n** goods, wares, merchandise
warm (ä) warm(ly) (S4)
die **Wärme** warmth; heat
warnen (vor + *dat.*) to warn (against)
warten to wait; **~ auf** (+ *acc.*) to wait for (10.G); **Warten Sie!** Wait! (7.1)
Wart's ab! *(coll.)* Just wait!
die **Wartungskosten** *(pl.)* maintenance costs
warum? why? (2.2)
was? what? (S2,2.G); **~ für (ein)?** what kind of (a)? (2.1); **~ für ein(e) . . . !** What a . . . ! (11.1); **so ~** s.th. like that
das **Waschbecken, -** sink
die **Wäsche** laundry
die **Waschecke, -n** corner reserved for washing
(sich) **waschen (wäscht), wusch, gewaschen** to wash (o.s.) (6.19.G)
der **Waschlappen, -** washcloth (*fig., coll.* wimp)
die **Waschmaschi'ne, -n** washing machine
das **Waschmittel, -** (washing) detergent
das **Wasser** water (2.1)
der **Wassermann, ¨er** Aquarius
der **Wasserski, -er** water ski; **~ laufen*** to water ski; **~laufen gehen*** to go water skiing
das **Watt(enmeer)** tidal flats
die **Webseite, -n** Web page
die **Website, -s** Web page
der **Wechsel** change
der **Wechselkurs, -e** exchange rate
wechseln to (ex)change (7.1)
die **Wechselstube, -n** exchange bureau
wecken to wake s.o. up
der **Wecker, -** alarm clock
weder . . . noch neither . . . nor (10.2)
weg away, gone
der **Weg, -e** way, path, trail (5.1); route; **nach dem ~ fragen** to ask for directions
wegen (+ *gen.* / [+ *dat.*]) because of (8.G)
weg·werfen* to throw away
wehen to blow (wind)
weh·tun* to hurt (9.1); **Mir tut (der Hals) weh.** My (throat) hurts. I have a sore throat. (9.1)
weich soft
weichen, wich, ist gewichen to give way to
die **Weide, -n** willow; pasture
(das) **Weihnachten: zu ~** at / for Christmas (4.1); **Frohe / Fröhliche ~!** Merry Christmas!
der **Weihnachtsbaum, ¨e** Christmas tree
das **Weihnachtsessen** Christmas dinner
das **Weihnachtslied, -er** Christmas carol
der **Weihnachstmann, ¨er** Santa Claus
weil *(conj.)* because (4.G)
die **Weile: eine ~** for a while
weilen *(poetic)* to stay, be
der **Wein, -e** wine (2.1); **Tafel~** table wine; **Qualitäts~** quality wine; **Qualitäts~ mit Prädikat** superior wine
der **Weinberg, -e** vineyard
weinen to cry (10.1)
weinrot wine-red
die **Weinstube, -n** wine cellar, tavern
die **Weintraube, -n** grape
weise wise
die **Weise: auf diese ~** (in) this way (13.2)
der **Weise (ein Weiser) / die Weise, -n, -n** wise man /woman
weiß white (S2)
weit far (5.1)
die **Weite** distance; wide-open space(s)
weiter: und so ~ (usw.) and so on (etc.); **~ draußen** farther out; **Wie geht's ~?** How does it go on? What comes next?
weiter- additional
Weiteres *here:* additional words and phrases
weiter·fahren* (ist) to drive on, keep on driving (8.2); to continue the trip
weiter·geben* to pass on
weiter·gehen* (ist) to continue, go on; **im Weitergehen** while passing
weiterhin still
welch- which (7.G); **Welche Farbe hat . . . ?** What color is . . . ? (S2)
die **Welle, -n** wave
das **Wellenreiten** surfing
der **Wellensittich, -e** parakeet

die **Welt, -en** world (11.2); **aus aller ~** from all over the world
weltoffen cosmopolitan
wem? (to) whom? (3.G)
wen? whom? (2.G)
wenig- little (not much), few (10.G); **immer ~er** fewer and fewer
wenigstens at least
wenn (*conj.*) if, (when)ever (4.G, 11.G); **selbst ~** even if
wer? who? (1.G); who(so) ever
die **Werbung** advertisement (10.1)
werden (wird), wurde, ist geworden to become, get (3.G); **es wird dunkel** it's getting dark; **Was willst du ([ein]mal) ~?** What do you want to be (one day)? (12.1); **Ich will . . . ~.** I want to be a . . . (12.1)
werfen, (wirft), warf, geworfen to throw (15.1); **weg·~** to throw away (15.1
das **Werkzeug** tool(s)
der **Wert, -e** value; worth
wertvoll valuable
weshalb (that's) why
wessen? whose? (8.G)
der **Wessi, -s** *(derogative nickname)* West German
die **Weste, -n** vest
der **Westen: im ~** in the west (1.1)
westlich von west of
die **Westmächte** *(pl.)* Western Allies
der **Wettbewerb, -e** contest
das **Wetter** weather (S4)
wichtig important (1.2)
wickeln (in + *acc.*) to wrap (into)
der **Widder, -** ram; Aries
widersteh'en* (+ *dat.*) to withstand
wie? how? (S1); like, as; **~ sagt man . . . ?** How does one say . . . ? (S2); **~ bitte?** What did you say, please? (S5); **so . . . ~** as . . . as (1.2); **~ lange?** how long? (4.1); **~ gesagt** as I (you, etc.) said
wieder again (S4); **schon ~** already again (S4); **immer ~** again and again, time and again (12.G); **Da sieht man's mal ~!** That just goes to show you. (15.1)

der **Wiederaufbau** rebuilding
wieder auf·bauen to rebuild
die **Wiedergeburt** rebirth
wiederho'len to repeat (S2)
die **Wiederho'lung, -en** repetition, review
wieder·hören to hear again; **Auf Wiederhören!** Good-bye. (on the phone) (6.1)
wieder·sehen* to see again; **Auf Wiedersehen!** Good-bye (S1)
(wieder)·vereinigen to (re)-unite
die **(Wieder)vereinigung** (re)-unification (14.2)
wiegen, wog, gewogen to weigh; **Lass es ~!** Have it weighed.
der **Wiener, -** the Viennese
die **Wiese, -n** meadow
Wieso' (denn)? How come? Why? (13.1)
wie viel? how much? (S3, 3.1)
wie viele? how many? (S3, 3.1)
wild wild(ly)
der **Wille, -ns, -n** will; **Wo ein ~ ist, ist auch ein Weg.** Where there's a will, there's a way.
willkom'men sein* to be welcome
willkür'lich at random
die **Wimper, -n** eyelash
der **Wind, -e** wind
windig windy (S4)
die **Windmühle, -n** wind mill / turbine
das **Windrad, ¨er** wind mill / turbine
windsurfen gehen* to go wind surfing
der **Winter, -** winter (S4); **im ~** in (the) winter (S4)
das **Winzerfest, -e** wine festival
winzig tiny
wirken to appear
wirklich really, indeed (S4)
die **Wirklichkeit** reality
die **Wirtschaft** economy
wirtschaftlich economical (ly)
der **Wirtschaftsprüfer, -** accountant
die **Wirtschaftswissenschaft** economics; economic science
das **Wirtschaftswunder** economic boom (*lit.* miracle)

wissen (weiß), wusste, gewusst to know (a fact) (6.G); **Ich weiß (nicht).** I (don't) know. (S5); **soviel' ich weiß** as far as I know
das **Wissen** knowledge
die **Wissenschaft, -en** science, academic discipline (13.1); **Natur'~** natural science(s) (13.1)
der **Wissenschaftler, -** scientist, scholar (12.1)
wissenschaftlich scientific(ally), scholarly
wittern to sense
der **Witz, -e** joke; **Mach (doch) keine ~e!** Stop joking! You're kidding!
witzig witty, funny
wo? where? (S2,6.G)
woan'ders somewhere else
wobei' where
die **Woche, -n** week (S4); **diese ~** this week (8.G); **zwei ~n** for two weeks (8.G)
das **Wochenende, -n** weekend; **am ~** on the weekend (4.1); **(Ein) schönes ~!** Have a nice weekend! (4.1)
wochenlang for weeks
wöchentlich weekly (8.G)
-wöchig weeks long
woher'? from where? (1.1)
wohin'? where to? (6.G)
das ***wo*-Kompo'situm, Kompo'sita** *wo*-compound
wohl *flavoring particle expressing probability*
das **Wohlbefinden** well-being
wohlriechend fragrant
der **Wohlstand** affluence
die **Wohngemeinschaft, -en = WG, -s** group sharing a place to live
wohnen to live, reside (1.2)
das **Wohnsilo, -s** (*coll.*) (high-rise) apartment (cluster)
der **Wohnsitz, -e** residence
die **Wohnung, -en** apartment (6.1)
der **Wohnwagen, -** camper
das **Wohnzimmer, -** living room (6.1)
der **Wolf, ¨e** wolf
die **Wolke, -n** cloud
die **Wolle** wool; **Baum~** cotton
wollen (will), wollte, gewollt to want to (5.G)
das **Wort, -e** (connected) word; **mit anderen ~en** in other words; **rührende ~e**

heartfelt words; **mit eigenen ~en** in your own words

das **Wort, ¨er** (individual) word; **vorher'gehende Wort** antecedent; **zusam'mengesetzte ~** compound noun

das **Wörtchen, -** little word

das **Wörterbuch, ¨er** dictionary

der **Wortschatz** vocabulary

das **Wunder, -** wonder, miracle

wunderbar wonderful(ly) (S1)

sich **wundern** to wonder; **~ Sie sich nicht!** Don't be surprised.

wunderschön very beautiful (14.1)

der **Wunsch, ¨e** wish (11.1); **~traum, ¨e** ideal dream

(sich) **wünschen** to wish (4.1)

die **Wunschwelt** ideal world

die **Wurst, ¨e** sausage (2.1); **Das ist (mir) doch ~!** I don't care.

das **Würstchen, -** wiener, hot dog (2.2)

würzen to season

die **Wut** anger

Z

die **Zahl, -en** number (S3); **Ordinal'~** ordinal number (4.1)

zählen to count (S3)

der **Zahn, ¨e** tooth (9.1); **sich die Zähne putzen** to brush one's teeth (9.G); **die dritten Zähne** dentures

der **Zahnarzt, ¨e / die Zahnärztin, -nen** dentist (12.1)

die **Zahnbürste, -n** toothbrush

die **Zahnmedizin'** dentistry

die **Zahnpasta, -pasten** tooth paste

die **Zahnradbahn, -en** rack-railway

der **Zahntechniker, -** dental technician

die **Zange, -n** pliers

zart tender

zärtlich affectionate(ly) (11.1)

die **Zärtlichkeit** affection

der **Zauber** magic (power)

der **Zauberspruch, ¨e** magic spell

der **Zaun, ¨e** fence

z. B. (zum Beispiel) e.g. (for example)

die **Zehe, -n** toe

das **Zeichen, -** signal, sign, indication

der **Zeichentrickfilm, -e** cartoon, animated movie

die **Zeichnung, -en** drawing

der **Zeigefinger, -** index finger

zeigen to show (5.1); **Zeig mal!** Show me (us, etc.)!

die **Zeile, -n** line

die **Zeit, -en** time (S5); tense; **die gute alte ~** the good old days

die **Zeitform, -en** tense

zeitgenössisch contemporary

zeitlos timeless

die **Zeitschrift, -en** magazine (10.1)

die **Zeitung, -en** newspaper (10.1); **Wochen~** weekly newspaper

zelebrie'ren to celebrate

die **Zelle, -n** cell, booth

das **Zelt, -e** tent

zelten to camp

der **Zentner, -** centner (50 kg)

zentral' central(ly)

das **Zentrum, Zentren** center; **im ~** downtown

zerbomben to destroy by bombing

zerbrechen* to break

zermatschen to squash

zerschlagen* to break, smash

zerstören to destroy (15.1)

die **Zerstörung** destruction

zerstreuen to disperse

das **Zeugnis,-se** report card; certificate

die **Ziege, -n** goat

ziehen, zog, gezogen to pull (11.2); to raise (vegetables, etc.)

ziehen, zog, ist gezogen to move (relocate)

das **Ziel, -e** goal, objective; destination

ziemlich quite, fairly (6.1)

die **Zigeu'ner, -** gypsy

das **Zimmer, -** room (S2)

der **Zimmernachweis, -e** room-referral service

die **Zimmervermittlung** room-referral agency

der **Zimt** cinnamon

das **Zitat', -e** quote

die **Zitro'ne, -n** lemon (2.1)

die **Zitro'nenlimona'de** carbonated lemonade

der **Zitro'nensaft, ¨e** lemonade

zittern to tremble, shake

zittrig shaky

zögern to hesitate

der **Zoll** customs; toll

die **Zone, -n** zone, area

der **Zoo, -s** zoo

der **Zorn** anger

zu- closed (7.G)

zu (+ *dat.*) to, in the direction of, at, for (purpose) (3.G); too (S3); closed (2); (+ *inf.*) to (9.G); **~ mir** to my place

zu·bereiten to prepare

zu·bleiben* (ist) to stay closed

der **Zucker** sugar (3.1)

zu·decken to cover

zuerst' (at) first (9.1)

zu·geben* to admit

der **Zufall, ¨e** coincidence; **So ein ~!** What a coincidence!

zufällig by chance; accidental(ly)

zufrie'den satisfied, content

der **Zug, ¨e** train (8.1); **mit dem ~ fahren*** to go by train (8.1)

zu·geben* to admit

zu·halten* to hold closed

das **Zuhau'se** home

zu·hören to listen (7.G); **Hören Sie gut zu!** Listen well / carefully.

der **Zuhörer, -** listener

die **Zukunft** future (12.1)

zukunftsorientiert' future-oriented

zuletzt' last (of all); finally

zu·machen to close (7.G)

zunehmend increasing(ly)

die **Zunge, -n** tongue

der **Zungenbrecher, -** tongue twister

zurück'- back (7.G)

zurück'·bleiben* to stay behind

zurück'·bringen* to bring back

zurück'·fliegen* to fly back

zurück'·geben* to give back, return

zurück'·halten* to hold back

zurück'·kommen* to come back, return (7.G)

zurück'·nehmen* to take back

zurück'·sehen* to look back

zurück'·weichen* to with-draw

sich **zurück'·ziehen*** to withdraw

zusam'men together (2.1); **alle ~** all together; **~gewürfelt** thrown together

zusam'men·arbeiten to work together, cooperate

der **Zusam'menbruch** collapse

zusam'men·fassen to summarize

die **Zusam'menfassung, -en** summary

die **Zusam'mengehörigkeit** affiliation; solidarity

zusam'men·wachsen* to grow together (15.2)

der **Zuschauer, -** spectator (10.2)

zu·schließen* to lock

zu·sehen* to watch; see to it

der **Zustand, ¨-e** conditions

zuständig für responsible for

zu·stimmen to agree

zuverlässig reliable, reliably (11.1)

die **Zuverlässigkeit** reliability

zuvor' previously; **wie nie ~** as never before

die **Zuwanderung** immigration

zwar though

die **Zwiebel, -n** onion

der **Zwilling, -e** twin; Gemini

zwischen (+ *acc. / dat.*) between (6.G); **in~** in the meantime; **~durch** in between

die **Zwischenlandung, -en** stop over

die **Zwischenzeit** time in between; **in der ~** in the meantime, meanwhile

zwitschern to chirp

(das) **Zypern** Cypres

der **Zypriot', -en, -en** Cypriot

zypriscn Cypriot

English– German Vocabulary

Except for numbers, pronouns, and **da-/wo-** compounds, the English–German Vocabulary includes all ACTIVE words presented in this book. If you are looking for certain idioms, feminine equivalents, or other closely related words, use the key word given and look it up in the German–English vocabulary. Irregular *t*-verbs ("irregular weak verbs") and *n*-verbs ("strong verbs") are indicated by an asterisk (*); check their forms and auxiliaries in the list of principal parts in the Appendix.

A

able; to be ~ können*
about (approximately) ungefähr, etwa
above über (+ *dat.* / *acc.*); **~ all** vor allem
abroad im/ins Ausland
academic discipline die Wissenschaft, -en
to **accept** an·nehmen*
ache: I have a (head)~. Ich habe (Kopf)schmerzen.
acquaintance der Bekannte (ein Bekannter) / die Bekannte, -n, -n
across (from) gegenüber (von + *dat.*)
actor der Schauspieler, -
actual(ly) eigentlich
ad die Anzeige, -n
address die Adresse, -n; **return ~** der Absender, -
advertising die Werbung
advice der Rat
affectionate zärtlich
afraid: to be ~ (of) Angst haben* (vor + *dat.*)
after (time) nach (+ *dat.*); **(conj. + past perf.)** nachdem
afternoon der Nachmittag, -e; **this ~** heute Nachmittag; **tomorrow ~** morgen Nachmittag; **yesterday ~** gestern Nachmittag; **in the ~** nachmittags, am Nachmittag; **every ~** nachmittags
afterwards danach
again wieder, noch (ein)mal; **Could you say that ~?** Wie bitte?; **~ and ~** immer wieder
against gegen (+ *acc.*)
ago vor (+ *dat.*); **a week ~** vor einer Woche
ahead: straight ~ geradeaus
aid die Hilfe
air die Luft
airplane das Flugzeug, -e
airport der Flughafen, ¨
all all-, alles (*sg.*); **That's ~.** Das ist alles.; **above ~** vor allem; **after ~** schließlich; **~ right** Na gut.; **~ sorts of** allerlei
to **allow** erlauben
allowed: to be ~ to dürfen*
almost fast
alone allein
along (prefix) mit-; **(adv.)** entlang
already schon
also auch, ebenfalls
although (conj.) obwohl
always immer
America (das) Amerika
American (adj.) amerikanisch; **(person)** der Amerikaner, -
among unter (+ *acc.* / *dat.*)
and und
angry: to get ~ about sich ärgern über (+ *acc.*)
animal das Tier, -e
annoyed: to get ~ about sich ärgern über (+ *acc.*)
another noch ein
to **answer** antworten
answer die Antwort, -en
anyhow sowieso
anyway sowieso
apart auseinander
apartment die Wohnung, -en
to **appear (to be)** scheinen*, aus·sehen*
to **applaud** klatschen
apple der Apfel, ¨
to **apply (for)** sich bewerben* (um)
approximately ungefähr, etwa
April der April; **in ~** im April
architect der Architekt, -en, -en
area das Gebiet, -e, die Gegend, -en
area code die Vorwahl, -en
arm der Arm, -e
armchair der Sessel, -
around (prefix) um-; (*prep.*) um (+ *acc.*)
arrival die Ankunft
to **arrive (in)** an·kommen* (in + *dat.*)
art die Kunst, ¨e
artist der Künstler, -
as wie; **~ . . . ~** so . . . wie
to **ask** fragen, bitten* (um); **to ~ a question** eine Frage stellen
at (the side of) an (+ *dat.*); **(o'clock)** um . . . (Uhr); **(the place of)** bei (+ *dat.*); **(a store, etc.)** bei
athletic sportlich; **un~** unsportlich
ATM machine der Geldautomat, -en, -en (7.1)
attention: to pay ~ auf·passen
attractive attraktiv, hübsch
attribute die Eigenschaft, -en
August der August; **in ~** im August
aunt die Tante, -n
Austria (das) Österreich
Austrian (language) österreichisch; **(person)** der Österreicher, -
author der Autor, -en
available frei
away (prefix) ab
awesome: (That's) ~! Wahnsinn!

B

back (prefix) zurück-
bad(ly) schlecht; schlimm; **too ~** schade
bag die Tasche, -n
baggage das Gepäck
to **bake** backen*
bakery die Bäckerei, -en
balcony der Balkon, -s / -e

ballet das Ballett
banana die Banane, -n
bank die Bank, -en
banknote der (Geld)schein, -e
barely kaum
to **bathe** baden
bath(room) das Bad, ¨-er; **to take a ~** sich baden
to **be** sein*; **(become)** werden*; **Be . . . !** Sei (Seid, Seien Sie) . . . !
bean die Bohne, -n
beautiful (wunder)schön
because (conj.) weil, denn; **~ of** wegen (+ *gen.* / [*dat.*])
to **become** werden*
bed das Bett, -en; **~room** das Schlafzimmer, -
beer das Bier, -e
before vor (+ *acc.* / *dat.*); **(conj.)** bevor; **not ~ (time)** erst; **(adv.)** vorher
to **begin** beginnen*, an·fangen*
beginning der Anfang, ¨-e; **in the ~** am Anfang; **at the ~ of the week** Anfang der Woche
behind hinter (+ *acc.* / *dat.*)
to **believe (in)** glauben (an + *acc.*); **(things)** Ich glaube es.; **(persons)** Ich glaube ihm/ihr.; **You better ~ it!** Und ob!; **That's hard to ~!** (Das ist doch) unglaublich!; **I don't ~ it!** Das gibt's doch nicht!
belly der Bauch, ¨-e
to **belong to** gehören (+ *dat.*)
below unter (+ *acc.* / *dat.*)
beside neben (+ *acc.* / *dat.*)
besides außer (+ *dat.*); **(adv.)** außerdem
best best-; **it's ~** am besten; **All the ~!** Alles Gute!
bet: you~! Und ob!
better besser; **You ~ believe it!** Und ob!
between zwischen (+ *acc.* / *dat.*)
bicycle das Fahrrad, ¨-er
to **bicycle** mit dem Fahrrad fahren*
big groß (ö)
to **bike** mit dem Fahrrad fahren*
bill die Rechnung, -en
billion (US) die Milliarde, -n
bird der Vogel, ¨-
birthday der Geburtstag, -e; **on/for the ~** zum Geburtstag; **When is your ~?** Wann haben Sie Geburtstag?; **My ~ is on the . . .** Ich habe am . . .(s)ten Geburtstag.; **My ~ is in . . .** Ich habe im . . . Geburtstag.; **Happy ~!** Alles Gute/ Herzlichen Glückwunsch zum Geburtstag!
bit: a little ~ of ein bisschen
black schwarz (ä)
blackboard die Tafel, -n
blouse die Bluse, -n
blue blau
boarding house die Pension, -en
body der Körper, -
book das Buch, ¨-er
bookstore die Buchhandlung, -en
border die Grenze, -n
bored: to get (or be) ~ sich langweilen
boring langweilig
born geboren (ist); **I was ~ May 3, 1968, in Ulm.** Ich bin am 3. 5. 68 in Ulm geboren.
both (things, sg.) beides; **(pl.)** beide
bottle die Flasche, -n; **a ~ of . . .** eine Flasche . . .
boy der Junge, -n, -n
bread das Brot, -e
breakfast das Frühstück; **(What's) for ~?** (Was gibt's) zum Frühstück?; **to eat ~** frühstücken
bridge die Brücke, -n
bright (light) hell; intelligent
to **bring** bringen*; **to ~ along** mit·bringen*
brother der Bruder, ¨-; **~s and sisters** die Geschwister (*pl.*)
brown braun
to **brush (one's teeth)** sich (die Zähne) putzen
to **build** bauen, auf·bauen; **to re~** wieder auf·bauen; **to be built** entstehen*; **building** das Gebäude, -; der Bau, -ten
bus der Bus, -se
business das Geschäft, -e
businessman der Geschäftsmann, ¨-er
business management: graduate in ~ Betriebswirt, -e
businesspeople Geschäftsleute
businesswoman die Geschäftsfrau, -en
but aber; doch; **not only . . . ~ also** nicht nur . . . , sondern auch
butter die Butter
to **buy** kaufen
by (prefix) vorbei-; **(prep.)** von (+ *dat.*)

C

café das Café, -s
cafeteria (student) die Mensa
cake der Kuchen, -
to **call** rufen*; **to ~ (up)** an·rufen*, telefonieren; **to ~ (name)** nennen*; **to be ~ed** heißen*
campground der Campingplatz, ¨-e
can können*
Canada (das) Kanada
Canadian (adj.) kanadisch; **(person)** der Kanadier, -
candle die Kerze, -n
capital die Hauptstadt, ¨-e
car das Auto, -s, der Wagen, -; **railroad ~** der Wagen, -
card die Karte, -n; **post ~** die Postkarte, -n; **telephone ~** die Telefonkarte, -n
cardigan die Jacke, -n
to **care: Take ~!** Mach's gut!
Careful! Vorsicht!
carpet der Teppich, -e
carrot die Karotte, -n
to **carry** tragen*
case: in any ~ jedenfalls
cash das Bargeld; **~ register** die Kasse, -n
cashier's window die Kasse, -n
cat die Katze, -n
cathedral der Dom, -e
to **celebrate** feiern
celebration das Fest, -e, die Feier, -n
cellular phone das Handy, -s
cent der Cent, -s
center die Mitte
certain(ly) bestimmt, sicher(lich)
certificate der Schein, -e
chair der Stuhl, ¨-e; **arm ~** der Sessel, -
chalk die Kreide
champagne der Sekt
change das Kleingeld

to **change** (sich) ändern, (sich) verändern; **(clothing)** sich um·ziehen*; **(money, etc.)** wechseln, um·tauschen; **(trains)** um·steigen*
channel das Programm, -e
characteristic die Eigenschaft, -en
charming charmant
cheap billig
check der Scheck, -s; die Rechnung, -en
cheese der Käse, -
chic schick
child das Kind, -er
choice (of) die Auswahl (an + *dat.*)
choir der Chor, ⸚e
Christmas (das) Weihnachten; **at/for ~** zu Weihnachten
church die Kirche, -n
citizen der Bürger, -
city die Stadt ⸚e; **~ hall** das Rathaus, ⸚er; **~ map** der Stadtplan, ⸚e
civil servant der Beamte (ein Beamter) / die Beamtin, -nen
to **clap** klatschen
class (group) die Klasse, -n; **(time)** die Stunde, -n; **(instruction, school)** der Unterricht; **(instruction, university)** die Vorlesung, -en
clean sauber
to **clean** putzen
clerk der Angestellte (ein Angestellter) / die Angestellte, -n, -n; **(civil servant)** der Beamte (ein Beamter) / die Beamtin, -nen; **(salesman)** der Verkäufer, -
clock die Uhr, -en; **o'clock** Uhr
to **close** zu·machen
closed (prefix) zu-; **(prep.)** zu, geschlossen
closet der Schrank, ⸚e
clothing die Kleidung
coat der Mantel, ⸚
coast die Küste, -n
coffee der Kaffee
cola drink die Cola
cold kalt (ä)
cold: to catch a ~ sich erkälten
to **collect** sammeln
color die Farbe, -n; **What ~ is . . . ?** Welche Farbe hat . . . ?
colorful bunt; diverse
to **comb** (sich) kämmen
to **come** kommen*; **to ~ along** mit·kommen*; **to ~ back** zurück·kommen*; **to ~ in** herein·kommen*; **That comes to . . . (altogether).** Das kostet (zusammen) . . . ; **Oh, ~ on!** Ach was!
comfortable bequem, gemütlich; **un~** ungemütlich, unbequem
comical komisch
compact disc, CD die CD, -s
company die Firma, Firmen; **large ~** das Unternehmen, -
to **compare** vergleichen, verglich, verglichen
to **complain (about)** (sich) beschweren (über + *acc.*)
complicated kompliziert; **un~** unkompliziert
composer der Komponist, -en, -en
concern die Sorge, -n
to **be concerned (about)** sich Sorgen machen (um)
concert das Konzert, -e
condo die Eigentumswohnung, -en
congenial sympathisch; **un~** unsympathisch
to **congratulate** gratulieren
congratulation der Glückwunsch, ⸚e; **~s!** Herzliche Glückwünsche!; **~s on your birthday!** Herzlichen Glückwunsch zum Geburtstag!
to **connect** verbinden*
construction der Bau
container der Behälter, -
to **continue** weiter·gehen*, weiter·machen
convenient bequem
convivial gemütlich
to **cook** kochen
cookie das Plätzchen, -
cool kühl
corner die Ecke, -n
correct richtig
to **cost** kosten
council der Rat
to **count** zählen
counter der Schalter, -
country das Land, ⸚er; **into the ~(side) / in the ~(side)** aufs / auf dem Land
couple: a ~ of ein paar
course der Kurs, -e; **(~ of study)** das Studium; **of ~** natürlich; (na) klar
cousin der Cousin, -s / die Kusine, -n
cozy gemütlich
crazy verrückt; **(That's) ~!** Wahnsinn!
credit card die Kreditkarte, -n
to **cry** weinen
cucumber die Gurke, -n
cup die Tasse, -n; **a ~ of . . .** eine Tasse . . .
cupboard der Schrank, ⸚e
cultural(ly) kulturell
curtain der Vorhang, ⸚e

D

daily täglich
to **damage** schaden
to **dance** tanzen
danger die Gefahr, -en
dangerous gefährlich
dark dunkel
date (calendar) das Datum, Daten; **What ~ is today?** Welches Datum ist heute?
daughter die Tochter, ⸚
day der Tag, -e; **during the ~** am Tag; **one ~** eines Tages; **all ~ long, the whole ~** den ganzen Tag; **each ~** jeden Tag; **in those ~s** damals
dear lieb-
December der Dezember; **in ~** im Dezember
to **decide (on / about)** sich entscheiden* (für / gegen)
decision die Entscheidung, -en
definitely unbedingt
degree der Abschluss, ⸚e
dentist der Zahnarzt, ⸚e / die Zahnärztin, -nen
to **depart** (from) ab·fahren*
departure die Abfahrt, -en
to **depend: That ~s.** Das kommt darauf an.
dependent unselbstständig
to **describe** beschreiben*
desk der Schreibtisch, -e
dessert der Nachtisch
to **destroy** zerstören
to **develop** (sich) entwickeln; **~ apart** sich auseinander entwickeln
to **die** sterben (stirbt), starb, ist gestorben
difference der Unterschied, -e

different(ly) verschieden, anders; **Say it ~!** Sagen Sie es anders!; **s.th. ~** etwas anderes
difficult schwer, schwierig
dining room das Esszimmer, -
dinner das Mittagessen, das Abendessen
diploma der Abschluss, ¨-e
dirt der Schmutz
dirty schmutzig
to **discard** weg·werfen*
dishonest unehrlich
to **divide** teilen
divorce die Scheidung, -en
divorced geschieden
to **do** tun*, machen
doctor der Arzt, ¨-e / die Ärztin, -nen
dog der Hund, -e
dollar der Dollar, -(s)
done fertig
door die Tür, -en
dorm das Studentenwohnheim, -e
downstairs unten
to **dream (of)** träumen (von)
dress das Kleid, -er
dressed: to get ~ (sich) an·ziehen*; **to get un~** (sich) aus·ziehen*
dresser die Kommode, -n
to **drink** trinken*
to **drive** fahren*; **to ~ on (keep on driving)** weiter·fahren*; **to ~ up** hinauf·fahren*
drugstore die Drogerie, -n
dull langweilig
during während (+ *gen.*)
DVD die DVD,-s
dynamic temperamentvoll

E

each jed-
ear das Ohr, -en
earlier früher
early früh
to **earn** verdienen
earth die Erde
east der Osten; **~ of** östlich von
Easter Ostern; **at/for ~** zu Ostern
East German der Ostdeutsche (ein Ostdeutscher) / die Ostdeutsche, -n, -n; *(derogatory nickname)* der Ossi, -s
easy leicht
to **eat** essen*
economy die Wirtschaft
educated gebildet; **un~** ungebildet
education die Ausbildung
egg das Ei, -er
e-mail die E-Mail, -s
employee der Angestellte (ein Angestellter) / die Angestellte, -n, -n
empty leer
end das Ende; **in the ~** am Ende, schließlich; **at the ~ of the week** am Ende der Woche
to **end** auf·hören
engaged verlobt; **to get ~ (to)** sich verloben (mit)
engineer der Ingenieur, -e
England (das) England
English *(adj.)* englisch; **in ~** auf Englisch; **(language)** Englisch; **Do you speak ~?** Sprechen Sie Englisch?; **(person)** der Engländer, -
to **enjoy: ~ your meal.** Guten Appetit!
enough genug; **That's ~!** Jetzt habe ich aber genug!
to **enter** herein·kommen*
enterprising unternehmungslustig
entertainment die Unterhaltung
entire(ly) ganz
entrance der Eingang, ¨-e
environment die Umwelt
environmentally aware umweltbewusst
equal gleich
especially besonders, vor allem
etc. = et cetera usw. = und so weiter
euro der Euro, -s
European europäisch
European Union die Europäische Union
even sogar
evening der Abend, -e; **this ~** heute Abend; **tomorrow ~** morgen Abend; **yesterday ~** gestern Abend; **in the ~** abends, am Abend; **every ~** jeden Abend; **Good ~!** Guten Abend!
evening meal das Abendessen
every jed-; **~ three years** alle drei Jahre
everything alles
everywhere überall
exact(ly) genau
exam die Prüfung, -en; **to pass an ~** eine Prüfung bestehen*; **to flunk an ~** bei einer Prüfung durch·fallen*; **take an ~** eine Prüfung machen
excellent ausgezeichnet
except for außer (+ *dat.*)
exchange der Umtausch
to **exchange** um·tauschen, aus·tauschen, wechseln
exciting spannend
to **excuse** sich entschuldigen; **~ me!** Entschuldigen Sie bitte! Entschuldigung! Verzeihung!
exit der Ausgang, ¨-e
expensive teuer
to **experience** erleben
experience die Erfahrung, -en
to **explain** erklären
extremely (loud) unheimlich (laut)
eye das Auge, -n

F

face das Gesicht, -er
fairly ziemlich
fairy tale das Märchen, -
to **fall** fallen*; **to ~ in love (with)** sich verlieben (in + *acc.*)
fall der Herbst, -e; **in (the) ~** im Herbst
false falsch
family die Familie, -n
famous berühmt
fantastic fantastisch, toll
far weit
fast schnell
fat dick; **to be ~tening** dick machen
father der Vater, ¨
fear die Angst, ¨-e
to **fear** Angst haben* vor (+ *dat.*)
February der Februar; **in ~** im Februar
to **feel (a certain way)** sich fühlen; **How are you (feeling)?** Wie geht es Ihnen? Wie geht's?; **I'm (feeling) . . .** Es geht mir . . . ; **to ~ like (doing s.th.)** Lust haben* (zu + *inf.*)
to **fetch** (sich) holen
few einig- *(pl.)*; wenig-; ein paar

fiancé(e) der Verlobte (ein Verlobter) / die Verlobte, -n, -n
field das Feld, -er; **(~ of study)** das Fach, ¨er; **(of specialization)** die Fachrichtung, -en; **(major)** das Hauptfach, ¨er, das Schwerpunktfach, ¨er; **(minor)** das Nebenfach, ¨ -er
to **fill out** aus·füllen
film der Film, -e
finally endlich
to **finance** finanzieren
to **find** finden*
fine gut (besser, best-), schön
finger der Finger, -
finished fertig
firm die Firma, Firmen
first erst-; **~ of all, at ~** (zu)erst
to **fish** angeln; **to go ~ing** angeln gehen
fish der Fisch, -e
flavoring particle for: admiration aber; ***(curiosity/interest)*** denn; ***(concern, impatience, assurance)*** doch; ***(emphasis)*** ja
flight (plane) der Flug, ¨e
to **fly** fliegen*
floor: on the first / ground ~ im Parterre; **on the second ~** im ersten Stock
flower die Blume, -n
to **follow** folgen (ist) (+ *dat.*); **~ing** folgend
food das Essen; **Enjoy your ~!** Guten Appetit!
foot der Fuß, ¨e
for für (+ *acc.*); **(since)** seit (+ *dat.*); **(conj.)** denn
to **forbid** verbieten*
forbidden verboten
foreign ausländisch
foreigner der Ausländer, -
forest der Wald, ¨er
to **forget** vergessen*
fork die Gabel, -n
formerly früher
France (das) Frankreich
free frei
French (adj.) französisch; **in ~** auf Französisch; **(language)** Französisch; **Do you speak ~?** Sprechen Sie Französisch?; **(person)** der Franzose, -n, -n / die Französin, -nen
(French) fries die Pommes (frites) *(pl.)*
fresh frisch
Friday (der) Freitag; **on Fridays** freitags; **~ night** Freitag Abend; **~ nights** freitagnachts
friend der Freund, -e
friendly freundlich; **un~** unfreundlich
friendship die Freundschaft, -en
from von (+ *dat.*); **(a native of)** aus (+ *dat.*); **I'm ~ . . .** Ich bin aus . . . , Ich komme aus . . .; **(numbers) ~ . . . to** von . . . bis; **(place) ~ . . . to** von . . . zu/nach
front: in ~ of vor (+ *acc. / dat.*)
fruit das Obst
full voll
fun der Spaß; **to be ~** Spaß machen; **to make ~ (of)** sich lustig machen (über + *acc.*)
funny lustig, witzig; komisch
furniture die Möbel *(pl.)*
future die Zukunft

G

game das Spiel, -e
garage die Garage, -n
garbage der Abfall, ¨e
garden der Garten, ¨
gate das Tor, -e
gentleman der Herr, -n, -en
genuine(ly) echt
German (adj.) deutsch; **in ~** auf Deutsch; **(language)** Deutsch; **Do you speak ~?** Sprechen Sie Deutsch?; **(person)** der Deutsche (ein Deutscher) / die Deutsche, -n, -n
Germany (das) Deutschland
to **get (become)** werden*; **(fetch)** holen; **(receive)** bekommen*; **to ~ off** aus·steigen*; **to ~ on *or* in** ein·steigen*; **to ~ up** auf·stehen*; **to ~ to know** kennenlernen; **to go and ~** (sich) holen; **to ~ used to** sich gewöhnen an (+ *acc.*); **~ well soon!** Gute Besserung; **to ~ together** sich treffen*
girl das Mädchen, -
to **give** geben*; **(as a present)** schenken
glad froh
gladly gern (lieber, liebst-)
Glad to meet you. Freut mich.
glance (at) der Blick (auf + *acc.*)
glass das Glas, ¨er; **a ~ of . . .** ein Glas . . .
to **go** gehen*; **to ~ by (bus, etc.)** fahren* mit; **to ~ by plane** fliegen*; **to ~ out** aus·gehen*; **to ~ up** hinauf·fahren*
going: What's ~ on? Was ist los?
good gut (besser, best-); **~-looking** gut aussehend
Good-bye! Auf Wiedersehen! Tschüss!; **(on the phone)** Auf Wiederhören!
goodness: My ~! Ach du meine Güte!
grade die Note, -n
to **graduate** das Studium ab·schließen*
grandfather der Großvater ¨
grandmother die Großmutter, ¨
grandparents die Großeltern *(pl.)*
gray grau
great (size) groß; **(terrific)** prima, toll, herrlich, klasse, spitze
green grün
greeting der Gruß, ¨e
grief: Good ~! Ach du meine Güte!
groceries die Lebensmittel *(pl.)*
ground level das Erdgeschoss
to **grow** wachsen*; **to ~ together** zusammen·wachsen*
to **guarantee** garantieren
guest der Gast, ¨e
to **guide along** vorbei·führen (an + *dat.*)
guitar die Gitarre, -n

H

hair das Haar, -e
half halb; **in ~ an hour** in einer halben Stunde
hallway der Flur
hand die Hand, ¨e
to **hang (up)** hängen
to **hang (be hanging)** hängen*
to **happen** geschehen*, passieren (ist)
happy glücklich, froh; **I'm ~ for you.** Ich freue mich für dich.
hard (difficult) schwer; **~-working** fleißig

hardly kaum
to **have** haben*; **to ~ to** müssen*
head der Kopf, ¨-e
health die Gesundheit
healthy gesund (ü)
to **hear** hören
heavy schwer
Hello! Guten Tag!
help die Hilfe
to **help** helfen* (+ *dat.*)
her ihr
here hier
Hi! Guten Tag! Hallo!
high hoch (hoh-) (höher, höchst)
to **hike** wandern (ist)
hiker der Wanderer, -
his sein
historical(ly) historisch
history die Geschichte
hobby das Hobby, -s
to **hold** halten*
holiday der Feiertag, -e
home: at ~ zu Hause; **(toward) ~** nach Hause; **at the ~ of** bei (+ *dat.*); **(homeland)** die Heimat
honest ehrlich
to **hope** hoffen; **I ~** hoffentlich
hoffentlich hopefully
horse das Pferd, -e
hot heiß
hotel das Hotel, -s, der Gasthof, ¨-e, die Pension, -en
hour die Stunde, -n; **for ~s** stundenlang
house das Haus, ¨-er
household der Haushalt
househusband der Hausmann, ¨-er
housemate der Mitbewohner, -
housewife die Hausfrau, -en
how wie; **~ much?** wie viel?; **~ many?** wie viele?; **~ much is / are . . . ?** Was kostet / kosten . . . ?; **~ come?** wieso?; **~ are you?** Wie geht's?, Wie geht es Ihnen?
however aber, allerdings, doch, jedoch
human being der Mensch, -en, -en
hunger der Hunger
hungry: I'm ~. Ich habe Hunger.
to **hurry** sich beeilen
to **hurt** weh·tun*; **My (throat) hurts.** Mir tut (der Hals) weh; **(to damage)** schaden
husband der Mann, ¨-er

I

ice, ice cream das Eis
ID der Ausweis, -e
idea die Idee, -n; **(I have) no ~!** Keine Ahnung!
identification der Ausweis, -e
if (conj.) wenn; ob
ill krank (ä)
to **imagine** sich vor·stellen; **I ~ that . . .** Ich stelle mir vor, dass . . .
immediately sofort
impatient ungeduldig
important wichtig
impossible unmöglich; **That's ~!** Das gibt's doch nicht!
in in (+ *dat. / acc.*)
income das Einkommen, -
inconvenient unbequem
incredible einmalig, unglaublich
independent selbstständig
individual(ly) einzeln
inexpensive billig
indeed wirklich, doch
industrious(ly) fleißig
inn der Gasthof, ¨-e
insecure unsicher
inside in (+ *dat. / acc.*)
in spite of trotz (+ *gen. / [dat.]*); **~ that** trotzdem
instead of (an)statt (+ *gen.*)
intelligent intelligent
interest (in) das Interesse (an + *dat.*)
interested: to be ~ in sich interessieren für
interesting interessant; **really ~** unheimlich interessant
internship das Praktikum, Praktiken
to **invite (to)** ein·laden (lädt ein), lud ein, eingeladen (zu)
island die Insel, -n
isn't it? nicht wahr?
Italian *(adj.)* italienisch; **in ~** auf Italienisch; **(language)** Italienisch; **Do you speak ~?** Sprechen Sie Italienisch?; **(person)** der Italiener, -
Italy (das) Italien
its sein, ihr

J

jacket die Jacke, -n
jam die Marmelade, -n
January der Januar; **in ~** im Januar
jeans die Jeans *(pl.)*
job die Arbeit; **(position)** die Stelle, -n
joint(ly) gemeinsam
juice der Saft, ¨-e
July der Juli; **in ~** im Juli
to **jump** springen*
June der Juni; **in ~** im Juni
just gerade; **~ like** genau(so) wie; **~ when** gerade als

K

to **keep** behalten*; **to ~ in shape** sich fit halten*
key der Schlüssel, -
kind nett; **what ~ of (a)?** was für (ein)?
king der König, -e
kitchen die Küche, -n
knee das Knie, -
knife das Messer, -
to **know (be acquainted with)** kennen*; **(a fact)** wissen*; **(a skill)** können*
knowledge die Kenntnis, -se
known: well-~ bekannt

L

lab(oratory) das Labor, -s (*or* -e)
lacking: to be ~ fehlen
lady die Dame, -n; **old ~** die Alte, -n, -n
lake der See, -n
lamp die Lampe, -n
to **land** landen (ist)
landscape die Landschaft
language die Sprache, -n
large groß (ö)
last letzt-
to **last (duration)** dauern
late spät; **How ~ is it?** Wie spät ist es?, Wie viel Uhr ist es?
later später; **See you ~.** Bis später!
to **laugh** lachen
lawyer der Rechtsanwalt, ¨-e / die Rechtsanwältin, -nen
to **lay (down)** legen
lazy faul; **to be ~** faulenzen
to **lead** führen
to **learn** lernen
to **leave (behind)** lassen*; **~ from** ab·fahren*; **(a place)** verlassen*
lecture die Vorlesung, -en; **~ hall** der Hörsaal, -säle
left links; link-
leg das Bein, -e

leisure time die Freizeit
lemonade die Limonade, -n
to **let** lassen*
letter der Brief, -e
lettuce der Salat
library die Bibliothek, -en
to **lie (to be located)** liegen*; **to ~ down** sich (hin·)legen
life das Leben
light (weight) leicht; **(bright)** hell
likable sympathisch; **un~** unsympathisch
like wie; **just ~** genau(so) wie; **s.th. ~** so etwas wie
to **like** gefallen*; **I ~ it.** Es gefällt mir.; **I would ~ (to have)** ich möchte, ich hätte gern
likewise ebenfalls
to **link** verbinden*
to **listen** zu·hören (+ *dat.*); **to ~ to** sich an·hören
little klein; **(amount)** wenig, ein bisschen; **(some)** etwas
to **live** leben; **(reside)** wohnen
living room das Wohnzimmer, -
long (adj.) lang (ä); **(adv.)** lange; **how ~?** wie lange?; **So ~!** Tschüss! Bis später!
to **look** sehen*; **to ~ (like)** aus·sehen* (wie + *nom.*); **to ~ at** sich an·sehen*, sich an·schauen; **to ~ for** suchen; **to ~ forward to** sich freuen auf (+ *acc.*); **~!** Schau mal!
to **lose** verlieren*
loud(ly) laut
love die Liebe; **to be in ~ (with)** verliebt sein* (in + *acc.*); **to fall in ~ (with)** sich verlieben (in + *acc.*)
to **love** lieben
luck das Glück; **tough ~** das Pech; **Tough ~!** Pech gehabt!
lucky: to be ~ Glück haben*; **I was (you were, etc.) ~.** Glück gehabt!
luggage das Gepäck
lunch das Mittagessen, -; **for ~** zum Mittagessen

M

mad: That makes me ~. Das ärgert mich.
magazine die Zeitschrift, -en
mail die Post
mailbox der Briefkasten, ¨
mainly vor allem
major (field of study) das Hauptfach, ¨er
to **make** machen
man der Mann, ¨er; **(human being)** der Mensch, -en, -en; **gentle~** der Herr, -n, -en; **old ~** der Alte (ein Alter)
many viele; **how ~?** wie viele?; **~ a** manch-
map die Landkarte, -n; **(city ~)** der Stadtplan, ¨e
March der März; **in ~** im März)
market der Markt, ¨e
marmalade die Marmelade, -n
marriage die Ehe, -n
married verheiratet; **un~** unverheiratet
to **marry, get married** heiraten
matter: (That) doesn't ~. Das ist doch egal. (Das) macht nichts.; **What's the ~?** Was ist (denn) los?
may dürfen*
May der Mai; **in ~** im Mai
meal das Essen, -; **Enjoy your ~.** Guten Appetit!
to **mean (signify)** bedeuten; **(think)** meinen
meanwhile inzwischen
meat das Fleisch
to **meet (get to know)** kennenlernen; **Glad to ~ you.** Freut mich (sehr, Sie kennenzulernen); **to ~ with friends** sich mit Freunden treffen*
menu die Speisekarte, -n
merry:~ Christmas! Frohe/Fröhliche Weihnachten!
middle die Mitte; **in the ~ of** mitten in/auf (+ *dat.*); **in the ~ of the month** Mitte des Monats
milk die Milch
millennium das Jahrtausend, -e
minor (field of study) das Nebenfach, ¨er
minus minus
minute die Minute, -n; **See you in a few ~s!** Bis gleich!
missing: to be ~ fehlen
Monday (der) Montag; **~ morning** Montagmorgen; **on ~s** montags; **~ mornings** montagmorgens
money das Geld; **to make ~** Geld verdienen; **to spend ~** Geld aus·geben*
month der Monat, -e; **per ~** im Monat, pro Monat; **for one ~** einen Monat
monthly monatlich
monument das Denkmal, ¨er
more mehr; **once ~** noch (ein) mal; **~ and ~** immer mehr
morning der Morgen; **early ~** früh (morgen); **mid-~** der Vormittag; **this ~** heute Morgen; **tomorrow ~** morgen früh; **yesterday ~** gestern früh; **in the ~** morgens, am Morgen; **every ~** jeden Morgen; **Good ~!** Guten Morgen!
most meist-; am meisten
mostly meistens
mother die Mutter, ¨
mountain der Berg, -e
mouth der Mund, ¨er
movie (film) der Film, -e; **(theater)** das Kino, -s
Mr. Herr
Mrs. Frau
Ms. Frau
much viel (mehr, meist-); **how ~?** wie viel?
museum das Museum, Museen
music die Musik
musical musikalisch; **un~** unmusikalisch
must müssen*
my mein

N

name der Name, -ns, -n; **What's your ~?** Wie heißen Sie?; **My ~ is . . .** Ich heiße . . . , Mein Name ist . . .
to **name** nennen*
napkin die Serviette, -n
nation das Volk, ¨er
natural science die Naturwissenschaft, -en
nature die Natur
nature preserve das Naturschutzgebiet, -e
near (distance) nah (näher, nächst-); **(vicinity)** bei (+ *dat.*), in der Nähe von (+ *dat.*)
neat prima; schick
neck der Hals, ¨e
to **need** brauchen
neighbor der Nachbar, -n, -n

neither . . . nor weder . . . noch
never nie; ~ **before** noch nie
nevertheless trotzdem
new neu; **s.th.** ~ etwas Neues; **nothing** ~ nichts Neues; **What's ~ ?** Was gibt's Neues?
New Year's Eve Silvester; **at/on** ~ zu Silvester
news die Nachricht, -en
newspaper die Zeitung, -en
next nächst-; ~ **to** neben (+ *dat.* / *acc.*); **What comes ~?** Wie geht's weiter?
nice schön, nett
nickname der Spitzname, -ns, -n
night die Nacht, ¨-e; **to~** heute Nacht; **last** ~ gestern Nacht, heute Nacht; **Good ~!** Gute Nacht!; **at/during the** ~ nachts, in der Nacht; **every** ~ jede Nacht; **to spend the** ~ übernachten
no nein
nobody niemand
noisy laut
nonsense der Quatsch
no one niemand
noodle die Nudel, -n
noon der Mittag, -e; **today at** ~ heute Mittag; **tomorrow at** ~ morgen Mittag; **at** ~ mittags; **after~** der Nachmittag, -e
north der Norden; **in the** ~ im Norden; ~ **of** nördlich von
nose die Nase, -n
not nicht; ~ **any** kein; ~ **only . . . but also** nicht nur . . . , sondern auch; ~ **yet** noch nicht; ~ **ever** noch nie; ~ **at all** gar nicht
notebook das Heft, -e
nothing (to) nichts (zu); ~ **special** nichts Besonderes
novel der Roman, -e
November der November; **in** ~ im November
now jetzt, nun; **just** ~ gerade
number die Nummer-n, die (Ordinal)zahl, -en
nurse (male) der Krankenpfleger, -; **(female)** die Krankenschwester, -n

O

o'clock Uhr
October der Oktober; **in** ~ im Oktober
of course natürlich; doch
off ab-
to **offer** an·bieten*
office das Büro, -s
often oft
oh ach; ~, **I see!** Ach so!; ~, **come on!** Ach was!; ~ **dear!** Ach du meine Güte!
okay: That's ~. Das geht. Das macht nichts. Na gut.; **That's not ~.** Das geht nicht.
old alt (ä); ~ **man** der Alte (ein Alter); ~ **lady** die Alte, -n, -n; ~ **people** die Alten; ~ **things** das Alte
on (top of) auf (+ *acc.* / *dat.*); **(vertical surface)** an; ~ **the first of July** am ersten Juli
once einmal; ~ **more** noch (ein)mal; ~ **in a while** manchmal; **(formerly)** einst, früher
one (people, they) man
only nur; **(not before)** erst; **not ~ . . . but also** nicht nur . . . , sondern auch
open (prefix) auf-; **(adj.)** ~ auf, offen, geöffnet
to **open** öffnen, auf·machen
opera die Oper, -n
opinion: to be of an ~ halten von
opposite das Gegenteil, -e
or oder
oral presentation das Referat, -e; **to give an** ~ ein Referat halten*
orange die Orange, -n; **(color)** orange
orchestra das Orchester, -
order: in ~ to um . . . zu *(+ inf.)*
to **order** bestellen
other ander-; ~**s** andere; **the ~s** die anderen; **s.th.** ~ **(quite different)** etwas (ganz) anderes; **in ~ ways** anders
our unser
out of aus *(+ dat.)*
over (location) über *(+ acc. / dat.)*; **(finished)** vorbei; **~there** da drüben
own (adj.) eigen-

P

to **pack** packen
package das Paket, -e
page die Seite, -n; **on/to ~ . . .** auf Seite . . .
pain der Schmerz, -en; **to have** ~ Schmerzen haben*
to **paint** malen
painting das Gemälde, -
palace das Schloss, ¨-er
pants die Hose, -n
paper das Papier, -e; **(term ~)** die (Semester)arbeit, -en
parcel das Paket, -e
parents die Eltern *(pl.)*
to **pardon: ~ me!** Entschuldigung! Entschuldigen Sie! Verzeihung!
park der Park, -s
part der Teil, -e; **to take ~ (in)** teil·nehmen* (an + *dat.*)
to **participate (in)** teil·nehmen* (an + *dat.*)
partner der Partner, -
party die Party, -s; die Feier, -n
to **pass (an exam)** bestehen*; **to ~ by** vorbei·gehen* (bei + *dat.*), vorbei·kommen*, vorbei·fahren*, vorbei·führen (an + *dat.*)
passport der Pass, ¨-e
past (*prefix*) vorbei-; **in the** ~ früher
patient geduldig
to **pay (for)** (be)zahlen
pea die Erbse, -n
peace der Frieden
pen der Kuli, -s
pencil der Bleistift, -e
people die Leute *(pl.)*; **(human being)** der Mensch, -en, -en; **(as a whole or nation)** das Volk, ¨-er
pepper der Pfeffer
per pro
performance die Vorstellung, -en
perhaps vielleicht
person der Mensch, -en, -en
pharmacy die Apotheke, -n
to **phone** an·rufen*, telefonieren
physician der Arzt, ¨-e / die Ärztin, -nen
piano das Klavier, -e; **to play the** ~ Klavier spielen
to **pick up** (sich) holen
picture das Bild, -er; **to take ~s** fotografieren
piece das Stück, -e; **(of music or ballet)** das Stück, -e
pink rosa
pizza die Pizza, -s
place (location) der Platz, ¨-e; **at our** ~ bei uns; **in your** ~ an deiner Stelle
plan der Plan, ¨-e
to **plan** planen, vor·haben*
plane das Flugzeug, -e

plate der Teller, -
platform der Bahnsteig, -e
play das Stück, ¨-e
to **play** spielen; **(checkers)** Dame spielen; **(chess)** Schach spielen; **(tennis)** Tennis spielen
pleasant gemütlich; **un~** ungemütlich
to **please** gefallen*
please bitte
pleased: ~ to meet you. Freut mich.
pleasure: My ~. Nichts zu danken!
P.O. box das Postfach, ¨-er
pocket die Tasche, -n
police (force) die Polizei; **~man** der Polizist, -en, -en; **~woman** die Polizistin, -nen
pollution die Verschmutzung
poor arm (ä)
population die Bevölkerung
position die Stelle, -n
possible möglich; **That's im~.** Das ist doch nicht möglich!
postcard ***(w. picture)*** Ansichtskarte, -n
post office die Post
potato die Kartoffel, -n
pound das Pfund, -e; **a ~ of . . .** ein Pfund . . . ; **two ~s of . . .** zwei Pfund . . .
power die Macht, ¨-e
practical(ly) praktisch
precise genau to
prefer lieber tun*; vor·ziehen*
to **prepare** vor·bereiten; **~ o.s. (for)** sich vor·bereiten (auf + *acc.*)
present (gift) das Geschenk, -e
preservation die Erhaltung
pretty hübsch
private privat
probably wahrscheinlich
problem das Problem, -e; **(That's) no ~.** (Das ist) kein Problem.
profession der Beruf, -e; **choice of ~** die Berufswahl
professor der Professor, -en
program das Programm, -e; die Sendung, -en
prohibited verboten
to **promise** versprechen*
to **protect** schützen, schonen
protection der Schutz
proud (of) stolz (auf + *acc.*)
pub die Kneipe, -n
public öffentlich
pudding der Pudding, -s
to **pull** ziehen*
pullover der Pullover, -; Pulli, -s
purple lila
to **put (set down)** setzen; **(stand upright)** (hin·)stellen; **(lay down)** (hin·)legen; **(hang up)** (hin·)hängen; **to ~ on (clothing)** (sich) an·ziehen*; **~ up** (auf·)bauen

Q

quarter das Viertel; **a ~ to** Viertel vor; **a ~ past** Viertel nach; **in a ~ of an hour** in einer Viertelstunde; **(university ~)** das Quartal, -e
queen die Königin, -nen
question die Frage, -n; **to ask a ~** eine Frage stellen
quick(ly) schnell
quiet(ly) ruhig, leise
quite ziemlich

R

radio das Radio, -s
railway die Bahn, -en
to **rain** regnen; **It's raining.** Es regnet.
rather lieber; ziemlich
to **read** lesen*
ready fertig
really wirklich; echt
to **rebuild** wieder auf·bauen
to **receive** bekommen*
to **recognize** erkennen*
to **recommend** empfehlen*
to **recuperate** sich erholen
red rot (ö)
refrigerator der Kühlschrank, ¨-e
region die Gegend, -en; das Gebiet, -e
regular normal
relationship die Beziehung, -en
to **relax** sich entspannen
reliable zuverlässig; **un~** unzuverlässig
to **remain** bleiben*
to **remember** sich erinnern (an + *acc.*)
to **remind (of)** erinnern (an + *acc.*)
to **renovate** renovieren
rent (*n.*) die Miete
to **rent** mieten; **to ~ out** vermieten
to **repeat** wiederholen
to **report** berichten
reporter der Journalist, -en, -en
to **request** bitten* (um)
to **rescue** retten
to **reserve** reservieren
to **reside** wohnen
responsibility die Verantwortung, -en
responsible verantwortungsvoll
to **rest** sich aus·ruhen
restaurant das Restaurant, -s
to **restore** restaurieren
to **return** zurück·kommen*
return address der Absender, -
(re)unification die (Wieder)-vereinigung
rice der Reis
rich reich
right rechts, recht-; **(correct)** richtig; **You're ~.** Du hast recht.; **isn't it (~)?** nicht wahr?; **(That's) ~.** (Das) stimmt.; **~ away** sofort
river der Fluss, ¨-e
roll das Brötchen, -
room das Zimmer, -; **bed~** das Schlafzimmer; **bath~** das Bad, ¨-er (Badezimmer); **dining ~** das Esszimmer, **living ~** das Wohnzimmer; **guest ~** das Gästezimmer; **single ~** das Einzelzimmer; **double ~** das Doppelzimmer, -
roommate der Mitbewohner, -
round-trip ticket die Hin- und Rückfahrkarte, -n
row house das Reihenhaus, ¨-er
to **run** laufen*

S

sad traurig
safe sicher; **un~** unsicher
safety die Sicherheit
salad der Salat, -e
salt das Salz
same gleich; **the ~ to you** gleichfalls; **It's all the ~ to me.** Es ist mir egal.
Saturday (der) Samstag; **on ~s** samstags
sausage die Wurst, ¨-e
to **save (money or time)** sparen; **(rescue)** retten
to **say** sagen; **Could you ~ that again? What did you ~?** Wie bitte?; **How does one ~. . . ?** Wie sagt man . . . ?
scared: to be ~ (of) Angst haben* (vor + *dat.*)

scarcely kaum
scenery die Landschaft
schedule (transportation) der Fahrplan, ¨-e
scholarship das Stipendium, Stipendien
school die Schule, -n
science die Wissenschaft, -en; **natural ~** die Naturwissenschaft, -en
scientist der Wissenschaftler, -
second die Sekunde, -n
secretary der Sekretär, -e
secure sicher
security die Sicherheit
to **see** sehen*; **Oh, I ~.** Ach so!
to **seem** scheinen*
selection (of) die Auswahl (an + *dat.*)
self-employed selbstständig
to **sell** verkaufen
semester das Semester, -
seminar das Seminar, -e
to **send** schicken
sentence der Satz, ¨-e
to **separate** trennen
September der September; **in ~** im September
server die Bedienung
service (in store or restaurant) die Bedienung
to **set (down)** setzen
several mehrer- *(pl.)*
to **share** teilen
shared gemeinsam
to **shave o.s.** sich rasieren
shelf das Regal, -e
to **shine** scheinen*
shirt das Hemd, -en
shoe der Schuh, -e; **in your/his ~s** an deiner / seiner Stelle
shop das Geschäft, -e
to **shop** ein·kaufen; **to go ~ping** einkaufen gehen*
short klein; kurz (ü)
to **show** zeigen; **That goes to ~ you.** Da sieht man's mal.
shower die Dusche, -n; **to take a ~** (sich) duschen
siblings die Geschwister *(pl.)*
sick (adj.) krank (ä); **~ person** der Kranke (ein Kranker) / die Kranke, -n, -n
to **sign** unterschreiben*
to **sign up for** belegen
to **signify** bedeuten
silly dumm (ü)
simple, simply einfach
since (time) seit (+ *dat.*)
to **sing** singen*
single (unmarried) unverheiratet, ledig
sister die Schwester, -n; **~s and brothers** die Geschwister *(pl.)*
to **sit (be sitting)** sitzen*; **to ~ down** sich (hin·)setzen
to **ski** Ski laufen*; **to go ~ing** Ski laufen gehen*
skill die Kenntnis, -se
skinny dünn
skirt der Rock, ¨-e
slacks die Hose, -n
slender schlank
to **sleep** schlafen*
slim schlank
slow(ly) langsam
small klein
to **smile** lächeln
to **snow** schneien
soccer: to play ~ Fußball spielen
sofa das Sofa, -s
soft drink die Limonade, -n
some etwas *(sg.)*; einig- *(pl. only)*; **(many a)** manch-; **(a couple of)** ein paar; **(a little bit of)** ein bisschen
somebody jemand
someone jemand
something (to) etwas (zu)
sometimes manchmal
son der Sohn, ¨-e
song das Lied, -er
soon bald; **See you ~!** Bis bald!; **as ~ as** sobald
sore: I have a ~ throat. Mir tut der Hals weh.
sorry: I'm ~. Es tut mir leid.
sort: all ~s of allerlei
so that (conj.) sodass
soup die Suppe, -n
south der Süden; **in the ~** im Süden; **~ of** südlich von
Spain (das) Spanien
Spanish (adj.) spanisch; **in ~** auf Spanisch; **(language)** Spanisch; **Do you speak ~?** Sprechen Sie Spanisch?; **(person)** der Spanier, -
to **speak** sprechen*; **~ up (louder)!** Sprechen Sie lauter!
special: s.th. ~ etwas Besonderes; **nothing ~** nichts Besonderes
spectator der Zuschauer, -
speech die Rede, -n
to **spend (money)** aus·geben*
to **spin** spinnen, spann, gesponnen
spoon der Löffel, -
sport(s) der Sport; **to engage in ~** Sport treiben*
sporty sportlich
spring der Frühling, **in (the) ~** im Frühling
square der Platz, ¨-e
stamp die Briefmarke, -n
to **stand (upright), be standing** stehen*
to **start** an·fangen*
start der Anfang, ¨-e
state der Staat, -en
to **stay** bleiben*
stay der Aufenthalt, -e
still noch
stomach der Bauch, ¨-e
stop (for buses etc.) die Haltestelle, -n
to **stop (doing s.th.)** auf·hören (zu + *inf.*)
to **stop (in a vehicle)** halten*; **~!** Halt!
stopover der Aufenthalt, -e
store das Geschäft, -e, der Laden, ¨-; **department ~** das Kaufhaus, ¨-er
story die Geschichte, -n; **detective ~** der Krimi, -s
straight gerade; **~ ahead** geradeaus
strange komisch
strawberry die Erdbeere, -n
street die Straße, -n; **main ~** die Hauptstraße, -n
streetcar die Straßenbahn, -en
strenuous anstrengend
strict(ly) streng
to **stroll** bummeln (ist)
student der Student, -en, -en / die Studentin, -nen
study das Studium, Studien; **(course of ~)** das Studium; **(room)** das Arbeitszimmer, -
to **study** lernen; **(a particular field, be a student at a university)** studieren (an + *dat.*)
stupid dumm (ü)
subject das Fach, ¨-er
subway die U-Bahn
such so ein *(sg.)*; solche *(pl.)*
sudden(ly) plötzlich
sugar der Zucker
suitcase der Koffer, -
summer der Sommer, -; **in (the) ~** im Sommer
sun die Sonne; **The ~ is shining.** Die Sonne scheint.

Sunday (der) Sonntag; **~ early in the morning** Sonntag früh; **on ~s** sonntags
superb super
supermarket der Supermarkt, ¨-e
supper das Abendessen; **for ~** zum Abendessen
to **suppose** an·nehmen*
sure sicher; doch; (na) klar; **for ~** bestimmt
surely bestimmt, sicher(lich)
surprise die Überraschung, -en; **What a ~!** Was für eine Überraschung!
to **surprise** überraschen
surroundings die Umgebung *(sg.)*; **(ecology)** die Umwelt
suspenseful spannend
system das System, -e
sweater der Pullover, -; der Pulli, -s
sweatshirt das Sweatshirt, -s
to **swim** schwimmen*, baden
Swiss (person) der Schweizer, -; **(adj.)** Schweizer, schweizerisch
Switzerland die Schweiz

T

table der Tisch, -e
to **take** nehmen*; **to ~ along** mit·nehmen*; **to ~ off (clothing)** (sich) aus·ziehen*; **to ~ off (plane)** ab·fliegen*; **(last)** dauern; **to ~ (a course)** belegen; **to ~ an exam** eine Prüfung machen; **~ care!** Mach's gut!
talented talentiert; **un~** untalentiert
to **talk (to)** reden, sprechen* (mit); **to ~ about / of** reden über (+ *acc.*) / von
to **taste** schmecken; **That tastes good.** Das schmeckt (gut).
taxi das Taxi, -s
tea der Tee, -s
to **teach** lehren
teacher der Lehrer, -
to **tear down** ab·reißen*
telephone das Telefon, -e
tell sagen, erzählen (von + *dat.*)
tennis Tennis
term paper die Arbeit, -en
terrible, terribly furchtbar, schrecklich
terrific toll, super
test die Prüfung, -en; **to take a ~** eine Prüfung machen
text message die SMS,-
than *(after comp.)* als
to **thank** danken (+ *dat.*); **~ you!** Danke!; **~ you very much.** Danke schön! Vielen Dank!; **~ God!** Gott sei Dank!; **~s, the same to you!** Danke, gleichfalls!
that das; **(conj.)** dass; **so ~ (conj.)** sodass
the . . . the je (+ *comp.*) . . . desto (+ *comp.*)
theater das Theater, -; **movie ~** das Kino, -s
their ihr
then dann; **(in those days)** damals
there da, dort; **over ~** da drüben; **to ~** dorthin; **~ is/are** es gibt
therefore deshalb, darum
thick dick
thin dünn
thing das Ding, -e
things: all sorts of ~ so einiges; **old ~** das Alte
to **think (of)** denken* (an + *acc.*); **(be of an opinion)** glauben, meinen, halten* von; **I ~ it's . . .** Ich finde es . . . ; **I ~ so, too.** Das finde ich auch.; **If you ~ so.** Wenn du meinst.; **Don't you ~ so?** Oder?
thinker der Denker, -
thirst der Durst
thirsty: I'm ~. Ich habe Durst.
this dies-
thought der Gedanke, -ns, -n
throat der Hals, ¨-e
through durch (+ *acc.*)
to **throw away** weg·werfen*
Thursday (der) Donnerstag; **~ evening** Donnerstag Abend; **on ~s** donnerstags; **~ evenings** donnerstagabends
ticket die Karte, -n; **(bus, etc.)** die Fahrkarte, -n; **(round-trip ~)** die (Hin- und) Rückfahrkarte, -n; **~ window** der Schalter, -
to **tie together** verbinden*
time die Zeit, -en; **What ~ is it?** Wie spät ist es? Wie viel Uhr ist es?; **at what ~?** wann?; **in the mean~** inzwischen; **one ~** einmal; **the first ~** das erste Mal; **for the first ~** zum ersten Mal
tired müde
to (prefix) an-; **(prep.)** zu (+ *dat.*); an (+ *acc.*); **(a country, etc.)** nach
today heute
together (prefix) mit-; **(adv.)** gemeinsam, zusammen; **~ with** mit (+ *dat.*)
toilet die Toilette, -n
tomato die Tomate, -n
tomorrow morgen; **the day after ~** übermorgen
too (also) auch; **~ much** zu viel; **me ~** ich auch
tooth der Zahn, ¨-e
to **tour** besichtigen
tour guide der Reiseleiter, -
tourist der Tourist, -en, -en
toward the speaker (prefix) her-
tower der Turm, ¨-e
town die Stadt, ¨-e
townhouse das Reihenhaus, ¨-er
toxic waste der Giftstoff, -e
track das Gleis, -e
traffic der Verkehr
trail der Weg, -e
train der Zug, ¨-e, die Bahn, -en; **~ station** der Bahnhof, ¨-e
training die Ausbildung; **practical ~** das Praktikum, Praktiken
trash der Abfall, ¨-e
to **travel** reisen (ist)
travel agent der Reiseleiter, -
tree der Baum, ¨-e
tremendously unheimlich
trillion (American) die Billion, -en
trip die Reise, -n, die Fahrt, -en; **to take a ~** eine Reise machen
true richtig, wahr; **(That's) ~.** (Das) stimmt.; **isn't that ~?** nicht wahr?; **That can't be ~!** Das kann doch nicht wahr sein!
to **try** versuchen
T-shirt das T-Shirt, -s
Tuesday (der) Dienstag; **~ at noon** Dienstagmittag; **on ~s** dienstags; **on ~s at noon** dienstagmittags
TV (medium) das Fernsehen; **(set)** der Fernseher, -; **to watch ~** fern·sehen*
typical(ly) typisch; **That's ~ of you.** Das sieht dir ähnlich.

U

ugly hässlich
unathletic unsportlich
unbelievable unglaublich; **That's ~!** (Das ist doch) unglaublich!, Wahnsinn!

uncle der Onkel, -
under unter (+ *acc.* / *dat.*)
to **understand** verstehen*
undoubtedly sicherlich
unemployed arbeitslos
unemployment die Arbeitslosigkeit
unexpected(ly) unerwartet
unfortunately leider
unification die Vereinigung
united vereint, vereinigt
United States (US) die Vereinigten Staaten (USA) *(pl.)*
university die Universität, -en; die Uni, -s *(coll.)*
unlucky: to be ~ Pech haben*; **I was (you were, etc.) ~.** Pech gehabt!
unique einmalig
until bis; **not ~** erst
up (prefix) auf-
upset: to get ~ about sich ärgern über (+ *acc.*)
upstairs oben
usual(ly) gewöhnlich, meistens
to **use** gebrauchen, benutzen, verwenden
used: to get ~ to sich gewöhnen an (+ *acc.*)
to **utilize** gebrauchen, verwenden

V

vacation die Ferien *(pl.)*
various verschieden
vegetable(s) das Gemüse, -
versatile vielseitig
very sehr; ganz
view (of) der Blick (auf / in + *acc.*)
viewer der Zuschauer, -
village das Dorf, ¨er
to **visit** besuchen; **(sightseeing)** besichtigen

W

to **wait (for)** warten (auf + *acc.*)
waiter der Kellner, -; der Ober, -; **~ !** Herr Ober!
waitress die Kellnerin, -nen; **~!** Bedienung!
to **walk** zu Fuß gehen*, laufen*; **to go for a ~** spazieren gehen*
wall die Wand, ¨e; **(thick)** die Mauer, -n
to **want to** wollen*, möchten*
war der Krieg, -e
warm warm (ä)
to **wash (o.s.)** (sich) waschen*
waste der Abfall, der Müll; **toxic ~** der Giftstoff, -e
waste separation die Mülltrennung
watch (clock) die Uhr, -en
to **watch: (TV)** fern·sehen*; **(pay attention)** auf·passen; **(look at)** (sich) an·schauen; **~ out!** Passen Sie auf!
water das Wasser
way der Weg, -e; **by the ~** übrigens; **this ~** auf diese Weise
to **wear** tragen*
weather das Wetter
wedding die Hochzeit, -en
Wednesday (der) Mittwoch; **~ afternoon** Mittwochnachmittag; **on ~s** mittwochs; **~ afternoons** mittwochnachmittags
week die Woche, -n; **all ~ long** die ganze Woche; **this ~** diese Woche; **Have a nice ~end!** (Ein) schönes Wochenende!
weekly wöchentlich
weird komisch
welcome: You're ~. Bitte (bitte)!, Bitte schön!, Nichts zu danken!
well (adv.) gut; **~** also, na ja, nun; **Get ~ soon!** Gute Besserung!
west der Westen; **in the ~** im Westen; **~ of** westlich von
what? was?; **~ did you say?** Wie bitte?; **~'s there to ...?** Was gibt's zu ...?; **~'s new?** Was gibt's (Neues)?; **~'s on ...?** Was gibt's im ...?; **So ~?** Na und?; **~ kind of (a)?** was für (ein)?
when (at what time?) wann?; **(at the time ~) (conj.)** als; **~(ever) (conj.)** wenn; **just ~ (conj.)** gerade als
where? wo?; **from ~?** woher?; **~ to?** wohin?
whether (conj.) ob
which? welch-?
while (conj.) während
white weiß
who? wer?
whole ganz
whom? wen?, wem?
whose? wessen?
why? warum?, wieso?
wife die Frau, -en
wild wild
to **win** gewinnen*
window das Fenster, -; **ticket ~** der Schalter, -
windy windig
wine der Wein, -e
winter der Winter, - **in (the) ~** im Winter
to **wish** (sich) wünschen
wish der Wunsch, ¨e; **Best ~es!** Herzliche Glückwünsche!
with (prefix) mit-; **(prep.)** mit (+ *dat.*); **(at the home of)** bei (+ *dat.*); **~ me (us ...)** bei mir (uns ...)
without ohne (+ *acc.*)
woman (Mrs., Ms.) die Frau, -en
to **wonder** sich fragen
wonderful(ly) wunderbar, prima, herrlich
woods der Wald, ¨er
word das Wort, ¨er
work die Arbeit
to **work** arbeiten; **That won't ~.** Das geht nicht.
worker (blue-collar) der Arbeiter, -
world die Welt, -en
worry die Sorge, -n
to **worry (about)** sich Sorgen machen (um)
to **write** schreiben*; **to ~ to** schreiben* an (+ *acc.*); **to ~ about** schreiben* über (+ *acc.*); **to ~ down** aufschreiben*; **How do you ~ that?** Wie schreibt man das?
wrong falsch; **You are ~.** Du hast unrecht.

Y

year das Jahr, -e; **all ~ long** das ganze Jahr; **next ~** nächstes Jahr; **Have a good New ~!** Ein gutes neues Jahr!
yellow gelb
yes ja; doch
yesterday gestern; **the day before ~** vorgestern
yet doch; **not ~** noch nicht
yogurt der Jog(h)urt, -s
young jung (ü)
your dein, euer, Ihr
youth die Jugend
youth hostel die Jugendherberge, -n

Z

zip code die Postleitzahl, -en

Index

This index is limited primarily to grammatical entries.

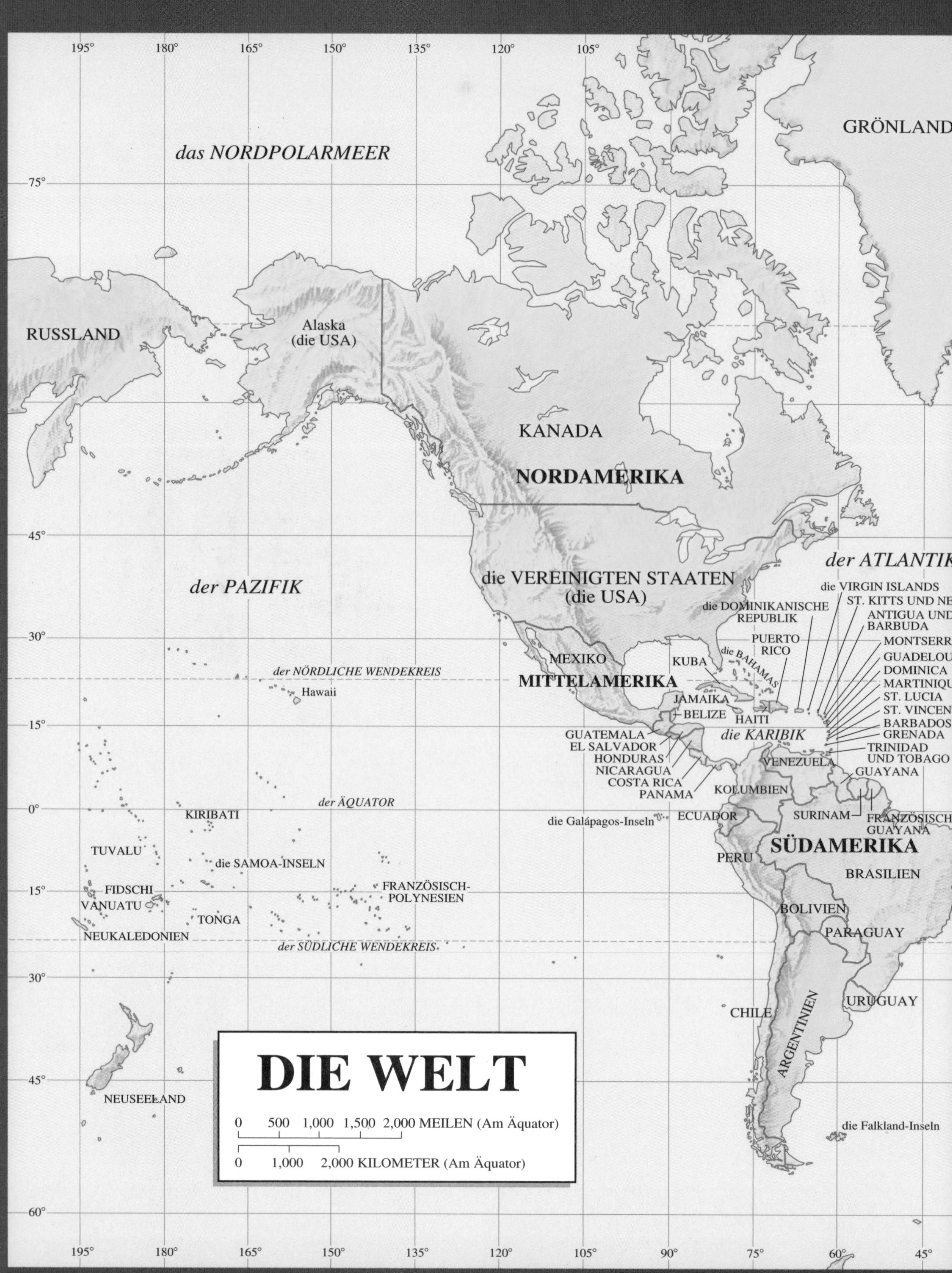

DIE WELT
das NORDPOLARMEER
GRÖNLAND
RUSSLAND
Alaska
(die USA)
KANADA
NORDAMERIKA
der PAZIFIK
die VEREINIGTEN STAATEN
(die USA)
der ATLANTIK
die VIRGIN ISLANDS
ST. KITTS UND NE
ANTIGUA UND
BARBUDA
MONTSERR
GUADELOU
DOMINICA
MARTINIQU
ST. LUCIA
ST. VINCEN
BARBADOS
GRENADA
TRINIDAD
UND TOBAGO
die DOMINIKANISCHE
REPUBLIK
PUERTO
RICO
die BAHAMAS
KUBA
MEXIKO
MITTELAMERIKA
JAMAIKA
BELIZE
HAITI
die KARIBIK
GUATEMALA
EL SALVADOR
HONDURAS
NICARAGUA
COSTA RICA
PANAMA
VENEZUELA
GUAYANA
KOLUMBIEN
SURINAM
FRANZÖSISCH
GUAYANA
ECUADOR
die Galápagos-Inseln
PERU
SÜDAMERIKA
BRASILIEN
BOLIVIEN
PARAGUAY
CHILE
ARGENTINIEN
URUGUAY
die Falkland-Inseln
der NÖRDLICHE WENDEKREIS
Hawaii
der ÄQUATOR
KIRIBATI
TUVALU
die SAMOA-INSELN
FIDSCHI
VANUATU
TONGA
NEUKALEDONIEN
FRANZÖSISCH-
POLYNESIEN
der SÜDLICHE WENDEKREIS
NEUSEELAND
0 500 1,000 1,500 2,000 MEILEN (Am Äquator)
0 1,000 2,000 KILOMETER (Am Äquator)
195° 180° 165° 150° 135° 120° 105° 90° 75° 60° 45°
75° 45° 30° 15° 0° 15° 30° 45° 60°